THE HANDBOOK

The Unofficial and Unauthorised Guide to the Production of DOCTOR WHO

THE HANDBOOK

The Unofficial and Unauthorised Guide
to the Production of DOCTOR WHO

David J Howe

Stephen James Walker

Mark Stammers

TELOS
.co.uk

First published in England in 2005 by

Telos Publishing Ltd
61 Elgar Avenue, Tolworth, Surrey, KT5 9JP, England
www.telos.co.uk

Telos Publishing Ltd values feedback. Please e-mail us with any comments
you may have about this book to: feedback@telos.co.uk

Previously published in a different form in seven volumes
by Virgin Publishing Ltd, 1992, 1993, 1994, 1995, 1996, 1997.

ISBN: 1-903889-59-6 (paperback)
Text © 2005 David J Howe, Stephen James Walker & Mark Stammers

ISBN: 1-903889-96-0 (deluxe hardback)
Text © 2005 David J Howe, Stephen James Walker & Mark Stammers

The moral rights of the authors have been asserted.

Font design by Comicraft. Copyright © 1998 Active Images/Comicraft
430 Colorado Avenue # 302, Santa Monica, Ca 90401
Fax (001) 310 451 9761/Tel (001) 310 458 9094
WEB: www.comicbookfonts.com; EMAIL: orders@comicbookfonts.com

Internal design, typesetting and layout by Arnold T Blumberg
www.atbpublishing.com

Printed in India.

Hardback bound in England
Antony Rowe Ltd, Bumper's Farm Industrial Estate, Chippenham, Wiltshire, SN14
6LH

1 2 3 4 5 6 7 8 9 10 11 12 13 14 15

British Library Cataloguing in Publication Data.
A catalogue record for this book is available from the British Library.

The seven volumes that comprised the original Handbook series were dedicated to a number of people. We feel it is only right to repeat those dedications here. So this book is dedicated to:

Ian K McLachlan, David Auger, Tony and Nikki Jordan, Martin Wiggins, the memory of Jon Pertwee, Ted, Sheila, Alan, Robert and Caroline, Alison, Anita Cotis, Mark Stammers, Andrew Pixley, Susan, Julie, Teresa and Kimberlie, everyone who ever contributed to *The Frame*, Nicole Adams (aka Suki), Claire.

ACKNOWLEDGEMENTS

First Doctor: For this incredible feat of researching the past we are, as always, indebted to numerous people who helped along the way. This time thanks must go to Keith Barnfather and Reeltime Pictures, David Auger, Michael Imison, Dallas Jones, Barry Newbery, Andrew Pixley, Marc Platt, Paul Scoones, Neil Somerville and Trevor White of the BBC Written Archives Centre, Martin Wiggins, John Wiles and all unsung *Doctor Who* fanzine editors and writers everywhere.

Second Doctor: For help in delving into the era of the second Doctor we are grateful to Andrew Pixley (as always), and also Keith Barnfather, Bobi Bartlett, Martin Baugh, David Brunt, Terrance Dicks, Sean Gaffney, Sean Gibbons, David Auger, Christopher Heer, Evan Hercules, Susan James, Sylvia James, Dallas Jones, Lighthope, Peter Ling, David Maloney, Ian McLachlan, John Peel, Jon Preddle, Darren Primm, Steve Roberts, Alex Rohan, Paul Scoones, Damian Shanahan, Roger Stevens, Jan Vincent-Rudzki, Patrick White, Martin Wiggins, the BBC Written Archives Centre and all *Doctor Who* fanzine editors everywhere.

Third Doctor: For help in delving into the era of the third Doctor we are grateful to, as always, Andrew Pixley, and also to James Acheson, Keith Barnfather and Reeltime Pictures, Bobi Bartlett, Jeremy Bentham and *In-Vision*, Paul Bernard, Richard Bignell, Allister Bowtell, David Brunt, Terrance Dicks, Sandra Exelby, David Auger, Gary Gillett, Simeon Hearn, Richard Hollis, Caroline John, David Myerscough-Jones, Barbara Kidd, Barry Letts, Jon Pertwee, Jon Preddle, Christine Rawlins, Tim Robins, Gary Russell, the Skaro Team, Elisabeth Sladen, Mark Stammers, Ken Trew, Jan Vincent-Rudzki, Martin Wiggins and all *Doctor Who* fanzine editors everywhere.

Fourth Doctor: Sincere thanks to Justin Richards and Peter Anghelides, editors of the *Doctor Who* reference work *In-Vision*, for permission to quote from their releases. Also to Andrew Pixley for assistance above and beyond…, Guy Daniels and Richard Bignell of *Private Who*, John Freeman and Gary Russell of *Doctor Who Magazine*, Gary Leigh of *Dream Watch Bulletin*, Christopher Barry, Barry Newbery, Terrance Dicks, Jack Weller, David Auger and Rosemary Howe. Thanks also to all those unsung *Doctor Who* fanzine editors and writers for providing many happy hours of entertainment and education.

Fifth Doctor: For help in delving into the era of the fifth Doctor we are grateful to, as always, Andrew Pixley, and also to Martin Wiggins, David Auger, Jon Preddle, the *Skaro* Team, Jan Vincent-Rudzki, Peter Moffatt, John Brace, Mark Stammers, Patricia Holmes, Richard Hollis, Johnny Byrne, Richard Bignell, Anthony Brown and *In-Vision*, Gary Russell, Simeon Hearn and all *Doctor Who* fanzine editors everywhere.

Sixth Doctor: We are indebted this time around to: Colin Baker for his support and enthusiasm, Richard Bignell, John Brace, Austen Atkinson Broadbelt, Nicola Bryant for her long-distance assistance, David Auger, Pat Godfrey, Graeme Harper, John Nathan-Turner for all his help in the past, Barry Newbery, Alister Pearson, Andrew Pixley for again allowing us to draw on his encyclopaedic memory, Jon Preddle, Gary Russell of *Doctor Who Magazine*, Eric Saward, Paul Scoones, Alan Spalding, Patrick White, Martin Wiggins for supplying us with so much helpful reference material, and Graeme Wood. Thanks also to all those unsung *Doctor Who* fanzine editors and writers for providing many happy hours of entertainment and education.

Seventh/Eighth Doctor: Our thanks go this time first and foremost to our good friend and fellow researcher Andrew Pixley, who has selflessly offered advice and shared his incredible knowledge with us throughout the preparation of this series of Handbooks.

Special thanks to those few knowledgeable and generous souls who have provided sections for the 'Selling the Doctor' chapter: Ian Wheeler, who took on the bulk of this work, and Michael J Doran, Robert D Franks, David Robinson, Richard Prekodravac, Paul Scoones, Damian Shanahan and Dallas Jones. Thanks too to Rosemary Howe, who spent many, many hours reading all seven Handbooks in order to create the incredible (and hopefully useful) index that appears herein.

A big thank you to Sophie Aldred for the introduction and for her help in general.

Thanks also to Mark Ayres, Jonathan Blum, David Brunt, Mary Carroll, Michael J Doran, Gary Gillatt and *Doctor Who* Magazine, David Golding, Susan James, Misha Lauenstein, Lance Parkin, Gary Russell, Philip Segal, Mark Stammers, Martin Wiggins and all *Doctor Who* fanzine editors past and present.

For the corrections to earlier volumes, we are grateful to the following people: David Brunt, Michael J Doran, Chris Fieldhouse, Rosemary Howe, Dan Kukwa, Steve Manfred, John Molyneux, Paul Scoones and Martin Wiggins.

Finally, we would like to raise our collective glasses to our editor-in-chief at Virgin Publishing, Peter Darvill-Evans. It was he who encouraged us to submit ideas to him back in 1990, and this series of seven Handbooks would never have happened, and may never have been completed, if it had not been for Peter's faith in us and in the show that we all love.

To Peter, and also to Virgin editors past and present Rebecca Levene and Simon Winstone, we say, thanks for your advice, for your enthusiasm and for your trust. We hope we've repaid it.

AUTHORS' NOTE TO THE TELOS EDITION

The Handbook series, originally published by Virgin Publishing in the 1990s, was a great success, not only for us as authors, but also for the publishers. For the first time, we had the scope to delve into some of the minutiae and detail of the production of the *Doctor Who* series, and collect it all together in a series of books that, we hoped, would complement our larger format, illustrated volumes, collectively known as the 'decades' books.

In 2003, Telos Publishing released a new and updated edition of *The Television Companion*, a programme guide that collected together as much information about the actual televised *Doctor Who* stories as possible: the plots, the cliffhanger endings, cast and crew, location and recording information, and review commentaries. Into that volume we added material from the 'Stories' sections of the seven original Handbooks, to make it even more comprehensive. That material is therefore omitted here, to avoid excessive duplication between the two books.

For this book, we have not extensively re-worked the remainder of the material from the original Handbooks; we have presented it in the same Doctor-by-Doctor format as before. Some corrections and updates have been made to the text to remove inadvertent mistakes, small instances of repetition etc. Also, some material cut from the published versions of those earlier volumes for reasons of space has been reinstated here. Most notably, there is the entire 'Script to Screen' section on the first Doctor story *The Ark*, which appeared only in heavily truncated form in the original Handbook. The extensive Production Guide to the first Doctor's era also has several more entries this time, and some of the other chapters have small embellishments to them as well. We have not, however, added large amounts of material to cover new developments that have occurred since the original volumes were written – such as the production of new audio adventures of the fifth, sixth, seventh and eighth Doctors by Big Finish – as these have already been comprehensively documented elsewhere.

At the time of writing this introduction, there is also a new series of *Doctor Who* due for transmission on BBC1 in 2005 ... something we've been awaiting with bated breath since 1989! Again, this book does not cover the production of the new series – look out for another Telos Publishing title, *Back to the Vortex*, for information on that.

Our aim here is to complete the picture with regard to *Doctor Who* on television from 1963 to 1996, and provide a complement to *The Television Companion* by chronicling the behind-the-scenes history of the first eight Doctors. We hope you enjoy reading, or re-reading, it as much as we enjoyed writing it.

David J Howe
Stephen James Walker
Mark Stammers

DOCTOR WHO STORY CHECKLIST

SEASON ONE [1963-1964]
The Doctor played by William Hartnell
100,000 BC (A)
The Mutants (B)
Inside the Spaceship (C)
Marco Polo (D)
The Keys of Marinus (E)
The Aztecs (F)
The Sensorites (G)
The Reign of Terror (H)

SEASON TWO [1964-1965]
Planet of Giants (J)
The Dalek Invasion of Earth (K)
The Rescue (L)
The Romans (M)
The Web Planet (N)
The Crusade (P)
The Space Museum (Q)
The Chase (R)
The Time Meddler (S)

SEASON THREE [1965-1966]
Galaxy 4 (T)
Mission to the Unknown (T/A)
The Myth Makers (U)
The Daleks' Master Plan (V)
The Massacre of St Bartholemew's Eve (W)
The Ark (X)
The Celestial Toymaker (Y)
The Gunfighters (Z)
The Savages (AA)
The War Machines (BB)

SEASON FOUR [1966-1967]
The Smugglers (CC)
The Tenth Planet (DD)
The Doctor played by Patrick Troughton
The Power of the Daleks (EE)
The Highlanders (FF)
The Underwater Menace (GG)
The Moonbase (HH)

The Macra Terror (JJ)
The Faceless Ones (KK)
The Evil of the Daleks (LL)

SEASON FIVE [1967-1968]
The Tomb of the Cybermen (MM)
The Abominable Snowmen (NN)
The Ice Warriors (OO)
The Enemy of the World (PP)
The Web of Fear (QQ)
Fury from the Deep (RR)
The Wheel In Space (SS)

SEASON SIX [1968-1969]
The Dominators (TT)
The Mind Robber (UU)
The Invasion (VV)
The Krotons (WW)
The Seeds of Death (XX)
The Space Pirates (YY)
The War Games (ZZ)

SEASON SEVEN [1970]
The Doctor played by Jon Pertwee
Spearhead From Space (AAA)
Doctor Who and the Silurians (BBB)
The Ambassadors of Death (CCC)
Inferno (DDD)

SEASON EIGHT [1971]
Terror of the Autons (EEE)
The Mind of Evil (FFF)
The Claws of Axos (GGG)
Colony In Space (HHH)
The Dæmons (JJJ)

SEASON NINE [1972]
Day of the Daleks (KKK)
The Curse of Peladon (MMM)
The Sea Devils (LLL)
The Mutants (NNN)
The Time Monster (OOO)

SEASON TEN [1972-1973]
The Three Doctors (RRR)
Carnival of Monsters (PPP)
Frontier In Space (QQQ)
Planet of the Daleks (SSS)
The Green Death (TTT)

SEASON ELEVEN [1973-1974]
The Time Warrior (UUU)
Invasion of the Dinosaurs (WWW)
Death to the Daleks (XXX)
The Monster of Peladon (YYY)
Planet of the Spiders (ZZZ)

SEASON TWELVE [1974-1975]
The Doctor played by Tom Baker
Robot (4A)
The Ark in Space (4C)
The Sontaran Experiment (4B)
Genesis of the Daleks (4E)
Revenge of the Cybermen (4D)

SEASON THIRTEEN [1975-1976]
Terror of the Zygons (4F)
Planet of Evil (4H)
Pyramids of Mars (4G)
The Android Invasion (4J)
The Brain of Morbius (4K)
The Seeds of Doom (4L)

SEASON FOURTEEN [1976-1977]
The Masque of Mandragora (4M)
The Hand of Fear (4N)
The Deadly Assassin (4P)
The Face of Evil (4Q)
The Robots of Death (4R)
The Talons of Weng-Chiang (4S)

SEASON FIFTEEN [1977-1978]
Horror of Fang Rock (4V)
The Invisible Enemy (4T)
Image of the Fendahl (4X)
The Sun Makers (4W)
Underworld (4Y)
The Invasion of Time (4Z)

SEASON SIXTEEN [1978-1979]
The Ribos Operation (5A)
The Pirate Planet (5B)
The Stones of Blood (5C)
The Androids of Tara (5D)
The Power of Kroll (5E)
The Armageddon Factor (5F)

SEASON SEVENTEEN [1979-1980]
Destiny of the Daleks (5J)
City of Death (5H)
The Creature from the Pit (5G)
Nightmare of Eden (5K)
The Horns of Nimon (5L)

SEASON EIGHTEEN [1980-1981]
The Leisure Hive (5N)
Meglos (5Q)
Full Circle (5R)
State of Decay (5P)
Warriors' Gate (5S)
The Keeper of Traken (5T)
Logopolis (5V)

SEASON NINETEEN [1982]
The Doctor played by Peter Davison
Castrovalva (5Z)
Four To Doomsday (5W)
Kinda (5Y)
The Visitation (5X)
Black Orchid (6A)
Earthshock (6B)
Time-Flight (6C)

SEASON TWENTY [1983]
Arc of Infinity (6E)
Snakedance (6D)
Mawdryn Undead (6F)
Terminus (6G)
Enlightenment (6H)
The King's Demons (6J)

TWENTIETH ANNIVERSARY SPECIAL [1983]
The Five Doctors (6K)

SEASON TWENTY-ONE [1984]

Warriors of the Deep (6L)
The Awakening (6M)
Frontios (6N)
Resurrection of the Daleks (6P)
Planet of Fire (6Q)
The Caves of Androzani (6R)
The Doctor played by Colin Baker
The Twin Dilemma (6S)

SEASON TWENTY-TWO [1985]

Attack of the Cybermen (6T)
Vengeance On Varos (6V)
The Mark of the Rani (6X)
The Two Doctors (6W)
Timelash (6Y)
Revelation of the Daleks (6Z)

SEASON TWENTY-THREE [1986]

The Trial of a Time Lord (7A/7B/7C)

SEASON TWENTY-FOUR [1987]

The Doctor played by Sylvester McCoy
Time and the Rani (7D)
Paradise Towers (7E)
Delta and the Bannermen (7F)
Dragonfire (7G)

SEASON TWENTY-FIVE [1988-1989]

Remembrance of the Daleks (7H)
The Happiness Patrol (7L)
Silver Nemesis (7K)
The Greatest Show in the Galaxy (7J)

SEASON TWENTY-SIX [1989]

Battlefield (7N)
Ghost Light (7Q)
The Curse of Fenric (7M)
Survival (7P)

THE TELEVISION MOVIE [1996]

The Doctor played by Paul McGann
Doctor Who

The First Doctor

by
David J Howe
Mark Stammers
Stephen James Walker

FOREWORD

The arrival of the elderly figure of the Doctor in a junkyard at 76 Totter's Lane heralded the start of a ground-breaking British television success story that would continue from the transmission of that first episode on Saturday 23 November 1963 right up to the present day.

The seeds of this success were sown in the spring of 1962, when the idea of mounting an ongoing science fiction series was first mooted within the BBC. The BBC's television service was not long out of its infancy then. Less than sixteen years had passed since it was reinstated after its wartime hiatus, and less than seven since it first encountered competition in the form of the new ITV network. The launch of its second channel, BBC2, was still some two years away. Over the past decade, it had however made enormous technical advances; had come to rival and then overtake the radio service in terms both of its popularity and of its resources; and had firmly established itself as one of the foremost programme-making institutions in the world.

The advent of ITV, and its initial ratings triumph, had acted as a catalyst that had caused the BBC completely to re-evaluate its output, aiming to broaden its popular appeal whilst retaining its commitment to quality. The Sixties was to be one of its most artistically successful decades as, under Director-General Hugh Carleton Greene, it cast off its former, rather stuffy, highbrow image and became a creative hothouse turning out a multitude of innovative, challenging and highly-acclaimed programmes across its entire range of production.

One way in which it did this was to bring in visionary new personnel such as the charismatic Canadian producer Sydney Newman, whose recent achievements at the independent ABC TV had included the popularisation of an entirely new style of drama – 'kitchen sink drama', as the critics dubbed it – dealing with contemporary social issues of relevance to ordinary working-class viewers; not to mention the creation a number of highly successful individual series such as, most notably, *The Avengers*.

It was under Newman's guidance, and with his active contribution and participation, that the format of *Doctor Who* was devised. It was a perfect example of the new style of programming for which he was striving; a style that eschewed the tried-and-trusted in favour of the innovative and the experimental; a style that matched the spirit of the bright new decade.

The Sixties was to be a period of great change and success for Great Britain. British pop music – especially the Mersey-beat groups led by the Beatles – would end America's domination of 'rock 'n' roll.' The fashionable would no longer look only to Paris for their clothes but also to London's King's Road and Carnaby Street, to new designers like Mary Quant and Biba. Attitudes towards the roles of the sexes were fast changing as people questioned long-established social codes, whilst the ever-present threat of nuclear war between the two super-powers, the Soviet Union and the United States of America, was leaving its mark on the collective psyche. Mankind was also taking its first faltering steps into space, turning what had so recently been science fiction into fact. If Man could now leave the Earth, surely he might one day walk on other worlds?

It was against this background and into this context that *Doctor Who* was born, to take its place – alongside its most famous monsters, the Daleks – as one of the greatest products and most widely-recognised icons of British popular culture.

Join us for a journey back in time to the swinging Sixties, and to the golden age of television.

WILLIAM HARTNELL: IN HIS OWN WORDS

ON HIS EARLY LIFE:

'All my spare coppers were spent on visits to the cinema. I revelled in the serials of Pearl White and the exploits of Tarzan. But my real guiding star was Charlie Chaplin. He influenced me more than any other factor in taking up acting as a career.'
Quoted by Peter Haining in *Doctor Who – A Celebration*, original source unknown.

'I was born in North Devon. Little place called Seaton.* A very old family. 300 years of us.

'I ran away from school at an early age. I had written to Stanley Wootton, at Treadwell House, Epsom, got myself a job as an apprentice with him to ride and become a jockey. After … I suppose it was a year or so, I suddenly started to put on weight and Stanley Wootton said it wouldn't do and he thought I ought to get out and take up another profession. Yes. So my second desire, immediate desire, was the theatre. Naturally I wanted to couple the two, but there it was – I was unable to do so.

'I suppose I associated myself with a lot of reading matter over a period. Shakespeare and other playwrights. And I was always in the school concerts and things like that. I was just mad keen on the theatre and horses, and those were the two things that I wanted in life, and unfortunately it didn't turn out that way.

'My first job in the theatre was luckily to be with Sir Frank Benson, a wonderful Shakespearean actor and teacher whom we all of course called at that period Pa Benson.

'After leaving the Benson company I was like any other actor, I suppose. I had to take a job on tour and earn my living the best way I could, which I did. I was on tour doing once-nightly and twice-nightly shows for fourpence a week and living in back rooms.

'My first appearance in the West End was a very modest entrance on my part, I think. I was understudy when I first appeared and, you know, sort of general dog's body. I understudied such personalities as Ernest Truex in *Good Morning Bill*, which was a Robert Courtneidge production, and Ralph Lynn in his light comedies and farces. Charles Heslop, who was in musicals, and also a farcical actor. And Bud Flanagan, Chesney Allen. And a well-known actor when I was a boy, Lawrence Grossmith.'
Interviewed by Roy Plomley on 2 August 1965 for BBC Radio's *Desert Island Discs*.

'Sir Frank Benson's Company was good training. Not only in Shakespeare, but in keeping fit! Sir Frank Benson believed in keeping his actors in good health and we were organised into hockey teams and cricket sides.'
Quoted by Peter Haining in *Doctor Who – A Celebration*, original source unknown.

---

* It is now known that this was untrue. Hartnell was born in London, the illegitimate son of a single mother, but concealed this fact from journalists throughout his later life.

'In 1924 I ran away from school to join Sir Frank Benson's Shakespearean Company. I later persuaded my parents to allow me to go on tour; at that time I was just seventeen. After I left Benson's Company, I stayed on the road for another six years, touring with various modern productions, old and new. In the years 1928-29 I did a tour in Canada, came back to England and found things pretty tough so crashed into pictures, but as I was unknown as a film actor I had to start all over again. And many of the agents who saw me so often in their offices began to think that I was quite a comic. They roared and laughed at my persistence and confidence.'
William Hartnell writing in 1946 for *British National's Film Review*.

'I reasoned that my light comedy style was much more fitted for British talkies than their American counterparts, so I returned to England. But now I think that decision was completely wrong.

'I often hovered near directors so that I could learn the business of film-making. I was always on hand, too, in case another actor was suddenly needed. Although this strategy worked on occasions, and I did get bigger "bit" parts, it did not lead to stardom. In fact, after crowd work for two years, I was told by a casting director that I had not got a "film face". I remember, incidentally, that Laurence Olivier was also a neighbour at the film casting offices as we all sought vainly for work.'
Quoted by Peter Haining in *Doctor Who – A Celebration*, original source unknown.

ON HIS EARLY FILM ROLES:
'I can't remember my very first film appearance. But I must admit that I was two years in crowd scenes before I was ever allowed to appear in a film. I was then in numerous films, "Quickies" of those days, where if you had ten pages of dialogue in one take and if you fluffed, well, you had to ad lib and then carry on. No retakes. Couldn't afford it.'
Interviewed by Roy Plomley on 2 August 1965 for BBC Radio's *Desert Island Discs*.

'One day I found myself playing in a comedy lead in a "Quickie" called *I'm an Explosive*, directed by Adrian Brunel. Other leads at this period were *Follow the Lady* (Fox), *Seeing is Believing* (Paramount), *Nothing Like Publicity* (Radio). On my discharge from the Army I had to pick up anew the threads of my career. I kicked off again playing a valet-cum-thief opposite Oliver Wakefield in *The Peterfield Diamond*, then an old London taxi-cab driver in *Flying Fortress* (which I enjoyed very much as it was a character part). Then came a small cameo in *Sabotage at Sea*, and a comedy lead in *The Dark Tower*, from there to Ealing Studios to play *The Bells Go Down*, directed by Bill Dearden. I played Dallow in *Brighton Rock* at the Garrick Theatre. This play certainly helped me up a few rungs. During its run, Carol Reed tested me for the part of the Sergeant in *The Way Ahead*. Since then I have starred in four pictures made by British National Limited; *Strawberry Roan*, and *The Agitator*, *Murder in Reverse*, and *Appointment with Crime*.'
William Hartnell writing in 1946 for *British National's Film Review*.

ON HIS DISCHARGE FROM THE ARMY:
'The strain of training was too much. I spent twelve weeks in an army hospital and came out with a terrible stutter. The Colonel said, "Better get back to the theatre. You're no

bloody good here." I had to start all over again. I was still only a spit and a cough in the profession and now I had a stutter which scared the life out of me!'
Interviewed in 1965 for the *Sunday Mirror.*

ON HIS 'TOUGH GUY' ROLES:

'Anyone can be horrific by gumming on lumps of hair and wax and by putting cotton wool up their nostrils to look like an ape, but I think the real shudder-creating villain is the one who looks the same as other men, except for the eyes, and the eyes ought to reveal just how rotten to the core the heavy is, with subtle graduations such as "forced into crime by mental instability" or "gone to the bad through evil surroundings" or "not a bad chap at heart but just lacking in strength of character." It's a fascinating study.'
Quoted by Peter Haining in *Doctor Who – A Celebration*, **original source unknown.**

'I'm tired of being the eternal "tough guy" of British films. Asking me to play this type of role in the first place was about as practical as asking Danny Kaye to play Napoleon on Elba!

'Somehow I've managed to scrape through, but after five years of it I can clearly see the danger signal ahead. I'm certain picturegoers are sick and tired of seeing me pull horrid faces before the cameras, and that if I don't change my style very soon, I shall soon find myself a has-been!

'It's not generally realised that forty-five of my sixty films are comedies and that I was a leading "Quota Quickie" funny man.'
Interviewed by D McFadden for *Picturegoer*, **edition dated 26 May 1945.**

'I got fed-up playing the bullying sergeant-major. People, complete strangers, would come up to me in pubs and bellow "Get yer 'air cut!"'
Interviewed for *Reveille*, **edition dated 7-13 January 1965.**

ON HIS ROLE AS SERGEANT MAJOR BULLIMORE IN *THE ARMY GAME*:

'I stayed with that series for the first year, and then I thought I would give it a rest and try and do something else. I was away from it for two years, back making films. And then I quite by accident met the producer again in a train going home one evening, and he asked me if I'd come back to the show. So I said yes, at a price. And he agreed and I went back for another year. Then I thought, well, I'd better leave now before I do go into a mental home.'
Interviewed by Roy Plomley on 2 August 1965 for BBC Radio's *Desert Island Discs.*

ON BEING CAST AS THE DOCTOR:

'All my life I've wanted to play an older character part in films, or in a play, and I've never been allowed to. Except just on one occasion prior to being offered this part, Doctor Who. After a second reading for Lindsay Anderson I was given the part of an old boy in *This Sporting Life*, where the lead was played and shared by Richard Harris and Rachel Roberts, both superb artists. And I was just playing this sort of bone idle, out of work, on the dole, ill old man called Dad who had a great ambition in life in earlier days to be a rugger player, and to be a good professional player, make a success of his life.

Unfortunately he ended up, as it were, in the gutter, and rather an ill and useless old man, but in this young boy he saw something; he saw something of himself. Yes. And therefore he ... I think he used his influence with the club managers and associates to get this boy a chance, give him a chance.

'And playing this part, strangely enough, led to the part of Doctor Who. Because it turned out that after I had played Doctor Who for several months Verity Lambert, my producer, a very charming and lovable person, finally confessed to me that she'd seen this film and she had decided that there was her Doctor Who.'
Interviewed by Roy Plomley on 2 August 1965 for BBC Radio's *Desert Island Discs.*

'I was "resting" when my son-in-law, who is also my agent, approached me about playing the part. I hadn't worked for the BBC since steam radio twenty-five years ago, and I didn't fancy the idea of returning to state control so late in life.

'My son-in-law – Terry Carney, son of George Carney, the variety artist – was quite right, the role was exactly me. For only the second time in thirty-seven years – the film *This Sporting Life* was the last – I had the opportunity to play an old man.

'What's more, the part required some thought, unlike *The Army Game* and most of the other rubbish I've been associated with in the past. I've not been offered the sort of work I've wanted, due I think to past disagreements I've had with producers and directors over how parts should be played.

'Financially and otherwise I am much better off now. I didn't like the initial script and I told them so. It made the old man too bad tempered. So they gave me carte blanche to introduce more humour and pathos into the part.

'I can hardly believe the break from playing servicemen has come, but now that it has happened, it's for good. I'll never play a uniformed part again.'
Interviewed in 1964 for syndication in local newspapers.

'I wanted to get away from military roles. That's why I was so pleased to be offered Dr Who.'
Interviewed for the *Daily Mirror*, edition dated 23 April 1966.

'The moment this brilliant young producer, Miss Verity Lambert, started telling me about *Doctor Who* I was hooked.'
Quoted in *The Making of Doctor Who* by Malcolm Hulke and Terrance Dicks, original source unknown.

ON THE MAGIC OF *DOCTOR WHO*:
'Apart from there being no sex or swearing, the treatment is very adult. But aiming it at the kids first was a masterstroke. Around tea time it's the children who decide what is seen on TV, not the parents. On the other hand, it is something mums and dads can watch as well without cringing.'
Interviewed in 1964 for syndication in local newspapers.

'The programme is a success because we keep it as a children's programme.

'The scriptwriters sometimes try to make Dr Who use expressions like "centrifugal force," but I refuse. If it all gets too technical, the children don't understand and they

lose interest. After all, it's an adventure story, not a scientific documentary. And Dr Who isn't a scientist. He's a wizard.'
Interviewed for *Reveille*, edition dated 7-13 January 1965.

'After we remade the first episode, I decided that the show would run for five years. That was my assumption then, two-and-a-half years ago, and I think my assumption is still pretty right.

'If it does continue for that long, then I shall have had enough.

'I hope that before we finish the series that we shall be able to make it in colour. I feel this would enhance the programme.'
Interviewed for the *Western Daily Press and Bristol Mirror*, edition dated 14 December 1965.

'To me, kids are the greatest audience – and the greatest critics – in the world. When I knew it was a children's programme, I thought "I must really make something of this."'
Interviewed for the *Daily Mirror*, edition dated 23 April 1966.

'I predicted it would run for at least five years. I was universally scoffed at – by the press and the producers.

'It was magical. Children don't think of space as magical any more.'
Interviewed by Michael Wynn Jones for the *Radio Times*, edition dated 30 December 1972 – 5 January 1973.

'It may look like hindsight now, but I knew – I just knew – that *Dr Who* was going to be an enormous success. Don't ask me how. Not everybody thought as I did. I was laughed at and mocked a good deal for my initial faith in the series. But I believed in it. I remember telling producer Verity Lambert right at the start: "This is going to run for five years." And now it's ten years old.

'We did it forty-eight weeks a year in those days. You know, I couldn't go out into the High Street without a bunch of kids following me. I felt like the Pied Piper.

'People really used to take it literally. I'd get letters from boys swotting for O Levels asking complicated questions about time-ratio and the TARDIS. Dr Who might have been able to answer them. I'm afraid I couldn't.

'But *Dr Who* is certainly a test for any actor. Animals and children are renowned scene-stealers and we had both – plus an assortment of monsters that became popular in their own right. Look at the Daleks. They started in the second series and were an immediate success.

'I remember once when I was asked to open a local fete I dressed in my *Dr Who* clothes and turned up in an old limousine owned by a friend. I'll never forget the moment we arrived. The children just converged on the car cheering and shouting, their faces all lit-up. I knew then just how much *Dr Who* really meant to them.'
Interviewed by David Gillard for the *Radio Times Doctor Who* special, published 1973.

'I think that if I live to be ninety, a little of the magic of *Doctor Who* will still cling to me.'
Quoted in *The Making of Doctor Who* by Malcolm Hulke and Terrance Dicks, original source unknown.

ON PLAYING THE DOCTOR:

'With rehearsals every day, it's just like being on tour. I live in digs near the studios all week and only go home at weekends.

'I give the rest of the cast my experience and they help me memorise my lines.

'I hope the series runs for another five years, because that is about as long as I give myself in this business. After that, I shall retire. After all, I'm not 21 any more.'

Interviewed in 1964 for syndication in local newspapers.

'I see Dr Who as a kind of lama. No, not a camel. I mean one of those long-lived old boys out in Tibet who might be anything up to eight hundred years old, but look only seventy-five.'

Interviewed for *Reveille*, edition dated 7-13 January 1965.

'I'm the High Lama of the Planet. Although I portray a mixed-up old man, I have discovered I can hypnotise children. Hypnosis goes with the fear of the unknown. I communicate fear to children because they don't know where I'm going to lead them. This frightens them and is the attraction of the series.

'I am hypnotised by *Dr Who*. When I look at a script I find it unbelievable, so I allow myself to be hypnotised by it. Otherwise I would have nothing to do with it.

'Everyone calls me Dr Who and I feel like him. I get letters addressed to me as "Mr Who" and even "Uncle Who". But I love being this eccentric old man. I love it when my grand-daughter, Judith, calls me "barmy old grandad".

'I can see this series going for five years at least. It has already been sold in Australia, New Zealand and Canada, so my audience is getting bigger every week.

'I am getting more money than I've ever earned in my life.'

Interviewed for the *Sunday Mirror*, edition dated 7 February 1965.

'I am fortunate to be given *carte blanche* with the role. This allows me tremendous range to improve and build on the original outline of Dr Who.

'I think I represent a cross between the Wizard of Oz and Father Christmas. Yet I am always adding fragments to the part, always trying to expand it.'

Interviewed for the *Daily Express*, date unknown.

'Last year I was invited by Whitehall to be VIP guest of honour at a Battle of Britain display near Doncaster. I put on my Doctor Who clothes and appeared in a colourful battle of the Daleks – with planes dropping bombs etc. There were 11,000 people there. Kids smashed barriers to get near me. But the greatest moment for me was to be entertained afterwards by 150 of Britain's most famous flyers.'

Interviewed in 1966, source unknown.

'I love playing to children, because you can't pull the wool over their eyes. And when they write to me, you know, it's the truth, the whole truth and nothing but the truth.

'I don't mind being typecast again, even if it's in a bath-chair for the rest of my life.

'They give me pretty well *carte blanche*; and as a matter of fact Verity has said that when the time comes they will give me a bath-chair free. So I said I might take her up on that one day.'

Interviewed by Roy Plomley on 2 August 1965 for BBC Radio's *Desert Island Discs*.

'When children write to me they demand sometimes over and above what I can provide, but I send them a photograph and sign it and answer some of their letters. One little child wrote to me not so long ago, which is rather charming, she told me in her letter how much she liked the show, and she ended up by saying "When I grow up I will marry you" – aged 4?!'
Interviewed by Roy Plomley on 2 August 1965 for BBC Radio's *Desert Island Discs*.

'I find there is a great appeal in playing older parts. In this story I am 750 years old, because I am a man from the future, and I label myself "The High Lama of the Planets". To the viewer, I appear as a man between 60 and 70.'
Interviewed for the *Western Daily Press and Bristol Mirror*, edition dated 14 December 1965.

'I'm signed up until next October. And the BBC have flatteringly said that they'll keep it on as long as I'm willing to continue. But I want a change in conditions. It's not a question of money, the BBC pay me very well, though I work bloody hard for it.

'But you can never escape from the character – that's the agony of being Dr Who.

'When I was in films, you worked hard for twelve or sixteen weeks, but when you'd finished, it was gone, in the bag.

'Dr Who has given me a certain neurosis – and it's not easy for my wife to cope with. I get a little agitated, and it makes me a little irritable with people.

'In fact, Dr Who seems to be taking over.

'I get nine weeks off a year. But it takes me two weeks to unwind from the part. What I would like for the next contract is something like Dr Finlay. He runs for twenty-six episodes and then gets a twenty-six-week break.

'Once or twice I've put my foot down with a new director and told him "I know how to play Dr Who and I don't want you to intrude on it or alter it."'
Interviewed for the *Daily Mirror*, edition dated 23 April 1966.

'It was like manna from heaven to get away from uniformed parts. The original Doctor was pig-headed and irascible, certainly, but there was also an element of magic in him – and that was what I tried to bring out.'
Interviewed by Michael Wynn Jones for the *Radio Times*, edition dated 30 December 1972 – 5 January 1973.

ON MAKING STORY SUGGESTIONS:
'The idea of doing a Western story was my idea. Children will always adore cowboys and Indians. And I'd like to see characters from children's books come into the series.'
Interviewed for the *Daily Mirror*, edition dated 23 April 1966.

'Your letter to me I found very interesting but first let me say you could not have two Doctor Whos.

'I myself suggested this some four years ago by having a son. The idea was for me to have a wicked son, both looked alike and both had a TARDIS and travelled in time and space. In fact I would have had to play a dual role when meeting up with him.

'This idea was not acceptable to the BBC so I forgot it very quickly. But I still think

it would have worked and been exciting for the children.'
William Hartnell writing in July 1968 in a letter to fan Ian McLachlan.

ON HIS DEPARTURE FROM *DOCTOR WHO*:

'I think three years in one part is a good innings and it is time for a change.'
Quoted in a BBC press release dated 6 August 1966.

'Basically I left *Dr Who* because we did not see eye to eye over the stories and too much evil entered into the spirit of the thing. *Dr Who* was always noted and spelled out to me as a children's programme, and I wanted it to stay as such, but I'm afraid the BBC had other ideas. So did I, so I left. I didn't willingly give up the part.'
William Hartnell writing in July 1968 in a letter to fan Ian McLachlan.

'It is a long time ago now, and I think my hurt has healed, although I must say the events of those last few months are engraved on my heart.'
Quoted by Peter Haining in *The Doctor Who File*, purportedly from an interview conducted in April 1969 by John Ball, actual provenance uncertain.

'I was upset at coming out of *Dr Who*. But I didn't agree with what was happening to him. There was too much violence creeping into the series.
'It's too adult. It's meant for children, not grown-ups.
'There are lots of things you could learn from it now to start a major war.
'I've stopped watching. So have a lot of children – that's what I hear. They keep saying to me, "When are you coming back?"
'But it's all so different now.'
Interviewed in 1970 for a newspaper, details unknown.

ON OUTER SPACE:

'Space travel? Quite honestly it scares me stiff. I haven't the slightest wish to get in a rocket and zoom through the stratosphere. Somebody else can be the first man on the moon. It doesn't interest me at all.
'If God had wanted us to live on Mars, he'd have put us there in the first place. I prefer life on Earth.'
Interviewed for *Reveille*, edition dated 7-13 January 1965.

'Certainly I believe there is life on other planets – and they know there's life here but don't have the technology to get through.'
Interviewed by Michael Wynn Jones for the *Radio Times*, edition dated 30 December 1972 – 5 January 1973.

ON HIS HOME LIFE:

'My favourite pastimes are work, recreation, fishing, horse-riding and reading.'
William Hartnell writing in 1946 for *British National's Film Review*.

'My leisure interests before getting the part of Dr Who were strictly down to earth – gardening, fishing, sitting down and horse racing.

'I've been married thirty-nine years, and all of them to the same woman.'
Interviewed in 1964 for syndication in local newspapers.

'My grand-daughter Judith, who is seven, will probably be a TV producer one day. With Doctor Who in the middle of some terrible global disaster she'll ask me what I've done with that pretty tall hat I was wearing in the previous scene.

'I'm a countryman at heart. I love fishing, especially sea fishing for bass. I have a couple of rods down at Newhaven and go there whenever I get the chance.

'My favourite exercise is chopping wood.

'My wife and I are both keen bird-watchers. During the big freeze a few winters back, you'd be amazed at all the different birds which came to visit us. We kept them alive during that cold weather.

'We found out what food each bird liked, and got it for them somehow.

'Everyone has to escape somehow. Some people do it through TV. My escape is the English countryside, which I love.

'Nothing would ever make me leave it to explore life on some other planet.'
Interviewed for *Reveille*, edition dated 7-13 January 1965.

ON LIFE AFTER *DOCTOR WHO*:

'How lovely to be interviewed for a television feature. I thought people had forgotten me.

'Before I went into *Dr Who* I was always given sergeant-major parts like the one in *The Army Game*. I thought playing Dr Who would break my image. It didn't people still think of me as Dr Who or a bad-tempered sergeant major.

'Recently I was in *Softly, Softly* playing an ordinary old man. You've no idea how marvellous that was for a change.

'I read a lot of play-scripts. When I find the right one, I'm hoping I'll be able to put it on in the West End.'
Interviewed in 1968 for a newspaper, details unknown.

'For your information, the original Dr 'Who', which I think is me, is still running, and has reopened in New Zealand, Iran and Jamaica.

'My fan mail is still coming along, also, some from Australia, posted to the BBC.

'Of course you may use our names on the Fan Club notepaper, but keep my address to the blackout, in other words, to yourself.

'Also, let me add, I have had a nervous breakdown which has lasted nearly two years and am only just getting on my feet again. My wife has had to take the brunt of my illness, and no better nurse I can assure you.

'At the moment on holiday in Ireland.

'It was my own fault, much too long without a proper rest.

'A lot of parts come my way but, of little use to an ill man. Anon.

'Carry on and bless you together with fans.'
William Hartnell writing in a letter dated 11 August 1969 to *Doctor Who* Fan Club Secretary Graham Tattersall.

ON HIS RETURN TO TV IN THE ITV PLAY *CRIME OF PASSION*:

'I was ill for eighteen months. It was a double affair – pleurisy and a nervous breakdown.

'Now I'm back in the acting business. But I don't say "Yes" to everything. I turn things down if I don't think they're right.

'I would like to get back to more TV, but it is difficult because you don't always get the parts you want.

'And, of course, they fight shy about engaging expensive actors.'

Interviewed in 1970 for a newspaper, details unknown.

WILLIAM HARTNELL: AS OTHERS SAW HIM

CHRISTOPHER BARRY (DIRECTOR):

'I remember, unfortunately, that William Hartnell had a rather old fashioned attitude to race. Also, by the time I came back to work with him on some of the later episodes, he thought he was "the Doctor", not William Hartnell. But all the cast had assumed their characters' personalities, and it's a great short-cut on any series or serial if the actors know their roles. They will then tell the director, "This is what I ought to be doing," or "ought not," and if you disagree with them it's up to you to convince them. That's perfectly healthy – you stop rehearsal and talk about it.'

Interviewed by David J Howe and Rosemary Howe in 1987 for *The Frame* Issue 1.

IAN STUART BLACK (WRITER):

'I thought he was an excellent actor. I think I first became aware of him when I saw a little scene he had done in a British film called *Odd Man Out*. He was on screen for only about two or three minutes in a ninety-minute picture, playing the part of a bartender who was under great strain, and in that short space of time he really caught my attention and impressed me with his abilities. Then of course my children used to watch him in *Doctor Who*. So when I came to write for him I was very pleased.

'I've heard it said that Hartnell could be irritable, and that's true. Certainly he could be irritable with some of the younger actors and actesses in *Doctor Who* whom he didn't consider to be totally professional. You have to remember that the series was taking people who at the time were fairly unknown and still learning the business, although some of them became stars later on, and I think that every now and again he felt mildly irritated. In a sense he was carrying some of them. As far as I was concerned, though, his professionalism excused any sort of personal attitude he might have had. I didn't know him very well, but I liked him. He just took the script and he acted it.'

Interviewed by Stephen James Walker in 1992 for *The Frame* Issue 23 & 24.

DOUGLAS CAMFIELD (DIRECTOR):

'To be perfectly honest, Bill could be difficult to work with. He was cantankerous, wilful, dogmatic and never suffered fools gladly. But life was never dull in his company and he was generous and encouraging if he knew that, like him, you put the good of the programme above all. He had "star quality" in abundance, and brought a special magic to the part. He "created" the Doctor and provided the yardstick against which every other actor who plays the part is measured. He helped me to get started as a director

and I owe him a great deal. He was a remarkable man and I shall never forget him.'
Interviewed by Gary Hopkins in 1979 for *The Doctor Who Review* Issue 1.

ANN CARNEY (DAUGHTER):

'His grandchildren had given him a new interest in the younger generation, as they always do older people. He never had a son, so I was the only one, and Paul (his grandson) had stimulated a different approach to children. Their interest in the modern space age etc was reflected in his interest in that type of programme.'
Interviewed for *The Time Scanner* Issue 2, published in 1985.

FRANK COX (DIRECTOR):

'William Hartnell seemed to me to hate rehearsing. He had a great problem learning the lines, and if he found a biggish speech, of half a page or so, he would say "Christ. Bloody *Macbeth*!" My impression was that he loved being the Doctor, especially when it involved opening bazaars etc., but that he was insecure about his ability to do the work. William Russell was a great help to me, mediating between the irascible old Hartnell and the trembling novice director, Cox. It was all a nightmare quite honestly.'
Interviewed by Ian K McLachlan for *TARDIS* Volume 7 Number 1.

MICHAEL CRAZE (ACTOR):

'Mr Hartnell, god rest his soul, was a devil! He was a bit overpowering, quite frankly. I found him just difficult to work with. I don't think he wanted to leave. I think the powers-that-be got fed up and said "Let's change the whole format," and they redrafted the whole thing.'
Interviewed by Gordon Roxburgh for *TARDIS* Volume 7 Number 4.

RAYMOND CUSICK (DESIGNER):

'Bill Hartnell took acting very seriously, and was desperate as an actor to do *Doctor Who* – and then all the mail that came in was for the Daleks, some fibreglass model! I remember him telling me that the company which manufactured the Dalek playsuits sent a representative down to his house to give him one of them. He said, "I don't know why they brought this bloody thing down to me. What do I want a bloody Dalek for?"

'He was funny, Bill Hartnell, but on the face of it he didn't appear to have any sense of humour. For instance, we were all sitting around drinking coffee one day and reminiscing about our time in the theatre, recalling all the embarrassing things which had gone wrong during shows we'd been involved with, and he couldn't understand why we thought these things were funny!

'He started telling us a story, very seriously. Apparently he had been touring in a play with an actor-manager who was an alcoholic – a Henry Irving type, a real ham. In one scene, the actor-manager's character was supposed to have an argument with Hartnell's character and then leave the room through a door, where he would meet two other characters and they would discover what was happening – this was the denouement of the play. Anyway, one night, when the actor-manager came to make his exit, instead of going through the door he opened a big wardrobe next to it and went in! Hartnell stood there waiting for him to come out, because it didn't lead anywhere, but he didn't come out. The two actors outside were given a cue and came in, and they just had to busk it

– to make it up as they went along! After the curtain came down, they all rushed over to the wardrobe, opened the door, and there he was, fast asleep! "What happened?" they asked him. "Well, my dears, I came inside here, shut the door, and suddenly it was dark. So I thought I'd sit down and have a rest." Hartnell was absolutely serious when he told us this but, by the time he'd finished, we were falling about, it was so funny.'
Interviewed by Stephen James Walker and David J Howe in 1991 for *The Frame* **Issue 21 & 22.**

GERRY DAVIS (STORY EDITOR):

'I got on well with Billy Hartnell. I discovered it was no good confronting him, because as soon as you did he'd get angry. There was a lot of anger in him. What I would do was, having the necessary knowledge, talk about something to do with his past.

'For example, there was the occasion of the chair. He came onto the set, took one look at this chair, and said, "This is ridiculous – I can't sit in this chair, it's wrong! Take it away – and I won't do anything until it's taken away." They used to send for me, and I'd come down and say, "What's the matter?" He said, "Look at this. It's an insult, and completely wrong for the scene." So I replied, "Doesn't it look familiar to you? When Barrymore played his 1925 *Hamlet* he used a chair identical to that!" And Hartnell paused, thought, and then said, "Oh yes, I saw him." So we talked about Barrymore for five minutes, and then I said, "Well, sorry to disturb you, you'd better get on with the scene. But first we must get rid of that chair!" And he looked at me and said, "Oh no, that's fine, nothing wrong with that!"

'He was very nice to me and took a great interest in me, always asking after my daughters. It was the make-up and costume people he bullied.'
Interviewed by Richard Marson in 1987 for *Doctor Who Magazine* **No. 124.**

MICHAEL FERGUSON (DIRECTOR):

'I liked him a lot and got on quite well with him, possibly because I had already worked with him as an assistant floor manager. The AFM really has to get on well with everyone, otherwise it can make life very difficult. I had always looked after Bill on *The Mutants* and I found him very co-operative. He could be cantankerous, he could be snappy, he could be a bit huffy sometimes, but that was something I found not particularly remarkable then and I find even less remarkable now when I think of the burdens borne by the lead actor of a major and popular series.'
Interviewed by Stephen James Walker in 1991 for *The Frame* **Issue 18.**

HEATHER HARTNELL (WIFE):

'The cast all got on awfully well. Of course he had his favourites. He loved Bill Russell, who was the first of his assistants, and Peter Purves who joined later. He got on awfully well with Bill Russell and Jackie Hill and Carole Ann Ford, who was his grand-daughter in the beginning. Oh! They all got on well together. Well, they had to, because they were making it in a very tiny studio and they were all on top of each other; they had to get on well together or else they would have come to blows I would imagine!

'He loved the historical stories because, like all actors, he loved dressing up in great gay clothes. He loved stories like the French Revolution one and *Marco Polo* and things like that, because they all had gorgeous, glamorous clothes. I don't know what his favourite story was. Perhaps *Marco Polo*, because they had great fun doing that. But of course his favourite monster had to be the Daleks. The point was that somehow he could get the better of all the other monsters, but the Daleks always popped up again! And William felt that he was never going to get the better of them.

'The performances that he was really proud of were in films, particularly a film called *The Way Ahead* and a film called *The Yangtse Incident*, they were service films. He loved doing *Doctor Who*, though. He absolutely adored it, because he always loved children and always had a way with them. He used to stay five nights a week in a little flat in London and then come home to Mayfield, where we lived, at the weekend. I used to drive over and meet him at Tunbridge Wells station, and the local children got to know that he'd arrive at Tunbridge Wells on a Saturday morning and they'd be waiting for him. It was very like the Pied Piper of Hamlyn, walking through the streets down to the car park. They knew it was him, and if he went into a shop they would wait outside, then follow him again. Well of course he loved it because they were children; he loved children.'
Interviewed for *No, Not the Mind Probe* Issue 1, published January 1985.

WARIS HUSSEIN (DIRECTOR):

'William Hartnell was Verity Lambert's idea for the role of the Doctor, but at first he was quite reluctant to accept it. We took him out to lunch one day and I had to talk literally non-stop to try to convince him. He had a number of worries. He had recently done a series – *The Army Game* – and didn't really want to get involved with something else which took up so much of his time. Also, he didn't quite know if he wanted to play such a peculiar character. He seemed to think that, by asking him to play the part of an eccentric, we were implying that he was eccentric himself – which of course he was! Ultimately, though, he agreed, and that was due largely to these diplomatic approaches from Verity and me, so I feel fairly strongly that I was very influential there.

'William was very much a prejudiced person, and I had a strong suspicion that he was prejudiced about me to start with. What was interesting, though, was that he never allowed it to interfere with his work, and gradually he came to like me a great deal, so in a way you could say there was something achieved through that! Once he realised that I knew what I was doing he really was supportive. He never, ever made things difficult for me, which he could have done if he'd wanted to. I had a lot of respect for the man. I think everyone's entitled to their opinions; but if you can change some of them, all for the better.'
Interviewed by Stephen James Walker and David J Howe in 1990 for *The Frame* Issue 16.

INNES LLOYD (PRODUCER):

'Bill had been in the role for a long time. He was getting on and he was getting tired. I thought that the tiredness and the irascibility were not going to be good a) for the show and b) for him – for him, mostly – and I would always have advised him to leave. I remember taking him home after the party on his last night, at about one in the morning. I told him "Bill, now you can have a rest" and he said "Yes, I'll be very pleased."

'I also recall him saying to me – though I don't know if he said it to anyone else – "There's only one man in England who can take over, and that's Patrick Troughton"! I think he was happy when he heard that Pat would be doing it.'
Interviewed by Stephen James Walker and Peter Linford in 1990 for *The Frame* Issue 14.

RICHARD MARTIN (DIRECTOR):
'William Hartnell disliked quite a lot but worked like a white man and worried like Reagan's bodyguard.'
Interviewed by Ian K McLachlan in 1983 for *TARDIS* Volume 8 Number 2.

DEREK MARTINUS (DIRECTOR):
'Hartnell was very quick to size me up; he did that with all the new directors. He was a pretty formidable figure, with a good track record in films, and he liked to present himself as an imposing, knowledgable sort of guy. He definitely liked to be the star.

'I remember Hartnell saying to me during one of the earlier episodes that he had been told he could go on as the Doctor for as long as he liked, that he had *carte blanche* over the scripts, and that when he finished the series was finished. He really believed he was the series, poor chap. He could not envisage it existing without him. He said "How can they replace Doctor Who? It's called *Doctor Who*, and if I don't do it, that's the end of it. They keep asking me to carry on, but I don't know how long I'll do it."'
Interviewed by Stephen James Walker and David J Howe in 1991 for *The Frame* Issue 21 & 22.

PETER PURVES (ACTOR):
'I liked Bill a lot. I thought he was a smashing bloke. Very difficult to work with, but he was a perfectionist in his own way and it came out as rattiness with directors and producers. He had a strong sense of what was wrong and what was right. He did have a bit of trouble learning his lines sometimes and used to get them wrong on takes, but that sort of thing happens and I still think he was the best Doctor by a long way. I had a very good relationship with Bill and he used to take me and my wife out for meals. He was a lovely man. Very entertaining and, I think, a very good actor.'
Interviewed in 1986 for *Flight Through Eternity* No. 2.

'Television acting is really quite confined, and he would always hold his hands up in front of his chest, because if they were down by his sides and he was in close-up you wouldn't see them. If he made a gesture it wouldn't be a big one, because again that would take his hands out of shot. Instead, he used to make all those neat little gestures of his.'
Interviewed in 1990 for the British Satellite Broadcasting *Doctor Who* weekend.

WILLIAM RUSSELL (ACTOR):
'Billy was marvellous, very professional. He had all the switches in the TARDIS marked out exactly in his mind, and he thought up the idea about the Doctor always getting my name wrong. Billy wasn't at all like the Doctor off set. He was a very professional actor who just did his job, in his own way.'
Interviewed by Graeme Wood, John Brand and Andy Lennard in 1984 for *The Merseyside Local Group Megazine* Volume 2 Issue 17.

JULIA SMITH (DIRECTOR):
'Mr Hartnell was a terrific professional and totally dedicated to the part he was playing. At times I think he honestly believed he was Doctor Who. Any actor supporting a series over a number of years gets very weary, and his age must have added to this. He was

finding it difficult to remember lines, which was one of the reasons he was given two companions instead of one. He was also given very athletic things to do by a lot of the writers and, as a director, one had to save him as much as possible.'
Interviewed in 1982 by Ian K McLachlan for *TARDIS* Volume 7 Number 2.

DONALD TOSH (STORY EDITOR):

'Bill was a hardened old pro, but he was also getting on in years. Time and time again he had the weight of the explanation to do, so as to make the whole thing acceptable and believable. He would stray away from the script and bumble and ad-lib his way through so that at times we tore our hair and there were some great old fights. However, usually when we came to look at the finished product, Bill had made it make sense and it looked fine.

'John Wiles and I had many battles royal with him, but that is true of any long-running programme – there are always arguments with the star. Bill cared very, very deeply for the programme. He was desperately sorry when the time came and he had to give it up. The success that *Doctor Who* has lived on since it began is greatly due to what Bill Hartnell brought to the programme.

'I think towards the end he almost began to lose the dividing line between his own reality and the fantasy reality of the Doctor. There were times when one knew he was going to be difficult and one had to head off trouble if one could, for our schedule was terribly tight and time was always at a premium. I recall once at a read-through Bill had a long and complicated speech which was absolutely vital, and I knew that he was going to ask for it to be rewritten or cut. As soon as the read was over I rushed across and congratulated him. I told him that it was a vital speech and he had read it quite beautifully, and that I had written it especially for him. Everyone likes sudden and surprising flattery so he was slightly taken aback, then smiled, said "Thank you" and went away and learned every word, and on transmission delivered it absolutely perfectly.'
Interviewed by Jan Vincent-Rudzki, Stephen Payne and Ian Levine in 1978 for *TARDIS* Volume 3 Number 3.

EDMUND WARWICK (ACTOR WHO DOUBLED FOR HARTNELL):

'He was incredibly kind. He wanted me to be good in the part, obviously, and so when we weren't rehearsing he spent a lot of his spare time showing me exactly how he held his head and how he stood, which was very generous of him really because actors are not all that kind as a rule.

'He could be tetchy, but when he wanted to help he was most helpful. The thing that made him tetchy was when scripts were not up to scratch.
'When Hartnell was there, he really was the most important person of the lot. Things went according to the way Hartnell wanted them to go, rather than anything else.'
Interviewed by John Bowman in 1989 for *The Frame* Issue 10.

JOHN WILES (PRODUCER):

'He wasn't as old as he thought he was. When he was with me he treated himself almost as a 75 year old. It may well have been that he was physically not in the best of health and so could not learn lines. Consequently, studio days could be absolute purgatory for everybody. If Bill was in an unhappy state then it put everyone into a terrible state.

'Eventually my directors devised a code for me. They would turn to their production assistant and say, "You had better phone the designer," which meant, "Get John down here quick," so that Bill wouldn't know I'd been summoned.

'One day I got a call from the studio to say that all the dressers had come out on strike! Now this was a cataclysmic start to a day in the studio where you depend on all your back-up all the time. Bill had simply offended his dresser, who had then complained, and so the entire staff had walked out. And this was on the *one* day you had to get an entire episode recorded. So there were those kind of pressures all the time.

'Peter Purves was very supportive and helped as much as he could. I imagine it must have been very nerve-wracking for him, in that he never knew from one day to the next what was coming from Bill.

'The feeling from above was that the show worked as it was, and would continue to run as long as Bill Hartnell played the Doctor. So perhaps I was mad for wanting to change it. But our audience research had shown the production office that many adults watched the show and so I felt we could do better than we were doing.

'I do remember suggesting to Bill once that we take the TARDIS to a planet where there is no gravity and no oxygen – where he would have to wear a spacesuit. You never heard such an uproar in all your life …'
Interviewed by Jeremy Bentham in 1983 for *Doctor Who Monthly* **Winter Special 1983/84.**

ANNEKE WILLS (ACTRESS):
'As you have probably heard from other people, Bill Hartnell was a very tricky character. Very, very tricky. So the rest of the cast would stick together, and have a sort of reality check! His departure was all pretty emotional, I think, and rather difficult.'
Interviewed by Stephen James Walker in 1991 for *The Frame* **Issue 20.**

CHARACTER – THE FIRST DOCTOR

The character of the Doctor was devised by BBC Head of Drama Sydney Newman in April 1963. His staff had by this point already done a considerable amount of work on developing a proposed new science fiction series, but it was Newman himself who decided that the central character ought to be, as he later put it:

> A man who is 764 years old – who is senile but with extraordinary flashes of intellectual brilliance. A crotchety old bugger – any kid's grandfather – who had, in a state of terror, escaped in his machine from an advanced civilisation on a distant planet which had been taken over by some unknown enemy. He didn't know who he was any more, and neither did the Earthlings, hence his name, Dr Who. He didn't know precisely where his home was. He did not fully know how to operate the time-space machine.
>
> In short, he never intended to come to our Earth. In trying to go home he simply pressed the wrong buttons – and kept on pressing the wrong buttons, taking his human passengers backwards and forwards, and in and out of time and space.

The earliest contemporary description of the Doctor's character appeared in a format document prepared during the early part of April 1963 by BBC staff writer/adaptor C E Webber, in consultation with Newman and with the Head of the Script Department, Donald Wilson. It read as follows:

> DR WHO
> A frail old man lost in space and time. They give him this name because they don't know who he is. He seems not to remember where he has come from; he is suspicious and capable of sudden malignance; he seems to have some undefined enemy; he is searching for something as well as fleeing from something. He has a 'machine' which enables them to travel together through time, through space, and through matter.

The same document later went on to give a description of the part that the Doctor would play within the continuity of the stories:

> He remains a mystery. From time to time the other three discover things about him, which turn out to be false or inconclusive (i.e. any writer inventing an interesting explanation must undercut it within his own serial-time, so that others can have a go at the mystery). They think he may be a criminal fleeing from his own time; he evidently fears pursuit through time. Sometimes they doubt his loss of memory, particularly as he does have flashes of memory. But also, he is searching for something which he desires heart-and-soul, but which he can't define. If, for instance, they were to go back to King Arthur's time, Dr Who would be immensely moved by the idea of the Quest for the Grail. That is, as regards him, a Quest Story, a Mystery Story, and a Mysterious Stranger Story, overall.
>
> While his mystery may never be solved, or may perhaps be revealed slowly over a very long run of stories, writers will probably like to know an answer. Shall we say:
>
> *The Secret of Dr Who*: In his own day, somewhere in our future, he decided to search for a time or for a society or for a physical condition which is ideal, and having found it, to stay there. He stole the machine and set forth on his quest. He is thus an extension of the scientist who has opted out, but he has opted farther than ours can do, at the moment. And having opted out, he is disintegrating.
>
> One symptom of this is his hatred of scientists, inventors, improvers. He can get into a rare paddy when faced with a cave man trying to invent a wheel. He malignantly tries to stop progress (the future) wherever he finds it, while searching for his ideal (the past). This seems to me to involve slap up-to-date moral problems, and old ones too.
>
> In story terms, our characters see the symptoms and guess at the nature of his trouble, without knowing details; and always try to help him find a home in time and space. Wherever he goes he tends to make ad hoc enemies; but also there is a mysterious enemy pursuing him implacably

every when: someone from his own original time, probably. So, even if the secret is out by the fifty-second episode, it is not the whole truth. Shall we say:

The Second Secret of Dr Who: The authorities of his own (or some other future) time are not concerned merely with the theft of an obsolete machine; they are seriously concerned to prevent his monkeying with time, because his secret intention, when he finds his ideal past, is to destroy or nullify the future.

If ever we get this far into Dr Who's secret, we might as well pay a visit to his original time. But this is way ahead for us too. Meanwhile, proliferate stories.

Sydney Newman, when presented with a copy of Webber's document, made a number of handwritten annotations to it, indicating that he was less than happy with some of these suggestions for the Doctor's character. Beside the section headed 'The Secret of Dr Who' he wrote:

Don't like this at all. Dr Who will become a kind of father figure – I don't want him to be a reactionary.

Beside 'The Second Secret of Dr Who' he commented simply:

Nuts!

Newman's idea for the character was that he should be an old man who, although grumpy and partly senile, would have a heart of gold; and who, far from hating scientists and inventors, would regard 'science, applied and theoretical, as being as natural as eating.'

The next version of the format document, dated 15 May 1963, contained the following revised description of the Doctor's character and of his relationship with his companions (one of whom was to have been called Cliff):

DR WHO

About 650, a frail old man lost in space and time. They give him this name because they don't know who he is. He seems not to remember where he comes from, but he has flashes of garbled memory which indicated that he was involved in a galactic war, and still fears pursuit by some undefined enemy. He is suspicious of the other three, and capable of sudden malignance. They want to help him find himself, but Cliff never quite trusts him.

All the other suggestions, including the 'Secrets of Dr Who' had by this point been dropped.

The character was further refined over the following weeks. The finalised version of the format document, produced by story editor David Whitaker around early July 1963 and sent out to freelance writers to invite them to submit ideas to the series, contained the following description:

DOCTOR WHO:

A name given to him by his two unwilling fellow travellers, Barbara Wright and Ian Chesterton, simply because they don't know who he is and he is happy to extend the mystery surrounding him. They do know that he is a Doctor of Science and that he is over sixty. He is frail-looking but wiry and tough like an old turkey and this latter is amply demonstrated whenever he is forced to run away from danger. His watery blue eyes are continually looking around in bewilderment and occasionally suspicion clouds his face when he assumes his decisions are being opposed by his earthly 'passengers'. He can be enormously cunning once he feels he is being conspired against and he sometimes acts with impulse more than reasoned intelligence. He can be quite considerate and wise and he responds to intelligence eagerly. His forgetfulness and vagueness alternate with flashes of brilliant thought and deduction. He has escaped from the 50th Century because he has found life at that time to be unpleasant and he is searching for another existence into which he can settle. Insofar as his operation of the 'ship' is concerned he is much like the average driver of a motor car in that he is its master when it works properly and its bewildered slave when it is temperamental. Because he is somewhat pathetic, his grand-daughter and the other two continually try to help him find 'home' but they are never sure of his motives.

It was during July 1963 that William Hartnell was cast as the Doctor. Unlike some of his successors, he had little initial input into the development of the character, being content to be guided by the requirements of the scripts and by the wishes of his producer and directors. He did however recall in a later interview that he considered the Doctor to be 'too bad tempered' as depicted in the series' untransmitted pilot episode, and that he told the production team as much. Sydney Newman also disliked the rather arrogant, supercilious Doctor of the pilot, feeling that he was not 'funny' or 'cute' enough, and asked that the character be softened in the remount for transmission.

The Doctor's costume was also changed between the pilot and the remount, from a plain dark suit and tie to a more eccentric outfit with a high wing collar and cravat. These formal, Edwardian-style clothes, together with the wig of long white hair that Hartnell was asked to wear for the role, helped to set the Doctor apart from the norm of paternal, lab-coated boffins who had been a stock feature of children's adventure serials in the past. Even more innovative was the fact that he was an alien time traveller from an advanced civilisation. While it was hardly unexpected for a science fiction series to involve extraterrestrial life-forms, to have an alien as the central figure was a very novel idea indeed. This aspect of the Doctor's background was first made clear to viewers in the following speech that he delivered in the first transmitted episode, *An Unearthly Child*:

'Have you ever thought what it's like to be wanderers in the fourth dimension? Have you? To be exiles? Susan and I are cut off from our own planet, without friends or protection. But one day we shall get back. Yes, one day, one day.'

This is one of the few references ever made to the Doctor's desire, as mooted in the early format documents, to return 'home'. His principal motivation in the transmitted stories seems to be, rather, to explore the universe and to see its many wonders. Whenever his 'ship', the TARDIS, materialises in a new location, he is always eager to venture outside and find out what fresh mysteries and wonders lie in store. This passion for discovery appears to be, at times, almost a compulsion; in the opening episode of the second story, *The Mutants* (sometimes referred to as *The Daleks* to avoid confusion with the Third Doctor story of the same title), it leads him to play a deception on his three travelling companions – Ian, Barbara and his grand-daughter Susan – so that they will be forced to go along with his plan to visit a mysterious city that he has seen in the distance.

Plainly he likes to get his own way; and his confidence in his own abilities is such that it occasionally borders on the arrogance of the untransmitted pilot. 'The mind will always triumph,' he announces at one point during *The Mutants*. 'With me to lead them, the Thals are bound to succeed'. In the early part of the first season, he can indeed be regarded more as an anti-hero than as an out-and-out hero. While he is essentially a kindly, sentimental, compassionate character, and while he certainly mellows quite considerably with the passage of time, he can often be brusque and irritable, and at times even violent – displaying perhaps the flashes of 'sudden malignance' described in early versions of the series' format document.

This Doctor is not one who sees himself as some sort of crusader against universal evil, nor one who goes looking for trouble. Certainly he is a humane man, who regards life in all its various forms as something to be valued and respected and who consistently sides with the wronged and the oppressed against the forces of tyranny and evil; but he does not actively court confrontation and conflict. His concern for the safety of himself and Susan, and later for that of his human travelling companions, means that he is quite content on occasion to withdraw from a dangerous situation and let discretion be the better part of valour.

Nor does he seek to stand out from the crowd; on the contrary, he prefers to remain in the background and keep a low profile. Whether he be on an alien planet like Marinus or Xeros or on Earth in a historical period such as the French Revolution or the American Wild West era, he always endeavours to assimilate the local customs and win the acceptance of the indigenous population. He is, in short, an observer rather than an active participant – unless forced by circumstances to become involved.

The necessity for the Doctor to remain an observer arose largely out of the attitude that producer Verity Lambert and story editor David Whitaker took towards the concept of time travel. This was set out by Whitaker in a reply of 1 May 1964 to a letter received from a viewer, Mr R Adams of Quinton, Birmingham:

> Undoubtedly one must look at time as a roadway going up hill and down the other side. You and I are in the position of walking along that road, whereas Doctor Who is in the position of being placed on top of the hill. He can look backward and he can look forward, in fact the whole pattern of the road is laid out for him. But you will appreciate of course that he cannot interfere with that road in any way whatsoever. He cannot divert it, improve it or destroy it. The basis of time travelling is that all things that happen are fixed and unalterable, otherwise of course the whole structure of existence would be thrown into unutterable confusion and the purpose of life itself would be destroyed. Doctor Who is an observer. What we are concerned with is that history, like justice, is not only done

but can be seen to be done. Where we are allowed to use fiction, of course, is that we allow the Doctor and his friends to interfere in the personal histories of certain people from the past. We can get away with this provided they are not formally established as historical characters. We cannot tell Nelson how to win at the Battle of the Nile because no viewer would accept such a hypothesis. However, we can influence one Captain on board a minor ship in Napoleon's armada.

As far as going into the future, learning facts, and returning to relay them, I am not sure that society is prepared to accept something until it is ready for it. There have been many long-sighted predictions in the world which have been ignored. Much of science fiction as written in the twenties and thirties is now established scientific fact today; such as space travel, for example; and H G Wells in *The War of the Worlds* came very near to future truths.

This rationale of time travel came to the fore on a number of occasions during the series' first season, most notably in *The Aztecs* when Barbara was seen to discover the futility of attempting to overturn the Aztecs' tradition of human sacrifice. Dennis Spooner, when he took over from David Whitaker as story editor, adopted a rather more flexible approach, indicating in his story *The Time Meddler* that the Doctor's opposition to changing established history was a matter of personal policy rather than a belief that to do so was impossible. The whole concept of the Monk character introduced in that story depended upon the fact that history could indeed be altered and redirected onto a new course. Even under this more flexible regime, however, it remained the case that the Doctor was fiercely opposed to such meddling, as evidenced in his attitude towards the Monk – who, apart from Susan, was the only other character from the Doctor's own planet to be seen during this era of *Doctor Who*.

Further evidence of David Whitaker's philosophy – which was of particular importance in the early development of the Doctor's character – can be gleaned from the following essay, entitled 'Who is Dr Who?', written for the *Dr Who Annual* published in 1965:

After Sir Isaac Newton came Dr Albert Einstein. After Einstein came Dr Who. His is the master-mind that spans all spatial infinity and all temporal eternity in his strange small ship, the TARDIS.

No one knows where he came from. He is human in shape and speech and manner. He appears to be old and feeble and at the same time young and strong and active, as though the normal processes of ageing had passed him by.

Inclined to be absent-minded and forgetful, he is also very much subject to fits of impatience whenever his will is thwarted and whenever his ideas are doubted. He likes his own way all the time and can sulk like any baby when he doesn't get it. He is, after all, a citizen of all Space and Time and that must make a man feel there's nothing much he doesn't know.

He is mostly very gentle and kind-hearted and he has the utmost respect for life of any kind, small and feeble or monstrous and mighty. He has seen more specimens of living creatures than any other person in the history of all the worlds and his heart is big enough to respect every one of the countless forms life has taken in all the ages and all the worlds.

A planet in our galaxy would seem to have been his original home, but he has journeyed so many millions of miles and covered so many millions of years back into the past and forward into the future, that perhaps even the good Doctor himself does not much remember his origins ...

The TARDIS holds within itself many marvellous inventions which would be scientific miracles in many of the spheres Dr Who has visited. To him, they are commonplace tools and instruments, methods of doing what he wants to do.

Headlong he passes, in his TARDIS, through all of Space and Time. Where is he going? What is his objective? What goal draws him on through the endless spheres, the millions of ages? No one knows. Perhaps he himself has long forgotten, so distant, in our years, is the time when he first set out on his odyssey. Are his voyages haphazard and merely satisfying the urge to travel everywhere and see everything, or is he seeking something definite? Again, no one knows.

Ceaselessly and restlessly he moves on, along the infinite strands of energy that criss-cross all Space-Time. There is the deep and always unsatisfied curiosity of the scientist in him. There is the love of all life which fights against its surroundings.

Strange as his many adventures and experiences have been, how strange will be that time and place, no matter how far away or how distant in time, that point in Infinity-Eternity when, at long last, Dr Who will reach his final goal and find that for which he is searching.

Mysterious and other-worldly though his origins may be, the Doctor's physical capabilities appear to be not much greater than those of a human being from Earth. He is actually rather frail, suffering all the aches and pains of old age, and often carries a walking stick given to him by Kublai Khan, a fellow sufferer, in the first season story *Marco Polo*. Mentally, however, his powers are somewhat superior. He delights in his ability to outwit his opponents, such as when, in *The Space Museum*, the Morok Governor of the museum tries to interrogate him with a mind-reading device and he projects an extraordinary series of false images onto the screen. He can even sense sometimes when an evil presence is nearby, as he indicates in *The War Machines*, and it is revealed in *The Sensorites* that he has a certain degree of telepathic ability.

At times, it must be said, his successes appear to result more from luck than from good judgment. He tends to muddle his way through situations, and often has a slightly bewildered air about him. If he seems a near-charlatan in some of his earlier stories, then in some of the later ones he could even be thought slightly senile, as Ian actually speculates in *The Rescue*. Indeed, there are aspects of his behaviour – such as his occasional bursts of almost hysterical laughter – that appear positively manic.

This trait of endearingly absent-minded bumbling was largely William Hartnell's contribution to the role. Hartnell regarded *Doctor Who* as a children's programme first and foremost, and was always looking for ways of making the Doctor more appealing to that audience. It was he who, for instance, came up with the idea that the Doctor should often get his companion Ian's surname wrong: so instead of saying 'Chesterton' he would call him anything from 'Chesserman' (in *The Mutants*) to 'Chatterton' (when remembering him in *The Massacre of St Bartholomew's Eve*). It was he, too, who gave the Doctor his indignant 'humphs!' and his frequent high-pitched chuckles. As his widow Heather later recalled, 'I know Bill would have liked to have put more comedy into the part, and to a degree he did try with those exasperated little coughs and splutters.'

Hartnell saw the Doctor as a wizard-like figure rather than a scientist. He was convinced that he knew better than the series' writers how the character should be played, and would actively resist the inclusion of obscure or technical terms in his dialogue. Writer Donald Cotton recalled sharing a taxi with him on one occasion and being asked if, instead of writing lines for the Doctor, he could in future simply give an indication of what he wanted the character to say and leave it to the actor to come up with the actual words.

Part of Hartnell's motivation in this regard may well have been to lessen the very considerable burden of dialogue that he, as the series' lead, had to carry in each episode. He was by this stage of his career finding it increasingly difficult to memorise his lines, and he lacked the advantage afforded to actors in later years of being able to stop for frequent retakes (video editing being a technically difficult and expensive process to achieve in the mid-Sixties.) There is however no doubt that he had very strong views as to how the Doctor should speak and behave, and that much of the character's on-screen appeal, which made him a hero to millions of children worldwide, was down to the actor's own skilful and engaging performance.

Aside from the aforementioned mellowing, and the refinements of interpretation made by Hartnell in his performance, no radical changes in the characterisation of the Doctor occurred during the three years of the actor's tenure in the role. The description given in the format guide sent out to writers towards the end of the first Doctor's era was much the same as that in the one prepared by David Whitaker in 1963 – and in some respects harked back to the even earlier C E Webber version. It read as follows:

> DR WHO
>
> A name given by the first travelling companions because neither he nor they knew who he was. He is 650 years old. Frail but wiry and tough like an old turkey – this is demonstrated when he is forced to run from danger. He has an air of bewilderment and occasionally a look of utter malevolence clouds his face as he suspects his travelling companions of being part of some giant conspiracy he cannot understand. He has flashes of garbled memory which indicate he was involved in a galactic war and still fears some undefined enemy. Because he is somewhat 'pathetic' his friends continually try to help him but are now and again bewildered by his mental agility and superior intellect – they are never quite sure of his 'motives' in dealing with a situation. He is vague – inquisitive. Has an interest in people and problems to do with people and civilizations. His ability to deal with highly complex problems, both scientific and menacing, comes, not really from intellect, but from experience and great age.
>
> He and his two companions must be the pivot around which any story revolves – their relationship in the different ways they deal with the situation.

He is fond, in an uncle's way, of his two companions. Ben he finds somewhat meddlesome, and irritating in the expressions he uses (Cockney), amusing because of his cautiousness.

Polly represents much that he finds annoying in modern girls – her flippancy, independence and her impulsiveness. Nevertheless he feels protective towards her.

Even in his last story, *The Tenth Planet*, the Doctor has lost none of his restlessness and curiosity, ushering his companions out of the TARDIS to investigate even though he knows that they have arrived in 'the coldest place on Earth' – Antarctica. Nor has his moral courage diminished, as is evident from the outrage he expresses at the Cybermen's unfeeling nature: 'Love, pride, hate, fear! Have you no emotions, sir?' However, when he collapses part-way through the story, apparently exhausted, and later speculates that his old body might be 'wearing a bit thin', it becomes clear that something very unusual is happening. This is confirmed in the closing moments of the final episode, when he demonstrates perhaps his most remarkable and unexpected ability of all and undergoes a complete transformation of his physical appearance …

ESTABLISHING THE MYTH

Every era of *Doctor Who* brings new elements to the series' developing mythology. Story after story, new facts are invented by the programme's writers and added to what is already known of the Doctor's universe. Some new pieces of this ever-growing jigsaw puzzle interlock neatly with what has gone before, while others fit so poorly that the viewer is forced to start rebuilding the picture from scratch. Many hard-core *Doctor Who* fans expend great amounts of time and energy trying to find an order that gives all the seemingly contradictory facts and storylines some kind of logical continuity.

The three most enduring elements of *Doctor Who*'s mythology were all introduced within the space of the first two stories. These were the TARDIS, the Daleks and of course the good Doctor himself.

Of the three, the Doctor is by far the most mysterious. There are however a number of tantalising clues given during the first Doctor's era which reveal some insights into the time traveller's background.

One of the most enigmatic aspects of the character is his name. Susan refers to him as 'Grandfather' or occasionally, when speaking to others, as 'the Doctor'. When Ian, one of Susan's teachers at Coal Hill School, addresses him as 'Doctor Foreman' in *100,000 BC*, the Doctor's brow creases as he mutters 'Eh? Doctor who? What's he talking about?', leaving little doubt that this is not his name – Susan has apparently taken the surname Foreman for the purposes of the school records, presumably because 'I M Foreman' is the name on the doors of the junkyard where the TARDIS stands. The only instance of the Doctor being called 'Doctor Who' is in *The War Machines*, where the computer WOTAN and its controlled human slaves use the term; although, in *The Gunfighters*, when Bat Masterson asks him 'Doctor who?', the Doctor does respond 'Yes, quite right!'

In *The Dalek Invasion of Earth*, the Doctor berates the human resistance fighter Tyler for calling him 'Doc': 'I prefer "Doctor",' he explains to the weary rebel. The Doctor also tells his companion Steven not to use this diminutive form, but it takes the astronaut slightly longer to get used to the idea.

The term 'Doctor' does not denote a medical qualification. In *100,000 BC*, he says, 'I'm not a Doctor of medicine'; in *Marco Polo* he tells Kublai Khan the same thing; in *The Aztecs*, he corrects the assumption that he is a medical man by explaining that he is 'a scientist and an engineer – a builder of things, not a healer'; and in *The Rescue* he tells Ian, after giving him a cursory medical examination, 'It's a pity I didn't get that degree, isn't it?'

Equally mysterious is the character's background. First of all there is his grand-daughter, Susan. There is little doubt that she is indeed his grand-daughter, and that this is not simply an unusual term of affection. In *Inside the Spaceship* he refers to himself as being Susan's grandfather and in *The Sensorites* he again clearly states that she is his own grand-child. He also demonstrates obvious familial affection for the girl. What is never explained is the whereabouts of the Doctor's own son or daughter – as, if he has a grand-daughter, he must have had at least one child of his own. This of course assumes that his race reproduces in the same way as ours, but there is never any suggestion to the contrary. The Doctor's decision to leave Susan on Earth with David Campbell at the end of *The Dalek Invasion of Earth* could otherwise seem rather thoughtless; or, at any rate, could leave David in for a shock if he and Susan ever decided to have children!

What is known for sure is that the Doctor and Susan are not from Earth. 'Susan and I are cut off from our own planet, without friends or protection,' the Doctor tells Ian and Barbara in *100,000 BC*. Susan adds that she was 'born in another time, another world'; and in *Marco Polo*, when asked how far away her home is, she says that it is 'as far as a night star'. In *The Sensorites*, she confirms: 'Grandfather and I don't come from Earth. It's ages since we've seen our planet. It's quite like Earth, but at night the sky is a burnt orange, and the leaves on the trees are bright silver.' At the end of the same story, she asks the Doctor when they will return to their own planet, and her tells her, 'I don't know, my dear, this old ship of mine seems to be an aimless thing.'

There are other pointers to their alien origins, too, like the Doctor not knowing what cricket is when the TARDIS materialises in the middle of a Test Match at the Oval in *The Daleks' Master Plan*. In *The Mutants*, he states, 'I was once a pioneer amongst my own people'; and, again, in *The Daleks' Master Plan*, he describes himself as 'a citizen of the universe – and a gentleman to boot!' In *The Rescue*, Barbara tells Vicki that the Doctor is 'from a different age, a different planet altogether.'

This is about all we ever learn of the origins of the Doctor and Susan, although Carole Ann Ford (who played Susan) once revealed that the cast had developed their own ideas as to why the pair were travelling about as they were. They had postulated that their own planet had undergone some violent natural catastrophe, like an earthquake or a volcano, and that they had fled in order to survive. No reference was made to this in the televised stories, however, and in fact it was arguably contradicted by the Doctor's meeting with another of his race – the Monk in *The Time Meddler*. The Monk, like the Doctor, is a renegade in search of excitement – but in his case the excitement is derived not from exploring the universe and seeing its wonders but from interfering with the course of history for the sake of his own amusement. The Monk crosses paths with the Doctor once more in *The Daleks' Master Plan*, and is still meddling and interfering; but no other members of the Doctor's race appear or are mentioned during the era of the first Doctor.

At the start of the series, the Doctor and Susan have been living in 20th Century England for five months, and Susan is distraught at the prospect of having to leave. The suggestion is that she and her grandfather have previously led a very unsettled, nomadic life to which she has little wish to return. In *Marco Polo*, she says 'One day we'll know all the mysteries of the skies, and we'll stop our wanderings.' During the course of the transmitted stories, details of a number of their earlier adventures are revealed. These include a visit to the planet Quinnis in the fourth universe, where they nearly lost the TARDIS (this was four or five journeys prior to *Inside The Spaceship*); a meeting with Gilbert and Sullivan (from whom the Doctor acquired the coat borrowed by Ian at the end of *Inside the Spaceship*); witnessing the metal seas of Venus (as mentioned by Susan in *Marco Polo*); and a trip to the planet Esto, where the plants communicate by thought transference (*The Sensorites*).

The Doctor has met Pyrrho, the inventor of scepticism (*The Keys of Marinus*); travelled to Henry VIII's court, where he threw a parson's nose at the King in order to be sent to the Tower of London and thereby regain the TARDIS (*The Sensorites*); and encountered Beau Brummell ('He always said I looked better in a cloak.') (*The Sensorites*). He claims to have taught a boxer (or possibly wrestler) called the Mountain Mauler of Montana (*The Romans*) and seems to be well-known in contemporary London, being accepted without question by senior civil servant Sir Charles Summer and by the scientific community working on the WOTAN project (*The War Machines*). It can also be surmised that he has previously visited Earth at the time of the French Revolution, as Susan asserts in *The Reign of Terror* that this is his favourite period in the planet's history – a fact that might explain her own desire in *100,000 BC* to borrow a book on the subject from Barbara, and her subsequent assertion that details in it are incorrect.

Despite his alien origins, the Doctor seems to have a physiology very much akin to that of a man from Earth. In *Inside the Spaceship*, he cuts his head when thrown to the floor of the TARDIS and, although the viewer never actually sees any blood or (this being the era of black and white TV) what colour it is, there are no comments of surprise from Barbara when she dresses the wound. In *The Mutants*, the Doctor appears to be at least as susceptible as his companions to radiation sickness, if not more so. In *The Sensorites*, he is attacked by an unseen assailant and knocked unconscious by a blow above his heart, suggesting that his internal organs are akin to a human's, too. His respiration seems to act in the same way as ours – he is quickly overcome by fumes in a burning farmhouse in *The Reign of Terror* and even dislikes London's night air, judging from his protective handkerchief and the cough he gives the first time he is seen in *100,000 BC*. Of course, the cough could be the result of smoking too much, as later in the same story he produces a pipe and matches; but as he is never again seen to smoke after he loses these in the Stone Age, perhaps it is not a regular habit.

In *The War Machines*, the character Professor Brett speaks of the Doctor's brain as being 'human', and in *The Sensorites* the Doctor actually refers to himself and his companions as 'we humans' when speaking of the difference between their eyes and those of cats. Similarly, in *The Savages*, he tells a guard harassing a defenceless Savage: 'They are men; human beings, like you and me.' In this context however he is clearly using the term 'human' as a figure of speech, or as shorthand for 'humanoid', rather than as a reference to a native of the planet Earth.

The Doctor appears to be elderly, and all the evidence is that this is exactly what he is. He has bad eyesight, needing the use of either pince-nez glasses or a monocle for close-up work. He also tires quickly, needs sleep and rest in order to recover and uses a walking stick to aid his progress. He even faints on several occasions. He complains of rheumatism in *Marco Polo*, and again in *The Space Museum* when he is subjected to the Moroks' freezing process. He tells Ian that he always gets rheumatism when cold, and yet also comments that throughout the freezing process his mind stayed active and alert – a clear difference between himself and his human companion.

If the Doctor's body seems weak and frail, then his mind is anything but. He displays an enormous intellect and a great wealth of knowledge on a wide range of different subjects. In *The Sensorites*, for example, he can reel off from memory the melting points of steel and molybdenum, and knows not only that the antidote to atropine poison is caffeine citrate but also how to make it. In *The Ark*, he even concocts a cure for the common cold virus.

He works out how to operate a complicated mechanism to escape from a Dalek cell in *The Dalek Invasion of Earth*, and frequently bamboozles his opponents with his wit and charm, always leaving himself with the advantage. Despite all this, there is no mention at all of the Doctor's age or of any special alien powers – unless one includes the implication in *The Sensorites* that he and Susan are both partially telepathic.

In fact the first suggestion of any special abilities comes in *The Web Planet*, when the Doctor uses his large, blue-stoned ring to open the TARDIS doors. 'This ring isn't merely decorative,' he explains to Ian. In *The Daleks' Master Plan*, he puts the ring to a similar purpose to overcome the Monk's jamming of the TARDIS lock mechanism. Later, in *The War Machines*, he uses it to help him hypnotise Dodo, leading one to believe that he has some aptitude in that direction.

Of course, the most startling ability of all is revealed right at the end of the first Doctor's era, when at the conclusion of *The Tenth Planet*, he collapses on the floor of the TARDIS and undergoes a complete change of physical appearance – a feat no human could possibly achieve. The result of this remarkable metamorphosis is the second Doctor, who subsequently comments that without the TARDIS, he couldn't have survived the process.

Like the Doctor, the TARDIS keeps many of its secrets to itself, but during the first Doctor's era viewers do learn a surprising amount about its properties, size and facilities.

The ship's name is revealed in the first episode of *100,000 BC* to be an acronym made up by Susan from the initials of Time And Relative Dimension In Space – a term that apparently describes the craft and what it does. The inference is that this is the only 'TARDIS' (and the name does not enter into regular use until the fifth story, *The Keys of Marinus*, the more usual appellation being simply 'the ship'). Nothing is said in *The Time Meddler* to contradict this, as the Monk's vessel is referred to both by the Doctor and by the Monk as a time-ship, and not as a TARDIS – it is the Doctor's companions Vicki and Stephen who assume that its name is the same. In *The Daleks' Master Plan*, however, the Doctor does himself refer to the Monk's machine as a TARDIS.

The fact that the ship is dimensionally transcendental – bigger inside than out – is established from the outset, but exactly how this paradox is achieved is left to the viewer's imagination.

Also quickly established is the fact that the police box exterior is simply a disguise. When the travellers leave the ship to explore the Stone Age in *100,000 BC*, the Doctor and Susan both remark upon its failure to change its appearance. Susan later explains that the ship's exterior should change to suit its surroundings wherever it lands. It has in the past been an ionic column and a sedan chair, amongst other things. The implication is that this is the first time this particular malfunction has occurred – the TARDIS had disguised itself as a police box as this was a commonplace sight in London in 1963.

The precise details of the ship's interior lay-out and of its instrument panels and contents vary from story to story, suggesting that its dimensions may be in some way unstable.

Inside the Spaceship reveals more of its secrets than perhaps any other story. From the main control room – which is the first room one enters from the external doors – there is a connecting lobby area, with at least two adjoining bedrooms. In the main control room, one wall is taken up with the fault locator – a bank of computers monitoring and checking the operation of the ship. Each component has a reference number, and the numbers of failed components appear on a read-out (K7, for example, is the fluid link).

The centre of the room is dominated by a hexagonal control console, at the apex of which is a transparent, instrument-filled column, which rises and falls during flight (and also rotates on occasion, usually with the ship is at rest). The heart of the TARDIS is held under the column, and when the column rises it shows the extent of the power thrust. Should the column come all the way out, then the power would escape; and the Doctor comments that even if a small fraction of it were to escape, then it would blow the occupants to atoms. Exactly what the power is and how it is contained is unclear, however.

The control room also has a monitor screen, which gives a black and white picture – the Doctor explains in *The Keys of Marinus* that he has a colour screen but that it is temporarily out of order. In *Planet of Giants*, the screen explodes, requiring a hasty – and unseen – replacement for the following adventure. There are also chairs, ornaments and other bits and pieces dotted about the control room.

In the lobby there is a food machine which, as revealed in *The Mutants*, can supply any food in any combination in a form that looks like a small, foil-wrapped chocolate bar. The machine also supplies water that comes sealed in a plastic bag (although in *The Space Museum* it arrives in a glass tumbler, which Vicki promptly breaks). The bedrooms have contoured sleeping couches, which swing down from the walls; and the presence of six buttons on a wall panel suggests that there are either six beds, or three beds that each have one button to lower and one to raise them.

In *The Web Planet*, the viewer sees for the first time the 'fourth wall' of the TARDIS control room. It seems to house two alcove-like spaces full of ornaments and clutter; and it is here that the Doctor operates the doors by passing his ring in front of a light on one of the pieces of equipment. Also in *The Web Planet*, the central console is seen to spin round, and the TARDIS doors open and close apparently of their own volition. When an inquisitive Zarbi ventures inside, it is repelled by some unknown force.

In *Inside the Spaceship*, Susan remarks upon the fact that the TARDIS is silent, implying that this is highly unusual and that it is normally active all the time. There is a faint vibration inside when it is in flight and this ceases when it arrives at its destination. As Ian and Barbara discover in *100,000 BC*, the exterior vibrates slightly while at rest. Perhaps the most intriguing suggestion is that TARDIS may actually be sentient. This comes in *Inside the Spaceship* when the ship itself attempts to warn the Doctor of the peril into which he has inadvertently placed himself and his fellow travellers. Although the Doctor is initially adamant that the machine cannot think for itself, he is later forced to consider the possibility that it might.

One area of initial inconsistency in the depiction of the TARDIS concerns the noise it makes on leaving one location and arriving in another. When it departs from London in the first episode of *100,000 BC*, a strident roaring is heard inside the control room. This gives way to a raucous cacophony during flight and fades out altogether on arrival in the Stone Age. When the ship dematerialises again at the end of the story, the roaring is heard outside but there is no subsequent materialisation noise inside – just the tail end of the dematerialisation whine, as before. In line with this, when the Doctor sets the controls to dematerialise in the first episode of *The Mutants*, the initial phase of the noise is heard inside (although the take off is subsequently aborted due to an apparent malfunction). The dematerialisation noise is also heard outside the ship at the end of this story. At the beginning of *The Keys of Marinus*, *The Reign of Terror*, *Planet of Giants* and *The Dalek Invasion of Earth*, however, no noise is heard outside when the TARDIS materialises; and its dematerialisation is also silent at the end of *The Keys of Marinus* and *Planet of Giants*. (No dematerialisation occurs at the end of *The Reign of Terror*). It is not until the end of *The Dalek Invasion of Earth* that a fairly consistent pattern emerges whereby the roaring noise is heard both inside and outside the ship, both when it materialises and when it dematerialises.

Amongst the other titbits of information revealed about the TARDIS during the first Doctor's era are: that it is impossible for the ship to crash (*Inside the Spaceship*); that it has a defence mechanism (*Inside the Spaceship*); that it has a memory bank to record all its journeys (*Inside the Spaceship*); that its doors should never open in flight (*Inside the Spaceship* and *Planet of Giants*); that its danger signal sounds like a fog horn or klaxon (*Inside the Spaceship* and *Planet of Giants*); that the interior is susceptible to movement of the exterior (*Inside the Spaceship*, *The Romans*, *The Web Planet*); that the outer shell is light enough to be lifted by several men and carried on a wooden cart (*Marco Polo*); that the external doors cannot be forced open from outside as this would 'disturb the field of dimensions inside the ship' (*The Sensorites*); that the lock is 'an electronic miracle' (*The Sensorites*), requires not only a key but also 'knowledge' to operate (*Marco Polo*) and has twenty-one different positions, only one them correct, so that if the wrong combination is used the whole lock fuses (*The Mutants*); that the ship can materialise inside a moving object (*The Sensorites*) and travel through solid matter (*The Rescue*); that it has some kind of loudspeaker system enabling the Doctor to address someone outside (*The Dalek Invasion of Earth*, *The Daleks' Master Plan*); and that anyone can operate the controls if properly instructed (*The Daleks*, *The Rescue* and *The Daleks' Master Plan* to name just three stories in which examples occur).

The Monk's ship is said in *The Time Meddler* to be a 'Mark Four' and to have originated some fifty years later than the Doctor's, from which it differs in that for example its control console stands on a raised dais and that it has an automatic drift control which allows it to stay suspended in space with absolute safety. When at the end of the story the Doctor removes its dimensional control, its interior dimensions contract to occupy the same space as the exterior. Components from the Monk's ship are only partly compatible with the Doctor's, however, as is demonstrated in *The Daleks' Master Plan* when the Doctor attempts to wire the Monk's directional control into his own control console and causes an explosion.

The other major element of *Doctor Who* mythology established right at the start of the first Doctor's era was the Daleks. In their first story, it is revealed that they are the mutated survivors of a civil war on the planet Skaro, which finished some 500 years beforehand when a neutron bomb was detonated. The Doctor deduces that the Daleks – then called Dals – were teachers and philosophers while the Thals, their opponents in the war, were warriors. After the bomb was dropped, both races underwent a cycle of mutation. In the Thals' case this came full circle, so that they are now a race of physically handsome humanoids, dedicated to farming and peace. The Daleks, on the other hand, retreated into their city and built machines in which to live and travel. They became the warriors.

The Thals seem now to have lost most of their technological skills – that is assuming they ever had any – although they are obviously able somehow to make the anti-radiation drugs that they give to the time travellers. The Daleks on the other hand have flourished in this respect. Their city is constructed from gleaming metal and glass, and the machines in which they live are powered by static electricity picked up from the floors. They are able to grow food and to analyse and synthesise drugs. They have cameras that can produce both moving and still pictures; vibration detectors; and a nuclear reactor that provides the power for their city.

The Daleks' casings are themselves also very advanced. They each have an eye-stalk with a dilating lens; a sucker arm that can operate machinery, open doors via a swipe mechanism and hold paper and trays with ease; and a gun that can either paralyse or kill, depending on its setting, and that is powerful enough to scorch metal.

Only once is a brief glimpse afforded of the creature inside the casing. When the Doctor and Ian remove the top of one of the machines, they hear a moist sucking sound and see a sight that brings a look of extreme distaste to both their faces. They then remove the creature from its casing, wrap it in a cloak and throw it onto the floor nearby, where a withered, claw-like appendage pushes its way into view.

Further evidence of what the creature is like can be gleaned from the fact its casing is sufficiently spacious for Ian to climb inside in its place, and from the nature of the equipment that he finds once there. He discovers that there are numerous levers and switches; and, when the eye lens has been cleared of the mud placed on it to trap the creature in the first place, he is able to see out, suggesting some sort of screen or periscope device. His voice is also synthesised into a Dalek-like grate, suggesting that the Dalek speaks aloud. Logically therefore these creatures must have limbs, eyes, a mouth (with lips and tongue, both needed to form words), vocal cords and possibly also lungs.

At the conclusion of the story, the Daleks are deactivated and left on Skaro, apparently dead. When they next appear, in *The Dalek Invasion of Earth*, the Doctor speculates that this is a million years in their past, in the 'middle period' of their history when they are a space-faring race and have invaded Earth in the 22nd Century. If this is indeed the case – and it is possible the Doctor may be mistaken – one can only presume that the planet Skaro must have undergone several rises and falls of civilisation in its history.

What is most telling is that in *The Dalek Invasion of Earth*, the Daleks have gone from being just one of a number of alien races that the Doctor encountered during the series' first season – others being the Sensorites, the brain creatures in the city of Morphoton, the Voords and the Thals – to being the most evil race in the universe. In behind-the-scenes terms, this change was of course prompted by the massive surge of popularity that the Daleks had enjoyed since their debut appearance, which required them to be developed from one-off characters into recurring villains.

In *The Dalek Invasion of Earth*, the viewer learns that the Daleks can now (or could then, depending on one's perspective) travel through space; move on non-metallic surfaces; and condition humans to work for them. They seem also for the first time to have a hierarchy, based on the colour scheme of their casings. One, possibly the captain of their space ship, has a shaded dome and alternately shaded panels on its base unit, and another, apparently the commander of the entire invasion force, has a black dome and base unit and is referred to as 'the Dalek Supreme' or, on occasion, 'the Black Dalek'. All the Daleks in this story are mounted on a wider skirt section than in *The Mutants* and have on their backs a saucer-shaped attachment, which Ian suggests could account for their greater mobility.

Also seen in this story is the Slyther – a 'pet' of the Black Dalek, used to keep guard in their mine. It is revealed that the Daleks have direct communication with each other and that they are light enough to be lifted up by several humans. In the process it is seen that they have a smooth, flat base – with no wheels – suggesting some form of hover or anti-gravity capability.

By the time of their third story, *The Chase*, the Daleks have a time machine and are able to follow the Doctor's progress through time and space in an attempt to destroy him. Then, in *The Daleks' Master Plan*, they are seen to have formed a temporary alliance with a number of other races in a plan to take over the Earth's galaxy using a powerful weapon known as the Time Destructor. When the Doctor turns this weapon against them at the end of the story, time runs backwards and their casings split open, leaving the embryonic Dalek creatures – looking something akin to star-fish – floundering on the surface of the planet Kembel.

Like *The Mutants* and *The Dalek Invasion of Earth*, *The Daleks' Master Plan* reveals more about the Daleks than is actually seen on screen. It is now clear that they are in fact one of the dominant forces in the universe, with a large and effective power base. In the light of this, it is perhaps not surprising that the Doctor keeps crossing paths with them. This, however, was to be the last of the first Doctor's battles with the creatures from Skaro, and further revelations would have to await later eras of the series' history.

Of the other creatures and aliens that appeared in *Doctor Who*'s first three years, many had the potential to develop into recurring adversaries. The Zarbi and the Menoptra from *The Web Planet*, for example, featured in stories in the *Doctor Who* annuals and in comic strips in *TV Comic*. None, though, flourished as the Daleks had done. In fact, apart from the Daleks, the Meddling Monk was the only adversary who returned for a second TV appearance during the first Doctor's era. As that era drew to a close, however, another monster race appeared that was ultimately to rival the Daleks in popularity: the Cybermen.

In *The Tenth Planet*, it is revealed that the Cybermen were originally humanoids from the planet Mondas – Earth's 'twin planet'. Aeons ago, Mondas drifted away from the solar system on a journey through space. During this journey, the inhabitants started experimenting with cybernetics and replacing their limbs and organs with machine parts. Now Mondas has returned to the solar system and is drawing energy away from the Earth. The Cybermen intend to destroy the Earth to safeguard their own planet's existence, and to take with them the occupants of a South Pole space tracking station for conversion into further Cybermen.

Like the Daleks, the Cybermen would go on to make many return appearances in later eras of *Doctor Who*'s history. It also appears that the Doctor may have encountered them prior to *The Tenth Planet*, as he knows in advance that the planet approaching the Earth will be its twin, and that the tracking station will shortly be receiving visitors.

During the era of the first Doctor, all the most important elements of *Doctor Who's* enduring mythology were established and developed. As a basis from which to progress, it provided an almost perfect formula: a mysterious stranger, a powerful and unpredictable time machine and a race of evil killers who would stop at nothing to achieve their aims.

PRODUCTION DIARY

This chapter takes the form of a diary chronicling the production of *Doctor Who* during the first Doctor's era, concentrating in particular on the steps that led up to the series' BBC TV debut in 1963 and on its formative and highly turbulent first year, when it had not only to establish itself with the viewing public but also to contend with considerable hostility from certain quarters within the BBC itself. All passages reproduced from contemporary memos and correspondence are quoted verbatim, save for spelling and clarificatory changes of a minor nature. The sender and the main recipient are always identified but, for reasons of space, details of other copy recipients are generally omitted.

The story begins in the spring of 1962 when responsibility for making all the BBC's plays, series and serials rested with the Drama Department, within which a large number of staff producer/directors were employed to take charge of individual projects. The scripts, on the other hand, were the province of the Script Department, which had the task of commissioning and developing material to meet the needs not only of Drama but also of many of the other production departments.

Acting Head of Drama at this time was Norman Rutherford. He had been temporarily promoted to the post in September 1961 pending the arrival of a permanent successor to the long-serving and highly-respected Michael Barry, who had left the BBC earlier in the year. Head of the Script Department was fifty-one year old writer, producer and director Donald Wilson, who had joined the BBC in 1955 after a successful career in the film industry.

Wilson's principal staff consisted of eight script editors – each responsible for a specific area of programming – and ten writer/adaptors, supported by a team of more junior readers and researchers. The Department was always on the lookout for fresh source material for television adaptation, and in May 1960 Wilson had established the Monitoring Group, later known as the Survey Group, the objective of which was 'to cover and report on current work in other media, in order that we may keep ourselves fully informed about writing and writers likely to be useful to us here.' The media covered were radio, films, stage plays, books and commercial television. The Group reported its findings at regular Script Department meetings, and the practical pursuit of new talent was then delegated to the editor concerned.

It was around March 1962 that Eric Maschwitz, the Head of Light Entertainment for BBC TV, asked Donald Wilson to have the Survey Group prepare a report on the literary genre of science fiction, the aim being to determine whether or not this would constitute a suitable source for 'a series of single-shot adaptations.' The task was delegated by Wilson to Donald Bull, the script editor for drama, and his colleague Alice Frick; and it is to their report that *Doctor Who*'s earliest roots can be traced …

APRIL 1962

Wednesday 25: Alice Frick sends Donald Wilson two copies of the report that she and Donald Bull have prepared. She suggests to his secretary Gwen Jones that one of them be retained for duplication and circulation with the next Survey Group minutes, and that the other be passed direct to Eric Maschwitz.

The report is three-and-a-half pages long. It describes the survey's scope as follows:

> In the time allotted, we have not been able to make more than a sample dip, but we have been greatly helped by studies of the field made by Brian Aldiss, Kingsley Amis and Edmund Crispin, which give a good idea of the range, quality and preoccupations of current SF writing. We have read some useful anthologies, representative of the best SF practitioners, and these, with some extensive previous reading, have sufficed to give us a fair view of the subject. Alice Frick has met and spoken with Brian Aldiss, who promises to make some suggestions for further reading. It remains to be seen whether this further research will qualify our present tentative conclusions.
>
> After making the general observations that 'SF is overwhelmingly American in bulk' and 'largely a short story medium' in which 'the interest invariably lies in the activating idea and not in character drama', the report goes on to describe a number of distinct sub-genres: 'the simple adventure/thriller'; the more sophisticated type of story which 'takes delight in imaginative invention, in pursuing notions to the farthest reaches of speculation'; 'the large field of what might be called the Threat to Mankind, and Cosmic Disaster'; and finally 'satire, comic or horrific, extrapolating current social trends and techniques'. Of these sub-genres, the report identifies 'Threat and Disaster' as being the one most commonly exploited by British writers and the one most suitable for TV adaptation.
>
> We thought it valuable to try and discover wherein might lie the essential appeal of SF to TV audiences. So far we have little to go on except *Quatermass*, *Andromeda* and a couple of shows Giles Cooper did for commercial TV. These all belong to the Threat and Disaster school, the type of plot in which the whole of mankind is threatened, usually from an 'alien' source. Where the threat originates on Earth (mad scientists and all that jazz) it is still cosmic in its reach. This cosmic quality seems inherent in SF; without it, it would be trivial. Apart from the instinctive pull of such themes, the obvious appeal of these TV SF essays lies in the ironmongery – the apparatus, the magic – and in the excitement of the unexpected. *Andromeda*, which otherwise seemed to set itself out to repel, drew its total appeal from exploiting this facet, we

consider. It is interesting to note that with *Andromeda*, and even with *Quatermass*, more people watched it than liked it. People aren't all that mad about SF, but it is compulsive, when properly presented.

Audiences – we think – are as yet not interested in the mere exploitation of ideas – the 'idea as hero' aspect of SF. They must have something to latch on to. The apparatus must be attached to the current human situation, and identification must be offered with recognisable human beings.

As a rider to the above, it is significant that SF is not itself a wildly popular branch of fiction – nothing like, for example, detective and thriller fiction. It doesn't appeal much to women and largely finds its public in the technically minded younger groups. SF is a most fruitful and exciting area of exploration – but so far has not shown itself capable of supporting a large population.

This points to the need to use great care and judgment in shaping SF for a mass audience. It isn't an automatic winner. No doubt future audiences will get the taste and hang of SF as exciting in itself, and an entertaining way of probing speculative ideas, and the brilliant imaginings of a writer like Isaac Asimov will find a receptive place. But for the present we conclude that SF TV must be rooted in the contemporary scene, and like any other kind of drama deal with human beings in a situation that evokes identification and sympathy.

The report goes on to conclude that 'television science fiction drama must be written not by SF writers, but by TV dramatists' and that 'the vast bulk of SF writing is by nature unsuitable for translation to TV'. It adds that Bull and Frick 'cannot recommend any existing SF stories for TV adaptation', but that 'Arthur Clarke and John Wyndham might be valuable as collaborators' on any future projects.

Friday 27: Having obtained Donald Wilson's agreement, his secretary Gwen Jones sends a copy of the report to Eric Maschwitz.

MAY 1962

Tuesday 1: Donald Bull writes to Jean LeRoy of the literary agency David Higham Associates Ltd, thanking her for sending him some science fiction stories by her client John Christopher. Bull's letter reflects the conclusions of the Survey Group report, asserting that the broad TV audience is not yet ready for 'the more fanciful flights of SF' in stories such as the author's *Christmas Roses*, but that there are 'considerable immediate opportunities … for using John Christopher's specialised knowledge and talent in conjunction with our future schemes, possibly in collaboration with a skilled TV dramatist …'

Monday 14: Donald Baverstock, the Assistant Controller of Programmes for BBC television, sends Eric Maschwitz a memo of thanks for letting him see the Survey Group report:

You describe it as interesting and intelligent. I would go further and say that it seems to me exactly the kind of hard thinking over a whole vein of dramatic material that is most useful to us.

I gather that Donald Bull and Alice Frick were responsible for it and I hope HSDTel will thank them.

Tuesday 15: Maschwitz forwards Baverstock's memo to Donald Wilson (HSDTel in the BBC's internal shorthand) after adding a handwritten note conveying his own 'admiring thanks'.

A few days later, following further discussion of the report, Alice Frick and Script Department colleague John Braybon are asked to prepare a follow-up, identifying some specific science fiction stories suitable for TV adaptation.

JUNE 1962

Saturday 9: The BBC transmits in its early evening slot the first of six weekly, half-hour episodes of a science fiction serial entitled *The Big Pull*, written specially for TV by Robert Gould. The story concerns an alien invasion precipitated by the return to Earth of a manned American space capsule which has passed through the Van Allen belt of deadly radioactive particles. The serial's producer/director is Terence Dudley.

Sunday 24: ABC TV, one of the ITV companies, screens an hour-long science fiction play entitled *Dumb Martian*, adapted from a story by John Wyndham, in its regular *Armchair Theatre* slot. It is presented as a prelude to a new thirteen-part anthology series, *Out of this World*, due to begin the following Saturday.

Thursday 28: A new BBC science fiction serial entitled *The Andromeda Breakthrough* – a sequel to the previous year's *A for Andromeda* – begins its run with the first of six weekly, forty-five- to fifty-minute episodes.

Saturday 30: ABC's *Out of this World* begins, becoming the first science fiction anthology series ever screened on British TV. It has been given the go-ahead by ABC's drama supervisor, Sydney Newman, who is a lifelong fan of science fiction and has previously produced a number of children's serials in that genre, including one based partly on Jules Verne's *Twenty Thousand Leagues under the Sea* for CBC in his native Canada, and the popular *Pathfinders in Space* and its two sequels for ABC. He is currently being forced to serve out the final months of his contract with ABC before leaving to join the BBC as their new Head of Drama, having accepted an invitation to do so shortly after Michael Barry's departure in the autumn of 1961.

JULY 1962

Saturday 14: *The Big Pull* finishes its run in the BBC's early evening slot.

Wednesday 25: John Braybon and Alice Frick present their report to Donald Wilson. The introduction reads:

It is not the purpose of the comments below to suggest that a science fiction series should, or should not, be undertaken. However, during the course of the past eight weeks, we have read some hundreds of science fiction stories; in general, they have been of the short story variety, so beloved by the current science fiction generation of authors. Included in the attached list are a number of titles each together with a brief synopsis. They have been chosen as potentially suitable for adaptation to television because they fulfil one, or all, of the following requirements:

1. They do not include Bug-Eyed Monsters.

2. The central characters are never Tin Robots (since the audience must always subconsciously say 'My goodness, there's a man in there and isn't he playing the part well')

3. They do not require large and elaborate science fiction type settings since, in our considered opinion, the presentation of the interior of a space-ship, or the surface of another planet, gives rise to exactly the same psychological blockage as the above-mentioned Robots and BEMs. (In our opinion, this has already resulted in the failure in the current ITV series, which has included *The Yellow Pill*, *Dumb Martian* and *Little Lost Robot*.)

4. They do provide an opportunity for genuine characterisation and in most cases, they ask the audience to suspend disbelief scientifically and technologically on one fact only, after which all developments follow a logical pattern.

Because of the above restrictions, we consider that two types of plot are reasonably outstanding, namely those dealing with telepaths, see *Three to Conquer* in the attached list, and those dealing with time travelling, see *Guardians of Time*. This latter one is particularly attractive as a series, since individual plots can easily be tackled by a variety of script-writers; it's the *Z Cars* of science fiction.

The stories covered by Braybon and Frick in the main body of their report are *Guardians of Time* by Poul Anderson, *Three to Conquer* by Eric Frank Russell, *Eternity Lost* by Clifford Simak, *Pictures Don't Lie* by Catherine MacLean, *No Woman Born* by C L Moore, *The Cerebrative Psittacoid* by H Nearing Jnr and *The Ruum* by Arthur Forges. The report concludes:

An SF serial or series is a possibility. A number of possible stories have already been tackled (with varying degrees of success) by ITV; e.g. *The Imposter*, *Dumb Martian*, *The Cold Equations*. Best bets are: *Three to Conquer* (rights are available, we're told) and *Guardians of Time*.

AUGUST 1962

Donald Wilson appoints Vincent Tilsley as Drama Script Supervisor to achieve a stronger liaison and better co-operation between the Script Department and the Drama Department.

NOVEMBER 1962

Thursday 8: A science fiction serial entitled *The Monsters* begins its run on BBC TV. Its four, forty-five- to fifty-minute weekly episodes are written by Vincent Tilsley with playwright Evelyn Frazer. The story, inspired by a *Panorama* documentary about the Loch Ness Monster, concerns the exploits of a honeymooning zoologist who sets out to investigate some reported sightings of strange creatures in a remote English lake and ends up uncovering a threat to the very survival of mankind. The serial's director is Mervyn Pinfield.

Thursday 29: The final episode of *The Monsters* is transmitted.

DECEMBER 1962

Wednesday 12: Sydney Newman finally takes up post at the BBC, beginning his five year contract as Head of Drama. The appointment of this charismatic, highly outspoken Canadian is viewed with considerable scepticism by some of the more traditional elements within the BBC, where senior posts have traditionally been the preserve of upper-class establishment types. His superiors meanwhile are looking to him to revitalize his Department's output in much the same way as he did at ABC; and this is no easy task, as he will recall in a later interview:

> 'I'll be perfectly frank. When I got to the BBC and I looked my staff over, I was really quite sick, because most of the directors there were people whose work I just did not like. I thought it was soft and slow and had no edge. Believe me, I had a bad Christmas, because I didn't know what to do – how to change those people who were stuck in their old ways, many of them having done their first television work at Alexandra Palace in 1938! Nice guys, willing guys, but most of them were just rigid!'

JANUARY 1963

Early in the new year, Newman receives some welcome news from the BBC's Controller of Programmes:

> 'When I turned up early in January 1963, after the Christmas week, I was called into Kenneth Adam's office, and Kenneth said "Sydney, I've got some great news. DG" – that is Hugh Carleton Green, the Director General – "has convinced the Government to allow the BBC to do a second channel, and we're going to go on the air one year from now. So

you have an increase in budget of 40 per cent!"

'Of course, that opened the door – I could then hire people whose work I liked. So I put the word around, and many of the directors and writers who had worked for me at ABC – Philip Saville, Ted Kotcheff, Peter Luke and so on – came over to join me at the BBC.'

During the course of this month, Sydney Newman disbands the BBC Children's Department. For the forseeable future all children's drama programmes would be made by the Drama Department.

FEBRUARY 1963

Newman puts in hand some radical changes to the organisation and working methods of the Drama Department, which now becomes the Drama Group:

'When I got to the BBC and saw the whole of it, I thought "I can't control all this by myself." So I broke the Drama Group down into three separate departments – Series, Serials and Plays – and appointed to each of them a Head who would exercise the direct control and do my bidding.'

One of the most important changes initiated by Newman is the phasing out of the traditional producer/director role in favour of the production team approach already established in a number of the ITV companies but hitherto adopted only infrequently within the BBC. The producer will now be invariably an executive rather than a director and will have full artistic and financial control over a particular project. Staff or freelance directors will be brought in to handle individual programmes or episodes on a one-off basis. The other permanent member of the production team will be a relatively junior story editor, who will have responsibility for finding and working with writers to provide the scripts.

These changes, which will take place over the following three months, will render the Script Department largely obsolete, and it will consequently be abolished.

MARCH 1963

Sydney Newman discusses with Donald Baverstock, now designated Chief of Programmes for BBC1, and Joanna Spicer, the Assistant Controller (Planning) Television, the requirement for a new drama serial to fill the early Saturday evening slot between the sports round-up *Grandstand* and the pop music show *Juke Box Jury*. What is needed is something that will appeal equally well to the respective audiences of both these highly popular programmes and so bridge the gap between them. Previously the slot has been filled with a wide variety of different shows such as the science fiction serial *The Big Pull*, a Francis Durbridge thriller and the comedy antics of *The Telegoons*.

Newman has considered a number of different possibilities – including, according to his later recollection, a series about two boys in a boys' school – but eventually decided on a science fiction idea. (It is possible he may have been involved in developing a series along these lines just before he left ABC; Howard Thomas, the Managing Director of that company, will later incorrectly assert in his autobiography *With an Independent Air* that *Doctor Who* was actually conceived while Newman was working there.)

Newman outlines his idea in general terms to Baverstock and Spicer, and they react very favourably. He then asks Donald Wilson, at this point still serving as Head of the Script Department, to come up with suggestions for a suitable format for a 52-week science fiction series comprised of a number of shorter serials.

Tuesday 26: Wilson convenes a meeting in his office to discuss ideas for the proposed new series, taking as a starting point the Survey Group reports on science fiction prepared in 1962. Present are John Braybon, Alice Frick and another Script Department writer/adaptor, Cecil Edwin Webber. Webber – generally referred to by the nickname 'Bunny' – has been on the Department's staff for some time and has previously been responsible for many successful children's dramas, including some popular adaptations of Richmal Crompton's *Just William* books.

Wednesday 27: John Mair, who as Senior Planning Assistant (I) is responsible for the allocation of studio time within the BBC's television service, sends a memo to Joanna Spicer seeking details of the proposed new series.

Friday 29: Alice Frick sends Donald Wilson a note recording the main points of the meeting held three days earlier:

> The following devices were discussed:
>
> 1. Time Machine: Donald Wilson suggested if this were used, it should be a machine not only for going forward and backwards in time, but into space, and into all kinds of matter (e.g. a drop of oil, a molecule, under the ocean, etc.)
>
> 2. Flying Saucer: Alice Frick thought this might be a more modern vehicle than a time machine, much discussed at present, and with a considerable body of literature concerning it. It would have the advantage of conveying a group of people (i.e. the regular cast of characters.)
>
> 3. Computer: Donald Wilson thought this should be avoided, since it was the *Andromeda* device.
>
> 4. Telepathy: This is an okay notion in modern science, and a good device for dealing with outer space inhabitants who have appropriated human bodies (e.g. *Three to Conquer* by Eric Frank Russell).
>
> 5. John Braybon suggested that the series should be set in the future, and that a good device would be a world body of scientific trouble-shooters, established to keep scientific experiments under control for political or humanistic reasons.

Ideas:

A good many possible (and probably some impracticable!) ideas for themes and content were discussed, among them some published works – *Guardians of Time* by Poul Anderson and *Three to Conquer* by Russell.

Some recent scientific discoveries or developments whose uses are still not known nor explored were mentioned, e.g. the Laser Beam. We all thought that the use of seven or eight such 'new' ideas, one for each short serial, could make a 52-week series.

Bunny Webber brought forward the idea of the continuance of thought; the idea that great scientists of the past might continue in some form of existence and could be contacted to discover further advances they had made, ideas they might bring to current discoveries, thought, etc.

Donald Wilson introduced a discussion of human creativity, the presence in the world of the human capacity to initiate original thought, to create new concepts, ideas, etc, the immeasurable and inexplicable work and productivity of genius. This led on to a discussion of energy, the difference between scientific energy, which can be measured, and human energy, which cannot.

Format:

Donald Wilson said that the series must be based on a group of regular characters, some of whom would be employed in major roles in one limited serial, others in the next, according to the needs of the different stories. He felt this was essential to establishing a loyalty audience. He suggested that, for the time-slot, two young teenagers should be included. Alice Frick advanced the opinion that children of that age were more interested in characters who are older than themselves, in the early twenties. Braybon and Webber supported this idea. Young children could be introduced occasionally, but should not be among the regulars.

The major problems in format are, how to involve a part of a permanent group in widely differing adventures, and how to transport them believably to entirely disparate milieux.

The meeting ended with Alice Frick assigned to making this report and Bunny Webber asked to suggest a cast of viable characters, which is attached hereto.

Webber's note, headed 'Science Fiction', begins as follows:

Characters and Setup

Envisaged is a 'loyalty programme', lasting at least 52 weeks, consisting of various dramatised SF stories, linked to form a continuous serial, using basically a few characters who continue through all the stories. Thus if each story were to run six or seven episodes there would be about eight stories needed to form fifty-two weeks of overall serial.

Our basic setup with its loyalty characters must fulfil two conditions:

1. It must attract and hold the audience.

2. It must be adaptable to any SF story, so that we do not have to reject stories because they fail to fit into our setup.

Suitable characters for the five o'clock Saturday audience.

Child characters do not command the interest of children older than themselves. Young heroines do not command the interest of boys. Young heroes do command the interest of girls. Therefore, the highest coverage amongst children and teenagers is got by:

THE HANDSOME YOUNG MAN HERO (First character)

A young heroine does not command the full interest of older women; our young hero has already got the boys and girls; therefore we can consider the older woman by providing:

THE HANDSOME WELL-DRESSED HEROINE AGED ABOUT 30 (Second character)

Men are believed to form an important part of the five o'clock Saturday (post-*Grandstand*) audience. They will be interested in the young hero; and to catch them firmly we should add:

THE MATURER MAN, 35-40, WITH SOME 'CHARACTER' TWIST (Third character)

Nowadays, to satisfy grown women, Father-Figures are introduced into loyalty programmes at such a rate that TV begins to look like an Old People's Home: let us introduce them ad hoc, as our stories call for them. We shall have no child protagonists, but child characters may be introduced ad hoc, because story requires it, not to interest children.

Under the heading 'What are our three chosen characters?', Webber's note goes on to propose that the regulars should be 'the partners in a firm of scientific consultants' known as:

'THE TROUBLESHOOTERS'

Each of them is a specialist in certain fields, so that each can bring a different approach to any problem. But they are all acutely conscious of the social or human implications of any case, and if the two men sometimes become pure scientist and forget, the woman always reminds them that, finally, they are dealing with human beings. Their Headquarters or Base illustrates this dichotomy: it consists of two parts: 1. a small lab fitted with way-out equipment, including some wondrous things acquired in previous investigations and 2. an office for interviews, homely, fusty, comfortable, dustily elegant: it would not have been out of place in Holmes's Baker Street.

After a brief discussion of the series' villains, suggesting that these be created on an ad hoc basis unless a recurring adversary should happen to emerge in the development of the stories, Webber's note concludes with a section headed 'Overall Meaning of the Serial.' This echoes the reports prepared in 1962 in stressing that science fiction on TV should be much more character-based than in literature; should have some 'feminine interest' added; and should 'consider, or at least firmly raise' serious moral and philosophical questions.

APRIL 1963

Sydney Newman considers the notes by Frick and Webber, which have been passed on to him by Donald Wilson, and makes a number of handwritten annotations to them. He dislikes Frick's idea of featuring a flying saucer, expressing the view that it is 'Not based in reality – or too Sunday press.' He also summarily rejects the idea of a future team of scientific troubleshooters, writing simply 'No' against this point in Frick's note. In the margin beside Webber's suggestions on possible characters he writes: 'Need a kid to get into trouble, make mistakes.' Concerned that the series should be partly educational, he notes that within the proposed team of scientists 'no-one has to require being taught.' He also criticises Webber's suggestions on villains as being 'corny.'

Newman's overall reaction to the ideas put forward by Wilson's team is that they are too highbrow and unimaginative, very much in the mould of old-fashioned BBC family drama from which he is keen to break away. He himself favours a format more akin to that of the *Pathfinders...* serials he produced at ABC, following in the long tradition of children's cliff-hanger adventures pioneered in the cinema and on radio and since continued on television – an area of science fiction completely overlooked in the Script Department reports of 1962, even though the BBC had itself produced a number of earlier serials in this vein, such as *Stranger from Space* (two seasons, 1951 and 1952), *The Lost Planet* (1954) and *Return to the Lost Planet* (1955).

Newman does however approve of the idea of a time-space machine, which will carry a group of contemporary characters 'backwards and forwards in time and inward and outward in space,' as he will later recall:

> All the stories were to be based on scientific and historical facts as we knew them at that time.
>
> Space also meant outer space, intergalactic travel, but again based on understood fact. So no bug-eyed monsters, which I had always thought to be the cheapest form of science fiction.
>
> Re time. How wonderful, I thought, if today's humans could find themselves on the shores of England seeing and getting mixed up with

Caesar's army in 54 BC, landing to take over the country; be in burning Rome as Nero fiddled; get involved in Europe's tragic Thirty Years War; and so on.

That was the scheme, so how to dress it up?'

Although content to go along with Webber's 'Handsome Young Man Hero' and 'Handsome Well-dressed Heroine', Newman insists that a young teenager be added to the regular team. And in place of Webber's 'Maturer Man', he devises the character who will become the focal point of the series: a frail and grumpy old man called the Doctor, who has stolen the time machine from his own people, an advanced civilisation on a far-distant planet.

As Newman later recalls (although no contemporary documentation exists to confirm this), he conveys these ideas in a memo to Donald Wilson.

Following the demise of the Script Department, Newman has now appointed Wilson as Head of the new Serials Department – the Department that will be responsible for making the series.

Friday 26: Drama Group administrator Ayton Whitaker replies on Donald Wilson's behalf to the memo that John Mair sent Joanna Spicer on 27 March. Noting that the new series is due to be recorded in Studio D at the BBC's Lime Grove Studios in west London, he goes on to describe the intended production and transmission dates and the requirements for special facilities such as back projection (BP):

> I understand that facilities are available for recording the Saturday serial weekly in Studio D on Fridays, starting from 5 July (Week 27), the first transmission to be in Week 31 on Saturday 27 July.
>
> The serials, which will in all run for 52 weeks, will average six episodes, and each serial will require one week's filming at the Television Film Studios. For the most part this filming will be confined to special effects, but artists, with therefore attendant wardrobe and make-up facilities, will be required on occasions. The first two serials are each of four episodes. Serial 1 will be recorded from Weeks 27-30 (transmitted Weeks 31-34), Serial 2 recorded Weeks 31-34 (transmitted Weeks 35-38), Serial 3 recording to start Week 35 (transmitted Week 39 onwards). A week's filming at the Television Film Studios will therefore be required in Weeks 26, 30 and 34.
>
> Moving and Still BP will be required in the studio on all recording days, so there should be a block booking for 52 weeks, starting on the Friday of Week 27. Inlay and overlay will also be required as a regular facility.
>
> The serials will cost £2,300 per episode, and an additional £500 will be needed to build the space/time machine which will be used throughout the 52 weeks.

Whitaker is informed that the Design Department should have sufficient capacity to handle the new series, provided that the work involved does not exceed 500 man-hours on the first episode and 350 man-hours on subsequent episodes.

MAY 1963

Around the beginning of May, staff producer/director Rex Tucker is asked to take charge of the series pending the appointment of a permanent producer under Sydney Newman's new production team regime. Tucker – a veteran who joined BBC radio in the thirties and transferred to TV in the fifties, specialising in children's drama and classic serials – is summoned to a meeting in Newman's office, where the format of the new series is explained to him. Also present is Richard Martin, an inexperienced young director who has just been assigned to the newly-established Serials Department after completing the internal directors' training course. It is expected that Tucker will direct the first story and that Martin will direct some of the other early episodes.

In subsequent discussions, the series is given the title *Doctor Who*. (Actor and director Hugh David, a friend of Tucker's, will later assert that it was Tucker who came up with the title. Tucker himself, however, will maintain that it was Newman.)

As the organisational changes initiated by Newman steadily reach fruition, the remains of the old Script Department are redesignated as the Television Script Unit. Bunny Webber, meanwhile, continues to be involved in *Doctor Who*'s development. Early in the month, he drafts a document headed 'General Notes on Background and Approach', intended primarily as a guide for prospective writers. It begins by setting out the basic format now established for the series:

> A series of stories linked to form a continuing serial; thus if each story ran six or seven episodes there would be about eight stories needed for fifty-two weeks of the serial. With the overall title, each episode is to have its own title. Each episode of 25 minutes will begin by repeating the closing sequence or final climax of the preceding episode; about halfway through, each episode will reach a climax, followed by blackout before the second half commences (one break).
>
> Each story, as far as possible, to use repeatable sets. It is expected that BP will be available. A reasonable amount of film, which will probably be mostly studio shot for special effects. Certainly writers should not hesitate to call for any special effects to achieve the element of surprise essential in these stories, even though they are not sure how it would be done technically: leave it to the Effects people. Otherwise work to a very moderate budget.

The document goes on to give a brief description of each of the series' four regular characters. Apart from the one for 'Dr Who' himself, these are:

BRIDGET (BIDDY)

> A with-it girl of 15, reaching the end of her Secondary School career, eager for life, lower-than-middle class. Avoid dialect, use neutral accent laced with latest teenage slang.

MISS MCGOVERN (LOLA)

24. Mistress at Biddy's school. Timid but capable of sudden rabbit courage. Modest, with plenty of normal desires. Although she tends to be the one who gets into trouble, she is not to be guyed: she also is a loyalty character.

CLIFF

27 or 28. Master at the same school. Might be classed as ancient by teenagers except that he is physically perfect, strong and courageous, a gorgeous dish. Oddly, when brains are required, he can even be brainy, in a diffident sort of way.

Webber next summarises some of the other main aspects of the series:

QUALITY OF STORY

Evidently, Dr Who's 'machine' fulfils many of the functions of conventional science fiction gimmicks. But we are not writing science fiction. We shall provide scientific explanations too, sometimes, but we shall not bend over backwards to do so, if we decide to achieve credibility by other means. Neither are we writing fantasy: the events have got to be credible to the three ordinary people who are our main characters, and they are sharp-witted enough to spot a phoney. I think the writer's safeguard here will be, if he remembers that he is writing for an audience aged fourteen ... the most difficult, critical, even sophisticated, audience there is, for TV. In brief, avoid the limitations of any label and use the best in any style or category, as it suits us, so long as it works in our medium.

Granting the startling situations, we should try to add meaning; to convey what it means to be these ordinary human beings in other times, or in far space, or in unusual physical states. We might hope to be able to answer the question: 'Besides being exciting entertainment, for 5 o'clock on a Saturday, what is worthwhile about this serial?'

DR WHO'S 'MACHINE'

When we consider what this looks like, we are in danger of either science fiction or fairytale labelling. If it is a transparent plastic bubble we are with all the lowgrade spacefiction of cartoon strip and soap-opera. If we scotch this by positing something humdrum, say, passing through some common object in the street such as a night-watchman's shelter to arrive inside a marvellous contrivance of quivering electronics, then we simply have a version of the dear old Magic Door.

Therefore, we do not see the machine at all; or rather it is visible only as an absence of visibility, a shape of nothingness (Inlaid, into surrounding picture). Dr Who has achieved this 'disappearance' by covering the outside with light-resistant paint (a recognised research project today). Thus our characters can bump into it, run their hands over its shape, partly disappear by partly entering it, and disappear entirely when the door closes behind them. It can be put into an apparently empty van. Wherever they go, so contemporary disguise has to be found for it. Many visual possibilities can be worked out. The discovery of the old man and investigation of his machine would occupy most of the first episode, which would be called:

NOTHING AT THE END OF THE LANE

The machine is unreliable, being faulty. A recurrent problem is to find spares. How to get thin gauge platinum wire in BC 1566? Moreover, Dr Who has lost his memory, so they have to learn to use it, by a process of trial and error, keeping records of knobs pressed and results (this is fuel for many a long story). After several near-calamities they institute a safeguard: one of their number is left in the machine when the others go outside, so that at the end of an agreed time, they can be fetched back into their own era. This provides a suspense element in any given danger: can they survive till the moment of recall? Attack on recaller etc.

Granted this machine, then, we require exciting episodic stories, using surprising visual effects and unusual scenery, about excursions into time, into space, or into any material state we can make feasible. Hardly any time at all is spent in the machine: we are interested in human beings.

OVERALL CONTINUITY OF STORY

Besides the machine, we have the relationship of the four characters to each other. They want to help the old man find himself; he doesn't like them; the sensible hero never trusts Dr Who; Biddy rather dislikes Miss McGovern; Lola admires Cliff ... these attitudes developed and varied as temporary characters are encountered and reacted to. The old man provides continuing elements of *Mystery*, and *Quest*.

The document continues with a more detailed discussion of the Doctor's function within the stories and proposes two 'Secrets of Dr Who'. It then concludes as follows:

The first two stories will be on the short side, four episodes each, and will not deal with time travel. The first may result from the use of a micro-reducer in the machine which makes our characters all become tiny. By the third story we could first reveal that it is a time-machine; they witness a great calamity, even possibly the destruction of the Earth, and only afterwards realize that they were far ahead in time. Or to think about Christmas: which seasonable story shall we take our characters into? Bethlehem? Was it by means of Dr Who's machine that Aladdin's palace sailed through the air? Was Merlin Dr Who? Was Cinderella's Godmother

Dr Who's wife chasing him through time? Jacob Marley was Dr Who slightly tipsy, but what other tricks did he get up to that Yuletide?

On receiving a copy of this latest format document, Sydney Newman again records his reactions by making a number of handwritten annotations to it. At the end of the opening paragraph he notes that each episode should close with a 'very strong cliff-hanger.' Much of the section headed 'Quality of Story' he considers 'not clear.' He is concerned that the proposed depiction of the Doctor's time machine is 'not visual', adding that a 'tangible symbol' is needed. He is pleased with the paragraph discussing the unreliability of the time machine, but greatly dislikes the description of the Doctor's role within the stories. As before, his overall reaction is largely negative:

> I don't like this much – it all reads silly and condescending. It doesn't get across the basis of teaching of educational experience – drama based upon and stemming from factual material and scientific phenomena and actual social history of past and future. Dr Who – not have a philosophical arty-science mind – he'd take science, applied and theoretical, as being as natural as eating.

Thursday 9: Owen Reed, Head of Children's Programmes for BBC Television, sends a memo to Donald Wilson strongly recommending Leonard Chase as a director for *Doctor Who?* [sic]. He points out that Chase 'has worked closely with Webber and has exactly the right flair for bold and technically adventurous "through the barrier" stuff.'

Monday 13: Ayton Whitaker circulates a memo indicating that the start of the new Saturday serial has been postponed by four weeks, and that recording will now begin on Friday 2 August.

Wednesday 15: After further discussion with colleagues involved in the project, Bunny Webber completes a revised draft of the format document. This is essentially a precis of the previous version – running to one-and-a-half pages rather than three-and-a-half – but takes Newman's comments into account. All the material under the heading 'Overall Continuity of Story', including the 'Secrets of Dr Who', has now been dropped. The young girl is no longer named Biddy; instead, Webber suggests a number of different names – Mandy, Gay, Sue, Jill, Janet and Jane – of which he appears to consider Mandy and Sue the front runners. The most significant changes of substance occur in the description of the Doctor's time machine, which now reads as follows:

THE MACHINE

> Dr Who has a 'machine' which enables them to travel together through space, through time and through matter. When first seen, this machine has the appearance of a police box standing in the street, but anyone entering it is immediately inside an extensive electronic contrivance. Though it looks impressive, it is an old beat-up model which Dr Who stole when he escaped from his own galaxy in the year 5733; it is

uncertain in performance and often needs repairing; moreover, Dr Who has forgotten how to work it, so they have to learn by trial and error.

The new idea for the ship's outward appearance has been suggested by Anthony Coburn, another BBC staff writer whom Donald Wilson has allocated to work on the series. Coburn has had the idea after seeing a police box while out walking near his office.

Also rather different in this version of Webber's document is the proposed outline for the first story:

THE FIRST STORY

Mandy/Sue meets the old man wandering in fog. He takes her to a police box in street. Entering the box, she finds herself inside this large machine; directly she leaves it she is again in street outside police box. Cliff and Lola, who have been to a late meeting at the school, come across Mandy/Sue and the old man. She shows them the machine. They are all reduced in size, to about one-eighth of an inch tall, and the story develops this situation for four episodes within the school science laboratory. The next story will begin with their regaining normal size, and at once start them on another adventure.

On this occasion it is Donald Wilson who makes handwritten annotations to Webber's work. These consist mainly of minor changes of wording, although he puts a cross right through the description of the Doctor's character, indicating that he considers this in need of more extensive revision. He also chooses the name Sue for the young girl character, striking out Webber's other suggestions, and changes the heading of the paragraph about the Doctor's time machine from 'The Machine' to 'The Ship'.

Thursday 16: Another draft of the format document is produced. Again Wilson makes some handwritten annotations to it, and a further draft is typed up the same day to incorporate these changes. The document then reads as follows:

'DR WHO'

General Notes on Background and Approach for an Exciting Adventure-Science Fiction Drama Series for Children's Saturday Viewing.

A series of stories linked to form a continuing 52-part serial; each story will run from between 4 and 10 episodes. Each episode of 25 minutes will have its own title, will reach a climax about halfway through, and will end with a strong cliffhanger.

APPROACH TO THE STORIES

The series is neither fantasy nor space travel nor science fiction. The only unusual science fiction 'angle' is that four characters of today are projected into real environments based on the best factual information of situations in time, in space and in any material state we can realise in practical terms.

Using unusual exciting backgrounds, or ordinary backgrounds seen unusually, each story will have a strong informational core based on fact. Our central characters because of their 'ship' may find themselves on the shores of Britain when Caesar and his legionnaires landed in 44 BC; may find themselves in their own school laboratories but reduced to the size of a pinhead; or on Mars; or Venus; etc etc.

The series, by the use of the characters in action stories, is designed to bridge the gap between our massive audience who watch sport on Saturday afternoon and those teenagers who watch *Juke Box Jury*.

CHARACTERS

Our four basic characters:

SUE

15, working-class, still at school; a sharp intelligent girl, quick and perky. She makes mistakes, however, because of inexperience. Uses the latest teenage slang. Has a crush on Cliff and regrets that his name is the same as Cliff Richard whom she now thinks is a square.

CLIFF

27, red-brick university type, the teacher of applied science at Sue's school. Physically perfect, a gymnast, dexterous with his hands.

MISS MCGOVERN

23, a history mistress at the same school. Middle class. Timid but capable of sudden courage. Admires Cliff, resulting in undercurrents of antagonism between her and Sue.

These are the characters we know and sympathise with, the ordinary people to whom extraordinary things happen. The fourth basic character remains always something of a mystery ...

DR WHO

A name given to him by his three earthly friends because neither he nor they know who he is. Dr Who is about 650 years old. Frail looking but wiry and tough like an old turkey – is amply demonstrated whenever he is forced to run from danger. His watery blue eyes are continually looking around in bewilderment and occasionally a look of utter malevolence clouds his face as he suspects his earthly friends of being part of some conspiracy. He seems not to remember where he comes from but he has flashes of garbled memory which indicate that he was involved in a galactic war and still fears pursuit by some undefined enemy. Because he is somewhat pathetic his three friends continually try to help him find his way 'home', but they are never sure of his motives.

THE SHIP

Dr Who has a 'ship' which enables them to travel together through space, through time, and through matter. When first seen, this ship has the appearance of a police telephone box standing in the street, but anyone entering it finds himself inside an extensive electronic contrivance. Though it looks impressive, it is an old beat-up model which Dr Who stole when he escaped from his own galaxy in the year 5733; it is uncertain in performance; moreover, Dr Who isn't quite sure how to work it, so they have to learn by trial and error.

FIRST STORY

The Giants

Four episodes of turbulent adventure in which proportion and size are dramatized

Leaving the secondary modern school where they work at the end of Parents Day, the applied science master, Cliff, and the history mistress, Miss McGovern, come across Sue in the fog. She asks them to help her find the home of a strange old man (Dr Who) who is lost.

To their surprise they find that his home is apparently a police box. To their further amazement they discover that its shabby exterior conceals a vast chromium and glass interior of a kind of space ship. They become locked in. Through the pressing of wrong buttons the ship convulses itself, breaking away from its moorings (no exteriors of this, please). More wrong buttons pressed and they discover that the ship has the capacity to transport them into time, space and other seemingly material worlds. In fact they get a preview of this.

The first episode ends when they find themselves in Cliff's own school laboratory. To their horror they have been reduced to the size of pinheads. 'All we have to do' says Sue 'is to get back to the ship.' Miss McGovern (somewhat hysterically) 'That's all! At our present size the door is equivalent to two miles away!'

Three more episodes follow to complete this first story in which their dreaded enemies turn out to be the other students and teachers who are of normal size and who might step on them at any moment. This adventure ends about two-thirds through the fourth episode and a new adventure begins.

Prepared by:
Donald Wilson
C E Webber
Sydney Newman

16 May 1963

Monday 20: Sydney Newman, now satisfied with the format document, sends a copy of it to Chief of Programmes Donald Baverstock with the following memo:

> This formalises on paper our intentions with respect to the new Saturday afternoon serial which is to hit the air on 24 August. As you will see, this is more or less along the lines of the discussion between you and me and Joanna Spicer some months ago.
>
> Those of us who worked on this brief, and the writers we have discussed assignments with, are very enthusiastic about it. If things go reasonably well and the right facilities can be made to work, we will have an outstanding winner.

Baverstock later tells Newman that the series is 'looking great.'

Tuesday 21: Ayton Whitaker sends John Mair a memo indicating that, owing to the previously notified four week postponement in recording of the series' first episode, the planned pre-filming at the BBC's Television Film Studios in Ealing should also be put back by four weeks. Filming for the first story should therefore take place in week commencing Saturday 20 July (Week 30 in BBC production terms).

Later the same day, Whitaker sends Mair another memo, requesting that filming for the first story now be brought forward by two weeks to week commencing 6 July as there is to be an experimental pilot episode of the series recorded on Friday 19 July. If this pilot proves successful, it will form the first transmitted episode on Saturday 24 August; if it proves unsuccessful, however, there will be two weeks remaining in which to resolve any technical problems before the previously scheduled first recording date of Friday 2 August.

Tuesday 28: Rex Tucker sends a memo to Donald Wilson expressing the view that the facilities available at Lime Grove Studio D will be inadequate for recording of such a technically complex production as *Doctor Who*.

Friday 31: Donald Wilson discusses Rex Tucker's memo of 28 May with Ian Atkins, who as Controller of Programme Services for Television has overall responsibility for the BBC's studio facilities. Ayton Whitaker is also present and later in the day produces a note of the meeting. Atkins agrees that, with its 'old fashioned lighting equipment,' Studio D is 'virtually the worst possible studio for such a project.' Other options are considered, including using either TC2 or TC5 at Television Centre which, because of their smaller size, would require recording over two days rather than one, with a concomitant increase in artists' fees. Donald Wilson decides that this is unacceptable and that the larger TC3 or TC4 should be used for the first serial – unless TC2 and TC5 can both be used together on the same day, with the artists moving between them as required. It is also agreed that Studio 2 at Riverside could be acceptable for the second serial, provided that new inlay equipment has been installed by then as anticipated.

By the end of May, *Doctor Who*'s production team has gained an additional member in the person of associate producer Mervyn Pinfield. Pinfield has worked in the BBC's television service since its earliest days in the thirties and is particularly expert in technical matters. His job will be to co-ordinate and advise on the technical aspects of *Doctor Who*'s realisation, drawing in part on his experience of directing the science fiction serial *The Monsters* the previous November.

JUNE 1963

Whilst development of the series' format has been progressing, Rex Tucker has been turning his attention to other aspects of the production. He has approached composer Tristram Cary to see if he would be willing to provide both the theme tune and the incidental music for the first serial, and has asked Hugh David if he would be interested in taking on the role of the Doctor. David however has declined, disliking the high public profile he has gained as a result of a recent stint as a regular in the Granada TV series *Knight Errant*.

Anthony Coburn has meanwhile started work on the series' second story, another four-parter, in which he proposes that the Doctor's time machine should journey back to the Stone Age. Coburn – full name James Anthony Coburn – has been on staff at the BBC ever since coming to England from his native Australia, where he worked as a butcher's assistant before turning to writing.

Tuesday 4: Donald Wilson sends Sydney Newman a full synopsis for Webber's story *The Giants*, promising that draft scripts for the first two episodes will be ready by the end of the week.

Webber's synopsis refers back to the 16 May format guide for the opening part of the first episode. It goes on to describe how in the later episodes the four travellers find themselves back in Cliff's classroom but reduced to one-sixteenth of an inch tall. A biology class is in progress and Cliff and Sue, having become separated from Lola and the Doctor, face a variety of dangers including a caterpillar, a boy carving his initials in a desk with a compass point, and a spider in a matchbox. They eventually make their way over to a microscope and position themselves under the lens, where they are spotted first by the pupils and then by the teacher.

By recording their voices onto tape and playing them back at a slower speed, so as to compensate for the change in pitch resulting from their miniaturisation, Cliff and Sue are able to communicate with the 'giants' and explain their predicament. The 'giants' and the 'minis' then co-operate in rescuing Lola, who has set out on a valiant but hopeless attempt to find Sue and Cliff. The travellers are returned to the police box just in time to avert an impending danger (which Webber suggests might be the threat of the ship being eaten by a mouse).

Friday 7: Sydney Newman briefly discusses with Donald Wilson and John Mair the problem regarding the unsuitability of Lime Grove D for recording of *Doctor Who*. It now appears that this will be the only studio available on the dates required for the first two serials. It is agreed that Mair will talk to Ian Atkins to ascertain how difficult it would be to have the facilities there adapted to make them more suitable.

Monday 10: Sydney Newman, having made a number of handwritten annotations to Bunny Webber's synopsis of *The Giants*, returns it to Donald Wilson with a memo summarising his reactions. He comments that 'the four episodes seem extremely thin on incident and character' and that Webber has 'forgotten that his human beings, even though miniscule, must have normal sized emotions.' The memo continues:

> Items involving spiders etc get us into the BEM school of science fiction which, while thrilling, is hardly practical for live television. In fact what I am afraid irritated me about the synopsis was the fact that it seemed to be conceived without much regard for the fact that this was a *live* television drama serial. The notion of the police box dwindling before the policeman's eyes until it's one-eighth of an inch in size is patently impossible without spending a tremendous amount of money.
>
> There are also some very good things in the synopsis, like the invention of the use of the microphone and microscope to enable our central characters to communicate with the normal size people.
>
> I implore you please keep the entire conception within the realms of practical live television.

(Newman's comments about 'live television' here are presumably figurative rather than literal, referring to the fact that the series is to be recorded largely continuously, as if live. *Doctor Who* has been planned from the outset as a recorded programme – a fact that Newman recognizes in earlier correspondence.)

Bunny Webber has by this time completed draft scripts for the first two episodes of *The Giants*. On the basis of these, however, Donald Wilson and Rex Tucker have decided to reject the story. This is partly because they realise that even radical reworking will fail to overcome Newman's objections (Tucker will later offer the opinion that Webber was too good a writer to 'write down to the level required') but mainly because the necessary 'giant' effects will now be impossible to achieve given that the production is to be restricted to Studio D, where amongst other problems the cameras cannot take either wide-angle or zoom lenses.

Wilson has concluded that, in view of the shortage of time now remaining before the planned recording dates, Anthony Coburn's story should be moved forward from second place to first in the running order. He has asked Coburn to adapt the first episode of his story accordingly, drawing on Webber's draft for ideas. He has also given him the task of writing in due course a replacement second story, again in four episodes.

Ayton Whitaker sends a memo to John Mair summarising the planned production dates and budgets for these first two serials. He ends with the following note headed 'Subsequent Serials':

While the first two serials of this 52 week series of serials can be produced in Studio D, a change of studio will almost certainly be required for some of the later ones. This change should be to (in order of preference): (i) TC2 & TC5; (ii) TC3 or TC4; (iii) Riverside 2. We would be glad if this change could be made in time for recording the third serial.

Tuesday 11: Donald Wilson goes on leave to take a holiday in Norway.

Rex Tucker sends Ayton Whitaker a 'blocked-out schedule' for production of the first serial, starting with pre-filming for the pilot episode in week commencing 6 July and ending with recording of the fourth and final episode either in week commencing 10 August or in week commencing 17 August depending on whether or not the pilot episode has proved acceptable for transmission. In his covering memo, Tucker notes that he has taken 19 July as the optimum date for recording of the pilot episode but that if the whole schedule is shifted 'a day or two earlier or (*preferably*) later' it would not matter as there is a week in hand at the end before he is due to go on leave. He adds:

> The post-recording of the special music on the video tape *after* the latter is made (a special and essential facility Donald Wilson agreed with me) prevents the pilot (1) date coming much closer to the second recording date than the fortnight which (for other reasons) I know you consider necessary.
>
> The playback immediately following recordings is for me to brief the composer. It is essential for the pilot (1) recording and very desirable after the others.

Wednesday 12: John Mair and Ian Atkins discuss the continuing problem of *Doctor Who*'s studio allocation. It is suggested that specialist inlay equipment could be transferred from TC2 to Riverside 2 to enable the series to be made in the latter.

Thursday 13: John Mair sends a memo to Ian Atkins. He reports that Donald Baverstock is unwilling to have inlay equipment transferred from TC2 to Riverside 2 as suggested, as this would deprive the popular satirical show *That Was the Week That Was* of the facility. He also reports that the Drama Group have now agreed that the first eight episodes of *Doctor Who* can be made in Lime Grove D and that Baverstock wishes to see how this works out before deciding whether or not a move is necessary. Baverstock does wish to know, however, what the cost and other implications would be of installing specialist inlay equipment in Riverside 2; if the answers are satisfactory, he might reconsider that studio being used on a permanent basis.

Richard Levin, the Head of Television Design, sends a memo to Joanna Spicer for the attention of John Mair, protesting at the demands which the new series will place on his Department:

> So far there are *no* accepted scripts for the series – at least if there are we

have not seen any.

The designer allocated for the series – and I have no substitute – does not return from leave until Monday of Week 26 and I am not prepared to let him start designing until there are four accepted scripts in his hands. The first filming cannot take place within four weeks of this.

I also understand that the series requires extensive model-making and other visual effects. This cannot be undertaken under four weeks' notice and, unless other demands are withdrawn, I estimate the need would be for an additional four effects assistants and 400 sq ft of additional space.

To my mind, to embark on a series of this kind and length in these circumstances will undoubtedly put this Department in an untenable situation and, as a natural corollary, will throw Scenic Servicing Department for a complete 'burton'. This is the kind of crazy enterprise which both Departments can well do without.

Ayton Whitaker sends a memo to Sydney Newman's deputy, Assistant Head of Drama Group Norman Rutherford – Newman himself having, like Donald Wilson, gone away on leave at this point – recommending that if the series' previously-stated production requirements cannot be met, as would appear to be the case from Richard Levin's comments, then the Drama Group should make no further compromise in its attempts to meet the planned first transmission date of 24 August but should 'ask for postponement … until such time as *we* are ready.'

By the end of the week, another major development has occurred with the arrival at Television Centre of *Doctor Who*'s permanent producer, Verity Lambert. She has been appointed to the post by Sydney Newman after his first choice, Don Taylor, turned it down. As Newman will later recall, she is exactly the kind of young, go-ahead person he wants in charge of the series:

When Donald Wilson and I discussed who might take over the responsibility for producing the show, I rejected the traditional drama types, who did the children's serials, and said that I wanted somebody, full of piss-and-vinegar, who'd be prepared to break rules in doing the show. Somebody young with a sense of 'today' – the early 'Swinging London' days.

I phoned Verity Lambert, who had been on my *Armchair Theatre* staff at ABC. She had never directed, produced, acted or written drama but, by god, she was a bright, highly intelligent, outspoken production secretary who took no nonsense and never gave any. I offered her the job and after Donald Wilson met her she joined us. I have a vague recollection that Donald Wilson at first sniffed at Verity Lambert's 'Independent' ways. Knowing both of them, I knew they would hit it off when they got to know one another better. They did.

Lambert's office is in Room 5014 on Television Centre's fifth floor (the floor allocated for use by the Drama Group), where she begins to acquaint herself with the work already carried out on the series. She has been sent in advance by Newman a copy of the format document and also a copy of a report published by ABC describing the results of a study carried out by two educationalists into children's reactions when viewing episode seven of *Pathfinders to Venus.*

Staff director Waris Hussein is also assigned to *Doctor Who* around this time to handle the second story.

Monday 17: A meeting takes place between production and servicing personnel with a view to reaching agreement over *Doctor Who*'s requirements. A two week postponement in production has now been decided upon, with initial pre-filming for the pilot episode put back to week commencing 20 July. Anthony Coburn's draft script for the first episode of serial one is now available, and those for the other three are confidently expected to be completed by 26 June. It is agreed that the series' filming, costume and make-up requirements can all be met without difficulty, both in the short term and in the long term. Although Richard Levin has specified that scenic design work for serial one cannot get underway until all four scripts are available, this should cause no difficulties provided that their completion is not delayed. To meet Levin's request for an extra four effects assistants and 400 square feet of space, however, would add approximately £40 to the cost of each episode. James Bould, the Design Manager, points out that the design and construction of the space/time machine will be particularly time consuming.

Tuesday 18: John Mair sends Joanna Spicer a memo recording the outcome of the previous day's meeting. He concludes:

> 1. It is clear … that provided the script dates are met we could handle recording on a weekly basis from Week 33 of the first two serials, carrying us up to Week 40, all in Studio D.

> 2. The question to be decided is whether to do this before the long-term studio problem has been solved. It seems unlikely that this can be done by June 26; and it seems therefore that we can either:

> (a) Ask Head of Drama Group to accept D on a continuing basis for the present, with an assurance that we will try to provide Riverside 2 as and when possible, but no certainty that in fact it can be done. Transmission would then start in Week 37;

> (b) Postpone the start of production for, say, another six weeks, and decide the Riverside 2 issue before we launch out on a continuing basis. If we did that, transmission would not start before Week 43. We should have to fill with further repeats – e.g. *Dark Island.*

> 3. My own feeling is that the long-term studio basis should be settled first, and that we should do all we can to do this before June 26, or as soon thereafter as we possibly can.

Ian Atkins speaks to D M B Grubb – designated Senior Assistant, Planning, Television – who agrees to report by 26 June on the implications of specialist inlay equipment being installed in Riverside 2.

Ayton Whitaker sends a memo to Terence Cook, the Acting Drama Organiser for Television, requesting that arrangements be made for an experimental session to take place in Lime Grove D between 10.30 am and 5.30 pm on Friday 19 July. The purpose of this session is to test the viability of achieving the dematerialisation of the Doctor's ship without recourse to inlay, using the previously untried 'roll back and mix' technique of rewinding the videotape between shots and performing a mix between two separately recorded images:

> In all aspects our requirements are minimal, i.e. design: a police or 'phone box, plus a little additional stock; technical requirements: two cameramen, simple lighting. We shall also require one vision mixer and one scene hand.

> NB This experimental session is for technical purposes and is quite distinct from the pilot recording two weeks later.

Whitaker also sends a memo to Bill Patterson, Assistant Head of Studio Management, requesting on Rex Tucker's behalf that Noel Lidiard-White be assigned as the vision mixer for the first serial, or Rachel Blayney if he is not available.

Other preferences expressed by Tucker for the first serial are to have Crew 1 or 4 as the camera crew, Graham Sothcott as Technical Operations Manager, Jack Brummett or Jack Clayton as Sound Supervisor and, in order of preference, Sam Barclay, Gerry Millerson, Geoff Shaw or Phil Ward as Lighting Supervisor.

Thursday 20: Donald Baverstock, Joanna Spicer and John Mair meet to discuss the problems regarding the servicing of the new series.

James Mudie, the Head of Scenic Servicing for Television, sends Mair the following memo:

> The present late information/drawing/properties plot situation is so bad that I feel you should think twice before proceeding with a weekly series of this nature. If you decide to proceed and the series falls in arrears with scripts, can I have an assurance that it will be withdrawn? If you cannot give this assurance and you decide to proceed as planned, I consider you are likely to endanger the rest of the planned output.

Friday 21: Mair sends Spicer a memo informing her that since the previous day's meeting he has heard from Assistant Head of Drama Group Norman Rutherford that Baverstock has now given his agreement for the new series to be started once four scripts are available. As previously stated, this should be by 26 June. In the event of a delay, further repeats can be scheduled as a stop-gap. He also reports that he has now heard it will be a year before specialist inlay equipment can be installed in Riverside 2, and that the cost would be £5,000. He continues:

> I am frankly not very happy about the idea of starting this series without

Drama knowing the continuing studio basis on which they are to operate. I suspect that unless we tell them they will instruct their script-writers – and they are struggling to get some scripts written – to write on the assumption that they can use extensive visual effects, tricks etc. For the same reason I feel we have to let them know whether additional Effects Assistants are likely to be available in the long run or not.

Monday 24: By the beginning of this week, the final member of *Doctor Who*'s production team has been appointed in the person of David Whitaker. He has spent the past six years on the staff of the recently-abolished Script Department, most recently as the assistant script editor responsible for Sunday plays, and is already fully conversant with the background to *Doctor Who*. His office, which he shares with fellow BBC story editor Barry Thomas, is in a caravan parked outside Television Centre.

Spicer sends Baverstock a memo, attaching the one of 20 June from Mudie to Mair:

> This had not arrived when we had our discussion last Thursday: but it supports my statement to you that I feel we ought not to embark on this series until there are an agreed number of scripts completed and accepted for servicing requirements.
>
> A.H.D.G.(Tel) [Assistant Head of Drama Group Norman Rutherford] informed S.P.A.(I) [Mair] after our meeting with you that you had accepted the series subject to the availability of four scripts. I hope you will agree that, before we give pre-recording facilities, these scripts must have reached the servicing departments and have been fully discussed with them and then with us.
>
> I think the real danger is that scripts will fall behind again after this delivery of the first four. From our meeting, however, I understood that you would be prepared to drop the series after eight if things go badly.
>
> A.C.P.S.(Tel) [Ian Atkins' assistant, Leonard Miall] has informed S.P.A.(I) that it would cost £5,000 to buy specialist inlay equipment for Riverside 2 and that the equipment would have to be installed in a room adjacent to the gallery, not in the gallery itself.
>
> It seems definite therefore that we must inform H.S.D. (Tel) [Donald Wilson] that all the episodes which they are now planning must be written for Studio D.

Tuesday 25: Terence Cook replies to Ayton Whitaker's memo of 18 June, telling him that as 'the whole production is awaiting the arrival of four scripts, and there is a stand-still on all facilities pending this moment,' no progress can be made on arranging the requested experimental session for 19 July.

Coburn has now completed a draft script for the second episode of serial one, which he has decided to assign the working title *The Tribe of Gum*. He has given the male schoolteacher the new name Mr Chesterton and has amended the young girl's name to Susan Forman. The script contains no dialogue for the Stone Age characters as the intention is that they will communicate merely by grunts. He sends the script to David Whitaker with the following letter:

I meant you to have this on Monday morning, but I have found out one thing about the cave man that you might pass on to any learned anthropologists you know – and I am sure you number many amongst your closest friends – and it is this. They must have been very much smaller than ourselves. This fact I deduce, not from a close study of their implements, nor by using my Scobonomometer in Hachendorff's Test of the Plutonium content of their left elbows ... but by knowing how bloody difficult it is to get into their skins.

And lastly, I rather think that, wordwise, this one might be a little too long. I'm a lousy timer. See what you think.

Son of the son of the son of the son of the son of the ad infinitum, firemaker,

Tony

Verity Lambert has a meeting with Head of Design Richard Levin and Design Manager James Bould. Levin backs down from his previous stand and agrees that scenic design work can now go ahead on the basis of just the two scripts currently available, given that no new sets are to be required for the other two episodes of the story.

D M B Grubb sends a memo to Ian Atkins explaining that the reason no inlay equipment can be installed in Riverside 2 until the following year is that all resources are currently tied up in providing the additional studios and facilities required for the forthcoming launch of BBC2. He indicates that the cost of the new equipment would be (contrary to the figure previously quoted) around £3,500.

Rex Tucker holds auditions in Television Centre Room 2119 for the roles of Susan Forman and Miss McGovern. The audition list reads:

Susan: Maureen Crombie, Anna Palk, Waveney Lee, Anneke Wills (not seen), Heather Fleming, Christa Bergman (to be considered in her absence), Camilla Hasse, Ann Casteldini.

Miss McGovern: Phillida Law, Penelope Lee, Sally Holme.

Tucker will many years later recall that he decided to cast 'an Australian girl' as Susan.

Wednesday 26: Coburn has now completed a draft script for the third episode of *The Tribe of Gum*, but the fourth is not expected to be ready until Friday 28.

Verity Lambert and David Whitaker both dislike Coburn's story and, despite the problems already caused by the unavailability of scripts, seriously consider rejecting it. Coburn is asked to carry out a substantial rewrite. Around the same time, Lambert approaches Terence Dudley – the producer responsible for the earlier Saturday serial *The Big Pull* – to see if he would be willing to write a replacement first story, but he declines.

Lambert sends a memo to Pauline Mansfield-Clark, Head of Artists' Bookings, to set out the basis on which the series' cast should be engaged:

Will you please note that the four principals in the above series, i.e. Dr Who, Mr Chesterton, Miss McGovern, Susan Foreman, should be booked on the following basis: for the pilot to be recorded on Friday 2 August (rehearsals to start on 26 July) on a two thirds payment to be made up to a full payment if it is transmitted, with an option for 51 weekly episodes, the first to start rehearsals on Monday 14 August, with a further option for one extra week should the pilot not be transmitted. To confirm our telephone conversation, there will be no recording or rehearsals during Christmas week, which will mean adding a week on to the total.

Will you please note that all the small parts for the first four episodes should be booked for the pilot on a two thirds payment, to be made up to a full payment on transmission, and for three weekly episodes (rehearsals to start on Monday 14 August) at full payment with an option for a further week at the end of this period should the pilot not be transmitted.

Artists may be required from time to time to do pre-filming, and bookings for this should be taken direct from the director concerned.

It will subsequently be agreed that the fifty-two week contracts for the regulars should be subdivided into four option periods of eight weeks, twelve weeks, sixteen weeks and sixteen weeks respectively, rather than two periods of one week and fifty-one weeks as Lambert has suggested.

Thursday 27: Sydney Newman, having now returned from leave, learns of the behind-the-scenes wrangling that has gone on in his and Donald Wilson's absence. He has a heated phone conversation with Joanna Spicer in which Spicer alleges that the Serials Department has failed to follow correct BBC procedures in setting up the new series; that the production team has been carrying out auditions and making other preparations without her authorization; and that the series' ambitious nature will place unreasonable demands upon the servicing departments. Later in the day, Newman sends Spicer a memo headed '*Dr Who* Hassle', which begins as follows:

Your comments of today on the 'phone absolutely flabbergasted me and I take exception to most of what you said. We are trying to get a new children's serial out economically and quickly and from what I can see the Serials Department of this Group has acted in complete accordance with all the standard Corporation procedures.

The memo then summarises some of the key steps in the development of the series to date, before concluding:

In view of the above, and since the first recording date is only five weeks away, do you wonder that we are anxious not to be held up? We have got to cast four people who must wear well over something like 52 episodes.

I cannot understand from the mass of correspondence that has gone on about this project why permission is still required from your office. At no time have I received from Ch.P.(1). [Baverstock], or anybody else, the notion that the project was ever even vaguely in doubt. Especially as we have in the main held to the limitations stated on 26 April. While I may be ignorant of some of the finer points of Corporation routine, it is apparent that Ayton Whitaker and others in my Group are not. I am, therefore, surprised at what seems to me a last minute hold up. After all, it was only H.Tel.Des. [Levin] who dug his heels in about the scripts and he changed his mind two days ago.

You may assume only that I intend to get drama programmes out on time and within budget. That my attitude to you and to Corporation routine will never be less than correct.

Spicer subsequently has a meeting with her Head of Department and Donald Baverstock in which a change is agreed to the early Saturday evening schedule: instead of two twenty-five minute children's programmes, broadcast between 5.00 pm and 5.50 pm, there will in future be only one half hour one, broadcast between 5.20 pm and 5.50 pm. This change will take place on 28 September and the new slot will be filled initially with the cartoon series *Deputy Dawg*, *Doctor Who* will then take over from 9 November onwards.

Friday 28: John Mair's deputy Alan Shallcross sends Spicer a memo reporting that Richard Levin and the Design Manager have now studied the first three scripts for *The Tribe of Gum* and have confirmed that they can meet the servicing requirements based on the previously agreed production dates. They are however unable to accept the requested experimental session on Friday 19 July.

Spicer, meanwhile, sends Baverstock a memo noting the outcome of their meeting the previous day. She also has a meeting with Sydney Newman and Kenneth Adam, the Controller of Programmes for Television, and later sends Newman a memo recording the decisions taken. In view of the change in the Saturday evening schedule, production of *Doctor Who* is to be postponed for a further eight weeks and the episode length increased from 25 minutes to 30. The pilot episode is to be recorded on Friday 27 September and the subsequent episodes weekly from Friday 18 October, all in Lime Grove D. The budget per episode is set at £2,300 and Newman is asked to make a formal request if the producer still wishes to use extensive visual effects which will entail the cost of extra staff, space and equipment. In addition, Newman is asked to confirm that the 'space time machine which is to be used throughout the series' cannot be financed on the standard budget.

Later in the day, at a Programme Management Board meeting, Sydney Newman protests at the change of episode length, pointing out that it has always been planned as 25 minutes. Ronald Waldman, the General Manager of Television Enterprises, also favours that length as it is better for overseas sales purposes. It is agreed that the episode length should be the subject of further discussion.

JULY 1963

Monday 1: The production team are informed of the postponement of the series. They quickly realise that Rex Tucker will no longer be able to direct *The Tribe of Gum* as the new production dates cut across the period when he is due to take a holiday in Majorca. It is therefore agreed that Waris Hussein will now direct the first story and Tucker the second.

Tucker subsequently phones composer Tristram Cary to tell him that, as a result of this change of plan, he will no longer be required to provide the music for *The Tribe of Gum*.

Verity Lambert and Waris Hussein dislike Tucker's casting ideas for the four regulars and, during the course of July, set about making their own choices. Actors considered for the role of the Doctor include Cyril Cusack (who is David Whitaker's suggestion) and Leslie French (who is favoured by Mervyn Pinfield and by Lambert herself). Lambert eventually decides to approach fifty-five year old character actor William Hartnell, having been impressed by his performances in the Granada TV comedy series *The Army Game* and in the film *This Sporting Life*. She contacts his agent – Hartnell's own son-in-law, Terry Carney, of the Eric l'Epine Smith agency – who, although a little reluctant to recommend a part in a 'children's programme', realises that this might be just the thing the actor needs to break out of his type-casting as a tough guy army officer or crook. Carney visits Hartnell at his home in Mayfield, Sussex and discusses the idea with him, taking along a copy of the draft first script for his perusal. Hartnell's reaction is initially quite positive, and he agrees to a meeting with Lambert and Hussein. His remaining reservations are then overcome, and he accepts the role of the Doctor.

The role of Ian goes to Russell Enoch, who uses the stage name William Russell. He is another actor whom Verity Lambert has admired for some time and is well known for his portrayal of Sir Lancelot in the Sapphire Films series *The Adventures of Sir Lancelot*. His BBC credits include *Suspense: The Patch Card, Moonstrike, Jane Eyre* (directed by Rex Tucker), *A Song of Sixpence, Nautilus* and *Adventure Story*.

Jacqueline Hill, a former model whose BBC credits include *Maigret, The Man from Room 13, The Watching Cat* and *The Six Proud Walkers* and whose husband, Alvin Rakoff, is an old friend of Verity Lambert's, is cast as Barbara after Lambert sees her at a party.

A number of actresses are considered for the role of Susan. These include Jackie Lane (then working under the name Jackie Lenya), whom Lambert and Hussein have seen appearing in recent episodes of the soap opera *Compact*. Lane loses interest however when she learns that the series is to run for a year, being disinclined to commit herself to one job for that length of time. The role eventually goes to twenty-three year old Carole Ann Ford after Hussein spots her on a monitor at Television Centre and recommends her to Lambert. Ford has been acting since an early age. She has appeared in a number of films, including *Mix Me a Person* and *Day of the Triffids*, and in TV series including ATV's *Emergency Ward 10* and, for the BBC, *Moonstrike, Compact* and *Man on a Bicycle*.

Tuesday 2: Ayton Whitaker sends a memo to John Mair setting out proposed new dates for filming at Ealing for the first three stories. He adds that an additional £500 will still be needed for building of the space/time machine and that a one day experimental session is still desired for Friday 19 July.

Ayton Whitaker also phones Design Manager James Bould and points out that the production team are awaiting the allocation of a designer so that they can explain their requirements for the space/time machine.

Wednesday 3: Ayton Whitaker sends a further memo to John Mair explaining that as the Design Department are unable to service the experimental session planned for 19 July, and as the technical adviser for the session is due to go on leave on 20 July, it should be postponed until Friday 13 September.

Anthony Coburn has left the staff of the BBC at the end of June following the demise of the Script Department. David Whitaker therefore briefs the Copyright Department to commission him to continue working on his two stories on a freelance basis. It has been agreed that the second story, with the working title *The Robots*, will now be a six-parter rather than a four-parter.

Friday 5: Head of Copyright R G Walford sends Coburn a contract for his ten episodes. At David Whitaker's request, it is made clear in the contract that the initial idea of *Doctor Who* and its four basic characters are the property of the BBC. Coburn is to receive the standard script fee of £225 for each of his episodes. Walford's letter continues:

> I understand that in this case you would like the payments for the initial fees for the ten programmes to be paid in the form of twelve monthly payments beginning on 1 August 1963 (so that in effect they will replace payments which you would have had in your staff contract as a scriptwriter/adaptor which has recently been terminated).

Donald Baverstock confirms that the episode length of *Doctor Who* will, after all, be 25 minutes. Sydney Newman conveys this information in a memo to Donald Wilson.

During the course of this week, both Verity Lambert and Mervyn Pinfield have made further calls to James Bould to enquire if he is yet in a position to allocate a designer to *Doctor Who*. He has told them that he may be able to do so on the following Monday.

Monday 8: Coburn receives his contract and signs it 'James A Coburn.'

Shortly after this, Coburn delivers to David Whitaker a revised script for the first episode of *The Tribe of Gum*. Concerned at the possible sexual connotations of a young schoolgirl travelling alone with an old man, he has suggested making Susan an alien of royal blood from the same planet as the Doctor and renaming her Suzanne.

David Whitaker passes the script on to Verity Lambert with the following note:

> Tony has improved episode one very much – particularly regarding CHESTERTON.
>
> He agrees to the change of any names we wish.
>
> I have discussed the whole business with him and we have agreed he shall push on and finish all four of the scripts before we get down to going through each one with the minor changes.
>
> He feels that the 'Gums' ought to talk.
>
> I have some reservations about this episode, this newly rewritten one, but all in all it flows much better. Tony has inserted some details about Suzanne regarding her own existence which we ought to consider, for they are important. Doctor Who, as you will read, tells that (or hints that) Suzanne has some sort of royal blood. This gives Dr Who and Suzanne good reason to leave their own environment, of course, but I think we must discuss this carefully with Tony when we go through the scripts with him.
>
> Regarding Doctor Who, I feel that he should be more like the old Professor that Frank Morgan played in *The Wizard of Oz*, only a little more authentic. Then we can strike some of the charm and humour as well as the mystery, the suspicion and the cunning. Do you agree with this idea?

The insertion of Suzanne as a princess or whatever can be carried off quite well but I think it ought to be done in a rather lighter way. Also I think Chesterton is a couple of shades too beefy in attacking Doctor Who.

Minor reservations then, but this is a better script. The cliff-hanger isn't as good as Tony's earlier one.

In subsequent discussions with Coburn, the idea of Suzanne being a princess is dropped. Instead, it is decided that she should be the Doctor's grand-daughter. Her name is finally fixed as Susan Foreman, and those of the two teachers as Ian Chesterton and Barbara Wright. It is however agreed that the Stone Age tribe should have dialogue. Whitaker will later describe this as 'the hardest decision we had to make' with regard to the tribe.

Tuesday 9: David Whitaker briefs the Copyright Department to commission Canadian writer John Lucarotti to provide the series' third story, a seven-parter with the working title *A Journey to Cathay*. Lucarotti has been suggested as a potential contributor to *Doctor Who* by Sydney Newman, who is an old friend of his. He lives and works in Majorca and makes only occasional visits to England, so most of his subsequent discussions with David Whitaker will be conducted over the phone. Waris Hussein has been assigned to direct Lucarotti's story.

Wednesday 10: Verity Lambert again phones James Bould about the allocation of a designer to the series, and is told that Peter Brachacki has been detailed to handle the first four episodes and the design of the space/time machine. At present, however, Brachacki is largely tied up on other programmes.

In the afternoon, Lambert, Mervyn Pinfield and Waris Hussein have a preliminary meeting with Brachacki. Brachacki can spare only half an hour and informs the production team that he will be completely unavailable for the next two weeks.

Friday 12: Verity Lambert asks the Music Copyright Department to contact the New York agent of the avant-garde French electronic music composers Jacques Lasry and Francois Baschet with a view to commissioning them and their group, Les Structures Sonores, to provide fifteen to twenty seconds of opening title music for *Doctor Who*. Les Structures Sonores typically create their music by such techniques as playing glass rods mounted in steel.

David Whitaker has by this time prepared a revised version of the series' format document. This is based on the 16 May version but has been updated to take account of more recent developments. The following new paragraphs have been added to the section headed 'Approach to the Stories':

> It is emphasised that the 'ship' may transport the four characters backwards or forwards, sideways into lesser or greater dimensions or into non-gravitational existence or invisibility etcetera, but once arrived into the different place and time the four characters have only their intelligence and ingenuity upon which to rely. They cannot produce a 'ray gun' to reduce a horde of Picts and Scots, nor can they rely upon specialised drugs to cure a Greek philosopher.

It is also emphasised that the four characters cannot make history. Advice must not be proffered to Nelson on his battle tactics when approaching the Nile, nor must bon mots be put into the mouth of Oscar Wilde. They are four people plunged into alien surroundings armed with only their courage and cleverness.

The character outline for Doctor Who now states that he is aged 'over sixty' rather than 'about 650' and the one for Susan has been amended to read as follows:

The Doctor's grand-daughter, aged fifteen. She is a sharp, intelligent girl, quick and perky. She makes mistakes, however, because of inexperience. Addicted to 20th Century contemporary slang and likes pop records – in fact, she admires the life teenagers enjoy in 1963. At the beginning of the story, she has persuaded her grandfather to stay in 1963 so that she can go to school and create at least one complete section of experience. Since she has been visiting all sorts of existences and places with her grandfather, Susan has a wide general knowledge and on some subjects can be brilliantly factual. On other matters, she is lamentably ignorant. She has something of a crush on Ian Chesterton.

The paragraph on the Doctor's ship has also undergone substantial revision, and now reads:

Doctor Who has a 'ship' which can travel through space, through time and through matter. It is a product of the year 5733 and cannot travel forward from that date (otherwise the Doctor and Sue could discover their own destinies), the authorities of the 50th Century deeming forward sight unlawful. This still enables Ian and Barbara (and the audience) to see into environments and existences far beyond the present day. The ship, when first seen, has the outward appearance of a police box, but the inside reveals an extensive electronic contrivance and comfortable living quarters with occasional bric-a-brac acquired by the Doctor in his travels. Primarily, the machine has a yearometer, which allows the traveller to select his stopping place. In the first story, however, the controls are damaged and the 'ship' becomes uncertain in performance, which explains why Ian and Barbara, once set upon their journey, are never able to return to their own time and place in their natural forms.

The revised document continues as follows:

The first story of four episodes, written by Anthony Coburn, begins the journey and takes the four travellers back in time to 100,000 BC to mid-Palaeolithic man, and it is in this story that the 'ship' is slightly damaged and forever afterwards is erratic in certain sections of its controls.

The second story of six episodes, written by Anthony Coburn, takes the travellers to some time approximately near the 30th Century, forward to the world when it is inhabited only by robots, where humanity has died away. The robots themselves, used to a life of service, have invented a master robot capable of original thought but, realising the dangers, have rendered their invention inoperative, even though it means they must sink into total inertia. The travellers, unaware of this situation, bring the robots and then the new invention 'to life' and face the dangers inherent in a pitiless computer.

Since this is primarily a series of stories concerning people rather than studio effects, and the original characters and backgrounds have been prepared already, the writer will be asked to submit a storyline from which he will be commissioned. This need not go into fractional detail – three or four pages of quarto ought to be sufficient to express the idea.

Technical advice is available insofar as what may or may not be achieved in the studio, but every endeavour will be made to meet the requirements of your story. There is a certain film budget, not extensive but sufficient to cover most contingencies, and the episodes will be Ampexed so that a 'stop and start' may be achieved if desired.

Writers may consult the story editor who will work out their plots and situations with them and arrange meetings with the associate producer who acts as the arbiter on technical and factual detail.

David Whitaker has sent this revised document to a number of freelance writers and writers' agents. 'They were all friends,' he will later recall, 'or otherwise friends of friends, who were then recommended to me … People I knew I could trust not only to produce a good story within the restrictions we had, but also who could produce their story to a very tight deadline.'

Writers so far invited to submit storylines are: Malcolm Hulke, Peter Yeldham, Robert Stewart (who will later write under the name Robert Banks Stewart), Terry Nation, Alan Wakeman, John Bowen and Jeremy Bullmore, and Barbara Harper.

Monday 15: Ayton Whitaker sends John Mair a memo listing the working title, director and number of episodes for each of the first three stories. He confirms that the second and third stories will each require five days' filming at Ealing, in weeks commencing 26 October (Week 44) and 7 December (Week 50) respectively, and concludes:

> In the event of the pilot recording in Week 39 being considered suitable for transmission, we will record part two of *The Tribe of Gum* in Week 42 and bring all subsequent recordings forward by one week until the Friday of Week 51 when we should record part one of *A Journey to Cathay*. We would then not record in Christmas week (Week 52), but record part two of *A Journey to Cathay* on the Friday of Week 1, as already planned. This arrangement cannot be put into effect until after the pilot recording has been assessed.
>
> I understand that Studio D will probably be going out of commission for conversion in December; I would be glad to know as soon as possible which will be the replacement studio for *Dr Who* as it will clearly have a bearing on facilities available for *A Journey to Cathay*.

Tuesday 16: C E Webber is paid a staff contribution fee of £187 10s 0d for the two scripts he wrote for his rejected story *The Giants*.

Wednesday 17: Verity Lambert sends Donald Wilson a memo recording her concern that the limited availability of designer Peter Brachacki has so far made it impossible to discuss with him in detail the requirements for the design of the first story and of the Doctor's time/space machine. She concludes:

> As we have been prepared to discuss in detail the design of the machine as from 2 July, I hope we will not be asked to make any compromises owing to shortage of effort in the Design Department.

Donald Wilson subsequently writes to Richard Levin, the Head of Design, conveying the substance of Lambert's memo and continuing:

> I should add that at the beginning of June, before I went away, I saw James Bould and told him of the special problems involved in *Dr Who*. We discussed possible designers and he told me there would be difficulty in obtaining the ideal man at that moment. There was no doubt in my mind when I heard of the postponement of the programme that a designer would be made available in time, particularly as everyone clearly understood the necessity for your Department to design and execute the space machine as early as possible.
>
> If the circumstances are as reported in Miss Lambert's note, it seems to me that this project, which is designed to run for 52 weeks, is not getting the necessary attention. We are constantly being asked for earlier information to help in design problems; the information is available, and has been available for some time. I would like to ask you now that one designer for the whole project of 52 weeks be agreed with Miss Lambert, with whatever assistance may be required, because we shall wish to maintain the same style of design throughout, however varied the different stories may be.

Monday 22: Donald Wilson holds a meeting with Richard Bright, the Television Publicity Organiser, to discuss promotion of *Doctor Who*.

David Whitaker is continuing to liaise with Anthony Coburn on his scripts for the first two stories. No-one on the production team is particularly enthusiastic about *The Tribe of Gum*, but it is too late for a replacement story to be found. Coburn's other story, which he has given the title *The Robots*, has undergone a number of revisions, and is now set on an alien planet rather than on a future Earth.

Tuesday 23: Richard Bright circulates a memo to his publicity colleagues attaching a copy of the format document for *Doctor Who* and reporting on the previous day's meeting with Donald Wilson. Likening the format to that of *Tim Frazer*, an earlier BBC drama which also consisted of a series of serials, he notes:

This is the first time we have undertaken a 52-part serial. It will be rather on the *Tim Frazer* pattern – a series of stories of varying lengths, each one starting during the last episode of the previous one. It will go on the air at 5.20-5.45 on Saturdays and is planned for family viewing with special attention to the 11-14 group.

After briefly summarising the intended transmission and production dates and the subject matter of the first three stories and giving the names of the four principal cast members, Bright continues:

Of the production team the producer, Verity Lambert, is a twenty-seven year old girl who has done a lot of commercial TV over here and has worked in the USA for David Susskind. She has been put on programme contract for a year to handle this serial. The two directors, Waris Hussein and Rex Tucker, will be in charge of alternate stories beginning with Hussein on No. 1. Anthony Coburn is writing the first two stories and the third will be written by John Lucarotti who has written a lot of television in the USA, Canada and commercial over here.

…

This would obviously be an important part of C.P Tel's [Kenneth Adam] autumn plans announcement and A.H.P. [the Assistant Head of Publicity] may decide to have a press launching when the first episode has been finally approved.

John Mair sends Sydney Newman and Donald Wilson a memo explaining that, due to previously unanticipated coverage of an athletics meeting in Moscow the previous Saturday, transmission of both *Deputy Dawg* and *Doctor Who* has been put back a further week. The first episode of *Doctor Who* is now therefore due to go out on Saturday 16 November.

Ronald Waldman, the General Manager of Television Enterprises, sends R G Walford, the Head of Copyright, a memo informing him of a dispute which has arisen with a company called Zenith Film Productions Ltd. Zenith have for some time been trying to interest the Children's Department and latterly Television Enterprises in commissioning a proposed new puppet series called *The Time Travellers*, devised by Martin and Hugh Woodhouse, the principal writers of the first season of Gerry Anderson's *Supercar* in 1959/60, but Waldman has turned the proposal down as being 'much too similar for comfort' to *Doctor Who*. Zenith are now claiming that the idea for *Doctor Who* has been stolen from them.

Thursday 25: Walford writes to Kenneth Cleveland, the legal adviser to Zenith, denying that the idea for *Doctor Who* has been taken either directly or indirectly from *The Time Travellers*:

The first important point which I must make is that this *Dr Who* series was devised jointly by Sydney Newman and Donald Wilson and I have ascertained that at the time when they worked it out they had no knowledge whatever of the suggested puppet series *The Time Travellers*. The scriptwriter of the first ten episodes of *Dr Who* is Anthony Coburn who likewise had no knowledge whatever of *The Time Travellers*. He was commissioned in the usual way as an outside writer to write scripts on the basic format which Sydney Newman and Donald Wilson devised and which of course the BBC owns.

Ronnie has already told you that he himself had no knowledge of *Dr Who*. *Dr Who* was of course never thought of in terms of a puppet series, and as Ronnie said in his letter of 16 July 'this is a large organisation and many things happen in the area of the creation of programme ideas which take a long time to come to the surface.'

The next important point to emphasise is that while, as Ronnie stated, *the idea* of the two programmes is similar, i.e. the idea of crossing time barriers, the two series are themselves completely different, one being for puppets and the other for live actors, and there could be no possibility of there being plagiarism of any sort.

Walford goes on however to offer Zenith 'a special *ex gratia* payment of 100 guineas, this being without prejudice and on the understanding that while we admit no legal liability we make the offer as a gesture of goodwill.'

Ian Atkins' assistant Leonard Miall sends him a memo to let him know that John Mair has now indicated that *Doctor Who* will be recorded in Lime Grove D on a permanent basis, and that the scripts will be tailored accordingly.

Tuesday 30: Donald Wilson circulates his own note of the preliminary promotion meeting held on 22 July. This summarises in more detail the points recorded by Richard Bright in his memo of 23 July and includes the revised first transmission date of 16 November.

Wednesday 31: The four regular cast members are issued with their contracts for the series.

David Whitaker briefs the Copyright Department to commission from writer Terry Nation a six-part story entitled *The Mutants*. This is on the strength of a detailed storyline that he has submitted under the earlier working title *The Survivors*. Nation's agents, Associated London Scripts, have negotiated a higher-than-usual fee of £262 per episode. His story is intended as the fourth in the series' running order, to be directed by Rex Tucker.

Whitaker also circulates a note giving a brief summary of the plot of each of the first four stories:

> Sufficient information is given of the flavour of each story to avoid possible future duplication of periods of history or environments by Saturday evening films, US or foreign television shows and so on, securing for *Doctor Who* an additional strength in its constantly varying locales, costumes and motivations.

Around this time, writer Alan Wakeman is also commissioned to write one episode as a pilot for a story entitled *The Living World*, the production team having been unable to decide on the basis of his storyline whether or not it might be suitable for the series. In the event, nothing comes of this. Wakeman is paid a fee of £75 for the work he has carried out.

By the end of the month, the idea of commissioning Les Structures Sonores to provide the series' opening music has been abandoned. At the suggestion of Lionel Salter, Head of TV Music, Verity Lambert has since had a meeting with Desmond Briscoe, Head of the Radiophonic Workshop, and explained that what she is seeking is something radiophonic, with a strong beat, which will sound 'familiar but different.' She has also expressed a desire for the theme to be written by Ron Grainer – a top TV composer who has provided memorable signature tunes for series such as *Maigret* and *Steptoe and Son*. Briscoe has been able to arrange this without difficulty as Grainer has only recently finished collaborating with the Workshop on *Giants of Steam*, a programme about railways.

AUGUST 1963

Thursday 1: Kenneth Cleveland of Zenith Films replies to R G Walford's letter of 25 July. He argues that plagiarism is not ruled out simply by the fact that *The Time Travellers* is intended for puppets and *Doctor Who* for live action, and requests a round table meeting between his clients and Sydney Newman, Donald Wilson and Ronald Waldman.

Friday 2: Mervyn Pinfield goes on leave.

Verity Lambert sends E Caffery, the BBC's Assistant Head of Copyright, a memo confirming that Ron Grainer is to provide the opening and closing music for *Doctor Who* in conjunction with the Radiophonic Workshop:

> Perhaps you could arrange a contract for him to compose approximately one minute of music at the opening and one minute of music at the closing, making a total of two minutes in all. I understand from Mr Grainer that because he will be working in conjunction with the Radiophonic Workshop, the BBC will automatically have some rights in any music produced.

Wednesday 7: William Hartnell visits Television Centre to have a make-up test and be measured for his costume.

Thursday 8: R G Walford replies to Kenneth Cleveland's letter of 1 August, reiterating that *Doctor Who* has been developed completely independently of Zenith's *The Time Travellers*.

> I am not saying that because one series related to puppets and the other to actors there could be no plagiarism, but simply that in this particular case the facts were such that neither series could possibly have been derived directly or indirectly from the other, so that any similarities that there may be could only be the result of coincidence, and such coincidences would not of course amount to plagiarism.

Walford goes on to reject Cleveland's request for a meeting.

David Whitaker sends the following memo to Ayton Whitaker arguing that the recording of *Doctor Who* in Lime Grove D on a permanent basis will 'badly restrict the variation of stories so necessary for the maintenance of the entertainment level':

> We badly need a serial about our four running characters being reduced in size. This requires inlay and could make effective use of overlay. I know the difficulties of black and white separation are not lost upon you nor the fact that these can be overcome in the right studio. I have had great experience of these techniques, having worked with Graeme Muir on over forty different productions employing inlay for which I wrote the scripts. I am very loathe to abandon the idea of a 'miniscule' adventure for *Doctor Who* without asking you what chances there are of eventual transfer from D to a studio capable of handling the visual effects which are, after all, an integral part of this project.

David Whitaker also sends E Caffery a memo stating that Terry Nation's story *The Mutants* is to be extended from six episodes to seven:

> Group producer Miss Lambert and I agree that Mr Nation's story is better expressed with the additional episode.

Around this time, Terry Nation delivers his first draft scripts to David Whitaker. The working title of the story has at this point been changed to *Beyond the Sun*, although it subsequently reverts to *The Mutants*. The production team consider the scripts and Whitaker discusses them with Nation, making a number of suggestions for rewrites. Consideration is given to dropping this story back to fifth in the running order, subject to obtaining the necessary facilities to mount a 'miniscules' story in the fourth slot.

Verity Lambert sends a memo to Jack Kine, one of the Heads of the Visual Effects Department (a separate unit within the Design Department), requesting that he provide a model of a 'Frank Lloyd Wright type of building' for filming on 28 October. This is to appear at the close of the final episode of *The Tribe of Gum*, in the scene leading into *The Robots*, to depict the travellers' new arrival point.

Monday 12: Waris Hussein contacts the BBC Radiophonic Workshop to brief them on the series' special sounds requirements. The man assigned to meet these requirements is Brian Hodgson. His biggest challenge on this first story is the sound effect to accompany the dematerialisation of the Doctor's ship, which Anthony Coburn has now named TARDIS – standing for Time and Relative Dimension in Space. He is inspired with an idea while out visiting a local cinema and later creates the effect by recording and then manipulating the sound of him scraping his front door key along the strings of an old upright piano at the Workshop.

Donald Wilson sends Sydney Newman a memo conveying his continuing dissatisfaction with *Doctor Who*'s studio allocation. Although it has previously been accepted that the series should be made in Lime Grove D, and the first four stories have been tailored accordingly, Wilson argues that a better result could be achieved with more advanced facilities:

These four stories cover a wide variation in time (100,000 BC to 30,000 AD) and space, but for so long as we are operating from D we shall not be able to introduce the third variant, that of size. I am particularly anxious that we should mount the 'miniature' adventure of *Dr Who*. Ideally this should be No. 4 in the series (starting recording on Friday 14 February 1964). Would you support an application for TC3, TC4 or Riverside 1 to be made available to us for Friday 14 February 1964 and the five successive Fridays? Of course if we could have one of these studios for story No. 3 (20 December 1963) and continue on a permanent basis, so much the better.

I feel most strongly that *Dr Who* must from time to time explore the full range of technical resources, otherwise we shall lay ourselves open to criticism for lacking in imagination and boldness.

Tuesday 13: Newman replies to Wilson's memo of the previous day:

You've got me wrong man! When I agreed to Studio D, I was led to believe that this studio contained all the technical facilities *Dr Who* required. It was only after the realisation that Studio D was inefficient for our purposes that I suggested we tried to 'live with it' for a while.

I'll do the best I can about getting the proper 'inlay, overlay' studio for the 'diminutive' size *Doctor Who*.

Thursday 15: Carole Ann Ford has a make-up test and costume fitting at Television Centre.

Saturday 17: Carole Ann Ford appears as a guest on the pop music programme *Juke Box Jury*.

Monday 19: Mervyn Pinfield returns from leave.

Tuesday 20: The first filming for *Doctor Who* – the creation of the series' opening title sequence – takes place on Stage 3A at the BBC's Television Film Studios in Ealing. The sequence has been designed by Bernard Lodge of the BBC Graphics Unit and makes use of a technique known as howl-around, which involves pointing a TV camera at a screen displaying the camera's own output and then filming the resultant feedback patterns. As Lodge recalls in a later interview, he has been inspired to use this technique by the pioneering work of a man named Ben Palmer:

'Quite a lot of howl-around footage already existed as a technical guy called Ben Palmer had been experimenting and had produced these patterns for a drama called *Amahl and the Night Visitors*. Although the pattern generation was a purely electronic process it had been recorded on film. They had yards and yards of this experimental footage and I was asked to go down to Ealing and watch through it all with Verity Lambert.'

Lambert's initial idea was that Lodge should create some animated lettering of the words 'Doctor Who' to be superimposed over the existing footage, but Lodge convinced her that the studio should be set up again so that the words could be fed into the picture electronically:

> 'What I didn't realise was that the simple shape of the words, the two lines of fairly symmetrical type, would actually generate its own feedback pattern. We shot a whole lot of new cloudy abstract stuff as well, but in the end I think we used one piece from the old *Amahl* footage – the very nice opening line which comes up the screen then breaks away. I can't take credit for that.'

The generation of the howl-around effect for this studio session has been supervised by a technician named Norman Taylor. Lodge subsequently takes the completed footage away and has it edited together into the finished sequence.

Having agreed with Lodge a rough timing for the sequence, Ron Grainer has meanwhile been working on his theme music. He has written a fairly simple score while on holiday in Portugal and has since discussed it with Delia Derbyshire, the Radiophonic Workshop composer assigned the task of committing it to tape. Keen that the music should be in keeping with the visuals, he has used expressions like 'windbubble and clouds' when describing the sort of sounds he envisages. Derbyshire and her assistant, Dick Mills, have created these sounds using sine and square wave generators, a white noise generator and a special beat frequency generator. The tune has been put together virtually note by note – each 'swoop' in the music being a carefully-timed hand adjustment of the oscillators – and the sounds have been cut, shaped, filtered and manipulated in various ways to prepare the tracks for mixing and synchronization.

Wednesday 21: Jacqueline Hill has a make-up test and costume fitting at Television Centre.

Verity Lambert discusses the first story's design requirements in detail with Peter Brachacki, who is now free of his other commitments.

Thursday 22: Verity Lambert sends a memo to James Bould, the Design Organiser, noting that *Doctor Who*'s fourth story will be either a futuristic one or an adventure concerning 'people who are greatly reduced in size', and that 'extensive use of electronic and scenic effects' will be required. She continues:

> I understand that George Djurkovic has made a detailed study of the Swedish entry for the Montreaux Festival, which concerned new techniques in this field. In the circumstances, I think George Djurkovic would be particularly useful to us on either of these two stories, and, if he is available, I would like to request that he be allocated to us.

Lambert now has a new office in Room 5017 of Television Centre, just two doors along from her old one. She has also been assigned a secretary, who is in Room 5016.

Friday 30: Rex Tucker goes on leave to take his holiday in Majorca. It has however been decided by this stage that when he returns on 23 September he will no longer be involved with *Doctor Who*. He has never been entirely happy working on the series and has now been reassigned to direct a prestigious Giles Cooper adaptation of Flaubert's *Madame Bovary* for transmission in March 1964. 'Much more the sort of thing I had done in the past,' he will later recall.

SEPTEMBER 1963

Monday 2: David Whitaker receives from writer Malcolm Hulke proposed outlines for two six-part stories: one set in Roman-occupied Britain around 400 AD and the other, entitled *The Hidden Planet*, set on a planet in the same orbit as the Earth but out of view on the opposite side of the sun.

Monday 9: By the beginning of this week, the first transmission of *Doctor Who* has been postponed again, to Saturday 23 November.

Tuesday 10: Revised versions of the scripts for episodes one and three of *The Tribe of Gum* are sent out to the cast, who previously received drafts of all four episodes.

Tuesday 12: Verity Lambert sends a memo to R W Bayliff, the Head of Technical Operations for Television Studios, requesting permission for Norman Taylor to be given a credit on the pilot episode for his electronic howl-around effects.

Friday 13: The experimental session originally scheduled for 19 July finally takes place in Lime Grove D, the purpose being to try out the effect of the dematerialisation of the Doctor's ship. A problem immediately arises when it is discovered that the police box prop is too tall to fit into the service lift by which scenery is transported up to the studio.

Monday 16: David Whitaker circulates a note containing synopses of the stories now planned to fill the first six slots in the series' running order. The first three are, as before, *The Tribe of Gum*, *The Robots* and *A Journey to Cathay*. The fourth, however, is now a four-part 'miniscules' story by writer Robert Gould, and is described by Whitaker as follows:

> 'Tardis' transports Doctor Who and his party back to 1963 but reduced down to one sixteenth of an inch in size. One room becomes a world of frightening proportions, one carpet an impenetrable jungle, where 'dust storms' are minor concerns. The immense difficulties of finding food and water, the death that can result from the sudden falling cigarette ash, the terrifying creatures that inhabit the new world in which they find themselves make up an unusual and thrilling adventure.

The fifth slot is now occupied by Terry Nation's *The Mutants*, while the sixth has been set aside for one of the Malcolm Hulke stories, summarised by Whitaker in the following terms:

> The travellers are set down in a Britain of 400 AD, when the Romans are just about to retire from the island. The Romans leave behind them an

authority which intends to carry on their civilisation but this is opposed by a group of people who see profit in destruction and disorder. This latter group are excellent allies for invading Saxons, completely opposed to anything Roman. Doctor Who and his friends are involved in a struggle at a time when the blank pages of history occur, in an adventure full of excitement and action.

Waris Hussein is still expected to direct the first, third and fifth stories, while Christopher Barry – a young but experienced staff director who joined the BBC in 1955 after starting his career in the film industry – has been pencilled in for the second and sixth and Richard Martin for the fourth. Whitaker concludes:

> These six stories, covering thirty-four episodes, are, as has already been stated, not finalised – however they do provide a statement of flavour and intention. The first, second, third and fifth serials have been commissioned and are in various stages of development – the first being complete, the second being half written in draft, the third in preparation and the fifth delivered in draft. Serials four and six are in discussion stages.

Waris Hussein is definite for the first and third serials but the actual deployment of Christopher Barry and Richard Martin has yet to be finalised.

Wednesday 18: R W Bayliff replies to Verity Lambert's memo of 12 September declining permission for Norman Taylor to receive an on-screen credit. This is on the grounds that his electronic effects fall short of meeting the established policy requirement of being 'both artistic and substantial, or of significant interest to viewers.'

Composer Norman Kay, conducting a group of seven musicians, records the incidental music for *The Tribe of Gum* between 6.00 pm and 10.00 pm in the Camden Theatre.

Thursday 19: A day of filming is carried out on Stage 3A at Ealing for the first story.

Friday 20: The series' regular cast take part in a *Radio Times* photocall at Television Centre, on a mock-up of the junk yard set for the pilot episode. It begins at 3.00 and is due to last an hour.

Editing of the Ealing film footage is carried out for the pilot episode. This is to be continued on the first three days of the following week.

Saturday 21: Waris Hussein and the cast begin rehearsals for the pilot episode, *The Tribe of Gum: An Unearthly Child*. The venue is a Drill Hall at 117 Walmer Road, London W2 – one of a number of West London halls used regularly by the BBC for rehearsal purposes.

Monday 23: A further four days' preliminary rehearsal begins for the pilot episode.

By the beginning of this week, Verity Lambert and David Whitaker have decided that Anthony Coburn's *The Robots* and Terry Nation's *The Mutants* should swap places in the planned running order. This is mainly because design work now needs to get underway on the second story and Nation's scripts are the only ones ready. The production team are dissatisfied with the work so far carried out by Coburn on *The Robots* and have asked for further rewrites.

The current intention is that, after the six-part Malcolm Hulke story pencilled in as the sixth in the running order, the remainder of the 52-week season should be broken down into two seven-parters and one four-parter. Terry Nation is to be asked to contribute the second of the seven-parters – a historical story entitled *The Red Fort* – but the other two slots remain to be filled.

During the course of this week, it is decided that only the individual episode titles will appear on screen and not the overall story titles, which will now be used for production purposes only.

Tuesday 24: Terry Nation is commissioned to write *The Red Fort*. This is to be a seven-part historical story set during the Indian Mutiny and will see the four time travellers becoming involved in events which took place on 11 May 1857 at the so-called Red Fort in Delhi. The target delivery date for the scripts is 16 December.

Friday 27: The pilot episode is camera rehearsed and recorded in Lime Grove D. The total cost of the episode (estimated at 18 November 1963) is £2,143 3s 3d.

It has yet to be decided how *Doctor Who*'s visual effects requirements will be serviced on a long-term basis, so the interior of the Doctor's ship has been constructed from Peter Brachacki's designs by a firm of freelance contractors, Shawcraft Models (Uxbridge) Ltd. The set has a number of unusual aspects, including its size – it takes up almost half the studio – and a large hexagonal unit suspended from the ceiling. The central control console is the dominant feature, with its six instrument panels and transparent central column. Brachacki's reason for having a console of this sort is that the ship is supposed to be capable of operation by a single pilot. He initially hoped to create special controls, moulded to the pilot's hands, but this proved too expensive so standard switches and dials have been used instead. Budgetary restrictions have also ruled out some of the designer's other ideas, such as having translucent wall panels that would pulsate during flight. One feature that has been afforded, however, is a distinctive pattern of indented circles on the walls. Brachacki's intention in using a geometric shape is to create a timeless feel, and he has chosen circles simply due to the fact that the plastic from which he made his original design model of the set happened to have circles on it. The central column of the control console is designed to rise, fall and rotate, but it frequently jams in the studio, causing hold-ups during camera rehearsals. The doors of the set also prove very difficult to open and close.

The costume supervisor assigned to the first story is Maureen Heneghan and the make-up supervisor Elizabeth Blattner.

Monday 30: By the beginning of this week, Sydney Newman has arranged to view a recording of the pilot episode. He jots down a number of comments on the back of two pages of the script. These range from technical instructions (such as 'Music to be very loud' at the start of the episode, 'Tremble camera' with reference to the scene of the dematerialisation of the Doctor's ship and 'End credits too big and roll credits faster' at the close), through relatively minor observations on the direction and scripting ('Bad profile of girl – can she be more cheeky? – too dour,' 'Lay off her profiles' and 'What does she draw?') to more substantive criticisms ('Old man – not funny enough,' 'They don't act as if he's locked her in box' and, again, 'Old man ain't cute enough.')

Newman subsequently takes Verity Lambert and Waris Hussein out to lunch and tells them that the pilot is unacceptable for transmission. The episode will therefore have to be remounted, as already planned on a contingency basis.

A meeting is held in Lambert's office to discuss special effects requirements for *The Mutants*. Present are Lambert, Mervyn Pinfield, David Whitaker, Christopher Barry (who has now been assigned to direct this story), designer Barry Newbery, lighting supervisor Geoff Shaw and secretary Susan Pugh.

Although *Doctor Who* has always been planned as a fifty-two week series, Chief of Programmes Donald Baverstock has yet to give his formal approval for it to continue beyond the first four episodes.

OCTOBER 1963

Wednesday 2: H Wilson, designated Film Operations Manager II, makes arrangements at Verity Lambert's request for a show copy of the pilot episode to be made available for the remount on 18 October.

Tuesday 8: Production assistant Douglas Camfield learns that scenery due to be delivered the previous day to the Television Film Studios at Ealing has yet to arrive. On making enquiries, he discovers that this is due to a lack of transport and a lack of staff at Television Centre to load it onto a van. The scenery eventually arrives at 3.40 pm and Camfield authorises the scene crew to work overtime to get it ready for the start of filming the following day.

Wednesday 9: Three days' filming begins at Ealing to complete all the film inserts required for the second, third and fourth episodes of *The Tribe of Gum*. Camfield directs some of these scenes himself, on Waris Hussein's behalf.

Thursday 10: Donald Wilson sends a lengthy memo to Donald Baverstock, Joanna Spicer, Sydney Newman and Richard Levin about the 'special effects effort' required on *Doctor Who*. After summarising discussions and correspondence to date on this issue, he protests that no extra visual effects staff have yet been provided for the series and that Programme Services are working on the basis that it is 'to be tailored to normal Saturday afternoon series level.' He continues:

> I do not know what 'normal Saturday afternoon series level' may mean, but if it means that the effort required to build the space ship for *Dr Who* is abnormal, then it seems to me that I should have been told so and I would then have informed everybody that the serials could not be done on these terms and we should therefore have to withdraw the project.
>
> What happened in fact was that a certain amount of effort was bought outside to make it possible for the pilot to be recorded on 27 September. The work was defective and this was one of the reasons why we determined that the pilot episode could be very much improved if it was

done again. It was not until the deficiencies appeared that I myself realised that the effort we had asked for was not being provided and could not be provided in the future without a large weekly sum of money over and above the agreed budget.

Wilson goes on to argue for an immediate decision to be taken on the continuation of the series beyond the first four episodes:

> As a result of the pilot, we have engaged the artists for the four running characters according to the option terms set out in their contracts, and have two further serials in writing.
>
> If we begin recording weekly on 18 October without a decision being made about the continuation we will be able, given the £800 promised by A.C.(Planning), to complete the first four episodes and the filming of the special effects for the second serial, but if we do not make a decision until after the third recording there will not be time enough to have the design effort and building ready for continuous production after number four. In other words, we would have to cease production for a period of three weeks after the decision is made, during which time we would have to continue paying the four running artists at the rate of £550 a week. We would also be unable to cast the second serial.
>
> To sum up, I think we should commit ourselves to at least eleven episodes on the basis of the existing pilot. (Eighteen episodes would be more satisfactory from the budgeting point of view.) We know that subsequent episodes will be better than this pilot if the effort is available and in view of the changes we have now made in script and characterisation. But in my professional opinion what we have here is something very much better both in content and in production value than we could normally expect for this kind of money and effort.

Friday 11: Christopher Barry sends David Whitaker a note of his initial thoughts on the scripts for *The Mutants*. He begins:

> Here are some general comments on the serial, but there are two important facets of the Thals' and the Daleks' characters which should be borne in mind throughout all re-writing.
>
> The Thals should have a death urge – or, at any rate, little will to live – in contrast to the Daleks who, hideously mutilated though they are, wish to survive, dominate, and perpetuate their ghastly species. They should be frightened for their ability – or lack of ability – to survive, and it is this fear that drives them to suspicious hatred of strangers.
>
> The Thals should be absolutely unable to take command of their own destiny, or even of any situation in which they find themselves, until our four come along and befriend/are befriended by them.

Barry then goes on to give a number of detailed comments on points of dialogue and description in Terry Nation's scripts.

Monday 14: Four days' preliminary rehearsal begins for the remount of *The Tribe of Gum: An Unearthly Child*. The venue for the series' rehearsals has now been changed to a Drill Hall at 239 Uxbridge Road, just a few minutes' walk from Lime Grove Studios.

Wednesday 16: Donald Baverstock decides on the basis of the pilot episode, which he has now viewed, that he is willing to give the go ahead to thirteen episodes of *Doctor Who*. John Mair, whose official designation has now changed from Senior Planning Assistant (I) to Planning Manager (Forward), is asked to 'state what extra programme allowance will be required to finance the special effects requirements and the operating effort needed to work them in the studio' so that Baverstock can decide by the end of the week whether or not he can agree to the consequent increase in the series' budget.

Friday 18: The remount of *The Tribe of Gum: An Unearthly Child* is camera rehearsed and recorded in Lime Grove D. Its total cost is £2,746.

It has by this point been decided that Peter Brachacki is unsuited to working on *Doctor Who*, and Verity Lambert has asked for a different designer to be allocated to the series. (Brachacki is in any case unwell and is soon to be admitted to hospital for an operation.) Two designers, Barry Newbery and Raymond P Cusick, have been asked to take over from Brachacki, handling stories on an alternate basis. Newbery's first task on *The Tribe of Gum* has been to have all the sets for the first episode rebuilt from Brachacki's plans as – despite Lambert's instructions to the contrary – only the set of the interior of the Doctor's ship has been retained from the pilot recording, the others having all been junked.

Director Christopher Barry sends David Whitaker a memo of further, more considered comment on the scripts for the first two episodes of *The Mutants*. He concludes:

> It seems that Terry Nation feels that once he has told the audience something the characters need no longer react to the situation. He is continually having them accept a situation in a most undramatic manner, and therefore losing a lot of potential value.
>
> I shall in due course be reading more carefully the remaining five scripts, but thought you would rather have what comments I have been able to produce so far in time for the weekend.

A major crisis arises for *Doctor Who* when Donald Baverstock sends Donald Wilson the following memo just before going on leave for three weeks:

> I am told that a first examination of your expenditure on the pilot and of your likely design and special effects requirements of later episodes, particularly two, three and four, shows that you are likely to overspend your budget allocation by as much as £1,600 and your allocation of man-hours by as much as 1,200 per episode. These figures are arrived at by averaging the expenditure of £4,000 on the spaceship over thirteen episodes. It also allows for only £3,000 to be spent on the expensive space creatures and other special effects. It does not take account of all the extra

costs involved in the operation of special effects in the studio.

Last week I agreed an additional £200 to your budget of £2,300 for the first four episodes. This figure is now revealed to be totally unrealistic. The costs of these four will be more than £4,000 each – and it will be even higher if the cost of the spaceship has to be averaged over four rather than thirteen episodes.

Such a costly serial is not one that I can afford for this space in this financial year. You should not therefore proceed any further with the production of more than four episodes.

I am asking A.C.(P) Tel. [Joanna Spicer] and P.M.F. [John Mair] to examine with everyone concerned the exact realistic costs of this serial so far and the costs we should have to face if it were to continue.

In the meanwhile, that is for the next three weeks while I am away, you should marshall ideas and prepare suggestions for a new children's drama serial at a reliably economic price. There is a possibility that it will be wanted for transmission from soon after Week 1 of 1964.

Sydney Newman receives a copy of this memo and immediately notes that the cost of the Doctor's ship was supposed to be £3,000 spread over fifty-two weeks, not £4,000 spread over thirteen.

Monday 21: Four days' preliminary rehearsal begins for *The Tribe of Gum: The Cave of Skulls.*

Tuesday 22: The implications of Donald Baverstock's memo of the previous Friday are now being considered. At Joanna Spicer's request, John Mair sends her a memo detailing some of the background to *Doctor Who*'s production, focusing in particular on its budget and costs. With regard to the interior of the Doctor's ship, he notes that 'this was originally to cost £500; the producer was told it would cost £3,000; in the event it appears to have cost nearly £4,000' but that Donald Wilson had always planned its cost to be spread over the full fifty-two episodes and kept within the original £2,300 budget.

Spicer subsequently holds a meeting with Mair, Donald Wilson, Verity Lambert, James Bould, Jack Kine and others to discuss the situation. She explains that Baverstock would be prepared to accept a run of thirteen episodes of *Doctor Who*, but only if he can afford it. She asks Wilson and Lambert to examine the possibility of making thirteen episodes within a budget of £2,500 each (£32,500 in total), from which £75 per episode (£975 in total) would go towards the cost of interior of the Doctor's ship, £200 per episode (£2,600 in total) would be used to employ an outside contract scenic effects firm and £500 per episode (£6,500 in total) would be the Design Department's budget allocation (DDBA in BBC terminology). The man-hours allocation would be 500 per episode (6,500 in total) and Lambert would have to gain clearance from James Mudie, Head of Scenic Servicing, if an unusually large proportion of the total was to be used up on any one episode. A special allocation would be made to pay off the remainder of the cost of the set of the Doctor's ship.

Wilson and Lambert are confident that the series can be produced within these limits. They agree to consider the matter in more detail and respond shortly. This marks the beginning of a week of intensive meetings and discussions between Wilson, Lambert and other members of the production team.

During the course of the week, David Whitaker prepares a new story listing, which indicates that the plans for the year-long run are now as follows: *The Tribe of Gum* (four episodes) by Anthony Coburn; *The Mutants/Beyond the Sun* (seven episodes) by Terry Nation; *Marco Polo/A Journey to Cathay* (seven episodes) by John Lucarotti; an untitled 'miniscules' story (four episodes) by Robert Gould; *The Robots/The Masters of Luxor* (six episodes) by Anthony Coburn; an untitled historical story (seven episodes) by Whitaker himself; *The Hidden Planet* (six episodes) by Malcolm Hulke (this having been substituted for Hulke's historical story set in Britain around 408 AD); *The Red Fort* (seven episodes) by Terry Nation; and a futuristic story (four episodes) still to be decided.

It is subsequently concluded that, given Donald Baverstock's decision to accept only thirteen episodes for the time being, a two-part story will have to be slotted in after *The Mutants*. This will have to be written by Whitaker himself as it is now too late for a suitable story to be found and commissioned from a freelance writer. It will also have to be confined to the interior of the Doctor's ship as there is no money available for additional scenery to be designed and constructed.

Also around this time, a less significant development occurs when the title of the first story is changed from *The Tribe of Gum* to *100,000 BC* (the likely reason being that the Palaeolithic tribe is no longer given a name in the final version of Anthony Coburn's scripts). As it has previously been decided that only the individual episode titles are to appear on screen and not the overall story titles, this creates no difficulty with regard to the recording already carried out.

It has now been agreed that Christopher Barry and Richard Martin should share responsibility for directing *The Mutants*. Directors for the later stories have yet to be assigned at this point.

Richard Martin sends the following memo to Verity Lambert, Mervyn Pinfield, David Whitaker and Christopher Barry:

> At the back of my mind there is a worry. This is the vagueness of the ship itself, whose qualities and possibilities *must*, I think, be understood and accepted by the audience before the adventures of its occupants are given credence. Therefore here is some phoney science for your agreement/disagreement.
>
> The ship is out of time but in space. The entrance is in both time and space. This entrance (the phone box) can best be described as a time/space ship gangplank. Or compression-decompression (comparison-decomparison) chamber.
>
> The only way to pass down the gangplank is by an effort of will. Therefore if you are afraid or doubtful all you would find is the inside of a phone box, and if you stayed inside you would have a bad headache from the intercellular electronic pulses forming the mental link. Therefore it is not easy to get in and out of the ship. For those unused to it, traumatic.
>
> The unit producing the band waves which form the time/space penetrator beams and the electronic computer to control this force are the two main pieces of machinery, the third being a service unit to take humans with it in their environment – oxygen, food etc. This is of strictly

limited dimensions as every square foot supported out of time and space needs great energy!

The outside appearance of the machine is a police box because when the machine is made and before it goes critical it is given an anchor in a definite age and space, without which there can be neither past nor future, and the time/space traveller would go mad – or meet God. Therefore its occupant must tie the machine to some definite anchor. This is the most complete of all its functions and one which Dr Who has only dared to do once when he originally escaped. When he does this again it could well be the end of the series – or at least a good reason to alter the external shape if desired.

Agreement on these basic rules I feel is necessary to the right use of the ship – the internal limit of it and the handling and mending of the controls and their appearance.

None of these ideas is taken up by the production team.

Wednesday 23: John Mair sends Donald Wilson a memo recording the main points of the previous day's meeting chaired by Joanna Spicer.

Friday 25: *100,000 BC: The Cave of Skulls* is camera rehearsed and recorded in Lime Grove D. Its total cost is £4,307.

Spicer sends Wilson a memo setting out in detail the financial basis on which she has asked him and Lambert to consider making *Doctor Who.*

Monday 28: Four days' preliminary rehearsal begins for *100,000 BC: The Forest of Fear.* Five days' shooting of film inserts for *The Mutants* begins at Ealing.

Tuesday 29: Mair sends Spicer the following memo:

As a result of further intensive discussions the costs of *Dr Who* appear to come out as follows:

Part I (four episodes)

Actual costs are not yet available for all four episodes, but on present reckoning it seems that:

(a) The spaceship cost £4,328 in all. The programme budget can contribute 14 x £75 = £1,050. Net sum to be met from special funds is therefore £3,278.

(b) The pilot, and episodes one and two together, cost a total, above the budget and above a sum equivalent to the original allocation of 350 man-hours, of £782. It is thought however that when the costs of the remaining two episodes come in, they will be well below the man-hour allocation, and much of this £782 can be paid for from DDBA.

Part II (seven episodes)
There is every hope that this can now be managed within a budget of £2,500 and 500 man-hours per episode.

Wilson and Lambert have a meeting with Spicer in which they agree to *Doctor Who* being taken forward on the basis proposed on 22 October.

Wednesday 30: James Mudie writes to Joanna Spicer drawing her attention to the memo he sent John Mair on 20 June protesting at the demands placed on his Department by *Doctor Who*'s scenic servicing requirements. He adds that the design drawings for the second story, which were due on 24 October, have yet to be received, and concludes:

> In these circumstances, you may wish to call a halt to the series before the output of the service as a whole is jeopardised by this production.

Spicer, meanwhile, sends the following memo to Kenneth Adam and (to be seen on his return) Donald Baverstock:

> I held a detailed discussion of the problems of, and future plans for, *Dr Who* on 22 October on the basis of Ch.P.BBC1's [Baverstock] wish to schedule thirteen programmes in this serial, as an initial stage, subject to a proper method of servicing being found and subject to acceptable cost.
> H.Serials.D.Tel. [Donald Wilson] and Miss Lambert followed up this meeting by further detailed discussions and came to see me yesterday with the position as it now appears.
> The details are as follows; and I recommend that these episodes are acceptable on this basis:
>
> 1. The pilot programme was made on an allocation of £2,300 which has already been covered in the BBC1 Pilot Fund for this financial year.
>
> 2. Thirteen episodes of *Dr Who* are offered to us in three parts of four episodes, seven episodes and two episodes respectively.
> The allocation for each programme would be £2,500; and in addition a special grant of £3,278 would be made for the provision of the special model space machine.
> Out of her £2,500 allocation per episode the producer will contribute £75 for this model. She will also set aside £200 per episode within which her requirement for scenic effects will be met by employment of the outside contract firm.
> The producer also intends to set aside £500 a week for the cost of sets etc, in the studio and for the filming sessions.

3. Each episode will be allocated seven days' designer effort and five hundred man-hours. The producer is fully informed about the use of man-hours and states that the programme can be successfully planned on this basis.

She will expect the designer to inform her if on any occasion the script, as first presented to him, requires more effort than this. It is then open to the producer to ask for an increase from within her programme allocation, subject always to H.S.S.Tel. [James Mudie] being able to handle this.

I hope it can now be agreed that H.Serials.D.Tel. can plan the serial on this basis. These thirteen episodes would thus run weeks 48-7 inclusive; and discussions could be held in good time about a continuation of the serial.

Approval is subsequently given for production to proceed on this basis, resolving the crisis that has threatened *Doctor Who* with cancellation before the first episode has even been transmitted. One consequence of the agreement reached is that the BBC's Visual Effects Department will have only minimal involvement in *Doctor Who* during the first Doctor's era. Instead, all the series' special props and effects will be designed by the scenic designer and realised by specialist freelance contractors such as Shawcraft.

Thursday 31: Richard Martin sends David Whitaker a three-page memo of comment on the script for the fifth episode of *The Mutants*.

A short video insert is recorded for *100,000 BC: The Forest of Fear* in Lime Grove D. This is for the scene where the caveman Za is attacked by a tiger (unseen).

NOVEMBER 1963

Friday 1: *100,000 BC: The Forest of Fear* is camera rehearsed and recorded in Lime Grove D. Its total cost is £2,181.

A meeting is held between Controller of Programme Services Ian Atkins, Head of Scenic Servicing James Mudie, Assistant Head of Scenic Servicing Tony Reeves, Assistant Head of Design I Beynon-Lewis and designer Raymond Cusick to discuss the sets for *The Mutants*. Atkins decides that the interior of the Doctor's ship should be redesigned as it is currently too heavy and too difficult to put up and take down in the studio. Reeves later conveys this decision to Verity Lambert, who replies that although she has no objection to the set being redesigned in this way, the costs should be borne by the Design Department rather than by the series itself as the fault lies with the original designer, Peter Brachacki.

The same day, Lambert produces an amended version of the Donald Wilson promotional note of 30 July, taking account of the changes agreed over the previous fortnight. The note no longer refers to the series running for fifty-two weeks but lists the first three stories, *100,000 BC*, *The Mutants* and *Inside the Spaceship*, the latter of which it describes with the single sentence: 'Dr Who and his companions find themselves facing a terrifying situation within the ship itself.' The note goes on to name the writers and directors for the three stories, indicating that Paddy Russell has been assigned to direct *Inside the Spaceship*, and concludes:

NB It is absolutely essential that the fact that the spaceship, from the exterior, looks like a police telephone box, should remain completely confidential.

Monday 4: Four days' preliminary rehearsal begins for *100,000 BC: The Firemaker*.

Tuesday 5: Donald Wilson is informed that plans to publicise the first episode of *Doctor Who* with a photograph on the front cover of the BBC's listings magazine *Radio Times* have been dropped, partly due to a lack of confidence in the series on the part of Controller of Programmes Kenneth Adam (C.P.Tel.). Wilson sends the following memo to the editor of *Radio Times*:

> I am unhappy to hear today that the proposal to give *Dr Who* the front page of *Radio Times* had now been abandoned. It was particularly · distressing to hear that one reason given was lack of confidence in the programme at Controller level. I assure you that this does not exist and if you have a word with C.P.Tel. I know he will express enthusiasm. I myself believe that we have an absolute knock-out in this show and that there will be no question but that it will run and run.
>
> I would be most grateful, if it is not too late, for the decision against it to be reversed, and that will help me to get this show off to a good start.

The *Radio Times* cover photo for the week 23-29 November will in the event be of Kenneth Horne from the radio comedy series *Beyond our Ken*, although *Doctor Who* will be prominently mentioned in the cover text and will be featured within the magazine in the form of two photographs and a short article. The series will also be promoted in the previous week's edition as a forthcoming attraction.

Wednesday 6: James Mudie sends Beynon-Lewis a memo reminding him of Ian Atkins' decision that the interior of the Doctor's ship should be redesigned and asking him to take this forward as a matter of urgency 'as in its present form it is obstructing the night setting operations for the whole of the Television Service.'

Thursday 7: Joanna Spicer responds to Mudie's memo of 30 October. She notes the developments that have occurred since the meeting she chaired on 29 October and expresses the hope that 'the situation in which your memo of 30 October was written no longer obtains.'

Raymond Cusick queries with Verity Lambert the instructions he has been given to redesign the interior of the Doctor's ship and shows her a copy of the previous day's memo from Mudie to Lewis. Lambert speaks to Design Manager James Bould and asks where the money and man-hours are to be found for this, reiterating her strong view that they should not come out of *Doctor Who*'s own allocation. She also sends a memo to Donald Wilson informing him of these developments and concluding:

> I would like to mention that I only found out about the redesign of the spaceship having been put into operation because the designer called me to check. No copy of Mr Mudie's memo was sent to me and instructions

were issued to the designer without reference to me in spite of the fact that no provision of man-hours or money has been made for this by anybody up to the present time.

Friday 8: *100,000 BC: The Firemaker* is camera rehearsed and recorded in Lime Grove D. Its total cost is £2,316.

Monday 11: Four days' preliminary rehearsal begins for *The Mutants: The Dead Planet*.

Friday 15: *The Mutants: The Dead Planet* is camera rehearsed and recorded in Lime Grove D.

This episode is the first to feature costumes designed by Daphne Dare, who has now been assigned as *Doctor Who*'s regular costume supervisor. The make-up is designed, as for *100,000 BC*, by Elizabeth Blattner. Subsequent make-up designers for the first year of stories will be Ann Ferriggi, Jill Summers and Sonia Markham, the latter of whom will go on to handle the make-up for the great majority of the first Doctor's stories.

Sydney Newman sends the following memo, marked 'Strictly Confidential', to Donald Wilson:

> I talked to Donald Baverstock this morning about *Dr Who* and am happy to tell you he is very keen about what he has heard about the serial.
>
> He is worried about money and was unable to commit himself at this time to the continuation of the serial beyond thirteen. I would suggest that some time next week you give him a ring and ... go and see him for a decision. If you handle him right I am sure everything will be OK.

Saturday 16: A trailer for *100,000 BC: An Unearthly Child* is transmitted at 5.40 pm on BBC TV.

Monday 18: Four days' preliminary rehearsal begins for *The Mutants: The Survivors*.

Verity Lambert sends Donald Wilson a memo giving estimated total cost figures, and actual design cost figures, for all four episodes of *100,000 BC*. These indicate that the series is operating well within budget and should certainly be able to pay off its outstanding commitment to the cost of the Doctor's ship by the end of the initial thirteen episodes.

The *Doctor Who* production office has now been moved to Room 512 of Threshold House, a BBC-owned building overlooking Shepherd's Bush Green in west London.

Tuesday 19: A serious problem has by this point been discovered with the previous Friday's recording of *The Mutants: The Dead Planet*: talk-back from the production assistant's headphones (i.e. the sound of messages relayed to him from the director in the control gallery) has been picked up by the studio microphones and is clearly audible on the soundtrack of the episode. Having viewed the episode, Donald Wilson has decided that this 'induction' is 'so bad as to made the recording unsuitable for transmission.' It is agreed that the episode will have to be completely re-recorded on 6 December, in the slot originally intended for recording of the fourth instalment of *The*

Mutants. All subsequent episodes will therefore be put back one week, but recording will still be six clear weeks ahead of transmission. This change of plan will also allow for model filming of the Dalek city to be redone, as the production team were unhappy with the model that Shawcraft built for the original recording of the episode.

Thursday 21: David Whitaker sends Donald Wilson a memo, headed 'Confidential', to convey some information he feels he is unable to give to Verity Lambert 'because of a personal friendship between her and Jacqueline Hill':

> Jackie told me in confidence that she has been offered a film which will begin immediately after her current engagement on *Doctor Who* is terminated, with the proviso that the BBC have an option on her services. Apparently the problem is that with the re-recording of episode one of Serial B, because the talk-back interfered, this will add another week on to the current contract, but from what I gather, no additional week's contract has been arranged by the Corporation with her.
>
> She told me that she was informed that there would be an extra week added on to the current commitment and felt that Verity would only ask her to do this because of their personal friendship, and she told me that she was not prepared to sacrifice her film simply for one extra week. It is not for me to decide whether or not this is reasonable, and neither do I wish to raise any mountains where mole hills exist, but it is surely right to let you know so that you can anticipate the situation. I hope I can be kept out of it.
>
> It may be symptomatic of a gradual lessening of confidence that the four contracted actors and actresses have in the serial itself. I think they are afraid that it is going to be taken off, and what worries me is that it will eventually affect their performances. Already I sense a certain laissez-fair attitude, and I would dearly love to stop this at birth. The only solution I can see is, of course, to tell them that the serial will continue after thirteen weeks, or not, as the case may be. Perhaps it is the indecision which is really making them feel insecure.
>
> I hope I am right in writing to you on this subject, which I hope you will treat in confidence.

After receiving this memo, Wilson recommends to Donald Baverstock that a further thirteen episodes of *Doctor Who* be given the go-ahead.

A press conference to launch the series is held at 5.00 pm in Room 222 at the Langham, a BBC-owned building opposite Broadcasting House in London's West End. Present are Wilson, Whitaker, Lambert and the four regular cast members.

Friday 22: Baverstock accepts Wilson's recommendation and sends him a memo authorising him to take up options for a further thirteen episodes, with a budget of £2,300 each. He adds:

> It is likely that I should be able to make a decision on the option to take up

another thirteen, making thirty-nine in all, sometime early in the New Year.

The Mutants: The Survivors is camera rehearsed and recorded in Lime Grove D. Its total cost is £2,796. The cast and crew are shocked to learn of the assassination of US President John F Kennedy in Dallas, Texas.

The set of the interior of the Doctor's ship has now been redesigned and is somewhat simpler than before, omitting altogether the large hexagonal unit that previously hung from the ceiling between the central console and the main doors.

Saturday 23: *100,000 BC: An Unearthly Child* is transmitted on BBC TV. Viewers in certain areas of the country are unable to receive the transmission due to a widespread power failure.

Monday 25: Four days' preliminary rehearsal begins for *The Mutants: The Escape*.

Tuesday 26: An additional day's shooting of film inserts for *The Mutants* takes place on Stage 2 at Ealing.

Wednesday 27: Donald Wilson sends the following telegram to Sydney Newman, who is currently staying at the Warwick Hotel in New York, USA:

DOCTOR WHO OFF TO A GREAT START EVERYBODY HERE DELIGHTED REGARDS DONALD

Friday 29: *The Mutants: The Escape* is camera rehearsed and recorded in Lime Grove D. Its total cost is £2,232.

Saturday 30: *100,000 BC: The Cave of Skulls* is transmitted on BBC TV. It is preceded by a repeat of *100,000 BC: An Unearthly Child*, which has been slotted into the evening's schedule for the benefit of those viewers affected by the power cut on 23 November.

DECEMBER 1963

Monday 2: Four days' preliminary rehearsal begins for re-recording of *The Mutants: The Dead Planet*.
One day's shooting of film inserts for *The Mutants* takes place at Ealing.
David Whitaker briefs the Copyright Department to commission the scripts for the six part story *The Hidden Planet* from writer Malcolm Hulke.

Tuesday 3: Verity Lambert sends a memo to Head of Artists' Bookings Pauline Mansfield-Clark enquiring if there is any possibility of changing the option terms of the regular cast's contracts:

At present we have taken up the first option for eight and the second option for twelve weeks; our next two options are for sixteen weeks each.

Ideally if we could issue a third option to run six weeks, bringing us to a total of twenty-six, and two further options to run thirteen weeks each, this would bring us into line with the Planning Department. I do not see any reason why the money should be altered, but this is something that probably you will have to go into in detail with the agents.

Lambert goes on to ask if separate contracts could be issued to extend the second option period from twelve weeks to thirteen in order to allow for the re-recording of *The Mutants: The Dead Planet*.

Thursday 5: Lambert sends Controller of Programme Services Ian Atkins a memo reminding him of the difficulties presented for *Doctor Who* by the antiquated facilities and lack of space in Lime Grove D and requesting that the studio be allocated four ring pedestal cameras rather than, as at present, two ring pedestals and two of the more cumbersome ordinary pedestals, which 'are heavy to move and ... cannot easily move up and down in vision, thereby imposing further restrictions on both director and cameraman and end product.'

Friday 6: *The Mutants: The Dead Planet* is re-recorded in Lime Grove D. This re-recording was not budgeted for; however, the cost – £2,817 – is largely confined to the artists' fees as all scenery etc can be reused from the original recording.

Saturday 7: *100,000 BC: The Forest of Fear* is transmitted on BBC TV.

Monday 10: Four days' preliminary rehearsal begins for *The Mutants: The Ambush*.

Friday 13: *The Mutants: The Ambush* is camera rehearsed and recorded in Lime Grove D. Its total cost is £2,641.

The recording medium on this occasion is 35mm film rather than videotape; a departure from the norm requested by the production team in order to facilitate the unusually complex editing required.

Saturday 14: *100,000 BC: The Firemaker* is transmitted on BBC TV.

Monday 17: Four days' preliminary rehearsal begins for *The Mutants: The Expedition*.

Thursday 19: *Junior Points of View* shows a clip of the fight scene between Kal and Za from *100,000 BC: The Fire Maker*, but overdubbed with a wrestling commentary by Kent Walton.

Friday 20: *The Mutants: The Expedition* is camera rehearsed and recorded in Lime Grove D. Its total cost is £2,223.

Saturday 21: *The Mutants: The Dead Planet* is transmitted on BBC TV.

Monday 23: A photo shoot with the Daleks is carried out around Shepherd's Bush in London.

Saturday 28: *The Mutants: The Survivors* is transmitted on BBC TV.

Monday 30: Four days' preliminary rehearsal begins for *The Mutants: The Ordeal*.

Tuesday 31: Chief of Programmes Donald Baverstock sends Donald Wilson a memo committing himself to accepting a further ten episodes of *Doctor Who* after the twenty-six already accepted. The budget per episode will remain at £2,300. Baverstock continues:

> I mentioned that I need from you now an outline of the future storylines with their locations in space and time. I hope that in these you will brighten up the logic and inventiveness of the scripts. In the episodes already recorded we have seen Dr Who and his daughter, though ageless and miraculously clever, reduced to helpless unscientific ordinariness once they left their spaceship, whereas even the two lay characters should have appeared incredibly knowledgeable to such people as the Cave Dwellers and the Country Dwellers outside the blasted city. Any ordinary man of the mid-20th Century returning to, say, the Marco Polo age could hardly help making assertions all the time which would sound to the 14th Century Chinese or Venetians like mad ludicrous prophesies. Likewise, the characters of the past and the future should also have appeared more strikingly and differently ingenious – the one more often reminding us of lost simple knowledge; the other of credible skills and capacities that can be conceived likely in the future.
>
> I suggest that you should make efforts in future episodes to reduce the amount of slow prosaic dialogue and to centre the dramatic movements much more on historical and scientific hokum.

JANUARY 1964

Friday 3: *The Mutants: The Ordeal* is camera rehearsed and recorded in Lime Grove D. Its total cost is £1,919.

Saturday 4: *The Mutants: The Escape* is transmitted on BBC TV.

Monday 6: Four days' preliminary rehearsal begins for *The Mutants: The Rescue*.
Sydney Newman sends Verity Lambert a memo of comment after watching *The Mutants: The Escape*. Despite reservations about the Daleks' adversaries, the blond-haired Thals, his reaction is very positive:

> Congratulations are due to you and those working with you on the splendid progress being made on *Doctor Who*. Many, many people have told me how much they enjoy it.
>
> Despite the blond faeries this last episode, *The Escape* contained one very marvellous thing which you should attempt to duplicate as often as possible. I am referring to the *demonstration* of intelligence by our four

heroes – you know the way they figured out how the Daleks operated their machines and how to disable them.

Tuesday 7: Donald Wilson sends Donald Baverstock a memo containing synopses of the next three stories due into production, which at this point are *Inside the Spaceship* (now to be directed by Richard Martin rather than by Paddy Russell or by Mervyn Pinfield who had been suggested as her replacement), *Marco Polo* (to be directed by Waris Hussein) and *The Hidden Planet* (to which a director has still to be assigned). The concluding scenes of *Marco Polo*, leading into *The Hidden Planet*, are described as follows:

> ...the travellers repossess their ship and land in a country which, at first sight, could well be England: The cycling policeman they see on their scanner screen however, once out of sight, behaves in a most extraordinary fashion, a way which leaves no doubt that wherever the TARDIS has landed, it is certainly not 20th Century England.

The Hidden Planet itself is then summarised as follows:

> Without knowing it, the space and time travellers have landed on a planet identical to Earth; the Tenth Planet on the other side of Earth's sun. The glass of fashion has a different reflection, the mould of form an altered pattern, yet both have sprung from the same roots as their counterparts on Earth. Thus, Doctor Who and his friends find themselves in a world where every parallel is in fact a paradox that comforts whilst it mocks. Primarily, the male sex is insisting on equality and the vote. The leader of the ruling (and female) class is, to all intents and purposes, Barbara's double. When Barbara is kidnapped by the male rebels, she is forced to assume her double's identity, while Doctor Who, Susan and Ian find themselves caught up not only in the violent struggle for male suffrage but in a web of intrigue and suspicion.

Thursday 9: J J Stringer, an administrator in Programme Planning, sends Donald Wilson a memo informing him that while it is acceptable within any given financial year for savings on one episode to be carried forward to help finance others, 'it is not possible to carry forward savings from one year to the next.' This means that the first eighteen episodes of *Doctor Who* – i.e. those currently due to be transmitted before week commencing 4 April 1964 (Week 14) – must be 'financially self-balancing, as no savings on these can be carried forward, neither can overspending be offset by savings in the following year.' He goes on to note that as the series' allocated budget up to the end of 1963 was fully spent, 'expensive programmes in January/March must be financed by savings within the same quarter.'

It has now been decided that Waris Hussein should direct all seven episodes of *Marco Polo*. Previously, Richard Martin has been due to direct episodes four and six.

William Hartnell appears on *Junior Points of View* in an interview about the Daleks recorded the previous day.

Friday 10: *The Mutants: The Rescue* is camera rehearsed and recorded in Lime Grove D. Its total cost is £2,634.

This episode is the first to utilise the 'roll back and mix' technique experimented with on 13 September 1963 for the effect of the police box dematerialising. The effect proves very difficult to achieve and will be used less than half a dozen times on *Doctor Who* during the sixties.

Saturday 11: *The Mutants: The Ambush* is transmitted on BBC TV.

Monday 13: Four days' preliminary rehearsal begins for *Inside the Spaceship: The Edge of Destruction*.

Five days' shooting of film inserts for *Marco Polo* begins on Stage 3B at Ealing.

A permanent production office has by this time been set up for *Doctor Who* in Rooms 505, 506 and 507 of Union House – the building directly adjoining its previous location, Threshold House.

Wednesday 15: At Verity Lambert's request, David Whitaker sends Donald Wilson a memo setting out audience size and audience reaction figures for *100,000 BC* and for each of the first three episodes of *The Mutants*. *100,000 BC*, including the repeat of the first episode, has registered an average audience of 12% (i.e. 6 million viewers) and an average audience reaction figure of 58.25; *The Mutants* has so far done even better, reaching by the third episode an audience of 18% (9 million viewers) and an audience reaction figure of 62.

Friday 17: *Inside the Spaceship: The Edge of Destruction* is camera rehearsed and recorded in Lime Grove D. Its total cost is £1,480.

Saturday 18: *The Mutants: The Expedition* is transmitted on BBC TV.

Monday 20: Four days' preliminary rehearsal begins for *Inside the Spaceship: The Brink of Disaster*.

Tuesday 21: The production team have by this point decided to abandon Terry Nation's historical story *The Red Fort*. They ask him instead to write a six-part replacement story with a futuristic theme. Nation agrees that, in view of the shortage of time remaining before the planned production dates, he will complete and deliver his scripts within the space of four weeks. Whitaker arranges to help him with weekly or bi-weekly discussions.

Friday 24: *Inside the Spaceship: The Brink of Disaster* is camera rehearsed and recorded in Lime Grove D. Its total cost is £1,506.

Saturday 25: *The Mutants: The Ordeal* is transmitted on BBC TV.

Monday 27: Four days' preliminary rehearsal begins for *Marco Polo: The Roof of the World*.

Friday 31: *Marco Polo: The Roof of the World* is camera rehearsed and recorded in Lime Grove D. Its total cost is £2,687.

FEBRUARY 1964

Saturday 1: *The Mutants: The Rescue* is transmitted on BBC TV.

Monday 3: Four days' preliminary rehearsal begins for *Marco Polo: The Singing Sands.* William Hartnell is ill and unable to take part.

David Whitaker visits Terry Nation's home for a script conference on the writer's new six-part story, which he has decided to call *The Keys of Marinus.* They discuss the first four episodes in depth and work out the set, filming and casting requirements as far as possible.

Tuesday 4: Whitaker sends William Hartnell a letter wishing him a speedy recovery.

Whitaker also has a meeting with writer Robert Gould in which they discuss at length the difficulties of the 'miniscules' idea. Whitaker asks Gould to submit another story proposal instead. Gould says that he has had an idea about a planet where plants treat people the way that people normally treat plants, and that he will let Whitaker know if this works out.

Two of the four Dalek props made by Shawcraft for *The Mutants* have now been put into storage, along with the control panels from their city, in the BBC's special effects store at Ealing. Jack Kine of the Visual Effects Department has decided that there is no room for the other two to be stored so, rather than let them be broken up, the production team decide to donate them to Dr Barnardo's children's homes.

Thursday 6: David Whitaker collects from Terry Nation's home the draft script for the first episode of *The Keys of Marinus.*

Friday 7: *Marco Polo: The Singing Sands* is camera rehearsed and recorded in Lime Grove D. Its total cost is £1,618.

Saturday 8: *Inside the Spaceship: The Edge of Destruction* is transmitted on BBC TV. A scene in which Susan violently and repeatedly stabs a pair of scissors into the mattress of her bed will subsequently be criticised internally at the BBC on the grounds that it could easily be copied by children. Verity Lambert will admit that its inclusion was a mistake and give an undertaking that nothing similar will occur in future.

Sunday 9: Robert Gould sends Whitaker a card to let him know that he has decided against proceeding with his idea for a story about a planet where the roles of people and plants are reversed.

Monday 10: Four days' preliminary rehearsal begins for *Marco Polo: Five Hundred Eyes.*

Tuesday 11: Whitaker collects from Nation's home the draft script for the second episode of *The Keys of Marinus.*

Wednesday 12: David Whitaker sends Assistant Head of Copyright E Caffery a memo seeking advice about a request made to the production office by A R Mills, Deputy Editor of publishers Frederick Muller Ltd, for permission to produce novelisations of 'several of the *Doctor Who* stories.' Mills had previously contacted writer Terry Nation about this 'but now thought it better to come to the fountain head, so to speak.' Whitaker has explained to Mills that *Doctor Who* is the property of the BBC and that he is unable to release any copies of scripts at this stage. 'I closed the meeting,' Whitaker notes, 'by saying that I would endeavour to find out, in the next few days, if the BBC was willing to grant permission for publication.'

Frederick Muller Ltd will later publish three novelisations: *Doctor Who in an exciting adventure with the Daleks* by David Whitaker (1964), *Doctor Who and the Zarbi* by Bill Strutton (1965) and *Doctor Who and the Crusaders* by David Whitaker (1966).

Thursday 13: Donald Baverstock, at a meeting with Donald Wilson to discuss the Serials Department's offers for the July/September quarter, agrees in principle that *Doctor Who*'s four regular cast members can now be firmly engaged right up to the end their fifty-two week contracts. Production is to continue uninterrupted and Baverstock will consider at a later date a proposal made by Wilson for a six week break in transmission at some point during the run. Baverstock agrees a budget for the last sixteen episodes of £2,380 per episode if outside stock film hire is involved or £2,300 per episode as before if film requirements can be serviced from within the BBC. He also agrees to consider separately a bid by Wilson for extra money to make a four part 'miniscules' story.

Friday 14: *Marco Polo: Five Hundred Eyes* is camera rehearsed and recorded in Lime Grove D. Its total cost is £1,958.

Saturday 15: *Inside the Spaceship: The Brink of Disaster* is transmitted on BBC TV.

Monday 17: Four days' preliminary rehearsal begins for *Marco Polo: The Wall of Lies*.
Terry Nation delivers to David Whitaker his draft scripts for the third and fourth episodes of *The Keys of Marinus*.

Tuesday 18: Donald Baverstock sends Donald Wilson a memo recording the points agreed at their meeting on 13 February.
The BBC's two remaining Daleks appear on *Hi There!*, a BBC programme starring popular Australian entertainer Rolf Harris.

Thursday 20: Sydney Newman is sent a memo by the Head of Business for Television Enterprises, who asks how long *Doctor Who* is due to continue and whether or not there are any plans to resurrect the phenomenally popular Daleks.

Friday 21: *Marco Polo: The Wall of Lies* is camera rehearsed and recorded in Lime Grove D. Its total cost is £2,317.

Saturday 22: *Marco Polo: The Roof of the World* is transmitted on BBC TV. It is promoted with a photograph on the front cover of this week's edition of *Radio Times* – the first time *Doctor Who* has been accorded this privilege. The photograph shows the Doctor (William Hartnell) with Marco Polo (Mark Eden) and the Mongol warlord Tegana (Derren Nesbitt).

Sunday 23: William Russell writes to his agent, T Plunkett Green, raising a number of grievances about his role in the series.

Monday 24: Four days' preliminary rehearsal begins for *Marco Polo: Rider from Shang-Tu*.

Donald Wilson replies on Sydney Newman's behalf to the memo of 20 February from the Head of Business for Television Enterprises. He informs him that there is now a firm commitment to fifty-two weeks of *Doctor Who* and continues:

> We have in mind, of course, to try and resurrect the Daleks, but with the writing we at present have in hand it is hardly likely to happen until well on in the summer.
>
> I am asking Verity Lambert to keep you informed both of the continuation dates for the programme and of any possible exploitation ideas, including the return of the Daleks.

T Plunkett Green writes to Wilson conveying the grievances that his client William Russell has raised with him. First, Russell is irritated that two of the guest cast rather than the regulars were pictured with William Hartnell on the previous week's *Radio Times* front cover; secondly, he feels that recent scripts have given him, and his fellow regulars, an insufficiently substantial role in the action; thirdly, he is concerned that a six minute scene, largely involving him, was added to *The Wall of Lies* only the day before the episode was recorded, leaving him very little time to learn and rehearse it.

Tuesday 25: Terry Nation has now completed his draft scripts for all six episodes of *The Keys of Marinus*, and these have been formally accepted by the production team.

At David Whitaker's request, Assistant Head of Copyright E Caffery writes to Malcolm Hulke's agent, Harvey Unna, to inform him that the scripts for *The Hidden Planet* are unacceptable in their present form and will have to be abandoned unless Hulke is prepared to rewrite them completely.

Whitaker also briefs the Copyright Department to commission from writer John Lucarotti a four-part historical story entitled *The Aztecs*.

Wednesday 26: John Crockett, a BBC staff director who has been brought in to handle episode four of *Marco Polo* before taking full responsibility for *The Aztecs*, sends David Whitaker a list of ideas for subsequent historical stories. The list reads as follows:

Jack Cade/Peasants' Revolt/Pilgrimage of Grace

Viking Raids on Britain

The '45 and Bonnie Prince Charlie

Drake/Armada

Raleigh/Colonisation

Globe Theatre/Burbage/Alleyne/Plague/Puritans

Australian Convict Settlement

Roman Invasion of Britain
Or   } c.f. Alfred Duggan
Defeat of Romans in Britain

Crusades/Richard I

Akhnaton/and his downfall

Guelphs & Ghibellines

Medici (Leonardo, Michelangelo, Savanarola) or Borgias } Florence

Benvenuto Cellini

Covered Wagons

18th to early 19th Century Cornish smugglers and wreckers

Boadicea

Friday 28: *Marco Polo: Rider from Shang-Tu* is camera rehearsed and recorded in Lime Grove D. Its total cost is £2,821.

Donald Wilson replies in apologetic terms to T Plunkett Green's letter of 24 February. He explains that many shots of the four regulars were taken at the *Radio Times* photocall for *Marco Polo* and that the production side had 'confidently expected' one of these to be used on the cover. The magazine makes its own decisions, however, and Wilson can only complain after the event – which he is now doing. On the question of the series' scripts, he continues:

> I know that Verity Lambert has discussed all this very thoroughly in the last two days with all four principals and I believe that now they are feeling much happier about what she has been able to tell them of our future plans. As you will now know, it is agreed that we should continue *Dr Who* for at least fifty-two weeks. This gives us a chance to work much further ahead on scripts and make sure that we do not again have to plunge into an unprepared job.
>
> I assure you that I will, myself, be watching very carefully to make sure that neither William Russell's or our own interests suffer from scripts which do not use his talents to the maximum.

Lambert sends Wilson a memo informing him that up to the end of the financial year the production team will have had to write off one script by Alan Wakeman (the trial episode of *The Living World*) and six by Malcolm Hulke (*The Hidden Planet*). If *Doctor Who* were to be discontinued after its initial fifty-two week run they would also have to write off 'a six-part serial by Anthony Coburn which has been accepted but which needs further work on it' (*The Masters of Luxor*). She adds that they are currently considering commissioning a four-part serial from writer Margot Bennett to act 'as a cover' in case TC1 proves unavailable or 'the "miniscule" story falls through,' and that this might also have to be written off if the series were to be discontinued.

David Whitaker has by this point commissioned a six-part future-based story entitled *The Sensorites* from writer Peter R Newman and has himself undertaken to write a six-part historical story set in 16th Century Spain after the Armada. Terry Nation has also agreed to write a six-part story concerning a future Dalek invasion of Earth, thus meeting the ever-growing demand for a return appearance by the series' most popular monsters. Moris Farhi is another writer currently in discussion with the production team.

The planned running order for the stories after *Marco Polo* is now: *The Keys of Marinus* (six episodes) by Terry Nation, to be directed by John Gorrie; *The Aztecs* (four episodes) by John Lucarotti, to be directed by John Crockett; *The Sensorites* (six episodes) by Peter R Newman, to be directed by Mervyn Pinfield; David Whitaker's historical story (six episodes), to be directed by Gerald Blake; a 'miniscules' story (four episodes), yet to be commissioned, to be directed by Richard Martin; and Terry Nation's Dalek story (six episodes), director yet to be assigned.

Saturday 29: *Marco Polo: The Singing Sands* is transmitted on BBC TV.

MARCH 1964

Monday 2: Four days' preliminary rehearsal begins for *Marco Polo: Mighty Kublai Khan*.

Harvey Unna writes to E Caffery to convey his client Malcolm Hulke's concern at being asked to make substantial revisions to his scripts for *The Hidden Planet*. He points out that the scripts adhere closely to the storyline, which was agreed with the production team in advance, and that the requested revisions constitute an unreasonable departure from this.

Friday 6: *Marco Polo: Mighty Kublai Khan* is camera rehearsed and recorded in Lime Grove D.

Saturday 7: *Marco Polo: Five Hundred Eyes* is transmitted on BBC TV.

Monday 9: Four days' preliminary rehearsal begins for *Marco Polo: Assassin at Peking*.

Tuesday 10: Caffery replies to Unna's letter of 2 March, refuting the assertions made by Hulke about the requested revisions to his scripts for *The Hidden Planet*:

In our opinion, and subject to the suggestions already made about it, there is nothing basically wrong with the storyline. It is the scripts – and their treatment of the storyline – which proved unacceptable and which need completely rewriting to bring them up to acceptance standards. Given Mr Hulke's contention that we are not adhering to the storyline and that he has already done what he was asked to do – a contention with which we cannot agree – is there really any point in continuing? In view of this impasse, is not the only sensible and practical solution to pay Mr Hulke for the work he has done and call the whole project off? Whilst Mr Hulke is free to rewrite the scripts on the basis proposed in my letter of 25 February, there can surely be no useful point in continuing in the face of such fundamental disagreement between the production unit and the writer.

Hulke subsequently agrees to continue working on his scripts and rewrite them as suggested by the production team. Episode two of the story subsequently acquires the working title *Year of the Lame Dog*.

Friday 13: *Marco Polo: Assassin at Peking* is camera rehearsed and recorded in Lime Grove D. The start of the day's work is delayed when the lift required to transport a camera dolly to the studio breaks down and has to be hastily repaired. A further fifteen minute hold up occurs when the studio fireman refuses to let camera rehearsals get underway due to his concern over a clutter of electrical equipment left in the fire gangways. A compromise is eventually reached on this.

Saturday 14: *Marco Polo: The Wall of Lies* is transmitted on BBC TV.

Monday 16: Four days' preliminary rehearsal begins for *The Keys of Marinus: The Sea of Death*.

Writer John Lucarotti is making good progress on his scripts for *The Aztecs*, but illness prevents him from bringing them in to the production office as he had planned. He agrees to come in the following day instead.

David Whitaker makes an appointment to see writer Dennis Spooner at 11.00 am on 18 March to discuss the possibility of him contributing a story about the French Revolution. This would act as a replacement for Whitaker's own Spanish Armada story.

Whitaker also visits rehearsals. He later reports to Verity Lambert, who is absent from the office this week, that they are going well and that the cast like director John Gorrie.

In addition, Whitaker sends some stills from *Doctor Who* to A R Mills of Frederick Muller Ltd, who are taking forward their plans to publish novelisations based on the series. Mills promises to return them by the end of the week.

Tuesday 17: David Whitaker briefs the Copyright Department to commission Terry Nation's new Dalek story, which at this point is referred to as *The Daleks*. It will shortly afterwards be given the new working title *The Return of the Daleks*. The target delivery date for the scripts is 19 June 1964.

John Lucarotti spends the day at the production office. His scripts for *The Aztecs* are two-thirds finished, and he works all day on the remainder.

Whitaker, meanwhile, completes some rewrites on episode four of *The Keys of Marinus* to remove the Doctor from the plot and thereby allow William Hartnell a week's holiday.

The BBC are currently considering a proposal from the *Daily Express* newspaper to run a regular cartoon strip based on *Doctor Who*. Jacqueline Hill, however, has considerable reservations about her likeness being used for this.

Wednesday 18: Whitaker meets Dennis Spooner to discuss the French Revolution idea. Spooner agrees to submit a storyline in two weeks' time.

Whitaker also sends copies of the completed scripts for *The Aztecs* to Design Manager James Bould.

Donald Wilson attends rehearsals to see a run-through of the episode due to be recorded in two day's time. He has only three minor comments on the dialogue, and Whitaker agrees to take these on board. Subsequently Wilson talks to Jacqueline Hill and the rest of the regular cast about the *Daily Express* proposal for a *Doctor Who* cartoon strip.

Whitaker speaks to William Russell about giving him a holiday from the series and suggests that this could fall during the French Revolution story, due to be made in July and August. Russell agrees to leave it to him.

Whitaker also makes arrangements with John Gorrie for Carole Ann Ford to be released from rehearsals on 13 April as she will be needed at Ealing for the shooting of some film inserts for *The Aztecs*. These are designed to cover for Ford's planned absence on holiday during the period when episodes two and three of that story are in production.

Mervyn Pinfield sends Wilson a memo explaining the reasons for the late start of recording the previous Friday. He notes that the problem of electrical equipment is an old and continuing one, as 'a certain quantity of equipment is permanently allocated to Studio D and it has to be kept in the studio, there being absolutely no other area to accommodate it.' He adds that this problem is particularly acute 'when the studio is chock full of sets' and concludes:

> Of course, the only real remedy is not to fill the studio area with sets and to leave a reasonable amount of room for this lighting equipment, but last Friday's production was, perhaps, the most complicated set-wise that we have yet had in the *Doctor Who* series.
>
> With the aim of reducing the possibility of a future delay of this description, perhaps the designers could be made more aware of this aspect of the problem.

Friday 20: *The Keys of Marinus: The Sea of Death* is camera rehearsed and recorded in Lime Grove D.

Saturday 21: *Marco Polo: Rider from Shang-Tu* is transmitted on BBC TV.

Monday 23: Four days' preliminary rehearsal begins for *The Keys of Marinus: The Velvet Web*.

David Whitaker briefs the Copyright Department to commission from writer Louis Marks a storyline for a possible 'miniscules' story to replace Robert Gould's.

Thursday 26: Whitaker sends Donald Wilson a memo refuting a charge made by Gould that Terry Nation's script for *The Screaming Jungle*, the third episode of *The Keys of Marinus*, plagiarises his idea for a story about a planet where plants treat people the way that people normally treat plants. Whitaker sets out the key stages in the development and writing of Nation's story and continues:

> I spoke to Terry Nation this morning on the telephone and a summary

of his words is as follows:

That the conception of an episodic serial (three or four different adventures in one serial) arose from combined discussions.

That episode one was entirely his creation, with only minor suggestions.

That episode two arose out of combined discussion – the 'throwing' of ideas back and forwards.

That episode three began with a suggestion from me that he wrote a 'House that Jack Built' story – some house or place that was full of booby-traps. Since episodes one and two had been basically interior sets, he wished to tell a story more 'out in the open' to give the designer a chance for different settings. It was his own idea to speed up Nature's process and have some of our principal artists battling with vegetation rather than with alien people.

Episode four started with an idea from me to change the climate (from the hot jungle of episode three to a snow region). The rest came out of general discussion.

Episodes five and six arose out of general discussion, although episode six was totally the author's.

Terry Nation is prepared to write to you himself with the relevant dates in confirmation of this, if necessary.

In conclusion, I can only say that Robert Gould at no time discussed his idea in any detail with me. My reaction after our meeting on 4 February was to repeat his 'plants treating people as people treat plants' comment to Miss Lambert, who agreed with me that it might be too near *The Day of the Triffids* by John Wyndham but that we would wait to see the storyline.

Friday 27: *The Keys of Marinus: The Velvet Web* is camera rehearsed and recorded in Lime Grove D.

Saturday 28: *Marco Polo: Mighty Kublai Khan* is transmitted on BBC TV.

Monday 30: Four days' preliminary rehearsal begins for *The Keys of Marinus: The Screaming Jungle*.

APRIL 1964

Thursday 2: David Whitaker briefs the Copyright Department to commission from Dennis Spooner the six scripts for his French Revolution story, now entitled *The Reign of Terror*.

Friday 3: *The Keys of Marinus: The Screaming Jungle* is camera rehearsed and recorded in Lime Grove D. Severe problems are encountered with the scenery during the recording of this episode. Head of Scenic Servicing James Mudie later puts this down to lateness of the design drawings, which was due in turn to lateness of the scripts.

Saturday 4: *Marco Polo: Assassin at Peking* is transmitted on BBC TV.

Monday 6: Four days' preliminary rehearsal begins for *The Keys of Marinus: The Snows of Terror*.

Tuesday 7: Verity Lambert sends Donald Wilson the following memo:

> As we discussed, I would like to put forward the following suggestion for a break in transmission of *Doctor Who* for the six weeks of 1 August to 5 September inclusive.
>
> We would, of course, continue recording *Doctor Who* during this period and, therefore, when transmissions commenced again on 12 September, we would be ten weeks in hand. This would mean that, if the series should continue for the following year, we would be able to have a break in recording of five weeks after 23 October (Week 43), and we would commence recording again in Week 48 with five weeks in hand.
>
> For the six weeks that we are not transmitting *Doctor Who*, we will provide a six part serial at approximately the same budget as *Doctor Who* to be recorded from Weeks 27 to 32 inclusive. David Whitaker and I are, at present, discussing ideas for this and we hope to let you have something definite by the end of next week.

Friday 10: *The Keys of Marinus: The Snows of Terror* is camera rehearsed and recorded in Lime Grove D.

Sydney Newman sends Verity Lambert the following memo:

> May I encourage you to do something in future episodes of *Doctor Who* to glamorize the title, occupation etc of an engineer.
>
> Nowadays for a kid to want to become a scientist is really hot stuff, but to become a technologist or an engineer – which the country needs in millions – is without prestige. Engineers, of course, are people who repair cars, aeroplane engines, run atomic energy plants etc. Another way of putting it is an emphasis on the applications of science rather than on pure science by itself.
>
> If you can help do this I think it will do the country a lot of good.

Nothing comes of this suggestion.

Saturday 11: *The Keys of Marinus: The Sea of Death* is transmitted on BBC TV.

Monday 13: Four days' preliminary rehearsal begins for *The Keys of Marinus: Sentence of Death*.

Film inserts for *The Aztecs* are shot at Ealing.

Tuesday 14: David Whitaker sends Verity Lambert a memo setting out his ideas for the second season of *Doctor Who*, on the assumption that the series 'will be renewed for a full fifty-two week period':

The first thing of importance to say is that the fewer writers we employ the better. It is quite obvious that Terry Nation, for example, has improved his approach to the serial and to the four running characters, although he had to write his second serial very speedily. I think a nucleus of writers would ensure that the characters did have growth and added dimension.

This is the way I suggest the future fifty-two weeks to be set up:

Serial A	Past	Spanish Armada	6 parts
Serial B	Future	(Possibly Malcolm Hulke)	6 parts
Serial C	Past	Egyptian	4 parts
Serial D	Future		6 parts
Serial E	Sideways		4 parts
Serial F	Future	(Possibly Tony Coburn)	6 parts
Serial G	Past	American Civil War	6 parts
Serial H	Future		4 parts
Serial I	Past	Roman	4 parts
Serial J	Future		6 parts

What I suggest is this. That at some time in the summer when the plans are clear, we ask two or three writers to attend a planning conference. That we discuss which characters are going to continue in *Doctor Who*; the way they are to develop; and the subjects we would like treated. (Obviously the above list is merely a suggestion.) Then I think we should put authors' names beside certain serials and in this way we can have a grand plan of operations. Writers will be able to see a year's work ahead of them and will know in plenty of time what their delivery date situation is, and their subject, and finally it will be very much easier to devise the ending and the beginning of new serials when the writers are able to co-operate with each other. At the moment I am entirely responsible for the linking of one serial into another, and while this may work well enough I feel that the more original ideas we have the better. If we are guaranteeing a year's work in the shape of, say, a promise of two serials to a writer, then he is going to be prepared to contribute ideas to the project as a whole.

I recommend that we make Terry Nation the senior writer, insofar as future subjects are concerned. He has worked very well for us and his writing is obviously improving. His figures are certainly the highest so far of all the writers and my suggestion is that he be offered three serials in the new fifty-two weeks. Secondly, I suggest that there be a senior 'past' writer who is offered two serials. This will then leave five serials only, and I suggest that they are split up between no more than four writers.

As you can see from my list above, I have suggested places where we can use scripts we have bought, like the Malcolm Hulke future serial, and Tony Coburn's robot serial.

Wednesday 15: Evelyn M Thomas, designated Editorial Assistant Publicity, sends the BBC's Publications Executive a memo confirming that, 'subject to the usual agreement being reached concerning the BBC's right to approve content and format', there is no objection in principle to a proposal from Souvenir Press Ltd to publish a *Daleks Annual*, based on contributions from Terry Nation and BBC illustrations, or to the proposal from Frederick Muller Ltd to produce *Dr Who and the Daleks*, written by David Whitaker based on Terry Nation's scripts. The Head of Films Television has agreed that reasonable facilities may be granted to Souvenir Press to view telerecordings of episodes and arrange for stills to be taken from them.

These are just the first of many product proposals that will soon see a whole host of *Doctor Who*-related and, in particular, Dalek-related merchandise appearing in the nation's toyshops.

Thursday 16: Chief of Programmes Donald Baverstock sends Donald Wilson the following memo regarding the continuation of *Doctor Who* beyond its initial fifty-two week production run:

> Present commitments, as I understand them, commit us to transmission of *Doctor Who* until the end of October this year. Provided you can assure me that, after a full examination of the problems ahead, you will find it possible to obtain a sufficient variety of good new storylines, I am willing to agree in principle that *Doctor Who* should continue for three months beyond the end of October. In contracting the four artists for this period I suggest you should also obtain options at the same fees for a further three months.

Friday 17: *The Keys of Marinus: Sentence of Death* is camera rehearsed and recorded in Lime Grove D.

Saturday 18: *The Keys of Marinus: The Velvet Web* is transmitted on BBC TV.

Monday 20: Four days' preliminary rehearsal begins for *The Keys of Marinus: The Keys of Marinus*.
BBC2 begins transmission.

Friday 24: *The Keys of Marinus: The Keys of Marinus* is camera rehearsed and recorded in Lime Grove D.

Saturday 25: *The Keys of Marinus: The Screaming Jungle* is transmitted on BBC1.

Monday 27: Four days' preliminary rehearsal begins for *The Aztecs: The Temple of Evil*.

Tuesday 28: Kenneth Adam, the Director of Television, sends a memo to Stuart Hood, the Controller of Programmes for Television, conveying the concerns of fellow members of the BBC's Board of Management about the direction *Doctor Who* is taking:
The 'creepiness' is laid on rather thick and there are so many refugees from Attica or, if you prefer, the Eisteddfod wandering about. If it is to survive, it needs a touch of discipline – especially in the writing; they couldn't really be so stupid by now as always

to split up the way they do when danger threatens. Even my 3 year old grand-daughter remarked on it on Saturday.

Hood subsequently passes a copy of this memo on to Sydney Newman, and Newman raises the matter with Donald Wilson.

Thursday 30: John Mair, Planning Manager (Forward), responds to a request from Joanna Spicer, Assistant Controller (Planning) Television, for recommendations regarding 'the Studio D situation with particular reference to *Dr Who*.' He explains that there are two problems currently faced by the production: first, the studio is to be taken out of service from 1 to 16 August inclusive to allow for work to be carried out on the sound equipment and to meet requests from the electricians' trade union for improved ventilation at studio gallery level; secondly, the lack of storage facilities for technical equipment means that space has to be allowed for this on the floor of the studio itself, leading to setting and rigging difficulties and potential union demarcation disputes.

Mair goes on to note that *Doctor Who*'s claim to one of the big Television Centre studios has previously been thought unjustified, but that he undertook some time ago to try to transfer it to the Centre during the summer months due to the excessive heat in Studio D. Consequently the series is due to be in TC4 for the six Fridays from 7 August to 11 September inclusive. Donald Wilson has also agreed that it can be moved into Lime Grove G for the four weeks prior to that, and Mair is hopeful that Verity Lambert will be prepared to accept this studio on a longer-term basis. The series could be moved to a larger studio if an exchange could be arranged with another show that similarly recorded just one day a week, but the only shows which follow that pattern are situation comedies and BBC2's *Thriller* serial, which are unsuited to being made in Studio D. He concludes:

> Given all these complexities, my recommendations would be:
>
> a) that we make TC3/4 available to *Dr Who* in the immediate future as and when possible, and subject to a guarantee that no last minute move will be made later than four weeks before production;
>
> b) that we put *Dr Who* into G and then TC3/4 as already agreed up to Week 37; and
>
> c) that we review the whole position in the light of autumn needs (which will by then be more clearly known) about two months before *Dr Who* is due to move out of the Centre in Week 38, unless we can do so earlier.

MAY 1964

Friday 1: *The Aztecs: The Temple of Evil* is camera rehearsed and recorded in Lime Grove D.

Saturday 2: *The Keys of Marinus: The Snows of Terror* is transmitted on BBC1.
Monday 4: Four days' preliminary rehearsal begins for *The Aztecs: The Warriors of Death*.

Wednesday 6: Donald Wilson sends Sydney Newman the following response to Kenneth Adam's memo of 28 April:

> I myself have been concerned about D.Tel.'s [Adam] points, particularly his last one, and some three weeks ago I urged on Verity the necessity for making sure a) that our leading characters don't appear to be simply stupid and b) that the thrills should be genuine and lead directly out of a strong situation and not be added for kicks. When I last spoke about this serial to you if you remember I made the point that the kind of writers with the necessary invention are not always necessarily the best in terms of characterisation and dialogue, but we must keep trying.
>
> I made a copy of D.Tel.'s note and will make sure that both Verity and David Whitaker see it.

Friday 8: *The Aztecs: The Warriors of Death* is camera rehearsed and recorded in TC3.

Sydney Newman sends Stuart Hood the following memo about the points raised by Kenneth Adam:

> Donald and I were on to this three or four weeks ago and rather forcefully brought these to Verity's attention. The scripts are what is difficult!

Saturday 9: *The Keys of Marinus: Sentence of Death* is transmitted on BBC1.

Monday 11: Four days' preliminary rehearsal begins for *The Aztecs: The Bride of Sacrifice.*

Wednesday 13: Verity Lambert sends Donald Wilson a memo commenting on John Mair's suggestion that Lime Grove G could become *Doctor Who*'s regular studio. She informs him that neither *The Aztecs* nor *The Sensorites* could be made there as they will require large composite sets and cannot be radically rewritten at this late stage. Although Studio G is larger in area than Studio D, it is long and narrow in shape and therefore accommodates only simple box sets. This makes it unsuitable for a drama series like *Doctor Who*, which depends greatly on having solid and sizeable sets – particularly for the historical stories. She concludes:

> If we were to move into Studio G, which certainly is inadequate for our design requirements, we would have to impose even more severe restrictions on our writers than we are doing at the moment. I can only say that this will obviously be detrimental to the series as a whole.
>
> As you already know, I am certainly not in favour of staying in Studio D, even if we are allowed to do so. The restrictions in D involve technical facilities and working conditions. We have struggled along for six months in this studio and have made compromises of all kinds. The sound equipment is inadequate, old fashioned and worn out. The cameras do not take any wide angle lenses or any zooms. The lighting equipment makes life almost impossible for the lighting supervisor and, because of

the heat, unbearable for everybody else in the studio.

Friday 15: *The Aztecs: The Bride of Sacrifice* is camera rehearsed and recorded in TC3.

Saturday 16: *The Keys of Marinus: The Keys of Marinus* is transmitted on BBC1.

Tuesday 19: Three days' preliminary rehearsal begins for *The Aztecs: The Day of Darkness.* (The rehearsal room has been closed on Monday 18 as it is Whit Monday.)

Wednesday 20: Sydney Newman sends Chief of Programmes Donald Baverstock a memo in which he outlines the problems currently facing *Doctor Who* and proposes a six week break in transmission after the conclusion of *The Sensorites* on Saturday 25 July:

> (1) The contracts of the main lead characters expire on 24 October. It is urgent that we renew on the basis of run-of-programme. In short, they should be contracted for as long as the programme continues, subject to our giving them between six and twelve weeks' notice. May I urgently request that you agree with this on the understanding that we will continue *Dr Who* until such time as you give us warning that it should stop – such warning to be as short a period of cancellation time as we can negotiate with the four stars.

> (2) On the assumption that you agree generally with the above it is proposed that we stop producing *Dr Who* for six weeks at the expiry of the present contracts. Since this comes at very much of a peak time of the year, I would like to recommend that we take *Dr Who* off the air from Weeks 32 to 37 inclusive, but continue the recordings to enable programmes to continue from the resumption in Week 38 during the winter months.
>
> Relating to an earlier conversation on this problem, we have found it impossible to plan the production of another serial to fill in the six-week summer gap, due largely to the shortage of studio facilities and production staff.

> (3) The most vexing problem of all is studio facilities. Studio D has worked against the best interests of *Dr Who*, has tired the cast, has not allowed for sufficient camera rehearsal, the heat is unbearable, it has no proper technical gimmicks, and so on. At any rate, I understand the deficiencies of the studio have been recognised and it is being withdrawn for use as a drama studio. Studio G, because of its somewhat ridiculous proportions, is unacceptable. Riverside 1 or the Television Centre studios are what remain as being suitable. I have gone into the question of seeing what single play series or weekly series can be switched about to make room for *Dr Who* and have come to the irrevocable conclusion that none can. Unless the proper studio can be allocated for *Dr Who* from Week 38 (the start of *The Return of the Daleks*) I think it would be better that I

recommended its cancellation. I can't bear to see this potentially marvellous programme go down the drain through inadequate support.

In general, Donald, I am proposing going off the air for six weeks in the summer in order to achieve a six-week break in the autumn. This will enable us to lick our wounds, consider the future with possible changes in cast, script, etc so that we can go on with the series with more promise than any idea we have yet thought of.

Baverstock subsequently approves a break in transmission, but stipulates that this must last for only four weeks and start from week commencing 12 September (Week 38) rather than from week commencing 1 August (Week 32). Dennis Spooner's French Revolution contribution, *The Reign of Terror*, will therefore form the closing story of the first season rather than the opening story of the second. Baverstock is furthermore unwilling to renew the series on an indefinite basis, agreeing only that it can continue transmission up to the end of January 1965.

Over the next few weeks, the production team discuss this situation and convey their thoughts to Donald Wilson. They have been considering making changes to the series' format and cast for its second year – in particular, they have been thinking of dropping the character of Barbara, thus reducing the number of regulars from four to three, and replacing Susan with another, younger girl – but Baverstock's indecision over the series' long-term future raises doubts as to whether or not this is worthwhile. Wilson summarises these considerations in the following discussion document:

We intend to continue recording until Week 43, then break recording for four weeks. This arrangement puts back our final transmission date of the current programme to Week 51 so only one more six-part serial will be required to take us up to the end of January. It is quite clearly not worth rethinking in terms of cast or format for one more six-part serial. I doubt even if the break in recording is necessary after Week 43. Moveover, there is no point in obtaining new scripts beyond the present limit unless and until we have decided on any changes in format and cast. One of our troubles has always been (from a design point of view) in getting scripts early enough. If we are to make changes starting with the first recording date of the new series, which date is in Week 48, i.e. week commencing 21 November, we must have the scripts for the first new serial completed by 1 October. I estimate, therefore, that the latest commissioning date for this serial … must be not later than 7 July. At this date we shall have the artists engaged only up to the end of the present recording period, namely 23 October.

If we are to lose any members of the cast – and our present thinking is that we may well drop the Jackie Hill character altogether and replace Carole Ann Ford with another younger girl – this must be decided upon in time so that we can write into *The Return of the Daleks* serial (the last in the first year's programme) the scenes which will make these changes work from then on. This serial is at present being written by Terry Nation and he is naturally anxious for an early decision.

In short, if we are to continue only to the end of January we will not make any changes in format or cast because it won't be worthwhile. If we are to change the format and cast we must decide to do so not later than 7 July.

Wilson is in one respect mistaken in this memo: the number of episodes required to take transmission up to the end of January 1965 would be seven, not six.

Thursday 21: John Mair sends Joanna Spicer a further memo about *Doctor Who*'s studio allocation. He begins:

> As spoken, in discussion with H.Serials.D.Tel. [Wilson] yesterday he explained that Serial G of *Dr Who* (production Weeks 22-27) is really too close to be rewritten for Studio G.
>
> He is having difficulty in any case with one or two of the storylines and he would prefer to accept D in certain weeks, even given the problems there, than to risk further disruption by trying to get the whole rewritten in terms of sets.
>
> On the other hand, I am sure we must not because of union problems leave it in D any more than is essential. I have therefore said that I would recommend:

Weeks 22, 23	TC3
Week 24	D
Week 25	TC4
Week 26	D
Week 27	D unless, as seems possible, the producer can manage G for this particular production. This she will confirm.

> You accepted that in the circumstances we should work on this basis.

Mair goes on to note the previously-agreed arrangement that the first four episodes of Serial H – *The Reign of Terror* – will be made in Studio G and the other two in TC4, and that all four episodes of Serial J – the 'miniscules' story – will be made in the latter.

The scripts for the four-part 'miniscules' story have now been commissioned from writer Louis Marks. It is known for a time simply as *The Miniscules*, but is later given the title *Planet of Giants*.

Friday 22: *The Aztecs: The Day of Darkness* is camera rehearsed and recorded in Lime Grove D.

Saturday 23: *The Aztecs: The Temple of Evil* is transmitted on BBC1.

Monday 25: Four days' preliminary rehearsal begins for *The Sensorites: Strangers in Space*.
Friday 29: *The Sensorites: Strangers in Space* is camera rehearsed and recorded in TC3.

Saturday 30: *The Aztecs: The Warriors of Death* is transmitted on BBC1.

JUNE 1964

Monday 1: Four days' preliminary rehearsal begins for *The Sensorites: The Unwilling Warriors.*

Thursday 4: Discussions have been continuing over the past fortnight with regard to *Doctor Who*'s long-term studio allocation. Sydney Newman has asked Donald Wilson and Verity Lambert to consider the possibility of using the small Television Centre studio TC2 and compensating for the reduction in space by recording each episode over two days rather than one (an idea first proposed as early as the end of May 1963). Lambert sends Wilson a memo pointing out that this would mean spending one day shooting on a large composite set and the other on all the more minor sets, therefore doubling the number of occasions on which scenery had to be put up and taken down in the studio. She adds that under the terms of the BBC's agreement with the actors' union Equity it would mean paying some £250 extra in fees to the cast for each episode. It would also necessitate an increase in camera rehearsal and recording time. She ends:

> The above-the-line costs of a two day operation are, in fact, not great, but I think that the below-the-line costs will be quite considerable.
> My own feelings are that this would be a very unsatisfactory way of doing *Doctor Who* from both a monetary and an artistic point of view.

It is subsequently agreed that *Doctor Who* will continue to be recorded one day per week and that Studio 1 at Riverside will be made available for it from the start of *The Return of the Daleks.*

Friday 5: *The Sensorites: The Unwilling Warriors* is camera rehearsed and recorded in TC3.

Saturday 6: *The Aztecs: The Bride of Sacrifice* is transmitted on BBC1.
Dalek actor Kevin Manser opens a fete for Dr Barnardo's in one of the Daleks donated to them by the BBC.

Monday 8: Four days' preliminary rehearsal begins for *The Sensorites: Hidden Danger.*

Friday 12: *The Sensorites: Hidden Danger* is camera rehearsed and recorded in Lime Grove D.

Saturday 13: *The Aztecs: The Day of Darkness* is transmitted on BBC1.

Monday 15: Four days' preliminary rehearsal begins for *The Sensorites: A Race Against Death.*
Doctor Who's first ever location filming takes place on a poplar-lined lane at White Plains, Tile House Lane, Denham, Buckinghamshire and on a lane and field at Isle of Wight Farm, Gerrards Cross, Buckinghamshire. The filming consists of some silent inserts for *The Reign of Terror* of the Doctor walking towards Paris. The Doctor, seen only from a distance, is played by Brian Proudfoot, who has spent most of the previous Friday learning to imitate William Hartnell's walk.

Tuesday 16: Three days' shooting of film inserts for *The Reign of Terror* begins on Stage 3A/B at Ealing. The first two days are devoted to live action work and the third, Thursday 18 June, to model shots of a farmhouse burning down for the end of the first episode.

Friday 19: *The Sensorites: A Race Against Death* is camera rehearsed and recorded in TC4.

Saturday 20: *The Sensorites: Strangers in Space* is transmitted on BBC1.

Monday 22: Four days' preliminary rehearsal begins for *The Sensorites: Kidnap*.

Friday 26: *The Sensorites: Kidnap* is camera rehearsed and recorded in Lime Grove D.

Saturday 27: *The Sensorites: The Unwilling Warriors* is transmitted on BBC1.

Monday 29: Four days' preliminary rehearsal begins for *The Sensorites: A Desperate Venture*.

JULY 1964

Friday 3: *The Sensorites: A Desperate Venture* is camera rehearsed and recorded in Lime Grove D.

Saturday 4: No episode of *Doctor Who* is scheduled for this evening as the sports programme *Grandstand* is extended to cover the cricket Test Match between England and Australia and the finals of the Wimbledon tennis tournament. The gap between recording and transmission is therefore restored to the position before *The Mutants: The Dead Planet* had to be remounted.

Monday 6: Four days' preliminary rehearsal begins for *The Reign of Terror: A Land of Fear*.

Friday 10: *The Reign of Terror: A Land of Fear* is camera rehearsed and recorded in Lime Grove G.

This is the first episode since the pilot to feature sets designed by someone other than Barry Newbery or Raymond Cusick. Roderick Laing has been brought in to handle *The Reign of Terror* in order to ease the workload on the two regulars.

Saturday 11: *The Sensorites: Hidden Danger* is transmitted on BBC1.

Monday 13: Four days' preliminary rehearsal begins for *The Reign of Terror: Guests of Madame Guillotine*.

Friday 17: *The Reign of Terror: Guests of Madame Guillotine* is camera rehearsed and recorded in Lime Grove G.

Saturday 18: *The Sensorites: A Race Against Death* is transmitted on BBC1.

Monday 20: Four days' preliminary rehearsal begins for *The Reign of Terror: A Change of Identity*.

Friday 24: *The Reign of Terror: A Change of Identity* is camera rehearsed and recorded in Lime Grove G. Director Henric Hirsch collapses outside the studio control room shortly before recording is due to begin, and John Gorrie is hastily brought in to take over from him for the rest of the evening.

Saturday 25: *The Sensorites: Kidnap* is transmitted on BBC1.

Monday 27: Four days' preliminary rehearsal begins for *The Reign of Terror: The Tyrant of France*.

Thursday 30: One day's shooting of film inserts for *Planet of Giants* takes place at Ealing.

It has now been over two months since Sydney Newman first raised with Donald Baverstock the question of *Doctor Who*'s long-term future, and still no decision has been taken. The start of the series' second season has meanwhile been put back to 31 October, three weeks later than originally planned. The production team have concluded that, if there remains a real possibility of the series being discontinued at the end of January 1965, a four part story will be required for transmission after *Planet of Giants* and *The Return of the Daleks*. This presents them with a number of difficulties, not least of which is that there is no four-part story currently commissioned; they have been thinking of using Malcolm Hulke's *The Hidden Planet*, now rewritten as a five-parter, to launch the new production block.

The production team have now abandoned the idea of writing Barbara out of the series but still intend to replace Susan with another, younger girl. To this end they have prepared the following document headed 'Proposed Elimination of Susan from *Doctor Who* Series':

> Doctor Who and his group return to Earth in the year 2042. They find the planet occupied by the Daleks. The plague and famine that preceded the invasion destroyed 90% of the Earth's population. Nearly all who survived are prisoners in Dalek working parties.
>
> In London one small group is attempting to overthrow the invaders. Doctor Who and his party become involved with this group. Prominent amongst them is David Somheim. In an early battle Susan becomes his companion.
>
> The enormity of the world catastrophe has a marked effect on Susan's character. She grows more adult as she realises that the *individual* is the society. She begins to find her place in time and space. David Somheim is dedicated to overthrowing the Daleks in order to build a new world. Some of his feeling is transmitted to Susan who, no longer a child, is unwittingly seeking an objective.
>
> David and Susan fall in love. For Susan this presents another problem. She knows that sooner or later the space travellers must move on and that she must go with them. She must leave David behind. And she must

forget her ideals of a new world. She is bound too tightly to her grandfather to think of leaving him.

However, Doctor Who is aware of her growing womanhood. He knows that he must make the decision as to whether she continues to travel with him or not.

In the closing scenes of the final episode, Susan prepares to leave with her grandfather. Inside the ship Barbara, Ian and Doctor Who prepare for their journey. Doctor Who watches Susan and David on the scanner, and then presses the control to close the doors. He talks to Susan telling her that she has grown up and that she no longer needs him. Susan, in spite of her sadness at saying goodbye to her grandfather, is happy to remain with David and to start her new life.

Inside the ship Doctor Who's sadness at leaving Susan is obvious to the others. They leave as soon as possible. During the course of their new journey the discover that there is a stowaway aboard, a fifteen year old girl whom they have already befriended. In spite of their concern, they know that there is no going back. In any case Ian and Barbara both realise that in time she may help Doctor Who to forget the loss of Susan.

Friday 31: *The Reign of Terror: The Tyrant of France* is camera rehearsed and recorded in Lime Grove G.

AUGUST 1964

Saturday 1: *The Sensorites: A Desperate Venture* is transmitted on BBC1.

Monday 3: Four days' preliminary rehearsal begins for *The Reign of Terror: A Bargain of Necessity*. The regular venue for the series' rehearsals has now been changed to the London Transport Assembly Rooms, a training establishment opposite Television Centre, as the Drill Hall at 239 Uxbridge Road has been criticised by cast and production team alike for its poor facilities.

Thursday 6: Verity Lambert sends the Serials Department Organiser a memo with the heading 'Renewal of Artists' Contracts for *Doctor Who*' in which she points out that the need for a decision on *Doctor Who*'s long-term future is becoming increasingly pressing:

> If we could get an OK for a further thirteen weeks from 2 January, I would at least be able to take out contracts for thirteen weeks with an option for a further thirteen. I have a feeling that, if we wait for much longer, we will find ourselves in the position of losing our artists, which can only lead to a certain amount of chaos at the end of our next serial.
>
> We will not be renewing Carole Ann Ford's contract, but I would like to retain the other three principals. I therefore would be most grateful if we could have a decision on the continuance of *Doctor Who* as soon as possible.

Friday 7: *The Reign of Terror: A Bargain of Necessity* is camera rehearsed and recorded in TC4.

The recording of this episode is covered by a film crew working on a documentary called *Short Circuit – The Park*.

Saturday 8: *The Reign of Terror: A Land of Fear* is transmitted on BBC1.

Monday 10: Four days' preliminary rehearsal begins for *The Reign of Terror: Prisoners of Conciergerie*.

The BBC's two remaining Daleks are lent out this week to appear in a recording of a BBC light entertainment show starring comedian Roy Kinnear.

Tuesday 11: Verity Lambert follows up her memo of the previous Thursday by preparing the following discussion document:

> NOTES
>
> On the effect of not having a decision as to whether we continue after the end of January.
>
> 1. If we continue to the end of January, we have to provide a four week serial, since the last transmission of the Daleks is on 2 January.
>
> a) I really do not see what kind of an approach I can make to artists' agents at this point on the basis of a four week extension.
>
> b) William Hartnell has already had an offer. William Russell's agent is going ahead on the understanding that his client's contract finishes on 23 October. The best offer I can make at this point is a four week extension with no guarantee of the serial continuing thereafter.
>
> *CONCLUSIONS:*
>
> If a four week extension is the best that Baverstock can offer us, I feel that we should terminate *Doctor Who* at the end of this present series.
>
> 2. We had intended to write the character of Susan out, and this has been done in the Dalek serial, the first recording of which is on 18 September. Filming for this serial takes place on 23 August to 28 August. If we are only continuing for four weeks, or if we finish at the end of this series, there does not seem to be any point in writing Susan out.
>
> a) We, therefore, have to rewrite the serial which goes into production in five weeks' time.
>
> b) If the series is to continue, we have to develop a character in this serial which we intend to take Susan's place. This means that, in the next week to ten days,

we have to look for and cast somebody who, to all intents and purposes, may continue at least for six months next year. We cannot approach any artist on the basis of a six weeks' engagement if, in fact, we are intending a six months' engagement. We, therefore, have to take out options.

CONCLUSIONS:

If we do not have a decision within the next two weeks as to at least a thirteen week extension, we will not be able to write Susan out and we will be stuck with the prospect of renewing her contract for next year when we have no desire to do so. The best we can do under the circumstances is to write the part of the new girl out of the present serial. This will involve considerable rewriting and it will also present us with the problem of introducing the new girl.

3. We also have the problem of commissioning a four part serial when we do not want to. We have a five part serial which we would have put in. It means that we have now the prospect of commissioning a serial in which we may have to introduce the new girl or we may not have to introduce the new girl: we may have to write in the part of Susan or we may not have to write in the part of Susan.

The information for this serial will be required eight weeks before our first recording date, which is scheduled for Week 50, i.e. 4 December 1964. This means that the information for the serial will be required at the latest by 12 September. This, of course, means commissioning it now.

I think this is an absolutely insoluble problem unless we can get a decision one way or another.

Wednesday 12: Verity Lambert sends Planning Manager (Forward) John Mair a memo summarising the problems set out in her discussion document. She ends:

I am really not trying to force a decision on this, but I think it would be a pity to jeopardise scripts if, in fact, there is any intention at all to carry on *Doctor Who* after the end of January.

John Mair subsequently sends Chief of Programmes Donald Baverstock a memo describing the problems put to him by Verity Lambert and concluding:

There appear to be three possible lines you could take.

a) You could stop transmission after Serial K, in Week 1. This would save possible contractual trouble with the artists, but would mean rewriting Serial K at short notice to make it suitable for a 'farewell' one. Replacement would be difficult at such short notice.

b) You could stop at end January. This would involve the problems described above.

c) You could continue to end March.

My own feeling is that an equivalent audience-puller will be difficult to find and a new series in any case unwise to launch in the middle of a winter when audience figures are particularly important, and that *Dr Who* should now go on till end March.

(Sample audience figures are attached. The series is doing less well than it did during last winter, but the drop may be at least partly seasonal.)

The search for a replacement should begin now, so that you are able to make a choice by say November/December on what to put in after March 1965.

Mair also sends Sydney Newman a memo briefly outlining the problems. He explains that Baverstock would like the cast's existing contracts to be extended by four weeks but that 'Verity Lambert is afraid that the agents will either ask exorbitant sums or refuse.' He adds that he has asked Lambert to get the agents' reactions, after which he will report back to Baverstock.

Thursday 13: A further day's shooting of film inserts for *Planet of Giants* takes place at Ealing.

Friday 14: *The Reign of Terror: Prisoners of Conciergerie* is camera rehearsed and recorded in TC4.

Donald Baverstock has a meeting with Verity Lambert in which he finally agrees to renew *Doctor Who* for thirteen weeks, with the possibility of a further thirteen after that. Later the same day, he sends her a memo recording the outcome of the meeting. With regard to the regular cast, he notes:

I agreed that you should renew contracts for three of the principals (and negotiate a new one for the artist who will now play the fourth) for a further thirteen weeks, with an option on thirteen more beyond that. This will take transmissions to 21 March. It is important that you should not assume the necessity for an automatic increase in fees. Negotiations should aim initially at no increase. If increases are demanded, I would like to be informed so that I can decide whether or not to agree them ...

No plans should be made, please, which might involve commitment to productions beyond these thirteen (other than options for us to decide) without prior discussion with me.

Music for episodes one and two of *Planet of Giants* is recorded.

Saturday 15: *The Reign of Terror: Guests of Madame Guillotine* is transmitted on BBC1.

Monday 17: Four days' preliminary rehearsal begins for *Planet of Giants: Planet of Giants*.

Following Donald Baverstock's agreement to renew *Doctor Who* for at least thirteen weeks, Verity Lambert chooses actress Pamela Franklin to replace Carole Ann Ford as the series' fourth regular cast member. Franklin is to be introduced in Terry Nation's Dalek story, now retitled *The Dalek Invasion of Earth*, playing a human resistance fighter named Jenny (originally called Saida).

Lambert sends Head of Artists' Bookings Pauline Mansfield-Clark a memo asking her to offer William Hartnell, William Russell and Jacqueline Hill new contracts on the basis agreed by Baverstock, and to offer Pamela Franklin a contract on the same basis but also covering the six episodes of *The Dalek Invasion of Earth*. She requests that Mansfield-Clark let her know if the established regulars' respective agents demand an increased fee, or if Franklin's agent asks for a higher fee than Carole Ann Ford's.

Derek Hoddinott of the Publicity Department has informed Lambert that he has seen in a newspaper that there is a beat group calling itself 'Doctor Who and the Daleks.' He is told that this is not a breach of copyright and that Lambert thinks it would be good publicity for the programme.

Wednesday 19: Lambert sends Baverstock a memo reporting the outcome of the approaches made to the regulars' agents:

> WILLIAM HARTNELL has turned down the offer completely. He would like a six months' contract with no options at 250 guineas per episode. This is 25 guineas more than he is getting at the present time.
>
> WILLIAM RUSSELL'S agent is away on holiday. In his absence, the contract for thirteen with an option of a further thirteen would be acceptable on the following terms. William Russell feels that his fee should be brought into line with William Hartnell's. He is, at the present time, getting 150 guineas a week and this would mean a raise in salary of approximately 75 guineas.
>
> JACQUELINE HILL would accept the offer of thirteen programmes with an option of a further thirteen at a salary of 200 guineas per episode. Her present salary is 105 guineas per episode and this would mean a raise of 95 guineas (I think there would be some room for negotiation in this particular case.)
>
> We have not tried to negotiate on any of the above. As you can see, it would mean a considerable increase in money.

Baverstock calls a meeting with Lambert to discuss the situation and then sends her the following memo recording his reactions:

> 1) That as a first step you should talk with the three principals and mention that if they were to hold to their demands for such very large increases, you might have difficulty in recommending a continuation of the series beyond January, with the same cast. Of the three, Hartnell and

Russell would be more valuable to you than Jacqueline Hill. But you thought it possible that none of them might prove indispensable. If the two men were to show willingness to sign again for their present fees (or with only a nominal increase), I mentioned to you that I would be willing to consider a commitment for six months, rather than for three with an option for three.

2) That I would agree to face the replacement of *Dr Who* for a period of six weeks, from 2 January, with another short serial (preferably science fiction) if you would need this time to restore *Dr Who* with a totally new or partly new group of principals after the end of the run which finishes in January.

3) That it would be unwise to attempt to establish the new girl as a permanent member of the cast in the last episode of the present series already booked.

Baverstock goes on to inform Lambert that he has decided, on reflection, that it would be wrong of him to act as her adviser 'on matters of negotiations and of such professional details', and that she should consult instead with Elwyn Jones, the BBC's Head of Series. Jones is currently deputising for Sydney Newman as both Newman and Donald Wilson are away from the office on holiday.

Later in the day, Lambert has a discussion with Jones and then sends him the following memo:

After careful consideration, I have decided, based on the premise that we can get permission to continue *Doctor Who* for six months, that it would be best to meet William Hartnell's demand for six months' contract at 250 guineas per episode.

As far as William Russell and Jacqueline Hill are concerned, we will try and negotiate contracts with them on the basis of a nominal rise of between £10 and £20 per episode. If this is not acceptable, we will write these two artists out at the end of the present series.

Bearing in mind that negotiations with the latter two artists may take a little time, I think, if we could keep the six weeks' break which Chief of Programmes BBC1 agreed with me this morning, this would alleviate the situation as to commissioning future scripts.

Thursday 20: Verity Lambert, director Richard Martin and a group of Daleks spend the morning visiting well-known London landmarks – including the Planetarium and Westminster Bridge with the Houses of Parliament in the background – for a press photocall. The aim is to publicise the Daleks' imminent return and also the fact that *The Dalek Invasion of Earth* is to be the first *Doctor Who* story to feature extensive location shooting.

Lambert later has a further discussion with Elwyn Jones about the situation regarding the regular artists' contracts. Jones supports most of the proposals she has made, but is unwilling to recommend a six week break in transmission after *The Dalek Invasion of*

Earth. Instead, he suggests that if William Russell and Jacqueline Hill have to be written out, William Hartnell should carry the main burden of the action on his own for three or four episodes. Lambert confirms that this would be possible and Jones then conveys their conclusions in a memo to Donald Baverstock, recommending that he now 'concede the existence of this programme for six months rather than for three with an option for three.'

In the light of the decisions already taken, Lambert has by this time requested that *The Dalek Invasion of Earth* be rewritten so that Jenny is no longer established as a regular character but relegated to a more minor, one-off role (which will eventually be played by actress Ann Davies). The new regular will now be introduced in the first story of the new production block, but Pamela Franklin is no longer in the running for the role.

Friday 21: *Planet of Giants: Planet of Giants* is camera rehearsed and recorded in TC4.
Elwyn Jones sends Verity Lambert a memo informing her that Donald Baverstock, in accordance with the recommendation put to him the previous day, has now agreed to renew *Doctor Who* for six months, rather than for three with an option for three as before.

Saturday 22: *The Reign of Terror: A Change of Identity* is transmitted on BBC1.

Sunday 23: Six days' pre-filming begins for *The Dalek Invasion of Earth.* The first five days are on location in London – the first major location shoot ever carried out for *Doctor Who.*

Monday 24: Four days' preliminary rehearsal begins for *Planet of Giants: Dangerous Journey.*
Verity Lambert sends Head of Artists' Bookings Pauline Mansfield-Clark a memo informing her the decision taken by Donald Baverstock the previous Friday and asking her to negotiate contracts with Jacqueline Hill and William Russell on the basis that they can be offered a raise of between ten and twenty-five guineas per episode each, but no more. She adds:

> As far as the options are concerned, we will leave it to you to do the best
> deal you can with their agents, but I am not averse to tying them both up
> for 26 weeks with no option.

Lambert also writes to Donald Wilson at his holiday home in Southwold, Suffolk, to inform him of the conclusions reached 'after the dramas of the last ten days.' She apologises for having disturbed him in the middle of his leave, but notes that 'things were a bit fraught here.'

Tuesday 25: Music for episodes three and four of *Planet of Giants* is recorded between 6.30 pm and 10.30 pm in studio 2 at Maida Vale.
Friday 28: *Planet of Giants: Dangerous Journey* is camera rehearsed and recorded in TC4.

Saturday 29: *The Reign of Terror: The Tyrant of France* is transmitted on BBC1.

Monday 31: Four days' preliminary rehearsal begins for *Planet of Giants: Crisis*.

David Whitaker, now starting to look for stories to use in the series' second production block, briefs the Copyright Department to commission from writer Dennis Spooner the scripts for a four-part historical adventure entitled *The Romans*.

SEPTEMBER 1964

Friday 4: *Planet of Giants: Crisis* is camera rehearsed and recorded in TC4.

Saturday 5: *The Reign of Terror: A Bargain of Necessity* is transmitted on BBC1.

Monday 7: Four days' preliminary rehearsal begins for *Planet of Giants: The Urge to Live*.

Friday 11: *Planet of Giants: The Urge to Live* is camera rehearsed and recorded in TC4.

Saturday 12: *The Reign of Terror: Prisoners of Conciergerie* is transmitted on BBC1.

Monday 14: Four days' preliminary rehearsal begins for *The Dalek Invasion of Earth: World's End*.

Camera tests are held at 11.15 am for the role of the new companion to replace Susan. The two actresses under consideration are Maureen O'Brien – one of whose former teachers at the Central School of Speech and Drama, now working at the BBC, has brought her to Verity Lambert's attention – and Denise Upson. The part eventually goes to the former. O'Brien has most recently been working as one of the founder members of the Everyman Theatre in her native Liverpool. She is initially reluctant to accept the *Doctor Who* role, but does so partly to be with her London-based boyfriend (later her husband).

Friday 18: *The Dalek Invasion of Earth: World's End* is camera rehearsed and recorded. This is the first episode to be recorded in *Doctor Who*'s new regular studio, Riverside 1. Assistant floor manager Christina Lawton subsequently prepares the following report on the day's proceedings:

> Only the marvellously efficient and willing co-operation of the scene crew made the day possible – complex and exceptionally filthy sets to handle with a lot of reconstruction of trick pieces. Only one run achieved before recording time. Three scheduled recording breaks plus two extra arising from the transposing of shot 56. Very slow start to camera rehearsal until it was proved that planned tracking lines had some validity. Floor Assistant Ray Day was most reliable and quick.

Production assistant Jane Shirley adds the following summary of the retakes required during the evening's recording:

> Shot 56 Taken out of seq at actor's request. Producer's agreement. Retake – actor missed cue.
> Shots 24-26 Actor out of pos.

Shot 32 on Re-start – actor jumped cue.
Shot 42 on Re-start here. 1. Actor dried. 2. Box did not fall.
Shot 59 Retake – 1. Camera didn't make position in time – actor off marks. 2. Extra long pause interpreted as dry!
Shots 69A-73 Telecine mistimed.
Shot 74 Camera off pos.

Monday 21: Four days' preliminary rehearsal begins for *The Dalek Invasion of Earth: The Daleks*.

Thursday 24: David Whitaker has by this time got down to work in earnest on finding and commissioning stories for *Doctor Who*'s second production block. It has been agreed that he himself should write the first of these, a two-parter which will introduce the Doctor's new companion. An early name considered for the character is Tanni, and Whitaker's draft scripts will bear the title *Doctor Who and Tanni* before the story is subsequently renamed *The Rescue*.

This story will mark Whitaker's own departure from the series' production team, as he has now decided to move on to other work. His successor is to be Dennis Spooner, whose *The Romans* is to be the second story of the new production block and who on 6 August began a period of trailing Whitaker to 'learn the ropes' of the story editor's job. Spooner has been working as a freelance writer since the early fifties, when he abandoned an unsuccessful career as a stand-up comic. His earliest TV scripts were for half-hour sitcoms, but he has since gone on to work prolifically on a wide variety of different shows including *Hancock*, *The Avengers*, *No Hiding Place* and Gerry Anderson's puppet series *Fireball XL5* and *Stingray*.

It has now been decided that Malcolm Hulke's *The Hidden Planet* should be finally written off as unsuitable. Whitaker sends Hulke's agent, Harvey Unna, a letter in which he explains the reasons as follows:

> Considerable re-writing would be necessary because Carole Ann Ford is leaving the cast, and I think also that the science fiction series that have been most successful in the past year have been those with mechanical or alien monsters in them. Mac's idea is based upon similarities of Earth and his invented planet. In the future we would rather give the audience more monsters and more truly science fiction creations.
>
> I am sorry about this after all the hard work Mac has put into it and, of course, it is not his fault that climates of opinion and styles of approach change as a serial like *Doctor Who* progresses.

Another story rejected by Whitaker on this date is Victor Pemberton's *The Slide*, about which he sends Donald Wilson the following memo:

> This is rather a stew pot of all the other science fiction serials we have ever done, with bits of Nigel Kneale scattered about. I don't think the dialogue is very good and I am quite sure it is not right for *Doctor Who*.

(Pemberton will in later years go on to become *Doctor Who*'s script editor himself, and to write a highly-acclaimed six-part story entitled *Fury from the Deep* based in part upon *The Slide*. *The Slide* itself will meanwhile have been turned into a successful science fiction serial for BBC radio.)

Friday 25: *The Dalek Invasion of Earth: The Daleks* is camera rehearsed and recorded in Riverside 1. During the course of the day, Jacqueline Hill sustains a minor injury to her hand.

Monday 28: Four days' preliminary rehearsal begins for *The Dalek Invasion of Earth: Day of Reckoning*.

David Whitaker briefs the Copyright Department to commission from writer Bill Strutton a six-part story entitled *The Web Planet*. The target delivery date is 13 November 1964.

OCTOBER 1964

Friday 2: *The Dalek Invasion of Earth: Day of Reckoning* is camera rehearsed and recorded in Riverside 1. William Hartnell is injured during camera rehearsals when the supports of the Dalek spaceship's entry ramp, down which he is being carried on a stretcher, suddenly collapse. He falls awkwardly on his spine, and for a while is paralysed, but X-Rays show no permanent damage and he recovers sufficiently to take part in the evening's recording. It is however agreed that he should be given the following week off to recover fully.

Monday 5: Four days' preliminary rehearsal begins for *The Dalek Invasion of Earth: The End of Tomorrow*, with William Hartnell absent. The episode is rewritten so that the Doctor – to be played by stand-in Edmund Warwick with his face out of vision – falls unconscious at the beginning and plays no further part in the action.

Tuesday 6: Dennis Spooner briefs the Copyright Department to commission from Terry Nation the scripts for a new six-part story with which it is intended to conclude the second production block. The target delivery date is 30 January 1965.

Thursday 8: Verity Lambert is sent a memo by Christopher Barry, who has been assigned to direct both *The Rescue* and *The Romans*. Barry requests a planning meeting with the production team before rehearsals begin; expresses the view that there has been insufficient rehearsal in the past, and that he would like therefore to rehearse from 10.00 am to 5.00 pm each day during the rehearsal period; and requests that the cast be asked to attend a script conference before work starts in earnest on *The Rescue*.

Friday 9: *The Dalek Invasion of Earth: The End of Tomorrow* is camera rehearsed and recorded in Riverside 1.

Verity Lambert replies as follows to the previous day's memo from Christopher Barry:

> As far as I am concerned I am quite happy to have planning meetings for
> the episodes you have prepared before you go into rehearsal.

I think it is up to you to discuss with the actors a possible 10.00 am to 5.00 pm rehearsal period. I do not think that they are particularly against this. The only day that we have regularly had an 11 o'clock start is Monday, as Bill Hartnell travels up from the country on that day and cannot get to rehearsal before 11.00 am.

I am afraid it is not possible to get the cast together for a script conference before we go into rehearsal. They have been working regularly for 52 weeks and I feel, from their point of view, they must have a complete break away from the show.

I agree with you it is quite possible that we are, perhaps, rehearsing too little. Most directors during the past few weeks and months have not rehearsed on Thursday afternoons. The cast have now got to feel that Thursday afternoon is an afternoon free. However, this is not so and, if fact, should you wish to rehearse Thursday afternoons, with them, they are being paid for it.

As you know, we can, in fact, rehearse for six hours. If you are not with the actors till 11.30 am or 12.00 am on a Wednesday, you have an extension till 7.00 pm. There is no reason, in fact, not to rehearse after the script conference (or to have a late run-through, as discussed this morning).

Barry subsequently agrees that rehearsals can continue to begin at 11.00 am on Mondays.

Monday 12: Four days' preliminary rehearsal begins for *The Dalek Invasion of Earth: The Waking Ally.*

Friday 16: *The Dalek Invasion of Earth: The Waking Ally* is camera rehearsed and recorded in Riverside 1.

Monday 19: Four days' preliminary rehearsal begins for *The Dalek Invasion of Earth: Flashpoint.*

Tuesday 20: Verity Lambert sends Donald Wilson a memo informing him that the total fees paid out to Malcolm Hulke for his ultimately unused story *The Hidden Planet* amounted to £1,612 10s 0d.

Donald Wilson sends Sydney Newman the following memo:

> As spoken yesterday, I am arranging to reduce the four-part serial entitled *Planet of Giants* to three parts. This is the 'miniscule' story with which we must begin our new season and I am not satisfied that it will get us off to the great start that we must have if it runs to its full length. Much of it is fascinating and exciting but by its nature and the resources needed we could not do everything we wanted to do to make it wholly satisfactory. I would, of course, have preferred to start with the Dalek serial but at the end of this one Carole Ann Ford is written out and we cannot, therefore, have her appearing afterwards in *Planet of Giants.*

Wilson goes on to say that, to make up for the lost episode, the Terry Nation serial with which it is planned to end the new twenty-six week production block will be extended from six episodes to seven. This idea will later be abandoned, however.

The reduction of *Planet of Giants* from four episodes to three is subsequently accomplished by the editing together of the final two episodes, with around half the recorded material from each being discarded.

A party is held in the Bridge Lounge at Television Centre to celebrate the impending completion of the first 52 episodes.

Friday 23: *The Dalek Invasion of Earth: Flashpoint* is camera rehearsed and recorded in Riverside 1. The recording overruns its allotted time by some fifteen minutes, finishing at around 10.30 pm. This is due partly to the fact that around twenty minutes has to be spent resetting scenery during the course of the evening, and partly to a number of problems that arise during recording of the last few minutes of the episode: a brief camera failure; a longer sound failure; a retake necessitated by William Hartnell fluffing his lines in the final scene; and a further retake required to rectify an unsatisfactory inlay shot.

This is Carole Ann Ford's last regular episode as Susan, and she subsequently writes to Sydney Newman to express her gratitude for having been given the opportunity to appear in the series.

Wednesday 28: Sydney Newman replies to Carole Ann Ford's letter as follows:

> Are you kidding – expressing your appreciation for appearing in *Doctor Who*! Fact is, we are greatly indebted to you. You have done a fine job for us in the BBC and we are deeply appreciative of your work.
>
> May I wish you the very best of luck in your future career, and hope to see you time and time again on the BBC screen in roles other than that of the 'waif from Outer Space' (what a title!)

Saturday 31: *Planet of Giants: Planet of Giants* is transmitted on BBC1.

David Whitaker's engagement as story editor formally ends at this point as he completes his hand-over to Dennis Spooner. Writers currently under consideration to work on the series are: William Emms, who is due to meet Verity Lambert to discuss his ideas; John Lucarotti, who may contribute another historical story; Brian Hayles, who has had one submission rejected but been asked to submit another; Alex Miller, who has likewise had two ideas rejected but been asked to try again; Hugh Whitemore, a writer on the soap opera *Compact*, who is to visit the production office to discuss the possibility of submitting some storylines; and Keith Dewhurst, a Manchester-based writer who has been approached through his agent but has yet to respond.

Also on the point of leaving the series' production team at this time is Mervyn Pinfield. Verity Lambert is by now well able to cope with the demands of the producer's job, and there is now no need for an associate producer. Pinfield will however continue to be credited on screen for the first two stories of the new production block.

NOVEMBER 1964

Thursday 5: Verity Lambert sends Drama Serials Organiser Terence Cook the following memo:

> With the approach of Christmas and also the fact that we are doing another Dalek serial, I have the feeling that we are going to be inundated once again with requests from various organisations to borrow Daleks.
>
> I have spoken to Perry Guinness in Publicity, who has been handling, so far, all the correspondence re borrowing Daleks. He tells me that he was, at one time, going to have two made for publicity purposes. This project fell through because he could not get permission from his Head of Department to put an order in.
>
> However, we now have four Daleks stored at Ealing. I am perfectly prepared to loan two of these Daleks to be used for publicity purposes if we have a guarantee that the Publicity Department will make good any damage which is incurred at the time of their use for publicity purposes.
>
> It obviously is not a problem of copyright, because Publicity Department were going to make two. Anyway, I do not know whether this seems to be a reasonable solution to this whole problem from everybody's point of view, but perhaps you could deal with it.

Saturday 7: *Planet of Giants: Dangerous Journey* is transmitted on BBC1.

Thursday 12: Verity Lambert sends Dennis Spooner, Mervyn Pinfield and Christopher Barry a memo stating that the name now decided upon for the new companion is Lukki (pronounced Lucky). Aside from Tanni, other names previously considered for the character have included Millie (which has been discounted because of possible associations with the *That Was the Week That Was* comedienne Millicent Martin) and Valerie.

Friday 13: Christopher Barry returns to composer Tristram Cary three tapes of incidental music from *The Mutants*, two of which Cary has lent him and the other of which he has found in the recording studio. Barry intends to re-use a number of pieces of this music for *The Rescue*.

Saturday 14: *Planet of Giants: Crisis* – the amalgamated version of the original *Crisis* and *The Urge to Live* – is transmitted on BBC1.

A BBC Wales programme about automation features two Daleks – speaking in Welsh! They have been loaned out by the *Doctor Who* office and have drawn tumultuous crowds when paraded through the streets of Cardiff on 7 December, prior to the programme's recording on 11 December.

Monday 16: Two days' filming of model sequences for *The Rescue* begins at Ealing.

Tuesday 17: Two days' shooting of film inserts for *The Romans* begins on Stage 3A/B at Ealing. On the second day, Wednesday 18, the Doctor is played by stand-in Albert

Ward, wearing a Roman toga and with his face kept out of shot.

Friday 20: By this time the name of Maureen O'Brien's character has been fixed as Vicki.

Saturday 21: *The Dalek Invasion of Earth: World's End* is transmitted on BBC1.

Tuesday 24: Dennis Spooner has been carrying out extensive rewrites on David Whitaker's scripts for *The Rescue*, and revised versions are now sent out to principal cast members.

Wednesday 25: Raymond Jones's incidental music for *The Romans* is recorded at Broadcasting House. It is played by five musicians, supplied by Alec Firman.

Thursday 26: Verity Lambert and William Russell record an interview for the BBC's *Points of View* programme.

Friday 27: Verity Lambert's secretary, Valentine Spencer, sends her the following note reporting some grievances on the part of two of the series' designers, Raymond Cusick and Spencer Chapman (the designer of *The Dalek Invasion of Earth*):

> Raymond Cusick would be most grateful if you would ring him.
>
> He wants to talk about the exploitation of the Daleks. He is 'rather sore' about it, as he is not getting anything out of it.
>
> He also told me that during rehearsal of Serial K, some people came into the studio and tried to start measuring up the Robomen's head pieces. Spencer Chapman found out they hadn't got permission to do this and asked them to leave. Ray thinks they may have been something to do with Press Department.
>
> Design Department is worried about both the above and have been having a Departmental meeting about these two things.

Cusick is later paid a bonus of £100 for having designed the Daleks. He regards this sum as derisory.

Saturday 28: *The Dalek Invasion of Earth: The Daleks* is transmitted on BBC1.

Monday 30: Four days' preliminary rehearsal begins for *The Rescue: The Powerful Enemy*.

DECEMBER 1964

Tuesday 1: A photocall is held to introduce Maureen O'Brien as Vicki to the press.

Wednesday 2: Val Spencer writes the following note:

> Derek Hoddinott in Publicity rang, asking Dennis Spooner to write a short piece on John Qualtrough, the 14 year old Liverpool boy who sent

in the story *Doctor What Strikes Again*, to give to the press, as the boy may be appearing on *Points of View* tomorrow.

Dennis Spooner wrote the following:

'The *Doctor What Strikes Again* script (subtitled *Doctor What and the Luxury Liner*) is a very funny send-up of the *Doctor Who* show.

'I'm certain that if the *Doctor Who* series runs long enough, Stephen John Qualtrough will become a serious contributor to the *Doctor Who* series – unless *That Was the Past That Was* claims him first.

'The dialogue, and the joke construction are near perfect, and it is astounding to find that somebody so young has such a penetrating sense of humour, and the ability to get it across.'

The above was dictated over the telephone to Derek Hoddinott. He asked if he could quote Dennis Spooner as having said this. Dennis Spooner agreed.

Thursday 3: At Publicity's request, William Hartnell attends a photocall with schoolboy Stephen John Qualtrough in studio Presentation A at Television Centre.

Friday 4: *The Rescue: The Powerful Enemy* is camera rehearsed and recorded in Riverside 1. Sound recordings of Jacqueline Hill screaming and of Ray Barrett (as the character Bennett) delivering the line 'You can't come in!' are made at 3.00 pm, as these are required to be played in on tape during the episode.

The Government's Central Office of Information borrow two Daleks to appear in one of their programmes.

Earlier in the year, David Whitaker approached John Wyndham to see if he would be interested in writing for the series, and today his agent replies that he is too busy working on a book.

Saturday 5: *The Dalek Invasion of Earth: Day of Reckoning* is transmitted on BBC1.

A number of Daleks appear on the BBC light entertainment programme *The Black and White Minstrel Show*.

Monday 7: Four days' preliminary rehearsal begins for *The Rescue: Desperate Measures*.

Friday 11: *The Rescue: Desperate Measures* is camera rehearsed and recorded in Riverside 1.

Saturday 12: *The Dalek Invasion of Earth: The End of Tomorrow* is transmitted on BBC1.

Monday 14: Four days' preliminary rehearsal begins for *The Romans: The Slave Traders*. Two Daleks appear on the BBC magazine programme *Late Night Line-up*.

Wednesday 16: The six-part story commissioned from Terry Nation on 6 October 1964 has been abandoned. However, Dennis Spooner now briefs the Copyright Department to commission from Nation a replacement story, again a six-parter, featuring the Daleks. The target delivery date remains 30 January 1965. The story has the working title *The Pursuers*.

Friday 18: *The Romans: The Slave Traders* is camera rehearsed and recorded in Riverside 1.

Saturday 19: *The Dalek Invasion of Earth: The Waking Ally* is transmitted on BBC1.

Monday 21: Dennis Scuse, Ronald Waldman's successor as General Manager of Television Enterprises, sends Sydney Newman a memo informing him that the recent sale of *Doctor Who*'s first fifty-two episodes to CBC in Canada was placed in jeopardy by the substandard telerecordings made from the 405-line videotapes:

> As you may or may not know, we have recently concluded a fairly substantial deal in Canada for the *Dr Who* series. The correspondence which I attach is largely self-explanatory and the problems which are mentioned arise from a considerable amount of low-key lighting used in the production. This is extenuated by the inevitable degradation of tape transfer and 16mm telerecording.
>
> There may not be very much that can be done but I would be grateful if these problems could be brought to the attention of the producer and the situation borne in mind for the future.
>
> I need hardly add that a success with *Dr Who* in Canada could be extremely lucrative not only directly but also indirectly through merchandising activities.

Wilson subsequently brings this memo to Verity Lambert's attention.

Tuesday 22: Lambert sends Wilson a memo about future plans for *Doctor Who*. She notes that the last scheduled recording in the series' second, twenty-six week production block is due to take place on 4 June 1965, and the last scheduled transmission on 26 June 1965. She goes on:

> Should *Doctor Who* be continued after this date, I would like to suggest that we break transmission throughout July and August. This would involve nine weeks (Weeks 27 to 35 inclusive). We could then start transmission again on 4 September 1965 (Week 36).
>
> We could start recording on 30 July (Week 30), which would give us five weeks in hand and a break of eight weeks in recording.
>
> I know that nine weeks seems a long break in transmission, but I think that July and August are bad months from our point of view.

Saturday 26: *The Dalek Invasion of Earth: The End of Tomorrow* is transmitted on BBC1.

Monday 28: Four days' preliminary rehearsal begins for *The Romans: All Roads Lead to Rome*.

Carole Ann Ford makes a public appearance at a *Doctor Who* exhibition at the *Daily*

Mail Boys and Girls Exhibition at London's Olympia.

JANUARY 1965

Friday 1: *The Romans: All Roads Lead to Rome* is camera rehearsed and recorded in Riverside 1.

Saturday 2: *The Rescue: The Powerful Enemy* is transmitted on BBC1.

Monday 4: Four days' preliminary rehearsal begins for *The Romans: Conspiracy.*
    Pre-filming begins for *The Web Planet* on Stage 2 at the BBC's Television Film Studios in Ealing. It is scheduled to be completed by Friday evening but overruns so that a number of scenes have to be held over to the following Monday. The only member of the regular cast required for the filming is Jacqueline Hill. Most of her scenes are shot on Wednesday 6 January and the remainder on the following day, and she is released from rehearsals for *The Romans: Conspiracy* to enable this to be done.

Tuesday 5: Three days' shooting of film inserts for *The Web Planet* begins at Ealing.

Friday 8: *The Romans: Conspiracy* is camera rehearsed and recorded in Riverside 1. The total cost of the episode is £2,383.

Saturday 9: *The Rescue: Desperate Measures* is transmitted on BBC1.

Monday 11: Four days' preliminary rehearsal begins for *The Romans: Inferno.*
    During the course of this week, David Whitaker draws up a revised schedule for the series' second production block, which indicates that the planned running order for the stories after *The Romans* is now: *The Web Planet* (six episodes) by Bill Strutton; a historical story (four episodes) by Whitaker himself; *The Space Museum* (four episodes) by Glyn Jones; and Terry Nation's new Dalek story (six episodes). No recordings are planned for 25 December (Week 52) or for 2 April (Week 13), as these are public holidays.
    Shortly after this, the proposals in Verity Lambert's memo of 22 December 1964 to Donald Wilson are rejected. It is agreed instead that the closing episode of *Doctor Who*'s second season should be transmitted on 24 July 1965 and the opening episode of the third on 11 September 1965, leaving a six week break in between. The series' second production block is to be extended from twenty-six episodes to thirty-five, with the last recording taking place on 6 August 1965, so that there will still be five episodes in hand when the break occurs. There will however be only a five week break in recording, with the first studio session of the third production block taking place on 17 September 1965.

Friday 15: *The Romans: Inferno* is camera rehearsed and recorded in Riverside 1. The total cost is £2,221.

Saturday 16: *The Romans: The Slave Traders* is transmitted on BBC1.

Monday 18: Four days' preliminary rehearsal begins for *The Web Planet: The Web Planet.*

Thursday 21: Christopher Barry sends the following memo to Raymond Cusick, who after *The Romans* is ending his regular assignment as a *Doctor Who* designer:

> Thank you for such lovely sets on *Dr Who*. I hope you enjoy your other work that you have now gone on to.
>
> Don't breathe a word but there's a vague chance that I may do another Dalek serial later in the year and if so I hope you would not mind working on it if it can be arranged.

Cusick will later work on three further *Doctor Who* stories, all featuring the Daleks, but from this point onwards it will generally be the case that scenic designers are asked to handle stories on a one-off basis rather than as part of a longer-term attachment to the series.

Friday 22: *The Web Planet: The Web Planet* is camera rehearsed and recorded in Riverside 1. The total cost is £3,033.

Saturday 23: *The Romans: All Roads Lead to Rome* is transmitted on BBC1.

Monday 25: Four days' preliminary rehearsal begins for *The Web Planet: The Zarbi*.

Friday 29: *The Web Planet: The Zarbi* is camera rehearsed and recorded in Riverside 1. The total cost is £2,428. The recording overruns its allotted time by sixteen minutes.

Saturday 30: *The Romans: Conspiracy* is transmitted on BBC1.

FEBRUARY 1965

Monday 1: Four days' preliminary rehearsal begins for *The Web Planet: Escape to Danger.*

Tuesday 2: Verity Lambert sends Serials Department Organiser Terence Cook a memo explaining the reasons for the overrun on the previous Friday's recording. After describing the seven retakes required, she concludes:

> This was an extremely difficult episode to do technically, in that there had to be a tremendous amount of scenery in the studio, and apart from the breaks necessary because of scene changes, there was the added problem that we had not used the Zarbi, except briefly in episode one, and it was impossible to tell until we got into the studio the kind of difficulties we would run into with dressing them and moving them from one scene to another. As it turned out we had to put in sufficient recording pauses to allow them to reposition from scene to scene.
>
> Finally, I would say that this was probably the most difficult episode of any we have attempted so far, and it certainly was the most complicated one of this particular six.

Hilary Bateson of the BBC's Publicity Department writes to D D'Vigne of Belle Vue Zoo Park (Manchester) Ltd to inform him that two Daleks which have been loaned to him for promotional purposes must be returned rather earlier than expected, on either 1 or 2 March. This is because they will be required for the new Dalek story, which is to begin recording in May.

Friday 5: *The Web Planet: Escape to Danger* is camera rehearsed and recorded in Riverside 1. The total cost is £2,196. This studio day proves to be one of the most problematic since the series began, and the recording overruns its allotted time by thirty-seven minutes. The start of camera rehearsals is delayed until 11.10 am as two sets – the TARDIS laboratory and the landscape of the planet Vortis – have yet to arrive in the studio, and a third – the Zarbi's Carsenome base – has yet to have its floor painted. This leads to further problems as the lighting supervisor has been unable to light the sets in advance and has to continue repositioning lights right up to and even during the evening recording period. Further delays occur during recording owing to a number of technical faults – one camera breaks down altogether and has to be dispensed with – and to the resultant nervousness of the cast.

Saturday 6: *The Romans: Inferno* is transmitted on BBC1. This is the last episode on which Mervyn Pinfield receives a credit as associate producer. The episode is followed by a short trailer for *The Web Planet*, consisting of a compilation of shots from the early episodes of the story and an accompanying voice-over.

Monday 8: Four days' preliminary rehearsal begins for *The Web Planet: Crater of Needles*.

Director Richard Martin sends Verity Lambert a memo about the trailer transmitted the previous Saturday for *The Web Planet*. He protests that, particularly in its use of long shots, it gave away too much, leaving him feeling 'like a conjurer about to do an elaborate two and a half hour trick when all the audience know the secrets already.' Lambert responds that she was responsible for the way in which the story was promoted, and that it was 'done with the specific purpose of taking the curse out of the Zarbi'; i.e. making them seem less horrific.

Tuesday 9: Lambert sends Martin the following memo headed 'Rewrites':

> I am very concerned about the amount of *line changing* that is going on during rehearsal of *Dr Who* scripts. I am not against rewrites, particularly if they improve the finished product. If, however, artists are continually changing lines purely because they can't remember what they are supposed to be saying this does not end up as an improvement. I feel that it is your responsibility as a director to exercise control over this.
>
> We have a reading on Wednesday, at which major points should come up. Odd line changes should take place on the Monday when you are blocking the show. By the Monday evening, save in exceptional circumstances, the script should be set and no changes should be made after that time. In this way the artists have a chance of learning their lines and going into the studio in control of the situation. If you allow them

to keep on changing lines they will do so, and we have nobody but ourselves to blame if they don't know the script. As you know, Dennis is always available to come down to rehearsal for rewrites, and if you do have major problems of course he can come after the Monday, but in general all script changes should be made by Monday evening.

This note is for you to act on as you think fit, but I would strongly advise against making any kind of general announcement of its contents to the cast; as you know already, this only causes unpleasantness. I suggest possibly trying to have a chat with Bill on his own if you find it difficult to stop the constant changing in rehearsal.

If you would like to discuss this with me, or if you would like me to put the point to Bill, I would be delighted to do so!

Friday 12: *The Web Planet: Crater of Needles* is camera rehearsed and recorded in Riverside 1. The total cost is £2,850.

Saturday 13: *The Web Planet: The Web Planet* is transmitted on BBC1.

Monday 15: Four days' preliminary rehearsal begins for *The Web Planet: Invasion*.

Tuesday 16: Three days' shooting of film inserts for *The Crusade* begins at Ealing.

Friday 19: *The Web Planet: Invasion* is camera rehearsed and recorded in Riverside 1. The total cost is £2,676.

Saturday 20: *The Web Planet: The Zarbi* is transmitted on BBC1.

Monday 22: Four days' preliminary rehearsal begins for *The Web Planet: The Centre*.

Thursday 25: Verity Lambert sends the draft scripts for Terry Nation's new Dalek story, *The Chase*, to Richard Martin, who has been assigned to direct it. She notes that she is 'really very happy with it as far as the movement and action in the story are concerned,' and that 'it is slightly tongue-in-cheek and obviously is purely an adventure story, but ... there are lots of opportunities for imagination and for excitement.' She does however have a number of reservations. She is concerned about how two new monsters – the Mire Beast and the Fungoid – will be realised, particularly in view of problems experienced with the design of the Slyther creature in *The Dalek Invasion of Earth*, and considers that another alien race, the Aridians, are too 'unpleasant looking' as described by Nation. She feels that an episode involving Frankenstein's monster is out of keeping with *Doctor Who*'s usual style and could suggest a lack of imagination, and is considering asking Nation to replace it with something else – a suggestion to which he is quite amenable.

It has by this point been established that William Russell will be leaving *Doctor Who* when his contract expires at the end of *The Chase*. Terry Nation has therefore introduced in the final episode of his story a new character, an astronaut called Bruck, who will become the Doctor's new male companion.

Nation has meanwhile been discussing with Verity Lambert and Dennis Spooner ideas for a further six-part Dalek story to be made during the series' third production block. They agree that this new story should be preceded by a single episode 'trailer' in which none of the regular characters appear, allowing the cast a week's holiday. Spooner briefs the Copyright Department to commission from Nation the script for this trailer, referred to as *Dalek Cutaway*.

Friday 26: *The Web Planet: The Centre* is camera rehearsed and recorded in Riverside 1. The total cost is £3,342.

Dennis Spooner briefs the Copyright Department to commission from writer Brian Hayles a storyline for a story entitled *The Dark Planet*. This will ultimately be rejected.

Saturday 27: *The Web Planet: Escape to Danger* is transmitted on BBC1.

Monday 29: Four days' preliminary rehearsal begins for *The Crusade: The Lion*.

MARCH 1965

Wednesday 3: Richard Martin has gone on holiday abroad following completion of *The Web Planet*. Verity Lambert sends him a memo to see on his return, listing the scenes from *The Chase* that she has agreed with the Design Department should be done as film inserts. She ends:

> Your filming schedule will be heavy, although it will not involve location shooting, but your model making etc will be most expensive. I do implore you to keep your studio settings down in cost. I shall be away on your return, but you will no doubt find out that you have exceeded your budget on the Zarbi story by something in the region of £1,000. I do not want this to happen again.
>
> Will you please work to a budget of £2,750 per episode. If you should require more on this serial, will you please notify my office.
>
> The budget allocated to *The Chase* is higher than the standard £2,500 as it is regarded as one of the more prestigious stories of this production block; savings will have to be made on some of the other stories to compensate.

It will later be decided that story should in fact have one day of location filming for some scenes set on the planet Aridius in the first two episodes.

Friday 5: *The Crusade: The Lion* is camera rehearsed and recorded in Riverside 1. The total cost is £3,515.

Saturday 6: *The Web Planet: Crater of Needles* is transmitted on BBC1.

Monday 8: Four days' preliminary rehearsal begins for *The Crusade: The Knight of Jaffa*.

Thursday 11: One day's shooting of film inserts for *The Space Museum* takes places at Ealing. Verity Lambert has by this time decided to leave *Doctor Who* at the end of the second production block and move on to other work, but her successor has yet to be chosen. She sends Donald Wilson the following memo, headed '*Doctor Who*: Serial S', requesting permission to take the unusual step of commissioning story editor Dennis Spooner to write the story that will follow *The Chase* in the season's running order:

> As you know, I agreed with you last week that we should contract Dennis Spooner to write this serial. This is because we will not have, at this point, finalised negotiations with Jacqueline Hill and Maureen O'Brien. This will make it impossible to commission an outside writer.
>
> This serial has to be ready for design information by the last week in April and, as I mentioned to you, we will not know about Jacqueline Hill until the new producer has been decided upon.
>
> I think it would be a great risk to try an outside writer on this serial for the following reasons:
>
> 1) He will not be able to start writing it until he knows the characters.
>
> 2) None of the writers we have used so far are available and this would mean trying a completely new writer.
>
> 3) Of necessity, this serial has to be written fairly economically and I would not have the same control over an outside writer.
>
> 4) I also have had to agree with Bill Hartnell's agent to let him have one week out of this serial. Obviously this complicates matters still further.
>
> 5) Using an outside writer, it could quite well be that the serial will necessitate some considerable rewriting. This will put us in a very awkward position as far as design information is concerned.
>
> Because of these points, I will be most grateful if you can confirm to me that I can commission Dennis Spooner to write this serial.

Friday 12: *The Crusade: The Knight of Jaffa* is camera rehearsed and recorded in Riverside 1. From this episode, *Doctor Who*'s budget per episode is increased from £2,330 to £2,500. The total cost of *The Knight of Jaffa* is £2,300.

Saturday 13: *The Web Planet: Invasion* is transmitted on BBC1.

Monday 15: Four days' preliminary rehearsal begins for *The Crusade: The Wheel of Fortune*.
Verity Lambert begins two weeks' holiday.
Donald Wilson agrees that Dennis Spooner can be commissioned to write Serial S.

Friday 19: *The Crusade: The Wheel of Fortune* is camera rehearsed and recorded in Riverside 1. The total cost is £2,150.

Saturday 20: *The Web Planet: The Centre* is transmitted on BBC1.

Monday 22: Four days' preliminary rehearsal begins for *The Crusade: The Warlords*.

Friday 26: *The Crusade: The Warlords* is camera rehearsed and recorded in Riverside 1. The total cost is £2,065.

Saturday 27: *The Crusade: The Lion* is transmitted on BBC1.

Monday 29: Four days' preliminary rehearsal begins for *The Space Museum: The Space Museum*.

APRIL 1965

By the beginning of this month, Dennis Spooner has – like Verity Lambert – decided to move on from *Doctor Who* when his contract expires later in the year. Spooner's replacement is to be Donald Tosh, a BBC staffer who has just completed an eighteen month assignment as story editor on *Compact*. Although he will be present during production of *The Chase*, his first on-screen credit will be for the following story, Dennis Spooner's four-parter, now entitled *The Time Meddler*. Lambert's successor has also been chosen now and is to be John Wiles, who has been on the staff of the BBC since the early fifties as a writer/adaptor and story editor and who has recently been promoted to producer by Head of Serials Donald Wilson.

To help acquaint the newcomers with the background to the series, Lambert and Spooner provide them with a note headed 'The History of *Doctor Who*', which gives a brief story-by-story summary up to the end of the second production block. The introduction reads as follows:

> You will find listed below a thumbnail sketch of the serials transmitted and/or commissioned for *Doctor Who*. I think it is a point to bear in mind that any stories that are commissioned and are set in the future will have to be checked from their date point of view. Serials G, K and L involve the Earth in some way, so any given date must not clash with these. The Dalek serials have also to be watched with this in mind, as in the first Dalek serial (Serial B) Doctor Who did in fact wipe out the Dalek race. With a time machine at his disposal this is not as disastrous as it sounds, as he can go back to any point in their history; but one has to be careful in Serial B, K, R and in the Dalek story to come that they are true to the Dalek history calendar.
>
> Another further note is that most writers call Doctor Who 'Doctor Who'. In fact he does not admit to this name, just the 'Doctor' part, and is never referred to as 'Doctor Who'. This is just the title of the show.
>
> Doctor Who comes from a planet that we have never named. Various references to it have been made in the scripts as the show has gone along, but I personally have not gone back looking for them all.
>
> Vicki's background was covered in Serial L, should you wish to go back

and find this, and our new character, tentatively called Michael, was covered in episode six of Serial R, and further developed in Serial S.

Friday 2: *The Space Museum: The Space Museum* is camera rehearsed and recorded in TC4. The total cost is £2,643.

Dennis Spooner rejects Malcolm Hulke's *The Hidden Planet* and *Britain 408 A.D.*, which Hulke has re-submitted to the production office following David Whitaker's departure.

Saturday 3: *The Crusade: The Knight of Jaffa* is transmitted on BBC1.

Monday 5: Four days' preliminary rehearsal begins for *The Space Museum: The Dimensions of Time*.

Friday 9: *The Space Museum: The Dimensions of Time* is camera rehearsed and recorded in TC4. The total cost is £2,394.

One day of location filming for *The Chase* is carried out in Camber Sands, East Sussex.

Saturday 10: *The Crusade: The Wheel of Fortune* is transmitted on BBC1.

Monday 12: Four days' preliminary rehearsal begins for *The Space Museum: The Search*.

Four days' shooting of film inserts for *The Chase* begins on Stage 3A/B at Ealing.

Friday 16: *The Space Museum: The Search* is camera rehearsed and recorded in TC4. The total cost is £2,028.

Saturday 17: *The Crusade: The Warlords* is transmitted on BBC1.

Monday 19: Four days' preliminary rehearsal begins for *The Space Museum: The Final Phase*.

Tuesday 20: The first of two sessions is held between 2.00 pm and 6.00 pm at the Olympic Sound Studios to record Dudley Simpson's incidental music for *The Chase*. Simpson conducts an ensemble of five musicians, and the instruments used are: an electronic organ; a celeste; three tymps (one pedal); a xylophone; a marimba; and a vibraphone.

Director Richard Martin and film editor Norman Matthews begin three days' film editing work on sequences for *The Chase*.

Thursday 22: The second of the two music recording sessions for *The Chase* is held between 1.30 pm and 5.30 pm at the Olympic Sound Studios. The personnel and instruments used are the same as on Tuesday.

Friday 23: *The Space Museum: The Final Phase* is camera rehearsed and recorded in TC4. The total cost is £1,636.

Writer Robert Holmes meets Donald Tosh to discuss possible story ideas for *Doctor Who*. Tosh explains that he and John Wiles are intending to bring a new, more sophisticated style to the series.

Saturday 24: *The Space Museum: The Space Museum* is transmitted on BBC1.

Sunday 25: Following their meeting the previous Friday, Robert Holmes sends Donald Tosh a letter containing a storyline for a proposed four-part story. (Nothing comes of this idea now, but Holmes will resubmit it five years later under the title *The Space Trap* and it will eventually be made as *The Krotons* in *Doctor Who*'s sixth season.)

Monday 26: Four days' preliminary rehearsal begins for *The Chase: The Executioners*. Rehearsals this week and next take place in a Drill Hall at 58 Bulwer Street, London W12.

The film sequences for *The Chase* are dubbed with music and sound effects.

It has by this point been decided that the new companion character introduced in *The Chase* should be called Michael rather than Bruck.

Friday 30: *The Chase: The Executioners* is camera rehearsed and recorded in Riverside 1. The total cost is £6,083. Recording overruns its allotted time by ten minutes. This is a knock-on effect from delays caused earlier in the day by the fact that a special effect commissioned from Shawcraft was unavailable; the Shawcraft effects man had been asked to make a short trip back to their workshop on *Doctor Who* business but failed to return, having been sent out for the rest of the afternoon on another job. Verity Lambert later asks designer Raymond Cusick to register a protest with Shawcraft, as they are paid to have a man working on *Doctor Who* for the whole of the studio day.

MAY 1965

Saturday 1: *The Space Museum: The Dimensions of Time* is transmitted on BBC1.

Monday 3: Four days' preliminary rehearsal begins for *The Chase: The Death of Time*.

Wednesday 5: Graphics and Effects Manager Tony Foster sends Verity Lambert a memo informing her that he has taken up with Shawcraft 'in the strongest possible terms' their failure to provide a proper service for the previous Friday's studio work, and that he has received an assurance that it will not happen again. Shawcraft's labour charge for the episode is to be reduced accordingly.

Thursday 6: Director Douglas Camfield and a BBC photographer meet Jacqueline Hill and William Russell at 2.00 pm in the main reception area at Television Centre. They then visit a number of London locations, including Trafalgar Square and Hyde Park, to take stills for inclusion in a montage sequence showing Barbara and Ian back on Earth after parting company with the Doctor at the end of *The Chase* – Hill having by this point decided, like Russell, to leave the series when her current contract expires.

Friday 7: *The Chase: The Death of Time* is camera rehearsed and recorded in Riverside 1. The total cost is £2,441. The recording overruns its allotted time, almost entirely due to problems cutting from telecine film to live action and the time needed to rewind the telecine for retakes.

Saturday 8: *The Space Museum: The Search* is transmitted on BBC1.

Monday 10: Four days' preliminary rehearsal begins for *The Chase: Flight Through Eternity*. This week and next, rehearsals take place in the Territorial Army Centre at Artillery House, Horn Lane, London W3.

Two further film inserts for the final episode of *The Chase* are completed at Ealing. The first, shot on Stage 3A/B in front of a back-projection screen, shows Ian and Barbara on a double decker bus following their return to Earth at the end of the story. The second, shot between 2.00 pm and 3.30 pm just outside a maintenance garage behind Stage 3A/B, is a slightly earlier scene of the two companions running away from the building where the Daleks' time machine has deposited them, with an explosion (in truth a simple lighting effect) then occurring beyond the garage doors. These scenes are directed by Douglas Camfield and designed by Barry Newbery, effectively being made as part of the following production, Dennis Spooner's *The Time Meddler*. Ealing film inserts for the latter story, showing the TARDIS on a beach beside a rugged cliff-face, are also shot on this date.

Friday 14: *The Chase: Flight Through Eternity* is camera rehearsed and recorded in Riverside 1. The total cost is £2,614. The recording again overruns its allotted time, for the same reasons as did the previous week's. During the course of the day, Verity Lambert and Dennis Spooner ask Peter Purves, who has been cast as the American hillbilly character Morton Dill, if he would like to play the Doctor's new companion, Michael Taylor, who is to be introduced in the final episode of the story. Purves readily agrees.

Terry Nation has by this point delivered his script for the *Dalek Cutaway* episode and started work on the new six-part Dalek story it foreshadows.

Saturday 15: *The Space Museum: The Final Phase* is transmitted on BBC1.

Monday 17: Four days' preliminary rehearsal begins for *The Chase: Journey into Terror*.

Friday 21: *The Chase: Journey into Terror* is camera rehearsed and recorded in Riverside 1. The total cost is £2,658. The recording overruns its allotted time owing to its exceptionally complicated nature and to the fact that the start of camera rehearsals was delayed by the need to wait for paint to dry on a piece of scenery.

Saturday 22: *The Chase: The Executioners* is transmitted on BBC1.

Monday 24: Four days' preliminary rehearsal begins for *The Chase: The Death of Doctor Who*. Rehearsals this week take place in the Drill Hall at 239 Uxbridge Road.

Wednesday 26: Verity Lambert sends a memo to Barry Learoyd, Chief Designer (Drama), complaining about the poor quality of the walls for the Empire State Building set featured in the *Flight Through Eternity* episode.

Thursday 27: The Copyright Department is briefed to commission from writer Paul Erickson the scripts for a four-part story entitled *The Ark*.

Friday 28: *The Chase: The Death of Doctor Who* is camera rehearsed and recorded in Riverside 1. The total cost is £2,529. A fight scene between the Doctor and his robot double (played in some shots by Edmund Warwick) is pre-recorded between 3.00 and 3.30 in the afternoon as William Hartnell finds such scenes tiring and needs time to recover before the main recording in the evening.

Gerald Savory, Donald Wilson's successor as Head of Serials, has now asked Verity Lambert to make the next season's Dalek story a twelve-parter rather than a six-parter. Lambert sends Savory the following memo in response:

> Re your request to make Serial V (Dalek serial) a twelve-part serial instead of a six. I have put into motion the following, subject to negotiations with Terry Nation's agent and Dennis Spooner's agent. It will be possible to have a twelve part Dalek serial written jointly by Terry Nation and Dennis Spooner. The first recording for this will be on 15 October 1965 (Week 41) and it would continue up to and including 7 January 1966 (Week 1). At the moment we have one week's filming allocated to us in Week 39. We shall now require two weeks' filming and this ideally should be in Weeks 38 and 39.
>
> I am not able at this point to say if these serials can be done for less than £3,000 an episode, which as you know is what we have spent on the last two Dalek serials. I have asked Terry and Dennis to try to keep the overall cost as low as possible. However until they have been able to get together and work out a storyline it is not possible for me to commit myself.

The start of the third production block will subsequently be put back by one week. Recording of the twelve-part story will therefore begin on 22 October, and pre-filming at Ealing will take place over Weeks 39 and 40.

John Wiles later confirms that it will be impossible to mount the story on the usual budget of £2,500 per episode. An additional, one-off allocation of £3,500 is then made to the programme, which he elects to split equally between the first two episodes of the story.

Saturday 29: *The Chase: The Death of Time* is transmitted on BBC1.

Monday 31: Four days' preliminary rehearsal begins for *The Chase: The Planet of Decision*.

JUNE 1965

Friday 4: *The Chase: The Planet of Decision* is camera rehearsed and recorded in Riverside 1. The total cost is £2,285.

Saturday 5: *The Chase: Flight through Eternity* is transmitted on BBC1.

Monday 7: Four days' preliminary rehearsal begins for *The Time Meddler: The Watcher*. This story's rehearsals take place in the Drill Hall at 239 Uxbridge Road.

Wednesday 9: Director Richard Martin sends the following memo of appreciation to designers Raymond Cusick and John Wood for their work on *The Chase* and, in Wood's case, also *The Web Planet*:

> Thank you both very much for a highly successful six episodes of *Dr Who*. As we all know the difficulties under which this programme labours – the impossible task of its visual realisation – and as you are seldom there when the bits are swept up late on a Friday and congratulations seem in order, I would like it on record that you both worked extremely hard and contributed in a very great measure to any success that the programme may have obtained.
>
> For Mechanoids and mizzens; not to mention ants and animi of foregone worlds; for the sweat of your brows and the sweep of your brushes, my thanks.

Barry Learoyd replies to Verity Lambert's memo of 26 May, saying that the Empire State Building set looked satisfactory to him on transmission and pointing out that continual late information from the production office and consequent late design drawings mean that construction work is often rushed, leaving additional tidying up for the designers and studio staff to do on the recording day.

Incidental music for *The Time Meddler* is recorded in Lime Grove Studio R, featuring drums played by Charles Botterill. (Other music for this serial is to come from stock.)

Friday 11: *The Time Meddler: The Watcher* is camera rehearsed and recorded in TC4. The total cost is £1,949. The recording overruns its allotted time by seven minutes. This is due partly to the fact that a technical fault causes it to start four minutes late and partly to the fact that an entire sequence has to be reshot as it has used more stock music than can be cleared for copyright purposes – a fact not discovered until the end of the day.

Saturday 12: *The Chase: Journey into Terror* is transmitted on BBC1.

Monday 14: Four days' preliminary rehearsal begins for *The Time Meddler: The Meddling Monk*.

Wednesday 16: Verity Lambert replies to Barry Learoyd's memo of the previous Wednesday, asserting that the only reason the Empire State Building set looked satisfactory was that the director changed some of his shots to disguise its deficiencies, and that scripts and design discussions for *The Chase* were on time.

Friday 18: *The Time Meddler: The Meddling Monk* is camera rehearsed and recorded in TC3. The total cost is £1,803. A fight scene featuring stuntmen Fred Haggerty and Tim Condren is recorded out of sequence before the main recording of the episode.

Saturday 19: *The Chase: The Death of Doctor Who* is transmitted on BBC1.

Monday 21: Four days' preliminary rehearsal begins for *The Time Meddler: A Battle of Wits*. During the course of this week, shooting of film inserts for *Galaxy 4* is carried out at Ealing.

Thursday 24: A photocall for *Galaxy 4* takes place at Ealing featuring the Drahvins and Chumblies.

Friday 25: *The Time Meddler: A Battle of Wits* is camera rehearsed and recorded in TC4. The total cost is £1,677. During camera rehearsals, actor Michael Miller, playing Wulnoth, is asked to make a sound recording of one line of dialogue to facilitate cueing in the main recording that evening.

Saturday 26: *The Chase: The Planet of Decision* is transmitted on BBC1. This is the last episode on which Dennis Spooner is credited as story editor.

Monday 28: Four days' preliminary rehearsal begins for *The Time Meddler: Checkmate*.

JULY 1965

Friday 2: *The Time Meddler: Checkmate* is camera rehearsed and recorded in TC4. The total cost is £1,728.

Saturday 3: *The Time Meddler: The Watcher* is transmitted on BBC1.

Monday 5: Four days' preliminary rehearsal begins for *Galaxy 4: Four Hundred Dawns*. By this point, John Wiles has in effect taken over the day-to-day production of *Doctor Who* from Verity Lambert.
  Donald Tosh briefs the Copyright Department to commission from Dennis Spooner the scripts for his six scripts for the new twelve-part Dalek story, now entitled *The Daleks' Master Plan*. (Spooner has still not fully relinquished the story editor's post but is unable to commission himself as this would breach BBC restrictions on story editors writing for their own shows.)

Friday 9: *Galaxy 4: Four Hundred Dawns* is camera rehearsed and recorded in TC4. The total cost is £3,100.
  Donald Tosh briefs the Copyright Department to commission from John Lucarotti a new four-part historical story about the massacre of the Huguenots in Paris, 1572. This subject matter is the production team's suggestion; Lucarotti originally proposed to write a story about Eric the Red discovering Newfoundland.

Saturday 10: *The Time Meddler: The Meddling Monk* is transmitted on BBC1.

Monday 12: Four days' preliminary rehearsal begins for *Galaxy 4: Trap of Steel*.

Friday 16: *Galaxy 4: Trap of Steel* is camera rehearsed and recorded in TC4. The total cost is £2,094.
  Dennis Spooner briefs the Copyright Department to commission from Terry Nation his six scripts for *The Daleks' Master Plan*.

Saturday 17: *The Time Meddler: A Battle of Wits* is transmitted on BBC1.

Monday 19: Four days' preliminary rehearsal begins for *Galaxy 4: Airlock*.

Tuesday 20: Douglas Camfield, who has been assigned to direct the forthcoming twelve-part Dalek story now entitled *The Daleks' Master Plan*, writes to composer Tristram Cary to ask if he would be willing to provide the incidental music for it:

> As a matter of interest, we met when I was production assistant to Waris Hussein on the *Marco Polo* story …
>
> My serial – to be written by Terry Nation and Dennis Spooner – will range far and wide in Space and Time. The basic idea is one concerning the Daleks' attempt to conquer the Universe in the year 4,000 AD. but we shall take in the Planet of Mists, a planet which is a kind of galactic Devil's Island, Ancient Egypt, Hollywood in the '20s, the Daleks' outer planet of Varga and so on and so forth. Being a twelve-parter, the story will be a complex and far-ranging one.
>
> One thing we shall be doing is to give back to the Daleks their former menace, plus trying, in general, to sharpen up the pace of the storytelling.
>
> The music, I think, should be largely electronic – weird and compelling. The first episode is to be called *The Nightmare Begins* and that should give some indication of the feeling I'm after. For the historical episodes, we could lose the electronic music and go after something else. Without scripts I cannot be more specific than that!
>
> I do hope that you will agree to work on this project. I thought your music for *Marco Polo* was excellent and I think this serial is right up your street!

Friday 23: *Galaxy 4: Air Lock* is camera rehearsed and recorded in TC4. The total cost is £2,293.

Saturday 24: *The Time Meddler: Checkmate* is transmitted on BBC1.

Monday 26: Four days' preliminary rehearsal begins for *Galaxy 4: The Exploding Planet*.

Friday 30: *Galaxy 4: The Exploding Planet* is camera rehearsed and recorded in TC3. The total cost is £2,463.

AUGUST 1965

Monday 2: Four days' preliminary rehearsal begins for *Dalek Cutaway: Mission to the Unknown*.

Friday 6: *Dalek Cutaway: Mission to the Unknown* is camera rehearsed and recorded in TC3. The total cost is £2,440.

SEPTEMBER 1965

Wednesday 1: One day of location filming is carried out for *The Myth Makers*.

Tuesday 7: John Wiles sends Terry Nation the following letter conveying comments by director Douglas Camfield and others on the draft scripts for the early episodes of *The Daleks' Master Plan*:

> Douglas has come up with some very exciting ideas for the serial which I do hope you will consider. One of his fears is that as far as he himself is concerned he would like to try to get more into the production indicative of the year 4,000 AD.
>
> We have had a lot of talks about this and some of the things we feel for example concern names of people. We both feel that, just as our names have changed a great deal since the time of Christ, so too in another 2,000 years a lot of names, now in use (and, in fact, used in your script) will have been corrupted into something else. This might happen by the dropping of consonants or the changing of vowels, e.g. ROALD instead of RONALD, VYON instead of WALTON. He also feels – and I think this is an interesting idea – that we may return to a kind of heraldry whereby the basic names in English reappear, e.g. BORS for one of the convicts on Desperus.
>
> In this connection also, it seems possible that words will emerge meaning 'SPACE VESSEL'. Donald has suggested a vehicle called a *FLIPT* (Faster than light inter-planetary transporter) and a *SPAR* (Space car): terms like this can easily be explained in the scripts and will add to the possible vernacular of the period. We are a little worried also about Vitaranium. Bill Hartnell will certainly have great difficulty in saying it. May we for certain occasions change it to VX 2?
>
> Some of the people who have read the scripts have also been a little worried by the reference to New Washington. They feel that in the year 4,000 the world will possibly be a single country owing allegiance to nothing that we know today. One suggestion is that we refer to it as Communication Centre Earth, which gives us the feeling that the whole world may be one giant built-up area where nationalities have ceased to exist.
>
> How do you feel about these ideas?
>
> This possibly sounds as if my only reaction to the scripts is to suggest amendments – far from it! I think there are some most exciting things in the story. But if we can help Douglas realise his ambitions for it we will get an even more exciting result.

Terry Nation replies later in the week indicating that he has no objection to most of the changes suggested by Wiles. He dislikes the substitution of 'VX 2' for 'Vitaranium', however, and suggests 'Vita' as a possible alternative. He also asks that the names of two of his characters, Mavic Chen and Sara Kingdom, be left unchanged.

Saturday 11: *Galaxy 4: Four Hundred Dawns* is transmitted on BBC1.

Monday 13: John Wiles writes again to Terry Nation, thanking him for his co-operation over the changes suggested the previous week and assuring him that there is no intention to change the names Mavic Chen and Sara Kingdom. He continues:

> 'Vita' and its derivatives worries us slightly because of its association with vitamins. Would you wear TARANIUM as a contraction of your original word? I am sure the Daleks would make it sound most sinister.

Four days' preliminary rehearsal begins for *The Myth Makers: Temple of Secrets*. This story's rehearsals take place at North Kensington Community Centre.

Maureen O'Brien, returning from holiday for the start of the new production block, is taken aback to learn that she is to be dropped from the series at the end of *The Myth Makers*. John Wiles' intention has been to replace Vicki with a new character, Katarina, whom he has had written into the last two episodes of the story as a late addition. He and Donald Tosh have quickly realised however that this character, a handmaiden to the prophetess Cassandra, would pose enormous difficulties for the series' writers, owing to her lack of modern knowledge. They have therefore decide to kill her off in the following story, *The Daleks' Master Plan*, and to use as another short-term companion Terry Nation's character Sara Kingdom, who will also be killed off at the end of that story. Adrienne Hill is subsequently cast as Katarina, and Jean Marsh as Sara.

Friday 17: *The Myth Makers: Temple of Secrets* is camera rehearsed and recorded in Riverside 1. The total cost is £3,327.

Saturday 18: *Galaxy 4: Trap of Steel* is transmitted on BBC1.

Monday 20: Four days' preliminary rehearsal begins for *The Myth Makers: Small Prophet, Quick Return*.

Friday 24: *The Myth Makers: Small Prophet, Quick Return* is camera rehearsed and recorded in Riverside 1. The total cost is £2,566.

Saturday 25: *Galaxy 4: Air Lock* is transmitted on BBC1.

Monday 27: Four days' preliminary rehearsal begins for *The Myth Makers: Death of a Spy*.

Five days' shooting of film inserts for *The Daleks' Master Plan* begins on Stage 3A/B at Ealing. The first scene to be shot is the death of Katarina for episode four – ironically, actress Adrienne Hill's first work on the series. As the story's scripts are still undergoing revision, director Douglas Camfield has to improvise some of the action based upon the agreed storyline. Problems occur all week due to the late delivery, and in some cases non-delivery, of props and scenery. A number of model shots due to be done on Friday are held over for completion the following Monday.

OCTOBER 1965

Friday 1: *The Myth Makers: Death of a Spy* is camera rehearsed and recorded in Riverside 1. The total cost is £2,230.

Saturday 2: *Galaxy 4: The Exploding Planet* is transmitted on BBC1.

Monday 4: Four days' preliminary rehearsal begins for *The Myth Makers: Horse of Destruction*.

A further five days' shooting of film inserts for *The Daleks' Master Plan* begins on Stage 3A/B at Ealing. The morning of the first day is spent completing the model shots held over from the previous Friday. Filming then continues with scenes of a battle between Daleks and Ancient Egyptians. Extras hired from the Denton de Gray agency to play non-speaking Egyptian soldiers are judged by director Douglas Camfield and production assistant Viktors Ritelis to be very poor, and a number of shots involving them are dropped. Problems again arise with scenery, and in particular with a model pyramid that takes one-and-half hours to erect on the morning of Wednesday 6 October after Shawcraft have worked all through the night to complete it. Bill Roberts, the manager of Shawcraft, tells Ritelis that he would be happy for some of the specialist prop and model work on *Doctor Who* to be put out to some other firm in future, as his team are overstretched.

Friday 8: One of the final pieces of filming for *The Daleks' Master Plan* at Ealing is a model shot of an erupting volcano, utilising steam and compressed air to achieve the effect of the magma. This proves unsatisfactory, however, as the volcano is out of scale with the model TARDIS required to materialise on it. A decision is taken to remount it at a later date.

The Myth Makers: Horse of Destruction is camera rehearsed and recorded in Riverside 1. The total cost is £2,091.

Saturday 9: *Dalek Cutaway: Mission to the Unknown* is transmitted on BBC1. This is the last episode on which Verity Lambert receives a credit as producer.

Wednesday 13: Composer Tristram Cary's incidental music for the first six episodes of *The Daleks' Master Plan* is recorded between 6.30 pm and 10.30 pm at the IBC Studios, at 35 Portland Place, London W1A. The instruments, played by an ensemble of musicians led by Eddie Walker, are: horn, cello, percussion, flute, oboe and vibraphone.

Friday 15: *Doctor Who*'s budget is set for the financial year beginning 1 April 1966 at an average of £2,750 per episode.

Saturday 16: *The Myth Makers: Temple of Secrets* is transmitted on BBC1.

Monday 18: Four days' preliminary rehearsal begins for *The Daleks' Master Plan: The Nightmare Begins*. The venue for this story's rehearsals is the Drill Hall at 58 Bulwer Street.

The volcano model shot initially attempted on Friday 8 October is remounted on Stage 2 at Ealing, this time using a high speed camera to increase its effectiveness. Again however it proves unsuccessful, this time because the rushes show strobing and an occasional sideways kick on the picture. It will therefore have to be remounted again.

John Wiles prepares a memo to be given to all the series' directors and their teams, setting out some standing orders for the production. Reiterating the contents of two earlier notes used by Verity Lambert for the same purpose, it stipulates that in order to facilitate overseas sales, each episode must have a 'fade to black' included immediately after the opening titles, or alternatively immediately after the reprise from the previous week, and another around half-way through (this is so that commercial breaks may be inserted); and that no more than five recording breaks should normally be scheduled for each episode. It goes on to state that artists who have appeared in previous *Doctor Who* stories should not be used again without approval first being obtained from Wiles; and that, in accordance with a ruling by Sydney Newman, no episode should have a duration of more than 24' 45" or of less than 23' 45". It also sets out the standard billing for *Radio Times* and explains the circumstances in which credits may be given for designers and members of the technical staff.

Thursday 21: The volcano model shot is again attempted at Ealing, but once more proves unsuccessful as the same picture fault occurs as on Monday.

Friday 22: *The Daleks' Master Plan: The Nightmare Begins* is camera rehearsed and recorded in TC3. The budget is initially set at £4,250 – the standard £2,500 plus half the additional one-off sum of £3,500 allocated to this story. It is subsequently increased to £4,310. The total cost is £5,318.

A press photocall takes place at 3.45 pm on the set, featuring William Hartnell and the actors playing characters called Technix, who are required to have their heads shaved for the production.

Saturday 23: *The Myth Makers: Small Prophet, Quick Return* is transmitted on BBC1.

Monday 25: Four days' preliminary rehearsal begins for *The Daleks' Master Plan: Day of Armageddon.*

Tuesday 26: John Wiles sends make-up supervisor Sonia Markham a memo pointing out that in *The Nightmare Begins*, the beard worn by actor Brian Cant, playing the character Kurt Gantry, differed noticeably between the pre-filmed inserts and the studio recordings, and that the hair-lace on William Hartnell's wig was showing badly in close ups. He concludes:

> I would be grateful if you could look into these points. The make-up on the whole in the programme is so good that I think it a pity when something lets it down.

Wednesday 27: Sonia Markham replies as follows to John Wiles's memo of the previous day:

> Thank you for your memo of 26 October. I have noted the contents. I appreciate your remarks and can only apologise for the lack of continuity on the make-up of Brian Cant.
> Regarding the hair-lace on Mr Hartnell's wig, owing to different lighting and change of positions on various sets, this does sometimes occur, especially in big close-ups, and this is almost unavoidable.

Friday 29: *The Daleks' Master Plan: Day of Armageddon* is camera rehearsed and recorded in TC3. The budget for this episode is £4,250, the total cost £4,031.

Saturday 30: *The Myth Makers: Death of a Spy* is transmitted on BBC1.

NOVEMBER 1965

Monday 1: Four days' preliminary rehearsal begins for *The Daleks' Master Plan: Devil's Planet*.

Friday 5: *The Daleks' Master Plan: Devil's Planet* is camera rehearsed and recorded in TC3. From this episode, the budget reverts to £2,500 per episode for the remainder of the story. The total cost of *Devil's Planet* is £2,268.

Saturday 6: *The Myth Makers: Horse of Destruction* is transmitted on BBC1.

Monday 8: Four days' preliminary rehearsal begins for *The Daleks' Master Plan: The Traitors*.

Friday 12: *The Daleks' Master Plan: The Traitors* is camera rehearsed and recorded in TC3. The total cost is £2,448.

Saturday 13: *The Daleks' Master Plan: The Nightmare Begins* is transmitted on BBC1.

Monday 15: The volcano model shot attempted on 8, 18 and 21 October is remounted again on Stage 3B at Ealing, and finally proves satisfactory.
   Four days' preliminary rehearsal begins for *The Daleks' Master Plan: Counter Plot*.

Tuesday 16: Donald Tosh briefs the Copyright Department to commission from writer Brian Hayles the storylines for two stories, entitled *The White Witch* and *The Hands of Aten*.

Wednesday 17: John Wiles sends Serials Department Organiser Terence Cook the following memo:

> I have been told by our designer, Barry Newbery, that when the large SFX units arrived at Ealing for storage after last week's recording, they were found to be so seriously damaged that one of them, required for this week, cannot be used at all, and repairs to both are going to be very extensive. Enquiries have not elicited who or what was responsible for the damage; all that is certain is that a most valuable piece of SFX equipment, costing a great deal of money, has been smashed by inefficiency and indifference, and another considerable amount will be needed to put it right, in the meantime creating immense difficulties for the director and his designers. I am told that there is great uncertainty as to whose is the responsibility for the safe transportation and storage of all special effects, but may we register a very strong protest at having to be the ones to

suffer for it. It is unforgivable that a director should be deprived within three days of recording of a vital piece of equipment because of inefficiency for which nobody will answer.

Friday 19: *The Daleks' Master Plan: Counter Plot* is camera rehearsed and recorded in TC4. The total cost is £2,194.

Barry Learoyd, the Chief Designer (Drama), sends John Wiles the following memo:

> *Dr Who* Serial V is proving a near disaster. I understand that the director is doing all possible to meet his dates but that his commitment to twelve consecutive episodes has made this virtually impossible. Scripts or near-complete scripts are often available but planning the design and shooting arrangements for these is entirely haphazard. The director has declared his availability to the designers, but in practice this means the designer designs to the script, presents the prepared design and gets an OK from the director in a meeting lasting perhaps five minutes. The result being that when he (the director) reaches the stage where he can plan his shots, he must use what is done – or whatever 'bits' of what is done that now fit in with his production ideas. This very often means large areas of unwanted and wasted scenery.
>
> I give you this summary, despite the fact that this Serial V will almost certainly continue in this same way, in order that you may make quite sure that the following four episode parts allow proper planning with the designers and directors together and so that you may fight wholeheartedly against any recurrence of more than six episodes being given to one director and in order that you take some action to ensure that the addition of the Christmas holiday period to the problem does not lead to real disaster.

Saturday 20: *The Daleks' Master Plan: Day of Armageddon* is transmitted on BBC1.

Monday 22: Four days' preliminary rehearsal begins for *The Daleks' Master Plan: Coronas of the Sun.*

Tuesday 23: John Wiles responds as follows to Barry Learoyd's memo of 19 November:

> Thank you for your memo. Once again I am sorry that script difficulties on the … serial have caused so much trouble to our designers. Nevertheless, I have no hesitation in affirming that I think the results to date have been first class, and a credit to all concerned with the programme. I am sorry that you consider some of the director's shooting to be wasteful as far as sets are concerned, this hadn't occurred to me, nor do I believe I agree with you. Your point about any director working for more than six consecutive episodes is valid and I agree. Personally, I am planning no serial of more than four episodes. The director of Serial W joins me at the end of this week and will be available for discussions with

her designer thereafter, and the director of Serial X will join me when he returns from leave in about two weeks' time. Consequently, I am hopeful that the same situation will not arise in the immediate future.

Wiles also sends Douglas Camfield a memo expressing his gratitude for the fact that the early episodes of *The Daleks' Master Plan* have been achieved within budget.

Friday 26: *The Daleks' Master Plan: Coronas of the Sun* is camera rehearsed and recorded in TC4. The total cost is £1,914.

Saturday 27: *The Daleks' Master Plan: Devil's Planet* is transmitted on BBC1.

Monday 29: Four days' preliminary rehearsal begins for *The Daleks' Master Plan: The Feast of Steven*.

DECEMBER 1965

Friday 3: *The Daleks' Master Plan: The Feast of Steven* is camera rehearsed and recorded in TC3. The total cost is £2,562.

Saturday 4: *The Daleks' Master Plan: The Traitors* is transmitted on BBC1.

Monday 6: Four days' preliminary rehearsal begins for *The Daleks' Master Plan: Volcano*.

Friday 10: *The Daleks' Master Plan: Volcano* is camera rehearsed and recorded in TC3. The total cost is £2,265.

Saturday 11: *The Daleks' Master Plan: Counter Plot* is transmitted on BBC1.

Monday 13: Four days' preliminary rehearsal begins for *The Daleks' Master Plan: Golden Death*.

Friday 17: *The Daleks' Master Plan: Golden Death* is camera rehearsed and recorded in TC3. The total cost is £2,398.

Saturday 18: *The Daleks' Master Plan: Coronas of the Sun* is transmitted on BBC1.

Friday 23: An extra day's shooting of film inserts for the final episode of *The Daleks' Master Plan* takes place on Stage 2 at Ealing.
Saturday 25: *The Daleks' Master Plan: The Feast of Steven* is transmitted on BBC1.

Monday 27: Four days' preliminary rehearsal begins for *The Daleks' Master Plan: Escape Switch*.

Friday 31: *The Daleks' Master Plan: Escape Switch* is camera rehearsed and recorded in TC3. The total cost is £2,391.

JANUARY 1966

Saturday 1: *The Daleks' Master Plan: Volcano* is transmitted on BBC1.

Monday 3: Four days' preliminary rehearsal begins for *The Daleks' Master Plan: The Abandoned Planet.*
Four days' shooting of film inserts for *The Massacre of St. Bartholomew's Eve* – John Lucarotti's four-part historical set in Paris 1572 – begins at Ealing.

Wednesday 5: Chief Designer (Drama) Barry Learoyd sends John Wiles a memo following on from their correspondence the previous November about *Doctor Who*'s scenery requirements:

> I was sorry to learn from the designer in the studio that there has been a bit of misunderstanding about our attitude to 'wasted' scenery. It is never our contention that a director should 'show the set' except where this is an integral part of his conception of the production.
>
> Our only interest in this respect is that he does not ask for more set than he is going to use. In Serial V, where the director had not the time available to plan productions with the designer in advance, and had no alternative therefore but to accept what was given to him, our interest was that he should shoot his action within these bounds, to the best advantage of the production.

Friday 7: *The Daleks' Master Plan: The Abandoned Planet* is camera rehearsed and recorded in TC3. The total cost is £1,919.
One day of location filming is carried out for *The Massacre of St. Bartholomew's Eve.* This is for a scene at the end of the story where a young girl named Dodo enters the TARDIS, subsequently to become the Doctor's new female companion. The production team's original intention was that the Huguenot character Anne Chaplet, played by Annette Robertson, should be taken on board the TARDIS at the end of this story. However, they have now reached the conclusion that to have a companion originating from Paris 1572 would pose the same problems of lack of modern knowledge as had been envisaged with Katarina. They have therefore decided to introduce instead a present-day character, Dorothea 'Dodo' Chaplet, descended from Anne. The actress cast as Dodo is Jackie Lane.

Saturday 8: *The Daleks' Master Plan: Golden Death* is transmitted on BBC1.

Monday 10: Four days' preliminary rehearsal begins for *The Daleks' Master Plan: Destruction of Time.*

Friday 14: *The Daleks' Master Plan: Destruction of Time* is camera rehearsed and recorded in TC3. The total cost is £1,888. The recording overruns its allotted time owing to the fact that the roller caption for the closing credits keeps sticking, requiring numerous retakes of the final scene. A further retake proves necessary when a stage hand appears in shot during the roller caption sequence, incurring director Douglas Camfield's wrath.

During production of *The Daleks' Master Plan*, John Wiles and Donald Tosh have both decided to quit the *Doctor Who* production team early in the new year. Wiles has never been entirely happy working as a producer, feeling more at home as a writer and a director, and he has had a very strained working relationship with William Hartnell. He has indeed proposed replacing Hartnell with another actor, but this has been overruled by Head of Serials Gerald Savory. Tosh has decided to leave partly out of loyalty to Wiles and partly due to a desire to move on to other work.

The man appointed as Wiles' replacement is Innes Lloyd, who has been on staff at the BBC since 1953 and has worked on a wide variety of different programmes. He has been chosen for the job by Sydney Newman, but accepts it with some reluctance as he is not a fan of science fiction. Tosh's successor is Gerry Davis, who has asked to be transferred to *Doctor Who* after a stint on the football team soap opera *United!*.

A number of stories have already been commissioned for the latter part of the third production block, including *The Ark* by Paul Erickson, *The Toymaker* by Brian Hayles (Tosh having now decided against using Hayles' other submissions, *The White Witch* and *The Hands of Aten*) and *The Gunfighters* by Donald Cotton. Accomplished writer Ian Stuart Black is also due to submit a storyline to the production office. *The Toymaker* – the story in which it was proposed that Hartnell might be written out – is currently being heavily rewritten by Tosh from Hayles' scripts as, partly because of their extensive special effects requirements, these were considered unsuitable for production. It will therefore be some time before the influence of Lloyd and Davis will be fully felt.

Saturday 15: *The Daleks' Master Plan: Escape Switch* is transmitted on BBC1.

Monday 17: Four days' preliminary rehearsal begins for *The Massacre of St Bartholomew's Eve: War of God*. This story's rehearsals take place in the Drill Hall at 58 Bulwer Street.

Donald Tosh has by this point left the production office after completing his rewrites on Brian Hayles's *The Toymaker* (which will shortly undergo a change of name first to *The Trilogic Game* and then to *The Celestial Toymaker*). In consultation with John Wiles and director Bill Sellars, he has removed a number of impractical effects sequences – including some scenes set in a maze – and substituted two new games of his own, one of these being the Trilogic Game.

Tosh has now also formally rejected Hayles's storylines for *The Witch Planet* and *The Hands of Aten*; but Gerry Davis will subsequently commission from the writer a four-part historical adventure entitled *The Smugglers*, which will be made as the last story of the series' third production block.

Davis himself has meanwhile rejected an idea entitled *The New Armada* by the series' first story editor, David Whitaker, and returns it to him with the following letter:

> Enclosed please find your storyline entitled *The New Armada* which was passed on to me by Donald Tosh.
>
> Sorry, but I don't feel that this is quite in line with the direction set down by the Head of Serials for *Doctor Who*.

We are looking for strong, *simple* stories. This one, though very ingenious, is rather complex with too many characters and sub-plots. To simplify it, as it stands, would reduce the plot to the point when it would virtually be a new creation.

I should very much like to hear from you. Perhaps we could meet for a chat in the near future. Could you bring over a number of storylines in embryo form we could take a look at?

Tuesday 18: John Wiles sends the following letter to Donald Tosh:

I have now had a chance of reading episode four of *The Toymaker* and I think it goes extremely well. Bill Sellars is also very pleased with it and a set of the scripts is now with the designer to start preliminary work. It is possible that it may be a bit short and I have agreed with Bill that I will look at all the episodes: in the event of one, three and four I'll try and work in sufficient business to give us an extra two or three minutes per episode and for episode two I will try and find another four minutes. I have discussed all this with Innes and Bill; I hope to do this as painlessly as possible, anyway don't worry, I shall respect the 'fabric' as if it were of Westminster Abbey itself. I gather … that you are sending back the Hayles versions of episodes one and two. I do appreciate this as it may help me to find the extra stuff, which I want to do early next week.

Things go well here. Ian Stuart Black has brought in a very exciting synopsis and we are going ahead with Serial AA. Douglas has even finished his editing and has lost ten years!

In conclusion I must thank you for everything you have done for the programme, not only in the immense amounts of rewriting which you have done, always so cheerfully and efficiently, but also for your constant encouragement and support in everything we have undertaken. Your help to me personally was quite fantastic and deeply appreciated and I hope that we shall continue to work together many times in the future. Have a splendid holiday and come and see us as soon as you get back.

Friday 21: *The Massacre of St Bartholomew's Eve: War of God* is camera rehearsed and recorded in Riverside 1.

The production team have now formally adopted a system of setting a budget for each episode according to its own particular requirements, rather than using the standard budget figure throughout. In future, the opening episode of each story will always be allocated a larger proportion of the total budget than the others, as this is the episode for which the new sets, monsters etc have to be made. It will however remain the case that if the total cost of a story exceeds the standard budget for the number of episodes it contains, savings will have to be made on other stories within the same financial year so that, at the end of the day, the books balance.

The budget for *War of God* is £2,825, the total cost £3,576.

Saturday 22: *The Daleks' Master Plan: The Abandoned Planet* is transmitted on BBC1.

Monday 24: Four days' preliminary rehearsal begins for *The Massacre of St Bartholomew's Eve: The Sea Beggar*.

Wednesday 26: Innes Lloyd sends copies of the draft scripts for the first two episodes of Donald Cotton's *The Gunfighters* to Rex Tucker, who has been assigned to direct it. The third episode is currently being rewritten as it 'came through with precious little action and nine sets,' and the fourth has yet to be delivered.

Friday 28: *The Massacre of St Bartholomew's Eve: The Sea Beggar* is camera rehearsed and recorded in Riverside 1. The budget is £2,425, the total cost £2,041.

Saturday 29: *The Daleks' Master Plan: Destruction of Time* is transmitted on BBC1.

Monday 31: Four days' preliminary rehearsal begins for *The Massacre of St Bartholomew's Eve: Priest of Death*.

FEBRUARY 1966

Friday 4: *The Massacre of St Bartholomew's Eve: Priest of Death* is camera rehearsed and recorded in Riverside 1. The budget is £2,425, the total cost £2,632.

Saturday 5: *The Massacre of St Bartholomew's Eve: War of God* is transmitted on BBC1.

Monday 7: Four days' preliminary rehearsal begins for *The Massacre of St Bartholomew's Eve: Bell of Doom*.

Friday 11: *The Massacre of St Bartholomew's Eve: Bell of Doom* is camera rehearsed and recorded in Riverside 1. The budget is £2,425, the total cost £2,019.

Saturday 12: *The Massacre of St Bartholomew's Eve: The Sea Beggar* is transmitted on BBC1.

Monday 14: Four days' preliminary rehearsal begins for *The Ark: The Steel Sky*. Although John Wiles will receive the on-screen credit as producer of *The Ark*, Innes Lloyd has by this point taken over full responsibility for the day-to-day production of the series.

Friday 18: *The Ark: The Steel Sky* is camera rehearsed and recorded in Riverside 1. The budget is £2,700, the total cost £5,678.

Saturday 19: *The Massacre of St Bartholomew's Eve: Priest of Death* is transmitted on BBC1. This is the last episode on which Donald Tosh is credited as story editor.

Monday 21: Four days' preliminary rehearsal begins for *The Ark: The Plague*.

Tuesday 22: Director Rex Tucker has by this time received draft scripts for all four episodes of *The Gunfighters*, but has expressed to Gerry Davis a number of reservations about them. Innes Lloyd sends him the following letter:

Gerry Davis has told me that he was able to talk to you yesterday about episodes three and four of *The Gunfighters*, and he will look at them again in the light of your criticisms.

Whilst they are not the greatest scripts, I believe and hope that there is a great deal of humour and adventure that can be got out of them. I am sure you will agree that it would be absurd to try and make a traditional western – I would suggest that the approach might be more on the lines of *Cat Ballou* – tongue in cheek – heroes and villains well defined. Perhaps before you do the casting we could have a talk about it. One of the things I believe we should look for is either American actors in London suitable to play parts in it, or English actors with really authentic accents.

...

We will let you have the revised scripts as soon as they are available. I look forward to seeing you after you have finished editing *A Farewell to Arms*.

Friday 25: *The Ark: The Plague* is camera rehearsed and recorded in Riverside 1. The budget is £2,400, the total cost £1,945.

Gerry Davis has by this point completely rewritten the scripts for *The Celestial Toymaker* as Head of Serials Gerald Savory has objected to Tosh's inclusion of two characters, George and Margaret, whom he himself created for his successful West End play *George and Margaret* (the gimmick of which was that the title characters never actually appeared). On seeing the rewritten scripts, John Wiles sends a memo of protest to Savory, pointing out that he might otherwise be open to criticism for wasting money on Hayles's originals. He stresses that the story was supposed to have been one of great menace – although arising from a battle of wills between the Doctor and the Toymaker character, rather than from ray guns and monsters – and that this was what had given it its relevance to *Doctor Who*. He expresses the view that this has now been lost, as the Toymaker has been reduced virtually to a bystander and his conflict with the Doctor downplayed. He ends by expressing his regret that the story is going ahead at all now that the producer and story editor who commissioned it have both left.

Saturday 26: *The Massacre of St Bartholomew's Eve: Bell of Doom* is transmitted on BBC1.

Monday 28: Four days' preliminary rehearsal begins for *The Ark: The Return*.

MARCH 1966

Thursday 3: One day's shooting of film inserts for *The Celestial Toymaker* takes place at Ealing. Also carried out is a sound recording of William Hartnell for the scenes in episode two where the Doctor is invisible and heard only as a disembodied voice. Hartnell himself will be on holiday for the studio recording of that episode and of episode three.

Friday 4: *The Ark: The Return* is camera rehearsed and recorded in Riverside 1. The budget is £2,400, the total cost £1,939.

Saturday 5: *The Ark: The Steel Sky* is transmitted on BBC1.

Monday 7: Four days' preliminary rehearsal begins for *The Ark: The Bomb*.

Tuesday 8: Gerry Davis briefs the Copyright Department to commission from Brian Hayles the storyline for a story entitled *The Nazis*.

Friday 11: *The Ark: The Bomb* is camera rehearsed and recorded in Riverside 1. The budget is £2,400, the total cost £1,597.

Saturday 12: *The Ark: The Plague* is transmitted on BBC1.

Monday 14: Four days' preliminary rehearsal begins for *The Celestial Toymaker: The Celestial Toyroom*. This story's rehearsals take place in the Drill Hall at 58 Bulwer Street.

Tuesday 15: Gerry Davis briefs the Copyright Department to commission from Ian Stuart Black the scripts for a further four-part story, working title *The Computers*, which will be transmitted immediately after *The Savages*. The basic scenario for this story, involving an attempt by a computer to take over the world from its base in the newly-constructed GPO Tower, has been suggested by scientist Dr Kit Pedler in discussion with Davis. It has been further developed in a storyline accepted from writer Pat Dunlop, who has since had to withdraw from the project as the proposed delivery dates for the scripts clashed with work he was already committed to doing on another BBC serial called *United!* Dunlop will subsequently be paid £50 for his contribution to the story. Pedler will meanwhile strike up a firm friendship with Davis and become *Doctor Who*'s unofficial scientific adviser.

It has by this point been decided that Steven will be written out of the series at the conclusion of *The Savages*. Peter Purves has been dissatisfied for some time with what he sees as a lack of development of Steven's character, and Innes Lloyd and Gerry Davis feel that the time is right for a change. The intention is that *The Computers* will introduce a replacement character called Richard, or Rich for short, who will join the Doctor and Dodo on their travels after meeting Dodo at a discotheque.

Friday 18: *The Celestial Toymaker: The Celestial Toyroom* is camera rehearsed and recorded in Riverside 1. The budget is £2,700, the total cost £3,686.

Saturday 19: *The Ark: The Return* is transmitted on BBC1.

Monday 21: Four days' preliminary rehearsal begins for *The Celestial Toymaker: The Hall of Dolls*.

Tuesday 22: Rex Tucker views the cinema film *Gunfight at the OK Corral* as part of his preparatory work for *The Gunfighters*.

Friday 25: *The Celestial Toymaker: The Hall of Dolls* is camera rehearsed and recorded in Riverside 1. The budget is £2,350, the total cost £2,535.

Saturday 26: *The Ark: The Bomb* is transmitted on BBC1. This is the last episode on which John Wiles is credited as producer.

Monday 28: Four days' preliminary rehearsal begins for *The Celestial Toymaker: The Dancing Floor*.
  Four days' shooting of film inserts for *The Gunfighters* begins on Stage 3A/B at Ealing.

Thursday 31: Innes Lloyd sends Drama Serials Organiser Terence Cook a memo in which he reports that Barry Newbery's design drawings for episodes two and three of *The Gunfighters* will be unavoidably late. There are two reasons for this: first, the production team have 'had much trouble with scripts, due to rewrites and an uncontactable author'; and, secondly, Newbery has been tied up with work on *The Ark*, due in particular to the unusually extensive special effects requirements of that story.

APRIL 1966

Friday 1: *The Celestial Toymaker: The Dancing Floor* is camera rehearsed and recorded in Riverside 1. The budget is £2,475, the total cost £1,716.

Saturday 2: *The Celestial Toymaker: The Celestial Toyroom* is transmitted on BBC1.

Monday 4: Four days' preliminary rehearsal begins for *The Celestial Toymaker: The Final Test*.
  Gerry Davis rejects two storylines, *The Ocean Liner* and *The Clock*, submitted to the production office by David Ellis, and one, *The Evil Eye*, by Geoffrey Orme.

Tuesday 5: A sound recording session takes place between 1.30 pm and 6.00 pm at Riverside Studios for *The Ballad of the Last Chance Saloon* – a song, written by Tristram Cary and Donald Cotton, which is to be featured throughout all four episodes of *The Gunfighters*. The singer is Lynda Baron and the pianist Tom McCall. The recording goes badly, however, as Baron has difficulty mastering the tune, and it is decided that a further session will be required the following week.

Friday 8: *The Celestial Toymaker: The Final Test* is camera rehearsed and recorded in Riverside 1. The budget is £2,475, the total cost £1,449.

Saturday 9: *The Celestial Toymaker: The Hall of Dolls* is transmitted on BBC1.

Monday 11: Four days' preliminary rehearsal begins for *The Gunfighters: A Holiday for the Doctor*. Rehearsals for this story take place in the Drill Hall at 58 Bulwer Street.

Tuesday 12: A further sound recording session takes place between 7.00 pm and 11.00 pm at Riverside Studios to finish work on *The Ballad of the Last Chance Saloon*.

Friday 15: *The Gunfighters: A Holiday for the Doctor* is camera rehearsed and recorded in TC4. The budget is £3,205, the total cost £4,065.

Saturday 16: *The Celestial Toymaker: The Dancing Floor* is transmitted on BBC1.

Monday 18: Four days' preliminary rehearsal begins for *The Gunfighters: Don't Shoot the Pianist.*

Friday 22: *The Gunfighters: Don't Shoot the Pianist* is camera rehearsed and recorded in Riverside 1. The budget is £2,575, the total cost £2,142. Rehearsal is delayed by the late arrival of the prop guns required for the action.

Saturday 23: *The Celestial Toymaker: The Final Test* is transmitted on BBC1.

Monday 25: Four days' preliminary rehearsal begins for *The Gunfighters: Johnny Ringo*.
Michael Ferguson, the director assigned to handle *The War Machines*, visits Theatre 3 at Lime Grove Studios from 10.30 am to 11.30 am to view a film entitled *Machines Like Men*, which he hopes may provide some inspiration for his realisation of the story.

It has by this point been decided that Dodo will be written out of the series in the second episode of *The War Machines*, Innes Lloyd and Gerry Davis having concluded that a younger and more sophisticated female companion is required. *The War Machines* will therefore introduce two new companions, whom the production team have decided to call Ben (replacing the character Rich in writer Ian Stuart Black's original storyline) and Polly.

The latest version of *Doctor Who*'s format document, sent out to prospective writers to explain the background and approach to the stories, describes the newcomers as follows:

> *General notes about Ben and Polly:*
> They must have a *positive* and *active role to play in any story*. (From a production practicability point-of-view – they should be written *to share quite a proportion of the stories with the Doctor* – this is so that the load isn't so great!)
>
> They are not merely *the Doctor's acolytes but thinking human beings from this age, capable of individual thought and action*. They do not always agree with one another or with the Doctor – they are people with all the *strengths and frailties – inhibitions and forms of expression of which individuals are capable*. They are thrown together with the Doctor – Ben as a reluctant traveller, who feels that he has been Shanghaid into the TARDIS and *always trying to get back to the present day and the Navy,* Polly, also reluctant, but *enjoys the excitement of the unpredictable* travel although *when very frightened wishes herself back in the security of her friends and London.* NEITHER OF THEM MUST EVER LOSE A SENSE OF AWE AND AMAZEMENT AT THE FORM OF TRAVEL THEY FIND THEMSELVES UNDERTAKING. e.g. *They are real people transported into real situations in incredible adventures in Space and Time.* They are ordinary people, with whom we sympathise, to whom extraordinary things happy.

As a general rule, Polly should find herself in dangerous situations from which either Ben or the Doctor, or both, rescue her. *She is our damsel in distress.*

BEN:
24, Able Seaman (Radar), Cockney. Father, now dead, was wartime sailor and peacetime dock-crane driver. Mother married again to unsympathetic step-father. Ben trained at sea school from age of 15, having previously stowed away on cargo ship for adventure to get away from unhappy home. He enjoys the Navy and all it has to offer. Enjoys all sport, especially boxing and athletics – interested in all things mechanical and electrical and in true Navy fashion can turn his hand to most things, including basic cooking and sewing.

Temperament:
A realist, down to Earth, solid, capable and cautious. Inclined, on occasions, to be shy. He is slow to anger but somewhat thin skinned about his Cockney accent. (He thinks, mistakenly, that Polly looks down on him because of this.) He is also sensitive to Naval allusions made in fun – such as 'What ho, my Hearties' – 'Shiver me timbers' etc. He is intensely loyal and will risk anything for his two companions but won't take any nonsense from either.

Attitudes:
Wants to get back to his ship in Navy and resents Doctor Shanghai-ing him in the TARDIS – also resentful of Polly for getting him into TARDIS in the first place. Apart from this he respects Doctor but thinks him impractical – i.e. the way he cannot predict where the TARDIS is going in Time and Space. Rises to Polly's jokes about the Navy and the Doctor's cracks about his 'quaint accent.'

POLLY:
21, Private Secretary to scientist. Father, country doctor in Devon, four brothers (one older – three younger). Happy and conventional middle class background, she has never been tied to her mother's apron strings – they never know when to expect her home but when she arrives they are happy to see her. Has been, in turn, a travel courier, done a small amount of modelling (which she found irksome to her intelligence and feet) and when we meet her she is secretary to chief scientist on computer programme. She lives in a self-contained Gloucester Road flat.

She loves sports cars, watching motor racing, ski-ing, clothes, swimming – pet hates: pomposity, deb's delights, conforming and officials (police to ticket collectors). She is always ready to lose herself in a new pursuit – if it offers excitement.

Temperament:

Intelligent, imaginative, impulsive, inclined to act first, think later. Gets terribly frightened by unimportant things but is stoic about larger dangers. Sometimes forgetful and unpredictable. She is a sucker for lame ducks. Her warm-hearted sympathy for the under-dog, coupled with her impulsiveness, sometimes lands her and her companions in trouble. She is totally undomesticated – cannot sew, knit or cook.

Attitudes:

Has sisterly affection for Ben, though relies on him when they are in a tight spot. Teases him about the Navy. Resents Ben's domestic practicability. The Doctor represents a father figure but irritates her at times when he is being pompous or mysterious. She is also inclined to tease him as well.

A number of actresses have attended auditions for the role of Polly, at which they have been required to read the following speech:

(SENTENCES IN CAPS SPOKEN TO PERSON IN ROOM)

POLLY: (INTO PHONE) Hello, yes right I'll hold on. (TO FRIEND IN ROOM) A LONG DISTANCE CALL – DUNDEE. NO HAVEN'T THE FOGGIEST. WHO LIVES IN DUNDEE ANYWAY? (TO PHONE) Oh, yes. (TO ROOM) HE'S COMING ON NOW!

Who's that? Doctor? Doctor, who? I didn't catch your last name, oh, I see. (TO ROOM) I WASN'T MEANT TO. (MAKES A FACE) Look are you sure you haven't got the wrong number of something?

Yes, my name is Polly Wright. But?... Oh, I see, a friend of my uncle's. But which uncle? Charles? Haven't seen him for ages – don't think he quite approves of me.

What! He's been kidnapped! You're joking! Who'd want to kidnap Uncle Charles? Oh I see!

(HAND ON PHONE – TO ROOM) HE SAYS THAT UNCLE CHARLES HAS BEEN KIDNAPPED BY DALEKS OR SOMETHING. HE MUST BE A NUT OF SOME KIND

Look, I think you'd better tell the police hadn't you, I mean ... Oh!

(TO ROOM) HE SAYS I'M HIS ONLY HOPE

I'm very flattered Doctor whatever your name is but ... Oh. He's in danger. You don't know Uncle Charles. They're in danger not him. He'll bore them to death. What's that? I'm in danger as well. Oh now, a joke's a joke but this ... (TO ROOM) HE SOUNDS QUITE SINCERE ABOUT IT

But who is threatening me? – What! But he's right here I (BACKING AWAY PHONE IN HAND) ROGER DON'T FOOL AROUND WITH

THAT KNIFE. STAY WHERE YOU ARE …

On the basis of these auditions, the role of Polly is this month awarded to Anneke Wills, who began her acting career in 1954 at the age of eleven and has since appeared in several films and numerous TV plays and series. She came to the production team's attention earlier in the year when her husband, actor Michael Gough, portrayed the Celestial Toymaker. Michael Craze, who began acting as a boy soprano in the fifties and has since won a number of TV parts, is cast as Ben. Contracts have been agreed under which Wills is to receive £68 5s 00d per episode and Craze £52 10s 00d per episode. (William Hartnell is by this point receiving £315 per episode.)

Wednesday 27: Two day's shooting of film inserts for *The Savages* begins at Ealing.

Friday 29: *The Gunfighters: Johnny Ringo* is camera rehearsed and recorded in Riverside 1. The budget is £2,575, the total cost £2,196.

Saturday 30: *The Gunfighters: A Holiday for the Doctor* is transmitted on BBC1.

MAY 1966

Sunday 1: Rex Tucker carries out one day of location filming at Virginia Water for a scene in episode four of *The Gunfighters* where a fur-clad Savage is seen on the TARDIS scanner screen. The Savage is played by walk-on John Raven.

Monday 2: Four days' preliminary rehearsal begins for *The Gunfighters: The OK Corral*.

Friday 6: *The Gunfighters: The OK Corral* is camera rehearsed and recorded in Riverside 1. The budget is £2,575, the total cost £2,012. Rehearsal is again delayed by the late arrival of prop guns, causing vociferous complaints from members of the cast required to use them.

Saturday 7: *The Gunfighters: Don't Shoot the Pianist* is transmitted on BBC1.

Monday 9: Four days' preliminary rehearsal begins for *The Savages* episode one.

Friday 13: *The Savages* episode one is camera rehearsed and recorded in Riverside 1. The budget is £3,205, the total cost £4,542.

Saturday 14: *The Gunfighters: Johnny Ringo* is transmitted on BBC1.

Monday 16: Four days' preliminary rehearsal begins for *The Savages* episode two.

Friday 20: *The Savages* episode two is camera rehearsed and recorded in Riverside 1. The budget is £2,575, the total cost £2,806.

Saturday 21: *The Gunfighters: The OK Corral* is transmitted on BBC1.

Sunday 22: Location filming for *The War Machines* takes place between 10.00 am and 5.00 pm in Berners Mews, Newman Passage, Fitzroy Square, Charlotte Place and Bedford Square, all in the vicinity of the GPO Tower in central London. A prop police box is set up in Bedford Square for scenes of the TARDIS arriving at the beginning of the story and leaving again at the end. The GPO have refused permission for filming to take place from the Tower itself – this is the first weekend after the public opening of the Tower and they are concerned that there would be too much disruption – so panoramic high angle shots of the area are taken instead from the Centre Point building on Tottenham Court Road and the Duke of York pub in Charlotte Place.

Monday 23: Four days' preliminary rehearsal begins for *The Savages* episode three.

Three days' shooting of film inserts for *The War Machines* begins at Ealing. The first two days are spent on Stage 3A/B, filming scenes of a warehouse where the War Machines are constructed. Wednesday 25 May sees the crew moving outside onto the studio lot for scenes of army troops storming the warehouse.

Thursday 26: A second day of location filming takes place for *The War Machines*, this time in the Covent Garden and Kensington areas, including Cornwall Gardens. Some high-angle shots are taken from a house at 50F Cornwall Gardens.

Friday 27: *The Savages* episode three is camera rehearsed and recorded in Riverside 1. The budget is £2,575, the total cost £2,252. Also recorded today are the first eight scenes of episode four, which involve smoke effects.

Saturday 28: *The Savages* episode one is transmitted on BBC1.

Monday 30: Four days' preliminary rehearsal begins for *The Savages* episode four.

JUNE 1966

Friday 3: *The Savages* episode four is camera rehearsed and recorded in Riverside 1. The budget is £2,575, the total cost £1,931.

Saturday 4: *The Savages* episode two is transmitted on BBC1.

Monday 6: Four days' preliminary rehearsal begins for *The War Machines* episode one. Rehearsals for this story take place in the Drill Hall at 58 Bulwer Street.

Friday 10: *The War Machines* episode one is camera rehearsed and recorded in Riverside 1. The budget is £3,205, the total cost £5,098.

Saturday 11: *The Savages* episode three is transmitted on BBC1.

Monday 13: Four days' preliminary rehearsal begins for *The War Machines* episode two.

Wednesday 15: Gerry Davis rejects the following storylines: *The Nazis* by Brian Hayles,

The People Who Couldn't Remember by David Ellis and *The Herdsmen of Aquarius* by Donald Cotton.

Friday 17: *The War Machines* episode two is camera rehearsed and recorded in Riverside 1. The budget is £2,575, the total cost £2,355.

Saturday 18: *The Savages* episode four is transmitted on BBC1.

Sunday 19: Five days' location shooting for *The Smugglers* begins in Cornwall. The regular cast are needed only for the first day. They then return to London to continue work on *The War Machines*.

Monday 20: Four days' preliminary rehearsal begins for *The War Machines* episode three. Innes Lloyd sends Jackie Lane a letter following her departure from the series:

> I'd like to thank you for all the hard work that you have put in since you have been playing Dodo. I am very sorry that because of the background etc., you were a victim of circumstance. Anyhow, let's hope that your time with us has not been wasted, and that from it you may receive a tempting offer.
>
> Should you want any photographs or anything, please do not hesitate to contact us; do come in and see us when you can.

Thursday 23: Michael Craze and Anneke Wills are presented to the press at a photocall beginning at 2.30 pm in Television Centre.

Friday 24: *The War Machines* episode three is camera rehearsed and recorded in Riverside 1. The budget is £2,575, the total cost £2,069.

Innes Lloyd sends Gerry Davis a memo confirming that William Hartnell will be unable to appear in episode three of Serial HH (yet to be commissioned), which is due to be recorded on Saturday 11 February 1967.

By this point, however, moves are afoot to write Hartnell out of the series altogether and replace him with another actor. Hartnell has been finding his role as the Doctor increasingly taxing and has now become extremely difficult to work with. Lloyd has decided that a change would be good both for the series and for Hartnell himself, and has won agreement to this from his superiors. He is already in discussion with well-known character actor Patrick Troughton to establish if he would be willing to take over from Hartnell. Other actors previously considered for the role of the second Doctor have included Michael Hordern and Patrick Wymark.

Saturday 25: *The War Machines* episode one is transmitted on BBC1.

Monday 27: Four days' preliminary rehearsal begins for *The War Machines* episode four.

Wednesday 29: Michael Craze carries out a sound recording for *The War Machines* episode four at Lime Grove R.

JULY 1966

Friday 1: *The War Machines* episode four is camera rehearsed and recorded in Riverside 1. The budget is £2,575, the total cost £2,090.

Saturday 2: *The War Machines* episode two is transmitted on BBC1.

Monday 4: Four days' preliminary rehearsal begins for *The Smugglers* episode one.

Friday 8: *The Smugglers* episode one is camera rehearsed and recorded in Riverside 1. The budget is £3,213, the total cost £4,261.

Saturday 9: *The War Machines* episode three is transmitted on BBC1.

Monday 11: Four days' preliminary rehearsal begins for *The Smugglers* episode two.

Friday 15: *The Smugglers* episode two is camera rehearsed and recorded in Riverside 1. The budget is £2,580, the total cost £2,299.

Saturday 16: *The War Machines* episode four is transmitted on BBC1. William Hartnell – having as usual returned for the weekend to his family home at Old Mill Cottage, Old Mill Lane, Mayfield, Sussex from his weekday digs at 98 Haven Lane, Ealing – tells his wife Heather than he has agreed to give up the role of the Doctor and that his final appearance will be in October. This will be in a story entitled *The Tenth Planet*, written by Kit Pedler with story editor Gerry Davis, which will be the first of the series' fourth production block.

Monday 18: Four days' preliminary rehearsal begins for *The Smugglers* episode three.

Friday 22: *The Smugglers* episode three is camera rehearsed and recorded in Riverside 1. The budget is £2,580, the total cost £1,552.

Monday 25: Four days' preliminary rehearsal begins for *The Smugglers* episode four.

Friday 29: *The Smugglers* episode four is camera rehearsed and recorded in Riverside 1. The budget is £2,580, the total cost £2,369. This brings to an end the recording of *Doctor Who*'s third production block.

AUGUST 1966

Monday 22: Director Derek Martinus sends the scripts for *The Tenth Planet* to William Hartnell, who is currently on holiday in Cornwall:

> We've done quite a lot of work on these and I think the end result moves along at a real pace and has a lot of action. We've got a very good supporting cast for you headed by Bob Beatty as General Cutler. It would be very useful indeed if we could have a read through of all four episodes on the first

Tuesday morning so that any inconsistencies can be ironed out and the new people get a perspective on the development of their characters. If we do this, it shouldn't be necessary for you to come in until after lunch on succeeding Tuesdays. I know you'll want to come up from the country, so can we say 10.45 for the first Tuesday morning (13 September)?

I hope you are having a wonderful rest in Cornwall, I very much look forward to working with you once more.

Rehearsals for this story are to start on the Tuesday of each week rather than, as in the past, on the Monday due to the fact that *Doctor Who*'s regular studio recording day has now been changed from Friday to Saturday, and the rest of the schedule has had to be adjusted accordingly.

Wednesday 24: Martinus holds a planning meeting for *The Tenth Planet*.

Hartnell replies as follows to Martinus's letter of 22 August:

The script arrived safely, thank you indeed.

I am extremely glad to hear that we have Bob Beatty with us, a good actor and an extremely pleasant fellow.

Forgive the repetition. We know each other well.

One important factor to me, at this boy's club, there are two ping-pong tables in the outer room where I would like to sit and compose my thoughts, therefore, I would ask you to forbid the rest of the cast playing at these tables during our working hours.

I find it most distracting trying to concentrate.

It will be my last four weeks with, or as, Dr 'Who', then I turn to pastures new.

My wife and I are certainly enjoying the rest together with beautiful surroundings and perfect peace.

Tell Innes, the fishing is superb.

Finally, let me add my thanks to you for the considerate after lunch calls, so much easier at that awkward place.

My affection and regards to all those concerned.

Tuesday 30: Four days' shooting of film inserts for *The Tenth Planet* begins on Stage 3A/B at Ealing. The first day is devoted to model shots.

SEPTEMBER 1966

Tuesday 6: Martinus sends a further letter to Hartnell's holiday address in Cornwall:

Thank you very much for your nice letter – I am glad you think Bob Beatty is a good idea. I have worked with him myself before in the theatre and, as you say, he is both a very good actor and a very nice chap.

I am still not completely happy with the scripts though we are in the process of making one or two minor changes. However, I shall do my utmost to let you have a complete corrected set by the end of the week.

You will be glad to know that we have found a much better rehearsal room at St Helen's Hall. I very much look forward to seeing you on Tuesday at 10.45 am.

Saturday 10: *The Smugglers* episode one is transmitted on BBC1.

Tuesday 13: Four days' preliminary rehearsal begins for *The Tenth Planet* episode one at St Helen's Hall, St. Helen's Gardens, London W10.

Saturday 17: *The Smugglers* episode two is transmitted on BBC1.
The Tenth Planet episode one is camera rehearsed and recorded in Riverside 1. The budget is £3,215, the total cost £4,835.

Tuesday 20: Four days' preliminary rehearsal begins for *The Tenth Planet* episode two.

Saturday 24: *The Smugglers* episode three is transmitted on BBC1.
The Tenth Planet episode two is camera rehearsed and recorded in Riverside 1. The budget is £2,585, the total cost £2,355.

Tuesday 27: Four days' preliminary rehearsal begins for *The Tenth Planet* episode three. William Hartnell fails to arrive, informing the production team that he is ill. Story editor Gerry Davis rewrites the script so that the Doctor is unconscious for the entire episode and seen only briefly from behind, played by a double, Gordon Craig.
Thursday 29: Derek Martinus sends Hartnell the following letter:

> Very sorry to hear you are so poorly, but please don't worry about the show. Gerry has been very clever and managed to write around you.
>
> Everybody sends their warmest regards and we all hope you will be fit to do battle on the last one.

OCTOBER 1966

Saturday 1: *The Smugglers* episode four is transmitted on BBC1.
The Tenth Planet episode three is camera rehearsed and recorded in Riverside 1. The budget is £2,585, the total cost £2,171.

Tuesday 4: Four days' preliminary rehearsal begins for *The Tenth Planet* episode four.

Saturday 8: *The Tenth Planet* episode one is transmitted on BBC1.
The Tenth Planet episode four is camera rehearsed and recorded in Riverside 1. The budget is £2,585, the total cost £2,453. The transformation from William Hartnell to Patrick Troughton is recorded first, from 6.30 pm to 7.00 pm, having earlier been rehearsed for an hour. Following the dinner break from 7.00 pm to 8.00 pm, the remainder of the episode is then recorded between 8.30 pm and 10.00 pm. Recording

slightly overruns its allotted time as Anneke Wills, Michael Craze and Gregg Palmer (playing a Cyberman) are required to do a retake of one scene in which technical problems occurred. This takes place between 10.00 pm and 10.15 pm.

After completion of the recording, the principal cast and members of the production team attend a farewell party for William Hartnell at Innes Lloyd's flat. Lloyd later drives Hartnell home.

Tuesday 11: Video editing is carried out between 7.30 pm and 10.30 pm on episode four of *The Tenth Planet*, bringing to an end the production of the first Doctor's era.

In the months between July and October 1966, following Patrick Troughton's agreement to take over from William Hartnell, the production team carried out a considerable amount of work on formulating the new Doctor's character and commissioning and developing scripts for the remainder of the fourth production block.

The Tenth Planet episode two was transmitted on BBC1 on 15 October 1966, episode three on 22 October 1966 and episode four on 29 October 1966, concluding the first Doctor's era on screen.

FROM SCRIPT TO SCREEN: THE ARK

Introduction

To try to analyse comprehensively the development of a *Doctor Who* adventure is not an easy matter. A television production is the result of many months' work by a large number of people, and what is ultimately seen on screen may have been affected and influenced in greater or lesser degrees by all of them.

Unless one is afforded a fly's eye view of every meeting and every aspect of the creative process, then any attempt to try to dissect the production is limited by the memories and personalities of those people to whom one speaks.

Bearing all this in mind, this chapter presents an in-depth look at just one of the first Doctor's stories. In doing so it reveals the process of making *Doctor Who* at this point in the series' history and – a factor common to every story – some of the behind-the-scenes discussions and thought which go into a production.

The production chosen for this case study is *The Ark*, a story transmitted mid-way through the third season in 1966.

The Ark was made during a period of transition for *Doctor Who*. Producer John Wiles and story editor Donald Tosh were both on the point of leaving the series, and their respective successors Innes Lloyd and Gerry Davis had yet to take over full responsibility from them. Consequently, Wiles, Tosh, Lloyd and Davis were all left with very few memories of this particular production. The story's writer, Paul Erickson, died in 1991, and as far as we know, never gave an in-depth interview about his work on it. For our view of the production we have therefore turned primarily to director Michael Imison – giving his first ever *Doctor Who* interview – and to designer Barry Newbery, who recall, scene by scene, the work that went into it. We have however incorporated a few comments from other participants, including some recollections from Paul Erickson taken from on-stage interviews given at two *Doctor Who* conventions in the eighties.

The Scripts

Every *Doctor Who* adventure that appears on screen starts life as an idea. This idea may be in the mind of a writer, it may come from the producer or the script editor, or, as is more often the case, it may develop out of a discussion between two or more of these people.

Once the initial contact has been made, a story outline or synopsis will generally be commissioned from the writer. Assuming that all is well when that is delivered, one or more of the actual scripts themselves will then be commissioned. Depending on the status of the writer, these stages may be compacted or expanded accordingly. In the case of *The Ark*, the idea of setting a story on board a giant travelling spaceship was one that the producer, John Wiles, was keen to develop. 'I loved the idea of the Ark,' Wiles remembers. 'It's always been one of my joys to imagine the world as a giant spaceship travelling on and on and on.' Wiles discussed this idea with story editor Donald Tosh who contacted Paul Erickson to see if he would be interested in submitting a story outline based on the concept. Tosh and Erickson then worked on the story outline together to develop the idea into final scripts.

Erickson was formally commissioned to write *The Ark* on 27 May 1965, at which time the story was assigned serial code 'Y'. Erickson was required to deliver the scripts for the first two episodes on 1 September 1965 and for the final two on 1 November 1965, for a production date of 5 March 1966. Erickson was paid through his agents a fee of £250 per episode.

There seems to have been a degree of wariness on the part of Erickson and his agents over the precise terms of the agreement to provide the scripts. Their concern revolved around whether or not there would be any fee payable if the scripts were ultimately rejected by the BBC. On 9 June, Erickson's agents arranged for a revised schedule of delivery dates, together with an assurance from Donald Tosh that he would advise promptly of the acceptance/non-acceptance of each script as it was delivered. The necessity for this assurance was that Erickson did not wish to work on any further episodes unless he was happy that they would be accepted. The revised delivery dates made provision for this. Episode one was now due on 18 August, episode two on 1 September, episode three on 30 September and episode four on 1 November.

Meanwhile, plans for the season as a whole were shaping up, and the extension of *The Daleks' Master Plan* from a six-parter to a twelve-parter meant that one story was effectively lost from the production order. Therefore, on 4 June 1965, *The Ark* was assigned the new serial code 'X'.

Erickson signed his writer's contracts on 14 June 1965 and subsequently delivered his draft scripts for episodes one and two on 7 September. John Wiles and Donald Tosh then discussed them with him, and the latter requested that he make some revisions. The revised versions of these first two episodes, together with the first drafts of episodes three and four, were all delivered on 18 November.

On 4 January 1966, Tosh accepted the scripts and authorised the full payment of all the moneys due to Erickson.

On 20 January 1966, Erickson's agent then contacted Tosh to ask that the final writer's credit be shared between Erickson and a woman named Lesley Scott, although he accepted that no further money would be due as a result. Up to this point, Erickson's had been the sole name on all documentation pertaining to the writing of the story. When asked about this in later years, Erickson replied that Scott – who was in fact his wife at the time – made no contribution whatsoever to the scripts. 'It was a personal arrangement I had with her,' he explained, 'which was my own personal business at the time. The circumstances went into history. I need say no more than that.'

The scripts for the first two episodes had a number of amendments made to them by Donald Tosh, and further input into all four episodes was made by the director, Michael Imison.

'I was brought in and given the scripts,' recalls Imison. 'Then I worked with the scriptwriters on them.'

Imison was not particularly impressed with the scripts at first. 'I didn't think they were wonderful! The Monoids were my idea. I can't remember what they were called originally. They were fairly indefinite creatures, but I had this idea, which I thought was brilliant, of having actors with ping pong balls in their mouths so that they could play these one-eyed creatures that would appear to have a living eye. I thought this would be a great thing for BBC Enterprises to market, but of course it was a total damp squib! I don't remember what else I got them to change. Having worked quite a lot as a script editor, I was quite happy to get people to rewrite.'

Pre-production

Michael Imison was a director new to *Doctor Who*, who had started his career at the BBC working for the Script Department.

'I applied for a general trainee scheme, which took half a dozen people straight from university and circulated them around the BBC with the idea of training top administrators. I thought that I would possibly be an administrator because my university experience, on the whole, though I'd done some directing, was as a student administrator. I didn't get the job, but I think they felt they ought to do something for me, and as I was clearly interested in drama, they sent me to the Drama Department in 1961. They employed me, first of all, as a script editor, and I worked on various plays and programmes under the overall control of Donald Wilson as Head of Script Department and Michael Barry as Head of Drama.

'There was pool of us who, when we weren't working on a particular programme, carried out a sort of general survey of what writing was available. It meant for instance that I could go to the theatre a good deal at the BBC's expense! Which I was very happy to do as the theatre has always been my main love.

'I worked on a programme called *Compact*, which I was script editor of for quite a time, and was getting a bit fed up with this when a directing course became available. After I'd done the course, I started by directing some poetry programmes, which were a sort of summer replacement for the arts programme *Monitor*. Then I became one of the regular directors on *Compact*. From there, I went on to do classic serials, the most important of which was a version of *Buddenbrooks* by Thomas Mann. That was really quite a big undertaking, nine episodes, of which I was rather proud, but at that time the departments were split up and there was a new department head and he didn't like what I'd done on *Buddenbrooks*.'

Buddenbrooks was the third classic serial that Imison had directed, and then out of the blue he was assigned to work on *Doctor Who*, a job he saw as being a kind of penance. 'I thought I'd gone on to bigger things!'

Also assigned to the production was designer Barry Newbery, who had worked on *Doctor Who* since the very beginning, initially alternating on stories with Raymond P Cusick. Newbery had yet to design a science-based story for the series, although he had handled some episodes of *The Daleks' Master Plan*, and *The Ark* was to be his first such *Doctor Who*.

Unfortunately, Newbery does not have very happy memories of working on this story. 'One of the problems was that I didn't feel that the director was happy directing science fiction. Looking at it now, I can see that Michael was into the story and understood it and did a good job. You had so little time designing *Doctor Who* in those days, and you needed a director who was really proactive when it came to the nitty gritty of getting the programme made. When you're working to such a tight deadline, you've got filming and studio work to plan and you give a director an outline that you hope he will understand. You do sketches and plans of the sets for him, and you want to know which he wants to shoot in the studio and which on film. The clock goes round ever so quickly, and you need someone who comes up with the answers you want and need quickly.

'I was usually terribly enthusiastic about my work, and I probably gave myself too much to do in the alotted time. When you've got all the balls in the air and at the same time are trying to get sense from the director, and he is likewise trying to get sense from you and doesn't understand what you're talking about, then you get a terrible feeling of frustration. And I got that with Michael Imison. Mind you, I am talking about my troubles, but he had his troubles too.'

A part of this frustration was no doubt due to the fact that Imison was not happy to have been assigned to *Doctor Who* in the first place, but that he was nevertheless determined to make his mark with the show.

'I think I was deliberately trying to show off,' he admits. 'I can see I had a pretty ambitious camera script, not all of which was achieved! I did feel that one of the things *Doctor Who* should be doing was to have as much science and and as many effects as one could manage. It was very complex, and I think over-ambitious.

'I remember vividly, because of the circumstances, that while I was recording the first episode, the Departmental Organiser, Terry Cook, appeared in the gallery and sat behind me. As a courtesy I said, "We're on page twelve," and indeed we'd been on page twelve for quite a time. "I was beginning to wonder if there was any other page!" he commented. So yes, it was quite complex.'

The Ark was the first full story for Jackie Lane, who played Dodo. Michael Imison remembers having to introduce her, as well as working with William Hartnell and Peter Purves, 'I had quite a lot to do with deciding what she was going to be like. Bill of course was very set in his ways and, as you can see in the finished episodes, was never very certain of his lines, and had to be handled with kid gloves. It was made very clear to me that I had to be very careful with him. Peter was very jolly. I liked him.'

The costumes for the Monoids were designed by BBC costume supervisor Daphne Dare and constructed by freelancers Jack and John Lovell. Dare recalls that the costumes were particularly challenging for the actors who had to wear them: 'The Monoids were a classic example of a monster that came together on the day. You see, we had so little time to practice the make-up and putting things together. The Monoids' Beatle wigs were more or less there to conceal the air holes in their heads. The costumes were very hot and uncomfortable, as they were made from latex and rubber. The actors would always wear cotton T-shirts underneath, which were absorbent, and then would put the costume on only at the last moment before rushing onto the set so that they were less likely to faint or expire!'

The novel aspect of the creatures was, as Michael Imison points out, the fact that they had only one eye. This detail is recalled by Jack Lovell: 'The eye was a ping-pong ball level with the actor's tongue. The actors looked out through holes in the mask, which is maybe why the upper part of the mask was covered with hair to conceal the holes, because I'm certain they were originally never meant to have hair.' John Lovell further recalls that the hair was actually yak hair.

During the sixties, the use of stock rather than specially-composed incidental music was a common practice, and it was one that Imison elected to follow for *The Ark*.

The music chosen was a combination of extracts from Tristram Cary's score for the season one story *The Mutants*, some of which had been reused on *Doctor Who* twice since, and some stock drum music by Robert Farnon (the track was actually called 'Drum-dramatics No. 11'). The latter was used as backing for the Monoid funeral in episode two, and also in episode four.

All the music and the new sound effects – which were provided as usual by Brian Hodgson at the BBC's Radiophonic Workshop – were pre-recorded onto tape and then 'played in' during the actual recording of the episodes in the TV studio. This meant that the cast and crew could hear the music and effects as they performed; and if a re-take was necessary, the tapes would need re-setting accordingly. This is one of the reasons why recording tended to be continuous, as the complexity of fitting together all the elements often precluded a retake if the only thing that was wrong was an actor fluffing a line and then recovering from it.

In Studio

Eventually, the programme went into the studio. By the time of the third season, recording of *Doctor Who* was being split between the facilities at Riverside Studios on the south bank of the Thames at Hammersmith and those at Television Centre in White City. *The Ark* was recorded entirely in Riverside Studio 1, with shooting of film inserts taking place beforehand at the BBC's Television Film Studios in Ealing.

The four episodes of *The Ark* were camera rehearsed and recorded on 18 February, 25 February, 4 March and 11 March 1966 respectively. There was also apparently a single piece of recording completed on 24 January (between the recording of episodes one and two of *The Massacre of St. Bartholomew's Eve*) with actor David Greneau playing a Guardian. It is not known exactly what this extra recording was, or why it was scheduled for a non-recording day rather than for one of the adjacent recording days. It is possible that it was a session with a photographer to take the still required for the shrinking sequence in episode one.

Rehearsals for *The Ark* took place in a Territorial Army Drill Hall at 58 Bulwer Street, London W12. The cast would start rehearsing each episode on a Monday morning with a read-through of the script. This would be followed by initial rehearsals, with full rehearsals taking place from Tuesday to Thursday. Wednesday morning would normally be devoted to a first read-through of the *following* week's episode, so that the story editor would then have time to take it away and, in consultation with the writer, iron out any problems identified.

On the Thursday morning there would be a 'producer's run', for which the producer and story editor would be present and any final adjustments would be made to the script and the performances before the cast and crew moved into the studio on the Friday morning.

During the day on Friday, a final series of rehearsals would take place on the sets (these having been erected overnight), for the benefit not only of the director and his cast but also of the cameramen, lighting and other technical personnel. By about 7.00 pm, all would have to be ready for the episode to be recorded. After an hour's dinner break, the half-hour between 8.00 pm and 8.30 pm would be spent on line up – i.e. making sure that that cast and crew were all in their correct positions and that all technical equipment was ready. The recording itself would then be scheduled to take place between 8.30 pm and 9.45 pm (although in the case of *The Ark* there were a few variations from the norm, as the recording of episodes one and three was scheduled to last from 8.30 pm to 10.00 pm, and that of episode two from 8.15 pm to 9.45 pm, the dinner break in the latter case having taken place between 6.45 pm and 7.45 pm and line-up between 7.45 pm and 8.15 pm.)

Recording had to finish by 10.00 pm if the production was not to go into overtime and incur additional costs. In the case of *The Ark*, this deadline was passed for some of the episodes.

'Producer's runs were very important,' confirms Michael Imison. 'I always liked to have several of them if I could. The problem was that it was all so fast-moving; people had to have the opportunity of remembering where they were supposed to be next. Very often, although there are scene breaks on the screen, we just carried on recording and the cast were rushing round behind the scenes getting ready for their next entrance.'

Typically in the sixties, stories would be recorded in the same scene order as would be seen on transmission. As videotape was very difficult to edit, recording breaks would be scheduled only if absolutely necessary – to allow cast to change costume or make-up for example, or to move from one set to another where this could not be achieved by way of a 'bridging' scene featuring other cast members. These scheduled breaks were kept to a minimum, with an upper limit of five normally permitted in any one episode.

In a complete departure from the normal course of events, however, *The Ark* saw the first use in *Doctor Who* of full out-of-scene-order recording. This was for the final episode of the story, and was required because of the difficulty involved in moving the single full-size space shuttle pod prop from one set to another.

The scenes in the final episode were recorded in the following order:

- The closing TARDIS scenes were recorded first, with the cast in their costumes for the following story, *The Celestial Toymaker*. William Hartnell was on a separate set to allow him to fade from view as the episode ended.

- The closing credits for the episode were then recorded from the caption roller.

- There was then a recording break to allow the regular cast to change into their costumes for *The Ark*.

- Recording continued from the start of the episode up until the first scene in the Refusian castle. Then all later scenes in the castle were recorded together.

- The scenes involving the escape of Steven and the Guardians from the kitchen were then recorded, as were all the scenes on the Ark involving the launcher.

- Next, the launcher prop was moved to the Refusis II set and all the scenes of the launcher on the planet were recorded.

- Finally, the remaining scenes were recorded in order.

Michael Imison also remembers doing storyboards for the episodes, planning out what the shots would look like when recorded and cut together. These storyboards would be used to help the designers and technical personnel to understand what the director was expecting. They were produced prior to the rehearsals, and then amended, if necessary, during the rehearsal process.

To indicate some of the considerations involved in making a *Doctor Who* story during the William Hartnell era, what follows is a scene-by-scene summary of *The Ark*, with comments from Michael Imison and Barry Newbery as appropriate, together with some contributions from Jackie Lane taken from a video interview.

The Steel Sky

A forest floor. A lizard sits motionless. Suddenly, with a raucous cry, a toucan flaps in and alights by the lizard.

Michael Imison: That shot was a failure, I have to say. You can see that it's a lizard. I wanted it to look like a huge monster but the cameraman couldn't find a lens that would do that, or misunderstood what I wanted.

Nearby, a scaly humanoid figure (Eric Blackburn) stands. When the creature turns we see that it has only one eye, which restlessly surveys its surroundings. It moves off through the jungle.

MI: He did manage to move the eye a bit there. One of the problems was that a lot of the Monoids were extras and you're not allowed to give extras specific direction, so I wasn't allowed to get them to do the sort of Monoid-y things that I'd hoped would make it a popular monster.

Barry Newbery: This looks quite a big jungle, doesn't it? It filled more than half of one of the stages at Ealing. At the very back there is a painted cloth. It's from stock, painted with Dylon, and it's been used so often that it's faded. It worked exceedingly well because it gave the impression of a tremendous distance, which doesn't come over too well on the black-and-white recording.

The boles of the trees are constructed scenery. The tops go out of frame. But all the foliage is from real trees. There's a great mixture of plants and trees from England and from elsewhere in the world.

A smoke machine was used in the jungle as well, and dry ice too.

All the greenery was hired from a firm called Greenery who were based at Hampton. They'd supply all the raw materials and we'd put peat and sawdust on the floor, marsh grasses and grass sods around, and then place all the trees and leaves to complete the effect.

The animals were all hired from a specialist firm and then looked after by minders. They'd put them into the shots where we'd need them. I remember one shot where we had the camera mounted on a mole crane and tracked along about sixty foot of camera track, then came down and stopped in close-up on a python moving over some dead tree branches. The sequence must have been dropped because I don't see it in this recording.

Elsewhere in the jungle, the TARDIS arrives. Dodo (Jackie Lane) emerges and promptly sneezes. Steven (Peter Purves) follows her out and berates her for leaving the ship.

MI: I'm trying to remember if I did that high shot with a mirror; shooting up into a mirror and seeing the image reflected. I think I may have done. That was one way to get around using a camera mounted on a very high crane.

Jackie Lane: The black and white tabard costume wasn't my favourite. It wasn't very flattering. The idea was that Dodo was an inquisitive character and they'd got this vast wardrobe in the TARDIS that they could use for wherever they happened to be, and Dodo just picked what she wanted at that particular moment whether she was in the right setting or not.

Dodo thinks that they have arrived at Whipsnade Zoo, just outside London, but she doesn't remember it as being quite so noisy.

MI: The soundtrack of birds was played in live, so the jungle would really have been that noisy!

The Doctor (William Hartnell) emerges from the TARDIS and suggests that Dodo might be right about their landing point. He returns to the TARDIS to continue checking his instruments as an alien reptilian hand pushes aside the greenery by the ship.
In a large control room, a report comes off a machine and is handed by a reptile creature to the Commander (Eric Elliott) who is presiding over a court of judgment.

BN: What's the date of this recording? That's a fax machine!

The Commander pronounces the prisoner (David Greneau) guilty of extreme carelessness in leaving open a valve in a heat exchange unit. This threatened the safety of the ship, and also of the Monoids. He passes a sentence of miniaturisation, to be carried out immediately. The prisoner will be reconstituted in 700 years' time when he will be of no further threat.
The Commander's daughter, Mellium (Kate Newman), pleads for clemency, but the Commander states that the only other option would have been expulsion. The defence counsel Manyak (Roy Spencer) and prosecution Zentos (Inigo Jackson) – on behalf of the Monoids –

accept the sentence, and it is carried out.

MI: There are children present on the Ark because this was meant to be a community travelling for many years through space and we wanted to suggest that.

BN: The costumes were pastel colours, pink and white stripes for the females and blue and white for the males. I think the Commander may have had some red in his costume to designate his rank.

The prisoner is taken to a minifier cabinet and placed inside. He crouches on the floor and suddenly shrinks until he cannot be seen. A tray is removed from the floor of the cabinet, and Zentos, on behalf of the Monoids, thanks the Commander for the care he takes of them all.

BN: That miniaturisation shot was achieved with inlay. The shot of the man had to be lined up with the base of the cabinet, and the base of the cabinet had to be lined up with the bottom of the screen. That was the only way that the effect of him shrinking could be done. In order to make him shrink, the camera pulls back while keeping him central at the bottom of the screen. Then, when that shot is married to the static shot of the cabinet, it looks as though he shrinks within the cabinet while remaining on its floor.

MI: We took a photograph of the actor crouching down and we got a camera on a track to focus on the photograph, and I said 'If you go on a 24 degree lens and tilt up 12 degrees, the photograph will sit on the bottom of the frame, and as you track back it will appear to reduce.' Which it did.

Back in the jungle, Dodo sees an elephant coming towards them. She finds some bananas hanging in a bunch and offers a couple to the elephant. The Doctor recognises the elephant as being from India, which just adds to the strangeness: all the animals here are from different countries.

JL: All the elephant's scenes were done in one day in a film studio. Her name was Monica and she behaved beautifully throughout.

BN: It's not a full-grown elephant, more of a baby really. I think the jungle was something like fifty feet wide. The banana trees are in tubs, with rhododendron-like foliage to hide the containers.

MI: I insisted that we had shots of the cast actually touching the elephant, because I'd gone to the trouble of getting a real animal in rather than using some stock footage. I actually had the elephant in a van outside my flat overnight because he had to be driven down from somewhere in the north of England and the BBC wouldn't give the driver anywhere to park on the premises. The driver fed it and then went off to some hotel and he asked if I could keep an eye on it.

The Doctor's puzzlement is complete when he points out that as well as the mixture of animals, there is no sky, and the ground is trembling slightly.

BN: For the shot when they look up and see the roof, I got a very nice bonsai plant and set it up in front of a scaled-down painting of the roof. With a wide-angle lens on the camera, the bonsai looked like a full sized tree and the effect was quite convincing. However, the shot we see here isn't the one I set up. I've no idea why.

The metal roof was also seen as a painted cloth. I asked the scenic artist to paint it in such a way that it appeared to curve downwards, giving the impression that the Ark was spherical. You see, I had decided – whether rightly or wrongly – that since the ship obviously had artificial gravity it must be spinning like a ball in order to create this. Actually, having since given it some further thought, I now realise that the characters would have had to have been standing on the inner surface of the sphere for this to have worked, so the roof/sky wouldn't have looked like that at all.

The Doctor postulates that they might be in an indoor nature park. Dodo sneezes again and the Doctor berates her for not using a handkerchief. They move off for a last look around. Behind them, a Monoid emerges from the foliage and follows them.

In the main control room, a Monoid arrives and communicates in sign language to Zentos. A group of children are dancing in a ring and another Monoid is driving an electric transporter across the floor. The place is bustling with activity.

MI: This is 'page 12'! There were problems in getting the high angle, and I seem to recall difficulties in steering the vehicle round the sets as well. It's also all one shot from the start of the scene, with the Monoid coming round the corner and the camera pulling back and up.

BN: The trolley was a BBC scenery trolley. They were used to take goods around from stores to where the carpenters and painters were working on the set, and I borrowed one for the show and used some additional dressing to disguise it.

Zentos informs the Commander that the Monoids have located some intruders in the jungle. An image of the Doctor and Steven is displayed on a large screen in the wall of the control room. The Commander asks for the humans to be found and brought to him – not arrested, but invited.

BN: That is a back projection screen. Since the two scenic artists' cloths at the very back of the set are mounted on curves, that meant there was room in the very corner of the studio for a projector and, in another corner, space for the back projection mirror, which was needed to reflect the projected beam because of the shortage of space.

MI: I think the picture on the big screen was provided using inlay, because if it had been back projection, then I would probably have had my camera moving.

Dodo has found some paintings on a rock face in the jungle, which appear to represent zebras with two heads! The Doctor and Steven look at her discovery. An alarm echoes through the jungle and Steven sees that a group of Monoids have found the TARDIS. Dodo points out a cave and the travellers hide inside. When the aliens have gone, they try to get back to the TARDIS and see a huge city or factory in the distance. The Doctor realises that they are on

board a spaceship. Suddenly they are surrounded by Monoids.

BN: That's a bad bit of camera-work! [A shot of Steven has wobbled all over the place]. Now this must be in the studio because if it had been on film, they would have re-shot it.

In order to match footage shot on film with material recorded in electronic studios, you had to have something that linked and matched the shots together, allowing you to cut between them. In the days when this was made, you couldn't cut the film or tape together afterwards. The film sequences, or telecine, were 'run in' live and it took nine seconds for the film to get to the point when you could cut to it, so it had to be planned very carefully, timing the action so that the telecine was actually to speed and playing the required scene to make a successful cut.

This meant that different telecine sequences couldn't have less than nine seconds between them unless you had two telecine machines. Then it got very complicated and time consuming.

Steven has been taken to the main control room, where he tries to explain how he and his fellow travellers arrived. The Commander disbelieves his story about time travel. He explains to Steven that the spaceship is travelling to the planet Refusis II as the Earth is dying. The Doctor and Dodo arrive and assure the Commander that they are human, and not Refusian spies as Zentos suspects.

The Doctor has been telling of some of his recent travels, all of which occurred, according to the Commander, in the first segment of time. They are now in the fifty-seventh segment, which the Doctor estimates to be at least ten million years since their last adventure.

The Commander informs them that they will arrive on Refusis in 700 years time. None of them will live to see the new world – that is a privilege reserved for their children's children.

BN: All those control consoles and equipment are built onto stock rostra. The columns were from stock with bits stuck on them. All the equipment is made. I put small pea-lights in the control panels, which didn't do anything except light up and look good. Other parts of this set were made from moulded PVC, which to me at the time was a brand new material and technique.

The Commander explains that the entire population of the Earth is held on the ship in a miniaturised form.

BN: It would have been far too expensive to have built a separate set for the shot of the cabinets containing the miniaturised humans, so I improvised. I used a couple of filing cabinets and two mirrors set up at angles to one another to give multiple reflections. The miniaturised humans were just painted cut-outs, made by a freelance designer called Peter Pegrum, who went on to manage the BBC's Visual Effects Department. However, these miniatures were not seen on screen and nor was a shot of a Monoid removing a tray. I don't know why, as I know it was recorded.

The Commander asks Mellium to show Steven and Dodo the spaceship's statue while the Doctor remains with their chief controller, Manyak, to talk about the ship itself. The statue is gigantic and is intended to be a human holding a globe. It is being constructed by hand from a material called gregarian rock, which will last forever.

BN: That platform upon which Dodo climbs to get a closer look at the feet of the statue is supposed to look as though it is hydraulic. There are nine sections and they were supposed to lift to about 2' 6" apart, giving a total lift of 22' 6". Despite that, Dodo has to get onto the hydraulic lift using a rather futuristic looking stepladder!

The feet of the statue went up about another three or four inches and were made from expanded polystyrene (jablite), which has been carved into shape.

An alarm sounds and the launching bay doors open.

BN: The door's on a hoist. All the scenery beyond the door is painted, all the landing shuttles and everything. There's no room round there, none at all.

A Monoid drives in, with another Monoid lying on the bed of the truck. A strange fever is spreading among the Monoids. The Commander suddenly collapses with the same fever, which Zentos proclaims to be a disease brought by the humans. Dodo asserts that it's just a cold. The Doctor points out to Steven that these people have no resistance to the cold virus and it might be fatal to them. The sick Monoid dies and Zentos has the strangers seized. He says that the strangers must be made to suffer for the crime they have committed. If they all now die, then it was pointless leaving the Earth in the first place.

On the monitor screen, the Earth is seen spinning past.

MI: That was a model of the Earth on a wire, I think. That is back projection this time.

End of *The Steel Sky*

The Plague

MI: Because each episode was recorded separately from the others, the reprise from the end of the previous episode was often re-recorded the following week. Therefore the camera shots and actions sometimes differ.

The Doctor, Steven and Dodo are placed in a cell. Dodo is feeling better but the Doctor is frustrated – if only the Guardians would release them, they might be able to help.

BN: This is a very simple set; a bench seat at the back. That's a good join between the two pieces of scenery making up the cell walls in the corner!

There was a firm, I think it was called Woollens, who stocked a lot of very modern and expensive furniture, and I would have gone to a place like that to choose the props. They also had some of the latest designs from Italy.

Back in the main control room, another Monoid death is reported. The Guardians watch on a monitor screen mounted in the control console as more Monoids collapse. No humans have

died yet, but nothing their microbiologists try seems to work against the virus.

BN: I would have asked the Technical Operations Manager on the show for a rack of eight or ten small monitors. He would have supplied me with their measurements so that I could ensure that the set was constructed to fit them.

MI: To get the effect of going from seeing the Monoid and the TARDIS on the monitor, to the same shot full on the screen, we simply ran the film, showed it on the monitor on the console, and then mixed to the film. It was quite a simple effect to achieve; it was just like going to another camera.

The Commander is in a sick bay being tended to by Mellium and a doctor, Rhos (Michael Sheard). Rhos explains that the data for this type of fever were lost in the primal wars of the tenth segment. The Commander gets Mellium to promise that if anything should happen to him, she make every effort to reach Refusis.

BN: That set was constructed from dark brown lathes against a cyclorama cloth round the back, illuminated so all you see are the lathes against the light.

Solemn drum beats ring out as four Monoids carry the shrouded body of one of their dead through the control room. They place it on a transporter and it is driven to the launching bay by a fifth Monoid. A hatch in the side of the space ship opens and the body is consigned to a space burial.

Zentos calls for a trial of the strangers before the illness gets too bad. Baccu (Ian Frost) will put the charges. Mellium and Manyak offer to defend the travellers.

Steven goes to speak at the trial, leaving the Doctor and Dodo in the cell watching on a monitor. As the trial progresses, Steven gets weaker. He tells the Guardians that the Doctor could help them if they would let him. Manyak argues that this is a reasonable approach. Baccu arrives with the news that a Guardian has died from the fever – the first Guardian to die. Two of the assembled Guardians (Paul Greenhalgh and Stephanie Heesom) call for the death of the prisoners, and this is picked up as a general cry. Zentos therefore condemns them to be cast from the ship by the Monoids. As the sentence is read, Steven collapses from the fever himself.

The Doctor argues that as one of his party has the fever, then they are as much victims as the Monoids and Guardians. The Commander recovers sufficiently to send an order from his sick bed that the travellers are to be released and allowed to try to find a cure, using Steven as a guinea-pig. After Dodo and Baccu have fetched some equipment from the TARDIS, the Doctor develops an antidote from natural animal membranes collected from two of the ship's specimens. Steven is treated, but rather than wait for the results, the Doctor goes ahead and treats everyone else as well.

The treatment works after about an hour, and Steven starts to recover.

As the Doctor and Dodo give Zentos and the other assembled Guardians the good news, the scanner shows the Earth boiling away as it spins through space.

BN: I didn't provide that effect. I suspect they went to Jack Kine at the Visual Effects Department for that.

MI: That shot was done on film at Ealing, but I don't recall how they got the smoke to come out.

The Doctor says his goodbyes to the Guardians, and a Monoid takes them back to the TARDIS on a transporter.

BN: That transporter is so noisy. I couldn't overcome the noise!

The TARDIS dematerialises, but moments later re-appears in what seems to be a slightly different part of the forest. The Doctor, Steven and Dodo emerge, puzzled at the fact that they appear to be in the same place.

BN: You see that tree there, the slanting one behind the TARDIS, that's made from fibreglass. It was built for Paul Bernard, another designer at that time when *Doctor Who* began. I had used it before in part three of *100,000 BC*.
They head for the control room, and Dodo notices that the statue has been completed – but it has the head of a Monoid and not of a human.

BN: That's a model with a good painting of the roof behind it. John Friedlander built the model.

MI: I had that model for a long time. It was about two feet high but it got thrown out eventually.

End of *The Plague*

The Return

The Doctor notes that 700 years must have passed as the statue is complete, and Steven deduces, by looking at a navigation chart displayed on the main screen in the control room, that the spaceship must be almost at Refusis II.

BN: The navigation chart is provided by back projection. If you wanted to use back projection, you had to book it in advance, as its availability was limited. Nowadays, you'd have to pay for it out of your programme budget, and you would have to work out whether you could afford it, but back then it was a 'below the line' cost.

The Doctor uses the monitor screens on the console to look at other parts of the ship.

BN: Those small monitor screens were just transparencies with lights behind them to give the effect.

The pictures appear on the large monitor as well, and the Doctor, Steven and Dodo watch as a Guardian, Maharis (Terence Woodfield), serves a drink to what appears to be a Monoid sitting in a high-backed chair.

BN: That's a BBC tea trolley there at the side of the Monoid's room!

Another image is of the kitchen where the Guardians are working. One of them accidentally knocks a pot to the ground and a scaly hand holding a gun is seen. The gun fires and the Guardian collapses to the ground.

MI: I cast all the smaller parts; that woman there [playing Venussa] was someone I had a personal connection with. She is Eileen Helsby, and her sister was my BBC secretary, Thelma Helsby.

The Doctor notes that the Monoids appear to have become overlords. His theorising is interrupted by the arrival of a group of Monoids and Guardians. One of the Monoids (Ralph Carrigan) – who wears a collar marked with the number two – demands to know who the travellers are, and Dodo notes that the creatures can now speak.

MI: The voices were created live in the studio using a similar process to that used on the Daleks. Obviously the voices were not spoken by the actors playing the Monoids as they had ping-pong balls in their mouths! There would have been a speaker on the studio floor so that the actors could hear the voices as well. The Monoid voices were all provided by Roy Skelton and John Halstead.

Monoid Two explains that his race are the masters, following a recent revolution. The Guardians work for the Monoids. Yendom (Terence Bayler), a subject Guardian, privileged to serve the Monoids directly, agrees with the Monoid's observation. Monoid Two takes the Doctor and his friends to see their leader, Monoid One.

MI: Terence Bayler was an actor I'd used before on other productions.

When they arrive, Monoid One (Edmund Coulter) views a recording of the travellers' earlier departure in the TARDIS.

MI: That is a film clip from the end of part two.

BN: I vaguely remember the chair that Monoid One is sitting in. I seem to recall slipping a false back over its existing back. I might even have had the chair made.

Monoid One has checked the ship's history scans and knows of the Doctor's previous visit, and of the illness. It transpires that a mutation of the fever sapped the will of the humans and allowed the Monoids to take over. Monoid One orders Monoid Two to take the travellers to the security kitchen.
In the kitchen, Dassuk (Brian Wright) and Venussa (Eileen Helsby) are discussing the new arrivals.

MI: I'd totally forgotten I'd cast Brian Wright as Dassuk. He was at Oxford with me, and I had used him in *Compact* and in one of the classic serials. He went on to write a series of very funny radio broadcasts called *The Penge Papers*.

The strangers are brought in to help with producing food for the Monoids. The Guardians also know the legend of the Doctor's previous visit, and are amazed that his party can travel in time.

BN: There's an upside-down telephone kiosk cover on the wall there. People wouldn't have recognised it at the time because that type of telephone was not common.

We were always having to break new ground. When doing science fiction, we all tried to make our designs look like the sort of thing that belonged to a different era. In addition, if you put commonplace items in a strange situation, then they tend not to be recognised for what they really are. For example, I used school desks in the kitchen, and they do look alien! Well, I hope they do!

You get to use a lot of different things in a kitchen. I'm pretty certain I used that thing, there in the corner on castors, in *Marco Polo*, where it was painted dark brown! It didn't have castors in the earlier story, it was just on the floor.

Back in the control room, the Monoids are discussing their imminent arrival on Refusis. Monoid One has a plan for when they finally settle there – a plan that will solve the problem of what to do with the Guardians. As an initial step, he intends to send a forward landing party to Refusis to see what is there.

In the kitchen, one of the Guardians throws a small capsule into a bowl and it transforms into a pile of potatoes.

MI: That transformation was done with overlay. You start with a picture of the bowl empty, then overlay a picture of it full. In fact, I think the empty bowl was overlaid first and when that image was removed, the potatoes were revealed.

The Doctor, Steven and Dodo discuss how they might overthrow the Monoids. Monoid Two arrives and, while it is distracted by Venussa, Steven tries to get the heat-prod weapon off it. Monoid Three arrives and the attempt fails, a Guardian being killed in the struggle.

MI: I think that effect of the gun firing was done by just turning up the contrast on the camera so the picture whited out. There was also a light at the end of the gun, and a small charge of flash-powder ignited to give a puff of smoke.

Monoid Two takes the Doctor and Dodo away. They are to make the first landing on Refusis, and Steven is to be held prisoner to ensure that they behave.

The launcher is prepared and the Doctor, Dodo, Yendom and Monoid Two set off for Refusis.

MI: This was a tiny model at Ealing. I went to Ealing myself and supervised all the filming of the models.

When the launcher arrives on Refusis, the door opens.

MI: That door was pretty awkward to open and shut.

BN: Yes, it was supposed to work smoothly but it ended up rather jerky.

The group leave the launcher and look around Refusis for the first time.

BN: All the bits of white draped on the trees are actually fibreglass rovings. At the time, we didn't know they are an irritant to the skin. Cotton wool would have been just as good, but rovings were fireproof.

This landscape had to have a totally different aspect, because it was a new world. The rocks were all carved from two inch thick jablite. I used lots of thin and spiky leafed plants as well as broom-type plants, on the stems of which I hung the fibreglass. My aim was to create a setting totally unlike any you could find on Earth. I also added some fibreglass rocks from stock and some grass and sawdust.

Behind them, an invisible entity enters the capsule. The controls appear to work themselves, and the door closes and opens by itself.

BN: The launcher prop was rigged up with wires and strings to make it seem to operate itself. There's actually someone underneath moving the switches.

Monoid Two is concerned that they haven't yet encountered any Refusians and wonders that perhaps their advance information was wrong. The Doctor suggests sending back a message to the ship to say that all is well, and Dodo agrees: the sooner they start getting the population down onto the planet, the better. Monoid Two comments that it may not take as long as they think. Dodo seizes on this statement, challenges the creature to admit that the Guardians will be left behind. Yendom is appalled – the Monoids promised that they would all settle on Refusis.

The Doctor has seen a castle-like structure in the distance. They decide to go there.

BN: That castle was a painted backcloth – it looks as though the structure is about twenty miles away!

Arriving at the castle, they find it lavishly furnished, but deserted.

BN: The main door has bits of hardboard stuck on it, and the floor has been painted with a stencil roller to create the pattern. Over at the back, you can see some wooden screens that I'd used previously in *The Crusade* for a part of Saladin's palace. The flowers in the vase on the table came from Japan. They were artificial, and I'd never seen anything like them before.

Monoid Two, by smashing a vase and throwing the flowers from a second vase to the floor, challenges the Refusians to appear. Suddenly a voice (Richard Beale) rings out, telling the Monoid to put the second vase down. Monoid Two's arm is grabbed and the vase is forced back to the table by an invisible presence. The flowers fly from where they have fallen on the floor and replace themselves in the vase.

BN: The flowers were filmed being pulled out of the vase on a wire, and then the film was reversed to give the effect of them leaping back into the vase like that.

Back on the ship, Monoid One and Monoid Three (Frank George) are plotting by the statue. They are concerned that they haven't yet heard from Monoid Two.

MI: That shot was done with a mirror to get the nice top-down angle.

Monoid One explains that a fission device has been hidden on the Ark to destroy the Guardians after the Monoids have left for Refusis. The bomb is hidden in the giant statue. Unknown to them, Maharis, another subject Guardian, has overheard them on a monitor screen, and he reports to Steven and the other Guardians in the kitchen. He admits however that he did not see where Monoid One indicated the bomb was hidden.

On the planet, the Doctor is chatting with the Refusian. The invisible creature explains that their incorporeal nature came about as a result of a giant solar flare. They cannot even see each other, although they can sense each other's presence. The Refusians would welcome the habitation of their planet once more and have built places like the castle for their visitors to enjoy.

Monoid Two kills Yendom when the human tries to prevent him from returning to the launcher. The Doctor and Dodo find the body. Monoid Two starts to make a report back to the Ark, but the Refusian approaches and the launcher explodes, killing Monoid Two.

MI: The explosion was done on film at Ealing, and we blew up a small model of the launcher.

Dodo is horrified. The Doctor states that the two of them will have to wait until another party arrives; and if no one does come, they will just have to stay on the planet.

End of *The Return*

The Bomb

Monoid Three asks Monoid One what they should do now, and Monoid One says that they should prepare for the main landings. Monoid Four (Edmund Coulter) is concerned that they don't know what Refusis is like. Monoid Three warns Monoid One that Monoid Four is questioning the wisdom of his leadership. Monoid One replies that if there is any problem, Monoid Four will be got rid of.

MI: Each of the Monoids has a communicator device around its neck. They move a slider to reveal a black dot at the front when they are speaking. I think that was to try and show which one was speaking at any given time, because it's not obvious otherwise.

The Refusian is concerned at the arrival of the Ark. They wish to have peace on their planet and do not want a war between humans and Monoids. The Refusian agrees to give the humans and the Monoids one day to try to resolve their problems.

MI: I wanted a 'god-like' voice for the Refusian, and I knew Richard Beale, who was a very good Shakespearean actor. I would have cast him because I thought he had the right sort of voice.

On the Ark, Steven is trying to work out how to escape from the kitchen. He and the Guardians decide to use Maharis without his knowledge.

The Monoids are forcing the Guardians to load trays of miniaturised Monoids into the launchers for transport to Refusis.

When Maharis enters the kitchen, Steven and Venussa distract him while Dassuk manages to slip through the door behind him. When Maharis has left, Dassuk opens the door from the outside and releases the captive Guardians.

The Monoids leave for Refusis. In the launcher, Monoid One informs Monoid Three that the bomb is timed to explode in twelve hours' time.

The launchers leave the Ark and head for Refusis.

MI: All those model launchers are on wires, and they've got little lights in them.

With the Monoids now out of the way, Steven and the Guardians start looking for the bomb.

The launchers arrive on Refusis and the Monoids disembark. They find the wreckage of the earlier launcher. The Doctor and Dodo watch from the undergrowth as Monoid Four expresses to another Monoid his discontent at Monoid One's decision to come to Refusis. The Monoid determines to challenge Monoid One and get back to the Ark before the bomb explodes. When they have moved on, the Doctor and Dodo get into one of the launchers.

Steven is growing dispirited at the lack of progress. He receives from the Doctor a message warning him about the bomb. An image of the Doctor is seen on the main screen.

MI: That image of the Doctor is inlay. When some of the Guardians move across it, their heads get cut off by the image!

The Doctor explains that he intends to try to glean from the Monoids the location of the bomb. He suggests that the Refusian pilots the launcher back to the Ark.

When the Doctor and Dodo move away from the launcher, they encounter Monoid Two and Monoid Sixty-Three, who take them off to see Monoid One. Behind them, the launcher leaves.

MI: That's a good model shot of the launcher leaving.

The launcher arrives on the Ark carrying the Refusian.

In the Refusian castle, the Doctor is questioned by Monoid One and denies having seen any Refusians. Monoid Four confronts Monoid One. Monoid One says that any of his people who are unhappy can return to the Ark. He tells them that the bomb is in the statue.

Monoid Four leaves with a group of Monoids sympathetic to his cause. Monoid One then reveals that he intends to destroy the rebels in the open. He and Monoid Two go to set an ambush.

On the Ark, Steven suggests that some of the Guardians should go to Refusis to try to preserve a proportion of humanity. Steven elects to stay on the Ark with Vanussa to try to find the bomb. Maharis has no wish to die for an ideal his forefathers thought of, so Vanussa suggests that he goes down to the planet with Dassuk and with two of the other Guardians.

Down on Refusis, Monoid One and his fellows ambush Monoid Four and his band of rebels on their way back to the launchers. There is a gun battle.

BN: This is quite a good illustration of the terrain I built. The basic shape was built up with rostra, then that was covered with rocks and foliage. That gives you different levels on the set. It's a very cheap and simple set to create.

The launcher from the Ark arrives.

MI: That is a forced perspective model shot. It's effective because you see a Monoid moving in the background as well as the full-sized launcher as the model touches down.

Maharis is the first to leave the shuttle, and he is immediately killed by one of the Monoids. The other humans leave the capsule as the Monoids fight. Dassuk makes for the castle and rescues the Doctor and Dodo, who return to the launcher. When they arrive, the gun battle is over, and Monoid Four seems to have won. The Doctor calls Steven on the radio to tell him where the bomb is hidden.
 Once it is known that the bomb is in the statue's head, the Refusian on board the Ark uses its great strength to move the statue into the launching bay.

MI: The model of the statue was lifted by someone holding its legs out of shot, and then shifting their grip to the head as it moved past the camera. That gave the effect of it being moved by an invisible creature.

Once it is in position, the statue is ejected into space where it explodes safely.

MI: The statue wasn't actually blown up as I kept it afterwards. The explosion was a separate piece of footage that was mixed in at the right point.

The danger over, the Refusian agrees to help the humans settle on Refusis, provided that they make peace with the Monoids first.
 The Doctor, Steven and Dodo say their goodbyes and make their way on an electric transporter back to the TARDIS.
 The TARDIS leaves.

MI: That dematerialisation is done with two photographs, as the background completely changes as the ship vanishes.

In the TARDIS control room, the TARDIS is arriving at a new destination. Dodo and Steven have changed their clothes. The Doctor coughs and vanishes from sight. Dodo postulates that this might have something to do with the Refusians, but the Doctor tells his companions it is something far more serious: it is some form of attack!

End of *The Bomb*

Post-production
While the recording of a *Doctor Who* adventure accounts for what is eventually seen on screen, the diary of a production does not end there. There is also post-production work carried out.

Far less time tended to be spent on post-production during the first Doctor's era than during later eras, simply because nearly all the work was done in pre-production and live in the studio. All that remained for the director to do was to supervise any editing required, and any final sound dubs. 'There would have been a certain amount of editing done the week after recording,' confirms Michael. 'That tended to take place on the Monday or Tuesday evening the following week.'

As previously mentioned, the number of edits tended to be minimised by having the story recorded in transmission order with few recording breaks – although *The Ark* was unusual in that it did involve a fair degree of out-of-order recording on the final episode. In addition, the recording of each episode was done only about two weeks' prior to its transmission. The director therefore had to split his time between the episode just completed, the episode to be rehearsed and recorded the following week, and, possibly, further episodes of the story being planned for subsequent weeks.

For Michael Imison, work on *The Ark* was overshadowed by the fact that he was told when he was mid-way through making the final episode that his services as a director were no longer required by the BBC.

'Before I went into the gallery to record the last episode,' he recalls, 'I was handed a note to say that my contract was not being renewed.'

Michael therefore went back to being a story editor. 'I had to find the job myself; I wasn't offered it. Some friends in the Plays Department employed me and, curiously, the fact that I had done *Doctor Who* helped. They were setting up a science fiction series called *Out of the Unknown* and needed someone who knew something about science fiction. I knew nothing about science fiction, but as I had done *Doctor Who*, they thought I might!

'After a crash course in science fiction, which I thoroughly enjoyed, I had a marvellous time. I attended the Trieste Science Fiction Film Festival in France as a BBC observer and was immediately put on the Grand Jury! They thought that to have someone English on the Jury would be a good idea. Then the next year we entered one of the *Out of the Unknown* episodes, *The Machine Stops*, and won, so that was rather fun.

'Then the man who had sacked me became Head of Plays, and I realised that my future at the BBC was going to be very limited. An actor friend whom I'd employed in *Buddenbrooks*, who was at the time represented by a large American agency in London, came to talk to me. His agency had lost their London agent to a rival company and they needed someone in a hurry to look after their American clients in England – the other agent had gone off with all the English clients!

'My friend arranged for me to be interviewed and they offered me twice the money the BBC was paying! So then I became an agent, and I must say I've never regretted it.'

Transmission

The Ark was eventually transmitted on consecutive Saturdays from 5 to 26 March 1966. It achieved ratings, in millions of viewers, of 5.5 (episode one), 6.9 (two), 6.2 (three) and 7.3 (four), all of which which were lower than the season average of 7.65.

Although the third season of *Doctor Who* had started successfully, enjoying audiences around the 10 million mark for most of the epic twelve part *The Daleks' Master Plan*, *The Massacre of St Bartholomew's Eve* had proved particularly unpopular, the ratings dropping off dramatically from 8.0 to 5.8 million. *The Ark* went some way towards improving the situation, and this trend was continued by *The Celestial Toymaker*, but *The Gunfighters* and *The Savages* proved less popular. In terms of position in the weekly TV chart, *The Ark* fared poorly. The highest placing it could manage was for episode two, which clocked in at 70th. For episode one, it dropped out of the top 100 shows altogether; the first time that *Doctor Who* had failed to appear in the top 100 since it started.

Part of the reason for *The Ark*'s poor figures was that most ITV regions were showing the highly popular music magazine show *Thank Your Lucky Stars* in the slot opposite *Doctor Who*. It seems that, against this competition, *Doctor Who* could command a really high audience only when the Daleks appeared.

Considering the problematic background of the third season as a whole, and also the limited technology and time available, *The Ark* stands up well as an example of *Doctor Who* in this period. It was a very ambitious project, achieved with much imagination and skill by all those involved.

CREDITS

Written by	Paul Erickson and Lesley Scott
Title Music by	Ron Grainer and the BBC Radiophonic Workshop
Title Sequence	Bernard Lodge
Incidental Music by	Tristram Cary (stock)
	Robert Farnon (stock)
Special Sound	Brian Hodgson
Production Assistant	David Maloney
Assistant Floor Manager	Chris D'Oyly-John
Assistant	Thelma Helsby
Floor Assistant	Ernest Skinner
TM2	Fred Wright
Grams	John Hurley
	Tony Bowes
Vision Mixer	Clive Halls
Crew	1
Film Cameraman	Tony Leggo
Film Editor	Noel Chapman
Costume Designer	Daphne Dare
Make-Up	Sonia Markham
Lighting	Howard King
Sound	Ray Angel
Story Editor	Gerry Davis (and Donald Tosh before his departure)
Designer	Barry Newbery
Producer	John Wiles (and Innes Lloyd after his arrival)
Director	Michael Imison

SELLING THE DOCTOR

MEDIA

One of the main bastions of public interest in *Doctor Who* was the BBC's own listings magazine, *Radio Times*. From the series' on-air debut in 1963 right through to the end of the first Doctor's era, each new story was heralded by a feature article, accompanied as often as not by a photograph. Occasionally features would appear part-way through a story's run as well. As *Radio Times* was published in regional editions, each giving details of programmes specific to its own particular region as well as of those transmitted nationwide, there would often be regional variations in the coverage given to the series. For example, the London edition might present a small feature while the Welsh one boasted a whole page plus a photograph.

The first story to be promoted with a front cover photograph in the magazine was *Marco Polo* in February 1964, although the Serials Department had been pushing for such coverage ever since the very first story. The same privilege was later accorded *The Dalek Invasion of Earth* and *The Web Planet* – the stories given perhaps the most publicity of any of the first Doctor's adventures.

Doctor Who's first mention in *Radio Times* was actually in the edition published the week *before* its debut episode was transmitted, when in the 'Next Week' preview column a photograph and 'teaser' text announced the start of the first story. The BBC's own in-house magazine, *Ariel*, also covered the event, this time with a photograph of associate producer Mervyn Pinfield, producer Verity Lambert and director Waris Hussein on the classroom set from *An Unearthly Child*. *Ariel* described *Doctor Who* as 'an ambitious space/time adventure serial consisting of a series of stories of a varying number of episodes. Each episode will end on a cliff-hanger.'

Clearly there was considerable interest in the new series but, as things turned out, the opening episode was transmitted in less than ideal circumstances. First, the assassination the previous day of US President John F Kennedy meant that many viewers were simply not in the mood to watch television – unless it was to see one of the special programmes hastily put together by the BBC and ITV to mourn Kennedy's passing. Then there was the fact that on that Saturday evening many viewers' homes were blacked out by a widespread power failure, denying them the opportunity to receive the transmission.

Those who did watch, however, apparently liked what they saw. 'William Hartnell, gazing from under locks of flowing white,' wrote Michael Gowers in the *Daily Mail* on 25 November, 'and the appealing Carole Ann Ford represent the Unknown Them, William Russell and Jacqueline Hill the ignorant, sceptical Us, and their craft is cunningly disguised as a police callbox. The penultimate shot of this, nestling, after a three-point touchdown, in a Neolithic landscape, must have delighted the hearts of the *Telegoons* who followed.'

It was due to the aforementioned power cuts that the first episode was repeated the following week, immediately prior to the second, launching *Doctor Who* on what had been announced as a fifty-two week odyssey through space and time.

The press were strangely silent during the run of the Daleks' introductory story, *The Mutants*, but the fact that Terry Nation's evil creations had caught the public's imagination did not go unregistered. On 4 February, just three days after the transmission of the story's final episode, Douglas Marlborough reported in the *Daily Mail*: 'Since the Daleks vanished from the series, hundreds of children have written to ask what would happen to them. Some suggested that they should be competition prizes. Now the future of two of the five-feet-tall fibreglass-and-wood robots has been decided. Today they go to children of Dr Barnardo's Homes.' Marlborough went on to explain that two more Daleks had been kept by the BBC in case they were needed 'for future TV appearances.'

Under the headline 'Do-it-yourself Daleks are coming,' the weekly newspaper *Reveille* reported on 2 April that the BBC was arranging for 'hundreds of do-it-yourself scale models of the robots to be put on the market.' The article went on to state that 'the eerie, clipped-voice robots which appeared in *Dr Who*, the BBC television serial, proved so popular that they are to be brought back to the screen again, probably in the autumn.'

During 1964 and 1965, the Daleks became a national cult, but they were not the only race of *Doctor Who* monsters that the BBC tried to promote. Another first season menace that received a fair amount of coverage was the Voords, who were revealed to the public by the *Daily Mail* on 11 April – the same day as the first episode of *The Keys of Marinus*, the story in which they featured, was transmitted.

'They bounce across BBC TV screens today in the first episode of a new DR WHO space series – and could rival the dreaded Daleks,' wrote the reporter. The article was accompanied by a photograph showing Carole Ann Ford in the clutches of a rubber-clad Peter Stenson.

Other aspects of *Doctor Who* also started to attract attention. Writer John Lucarotti was interviewed by Elsie M Smith for an unknown newspaper, in which he revealed that writing *Doctor Who* was 'five per cent inspiration and ninety five per cent perspiration.' Designer Raymond Cusick was also interviewed for the same publication.

1964 drew to a close with another Dalek-related report in the *Daily Mail* – the paper that had given *Doctor Who* the most coverage over the previous year. Hot on the heels of the conclusion of *The Dalek Invasion Of Earth*, they reported that Terry Nation was being asked to bring back the aliens once more, but that he didn't want to do so. 'I don't want to bring them back,' he explained to Douglas Marlborough. 'They've hit such a level of popularity that nothing they do can be quite as popular again. The Beatles and pop groups in general have dropped a bit, and the Daleks seem to have filled the gap. I can't see them hitting this level for much longer. But what can one do? I don't want the Daleks back. The BBC does. They've insisted on it.' Perhaps the fact that, as Marlborough reported, Nation was speaking from a '15-room £15,000 Elizabethan mansion near Teynham, Kent' had something to do with his being persuaded to write another Dalek story.

During the series' second season, Nation's finances continued to fascinate Douglas Marlborough, who on 11 March 1965 reported: 'The man who invented the Daleks has made a fortune out of his science fiction mechanical monsters. Mr Terry Nation, their 34-year old creator, last night declined to say how much. But the TV and film rights are believed to be worth £300,000.' Nation was quoted later in the article as saying 'There was a sudden need for money and so I did the series. It turned out to be the shrewdest move I've ever made.'

Reveille carried an interview with Verity Lambert around the same time, and revealed that Carole Ann Ford was to be replaced with Margaret O'Brien (sic). The ever-dependable *Daily Mail* also interviewed Lambert on 28 November 1964, as the second Dalek story finished its run. On 2 April 1965, the *Daily Mail* reported that Jacqueline Hill and William Russell had both asked to leave the series by June.

Monsters other than the Daleks continued to be mostly ignored by the press, with two notable exceptions: the Zarbi, who received almost full-page coverage in the *Daily Mail*, and the Mechanoids, who were afforded similar treatment.

After *Galaxy 4* went into the studio, newspaper readers were treated to the sight of a trio of attractive women wielding rather large guns. 'Enter Dr Who's new foes: The ray-gun blondes' screamed the headline to Brian Bear's feature in the *Daily Mail*. This was followed by 'UGH! It's the TV monsters' after *Mission to the Unknown* was recorded on 7 August. On 23 October, a sextet of bald men peered from the paper as the Technix from *The Daleks' Master Plan* were unveiled. On 4 December, Jean Marsh hit the headlines as 'A Touch of the Avengers: The New Girl Linking Up with Dr Who Tonight.' The feature, with an accompanying photograph, revealed that Marsh had been given 'a woollen cat-suit, black leather boots, expertise in judo and karate and a ray gun for when that suits the script writers better.' The Beatle-wigged monocular creatures of *The Ark* also appeared in the press when Jackie Lane was announced as the latest addition to the TARDIS' crew.

On 3 December 1965, the Manchester *Evening News* speculated that William Hartnell might be giving up the role of the Doctor. 'I've had a good innings,' he apparently explained to their reporter. Hartnell's agent, Eric L'Epine Smith, denied any such thing: 'I can assure you categorically that William Hartnell is not giving up. I have plans for him when he finishes the series.'

Of course, Hartnell did eventually leave, and, on 6 August 1966, newspapers reported that the BBC was searching for a new actor to take the role of the Doctor. 'I think three years in one part is a good innings and it is time for a change,' Hartnell was quoted as saying in *The Times*.

OVERSEAS SALES

England was not the only country to enjoy the first Doctor's era. By the beginning of 1977, according to an internal BBC listing, the following overseas sales had been registered:

100,000 BC
New Zealand, Australia, Canada, Singapore, Nigeria, Rhodesia, Cyprus, Mexico, Hong Kong, Uganda, Lebanon, Ghana, Zambia, Jamaica, Kenya, Thailand, Mauritius.

The Mutants
Canada (episodes two to seven only), New Zealand, Australia, Nigeria, Singapore, Rhodesia, Cyprus, Uganda, Ghana, Zambia, Jamaica, Venezuela.

Inside the Spaceship
Canada, Australia, New Zealand, Singapore, Thailand, Nigeria, Rhodesia, Cyprus, Hong Kong, Mauritius, Ghana, Zambia, Jamaica, Kenya, Tunisia, Mexico, Morocco, Saudi Arabia, Iran, Ethiopia, Algeria.

Marco Polo
Australia, Canada, New Zealand, Nigeria, Singapore, Hong Kong, Uganda, Ghana, Zambia, Jamaica, Cyprus, Kenya, Thailand, Mauritius, Rhodesia, Venezuela, Bermuda, Ethiopia.

The Keys of Marinus
Australia, Canada, New Zealand, Singapore, Nigeria, Rhodesia, Uganda, Ghana, Zambia, Jamaica, Cyprus, Lebanon, Hong Kong, Kenya, Bermuda, Mexico, Thailand, Venezuela, Mauritius, Morocco, Saudi Arabia, Ethiopia, Algeria.

The Aztecs
Australia, New Zealand, Singapore, Hong Kong, Nigeria, Saudi Arabia, Trinidad and Tobago, Zambia, Uganda, Cyprus, Jamaica, Mexico, Rhodesia, Venezuela, Mauritius, Tunisia, Thailand, Iran, Ethiopia.

The Sensorites
Australia, New Zealand, Singapore, Nigeria, Iran, Hong Kong, Arabia, Trinidad and Tobago, Ethiopia, Zambia, Uganda, Cyprus, Mexico, Jamaica, Caribbean, Rhodesia, Mauritius, Tunisia, Venezuela, Sierra Leone, Morocco.

The Reign of Terror
Australia, New Zealand, Singapore, Nigeria, Hong Kong, Trinidad and Tobago, Zambia, Uganda, Cyprus, Jamaica, Rhodesia, Kenya, Mauritius, Thailand, Ethiopia.

Planet of Giants
Australia, New Zealand, Singapore, Nigeria, Hong Kong, Trinidad and Tobago, Zambia, Uganda, Jamaica, Venezuela, Mexico, Rhodesia, Kenya, Mauritius, Tunisia, Thailand, Mexico, Morocco, Saudi Arabia, Iran, Ethiopia.

The Dalek Invasion of Earth
Cyprus, Singapore, Nigeria, Zambia, Uganda, Hong Kong, Australia, Trinidad and Tobago, Arabia, Jamaica, Rhodesia, Kenya, Caribbean, Venezuela, Thailand, Morocco, Ethiopia, Algeria.

The Rescue
New Zealand, Australia, Singapore, Nigeria, Hong Kong, Trinidad and Tobago, Arabia, Zambia, Uganda, Jamaica, Mexico, Venezuela, Caribbean, Rhodesia, Kenya, Lebanon, Mauritius, Thailand, Saudi Arabia, Ethiopia, Algeria.

The Romans
Australia, New Zealand, Gibraltar, Singapore, Nigeria, Zambia,

Caribbean, Mauritius, Sierra Leone, Jamaica, Ethiopia.

The Web Planet
Australia, Singapore, Nigeria, Zambia, Venezuela, Caribbean, Mauritius, Iran, Sierra Leone, Jamaica, Ethiopia.

The Crusade
Australia, Gibraltar, Singapore, Nigeria, Zambia, Caribbean, Mauritius, Sierra Leone, Jamaica, Ethiopia.

The Space Museum
Nigeria, Australia, New Zealand, Zambia, Venezuela, Caribbean, Mauritius, Mexico, Iran, Sierra Leone, Jamaica, Ethiopia.

The Chase
Australia, Gibraltar, Singapore, Nigeria, Zambia, Venezuela, Caribbean, Iran, Mauritius, Ethiopia.

The Time Meddler
Australia, New Zealand, Gibraltar, Singapore, Nigeria, Zambia, Caribbean, Mauritius, Jamaica.

Galaxy 4
Australia, New Zealand, Caribbean, Zambia, Sierra Leone, Singapore.

Mission to the Unknown
None.

The Myth Makers
Australia, New Zealand, Caribbean, Zambia, Sierra Leone, Singapore.

The Daleks' Master Plan
None.

The Massacre of St Bartholomew's Eve
Australia, New Zealand, Caribbean, Zambia, Sierra Leone, Singapore.

The Ark
Australia, New Zealand, Caribbean, Zambia, Sierra Leone, Singapore.

The Celestial Toymaker
Australia, New Zealand, Barbados, Zambia, Sierra Leone, Singapore.

The Gunfighters
Australia, Caribbean, Zambia, Sierra Leone, Singapore.

The Savages
Australia, New Zealand, Barbados, Zambia, Sierra Leone, Singapore.

The War Machines
Australia, New Zealand, Caribbean, Zambia, Sierra Leone, Singapore, Nigeria.

The Smugglers
Australia, New Zealand, Caribbean, Zambia, Sierra Leone, Singapore.

The Tenth Planet
Australia, New Zealand, Singapore.

On the basis of this list, therefore, *The Keys of Marinus* was the first Doctor story sold to the most countries in the sixties and early seventies, and *Mission to the Unknown* and *The Daleks' Master Plan* those sold to the least. (It appears that *The Daleks' Master Plan* may have been offered for sale only as an eleven-part story – presumably minus the off-beat Christmas Day episode *The Feast of Steven*.)

New Zealand
By Paul Scoones

New Zealand holds the distinction of being the first country outside the United Kingdom to screen *Doctor Who*. The New Zealand Broadcasting Corporation (NZBC) acquired the first three stories, *100,000 BC*, *The Mutants* (a.k.a. *The Daleks*), and *Inside the Spaceship*, in June 1964. All thirteen episodes were rated Y, which meant they were considered unsuitable for screening before around 8 pm.

A single film print of each episode was held by the NZBC necessitating the staggering of the schedules so that the films could be transported between New Zealand's four regional channels: Auckland (AKTV-2), Wellington (WNTV-1), Christchurch (CHTV-3) and Dunedin (DNTV-2).

The episodes were first screened in the Christchurch region from 18 September to 11 December 1964, then in Auckland from 30 October 1964 to 29 January 1965, Wellington from 6 November 1964 to 5 February 1965 and Dunedin from 5 March to 28 May 1965. The episodes were screened on Fridays across all regions, usually at 7.57 pm, although from 19 March 1965 the screening time moved to 8.07 pm in Dunedin.

The New Zealand screening rights for this first batch of thirteen episodes expired 16 June 1966 and the episodes were sent on to Denmark on 26 March 1968.

Marco Polo was received 27 May 1966 was rated G, after censor edits to all but the first two episodes. The serial was first screened in the Auckland region on Thursdays from 27 October to 8 December 1966, then in Wellington on Tuesdays from 1 November to 13 December 1966, Dunedin on Thursdays from 15 December 1966 to 26 January 1967 and Christchurch on Mondays from 20 March to 1 May 1967. The start times were mostly around 6.50 pm. The New Zealand screening rights for *Marco Polo* expired 19 November 1968, by which time the NZBC were only holding the five edited episodes of the story as the first two uncut episodes had been dispatched to Iran on 20 October 1967. The five remaining episodes were still held at the Wellington Hill Street film store in April 1970; their fate after this date is unrecorded. However, the reused film can that had previously contained the last episode, *Assassin at Peking*, was discovered by Graham Howard at a Television New Zealand film storage facility in Wellington in 1990.

A BBC Enterprises document from 1977, detailing overseas sales of *Doctor Who* stories, notes *The Keys of Marinus, The Aztecs* and *The Sensorites* as having been sold to New Zealand, but if this was the case, there is no evidence that these stories were ever received.

A batch of seven stories was received on 19 September 1967, including *The Reign of Terror, Planet of Giants, The Dalek Invasion of Earth, The Rescue, The Romans, The Web Planet* and *The Crusade*, however three of these were omitted from the 1977 document. All episodes of *The Dalek Invasion of Earth* were rated Y. Episodes 1 to 4 of *The Web Planet* and Episode 1 of *The Crusade* were also rated Y – although the remaining episodes of both stories gained G ratings. These three stories with Y-rated episodes were apparently held by the NZBC for some time with the intention of rescheduling them in a later post-8 pm time-slot, however this never happened.

The Reign of Terror, Planet of Giants, The Rescue and *The Romans* first screened in the Christchurch region from 26 January to 3 May 1968, then in Wellington from 8 March to 14 June 1968, Dunedin from 29 March to 5 July 1968 and Auckland from 24 May to 30 August 1968. The episodes played on Fridays across all regions, mostly around 5.30 pm.

After the transmissions, the episodes from this batch were retained at the Wellington Hill Street film store and were logged as held there on 1 April 1970. *The Reign of Terror* was subsequently destroyed on 18 June 1971 and *Planet of Giants* was destroyed on 14 July 1971. The first episode of *The Crusade, The Lion*, was still held in storage in Wellington in 1975, at which time it was scheduled to be destroyed. The 16mm film print was rescued from dumping by film collectors and was held in private hands until January 1999 when it was discovered in the collection of Auckland film buff Bruce Grenville by fans Neil Lambess and Paul Scoones, who arranged for the film to be loaned to the BBC.

A further batch of eleven Hartnell stories was received 23 September 1968, including *The Space Museum, The Time Meddler, Galaxy 4, The Myth Makers, The Massacre of St Bartholomew's Eve, The Ark, The Celestial Toymaker, The Savages, The War Machines, The Smugglers* and *The Tenth Planet*. Four stories were not purchased which were: *The Chase, Mission to the Unknown, The Daleks' Master Plan* and *The Gunfighters*. All eleven stories were rated G, however some censor edits were required to gain this rating. The film trims edited from *The Ark*, featuring several minutes of footage, were discovered by Graham Howard in New Zealand in 2002.

All eleven stories were screened in one transmission block and first aired in the Christchurch region from 27 October 1968 to 24 August 1969, then in Wellington from 24 November 1968 to 21 September 1969, Auckland from 5 January to 3 November 1969 and Dunedin from 12 January to 10 November 1969. The start time was initially mostly around 5.45 pm but later moved to around 6.10 pm in all regions from July 1969. The series screened on Sundays in all regions, however the series moved to Mondays in the Auckland region from 13 October and in Dunedin from 27 October 1969.

Following the transmissions, the episodes appear to have been stored in Wellington.

The last recorded location of *The Space Museum* was at the Wellington Hill Street store in April 1970. *The Time Meddler* was sent on to Nigeria on 2 March 1973, from where the film prints were subsequently returned to the BBC in 1985. Government censor documentation indicates that the cuts present in these recovered episodes were made in New Zealand. *Galaxy 4*, *The Myth Makers*, *The Massacre of St Bartholomew's Eve*, *The Ark* and *The Celestial Toymaker* were sent to Singapore on 20 September 1972. *The Savages*, *The War Machines*, *The Smugglers* and *The Tenth Planet* had all previously been sent to Singapore on 10 January 1972. *The War Machines* film prints, which had had censor cuts made in New Zealand, were later found in Nigeria and returned to the BBC in 1984.

Having been omitted twenty years earlier, *The Dalek Invasion of Earth* finally aired on New Zealand television in November 1988 when it was scheduled to launch Television New Zealand's *Doctor Who* twenty-fifth anniversary 'Silver Jubilee' week. The story was presented in an omnibus format with all six episodes edited together, beginning at midday on Saturday 19 November 1988. The story gained a viewer rating of 3.6%.

The Dalek Invasion of Earth was repeated on TV2, broadcast from 17 February to 24 March 1991 on Sundays, mostly around 9.15 am. This time, the six episodes were screened in a single-episode-per-week format. This story was followed by a repeat of three Season Six Troughton stories and then the first two Pertwee seasons in several short blocks. Then, directly after the Pertwee story *The Daemons*, *The Time Meddler* screened from 9 May to 30 May 1993 on Sundays at 11.30 am on TV2. The version of *The Time Meddler* screened was the almost complete version restored and screened by the BBC in early 1992. This may have prompted the sale of this story to New Zealand.

In May 2000, the UHF and satellite channel Prime Television began a screening of every complete story in order from the beginning. The episodes were initially screened five nights a week (Monday to Friday), and after the first three weeks, an extra episode was added to the schedules on Sundays. The start time was 6.25 pm. The screenings commenced on Monday 15 May 2000. The Hartnell transmissions on Prime included six stories that had never before screened in New Zealand: *The Keys of Marinus*, *The Aztecs*, *The Sensorites*, *The Web Planet*, *The Chase* and *The Gunfighters*. *The Time Meddler* episodes screened on this occasion were the unrestored versions recovered from Nigeria with the cuts made by the New Zealand censor in 1968 still in evidence. Some of the Hartnell episodes screened on Prime were edited to remove 'Next Episode' captions and some had end credits that had been made for US syndication. The Hartnell era screenings ended Sunday 13 August 2000 with the last episode of *The War Machines*, but the series continued the following day with the first episode of *The Tomb of the Cybermen*.

Australia
With thanks to Dallas Jones

Doctor Who first aired in Australia at 7.30 pm on Tuesday 12 January 1965, when ABW Channel 2 Perth, part of the Australian Broadcasting Commission (ABC) network, transmitted the opening episode of *100,000 BC*. As in New Zealand, programmes were transmitted on a regional basis rather than nationwide, as the film had to be physically taken from one region to the next. *Doctor Who*'s debut in other regions therefore came a few days later. In Sydney, for example, the first episode went out at 7.30 pm on Friday 15 January.

The Australian Censorship Board (ACB), by whom all TV programmes and films were required to be vetted and classified before they could be shown, had rated the first three *Doctor Who* stories as 'A', or Adults Only – hence the relatively late time slot. This initial batch of episodes had in fact been made available to Australia back in April 1964, but transmission had been delayed due to this unexpected hitch. When it came to *Marco Polo*, the ACB were prepared to rate some of the episodes 'G', or General, but only after certain cuts were made. This set a precedent whereby most of the other first Doctor episodes shown in Australia would be rated 'G' but subjected to minor cuts to remove supposedly objectionable shots.

Once weekly transmissions got underway, Australians were able to see *Doctor Who* regularly for sixty-seven weeks until the fourth and final episode of *The Crusade* was screened in Sydney on 22 April 1966 – one of the longest uninterrupted runs that *Doctor Who* has ever enjoyed anywhere in the world.

A further season began later in the year, on 3 October in Sydney, but now *Doctor Who* was being shown four nights a week (Monday to Thursday) rather than weekly, and at 6.30 pm rather than 7.30 pm. All the episodes in this season received a 'G' rating, but again cuts were made. Stories to suffer in this way included *The Chase, Galaxy 4, The Ark* (from which all close-ups of the Monoids were removed!) and *The Gunfighters. Mission to the Unknown* and three episodes of *The Daleks' Master Plan* were not cleared for transmission as it was considered impracticable to bring them within a 'G' rating by making cuts, the problem lying with the grim nature of the storyline itself. Consequently these two stories were not purchased for transmission in Australia.

The first *Doctor Who* repeat in Australia was of *The Reign of Terror*, beginning on 9 November 1966. This was followed by repeats of *Planet of Giants, The Romans, The Web Planet* and *The Crusade.* (*The Dalek Invasion of Earth* and *The Rescue* were omitted from this run due to their 'A' ratings.) After the repeats, the final batch of first Doctor stories were transmitted, starting on 31 March 1967 in Sydney. The final episode of *The Tenth Planet* – a story that, unusually, had escaped any cuts – went out on 14 June 1967.

Canada

Another country that saw *Doctor Who* at a very early stage was Canada. The first episode was broadcast by the Canadian Broadcasting Corporation (CBC) at 5.00 pm on Saturday 23 January 1965. Transmissions then continued weekly (excluding *The Mutants: The Dead Planet*, and with a two week break after *100,000 BC: The Cave of Skulls*) until 21 April 1965, when the programme's slot was moved to 5.00 pm. on a Wednesday. The final five episodes of *The Keys of Marinus* were shown in a daily 5.00 pm slot from 28 June to 2 July. After this, CBC never aired *Doctor Who* again.

MERCHANDISE

The overwhelming success of *Doctor Who* in the sixties can arguably be traced back to the seven part Terry Nation-scripted story *The Mutants*, which added two new words to the vocabulary of schoolchildren everywhere: 'Dalek' and 'Exterminate'.

The BBC, as reported in the press, were bombarded with letters asking when the Daleks would return, and the interest continued unabated for the following three years. It is easy to look back and come to the conclusion that the Daleks were an overnight success, as they quite obviously were, but what has been less well-documented is the fact that their meteoric rise to become *the* merchandise item of the mid-sixties owed a great deal to one man, Walter Tuckwell.

In the early Sixties, the BBC created a licensing department, BBC Exploitation, whose job it was to exploit the varied and numerous rights in BBC-owned characters and settings. The department was very small and came into being partially because of the demand for Dalek-related products. The rights to market the Daleks were eventually given to a character-licensing company with whom the BBC had done business before, thus relieving the BBC of much of the work involved in such dealings. This company was Walter Tuckwell Associates.

'When they made their first appearance in about the fifth episode of *Dr Who*, late in 1963, I rang the BBC and asked if they were going to be a big thing,' Tuckwell explained in an interview at the time. 'They said: "Forget it. Dr Who is going to finish them off after six episodes and then he is off to China with Marco Polo."

'But like Dick Barton just after the war, this was a scary programme that the kids loved. They enjoy being frightened when they know the goodies are going to win in the end. Before the end of that first series, youngsters were running round their school playgrounds growling "Ex-term-in-ate". It was bingo and nobody knew it.'

Tuckwell's job was to approach manufacturers and publishers and try to interest them in buying a license to use the Daleks in conjunction with their products. As this involved the companies being approached and given the idea, rather than the companies independently deciding to approach the BBC, Tuckwell met with a very favourable response. By Christmas 1964, there were numerous companies gearing up to release toys and games the following year. When the BBC announced that they were planning another Dalek story for Christmas 1965, interest grew even stronger, and by the end of 1965 around eighty-five different products had been released to tie in with *Doctor Who* and the Daleks.

This trend was reported by the press – how could they fail to notice? – and on 20 December the *Daily Mail* ran a story by Colin Reid discussing the problems parents faced in trying to keep Christmas presents secret from their kids: 'Have YOU ever tried to say "How much is that Dalek in the window?" just using your face and an occasional hiss? You have? That's the easy part.' The feature ended with Colin's kids finally finding the secret stash of Dalek toys and playing with them.

There was even a special BBC 'Interlude' film, set in a toyshop, during the course of which an army of Louis Marx Daleks was seen to be wiped out by a large, crawling doll.

Tuckwell's success at getting the Daleks into every toyshop, and from there into every child's Christmas stocking, was what really brought *Doctor Who* into the public eye. Without that marketing push, it is arguable that *Doctor Who* would not have become the hit it did.

There was even a fan following for the programme, and reviews of *Doctor Who* started to appear in science fiction fanzines of the period. A fan club for William Hartnell, concentrating on his role as the Doctor, was set up and run by a young fan who lived in Stoke-on-Trent. It provided occasional newsletters and sent out autographed publicity photographs of the regular cast members. This was the start of *Doctor Who* fandom, and fan organisations have continued to support and appreciate the series ever since.

SPIN-OFFS

Interest in *Doctor Who* spilled over into the theatre and onto cinema screens as the Daleks moved outside the boundaries of the television show that had spawned them.

24 June 1965 saw the release of the first full-length cinema film to feature the Daleks.

Dr Who and the Daleks was an instant hit with people of all ages, and preparations started almost immediately on a follow-up, *Daleks Invasion Earth 2150 A.D.* This second film was released in June 1966, but as the Dalek craze was dying down by then, it fared less well at the box office. Although both films were based on televised scripts (for *The Mutants* and *The Dalek Invasion of Earth* respectively), the Doctor was played by Peter Cushing and his assistants by Roy Castle, Jennie Linden and Roberta Tovey (first film) and Bernard Cribbins, Jill Curzon and Roberta Tovey (second film).

Both films generated a large amount of media attention, which was boosted in 1965 by the Daleks paying a visit to the Cannes Film Festival and by a major display of props and sets that was mounted initially in London's Selfridges department store and then went on tour around the country to other stores owned by the same parent company.

Producer Milton Subotsky's later claim that there were plans for a third film (reported to have been called *Doctor Who's Greatest Adventure*) seem to have no factual basis in the BBC documentation of the time, which indicates that although the contract for the first film allowed for the option on a second to be taken up, the contract for the second made no such provision for any further follow-ups.

Aside from the two cinema films, there was also a one-off stage play. *The Curse of the Daleks* was written by *Doctor Who*'s story editor, David Whitaker, and featured neither the Doctor nor the TARDIS, concentrating instead on the Daleks themselves. The plot of the play picks up on the Daleks' immobilisation at the end of *The Mutants* and depicts the reactivation of the creatures by an unwary archaelogical team, one of whose number has secret plans for them. The play was staged at the Wyndham's Theatre in London's Charing Cross Road and ran for two weeks from 21 December 1965.

Not content with taking part in the performing arts, the Daleks also had their own comic strip, which ran in *TV Century 21*, and their own annuals and books. They even made appearances at numerous promotional events and exhibitions, including the *Daily Mail* Boys' and Girls' Exhibition of 1964/65. This was the first major public appearance of the Daleks, and crowds packed the hall at London's Olympia exhibition centre to catch a glimpse of them as they patrolled the area, shrieking 'Ex-ter-min-ate' to general delight.

VIEWER REACTION

Doctor Who's first episode was watched by 4.4 million viewers. More and more people then tuned in as the weeks went by, until 10.4 million saw the end of *The Mutants*. The figure then hovered around the 9 to 10 million mark for a while before falling to around 7 million by the close of the first season.

The popularity of the Daleks peaked the following year, and it is perhaps unsurprising therefore to find that the second season gained the highest ratings for the series in the Sixties. It started well, with over 8 million viewers for *Planet of Giants*, but by the time *The Dalek Invasion of Earth* concluded, the figure had climbed to an impressive 12.4 million. The highest mark of the season, however, came with episode one of *The Web Planet*, which was watched by 13.5 million viewers.

From this point, the figures steadily fell, and the lowest audience of the first Doctor's era was recorded for episode three of *The Smugglers*, which managed only 4.2 million viewers.

Considering that far fewer people owned television sets in the Sixties than in later years, these ratings were not at all bad. *Doctor Who* was normally within the top fifty most watched shows each week, and *The Romans* episode one and *The Chase* episode six both climbed as high as number seven on the TV chart.

The series' audience appreciation figures were also generally good. These statistics were compiled by the BBC from a regular survey of a panel of viewers, whose comments would occasionally be used to write up more detailed Audience Research Reports on particular programmes. The Reports for *Doctor Who* provide a fascinating insight into how the series was perceived by the general public at the time of transmission.

'Tonight's new serial seemed to be a cross between Wells' Time Machine and a space-age Old Curiosity Shop, with a touch of Mack Sennett comedy,' commented one viewer, a retired Naval officer, after watching the opening episode of *100,000 BC*. There were occasional voices of discontent – 'A police box with flashing beacon travelling through interstellar space – what claptrap!' was one viewer's opinion – but on the whole the episode was regarded as 'an enjoyable piece of escapism, not to be taken too seriously, of course, but none the less entertaining and, at times, quite thrilling.'

By the time of *The Aztecs*, interest was apparently falling off. One viewer said he was 'afraid that this series has gone on far too long: the danger and escape therefrom fall into a never-varied pattern length and repetition – result, ennui.' And this was for the third episode of the sixth story to be transmitted! Others expressed a preference for the science fiction based adventures over the historical, but younger children seemed to have enjoyed *The Aztecs* more than their parents.

When the second season began with *Planet of Giants*, viewers welcomed the series' return – 'preposterous' though its concepts were. The most frequently-expressed view about the first episode of *The Dalek Invasion of Earth* was that there was not enough of the Daleks in it. Another comment was that the show was 'rather gruesome for young children to watch, with drowned bodies and daggered bodies.'

The Romans came under fire as being 'so ridiculous it's a bore!' Again there was criticism of the historical adventures in general, and one common comment was that the story lacked any realism – everything was 'transparently phoney.' *The Web Planet* was not liked either, being described as a 'third rate kiddies pantomime.' It was generally felt that the series had 'lost its entertainment value and should be either rested or "scrapped." Plainly, ideas were running out.' *The Space Museum* seemed to confirm this view as, after a promising start, it was thought to have deteriorated into 'a load of drivel.' Some viewers commented that William Hartnell seemed unsure of his lines – 'or,' said one, 'was it that Dr Who was given too many "um's", "ah-h-h's" and "er's" in the script?'

An interesting point to note here is that the stories that tended to attract the most criticism in the Audience Research Reports were those which received the highest ratings!

The Chase was very well received, with many positive comments being expressed. 'Full of adventure' and 'exciting, lively and quite convincing' were examples. However, a large minority seemed to hate *Doctor Who* with a vengeance, dismissing the programme as 'rubbishy, incredible and ridiculous – too ridiculous even for children.'

The Daleks' Master Plan elicited a wide variety of comments also, but the summation at the end of episode twelve was: 'It may be said that if adult viewers start by "tolerating" this serial for the sake of their children, it seems clear that they often find that it has its attractions and on this occasion there were, in fact, plenty who considered *Dr Who* excellent entertainment by any standards.'

Other, more ad hoc surveys of viewers' reactions were carried out from time to time by the BBC's audience researchers. During the run of *Marco Polo*, for instance, numerous comments were received to the effect that 'Dr Who seemed to be a great favourite, apart from one or two younger children who find it frightening,' but that 'the punch and excitement of the Dalek period has given way to boring details of maps and commentary,' and more generally that 'several children and their parents have said they prefer this series to look into the future rather than the past.' Again, the occasional more disparaging comment was made. Two 'professional class' fathers, for example, thought that Doctor Who was 'a bad and pernicious programme' for the BBC to be putting out. However, these views were very much in the minority.

Overall, Doctor Who had been a great success, and from humble beginnings had risen to a position of prominence in British popular culture unparalleled by any contemporary TV series.

FIRST DOCTOR STORIES IN ORDER OF AVERAGE VIEWING FIGURES
(Figures in millions of viewers)

The Rescue	12.5
The Web Planet	12.5
The Dalek Invasion of Earth	11.9
The Romans	11.6
Inside the Spaceship	10.15
Galaxy 4	9.9
Marco Polo	9.47
The Chase	9.4
The Crusade	9.38
The Daleks' Master Plan	9.3
The Space Museum	9.2
The Keys of Marinus	9.07
The Mutants	8.97
Planet of Giants	8.57
The Time Meddler	8.4
The Myth Makers	8.34
The Celestial Toymaker	8.3
Mission to the Unknown	8.3
The Aztecs	7.53
The Sensorites	6.92
The Tenth Planet	6.75
The Reign of Terror	6.73
The Ark	6.48
The Massacre of St. Bartholomew's Eve	6.43
100,000 BC	6.4
The Gunfighters	6.25
The War Machines	5.23
The Savages	4.91
The Smugglers	4.48

The Second Doctor

by
David J Howe
Mark Stammers
Stephen James Walker

FOREWORD

For the legions of fans who had been glued to the adventures of this irascible old character for the previous three years, Hartnell was Doctor Who and it was impossible to imagine the series without him. Yet on 22 October 1966, their hero lay gravely ill on the floor of his TARDIS, his features blurred and were replaced by those of another. The unthinkable had occurred, Hartnell was gone but the series would continue. Whilst the credits rolled at the end of *The Tenth Planet*, viewers were left to ponder whether or not the series would have much of a future with its new star, Patrick Troughton.

Doctor Who had succeeded in popularising science fiction with the British viewing public. Hartnell had found renewed fame amongst a new generation of young fans. The dwindling numbers of 'real life' police boxes had suddenly become universally recognised as the exterior of the Doctor's TARDIS, and the Daleks had become a massive craze in their own right, spawning hundreds of pieces of merchandise and two feature films. Yet virtually all this success had taken place within the series' first two years, and despite the efforts of the production team, public interest had since waned.

Many within the BBC had doubted the series' appeal from the beginning, only grudgingly admitting the obvious success it achieved. When the viewing figures began to trail off during the third season, similar voices began to say it had run out of steam and that it was perhaps time for something new.

Britain and the world had changed a great deal since the series had begun. Beatlemania and the Mersey sound, Mary Quant and the arrival of the permissive society had changed people's perceptions. The growing conflict in Vietnam and the cold war dominated the news reports, whilst the Americans and the Soviet Union pushed onwards in the race to put a man on the moon. Science fiction was quickly turning into science fact. The mid-Sixties was a great time to be young. Teenagers were better paid and more independent than their parents had even been. Fashion, music and entertainment changed in style to attract the affluent youth market.

In the face of so much change, it was natural to expect that *Doctor Who* would need to adjust its format to continue to attract audiences. The series' production team were keen to aim its storylines at a slightly older viewing audience. This, however, caused problems between successive producers and Hartnell. The actor strongly believed that the show should stick with its tried and tested mix of fantasy stories and pseudo-historicals aimed at the younger end of the family audience. As the only survivor from the original cast and crew, he believed that he knew better than anyone else how *Doctor Who* should be made. Producer Innes Lloyd was determined, however, and he reached an agreement with Hartnell that the actor would not continue in the role. The search for a replacement ended with the announcement of Patrick Troughton as the new Doctor.

But how could such a change of actor be explained? Would the series' regular viewers accept Troughton in the role, or would they simply turn off? Would a greater emphasis on action in the plots attract new and bigger audiences? The production team could do nothing but wait for the public's reaction.

Join us as we travel back to examine a pivotal period of the series' history. The end of historical stories. An influx of new monsters, including several that would menace the

Doctor in further adventures. A mammoth finale that would reveal the Doctor's origins. And an era packed with many stories that are still considered classics today.

@@@@@@@@@@@@@@@@@@@@@@@@@@@@@@@@@@@@@@@

PATRICK TROUGHTON: IN HIS OWN WORDS

ON HIS EARLY LIFE AND CAREER:

'I was born in Mill Hill, a suburb of London. I went to a sort of kindergarten there, and studied ballet dancing, under Pearl Argyle. She was in the film *Things to Come*. Anyway, I soon gave up the idea of becoming a ballet dancer – I must have been about six at the time. I went away later to boarding school at Bexhill-by-the-Sea. I did my O Levels at Mill Hill Public School, then my A Levels. Having got those, I went to the Embassy School of Acting. I was there for a couple of years, and received a scholarship to go to the school of the John Drew Memorial Theatre in East Hampton on Long Island in America. We did a whole lot of plays there, as well as a lot of hard work in our studies. I had a wonderful time; that is a wonderful part of the world.

'The day we broke up, we listened in to Neville Chamberlain announcing that we had declared war on Germany. My dad was a lawyer in a shipping firm, and he arranged me a trip back on a Belgian ship. We hit a mine off Portland Bill, coming back from Rotterdam. We had to take to the boats, and were picked up by a Greek steamer. We were taken into Weymouth, from where I phoned my dad to tell the family I was there. I was nineteen, so I did a bit of rep acting, to wait for my call-up. I had to wait till I was twenty-one, so I did some winter rep at Tunbridge with people like John Cullum, Googie Withers and others. I played Bottom in *A Midsummer Night's Dream*, apart from anything else! It was fun, but a bit sad really. One knew it was all coming to a grisly end when we joined up.

'I joined the Navy, and spent my first six months of the war up in the Highlands, at Loch Ewin. There, about five of us were chosen as commissioned candidates and sent to do three months' sea time before we could take our exams. We actually did six months, in fact, on the east coast convoy, on destroyers, working between Rosside and Sheerness. Then I was posted back to Scotland to train on Coastal Forces, which is what I wanted to do – small ships, motor torpedo boats, that sort of thing. I spent the rest of the war based in Great Yarmouth defending our convoys off the east coast against U-Boat and air attack. We also attacked the German convoys off the Dutch coast. We went generally looking for trouble, running up and down the convoy routes. That was all night work.

'Then we went down to Ramsgate, to bottle up the E-Boats off Ostend, to stop them coming out. I was given my own command, and sent back to Great Yarmouth. I spent the rest of the war picking Americans up out of the drink! This was when they returned in their Fortresses and Liberators. That was more or less my war ... It's very lovely having your own boat!

'After the war, I went back to rep work, in Amersham. I did three plays there, then I got into the Bristol Old Vic to do a whole season of Shakespeare and a few other plays. Then I decided that I didn't want to be away from home any longer, since I'd been away all the war. I was married by then, so I returned to London to try and find work. I went to the Mercury Theatre, where they were doing T S Eliot plays – *Murder in the*

Cathedral and *Family Reunion* – and did those for about two years. Then I got into the film of *Hamlet*, playing the player king, with Laurence Olivier. Later on, I was in *Richard III*, where I was Olivier's acting understudy. I was in an identical costume, identical make-up. I had to watch him rehearse a scene, then do it for him – exactly as he had done it, or I was in trouble! This was so that he could compose the picture (he directed as well as starred), then he would do the scene. We went to Spain to film the battle – heaven knows why! It looked like the Crusades. It should have been a foggy, wet day in England. I can't think why he did it! I started then with television, in 1948. I got in on the ground floor, and I've never stopped. I did live television for about fifteen years, then taped – or telecine as it was in those days.'
Interviewed by John Peel in 1986 for *Fantasy Empire*.

ON PLAYING TV'S FIRST ROBIN HOOD:

'It was a bit primitive in those days. For the forest we had back projection. This was a slide, on a screen behind the actors. The projectionists were from Pinewood Studios, because they had a machine, and we had to hire it from them. It was all live, of course. We had this scene where I first met Little John. We came on for the scene, there was a noise behind us where the back projection machine was – and they put the forest in sideways! Then there was a sort of muffled conversation behind us while we were doing the scene, and the trees disappeared – there was a white screen – and then they went in the right way up! This was all being broadcast; it was live, you see, and you couldn't stop! That was quite fun … It was a very good serial, though, despite that.'
Interviewed by John Peel in 1986 for *Fantasy Empire*.

ON WATCHING WILLIAM HARTNELL AS THE DOCTOR:

'We watched Billy as a family, and saw every single *Doctor Who* story through for his three years. We used to enjoy the ones where he went to the future and he met all kinds of creatures. We didn't so much enjoy the ones that were back in history, because they were so predictable. There was one, though, which explained the mystery of the *Mary Celeste* – which of course was Daleks! – that was rather fun. You can do anything you like on the show. You can move sideways, forwards or backwards in time. Billy was very keen, especially toward the end of his time, when there was some sort of alien presence or invasion, or when they were detected, to say in his character "Now, steady on. Don't let's think of them as a menace. Let's make contact with them". That's very important, really, because fear is a terrible thing.

'I tried to keep on Billy's idea that the aliens weren't necessarily enemies just because they were different.'
Interviewed by John Peel in 1986 for *Fantasy Empire*.

ON BEING CAST AS THE DOCTOR:

'[*Doctor Who*] had been going on about three years and I felt at the end of three years that, you know, it had gone on a long time and I didn't know how long the BBC were really thinking of keeping it. So, to be quite honest, I was very reluctant at first. To go and commit yourself to something out of the blue, which you really didn't know would go on … I had a feeling that in a way the joke was over and that it had gone on too long.'
Interviewed by Richard Landen in 1983 for *Doctor Who* Magazine No. 78.

'I didn't think it was a particularly good idea of the BBC to replace Billy. I thought it was pretty silly, really! I didn't see how anyone could follow him. The only way that you could do that was to copy him, like Dickie Hurndall did in *The Five Doctors*. But to make him a completely new person ... I thought that the difficulties of selling it to the audience – apart from selling it to poor old Ben and Polly! – were enormous, almost insurmountable. However, in the end, I was ... persuaded, over a week of negotiations, and I thought, "What the heck, let's do this for a while and see what happens". Then, after a rather stop-start beginning while the audience wondered who the heck it was taking over, they settled down and started to like me, then to love me. I settled down and had the three best years of my life.'
Interviewed by John Peel in 1986 for *Fantasy Empire*.

'I was making a film called *The Viking Queen* when they tried to get me to play Doctor Who. We were in Ireland and it was while I was filming. The phone kept on ringing, and they were saying "Come and play Doctor Who". And I said "No, no, don't want to play Doctor Who". And they went on phoning up and I said "No, no, I don't want to play it out. It wouldn't last more than six weeks more with me!" In the end, they kept on pushing the money up so much every day that at the end of the week I said "What am I doing? Of course I'll do this part! Yes!" So I decided to do it, thinking "Well, perhaps a couple of episodes and then they'll finish with it; that'll be the end, but it'll be just one job and I'll move on to another". Little did I know ...'
Interviewed by Ben Landman in 1984 for *Whovian Times* Volume 9.

ON HIS DOCTOR'S CHARACTER:
'We had to do something a bit different. My original idea was to black up, wear a big turban and brass earrings with a big grey beard; doing it like the Arabian Nights. The idea was that when I'd finished, I could shave the beard off and so on and no-one would know who I was and I wouldn't be type-cast'
Interviewed on *Pebble Mill at One* in 1973.

'The first idea was this windjammer captain with a sort of Victorian naval hat and brass buttons, but the Head of Drama Sydney Newman took one look at this costume and said "Whatever happened to the cosmic hobo?" He had the idea of making a sort of Chaplinesque character, a sort of tramp, in contrast to Billy Hartnell, and I suppose he must have known that I have a wicked glint in my eye for comedy, so we decided on that.'
Interviewed by Richard Landen in 1983 for *Doctor Who* Magazine No. 78.

'We went up to Bermans, the costumiers, and we just looked through all the old rubbish, really. We just got things out of hampers and had a look, and the costume evolved. It was sort of a ragged imitation of Billy Hartnell, I suppose, only a bit more way-out. To begin with, you see, I found myself playing it over-the-top, mostly because Sydney Newman kept on urging me to. But the Head of Serials, Shaun Sutton, who I think was a little bit wiser than Sydney Newman in many ways – in fact, considerably wiser! – said "No, no, just do it in your head, old chap, don't do all those stunts and so on". So I toned it down a bit after that, and it was warmer and a bit more successful.'
Interviewed on stage at the PanoptiCon VI convention in 1985.

'It worked very well when I first took it on, because one was saying to everybody ,"This is the way we're going to do it. It's going to be different. If you don't like it, you can lump it." So we were exaggerating it a bit, and afterwards we toned it down as we got more confident in what we were doing. It became more subtle, and the script writers began to get on our wavelength, which made a hell of a difference. They began to write for you rather than you having to change the script to fit what you wanted to do. Fortunately, that happened very quickly.

'As for the hat, well I think it was dear old Campbell Logan [a BBC producer], or it might have been Andy Osborn [the Head of Series], who said to me in the BBC club one evening, after they'd shown the first one, "Oh splendid. It'll go on for another three years. Have to get rid of the hat though." So the hat went!'
Interviewed by Richard Marson in 1984 for *Doctor Who Magazine* **No. 102.**

'I had young children of my own when I was doing it. My daughter was about twelve and my son maybe ten, and my other son about eight, so obviously I had them in mind when I was playing it – and I tailored it to that, really. I think perhaps if I'd had a grown-up family, it might have been a different character that emerged; but with them being young, one had that in mind – you didn't want to make it too frightening and all that. You know, I heard the other day – having decided to be a sort of ineffectual, or apparently ineffectual, genius who seemed to get it all wrong until the very end when he got it right – apparently that scared the hell out of children far more than being absolutely certain you've got to win! Because all the time, the fear that I showed and the apparent bungling got them worried. They had no faith in the fact that I was going to solve it in the end, although of course we always did. That was just the reaction of one child I met – who's now grown up, of course.'
Interviewed by Ben Landman in 1984 for *Whovian Times* **Volume 9.**

'I don't think he was a goody. He was a bit naughty, wasn't he? Of course, you've got to be on the right side when there's a villain about, but he was naughty all the same. If you're going to be totally moral it's boring, so you have to colour it a bit. Let's face it, it's a smashing part!'
Interviewed by Richard Marson in 1984 for *Doctor Who Magazine* **No. 102.**

ON THE DEMANDS OF THE *DOCTOR WHO* SCHEDULE:
'We're not creative, we just do it. We rehearsed Monday, Tuesday, Wednesday and half Thursday, doing the show on Friday. At the beginning, we were filming every other weekend as well. You didn't have time to luxuriate in things like creativity and all that. By and large, though, the directors were all fine. Very nice. People like Gerry Blake, Douglas Camfield and David Maloney. They were all good.

'We got very tired about half way through the run, because they wanted us to film at weekends too. It was silly really, so we had a sort of sit-down strike and said "You've got to alter it". Our boss Shaun Sutton, bless his heart, said "OK, we'll change it," and it was arranged that before each story, we would do a week's work with the new director and new cast doing all the filming necessary. Then we would do the studio stuff in the normal way. It gave us a chance to catch our breath. You had so little time to think, you needed your Saturday and Sunday off to cope.

'You got into a pattern of doing it, and if anyone upset that routine, you were very distressed. If a director came along and started rehearsal half an hour late or quarter of an hour early, it threw you off balance straight away. Working like that, at that pace, for three years, was like doing weekly rep. You got extremely tired and you wanted a definite routine to keep you going and make sure you knew exactly what you were supposed to be doing. Anything that varied from that was awkward and you had to try and get it back to the old way of doing things.'
Interviewed by Richard Marson in 1984 for *Doctor Who Magazine* **No. 102.**

'We used to have four weeks off every August, and starting again was rather like jumping on a running bus. I remember that feeling when we were filming in Wales for *The Abominable Snowmen.*'
Interviewed on stage at the PanoptiCon VI convention in 1985.

'We had three and a half days' rehearsal, which was done in a church hall. When we were not actually rehearsing, Frazer Hines, Debbie Watling and eventually Wendy Padbury and I played a card game called Aggravation – non-stop for three years. For sixpenny stakes! It was a game you sort of won and lost as the years went past ... Then we would get called to do a scene. If we were left playing cards too long, we would poke our heads around the door and yell "What's going on? We want to work!" But the fun was purely by the way. We were like squirrels on a wheel.

'The problem was fatigue, really. In the end, you got the giggles, you were so fatigued. That can get very distressing, when someone gets the giggles. Not on the part of the artists so much, but the directors get a bit annoyed.'
Interviewed by John Peel in 1986 for *Fantasy Empire.*

ON HAZARDS ENCOUNTERED DURING PRODUCTION:

'On one occasion I went onto the set of *The Moonbase* at Lime Grove and they had this Gravitron hanging from the ceiling of the studio on a couple of wires and a hook. I normally wander about the set before the day begins to say "That's there, this is here, that looks like that," and generally become accustomed to the set. I stood under the Gravitron, had a good look and thought "Yes, that looks very nice". I took two steps off the set and the whole thing, which must have weighed about two tons, crashed down! I'd have been flattened! I remember the director, Morris Barry, deciding he didn't like the look of the set and having it rebuilt on the studio day. I admired him for that, but he was able to keep the show going only because he had very wide experience of live television.

'Explosions tended to be not so much dangerous as loud. There's a super photo of me from *The Invasion* being exploded at. One's nerve was fairly ragged after doing it non stop, so those expressions were pretty realistic. The worst one was *The War Games*, which we filmed on Brighton rubbish tip. They'd used it for *Oh! What a Lovely War*, so there were already trenches and wire laid out. Visual Effects had these enormous explosions with great clods of earth all over the place. It was a bit alarming. By that stage we were all giggly, hysterical giggly. I just had to say "Jamie, Zoe" and we collapsed – that was it, finish.'
Interviewed by Richard Marson in 1984 for *Doctor Who Magazine* **No. 102.**

ON THE PLEASURES OF HIS TIME AS THE DOCTOR:

'My favourite role, I think, was Mr Quilp in *The Old Curiosity Shop* – but *Doctor Who* comes a very good second! I liked doing them all, but the first Yeti one was good fun.'
Patrick Troughton writing in November 1980 in a letter to fan Patrick Mulkern.

'It was a very happy show for a start. We were very fortunate in having super people like Frazer Hines. I acted with Frazer when he was twelve, a boy actor, so I've known him a long time. We just hit it off on the set, and when we ever had any time off the set, we liked each other there too. We found we could communicate acting-wise. He's a very good listener. Half the art of working with someone on a long-term basis was that you listened to what the other person was saying to you. This made a big difference to me.

'The producer, Innes Lloyd, was super too. Couldn't have a better producer than that – diplomatic, friendly and enthusiastic. Oh, we were very lucky.

'I'm sure Frazer has embellished a few of the stories that could be told. His favourite little jape was if we were off set or in the TARDIS, he'd say "cue" and I'd walk on, only to discover that it wasn't our cue at all. In fact, he's still doing that one!

'People do tend to romanticise, but it's part of our job to get people to do that. The more you do that the greater the compliment. In the end, of course, it's just a job. I'm a character actor, and I play a lot of characters. With *Doctor Who*, like a lot of work, you have enormous fun – more than usual even. But in the end it's still just a job.'
Interviewed by Richard Marson in 1984 for *Doctor Who Magazine* No. 102.

'It was a marvellous time. On a couple of occasions, standing in the TARDIS waiting for a cue to come on to the studio floor, Frazer Hines and I at a given signal would whip down Debbie Watling's pants just before we got the cue and then open the door and go out, and she'd be giggling away trying to struggle into her pants to get on the set! I don't know if that's printable, but there we are! That was the sort of thing – all very clean, you know, but great fun really! We had that sort of rapport, which was lovely.'
Interviewed by Ben Landman in 1984 for *Whovian Times* Volume 9.

'I loved playing the part! Playing one part for three years – I'd never done that in my life, you see. I'd gone from one character part to another, playing wildly different things: Saint Paul; Allan Breck in *Kidnapped*; the dwarf, Quilp, in *The Old Curiosity Shop*; the old Doctor Manet in *A Tale of Two Cities*; sometimes mad comedy; and just to come to one part for three years, which was happy, and people liked, was an absolute joy. It was wonderful! I had a young family at the time and it meant lots of pennies for them, and sending them to schools and that sort of thing. It was lovely, marvellous – just at the right moment, really!'
Interviewed by Ben Landman in 1984 for *Whovian Times* Volume 9.

ON MAKING SCRIPT SUGGESTIONS:

'One is inventing all the time, and it is either chucked out or accepted by the director. They have what is called a producer's run. This is the last run at a rehearsal. Peter Bryant was the producer after Innes and his little trick was that as the producer's run started, directly I opened my mouth, he started writing on his note pad. Frazer Hines and I had it down to a fine art. What we used to do was put in things we knew he wouldn't accept

but at the same time slip in things he probably wouldn't see or notice. This way, he would chuck out the obvious ones and retain the more subtle ones, and that's how we did it. Another dodge we had was, if Frazer and I thought the script was over long, on reading it through we used to read it very slowly. There is always the lady with the stopwatch timing it to the end, and if it was too long, they had to cut it. That way we didn't have so much to learn. They could always pad it out with action if necessary.'
Interviewed by Richard Landen in 1983 for *Doctor Who* Magazine No. 78.

ON HIS DEPARTURE FROM THE SERIES:
'Three years was long enough. I didn't wanted to get "typed" and one had to get out while the going was good. Peter Bryant asked me way back how long, and I said "Three years, no longer". You see, say it had gone on for ten years and then the BBC had dropped it. I would have been sunk, because after ten years, you can't walk into another play. They'll all say, "Oh look, it's Doctor Who" straight away. Even though before I did *Doctor Who* I had done a long line of character parts, thirteen years of one part, Doctor Who, would have been suicide, professionally. Unless of course you can go on forever, then that would have been all right, but there was no guarantee that the BBC were going to keep it on forever. So I had to say, "How long? Okay, three years and I'll have to get out".'
Interviewed by Richard Landen in 1983 for *Doctor Who* Magazine No. 78.

'I resent giving it up from the money point of view – but not any other, even though I enjoyed doing it very much. One can't stay in one part forever, especially a success, and I saw the writing on the wall ...!'
Patrick Troughton writing in January 1972 in a letter to fan Ian McLachlan.

ON *THE THREE DOCTORS*:
'Wasn't it for an anniversary of some sort? That was the reason I did it. They wanted us all together, and so I said "Yes, fine, great". And it was fun, it was lovely. Especially having Billy Hartnell there, even though he was only on film, trapped in a sort of bubble. A bit ga-ga, poor lad, but it was lovely seeing him there. Jon Pertwee and I developed quite a rapport, shall we say.'
Interviewed on stage at the PanoptiCon VI convention in 1985.

ON *THE FIVE DOCTORS*:
'It was wonderful! I fell into it at once! There's only one thing I regret, and that is that I didn't quite get the hair right – because my make-up lady, fifteen years ago, used to lift it with sort of curlers, you know, so it was fairly high, and I forgot that this time. So although the length and so on was right – it was my own hair, it wasn't a wig, although it looked like a wig I know – it wasn't quite the same. If I do it again, I'll lift it up a bit to look more like it used to.
'It was better than *The Three Doctors* in a way – it was more vivid. I don't know why.'
Interviewed by Ben Landman in 1984 for *Whovian Times* Volume 9.

ON *THE TWO DOCTORS*:
'*The Two Doctors* is a beauty. The Sontarans I'd never met on screen before, and they're

splendid. Colin Baker is super too. And Seville was fantastic. It was very hot, but we had a lovely swimming pool we could fall into. I read my script and dressed accordingly – no way would I have that fur coat!'
Interviewed by Richard Marson in 1984 for *Doctor Who Magazine* **No. 102.**

ON HIS RELUCTANCE TO GIVE PRESS INTERVIEWS:
'You're press. I heard you were coming. It's no good. I never give interviews. Never.
'Just tell them that I am that mystery man of television, Doctor Who.
'You see, I think acting is magic. If I tell you all about myself it will spoil it.
'People talk about television being in the sitting-room and becoming an everyday thing. But it is not true, especially for the children. It is still magic, and I hope it always stays that way.
'I've only talked to you because you're a girl. And I like girls.'
Interviewed by Margaret Pride and Gillian Mills in 1966 for *Reveille*, **edition dated 22-28 December.**

'It's like a conjuror showing you how he does his tricks. If you can see how it's being done, it takes away all the magic. I don't want people to see me. I want them to see the person the writer's spent so much time creating, brought to life.'
Quoted in 1987 in *Doctor Who – An Adventure in Space and Time: Season Six Special.*

ON CONVENTION APPEARANCES:
'I don't want to become too associated again with the part – in this country. Not too much. In America, that's different, because I don't appear over there, except in repeats and things. I enjoy going to the American conventions very much – the travel and so on. But over here, I don't want to do it too much. I love doing it, though. It's lovely.'
Interviewed on stage at the PanoptiCon VI convention in 1985.

'It's an ego trip. They love you so much. When I was on the show, you didn't have time for such things. You didn't have time to do anything but go home and go to sleep! I went to bed at nine o'clock every night for three years! I couldn't have existed otherwise.'
Interviewed by John Peel in 1986 for *Fantasy Empire.*

ON THE RELATIVE MERITS OF STAGE, FILM AND TV WORK:
'I don't like acting on the stage, because I like to work during the day and I like to go home during the evening and put my feet up and watch the telly. Also, if I do the stage, I never see my wife Sheelagh because she works all day; she'd go to work and come back and I'd be going to work and it would be impossible. I much prefer the technique and intimacy of television or film. It's my style of acting. I can do both, though, and I'd love to do a while of farce or comedy on the stage – I think that's where it's most successful, because you've got to build on the audience for comedy; you've got to build on the laughs and so on. I wouldn't mind doing that, but it would have to be a very happy play and a very happy part, and for a limited time – six months or something, at the most. But I prefer television, and I've been in it now since 1948. It's given me all my chances, and you naturally stay with what you like.'
Interviewed by Ben Landman in 1984 for *Whovian Times* **Volume 9.**

ON HIS HOME LIFE:

'I like working with my hands, making things and home decorating, also gardening.
'I suppose, at heart, I am a country person. I would like to have been a naturalist as long as it didn't get me involved with snakes and spiders.'
Interviewed by Margaret Pride and Gillian Mills in 1966 for *Reveille*, edition dated 22-28 December.

ON RELIGION:

'I'm interested that you are studying theology. I don't think I could ever have done that – in a conventional church. There seem too many stumbling blocks to me – though I know the private views of churchmen are sometimes very different from the 39 Articles etc.

'But if only the great difficulties had not been there, I might well have been a professional churchman myself, though not in the Church of England.

'It does seem to me that so much is just watered down medieval Christianity with no real attempt made to solve the problem, "Love or be damned". To me love can never reject, only fail to draw, and then only temporarily. I cannot get round the issue that Jesus seemed to believe in and advocate eternal torment – and that for no remedial reason.

'Either he's not the full embodiment of the Spirit of Christ of the Cosmos – or the record is sadly wrong. I think it is the latter; I think men may well get into torment and Jesus's reaction is always to get them out of it, but not, I'm afraid, in so many places in the Gospels. I wish he'd been a vegetarian too – not that I am – but Buddha was and I think that is more loving.'
Patrick Troughton writing in January 1972 in a letter to fan Ian McLachlan.

CHARACTER — THE SECOND DOCTOR

These days, the fact that the Doctor can from time to time 'regenerate' – take on a completely new physical appearance in order to escape death – is well known to the general viewing public. It has indeed become an integral part of *Doctor Who*'s basic mythology, arguably as important an element of the series' format as the TARDIS or the Daleks, and each successive change of Doctor generates a wealth of speculation and publicity. This was not always the case, however.

From the time *Doctor Who* made its on-air debut in November 1963 up until the autumn of 1966, William Hartnell was the Doctor and the Doctor was William Hartnell – the two were effectively inseparable in viewers' minds. Hartnell's memorable portrayal of the character as a stern but kind-hearted grandfather figure, complete with long white hair and dignified Edwardian clothes, had endeared him to millions and helped to make *Doctor Who* the great national and international success it had become. While it was not unknown for a leading character in an important programme to be recast – each of the BBC's three famous Quatermass serials of the Fifties, for instance, had seen a different actor in the central role of Professor Bernard Quatermass – it was very unusual in an ongoing weekly series, and inevitably a risky and potentially unpalatable step to take.

Clearly, then, the decision to replace Hartnell with another actor was a brave one on the part of *Doctor Who*'s third producer, Innes Lloyd. Such a move had been considered by his predecessor, John Wiles, but had at that time been effectively overruled by the then Head of Serials, Gerald Savory. In announcements to the press, it was diplomatically suggested that Hartnell had left the series to resume his career in the theatre. In truth, however, according to many of those who worked with him, the actor had become increasingly difficult to work with – due partly to ill health and partly to an increasingly dogmatic and proprietorial attitude on his part – and Lloyd considered that the change would be beneficial not only for the series but also for Hartnell himself.

The concept of the Doctor undergoing a total physical transformation (a process that would not actually be termed 'regeneration' until 1974) provided a means of incorporating the change of actor into the ongoing narrative of the series itself. It is uncertain exactly who first came up with this idea – Wiles had proposed simply having the Doctor's appearance changed by the Celestial Toymaker after a period of invisibility in the third season story named after that character – but the likelihood is that it emerged in discussions between Lloyd and his story editor, Gerry Davis. Others who may well have been involved in the discussions were Head of Serials Shaun Sutton and Dr Kit Pedler, *Doctor Who*'s unofficial scientific adviser, with whom Davis was working closely on the scripts for the first Doctor's final story, *The Tenth Planet*.

Although a number of other possibilities, including Sir Michael Hordern, were considered, the man eventually chosen as Hartnell's replacement was 46-year-old character actor Patrick Troughton (who had at one time been a contender for the guest role of gunslinger Johnny Ringo in the third season story *The Gunfighters*). As Lloyd later recounted, this was a choice of which Hartnell himself very much approved:

'I recall him saying to me – though I don't know if he said it to anyone else – "There's only one man in England who can take over, and that's Patrick Troughton."'

Lloyd's own view was that Troughton was 'an absolutely ideal choice':

'He had versatility going for him – he was a distinguished character actor with a great many varied roles behind him. He was always in demand. He was a popular actor with a great following. Most important of all, I think, was that he had a leading actor's temperament. He was a father figure to the whole company and hence could embrace it and sweep it along with him.'

Troughton was offered the role of the new Doctor during the third week of June 1966, while he was on location in Ireland for the Hammer film *The Viking Queen*. Although he felt that *Doctor Who* had perhaps been 'done to death', he was eventually persuaded to accept, in part because he realised that the regular income would help to pay for his sons' education. He signed his initial twenty-two episode contract on 2 August.

In an article published on 2 September under the heading '"Tougher" Doctor Who is chosen', the *Daily Telegraph* reported the views of the BBC's Head of Drama Sydney Newman on the recasting of the Doctor:

'Our problem in choosing the new Doctor Who was very difficult, because we have decided to make considerable changes in the personality of the character. We believe we have found exactly the man we wanted.'

Troughton had initially harboured considerable doubts as to whether or not the audience would actually accept him as the Doctor. It had however been agreed from the outset that he should not even attempt to copy the style of Hartnell's performance but should instead endeavour to bring to the role his own, completely different characterisation. The big question was, what should that new characterisation be?

The production team set out their initial ideas in a short note (drawing in part on an early draft of the series' original format, dated 16 May 1963, which suggested that the Doctor had begun his travels as a fugitive from an unknown enemy during a galactic war). This read as follows:

The New Doctor Who

Appearance. Facially as strong, piercing eyes of the explorer or Sea Captain. His hair is wild and his clothes look rather the worse for wear (this is a legacy from the metaphysical change which took place in the Tardis). Obviously spares very little time and bother on his appearance. In the first serial, he wears a fly-blown version of the clothes associated with this character.

Manner. Vital and forceful – his actions are controlled by his superior intellect and experience – whereas at times he is a positive man of action, at other times he deals with the situation like a skilled chess player, reasoning and cunningly planning his moves. He has humour and wit and also an overwhelmingly thunderous rage which frightens his companions and others.

A feature of the new Doctor Who will be the humour on the lines of the sardonic humour of Sherlock Holmes. He enjoys disconcerting his companions with unconventional and unexpected repartee.

After the first serial – the Daleks – (when the character has been established), we will introduce a love of disguises which will help and sometimes disconcert his friends.

To keep faith with the essential Doctor Who character, he is always suspicious of new places, things or people – he is the eternal fugitive with a horrifying fear of the past horrors he has endured. (These horrors were experienced during the galactic war and account for his flight from his own planet.)

The metaphysical change which takes place over 500 or so years is a horrifying experience – an experience in which he re-lives some of the most unendurable moments of his long life, including the galactic war. It is as if he has had the LSD drug and instead of experiencing the kicks, he has the hell and dank horror which can be its effect.

The task of writing the new Doctor's debut adventure had been entrusted to David Whitaker, who as *Doctor Who*'s original story editor had been one of the small group of individuals responsible for developing the series in the first place. He had since contributed several stories of his own and had recently been discussing a number of new ideas with Davis; consequently, he seemed a natural choice to tackle this important project.

The storyline that Whitaker came up with was entitled *The Destiny of Doctor Who* – a reference to the Doctor's transformation – and, as suggested in the production team's note, featured the ever-popular Daleks (the hope being that their presence would help to reassure viewers that this was still *Doctor Who* that they were watching, even though the Doctor himself now looked different). Davis approved this storyline and on 22 July 1966 commissioned Whitaker to write the complete scripts for the six part story, for a fee of £300 per episode, with a target delivery date of 8 August. A separate fee of £15 per episode was paid to the Daleks' creator, Terry Nation, for their use in the story.

'This was around the time William Hartnell was leaving,' Whitaker later observed, 'and so, aware that the idea was to replace him with another actor, I wrote the Doctor's part as sketchily as possible, so that it could be easily altered. I then concerned myself with the rest of the story and delivered my scripts just before I was due to go abroad for a time.'

Mindful as he was of the need to keep the characterisation of the Doctor relatively vague, Whitaker was nevertheless influenced to a certain degree by the production team's note. Consequently he made him a somewhat verbose and arrogant type, with a sardonic wit akin to that of Sherlock Holmes. These draft scripts proved a source of some concern to Troughton, as he told a convention audience in 1985:

'We had script conferences and there was a first script, which was sort of written for Billy but in a way it was written for, it struck me reading it, a very verbose, autocratic Sherlock Holmes type – who never stopped talking! I thought, "That's not going to do for me over three years every week," so I said that I didn't see my Doctor quite like that: I saw him really as a listener. I thought that this Doctor listened to everyone and totted it all up and then made his own decision about things. Then in comes Sydney Newman and he starts talking about a "cosmic hobo", who obviously wouldn't talk like an intellectual, autocratic Sherlock Holmes type at all. So I leapt at it: I said "What a good idea! … A man like that'd be more of a listener, wouldn't he? …" I was very keen on the idea of doing it as a cosmic hobo.'

Newman had overall responsibility for literally hundreds of programmes each year and would not normally concern himself with the day-to-day production of *Doctor Who*. He did however keep a watchful eye on the series – all the more so, many people believed, because it was to a large extent his own brainchild – and he would always have to be consulted about important developments such as major format or cast changes. Hence his involvement in the initial discussions concerning Troughton's portrayal of the Doctor.

Davis later described how the detailed characterisation had been arrived at:

'We had to change the concept of the Doctor. We spent a whole day – producer, Head of Serials, Patrick Troughton, me and some others – at a meeting. As the morning went on, it became chaotic. Everyone was giving ideas, but there was no real cohesion. I could see that Troughton was getting very irritated. He was very uneasy about taking the job anyway, thinking that he might be type-cast. At the end of the morning, I realised we were getting nowhere, so I ejected everyone else from the meeting and just Patrick Troughton and I worked out the character.

'Really it came mostly out of Troughton's own personality. In an odd sort of way, he was playing himself. He was hard to pin down, shifting, always eluding the issue. This was very different from the positive, dogmatic character of Hartnell. So at the end of the day, we went back and I said I thought we had it.

'I thought it would be very interesting to have a character who never quite says what he means, who, really, uses the intelligence of the people he is with. He knows the answer all the time; if he suggests something, he knows the outcome. He is watching, he's really directing, but he doesn't want to *show* he's directing like the old Doctor.'

Davis was inspired in part by the character Destry portrayed by film star James Stewart in the popular Western *Destry Rides Again* (a 1939 production by Universal); someone who when asked a question would always reply by way of a parable rather than give a straight answer.

Once the new Doctor's character had been worked out, Whitaker's scripts for his debut story – which had now been retitled *The Power of the Daleks* – had to be amended accordingly. As this was a last minute job, and as Whitaker did not have the time to do it himself, Davis contacted another former *Doctor Who* story editor, Dennis Spooner, to perform the rewrite, beginning with the first episode over the weekend of 8-9 October 1966. Spooner's fee for this work was £75 per episode. Whitaker agreed to the rewrite on condition that neither his own fee nor his overseas rights were affected, that the characterisation of the Daleks was left unchanged, and that he still received sole writer's credit.

'I rewrote the story from David's scripts,' Spooner later confirmed. 'Terry Nation had the rights to write all the Dalek stories, but he was busy and couldn't do this one. So he handed the task over to David to write it. David wrote it as a straight piece for *nobody*. You see, he knew it wasn't going to be William Hartnell, and he didn't know *who* it was going to be. So he wrote it as "the Doctor", and "the Doctor" was really not written at all. Nothing the Doctor said was important to the development of the story. The Doctor was on the sidelines of the plot.

'When they cast Pat Troughton, Gerry Davis didn't feel that he, as story editor, could do the amount of rewriting that was going to be involved. As story editor, you've got to liaise with Make-up, Costume and all the other departments; you've got to look after your producer; you've got to take the director in hand. He knew that if he took this story, he would have to go home for three weeks to do the amount of rewriting it needed, so he asked me to do it.

'I went in and met Pat Troughton and I said to Pat, virtually, "How do you see yourself as the Doctor?" That was obviously so I'd be able to write it as he wanted to play it. Basically, he saw it as Charlie Chaplin. So we went through it together, and his part expanded to just the right size.'

When it came to choosing the costume and make-up that Troughton would wear, a number of outlandish ideas were mooted. It was thought, for example, that he might 'black up' and put on curly-toed slippers and a turban (an image that in later interviews he would often liken to the one adopted by German star Conrad Veidt in the 1940 London Films movie *The Thief of Baghdad*), or perhaps adopt the guise of a sea captain in full Victorian-style naval uniform. A number of these ideas were actually tried out in test fittings; and each time Troughton was kitted out in a new look, Newman would be fetched to pass judgment. Newman's reaction was invariably negative and, as Troughton would later attest, he eventually asked, 'But whatever happened to the cosmic hobo?' Consequently, Troughton's eventual costume, designed by Sandra Reid, was – as foreshadowed in the production team's original note – a tramp-like, Chaplinesque parody of Hartnell's, with stove-pipe hat, spotted bow tie, disreputable old frock coat and enormously baggy checked trousers. At one point during the rehearsal process, Troughton proposed playing the part wearing a frizzy, Harpo Marx-type wig. In the end, however, after this was objected to by his fellow regular cast members, his own hair was simply cut into a Beatle-style mop.

It was on 29 October 1966 that the series' followers were given their first glimpse of the new Doctor, at the end of the closing episode of *The Tenth Planet*. The production team had originally thought that it would be impracticable for the actual physical transformation to be depicted on screen – they had envisaged that the old Doctor would simply collapse to the floor of the TARDIS with his cloak covering his face – but they had changed their plans after discovering that a suitable electronic effect could be achieved by vision mixer Shirley Coward. Troughton had consequently been asked to sign a separate contract for this episode, and had done so on 16 September. After the transformation scene, viewers had to wait another week to begin to discover just how different from the original the new Doctor was going to be (although, due to the need to allow time for the last-minute rewrite, there had actually been a two week break in production between *The Tenth Planet* and *The Power of the Daleks*, recording for the former having been completed on 8 October and that for the latter having got underway on 22 October).

The director appointed to handle *The Power of the Daleks* was Christopher Barry. Barry was a long-standing contributor to the series, having worked on the very first Dalek story amongst others, and he also knew Troughton of old:

'Patrick Troughton took to *Doctor Who* like a duck to water. I don't think Sydney Newman was entirely happy with the first appearance of him during rehearsal. I think we had to tone it down a little, to try and incorporate more of Troughton's youth and humour and whimsy. Hartnell was always the old professor, grandfather sort of figure, which was good, but Troughton was a sort of whimsical figure, more musical, and advantage could be taken of that.

'Troughton, like Hartnell, was a very experienced actor and a very resourceful person. I think he found depths in his own personality. He nearly always played very straight, stern roles, like Cromwell in *A Man for All Seasons*, and I think he relished the idea of the Doctor. He was that sort of warm-hearted, lovely person himself, and it was seldom that he got a chance to play that sort of role in television.'

In the opening scenes of *The Power of the Daleks*, as the Doctor starts to recover from his transformation, his companions Polly and Ben see that underneath his cloak he now has on different clothes and is somewhat smaller in stature. Although Polly is prepared reluctantly to accept that this is the Doctor, albeit in a different body, Ben remains highly sceptical, suspecting that an impostor has infiltrated the TARDIS. Their uncertainty (which would doubtless have been shared by many viewers at the time) is in no way lessened by the Doctor, as he continually refers to himself in the third person and – as in the following exchange – will give only vague or oblique answers to their questions:

> BEN: (PICKING UP THE OLD DOCTOR'S RING) The Doctor always wore this. If you are him it should fit. (HE TRIES THE RING ON THE DOCTOR'S FINGER, BUT IT IS FAR TOO BIG) That settles it.
>
> DOCTOR: I'd like to see a butterfly fit into a chrysalis case after it spreads its wings.
>
> POLLY: Then you *did* change.
>
> DOCTOR: Life depends on change, and renewal.

BEN: (SCEPTICAL) Oh, *that's* it, you've been renewed, have you?

DOCTOR: (HALF TO HIMSELF) Renewed? Have I? That's it, I've been renewed. It's part of the TARDIS. Without it I couldn't survive.

The new Doctor is initially characterised by his unpredictability and his resorting to foolery when faced with a difficult situation. At moments of stress, he often delves into his pocket and takes out a recorder (an item liberated from the TARDIS's storage trunk), proceeding to play a jaunty tune on it – and even, on occasion, dancing a little jig. It is only as the adventure progresses that Polly and Ben, and with them the series' viewers, come to realise that the new Doctor's clown-like facade masks a keen intelligence and highly developed powers of observation, and that the strong sense of morality that the first Doctor always manifested is equally apparent in his successor.

This Doctor likes to create a smokescreen, so that no-one realises exactly what he is up to. His unassuming, sometimes outlandish behaviour is soon seen to be a tactic adopted to keep his adversaries – and sometimes even his allies – off balance. He deliberately leads people to underestimate his capabilities and intellect, but in truth has a keen analytical mind and knows exactly what he is doing. This is well illustrated by a scene at the end of *The Power of the Daleks* in which he appears somewhat bewildered and embarrassed at having 'accidentally' wiped out the colony's power supply in the process of immobilising the Daleks. 'Did I do all that?' he innocently asks, before whisking his companions back to the TARDIS. To Polly's later assertion that he *did* know what he was doing, his response is merely a wry grin and a chirpy tune picked out on his recorder.

While *The Power of the Daleks* was still in production, Lloyd and Davis amended their original note on the new Doctor's character to take into account the changes that had since been decided upon. The revised version, intended for the information of prospective writers for the series, was dated 28 November 1966 and read as follows:

THE NEW DOCTOR WHO
(It must be emphasised that these notes are only a *supplement* to watching the Doctor in action on the screen and that *this* is the only way to a full understanding of the character.)

The new Doctor is younger than the former (Hartnell) characterisation. He is more of an enigma, using humour to gain his ends rather than direct confrontation. His clowning tends to make his enemies underrate him and his obsession with apparent trivialities, clothes, novelties of all kinds, etc, is usually a device merely to give him time to examine a newly-discovered clue.

With Ben, Polly and Jamie, he is cryptic, oblique and mysterious, preferring (like Sherlock Holmes) to keep his conclusions to himself and let the others theorise about the situation. However, we must feel that there is a keen purpose in all he does (if we can spot it!) and that he can flare into direct action and dominate the scene when necessary.

For some serials he uses disguise and appears in outfits ranging from an old woman to a German doctor of the 18th Century (these though must always be discussed with the story editor so we don't have him going into costume in every serial). His disguise is that of a Scarlet Pimpernel and used for the same purpose.

Perhaps his chief attribute is an avoidance of the cliché and obvious. His attitudes to any given situation are off-beat and unpredictable. Sometimes this leads to misunderstandings with his companions who consider him to be favouring the 'wrong side'. Ultimately we see his action to be the right one and understand his line of reasoning, but in the process he can revitalise many a familiar situation.

When he has achieved the desired result and is congratulated by the others, he invariably looks puzzled: Did he really do that? And if so 'how'? Perhaps the others can explain *how* he did it? His companions are therefore never quite certain if he has won a battle, etc, by accident or design and this sometimes leads to a 'Pied Piper' ending, with the people he has saved rejecting him because of his manner and his refusal to accept their gratitude. As with his fellow time travellers (and the viewers!), he wants them to think for themselves and stand on their own two feet, instead of putting a statue to their deliverer in the market place and making the same mistakes again.

The suggested disguises of 'an old woman' and 'a German doctor of the 18th Century' were actually seen to be adopted by the new Doctor in his second story, *The Highlanders*, which had been written by Davis himself (with a co-credit to Elwyn Jones, who had been originally due to write it). This story also saw the character taking on the guise of a Redcoat soldier; and the following one, *The Underwater Menace*, had him passing himself off as a gypsy musician in the Atlantean market place. Later, the season five story *The Enemy of the World* provided possibly the ultimate illustration of his talent for mimicry when he was seen to impersonate the tyrant Salamander, to whom he bore a remarkable physical similarly (not surprisingly, as this was a dual role for Troughton). By the time *The Enemy of the World* was transmitted, however, this character trait had been largely discarded. This was in line with the production team's rapidly-taken decision – based in part on adverse viewer reaction to *The Power of the Daleks*, as reflected in the BBC's internal Audience Research Report – to tone down the more outrageous aspects of the new Doctor's behaviour and make him an altogether less comical character. One illustration of this, as recalled by Sutton, is that the recorder prop played frequently by Troughton in his earliest episodes was hidden so that he was unable to use it.

The change of emphasis was reflected in the Doctor's costume, too, as the voluminous, loudly checked trousers in which he made his debut were altered and eventually exchanged for a much more conservative pair and the tall stove-pipe hat was dropped altogether, being seen for the last time in *The Underwater Menace*. Lloyd later claimed in interviews that the original trousers had in fact been taken in at the rate of an inch a week so that Troughton – who still feared type-casting and hoped that an outlandish costume would help him to avoid it – would fail to notice the difference. Troughton however denied this, arguing that he could not have been so easily fooled, and asserted that he was actually in full agreement with the overall mellowing of the character.

Following this change of approach, the second Doctor was still portrayed as someone who liked to fool people into underestimating his abilities – deliberately failing a simple intelligence test in the season six story *The Dominators*, for example – but the bizarre antics of his earliest episodes gave way to a gentle, quirky humour that counterpointed rather than eclipsed the drama and helped to diffuse the tension in some of the scarier scenes. Similarly, Davis's idea that the Doctor should achieve his objectives by subtle direction of others rather than by taking positive action himself was retained, but was now given a rather different slant whereby the character was seen to be somewhat manipulative.

Perhaps the prime illustration of this trait is provided by *The Evil of the Daleks*, the closing story of season four, in which the Doctor appears at times to be acting in a decidedly furtive and suspect manner. More so than at any other point since the early part of the series' first season, he seems an enigmatic and potentially dangerous figure with a distinctly dark side to his nature. His companion Jamie is on one occasion even moved to denounce him as being 'too callous' and to threaten to part company with him as soon as they reach their next destination – an echo of feelings expressed by the Doctor's original human companions, Ian and Barbara, in the early days of their travels in the TARDIS. The Doctor's dispassionate manoeuvring of individuals and events in order to bring about the Daleks' destruction – the sort of scheming now more commonly associated with his seventh incarnation than with his second – provides an effective reminder of his alien qualities. 'I am not a student of human nature,' he comments at one point, 'I am a professor of a far wider academy of which human nature is merely a part'.

Another notable instance of the Doctor's manipulation of others is offered by the next story, *The Tomb of the Cybermen*, in which he encounters a team of human archaeologists on the planet Telos and, largely without their realising it, gives them a crucial helping hand in gaining access to the base where the Cybermen are entombed – placing all their lives in considerable danger as a result. It would however be fair to acknowledge that these examples are somewhat atypical, and that the Doctor's knack of getting others to follow his agenda was generally portrayed in a rather less sinister light. This is certainly true of the numerous occasions on which the writers had him encountering inflexible authority figures – including Hobson in *The Moonbase*, the Commandant in *The Faceless Ones*, Clent in *The Ice Warriors*, Robson in *Fury from the Deep* and Bennett in *The Wheel in Space* – and gleefully confounding them with his shambolic manner and chaotic approach.

Troughton's interpretation of the Doctor became increasingly popular with viewers as time went by. The actor himself, though, found *Doctor Who*'s gruelling production schedule more and more difficult to cope with, and seriously considered declining to renew his contract after completing a second year on the series. In the end, he decided to stay on – even though the BBC had turned down a request he had made, at the suggestion of *The Enemy of the World*'s director Barry Letts, for a reduction in the number of episodes to be produced per season. The pressure on him was eased a little when he and his fellow regular cast members subsequently won an agreement that they should no longer be required to work at weekends as well as during the week. Early in his third year, however, Troughton made it known to the series' production team that he would not want to continue for a fourth. By this time, the strain of making the series was really beginning to take its toll.

'We were aware that Pat wanted to leave, of course,' says Derrick Sherwin, who worked as script editor and producer on his last season. 'He had had a hard slog – don't forget, we were doing about forty episodes a year in those days – and he was very, very tired. He had been consistently getting pretty shoddy scripts, too, and he was a perfectionist, he really wouldn't say poor dialogue. Consequently he was becoming very edgy towards the end, and there were a few rows. Eventually he decided that he had had enough. The Doctor had changed before, so we knew that we could change him again, and that's what we did.'

Director Paddy Russell also recalls the reputation that Troughton had acquired for being rather difficult to work with: 'Though I never directed a *Doctor Who* with Patrick Troughton, I knew him very well as an actor and had worked with him a lot ... It was interesting, because I talked to Pat about *Doctor Who* much later, when he was doing a classic serial for me. Having found him a superb actor to work with and not at all difficult, I found it extraordinary when I heard that he had begun to give himself a very bad reputation on *Doctor Who*. We were chatting away one day and I said I couldn't believe these stories, and he said, "Well, I couldn't believe what I was doing. That's in the end why I left. The part overwhelmed me and it almost gave me schizophrenia".'

The production team decided that Troughton's final story ought to be a particularly memorable one and that, in order to achieve this, it should take the bold step of dispelling some of the mystery that had always surrounded the Doctor's background. Apart from occasional, invariably vague mentions of his alien origins – including, in *The Tomb of the Cybermen*, a rare and oblique reference to his family – very little had ever been revealed about his life prior to the televised adventures. Now, however, all that was to change. In *The War Games*, writers Malcolm Hulke and Terrance Dicks (then the series' script editor) came up with the explanation that the Doctor was in fact a renegade member of an awesomely powerful race of time travellers called the Time Lords. They also had him giving his companions Jamie and Zoe an explanation as to why he had first embarked on his journeys in the TARDIS:

DOCTOR: I was bored!

ZOE: What do you mean, you were bored?

DOCTOR: Well, the Time Lords are an immensely civilised race. We can control our own environment; we can live forever, barring accidents; and we have the secret of space-time travel.

JAMIE: Well what's so wrong in all that?

DOCTOR: Well, we hardly ever use our great powers. We consent simply to observe and gather knowledge!

ZOE: And that wasn't enough for you?

DOCTOR: No, of course not. With a whole galaxy to explore? Millions of planets? Aeons of time? Countless civilisations to meet?

JAMIE: Well, why do they object to you doing all that?

DOCTOR: Well, it is a fact, Jamie, that I do tend to get involved in things ...

In order to explain Troughton's departure, Hulke and Dicks had the Time Lords in the closing episode of *The War Games* finally capturing the Doctor, placing him on trial for transgression of their law of non-interference in the affairs of other planets, returning his companions to their respective points of origin (in Jamie's case the Scottish Highlands in the aftermath of the Battle of Culloden, as seen in *The Highlanders*, and in Zoe's case the space station known as the Wheel, the setting of *The Wheel in Space*) and ultimately sentencing him to a period of exile on Earth – with a completely new appearance. Thus was the scene set for the era of the third Doctor ...

PRODUCTION DEVELOPMENT

Production of the early part of the second Doctor's era was overseen by the same team as had handled the latter part of the first Doctor's – namely producer Innes Lloyd and story editor Gerry Davis. Lloyd, who had been assigned to *Doctor Who* by the BBC's Head of Drama Sydney Newman, had accepted the posting only reluctantly, as science fiction had previously been of no great interest to him. He had however grown to enjoy the genre as time had gone by – particularly after he had worked through a number of stories inherited from his predecessor John Wiles and started to make his own mark on the series. Davis, by contrast, had always liked science fiction, and had actually asked to be transferred to *Doctor Who* from his previous assignment on the football team drama series *United!*.

Lloyd had been keen from the outset to update the style of *Doctor Who* – which in his opinion had previously been rather old-fashioned and whimsical – and to make the Doctor's adventures more action-orientated and 'gutsy'. The first real fruits of this had become evident in the season three story *The War Machines*, which had seen William Hartnell's Doctor in the unfamiliar setting of contemporary London, working alongside the British armed forces to combat a megalomaniac super-computer situated within the newly-completed GPO Tower (which was renamed the Telecom Tower in the early Eighties). Lloyd had also taken this opportunity to change the image of the Doctor's companions. The original intention had been that Dodo (played by Jackie Lane) should continue as a regular, with a new character called Richard, or Rich for short, brought in to replace Steven (Peter Purves), who had been written out in the previous story, *The Savages*. In the end, however, Lloyd had decided that Dodo should also be written out, leaving the way open for the introduction of a completely new male and female companion team: seaman Ben Jackson (Michael Craze) and secretary Polly Wright (Anneke Wills) (whose surname was never given on screen) – two up-to-date, 'swinging Sixties' characters, very much in line with the aim of bringing a greater degree of realism to the series.

Indicative of the seriousness with which the production team viewed this aim was the fact that they had engaged the services of an unofficial scientific adviser in the person of Dr Kit Pedler. Pedler's first contribution to the series had been to propose the basic ideas for the story that had ultimately become *The War Machines*. He had then gone on to create, with assistance from Davis, the Cybermen for the first Doctor's swansong, *The Tenth Planet* – which, with its suspenseful depiction of a multiracial team of scientists under siege in their advanced but isolated base, was typical of the type of story that Lloyd and Davis wanted to see presented in *Doctor Who*.

This basic scenario – an isolated community of humans, led by a strong-willed but misguided authority figure, being attacked and infiltrated by terrifying alien monsters – was indeed adopted as something of a standard format for Patrick Troughton's first two seasons as the Doctor. Stories that conformed to it to a greater or lesser degree included *The Power of the Daleks*, *The Moonbase*, *The Macra Terror*, *The Faceless Ones*, *The Tomb of the Cybermen*, *The Abominable Snowmen*, *The Ice Warriors*, *The Web of Fear* and *The Wheel in Space*. The perceived benefits of this approach were twofold: first, it made for some tense, claustrophobic and often very frightening dramatic situations; secondly, as Davis later explained, it meant that the series' relatively modest resources could be used particularly effectively:

'My basic premise for *Doctor Who* stories in that era of minuscule budgets was to forego the usual dozen tatty sets in favour of one major set around which we could concentrate all the money. This made a much more exciting and convincing central location for the drama.'

There were nevertheless a number of stories that departed from this approach. One of these was *The Highlanders*, Troughton's second outing as the Doctor, which was set in 18th-Century Scotland and – apart from the TARDIS and its occupants – featured no science fiction elements at all. This was to be the last historical story for many years, however, as the production team had decided that this genre – which had constituted an important part of the series' format since its inception – should now be dropped. One theory often advanced to account for this development is that the historical stories were less popular with viewers than the science-based ones. This indeed was the explanation given by Lloyd in a contemporary interview for the magazine *Television Today*:

'One change we have decided on is to drop the historical stories, because we found they weren't very popular. This doesn't mean we won't use historical *backgrounds* like those in *The Highlanders* by Elwyn Jones and Gerry Davis or *The Smugglers* by Brian Hayles, but we will not involve Doctor Who and his companions in events which cannot be changed because they really happened.'

An objective assessment of the series' ratings and audience appreciation figures in fact reveals very little evidence to support the contention that the historical stories were less popular than the science-based ones. The real reason for the dropping of the former may well have been not so much that they were unpopular with the viewing audience as that they were unpopular with the production team themselves, and out of line with their vision of the type of series that *Doctor Who* ought to be in 1967. Despite Lloyd's suggestion to *Television Today* that stories with historical *backgrounds* might continue to be produced, this proved not to be the case.

The Highlanders was also notable for marking the debut of a new companion character, Jamie McCrimmon (Frazer Hines), who would continue in the series until the end of the second Doctor's era – making him the longest-running in the series' history. The production team prepared a detailed note to explain the character to potential writers. This was dated 28 November 1966 and read as follows:

FRAZER HINES in the part of JAMIE
He is a piper, and the *character must be that of a simple but engaging Scot*. Although his smile disarms opposition, he is on occasions a man of action who will defend his friends or principles fearlessly. *He is cheerful, open,*

manly, flexible – more flexible in fact than Ben and Polly. *When either Ben or Polly are pulling his leg, he reacts with a grin.* Because of his romantic appearance, *he always wears the kilt* – his hair is longer and his shirt has a swashbuckling appearance: because of this and the attractive features of his character *he must assume the part of the Young Hero in each story.*

He must be constantly *AMAZED AND PERPLEXED* that he is wandering through Space and Time and is coming up against things, even common-place things, which he could never have dreamt of in his day. *The large things – planes, computers etc – rock him back on his heels* – he finds it hard to comprehend them all.

He brings many of the attributes of the Highlander of his period with him, being courageous, impetuous, superstitious and romantic. His impetuosity often provokes difficult situations for the time travellers, but his direct approach will sometimes help solve problems as well as create them.

His superstitious background enables him to relate the forces of evil fought by the Doctor to the witches, demons, goblins etc of his native land. Sometimes, in fact, this folklore gives him a deeper insight into the forces opposed to the travellers than the more scientific approach of the Doctor, Ben and Polly.

Attitudes to the Doctor, Ben and Polly.

TO THE DOCTOR:
The Doctor is a strange, loveable, wee chap to Jamie. He is obviously some sort of genial wizard or magician. He finds it hard to understand what his motives are or what he is doing when tackling a technical problem – but he knows he can help out with brawn, so he does. He doesn't question motives, he asks the question from interest and from a desire to know what is going on.

The Doctor enjoys Jamie as an oddity like himself. He also enjoys him as he knows that he has an appreciative and captive audience, and one that will laugh at his jokes. The Doctor is quick-witted with a supernatural intelligence, who will arrive at the answer to problems from the most unpredictable reasons ... Jamie has dash, but a scant education has only given him a sharpened instinct which he uses to approach a problem straightforwardly and solve it in a predictable way.

TO POLLY:
Jamie doesn't really know how to treat Polly. She is a girl and therefore all his experience tells him that she must be weak and gentle and therefore should be treated with chivalry. He goes out of his way to look after her, but is often confused by her 1966 attitudes and appearance. He is a little shy of her and all women, especially emancipated women. Polly is fascinated by Jamie's shyness and his Heroic aspect. She enjoys making Ben jealous, even though Ben's relationship has been that of bossy brother. She might have a 'thing' about Jamie if she didn't realise that it

might make time travelling with her companions tricky.

TO BEN:

Ben has complexes, Jamie has none. Ben is nervy, Jamie is calm. They both question ... Ben because he is suspicious of motives, Jamie because he genuinely wants to know. In adventurous escapades, they complement each other, Ben working out what a course of action should be and Jamie carrying it out. Ben is apt to take the mickey out of Jamie and is irritated when Jamie takes it good-humouredly – usually with a grin rather than a quip. Seeds of jealousy creep into Ben's character, having Jamie as a fellow time traveller. They don't always need to be seen to be negative emotions, but on occasions would motivate him to doing heroic actions to impress Polly and the Doctor and put him one up on Jamie.

After a period of relative stability for the series' production team, the end of May 1967 saw Davis relinquishing his post as story editor and going to work on another BBC show, *First Lady*. He had actually been asked to become producer of *Doctor Who* – Lloyd was now keen to move on, feeling that he had contributed all he could to the series – but had decided against this. Davis's departure also marked the end of Pedler's regular involvement as *Doctor Who*'s unofficial scientific adviser, although he would continue to provide storylines for Cyberman adventures throughout the remainder of the second Doctor's era. Davis and Pedler continued to work together as a team on other projects – most notably the highly popular *Doomwatch* series, which they created for the BBC.

Davis's successor as story editor was Peter Bryant – a former actor and radio writer, director and producer – who had been trailing him as an assistant since around January. Bryant was also seen as a potential replacement for Lloyd; he had looked after the show while Lloyd was on holiday for a week in January, and it had initially been thought that he would take the role of associate producer on the series, and he was actually credited as such on some episodes of *The Faceless Ones*. At the same time as he took over from Davis as story editor, Bryant brought in a new assistant of his own, namely his friend Victor Pemberton (who had previously had a small acting role in *The Moonbase*, at a time when he was working as a bit-part player while trying to obtain commissions as a writer).

The fourth season had been, all things considered, a successful one for *Doctor Who*. A critical change of lead actor had been well accomplished; a period of experimentation had led to the development of an effective new format; and, with the arrival of Jamie in *The Highlanders* and Victoria (Deborah Watling) in *The Evil of the Daleks*, two promising new companion characters had been introduced in place of Polly and Ben, who had made their final appearance in *The Faceless Ones*, a decision having been taken – apparently by Head of Serials Shaun Sutton – to write them out earlier than originally intended. The changes overseen by Lloyd and Davis had, in short, revitalised the series, which had won an increase in ratings from an average of around five million viewers per episode at the start of the season to an average of around seven million at the end, and an accompanying rise of around ten percentage points in its average audience appreciation figure, which now hovered at around the fifty-five mark. The task that Lloyd and Bryant faced for the fifth season was to consolidate and build upon that success.

Throughout this period, Lloyd remained keen to move on from the series, and it was not entirely coincidental that for the season opener, *The Tomb of the Cybermen* (which was actually made as the last story of the fourth production block), Bryant was temporarily elevated to the position of producer, while Pemberton took the story editor's credit. As Bryant later recalled, this came about after he simply asked Lloyd if could handle a story by himself:

'Innes knew that I wanted to be a producer, and by then I had a pretty solid background in the business, one way and another. I had all the qualifications one needs to be a producer. I'd done it all. So Innes said, "Yes, fine, sure". I think he may also have felt that since he wanted to leave the series at that point, if he had someone ready to take over from him, it would be a lot easier.'

The Tomb of the Cybermen was generally adjudged a great success within the BBC – Bryant recalls that Sydney Newman actually phoned him after the first episode was transmitted to say how much he had enjoyed it – but, nevertheless, the start of the fifth production block saw Lloyd continuing in the post of producer while Bryant reverted to story editor and Pemberton to uncredited assistant. Lloyd was still looking to leave the series at the earliest opportunity, however, and actively grooming Bryant as his successor.

One significant move that the two men made at this point was to start commissioning longer stories. During the previous production block, all but three of the stories had been in four episodes; for this one, six episodes was adopted as standard. The production team recognised that this extended length allowed for greater character development and a slower build up of suspense in the stories, but their motivation was nonetheless more financial than artistic. They knew that the fewer stories there were per season, the greater the proportion of the overall budget that could be allocated to each, and thus the higher the quality of the sets, costumes, visual effects and so on that could be obtained. The severe restriction of resources that had limited what could be achieved in the realisation of some of the stories of the fourth production block – most obviously those such as *The Underwater Menace* that had departed from Davis's favoured approach of having the action centred around a single main set and involving a relatively small cast – was therefore largely avoided during the fifth.

Location filming was also more affordable now, although the series' tight schedule still meant that only the first story to be made in the block could be accorded a major shoot; a whole week was spent in Snowdonia, North Wales, filming the exterior scenes for *The Abominable Snowmen*.

Another notable feature of the fifth production block was its conspicuous lack of Daleks – previously a staple ingredient of the series. Lloyd and Bryant did at one point toy with the idea of commissioning a story featuring both them and the Cybermen, but this was quickly vetoed by their creator, Terry Nation. Nation still harboured some hope of winning backing in the USA for the production of a separate series devoted to the Daleks (having failed to secure this from the BBC in discussions during 1966), and so in any case was unprepared to have them appearing in *Doctor Who* for the time being. It was this fact that had led to the development of the storyline in *The Evil of the Daleks* that had culminated in their apparent destruction at the end of the fourth season.

The unavailability of the Daleks left something of a vacuum, which the production team filled both by placing an increased reliance on the Cybermen – the series' second most popular monster race – and by taking steps to introduce a whole host of new creatures that they hoped would prove equally successful – an aim they came close to achieving with the Yeti and the Ice Warriors.

The Enemy of the World was Lloyd's last story as *Doctor Who*'s producer, as he had finally been granted his wish to move on to other projects. As planned, Bryant then took over from him. Pemberton, however, had by this time become aware that he was not cut out for the story editor's job, and had returned to freelance writing. That post consequently went instead to newcomer Derrick Sherwin, who had previously been an actor and a freelance writer. Terrance Dicks – another young freelance writer, who had previously worked for an advertising agency – was meanwhile invited by Sherwin, an acquaintance of his, to come in as a new assistant story editor.

'Sherwin had written to Shaun Sutton,' recalls Bryant, 'and Shaun had seen him and spoken to me about him. He'd said that there was this guy – an actor who'd done some writing as well – who wanted to come into the Beeb and work as a story editor, and would I like to meet him? So I did, and I said okay.'

It was in fact quite common for Sutton to put forward to the *Doctor Who* office the names of people that he thought might be suitable to work on the series – particularly directors.

'Shaun tried to encourage us to take people who possibly weren't getting the sort of beginnings or not getting quite as much work as they should have been. A lot of the first timers who came in, he wanted me to give 'em a go – and I did.'

The end of the fifth season saw another change occurring in the series' regular cast of characters. *Fury from the Deep* was Victoria's last full story (Watling having decided to bow out at this stage), and *The Wheel in Space* introduced a replacement in the person of Zoe Heriot (Wendy Padbury).

The making of season six was dogged by a number of behind-the-scenes problems. During this period, Bryant and Sherwin both became involved with other projects – perhaps most notably the military drama *S P Air*, produced by Bryant and written and co-produced by Sherwin, of which two pilot episodes were made in July and August 1969 and transmitted in November 1969 – and so were unable to give their full, undivided attention to *Doctor Who*.

On the scripting side, late changes were made to the number of episodes allocated both to *The Dominators* and to *The Mind Robber* (the former of which went out under the pseudonym Norman Ashby after writers Mervyn Haisman and Henry Lincoln demanded that their names be removed from it); and three of the seven transmitted stories – *The Krotons*, *The Space Pirates* and *The War Games* – were last minute replacements for others that had fallen through. The season did nevertheless achieve a far greater variety of settings and plots than the previous one, which had been largely Earth-bound and, with its heavy reliance on the 'isolated group of humans infiltrated and attacked by alien monsters' scenario, somewhat formulaic. As opposed to the previous season, this time there were only three stories – *The Invasion*, *The Krotons* and *The Seeds of Death* – that could really be considered traditional monster tales. Again, however, this was not so much an artistic decision as a matter of economic necessity. Although the production team continued to spread the series' costs as far as possible by commissioning stories with relatively high episode counts – including the eight-parter *The Invasion* – they found that the budget would simply no longer run to creating large numbers of convincing alien costumes and environments.

Bryant was in no doubt that the commercial success of *Doctor Who* relied to a large extent on its monsters. Seeing that the first episode of *The Krotons* had gained an audience of nine million viewers, compared with an average of under seven million for some recent stories, he wrote a memo dated 21 January 1969 to BBC Enterprises bemoaning the cost of creating such alien creatures and explaining that, as he had no money remaining, the next six months' worth of the series had been planned with no monsters at all. His point was that if Enterprises wanted to be able to market the series, they should be prepared to make some financial contribution towards creating its most marketable assets. His memo provoked no concrete reaction.

Bryant and Sherwin had in any case concluded at an early stage of the season's production that *Doctor Who* was no longer working in its current format and needed to be revamped.

'I think people get bored with seeing monsters all the time,' says Sherwin. 'They get bored with seeing funny planets and weird frogs and people with trees growing out of their ears. Going back into history as well – the historical bits were incredibly boring. The monsters were okay if you actually had a good monster, and the interplanetary stuff was fine as long as you had good models. But it was all expensive, and I personally felt that at that time it was absolutely essential to bring it down to Earth, to get the audience back and to make it a real show that they could watch; something that they could identify with.'

Bryant was very much in accord with this philosophy:

'I thought it was a good idea to do that, so that the kids could identify with what was going on. They'd know if a story was in the London Underground, because they'd know what an Underground station looks like. I didn't necessarily think there was anything lacking in the more fantastically-orientated stories, I just thought "Let's get back down to Earth again. Let's get somewhere where the kids can identify with the actors, with the characters".'

One of the main inspirations behind this idea was Nigel Kneale's three highly successful science fiction serials of the Fifties, in which Professor Quatermass and his scientific and military colleagues had been seen to battle a succession of alien menaces in near-contemporary England. In order to help meet his and Bryant's aim of remoulding *Doctor Who* in this image, Sherwin created the United Nations Intelligence Taskforce, or UNIT for short. This was to be an international military intelligence unit, established specifically to investigate UFOs and other strange phenomena, with which the Doctor could work while on Earth.

'The idea of it happening on Earth with real people who were involved in everyday lives was a good one,' asserts Sherwin, 'so I invented the United Nations Intelligence Taskforce and brought in some new characters.'

Having been impressed by the character Colonel Lethbridge-Stewart (played by Nicholas Courtney) in *The Web of Fear* – a story that had itself been somewhat influenced by the Quatermass serials – the production team decided (subject to the actor's availability) to bring him back as the commander of the British branch of UNIT.

'The character played by Courtney was a good foil for the Doctor,' observes Sherwin. 'A typical, type-cast, crass idiot from the Army, but nevertheless relatively intelligent and reliable and honest and straightforward. He was, well, limp.'

UNIT, with Lethbridge-Stewart promoted to Brigadier, made its debut in *The Invasion*; and, as Sherwin tells it, this was always intended as simply the first step in a process of moving towards a more permanent Earth-bound setting – something that he says would have happened even if Patrick Troughton had not made clear his intention to leave *Doctor Who* at the end of the season:

'The idea was always to bring it down to Earth gently and then to stay there for a long period of time. Quite apart from dramatic considerations, another factor was that budgets were being cut and we were being asked to do more. Don't forget that we were going from black and white into colour, which was an expensive exercise, and we had to have a run of productions that we could afford. We couldn't keep on creating spaceships and monster suits all over the place and going out to the back end of nowhere to film alien planets – it just wasn't on, with the financial restrictions that existed.'

By the time of the making of *The Invasion*, Sherwin had effectively become co-producer of *Doctor Who* with Bryant, leaving Dicks to take over as script editor (as the post of story editor had now been renamed). A young writer named Trevor Ray was later brought in to replace Dicks as assistant script editor. Bryant himself was now becoming less and less actively involved with *Doctor Who*, as he was in ill health.

Bryant's last credit as producer of *Doctor Who* was on *The Space Pirates*, for which Sherwin temporarily returned to script editing duties while Dicks was busy co-writing *The War Games* with Malcolm Hulke. The producer's credit on the latter story then went solely to Sherwin. At the beginning of October 1969, Bryant, Sherwin and Ray would all move on to troubleshoot an ailing BBC series entitled *Paul Temple*.

The conclusion of *The War Games*, with the Doctor being captured by the Time Lords and sentenced to a period of exile on Earth, was specifically designed to usher in the new format that Sherwin and Bryant had devised for *Doctor Who*. It was not to be until the following season, however, that that new format would finally come to fruition. The original intention had been that Bryant would return as producer for that season. In the end, however, he would be involved with only its first two stories and would then devote his time fully to *Paul Temple*. The producer's credit on the first story of the seventh season would go to Sherwin, and that on the second to Bryant's eventual successor – Barry Letts.

VISUAL EFFECTS

Visual effects is an aspect of *Doctor Who*'s production that has always attracted particular attention. Sometimes this has taken the form of derogatory remarks and mocking comments, but from more well-informed commentators there has been a recognition that, given the technical and financial constraints within which it was made, the series overall actually achieved very high standards in this area. It was often, indeed, a pioneer of new visual effects techniques within television.

At the series' inception back in 1963, responsibility for its visual effects was assigned not to the BBC's own Visual Effects Department – which had been established as a separate unit within the Design Department in 1954 and cut its teeth on the controversial Nigel Kneale adaptation of Orwell's *1984* starring Peter Cushing – but to the scenic designers. Barry Newbery, who designed the first story, *100,000 BC*, explains how this somewhat surprising state of affairs came about:

'The original producer, Verity Lambert, had approached the Visual Effects Department at an early stage to see if they wanted to handle the series' visual effects work – of which there was obviously going to be quite a lot – but they'd said that they couldn't do it unless they had four more staff and an extra four thousand square feet of space. The powers-that-be weren't prepared to go along with that, and so it was declared that the set designers would have to be their own visual effects designers. The only exception was where fire or explosives were concerned, which is why the Visual Effects Department received a credit on *100,000 BC*.

'This wasn't just a case of political manoeuvring by Visual Effects to avoid getting involved with the series. Jack Kine and Bernard Wilkie, who ran the Department, weren't like that at all. They were really enthusiastic about their work, and I'm sure they would have loved to have done *Doctor Who*. I mean, they may have exaggerated their requirements a bit – and seen this as a good opportunity to boost their resources – but they certainly couldn't have coped with their existing resources.

'Mind you, in later years, when the Visual Effects Department got bigger, the situation changed, and I think there was a good deal of jealousy then. Their people were understandably keen to get in on the act!'

Raymond Cusick, the other principal designer for the series' first season and the man responsible for the Daleks' distinctive appearance, puts his own perspective on this:

'When the idea of *Doctor Who* was first put forward, Jack Kine, the Head of the Visual Effects Department, said that he would need three more visual effects designers to cope with the extra workload of doing the show. He was told that he couldn't have them, so he said, "Right, I don't want anything to do with it. The whole thing goes out to contract, to Shawcraft Models in Uxbridge". He was basically being obstructive. His assistant, a chap called Bernard Wilkie, was more helpful. I used to go and ask his advice on bangs and explosions, how we could do that sort of thing – because what happened was that Barry Newbery and I, although we had been booked simply to design the sets, ended up having to design the visual effects and the special props as well. Our workload was doubled! Having to go backwards and forwards checking sets was one thing, but having also to run off down to Uxbridge all the time to check with Bill Roberts, the manager of Shawcraft, well … Bill Roberts was a nice chap, mind you, and very helpful. We were both stuck with the situation, and neither of us knew what we were doing, quite honestly.

'I'm sure Jack Kine – like everyone else, really – thought that *Doctor Who* would die a death, and that the constant demand for visual effects would kill it off within the BBC. He was quite right about the amount of work involved; he really would have needed the extra people. I think he got upset when the show was a success. This sort of thing often happens at the BBC: if something's successful, all the producers and heads of department step forward and claim credit, whereas if it's a wash-out, they all step back, push the others forward and say "You take the blame". I've worked on productions where I've never even seen the producer, but later, when there's been a big ballyhoo, he's been the one to go and pick up all the awards.

'The truth is that Jack Kine and the BBC Visual Effects Department made no real contribution to *Doctor Who* until about five years after it started. I've read Barry Newbery's comment that they used to take responsibility for scenes involving fire or explosives, but I'm not sure about that. In the first Dalek story, there was a sequence of the Daleks cutting through a door with oxyacetylene, and that was done at Ealing under the supervision of a freelance chap who worked for Bill Roberts. There might have been someone from Visual Effects standing by, overseeing it, but if so, I can't remember who it was.'

This situation had changed little by the start of the second Doctor's era: the series' scenic designers remained responsible for meeting the visual effects requirements of the stories to which they were allocated and, while the Visual Effects Department was now prepared to service some of the more basic and straightforward of these requirements, anything complex or ambitious still had to be put out to contract.

At an early stage in the production of each story, the director, usually in consultation with the designer, would go through the scripts and decide which aspects of them would need to be realised by way of visual effects. These requirements would then be notified to the Visual Effects Department. On *The Moonbase*, for instance, director Morris Barry's production assistant Desmond McCarthy sent to Jack Kine the following memo dated 2 January 1967 and headed 'Visual Effects: "Return of the Cybermen"' (*The Return of the Cybermen* being the story's working title):

As spoken to your office, herewith list of visual effects:

EPISODE 1:
Page 4:   Models
"   19:   Meter needle flicks
"   23:   Electronic box – hospital
"   29:   Spark from Cyberman

EPISODE 2:
Page 10:   Oscilloscope

EPISODE 3:
Page 1:   Cyberman weapon?
"   2:   Smoke from man
"   20:   Model
"   25:   Squirt jets (studio)
            Chest units disintegrating (film)
"   29:   Weapon (as page 1) (film)
"   32:   Bottle bursts on Cyberman's chest unit (film)

EPISODE 4:
Page 6-7: Bazooka (also 3/37) (film)
"   14-16: Dot on monitor (film)
"   26:   Boiling fluids, exploding bottles
"   30:)   Laser torches
"   33:)
"   37:   Saucer model

Scripts enclosed.

In subsequent discussions, it was decided that the oscilloscope effect proposed for the second episode should be dispensed with and that the shots of boiling fluids and exploding bottles destined for the fourth should be accomplished on film rather than in the recording studio. It was also established which of the effects could be handled internally by the Visual Effects Department and which would have to be bought in from an outside contractor – in this case, one of the series' regular suppliers, Bill King of Trading Post Ltd. On 12 January, McCarthy wrote to King at Trading Post's Factory Yard premises on the Uxbridge Road in London to detail what the commission involved:

> This is to confirm that we require the following visual/pyrotechnic effects for the above programme as discussed with our designer Colin Shaw:
>
> 1) Two Cyberman chest units to 'disintegrate/smoke' when fired upon by fire extinguisher – for film on 18 and 19 January and studio, episode three, on 18 February (discuss with designer how much needed for studio)
>
> 2) Bottle (from fire extinguisher) thrown at chest unit (as above) to burst and destroy it. For film on 18 January.
>
> 3) Smoke pours from the openings in man's clothes resulting from being fired upon by Cyberman's 'weapon' for studio, episode three, on 18 February (discuss with designer and wardrobe supervisor Miss Sandra Reid).

The series' continued reliance on outside contractors to meet requirements of this sort occasionally gave rise to problems. These came to a head during the filming of model shots for *The Faceless Ones*. Director Gerry Mill subsequently provided producer Innes Lloyd with a detailed note setting out what he considered to be a number of shortcomings in the work carried out for that filming by Shawcraft:

POINTS CONCERNING SHAWCRAFT
1. The actual making of the aircraft was satisfactory, but when one is told that they are professionals and advised to use their staff to suspend and animate the model, one would have expected them to work out the suspension of the aircraft and the strength of the wires holding the model. They had done neither, and when at one point the model was left suspended on one wire, the model fell and was broken. As it happened, they were able to mend it overnight and it did not hold up filming, as the aircraft shots had been completed for the day, but this need not have been the case.

2. As to the satellite, they knew this had to be flown, and once again we assumed they would give the matter some thought. We were amazed, however, to find their two suggested methods of suspension were:

a) an 'L' shaped tubular piece of scaffolding and

b) five or six strands of nylon thread, which was by no means a certified safe way of suspending the satellite and certainly from a filming point of view was completely unusable.

Eventually it was necessary, having used the scaffolding system, to take all light off the top of the model, thereby losing the whole effect of the satellite flying in space.

As to the finish of the satellite, the top section was reasonable, but the one and only working section, i.e. the 'bomb doors', was made of three-ply, which had neither been sand-papered nor sealed, and a MCU [i.e. medium close up shot] was taken of the doors opening, which has in fact proven to be unusable.

One's main complaint is that the Corporation appears to pay a large amount of money to Shawcraft for which one would expect a professional service, which is not forthcoming. Another small point, but very important nevertheless, is that at no time did they produce spare parts – e.g. when a lamp blew at the base of the satellite, at the end of a very frustrating day (i.e. waiting two and a half hours for the satellite to be slung), we then had to wait another half hour while the house electrician tried to find a suitable lamp!

This is not for my money a professional attitude. In addition, it is to be taken into consideration that we pay out of our budget an extra fee to the staff of Shawcraft to operate their special models (approx. £40 per day).

In addition, there is the added irritation that when a minor prop, for example the ray gun, was damaged on filming, there were no facilities for collecting or delivering the repaired ray gun from Shawcraft – and in fact there was a delay of three days, Shawcraft being 36 miles out of central London.

As a general point, it would seem to me that no one firm can be expected to make all the varying types of models that are needed for a programme like 'Doctor Who'.

Lloyd sent a copy of this note to Kine under cover of the following memo dated 17 March 1967:

> On the serial being filmed at the moment – KK – the director, Gerry Mill, went to considerable trouble to find an aeroplane model making firm as he wanted a) to produce a more specialised model than Shawcraft b) at a more economical price. I understand that he consulted you about it and that Shawcraft were eventually given the order. At Ealing, due to mishandling by Shawcraft's men, shooting in the morning was held up two and a half hours and the first shooting in the afternoon was at five o'clock – added to which the model which was suspended was too heavy and fell, thus being damaged in consequence. Due to all these troubles, it was necessary to reshoot the model scenes today.
>
> Whereas I understand that they give 'Doctor Who' a regular service, there have been gathering complaints recently by directors that their services are time consuming – things not working – or that their prices are exorbitant for the job they do. Is there a reason why we are not allowed to shop around to get better value for our money (we may not achieve this – but certainly in Gerry Mill's case he *found* such a company

who were willing and able to provide the exact sort of model effect for the money he could afford from his budget)?

As far as cost is concerned, the MACRA – the monster featured in our current serial – cost £500+, the same price as a cheap car. It can be seen in studio on this Saturday or Saturday 25 March and I fail to see how the cost can be anything like the price they are asking.

The reshooting of the model scenes on 17 March, referred to by Lloyd in his memo, was abortive, and a further reshooting was scheduled for 11 April. On 21 March, Mill's production assistant Richard Brooks sent a letter to Bill Roberts setting out with the aid of a diagram a number of detailed improvements that the production team would like to see made to the satellite model. These were as follows:

1. A smoke feed (from smoke gun) through black piping (diameter to be decided) to be fed into satellite via one of the low arms near the base.

2. *Flying*: Satellite to be suspended by wire hawser (as thin as possible allowing for weight of satellite). Hawser to be painted with a black matt finish. *Very* thin wires to be attached to the ends of the other three arms and run through screw eyes on the floor to minimise swing of satellite.

3. 'Bomb doors' at base to be thoroughly refurbished, i.e. given a bright *metallic*, very smooth sheen – *NB* they have to be seen in close up.

4. Flashing lights in base rim – these must be able to be wired to a dimmer in order to achieve a pulsating light as against an actual flash.

I shall be coming along to Shawcraft on either 3 or 4 April and any further details can be cleared up then.

Following the problems encountered on *The Faceless Ones*, it was agreed that the Visual Effects Department would finally take over responsibility for *Doctor Who*'s effects work. *The Evil of the Daleks* thus became the first story on which their designers received a credit since *100,000 BC*. The significance of this change was twofold: it meant first that the Visual Effects Department rather than the series' set designers would now carry out all effects design work for the series, working on the basis of a Visual Effects Requirements form agreed by the director, and secondly that although outside contractors would still sometimes be used to realise particular effects (as indeed was the case on *The Evil of the Daleks*, for which Shawcraft provided a number of models), it would now be Kine's staff rather than the production team who would carry out all direct liaison with them and be responsible for ensuring that their work was of an acceptable standard.

Unlike in later years, when a single Visual Effects Department designer would generally take charge of all the effects work for a given story, at this point in time, a number of assistants would usually collaborate to achieve the desired results. Hence, although one or two of these assistants would nominally have lead responsibility, the on-screen credit would always be to the Department as a whole rather than to any particular individuals.

The assistant with lead responsibility for effects on *The Evil of the Daleks* was Michealjohn Harris, who has particularly fond memories of the climactic civil war between the different Dalek factions:

'I know we had an absolutely marvellous time in that battle sequence, and we even had two radio-controlled model Daleks. We had a giant Mother Dalek in the studio, with a lot of hoses attached to it. We filled these up with all sorts of horrible mixtures, so that when they blew apart, the hoses swung through the air spewing filth. I know it caused a strike among the studio hands afterwards, clearing up the mess. In those days, we didn't have a model stage, and all those sequences were set up at Ealing. There was a model of the Dalek city seen from the mountains above; we did that as well. Compared with what was done in later years, it was fairly amateurish, but the great advantage was that it was on 35mm film, so what we lost in being amateurish, we gained in quality. I remember we built the whole city in various sorts of balsa wood and so on, and flooded it with dry ice fog as an opening sequence. We got a sort of rippling effect. Then the first explosions took place, and they were quite nicely sequenced using lines of running power … Considering the circumstances under which it was made and how early it was, I don't think it was too bad. It wouldn't stand comparison today, though. It's a museum piece.'

Harris also worked on the following story, *The Tomb of the Cybermen*.

'We built models of the cryogenic chambers and they were used quite effectively. We filmed the model sequences at Ealing, because it was the business of the deep frost disappearing and the Cybermen coming back to life, a slight movement, and so on; it was a case of building up more frost and then reversing the whole sequence on film. Then we cut to the full-sized set at Lime Grove. We had to sew two or three of the Cybermen up with various pyrotechnic effects; smokes and fizzes and flashes and things out of their machinery.

'A number of techniques were used all at once for the Cybermats. That's the beauty of television; you can do all sorts of things. I remember our heroes had gone to sleep and the Cybermats were crawling up to them. Obviously there is no way in which you can do that forward, so again we did it in reverse. It was very, very effective because, curiously enough, when you do a thing in reverse like that, it starts slowly and then darts forward as though it has sort of made an effort, creeps forward and jumps, and the effect is very, very good.

'I've got a feeling we probably made about a dozen Cybermats. This was in the early days of television recording, when you weren't supposed to cut the tape – the tape was running on, so if you went from one side of the studio to the other, from one set to another, you ran like hell! – and I can remember very well, even to this day, running full tilt across the studio, holding the remote control in my hand, flinging myself down on one shoulder and sliding in on my shoulder and arm underneath the cameras to get to a control point. Oh, it was great fun in those days, it really was.'

This story involved some location filming for scenes in which a team of human archaeologists find the gates to the Cybermen's city.

'We did that in a grand quarry in Gerards Cross,' recalls Harris. 'We used a matte model; the gates to the city were matted in about six feet from the camera and lined up on a quarry face on the far side … but of course you couldn't open the gates on that because you just got solid rock.'

The explosion that revealed the gates, though, was real.

'We had set up the charges quite early in the morning. We had pushed some of them down behind a great chunk of soft, gravelly sandstone, and there had been a delay – some reason why it couldn't be filmed – so we had gone on to do something else. The trouble was that, in the course of the day, with people walking past, the sand had dribbled in and dribbled in until it had filled the whole crack up – so it became a much more powerful explosion than was originally planned. It showered stone and sand and dust everywhere for miles!'

Harris's tasks for *The Abominable Snowmen* included creating the Yeti's metallic control spheres.

'The one that moved ran on two tiny trailing wheels, one single drive and one steering wheel that revolved around its own central axis. It was almost a complete sphere ... highly polished so that you couldn't tell whether it was rolling or not.'

The Yeti costumes were a joint effort between Visual Effects, who constructed the chest unit, and the Costume Department, who built the framework around the unit and covered the whole thing with fur.

'I remember the costumes being terrible things to wear,' says Harris. 'Awful. And the trouble was that there was filming in North Wales, and the actors inside them couldn't see their feet. They had to have three people to help them through each sequence! Terrible. The poor men kept falling down!'

Kine's resources were still very stretched during this period, and for season five's closing story, *The Wheel in Space*, it was decided that, in a throwback to the earlier system, all the required effects work should be handled by the set designer and bought in direct from an outside contractor – Bill King of Trading Post. It was however agreed that the extra costs that would inevitably result from this (given that such contractors naturally worked on a profit-making basis) would be underwritten by the Visual Effects Department rather than charged to *Doctor Who*'s budget. The same arrangement was then followed for *The Mind Robber*, *The Invasion* and *The Krotons*.

The *Doctor Who* production team were by this point becoming increasingly concerned with the situation. So too was the Drama Department's Chief Designer, Lawrence Broadhouse, who on 15 November 1968 sent to his boss, Head of Scenic Design Clifford Hatts, the following memo about the effects requirements for *The Seeds of Death*:

> The visual effects requirements in this 'Doctor Who' are extremely heavy and complicated. I have discussed with Jack Kine the situation arising from his statement to you that he cannot supply a visual effects designer at all, mainly owing to acute shortage of staff due to prior programme commitments and to sickness.
>
> The only solution he can offer is as follows: Bill King of Trading Post can undertake the work (I do not know if he has been told of the large amount required) but Jack Kine admits that King does not profess to design, although he says he has two 'designers'. The danger in this is that the scenic designer would have to devote considerably more time co-ordinating, if not actually designing, the visual effects than if an effects designer were allocated. But the scenic designer himself has a particularly heavy commitment in this serial.

The whole situation is tricky because of the difficult type of effects required, and the large number.

Having considered this memo on the day that it was sent, Hatts noted:

I agree with this memo and consider the situation extremely unsatisfactory and not acceptable to me.

Despite this, the effects for *The Seeds of Death* were eventually provided by Trading Post as Kine had suggested.

On 9 December, *Doctor Who*'s producer Peter Bryant sent the following memo to Kine about the effects requirements for the sixth season's last two stories, *The Space Pirates* and *The War Games*:

I would like to request strenuously that the special effects in Serials YY and ZZ be serviced internally.

YY is going to be complicated, and if not done internally very costly (even allowing for an underwrite). ZZ is a ten part serial, the last before the summer break in 1969, and again complicated.

Both the shows are going to require a fair proportion of special effects *design* effort, and I would think too much for the set designer to be able to cope with in addition to his other work.

This provoked the following memo of reply dated 16 December from I Beynon-Lewis, the Head of Design Services Television:

Further to your memo of 9 December and our telephone conversation, I am hopeful that the estimate to increase the staffing of Visual Effects Section will be presented to the Director of Television's Finance Meeting before the end of this month. At the same time, our accommodation problems should be considerably eased – at least on a temporary basis.

Coming back to YY and ZZ in the light of the above, it is almost certain that we shall be able to cope with ZZ internally. YY we are not so sure about, since even after the establishment has been increased, we are still left with the problem of recruitment and training of new staff. We may be lucky in our recruitment – I hope so – but we must face up to the fact that training in our methods will still be essential. In the light of this, YY may have to be put outside, but I am asking Jack Kine to confirm this, or not, nearer the time.

In the event, it transpired that not only was the Visual Effects Department unable to service *The Space Pirates* internally, but Trading Post were also unable to undertake the assignment. This posed a considerable dilemma, which could eventually be solved only by having the design, construction and filming of the models undertaken entirely by freelancers. The designer from whom this work was commissioned was John Wood, who when previously employed by the BBC had been responsible for the sets for a number of Hartnell-era stories. The models were made by Ted Dove of Magna Models, and Wood then supervised the shooting of them by the Bowey Group's Nick Allder and assistant Ian Scoones at Bray Studios.

'That really arose out of internal BBC planning,' confirms Wood. 'At the time, an attempt was being made to convince the powers-that-be that there was a need for a new effects designer post within the Visual Effects Department – up to that point, you see, all the effects people had been at assistant level, and there wasn't a fully-fledged designer there. The scenic designer on *The Space Pirates* was Ian Watson but, mainly to help demonstrate the need for this new post, I was asked to go in and collaborate with the designer on the modelwork.

'I designed all the spaceships from scratch and had them purpose-built by an outside contractor, Magna Models. I wanted them to be clean-looking: simple and uncluttered, with sharp lines and angles. The models were quite large and detailed. The V-Ship, for instance, measured about eight feet across and had a transparent perspex panel at the top through which you could see the various levels and galleries representing the ship's interior. It also had hinged panels on the wings, which opened up to form launching bays for one of the smaller ships. I was particularly pleased with how that turned out.

'The actual filming of the spacecraft scenes was done by a firm called Bowey Films, and I went out to their premises in Slough to supervise it. I was asked by the director, Michael Hart, to handle these scenes due to the constraints of time.

'Bowey Films had been working on *Thunderbirds* with Derek Meddings and people like that, and they were specialists in their area, so I was able to rely quite a lot on their expertise.'

On 10 January 1969, Bryant sent the following memo to Beynon-Lewis:

> With reference to your memo dated 16 December 1968, I now gather from Jack Kine that it is not going to be possible to service ZZ internally, and on current form it rather looks as though we are going to be in exactly the same situation that we have been with Serial YY.
>
> With the greatest goodwill in the world, I really cannot accept a repetition of this alarming state of affairs, when, with the unavailability of Bill King, it became apparent that this programme could not be serviced either internally or externally, and days of very precious time were lost until Jack Kine was able to come up with a solution – and a very costly one at that as well. Had this been a programme charge, it would have been quite impossible to have done the show at all, but being very properly charged as if serviced internally, the excess will be paid from a design source.
>
> Serial ZZ is in ten parts and in its own way as complicated as YY. It is a very important serial since it will be Patrick Troughton's exit from the programme, and the last we do before colour. I would be most grateful for some thoughts on this matter. Filming on ZZ begins on 23 March 1969.

In the light of this protest by Bryant, it was eventually agreed that the effects for *The War Games* would, after all, be overseen by a member of Kine's team – namely Harris – although the majority of the work would still be subcontracted out.

'First World War battle scenes?' muses Harris. 'Yes, I did that down at Brighton on the rubbish dump there, just after they'd done Attenborough's *Oh! What a Lovely War* in the same place. I remember poor old Patrick Troughton being a bit nervous on that one, and laying down the law very strictly: "If he presses the button for that explosion while my head is above ground, I shall walk off the shoot and never come back!"

'There was quite an interesting control room in the studio scenes, which I can't remember very much about except that it had circular television screens. Funny, the details that come back. I've got a feeling that we built war game tables as well, with symbols on them. My goodness, the things that come back when you start to delve into the memory – things I'd absolutely forgotten about!'

The relationship between the *Doctor Who* production team and the Visual Effects Department continued to worsen as the costing of the effects work for *The War Games* became the subject of a heated dispute. Bryant's deputy Derrick Sherwin, who produced the story, made his feelings on the matter clear in the following memo of 17 March 1969 to Kine:

> With reference to the costing of the special f/x commitment of the 'Doctor Who' serial ZZ, WAR GAMES.
>
> Our conversations regarding the costing of these shows have been somewhat confused by your attitude towards the method of costing. As I previously mentioned to you in a memo (dated 6 March 1969), we have been working on the basis of our previous arrangement, i.e. that our special f/x programme costs shall not exceed the estimated cost of the show being serviced from within the organisation, whether or not we use external or internal services. This is a principle agreed upon some time ago and one which, to my knowledge, has not been superseded by any other arrangement.
>
> On the telephone today, you were talking about 'new methods' of costing, and of applying these innovations to my show, Serial ZZ. This, it seems, is why the costs of this comparatively light show seem to be astronomically high! If this is the case, then I'm afraid I must object to these new costing innovations being thrust upon me at this critical stage of production. I am not arguing for or against this new system -- merely the timing of it. If a new system is to be brought into operation, then I feel we need considerable advance warning. This we have not had. Consequently I must insist that our previous arrangement stands, and that we cost the show accordingly.
>
> Our latest conversation regarding these costs, although your estimate dropped from the original £1500 to £900, is still to my mind well above reality. This is why, although I agreed to accept the latter figure as a basis for argument, I would like to see a *complete* breakdown of the f/x costing, so that we might judge each effect on its merit.
>
> I'm sorry to be so insistent about this costing business, but on a show which has a very tight budget, I must watch every single penny that is spent.
>
> I look forward to receiving the f/x costing breakdown from you.

This drew the following response of 20 March from Kine:

Thank you for your memo of 17 March. I have noted the contents and feel that in some degree I have contributed to your confusion by my reference to the new costing methods. As we stand at the moment, they are functioning *only* in Drama Plays, but will eventually cover all other productions. Basing the costings for 'Doctor Who' Serial ZZ on my original tariff, I enclose a breakdown showing actual external costings and internal costings.

Since costing is the purpose of this memo, I feel I must point out that over the past four 'Doctor Who's, Serials WW, XX, YY, ZZ, based on the internal-external differences in costing, the above four shows have cost Visual Effects £4,800. This shows that my own internal costing for *all* shows must have a built in loading in order that we can cover ourselves to pay for the difference in costing for all shows that we place to contract.

***

VISUAL EFFECTS BREAKDOWN FOR 'DOCTOR WHO' SERIAL ZZ

	Internal	External
1 Landing Stage, Control and Base.	£60 0s 0d	£140 0s 0d
2 Practical Stunguns.	£120 0s 0d	£265 12s 0d
4 Non-practical Stunguns.		
3 Battlefield Communicators.	£65 0s 0d	£130 5s 6d
1 Truth Machine.	£50 0s 0d	£110 10s 0d
4 Internal Alien Communicators.	£60 0s 0d	£150 0s 0d
1 Brain Washing Machine.	£52 0s 0d	£135 0s 0d
30 Map Symbols.	£22 0s 0d	£35 0s 0d
40 Magnetic Control Panel Symbols.	£15 0s 0d	£22 10s 0d
2 Perspex Maps for Cut-a-ways.	£35 0s 0d	£91 12s 0d
1 Sidrat Control Panel.	£15 0s 0d	£25 0s 0d
1 Fireplace Control Panel.	£32 0s 0d	£58 10s 0d
4 Gas Bottles and Valves.	£27 0s 0d	£60 0s 0d
Sonic Screwdriver Sequence.	£36 0s 0d	£59 15s 0d
Stop Motion Filming and Box.	£40 0s 0d	£95 10s 0d
Location Filming Battle Sequence.	£120 0s 0d	£200 0s 0d
Safe Explosion + 2 (effects).	£10 0s 0d	
	£759 0s 0d	£1,579 4s 6d
Contingency for Repairs over Serial (10 part)	£100 0s 0d	

Internal Total with Uplift   £920 0s 0d   £1,579 4s 6d

Difference to be paid by Effects   £659 4s 6d

Sherwin wrote back to Kine later the same day:

> Thank you for your memo of 20 March. I note your remarks concerning costing, but find your second paragraph still somewhat confusing.
>
> If all shows are to have a built in loading to overcome the effects of your differences in costing, why then should this particular serial appear to cost far more in comparison with previous shows? Your costing breakdown appears to be comparatively reasonable with the exception of one or two individual items.
>
> (1) *2 practical stun guns* at £120!? At £60 apiece this seems quite ridiculous! How can they cost this much internally?
>
> (2) *4 gas bottles and valves* can not cost £6 or £7 each!
>
> (3) *Stop motion filming and Box:* We were assured that this would cost us merely the price of the box plus the stock! This surely can't come to £40!?
>
> (4) *Location filming battle sequence:* Again, the price you personally gave us of £60 – how come it is now £120!?
>
> These are the four items that immediately strike me. I have not in fact had time to go through your costing breakdown in detail. However, it does strike me that all costings are above average by 10% at least, and that this show is being '*loaded*' quite unfairly.
>
> Despite your protestations that this set of shows is being treated on the basis of previous costing methods, I am still convinced that it is unrealistic. What, for instance, do you mean by '*uplift*'? The estimate of £100 for repairs to sf/x during the serial seems quite outrageous.
>
> It does seem to me that if we are to agree on a final figure and cease argument, you could quite safely drop your estimates by at least £150 to £200 and still come out on the right side, despite your 'uplift'!
>
> I sincerely hope we can come to some mutually acceptable arrangement over this issue, and if you can review your estimate and bring it to within £700 to £750, we shall have no difficulty in reaching an agreement.
>
> During the next two weeks I shall be away on location filming for this set of 'Doctor Who' stories. However, any comments or reaction to my suggestions will be communicated to me via my secretary. Should your reactions necessitate an immediate meeting, I shall of course return to London.

A rare note of harmony was sounded on 31 March when Michael Hart, the director of *The Space Pirates*, sent Kine a memo praising the effects work on that story. On 8 April, however, the dispute over *The War Games* continued, with Kine sending Sherwin the following memo:

> I have now obtained a copy of your memo of 20 March; for some reason I never received one.
>
> However, in brief I feel the time has come to wave the white flag. I could quite obviously do 'Doctor Who' or any show for the cost of the materials, but where would the capital come from to enable outside work to be paid for? This particular costing has been undertaken in close liaison with HDS Tel and I feel that I must refer to him before proceeding any further. He is at the moment on leave, but I should be able to contact him on his return on Monday 14 April. I imagine his reactions will be communicated to you via your secretary.

Sherwin, having heard nothing further in the interim, sent the following memo of 23 April to Beynon-Lewis:

> I have recently been 'fighting' a battle with Jack Kine re the costing of special effects for the 'Doctor Who' serial ZZ, '*War Games*'. Jack has now called a truce and referred the whole matter to you – hence this memo.
>
> To attempt to put this matter in a nutshell is quite impossible, so you must bear with me whilst I go into it in some length.
>
> The costing of special effects for this serial was, I presumed, going to be based on our previous agreements with you, i.e. that if Visual Effects could not cope with doing the show 'inside' then we should not suffer financially, as a programme, from it being subcontracted.
>
> However, this previous agreement appears to have been overlooked. When I tackled Jack about this, he murmured vagaries about there being a new costing system to allow for compensation of monies having been spent outside on subcontracts.
>
> This was new to me – and certainly to Peter Bryant. It would seem that we are being asked to pay far and above the cost of our special effects to accommodate this departmental malady. Can this be the case?
>
> In the case of the serial ZZ, I feel justified in insisting that costing methods should be as we previously agreed. Having budgeted a show on this basis, I feel it would be extremely unfair and indeed impractical to change your mind mid-stream.
>
> I have agreed with Jack that £900 should be a 'talking point' re the costing of special effects on ZZ. This is a drop from the original estimate of £1,500!! Even so, £900 is still excessive for the internal costing effort. It should be no more than £750 at most. He insists that this excess is a result of these 'mythical' new costing methods!
>
> What I want to know is: Do these new costing methods exist? If so, what are they? Why should they be suddenly applied to us without

warning? Do they apply to the new series of 'Doctor Who' being formulated now?

Peter Bryant is I know concerned about this new departure affecting his new series of 'Doctor Who' stories.

In short, I do feel that if there are to be new costing methods, we should be briefed before the event.

I shall be delighted to discuss Serial ZZ with you in detail if this be necessary.

Beynon-Lewis's response to this memo is unrecorded, as is the eventual outcome of the dispute over *The War Games*. In any event, this whole issue of the cost of external contractors would soon be largely overtaken by events as the extra staff and resources for which the Visual Effects Department had been pressing would finally be granted to them, and they would in future be able to service the great majority of *Doctor Who*'s requirements internally. Even with the Doctor's exile to Earth by the Time Lords, these requirements would remain extensive, and the Visual Effects Department would thus continue to make a vital contribution toward the series' successful on-screen realisation.

REWRITING THE MYTH

One of the most major developments during the Patrick Troughton era was the exploration of the nature of the Doctor himself. The first, and arguably most important, aspect of this was the fact that the Doctor could physically change his appearance.

When the Doctor's body succumbs to the ravages of old age (or, as the Doctor himself puts it: 'This old body of mine is wearing a bit thin') at the end of *The Tenth Planet*, a mysterious force from within the TARDIS aids him to renew himself. He falls to the floor of his ship and his features visibly re-arrange themselves. He regains consciousness as a more youthful man who shares few physical characteristics with his former self. This change goes beyond his appearance, as his personality and mannerisms also have been affected by the metamorphosis. As the new Doctor tells a sceptical Ben at the start of *The Power of the Daleks*: 'I've been renewed. It's part of the TARDIS. Without it, I couldn't survive.'

This explanation is, however, ambiguous. The TARDIS's role in the process is never made clear, although during the Doctor's transformation the ship appears to operate itself – the levers and switches move of their own accord – and the central column in the main control console falls and rises. It could be argued that the use of the word 'renewed' is evidence that the new Doctor is merely a younger version of the original. However, given not only the physical differences between the two incarnations but the shift in personality as well, this seems unlikely. The Doctor himself likens the change to that of a butterfly emerging from its cocoon, when he attempts to explain to Ben why his ring no longer fits on his finger. This suggests some form of total bodily change, rather than just a turning back of time, and implies that the Doctor could potentially change his physical form and abilities as radically as a butterfly is different from a caterpillar. The term that has become more commonly connected with this change in the Doctor's appearance – regeneration – was not coined until later in the series' history.

The new Doctor's nature strikes the viewer as being a great deal more relaxed than before. Aloofness and irascibility are replaced by an often childish yet friendly demeanour with hidden depths. This Doctor later states that he is 450 years old (*The Tomb of the Cybermen*), the first time that an actual age in human terms has been established for the character. We also discover that the Doctor's new form is the spitting image of the would-be Earth dictator Salamander (*The Enemy of the World*). The Doctor therefore manages to impersonate Salamander with ease, but is just as adept at taking on the guise of a German doctor (*The Highlanders*), a gypsy musician (*The Underwater Menace*) and an Earth Examiner (*The Power of the Daleks*), not to mention his vocal impersonation of the Karkus (*The Mind Robber*). The Doctor had previously assumed various roles during his adventures, and so perhaps this talent was always present, however it is within the era of the second Doctor that it comes to the fore.

With the fact that the Doctor is not human firmly established, we also learn in *The Tomb of the Cybermen* that he has a family. It had previously been stated that Susan was his granddaughter, and so the fact of the Doctor having other relations should come as no surprise. It is not, however, made clear whether he is referring to Susan or to a wife or even to parents. It is also possible that the Doctor's familial reminiscences are merely to ease his companion Victoria's pain following her father's recent death, and there may, in fact, be no family at all.

Susan's whole nature is called into question by the revelations during the Doctor's trial at the end of *The War Games*. She is not mentioned during the Doctor's trial, and this seems strange: the Time Lords are concerned to bring the Doctor to justice for his apparent interference in history, but appear happy to allow Susan to affect Earth's future development. One answer to this dilemma could be that Susan is not a Time Lord. Additional weight is given to this theory by the fact that, in the light of the Time Lords' longevity and ability to renew themselves, the Doctor's decision to leave Susan on Earth to marry the resistance fighter David Campbell in *The Dalek Invasion of Earth* seems in hindsight rather heartless. First, he would have known that she would outlive her future husband by centuries; and, secondly, without the TARDIS to aid her renewal, she would be condemned to die the first time she underwent this process.

Further revelations about the Doctor were to come, however. What had been shrouded in mystery from the very start of the series had been the reasons why the Doctor was travelling in his TARDIS in the first place. At the end of *The War Games*, we finally learn more about the Doctor's own people, the Time Lords, who had not previously been named.

We discover that the Doctor had the ability to contact his people whenever he chose to. The Doctor's reasons for fleeing his planet and its culture are also revealed. He simply became bored by his utopian world. The Time Lords had great powers but had strict laws against interfering with the affairs of others races. The Doctor therefore stole the TARDIS and left to see the wonders of the universe and to fight evil wherever he found it.

The Doctor's people appear to be very technologically advanced. We discover that they can live forever, barring accidents, can force a change of appearance upon another Time Lord, as they do to the Doctor, and that they can choose what their next incarnation will look like. The Time Lords also appear to have wide-ranging powers. The War Lord's and then the Doctor's trials are conducted without the aid of any visible control consoles: they can cause force fields to appear, can use a 'thought channel' to present images of what someone is thinking, and can affect the handling of a TARDIS at a distance. They are even able to remove a whole planet from time; and although they express a dislike of physical violence, they are ultimately prepared to erase life forms from history if their crimes are considered bad enough.

Along with revelations about the Doctor, his TARDIS too has several new facts established during this era. Up until this point, there had been only one ambiguous comment made by the Doctor (in *The Chase*) that suggested that he might have built the TARDIS himself; and Susan claimed to have named the machine from the initial letters of Time And Relative Dimension In Space. The Time Lords seen in *The War Games* also call their time machines TARDISes, which perhaps suggests, assuming Susan did devise the name, that she did so before her departure from her home world.

As well as previously established facts being confirmed – such as, for example, the ship's telepathic abilities, in that it can warn of danger by showing diverse images on the scanner (*The Wheel in Space*), and the use of mercury in the fluid links (*The Wheel in Space*) – other details are revealed, including the presence of an emergency exit out of the rear of the police box shell (*The Wheel in Space*), a power room (*The Mind Robber*) and a laboratory (*Fury from the Deep*) and the ability to present details of one of the Doctor's past adventures on the scanner (*The Wheel in Space*), this including events that the Doctor was not even present for and would therefore have no knowledge of. This could be explained as an extension of the TARDIS's telepathic abilities, which also allow it to show future events (*The Moonbase/The Macra Terror*) via the time scanner. Other minor revelations reinforce the invulnerability of the ship, in that it can temporarily survive being buried in hot lava (*The Mind Robber*) and that it has a special circuit called the Hostile Action Displacement System (HADS), which, if activated, will automatically move the ship if it is attacked (*The Krotons*).

At the conclusion of the Doctor's trial in *The War Games*, he is sentenced to exile on Earth, and Jamie and Zoe are, according to one of the Time Lords, returned to the point in time just before they started their travels in the TARDIS. It is also stated that they will remember only their first adventure with the Docor. This can be interpreted in one of two ways: that their subsequent adventures with the Doctor never happened, or that they had their memories of the incidents wiped. The latter seems the more likely explanation. When the Doctor watches Zoe back on the Wheel, we hear the TARDIS leaving, suggesting that his companions were returned just *after* the TARDIS departed, presumably with them on board. Therefore the only way they would remember just their first adventure would be if the Time Lords had tampered with their minds. This idea is reinforced by the fact that Zoe has a vague feeling of having forgotten something important.

The Doctor meets his oldest enemies, the Daleks, only twice during this era, and not much more is revealed about them. In *The Power of the Daleks*, the Daleks on board the crashed spacecraft on Vulcan still need static electricity to move about, but the creatures are shown being created for the first time, and the organic Dalek mutants are somewhat similar in appearance to those seen previously in the season three story *The Daleks' Master Plan*. The Daleks that invade Earth in 1866, as seen in *The Evil of the Daleks*, are summoned by the use of static electricity, but appear not to need it as a motive force. They also have a time machine, with which they are able to transport the Doctor and Jamie from 1966 back to 1866 and from there to Skaro. In the Dalek city on Skaro, we see for the first time the Dalek Emperor – a huge motionless machine that sits within a mesh of pipes connected to the rest of the city. The Daleks manage to identify and isolate 'the human factor' – the aspect of humanity that has allowed the species to defeat the Daleks on numerous occasions. This discovery leads to the creation of 'the Dalek factor', a set of opposing impulses that, when introduced into human subjects, turn them into organic Dalek slaves. At the conclusion of the adventure, the Doctor manages to engineer a civil war on Skaro between Daleks that have had 'the human factor' implanted into them, and those Daleks still loyal to the Emperor. As the Dalek city is razed to the ground, the Doctor believes that he is witnessing the creatures' final end.

With the Daleks appearing only twice, other monster races come to prominence during this period – and none more so than the Cybermen, who first appeared right at the end of the first Doctor's era. The Cybermen develop significantly during the second Doctor's tenure – in particular in terms of their appearances and voices, which differ to a greater or lesser degree in each of their stories. These changes, however, are never explained or commented on in the dialogue.

The Cybermen who invade the Earth's lunar weather control station in *The Moonbase* are from an era subsequent to the destruction of their home planet, Mondas, and – perhaps surprisingly, given his change of appearance – recognise the Doctor. They make use of an effective neurotropic virus, and are able to hypnotically control human subjects. At some point, they have colonised the planet Telos as a new home. . It is in *The Tomb of the Cybermen* that the Doctor visits Telos and meets the Controller, a massive silver figure visibly different from his fellow Cybermen. The Cybermen are held in a state of suspended animation in their tombs by being frozen – a curious fact, when one considers that they have been seen to be capable of operating on the icy lunar surface (*The Moonbase*) and will later be seen active in space (*The Wheel in Space*). No explanation is given for this apparent discrepancy.

In later stories we see Cybermen being 'hatched' from egg-like shells (*The Wheel in Space*) and webbing cocoons (*The Invasion*). Various new weaknesses are also established for the creatures: along with being exposed to radiation (*The Tenth Planet*), their susceptibilities include being subjected to a gravity beam (*The Moonbase*), having their chest units sprayed with plastic solvents (*The Moonbase*) or liquid plastic (*The Wheel in Space*), being fired on by an x-ray laser (*The Tomb of the Cybermen*), having their chest units physically battered (*The Tomb of the Cybermen*), being subjected to intense electrical energy (*The Wheel in Space*), having pure emotion directed at them (*The Invasion*), and coming under fire from the mortars and shells of an army battalion (*The Invasion*).

Some variations on the standard Cyberman are also introduced. These include the Cyber Planner (*The Wheel in Space*) and the Cyber Coordinator (*The Invasion*), both of which appear as a computer-like brain, and the Cybermats (*The Tomb of the Cybermen*, *The Wheel in Space*), small metallic rodents that they use to carry out tasks of infiltration and attack.

The Tomb of the Cybermen confirms and re-emphasises a motivation for the Cybermen that was initially established in *The Tenth Planet*: specifically, to create more Cybermen by finding other humanoid species and altering them. Victims of this process include, in *The Tomb of the Cybermen*, the mute servant Toberman, who is partially converted into a Cyberman, including the replacement of one of his arms; and, as seen in *The Invasion*, the industrialist Tobias Vaughn, who has his body replaced, while his head, brain and hands remain human, and several workmen at Vaughn's factory.

Despite their humanoid origins, the Cybermen also need power in order to survive, and their city on Telos contains a revivification room, which can be used to 'recharge' the creatures as they emerge from hibernation.

The second Doctor's era spawned some other enemies that would go on to become part of the series' established myth. Perhaps the most distinctive are the Ice Warriors, a race of humanoid bipeds with reptilian scaly green armour who originate from the planet Mars. The creatures' bodies are a curious mixture of organics and electronics, including an effective sonic weapon mounted into their arms.

In *The Ice Warriors*, they have been buried in a glacier on Earth for many centuries, having left Mars in search of a new planet to colonise, as their own was dying. They are discovered around the year 3000 AD; and yet, in *The Seeds of Death*, set in the 21st Century, Earth is again looked to by the creatures as suitable for colonisation. Presumably as the first expedition had failed to report back, the Martians felt it was worth another attempt.

In *The Seeds of Death*, the Martians have evolved a highly ordered society; a caste system is revealed in which the Warriors, who in the earlier mission had commanded in their own right, are now commanded by unarmed Martians of smaller stature and with a different style of helmet. Above these commanders is a Grand Marshal.

There was a final element in *Doctor Who*'s mythos that was introduced during the latter part of the Sixties, and that was to form the basis for many of the adventures in the following decade. This was an organisation called the United Nations Intelligence Taskforce, or UNIT for short.

The seed from which UNIT grew was established when the Great Intelligence attempted a second invasion of Earth, as told in *The Web of Fear*, this time using the London Underground system as the means to attack. Leading the regular army during this adventure is a soldier named Colonel Lethbridge-Stewart.

Lethbridge-Stewart is a somewhat straight-laced army man, who operates by the book on most occasions. After his success at freeing London from the attentions of the Intelligence, he is promoted to Brigadier and placed in charge of the British arm of UNIT, a specialist force created to handle any future alien insurgencies on Earth.

UNIT has control of numerous pieces of impressive hardware, including jeeps, helicopters and a flying control centre. Their artillery contains everything from hand-guns to rocket launchers, and they appear to have almost limitless resources.

The creation of UNIT in the story *The Invasion*, together with the revelations about the Doctor, were arguably the most important developments during the second Doctor's era. They paved the way for the continuation of *Doctor Who* as an Earth-based adventure series, and introduced new regular characters into the format who would become almost as important as the Doctor and his companions themselves.

FROM SCRIPT TO SCREEN: THE MIND ROBBER

Introduction
This chapter presents an in-depth look at just one of the second Doctor's stories. In doing so it reveals the process of making *Doctor Who* at this point in the series' history and – a factor common to every story – some of the behind-the-scenes discussions and

thought that go into a production.

The production chosen for this case study is *The Mind Robber*, a story in the series' sixth season in 1968. For our view of the production, we have turned primarily to director David Maloney, who recalls, scene by scene, the work that went into it. We have also had assistance from the main writer, Peter Ling; the designer, Evan Hercules; and the costume designer, Martin Baugh.

The Scripts

The Mind Robber started life as a story outline from Peter Ling, entitled *Manpower*.

Ling was a well known and respected television writer, children's writer and editor, who, with Hazel Adair, had devised one of the earliest television soap operas, *Compact*, and gone on to create the popular *Crossroads* series. He also worked on other popular shows including *The Avengers*, as well as productions for Associated Rediffusion and Lew Grade. The commission to write for *Doctor Who* was the result of a meeting on a train, as Ling recounted to *Doctor Who Magazine* in 1991:

'Terrance Dicks and Derrick Sherwin were working on *Crossroads* and *Doctor Who* at that time – although how they found time to do both, I don't know! During that time, when we were all commuting to Birmingham, I got to know them, and they suggested I write a *Doctor Who* story. My first reaction was, "Oh no, I couldn't possibly do that – it's not my cup of tea, and I don't know anything about science fiction." In the end, I did what must have been one of the least science fiction orientated stories they made.'

Of the initial ideas, Ling has only hazy memories: 'I outlined the vague notion of a planet inhabited by fictional characters, on the supposition that everything created has an existence of its own and must go on living somewhere, in some dimension of time, space, or thought. I suppose this arose from my own experience of soap-opera fans who have a strange kind of suspension-of-disbelief. They *want* to believe that somewhere there is a real Crossroads Motel. Sometimes we got letters from ladies applying for jobs not as actresses but as waitresses.'

Ling was commissioned on 21 December 1967 to prepare a detailed storyline and breakdown for a six-part *Doctor Who* serial, and the commission was agreed by his agent on 3 January 1968. Although the commissioning letter stated six episodes, Ling's initial, undated, breakdown was for the first episode of a four part story; and a letter of response from script editor Derrick Sherwin confirmed that Ling was indeed writing a four parter.

The original scene breakdown for the first episode of *Manpower* (which appeared as one word on the actual breakdown, although it also appeared as two words – *Man Power* – in other contemporary documentation) read as follows:

PART ONE: ANOTHER WORLD
The Doctor, Jamie and Zoe are travelling through space and time – there is a certain amount of friction between Jamie and Zoe, since he still misses Victoria and resents the newcomer who has taken her place. The Doctor tries to explain to him that Zoe's brilliant mathematical mind will be a great asset to them – her particular talent will be invaluable at plotting their course. Jamie is still not convinced, and when things start to go wrong, he immediately assumes that Zoe is at fault. The instruments are going haywire; Dr Who discovers that they are in the centre of a very powerful magnetic

storm which makes the control of the Tardis impossible.

Worse is to come; first of all the spacecraft is lurching and shuddering badly, and then bits of it begin to disintegrate. This is no accident; they realise that some powerful force is moving in on them, and they are helpless to prevent it. Gradually the Tardis breaks up, and the three time travellers are whirled away into space, spinning off in different directions.

The Doctor tries to reach the others, but he too is floating in freefall, and soon he is alone – expect for a bright point of light that seems to be rushing towards him. It gets nearer and nearer, dazzling him with its brilliance, and he finally collapses.

SCENE 2. THE FOREST

When he comes to, he finds himself miraculously unhurt, at the foot of what appears to be a tree, in a dense forest. But these are no ordinary trees; they are tall, smooth columns of various shapes, and he wanders through them as if in a maze.

There is no sign of Jamie or Zoe – he calls to them, and he can hear their voices in the distance, but cannot get through to them.

Suddenly he sees someone moving among the 'trees' , and finds a corner where he can take cover and watch.

The 'someone' turns out to be a strange semi-human monster with a sinister, uniform appearance. (NB: The exact form of the new 'monsters' is obviously something to be decided in conference, but as a suggestion, what about a faceless head – a simple 'brain centre' – and enlarged, sensitive hands capable of 'seeing' or 'hearing' by turning towards a sound or an object like a radar scanner?).

The Creature is joined by some similar monsters; they are clearly a kind of army unit, methodically searching – and it becomes apparent that they are searching for the Doctor. They know he must be there somewhere, but they cannot find him.

The leader of the unit points his cupped hand at the trees, slowly 'scanning' the scene; and we cut to –

Scene 3. CONTROL ROOM

A TV screen picking up his field of vision, slowly panning across the forest. A man we cannot see – (over the shoulder shot) – is watching the screen; and he gives orders to move on to another area; they are not to give up their search until the Doctor has been found.

Scene 4. THE FOREST

The army obediently move away, and Dr Who emerges from his hiding place – to find himself face to face with a stranger; a man of about thirty, in 18th Century costume (leather coat, buckled shoes, Tom Jones wig) who carries a musket, pointed at the Doctor. He accuses the Doctor of spying – who is he? Where has he come from? The Doctor tries to explain as best he can; the stranger understands very little of the explanation, but is at least slightly mollified, and says that he's by way of being a sort of time traveller himself – his travels have taken him far and wide, ever since he was born in 1726.

The Doctor tells him he has to find Jamie and Zoe, and the stranger advises him which way to go, speeding him on his way with a warning that there are many traps hereabouts. Then he vanishes, as inexplicably as he had appeared.

The Doctor makes his way through the trees and is suddenly confronted by two of the army unit. They point their cupped hands at him, and we see –

Scene 5. CONTROL ROOM

As before, but this time the Doctor is picked up on two TV screens from the different angles of the two 'hands'.

The controller-figure gives his orders: 'Question him. You know the form of interrogation.'

Scene 6. THE FOREST

The two 'soldiers' fire questions at him – simple, childish riddles and catch-questions. Bewildered, the Doctor replies to the best of his ability – but when he tries to ask questions in his turn, the two figures will not reply. Instead, one of them suddenly produces a sword, and menaces him with it, asking: "What can you make of a sword?"

The Doctor is baffled, and the sword gets closer, the blade at his throat. 'What else can you make of it?' repeats the 'soldier'. 'Rearrange it!'

'S W O R D,' the other 'soldier' spells it out. 'This is your last chance – rearrange!'

The Doctor sees the sword lifted and poised to strike, and says desperately: 'S W O R D – well, it's an anagram of – of – W O R D S – *words*!'

And he lifts his hands to ward off the blow, only to find himself holding not a sword but a book – a dictionary ... words ...

'You have answered correctly. You may be a suitable candidate,' the 'soldiers' tell him, and move away.

It is getting dark now, and a thick mist is creeping up. The Doctor hears Jamie calling him, somewhere quite close, and thinks he sees him through the mist. But when he gets to him, he finds it is a lifesize cutout portrait of Jamie. The mist is thicker, and there is an old-fashioned steel safe, beside a wishing well. The Doctor examines these objects warily; is this another trap?

Then, above his head, he sees two huge letters with diagonal strokes through them – an M and a T, floating in the mist; and between the safe and the well there is a giant hand, with a letter H in the palm, also crossed through.

The Doctor realises this is some form of rebus – picture-writing, as he called it when he was a child. He spells it out ... 'Jamie' (the picture) – 'Mist', less the M and the T – that makes 'is' ... 'Safe' ... 'Hand' without the H – 'and' ... 'Well' ... 'Jamie is safe and well'.

And as he solves the puzzle, Jamie appears; another test has been completed successfully.

The Doctor is of course delighted, and Jamie wants to know what has been going on – where are they? The Doctor *[missing words]* expected here – they have been brought here as part of a plan, and the plan involves putting the Doctor through various intelligence tests, all of them involving words or a play on words.

They resume their search for Zoe, and hear her calling for help. They come up against –

Scene 7. THE WALL

A thick wall in the middle of the forest, with a heavy iron-studded door in it. On the other side, ZOE is trapped, begging them to rescue her. But when they go to open the door, they discover it isn't real – it's only painted on the wall. The Doctor says it reminds him of something – when he was very young … something is clicking at the back of his mind …

The door and the wall melt away, and there is Zoe, inside a huge glass jar, like a biology specimen.

'Got it!' The Doctor shouts triumphantly. 'When is a door not a door? When it's a jar …!'

And suddenly Zoe is free. Another test is over.

At least they are all together again; but the big problem now is where to go. With no Tardis, there seems to be no escape. Perhaps if they were to try and find a way through the forest.

Scene 8. THE FOREST

They set off together, but the 'trees' seem to go on forever. Jamie volunteers to climb one of them, to try and see from the top if there is a clearing anywhere. With their help, he shins up, & says this is a very odd pillar; the top of it is a letter 'E', like the drawn out letters in a stick of rock, only recognisable as letters from the end. In fact all the pillars are letters – we pull out and up and look down to see that our three travellers are in a forest of words; words on a giant page.

But at least there is a margin in sight in the distance – a way out.

Jamie climbs down again, and they head in the direction he tells them. They meet the 18th Century stranger again; he is more friendly now, and the youngsters take a liking to him. He says he has been on this planet longer than he can remember, and he knows his way around. He explains to the Doctor that this period of initiation won't take long; 'they' have to test newcomers, so that everyone can be best fitted into the scheme of things. Who are 'they'? Oh – the master, up in the castle, and his assistants. There is really no need to be afraid of the Master – as long as you don't try to step out of line. Dr Who questions him about the 'Army' – are they human or electronic robots?

The stranger suddenly seizes up, and does not seem to understand. 'What army? I do not know what you mean.'

The Doctor tries to describe them – 'You must have seen them'.

But the stranger only says flatly: 'I cannot say more than I am given to know'. It is as if they were suddenly speaking different languages.

Then the 'Army' starts to come back; the Doctor hears them approaching, and asks the stranger to help them – to hide them. Our three heroes find a hiding-place, among the 'trees', and the stranger stays on guard.

The 'Army' moves in, still searching. The Stranger waits for a little, then turns to the Doctor's hiding-place and says calmly:

'You must have been mistaken. There are no soldiers here.'

At once the 'Army' rally round and encircle the Doctor and his companions, bringing them out of their hiding place. Jamie accuses the stranger of deliberate treachery – but he is bewildered and indignant. What soldiers? There are no soldiers.

The Doctor says 'Don't you understand, Jamie? He can't see or hear the soldiers. They are something he is not "given to know"!'

Sure enough, the stranger pleasantly wishes them a safe journey home and wanders off, leaving them in the hands of the enemy.

The 'soldiers' line up and advance, like beaters at a shoot, driving our heroes before them, until they reach the edge of the forest – now they have brought the trio out, it seems that their job is done. We cut to –

Scene 10. CONTROL ROOM
Where the 'Master' says approvingly: "Mission accomplished ... Now for the real test ..."

Scene 11. THE PLAIN
The trio are alone in the night. Where to go? Which way now?

In the distance they hear the sound of hoofs – galloping – coming nearer. A horse? No, not a horse; they see the creature at last, shining and white against the darkness ... A Unicorn. But no gentle storybook creature; its head lowered to charge, its sharp horn pointing straight at the Doctor – it comes on, faster and faster, and he is helpless to escape.

At the time that Ling submitted this outline, Sherwin and *Doctor Who*'s producer Peter Bryant were heavily involved in interviewing actresses for the part of the Doctor's new female companion to replace Victoria, played by Deborah Watling, who was leaving in *Fury from the Deep*, the penultimate story of the fifth season. The new actress was required imminently for the production of the fifth season's final story, *The Wheel in Space*. At this time a name for the new character had yet to be decided upon, and in his response to Ling's initial outline, dated 16 January 1968, Sherwin noted that he thought that they would gratefully adopt the name 'Zoe' for the companion. It therefore appears that this name was first suggested by Ling during early discussions about his story, or possibly by its inclusion in the outline.

Sherwin went on to give some suggestions and comments on the outline:

1) *Scene 1*: Before things start to go wrong with the Tardis, I think all three characters should be 'attacked' mentally, i.e. that they should suddenly start thinking and speaking erratically. The Doctor should be the last one to go 'under', insisting that they must all fight this cerebral aggressor with all their might.

2) *Scene 2*: We discussed this before, but I think it is sufficiently important to reiterate. Is it wise to show the 'soldier' so soon? It is always better to use innuendo and keep the full visual impact of the physical threat until as late as possible, in this instance, towards the end of this first episode.

3) *Scene 4*: Gulliver should speak only phrases written by Swift – possibly only Gulliver's dialogue.

4) *Scene 5*: Another note we also discussed previously. It might be fun to use children as the Interrogators and not the early on 'soldiers'; then introduce a 'soldier' as the Warrior, but the 'soldier' could be an actual mythological or fictional soldier. Perhaps the Doctor should recognise this mythical image as part of the test. At the end of the test, the voice could be disembodied or perhaps actual words across 'ye silver screen'.

5) *Scene 7*: Zoe's imprisonment – they hear her voice behind the door on echo.

6) *Scene 8*: Gulliver: Once again, Gulliver should talk in Swift's actual words. Here maybe the Doctor could recognise him and also recall some of Swift. His questioning would fall down eventually as he runs out of quotes, hence Gulliver is unable to answer his questions concerning the 'soldier'.

These are my main points concerning the breakdown. Now for just an overall note concerning the actual construction and writing of the episode. It is essential to maintain the adventure element within the story, both particularly and as far as the visual aspect is concerned.

The Sets: As our studio facilities are at present limited, we must consider doing anything that isn't in the wood or on the plain, on film at Ealing. Therefore, the ensuing sequence in the Tardis, its disintegrating and the noise within the Master's Control Hall must be considered to be part of our film effort. This will leave the entire studio free for the main body of the piece.

Peter and I are very enthusiastic about the idea, and I suggest that you now go ahead and complete the breakdown of the three remaining episodes. When you have done that, we can talk further and proceed with the scripts if all else is equal.

Ling was eventually commissioned on 31 January 1968 to provide scripts for a four part story. Ling recalled that some of the ideas came, 'from my vague thought that Gulliver was a traveller outside the boundaries of space and time, and the idea of making him a real character. Having been a children's script editor for such a long time, I think I was soaked in children's literature and knew a lot about it.

'The central villain was "the Master", somebody who had been churning out boys' adventure stories. He was partly based on the famous Frank Richards, who used to write things like *Magnet* and Billy Bunter stories. I think he turned out more words than almost any other writer. He was also partly based on myself in a way, because for six years I wrote an endless school serial in the comic *Eagle*, so I was putting myself in that spot.'

Problems with *The Dominators*, one of the other stories for the sixth season, meant that that story, also originally conceived as a six part adventure, was reduced by one episode during editing of its scripts. This left the season potentially one episode short, and the production team decided to get around that problem by extending *Manpower* to a five parter. The problem was that there was no additional budget to cover this increase in length, so Derrick Sherwin took on the task of writing the additional episode himself.

'The only way to fill the slot was for me to write an extra episode,' Sherwin explained. 'But, because we'd already spent all the money, I had no sets, no visiting characters and no new monsters. All I had was a white cyclorama, lots of smoke, the three regulars, the TARDIS prop and what was left of the tatty TARDIS interior set – and out of that, I had to construct an episode. I also used some old robot costumes that I found dumped in a storeroom.'

These robots had, in fact, been created by designer Richard Henry for an episode of the BBC2 science fiction anthology series *Out of the Unknown* called *The Prophet*, which had been completed late in 1966 and transmitted on 1 January 1967. These costumes had therefore lain unused for over a year.

To create the new opening episode, Sherwin drew on his own idea of the TARDIS crew being attacked mentally before their arrival in the forest of giant letters.

Ling's four episodes were delivered in first draft (still numbered one to four) as follows: episode one on 26 February 1968 and episodes two, three and four on 26 March. Following the decision to allocate a further episode to the story, which was taken in late March 1968, Ling's scripts were renumbered on 4 April. On 7 April, Sherwin gained official sanction to write the new opening episode himself. On 22 April, the story's title was changed from *Manpower* to *The Mind Robber*, and Sherwin issued an internal memo informing all recipients of copies of the rehearsal scripts of this fact.

Ling's melding of fact and fiction continued as a theme throughout the scripts, and, upon receipt of revised drafts of episodes three and four on 17 April, Sherwin questioned the use of the character 'Zorro' – a black-masked and caped avenger created by writer Johnston McCulley for a serial called *The Curse of Capistrano*, which first appeared in 1919 in *All-Story* magazine – as it may have resulted in copyright clearance problems, and Ling's usage of the first verse of Walter de la Mere's *The Traveller*, for similar reasons. Ultimately neither was featured in the completed story.

Pre-production

The director assigned to handle *The Mind Robber* was David Maloney. Maloney had started out as an actor and had worked as such from 1954 until 1961. With a wife and a young child to support, he had then started to look for a job with more security.

2 SECOND DOCTOR

'In 1960, I was working in the provinces doing repertory theatre, and I wanted something safer. I decided to join the BBC as a floor manager, and I rather cheekily told them that I'd done a lot of stage managing in repertory. I remember at my interview, when I was offered a temporary contract, they said to me, "Don't come in with the idea of ever directing. You will never be a director. Do you want to be a director?" And I said, "I want to work as a floor manager."

'After about 18 months as an assistant floor manager, BBC2 started up and I was promoted to a production assistant, a job that I did for the next six years. Over that period, I worked with a lot of interesting and exciting directors – both internal and freelance – and I gradually realised that some of these directors knew less about working with actors than I did. I started to think that maybe I could do this, and so when my chance came, I went on the BBC's directors' course and started to direct. I enjoyed it. I got a lot of good opportunities to do costume work, as well as working on shows like *The Newcomers* and *Z-Cars*.

'When Shaun Sutton, the BBC's Head of Serials, said, "Do you fancy doing a *Who*?" I said, "Yes please!" and so I was allocated. This *Doctor Who*, *The Mind Robber*, was the first *Doctor Who* that I directed, although I had worked on the show as an assistant with William Hartnell. I remember that first episode was a sort of buffer episode that was shot on a white stage against a white cyclorama, which was difficult. We couldn't make coloured marks on the floor for the actors' positions. I can't remember how we resolved this, but we obviously managed it.'

Joining Maloney as director was another for whom this was to be a first – and, in this case, only – *Doctor Who*. This was Australian designer Evan Hercules.

'Originally I came over to England from Melbourne to work in the theatre, as I thought that that was what you had to do. This was the early Sixties, and I left Australia because there wasn't much scope left for me there designing in theatre and I had been told by quite an eminent director that if I went to London, did a couple of shows and then came back, then he'd give me a job instantly. So I headed off to London ... where I stayed!

'At that time, the BBC was advertising for designers to work on BBC2, and I was lucky to be among the limited number chosen. We trained under Dick Levin, and one of the first things I did was *Doctor Finlay's Casebook*. As assistant designers, we were attached to a senior designer, and I was working with a wonderful lady called Fanny Taylor. Her voice would echo through the corridors of the BBC ... a darling lady. I worked as an apprentice with her, and eventually took over her shows, which included *Doctor Finlay's Casebook*. It was fun and gave me a taste for the process of getting the designs together and the system of getting your ideas into reality. We'd learned this in theory, but doing it was another matter.

'Having worked in the theatre, for which all the designs tend to be three-dimensional, working for television was different, in that your work was seen in only two dimensions. Also, although we were working in reality, it was a compressed reality, where you had to try and bring over the feel of whatever the show was within the designs for it. We would interpret the reality into a number of symbols and images and then try and incorporate those in the sets and in the overall design.

'Working on *Doctor Who* was curious, because it presented me with a dichotomy. The story was set in a land of total fantasy, and so here was a chance to be extravagant and imaginative, but at the same time, you had to discipline yourself, because the story demanded specifics like a unicorn and Princess Rapunzel. I'd not done any science fiction before – and haven't since, as it happens – so this was a first for me, and was a great learning experience. The *Doctor Who* came up simply because it was my turn.'

The other key designers assigned to work on the story were Martin Baugh handling the costumes, and Sylvia James looking after the make-up. Both Baugh and James had worked extensively on *Doctor Who* before this point. Baugh had been responsible for the costumes for the bulk of the fifth season, and his designs for the show included the Yeti, the Ice Warriors, the redesigned Cybermen in *The Wheel in Space* and the Quarks.

Casting

'My approach to casting was fairly standard,' explains Maloney. 'Particularly for young girls and boys, I would consider anyone put forward by agents, I'd go through *Spotlight* ... see dozens of people for the parts. For main parts, I'd draw up a short-list. First of all, when you had some idea of who you might like to cast, you'd check on their fee, to make sure that they weren't so expensive that you couldn't afford them. This was done through the Contracts Department, and they'd tell you what the person was paid the last time they worked for the BBC. Sometimes you could afford to use an expensive actor if you made sure that it was balanced out elsewhere in the artists' budget by using a couple of less-expensive ones elsewhere. Then you'd contact their agent to check on availability. If the person was free, in the case of a well known actor, you'd send them a script. Then they might want to meet you to make sure you were all right, say, over lunch.

'Once, when I went to Scotland to direct a play, I was allowed only one hospitality meal on the production, and as I was about to engage Gregor Fisher – who is well known now for playing Rab C Nesbitt – I invited him to lunch. But he said he'd rather have a couple of pints. And that was the end of my hospitality allowance!'

For *The Mind Robber*, Maloney used only one well-known actor, Emrys Jones, along with Bernard Horsfall, who had played the detective Campion in 1959/60, while the remainder of his small cast were made up of newer, up and coming actors and bit-part players.

On Location

The location work for *The Mind Robber* was not extensive. There were two sequences that required the use of locations: one where Jamie clambers up some rocks to escape from a toy soldier, and a second where a white unicorn is seen to charge at the Doctor, Jamie and Zoe.

As was usual, the location filming all took place before any studio recording was started for the story.

The film was edited before the studio recording, and then transferred onto video by running it in during the recording breaks in each episode. One exception to this during this story was for episode five, all the material for which was, for reasons unknown, put straight onto film, in which form the episode was eventually transmitted. It is most likely that this was done due to the complex nature of the editing that would be required in the episode.

In order to transfer the electronic images from the studio cameras onto 35mm film, a Film Recorder (also known as a Telerecorder outside the BBC, and a Kinescope in America) was used. This was, in essence, a film camera that took pictures from a television screen; however, in reality, it was a complex, purpose-built device consisting of: a) a special high-resolution flat cathode ray tube (CRT) and shaped-filter assembly;

b) a high precision clawbox to move, stop and position the film in an extremely short space of time; c) a high-quality optical system; and d) sophisticated electronics to synchronise the camera shutter to the television frame.

Film recording was the only way of preserving video material from around 1951 until the advent of the 2" video recorder at the BBC in about 1961, and it continued in use until much later. Shows that had a lot of editing work to be done in post production would often transfer to film because it was easier to edit than videotape (which had to be cut-edited until the late Sixties). Results were usually very good, with even 16mm systems managing to capture the full video bandwidth. Unfortunately, it is rare to see a first-generation recording, giving people the false impression that it was a poor-quality system.

In Studio

At this time in *Doctor Who*'s history, the programme was being recorded at the rate of one episode per week. To indicate some of the considerations involved in making a *Doctor Who* story during the Patrick Troughton era, what follows is a scene-by-scene summary of *The Mind Robber*, with comments from director David Maloney and designer Evan Hercules.

Episode One

Standing outside the TARDIS, the Doctor and Jamie realise that lava from the volcanic eruption caused by the detonation of the Dominators' rockets on the planet Dulkis, is headed directly for them. They hurry inside and prepare the ship to leave.

The lava rolls over the TARDIS, and the fluid links start to overheat. The Doctor manages to stop the mercury from vaporising, but they are stuck. The Doctor suggests that he could use an emergency unit, which would move the TARDIS out of reality. He fetches it from a cupboard under the console and fits it to one of the panels. He hesitates about using it, but Jamie pushes the unit home and the TARDIS vanishes from within the lava flow.

When the Doctor asks Zoe to check the meters, none of them is showing anything. The Doctor goes to the power room to work on the controls, and when Zoe asks him where the TARDIS has brought them, he replies that they are 'nowhere'. Jamie and Zoe head off to change their clothes.

David Maloney: Because we were still making the programme almost as if it were live, with continuous shots, there are lots of tiny mistakes. There was a shot just now where we cut to a camera that wasn't quite settled on the TARDIS's monitor screen, and so the picture jerks as you see it … Things like that. The vision mixer did all the cutting between the cameras. The model work of the lava was all shot earlier and played into the monitor at the right point. We also shook the camera to simulate turbulence as the ship took off. We did that a lot!

You can see how good Wendy Padbury is here. I didn't cast her, but she was brilliant. She had a sort of innocence. Simply marvellous. And Frazer was excellent for the children too. What's amazing is that Frazer's looks haven't changed in all these years. Witness *Emmerdale*. And I was a great admirer of Patrick. He was magical. In fact, after he had given up playing the Doctor, I cast him as an old sea-dog in a production of

Fennimore Cooper's classic period story *The Pathfinder* for the BBC.

Zoe, who has changed into a glittery cat-suit, joins the Doctor in the power room. The Doctor claims that he isn't worried, and tries to warn Zoe not to go outside the TARDIS. He tells her they must stay in the ship.

DM: The instrumentation in the background looks as if it comes from an old electricity generating station – it probably did!

Evan Hercules: We just brought in a couple of extra flats to make the power room, and I expect the bits of electronic equipment came from Trading Post, a props company that was used quite extensively.

Back in the control room, Jamie's attention is drawn to the scanner screen by the skirl of Highland bagpipes. He sees an image of what he believes to be his home.

DM: The image of the Scottish Highlands was simply a caption slide that was mixed in at the appropriate place. The same technique was used for when Zoe sees her home. The slides were obtained from a company called G M Studios.

Zoe enters and the image disappears. Jamie is convinced that they have landed, and he checks the console, where there is a device that warns to go elsewhere if there is any danger. Zoe sees her own home on the scanner, but it too vanishes. They rationalise that they must have landed, and Zoe is all set to go outside. Jamie advises getting the Doctor, and goes to do this. When he's gone, the image of Zoe's home reappears and, calling for the Doctor and Jamie to follow, she opens the doors and runs out into a featureless white void. The image on the scanner vanishes.

DM: We were lucky on this serial, because we got the very best camera crew. Crew 5, run by Dave Atkinson. They were very, very creative, and that's something that we had on our side. The lighting co-ordinator, Howard King, was also splendid.
There's a lot of talk in this story, but I don't think that audiences at the time would have objected to talk. The point is that talk is cheaper than action and effects, and as *Doctor Who* was regarded as a 'children's' series, it was never given the budget it needed.

EH: There was no dry ice there, where she runs out. She just fades away. Very nice.

Jamie finds the Doctor and tells him about the images. The Doctor hurries to the control room to find that Zoe has gone. The TARDIS sounds a 'first warning' and, despite the Doctor's protests, Jamie runs out after her.

DM: If you look at the side of the shot, you can see that the camera is locked off and there's a mix to make Jamie fade from sight as the Doctor comes into shot.

The TARDIS sounds a 'second warning' and the Doctor becomes aware of a presence in the ship. He sinks into a nearby chair and determines to fight.

In a white void, Jamie and Zoe call to each other.

DM: The lighting for these scenes was excellent. Howard King managed to bleach out the background and leave the characters prominent without resorting to any electronic trickery. It's nice camera work as well.

EH: It's the camera crew again. When you have a good crew, they actively seek good shots, and the results are better.

DM: Crew 5 were a Plays Department crew, and we couldn't book them easily for serials. They were permanently 'not available'. But I'd worked with them as a floor manager on plays, and so I asked if they'd come and do this *Doctor Who*. They agreed almost as a joke. I can, however, see the quality of the camera-work in this.

EH: We had to use Studio 1 at Television Centre for this episode, because we needed the sense of space, and we also had to get the cameras a long way away from the actors.

[NB: Although both Maloney and Hercules recall recording episode one in Studio 1 at Television Centre, and episode two in a smaller studio, both are documented as having been recorded in TC3. The original recording was due to take place in Lime Grove Studio D, but this was changed at a late date, possibly to accommodate the large white set and distant camera positions that Maloney wanted for the opening episode.]

Jamie and Zoe find each other but realise that they are lost. They decide to call out to the Doctor.
   In the TARDIS, the Doctor hears them calling, but believes it to be a part of the attack against him.
   Jamie and Zoe start to feel that they're being watched; and, unseen by them, several robots (John Atterbury, Ralph Carrigan, Bill Weisener, Terry Wright) are closing in on them through the void.

DM: Those robots make a noise like a slowed down fart! I wonder what it was really.

Zoe and Jamie see their homes again, but resist the temptation. They suddenly see the robots approaching.

DM: Wendy was excellent at being afraid, at acting scared. She was a great screamer as well.

The robots cluster round the two travellers, and Zoe screams as she sees images of herself and Jamie, dressed in white, beckoning them away. The Doctor, still in the TARDIS, also sees the images, and mentally warns them not to go.
   A voice (Emrys Jones) in the TARDIS tells the Doctor to follow them, but he refuses.
   The robots aim their chest-mounted guns at Jamie and Zoe and open fire.

EH: The effect of the robots firing their weapons was created by simply spinning a wheel, on which had been painted a pattern of concentric lines, in front of a camera, and the vision mixer combining that image with the main image of the gun. It was done live, at the time we wanted the effect.

The voice tells the Doctor that there is still time to save his companions, and he realises that he can't let them remain in peril. He leaves the ship, and finds himself standing outside a completely white police box exterior.

EH: We had to paint the outside of the police box white for these scenes, and, when we'd finished, we had to clean all the white paint off again.

The Doctor calls to Jamie and Zoe, and he sees the white-garbed versions coming towards him, followed by the robots. He urges his companions into the TARDIS, and when they won't move and the robots open fire once more, he pushes them in with his hands.

Once inside, they are suddenly wearing their normal clothes again, and the Doctor closes the doors and initiates dematerialisation. Jamie settles down for a rest and Zoe apologises for going out. The Doctor tells Zoe about the voice he heard, but he can't explain what happened. Jamie hears a horse neighing in his sleep. The Doctor finds the power booster on the console and operates it. Jamie awakens from a dream about a unicorn.

As Zoe notes the power rising, the Doctor notices a buzzing sound that seems to be getting more intense. Jamie and Zoe become aware of it too. The Doctor tells Zoe to continue to read off the readings as the sound gets louder and louder. He slips into a chair and closes his eyes to try and fight off the mental attack.

The TARDIS, floating in space, suddenly bursts apart, and Jamie and Zoe are left clinging to the spinning console. They see the Doctor floating away from them, still sitting in the chair, as the console descends into a bank of mist.

DM: This was done in the model studio at Ealing. There was a model TARDIS and a model console and we cut between them and the real ones to get the effect. The smoke was overlaid on as well.

End of Episode One

Episode Two

DM: Looking at this today, there seems to be too much re-capping between episodes; however, at the time, with a week in between, you could get away with it. The re-cap made up minutes of an episode that we had to take into account when timing the new story portions. We made the re-cap shorter or longer to adjust the overall time of the episode.

Jamie finds himself in a strange forest.

EH: The 'trees' were made from polystyrene, which was very expensive in those days. It was known by its trade name, jablite. It's a shame that you can't see that they're letters.

He suddenly spots a Redcoat (Philip Ryan) and attacks him with his knife.

DM: It's interesting here that Jamie has a knife. I doubt he would be allowed that in a serial like this today. The hero would simply not be permitted to carry such a weapon.

The soldier fires at point-blank range, and Jamie freezes into a photographic cut-out.

DM: When we started rehearsals for this episode on the Monday – each episode was rehearsed on the Monday to the Thursday and then recorded on the Friday – Frazer came in and said that he'd got chicken pox, and that they'd told him that he had to be in quarantine for a week and so he couldn't work. The first episode had been made, and so Derrick Sherwin came up with the very clever idea that in order to rescue Jamie, the Doctor had to make the face up from some cut-out parts, and he would get it wrong. He would build a different face, and out would jump another Highland warrior: not Jamie, but someone else. So we cast a substitute, a Scottish actor who simply played Jamie for the period that Frazer was not available. Then, later in the story, Jamie was again turned into a cut-out with a puzzle-face, and this time, the Doctor got it right and Frazer, having recovered from his chicken pox, took over playing Jamie once more.

EH: It's the sheer boldness of the idea as well. It's so full of interest, and an unexpected and interesting boldness.

Meanwhile, Zoe finds herself trapped by some castle walls where a door creaks open in front of her. Stepping through, she falls into darkness with a scream as the door closes behind her.

EH: I hired that door from Pinewood Film Studios.

In a control room, monitor screens show images of the castle door and the frozen Jamie. A figure (Emrys Jones) sitting before the screens, orders that the Doctor be found.

EH: We made the walls and ceiling out of mesh, as we wanted to get a sense of the galaxy around this fellow as he looks at his screens. The walls were a painted cyclorama cloth, and we also put a cloth over the top to give us a ceiling. The starfield was painted in black, blue and white. For this episode, we were in a smaller studio than for the first episode.

DM: The scenes being shown on the three monitors would have been fed through from the other cameras in the studio. We had five cameras available, and so the images from three of them would have been relayed to the monitors as the fourth camera shot the scene – notice it's all one take – and the fifth was positioned on Troughton for the following scene. All camera positions were plotted beforehand.

Emrys Jones, who played the Master, had been an absolutely first class juvenile actor in British films in the thirties, forties and fifties. I can't remember how I came across him, but I remember persuading him to take on the Master, which was really a character part for someone who had been a leading man in British films. I enjoyed working with him enormously, because he was a name and gave us such a marvellous character.

The Doctor awakens to find himself in the same forest as Jamie. He hears Jamie and Zoe calling to him, but he cannot find them.

Watching on the monitors, the Master requests that the lights be put on. The Doctor can now see what he's doing. The Doctor hides in one of the 'trees' as a squad of clockwork soldiers (Paul Alexander, Ian Hines, Richard Ireson) pass by, searching under the direction of the Master.

DM: Notice that the Master is wearing little devilish horns. I think that's the effect the producer intended to convey until we know more about him.

I can't imagine that we would have had the money to have constructed the costumes for the clockwork soldiers for this story.

When they have gone, the Doctor emerges, to be confronted by a stranger (Bernard Horsfall) who speaks an odd language. Settling on English, the Doctor makes friends with him after an initial misunderstanding.

Peter Ling: When I was writing the scripts, for the dialogue spoken by the stranger, I researched *Gulliver's Travels.* It wasn't something I knew backwards or anything, I just found the right dialogue. I did cheat a bit, however, and put together phrases quite unconnected in *Gulliver's Travels.* Most of the phrases were accurate, though.

DM: This was the first time that I cast Bernard Horsfall. I used him on two further occasions in *Doctor Who*, first as the Thal leader in *Planet of the Daleks* and then as the Doctor's opponent in *The Deadly Assassin*, because he was one of the few actors that I knew that was big enough to counter Tom Baker. I wanted a physical opponent who could match him. Here, playing Gulliver, it's interesting to note that all his lines are from the book, so whatever he's asked, he only quotes from the novel.

The stranger accuses the Doctor of being a traitor and claims that, by order of the Master, he is not permitted to help. He abruptly leaves.

The Doctor is suddenly surrounded by a group of children (Timothy Horton, Martin Langley, Sylvestra Le Touzel, Barbara Loft, Christopher Reynalds, David Reynalds), who shout riddles at him.

DM: The children came from the Barbara Speake stage school, and one of them was Sylvestra Le Touzel, now quite a well-known actress. I'd forgotten where I had worked with her. Then she mentioned it to me years later, and I couldn't remember her as the child.

Having solved the riddles, one of the children holds a sword at the Doctor's throat – he realises it's another test, and rearranges the letters in 'sword' to make 'words'. The sword, thrown into the air, falls as a dictionary. The children run off.

Jamie calls once more, and the Doctor finds the cardboard cut out.

EH: We took a photograph of Jamie and then blew it up to life size, which was something we used to do on *Z-Cars* quite a lot. We then mounted it on board and lit it so that at first you might think it was a real person.

The Doctor also finds a locked safe and a wishing well: it's a word puzzle, which he solves as 'Jamie is safe and well', at which point a jigsaw-type puzzle of Jamie's face appears. The

Doctor completes the puzzle and Jamie returns to life, but with a different face (Hamish Wilson) – the Doctor got it wrong!

DM: One of the cut-up pictures of the faces on the puzzle was of me, one was of Frazer and a third was of the new actor playing Jamie, Hamish Wilson. I think the fourth might have been of the director Douglas Camfield. Hamish Wilson is now a well known radio producer in Scotland. He was an actors' union representative for a long time. Hamish has an authentic Scots accent, unlike Frazer, who had an assumed accent.

The Doctor shows Jamie his face in a hand mirror to prove to him that he has changed. They head off and, solving yet another puzzle, find Zoe trapped in a giant jam jar.

DM: That shot of Zoe in the jar was on film. In the studio, you don't actually see the glass jar at all – just the rim of it.

EH: We couldn't have done a giant glass, as it would have been too expensive to have created a large, curved perspex surface.

They rescue Zoe and try and find a way out of the wood. Jamie suggests climbing one of the 'trees' to see if there is a way out. He does so, and discovers that what they thought was a forest of trees is actually a forest of letters and words that spell out proverbs and sayings.

EH: I had a great deal of trouble with the forest of words. They were never really what I wanted. They never had the graphic quality that they should have had, because you should be able to see letters and words from above, and we were not able to pull that off.

DM: We couldn't see the letters. We couldn't get up high enough, because the studio was too small. We should have got the camera above the set – maybe using a mirror – and seen everything widely. We could do something better these days with electronic effects.

Jamie is, however, able to see a way out.

EH: We contrived that shot so as to get a low-angle on Jamie, while not seeing any of the studio ceiling. We rigged it so that there was a backing cloth behind him as the camera looked up.

Jamie descends and, as they move off, they once again meet the travelling stranger. The Doctor tries to question him, but the answers make no sense. The Doctor mentions the army of soldiers, but the stranger appears not to know what he means. They hear the soldiers returning and, as the Doctor and his friends hide in the letters, the stranger keeps guard. However, once the soldiers arrive, the stranger calls to the Doctor that there is no army present. The Master orders the soldiers to round up the Doctor and his friends. The soldiers herd them off through the forest of letters.

When they arrive at the edge of the forest, they stop, and the soldiers vanish. The Doctor, Jamie and Zoe are left in a black void.

EH: The blackness was created with black velvet: on the floor and on a surrounding cyclorama.

Suddenly they hear a horse galloping and see a white unicorn coming towards them. Jamie remembers it from his dream. As the unicorn charges at them, the Doctor tells them not to run.

DM: We were assured by the property department that they had found a white circus horse for use as the unicorn. We intended to strap a horn on the horse's head. As we had such limited film time, we ended up at about one o'clock in the morning at an airfield south of Croydon on a very black night to film the sequence.

EH: The horn kept coming off. At first we tried to stick it on, but every time the pony shook its head, it came off. I can't remember how we ended up attaching it – perhaps by a strip around the pony's head.

Sylvia James: What we wanted was a white horse onto which we planned to attach a horn, which had been supplied by another department; and I had a small goatee beard to put on as well. When we got to this airfield in the middle of the night, the horse turned out to be a dark gold colour. Luckily someone had the idea of getting some 'blanko' from the RAF people stationed nearby, which was ideal as it was washable and would not harm the horse.

DM: This is a prime example of how we used to work in those days. We were so conscious that the thing wasn't working that, during the editing, we cut it as subliminally as we could, so that the viewer barely had a chance to see what was charging at the Doctor.

[The pony, whose name was 'Goldy', was supplied for filming on Sunday 9 June 1968 by Joan Roslaire of Willoughby Farm in Essex. The hire cost was 50 guineas]

End of Episode Two

Episode Three

The Doctor shouts to Jamie and Zoe to deny the existence of the unicorn, and it freezes into a cardboard cut-out.

DM: Of course, we couldn't get the unicorn and the actors in the same shot together, so the effect of it being there and charging at them was created through the editing.

The Master is watching on the monitors, and decides that the Doctor was 'a good choice'.
The soldiers reappear, and the Doctor and his friends run off. The Master lets them go, as they have no way of escaping.
The Doctor, Jamie and Zoe find themselves walking through a cobweb-strewn forest of twisted wood.

2 SECOND DOCTOR

DM: I remember Evan being very clever with all this, and using the cobweb stuff. It looks quite nasty and eerie, and I remember being impressed with what Evan had done.

They come to a building where a Redcoat shoots at Jamie once more. The Doctor knows what to do, and re-creates his face – correctly this time – causing the real Jamie to come back to life.
They enter the building, which is full of cobwebs and lit with candles.

EH: The spider-web there, with the spider in situ, was brilliant! We had a little wooden frame on which the web had been knitted. I think it'd been provided by Visual Effects. The idea behind the candles was a wonderful film by Jean Cocteau called *La Belle et la Bete* (*The Beauty and the Beast*), where there was a hand coming out of the wall holding the candelabra. These were very rich, rococo designs in brass. The effect of the candles being all melted down was achieved by us working with the candles beforehand.

The Doctor finds a ball of twine, and they realise that this is a labyrinth. Jamie ties the string to the door handle and they move into the maze, watched by the Master.

DM: The maze that the Master is looking at was simply a piece of perspex with three torches moving behind it to create spots of light.

The twine runs out, but Zoe believes she has worked out how to complete the maze. Jamie stays with the end of the twine while Zoe and the Doctor explore further. They eventually arrive at the centre of the maze, where there are piles of bones and animal tracks. Suddenly, roars ring out and the Minotaur (Richard Ireson) appears.

[The head of the Minotaur came from stock.]

Jamie hears the noise and runs to help, but is intercepted by a clockwork soldier. Realising that the solider 'sees' through a light on its hat, he covers it with his jacket. While the soldier (and therefore the Master) is blinded, he runs off.
The Doctor and Zoe shout that the Minotaur does not exist, and it vanishes. They return to where they left Jamie, but find that he has gone. The stranger appears once more, and the Doctor realises that he is Lemuel Gulliver, and that he can speak only the words that Swift wrote for him.

DM: Those lines are actually the opening lines of the book.

Jamie, still chased by the soldier, finds himself by some rocks, which he climbs to get away from it.

[The soldier was played by Ian Hines, Frazer Hines' cousin.]

DM: This location was south of Tunbridge Wells, and was the nearest place to London where you actually get rock that can be climbed. It was a youth training activity adventure centre with a rock face. We had to get a whole sequence – this – and the night filming of the unicorn completed in one day. So, we went down in the late morning, quickly shot the sequences of Jamie climbing the cliffs, and then, after an evening meal break, we travelled to Croydon to film the unicorn.

Looking up, Jamie wonders how he will ascend, when a rope is dropped down to him. He climbs the rope to a window in a castle turret, where he is met by a girl – he has actually been climbing up her hair! This is Princess Rapunzel (Christine Pirie).

S J: As the responsibility of the Make-up Department extended to the wigs and hair, we had to create this enormous long plait for Rapunzel. We got hold of a vast length of what must of been some sort of nylon hair, which we plaited and then sprayed with a blonde hairspray. This plait was so long that it went all the way round the make-up area – it was simply enormous. The actress, Christine Pirie, also had a blonde wig, and we attached this plait to the wig.

Rapunzel reluctantly agrees that Jamie can climb in the window. He does so, and finds himself in a hi-tech control room.

EH: This is perhaps the worst example of being able to see the joins in the set. I can't understand why it's so bad in these scenes. Perhaps I didn't have the time in studio to go round and cover up all the cracks.

On a large monitor is a page from the book Treasure Island, *while a ticker-tape machine prints out the continuing story of what the Doctor and Zoe are doing.*
   The Doctor and Zoe return to the heart of the labyrinth, where they find a statue of the Medusa (Sue Pulford). It starts to come alive. Jamie reads of their predicament. If they look at the Medusa's eyes, they'll be turned to stone.

[Sue Pulford played the Medusa only in long-shot in studio and for the scenes where her hand was seen approaching Zoe's face. All the animated shots of the head and shoulders of the creature were created in the visual effects studio by John Friedlander.]

The Doctor tries to get Zoe to disbelieve in the Medusa, but she cannot.

End of Episode Three

Episode Four

The Doctor remembers the mirror in his pocket, and they look at the image of the Medusa in that. It returns to stone.
   Jamie reads that the Doctor and Zoe have escaped, and tries to run himself, but an alarm sounds and he is trapped. Gulliver appears, closely followed by the robots from the void. Jamie hides, and the robots pass by.
   The Doctor and Zoe have left the labyrinth and see the citadel perched on top of a mountainous crag.

EH: That painting of the citadel came from the Design Department, but I didn't paint it myself.

Before they can make their way up, there is an explosion behind them, and the costumed figure of the Karkus (Christopher Robbie) appears in a flash. He challenges the Doctor, and Zoe informs him that the Karkus is a fictional character. The Karkus brandishes an anti-molecular ray disintegrator, which the Doctor claims is scientifically impossible, making it vanish. Enraged, the Karkus attacks the Doctor, and Zoe tells him that the Karkus has superhuman strength.

Zoe defends the Doctor and ends up beating the Karkus. He submits, and says he'll help them.

DM: I was most unhappy with this fight. I think I was sloppy on the day that we recorded it, and I should have had it re-taken, but I didn't.

[The fight arranger, B H Barry, was booked to coach Wendy Padbury in judo from 8 to 12 July 1968.]

Zoe explains that the Karkus appears in a strip cartoon from the hourly telepress in the year 2000. Reaching the door to the citadel, the Doctor rings the bell and imitates the Karkus to gain entry.

The Doctor and Zoe find Jamie, and he warns them about the alarm system – a photoelectric cell. The Doctor intends to see the Master, but Gulliver warns against this. The Doctor says he'll think about it, and Gulliver leaves. However, when he's gone, the Doctor says he intends to fight on. Jamie shows the Doctor the machine that was telling the story. The Doctor realises that the Master has been trying to turn them into fiction. Zoe is horrified, and accidentally activates the alarm. The robots arrive and silently herd them towards a doorway, where a voice welcomes them in.

EH: The sets are a lot better on this episode. I expect we'd had more time to get them set up properly.

They find themselves in the Master's control room. He is an old man who greets them warmly. He is connected from a skull-cap to a large, spinning computer behind him. He explains that he left England in the summer of 1926, having dozed off over his desk. He was writer of the adventures of Jack Harkaway which, for 25 years, appeared in the Ensign *magazine. It was because of this that he was selected to work in the Land of Fiction. His brain keeps the operation going. The Master explains that the Doctor is required to take his place in the running of the Land.*

Jamie and Zoe decide to sneak away as the Doctor keeps the Master talking. They find themselves in a huge library. They cannot get out, and the robots arrive, trapping them.
The Doctor refuses to cooperate, and the Master alternates between a harsh computer-voice (that of the Master Brain) and his own voice as he reveals that he has already written the fate of Jamie and Zoe, which has happened as predicted. He points to a screen, where the friends are seen to be fired upon by the robots before backing into the pages of a giant book. The book starts to close, squeezing them within.

EH: The book was mounted on enormous castors, and we had a couple of scene hands pushing it closed.

End of Episode Four

Episode Five

The Master explains that Jamie and Zoe have been turned into fiction. The Doctor still refuses to cooperate, and climbs up a bookshelf to escape. He arrives on the roof of the citadel.

EH: That set was based on Knowle House, a marvellous piece of architecture.

Jamie and Zoe appear, and the Doctor realises that they are now trapped.

The Doctor sees the master tape through a skylight and inadvertently calls on the Karkus to remove the glass panes. He then uses Rapunzel's hair to climb down to the typewriter, so that he can start to alter the fiction to his advantage.

The Master watches as the Doctor types in the next instalment: '... the enemy had been finally defeated by the Doctor'. Just in time, the Doctor realises that he cannot put this without turning himself into fiction. He climbs back onto the roof, where Jamie and Zoe have gone. The Karkus and Rapunzel are joined by Gulliver and the children, who all talk at once. Meanwhile, the Master writes that Jamie and Zoe realise that the Doctor is evil and must be punished. He sends them off to trap the Doctor.

The children are playing when they suddenly notice the TARDIS, from which Jamie and Zoe emerge. They usher the Doctor inside, and the external walls fall away to reveal that he is trapped within a perspex box, which fades away.

The Master writes the children out of the story, and the Doctor re-appears in the control room. The Master now intends to take over the planet Earth with the Doctor's co-operation, and has linked the Doctor to the Master Brain.

The Doctor realises that he now has equal power with the Master. He frees Jamie and Zoe from the book as the Master Brain calls for the white robots to enter the control centre. The Master orders the clockwork soldiers to destroy Jamie and Zoe.

DM: The monitor that they are watching this action on is called an Eidophore. It threw the picture onto a very large screen. We would book the Eidophore when we wanted a large, projected image in studio. It was used until the advent of Colour Separation Overlay (CSO), or Chromakey, when it was superseded.

EH: It was effectively a back-projection screen. We used them on *Z-Cars*. It had an arrangement of mirrors, which bounced the image about and made it larger.

DM: The difference was that a back-projection screen could take only a filmed picture, whereas the Eidophore could take a feed from one of the studio cameras and enlarge it. This process wasn't conceived by the Drama Department. It probably originated in one of the topical programmes or even *Top of the Pops*. We used to watch *Top of the Pops* regularly to pick up ideas and translate them into *Doctor Who*.

The Doctor calls on the Karkus to destroy the soldiers, which he does. The Master turns the Karkus on Jamie and Zoe, but the Doctor relates that his gun's energy has been used up. The Master then calls up Cyrano de Bergerac (David Cannon), and the Doctor counters this with D'Artagnan (John Greenwood). The two fictional swordsmen fight up on the roof.

DM: As an assistant, I worked on *The Spread of the Eagle*, three Shakespeare plays for the BBC, and John Greenwood arranged the fights. John and Bernard Hepton also did the fights for the Laurence Olivier film of *Richard III*. Greenwood was an excellent swordsman, and I cast him because of this.

Jamie and Zoe escape as the battle continues. The Master cancels Cyrano and substitutes Blackbeard the Pirate (Gerry Wain) instead. The Doctor cancels D'Artagnan and puts in Sir Lancelot (John Greenwood) in full armour.

DM: We used a real horse here for just one scene.

The Master Brain orders the Doctor destroyed, but the Master protests – the Doctor is the only person who can take his place. The Master Brain changes the white robots' weapons to destructor beams and sends them to remove the Doctor. The Doctor cannot save himself without writing himself into fiction. Jamie and Zoe decide to attack the computer in order to save the Doctor. They start pressing buttons at random, and the Master Brain overloads. The Doctor unplugs the Master from the computer as the robots open fire on Jamie and Zoe, who duck. The computer is hit.

DM: This is the point where we should have gone off in a new direction and done something fresh for the climax, but of course the endings are often forced on these *Doctor Who*s. You can see we're regurgitating some of the same effects again here. This is due to there being no more money and nowhere else to go except to blow the set apart.

The Doctor, Jamie and Zoe help the Master from the control room and out into a black void. A mist starts to appear and the Doctor hopes that the destruction of the computer will send them all back into reality.
The TARDIS re-forms in space.

DM: That was a reverse of the film sequence of the TARDIS breaking up.

End of Episode Five

[As an addendum to the story of *The Mind Robber*, the start of the script for the first episode of the following story, *The Invasion*, contains the following stage direction:

THE CAM. IS DEFOCUSED AND AS ITS PICTURE SHARPENS WE SEE THE DR SEATED IN HIS CHAIR WHERE WE LEFT HIM BEFORE THE TARDIS BROKE UP IN THE PREVIOUS STORY

This suggests that, aside from episode one of *The Mind Robber*, the remainder of the story was intended to be some sort of dream, or perhaps to have taken place only in the minds of the characters involved.]

Post-production

After the recording, very little remained to be completed on the show. 'One of the things that Sydney Newman changed when he became Head of Drama was the overruns in the studio,' explained Maloney. 'Many shows used to overrun their schedules, which cost money in overtime. So Sydney insisted there be a maximum of five recording breaks in a half-hour of drama. This meant that after recording the studio show, there were only five joins to make in the tape. That cut down editing time to the point where some directors didn't go to the editing – they just sent their assistant.

'This *Doctor Who* was a little more complex than that, however.'

One of the reasons for this was the way that the story had been constructed, both in planning and out of necessity.

The first thing to be completed for the story was the location filming, followed by all the model work (which included the stop-motion animation of the Medusa's head). Then, filming took place at Ealing Film Studios for sequences of the robots in the white void for episode one, plus several sequences for episode five including all the fights between the fictional characters.

Finally, selected sound recordings had to be made for the episodes, in particular for episode one, where the Doctor's thoughts were vocalised as he battled the Master Brain's invasion of the TARDIS. These took place at various times during the period of the recording of the episodes.

A final complication was Frazer Hines contracting chicken pox and having to be totally absent from the recording of the second episode. As a result of this, Hines' scenes at the very start of the episode were recorded before the scheduled start of recording for episode five.

Due to set requirements, the first three scenes of episode three (featuring the black void and the cut-out unicorn photograph) were recorded at the end of episode two. This allowed more space in studio for the other sets required for the second episode.

All this resulted in considerably more post-production editing and audio dubbing than was usual at this point in *Doctor Who*'s history.

Another note with regard to *The Mind Robber* is that, aside from in the final episode, there was no incidental music. Most stories of this era made use of stock music, while a few had scores especially provided by composers. The stock music in *The Mind Robber* was used only during the fight sequence between the fictional characters in the final episode and was a one minute and twenty-five second excerpt from Bruchner's 'Symphony No 7 in E Major'.

Perhaps the last word should go to David Maloney: 'Considering the crude conditions under which it was made, it's really quite slick.'

Transmission

The Mind Robber was transmitted on BBC1 from 14 September to 12 October 1968 and received an average audience rating of 6.86 million, which was just above the overall season average of 6.37. The ratings tailed off alarmingly at the end of the season, giving Troughton a less than auspicious end to his era.

The BBC also commissioned an audience research report for the final episode of *The Mind Robber*. There were 238 people surveyed to produce the report, and the compiler concluded that the overall reaction was not favourable.

'It seemed that this episode only served to confirm the growing feeling that the element of fantasy in *Dr Who* was getting out of hand,' the report said. 'This was one of the most far-fetched they had yet seen, most of the sample said, and, with the exception of a few who considered the ending a "bit of a let down" to a promising adventure, the remarks of those reporting also applied to the story as a whole.

'For many, *Dr Who* was clearly something watched "for the children's sake" rather than from personal inclination. Never one of their favourite programmes, it had now deteriorated into ridiculous rubbish which could no longer be dignified with the term science fiction, they declared. This latest adventure, with its weak story line, was too silly for words and, in their opinion, *Dr Who* had had his day.'

Only a third of those spoken to felt that the story was enjoyable, and these people also liked the idea of a 'master mind' having the ability to fictionalise real people. However, the report also had a down side to this: 'On the other hand, several who welcomed the theme as a refreshing departure from "the more usual punch-up" between the Doctor's party and their current enemies thought the action terribly disjointed and difficult to follow and, although they personally found the story one of the best for a long time, ended by condemning it as far too complicated for younger viewers – who were, after all, its main audience.'

The report went on to detail the reactions of those children who were among those surveyed.

'Among the children whose comments were reported, some of the older ones welcomed this adventure as "one of the best ideas ever thought of in this series", and there was plenty of evidence that *Dr Who* still had a legion of devotees among younger viewers, from the five-year-old for whom it was "a Saturday-evening ritual" to the rather older boy who dismissed it as "tripe" but, according to his mother, "secretly rather enjoys it". Nevertheless, the doubts expressed by some members of the sample regarding children's ability to follow the idea behind this story were confirmed to a certain extent by the reported comments of the youngsters. Although many parents said that *Dr Who* was a viewing "must" with their children (even if his fascination was "of the horrible variety"), they quite often added that, on this occasion, it was fairly obvious that they were rather "at sea" as far as the plot was concerned. The under-tens, especially, were reported as saying that they much preferred the episodes with "monsters" (Daleks, Yeti and so forth), and, although a few criticised it as "childish", it would seem to have been the lack of action which mainly accounted for their disappointment.'

All these comments would no doubt have been of particular interest to producer Peter Bryant and script editor Derrick Sherwin as they formulated plans to take *Doctor Who* in a new, more adult direction in the early Seventies.

CREDITS

Director	David Maloney
Producer	Peter Bryant
Script Editor	Derrick Sherwin
Assistant Script Editor	Terrance Dicks (ep 4)
Writer	Derrick Sherwin (ep 1)
	Peter Ling (eps 2-5)
Designer	Evan Hercules

Costume Designer	Martin Baugh (did not supervise ep 5 recording)
	Susan Wheal (ep 5)
Make-Up Artist	Sylvia James
Visual Effects	Jack Kine
	Bernard Wilkie
Production Assistant	John Lopes
Assistant Floor Manager	Edwina Verner
Assistant	Judy Shears
Floor Assistant	Gavin Birkett
Vision Mixer	Geoff Walmsley
Fight Arranger	B H Barry (ep 4)
	John Greenwood (ep 5)
Typist	Trish Phillips (ep 5)
Film Editor	Martin Day
Film Cameraman	Jimmy Court
Grams Operator	Pat Heigham
Crew	Five (eps 1-3)
	Six (eps 4-5)
Sound	John Holmes
Lighting	Howard T King
TM2	Fred Wright (eps 1-4)
	Neil Campbell (ep 5)
Title Music	Ron Grainer and the BBC Radiophonic Workshop
Title Sequence	Bernard Lodge
Telesnaps	John Cura
Special Sound	Brian Hodgson

SELLING THE DOCTOR

MEDIA

By the autumn of 1966, press interest in *Doctor Who* was waning. Newspaper and magazine editors had seemingly grown tired of reporting the show's many changes of cast, and the unexpected and extensive interest in the Daleks over the previous couple of years had now abated, leaving everyone looking for something new to report on.

The BBC's own listings magazine, *Radio Times*, was still a staunch supporter of the show, and during Patrick Troughton's time with the series, afforded three front covers to it (the first publicising *The Power of the Daleks*, the second doing likewise for *The Tomb of the Cybermen* and the third, which appeared while *The Enemy of the World* was being transmitted, prefacing an internal feature looking at *Doctor Who*'s monsters). Small internal articles continued to appear on a regular basis, usually accompanied by a photograph, and readers were never in doubt when *Doctor Who* was around. *Radio Times* continued to be published in regional editions with occasional differences to the amount of coverage given to the show by each edition. The issue carrying the feature on the monsters was also heavily promoted, with clips of Troughton, Frazer Hines and

Debbie Watling appearing in several TV trailers advertising the issue.

William Hartnell's forthcoming departure from the show was announced to the public on 6 August 1966, and a small item was carried by *The Times* indicating that the search was on for a new actor to play the Doctor. This actor was publicly named as Patrick Troughton on 2 September 1966. 'Actor Patrick Troughton, 46-year-old veteran of many "heavy" roles on the stage and TV, is to be the new Dr Who on BBC TV,' explained the *Daily Mirror*. 'He is taking over from William Hartnell who has given up the part of the long-haired scientist after three years. Troughton – he has twice played the part of Hitler in the theatre – will be seen battling the Daleks on Guy Fawkes Night. Dr Who will also have a changed personality – but the BBC is keeping this secret.'

When *The Power of the Daleks* made its debut on 5 November 1966, there was some coverage from the newspapers, most notably the *Daily Mail* and *The Times*, both of which ran short stories about it. Other items that gained press coverage included the return of the Cybermen in *The Moonbase*, the fish people in *The Underwater Menace*, and the Ice Warriors in *The Ice Warriors*.

Troughton has been described as an elusive and mysterious actor, and those newspapers that tried to give coverage to *Doctor Who* and its star found this to be the case. Troughton's dislike of interviews and publicity resulted in an almost total dearth of press coverage for the show. *Reveille* ran a full-page feature on *Doctor Who* in their Christmas 1966 edition, and found that while Anneke Wills, Frazer Hines and Michael Craze were happy to chat about their lives and what it was like to star in *Doctor Who*, Troughton was far more of a slippery customer. At the end of the interview, the reporter claimed that he said 'I've only talked to you because you're a girl. And I like girls,' before vanishing off to work. The piece ended with the reporter musing that Troughton was not the Doctor at all, but a leprechaun in disguise.

Kenneth Baily, writing in the *People* in September 1967, had more of a problem. He wanted to interview Troughton, but ended up being able to speak only with the people Troughton worked with. Baily claimed that in 20 years of appearing in TV roles, Troughton had never granted an interview – not strictly true, given that he had, at least, spoken to *Reveille* the previous year. The picture he painted was of a reclusive yet dedicated actor, much loved by all who worked with him.

Troughton maintained his privacy to the end of his time spent playing the Doctor, and beyond. The first 'major' interview about his time on the show came on the BBC's *Pebble Mill* programme in an interview to publicise *The Three Doctors*, a story celebrating *Doctor Who*'s tenth anniversary. Even in this interview, he said little, preferring to remain elusive when questioned about the series.

One rare occasion when Troughton did cooperate with publicity for the series came in December 1967, when he was pictured first helping to judge and then, in costume, with the winning entries to a competition launched by the BBC children's magazine show *Blue Peter* on 27 November to design a monster to beat the Daleks. According to *The Times* on 15 December 1967: 'BBC Television's *Blue Peter* programme received more than 250,000 entries when children were asked to design a blueprint for an original Dr Who-type monster. The winning designs were constructed by the visual effects department and went on parade at Lime Grove studios yesterday. Among top monster-makers were Stephen Thompson, aged 13, of Moira, near Burton-on-Trent, with his "aqua man", and Paul Worrall, aged eight, of Sheffield, with his "hypnotron".'

Troughton's appearance in costume was actually at the *Daily Mail* Boys' and Girls' Exhibition over the Christmas 1967 period, at which event the winning entries were also displayed.

Because of Troughton's low profile, the newspapers and other media, on the rare occasions when they did cover the series, tended to concentrate on other aspects. The companions, the monsters and the effect of the show on children were all topics discussed at different points during the late Sixties.

MERCHANDISE

Compared with the first three years of *Doctor Who*, the Troughton era was largely forgotten by merchandisers and publishers alike. From a boom of around 100 items in 1965 alone, the years 1967 to 1969 saw only nine items of merchandise released: three editions of World Distributors' *Doctor Who* Annual (1967, 1968 and 1969), two records ('Fugue for Thought' by Bill McGuffie (1967) which featured music from the second *Doctor Who* film, *Daleks Invasion Earth 2150 A.D.*, and 'Who's Dr Who?' by Frazer Hines (1968), at the time playing Jamie), a paperback edition of David Whitaker's novel *Doctor Who and the Crusaders* published by Green Dragon (1967) and two larger items: a Dalek Kiddie Ride produced by Edwin Hall and Co (1967); and a TARDIS climbing frame and playhouse produced by Furnitubes Associated Products (1968), of which only twelve are recorded as having been sold.

Perhaps the most significant activity for the era came when T Wall and Sons arranged a high profile *Doctor Who* promotion for their 'Sky Ray' ice lolly, which had just been re-launched in a 'new' shape. The promotion featured collectible cards given away with each lolly, and a special album could be obtained in which to keep them. There were television and cinema advertisements produced to promote the line (at least one of which was in colour) and in these, another actor appeared as the Doctor along with the Daleks. The Doctor was dressed in an outfit very similar to that worn by Patrick Troughton in his first few *Doctor Who* stories, and kept his face covered by his hands for the majority of his brief appearance. The 36 cards told the story of a Dalek invasion of the planet Zaos. The Doctor helps by bringing giant astro-beetles into the fray to fight against the Daleks. The album, called *Dr Who's Space Adventure Book*, contained 24 pages and, as well as a text story into which the collectible cards could be pasted, featured the 'inside secrets' of a Sky Ray Space Raider craft, pictures to colour, a cut-away Dalek into which readers could draw their own idea of what lived inside, and a 'mind mesmeriser'. The cover to the book was painted by Patrick Williams, who may also have painted the uncredited artwork that appeared on the cards themselves.

Only the Sky Ray promotion, the three *Doctor Who* Annuals and the ongoing comic strip in *TV Comic* featured the image of the second Doctor, and although there was some external interest shown in the Quarks (from *The Dominators*), a dispute between their creators and the BBC resulted in no products being licensed, although the robots did appear in several of the *TV Comic* strip stories. The Cybermen also appeared in the *TV Comic* strip.

OVERSEAS SALES

Continuing the practice of *Doctor Who* being sold for transmission abroad, the Troughton stories were picked up by several countries. These were documented in an internal listing produced by the BBC in February 1977. The listing is known to be incomplete – see the details of overseas transmissions in *New Zealand* that follow by way of example – and, in addition, prints would be passed on from one country to another, but what it presented was as follows:

	Australia	New Zealand	Singapore	Zambia	Hong Kong	Uganda	Nigeria	Gibraltar
The Power of the Daleks	•	•	•					
The Highlanders	•	•	•	•	•	•		
The Underwater Menace	•	•		•	•	•		
The Moonbase	•	•	•	•	•	•		
The Macra Terror	•	•	•	•	•	•		
The Faceless Ones	•	•	•	•	•			
The Evil of the Daleks	•	•	•		•			
The Tomb of the Cybermen	•	•	•		•			
The Abominable Snowmen		•	•	•	•		•	•
The Ice Warriors	•		•	•	•			•
The Enemy of the World	•	•	•	•	•		•	
The Web of Fear	•	•	•	•	•		•	
Fury from the Deep	•		•		•			•
The Wheel in Space	•		•		•		•	•
The Dominators	•		•		•		•	•
The Mind Robber	•		•		•			•
The Invasion	•		•		•			•
The Krotons	•		•		•		•	•
The Seeds of Death	•		•	•				•
The Space Pirates	•		•	•				•
The War Games	•		•	•	•			•

Whereas Hartnell-era stories had been sold to as many as twenty three countries in total, during the Troughton era that number dropped to only eight, with only three countries – Australia, Singapore and Hong Kong – taking the majority of stories at the time.

No Troughton-era adventures were sold to the USA until around 1985. This was partly because in the late Sixties, the BBC undertook a systematic programme of wiping the master video tapes of any shows felt at the time to have no further commercial potential. These included the vast majority of *Doctor Who* stories made to that point. When this practice was eventually stopped, several Hartnell- and Troughton-era stories were found to be still in existence in negative format, and others were slowly returned from overseas and from private collectors. In 1985, a package of those Hartnell- and Troughton-era stories that had been recovered were made available to the USA for the first time.

Australia
by Damian Shanahan

One of the main television providers in Australia is the Australian Broadcasting Corporation (ABC), the head offices of which are in Sydney. BBC Enterprises in Sydney would routinely provide the ABC with black and white 16mm film prints of *Doctor Who* serials as soon as they became available from the BBC in the UK. From there, stories would be sent to the Film Censorship Board (now the Office of Film and Literature Classification) for classification prior to transmission. The prints would then be passed around the country, eventually screening in all states, but not always premiering in the same region. When this circulation of material had finished, prints were either destroyed or passed on to other countries for further screening.

The following transmission details cover the screenings in Sydney, and while the dates differ considerably from those in other capital cities, the order of debut screening was essentially the same.

At 6.30 pm on Friday 21 July 1967, the first episode of *The Power of the Daleks* premiered in Sydney. This was followed by weekly transmissions up the end of *The Faceless Ones* on 26 January 1968. *The Evil of the Daleks*, the final story in Troughton's first season, was not purchased at this stage. Following transmission of *The Faceless Ones*, the ABC launched into an almost immediate run of repeats, starting on 12 February 1968, with all episodes from the William Hartnell story *The Chase* to *The Faceless Ones* (apart from *Mission to the Unknown* and *The Daleks' Master Plan*) shown Mondays to Thursdays at tea-time, and ending on 25 June. This effectively kept *Doctor Who* on Australian screens until the next season was ready to be shown.

At 6.05 pm on Friday 5 July 1968, Troughton's second season commenced its debut run. It continued until the end of *The Web of Fear* on 6 January 1969. The time slot had changed from Fridays to Sundays after the screening of *The Abominable Snowmen* concluded on 6 September 1968. This was followed by *The Evil of the Daleks*, which was screened weekly from 12 January 1969 to fill a gap created by delays in the censorship of *Fury from the Deep*, which was then screened from 2 March. *The Wheel in Space* was first transmitted from 13 April.

Meanwhile, the ABC took advantage of school holidays to utilise repeat rights, and *The Evil of the Daleks* was screened from 7 to 16 May. August school holidays saw repeats of *The Tomb of the Cybermen* and *The Abominable Snowmen*, and the Christmas vacation allowed for repeats of the remaining second season stories up to *Fury from the Deep*, concluding on 23 January 1970. *The Wheel in Space* was eventually repeated weekday afternoons from 31 August to 7 September 1970.

Troughton's third season commenced screening in April 1970 with *The Dominators*, which was followed by the remainder of the season up until *The Seeds of Death*. In January 1971, *The Dominators*, *The Mind Robber* and *The Invasion* were repeated. *The Space Pirates* and *The War Games* were eventually premiered from 11 April 1971.

The Space Pirates was repeated with *The Krotons* and *The Seeds of Death* in January 1972, while *The War Games* was repeated during the second week of May 1972, with the episodes shown in fifty minute blocks.

This was the last time that Troughton-era episodes were screened in Australia in the Seventies. Fourteen years later, in February 1986, *The Krotons* and *The Mind Robber* were repeated, following the first run of season twenty-two, and led into a complete run of Pertwee stories. The transmission of these two stories was the first time black and white episodes of *Doctor Who* had been screened since Australian television switched over to colour in 1975. While rights for two screenings of each of these stories were purchased, due to expire in 1988, they were not repeated. Clips from the first episode of *The Mind Robber* were used in promotional advertisements for the ABC shop throughout 1986.

Although all Troughton's stories had been screened, Australian viewers had not actually seen some of them as originally transmitted by the BBC. Because of the early time slot provided for the show by the ABC, each story was required to be rated 'G' – for General Audience. Hence, all stories had to be screened by Government censors who would make recommendations as to cuts required in certain episodes in order to bring them in line with the 'G' rating.

The following detail the cuts made to the stories.

The Highlanders was classified 'G' (for General) with minor cuts required to episode one. Reductions were made to Alexander McLaren's battle with a Redcoat at the beginning of the story, and to a hanging sequence featuring the Doctor, Ben, Jamie and Colin McLaren toward the end of the episode – about thirteen seconds in all.

The Underwater Menace had a total of 50 seconds of material removed, with each episode individually rated 'G with cuts'. The bulk of censoring concentrated on the sequences involving Polly's artificial gill operation from the first two episodes. Zaroff's spearing of Ramo in episode three and his own drowning sequence from the end of episode four were also reduced considerably.

Four separate cuts were made to *The Macra Terror* on 31 October 1967. Three of these were from the same scene, in which Ben and Polly first confront the Macra beast, with deletions made to Polly's screams and her being attacked by the creature. A small edit of a Macra claw approaching the Controller's neck was made to the end of episode two, and also to the reprise of this scene at the beginning of episode three. A total of just under half a minute of footage was excised from the story.

The Faceless Ones was viewed by the Censorship Board on 4 October 1967, and its Certificate of Registration was issued after consideration some three weeks later. One of the censors remarked: 'In my opinion this series is not suitable for 'G' classification, but could be passed 'A' with no cuts. I am sure that this would not please the ABC so I am referring at this stage to all episodes screened so far. I will review episode 6 later.' *The Faceless Ones* was eventually passed for general viewing with only episode 1 requiring cuts in order to grant it a 'G' rating, bringing it in line with the rest of the episodes. Five cuts totalling approximately half a minute were made, mainly to close-up shots of the faceless creatures.

The Tomb of the Cybermen was viewed at the Film Censorship Board on 10 January 1968 by three government censors, two of whom rated the serial 'A' (for Adult). One censor remarked that 'the serial is not suitable for children as it is violent, shows no regard for human life (or robot life) and is likely to terrify young children.' Another referred to *The Tomb of the Cybermen* as 'typical of the *Doctor Who* series – weird and wonderful! There are a number of aspects of the story which I would not want shown for General Exhibition so my opinion would be "A with cuts". There are a number of shots of deliberate violence or threats of violence.' Irritated by this attitude (which saw Hartnell's *The Daleks' Master Plan* rated 'unsuitable for general viewing' and hence unable to be screened), BBC Enterprises sought to appeal against this rating, which would as a consequence preclude a sale, as the ABC was only interested in purchasing *Doctor Who* that could be rated 'G'. BBC Enterprises issued a Notice of Appeal on 20 March 1968, which argued that the producers of *The Tomb of the Cybermen* 'took care to ensure that the material was in no way injurious to the psychology of children … This series of programmes was viewed by two world authorities on child psychology, Drs Pedler and Himmelweit, and both pronounced the series to be quite harmless.' The Appeals Censor informed the BBC that the appeal would be heard on Monday 6 May and that the films were required for viewing on that day. On 15 May, the BBC were informed that *The Tomb of the Cybermen* was now passed as 'G' with no cuts required, and that the Appeal fee of three guineas was refunded. This was an unusual back down by the Film Censorship Board, and a delighted Enterprises made use of this as a case study in later appeals (most notably for the third Doctor story *The Daemons*). It could however be said that the appeal was, in part at least, somewhat disingenuous, as the 'Dr Pedler' referred to was the story's co-writer, Kit Pedler, who, although a respected scientist, was not a world authority on child psychology! The appeal in fact seemed to be referring to a debate that had taken place on the BBC viewers' comment programme *Talkback*, in which both Pedler and Himmelweit had been involved (see below for further details).

Fury from the Deep had been offered to the ABC on 26 June 1968. The prints were auditioned and then sent to the Censorship Board for classification, but weren't viewed by the Board until late January 1969. One of the three censors rated the serial as 'A' throughout, which would have precluded screening in the allotted late afternoon timeslot. He was out-voted, however, and the episodes passed as 'G with cuts'. A total of seven cuts were required in episodes two, four and five in order to grant the 'G' rating. The longest of these lasted 54 seconds and involved the deletion of the entire sequence where Mr Oak and Mr Quill enter Mrs Harris' bedroom and breathe out toxic fumes, which cause her to collapse. The total time removed from the story was just under two minutes.

The ABC received audition prints of *The Wheel in Space* in August 1968. Censors viewed the story in March 1969 and rated it 'G and cut', ordering that the death sequence of the Australian character Duggan in episode four be reduced by four seconds, to edit his screams.

The Dominators was offered to the ABC as early as 29 August 1968, and auditioned by the Director of Drama and Controller of Programming within weeks, but it was not viewed by the Censorship Board until 10 April 1969. The Censorship Board passed *The Dominators* as 'G' with a total of three cuts required to episode four. The Quark's execution of Tensa, torture of Teel and the extended murder sequence of Educator Balan were removed from episode four, reducing it by approximately twenty seconds. The tail end of Balan's death was also excised from the beginning of episode five.

The Invasion created headaches for BBC Enterprises when the censors gave it an overall 'A' rating. Offered for purchase to the ABC on 24 December 1968, the films weren't sent for classification for almost a year. After some delay, the ABC indicated an urgency to have the material classified. The Censors replied, 'As you are aware, the Censor must see all episodes of a serial at one screening – the next *Doctor Who* serial VV *The Invasion*, has eight parts; we have tentatively scheduled it for censorship on 24th, 25th or 26th of February; i.e. the Censorship Schedule to be issued on 16th February. Please be assured that each serial will be scheduled for censorship as expeditiously as other programme pressures permit.' When BBC Enterprises learned of the 'A' rating, another appeal was lodged, and as with *The Tomb of the Cybermen* the serial was successfully reclassified 'G'. This time, though, cuts were required in episodes five, six and seven. A total of over thirty seconds was edited, which included the killing of a policemen in the sewers by a Cyberman and reductions to the sequence in which Professor Watkins fires a gun at Tobias Vaughn.

Vaughn's sinister appraisal of the Professor as being '… our insurance' was also removed.

The War Games was classified 'G' with two minor cuts required to reduce throttling and strangle holds in a battle sequence in episode four, which totalled ten seconds.

In 1984, Australian fan Dallas Jones first received information on the Film Censorship Board's cuts made to *Doctor Who*. In October 1996, following more research by Jones along with several other researchers, most notably Rod Scott, fellow Australian Damian Shanahan uncovered more detailed information relating to all the cuts made by censors, as well as locating the actual footage. Commensurate with Australian Government requirement to retain edited material, the strips of 16mm film physically removed from those episodes had been kept. On 8 January 1997, the BBC received a digital copy of these segments of film, in many cases from episodes of *Doctor Who* at that point missing from the BBC's archives.

New Zealand
by Paul Scoones

The Patrick Troughton era began on New Zealand television in August 1969 with *The Power of the Daleks*, which was the latest in a long uninterrupted run of stories that had commenced with *The Space Museum* in October 1968. The first three Troughton stories, *The Power of the Daleks*, *The Highlanders* and *The Underwater Menace* were acquired in March-April 1969.

A single film print of each episode was held by the New Zealand Broadcasting Corporation (NZBC) necessitating the staggering of the schedules so that the films could be transported between New Zealand's four regional channels, Auckland (AKTV-2), Wellington (WNTV-1), Christchurch (CHTV-3) and Dunedin (DNTV-2).

Christchurch was the first region to screen Episode 1 of *The Power of the Daleks*, on 31 August 1969, followed by Wellington on 28 September, Auckland on 10 November and Dunedin on 17 November 1969. In the Christchurch and Wellington regions the series initially screened on Sundays, but moved to Mondays from 6 October (in Wellington) and 20 October (in Christchurch). In the Auckland and Dunedin regions episodes screened on Mondays from the outset of the Troughton era. Start-times were mostly around 6 pm.

The Moonbase and *The Macra Terror* screened in Christchurch and Wellington, but for viewers in the Auckland and Dunedin regions the series stopped after *The Underwater Menace*. This staggered break in the schedule allowed for all four regions to stop screening the series within the space of a month, between 26 January and 23 February 1970. The film prints for both *The Moonbase* and *The Macra Terror* were then stored in Auckland until the two serials screened several months later; in Auckland from 26 June to 14 August 1970 and in Dunedin from 10 July to 28 August 1970, on Fridays at around 6 pm.

Some information is available on the fate of the first five Troughton stories. NZBC records show that following transmission, the 16mm film prints were stored at a facility in Hill Street in Wellington. *The Power of the Daleks* was sent on to a television station in Singapore in January 1972. *The Highlanders* film prints are noted as having been destroyed at some point after April 1970, the fate of *The Underwater Menace* is unrecorded and records show that *The Macra Terror* episodes were destroyed on 27 June

1974. The fate of *The Moonbase* is also unrecorded, but the reused film can that had previously contained Episode 3 of this story was discovered by Graham Howard at a Television New Zealand film storage facility in Wellington in 1990.

The next four Troughton stories were purchased from August to October 1969. *The Faceless Ones* was rejected by the censor as unsuitable for broadcast and as a result the story was returned to the BBC in July 1970. The remaining three stories, *The Evil of the Daleks, The Tomb of the Cybermen* and *The Abominable Snowmen*, were screened, first in Wellington from 19 June to 9 October 1970, then in Christchurch from 3 July to 23 October 1970, Auckland from 21 August to 11 December 1970 and finally Dunedin from 4 September 1970 to 1 January 1971. In these last two regions the new episodes followed on directly from the delayed screenings of *The Moonbase* and *The Macra Terror*. The episodes screened on Fridays at around 6 pm on all channels.

According to NZBC records, the screening rights expired for the three stories in May, July and August 1973 respectively. The seven episodes of *The Evil of the Daleks* are all noted to have been destroyed, but the fate of *The Tomb of the Cybermen* and *The Abominable Snowmen* is unrecorded.

The remaining five stories from Season Five were all purchased between October and December 1970, however two of the five were not screened as *The Ice Warriors* and *Fury from the Deep* were rejected by the censor and the programme purchasing viewing committee respectively. *The Enemy of the World, The Web of Fear* and *The Wheel in Space* were approved by the censor for viewing, although some cuts were made to all three stories. Film trims of some of the censored sections from the latter two stories were discovered by Graham Howard in New Zealand in 2002. These three stories screened first in Wellington from 3 May to 30 August 1971, then in Auckland from 10 May to 6 September, Christchurch from 17 May to 13 September and finally Dunedin from 24 May to 20 September 1971. All of the episodes screened on Mondays mostly around 5.45 pm. The rights to these stories expired by May 1974 and the fate of the film prints is unrecorded.

Following the screening of *The Wheel in Space* no episodes of the series were broadcast in New Zealand for three and a half years and when the series did return in March 1975 it was with Jon Pertwee's first story as no stories from Season Six had been purchased by the NZBC.

Episodes from Season Six were first screened in 1985. *The Mind Robber* and *The Krotons* were selected to begin a long run of a mix of first-run and repeated *Doctor Who* stories on Television New Zealand (TVNZ)'s second channel, TV2. *The Mind Robber* was billed as both "the very first *Doctor Who* story" and a repeat in promotional material, when in fact it was neither. The story was transmitted on Fridays from 12 April to 26 April 1985, followed by *The Krotons* from 26 April to 10 May 1985. Two episodes were screened back to back each week, from 6.30 pm. The middle closing and opening credits were removed, and the opening titles of the first episode screened were edited to remove the episode number, usually replaced by a still frame of the series logo. The closing credits of the last episode of *The Mind Robber* were removed, with a continuity announcer coming on to explain that the first episode of *The Krotons* would follow after the commercial break. Viewer ratings for these screenings show that the series got off to a strong start, with *The Mind Robber* rating 11.1%, making it the seventh most watched *Doctor Who* story between 1985 and 1989. *The Krotons* however saw a drop to 8.1%.

A third previously unscreened story from Season Six was first aired in 1988 as part of TVNZ's *Doctor Who* twenty-fifth anniversary 'Silver Jubilee' week. The Troughton era was represented by an omnibus version of all six episodes of *The Seeds of Death* on 19 November 1988. Placed in a 2.40 pm Saturday slot on TV2, the story gained a viewer rating of 2.4%. As had been the case with *The Mind Robber* and *The Krotons*, the story was billed as a repeat, when in fact this was its first-time appearance on New Zealand television. *The Seeds of Death* was advertised in some publications with a synopsis for *The War Games*, prompting a voiceover correction at the beginning of the story.

The Seeds of Death, *The Mind Robber* and *The Krotons* were repeated in this order on TV2, broadcast from 31 March to 30 June 1991 on Sundays, initially at 9.15 am and then at 9.35 am for *The Krotons*. This time, the stories were screened in an unedited, single-episode-per-week format, with the exception of the last two episodes of *The Krotons*, which were broadcast back-to-back on 30 June 1991 as a late change to the schedules. Episode Four had been scheduled to screen on 7 July 1991.

Every complete surviving Troughton story screened as part of a run of *Doctor Who* stories on the UHF and satellite digital channel Prime Television, in 2000. The episodes were screened six days a week (Sunday to Friday) at around 6.30 pm from 14 August to 21 September 2000. Following on directly from *The War Machines*, the Troughton stories began with *The Tomb of the Cybermen* followed by *The Dominators* – making its New Zealand television debut – *The Mind Robber*, *The Krotons*, *The Seeds of Death* and finally *The War Games*, also screening on New Zealand television for the very first time, more than thirty years after this story first screened in the UK.

JUNKING

by Andrew Pixley and Jan Vincent-Rudzki

It was during Patrick Troughton's tenure as the Doctor that the destruction of *Doctor Who* material began at the BBC. During the 1960s, it was policy to retain the master 405 line videotapes of programmes for a while, to allow for possible repeats. Then they would be erased by an electromagnet for re-use recording another show. Some episodes would be retained, however, generally as 16mm film recordings of the type used to sell BBC programming to other countries (film being an international standard whereas videotape was not).

On 13 December 1966, a Retain Order from Television Enterprises Sales was placed on all the *Doctor Who* serials up to and including *The Gunfighters* – this included the untransmitted pilot and a number of episode such as *The Waking Ally* that had been made on film. Around this time, Retain Orders were sent to the Videotape Library on an almost weekly basis to ensure that the most recently screened episodes – such as *The Power of the Daleks* and *The Highlanders* – were not wiped, at least not before 16mm films could be made of them. Although the paperwork is inconsistent (some episodes are listed for wiping more than once), it would appear that the first *Doctor Who* tapes to be wiped were those for *The Highlanders*, soon after 9 March 1967, barely a month after their BBC1 transmission. (*The Underwater Menace* episodes 1 and 2 were similarly labelled for wiping, but seem to have escaped erasure at this point.)

The first mass erasure of *Doctor Who* tapes appears to have been on 17 August 1967, less than a year after the initial Retain Order was issued. 80 episodes from the pilot to

The Gunfighters were targeted for wiping (although probably only 78 of these were erased at this point). Some entire stories were deleted at this time (e.g. *Marco Polo*, *The Romans*, *The Ark*) while others were partially wiped (e.g. *The Reign of Terror*, *The Dalek Invasion of Earth* and seven episodes of *The Daleks' Master Plan*, including *The Feast of Steven*). Part of the reason for this may have been the arrival of new technology; *Doctor Who* would be recorded on the higher definition 625 line tape from late 1967 onwards, starting with *The Enemy of the World* episode 3. BBC1 would continue to transmit on 405 lines up until November 1969, with the 625 line tapes standards converted for broadcast.

The only episode to be marked for wiping in 1968 appears to have been *The Abominable Snowmen* episode 4, on a document dated 4 March – although the wiping does not actually seem to have occurred at this time. However, other paperwork shows that the tapes of *The Evil of the Daleks* were erased in August 1968, just after their BBC1 repeats (and despite a Retain Order issued on 1 August that year). Most of the remaining Hartnell tapes were destined for the same fate on 31 January 1969, when 25 more were wiped (including the second episode of *Inside the Spaceship*, the fourth episode of *The Reign of Terror*, *Planet of Giants*, the third episode of *The Dalek Invasion of Earth*, the first and last episodes of *The Crusade*, the third episode of *Galaxy 4* and the first episode of *The Myth Makers*). Nine Troughton episodes were also marked for deletion, along with *The Tenth Planet* episode 4, yet it seems that all these tapes in fact survived for a few more months.

17 July 1969 saw authorisation to wipe *The Chase: The Executioners*, the last three episodes of *The Daleks' Master Plan*, and *The Mutants: The Expedition*. On 21 July, the tapes and films for a number of Troughton instalments from *The Underwater Menace* through to *The Space Pirates* (i.e. both 405 and 625 line tapes) were listed on a junking document – a sign that the age of monochrome for BBC1 was shortly to come to an end. September saw a few Troughton episodes that had escaped the July purge re-assigned to a new list (editions of *The Underwater Menace*, *The Faceless Ones*, *The Abominable Snowmen*, *The Ice Warriors*, *The Web of Fear* and all *The Tomb of the Cybermen*), with eight other shows joining them in October (*The Tenth Planet* episode 4, *The Ice Warriors* Five and Six, *The Enemy of the World* episode 1 and episodes 1, 3, 5 and 6 of *The Web of Fear*).

By the end of 1969, it appears that the only monochrome episodes of *Doctor Who* to exist on their original tapes were both versions of *100,000 BC: An Unearthly Child*, *Mission to the Unknown*, *The War Machines*, *The Macra Terror*, *Fury from the Deep* and *The War Games*. Thankfully, at this point, although the tapes had gone, the 16mm films for most episodes were generally still in circulation around the globe from BBC Enterprises.

VIEWER REACTION

During the late Sixties, viewers were increasingly given opportunities to comment on television in general. This was through the letters pages of the *Radio Times*, through internal BBC 'audience research' surveys, and also on several television talk shows designed to air comment about television itself.

Reaction to the change over of William Hartnell to Patrick Troughton was mixed, at least from readers of the *Radio Times*, whose views were printed in the magazine's

'Points from the Post' column. For example, G Howard from Leeds commented: 'I would like to send my heartiest congratulations to the production team of BBC1's *Dr Who*. Patrick Troughton and the superb character he has created have dragged the programme out of the unfortunate mess it had degenerated into. Given sensible scripts the programme could possibly emerge as one of the real successes of television science-fiction. I look forward to the time when *Dr Who* is performed for adults only.'

Mrs Estelle Hawken from Cornwall was, however, less impressed: 'What have you done to BBC1's *Dr Who*? Of all the stupid nonsense! Why turn a wonderful series into what looked like Coco the Clown? I think you will find thousands of children will not now be watching *Dr Who* which up to now has been the tops.'

Comments on the third episode of *The Power of the Daleks* from the BBC's viewing panel were recorded in an internal audience research report. 'Viewers in the sample who were enthusiastic about this episode ...' said the report, 'were confined to a minority, less than a quarter ... finding it appealing to an appreciable degree'. Amongst this group, it seemed the Daleks were the main attraction. 'This is supposed to be for the "kids",' commented a 'senior clerk', 'but I must confess that I found the programme quite gripping. As an ardent sci-fiction fan, I think the Daleks are the most sinister "aliens" I've come across'.

More often, though, 'viewers in the sample reported a very moderate degree of enjoyment, and a number were scarcely interested at all'. For some, even the Daleks had lost their appeal. 'They have made their impact, served their usefulness,' commented one malcontent, 'now they just seem hackneyed and more unreal than usual'.

If the production team had hoped that Patrick Troughton's arrival would give *Doctor Who* a boost, the initial signs were not encouraging. 'The series in general,' continued the report, 'is not as good as it used to be, in quite a few opinions – "At one time we used to hate to miss it; now we are quite indifferent"'.

Comments on the change of Doctor were more scathing: 'Once a brilliant but eccentric scientist, he now comes over as a half-witted clown,' complained a teacher. 'The family have really "gone off" Doctor Who since the change,' noted another viewer. 'They do not understand the new one at all, and his character is peculiar in an unappealing way'.

There was criticism, too, of Troughton's performance – although one person conceded that he 'seemed to be struggling manfully with the idiotic new character that Doctor Who has taken on since his change'. Typical opinions were that he was overacting, 'playing for laughs,' and making the Doctor into 'something of a pantomime character'. 'I'm not sure that I really like his portrayal,' was one verdict. 'I feel the part is over-exaggerated – whimsical even – I keep expecting him to take a great watch out of his pocket and mutter about being late like Alice's White Rabbit'. A number stated that they had preferred William Hartnell in the role.

There was however a recognition from a minority that Troughton had yet to settle down and that there was still time for him to become 'fully acceptable'. Perhaps the most positive comment came from a student, who said that 'Patrick Troughton, a brilliant actor, had improved the programme greatly'.

In the mid-Sixties, there was an increased awareness of the role of the viewing public as a commentator on the programmes that the BBC produced. With this in mind, two series started transmission that gave the public the chance to air their views. *Junior Points*

of View and *Talkback* gave *Doctor Who* a significant amount of coverage in the Sixties, in particular starting and then developing debates about whether or not the programme was too frightening for children.

'Please bring back the old Doctor Who. We don't like the new one, he looks as though he might be bad and never says "Now, now, my child,"' one concerned party wrote to *Junior Points of View*. Another commented: 'As *Doctor Who* is a programme for intellectuals, I suggest that the scriptwriter is replaced or forced to write something sensible for an actor on a great programme, too good to be wasted.'

The general feeling on this edition of *Junior Points of View*, which aired on 11 March 1967, was that 'it's not Patrick Troughton you don't like; it's the way he's made to play the part.' Some, however, did like Troughton, and favourable comments were reported along with the negative.

By 12 May, the show reported that 'letters praising far outnumber those against and it's now quite common to receive this sort of view from Corinna Duerden in Camberley: "We think the new Doctor Who is much better than the old one. At least he has more character and lets Polly and Jamie join in. Also it's not him alone who has the ideas. He's not such an old crank as the other Doctor Who."

When, in September, *Junior Points of View* transmitted comments from three Wiltshire schoolgirls who believed *Doctor Who* should be taken off air, the feedback the following week was swift and to the point. Viewers were horrified that no counter-argument had been presented, and continued to say that 'the lassies who objected to *Doctor Who* should have their minds brain-washed' and '*Doctor Who* is Dalektable'. They concluded with a brief poll: 'Let's see how the final voting went: for *Doctor Who* ... 278; against *Doctor Who* ... 31. And so by a substantial majority, *Doctor Who* is voted a hit!'

Concern over the horror content raised its head with the transmission of *The Tomb of the Cybermen*. The BBC programme *Talkback* covered this in its first transmitted edition on 26 September 1967. (It had also featured *Doctor Who* in its untransmitted pilot.) The transmitted edition was analysed by Trevor Wayne in issue 37 of the fan reference work *Doctor Who: An Adventure in Space and Time*. He related one mother's complaint thus: 'I was horrified at the violent scene on *Doctor Who* last Saturday evening,' she said, referring to the final episode of *The Tomb of the Cybermen*, 'where the coloured man, Toberman, bashes into the Cyberman with his metal claw and the camera concentrated on the Cybermen's innards oozing out. I can't think of anything more disgusting and revolting and unsuitable for children, and this programme is put out at a time when even small ones might be around.' Kit Pedler was in the studio to try and defend the show by placing it in context: '... horror perpetrated by non-human beings ...,' he said. However Wayne went on to report that the show featured many 'excitable' contributors from the general public, and that no one seemed too concerned to defend either *Doctor Who* or the BBC, although those contributors who were parents seemed to place all responsibility on what their children watched on the BBC, and responded badly to suggestions that there might be an element of parental control required as well. The show concluded with input from Doctor Hilda Himmelweit, who came down in favour of the BBC, *Doctor Who* and the concept that 'children like to be frightened – but not too much.'

Junior Points of View on 6 October featured comments on the *Talkback* show in defence of *Doctor Who*. 'One lady criticising *Doctor Who* said that she was disgusted when she saw the Cyberman killed by the coloured man and all the white liquid oozing out of the Cyberman's body. I am sure the lady would not complain if a man was shot and he had blood oozing out of his body,' wrote one ten-year-old. Another correspondent commented, sagely: 'The adult does not know how a child's mind works.'

Most of the audience research reports conducted during the Troughton period noted *Doctor Who*'s continuing strong appeal to children. For instance, the one commissioned for the final episode of *The Moonbase* revealed:

'Whether they enjoyed it or not, a number supplying evidence made it plain that *The Moonbase* – not to speak of every *Dr Who* story – delighted their children: "My daughter is a firm fan of the programme" (housewife); "Like the Gravitron – had pulling power for the children" (planner); "The children love every minute of it. They prefer the science fiction adventures to the historical ones"'.

The report on the final episode of *The Evil of the Daleks* continued this positive trend. The most commonly expressed view was that the story had been 'as amusing and exciting as ever'. For those who held this view, 'the entire *Dr Who* series, if undoubtedly "pure escapism", was nevertheless "good fun" and certainly utterly harmless'. It seemed however that there remained some amongst the 180-strong sample who harboured very negative feelings towards the series: 'A not inconsiderable minority ... hoped that, as this episode suggested, this was indeed the last of the Daleks – and, for that matter, Dr Who, the TARDIS and "the whole stupid, childish, silly boiling lot". In their opinion the series, which had always struck them as being "rubbishy" to a degree, had been "done to death"'.

The concluding instalment of *The Wheel in Space* drew very much the same cross-section of opinion from its sample of 214 viewers. 'The overall response to *The Wheel in Space*,' the report concluded, 'was favourable. There were, certainly, those who thought the whole thing ridiculous in the extreme and who could not imagine either children or adults finding much in it to appeal to them. Another group enjoyed it fairly well but felt that invention was, perhaps, beginning to flag. The stories were becoming repetitive; the series needed new ideas and new antagonists for Dr Who rather than Daleks, Cybermen and the like. This was a rather tame adventure, it was said, and there was too much use of pseudo-technical jargon that would be over the heads of most younger viewers. Whether they took it seriously or not, however, the bulk of the sample enjoyed Dr Who's encounter with his old enemies, two or three going on to say that they preferred his science fiction adventures to the historical ones'.

Attitudes seem to have changed, however, during the break between seasons five and six. A clear majority of the 185 viewers who commented on the opening episode of *The Dominators* considered that 'the continuing story of *Dr Who* had ceased to hold any interest or appeal. At first quite original and entertaining, it had been running far too long, they thought, and was now very much in a rut'.

'In the opinion of dissatisfied viewers,' it was noted, 'this particular episode ...: was typical of the recent trend in the series, by which the idea of going backwards in time to various historical events (which several much preferred) had been largely discarded in favour of concentrating on the science fiction stories. Consequently, in order to maintain interest, the non-human characters had become more and more fantastic and improbable, it was said, and at least three in ten of those reporting dismissed this latest story as absolute rubbish. The series had long since lost all element of surprise, they declared, as, apart from minor details, each adventure followed the same pattern ("they arrive, separate, someone gets captured and the rest of the story is taken up with their rescue"); the new Quarks were nothing but "square Daleks"; and the development of the plot was much too slow: "this sort of thing needs to get off to an exciting start'".

Only just over a third of the sample, who had long enjoyed *Doctor Who* as 'an entertaining "escapist" serial', felt that it 'continued to maintain a good level of inventiveness'; and some who had previously been regular viewers were now apparently starting to lose interest. 'Although I am a *Dr Who* fan of many years standing,' ran one typical comment, 'my enjoyment is steadily decreasing every week'.

It was the final episode of *The War Games* that attracted the most uniformly positive report for some time. Notwithstanding the story's epic length, the reaction of those viewers – roughly two thirds of the sample of 179 – who had seen all or most of the ten episodes was 'decidedly favourable'. Some were admittedly 'inclined to damn with faint praise', but the only really negative comment was that children seemed disappointed by the lack of monsters – and even this was balanced by the observation that 'not a few adult viewers' considered the story 'all the better for the absence of "inhuman creatures"'.

'Although there was little evidence of any great enthusiasm for this final episode of *The War Games*,' the report noted, 'nevertheless it is clear that the majority of the sample audience were very well satisfied. Certainly there were those, but in minority numbers only, who dismissed it as "the usual rubbishy nonsense", while others apparently found it disappointingly inconclusive. According to most, however, this exciting and action-packed episode had not only brought this adventure on the planet of the Time Lords to a most satisfactory ending, but also cleared up the mystery surrounding Dr Who's origin besides (most ingeniously) setting the scene for the "new" Dr Who'.

Despite these positive and reassuring comments, the show was failing badly in the ratings, and some possible reasons for this are discussed in the next section of this chapter. Despite the falling ratings, the memories that many adults today hold of the programme hail from this era of the show's history: Yeti in the Underground, Cybermen in the sewers, stinging seaweed and hissing Ice Warriors. This perhaps indicates that while fewer people were watching, the show was having a greater impact on those who did.

From a media point of view, it might be argued that *Doctor Who* needed this period of quieter contemplation. This allowed the initial furore created by the Daleks to die down, and for the show to establish itself as gripping and sometimes controversial teatime entertainment in which the Doctor was seen as the champion of good and order against all manner of monsters and creatures from space.

What is most interesting, however, is that just as mankind reached for the stars, and sent men to walk on the moon's surface in 1969, so *Doctor Who* was undergoing a re-vamp and was being planned as an Earth-bound series, forsaking the travels in space and time, for a far more fixed and recognisable setting.

RATINGS

Towards the end of the Hartnell era, the viewing figures for *Doctor Who* were at their lowest since the series began. From a peak of around 12.5 million in the second season, they had slumped to 4.5 million for *The Smugglers*, and, with the exception of the final

Hartnell story, *The Tenth Planet*, which saw an upturn to 6.75 million, all the stories at the tail end of the era received the lowest ratings that the series had yet seen.

The reasons for this can be partially explained by looking at the shows that were being scheduled against *Doctor Who* on the regional ITV channels. During most of the Hartnell era, the ITV regions tended not to schedule like against like, and so science fiction and adventure fans tended to watch *Doctor Who* rather than the light entertainment fare that was on at the same time opposite it. In addition, *Doctor Who* had the hook of being a continuing serial and thus demanding some degree of viewer loyalty, which one-off films and cartoons did not. It wasn't until the transmission of *Galaxy 4* in 1965 that ITV finally placed a science fiction show opposite *Doctor Who*. This was the imported Irwin Allen space adventure series *Lost in Space*, and *Doctor Who*'s ratings suffered a dip from the eleven million mark of *Galaxy 4: Air Lock* to 9.9 million for *Galaxy 4: The Exploding Planet* and 8.3 million for the single-episode Dalek story *Mission to the Unknown*.

When *The Power of the Daleks* began on 5 November 1966, ITV's 'secret weapon' in the ratings war was another imported American series called *Batman*. As the Troughton era continued, ITV offered *Doddy's Magic Box* (a variety show featuring comedian Ken Dodd), *Mike and Bernie's Music Hall* (more variety, this time with Mike and Bernie Winters), *F Troop* (an American film series) and *Opportunity Knocks* (a popular talent show hosted by Hughie Green). The net result of these opponents (although *F Troop* actually made no impact at all) was that *Doctor Who* lost two million viewers (although there is no proof that the ITV competition was the sole cause of this).

The following year, ITV continued to place a diverse array of material opposite *Doctor Who*. There were repeats of *Sir Francis Drake*, *Just Jimmy* (comedy with Jimmy Clithero), cartoons, another swashbuckling adventure series called *Sword of Freedom*, and, in one region, *Captain Scarlet and the Mysterons*.

When *The Dominators* started, however, there was minimal competition from the regions due to a strike by the technician's union ACTT, which had begun on 2 August 1968. However, once the strike ended, the ITV service began to attack *Doctor Who* with renewed vigour. Gerry and Sylvia Anderson's *Joe 90* was transmitted against *The Mind Robber* on the London Weekend Television (LWT) region, while Granada presented Irwin Allen's *Voyage to the Bottom of the Sea*, and Yorkshire and Anglia Television brought an imported high adventure series called *Tarzan* to the small screen. The cumulative effect of science fiction and adventure against *Doctor Who* contributed greatly towards a dramatic downturn in the BBC ratings.

Early in 1969, ATV and Southern transmitted Irwin Allen's *Land of the Giants*, and *Doctor Who* promptly lost a million viewers. A further million defected over the next fortnight. By 1 February, Yorkshire had started transmitting *Voyage to the Bottom of the Sea*.

As the sixth season of *Doctor Who* progressed, viewers appeared to forego *Doctor Who*, preferring the regional ITV fare of *Voyage to the Bottom of the Sea*, *Land of the Giants*, *Tarzan* and an imported series from Australia, *Woobinda, Animal Doctor*. At the end of the sixth season, individual episodes of *The Space Pirates* and the ambitious ten-part *The War Games* received the lowest ratings so far in *Doctor Who*'s history, with the final story not even managing on average to break the five million mark, and episode eight managing only 3.5 million, making it the lowest rated episode to date.

As the Doctor spiralled off into the void at the end of *The War Games*, the show's traditional Saturday evening slot was filled by a brand new imported American series. This was, like *Doctor Who*, a science fiction drama series, with regular characters, monsters and a distinctive spacecraft. It was called *Star Trek*.

PATRICK TROUGHTON STORIES IN ORDER OF AVERAGE VIEWING FIGURES
(Figures in millions of viewers)

The Moonbase	8.33
The Macra Terror	8.20
The Krotons	8.00
The Power of the Daleks	7.80
The Web of Fear	7.62
The Underwater Menace	7.48
The Enemy of the World	7.42
The Faceless Ones	7.38
The Ice Warriors	7.33
The Wheel in Space	7.25
The Seeds of Death	7.22
Fury from the Deep	7.20
The Highlanders	7.05
The Invasion	6.91
The Mind Robber	6.86
The Abominable Snowmen	6.85
The Tomb of the Cybermen	6.75
The Evil of the Daleks	6.43
The Dominators	6.16
The Space Pirates	5.93
The War Games	4.94

The Third Doctor

by

David J Howe

Stephen James Walker

FOREWORD

The close of the Sixties was an exciting time. Technological advances seemed to be coming thick and fast. No sooner had people become used to having black and white television, than colour television was just around the corner. Cars were becoming more sophisticated and, to cap it all, we put a man on the moon on 21 July 1969 – surely the greatest acknowledgement of our technological superiority.

With this final conquest of space, thoughts were again turning outwards. Were we drawing attention to the Earth from alien beings? The moon was proved to be dry, dusty and dead, but what of Mars? Or Venus? What wonders might we be able to witness on those worlds?

With this new attitude, the science fiction shows of the past started to look very dated. The concept of rockets travelling across the vast reaches of space powered only by a firework could no longer be sustained. The idea of alien creatures crawling out of every nook and cranny of every planet – and many of them looking like humans – was also a dated one.

Things had changed, and *Doctor Who* had to change with them.

Co-producers Derrick Sherwin and Peter Bryant had several problems on their hands during the making of the series' sixth season. They knew that for the following season, the show was to be made in colour – even though there was no additional budget to cover this – and the alien monsters and creatures that had been *Doctor Who*'s staple for many years were becoming prohibitively expensive to realise.

Faced with having to solve these problems, Sherwin felt that moving *Doctor Who* to a more Earth-bound setting was a sensible approach. It was easier and cheaper to go out on location to film something that was supposed to be on Earth than something futuristic or alien. In addition, the menaces fought by the Doctor could be more home-grown, removing the need for complex alien make-up and costume requirements.

With this in mind, Sherwin introduced the concept of UNIT in the sixth season story *The Invasion*. UNIT was a military organisation that was dedicated to the protection of Earth from alien forces, and that would deal with any situation that seemed out of the remit of the regular Army. Even if Patrick Troughton had not left the show, the Doctor would still have been exiled to Earth, with UNIT effectively becoming the Doctor's 'home'.

As it was, Troughton stepped down and Jon Pertwee was chosen to play the third incarnation of the Doctor. A popular radio comedian and character actor, Pertwee was to bring a sense of style and flair to the show, and update its image from an eccentric tea-time series to an engaging action/adventure romp, with gadgets worthy of James Bond, and a dynamic Doctor with a sexy young woman in mini-skirt and boots as his companion.

With the new format in place, Sherwin and Bryant left *Doctor Who* in the hands of new producer Barry Letts, while they moved on to look after another BBC serial, *Paul Temple*. Letts' vision for *Doctor Who* was not too dissimilar from that of Sherwin and Bryant, and he delivered an action packed show that allowed for alien invaders and visitors, whilst still keeping the Doctor more or less trapped on this planet.

Other events at the time included the capture of the Manson 'family' for the killing of Sharon Tate; famine in Biafra; the first publication of the New English Bible, which sold at over 20,000 copies a week; the splitting up of the Beatles; and the Tories' return to power led by Edward Heath.

During the era of the third Doctor, the public saw the introduction of decimal currency to the UK, hot pants were all the rage in the fashion scene, the first heart and lung transplant was carried out, the miners went on strike over pay and blacked out large portions of the country, Nixon surrendered to the scandal of Watergate, Princess Anne was married to Mark Phillips, and Harold Wilson and Labour were swept to power after the fiasco of the miners' strike, ousting Edward Heath, who was himself replaced by Margaret Thatcher as leader of the Tory party.

Jon Pertwee was a radical change from Patrick Troughton, and his era saw the introduction of several new foes. Foremost among them was the Master, played by Roger Delgado. This evil renegade from the Doctor's own race appeared several times to try to conquer the Earth and to destroy the Doctor. Viewers were also introduced to a number of new monster races, including the Axons, the Sea Devils, the Mutants and the Sontarans, and saw the return of some old ones, in the forms of the Daleks and the Ice Warriors.

In the following chapters, we look at the development of *Doctor Who* during the third Doctor's era. *Day of the Daleks* is examined as a typical example of *Doctor Who* during this period in the show's history. We look at Jon Pertwee through his own words, and explore the art of costume design. We also look at the series' developing mythology, and examine the promotion and marketing that surrounded the series.

Join us as we revisit the era of the third Doctor.

INTRODUCTION BY JON PERTWEE

As an actor, it is impossible to keep up with the many and intricate points of continuity that may occur when working on a long running drama show like *Doctor Who*. For a start, while I was working with the director on one story, the next couple of stories were already being discussed and planned by other directors. By the time I actually came to record a story, my main concern was to learn the lines, and if any major crimes of continuity had been committed, assuming I could spot them in the first place, I would usually try and suggest some easy way round them.

David J Howe and Stephen James Walker have bravely stepped through this continuity minefield and have pulled together an incredible number of facts and figures about my time as the Doctor. There are things in this book that I never knew and some, I'm sure, that no-one ever knew! Here you can discover in which story Nick Courtney wore that infamous eye patch; how and where I met the Drashigs, the Ogrons and the Ice Warriors; how my great friend Roger Delgado came to join us on the show; and many other fascinating and obscure pieces of information about the period when I played the Doctor.

In my book *I Am The Doctor*, I tell the story of that time from my own point of view. In this Handbook, you can find out more about the events that I was not party to.

It's an impressive book and I hope you enjoy it.

Jon Pertwee, April 1996

JON PERTWEE: IN HIS OWN WORDS

ON HIS EARLY LIFE:
'I was born in the Chelsea area of London on 7 July 1919. I have mixed blood. My father came from a French Huguenot family, and my real name is Jean Roland Perthuis de Leillevaux. We were Huguenots, who during the French Revolution escaped from France and set up in Essex. Anybody with the name Pertwee is a relation. There's Guy Pertwee in the Navy, and Admiral Jim Pertwee is my cousin. Bill Pertwee, the comedian from *Dad's Army*, is my cousin. Michael Pertwee, the playwright, is my brother. My father was Roland Pertwee, a famous actor, playwright, screenwriter – one of the top screenwriters in the world in the heyday of the movies.

'My father influenced me a great deal. He taught me to stand on my own two feet, to go out and earn my own living when I was sixteen and a half. He gave me a very good education, which I was hopeless at – I was expelled from a couple of schools, because I rebelled against ludicrous authority. I rebelled against spotty boys calling me back from my music lesson when I'd have to run about a quarter of a mile to their little rooms where they'd say: "Make me a piece of toast". I would say, "Why can't you make it yourself, are you crippled?", for which I'd be soundly beaten. I finally rebelled at the end of term after being beaten very unjustly and said to my fag master, "You threaten me with beating once more and I'll beat you within an inch of your life". He didn't believe me and sent me down into the quad, so I managed to grab a cane and, as he came round the corner, I gave him one across the face and opened it up like Errol Flynn slashing Basil Rathbone. That, of course, was the end of my career as a public schoolboy, because they did not "give the sucker an even break". It was tradition, tradition, play with a straight bat. Games were all-important. Human relationships and personality meant nothing. I was influenced by my father, a brilliant conversationalist and a wonderful man with words. He was intensely interesting, he could do anything … fisherman, actor, painter, writer.'
Interviewed by John Hudson and Stuart Money in 1975 for *Jon Pertwee Fan Club Newsletter* Issue 3.

'My parents always told me I was born in Innsbruck, Austria, and then when I got my birth certificate I found I wasn't – I was born in Chelsea. My mother was an Austrian and my father was of a French family, so we were a slightly mongrel family.'
Interviewed by Simon M Lydiard in 1984 for *Skaro* Volume IV Number 3/4.

'I had a strange sort of childhood. My mother and father parted just after I was born, and my father, who was a writer and originally an actor with [Sir Beerbohm] Tree and [Sir Henry] Irving, was rather wrapped up in himself and his own life. I was the youngest of three brothers and always felt a bit left out.

'We were brought up in the country, at Dulverton in the Exe Valley, near Tiverton, and I wish I'd appreciated how lucky we were in that. My father was a keen sportsman, and we had our own horses and rode to hounds and fished and shot. We had enormous physical freedom. Like my father, I had an ear for dialect and, living in the West Country, soon picked up the accent I now use for Worzel Gummidge.

'I went to several boarding schools, none of which I liked except the last, Frensham Heights in Surrey. That was better because it was co-educational and being of French extraction ... I was interested in girls from an early age. I was offered a wonderful education and I wish I had taken advantage of it, but I've never liked the role of student. I've always had a thirst for adventure though.'
Interviewed by Pamela Coleman in 1983 for the *Sunday Express*.

'I joined a circus and had to drive a converted Austin Seven on the Wall of Death, with a lion sitting on a platform behind me.

'It was a very old lion, mark you. So old, you'd have had to kick it where it hurt to make it roar. Only the boss didn't want it roaring. "Folks'll see it ain't got no teeth," he used to moan.

'Anyway, the act ended one afternoon when we were having a break inside the base of the Wall. You know, sort of "take five" – only the lion took forever. We had to dismantle the Wall to get rid of it!'
Interviewed in 1972 for *Motor Cycle*.

'My father was an overpowering man. He had so many talents. As well as his acting and writing abilities, he knew all sorts of quaint, unexpected things. For instance, he was a great fly-fisherman and he invented his own kind of imitation fly, which is still sold commercially.

'I admired him intensely, but he seemed to find it terribly difficult to show love.

'I will always remember the night of my first professional performance in rep in Brighton. My father had promised to be there, and when I looked through the curtains before the performance, there he was in the fifth row. "He'll be round after the performance," I told my friends. But he never came, and the others said he couldn't have been there.

'But I had seen him. So the next day I rang him up and asked him why he didn't come round. He said, "I'm terribly sorry, I was too busy, I couldn't get there." But I had seen him ...

'Yet he would work at being a father in his own strange way. One day, my brother and I were due to go fishing, and we understood the tackle would be waiting for us in a fishing hut by the river. When we arrived there was none, but by using our imaginations a bit, we were able to improvise tackle from things lying around the hut – bits of cane, twine etcetera.

'Then, later, it dawned on me that my father had carefully left everything necessary to build tackle in the hut. It was a planned exercise in initiative.'
Interviewed by Ian Cotton in 1974 for *TV Times*.

ON HIS TIME AT THE ROYAL ACADEMY OF DRAMATIC ART (RADA):

'I had a teacher of Greek drama who wanted me to be a Wind. She wanted me to stand on the side of the stage and make wind noises – go "Woooh". This was such a load of rubbish that I really couldn't be bothered with it and didn't take it seriously, so I was very much reprimanded by the principal. On top of that, I was accused of writing rude remarks about the principal and this teacher on the lavatory walls – something that I denied categorically, because I had *not* written rude remarks on the lavatory walls. I told my father, who was absolutely furious. He rang the principal up, saying that he was going to sue him for defamation of character, for libel and every other charge you can think of. He said he was going to employ the greatest graphologist – handwriting expert – he could find to prove that it was not my writing. The principal then realised that he'd bitten off more than he could chew and dropped the charges. But he hated me, and soon afterwards I was given my cards, so to speak, and told that I was not the sort of person they wanted.

'It was after this, just before I left RADA, that we were doing an end of term play. In the first act I was a man who was murdered, and in the second I was a detective who came in and found out who did the murder. Noel Coward was judging, so when the play was over, they asked him if he'd seen anyone he liked. He said, "Yes, there were two very, very promising performances, from the murder victim in the first half and from the detective in the second. Who were the two people who were playing them?" So they had to tell him it was actually *one* person, and I was introduced to him. He said, "Ah yes, Pertwee. You're Roland's son, no doubt." Which of course I was. "Very good, very promising." And this was about the person they'd just expelled because, as they said, I wasn't cut out for the theatre!'

Interviewed by John Hudson and Stuart Money in 1975 for *Jon Pertwee Fan Club Newsletter* Issue 5.

ON THE START OF HIS ACTING CAREER:

'After RADA came a tremendously happy period when I joined a travelling theatre company. We went round in an old bus and I drove it, put up the theatre, got the water to put in the carbide lights that dripped onto the crystals that made the gas that lit the stage. It was as primitive as that.

'Then I went into rep. The name Pertwee certainly opened doors, but it didn't get me jobs. My father didn't give me a lot of encouragement, and now I think that that is probably what motivated me. I took on anything and grossly overacted.'

Interviewed by Pamela Coleman in 1983 for the *Sunday Express*.

'I was 19 in 1938 and had just joined the Rex Leslie-Smith Repertory Company at the end of the West Pier in Brighton, a job that marked the end of a lean time.

'The company paid me the splendid remuneration of three pounds ten shillings a week, and I stayed with a Madame Penison in the Victoria Road. I had a very comfortable room with crisp, clean French linen and, because this was the summer season, fresh flowers by the bed. My room and board cost me thirty shillings a week.

'From the residue of my earnings, I ran a superb Ariel Square-Four motorcycle, paid for on HP at a few shillings a week. I smoked five Woodbines a day, drank a quantity of rough cider and found I still had enough left over to escort "lady friends" out for cups of tea, ice cream and to take them dancing at Sherry's Dance Hall and generally lead the life of Riley.'

Quoted in 1996 in the *Daily Mail*.

ON HIS RADIO ROLES:

'I was in Naval intelligence during the War, and they sent me down to see a radio show that Lieutenant Eric Barker was doing. It was rumoured to be insulting to leading figures in the Government, and I was sent to put a stop to any risqué jokes. I sat in the auditorium, and Eric said, "I want somebody to shout out these lines". I said, "I'll do it". He looked at me and said ,"Who are you?", and I replied, "I'm a spy!". I told him that I'd been sent to check up on him, but if he let me say the lines I'd be a very bad spy. So he let me say the lines. The lines were [in a broad Cockney accent], "Leave him alone, you're always picking on him, the poor perisher!". Eric's actress wife Pearl Hackney would then walk in and say, "Who's that?", to which Eric would reply, "That's the Minister for Education!" (who was a Cockney at the time) – it was precisely the sort of joke I was supposed to stop!

'After this, Eric asked me if I wanted to go back the following week, which I did, and that was my big break in showbusiness. That was my stepping stone from straight theatre to light radio, which was all-important then. I stayed with Eric for eight or nine years after that. We bought the rights to the show called *Mediterranean Merry-Go-Round*, and there were three versions for Army, Navy and Air Force. The Air Force one became *Much Binding in the Marsh*, the Army version became *Stand Easy* with Charlie Chester, and we became *Waterlogged Spa*, in which I played a postman (on whom I based the voice of the Worzel Gummidge character I play now).

'Much later, we did *The Navy Lark*, and I asked for two *names* alongside myself to appear, as I'm a great believer in teams. We got, originally, Leslie Phillips and Dennis Price. We took it in turns to top the bill each week. My voice man was Ronnie Barker. Michael Bates, Richard Caldicott and Heather Chasen were all beginners in radio and part of my team. Ronnie left after a while because he hadn't the time to keep doing it. He was becoming much too important in the business.'

Interviewed by Sheldon Collins, Robert Cope and Gary Leigh-Levy in 1988 for *Dream Watch Bulletin* Number 64.

'In spite of all my "voices" – and I used to use forty-two different ones in *Waterlogged Spa* – they aren't imitations. I adapt them from people I know. The "er, er, um, um-er" stutter is taken from the lady who used to serve in my school tuck shop. She used to try terribly hard to remember everybody's name as we all surged in for our daily bun and bottle of pop, and she'd mumble away to herself until she obviously couldn't go on saying "er, um" any longer, and she'd shout, "Next".

'Commander Highprice, my confidential spy, is based on my cousin. Cousin Hugh has a slight impediment to the roof of his mouth and he speaks quietly and confidentially to you as if every word were top secret. So I "borrowed" him.'

Interviewed by Val Marriott in 1973 for *Leicester Chronicle*.

'The BBC suggested doing a new comedy series based round the armed forces. They suggested the Air Force, but I said no, if it was any of them it had to be the Navy, and besides I was a Navy man. I did six years during the last war.

'A Navy man can get away with things that the other armed forces can't.

'The only people who've left *The Navy Lark* over the past fifteen years have been the late Dennis Price, who went after the first series, and Ronnie Barker. I'm rather glad that Ronnie left, not because I don't think that he is a super person – I do – but because it has given me a chance to do all the funny voices and not just the part of the Chief Petty Officer.

'The show has a sort of humour that doesn't really change. I've nostalgic feelings for it as well now.

'We do work to a script, but we're always flying off the page. This is a fantasy thing.

'I find it easy to imitate accents, but I can't copy people's voices. I have a set of gramophone records at home, and if I'm required to learn an accent, I put them on. It takes me only about fifteen minutes to pick up the way of speaking.'
Interviewed by John Kelleher in 1974 for *Cambridge Evening News.*

ON HIS FILM ROLES:

'My earliest film of any merit was *Murder at the Windmill,* which I made, I suppose, in the late forties, with Garry Marsh and Jimmy Edwards. It was about the Windmill Theatre and I played a detective. It was a very good little film and made an awful lot of money – in fact it's still making money in America.'
Interviewed by Simon M Lydiard in 1984 for *Skaro* **Volume IV Number 3/4.**

'I doubled for Danny Kaye in a film called *Knock on Wood.* Danny was double booked. He'd signed for something else in America. I didn't want to do it, but the film company were very persuasive. "This is a great opportunity," they said. "We'll get a lot of you on camera!" "You'll get my arse on camera!" The only way to put people off is to be ridiculously demanding. So I said to my agent, "I want a suite at the Savoy, I want a Rolls Royce hired, I want a Berkely caravan to use on location – the most expensive one you can buy – and at the end of the shooting I want it given to me. I want no publicity, I want all the clothes that I wear in the picture …" – and everything else I could think of! I asked "What are they offering?" and when told replied, "Don't be ridiculous, I want five times that!" I did everything I could to get them to say "Is he out of his mind?" They took one look at my demands and said, "OK. Agreed." So I hoisted myself on my own petard.

'On the opening night, the film was very well received. A little Irish journalist went up to Danny Kaye and introduced himself. "I thought Jon Pertwee did very well for you," he said. "Yes, Jon did a great job," came Danny's reply. "Thank you!" That was all he needed! A quote from Danny Kaye. "Danny's Double" next day in the headlines!

'The part that I had originated in the stage version of *A Funny Thing Happened on the Way to the Forum* was that of the brothel keeper, Lycus, but it was played in the film by Phil Silvers! "Jon Pertwee" meant nothing to the general public abroad, so they gave me a tiny part instead. My wife Ingeborg and I went out to Madrid, lazing around for a month. It would take only about a day to film, so this was a sort of sop to my ego, because 20th Century Fox felt sorry for me. I felt sorry for myself! I got out there and they said, "Could you play the brothel keeper tomorrow? Phil Silvers has got religious mania! He's jumping up and down on his bed relating the Lord's Prayer because nobody recognises him in Spain!" But a second assistant director – I could kill him when I come to think of it! – went to the director Dick Lester and said, "I can get Phil Silvers on the set for you tomorrow". "You can? Go to it, son! The world will be yours if you can do it!" So he went off and said to Phil Silvers, "Jon Pertwee is in town", to which Phil replied, "Who?" "He's the man who played Lycus on Broadway and in London, and if you aren't on the set by half-past six, he's taking over!" He was there! I could have killed that guy, because I don't think he would have appeared otherwise.'
Interviewed by Andrew Knight and Martin Guarneri in 1985 and transcribed by Paul Mount for *Doctor Who – An Adventure in Space and Time: Season Eight Special.*

ON HIS SECOND WIFE, INGEBORG:

'I met her in a place called Kitzbühel, an Austrian ski resort. I was there on holiday, and I broke my leg in half – a compound fracture – when I was out skiing. That's why I was hobbling around Kitzbühel doing nothing but sitting around in the sun, drinking cups of tea and coffee and chatting in the market. Anyway, when I got back, a married couple, friends of mine, wrote to her and invited her to come over to England and stay with them and get to know me. So that's how it all happened. Her name was Ingeborg Rhoesha, and her father was a very eminent financier in the West German government; she was born and bred in Berlin and later lived in Bonn.'

Interviewed by John Hudson and Stuart Money in 1975 for *Jon Pertwee Fan Club Newsletter* **Issue 3.**

ON HIS PORTRAYAL OF THE DOCTOR:

'I asked Shaun Sutton, Head of Drama at the BBC and an old friend of mine, how he wanted me to play Doctor Who. He said, "Well, as you". I said, "Yes, that's the problem: what is me?" Like Peter Sellers, I had always hidden myself under what's known in the theatrical business as a green umbrella. I'd always played character parts and eccentrics, I'd never allowed myself to be just myself ... So eventually I just decided to play him as I felt, so really what the Doctor liked was just an extension of what I like. I like rather outrageous clothes, speed-boats, gadgets, karate and so on. I don't know how he struck me as a man ... I don't think I went into it that deeply, to be frank.'

Interviewed by John Hudson and Stuart Money in 1975 for *Jon Pertwee Fan Club Newsletter* **Issue 3.**

'I said, "Why have you hired me if you don't want me to do what I've learnt to do over the years – and act?" The producer Barry Letts, bless his soul, said that it was the ultimate test of my acting ability, to see if I could take these predominant elements of myself and turn them into a character for the Doctor.

'If you think about it, it does take a lot of confidence to play as up-front a figure as the Doctor. Most of the time, actors can safely hide behind their art. With this part, I didn't have that kind of easy protection – there was no fall-back.'

Interviewed by Richard Marson in 1986 for *Doctor Who Magazine* **Number 113.**

'I got away with murder on *Doctor Who* ...

'I was just playing me for the first time really, and I made him a dashing bloke dressed in pretty clothes. This was in the Seventies when people were very clothes conscious and wore frilly shirts and colours. All that hooked at the right time. I put in the martial arts and my love of gadgetry, motorcycles, cars, Bessie, helicopters – these were things that I liked anyway, so I just adapted them into *Doctor Who*. Apart from being hard work, it was a piece of cake!'

Interviewed by Andrew Knight and Martin Guarneri in 1985 and transcribed by Paul Mount for *Doctor Who – An Adventure in Space and Time: Season Eight Special.*

'I leave Doctor Who in the studio. But Doctor Who *is* me.

'He is an extension of myself, a complete extension and therefore a completely believable character.

'I can't bring him home with me, though. Otherwise I'd be besieged by vast hordes of Daleks.

'And I'd be arriving home in the middle of the sitting room in a blue box. Whatever would Ingeborg say!

'Playing Doctor Who is a job. I am a working actor. But people see certain eccentricities in him which, as I've said, are extensions of myself.

'I suppose he shows a certain amount of intolerance to others on occasion, plus a keenness to get on with the job in hand and not just wait about.

'And I love playing him because he's so active and adventurous. Like me in many ways, I suppose.

'For example, I love gadgets. I've got a new machine in the kitchen that can turn out instant cold drinks. I'm all for anything new and extraordinary.'
Interviewed by John Deighton in 1973 for *New Reveille*.

'I've got the best job on television and I wouldn't drop it for the Royal Mint. For a major movie I'd drop it, but for the Royal Mint, certainly not.

'Of course the income is very nice. I get nine months a year steady work and I can carry on as long as I like.

'It may not be the heaviest show on TV, but then I'm far too old to worry about artistic integrity and all that.

'I play it for real … A send-up would be unforgivable.'
Interviewed by Patrick Stoddart in 1973 for *Evening Echo*.

ON HIS DOCTOR'S COSTUME:
'They asked me what I wanted to wear for *Doctor Who* and I had all sorts of ideas. Then I got an early photo call, so I found my grandfather's old Inverness cape, a smoking jacket I had, and a frilly shirt from Mr Fish. They thought it was marvellous. I said, "How can we explain the change from Pat Troughton's rags?" and that's why, in *Spearhead from Space*, they had me steal all the bits of clothing from the changing room in the hospital.'
Interviewed by Stuart Money in 1977 for *TARDIS* Volume 2 Issue 3.

ON THE *DOCTOR WHO* MONSTERS:
'I'm sure there must be things that would attract attention like the Daleks have, and we have tried hard to find them, but so far without success.

'The kids always go for something mechanical. They don't want to be a maggot, but they do want to be a machine. It's very easy to go around saying "Exterminate, exterminate", and great fun for them.

'The conditions inside the rubber suits we use for the monsters are almost intolerable. We almost killed one little midget gentleman who had a bad heart and all sorts of things wrong with him, and we didn't know and we put him in one of these things and he almost died.

'It gets so hot and so uncomfortable inside them that actors are allowed to wear the suits only for five minutes at a time, which poses a big problem for the director.

'We were doing one episode in which the Sea Devils appeared, and they were in full costume with big lizard heads. They were supposed to be sea creatures, and in one

sequence they had to swim out to sea and submerge. But the costumes were so bulky that they couldn't. The director was screaming at them to dive, but they just couldn't get under the surface. They were all wallowing and floundering about, and with the heads coming off and floating around it was a shambles.'
Interviewed by John Curzon in 1973 for *Western Mail*.

'I can't bear the Daleks. I find them very boring, because they're tatty. But the public loves them. Whenever we had a Dalek story, the ratings went straight up. I like the Draconians, which had marvellous warts all over their faces, and cock-comb tops. I like the Ogrons, the half-masks. I like the things that are humanoid. Alpha Centauri, the one with the tentacles, had that very bad eye-lid. I enjoyed the one where the spaceship landed outside the power station at Dungeness – *The Claws of Axos*. Remember the monsters they had in that one – fantastic rubberoid things that looked as if they were inside out. They were marvellous. I like the Exxilons, though the reflective material on the costumes didn't work as well as we'd hoped. To me, the Cybermen, although I've never seen them on the screen, always seem as if they were pieces of tin and pipe – don't they lack reality in some way?'
Interviewed by John Hudson and Stuart Money in 1975 and quoted in *TARDIS* Volume 1 Issue 3.

'Often a *Doctor Who* monster that looks good on screen will be laughably bad off it. The production team were always scratching something together from nothing. I remember one of the worst were the Primords in *Inferno*, which was partly directed by Douglas Camfield. The whole filming was going very nicely, we all thought, the script was a good one, full of frightening bits for the audience and lots of action for the Doctor. Then they unveiled these ridiculous werewolf things with great false teeth and fur-covered rubber gloves. They were *awful*.

'I remember asking Douglas if he was serious about using them, and although I don't think he was very happy about it, it was too late to do anything about it. Olaf Pooley, who was playing the main villain in the story, caused a great stir when he refused point blank to be made up as one of these things, and I have to admit, I saw his point.

'It's well known now, but my other pet hate is the Daleks. Couldn't bear the things and can't imagine how they could be so popular. They looked so primitive to me, trundling around in the studio, and it was a great fight for our directors to make them look anything more than a heap of old plywood on castors.

'It was just my luck that we did several Dalek stories, and I squirmed through each and every one of them.'
Interviewed by Richard Marson in 1986 for *Doctor Who Magazine* Number 113.

ON THE *DOCTOR WHO* STUNTS:
'I frequently hurt myself because I take risks, and I take tumbles.
'My latest injury is a punctured vein in the hip.'
Interviewed in 1972 for the *Sun*.

'It's the stuntmen themselves who bear the brunt of this. In *Inferno*, I hit Alan Chuntz – I hit him with Bessie at about forty miles an hour and put eighteen stitches in his leg!

He didn't get out the way quick enough, and it opened him right up from the knee down to the ankle-bone. And he never said a thing! He knew I was upset, so he came out of hospital back onto location saying, "I'm all right". We said, "Come on Chuntzy, don't be silly, go home". But he stood up and managed to get through about three shots before he passed out. He's such a tough guy, and a very fine stuntman. Black belt karate, as well. We had a fight in *The Green Death* where some guards attacked me in a sort of corridor, and these guys – Alan Chuntz and Billy Horrigan – fought each other and tried to make each other cry out, pinch each other, twist an arm. The amount of punishment they take is incredible. They do a superb job, and never really get a mention. They're some of the most dedicated guys in the business.'
Interviewed by John Hudson and Stuart Money in 1975 and quoted in *TARDIS* Volume 1 Issue 3.

'What we did in my *Doctor Who* was to try to combine two approaches. The Doctor would use physical violence only when and if he had to, but if he had to then, boy, did he sock it to them. I was very lucky to be backed by one of the best stunt teams in the business – men like Stuart Fell and my usual double Terry Walsh.

'Where I could, I would always do my own stunts, but on occasions one of the boys would take me to one side and say, "Look mate, this one is really too dangerous, let us do it, okay?", and then I would give way, because you just don't argue with the professionals.

'My other problem was my bad back. I've suffered an awful lot from it over the years, the result of all the wear and tear I've subjected it to during the course of my career, both in the Navy and in show business. When we were making *Doctor Who*, it was Katy Manning who used to come up with the best solution – massage. She had a very light touch, and before long I'd be back on the set, so when she left, I really felt it!'
Interviewed by Richard Marson in 1986 for *Doctor Who Magazine* Number 113.

ON THE WHOMOBILE:
'I'd suggested to Barry Letts that the Doctor ought to have a space age car that could fly, hover and so on, but Barry had said, "Forget it, the show wouldn't stand the budget". I still liked the idea, though, and consequently when I met Peter Farries – who designs custom cars – at a Ford Main Dealers shop opening in the Midlands, I put it to him. Together we worked out a practical design that would be both outer spaceish and street legal. Before that, everyone had estimated that the mould needed for the fibreglass body would need to be in at least eight sections. Pete did it in two. When fitted to the Bond Bug chassis, the car had a top speed of over 100 miles per hour.

'One of the great joys of driving the Whomobile was watching the astonished expressions on the faces of policemen who would periodically stop the car, surround it with tape measures and then have to go away nonplussed because, despite its shape, all the dimensions were in accordance with the law.'
Interviewed by Richard Landen in 1982 for *Doctor Who Magazine*'s Winter Special.

ON HIS FAVOURITE *DOCTOR WHO* STORIES:
'Undoubtedly the one we filmed at Aldbourne in Wiltshire – *The Dæmons*. That was a marvellous story, and Chris Barry's direction was really something. And it was an ideal

length – five episodes. I've always thought if you can't tell a story in five episodes, you can't tell it at all. But then of course, you've got to consider the budget of the show.'
Interviewed by Stuart Money in 1977 for *TARDIS* Volume 2 Issue 3.

ON MAKING AN INPUT TO THE SERIES' SCRIPTS:

'I didn't have any input at all into the storylines. There wasn't the time. If I'm going to finish shooting one story at the end of next week, and two days after that I'm going to be starting a new story – now that story's already been produced, cast, they've got the director, special effects men, make-up, and all these people are different from the ones I'm working with on the story I'm doing now, so that's all prepared. Come Monday, there are the director and the producer who come in and say, "We've discussed all this months ago – here we go". So naturally I can't have any input, because I can't work months ahead and do a show as well. The only thing that could happen was on the Monday read-through. I'd read the script through and, being a very perspicacious man, I could see where the flaws were, which scenes I didn't like and wouldn't be happy with. I'd say, "I don't like this, I'd rather do this, that or the other". The writers would be there with the okay, or they would say "No", and then we'd have little verbal punch-ups, but in the main they would see my reasoning and go away in a corner and rewrite over the lunch hour. Then it's fixed, and from the Tuesday onwards you stick to the script as arranged on the Monday. So that's the only input on the script.

'On the other hand, if I went to the Boat Show, as I did, and saw a miniature hovercraft, I would say to the fellow, "I play a character called Doctor Who. How would you like to have one of your machines on television?" The answer was usually, "You don't have to tell me, I know – and yes, anytime!" So this is why, right throughout my era, we had those jet-ski boats and so on – I mean, I own all of them, I've got them all out in my place in Spain. I no longer have the Whomobile, I gave that to a very sweet young man, but he lets me use it whenever I need it for events and things, and Bessie of course was BBC property, but all the jet-boats and motorbikes I bought. Of course, after giving them big publicity, I got them very cheap!'
Interviewed by Guy Wainer, Greg Jones, Neil John and David Greenham in 1990 for *Skaro* Volume 5 Number 2.

ON THE APPEAL OF HIS ERA AS THE DOCTOR:

'Like every other programme, *Doctor Who* has had to move with the times. The problems with which he now finds himself faced are very different from the ones he had when the programme first started.

'When *Doctor Who* began, no-one ever thought a man would walk on the moon, but that has now become commonplace, and people are much more aware of scientific terms and phraseology.

'Frequently I have to memorise pages and pages of long involved scientific explanations and, believe me, that's no joke when you've no idea what it's all about.

'But I am very fond of gadgets and love all the ones we use in the programme.

'*Doctor Who* appeals to all ages and all classes. A man might come up to me in the street and say, "My daughter always watches *Doctor Who*". I then ask him, "But what about you?" 'And he will say, "Oh, I never miss it either".'
Interviewed by Norrie Drummond in 1973 for *South Wales Argus*.

'One of the remarkable things about *Doctor Who* is that although it might occasionally seem a little banal, a little infantile, it is very seldom wrong. It is always scientifically true, and writers spend a great deal of time making sure of this. Every idea put forward is checked in our reference library or with scientists.

'I met a gentleman recently, the president of the British Boxing Board of Control, in Jamaica. He was a man of about 65, and his wife said that he was a most crashing bore because every Saturday night, no matter where they were or who they were with, he had to get to a television set to watch *Doctor Who*, and there are a lot of people in that age group like that.

'It's not a children's programme, it is a family show. Some of the dialogue is so technical and complicated that the kids can't follow it, in fact half the time I don't understand it myself. I've spouted two whole pages of script and I haven't the faintest idea what I'm talking about.

'But the kids have a much greater fantasy than we have and they can accept it overall without understanding every detail. I've got an eight year old boy and he's often confused scientifically but he gets the story dead right, and he asks a lot of pertinent questions that I just don't know the answers to, so I have to give him 50p to shut him up.

'I have a theory, which I use, that there's nothing more alarming than coming home and finding a Yeti sitting on your loo in Tooting Bec. If you find a Yeti in the Himalayas that's where you expect it to be, but if it's on the loo in Tooting Bec that's a real surprise. People didn't like us finding these creatures on Earth, they preferred us travelling about in time and space.'
Interviewed by John Curzon in 1973 for *Western Mail*.

'The standard of the stories was one of consistent excellence, rather than occasional peaks among the dross. There were very few poor stories – the odd script might have needed a bit of reworking in rehearsal, but generally I was very well served.

'Barry Letts was very keen on the moral message, and a lot of our scripts incorporated that philosophy so that we became instruments of different political and social arguments. We did one about sharing the planet we inhabit, we did one about pollution, and they all had a kind of truth that our directors would seek out and enlarge. I think this is the main reason why audience figures went up so significantly when I was on – I'd like to think it was solely because of me, but in reality it had a lot to do with the twin appeal of the scripts – they had the crash bang wallop for the kids and the inner message for the mums and dads. And, of course, they had Katy Manning in a mini-skirt!'
Interviewed by Richard Marson in 1986 for *Doctor Who Magazine* Number 113.

ON *DOCTOR WHO*'S SUITABILITY FOR CHILDREN

'*Doctor Who* does not harm children. It is pure fantasy. Children love fantasy. The monsters scare them a bit but only in the short term.

'I recently judged a competition for children's drawings of monsters. Some of them were utterly horrific.

'And you should have seen the hair-raising stories they wrote about them.

'Children do have this kind of imagination.

'You never actually see anyone stabbed with a spear or anything like that in *Doctor Who*. You just see somebody throwing the spear.

'It's the explicit James Bond kind of violence, messy and bloody, that I think is bad.'
Interviewed by Hilary Bonner in 1972 for *Reveille*.

'We admit our errors. But I am irritated by parents who complain that their children have nightmares after watching the serial. All they have to do is bend forward at an angle of 45 degrees and turn a knob.

'You've never seen me hit anyone to bloodlet, have you?

'There is no pain inflicted. People just disappear or wilt when I place two fingers on their chests. But that goes down as violence. For a time I was stopped from doing karate, or anything that could physically defeat Doctor Who's enemies.

'It got to the point where we were allowed only to trip up monsters. In the end, we said we could not carry on like that. It was just too ridiculous for words.

'Things are better now. I had a glorious wrestle in slow motion with the devil the other day. But it was not violent.

'We kept out all the karate chops to the neck, and that sort of thing, in case the kids try it. I feel that in comparison with other programmes, we are not in any way violent.'
Interviewed in 1973 for *Gloucester Citizen*.

'*Doctor Who* has been described as the most violent programme on television. That's rubbish. We're out to scare children because they love being scared. They'll hide behind settees with their hands over their faces – but they're still watching.'
Interviewed in 1973 for *Newcastle Journal*.

ON NICHOLAS COURTNEY AS THE BRIGADIER:

'Nick was and is one of the finest actors available for that mix of English reserve and pure irony. He was great to work with, because he was a lot of fun beneath a very cool exterior and he would always play the most serious of scenes with a detectable twinkle in his eye.

'I remember when we were on location filming for *The Dæmons* there were a series of delays, and it looked as if we might have to call it a day without getting what we wanted in the can. This would have been frustrating in itself, even had it not been for the long time we had all been standing around waiting for the command to do the scene. Well, on hearing this I hit the roof, using the most colourful language at my disposal and generally behaving in a most unprofessional manner. Nick was marvellous in fraught situations. He came up and stopped me in my tracks and made me laugh, which cooled the situation down. You can't resist a man with his sort of charm, and he was a super colleague to have in all those *Doctor Who* episodes we made together.'
Interviewed by Richard Marson in 1986 for *Doctor Who Magazine* Number 113.

ON ROGER DELGADO AS THE MASTER:

'Roger was one of the most gentle men I've ever known. He was the most courteous person – he had a temperament, but always pointed it at himself in rehearsals. He would go absolutely berserk with anger if he couldn't get something right, but always at himself, never at anyone else. He was charming, polite, kind and considerate. He and his wife Kismet were very close friends to Ingeborg and me, and we loved them very dearly. I was desperately shaken when he was killed. We looked after Kismet until she managed to get herself together, and we still see a lot of her. Roger played villains because of those marvellous, hypnotic eyes, and that beard – he always had the beard like that. He played villainous Arabs, villainous policemen in the Far East, villainous crooks.

'As time went on, the Master appeared less regularly in the series. We decided his regular appearance was a mistake, because I was always defeating him, which just made him look stupid. I think sometimes the Master should have defeated me temporarily at the end of a story – such as in *The Sea Devils*, but on a grander scale. It was suggested once by Nick Courtney that the reason we didn't kill each other was that fundamentally we knew there was some connection between us. Then we wanted it to turn out by a Time Lord giving the game away that we were, in fact, brothers, which would have been a rather clever idea. So Roger gradually faded from the scene a little. We brought him into only about two stories per season, which we found was better. I loved working with him, and still miss him tremendously.'

Interviewed by John Hudson and Stuart Money in 1975 for *Jon Pertwee Fan Club Newsletter* Issue 3.

ON HIS *DOCTOR WHO* COMPANIONS:

'In my opinion, Caroline John didn't fit into *Doctor Who*. I couldn't really believe in Liz as a sidekick to the Doctor, because she was so darned intelligent herself. The Doctor didn't want a know-all spouting by his side, he wanted someone who was busy learning about the world. Although Caroline and I worked well together, I don't think it did the series any harm when she left.

'Katy Manning was far and away my favourite girl, and she fitted in perfectly with the way I wanted to do the show. It was funny, Katy was by no means conventionally attractive, she was really quite a funny mix, but I still think she was incredibly sexy in the part, and certainly off-screen too.

'They tried to turn her into a bit of a swinging teenager in the series, but no way could they have shown the real Katy! She was enormous fun and exceptionally generous to work with, always a good steadying influence on my rather volatile temper. It was a very sad day when she married Stewart Bevan and left us.

'Lis Sladen was a very talented lady with tremendous looks and a smashing figure. I remember Barry Letts saying to me, "Come along and meet Lis," and as they were casting for Katy's replacement, I instinctively knew that this was the girl Barry had in mind. Anyway, he led me into his office and introduced us. We all stayed for coffee and some general conversation and little did Lis know that every time her back was turned, I was making thumbs-up signs to Barry who, when given the opportunity, was frantically returning them to me.'

Interviewed by Richard Marson in 1986 for *Doctor Who Magazine* Number 113.

ON LEAVING *DOCTOR WHO*:

'I felt the team was breaking up. It all seemed to be changing and I decided I would change with it.

'Perhaps it's a bad decision – *Doctor Who* would have been a certain bread ticket for another year. It's a gamble that I hope doesn't come amiss.

'I've enjoyed doing the part, but I like to keep in lots of media – a jack of all trades but a master of none.

'What I really want is a break. It doesn't mean to say I'll never be Doctor Who again. I would if the BBC wanted me.

'I have been out of the theatre for five years. It is time I went back.'
Interviewed by Tim Ewbank in 1974 for the *Daily Mail*.

'I have no vertebra between the fifth and sixth lumbars. I have been in permanent pain for the last two *Doctor Who* series and there are now certain things I cannot do, such as twist around easily or bend properly.

'I don't believe in pain killers. I have trained myself to live with the pain – to rise above it.

'The back business wasn't the only reason I left *Doctor Who*. I felt I had run the gamut for the time being, although if the chance ever came I would love to go back.

'*Doctor Who* was a marvellous experience. I became the godfather to groups of autistic children, under-privileged kids – all sorts of youngsters who needed the strength and protection Doctor Who personified.

'Nothing I could do in the future could give me the same kind of pleasure.'
Interviewed by Patrick Stoddart in 1974 for an unknown newspaper.

'For one thing, Roger Delgado, who played the Master, was a very dear friend of mine. We he died, I was terribly upset. Then the producer, Barry Letts, decided to leave. So did the script editor.

'And while Lis Sladen, who took over as my leading lady, is a lovely and very talented girl, it just seemed that the old team was falling apart. It was the end of an era.

'It has left me time to do *Whodunnit?*

'And I think it is a good idea to appear just as myself, so that people will stop thinking of me as Doctor Who.

'I hope to be back on television in about eighteen months. It's going to be an adult adventure serial with a difference.'
Interviewed by Margaret Forwood in 1974 for the *Sun*.

'I get rather sad sometimes when I think that it's all over and that I shan't be there for the new series.

'The following for the programme has been fantastic. I get hundreds of letters a week, many from underprivileged and autistic children who seem to have identified Doctor Who as a father figure.

'Schoolmasters have told me that the programme has a tremendous influence for the good, because the Doctor inspires confidence and trust – qualities children really need to understand.'
Interviewed by Graham Johnston in 1974 for *Lancashire Evening Post*.

ON *THE FIVE DOCTORS*:

'I was delighted to appear in *The Five Doctors* and I thought it was a great shame that Tom Baker declined to take part. Of course, it would have been nicer to have had a bit more to do, but that was necessarily a problem, considering the amount of characters Terrance Dicks was trying to cram into his script.

'Generally, I thought I was done justice, and I told the producer Nathan-Turner then that I wouldn't mind coming back again to do the odd special – only occasionally, as I'm a bit long in the tooth now for the kind of physical demands *Doctor Who* makes of one ...'
Interviewed by Richard Marson in 1986 for *Doctor Who Magazine* Number 113.

'One occasion that comes to mind is coming down a mountain at about eighty miles per hour. I was icy cold and my eyes were scarlet. (There's a BBC postcard of me from that show which, if you look, has got red eyes!) Then a cameraman said to Lis Sladen, "Would you mind slapping Jon's face?" She said, "Yes, I would, I'm very fond of him, why should I do that?" He said, "Jon's face has turned blue and that's the only way of getting some colour back into him!"

'How they got that whole story together, I'll never know. The director did an amazing job trying to control all of us, and it must have been very difficult trying to control Pat Troughton and me.'

Interviewed by Sheldon Collins, Robert Cope and Gary Leigh-Levy in 1988 for *Dream Watch Bulletin* Number 64.

'When we did *The Five Doctors*, Lis Sladen and I were concerned about how we were going to work together, not having done so for some years. We went up on top of a mountain in Wales and did our first scene and reeled it off in one take, with absolutely no problems at all. It was as if we had never stopped working. It was just an instinctive thing.'

Interviewed by Joe Nazzaro in 1991 for *Doctor Who Magazine* Number 170.

ON *THE ULTIMATE ADVENTURE* STAGE PLAY:

'I enjoyed the tour very much, but twelve weeks was plenty for me. At my age, living out of suitcases gets very exhausting after a bit. Luckily I had a wonderfully enjoyable company to work with, a lot of youngsters for whom this was their first job and who were superbly enthusiastic. They worked very well with very little kudos – because if you're in a Dalek or a Cyberman skin nobody can see your face, and thus nobody can say "Wasn't he good?".

'During its run, the play changed enormously. In a morning, we'd rehearse a whole new scene that would appear in that afternoon's performance. When you're doing a tour like that, all the time you're chopping and changing, and I would be making suggestions to the company manager and then we'd go ahead and do 'em.

'There were plans to take the show to Australia and the West End. I was going to have a couple of months off and then go on tour again for three months in Australia, then come back and do a Christmas season in London. But I wouldn't have gone to Australia – my wife decided that for me. "I hope you enjoy yourself in Australia," she said, "because I'm not going. I don't want to travel around any more." I've been dragging her around like a gypsy for years! I work a lot in America, a lot in Australia, and the last few years in New Zealand doing *Worzel Gummidge Down Under*. She said, "I've got a home and I'm never in it – what the hell's the point?" She's a writer, my wife, and at the time was working on a novel with a historical tone – a big book, taking an awful lot of work. I wasn't going on my own, so that was decided.

'Then the plan was to have a lovely long holiday and come back if we had a West End theatre. Whilst we were at Bristol, Ruey Benjamin, who runs the Palladium, sent his daughter to report on the play. Typically with someone really important like that, she arrived ten minutes late, which does not give one a very good opportunity of showing what the play is like. It just doesn't mean anything unless you see the beginning. The producer Mark Furness already had *'Allo, 'Allo!* on, which was an enormous success at the Palladium, and I think *Doctor Who* would have done great business during the

Christmas season. I'm sure of it. But it didn't happen.'
**Interviewed by Guy Wainer, Greg Jones, Neil John and David Greenham in 1990
for *Skaro* Volume 5 Number 2.**

'The performance had to be enlarged for a live audience. It couldn't be played down in
the way I do on television. I work to a television camera very much like I work to a
cinema camera, but the theatre technique is quite different. The performance had to be
bigger, in this show particularly, because we were playing very big theatres.

'We had a short rehearsal period really, so we had to get the script right before we went
to rehearsals. I got a very early copy and made copious notes, suggestions and cuts. The
writer Terrance Dicks and I have worked closely for years, so that presented no problem.
We agreed on many things.

'The script evolved as the show went on, but not a lot as I was hardly ever off the stage
and so certainly didn't want to do any rehearsing when we were on the road. The kids
in the cast did, because they were doubling up and playing five or six roles each. If
somebody got sick, then somebody would step in and take over, but I didn't rehearse
on the road at all. We got it more or less right.'
Interviewed by Joe Nazzaro in 1991 for *Doctor Who Magazine* Number 170.

ON SPARE TIME PURSUITS:

'Anything that is beautiful and pleases the eye appeals to me. That is why I collect
paintings and antiques – and love my garden.

'My only regret is that my acting career takes up seven days a week and finding time
to enjoy the treasures around me is a problem.

'Our favourite varieties of rose are "Blue Moon", "Peace" and "Piccadilly", but last
year we bought some bushes of "Opera".

'Design is very much my forte and what I have in mind is to put all the beds at one
end and have a large lawn where our children Dariel (11) and Sean (8) can play without
fear of damaging something important.'
Interviewed by Brian Gibbons 1973 for *Garden News*.

'I used to take my wife hunting around junk shops for antiques but she so obviously
hated it that I always felt I was keeping her from something she'd much prefer to be
doing. It inhibited me, so now I no longer drag her along on shopping jaunts. I make
snap decisions and they usually turn out right. If she makes a suggestion, "Let's paint
this wall orange", I say, "Tell you what, darling, let me paint a bit of it and leave it for a
week to see if you like it". Never fails. Once she sees the result, she knows it's wrong,
whereas I can usually judge without seeing the whole thing. We are both perfectly happy
with the way things are.

'She wanted this house in Barnes very much. I was not immediately attracted to it. I
like "cottagey" houses with low beams which make me feel secure, but Ingeborg loved
the space, the high ceilings, the tall windows of this house. I agreed for her sake and
grew to love it.

'I had always been mad on this village. It's the Beverly Hills of London, all the pros
live here, West End only minutes away. It still retains all the little shops, delivery boys
come round on bicycles and the milkman passes on messages: "Oh, when you get along

to Sylvia Syms, do tell her ..." – and he does.

'We made one mistake here. We put orange hessian on the staircase wall, which was good when the doors were painted white, but ghastly when the doors had been stripped down to the pine. We changed it to green instead of orange.

'And I'm not good at lighting. I find it difficult to achieve exactly the effect I want. Lighting and lamp-shades still present me with problems.

'My main love is primitive design, old oak furniture, simple classic things. I find some modern designs interesting. I don't like Victoriana or Edwardian things. I am really drawn to anything that smacks of antiquity and age.

'In most homes there has to be a compromise between appearance and practicability. I think a dishwasher, and gadgets like that, are essential to a happy home, and I wouldn't expect to burden my wife with endless chores on my behalf.

'Coming from a theatrical family, I have never had the desire to hang on to the theatrical way of life, as do many actors who come into the profession from outside and can't get over congratulating themselves for having made it. When I am not working, I like to get right away from everything connected with acting. I'm a great hobbies man.'
Interviewed by Shirley Flack in 1974 for *tvlife*.

'Relaxation is riding a motorbike, a bit of water-skiing, or a nice burn-up in the jet-boat. My wife thinks I'm demented.

'I was with some friends a few years ago in Australia, water skiing on the Hawkesbury River near Sydney, and I seem to remember that most of the people involved had been having a very good lunch and were well smashed. The pilot of a shark-spotting plane was there, complete with plane, and someone suggested I try for the world water ski speed record – towed by the plane.

'So we put eight ropes on and the pilot muttered something about it being all right as long as we avoided thermals, and off we went.

'We got up to about 60 mph and then we came to a bend in the river where the pilot hit a thermal and the plane went straight up in the air. This presented a problem: did I let go and risk breaking every bone in my body or did I hang on, take off, follow the pilot over the bank and try a water ski touch-down on land?

'I chose the river, let go and bounced along for about a mile. To my considerable surprise, I survived.'
Interviewed by Ian Cotton in 1974 for *TV Times*.

'There was recently an incident in Spain when I nearly lost my leg. It was badly cut by the prop of a speed boat. My matelot would never listen to the instructions I gave him, the boat kicked and threw him out.

'I was worried the boat would go rogue and run down a lot of kids, so, I tried to swim into the middle of its circle and grab ahold of the rope hanging from the bow and get into the boat.

'It didn't work, with the result I got myself into the splits with one foot one side and one foot the other with the engine in the middle and me hanging on. I had three choices: one was to be drowned, because the water was pouring over my head; another was to let go – the boat would come straight over and disembowel me.

'I took the third, which was to risk letting this foot go and pushing the boat off course.

As soon as I let it go, my foot went straight into the prop. I nearly copped it that time.

'When I was about fifteen or sixteen, I bought myself an SOS two-stroke, a trial bike, which was a swine of a bike that never went properly. The very first day I took it out, I drove it straight into a flint wall, and I've still got the scars to prove it.

'After the War, I got the bug for motor racing, but I realised that I wasn't cut out to be a really ace man. If you're not going to be an ace, don't touch it. So I started racing hydroplanes. I belonged to the British Outboard Racing Club, and I'm still an honorary president or something.

'I raced hydroplanes for quite a few years until that again became big money, and then I started messing around in karts before it all became very pricey and the sport feeling went out of it. I always get out when the thing becomes too heavy.'
Interviewed by John Bryan circa 1974 for an unknown magazine.

ON OUTER SPACE:
'I'm a great believer in all things being possible. I shouldn't be in the least disconcerted if I came face to face with a bug-eyed monster from outer space – I hope I do – and I've met ghosts and poltergeists many times. I'm convinced there is life on other planets. 'I only hope I'm around when they come visiting.'
Interviewed by Val Marriott in 1973 for *Leicester Chronicle*.

CHARACTER — THE THIRD DOCTOR

The principal responsibility for casting a new leading man to succeed Patrick Troughton in *Doctor Who* rested with the series' then producer Peter Bryant, in consultation with his deputy and script editor Derrick Sherwin.

'I went through *Spotlight*, the casting directory,' recalls Bryant, 'and thought and thought and thought about it. My first choice was Ron Moody, who had played Fagin in the musical *Oliver!*. I felt he would bring something special to the role. When I approached him, though, he turned it down.

'The other person I had in mind was Jon Pertwee. Again, that was on the basis that he was somebody who had the personality to bring something to this difficult, nebulous part, which on paper means nothing.'

'I was in a radio programme called *The Navy Lark*,' Pertwee later recalled, 'and one day one of the other actors, Tenniel Evans, said "Why don't you put yourself up to play Doctor Who? I understand that Patrick Troughton is leaving." I said "Why the hell would they want me? I'm a sort of eccentric character actor." He replied, "I think you would make a very good Doctor Who." So I rang my agent and told him, and there was a terrible pause. I said, "All right, forget it, I suppose it wasn't a very good idea." He answered, "No, no. It comes as a bit of a shock, that's all. I'll ring them up."

'He phoned the BBC, told them he had heard that Patrick Troughton was leaving and that he wanted to suggest one of his clients to take over. The producer said, "Who's that?" When my agent told him, there was a long pause. My agent said, "Sorry, we'll forget all about it!" The producer then said, "May I read you our short list?" So he read the list, and my name was second – and none of us had any idea! That was how I got the job.

'I went to see Shaun Sutton, who was Head of Drama at the BBC and a very old friend – we'd started in the business together. I said, "How do you want this played?" and Shaun replied, "Well – as you." I said, "What is me? I don't know what I am!" You see, I had always "hidden under a green umbrella" – meaning one has always played character parts. I had never played "me". He told me, "We know what you are, that's why you've been cast, and if you play it as you, it will come out all right." So Doctor Who was me!'

Bryant's expectation was that Pertwee would give the Doctor a lighter, more whimsical quality:

'I hadn't met Jon Pertwee before I cast him, but I knew a lot about his work and thought he would bring some comedy into the programme. It had been getting a bit heavy towards the end of Patrick Troughton's stint and I felt it badly needed lightening. He was such a multi-talented man, Jon. He could sing, he could play the guitar, he could do funny voices and he looked very good. All these things I thought he would contribute to *Doctor Who*. He had great authority, too, when he wanted to use it. He'd been in the business a long time; he knew his way around.'

In the event, although a few touches of whimsical humour would be apparent in his earliest episodes, Pertwee ultimately played the Doctor in a predominantly straight, serious vein, and his interpretation of the role was not at all as Bryant had envisaged.

Pertwee signed his contract for his debut season – *Doctor Who*'s seventh – on 21 May 1969, and was presented to the press at a special photocall held at the BBC Pictorial Publicity premises in Cavendish Place, just across the road from Broadcasting House in London's West End, on 17 June, four days after the recording of Troughton's final episode and four days before its transmission.

An early priority was to decide upon the new Doctor's regular outfit, a task that fell to BBC costume designer Christine Rawlins in consultation with Pertwee and the production team. The costume was made by distinguished tailor Arthur Davey, and the final details worked out in two fittings, which took place on 27 August and 4 September 1969 respectively.

New producer Barry Letts, who took over from Bryant and Sherwin shortly after this, had no involvement in Pertwee's casting but was nonetheless delighted with it, as he told *Doctor Who – An Adventure in Space and Time* in 1986:

'The role of Doctor Who demands an actor who genuinely possesses that much over-used, and often erroneously attributed, phrase "star quality". Jon would be the first to admit he is no classically-trained actor. He isn't another Laurence Olivier. But what he does have is an enormous amount of that "star quality", both on screen and off, and it's what I believe made him so absolutely perfect for the role.'

Letts was also completely in favour of the idea of Pertwee drawing to a large extent on his own personality in his portrayal of the Doctor, as he noted in a 1983 interview for *Doctor Who Monthly*:

'No actor playing the Doctor should be acting *all* the time. There has to be enough of his own personality showing on the screen. It makes life easier for him, for the script writers, in fact for everybody.'

In keeping with Pertwee's love of energetic sports, fast modes of transport and stylish clothes, the new Doctor's image was certainly much more dashing and action-orientated than those of his predecessors. This was also very much in line with the production team's general desire to steer *Doctor Who* in a more adult direction, away from science fantasy and toward science fiction, to which end they had already decided to change the series' format by having the Doctor exiled to near-contemporary Earth by his own people, the Time Lords.

Just as the rather quaint police box exterior of the TARDIS was abandoned for most of the seventh season in favour of the relatively technological-looking central control console, so the more whimsical aspects of the Doctor's character were gradually played down. He was placed in the position of being an expert or an adviser, a brilliant scientist called in to deal with problems too difficult for others to handle, and his standard costume was frequently discarded in favour of more commonplace clothing such as lab coats, space suits and overalls. Once his alien credentials had been established in his debut story *Spearhead from Space* – in which he is admitted to hospital after his arrival on Earth and the doctors discover that he has two hearts (later revealed in *Inferno* to have a normal beat rate of 170 per minute), an inhuman blood type and cardio-vascular system, and the ability to enter a self-induced recuperative coma – subsequent references to his origins usually took the form of humorous asides providing light relief from the action. Examples include his ability to communicate in Delphon by wiggling his eyebrows, as also demonstrated in *Spearhead from Space*, and his frequent name-dropping references to meetings with famous historical figures such as Raleigh (*The Mind of Evil*), Mao Tse-Tung (also *The Mind of Evil*), Napoleon (*Day of the Daleks*) and Nelson (*The Sea Devils*).

Parallels can indeed be drawn between the style of Pertwee's Doctor and that of the distinctly down-to-earth Jason King, the flamboyant, frilly-shirted author who was one of the central characters in ITC's *Department S* and who in 1971 would be given his own eponymous series. Another contemporary hero to whom Pertwee's Doctor bore some similarities was Simon King of the *Counterstrike* series, transmitted on BBC1 in 1969. King, an alien observer sent to Earth to monitor the activities of hostile invaders, attracts attention when he is admitted to hospital and is found to have non-human blood.

Programmes within the same genre often draw on the same stock settings, scenarios and character types, and similar hospital scenes can also be found in the opening episode of the 1966/67 BBC series *Adam Adamant Lives!*, the costume of whose central character was one of the main inspirations for the third Doctor's regular attire.

Much of the characterisation of the third Doctor during the early part of his era derived indirectly from the exile scenario, and in particular from the fact that this involved him entering into an uneasy alliance with the British branch of UNIT – the United Nations Intelligence Taskforce – under the command of Brigadier Lethbridge-Stewart. The writers had him making frequent attempts to escape from Earth – including stealing the TARDIS key back from the Brigadier after the latter confiscates it (*Spearhead from Space*); trying to repair the TARDIS control console (*The Ambassadors of Death* and *Inferno*) and its dematerialisation circuit (*Terror of the Autons* and others); and enlisting the help of his arch-enemy the Master to overcome the Time Lords' grounding of the ship (*The Claws of Axos*) – and much of his dialogue with the Brigadier consisted of verbal sparring signifying his resentment at being confined to one place and time and effectively being reduced to the level of, and worse still having to rely upon, humanity.

There are indeed times, particularly during these early stories, when the Doctor is depicted as a somewhat aloof and arrogant character. He is gratuitously rude and insulting – he calls the Brigadier a 'pompous self-opinioned idiot' in *Inferno*, for instance, and frequently rails against UNIT's military solutions to problems – and at times is blatantly patronising toward his assistant Liz Shaw and her successor Jo Grant. This serves both to point up his superiority over others – a purpose to which he also (somewhat hypocritically) puts his UNIT connections on some occasions when dealing with civilians, such as in *Doctor Who and the Silurians* when he states at one point "I have the authority to do precisely as I please" – and to emphasise the frustration he feels at his exile. On the rare occasions when he does actually manage to leave Earth, it is only on the Time Lords' terms, because they want him to carry out a mission on their behalf – a fact that appears if anything to add to his frustration. "It seems that I'm some sort of a galactic yo-yo," he fumes in *The Claws of Axos*, on learning that the Time Lords have programmed the TARDIS always to return him to Earth.

The production team's decision to have the Doctor's sentence of exile lifted in *The Three Doctors*, the opening story of the tenth season, meant that the character and the nature of his association with the Brigadier and UNIT had to change. There was now nothing to prevent the Doctor from leaving Earth if he wanted to do so. This presented less of a problem than it might have done, as during the course of seasons eight and nine the writers had in any case gradually mellowed the Doctor's attitude toward the Brigadier – and indeed his demeanour generally. Originally depicted as one of uneasy mutual convenience, their relationship was by this point being presented as one of obvious trust and respect. There was consequently no great strain placed on viewers' credulity by the suggestion that a bond of friendship had grown up between the two men, and that the Time Lord was now quite content to spend a proportion of his time on Earth voluntarily helping UNIT to defend the planet against alien attacks and other menaces. The implication was that his previous desperate attempts to get away had owed more to the fact that the Time Lords had removed his freedom to do so than to any positive desire on his part to sever his connections with UNIT.

In these later stories, the Doctor no longer insults the Brigadier but instead just occasionally pokes fun at him – as for example in *Planet of the Spiders* when he learns of his one-time romantic liaison with a woman called Doris. He even sometimes speaks in the Brigadier's defence when he is criticised by others, such as Professor Rubeish in *The Time Warrior*.

Similarly, the Doctor's attitude toward the Time Lords, initially depicted as one of great hostility and resentment, is by the latter part of his era being more commonly presented as one of allegiance and loyalty.

Certain aspects of the third Doctor's characterisation remained constant throughout. One example is his love of unusual modes of transport, first evidenced in *Spearhead from Space* when, as a condition for his continued co-operation with UNIT, he insists on being bought a vintage roadster similar to the one he appropriated from the hospital where he was treated after his arrival on Earth. In addition to this car, which he nicknames Bessie, he is also seen driving – amongst other things – a motorbike (*The Dæmons*), a three-wheeled trike (*Day of the Daleks*), a jet-ski (*The Sea Devils*), a Land Rover (*Day of the Daleks*, *Invasion of the Dinosaurs*), a milk float (*The Green Death*), a hydraulic lift (*The Green Death*), a futuristic hovercraft-like vehicle (*Invasion of the Dinosaurs* and *Planet of the Spiders*), a gyrocopter (*Planet of the Spiders*) and a miniature hovercraft (also *Planet of the Spiders*).

Gadgets are also a great source of fascination to this Doctor – another character trait drawn from Pertwee's own personality. Most notable is his trusty sonic screwdriver, which he presses into service far more frequently than in the past and uses for a variety of different purposes, including not only opening numerous doors but also hypnotising the planet Peladon's sacred beast Aggedor (*The Curse of Peladon*), detecting and detonating land mines (*The Sea Devils*), detecting anti-matter (*The Three Doctors*) and causing marsh gas explosions (*Carnival of Monsters*).

The third Doctor also retains throughout a notable pride in his appearance, which in *The Three Doctors* leads his first incarnation to brand him 'a dandy'. Typically he sports a velvet jacket over a frilly shirt and cravat or bow tie, sharply-pressed trousers and well-polished slip-on shoes. Frequently he also dons a cloak or a cape when venturing outdoors. Such is his concern with his appearance that in *Planet of the Daleks* he even finds time to change his clothes when trapped alone in the TARDIS faced with imminent suffocation! In keeping with his image of sartorial elegance, he is also a connoisseur of food and wine (*Day of the Daleks*) and can at times can be said to show a degree of vanity.

An athletic and physically active man, he is proficient in the use of Venusian aikido and – as seen in *The Sea Devils* – an excellent swordsman. Other previously unsuspected abilities include fluency in Hokkien (*The Mind of Evil*) and an apparent degree of precognisance, such as in *The Time Monster*, when he has a nightmare foretelling some of the events that are to occur later in that story, and in *The Dæmons* when he appears to realise that there is a problem at Devil's End before there is any indication of this.

Like his previous incarnations, the third Doctor has a strong sense of morality, is highly protective toward his human companions, and invariably exhibits great compassion for the oppressed and those in need of assistance.

The question of the Doctor's motivation was one to which the production team gave a great deal of thought, as Letts told *Doctor Who – An Adventure in Space and Time*:

'Terrance Dicks and I are great talkers and great listeners, and throughout our years together we were constantly striving to find a "rationale" for *Doctor Who*; an "ethic" if you prefer. I was very clear in my mind about what the Doctor would do and what he wouldn't do. He was a flawed knight in shining armour, but flawed only insofar as he was "human". In other words, he was a knight who had left part of his armour at home and had knocked the rest up out of old tin cans.

'In *The Time Monster*, the Doctor talks about his old teacher on the hillside who inspires him with his greed, a greed to experience all the wonders of these new worlds he goes to. There's nothing wrong with experiencing such wonders as an end, but what *is* wrong, and what is thus wrong in the Doctor's character, is the craving for it. *The Time Monster* paints him as an only semi-enlightened being – someone who sees more clearly into reality than we do, who sees more clearly into his own motivations than we see into ours, because he is further along the path, so to speak, but who is by no means fully enlightened. Unlike the old hermit, he is no Parsifal, no Buddha. On the contrary, the very fact that he stole the TARDIS in the first place, to escape and to satisfy his craving, is the key to the flaw that makes him fallible.'

This was a theme to which Letts returned in the third Doctor's swansong *Planet of the Spiders* – which, like *The Time Monster*, he co-wrote on an uncredited basis with Robert Sloman. On this occasion, the whole story was consciously conceived as a Buddhist parable addressing the Doctor's thirst for knowledge.

THIRD DOCTOR

'There is nothing wrong with the acquisition of knowledge in itself,' noted Letts, who also directed the story. 'Indeed it is the goal of any being who travels along a path of meditation towards enlightenment. What is wrong is having a greed for that knowledge, as greed presupposes a preoccupation with the self, the ego. We know that in the beginning the Doctor stole a TARDIS to satisfy his greed for knowledge, and in *The Green Death* he stole one of the blue crystals for precisely the same reason.

'The spiders in *Planet of the Spiders* represent the aspects of the ego – the false self with which we identify, including all the greed and the avarice, which causes us suffering in Buddhist terms. The individual spiders latch onto people like that, exteriorising the ego. Then, at the end of the story, the Doctor goes right inside the blue mountain. That symbolises him going right inside himself, even though he knows it will destroy him; just as somebody going right to the end of Zen is willing to allow himself to be destroyed, the false ego being destroyed to find the real self. He knows he will be destroyed, but knows also that he will be regenerated.

'What he is going to find is the Great One – the core of egoism, the central motivator of our lives, which wants to be in control of the world. The way it wants to do this is to increase the power of the thinking mind, as opposed to the experiencing mind. In other words, the mind is trying to become the Buddha, is trying to become the Uncreated, the Unborn, the Whole, which is impossible. If anyone tries it, ultimately they're going to destroy themselves. So the Doctor goes in, confronts this, and sees that it is an impossibility. In fact he warns the Great One in scientific terms that it is impossible. The old man is destroyed and the new man is regenerated. Yes, it was all a quite deliberate parallel.'

On 8 February 1974, between transmission of episodes four and five of *Invasion of the Dinosaurs*, the production team held a press conference to announce that Pertwee would be leaving *Doctor Who* at the end of the series' eleventh season. Pertwee later stated in interviews that he was given no choice but to go when Head of Drama Shaun Sutton reacted unfavourably to a request he had made for an increase in his fee. Others, however, recall that he was keen to move on, fearing that if he continued to turn down offers of alternative work, they might soon dry up. In the press, he was quoted as saying that he wanted a break and that a major factor in his departure was the sadness he felt over the recent death of his friend Roger Delgado (who had portrayed the Master) and the gradual break-up of his team on the series (Manning having left the previous year, Letts and Dicks having both decided to quit the production team, and the apparent phasing out of UNIT).

So ended another era of *Doctor Who*'s history, with the departure of the dashing man of action who had been the third Doctor.

REWRITING THE MYTH

Plot continuity has always been a bug-bear of long-running television series. It could be argued that good continuity is essential in a popular soap opera for the sake of believability, but is it really so vital in a series such as *Doctor Who?* Certainly Barry Letts and Terrance Dicks, the production team who oversaw most of the third Doctor's era, had little interest in sticking slavishly to the precise details of what had been established in the past, particularly where to do so would get in the way of telling a good story. They were however keen to keep faith with the series' regular viewers by avoiding any major contradictions, and indeed to make use of and develop the series' mythology where to do so would be advantageous, for example in providing the basis for new adventures. In this they were assisted by the fact that the Doctor had until recently been presented as a highly enigmatic character of unknown origins – he had only just been disclosed to be a Time Lord in the closing story of the series' sixth season – leaving them a virtually blank canvass with which to work.

Created by Dicks and writer Malcolm Hulke, the Time Lords were to constitute one of the most important elements in *Doctor Who*'s development during the Seventies. Initially, however, little was revealed about them. In their debut story, *The War Games*, they had been restricted to a brief appearance, and been presented as a mysterious and rather aloof race possessing awesome powers – including the power to exile the Doctor to Earth and transform his physical appearance. Nothing more was then seen of them until season eight's opening story, *Terror of the Autons*, when a Time Lord emissary dressed in a supposedly inconspicuous business suit, complete with bowler hat and brolly, materialises in mid air to warn the Doctor of the presence on Earth of another of their race – a renegade known only as the Master.

With the exception of the Master, who was conceived by Letts and Dicks as a regular arch-enemy for the Doctor, the Time Lords' presence is more felt than seen during the remainder of the eighth season and the whole of the ninth. Although *Colony in Space*, *The Curse of Peladon* (at least, if the Doctor's assumption is correct) and *The Mutants* all involve them sending the Doctor on missions to other planets, only in the first of these do they actually make another brief on-screen appearance (when it is revealed that the Master has stolen some of their files – as also mentioned later in *The Sea Devils*).

The fact that they need the Doctor to carry out missions on their behalf makes the Time Lords seem rather less all-powerful than was suggested in *The War Games* – and arguably also somewhat hypocritical, given that their reason for exiling the Doctor to Earth in the first place was that he had broken their cardinal law of non-interference in the affairs of other planets. This impression is confirmed in *The Three Doctors*, the opening story of the tenth season, which constitutes their most extensive appearance to this point.

On this occasion, they are even seen to be vulnerable to attack, albeit by one of their own kind – namely Omega, the engineer who, by arranging the detonation of a star, gave them the power they needed for time travel. Omega (whose robes are reminiscent of those of his fellow Time Lords) was thought to have been lost in the super nova and has long been regarded as one of his race's greatest heroes. In truth however he became trapped in the universe of anti-matter, where he now survives purely by force of will. His attack on the Time Lords – which involves draining the universe's cosmic energy into a black hole – is motivated by a desire for revenge for his apparent abandonment.

The Three Doctors sees the Time Lords portrayed as an essentially technocratic race, heavily reliant on science for their position of power. They are also shown to have a hierarchy, with a President and a Chancellor (who apparently has the power to overrule the President) taking charge of the emergency – an emergency that they fear could leave them as vulnerable as those they are 'pledged to protect', a rather surprising sentiment for a race supposedly committed to a policy of non-interference.

Other information to be gleaned from *The Three Doctors* includes the fact that the Time Lords have some sort of time scanner capability that enables them to observe the Doctor during his first and second incarnations; that they are able to bring all three Doctors together, although to do so is in breach of the First Law of Time; and that they can communicate with the first Doctor even when he is stuck in a 'time eddy'.

Still *The Three Doctors* fails to reveal any great detail about Time Lord society, leaving a residual air of mystery surrounding them. It is not in fact until season eleven's opening story, *The Time Warrior*, that viewers even learn the name of their home planet, Gallifrey (amended slightly from Galfrey in writer Robert Holmes's original storyline).

The only other Time Lord seen during the course of this era is K'anpo Rimpoche, who features in *Planet of the Spiders* – the third Doctor's swansong. He appears initially to be a Tibetan Abbot in charge of a meditation centre in the heart of the English countryside, but the Doctor recognises him as his one-time Time Lord guru – possibly the same person as the old hermit he once mentioned to Jo in *The Time Monster*. K'anpo is apparently killed during the course of the action, but is almost immediately reborn in the form of his deputy Cho-je – a projection of his own future self. For the first time, the Time Lords' ability to transform their appearance in this way is referred to here as 'regeneration'.

Throughout his third incarnation, the Doctor works on a semi-permanent basis with the British branch of the United Nations Intelligence Taskforce, or UNIT for short, and its commanding officer Brigadier Alistair Lethbridge-Stewart – a scenario set up in the season six story *The Invasion*. The alliance is initially an uncomfortable one, forced on the Doctor by his exile to Earth, but it becomes gradually less so as time goes by, and ultimately continues even after he has had his freedom to travel in time and space restored by the Time Lords.

Starting with the Brigadier, a character established in the Sixties stories *The Web of Fear* and *The Invasion*, the production team gradually built up a small ensemble of UNIT regulars. First was Sergeant Benton, who had also appeared in *The Invasion* – then holding the rank of Corporal – and was reintroduced in season seven's *The Ambassadors of Death*. Then, at the start of season eight, Captain Mike Yates was brought in as the Brigadier's second-in-command, a function previously fulfilled by a number of one-off characters – Captain Turner in *The Invasion*, Captain Munro in *Spearhead from Space* and Captain Hawkins in *Doctor Who and the Silurians* – and even by the relatively lowly Benton in *The Ambassadors of Death* and *Inferno*.

Another new regular, Corporal Bell, was more short-lived, appearing in only *The Mind of Evil* and *The Claws of Axos*; and other UNIT personnel, such as Major Cosworth in *The Mind of Evil* and Sergeant Osgood in *The Dæmons*, continued to be brought in on a one-off basis. Lethbridge-Stewart, Yates and Benton, however, went on to feature in many stories during the third Doctor's era.

The Brigadier comes across as a soldier of the old school, a stickler for military correctness, and often shows a lack of imagination when dealing with alien menaces, choosing to shoot first and ask questions later. He has no doubt where his loyalties lie and is willing to do whatever is necessary to safeguard the world as he knows it. He does however mellow with age, his manner becoming less formal – as evidenced by the gradual lengthening of his hair – and his relationship with the Doctor becoming less abrasive. In *Planet of the Spiders*, the Doctor even learns of a romantic tryst he once had in Brighton with a woman named Doris.

Captain Yates seems initially to be very much in the 'Boy's Own' mould of dashing army officers, debonair and athletic, but it soon becomes apparent that there is a more sensitive, romantic side to his nature. This eventually leads him, in *Invasion of the Dinosaurs*, to ally himself to the idealistic cause of Operation Golden Age, and in the process to betray his friends at UNIT. Allowed to resign quietly when his misguided actions are revealed, he is later seen, in *Planet of the Spiders*, to be developing the more spiritual side of his nature at K'anpo's meditation centre. This is perhaps more in keeping with his character than was his previous military lifestyle, although he seems to slip back quite comfortably into the role of a hero in the ensuing fight against the giant spiders of Metebelis 3.

Benton, meanwhile, is a relatively straightforward character; a solid and ever-dependable soldier who displays a strong loyalty to UNIT, the Brigadier and the Doctor.

UNIT has its main headquarters in Geneva, and has to liaise with the regular Army when carrying out its British operations. The Army even has the power to arrest UNIT officers and personnel in certain situations, as seen for example in *The Claws of Axos* and *Invasion of the Dinosaurs*. The British branch of UNIT appears to have a number of different headquarters buildings, including at least two in central London (*Spearhead from Space* and *The Mind of Evil*), one beside a canal (*Terror of the Autons*) and one set in large grounds (*The Three Doctors*) – or possibly it is simply subject to frequent relocations. It also has mobile headquarters units (*The Claws of Axos* and *The Dæmons*).

It is never stated in which years the UNIT stories are set: in many respects they appear to be contemporary to the time of their transmission, but in many other respects they appear to take place in the future; Britain, for instance, has a space programme that has succeeded in mounting manned missions to Mars (*The Ambassadors of Death*).

Doctor Who and the Silurians introduces a race of intelligent reptiles who ruled the Earth before the rise of humankind. They went into hibernation when a rogue planet approached and threatened to wreak destruction, and failed to wake up again when this threat failed to materialise, as the rogue planet went into orbit and became the moon. *The Sea Devils* features an amphibious strain of these reptiles, who have lain dormant in a base off the English coast, and the Doctor states that they hail from the Eocene era (their previous identification as Silurians in *Doctor Who and the Silurians* being incorrect).

Other previously unknown information about the Earth's history revealed during the third Doctor's era includes the fact that by the twenty-fifth century it will have become a pollution-ravaged and overcrowded nightmare from which groups of people will flock to colonise other worlds (*Colony in Space*); that by the twenty-sixth century it will have a powerful empire spanning half the galaxy (*Frontier in Space*); and that around the thirtieth century that empire will decline and fall, with many of its subject planets being granted independence (*The Mutants*).

The third Doctor's era also sees a considerable amount of new information being disclosed about the TARDIS, including the fact that the central control console can be taken outside the ship and operated independently of it, as seen in *The Ambassadors of Death*, *Inferno* and *Day of the Daleks*; that the dematerialisation circuit (a Mark I in contrast to the Master's Mark II) is vital to its function; and that the Time Lords are able to operate the ship by remote control. In *The Curse of Peladon*, the Doctor states that the TARDIS is indestructible. *The Time Monster* however brings the revelation that two TARDISes (in this case the Doctor's and the Master's) can materialise inside each other, and that if they are configured to occupy exactly the same position in space and time – a move known as time ram – this will result in their total annihilation.

The Time Monster introduces the TARDIS's telepathic circuits, by which the Doctor manages to communicate with Jo after being consigned to the time vortex. On the Doctor's instructions, Jo returns him to the ship by activating a unit marked 'extreme emergency' on the control console. In *The Three Doctors*, the Doctor uses this same unit to send a request for assistance to the Time Lords, and in *Planet of the Daleks*, he uses the telepathic circuits to send a further such request. Also in *Planet of the Daleks*, the control room is shown to contain a wall unit from which a medical bed can be made to slide out for use in an emergency; and the Doctor almost dies after the police box outer shell is completely coated in fungus and the emergency oxygen cylinders run out. In *Death to the Daleks*, the ship's power is drawn off by a living city on the planet Exxilon, causing its systems to shut down completely – even to the extent that the Doctor has to open the main doors with a mechanical crank handle.

A number of stories, including in particular *The Time Monster* and *Planet of the Spiders*, even give strong suggestions that the TARDIS might actually be akin to a sentient being.

In *Day of the Daleks*, the Doctor mentions to Jo the Blinovitch Limitation Effect – an idea devised by the production team to explain away the paradoxes they saw as inherent in the concept of time travel, and later mentioned again in *Invasion of the Dinosaurs*. Interviewed in 1983 for *Doctor Who Monthly*, Letts explained how the idea had come about:

'Terrance Dicks and I had endless discussions about this whole question of the time paradox. What happens if you go back in time and shoot your grandfather before he's met your grandmother? You can't be born because your father was never conceived and, if that is so, how then could you shoot your grandfather? In short, time travel is impossible, and so we had to think of reasons that would make it *seem* possible. This was particularly true where we had action taking place in two parallel times.

'In *Day of the Daleks*, guerrillas were coming back from the future to the present day in repeated attempts to blow up a peace conference. While this was going on, the Doctor had gone ahead into the future to try to sort things out there. So there was action going on it two places at the same time. Now why, we wondered, should these events be going on coincidentally? Why, if you travel forward in time for a day and then come back, do you find a day has elapsed in your own time too? It isn't necessary at all: you could come back the day before, if you wanted to, surely.

'In the end, this difficulty really got on top of us. Having had it at the forefront of our minds for so long, we eventually had Jo Grant say to the Doctor, in effect, "Why don't we go back to the day before and get it right this time?" There is no real answer to that, so what the Doctor said was something like "Ah well, that's the Blinovitch Limitation Effect." When Jo said that she didn't understand, the door opened and in came the guerrillas. So we never explained the Blinovitch Limitation Effect, but it provided us with a way out of time paradoxes.'

Arguably rather at odds with this concept, *Day of the Daleks* reveals that the Daleks have undertaken a second invasion of 22nd-Century Earth – the first having been seen in the season two story *The Dalek Invasion of Earth*. It also has them using a race of unintelligent ape-like creatures, the Ogrons, as guards for their human slave workers. They initially fail to recognise the Doctor as their old adversary (unlike when he previously changed his appearance, in *The Power of the Daleks*), but then confirm his identity by way of a mind probe that extracts images of his previous two incarnations.

The Ogrons appear again in *Frontier in Space*, and the Daleks turn out to be behind a plot by the Master to cause a war between the rival empires of Earth and Draconia – the two dominant powers of the galaxy. In the following story, *Planet of the Daleks*, the Daleks' huge army is seen held in suspended animation on the planet Spiridon, waiting for the invasion to begin – an event that, in the end, is forestalled by the Doctor. Amongst the new facts revealed about the Daleks in this story are that they have been experimenting with invisibility; that their casings emit an automatic distress signal if opened; and that they are susceptible to extreme cold.

Death to the Daleks, the last Dalek story of the third Doctor's era, sees the machine-creatures encountering problems with the same power drain that has affected the TARDIS. They remain able to move about – something that the Doctor puts down to the psycho-kinetic nature of their motive power – but their weapons are initially useless. They overcome this obstacle by fitting themselves with new projectile weapons, which they test out by firing at a small model police box!

The other established *Doctor Who* monsters to be brought back for return appearances during this era were the Ice Warriors, who had been previously seen in two second Doctor stories – *The Ice Warriors* and *The Seeds of Death*. *The Curse of Peladon* reveals them to have forsaken their traditional warlike ways and joined a peaceful planetary alliance called the Galactic Federation, which also counts Earth, Alpha Centauri and Arcturus amongst its members – although the Arcturan delegate on the committee to assess Peladon's suitability for admission to the Federation turns out to be a traitor. In the sequel, *The Monster of Peladon*, the Doctor encounters a breakaway faction of Ice Warriors, led by Commander Azaxyr, who want their race to return to its old ways. With the Time Lord's help, however, they are eventually defeated.

The Time Warrior sees the introduction of the Sontarans, who would go on to become one of the series' most popular alien races. In this story, Linx, a Commander of the Fifth Army Space Fleet of the Sontaran Army Space Corps, crash-lands his golfball-like ship in Medieval England. It is revealed that his race – three-fingered clones with huge domed heads – are locked in a near-perpetual war with the Rutans. They are dedicated to military efficiency, but do have one weak point – the probic vent at the back of their neck – which proves to be Linx's downfall. The Sontarans know about and have carried out a military assessment of the Time Lords – who they have concluded would be unable to withstand a sustained attack – and have their own, albeit relatively primitive, time travel capability achieved through the use of an osmic projector.

All in all, the third Doctor's era saw some significant changes taking place in, and some important additions being made to, the *Doctor Who* universe; a legacy that would remain with the series and be further built upon in later years.

THIRD DOCTOR

COSTUME DESIGN

Television is an essentially visual medium, and it should therefore go without saying that the success or failure of any programme will depend to a large extent on the visual realisation of the ideas worked out by the writer, director and production team. This is arguably all the more so in the case of a series such as *Doctor Who*, which relies for its impact on the willing suspension of disbelief by its audience. The on-screen depiction of the Doctor's fantastic and other-worldly adventures must be sufficiently convincing to enable the viewer to accept them as real – an illusion that can be very easily shattered by, say, a false-looking visual effect or a poorly executed monster. All too often, though, the role of the series' designers is overlooked or undervalued. This chapter aims to help redress the balance by highlighting one particular area of design – costume – that, along with others such as make-up and visual effects, makes a vital contribution toward the presentation of every *Doctor Who* story.

The usual practice during the 1960s had been for a particular costume designer to be allocated to *Doctor Who* on a semi-permanent basis, to handle a run of consecutive stories. This approach was continued at the start of the 1970s as newcomer Christine Rawlins was assigned to provide the costumes for all four stories of Jon Pertwee's debut season, season seven.

This assignment was not an entirely welcome one for Rawlins, as she was no great fan of science fiction in general or of *Doctor Who* in particular.

'I don't think I've ever watched the series before or since!' she commented in an interview for a 1988 issue of *The Frame*. 'To be honest, science fiction doesn't interest me particularly. When I was told I was doing *Doctor Who*, I did look at a few episodes but, no, it wasn't something that I'd thought that I'd want to do.'

An early priority was to design the new Doctor's costume; and although Pertwee would often state in interviews that this had come together more or less by accident, when he had decided to wear some of his grandfather's old clothes to attend a photocall, in Rawlins' recollection there was rather more to it than that:

'Around that time, there was a series called *Adam Adamant Lives!*. Adam Adamant was dressed in period costume, complete with cloak, and I remember thinking that something rather "romantic" like this would be a good contrast to the previous Doctor. That Jon Pertwee was thinking along the same lines was an agreeable coincidence, though whatever Jon had wanted, I'm sure the producer would have endorsed.

'Jon was extremely positive and professional and cared very much about the "look" of the whole production.

'Arthur Davey – a brilliant tailor – made the outfits for Jon.'

With the Doctor now exiled to Earth, season seven saw the Brigadier and his UNIT troops appearing as regular characters in the series. This initially entailed little extra work for Rawlins – for the first two stories, *Spearhead from Space* and *Doctor Who and the Silurians*, the UNIT uniforms created by Robina 'Bobi' Bartlett for the previous season's *The Invasion* were simply brought out of storage and reused, with extra copies made where necessary. Rawlins did however have to design all the outfits for the other new regular introduced at this point – the Doctor's assistant Liz Shaw, played by

Caroline John.

For *Spearhead from Space*, Liz wore a very distinctive jacket that Rawlins created with the benefit of experience gained during her earlier career as a teacher of fashion design.

'We'd been teaching our students about vacuum moulding, which the Royal College of Art were doing in quite a big way at that time. I designed Liz's jacket so that the panels at the front were vacuum-moulded, while the rest was a jersey material. The jersey eased, but the vacuum-moulded sections were rigid, so you got an interesting effect. I remember Caroline John was fascinated by the whole thing. She was lovely.'

It has often been suggested that the UNIT stories were supposed to be set at some point in the future, but this was not something that Rawlins was asked to reflect in her costumes.

'No. In fact, the general rule I worked to on this season was to make the costumes sort of indeterminate, so that you couldn't specify a time period. Take the Autons, for example, with their boiler suits. The thing about boiler suits is that they are simple, straightforward – dateless – and come in sizes to fit everyone. We put scarves on them to hide the awful join at the neck. The masks were made by Visual Effects, and of course Make-up was very much involved.'

A similar collaboration between departments took place on *Doctor Who and the Silurians*.

'I remember the Silurians quite well. The costumes were very uncomfortable to wear, and got very sweaty inside!

'Jim Ward of Visual Effects designed the heads and put the lights in, and I was responsible for the bodies. They were actually sent outside the BBC to be made. We were looking at dinosaurs and prehistoric animals, and so the scaly suit evolved.

'The costumes were made from sheets of moulded rubber – ghastly to wear! – and, as far as I remember, they weren't tailored to the individual actors. We just made some standard sizes and they had to fit: that was the only thing we could do, so far in advance.

'I remember Jon Pertwee being very anxious about the join between the head and the body, which he thought was too obvious. It wasn't absolutely ideal, but we had to be able to lift the actors out very quickly if anything went wrong, because they could hardly breathe in there. I think it looked better when we got into the more controlled situation of the studio, after the location work, because it could be covered up more easily there.'

For the following story, *The Ambassadors of Death*, one of Rawlins' main tasks was to design the advanced spacesuits worn by the astronauts.

'That was actually a problem, because the first moon landings had only just happened in 1969 – the idea of somebody actually walking on the moon was still considered astonishing – and yet for this story we had to assume that space travel was usual. The aliens' helmets and suits were supplied from outside the BBC by a freelance contractor, Jack Lovell. The suits were made of quilted material, so they were rather like protective jump suits or jogging gear. The helmets were simple, too, and the attachments were reduced to the minimum.'

'We did make those spacesuits that appeared in *The Ambassadors of Death*,' confirmed Jack Lovell's son John in a 1989 interview for *DWB*, 'although they were actually made for the film *Moon Zero Two* and the BBC hired them out from the costumiers Bermans and Nathans for that story.'

The next story, *Inferno*, had relatively straightforward costume requirements.

'There's nothing much to say about that one really,' noted Rawlins, 'except that I think it was a good story.

'I remember there was a requirement to put UNIT in battle dress type uniform. For the soldiers in the alternative world, we just used different epaulettes and so on. We also gave them a different, American-style beret.

'Olaf Pooley as Stahlmann wore a Nehru suit, with the high collar. I remember taking him to Bermans and Nathans to get that made. There again, it was dateless in a way, yet also rather fashionable at the time, with the Indian influences around.'

Looking back on her year with *Doctor Who*, Rawlins reflected that it was not a very happy experience. Quite apart from the fact that she encountered a rather strained working atmosphere on the series, she found it extremely problematic to have to design the costumes for four stories in succession so quickly.

'Just as you were getting into the studio with one story, you had to design the next one. You had two directors demanding your attention at the same time! It was tricky. I do think my design was pretty awful, for that reason. I was the last costume designer to do a whole year of *Doctor Who*. Afterwards, the BBC, in their wisdom, changed that policy.'

In line with this change of policy, the work on the five stories of season eight was split between four different costume designers. The season opener, *Terror of the Autons*, was handled by Ken Trew, whose tasks included creating costumes for two new series regulars: Roger Delgado as the Master and Katy Manning as Jo Grant.

'Roger and I sat down and talked about how he wanted to look,' recalled Trew in a 1989 interview for *Starburst*, 'and we developed the idea of a business suit with a difference. It was at the time that the Maharajah jackets were just coming in, so we based it on that design with an embroidered collar. With Katy Manning, there wasn't much actual designing as such. We would take her shopping for fashionable clothes, to places like Biba's.'

The Mind of Evil marked the return to *Doctor Who* of season six's principal costume designer, Bobi Bartlett.

'I actually had a very harrowing experience on that one,' she recalls. 'It was quite a nightmare! I had to provide an awful lot of costumes – hundreds in fact – including some traditional but modern Chinese uniforms, which had to be made up from scratch, for the delegates at the peace conference. Now, whenever I had needed to get military-style costumes made up for a programme in the past, I had always gone to a very talented young man at Bermans and Nathans. At this time, when I came to do *The Mind of Evil*, he had just gone freelance and set up his own business specialising in uniforms, and naturally I went to him just as usual – he had always done such a good job for me in the past. I gave him all my designs and instructions, and told him that he had about six weeks in which to get the job done. Unfortunately, it turned out that he was in dispute with his former employers, and actually ended up in prison! I could never get to the bottom of what the disagreement was about. All I knew was that he was making up these costumes specially from my designs, so he couldn't have been at fault there.

'I tried everything I could to get things straightened out, but without success, so obviously I was left with a big problem. The police had seized everything from the costumier's premises, so I had to go down to the police station and search through a whole pile of clothes in one of the cells, to try to find my costumes. I was saying, "Look, I'll have a heart attack if I don't find these costumes. I'm trying to dress a *Doctor Who* story and I really need them. They must be here somewhere!" I actually got the detectives to help me look for them, but we couldn't find them anywhere.

'In the end, I decided that the only other thing I could do was to go to the prison where the costumier was being held and try to get in to talk to him. So I took a taxi to the prison, told the driver to wait outside for me, and went up and banged on the door. At first they didn't want to let me in, as it wasn't visiting time, but I demanded to see the governor, and eventually they took me through to the yard and locked me in a sort of cage, which was normally used by press reporters. There were some phones in there, so I got permission to call the BBC and tell them what was happening. I was trying not to panic, and to give the impression that this was just an everyday experience for me. You know, I was determined not to be fazed by it! I expect the guards were having a good laugh at my expense, or else they simply didn't believe my story.

'Anyway, about ten minutes later, a guard came back, keys clanking, and let me out of this cage. He said that the governor had agreed to see me, and showed me into his office. The governor sat there, wide-eyed, as I told him "You're not going to believe this, but ..." I explained what had happened, and eventually he agreed that I could speak to the prisoner by phone from his office. So they let this poor man out of his cell and got him to a phone, so that I could speak to him! I said "I'm terribly sorry about what's happened to you, but I've got to ask you where those costumes are." And it turned out that he'd never actually had a chance to get them made up before he was arrested! This was now less than two weeks before filming was due to begin, and I had no costumes!

'Fortunately he was able to tell me where all the material was, so I cut the conversation short, thanked him, and said to the governor, "Look, can I make some more phone calls? I've got to arrange for these costumes to be made up immediately." I was taken back into the same cage with all the phones, and got in touch with another costumiers in Shaftesbury Avenue, who agreed to do it as a rush job. I had to pay over the odds, as they had to bring in extra people and work overtime – sometimes through the night – but fortunately they managed to get everything done in time. I remember that when filming finally got underway, everyone on the production was saying that I had performed a minor miracle – because by this time, of course, the story had got around about me going to this prison and making them let me in!'

To provide the Axon monster costumes for the next story, *The Claws of Axos*, producer Barry Letts went direct to an outside contractor, Jules Baker. The other costumes for *The Claws of Axos* were designed by Barbara Lane. This was her first assignment on the series, but she would go on to handle a further three stories – *The Dæmons*, *The Curse of Peladon* and *The Time Monster* – during the third Doctor's era. She recalled her *Doctor Who* work in 1973 in an interview for a special *Radio Times* publication to mark the series' tenth anniversary:

'I had done a little science fiction work before *Doctor Who*, with programmes like *Out of the Unknown*. But I like doing all sorts of design – everything from classic serials to light entertainment. *Doctor Who* always presents special problems. The script provides you with a framework to build your monsters round, so at least you know whether it's smooth or hairy, six-armed or two-armed. But the big problem is that the costume has to fit over a human shape and yet disguise the fact there's a man or a woman inside.

'Inspiration can come from many directions. Prehistoric monsters are always good for research, so I often go round the museums or look up books before starting a design. The people the Doctor found in Atlantis [in *The Time Monster*] were in costumes based on ancient Cretan wall-paintings.

'As for materials, I try to use anything new that comes on the market. Plastic materials normally used for industrial purposes prove very useful, because they can be moulded to many different shapes and they're light to wear. If you make costumes too heavy, you're likely to find people fainting in them – we had that with the early Cyberman costumes, which were so bulky they had to be held together with nuts and bolts. I often use latex rubber, and the large, solid costumes are usually hung around a cane frame. For hairy creatures I sometimes use a man-made fibre usually used for rugs.

'Costumes for the "ordinary" characters are easier. I wanted Katy Manning to look a little way out, yet be dressed in practical clothes because of all the chasing about she had to do. That's where a trouser suit comes in handy. Jon Pertwee came up with his own designs originally, but I wanted him to look a little trendier, so I designed him a rather smart smoking jacket and a tweed cloak – but still cut on Victorian lines.'

Four costume designers who notched up just a single credit each on *Doctor Who* were Michael Burdle for *Colony in Space*, Mary Husband for *Day of the Daleks*, Maggie Fletcher for *The Sea Devils* and Hazel Pethig for *Planet of the Daleks*. Far more significant was the contribution made by James Acheson, who handled a number of stories during the third and fourth Doctors' eras and later went on to a highly successful career in feature films, winning three Oscars in recognition of his achievements.

Acheson had long been an admirer of *Doctor Who* before he first came to work on it for the season nine story *The Mutants*. In general, however, the series was not highly regarded within the Costume Department.

'I think one of the reasons for that,' noted Acheson in a 1987 interview for *The Frame*, 'was that people were quite scared of doing it, because it asked you to be more imaginative. It also demanded that you worked not just with bits of silk chiffon and three yards of wool crepe, but with fibreglass and plastic. People got a bit wary if they'd been used to working with dress fabric all their lives. They thought fibreglass was a remote, chemical process that ought to be left to other people rather than embraced and used. I found that idea rather exciting.'

The Mutants offered plenty of scope to try out unusual techniques and materials.

'That was the first show I did on my own, god help me. How I got this break was that Barbara Lane, the costume designer who was doing it, fell ill. I think we had about three weeks to put it together.'

The biggest challenge on this story was posed by the Mutant creatures themselves, and Acheson decided to contract out the making of their head masks to freelancer Allister Bowtell.

'I got a call from Jim Acheson,' remembers Bowtell. 'I didn't actually recognise the name, but when he appeared at my front door, I realised that he had been a student at Wimbledon Art School when I had been a teacher there, and our paths had crossed then. Now here he was, working for the BBC, wanting to talk to me about making a *Doctor Who* monster.

'The nice thing about this job was that it was the first time I had discovered and used foam latex. It was very difficult to get hold of – we went direct to Dunlop. It consisted of a five part mix and involved a baking process, which we had to do in a domestic oven. It was all very crude, but the material was lovely and flexible and so we decided to use it. We had some success, although only a moderate amount as we had to cast something like ten masks to get four useable ones out.

'The carapaces and claws were done by the Costume Department; I just did the masks. I sculpted the head, made the mould and then cast the masks – the whole process. I also painted them, and Jim then repainted them. I think the total cost was about £60 each.'

'One of the loveliest things about *Doctor Who*,' noted Acheson, 'was the planning meetings, which were very extensive, often extremely complicated and involved all the departments. We would sit round a table and thrash out how we were going to create these miracles in the twenty-five minutes' screen time we'd got. One had to work very closely with the director, because everybody had to know all the elements that went into a story – whether it was Colour Separation Overlay, whether your monster could get through the door, and so on.'

These were still early days in Acheson's career and, despite receiving welcome support from Letts, he felt that he sometimes made mistakes – principal amongst which he considered to have been the four Gel Guards in *The Three Doctors*.

'What one had always been taught to believe in and to respond to was the script. I mean, that's your starting point. So if a writer writes down that strange, jelly-like blobs with an eye in the middle are devouring people at will, that's what you do. You go along with the author's conception. What one came to realise was that often a literary or mental idea of what a monster ought to look like is hugely impractical, and that often one has to throw out an author's concept. And that was where one learned one's lesson, because those particular monsters were a disaster – an absolute disaster.

'They were impractical from all points of view. You were asking somebody to blob along in rough terrain without showing their legs and wearing an extremely hot and uncomfortable costume. I'll never forget the first day – I think it was at Rickmansworth chalk pits – when the van arrived with these blobs. They were pulled out of the back of the van, and people just laughed. I mean people just laughed at these things. It's a terrible moment when something like that happens, because you then have to live with these mistakes for however long it takes to make a whole four part story. It's a chastening experience.'

As in the case of the Mutant masks, the Gel Guard costumes were contracted out to be made by Bowtell (who, on the strength of his work with Acheson, had been added to the BBC's list of *bona fide* suppliers, and would subsequently become involved in numerous other productions).

'The Gel Guards were basically tailored out of about two inch thick foam rubber,' explains Bowtell, 'covered with vacuum-formed hemispheres of different sizes and latex over the whole lot. The Effects Department made the special claw with lights running down it.

'We also made the mask for Omega, although not the costume.'

'For Omega,' noted Acheson, 'I looked at lots of Greek masks. It was sort of based on a Greek theatre mask. I remember there were some very nice Colour Separation Overlay tricks for the scenes where Omega takes the masks off and there is no head behind it. I loved learning about effects like that. There were a couple of real young boffins – Dave Jervis I think was one – who had managed to create a little department for themselves. When you think of what we have now, with the amount of video graphics and paintboxes – the whole development of video trickery – those guys were pioneers.'

Acheson used reference material to recreate the costumes of the first two Doctors, but decided to redesign totally the costumes of the other Time Lords.

'I can remember looking at some Time Lords from previous stories and not liking them very much. The cliché of costumes for *Doctor Who* – or *Star Trek*, *Star Wars*, you name it – is that everybody seems to wear what's called a patrol collar, a stand collar. I noticed that whenever anyone moved their head, the collar would always become very crumpled. So on the Time Lord costumes, we used a shoe lining material for the shoulder pieces. You soak this in acetate and can then mould it over bodies. In fact, we moulded it over dress dummies. It gave everybody a very clean, armoured look around the heads.'

Acheson had previously used the same material for the costumes of the Inter Minorians in *Carnival of Monsters* – which although transmitted immediately after *The Three Doctors* at the start of the series' tenth season had been made some months earlier at the end of the ninth production block.

'These gentlemen were originally going to be wearing grey masks covering the whole head,' he noted, 'but when they put them on, they couldn't talk or act, so they all ended up with bald heads! But that was a Visual Effects Department problem.'

The costume created by Acheson for the showman Vorg had posed an unusual difficulty: the transparent bowler hat had steamed up at regular intervals! The headgear for Vorg's assistant Shirna had proved more successful, however.

'These were supposed to be a couple of vaudeville entertainers lost in space. At the time, you could go into any kind of horrible gift shop and find these springy things with balls on the end. They were just decorative gifts, but I thought they looked like planets revolving around a solar system, so we made a silly head-dress out of them.'

Barbara Kidd was the costume designer assigned to *Frontier in Space* – the story made between *Carnival of Monsters* and *The Three Doctors*. Like Acheson, she was very pleased to have an opportunity to work on *Doctor Who*.

'*Doctor Who* was just brilliant,' she recalls, 'because you did drawings and actually designed things – things you thought up in your head rather than researched from books.'

Frontier in Space featured a number of different groups of characters, and consequently had relatively heavy costume requirements. Particularly memorable were the Draconians. The initial concept for the heads of these creatures was sketched out by director Paul Bernard, and the masks were then made by Visual Effects Department sculptor John Friedlander, who had previously worked on other creatures such as the Ogrons (for *Day of the Daleks*) and the Sea Devils. The rest of the costume, however, was Kidd's responsibility.

'There was just a pencil sketch of the head,' she confirms, 'and that was all I ever saw. The body of the Draconian was designed by me. The basis was a sort of Samurai look. Originally the shoes were made out of flip-flops; we stuck lots and lots together to give a platform effect. On the filming, though, they all broke, so we had to use something else. I can't remember what we used in the end.'

When designing futuristic costumes for human characters, Kidd tended to opt for simple, elegant styles reflecting a logical progression from contemporary fashions – a reaction against what she saw as the excesses of some other designers when assigned to science fiction productions.

'The futuristic costumes for *Frontier in Space* were inspired by the idea of comic book drawings,' she notes.

Kidd went on to work on three further third Doctor stories – *The Green Death*,

Invasion of the Dinosaurs and *The Monster of Peladon*. The latter featured the return of the Ice Warriors, but their costumes were simply taken from stock and sent out to be repaired by Bowtell.

'The Ice Warriors were incredibly uncomfortable things,' observes Kidd. 'They were just fibreglass shells that were bolted together, and once the guys were inside them, they couldn't get out – there was no release mechanism. They were incredibly hot, too. When they sat down between takes – and they always seemed to have to wait a long time for their scenes to be done – their heads disappeared into their bodies, and they would just sit there like that!'

Kidd's ambitious original design for the Vega Nexos character seen in the first episode of *The Monster of Peladon* had to be dropped in favour of a simpler approach when it proved too expensive to realise.

'I was always very disappointed with the BBC's attitude towards *Doctor Who*,' she asserts. 'It was watched by millions of kids and adults, but because it had already captured that audience, they couldn't see why they should spend any more money on it. That, to me, was just the wrong way of thinking. If you've got an audience of that size, then you should put money into it, because those people should have the best that's on offer.'

Season eleven's opening story, *The Time Warrior*, was another for which Acheson provided the costumes. The most notable innovation on this occasion was Linx the Sontaran, whose look he devised in collaboration with make-up designer Sandra Exelby.

'The Visual Effects people had designed the costume and the facial features of the Sontaran up to a point,' recalled Exelby in an interview for *The Frame*, 'but they couldn't do the whole thing, as they needed time to design the spaceship. At our first planning meeting, we all sat down and the director, Alan Bromly, tried to explain the kind of thing he wanted. I can't remember if it was I or James Acheson who suggested that he should look half man, half frog and have no neck. We thought the lack of a neck would enhance the impression of him being frog-like.'

'The head had been modelled by John Friedlander,' confirmed Acheson, 'I think before I joined the production. We just had this very silly idea that he should have a helmet and that, when he took the helmet off, the head should be almost the same shape.

'I often worked very closely with John. He was very, very clever. He was making people speak through rubber masks long before he had the right materials available.'

The Sontaran's helmet and collar were contracted out to be made by Bowtell, but not the mask itself.

'The actual making of the mask was the responsibility of Visual Effects,' explained Exelby, 'as at that time the Make-up Department didn't have any facilities for making prosthetics. (It can be classed as an early prosthetic as it did use a certain amount of foam.) They took a cast of the actor Kevin Lindsay's face, and I went to help them do this, as I don't think they had ever done face casting before. They then constructed the mask from latex and fibreglass (without the resin – just the glass matting used to build up the shape). The top lip actually went inside Kevin's own lip as a flap. The bottom lip was attached under his lip, so there was some movement there, and then I just painted his lip in the same sort of browny-green colour as the mask. I also had to attach the mask round his eyes, adding make-up there to blend it in.'

The final addition to the ranks of the series' costume designers during the third Doctor's era was L Rowland-Warne, who handled two stories – *Death to the Daleks* and

Planet of the Spiders. One of his challenges on the former of these was to create the look of the Exxilons, as he recalled in a 1988 interview for *Starburst*:

'The script said that they came out of the rocks, so I went to the location with the director and took Polaroid photographs of the sand dunes. Lots of these dunes had little ridges where the water had run down, and so I tried to incorporate that into the costumes. They were made from calico, onto which I laid torn terylene wadding that had been dipped in latex and silica. I used wood dyes in with the latex to give it colour, then created the texture by spraying on plastic paints. I designed the masks, which were then made by John Friedlander just before he left the BBC.

'Barry Letts made sure there was a logical reason for everything: the underground Exxilons were smaller than those on the surface because they had split away from the rest of their species generations earlier. To make them look different, we tried painting them with fluorescent paint, but that didn't do anything. In the end, we achieved luminous patterns on their bodies using a process called front axial projection. I contacted a company that make reflective road signs and got hold of some paint that reflects only when you are looking down the axis of the light. The studio cameras were fitted with a light source, which then lit up the fluorescent channels on the Exxilons' costumes.

'The subterraneans actually had to be glued into their costumes. There is a shot on the location filming of one of them looking over a hill, where we didn't glue the mask down, and you can see the back of it flapping in the wind. When we came to the studio, they were all sealed into their costumes, and were able to cool down only by removing the eye pieces.'

It was common practice for spare copies of costumes to be taken on location in case the originals became dirty or suffered unexpected damage, and Rowland-Warne recalled an incident during filming of the chase sequence for the second episode of *Planet of the Spiders* that illustrated the potential dangers of foregoing this precaution:

'The gyrocopter was being flown by a pilot wearing Lupton's jacket, which was tweed and I had found in BBC stock. Unfortunately the gyrocopter crashed. The pilot escaped without injury, but the jacket was in shreds on one side and I had no duplicate. I tried to buy another, but they had ceased to be made years before. So, on location, I had to make up the missing bits by taking out the turnings and sticking these onto the lining of an old anorak, which I then tacked onto the jacket. As it was a check jacket I joined all the pieces together and stuck them on with copydex.'

Rowland-Warne also recalled the recording of the regeneration scene at the story's conclusion:

'We had Jon Pertwee lying on the floor, which was then marked, and we moved in Tom Baker. The image was then rolled back and mixed. We always had a spare set of clothes for Jon in case one set got dirty, so Tom was dressed in these, as they were of similar build.

'I got on very well with Jon. We were both jokingly rude to one another, but he was lovely – a real professional. He took *Doctor Who* very seriously, but was wonderful with kids. We were filming the hovercraft chase from *Planet of the Spiders* never the Severn estuary, and he got very wet. We went back to the hotel and there were hundreds of kids who wanted his autograph. He got them all lined up, popped off to put on dry clothes and then came back down. We were all knackered, and yet he stayed and talked to them for an hour or so.

'Lis Sladen was also lovely. We mainly bought her stuff from Bus Stop, and we would go and choose from the new collection. I felt that she was an ordinary girl of the present day who would wear ordinary clothes.'

The arrival of the fourth Doctor marked the dawn of a new era for *Doctor Who* but, although many changes lay ahead, one thing would remain constant: the series' costume designers would continue to play a crucial role in the successful on-screen realisation of the Doctor's adventures.

PRODUCTION DEVELOPMENT

The start of the third Doctor's era coincided with a significant change of direction for *Doctor Who*, as co-producers Peter Bryant and Derrick Sherwin decided to have the Doctor exiled to Earth by the Time Lords and allied with UNIT under Brigadier Lethbridge-Stewart. In a contemporary interview, conducted toward the end of 1969, Sherwin explained his aims for the new format:

'What I want to do is to bring *Doctor Who* down to Earth. I want to mould the programme along the lines of the old Quatermass serials, which I found so compelling. I want to establish the concept of having things happen down on Earth, with people with everyday lives coming up against the unknown.'

The influence of writer Nigel Kneale's three ground-breaking BBC Quatermass serials – *The Quatermass Experiment* (1953), *Quatermass II* (1955) and *Quatermass and the Pit* (1958/59) – was certainly very apparent in the transmitted stories of season seven, which presented essentially the same scenario of a scientist (the Doctor) and his assistant (Liz Shaw) facing horrific alien threats, hindered by sceptical Earth authorities and with much of the action taking place in advanced laboratories, secret research establishments and sinister industrial complexes.

Of the four individual stories, *Spearhead from Space* is the one that most closely follows the narrative of a *Quatermass* plot. Here, just as in *Quatermass II*, a shower of hollow 'meteorites' brings to Earth a disembodied alien intelligence that takes over senior establishment figures and ultimately manifests itself as a hideous many-tentacled monster. *Quatermass* elements also feature in all the other stories. In *Doctor Who and the Silurians*, the discovery of aliens buried deep underground triggers a race memory in some human beings, a plot device also used in *Quatermass and the Pit*. *The Ambassadors of Death*, like *The Quatermass Experiment*, involves a missing space capsule later recovered with alien life on board. And in *Inferno*, as in *The Quatermass Experiment*, an infection gradually transforms men into vicious monsters.

The move to a near-contemporary Earth-bound setting and the conscious adoption of a more adult tone also gave *Doctor Who* something of the feel of a conventional action-adventure drama, the alien menaces encountered by the Doctor seeming all the more strange and unnerving for being seen in contrast with everyday settings – the 'Yeti on a loo in Tooting Bec' factor often cited by Jon Pertwee. Not only was this in accord with the artistic preferences of Bryant and Sherwin, but it also meant that the cost of creating fantastic alien settings and civilisations – something that had strained the series' budget to the limits during the latter part of the second Doctor's era – could be avoided. The increased use of location filming and the foregrounding of UNIT's military hardware, such as the 'Windmill' helicopter, also brought James Bond and war film connotations to the series, while UNIT itself recalled similarly-designated organisations such as UNCLE in the MGM/Arena series *The Man from U.N.C.L.E.*

The team of the Doctor, the Brigadier and Liz Shaw – a sophisticated assistant in contrast to the impetuous young companions of the past – followed the two-heroes-and-one-heroine set-up of many traditional action series, such as ITC's *The Champions, Randall and Hopkirk (Deceased)* and *Department S,* all of which were made at the tail end of the Sixties. Moreover, the fact that costume designer Christine Rawlins partly based the new Doctor's standard attire on Adam Adamant's period garb is only one of a number of respects in which the imagery of early-Seventies *Doctor Who* echoed that of the BBC's *Adam Adamant Lives!*. Another striking example lies in the fact that the Doctor was given a highly unusual car with a gimmick number plate, 'WHO 1', just as Adam Adamant had acquired a distinctive Mini Cooper S, number plate 'AA 1000'. In terms of its actual appearance, the Doctor's vintage roadster, Bessie, was very reminiscent of the cars driven by John Steed in *The Avengers,* the ITV series with which *Adam Adamant Lives!* had been designed to compete. The concept of the Doctor's exile to Earth, meanwhile, recalled the fate of comic strip superheroes such as DC's Superman and Marvel's Silver Surfer, a character who in his first adventure was deprived of his powers to travel through space and time and exiled to Earth for daring to defy his master.

Whilst acknowledging that the new format ushered in by Bryant and Sherwin dealt in the currency of conventional science fiction and fantasy-based action-adventure series, it would be wrong to suggest that it was completely dissimilar to Sixties *Doctor Who,* which had itself drawn on many of the same genres and traditions. It could indeed be seen as representing simply the culmination of a number of trends that had begun during the second Doctor's era, such as the increasing reliance on Earth as a setting and the proliferation of stories taking place in and around advanced scientific establishments presided over by misguided authority figures. The Quatermass influence had been very apparent in season five's *The Web of Fear,* and a number of late-Sixties stories, including *The Faceless Ones* and *The Enemy of the World,* had shown leanings towards a James Bond-type thriller style. UNIT itself had been carefully established in the season six story *The Invasion,* to which *Spearhead from Space* bore a number of similarities, even to the extent of including a near-identical battle sequence filmed at the same location. Season seven also followed the lead of season six in focusing on human evil as much as, if not more than, alien evil.

In terms of its realisation, too, this first season of the Seventies, despite boasting a higher location film content, had much in common with those of the late Sixties. Each of its four directors had worked on the series before, and had consequently become familiar with its techniques and conventions. Michael Ferguson's style of direction on *The Ambassadors of Death,* for instance, was very reminiscent of his work on the previous season's *The Seeds of Death.*

The departure of Bryant and Sherwin and the arrival of new producer Barry Letts, who formally took over with effect from *Doctor Who and the Silurians,* resulted in the series harking back even more strongly to its Sixties roots. Although pleased that the emphasis of the series had, as he saw it, moved away from science fantasy and towards science fiction, Letts disliked the stories being set almost exclusively on near-contemporary Earth and determined to have the Doctor journeying once more into space and time. In this, he was strongly supported by script editor Terrance Dicks, with whom he quickly developed a strong and effective working relationship. To achieve their aim, they came up with the idea of the Doctor being forced to undertake occasional missions for the Time Lords – a plot device first used in *Colony in Space*. They also felt that the series should become rather lighter in tone than had been the case in the recent past, with a greater focus on characterisation.

One element of season seven with which Letts and Dicks had been particularly dissatisfied was the character Liz Shaw. They felt that the independent, self-confident scientist had little need to rely on the Doctor for explanations, and so failed to fulfil the required dramatic functions of aiding plot exposition and acting as a point of audience identification. They therefore decided to drop the character and to introduce in season eight's first story, *Terror of the Autons*, a replacement more akin to the naive young 'screamers' of the Sixties.

The new companion was Josephine Grant – or Jo for short – an impetuous young woman assigned to UNIT as a result of some string pulling by an influential relative. Jo would frequently run into danger and require rescuing by the Doctor, who could take her under his wing in a way that would have seemed condescending with her predecessor. At the same time, she would provide the writers with an easy-to-use cipher for any plot information that they needed to convey to viewers.

The production team also decided at this point to enlarge the UNIT team by giving the Brigadier a new second-in-command more suited to his status than the relatively lowly Sergeant Benton. This was Captain Yates, who was also envisaged as a possible love interest for Jo – although, in the event, little came of this in the transmitted stories.

Another, arguably even more significant, innovation in *Terror of the Autons* was the introduction of a new villain in the person of the Master – a renegade Time Lord dedicated to evil – who would appear in every story of the eighth season. Dicks and Letts, when recalling how they came to create this character, generally cite Sherlock Holmes's great adversary Moriarty as their chief inspiration. The fictional concept of the arch-enemy goes back much further than Sir Arthur Conan-Doyle's novels, however, and was firmly established in many of the genres and individual sources upon which *Doctor Who* drew in its seventh and eighth seasons.

In the James Bond films, for example, Bond almost always finds himself pitted against some deranged yet brilliant super-criminal, intent on taking over or destroying the world by means of a fiendish – if highly convoluted and improbable – 'master plan'. The name and individual traits of the villain might sometimes change from one film to another, but the character fulfils essentially the same function every time – to act as Bond's arch-enemy.

Superheroes, too, need supervillains to battle against; and just as a superhero always has characteristic powers and special abilities, so too must his adversary. Batman, for instance, is aided by Robin, has the use of his utility belt, travels in the Batmobile and can call on the resources of the Batcave, while each of his regular foes – the Riddler, the Joker, the Penguin, Catwoman *et al* – has his or her own particular special abilities and trademarks.

In early Seventies *Doctor Who*, the Doctor is aided by Liz or by Jo, has the use of his electronic gadgets, travels in Bessie and can call on the resources of UNIT. He also has his own special powers and abilities: mastery of Venusian aikido; the ability to converse fluently in obscure dialects; a high resistance to G-forces; and even, in *The Ambassadors of Death*, the power to make an object vanish as if by magic and reappear a few minutes later, without any apparent technological aid. The Master, filling the previously-vacant role of the Doctor's arch-enemy/supervillain, quickly establishes some of his own trademarks: the use of a matter-condensing gun; the power to hypnotise people and force them to do things against their will; and the expert use of disguises.

The Master's name is itself evocative of similar characters in other series, such as Batman's aforementioned adversaries and Adam Adamant's recurring foe, the Face; and it had been used once before in *Doctor Who*, for the mysterious controller of the Land of Fiction in the season six story *The Mind Robber*. As Letts and Dicks recall, however, their main reason for choosing this name was that, in common with the Doctor's, it corresponded to an academic qualification.

The only humanoid villain to have appeared in more than one story prior to the introduction of the Master had been the Time Meddler – also a member of the Doctor's own race – in the mid-Sixties. He however had been a very different type of character, motivated by a mischievous sense of fun and a desire to 'improve' the course of history rather than by a genuinely evil disposition. A much closer antecedent to the Master in terms of character traits can be found in *The War Games* in the person of the War Chief, an evil renegade Time Lord cynically exploiting his alien 'allies' as part of a scheme to gain power for himself – something the Master would also attempt in stories such as *Terror of the Autons*, *The Claws of Axos* and *The Sea Devils*.

The Doctor's relationship with the War Chief was quite different from those with his previous adversaries. The two Time Lords were seen to discuss the pros and cons of their situation in an academic, almost detached manner, and for once, the Doctor appeared to regard his opponent as an intellectual equal. When the War Chief tried to strike a bargain, offering the Doctor a half-share of power in return for his help, viewers were left with serious doubts as to what the Doctor's reply would be. This curious rapport – an indefinable bond, perhaps, between two members of the same race, outcast amongst lesser beings – was also very apparent between the Doctor and the Master. The Doctor seemed actually to relish each new encounter with his arch-enemy, admitting at the end of *Terror of the Autons* that he was 'almost looking forward to it'; a perhaps surprising sentiment, given the death and destruction that the Master had just caused.

While the War Chief can be regarded as a direct forerunner of the Master in terms of his motivation and his relationship with the Doctor, the War *Lord* – another character in the influential season six story *The War Games* – was a much closer parallel in terms of appearance, with his bearded, saturnine countenance and his plain black suit, complete with Nehru-style high-collared jacket. The hypnotic powers displayed by the War Lord's race, the Aliens, similarly foreshadowed those of the Master.

Quite apart from fulfilling the function of an arch-enemy, the Master also provided the production team with a means of lending credibility to a situation – a rapid succession of seemingly unconnected threats to Earth's security – that would otherwise have become increasingly unbelievable. All the various alien invasion attempts presented in the eighth season were seen to be due purely to the Master's intervention, and the Master's interest in Earth due mainly to the Doctor's own presence there. The workability of the exile scenario was thus preserved, although at the cost of a certain degree of predictability in the stories. The production team soon realised that viewers would eventually lose patience with the inclusion of the Master as the major villain in every story and with the long list of alien beings seemingly queuing up to attack the Earth. They therefore decided to limit the Master to one or two appearances per season from that point onwards, in conjunction with their policy of moving the series away from a totally Earth-bound setting.

Another shift of dramatic emphasis that occurred after *Terror of the Autons* sparked off a wave of criticism from some commentators about the levels of violence and horror in the series.

'There were big leading articles in several newspapers complaining bitterly about what we'd done,' reflected Letts in an 1990 interview for *Doctor Who Magazine*. 'We even had a letter from Scotland Yard about the policemen who turned out to be Autons, saying "Please don't do it again".

'I think we did go over the top but, when you think of it, the most terrifying things are ordinary things that can't be trusted. If it's a monster, it's a monster, and you know where you are. But if a toy comes to life and tries to kill you, it's not so funny.

'The BBC kept a very close eye on us after that, and we made sure we didn't do that sort of thing again, although in stories like *The Dæmons* we came close to it.'

Season eight had in many respects laid down a template for the remainder of the third Doctor's era. The gritty realism of the previous year's stories and been discarded, and *Doctor Who* had been steered back more towards a family audience. UNIT continued to represent an important element of the format, but characterisation and humour had now been given precedence over military hardware and action set-pieces; and while in season seven the Doctor's relationship with the Brigadier had been one of uneasy mutual convenience, during season eight it had become one of obvious friendship. The Doctor himself had also mellowed, losing the harder edges of his rather arrogant season seven persona and becoming a debonair and reassuring uncle figure, albeit still a man of action. There had now been established a group of reassuringly familiar regular characters – the Doctor, the Brigadier, Jo, the Master, Yates and Benton – and the actors who portrayed them had bonded together into a highly effective team, their *esprit de corps* readily evident from the transmitted episodes. All these developments would be carried forward and built upon.

Season nine consequently saw *Doctor Who* enjoying a period of relative stability. It had the same production team and main cast as season eight and was made in much the same style, continuing the mixture of stories set on near-contemporary Earth, where the Doctor operated as UNIT's scientific adviser, and occasional forays to other worlds, where he acted as an agent of the Time Lords. The less frequent use of the Master, however, left the way clear for stories devoted to other adversaries; and the production team took this opportunity to bring back some of the traditional monsters for which *Doctor Who* had become famous in earlier years – a further nod toward the series' roots. The season thus saw stories featuring the Daleks, the Ice Warriors and the Sea Devils – amphibious counterparts to season seven's Silurians.

Season nine also saw the production team increasingly using the series as a vehicle to highlight some of their own interests and to comment obliquely on issues of current concern to them. Examples included *The Curse of Peladon*'s allegory of the UK's accession to the European Community (generally referred to at the time as 'the Common Market'), *The Mutants*' commentary on ecology, colonialism and apartheid, and *The Time Monster*'s exploration in one scene of the Doctor's motivation in Buddhist terms (Letts being a devotee of Buddhism). Letts, in particular, was keen that the stories should work on more than one level and have a moral message underlying the action.

'The morality question was important to me from two points of view,' he told *Doctor Who Monthly* in 1983. 'First, I believe television does exert a strong influence on people. I disapprove strongly of any sort of show – film or television – that says there is no morality; that it is purely accidental whether you're on the side of the goodies or the baddies, and the person who wins is the one who hits the hardest. Secondly, I feel something of the moral passion that George Bernard Shaw talks about. Now that's nothing to do with whether you're religious or not. I think that all humankind is looking for an order and a meaning to life, and a facet of that search is this quest for morality; finding it and then trying to live by it.

'To give you an example of this in *Doctor Who*, one of the first things I did editorially on the show was to alter the ending of *Doctor Who and the Silurians*. If you remember, it was the sequence where the Brigadier blows all the Silurians up. Now, in the script, after the Brigadier has done this act, the Doctor says something like, "What a terrible thing to do. Think of all the science they've got that we haven't," and so on. To me that was wrong, and I had it changed to, "But that is murder. Just because a race has green skin doesn't make them any less deserving of life than we are."

'Now talking about moral passion might sound a bit pompous, but being aware of it also makes for good storytelling. When people used to come up with a story, or Terrance and I thought of a story, and we couldn't quite see where we were going with it, we would say, "Let's go back to the basics and ask ourselves: what is the story about; what point is the story making?" If it's just an adventure chase-about, then it's very difficult to make a good story, because all you're doing is just inventing new incidents. On the other hand, if you go back to brass tacks and say to yourself, "The point of this story is, for instance, that just because a chap has green skin doesn't mean he should be treated as an inferior," then immediately things start to fall into place, so that if an incident arises within the plot, you can ask "Is this leading the story in that direction?" It is an enormous help in the structuring of stories to have a point or theme to the whole thing.'

The tenth anniversary season again saw *Doctor Who* looking back to and celebrating its own history. This was most readily apparent in the opening story, which continued the production team's practice of aiming to launch each new season with some sort of 'gimmick'. Previous gimmicks had been the introduction of the Master in *Terror of the Autons* and the return of the Daleks in *Day of the Daleks*. On this occasion, it was the teaming up of the third Doctor with the first and second in a story entitled, appropriately enough, *The Three Doctors*. This was also the point at which Letts and Dicks finally contrived to bring the Doctor's exile to Earth to an end, having the Time Lords restore his freedom as a reward for defeating the renegade Omega.

'A lot of people have asked me how we came to do *The Three Doctors*,' noted Letts in a 1981 interview for *Doctor Who Monthly*, 'but really, if you think about it, it's the most obvious plot device of all: to have a serial where all three of them come together. While I was producer of *Doctor Who*, hardly a week went by without somebody coming up to me and suggesting this idea. So, when we actually came to do the story for the anniversary year, it was more a case of bowing to pressure than divine inspiration.'

Other anniversary elements within season ten included the return of the Daleks, again aided by the Ogrons, in two linked six-part stories, *Frontier in Space* and *Planet of the*

Daleks, which together made up an epic tale recalling the twelve-part first Doctor story *The Daleks' Master Plan*.

This season was also notable however for marking the beginning of the end of the relatively stable period that the series had enjoyed since *Terror of the Autons*. The death of actor Roger Delgado shortly after the completion of the season's production meant that *Frontier in Space* would be the last third Doctor story to feature the Master – and there had in any event been plans to kill the character off after just one further appearance, to enable Delgado to pursue other work – while *The Green Death* saw the departure of Jo Grant as behind the scenes factors culminated in actress Katy Manning's exit from the series.

Season eleven's opening story, *The Time Warrior*, introduced a new regular character, Sarah Jane Smith, to accompany the Doctor on his travels. A different companion had originally been envisaged to fulfil this role but, as rehearsals began with the actress concerned (whose identity is currently unknown), it became clear that a rethink was called for. The production team then devised Sarah, who, as a freelance journalist, would have a plausible reason to get involved in dramatic situations and would also be capable and independent – attributes that Letts was particularly keen to see maintained, as he felt that the portrayal of earlier companions had left the series open to criticisms of sexism.

Sarah proved a worthy successor to Jo, but her introduction did nothing to stem the gradual break-up of the third Doctor's established behind-the-scenes team as Letts, Dicks and then finally Pertwee himself all decided to quit the series. Letts and Dicks both felt that they had contributed about as much as they usefully could on the production team, and that it was time for them to move on to other projects. They had already produced the adult science fiction series *Moonbase 3* for the BBC, and had indeed initially considered leaving *Doctor Who* some two years earlier, but had been persuaded by their BBC superiors to stay on and continue their highly successful run on the series.

'I think we did change the face of *Doctor Who* quite dramatically over the period when Jon Pertwee was the Doctor,' observed Letts in 1981. 'Certainly we attracted a much older age group to the show, as was proved one year when I had an audience survey conducted. The results showed that out of our total audience figure of nine million, 58% were over the age of fifteen. We pushed the technology of the BBC to its limits, using every new process we could lay our hands on, and, I think, introduced quite a few new elements into the stories.'

By the end of season eleven, however, it was clear to all concerned that *Doctor Who* would benefit from an injection of new blood; and that this would come with the appointment of a new producer and script editor and the casting of a new Doctor to take the series into the second half of the decade.

FROM SCRIPT TO SCREEN: DAY OF THE DALEKS

Introduction

This chapter presents an in-depth look at just one of the third Doctor's stories. In doing so, it reveals the process of making *Doctor Who* at this point in the series' history and – a factor common to every story – some of the behind-the-scenes discussions and thought that go into a production.

The production chosen for this case study is *Day of the Daleks*, the story that introduced the series' ninth season in 1972 and that saw the return of the Daleks to *Doctor Who* for the first time since their apparent demise at the end of *The Evil of the Daleks* in 1967.

For our view of the production, we have turned primarily to director Paul Bernard and to designer David Myerscough-Jones, who recall, scene by scene, the work that went into it. We have also spoken to producer Barry Letts and script editor Terrance Dicks.

The Scripts

The initial idea for *Day of the Daleks* came in the form of a story outline from Louis Marks entitled *The Ghost Hunters*.

Marks had already written one story for *Doctor Who*, *Planet of Giants*, transmitted in 1964, and since then had been busy working on other assignments, including as writer and story editor on *No Hiding Place* and subsequently on a series that he himself had created, called *Market in Honey Lane* (latterly *Honey Lane*). As it happened, Paul Bernard, the eventual director of *Day of the Daleks*, had also been working on *Market in Honey Lane*, as had regular *Doctor Who* writer Robert Holmes.

Bernard had started his career as a theatrical designer in the Fifties, working on opera, ballet and musicals. He was employed by the theatrical manager Emil Littler to work on several of his productions, including a version of *Kiss Me Kate*, and a number of pantomimes. His theatrical career culminated with an approach by Granada Television in 1958, when he was offered a contract with them. Bernard therefore moved to Granada and worked in television design until 1960, when he left to become a freelance television designer. He subsequently worked for Thames Television on productions such as *The Avengers* and *Armchair Theatre* and for the BBC on numerous plays, including the *20th Century Theatre* series, and also on the detective series *Maigret*.

He had worked for Granada on a series called *The Verdict is Yours*, a complex courtroom production that was transmitted live. This involved the planning and choreography of six cameras, as he had to ensure that the entire production ran smoothly and that his designs incorporated the requirements and the potential requirements of the director. This resulted, by 1962, in Bernard achieving a high profile as a designer who also understood the technicalities of television. He was therefore asked by the BBC, in 1963, if he would consider training as a director in order to work on the embryonic BBC2 channel. Bernard accepted this offer, and in 1965, following his training and working on shows such as *Z-Cars*, again returned to freelance work, this time as a director.

He accepted a rolling contract with ATV during which he worked on shows including *Love Story*, *Emergency Ward 10* and *This is … Tom Jones*. It was while working on *Honey Lane* that Bernard had introduced both Marks and Holmes to his own literary agent, who took them on. 'Robert, Louis and I had a very close working relationship on *Honey Lane*,' commented Bernard. 'We knew each other well and had a strong professional bond.

'Unknown to me, Louis had submitted a story idea to Barry Letts, who had just taken over as producer on *Doctor Who*. And both Robert and Louis knew that I was ambitious. I had spent some seven years at ATV as a drama director and was now looking for new challenges elsewhere. Obviously between Robert and Louis meeting Barry, and my coincidentally having directed a play written by Barry three or four years before, meant that he knew of my work. All this ultimately led to my getting a call from Barry asking if I would be interested in joining him on *Doctor Who*. Of course I said that I'd be delighted, as I knew that the challenge of working on *Doctor Who* would be more demanding of my creative talents.'

The outline for Marks' story underwent some discussion before Dicks was happy with it. In a letter to Marks dated 27 October 1970, Dicks commented that, 'the addition of the "going into the future" element gives it the added science fiction feeling that we need.' Dicks went on to explain that although he wanted to commission scripts, he was currently unable to do so because the go-ahead had not yet been received from 'the powers that be' for the season to be commissioned. He expected this to happen towards the end of 1970 or at the very start of 1971.

The storyline was eventually commissioned from Marks on 22 January 1971. Marks had at that time just started work for the BBC as script editor on a series called *Trial*. This caused some concern, in that he had worked out the storyline and it had been accepted by Dicks while Marks was still a freelance writer, and the terms and conditions for BBC personnel writing for a series like *Doctor Who* were different from those of a freelancer. Dicks pointed this out in an internal note dated 25 January, commenting that he and Letts were 'particularly keen to have this as our first 4-part serial of the next season.'

The storyline was scheduled to be delivered on 8 February, and by 23 February a four-part breakdown had been accepted by Dicks. Marks' four scripts for the story were accepted on 22 March 1971.

By this time, plans for the season as a whole were coming together, and, as with previous seasons, which had featured the introduction of the Doctor and the introduction of the Master respectively, Letts and Dicks were keen to make the most of the opening story for the ninth season.

'It's a curious thing about the Daleks,' explained Letts in a 1993 interview for Reeltime Pictures' *Myth Makers* series of video interviews. 'In general, directors don't like working with the Daleks – and writers as well. Even Terry Nation was finding it difficult to get new variations on the Dalek theme. The thing is that they are very limited, but everybody loved them. So we had quite happily made up our minds that we weren't going to have the Daleks. But then there seemed to be a groundswell of people wanting to know where the Daleks were, and when the Managing Director of Television asked us where they were, we thought that it was about time that we had the Daleks.'

'We held them back until there was a definite demand for them,' agreed Dicks in the same interview.

Dicks remembers that the idea was always to add the Daleks into Marks' scripts. 'We got Louis' scripts in,' he recalled, 'and it was a fine story with nothing wrong with it at all. However, it still didn't have that certain something that we felt it needed in order to open the season. We then hit upon the idea of including the Daleks, and hurriedly set about doing this.'

Dicks then recalls that they were contacted by Nation's agents. 'They said that they had heard we were doing a Dalek story, and that we needed permission to proceed. So Barry and I went to see Terry down at Pinewood, where he was making *The Persuaders!*

with Roger Moore and Tony Curtis, and, to try and get him on our side, asked if he would consider writing us a story for the following season. After some consideration, he was happy to do so, and we had no further problems on *Day of the Daleks*.'

Letts, however, believes that permission may have been sought before the Daleks were added, but that either way, he and Dicks were in contact with Nation, who gave his blessing to another writer using the Daleks.

On 14 April, Letts' secretary, Sarah Newman, wrote to the BBC's Head of Copyright, formally asking if they could check with Nation if it would be possible to include the Daleks in the season under preparation. On 22 April, ALS Management, replying on behalf of Nation, said that there was no problem about including the Daleks, subject to the usual negotiations as to this use.

As the decision had been made to include them in Marks' scripts, he was duly contacted about this.

'It simply meant putting the Daleks into the place of the other aliens I had envisaged ruling Earth in the future,' he explained in an interview for the fanzine *Matrix* in 1980. 'Once we got to work on it, we realised that the Daleks offered all sorts of other story possibilities.'

By this time, the story had been retitled *Years of Doom*, and around the start of June, Dicks produced a final scene breakdown, which featured the Daleks and which was all but identical to the story as it would be transmitted. He sent this breakdown to Marks on 8 June, so that the scripts could be revised accordingly. Letts confirmed that the Daleks were to be included in a memo dated 15 June to the BBC's Head of Copyright, asking them to formally clear the use of the Daleks with Nation. Nation was subsequently paid the sum of £25 per episode for their use.

On 5 July, Marks had revised and delivered all four scripts, and on 15 July, Dicks again wrote to let him know that the production team had decided to change the title from *Years of Doom* to *Day of the Daleks* – 'We thought we had better get them into the title,' he commented.

On the same date, Dicks sent copies of the scripts to Nation for his approval. In the accompanying letter, he mentioned that he was keen to set up a meeting to discuss with Nation the Daleks' *next* return in the following season.

Nation replied on 20 July, commenting that, 'It seems a very good and exciting batch of episodes.' He went on to say, 'I have a few suggestions for what (I think) will improve some of the Daleks' dialogue, and I'll let you have my notes quite soon. But you're the Script Editor and you can decide whether you think they're improvements or not.

'Look forward to talking to you about the second coming of the Daleks before very long.'

There is no record of what Nation's suggested changes were, or whether or not they were incorporated into the scripts.

'When I first saw the scripts,' Bernard recalled, 'the Daleks were definitely in. I never had any part in reinventing the storyline at all – in fact I never had any part in talking to Louis! Such was the lack of time. I was just delighted that my first script for *Doctor Who* was going to be by Louis Marks.

'I very seldom read a script all the way through and then go back and start again. As I read a script, I break it down into thumbnail sketches: either plan sketches from a directorial viewpoint as to what the mechanics of a scene are; or I do visuals – little scribbles. *Day of the Daleks* was made for these little visuals. My normal procedure would be that, having gone through the script and having linked it all together as a series of mechanics and visuals, I might then make some suggestions as to how certain scenes might be re-written to make them flow together. I can't be specific, but this is generally how I work.

'With this story, however, as I had been working with Louis and as he knew my style of directing, it is possible that there was not much that I needed to suggest as changes to the scripts.'

Casting

'In those days,' explained Bernard, 'unlike today, the director did his own casting. Certainly at the BBC. They had a department that booked the artistes once you had chosen them, but they didn't have someone who went away and then came back with recommendations. You told them specifically who you wanted, and they went away and came back to tell you how much this person would cost, when they were available, and so on.

'As I read through the scripts, I start to think of people who would be good for the parts. Many directors liked to use their own group of people with whom they had worked, and I was no exception. Some people simply fitted in with the thinking of the script.

'Aubrey Woods was like that. He always had a reputation for being an oddball, outside the conventional, and that was exactly what I was after for the part of the Controller. I can't recall thinking of anyone else for that part.

'Anna Barry was a discovery. I saw a lot of girls for the part of the lead guerrilla, Anat. There were half a dozen agents that I would let know what I was doing, give them outlines of the three or four characters I wanted, and spontaneously they would supply me with suggestions. You could almost complete the casting of a production with literally two or three phone calls.

'Anna Barry was the result of a search through agents for a suitable actress. She was the daughter of the BBC's ex-Head of Drama, Michael Barry, and hadn't really done any major television. I liked to cast people who were unknown on television. Wanda Moore in *The Time Monster* was cast for similar reasons, in that she had done lots of stage work but not much television.

'The person that I wanted to get was Valentine Palmer, who played Monia. He was very popular at the time, but for some reason later dropped out of acting. He was very much in demand in the early Seventies, and was an excellent actor and very pleasant to work with.'

Pre-production

The designer assigned to work on *Day of the Daleks* was David Myerscough-Jones, who had worked on two previous *Doctor Who* stories, *The Web of Fear* in 1968 and *The Ambassadors of Death* in 1970. He continued to work at the BBC up until 1991, when he left to work on the film *The Hawk* as well as other independent television and stage productions.

Myerscough-Jones had joined the BBC in the mid-Sixties as a designer, after spending time working in repertory theatres and at London's Mermaid Theatre as production designer.

'I always wanted to be a designer,' he explained. 'Ever since I was fourteen, I was influenced by film and theatre. I used to go to the theatre quite often in Liverpool and was passionate about theatre design – I still am. I was born in Southport in 1934 and, after the War, suffered a mixed education, but moved towards arts and design and spent three years at an arts school. Then I spent three years at the Central School of Arts, studying theatre design and painting. After finishing my studies, my first job was down at Perranporth in Cornwall, working in repertory theatre, and from there I travelled all over the country.

'I worked for three years at Glasgow's Citizen's Theatre, which was a marvellous experimental theatre. We had the ability to put on various plays in very adventurous ways, and it was a time of fermentation and great excitement. After that, I headed for London, and ended up working with Bernard Miles at the Mermaid Theatre for another three years. That too was adventurous and exciting, but my feeling at that time was that the nearer you got to London, the more conservative everyone was about theatre design. At the Citizen's, you could actually try things out, it was a great workhouse atmosphere, but in London everything seemed more standardised and economic. The Mermaid, however, was like a breath of fresh air, as Bernard was very supportive of anything new. I then got married, and realised that I needed to increase my income to live.

'I'd always had a fascination for television. It had a reputation among theatre-types of not being a 'true' medium, which I thought was rubbish. The regime that was there in the early Sixties was looking for a totally new concept of design for television. I have a huge admiration for Richard Levin, the BBC's Head of Design, who was an industrial designer, and yet he considered theatre and film sets to be some sort of invasion into television. An awful lot of people came into television whose backgrounds were in industrial design, and this resulted in a prejudice against certain design styles, which lasted for an awfully long time.'

Myerscough-Jones started at the BBC working for the Design Department as holiday relief, and was eventually made up to be a fully fledged designer around the mid-Sixties.

He was assigned to work on *The Web of Fear* as part of the normal allocations process, and among his work for that show were the Underground tunnel sets in which most of the action took place.

'We tried to get permission to use real London Underground stations for the story, but they wouldn't let us. We had to build them in the studios instead. They had to be multi-use sets, because there were so many different shots that had to be achieved. The set was constructed in sections so that they could be put together in different configurations to give the effect of the tunnels. We put them on rollers so that they could be swung round to form new curves and junctions and, with the addition of painted back-drops, we got the effect of tunnels going off into the distance.

'The tracks were made in lengths, and these too linked together and could be re-shuffled into different forms. One problem we had was that the contractor we used in London to make the tunnel sections couldn't cope, because they had also landed a theatre production for Covent Garden, and so we had to send out some of the sections to another contractor. The problem was that the two sets of sections didn't quite match up, and so we had to stick silver tape over the joins to try and get the lines continuous.'

Myerscough-Jones' next *Doctor Who* was *The Ambassadors of Death*. The opening scenes of this story demonstrated his desire to try and bring some wide-angle establishing shots into the programme.

'I always wanted to get away from the close-up and to open out the sets on a grand scale. There is an opening shot in *The Ambassadors of Death* of the interior of the Space Centre, where the director, Michael Ferguson, pulled the camera back into the farthest corner of the studio and shot the set with all the studio lights and equipment in the ceiling showing above. Then another camera was set up to point at a small model of the roof that we had constructed from straws and tracing paper cut into squares. It was a very laborious business to get the cameras lined up, and then the vision mixer combined the pictures from both cameras so that the model of the roof obscured the ceiling of the studio on the main picture. At that time, this sort of shot was rarely done, and many directors just went with standard shots of standard sets. It was a huge effort to try and get them to do anything else.'

For *Day of the Daleks*, Myerscough-Jones' work was divided into two distinct areas; the present day settings and those in the future, each of which posed particular and different problems for the designer and which are discussed in the detailed breakdown of the story.

'At that time, you tended to be allocated to work on productions, unless a producer or director specifically asked for you to work with them. We tended to be allocated to things that we were known for doing well, and I had been doing a lot of operas and more theatrical presentations. *Doctor Who* was something completely different, and was quite challenging and exciting to do. To work on *Doctor Who* was to be given a superb opportunity to extend the designer's range and vision. *Doctor Who* was a perfect vehicle for that, although, because of the way the stories were made, there was very little time to explore that aspect. Time in the studio was so tight that there was seldom the opportunity to experiment or to try something new.

'The whole time I worked at the BBC, I was always trying to extend the range of what we were doing in terms of design, and to try and get a different look to the productions. With *Doctor Who*, you could have a bit of fun and use materials and designs that you could not use elsewhere. It was a good show to do.

'When I got the scripts, the first thing I did was to look at the number of sheets of paper that made up the episode. *Day of the Daleks* had around 40 pages per episode, which was an incredible amount to get through in half an hour. Generally speaking, the more pages there were, then the more dialogue there was and the less action. Then I would look at the balance between dialogue and stage directions, and, again, *Day of the Daleks* had quite a lot of different locations.'

The next task of the designer was to break the script down into the different sets that were required and assess their complexity and importance to the story. For example, scenes set in the TARDIS were not normally a problem, as the sets already existed and the designer had only to consider if there was some specific prop or requirement for the console. In *Day of the Daleks*, the TARDIS interior was not required, but there were two main sets: Sir Reginald Styles' study and the hallway adjacent to it, and the main control room in the future. Less major, but nevertheless important, was the UNIT laboratory. Finally came less important sets, like the cellar in Styles' house, the interrogation room in the future, the tunnels through the railway arch and the guerrillas' hideout.

'I remember being generally very frustrated that I wasn't allowed to do as much as I wanted to do visually,' mused Myerscough-Jones. 'I think that's possibly a personal vanity, but it helps enormously to create shots that are visually impressive.'

In view of the fact that *Day of the Daleks* featured some complex effects work, and also in in order to draw on Bernard's experience on previous shows, Letts took the unusual step of booking a studio for an experimental session to carry out some tests using Colour Separation Overlay (CSO). This practice was later repeated for several other stories during this period, when particularly complex effects were required.

'At the time of my being asked to direct *Day of the Daleks*,' explained Bernard, 'the BBC, like most studios, used a blue background to "key-in" a required background to a shot. At an early meeting with Barry, before I was commissioned to direct *Day of the Daleks*, I pointed out to him that we had experimented and worked with other colours on the series *This is ... Tom Jones* at Elstree for ATV. One of the most successful in these early exchanges was a yellow. When you used blue, you tended to get a trail behind the subject if they moved, which meant that you couldn't pan or move the camera. The main advantage with the yellow was that this "halo" effect was very much minimised, and we had found that we could pan and have the subject moving. We arranged for a full exercise with different yellows in the studio to gain engineering agreement. We tried different lighting situations and different yellows until we found one that "held" and created a genuine highlight. This was adopted, and used for the first time on *Day of the Daleks*. When I later went to Thames Television, I managed to gain approval to use it for *The Tomorrow People*.

'What it meant was a total rethink in wardrobe colours. Now, the actors could wear blue, but the costume designers had to be careful with yellow. However, the fidelity of the tone we used meant that near-yellows – orange, primrose, gold, caramel or pale yellows – could be used. It also meant that people with blue eyes no longer looked like something out of *Dracula* in close up!'

According to BBC documentation, the session was scheduled to take place in Studio 4 at Television Centre on Tuesday 7 September, although Bernard remembers that a full two days of studio were booked for the session.

'We were given a studio and use of the BBC's engineering department, but the session was not fully scheduled in the true sense of the word. We had to use whatever was available on the days: if we could record on video, then we did that, but if we had to wait because engineering or the mixing desks were in use by another production, we had to wait. We had to fit in with whatever else was happening.'

The main purpose of the session was to confirm whether yellow was a better 'key' colour for the CSO process than blue. Three colours were tested: green, purple and yellow. Although the test was not specific to *Doctor Who*, Bernard also took the opportunity to try out some special effects explosions, and also some optical effects for the sequences when Jo travels through the time vortex and for when the guerrillas travel through time.

For these tests, the UNIT lab set was erected in the studio; and actor and fight arranger Rick Lester (who played an Ogron in the story) and actress Wendy Taylor stood in for the Doctor and Jo for the CSO tests. Lester was also costumed and made-up as an Ogron for those sequences requiring the 'monster'.

The following sequences were carried out:

1. Involving 'monster' guard, Jo, guerrilla and guns
2. Unit lab scene with Doctor and Jo
3. Vortex sequence
4. Time travel sequence
5. Unit lab, gun/dummy sequence
6. Other CSO effects

The result of the test was that a colour called 'golden yellow' was found to be best for the CSO 'key' colour, and also that certain parts of the set would need re-painting as a result. They were too close to that colour, and would therefore cause problems on the final recording if left unchanged.

On Location

Much of the action in *Day of the Daleks* centred on three main locations: a railway arch; a large country house; and a futuristic work centre.

Bernard recalled that the railway arch was suggested by a friend who was always asking about his work. 'One day I mentioned to him that I was looking for a derelict area that had a bridge, maybe over water, maybe over railway lines, and he told me about this place called Bull's Bridge in Hayes, where he used to play as a kid. I went out there in the car, and it was perfect. It had been a shunting yard owned by British Railways, and they were tearing up the railway lines and turning the area into a vast wasteland. It also had some underground passages, so we could have the characters appear to be going into and coming out of underground tunnels.

'I got quite excited about this, because it meant that we didn't have to dig any holes in the ground.'

A large house to use as the country home of Sir Reginald Styles was found by the production team in Dropmore Park in Buckinghamshire. 'That one was not my doing,' commented Bernard. 'It was most probably found by my PA, Norman Stewart.'

Agreement was secured to use these locations: £160 was paid to use Bull's Bridge while £75 per day was agreed for the use of Dropmore Park.

The final location was the futuristic work centre.

'I had remembered,' explained Bernard, 'because I drove in from Roehampton, seeing a set of office blocks against the sky, and how, with the sun behind them, they looked rather ominous, and we agreed that they could be utilised.'

These office blocks were situated in Green Dragon Lane, just beside Kew Bridge in London. The building, called Harvey House, and its underground car park, were felt to be suitable as the factory where the Doctor sees women and children working before he is captured and taken for interrogation.

In order to document all the details relating to location filming on a story, a filming diary was prepared. This showed who was required on which locations and to film which scenes in which order. In the case of *Day of the Daleks*, the filming diary is different from Bernard's own notes. According to Bernard's notes, the following was filmed on each of the four days allocated. The number in brackets after the brief description is the episode number.

DAY ONE (Monday 13 September)
Dropmore Park (House): Guerrilla appears and runs (1); Dusk shot of House (1); UNIT troops deployed at house (1); Shura sees Doctor in house (1); Yates and Benton realise the Doctor is missing (2); Ogrons attack house (2); Daleks and Ogrons attack (4).

DAY TWO (Tuesday 14 September)
Bull's Bridge (Tunnel Area): Guerrilla attacked by two Ogrons (1); UNIT soldiers find body (1).

Harvey House (Underground Car Park): Doctor sees workers (3); Guerrillas fight Ogrons and Dalek (4).

Harvey House (Flats Area): Doctor & Jo escape and see trike (3).

Dropmore Park (House): Delegates arriving (4); Delegates leaving (4).

DAY THREE (Wednesday 15 September)
Bull's Bridge (Tunnel Area): Guerrilla put in ambulance (1); Anat's party appears (1); Shura kills UNIT soldiers (1); Shura arrives back at tunnel and is attacked by an Ogron (2); UNIT search unsuccessful (4); Doctor and Jo emerge from tunnel (4); Daleks and Ogrons emerge from tunnel (4).

Bull's Bridge (Devastation Area): Monia enters hideout (3); Trike chased by Ogrons (3).

Bull's Bridge (Desolation Area): Doctor exits from tunnel (3); Doctor passes security camera (3).

DAY FOUR (Thursday 16 September)
Harvey House (Flats Area): Doctor enters building (3); Ogrons chase Doctor and Jo from building (3).

Bull's Bridge (Devastation Area): Doctor and Jo return to tunnel (4); Final scene with Doctor and Styles (4).

After filming completed on 16 September, it was back to London to start rehearsals for the first studio recording, which took place on Monday 4 October and Tuesday 5 October.

In Studio
At this time in *Doctor Who*'s history, the programme was being recorded two episodes every two weeks. This was a process instigated by Letts, in consultation with the production departments, from *Inferno* onwards. It meant that two episodes were rehearsed over a two week period, followed by a two-day studio recording block when

all scenes for those episodes were recorded, often in transmission order. There were some exceptions.In the case of *The Dæmons*, for example, there were only three studio days (because there was a great deal of location filming for the story, reducing the amount of material that had to be recorded in studio) with material for episodes 1 to 3 being recorded on the first day, material for episodes 2 to 4 being recorded on the second, and material for episodes 4 and 5 being recorded on the final day.

To indicate some of the considerations involved in making a *Doctor Who* story during the Jon Pertwee era, what follows is a scene-by-scene summary of *Day of the Daleks*, with comments from some of those involved in the production.

Episode One

A sentry stands by a door in a hallway in Auderly House. Miss Paget (Jean McFarlane) emerges from the room and tells the sentry that Sir Reginald Styles is not to be disturbed.

[The name of the house underwent several changes over the course of the production. It started as Austerley House in the rehearsal scripts and was then changed to Aulderley House, and finally to Auderly in the transmitted version.]

Paul Bernard: What I used for these initial shots was a floor camera – literally a camera on mountings only, on the floor. The idea was to get a shot that was a little sinister and different.

In his office, Styles (Wilfred Carter) is working at his desk when a wind blows the curtains. When Styles goes to close the window, there is a man dressed in guerrilla attire there. The guerrilla (Tim Condren) points a gun at Styles but then vanishes into thin air. Miss Paget enters, and sees Styles is flustered. He explains what he saw to her.

PB: I cast Wilfred Carter because I wanted someone who could play Styles as a slightly pompous character. Again, I had worked with him before.

David Myerscough-Jones: To dress a set like this, you would brief the prop buyer on what you wanted and then they would go out and hire in all the numerous bits and pieces that were required. Just about all the elements in this set were hired in. The prop buyer is terribly important, but they tend to not be credited for their contribution.

At UNIT HQ, the telephone rings and the Brigadier (Nicholas Courtney) speaks to the Minister (unknown), who tells him what happened at Auderly House. The Brigadier assures the Minister that he was about to put his best man on it.

PB: I enjoyed working with Nicholas Courtney a lot. Very enjoyable. A very professional actor.

DM-J: The telephones were from stock. They are simply telephones that were in use in 1971, which is when the story was being made.

The Doctor is putting the finishing touches to the TARDIS' dematerialisation circuit. The TARDIS console is standing in his lab at UNIT HQ, and the Doctor ducks down to fiddle with it. Suddenly, a pair of doors at the back of the room swing open to reveal another Doctor and Jo. After a few moments, a component on the console explodes with a flash, and the 'other' Doctor and Jo vanish.

DM-J: That sequence was actually recorded at the start of the day – before we began on that opening scene. It was then played into this scene. I had a massive argument with Paul over this scene. If you look closely, you can see that the yellow background when the Doctor's and Jo's doubles are there, does not extend down far enough. There was a problem that we couldn't extend the cloth to mask the patch at the base. We also had to paint the backs of the doors so that they didn't pick up the CSO key colour.

The cycloramas we used were made of felt so that they reflected an even colour.

PB: The problem with the floor was that I had to be able to see Katy, and so could not drop the camera down in order to hide the floor. The lesson learned was that we should have painted the floor yellow as well.

The Doctor explains to a perplexed Jo that this was a freak effect due to his tampering with the console. The Brigadier enters, and tries to persuade the Doctor to come and investigate the 'ghost' at Auderly House.

PB: Katy was very useful. She knew how to handle Jon Pertwee. I knew that at any critical moment on set, when there was some crisis going on, that I could sort things out and rely on Katy to calm Jon down. She was worth her weight in gold. Absolutely marvellous.

I was warned by several people, when I was about to start this story, that Pertwee could be difficult. I think that was the generalised phrase. Now, I had discovered in my working career, that those people who had been labelled like this, invariably I got on with. I found that it was no more than bloody-minded professionalism – and that, I respect. It turned out to be so. Pertwee was a perfectionist and a professional. It was difficult, but I eventually learned how to work with him and how to bend with him. All you had to do was to give him respect and understanding and he gave you a lot back.

Outside the house, the guerrilla appears once more.

PB: That pattern was simply projection of light onto a screen. We had no electronic effects in those days, and I had to invent these projected light effects. They were done by a company called EM-Tech, run by a young couple who had just come out of art school and who were putting on discos. I was introduced to them, and they had all these different light-projected patterns, and they went away and developed the patterns that I was after. The moving light pattern was then projected onto a screen about one metre by one and a half metres, and I then positioned a camera on the other side of the screen – like back-projection. We then mixed the image of the light with the image of the characters appearing and disappering..

The guerrilla hears a whistling noise and runs. Just beside a railway arch, he is attacked and knocked to the ground by an Ogron (Rick Lester). Another Ogron (Maurice Bush) appears, and they head into the railway arch.

PB: The look of the Ogrons came about through sketches that I did while reading through the scripts. I showed these sketches to Barry Letts and told him that these were my initial ideas of what the Ogrons should look like. I do recall that the word 'Alsation' had been used in an earlier version of the scripts: that these creatures were the Daleks' guard dogs. I said that I didn't want to pursue that line, and that I saw them as more ape-like. I had this idea that they should be big men, and that the actors who played them should be, at a minimum, six foot six tall. I made that a condition. They were frightening by their size as well as by their make-up and their faces.

My intention with the monsters was always to frighten the kids. Their introduction in that scene was meant to be frightening. We had to be careful not to go too far with it, but the idea was to frighten the kids without being too grotesque.

[The rehearsal scripts describe the monsters – the name Ogrons does not appear – as 'Savage. Larger than life. They are humanoid in shape, with alien heads and hands.']

In Styles' study, the Doctor speaks with Miss Paget about the events of the previous night. Styles enters, and insists that nothing happened. The Doctor, however, has noticed muddy boot marks on the floor. Styles is preparing to leave for the airport and gives permission for the Brigadier's men to search the grounds.

DM-J: You can see in this scene that the chandelier has a braille line attached to it. Lighting technicians generally hate chandeliers; they have to be hung from the lighting bars in the studio, as the sets do not generally have ceilings. You indicate on your floor-plan where the chandelier is to be, and they then set it in that position. There is a diagonal wire, as well as the vertical one, used for positioning, and the cameraman would usually make sure that viewers can't see the wires holding up the chandelier.

PB: As a designer, I always used what are termed 'headers' on sets. These are ceilings and front pieces, things on top of the walls of the sets. I always insisted on seeing a ceiling where a ceiling should be seen. I wanted that study set to have a lot of depth to it, and I wanted it to have a visible ceiling. As to why the braille line is in shot … well … it shouldn't have been.

The guerrilla is found by the arch, and the Brigadier gets Captain Yates (Richard Franklin) to order an ambulance. There is a futuristic-looking gun beside the body, and Sergeant Benton (John Levene) finds a black box hidden 50 feet inside the tunnel.

In a control room in the future, the two Ogrons report to the Controller (Aubrey Woods). They claim to have found and destroyed the enemy. The Controller orders them to intensify their search for the guerrillas.

DM-J: The script gave only a very brief description for this set: 'a small austere room … control panels … a centre plinth'. I used the idea of the technicians sitting on seats attached to tracks so that they could move around. The whole set was up against a cyclorama, which had a dappled lighting effect thrown on it. The panels at the back were made from transparent perspex and were lit with coloured lights. The idea here was deliberately to give the idea of space, in contrast to Styles' study, which was very cluttered.

The Controller's chair was definitely hired from one of the more flamboyant hiring companies that we used. I think they were called Roy Moore and used to import the most extraordinary modern designs from Italy and the continent. You could never afford to build a chair like that. Even if you wanted to, it would have been very expensive. Again, it's prop-buying, and where you have to hire in a prop that is central and important to the overall design, then that single item can dictate how the rest of your designs may turn out. It's very important.

Back in Styles' study, the Doctor and the Brigadier report to Styles. He leaves for the airport. The unconscious guerrilla is put in an ambulance and, accompanied by Benton, taken to hospital.

Back in the Doctor's lab at UNIT HQ, the Doctor tests the gun. It is an ultrasonic disintegrator, however it was made on Earth. The Doctor shows Jo and the Brigadier the box found in the tunnel and explains that it is a crude time machine. He places a small circuit, which looks like a version of his TARDIS' dematerialisation circuit, in the box, and it starts to operate.

The guerrilla in the ambulance vanishes before Benton's eyes.

In the future, the Controller is advised by a technician (Deborah Brayshaw) that a time transference has taken place. It stops before they can track it. A Dalek orders the Controller to report.

[In the rehearsal script, this scene started with an exchange between the Controller and the Ogrons:

CONTROLLER: Well?

MONSTER: We are still searching.

CONTROLLER: You haven't found their headquarters?

MONSTER: We believe they are concealed in the tunnels beneath the city – the area is large...

CONTROLLER: I don't want excuses. Find them. Time is short.

This dialogue was cut from this scene and the earlier scene with the Controller and the Ogrons included to replace it.]

DM-J: The way that the technicians were operating their consoles was a deliberate attempt to be futuristic. We reasoned that there wouldn't be buttons and switches, but that all the controls could be worked by touch-sensitive panels.

I remember I wanted to get some long shots of that set. We put some sheets of moulded plastic, which glistened like coalite, under the technicians' seats. I wanted to get a feeling of interplanetary movement, and to have the technicians spinning around in space, but we never got round to it.

The Doctor notes that the machine has blown a fuse. Benton reports to the Brigadier that the guerrilla has vanished. The Doctor decides to spend the night at Styles' house, in case the attackers return.

At the house, the Doctor and Jo settle down for the night. Jo is nervous, but the Doctor enjoys the food and wine from Styles' cellars. Jo provides some food for Benton, but Yates takes it instead, citing RHIP – Rank Has Its Privileges – as his excuse.

DM-J: The tapestries on the walls were hired in. We didn't have anything like that especially painted for this story. It's important when designing rooms to realise that hiring a tapestry is cheaper than building scenery.

The BBC used to have a substantial stock of furniture and drapes, which you used as much as possible because it was free. Nowadays you have to hire it all in, which is very expensive.

[The sequence where Jo offers Benton some cheese and wine only to have Yates take it instead is not in the rehearsal script but is present in the camera script.]

Outside the house, UNIT troops are all positioned. Down by the railway arch, three more guerrillas, Anat (Anna Barry), Shura (Jimmy Winston) and Boaz (Scott Fredericks) appear. Their leader, Anat, says that they will wait until light.

At first light on 13 September, the Doctor pulls back the curtains, waking Jo up. Two UNIT soldiers patrolling by the railway tunnel are disintegrated by Shura.

PB: Because the tunnel was alongside a canal, I hired a barge and we used that to film some of the scenes from.

At UNIT HQ, a message is received by a radio operator (Gypsie Kemp) concerning the international situation, and it does not look good. All UNIT personnel are placed on maximum alert.

DM-J: The table in the foreground breaks the rules about the 'fourth wall' that you never see on television. You can see the edge of the table at the front, and the camera should have been closer so that you couldn't see it. There is supposed to be a wall there, and yet it looks like the table is, for no apparent reason, sitting in the middle of the room.

PB: I can't remember who I got to do the voices on the radio in that scene, or the Minister who speaks to the Brigadier on the telephone. As I had a sound booth in the studio to do the Dalek voices, it was most likely the same two people who did these other voices. That would have made economic sense.

Shura enters the house and fights with the Doctor. The machine is operating on the table.
The Controller is advised that the time machine is operating again. The Controller reports to the Daleks that his underlings are trying to obtain the time/space co-ordinates.

PB: One of my requirements was to use CSO to key a picture onto a mock TV screen and then to be able to alter the composition of the shot with the screen in, without the image on the screen jumping all over the place. The engineers came up with a system – I think it was called Gaze – where two cameras were locked onto one master zoom control. They used it in *Top of the Pops* after us, and also in some sports programmes.

The Daleks (Murphy Grumbar, Ricky Newby, John Scott Martin; voices: Oliver Gilbert, Peter Messaline) order that whoever is operating the time machine must be exterminated.

DM-J: One way to get over the fact that you can't build miles of scenery, is to use screens of reflective material. You reflect one into the other all the way down a corridor, and give the illusion of depth when there isn't any present. On this occasion, unfortunately, the use of all the reflective surfaces doesn't really work, and the room that the Daleks are in looks small and cramped.

[The original idea in the rehearsal script was that the Daleks' operations room should be a vast hall, with twenty or thirty Daleks operating the equipment.]

End of Episode One

Episode Two

Anat and Boaz enter Styles' study with Jo, and order the Doctor to switch off the machine.
The Controller enters the Daleks' room and tells them that the trace has gone. The Daleks order him to find the rebels.

PB: I like the door, because it's quite ominous in the way it takes a long time to open. Not like those very clever jigsaw things that slide apart in a flash. I remember I wanted something that took its time.

DM-J: All the camera script said was 'the big door opens', and I decided to use it opening like some great hydraulic thing rather than a standard door. It was attached to wires, which were attached to hoists in the studio and lifted up.

The guerrillas assume that the Doctor is Sir Reginald Styles and prepare to kill him, until the Doctor points out their mistake. They all hide in the cellar when Benton and Yates come looking for the Doctor and Jo.

DM-J: You can see a skylight above them in the cellar. That is known as 'doing things cheaply'. The skylight would have come from stock, and you can't alter it, all you can do is shine a light through it. It works to give the impression of a skylight, but it is a very cheap and simple effect.

When they have gone, the guerrillas tie the Doctor and Jo up and return to the study.

PB: I think this sort of scene where Jo and the Doctor simply chatted formed a part of the character of *Doctor Who*, particularly with Pertwee playing it. His character fitted in with this kind of loose Chinese philosophy on life.

In the future, the Daleks attach a time vortex magnetron to the equipment. Anyone using the time transfer machine will now be diverted to the control centre.

PB: When we went and looked in the BBC's storeroom where all the old props from the series were kept, we could find only three and a half Daleks. We refurbished three of them, and I used the half-Dalek several times as a 'blown up' one. We simply didn't have the money to make any more, so bravely I said that I could make it work.

At the house, Anat cannot make contact with her base, due to interference in the time vortex. Shura returns to the tunnel to try and make contact from there. He encounters an Ogron but manages to kill it before hiding himself.

[In the rehearsal script, Shura hid himself in the tunnels, but in the transmitted scene he runs off back towards the house.]

Unable to find the Doctor and Jo, Yates and Benton report to the Brigadier. He telephones the house, and Anat gets the Doctor to answer the call. The Doctor alerts UNIT to the fact that all is not well by using the phrase 'Tell it to the marines'.

Jo manages to free herself and grabs the box. It operates, and she is transported into the control centre in the future.

[The effect of the time vortex was achieved with a stock lens fixed to a camera. The lens was a multi-image lens-rotating prism, which had previously been bought by technical manager Bernard Fox for a previous *Doctor Who*, at which time the cost had been shared with *Top of the Pops*.]

PB: The effect of Jo spinning was done in the studio. It was done using a 20:1 zoom lens, and we got the distance by shooting into a mirror mounted on the lighting gantry. Katy was lying on a black covered rostrum, and she simply waved her arms and legs about as we zoomed out from her image in the mirror, rotating the lens as we did it. The lighting effect also served to cover up the image around Katy, as much of the studio was visible.

The Controller is cordial and friendly, and gets Jo to tell him exactly where and on which date she left her time.

DM-J: The set is actually a lot bigger than it looks on screen. As a designer, you try and provide something that will look good and that will also suit the requirements of the director. Unfortunately, there is no requirement that says he has to show all your set!

With this information, the Daleks prepare an ambush in the railway tunnel. They intend to go themselves to ensure there are no mistakes.

The Doctor is tied up, but he frees himself. Anat and Boaz run as the house is attacked by Ogrons (Rick Lester, Maurice Bush, David Joyce, Frank Menzies, Geoffrey Todd, Bruce Wells).

DM-J: Visual Effects would have built the French windows and inserted them into the set for the scene where the Ogron smashes into the house. We had to make some effort to ensure that the interior of this room matched the windows on the outside of the house.

The Doctor manages to elude the Ogrons thanks to the timely intervention of the Brigadier, and follows the guerrillas to the railway tunnel, where he sees a Dalek.

End of Episode Two

Episode Three

After seeing the Dalek, the guerrillas and the Doctor are transported 200 years into the future to the 22nd Century.

[According to the rehearsal script, the guerrillas had come from the 24th Century.]

PB: That effect was not quite as successful as the last one. It's a little off-centre. Today they would be able to correct something like that electronically, but we had no such facilities. They're really spoilt these days.

The Doctor tells them that he knows of the Daleks, and they explain that the creatures have ruled Earth for more than a century. The Ogrons attack, and they split up and run off.

The Doctor finds a ladder and ascends out through a hatch onto an area of wasteland.

DM-J: I remember putting that hatch in. There was a hole in the ground, which was either dug for us or was there already, and the hatchway was made especially by us.

PB: We didn't dig the hole; it was there already.

The Controller reports to the Daleks that the rebels have escaped. When he mentions that Jo spoke of someone called the Doctor, the Daleks become agitated. They tell the Controller that he is an enemy of the Daleks and must be exterminated.

[The rehearsal script contains an additional scene prior to the above, in which two monsters give a report to the Controller that they have not found any of the rebels. One of the monsters also mentions that one of those who travelled to their time was dressed strangely and was called 'Doctor'.]

The Doctor makes his way to a work centre, where old men, women and children are toiling. He is seen on a security camera.

DM-J: The security camera was provided by Visual Effects. We supplied the huge door that the Doctor opens to get into the work centre.

Anat and Boaz are met by their leader, Monia (Valentine Palmer), at their hideout. Monia knows that Jo is in the control centre.

PB: Those were old buildings belonging to the abandoned British Rail goods yard. It was a wonderful location, with just about everything we wanted.

The Doctor is captured by Ogrons.

[According to the rehearsal script, just before the Doctor is captured, he sees one of the guards on a motor tricycle. This scene is emphasised in Bernard's own film schedule, but does not appear in the transmitted story.]
The Controller shares a meal with Jo. He is told that the Doctor has been captured, and assures Jo that he is safe and well.

DM-J: All those dishes and other tableware were especially made for the production. This is also the same set as the main control room, re-dressed and with different colours thrown onto the background.

The Doctor is being interrogated by the senior guard (Andrew Carr).

DM-J: The cell set is very simple. The bars at the back are standard stock set elements – something like P68 Stock Cell Units – which I positioned to give the idea of bars. Again, you can see the tops of the bars, and it would perhaps have been better if the shot had not been so wide, as it looks insecure.

The Centre Manager (Peter Hill) arrives and, once the senior guard has gone, tries to assure the Doctor that he is on the guerrillas' side. However, the Controller arrives and has the Doctor freed as his guest. The Manager transmits a report to Monia, telling him that the Doctor is important to the Daleks. Suddenly an Ogron smashes the Manager's transmitter.
Although the Controller is friendly, the Doctor is not prepared to listen to him. He knows that the Daleks rule in this time and that the Controller is a mere quisling. The Daleks plan to use a mind analysis machine on the Doctor to determine if he is their old enemy, as his appearance has changed. The Doctor and Jo knock their Ogron guard unconcious and escape on a three wheeled power-trike. They are, however, recaptured..

PB: Someone had told me about these little trikes that they were using on a 007 production at Pinewood – *Diamonds are Forever*, I think it was – and I thought this sounded like a great idea. I saw them on a documentary about the making of the film, and so we asked if we could get one. It was written in the script as a motor tricycle, and this balloon-wheeled vehicle was absolutely ideal.

During a publicity session for the story, Jon and Katy were like children. Every moment they could, they leaped onto it and drove it around. We all did.

DM-J: The trikes were brought into the production, and they really worked well. Although the chase is short, it is effective. It's all good, harmless stuff.

Monia decides that they must rescue the Doctor.
The Daleks place the Doctor under the mind analysis machine.

[Photographs of William Hartnell and Patrick Troughton were overlaid onto a sequence of graphics from the title sequence, representing the operation of the mind analysis machine on the Doctor. The image was keyed using CSO onto a yellow CSO board, which was suspended in the set.]

PB: I remember this scene being quite traumatic to do, because we had to make the image that appears on the CSO screen fit the picture. The image had to be created so that it filled the whole of the TV screen, but we were only 'seeing' a small strip of the image at the top. We had to make sure that the portion that was going to be seen had the correct patterns and pictures in it.

End of Episode Three

Episode Four

The Controller stops the Daleks from exterminating the Doctor and promises that he can get information from him.

[As scripted, the scene in which the Doctor is taken away starts with an extra exchange between the Doctor and the Daleks:

> DR WHO: I've defeated you before. I introduced the human factor into the Daleks on Skaro. There was a rebellion …
>
> DALEK 2: The rebellion was unsuccessful. The rogue Daleks were hunted down and exterminated.
>
> DR WHO: I defeated you here on Earth too. Your invasion failed.]

Monia, Anat and Boaz work out how best to rescue the Doctor.

[This scene was completely restructured for the studio recording. The following is the camera script version:

> (THE GUERRILLAS ARE PREPARING THEIR GEAR READY FOR THE ATTACK.

GUNS BEING INSPECTED)

BOAZ: (TO A GUERRILLA) Explosives?

(THE GUERRILLA HOLDS UP SOME POUCHES WHICH HE THEN PROCEEDS TO STUFF INSIDE HIS BATTLE DRESS)

Mind how you handle that stuff; it's still pretty unstable.

(BOAZ MOVES OVER TO WHERE MONIA IS DISCUSSING THE PLAN FOR THE ATTACK WITH ANAT. THEY HAVE VARIOUS PLANS LAID OUT BEFORE THEM

ANAT: Can't Jacob help us? He runs the Work Centre?

(BOAZ CROSSES TO JOIN THEM)
MONIA: Jacob was executed this afternoon.

ANAT: You mean when …

MONIA: That's right. They picked him up when he was contacting us about the Doctor.

ANAT: Oh no.

(A MOMENT)

BOAZ: Then how *do* we get through?

MONIA: The underground network of the old city. There's an exit just by this wall.

(THEY LOOK AT THE MAP)

ANAT: That network used to run under the whole town. Trains every few minutes. I've read about it.

BOAZ: Even as a ruin it has its uses.

MONIA: Come. Time is short.]

The Controller explains to the Doctor that Dalek rule started with 100 years of human war, which wiped out seven eighths of the population, leaving the Earth open to Dalek attack. The Daleks are using the Earth to provide raw materials for their ongoing war against all other life forms.

The guerrillas attack the centre to try and rescue the Doctor.

PB: When we came to film this sequence at the car-park, that rubbish skip was there and we couldn't do anything about it. I may have asked for it to be painted, but we just had to work around it.

DM-J: I remember that horrible yellow dustbin there. I should have done something about it. At the time, you think that no-one will notice it and that maybe it looks slightly futuristic.

Boaz is killed, but the Doctor and Jo are freed. The Doctor insists that the guerrillas leave the Controller alive as they make their escape.

[A short extra scene appeared in the camera script following this sequence. It was of the guerrillas arriving back at their underground bunker.]

Back in the 20th Century, UNIT are searching for the Doctor and Jo, but to no avail. [This scene featured a UNIT soldier with an Alsation dog. The dog was hired from a company called Zoo Animal Actors.]

[A scene where Shura emerges from hiding has been lost here.]

Monia and Anat explain to the Doctor and Jo that the wars started when Styles caused an explosion that destroyed the house in which the peace conference was taking place. The guerrillas therefore decided to kill Styles and allow the conference to go ahead. They now want the Doctor to return to kill Styles for them.

PB: I was pleased with this scene, because the guerrillas were being played by three good actors. As a director, it was satisfying to get them to settle down and emote rather than to just go through the motions and the lines.

Shura emerges from hiding and heads for the house. He breaks into the cellar and sets up the bomb he has been carrying.
  The Doctor realises that Shura is still in the past, and that Anat's party had some dalekanium explosive with them. It was Shura who caused the explosion – by trying to change history, they have created their own future.
  The Daleks set up an ambush in the tunnels to try and recapture the Doctor.

DM-J: Although this is the same set as in the earlier episode, the door to the section that the Daleks are in is completely different: it slides up on runners rather than being hinged at the top and hoisted on wires. The reason for this is that the sets for episodes three and four are in a different studio session from those for episodes one and two. Because of the need to put all the sets into the same studio, we didn't have room to put the full control room in: only a part of it was needed for these episodes, and the fabric of that set was being re-used for the area where the Doctor and Jo were being held. Therefore, what has happened is that the Daleks' room is there, but the control room is not. The door changed probably because there wasn't enough room in the studio to use the hinged door.

When the Doctor and Jo arrive in the tunnels in order to return to the 20thCentury to try and stop Shura, they are confronted by the Controller. The Doctor convinces him to let them go.

The Doctor and Jo run from the tunnel in the 20th Century, and Benton reports to the Brigadier that they have been found.

Unfortunately the senior guard witnessed the Controller's actions, and the Controller is exterminated by the Daleks.

[The Daleks' extermination effect, during which the picture goes into negative, was achieved using a technical device called a Complimentary Picture Amplifier (previously known as an NPA within the BBC).]

The senior guard becomes the new Controller. The Daleks decide to invade the past themselves, to ensure that the conference is destroyed and that war breaks out.

[A short camera-scripted scene is missing here, showing Shura priming the bomb.]

A newscaster (Alex MacIntosh) announces the arrival of Styles and the delegates at the house.

PB: Alex MacIntosh was a real-life news presenter but had retired from being on the front-line and was freelancing at the time we made this story.

[According to the BBC's files, a Rolls Royce (MWF 435F) and a Daimler (AWP 633H) that had been hired for filming were damaged by adhesive signs that were affixed to the doors. The BBC's insurance did not cover this damage as it was not considered to be accidental, and the production had to foot the bill for repairs, which came to £239. However, there are no insignia or logos visible on either of the two cars in the footage used in the episode.]

PB: I put nothing on those cars except a small flag on the bonnet. I saw no need to.

The Doctor arrives and manages to convince the Brigadier to evacuate the house, and all the delegates leave.

[Jean McFarlane was originally to have appeared in this scene as Styles' secretary, but the actress had fallen ill and was unavailable. Her lines were given to an aide instead.]

Daleks and Ogrons emerge from the tunnel and storm the house.

UNIT troops fight them but cannot stop them. The Doctor finds Shura in the basement and explains what is happening. The Daleks enter the house. Shura tells the Doctor and Jo to leave. He intends to destroy the house and the Daleks with it.

PB: The worst thing about the design of the Daleks was that they could only run on smooth surfaces. We therefore had to lay boards down over the ground that the Daleks were to cross. This meant that I had to be very careful with how I placed the camera, so that we didn't see the boards. Considering that we had only six Ogrons, three Daleks and about ten UNIT guys, it was a hard battle to make work on screen. I did have the benefit of film editing, which allowed me to cut the shots together so that they had a lot of dramatic impact.

The Doctor tells the Brigadier to let the Daleks pass, and the troops fall back. The Daleks move through the house, looking for Styles and the delegates, and Shura detonates the bomb. The house is completely destroyed.

DM-J: That is an incredibly good model of the house, and it matches the real house superbly. It's a brilliant explosion.

The Doctor tells Styles that the peace conference has been saved.

PB: The explosion that they see in the distance was done on the waste ground that we had been using.
[There is a final scene in the camera script, which does not appear in the finished production. It starts with the Doctor and Jo walking towards the UNIT lab and pushing open the doors to see another Doctor and another Jo inside. There then follows exactly the same exchange as seen in episode one, ending with the Doctor and Jo in the lab vanishing. The scene then continues:

DR WHO: There you are, they've gone!

(THE BRIGADIER ENTERS)

JO: Doctor, what happened?

DR WHO: Very complicated thing, time. Once you've begun tampering with it, the oddest things start happening.

BRIGADIER: Doctor, what's going on here?

DR WHO: Nothing for you to worry about old chap.

BRIGADIER: For one ghastly moment I thought I saw two of you!

DR WHO: (NOW JOKING AGAIN) Exactly.

BRIGADIER: You mean there *were* two of you?

DR WHO: That's right.

JO: But which of us was the real us?

DR WHO: Both.

(THE BRIGADIER SHAKES HIS HEAD TRYING TO WORK IT OUT)

JO: Doctor – that future we went to – with Daleks ruling Earth. Is it going to happen or isn't it?

DR WHO: Well. It is and it isn't.

BRIGADIER: Oh come along Doctor.

DR WHO: First it is – then it isn't. There are all kinds of futures, you know.

JO: Futures with Daleks in?

(DR WHO STOPS WORK FOR A MOMENT)

DR WHO: It's possible Jo.

BRIGADIER: But surely the Daleks were all destroyed …

DR WHO: I thought I'd destroyed them once before, but I was wrong. I must get the Tardis working again, Jo. I think I'm going to need it.

Although this scene was scripted, it is unlikely that it was actually recorded.

PB: I was never one for an anti-climax. Once you had reached the end, then that was it. The ending that the transmitted story has is much more my style, and I think that the addition of that final scene in the script does create an anti-climax. I suspect it was removed before we started filming and recording the story. It may also have been omitted because of a lack of time

Post-production

In the early Seventies, episodes of *Doctor Who* were recorded two at a time, and all the scenes for one episode were generally recorded in the order they would be transmitted, or else grouped by set, depending on technical requirements or director preference. All the film sequences were prepared in advance and then 'played in' at the appropriate time onto the videotape master. Much of the videotape editing for *Day of the Daleks* was also carried out 'in-camera' at the time of recording.

'By the time we got to record in the studio, all the film sequences would have been edited together,' explained Bernard. 'The shots were filmed and edited together based on my film script, but you would go at the end of the rehearsal day to see the film editor in order to check and approve what had been done.

'By the time you got into studio, the film sequences were ready, and you played them in to add the effects and links to the recorded material live in the studio. You were expected to end up with the show pretty much as it would be transmitted. All

THIRD DOCTOR

that was missing was the music and sound effects, assuming that we hadn't added them in live as well.'

Dudley Simpson was hired to compose and create the incidental music – as usual at this point in the series' history.

'Dudley and I got on very well,' remembered Bernard. 'When I joined Thames Television, I took him with me, and he created the music for *The Tomorrow People*. We worked together very closely. I used to sit with him and go through the story in order to plan out where the music would fall.

'My feeling was that music had been used too often and too much in *Doctor Who*, but there was this philosophy that *Doctor Who* had to be supported by music. I don't think I overused it in *Day of the Daleks*. Dudley was very, very talented, and he could watch a story with me, and then thirty six hours later return with a finished score to start recording the music.'

On this story, Simpson hired two further musicians to create the music, and the score was recorded on 25 October 1971.

At the same time as Simpson was composing the music, Brian Hodgson from the BBC's Radiophonic Workshop was working on the special sound effects. These were added to the edited videotape, together with the music, at dubbing sessions that took place on the following dates: 28 October 1971 (episode 1), 29 October 1971 (episode 2), 3 November 1971 (episode 3) and 4 November 1971 (episode 4).

'I think *Day of the Daleks* stands up very well,' commented Bernard. 'I think it's slow in parts, but that comes partly from the indoctrination of television in the Nineties, which is very fast and furious.

'I look back on the two years I was involved with *Doctor Who* and *The Tomorrow People* as perhaps the most creative period of my career. I was firing on five cylinders, and had to be. The amount of creativity that needed to be generated was massive. It was a very exciting time, and I'm very proud to have been involved with it.'

Transmission

Day of the Daleks was the first story in the ninth season, and was transmitted between 1 January and 22 January 1972.

It was heralded, as was each of the third Doctor's seasons, with a *Radio Times* cover. This was a painting especially commissioned from artist Frank Bellamy. Inside the magazine could be found a competition to win a Dalek of your own. The prizes were billed as 'mark 7' Daleks, and were in fact a number of specially commissioned Dalek toys. They were around two and a half feet tall and were operated by a control box mounted upon a stalk that projected from the rear of the Dalek. An edition of the BBC's regional news programme *Nationwide* on Tuesday 22 February 1972 featured a film report covering the delivery of a 'mark 7' Dalek to a winning junior school.

To enter the competition, readers were invited to complete a story that had been started by Terry Nation.

According to the *Radio Times*:

> Among the things that Dr Who most treasures is a crumpled and grubby piece of paper, a single page from the log of the Spaceguard patrol ship *Defender*. The edges of the page were charred by the fire that burned out

the *Defender* when she re-entered the atmosphere of Earth too fast after returning from her mission on the planet Destron.

The being who wrote these words is long dead or has not yet been born, for the event he describes may be in the past or the future. In deep space, time as we know it has no meaning.

The events of which this single page tells intrigued the Doctor for many years. Finally his curiosity overcame his natural caution and he could resist no longer. He set the controls in the TARDIS, and with Jo started for Destron. The moment they were under way he handed Jo the page from the log. If all goes well, Dr Who and Jo will reach Destron. They may face the same dangers as the crew of the *Defender*. Perhaps become involved in the great battle. Anything might happen …

The story was then started by Nation as the text of this note, and this described the planet Destron and explained the mission of the note's anonymous author: to stop Destron's weaponry from falling into the hands of the Daleks.

Following a cliff-hanger ending, entrants had to take up the story, telling it as though they were there. The story was to be concluded in less than 400 words, and three drawings were also to be included: a landscape of Destron; some of the monsters that inhabit it; and the battle between the crew of *Defender* and the Daleks.

Some of the competition entries were displayed at the Ceylon Tea Centre in London during March and April 1972, along with a small exhibition of *Doctor Who* props, including an Axon, Alpha Centauri, Aggedor, Arcturus and, of course, a Dalek. Everyone whose work was displayed received a special certificate to commemorate the fact.

A special trailer is reported to have been commissioned for *Day of the Daleks*, but no documentary evidence has been found to support this. This was allegedly filmed on location in central London and featured the Daleks patrolling many famous landmarks.

The story's transmission gained favourable ratings; the highest yet received by a third Doctor story. Despite this, the press were not kind in their criticism.

'Behind all the technological patter about ultrasonic disintegrators, *Doctor Who* appears to have been reduced to a single basic theme: the defeat of a world domination league,' complained Matthew Coady of the *Daily Mirror*, his feelings being echoed by Chris Kenworthy in the *Sun*.

Even Jon Pertwee made his dislike of the Daleks public, and subsequently singled out this particular show as one of the worst that he had done, although he was to revise this opinion shortly before his death in 1996.

Whatever the criticisms of the show, the Daleks had once more worked their magic, and the ninth season of *Doctor Who* was off to a flying start.

CREDITS

Director	Paul Bernard
Producer	Barry Letts
Production Assistant	Norman Stewart
Assistant Floor Manager	Sue Heddon
Assistant	Carolyn Driver

Floor Assistant	John O'Shaughnessy
Script Editor	Terrance Dicks
Production Secretary	Sarah Newman
Designer	David Myerscough-Jones
Costume Designer	Mary Husband
Make-Up Artist	Heather Stewart
Visual Effects	Jim Ward
Fight Arranger	Rick Lester
Film Editor	Dan Rae
Film Cameraman	Fred Hamilton
Assistant	Brian Easton
	Brian Johns
Sound Supervisor	Tony Millier
Sound Recordist	Chris King
Grams	Gordon Phillipson
TM1	Alan Horne
TM2	Derek Martin (eps 1, 2), Alan Arbuthnott (eps 3, 4)
Assistant	Norman Johnstone
Grips	Tex Childs
Vision Mixer	Mike Catherwood
Graphics	Sid Lomax
Crew	10
Title Music	Ron Grainer and the BBC Radiophonic Workshop
Incidental Music	Dudley Simpson
Special Sound	Brian Hodgson
Writer	Louis Marks
Daleks Originated by	Terry Nation

SELLING THE DOCTOR

MEDIA

Unlike any of the previous actors to have played the Doctor, Jon Pertwee was the media's darling. William Hartnell had neither the presence nor the trendiness, while Patrick Troughton had preferred to leave the character of the Doctor in the studio, and when he did consent to give an interview, it tended to be as an evasive and mischievous version of his on-screen persona.

Pertwee, on the other hand, actively courted the press. Here was an actor with many different facets to his character, whether they be in his professon as an actor, or his interest in gardening or motorcycling, or even a penchant for deep sea diving and an appreciation of moustache cups. When Troughton's intention to stand down from *Doctor Who* was announced in January 1969, there was minimal attention from the press. The previous changeover, from Hartnell to Troughton, had also been a low key affair; there had not even been a press call to announce the new Doctor, and therefore there had been few photographs and scant column inches given over to the event.

With Pertwee's arrival, however, there was much more excitement over the change-over.

The press launch in June 1969 to announce Pertwee's appointment was very well attended, and the idea of bringing in a Yeti for the proverbial 'photo opportunity' was inspired. This resulted in coverage in many of the national newspapers the following day.

The press seemed initially interested in the change in direction that the series would be taking: a move away from the outer space adventures of the past, with the Doctor being brought down to Earth with a bang. Comments were made about the fact that the stories were going to be more adult, that the new companions – the Brigadier and Liz Shaw – were more aimed at an adult audience, and that Pertwee himself was going to play the Doctor as a serious character. He even noted in one early interview that, 'It will be set on Earth in the 1980s. I won't be wearing the Victorian clothes that the other Doctor Whos have used. I will be in a modern day suit.'

The producer, Peter Bryant, also said, in another interview, 'The new stories will be more realistic, with a sort of Quatermass flavour. We have an audience now which is adult sophisticated.'

Even Shaun Sutton, the BBC's Head of Drama, commented, 'The Daleks marching down Piccadilly is much more horrifying than anything up in space. This is real science fiction.'

This intention of making *Doctor Who* more adult and realistic resulted in an unexpected backlash. *Spearhead from Space* showed shop dummies coming alive and attacking shoppers, while *Terror of the Autons* depicted lethal plastic daffodils, a toy troll doll coming alive and strangling someone, and, worst of all, a policeman revealed to be a faceless killer robot rather than a trustworthy figure of law and order. These two stories managed to redefine the way in which the media perceived *Doctor Who*. Up until that point, it had been a curiosity. A show that was looked upon as providing gentle thrills and spills for viewers of all ages. Now it was a subject of national concern, as Mrs Mary Whitehouse of the National Viewers and Listeners Association repeatedly condemned the show as a bad influence on children's minds.

This criticism of excessive violence and horror was levelled at *Doctor Who* time and again during Pertwee's time as the Doctor, and the actor consistently countered these arguments by asserting that the ratings were very good, that parents did know that there was an 'off' switch on their television sets, and that he had personally met many hundreds of children to whom *Doctor Who* had done no harm whatsoever. In fact, the production team almost came to welcome Mrs Whitehouse's comments, as they always got covered by the press and ensured that *Doctor Who* was rarely out of the public eye.

Throughout the first half of the Seventies, it was the BBC's own listings magazine *Radio Times* that remained the strongest supporter of the show. The opening episode of every season was afforded a front cover on the magazine, something that no other Doctor could claim – Hartnell had been granted three covers, as had Troughton, but after the end of the Pertwee era, the coverage in the *Radio Times* would drop off to the extent that the only other cover to be granted while *Doctor Who* was regularly on the air was for the twentieth anniversary show, *The Five Doctors*, in 1983.

Not only were there covers, but there were also a great many features to be found inside the magazine. These ranged from fairly standard features on the cast, to a special feature on the making of the show, which ran as *Inferno* started transmission in 1970, and a three page comic strip painted by Frank Bellamy for the start of *Colony in Space*. Mid way through Pertwee's tenure, Bellamy started to provide small artwork images, which were included with the television listing each week, and occasionally larger pieces for specific stories, including *The Dæmons*. Occasionally other artists would be commissioned for pieces in a similar style, as for *The Time Warrior*.

As previously mentioned, Pertwee was a media magnet. This meant that there were numerous opportunities for 'lifestyle' pieces revolving around his love for motor bikes, gardening, lavishly decorated homes and his family. Pertwee was a true 'action man', and he seemed to be forever opening fetes and shopping centres, dressed in his *Doctor Who* outfit and driving, first Bessie, and then his special *Doctor Who* car that was later dubbed 'the Whomobile'.

Doctor Who found itself being promoted on a great many other shows. These included, in 1970, *Junior Points of View*, which made unfavourable comparisons with *Star Trek*. *Junior Points of View* became *Ask Aspel* and in 1971, it reported some children as saying that *Doctor Who* was not as scary as it used to be, and made a comparison by showing clips from the first Troughton story *The Power of the Daleks* and from *Terror of the Autons*. *This is Your Life* came knocking on Pertwee's door in 1971, and on 21 October 1971 the Daleks made an appearance on *Blue Peter*, hinting that they would be back in the new season. In December of 1971, the *Young Observer* magazine reported on an event at London's Planetarium, which featured Pertwee and Barry Letts talking about *Doctor Who* and displaying various props and monsters from the series. This event was hosted by *Blue Peter* presenter Peter Purves, who had himself, of course, appeared in *Doctor Who* as the Doctor's companion Steven Taylor back in 1965 and 1966.

Following up the 'Win A Dalek' competition in the *Radio* Times, the BBC's local news programme, *Nationwide*, carried a feature on 22 February 1972 on the delivery of a Dalek to one of the winning schools. Pertwee was the guest on *Ask Aspel* on 5 March 1972. In addition, the two Dalek cinema films from the Sixties made their debut on television during the Pertwee era. The first film, *Dr Who and the Daleks*, was shown on 1 July 1972, and the second film, *Daleks Invasion Earth: 2150 A.D.*, was shown on 19 August the same year. The BBC's Special Effects Exhibition at the Science Museum in London featured a *Doctor Who* display, and ran from December 1972 until June 1973. Its opening was featured on the 7 December edition of *Nationwide*.

On 10 Jan 1973, *Pebble Mill* had as its guests Troughton and Pertwee talking about *The Three Doctors*; and on 28 May 1973, Pertwee presented *Disney Time*. *Nationwide* also covered Katy Manning's departure from the show on 22 June 1973; Pertwee and a selection of monsters attended the Lord Mayor's show on 10 November 1973; *Blue Peter* on 5 November 73 covered the forthcoming season and unveiled the Whomobile to the public; while on *Nationwide* on 14 December 73, script editor Terrance Dicks appeared to talk about *Doctor Who* winning a BAFTA award for its scripts. Finally in 1973, on 21 December, *Pebble Mill* again featured *Doctor Who*, this time with Troughton and visual effects designer Bernard Wilkie demonstrating some monsters and effects. On 6 January 1974, Billy Smart's Circus featured a guest appearance by Pertwee with his Whomobile.

THE TENTH ANNIVERSARY

Doctor Who's tenth anniversary fell in 1973, and to celebrate it, the production team decided to commission a special story that would feature all three Doctors. This act established a precedent that was to last for the next twenty years, as each major anniversary would be marked with a special story in which the Doctor's past incarnations came together to defeat some evil menace. *The Three Doctors* resulted in less publicity than had been hoped, perhaps because the press had by now become bored with always reporting the same thing: that *Doctor Who* was too violent. The angle of 'sex in the TARDIS' had not yet been discovered by the tabloids, and so, whereas in later years if the Doctor's assistant wore something revealing then it became practically front page news, back in the early Seventies, the costumes worn by Katy Manning as Jo Grant barely raised an eyebrow.

The anniversary was also marked by the *Radio Times* releasing a special magazine. The only piece of factual writing readily available at this time was Malcolm Hulke's and Terrance Dicks' *The Making of Doctor Who* (which had been released as a paperback book by Pan in 1972), and therefore the *Radio Times Tenth Anniversary Special* was a milestone in the history of *Doctor Who* publishing. It collected together information and photographs from the entire history of *Doctor Who*, putting it all in context and including interviews with the Doctors and companions, as well as a new story by the creator of the Daleks, Terry Nation, and, for all those budding engineers who had written in to the BBC asking how to build a Dalek, plans for doing just that.

The magazine was very well received, and firmly established that the series had a history that was every bit as important as the current show. As this was the first piece of commercially available material that detailed the early days of the programme, there were a number of mistakes made, most notably in the titles given to some of the Hartnell stories, which had not been afforded overall titles on their transmission. (Up until *The Gunfighters* in 1966, all *Doctor Who* episodes had individual titles.) In compiling the special, in many cases the title of the first episode of a story was taken as being the overall title of the story itself, resulting in much confusion over subsequent years as to what the overall titles actually were.

Concluding the celebrations, the production team held a party on 10 December 1973, to which cast and crew were invited, along with selected members of the press.

MERCHANDISE

No new merchandise was released in 1970 to tie in with Pertwee's debut season. The first items associated with his Doctor started to appear in 1971, as merchandisers began to catch on to the potential of his Doctor. An early promotional tie-in was for a Kellogg's breakfast cereal, Sugar Smacks. The Doctor was shown on the front of all the boxes over the promotional period, and six small metal badges were given away inside the packs. The 'tag line' for the promotion was that Sugar Smacks endowed the consumer with: 'The Timeless Energy of Doctor Who'. The badges were particularly of interest, as they appear to have been the first examples of metal badges released to tie in with *Doctor Who*. The Doctor was also used as the basis of a promotion for one of Nestlé's ranges of milk chocolate bars, with a series of 15 different wrappers being issued, collectively telling the story of the Doctor's battle against the Master's 'Masterplan Q'. The other items released in 1971 were a set of two *Doctor Who* jigsaws from Michael Stanfield Holdings, which featuring photographs of the Doctor, and an iron on transfer of a Dalek issued by Dodo Iron-Ons.

Although a *Doctor Who* Annual had not been produced by World Distributors for 1972 (the reason for this is unknown) it returned for a 1973 edition and featured a photographic cover showing the Doctor in the UNIT laboratory from *Terror of the Autons*. A further *Doctor Who* Annual was to be published for each of the remaining years that Pertwee played the Doctor.

1972 saw even more interest in the series, as a further two jigsaws were released in the Michael Stanfield Holdings range; *The Making of Doctor Who* by Hulke and Dicks was published by Pan through their children's imprint, Piccolo Books; a poster showing the Doctor menaced by a claw from *Colony in Space* was released, only to be hastily withdrawn at the request of Pertwee and replaced with a photograph of the Doctor and a Sea Devil instead; and the BBC Special Effects Exhibition at the Science Museum resulted in two more metal badges being issued, conferring on their wearer the rank of 'TARDIS Commander'.

Finally, in time for the Christmas market, Pertwee lent his vocal talents to a single called 'Who Is The Doctor', which was released on the Purple record label.

1973 saw the launch, in May, of the Target range of *Doctor Who* novelisations. Published by Allan Wingate in hardback and by Universal Tandem in paperback, the range kicked off with reprints of the three novels from the Sixties: *Doctor Who in an exciting adventure with the Daleks* (renamed to the simpler *Doctor Who and the Daleks*), *The Crusaders* and *The Zarbi*. These were followed in 1974 by newly commissioned novelisations of *Spearhead from Space* (called *The Auton Invasion*), *Doctor Who and the Silurians* (*The Cave Monsters*), *Day of the Daleks*, *Colony In Space* (*The Doomsday Weapon*), *The Dæmons*, *The Sea Devils*, *The Abominable Snowmen* and *The Curse of Peladon*. These books established the Target range and kicked off a publishing phenomenon that was to last for as long as the original *Doctor Who* series and beyond.

Also in 1973, the BBC finally re-issued the Ron Grainer *Doctor Who* theme on a single. Also made available in this format was a track called *The World of Doctor Who*, which appeared as the 'B' side to Dudley Simpson's title music for the BBC series *Moonbase 3* and included music from *The Mind of Evil* and the Master Theme from season eight. With the first of the BBC's *Doctor Who* exhibitions opening at Longleat House, another metal badge was released; another set of four jigsaws was produced, this time from Whitman Publishing; World Distributors published a *Doctor Who* colouring book; and the *Doctor Who* Space Mission Pad, a set of code sheets and carbon paper, was mad available by Naocraft Ltd.

Finally, Polystyle Publications, the publishers of *TV Comic*, which had been running a *Doctor Who* comic strip for many years, released in 1973 a *Doctor Who Holiday Special*. This featured *Doctor Who* comic strips and stories and a look behind the scenes at the story *Frontier in Space*. A second special was released in 1974.

FANDOM

There had been a *Doctor Who* Fan Club in existence since 1965, but by 1970, its new secretary, Graham Tattersall, found that he was running it almost single-handedly. The Club's magazine intended to range somewhat wider than *Doctor Who* in its content. It was printed on a Roneo duplicator and, as this method was expensive, Tattersall decided to abandon publication after only a few issues.

'In the end,' Tattersall comments, 'I found the whole project of running the Club not only expensive but also very time-consuming. My job was taking up much of my spare time, and I had no option but to give up the Club.'

This fact was discovered in late 1971 by a fourteen-year-old Edinburgh-based fan called Keith Miller, who had written to the BBC asking about *Doctor Who* fan clubs. Miller had tried to contact Tattersall, but to no avail, and in the end he had written again to the BBC, who found out that Tattersall was no longer interested in running the Club. On learning this, Miller asked Barry Letts's production secretary, Sarah Newman, if he could take over. Not realising how young he was, Newman agreed, and arranged for a box of miscellaneous items, including the addresses of approximately forty of Tattersall's members, to be sent to him.

Miller started up his revamped *Doctor Who* Fan Club on 30 December 1971, and initially the only service it provided was a monthly newsletter sent out entirely free of charge to the Club's members. After a couple of issues that Miller produced and published himself, he came to an arrangement with Newman that he would supply stencils and she would run off copies using the BBC's facilities. Miller feels that the Club would never have got off the ground if it wasn't for Newman's support and assistance.

Initially the newsletter was a relatively cheap publication, each issue consisting of a few A4 sheets of typewritten text duplicated on coloured pulp paper, stapled together in the top left-hand corner. From Issue 15 in April 1973, the newsletter – now called *DWFC Mag* – went bi-monthly, and Miller included more material on the history of the show and interviews with the cast. Although Pertwee was delighted that there was a *Doctor Who* Fan Club in existence, he encouraged a fan named Stuart Money to set up a Jon Pertwee Fan Club as well. Miller queried this arrangement, and Newman informed Money that the DWFC was the officially recognised club and that he should not set up a rival.

One of the most interesting aspects of Miller's newsletters were the frequent set reports that he presented. Although lacking in detail, the reports covered stories including *The Three Doctors* and *The Green Death* and were written with great enthusiasm.

OVERSEAS

1972 saw the first commercial sale of *Doctor Who* to America, with a batch of 72 episodes being made available by Time Life Films.

The original publicity brochure stated that *Doctor Who* was: 'Excellent access time programming – as a strip or once a week. Dramatising 13 complete, serialised adventure tales, each tale a complete story. Dr Who – part Who-dini, part Who-dunnit – travels around the universe encountering one incredible adventure after another – often aided by his capable, beautiful assistant, Jo Grant ... opposed by a cunning, sinister foe, the Master. Serialised dramas, each with gripping, cliff-hanging endings guaranteed to keep audiences coming back, again and again, to follow the adventures of ... Dr Who'

A page in *Broadcasting* magazine featured a photograph of Jon Pertwee from the show's title sequence with the heading: '72 half-hours with Dr Who and you're cured.' The main thrust of the advertisement was that *Doctor Who* could cure your TV station of flagging ratings 'and brings fast, fast, fast relief.'

The thirteen stories available were: *Doctor Who and the Silurians* (called *The Silurians* on the publicity brochure), *The Ambassadors of Death, Inferno, Terror of the Autons, The Mind of Evil, The Claws of Axos, Colony in Space, The Dæmons, Day of the Daleks* (called *The Daleks* on the information brochure), *The Sea Devils, The Curse of Peladon, The Mutants* and *The Time Monster*. These were shown repeatedly on those channels that had purchased them, and no new sales of *Doctor Who* were made to America until a batch of 98 Tom Baker episodes was purchased in 1978.

TV Ontario in Canada started airing specially selected *Doctor Who* episodes in 1976. They aired two 'seasons' of Pertwee serials. Each story was introduced by commentator Dr Jim Dator, who discussed various philosophical and scientific elements of the show as well as continuity with previously aired stories. TVO also published an educational viewers guide to *Doctor Who* in 1976.

Their first 'season' was broadcast from 18 September 1976 to 12 March 1977 and consisted of *The Three Doctors, Day of the Daleks, The Curse of Peladon, The Claws of Axos, The Mutants* and *The Time Warrior*. All of these bar *The Claws of Axos* and *The Time Warrior* were repeated in 1979

Their second 'season' was broadcast from 16 September 1977 until 25 March 1978 and contained *The Time Monster, The Green Death, Death to the Daleks, The Monster of Peladon* and *Planet of the Spiders*. *The Time Monster, The Green Death* and *The Monster of Peladon* were repeated in 1980

New Zealand
By Paul Scoones

The Pertwee era commenced in New Zealand with *Spearhead from Space* and *Doctor Who and the Silurians*, which were shown on Television One from 14 March to 23 May 1975 on Friday at around 6 pm for the first three weeks, and then moved back to around 5 pm for the remaining eight weeks. Although colour television had been introduced to New Zealand in October 1973, these episodes were broadcast from black and white 16mm film prints, which had been acquired 24 January 1975.

Soon after the arrival of New Zealand's second national television channel, South Pacific Television (SPTV), the series returned on this new second channel. Because SPTV was still in the process of setting up its transmitters around the country, some regions missed out on seeing some of the episodes. From this point *Doctor Who* was transmitted in colour. The first story screened was *Day of the Daleks* followed by *Carnival of Monsters, The Three Doctors* and *The Time Warrior* in this order from 1 September to 16 December 1975. *Day of the Daleks* screened on Mondays at around 6 pm, and the rest of the stories screened on Tuesdays at around the same time.

Death to the Daleks was screened as a stand-alone story eight months later, on Fridays at 8 pm on SPTV from 6 to 27 August 1976. After another long break, the final two stories of the Pertwee era, *The Monster of Peladon* and *Planet of the Spiders*, were screened on Sundays on SPTV at 6.35 pm for the first story and 6.15 pm for the second, from 20 March to 5 June 1977.

Well over half of the episodes from the Pertwee era were omitted during the initial screenings on New Zealand television. From Season Seven, both *The Ambassadors of Death* and *Inferno* had been omitted. All of Season Eight (*Terror of the Autons* to *The Daemons*) was unscreened, and *Day of the Daleks* was the sole transmitted representative of Season Nine. From Season Ten, *Frontier in Space*, *Planet of the Daleks* and *The Green Death* were all omitted. TVNZ programme traffic documents and a BBC Enterprises document from February 1978 listing overseas sales of all *Doctor Who* stories, both indicate that every purchased story was screened. It may be possible to attribute this to the BBC's junking of many Third Doctor episodes during the mid 1970s. Although as late as 1977 many of the omitted episodes were still screened in other countries, these appear to have been 16mm black and white film prints and colour NTSC video copies which were both unsuitable formats for PAL colour television in New Zealand.

The next Pertwee story screened was *The Green Death*, placed out of sequence between the Tom Baker stories *The Android Invasion* and *The Brain of Morbius* on Fridays at 6.30 pm on SPTV from 26 January to 2 March 1979. Jon Pertwee visited New Zealand in 1979 on a cabaret tour and his crime quiz show *Whodunnit* was popular with New Zealand viewers; these factors may have prompted the scheduling of *The Green Death* at this time.

A long run of *Doctor Who* stories on Television New Zealand (TVNZ)'s second channel, TV2 commenced in April 1985 with two previously unscreened Troughton stories, followed by an almost complete run of the entire Pertwee era. The episodes were initially screened on Fridays at 6.30 pm with two episodes back to back and the middle closing and opening credits removed. *Spearhead from Space* began on 10 May 1985, and the series ran without a break through to *The Three Doctors*. Most stories were screened in colour, except for: *Doctor Who and the Silurians*, *The Ambassadors of Death*, *Terror of the Autons*, *The Mind of Evil* and *The Daemons*. The last three episodes of *The Three Doctors* were screened back to back on 7 February 1986, followed by a month's break.

Viewer figures for this run of Pertwee episodes reveal that 12 July 1985 gained the greatest *Doctor Who* audience with *The Ambassadors of Death* Episode 7 rating 14.5% and its paired episode, *Inferno* Episode 1 increasing to 15%. 16 August 1985 received the second highest ratings, with Episodes Two and Three of *Terror of the Autons* both rating 13.5%. *Doctor Who and the Silurians* Episode 3, screened 31 May 1985, also rated 13.5%. *Terror of the Autons* was the highest-rated story with a 12% average.

Carnival of Monsters commenced on 11 March 1986, now in a single episode per week format on Tuesdays at around 5.30 pm on Television One. *Planet of the Daleks* Episode Three was screened in black and white, and the first episode of *Invasion of the Dinosaurs* was omitted as TVNZ had been supplied with a re-edited five part version with renumbered episodes. The Pertwee episodes screened during this period were supplied by the Australian Broadcasting Corporation and consequently in many cases had cuts that had been made by the Australian censor. From 18 November 1986, during *The Monster of Peladon*, the series was screened on Wednesdays as well as Tuesdays at the same time. The Pertwee era ended 24 December 1986 with the screening of *Planet of the Spiders* Part Six.

The highest rated Pertwee episodes for this period were *Planet of the Daleks* Episode Six and *The Time Warrior* Episode Two, each with 13% of the potential viewing audience. *Planet of the Daleks* was the highest-rated story with a 10.8% average.

Stories from the Pertwee era were next broadcast in 1991, following on from repeat screenings of selected Hartnell and Troughton stories on TV2. *Spearhead from Space* Episode 1 screened 28 July 1991 (rescheduled at short notice from 14 July), and the whole of Season Seven played on Sundays at around 11.30 am, ending with *Inferno* Episode 7 on 12 January 1992. *Doctor Who and the Silurians* and *The Ambassadors of Death* were again screened in black and white.

After a one month break, the series resumed in the same timeslot for a further ten weeks, with *Terror of the Autons* and *The Mind of Evil*, from 16 February to 19 April 1992. All ten episodes were screened in black and white. Another much longer break preceded the screening of *The Claws of Axos, Colony in Space* and *The Daemons* from 24 January to 2 May 1993, again on Sundays at 11.30 am on TV2. *The Daemons* was screened in black and white. *The Daemons* was followed by a screening of the Hartnell story *The Time Meddler* in the same timeslot.

The thirtieth anniversary of *Doctor Who* was marked by TV2 with a screening of *Day of the Daleks* from 28 November to 19 December 1993 followed by the 1992 documentary *Resistance is Useless* on 26 December 1993. The timeslot was 11.35 am on Sundays, and each week's instalment was introduced by BBC Enterprises' thirtieth anniversary montage of the faces of the seven Doctors that appeared on BBC *Doctor Who* videotapes released during 1993.

Other than two screenings of the Paul McGann TV movie, it was more than six years before *Doctor Who* returned to New Zealand television. The UHF and satellite channel Prime TV began screening the series from the beginning in May 2000, and by September had reached the Pertwee era. At this time, Prime was screening the series at the rate of an episode a day, six days a week – excluding Saturdays – at 6.30 pm. Every Pertwee episode was screened in the correct sequence and without a break. This run saw the New Zealand debut of *Invasion of the Dinosaurs* Part One, and the rest of this story was broadcast with correctly numbered episodes for the first time and, in addition, a slightly longer edit of Part Three.

A number of episodes that had previously screened in New Zealand in black and white were broadcast for the first time in colour on Prime, including *The Ambassadors of Death* Episode 5, and all of *Terror of the Autons* and *The Daemons* – all of which had been successfully restored to transmission-quality colour by the BBC in the early 1990s. Although BBC held a colour version of Episode 1 of *The Ambassadors of Death* and a colour-restored version of all seven episodes of *Doctor Who and the Silurians*, black and white recordings of these instalments were supplied to Prime. Also broadcast in black and white were Episodes 2, 3, 4, 6 and 7 of *The Ambassadors of Death*, *The Mind of Evil*, *Planet of the Daleks* Episode Three and *Invasion of the Dinosaurs* Part One.

From *Death to the Daleks* onwards, Prime doubled their *Doctor Who* screenings from six to twelve episodes per week by moving the start time to 6 pm and running two episodes per night back to back. These were presented with the middle closing and opening titles and recap removed. The Pertwee era ended on Prime on 8 February 2001 with the screening of Parts Five and Six of *Planet of the Spiders*.

VIEWER REACTION

When one considers the ratings for the first of Pertwee's five seasons, it is a wonder that the change in format was considered successful. From just over 8 million for *Spearhead From Space*, the viewing figures dropped alarmingly over the season, finishing with around 5.5 million for *Inferno*. In fact, *Doctor Who* had not seen regular average ratings this poor since the last few stories of Hartnell's era (*The Savages*, *The War Machines* and *The Smugglers*), while the *War Games* had averaged out at 4.9 million.

The start of the eighth season saw a return to the 8 million mark, but this time the viewing figures were consistent over the whole season, with *Colony In Space* peaking at nearly 9 million (partly because of a new time-slot, which removed a scheduling clash with Gerry Anderson's *UFO* series on many ITV regions) and *The Dæmons* just behind it. Things were looking even better for the ninth season, with *Day of the Daleks* coming in at over 9.5 million viewers. After this, however, the season tailed off again, ending at about 7.5 million for *The Time Monster*. Repeating the success of previous season openers, *The Three Doctors* managed to pull in 10.3 million on average, with *Planet of the Daleks* not far behind. The figures for *Planet of the Daleks* were inflated by an extremely good figure for episode one (11.0), no doubt due in part to the FA Cup Final being shown immediately before it. *The Green Death* was the disappointment here, with just under 8 million viewers. The figures stayed pretty much the same for the eleventh, and final season, with, for the first time, the opening story not performing the best. *The Time Warrior* managed only around 8 million, while *Invasion of the Dinosaurs* and *Death to the Daleks* brought in around 9.5 million each. The Doctor's swan song in *Planet of the Spiders* saw about 9 million viewers tuning in on average.

Somewhat strangely, the highest rated third Doctor transmission was the repeat showing of *The Dæmons*, which achieved a figure of 10.53 million, followed by the repeat of *The Green Death*, which managed 10.45 million. Aside from these repeats, the highest rated Pertwee story was, perhaps not surprisingly, *The Three Doctors*.

In the media, the show seemed to be universally liked, with few negative comments to be heard. 'Wins my vote as the best in the series so far,' wrote Matthew Coady in the *Daily Mirror* about *Spearhead From Space*. 'What keeps *Doctor Who* forever young ... is its absolute conviction,' Richard Last said in the *Daily Telegraph* about *The Three Doctors*. Writing about *The Green Death*, the same journalist later commented, '... an imaginative Christmas pudding script, taut direction, lavish filming and even a trendy ecological theme all contributed to the total effect, but what makes this venerable series tick is the complete conviction of all concerned.'

Where there were adverse comments, these tended to be inspired by the media's 'concern' for the violence and horror that was apparently contained within *Doctor Who*'s format – or else by a negative opinion of the Daleks. *Day of the Daleks* came in for some particularly harsh words: 'The series ... is beginning to acquire an exhausted air, of which the return yet again of the mechanical monsters is an unmistakable symptom,' muttered Coady, again in *The Daily Mirror*; and, '...it's about time the BBC exterminated them once and for all,' declared Chris Kenworthy in the *Sun*.

The lasting appeal of the series was summed up by Richard Boston in *The Observer*, when he said of *Planet of the Spiders*, 'It is, I suppose, beyond dispute that *Doctor Who*

3 THIRD DOCTOR

is the best thing that has been done on television, and now that the programme is ten years old and that the current incumbent of the title role is about to be recycled, it seems only appropriate to pay tribute to its colossal achievement.'

But what of the viewers? In the BBC's internal audience research report for the omnibus repeat of *The Sea Devils*, it was stated that the story had been 'received with rather mixed feelings'. The report noted that 'a sizeable minority did not care for the series (which, in their opinion had "outlived its entertainment value") and found this story particularly corny and far-fetched, saying they "only watched for the children's sake". On the other hand, a considerable number said they thoroughly enjoyed Dr Who and the Sea Devils, despite having seen it before, and the series as a whole was considered imaginative and "good fun".'

For *Planet of the Spiders*, it was noted that the ending 'met with a tolerant rather than enthusiastic response from most of the ... viewers who constituted the adult audience ... a minority of about one in three found it very enjoyable.'

The report went on to state that Pertwee was, according to long term viewers, 'the most likeable and subtle Doctor so far' and ended with a selection of comments from children, which make for interesting reading:

'My 10-year-old son says: very entertaining, liked the story, marvellous effects (the spiders looked revolting), quite well acted, made you want to make sure of seeing next episode.'

'I thought it was good and scary.' (age 9)

'Three boys (14, 11 and 8) enjoyed it, but the spiders don't have the impact of Daleks.'

'My three year old was frightened of some parts but liked to listen to the music at the beginning and end.'

'My daughter (10 and a half) thought this last adventure was fabulous, but was very upset when the Doctor changed.'

'They seem to enjoy it immensely, with enough creepy monsters to keep them on the edge of the seat.'

'Two small boys rooted to their seats, tea forgotten, deaf to all talk by grown-ups, and nearly in the box with the horrors on the screen!'

'Exciting, frightening, a must for Saturday. When will it come back, Mum?'

THIRD DOCTOR STORIES IN ORDER OF AVERAGE VIEWING FIGURES
(Figures in millions of viewers)

The Three Doctors	10.3
Planet Of The Daleks	9.7
Day Of The Daleks	9.6
Invasion Of The Dinosaurs	9.6
Death To The Daleks	9.4
The Curse Of Peladon	9.38
Carnival Of Monsters	9.2
Planet Of The Spiders	9.0
Colony In Space	8.5
The Dæmons	8.34

The Time Warrior	8.25
Spearhead From Space	8.2
The Sea Devils	8.17
Frontier In Space	8.0
Terror Of The Autons	7.95
The Mutants	7.8
The Green Death	7.72
Doctor Who And The Silurians	7.71
The Monster Of Peladon	7.7
The Mind Of Evil	7.6
The Claws Of Axos	7.4
The Time Monster	7.38
The Ambassadors Of Death	7.35
Inferno	5.6

3 THIRD DOCTOR

The Fourth Doctor

by

David J Howe

Mark Stammers

Stephen James Walker

FOREWORD

On Saturday 8 June 1974, at two minutes and sixteen seconds past six o'clock, the familiar features of the third Doctor melted away to be replaced by those of a stranger; the fourth Doctor. As the credits came up signifying the end of the eleventh season of *Doctor Who*, fans were left with a gap of six months to ponder what lay ahead.

If *Doctor Who* had been cancelled at this point, with the departure of Jon Pertwee, it would no doubt have been remembered as a very successful series of its type, which had been fronted by three excellent lead actors, spawned a number of highly memorable concepts and characters (most notably the dreaded Daleks) and given years of pleasure to a generation of Saturday tea-time viewers. As it was, of course, the series did not end there – it was doing far too well for that even to have been a consideration in the minds of BBC executives. Instead, Tom Baker embarked on what was to become an epic stint as the Doctor, lasting from 28 December 1974 to 21 March 1981, a period of six years, two months and 25 days; and during that period, *Doctor Who* would rise to a higher plane of popularity than at any time since its second season.

When asked about his reasons for leaving the series, Jon Pertwee has often cited the slow break-up of 'his team'. His long serving co-star Katy Manning had left at the end of season ten to be replaced by Elisabeth Sladen, and script editor Terrance Dicks and producer Barry Letts had also decided to move on. The tragic death in a car accident in 1973 of Pertwee's friend Roger Delgado, who had played the Doctor's arch enemy the Master throughout the era of the third Doctor, had also resulted in the series losing one of its most popular villains. But the decision whether to leave or stay was ultimately taken out of Pertwee's hands when his request for an increase in his fee was rejected by the BBC's Head of Drama, Shaun Sutton, and he was informed that he would not be required for the twelfth season. The BBC clearly felt it was time for a new Doctor, and the production office wasted little time in setting about the task of finding a replacement. After a lengthy period of searching, Tom Baker was introduced to the press as the fourth Doctor on 16 February 1974.

This new Doctor was born into a Britain emerging from the nightmare of oil shortages, which had led to the rationing of fuel for cars, sent huge numbers of the population's homes into the dark during frequent power cuts, and left more than a few irate young *Doctor Who* fans staring by candlelight at a blank TV screen that should have been filled with the latest adventures of their hero. Where the Daleks and the Cybermen had failed, a group of Middle Eastern countries that comprised OPEC had succeeded in temporarily defeating the Doctor – a dastardly plan of the Master's perhaps? 1974 also saw the departure of Edward Heath as Prime Minister and the return of Harold Wilson's Labour Government. West Germany won the World Cup, and ABBA took the Eurovision Song Contest, and then the pop charts, by storm. Joining the Swedish super-group in the charts were artistes such as Mud, Slade, Gary Glitter and The Bay City Rollers.

With the departure of Jon Pertwee, some TV pundits, and indeed some fans of the series, could have been forgiven for thinking that *Doctor Who* had run its course and that there was little new ground left for it to cover. After all, the series was already eleven years old, an almost unheard-of age for any drama production other than a soap opera.

Yet the next seven seasons would see *Doctor Who* establishing itself as a true British institution, and a worldwide hit with a reported 110 million viewers in some 43 countries, making it BBC Enterprises' biggest money-spinner. Its ratings attained their highest ever level and, for perhaps the only time in its history, it came to be accepted as a truly mainstream TV success – no longer could it be dismissed as simply a kid's show or a cult favourite. Tom Baker himself became not so much a star as a national hero.

In particular, this period saw *Doctor Who* break through into the American TV market. By the end of the fourth Doctor's era, it had gained an enormous cult following estimated at around 56,000 American fans, who could turn on their TVs at virtually any time and expect to find *Doctor Who* episodes playing on one or more of the Public Broadcasting Service (PBS) stations scattered across the United States.

One of the main reasons for the success of the fourth Doctor can be simply deduced. It was the enormously exciting and eccentric personality of Tom Baker himself. As well as the character of the Doctor, the style of the programme was very much influenced by its incumbent producer. There were four producers during the Tom Baker years, and they struggled with a variety of external factors that influenced their decisions, especially the growing criticism from and influence of pressure groups like the National Viewers and Listeners Association headed by Mrs Mary Whitehouse, and the newly formed fan group, the *Doctor Who* Appreciation Society.

If the Seventies were the years of your childhood, then this section should jog your memories of the thrill of travelling with the fourth Doctor. If you are too young to have been there at the time, then maybe this will give you a taste of what it was like to watch unfold before you possibly the most exciting era of *Doctor Who*.

TOM BAKER: IN HIS OWN WORDS

ON HIS EARLY LIFE:
'I was brought up in the Scotland Road area of Liverpool among Irish pubs and Irish priests, and brainwashed with a preoccupation with death. Which is perhaps why I still wander round graveyards collecting strange epitaphs.'
Quoted in 1979 in Marvel Comics' *Starburst* No. 10.

'One of my earliest memories is of my Auntie Chrissie. She was a street bookmaker before they legalised betting shops. She and my Uncle Willy and Uncle Terry took the betting slips on the street corner. My mother would pick up some of the bets standing in a graveyard while I was with her. It was the most discreet place she could think of.

'In those days people used to die of things like 'flu and TB so, as an altar boy, I went to about four or five funerals a week, especially in the winter. The relatives used to give you a sixpenny bit. Once I was standing at a graveside, and on this particular day the wind was biting and I was crying with the cold. This fella looked at my tears, squeezed my little arm and patted my little head, and gave me a two shilling piece. Two shillings! I mean, that was twenty-four ice creams. So after that I began to cry all over the place and I became a highly paid professional mourner, almost.'
Interviewed by William Marshall in 1979 for the *Daily Mirror*.

'I was always looking for a way out, but how was I to manage it? I was from a poor background: from a house with no books, and parents with no experience of how to form one's life. Here was a young man desperate to make his mark, fantasising and dreaming. Not clever at school. Rather overgrown and therefore odd to look at. "Good heavens! Is he only eleven? But he's six foot one!" people said. In addition I was skinny and had a curved back because I could hardly ever stand up straight.

'When people came to the school to talk about careers, I was always intensely interested. Then one day a man came and talked about monasticism. I was interested because having been brought up by a very devout Roman Catholic mother – my father was away at sea all the time – I was very preoccupied with religion. The man warned us that we would have to take a vow of chastity, poverty and obedience, but that didn't matter to me. The chastity was enforced by my age, the poverty was understood, and as far as obedience went – well, everybody kicked my backside. And it appeared that they fed you as well, and you had sheets on your bed. So at 15 I went into a monastery in Jersey, and later Shropshire, as a noviciate. But I must admit that I did it only to get away from my background.

'After six years I left, and six weeks later I was called up to do my National Service. It was in the Army that I gained the conviction that I could act and enjoy it. I had acted at school and had been offered a job at the Abbey Theatre in Dublin when I was 15, but my mother wouldn't let me go. But now I decided, "This is what I want to do." I've had some terrible moments of depression and sometimes I've felt really isolated and lost, but I've never wavered from that feeling.

'I was appearing in a late-night revue in York, playing a dog, when I was spotted by a talent scout from the National Theatre. Lord Olivier interviewed me and gave me a job. My first part was playing a horse. Sir Laurence encouraged me and helped me a lot. He was responsible for my getting the part of Rasputin in *Nicholas and Alexandra*. The film was made in Spain at a time when I was in two plays at the National and rehearsing a third. I was shuttled back and forth to Spain to film my bits. I was whisked about in limousines and first-class plane seats. It was heady stuff. I was asked, "How does a working-class boy like you adjust to an air-conditioned Cadillac?" I replied, "Terribly easily."'
Interviewed by Peter Dacre in 1978 for the *Sunday Express*, 12 March edition.

'Those years with the Brothers of Ploermel were terribly exciting and demanding. I enjoyed the suffering and deprivation and silence, although I haven't stopped talking since. I enjoyed the hysterical self-indulgence of feeling unworthy.

'I am absolutely certain that when men are together and deprived of women, they become homosexual. I wanted to embrace a young brother called Olivier-Jean so much that my bones used to *crack*. When you're young, it's very difficult to think about anything but lust. By the end of the six years, I was absolutely worn out by my sexual urges, and a priest advised me to get out.

'Once I was doing my National Service and encountering girls, I discovered sex, started practising it in a frenzy and rejected the Church very swiftly. It left me with a huge residue of guilt. Sometimes God knocks on the side of my head now and says, "Let's get back together." But I prefer guilt, lust, anxiety, lies and confusion. I prefer the uncertainties of life.'
Interviewed by Corinna Honan in 1992 for the *Daily Mail*, 28 March edition.

'I simply feigned idiocy right through my National Service and got away with murder. In my second year, I was able to turn up on muster parade in red leather slippers. Harmless dementia is considered something sacred as long as there's no violence in the unhingement. I went around saying preposterous things. I'd say, "I won't be shouted at by a bunch of professional murderers," and of course they'd shout at me, so I'd proceed to cry. And that simply unhinged them. Finally, they just left me alone because I was too much trouble.

'I was a terribly withdrawn, pained, skinny man, and the Army released me. I loathed Queen's Regulations. It was the enforced contact with people of disparate backgrounds that did it. I was coerced into a Unit show. When I discovered I could make people laugh, it gave me a new strength.'
Quoted in 1979 in Marvel Comics' *Starburst* **No. 10.**

ON BEING AN ACTOR:

'When I was starting out in the Fifties, I was anxious to get started and *so* nervous about trying to make my way. Most people will tell you they want to achieve something, learn something, build a pattern; to find a partner, have somewhere to live that's nice and where they can feel a bit safe; to have a couple of children and a car, collect a few books and go on holiday. That's what most people want, I think. And then there are actors.

'Concomitant with being an actor is that dreadful, exhausting state of being self-aware all the time, because you're marketing your appearance, you're marketing what you sound like. You're worried about whether you're ugly or going bald or getting fat. You're worried about dental bills or worried that no-one wants you. In other words you are *ill*. To want to be an actor, especially these days, is to be ill. It's a kind of illness – this terrible pernicious itch to want what threatens you most, which is insecurity. Performers, like other people, are mesmerised by what threatens them most. They have to learn to love it and live with it and create out of it.

'Performers create out of anxiety, they don't create out of jolliness or a happy song. They have to exorcise the most terrible memories of the last effort, to forget past failures and hope all the time that they're going to please someone. Actors are just professional pleasers, like waiters!'
Interviewed by John Freeman in 1991 for *Doctor Who Magazine* **Nos. 179-181.**

I'm feeling much jollier and philosophical about most things now. You see the other thing was that [*Doctor Who*] weighed on me, because no-one would employ me. I'd like to think that was because I was a huge success and therefore had no credibility as anything else. That's the way actors always justify it. And then the last two years, thanks to the BBC, again, with *The Law Lords* and *The Silver Chair*, and then *Medics* and *Cluedo*, suddenly things have looked up again.
Speaking at a press conference to publicise the release on video of *Shada*, **11 May 1992.**

ON FANTASTICAL CHARACTER ACTING:

'Everyone wants to do something amazing and have the funniest lines or the greatest costume or the best exit or entrance. I mean, we adore what's fantastic, don't we? People are obsessed with fantasy, whether they know it or not. Middle-aged paunchy men – I'm well past that! – dream of being the footballer Maradona or the cricketer Viv Richards.

4 FOURTH DOCTOR

I mean, Richards is just forty, and how many forty-year-old men look at him and wish they were him, and wouldn't dare tell their friends. Everyone has a heroic impulse, a desire towards being amazing, towards achieving, towards being heroic.'
Interviewed by John Freeman in 1991 for *Doctor Who Magazine* Nos. 179-181.

ON THE ATTRACTION OF PLAYING THE DOCTOR:

'To be honest, it was nothing about the character that influenced me at all, it was sheer necessity! I was desperately out of work and was terribly depressed by this. Suddenly, along came the possibility of playing Doctor Who. It was just relief to play a major part!

'Because I didn't watch *Doctor Who* much, I had no notion of what this would do. It just so happened that with the new scripts that Barry Letts (and later Philip Hinchcliffe) had commissioned, the directors, costume and set designers who moved in ... well, it all came together. I didn't know what was happening. I just responded to that, which I suppose is the great secret, isn't it?

'I was working very hard on a building site in Ebury Street, next door but one to where Mozart wrote his first symphony, when I got the job. The builders were actually very good to me, and I have a happy memory of that, but of course I didn't *want* to be on a building site, because I hadn't much skill. I wanted to be an actor.

'When I got the part, I had this feeling of just *huge* relief, and also one of great pride. I didn't tell my workmates I'd got the job. I had the day off and went to the BBC, and then it was in the first edition of the *Evening Standard*. I knew they all took that paper – and bang, all was revealed! So there they were, looking over the tops of their papers at me. It was a great moment of pleasure. They were very proud of me – and I was very proud of them.'
Interviewed by John Freeman in 1991 for *Doctor Who Magazine* Nos. 179-181.

ON HIS DOCTOR'S COSTUME:

'I think that the style of the costume represented my personal style of dress, which is rather casual. I was inspired by a designer called Jim Acheson, who was young and conscientious and very witty, I thought. I met several lovely designers at the BBC. June Hudson, latterly, was a designer I saw a lot of. But Jim Acheson and I went out to play for a few weeks and we gradually got this tatty costume together, which was a mixture of sort of scruffiness and elegance. Scruffiness in the way it was worn but elegance in the cut of the coat – and madness in the size of the scarf. The hat was Herbert Johnson. Yeah, I had some influence in it, but it was mostly Jim's inspiration really.'
Interviewed by Dave Dean in 1982. Published in *Private Who* Issue 3.

'Jim Acheson designed the scarf, bought the wool and gave it to someone's relation at the BBC called Begonia Pope, who was thrilled to be working for the Corporation. She didn't ask any questions; Jim gave her the design and she knitted up all the wool. Jim of course had no knowledge about knitting, except for colour. He bought ten times the amount of wool that was needed, and she knitted the lot! He omitted to say it was just a scarf, like the sort you'd see on the Left Bank in Paris. When I put it on, it was hilarious, and Jim instantly said, "Keep it, it's funny."'
Interviewed by John Freeman in 1991 for *Doctor Who Magazine* Nos. 179-181.

ON HIS DEBUT AS THE DOCTOR:

'I didn't know how I was going to do *Doctor Who*. I had no idea at all – not until the very first rehearsal, and even then I didn't know ... I just did it. I just played the script and something evolved and the audience liked the way I did it, obviously, so we kept it like that. But sometimes it was funny and sometimes not so funny and sometimes it was thrilling. It was just an accident, really.'

Interviewed by Dave Dean in 1982. Published in *Private Who* Issue 3.

ON BREAKING HIS COLLAR-BONE DURING RECORDING OF *THE SONTARAN EXPERIMENT*.

'When I fell, I banged my head as well, and I wasn't sure when I fell ... how badly I was hurt, because the pain was very bad and it was quite deep. In fact it was just a shock of the collar bone, which is the swiftest bone to mend but when it breaks it made you feel very sick. I thought, am I hurt badly? And it wasn't that I was afraid of dying. I mean I thought, how am I going to get on with the show? I was taken away for investigation, and when I came back, Barry Letts and Philip Hinchcliffe were looking all grey-faced in the pub, and I swanned in and had several large gins.'

Speaking at a press conference to publicise the release on video of *Shada*, 11 May 1992.

ON *DOCTOR WHO*'S UNIQUE FORMAT:

'I think if I bothered about the plots, I wouldn't get much done. The plots won't stand up to severe examination. The mass of our audience is children and they're only interested in the high spots of the Doctor's adventures anyway.'

Speaking on *Woman's Hour*, 12 January 1977.

'Given fundamental expertise from the producer downwards, the real gold of the thing is the formula. Given that you haven't got a bonehead at the top or a powerful subversive somewhere down the line, you couldn't really fail with it. The first reason we are so successful – the very first reason – is that we are incomparable. Nothing admits to comparison with *Doctor Who*. When people try to plagiarise our situations or our attitudes they fall down, because it's obvious plagiarism. They don't really start with this marvellous thing that the character's an alien, and the wonderful heroic comedy-thriller notion that he can travel in this daft box. That's why I think the formula, which is so wonderful, engages such a huge audience.'

Interviewed by John Fleming in 1980 for Marvel Comics' *Starburst* No. 19.

'I think the formula lent itself to Gothic areas, not because science fantasy should do that but simply because we have that long film background of Gothic horror, tension and fantasy, the tragi-comedy if you like. Do you remember the old Hammer films, especially the late-night ones when one had been drinking? You'd get gales of laughter from one particular section of the audience and the rest would be sat po-faced. It's rather like going to a theatre with a lot of actors or musicians, and they're picking up one thing and someone else is seeing it on another level.

'*Doctor Who* was like that. I was always, constantly trying to translate whatever was happening to me and add it to the role, drawing on other experiences. One of the reasons I spent so much time on the road promoting the programme was that I was

drawing on the children from the audience. What they told me they liked, I did more of, or else adapted it and did variations. I used to get hints of what they liked. So it might have appeared I was being very nice to them, but actually what I was doing was 'vampiring' them for ideas. It was quite shameless!'
Interviewed by John Freeman in 1991 for *Doctor Who Magazine* **Nos. 179-181.**

ON NOT WATCHING *DOCTOR WHO*:

'I didn't watch it before I was in it and I certainly didn't watch it while I was in it, because that would only make me unhappy. My reasoning was, "What is the point in watching it?", because we worked under such pressure; I always wished I could do it better, you see, and there was never any time, with a maximum of maybe two or three takes per scene. If there was any doubt, I sometimes deliberately used to blow it out on such a scale that they had to do a retake. Directors know about this!

'Occasionally I might have watched a sequence over which we'd had an argument, but I didn't watch it as a rule, because I would never have been pleased with it. I might watch it now out of curiosity after so long, but generally, if it's marvellous someone will tell me about it and if it isn't so marvellous I'll just be unhappy.'
Interviewed by John Freeman in 1991 for *Doctor Who Magazine* **Nos. 179-181.**

ON THE PLEASURES OF REHEARSALS:

'Most of the time it was a pleasure to get to work, to get off the street and out of the ghastly world of reality, away from the bloody TV news and into Rehearsal Room 603. It was just bliss.

'During rehearsals, we used to mime a lot and pretend the monsters were there. You'd get actors from other shows peeping in through the bullseye windows and laughing at us – not in a derisive way but with pleasure at all this over-acting. They were still enjoying it, and lots of people – lots of very distinguished actors – wanted to be in it and used to tell me so in the BBC canteen, which moved me very much. I remember polished actors like John Woodnutt being killingly funny about it, and there were others, like Bill Fraser, Freddy Trieves and George Baker.'
Interviewed by John Freeman in 1991 for *Doctor Who Magazine* **Nos. 179-181.**

ON AUDIENCE REACTION:

'One of the surprising things about *Doctor Who* is the range of the audience. Although I have always thought of it as a children's programme – not a childish programme, mind you – we have a big adult audience. And over the past two years, we have discovered that there are a lot of *Doctor Who* fan clubs at the universities. I was astonished to be invited to St John's and Somerville Colleges at Oxford, and I spoke to absolutely packed halls. If I accepted all the invitations, I could be going to the universities three or four times a week.

'Some actors get a bit neurotic when they are approached by people and called by the name of the character they play. I don't mind being called Doctor Who – which I am all the time. I can't tell you just how dull life was when I was just Tom Baker. Simply nobody recognised me.

'I must always remember that I do not have an existence as Tom Baker. Apart from my close friends and colleagues, everybody calls me Doctor Who. Even children in push-chairs point at me in the street. But I am very aware that they are looking not at Tom

Baker but at this image they have of this character. It is important to me, therefore, that I never disappoint people, especially children. I would never be seen being raucous in the streets, or plastered, or smoking cigars. When I want to go out to play, I do it discreetly in selected actors' bars or clubs. Even then there is sometimes no escape. A friend once took me to a select West End club. "We won't be bothered here," he said. We had not been there more than a few minutes when a chap raised his glass and said, "My dear Doctor, how nice to see you here." My friend was astonished, because the man was a judge.'

Interviewed by Peter Dacre in 1978 for the *Sunday Express*, 12 March edition.

'The programming of *Doctor Who*, in my view, is absolutely brilliant, because it follows the sports round-up, the brief news, sometimes a programme like *Basil Brush*, and it's then followed by *The Generation Game* or *The Duchess of Duke Street* or whatever it is; but that time on a Saturday vitally influences the attitude of the audience. I mean, if you pushed it on, rolling back the frontier to half past ten at night, the audience would be drunk! How are they going to follow our script? They can't possibly follow our script when they're stone cold sober, but if they go out and drink Red Barrel or some inflamatory drink like that, it scrambles people's heads!'

Speaking on stage in August 1979 at the *Doctor Who* Appreciation Society convention PanoptiCon III.

'Sometimes I enjoy being recognised. Especially by children. It gets very debilitating when you're accosted by adults all the time. But *children* – I love it, especially if I'm on the move. Going home from work on the train last night, I made three tube changes, and all the kids were coming back from Hyde Park with their mothers. They were so densely packed and I was threading my way through and, quite often, a child is actually being led towards me and he recognises me and he smiles and then he wonders why he smiled. And then it clicks, but by the time it's clicked, I've gone. It's terrific fun, that kind of contact. Great fun. I love it with the *small* children – it's amazing, that.

'You see, to use a very overworked word, it's a participatory programme. In your average family of a man and his wife and three children, with the children going in age from say nine to three, when it comes to Saturday night viewing it becomes a bit of a charade. Children are very quick to cotton on to some kind of regular routine. So, when they watch *Doctor Who*, several things happen. It's not passive in a two- or three-child family. The older child of nine or ten might be actually following the narrative very carefully and quite critically. His six year old brother, when the monsters come up, is wincing a bit. And the little fellow, getting in on the act, is behind the sofa or he's in the kitchen looking through the crack in the door. Now, the parents notice this and enjoy it. I've talked to hundreds of parents: they enjoy this. The moment you actually give children that attention – just like, indeed, adults – you get this marvellous response. When our music comes up – and the opening music to *Doctor Who* is absolutely *wonderful* – that's the signal for the weekly sit-down and the sharing.'

Interviewed by John Fleming in 1980 for Marvel Comics' *Starburst* No. 19.

'I love small children. By an accident of temperament I get on very well with them. I am perfectly happy to spend a lot of time with them. Wherever I go now, I get enormous

4. FOURTH DOCTOR

attention – from children and adults. Their response is so warm and generous that my life is different from most other people's. I would be lying if I didn't say that it gave me a huge amount of pleasure. I am one of the few men in England to whom "Don't talk to strange men" doesn't apply. When I bump into small children in the park, I can pick them up or embrace them and no policeman will come and move me on. Sometimes I see parents looking a bit anxious, but when they come over and see it is Doctor Who, they are as thrilled as their children. Nothing appeals to me more than *Doctor Who*.

'If I am in a bar alone, everybody feels they can talk to me. Sometimes it gets irritating. I am quite happy to stand alone with my gin and tonic trying to finish a crossword or reading.'
Interviewed by Dan Slater in 1979 for the *Sun*.

'People are quite kind to me; children are always wonderful. But I've had my share of rudeness. The trouble with becoming a "name" on TV is that you are licensed in the public's mind to play just one role. I have to behave like the Doctor. I'll put up with any pathetic, troublesome old drunk, simply because I could not bear the thought of him going home and telling his kids, "I saw Doctor Who today and he told me to sod off." As a viewer, I wouldn't like to see someone from a children's programme behaving badly. It would be like seeing Robin Day dancing on the table in a restaurant.'
Interviewed by Charles Catchpole in 1981 for unknown newspaper, 21 March edition.

ON COMPANION LEELA'S VIOLENT STREAK:

'I've forgotten the details of the character, but I do remember being *appalled* at her aggression, without me having the ammunition to put forward my side of the argument. There was a moral dimension, an ethical dilemma, because she *killed* things. It wasn't just my character, *I* was furious at the beginning. There was some facetious dialogue about it, some claptrap like "I don't really think you should do that." The point is that these gentle ironies are quite inappropriate when life and death are at stake. What I tried to give it was outrage and burning indignation – that if it didn't change, if *she* didn't change, the character would have to go. I don't mean Louise Jameson, but I would have to threaten Leela with this, because I could not coexist with someone whose solution to problems was to kill. So they modified that and Louise was very good and hugely successful. But I was very rattled by it.'
Interviewed by John Freeman in 1991 for *Doctor Who Magazine* Nos. 179-181.

ON THE TARDIS:

'I often felt, myself, that they didn't really pursue the wonderful, cosmically funny aspect of the TARDIS being bigger on the inside than on the outside. I couldn't understand why on the inside of the TARDIS there shouldn't be a whole market town with a cathedral, which we could keep the wellingtons in! Instead it was always just a control room – we occasionally went into other areas – but, in my view, no-one ever wrote a story that suggested the logic of dimensional transcendentalism; that inside the TARDIS is not just a console room but a whole *world*.

'It would be amazing, to go into the TARDIS and have the assistant say, "My god Doctor, look – there are thousands of sheep there!" And the Doctor would say "Good grief, so there are. I remember now ..." And of course he can't remember the exact details, but the sheep would have come in at some difficult time and he'd saved them, intending to transport them somewhere. Why *isn't* a world shown, instead of waving it away with some facetious, smart-assed remark? I mean, who cleans for the Doctor? Why isn't there someone suddenly bellowing, "Where have you been? I've been waiting. Don't you remember you took me on to clean for you?" To which the Doctor would say, "Did I? I really must get a hold of myself ..."'

Interviewed by John Freeman in 1991 for *Doctor Who Magazine* Nos. 179-181.

ON THE DOCTOR'S ROBOT DOG, K-9:

'I don't really have opinions about bits of metal ... I suppose it was a good idea to have K-9. It's an insufferable pun, but it did work. It worked very well, because of what John Leeson, who was the voice of K-9, did in rehearsals, which was much more interesting than K-9 itself. For instance, despite all the money we spent on him, K-9 couldn't run over a matchbox. He could be moved of course from a distance, by remote control, but what John Leeson did was much more interesting than K-9 ever was. So I had strong feelings for what John Leeson did, but not for that dreary metal dog.'

Interviewed by Dave Dean in 1982. Published in *Private Who* Issue 3.

'K-9 was a blasted hard thing to act with! Off-set there'd be John Leeson doing the voice, and because the thing is so small, all the dialogue shots had to be done at its level. We had tremendous technical problems with it as well. It was always breaking down, especially on location when we'd get annoyed because we were always running behind schedule, so that was just another hold-up.'

Interviewed by Richard Marson in 1984 for *Doctor Who Magazine* No. 92.

ON HIS FOUR *DOCTOR WHO* PRODUCERS:

'Barry Letts only produced my first one – although it was he who got me the job. Then Philip Hinchcliffe was with us for quite a while – he was a good, hard-working producer. Graham Williams came on and worked like a dog at a rather trying time for all of us when money was getting scarce and we were behind schedule. John Nathan-Turner did my last year and was very kind to me, very accommodating. I saw a lot of him socially – we were both bachelors at the time. He's good company and he cares so much for the programme. In their own ways, and as far as the series would allow, they were all trying to ring the changes, I suppose. They had their job and I had mine, and we worked quite closely together; the only conflict we ever had was professional, and that kind of conflict is essential.'

Interviewed by Richard Marson in 1984 for *Doctor Who Magazine* No. 92.

ON THE HORRIFIC CONTENT OF *DOCTOR WHO*:

'We often discuss the horror content, and they take it very seriously at our office, because they're experts at it. They're willing to listen to me of course – after all I go out and meet the children. On the other hand, there is often a scene when we're're shooting it that looks unbearably horrifying – but that won't be how it's edited. I don't do the editing, that's not my job. That's the director's brief. Then finally the producer and the head of the department decide how far to go. But it is very often an arbitrary thing. Only two people can decide. We've come under a lot of stick from Mrs Whitehouse especially. I understand that she won't even have lunch with me!

'I sometimes think that the stories are very frightening, but the consideration always

FOURTH DOCTOR

is that television takes place in a domestic context. And one can go further in terror. Children like to be terrorised. At home, they'll be watching the television and seeing something happening to me, and then they move their eyes through a very small arc and they see their fish fingers, or their mum, or their dad. It's a family event. You have the little ones behind the sofa. I know about this, I've spoken to hundreds of children. Little ones behind the sofa, or looking through fingers, or looking through cracks in doors. And the whole thing in many ways is rather diffused by that, because it is so obviously fictional.'
Speaking on *Woman's Hour*, 12 January 1977.

ON THE DOCTOR'S MORE HUMOROUS STYLE UNDER GRAHAM WILLIAMS:

'I don't know what Graham was told, but although he and I worked together and there were some successes in his time, he and I weren't really all that close. I was just responding to whatever was going there.

'I don't want to try to define what my style was; I just responded to the scripts and finally filtered them through me. As you know – I've been quoted many times – Doctor Who was not an acting part any more than James Bond is an acting part. By acting I mean an actor's definition of an acting job, which is when a character actually develops and discovers something so amazing that there is actually a transformation. Either that or there is a realisation that he has been entirely wrong. This isn't so with heroes. There's an utter predictability about playing heroic parts. Heroes, you *know* what side they'll come down on. Doctor Who isn't suddenly going to become obsessed with sex or money or gratuitous violence – he's predictably good, like an innocent child. Within that predictability, within all that certainty, the fun of doing it was, "How do you surprise the audience and hold them and make them want to watch again and again?"'
Interviewed by John Freeman in 1991 for *Doctor Who Magazine* Nos. 179-181.

ON TENSIONS DURING PRODUCTION:

'One grew to know what the difficulties were for the technical crew who had to realise the story, and one co-operated the best one could. I mean, I was often, I'm afraid, impatient and difficult. Not out of malice or intention, but I'm an anxious sort of actor and I'm easily thrown. I think sometimes I was impatient and difficult and I regret that but, I mean, it was with the best will.'
Interviewed by Dave Dean in 1982. Published in *Private Who* Issue 3.

'I found the schedule very hard, but then I find all acting difficult – it requires a huge amount of work before I'm really happy with my own performance, and on television you never have the time. I used to long for just a few extra days to get it exactly right, but we always had a punishing deadline to work to. As soon as one story was completed, I'd find another wad of scripts to learn for the next week, and so on. I did get tired, but I couldn't stop concentrating, because if I did, it wouldn't have worked at all. By the time I left, I was seven years older and consequently I didn't have the same resources of energy I'd had when I joined.'
Interviewed by Richard Marson in 1984 for *Doctor Who Magazine* No. 92.

'Sometimes things just didn't gel during recording, because I was very possessive and irrational about it. Sometimes I felt that this was *my* show, although when new actors came on it, I wanted to love them, albeit only for the duration of the production. I wanted them to be really *amazed* at this world they came into, so that when we started rolling the cameras, there would be this realistic element of people being constantly amazed by me and by what was going on around them.

'There was tension all the time, which I wanted, but sometimes when it didn't go as well as other times, I became very irascible. I read an article the other day that said how moody I was, and I said to my wife, "Moody? They say I'm moody! Am I moody?" And she said, "Well ..." I cut in with, "Well it's ridiculous, isn't it? *Me*? *Moody*? It's like saying I've got no manners!" So she said, "Well sometimes you're very moody, and often you've got the manners of a pig!".
Interviewed by John Freeman in 1991 for *Doctor Who Magazine* Nos. 179-181.

ON CONTRIBUTING IDEAS:

'The scripts were often dull. I didn't get a buzz of excitement after reading them. I always felt that the series gave you such free rein, such scope for imaginative plots, and that our writers were throwing the chance away with dramatic stereotypes. So I was shamefully badly behaved with the scripts – I maltreated our writers' reputations in rehearsal more than anything else, I found it so frustrating. It's not that they were really terrible scripts, but they weren't great either. We did so many as well; I'd get a huge pile of them to wade through every so often, and it was always the same – a bit of a let down.

'I was always suggesting this or that – maybe an extra line or a different situation – and the director would say yes or no. Generally they were very kind to me. They humoured some of my extravagances but took me seriously as well. That was nice – it gave us all a working respect for each other. And some of my ideas they kept in!'
Interviewed by Richard Marson in 1984 for *Doctor Who Magazine* No. 92.

'Over the years, I came to understand what the Doctor could and could not do better than any writer or director who has only one story to worry about. I used to spend a long time checking the scripts and dialogue to make sure they conformed to how the Doctor should be played. If I found any scenes that depicted him as being over-emotional or gratuitously violent, then I would argue very strongly for their removal.'
Quoted by Peter Haining in 1986 for W H Allen's *The Doctor Who File*.

'I don't want to give the impression that I claim too much authority. Obviously the writers did try to write for me and the producers did indulge me a great deal, because most of the time I was the one making the contact with the audience. Because I had been doing the thing so long, it became more and more impossible for me to accept any kind of guidance. I felt I knew it all. I was there week after week. I knew the shots, the set-ups; I knew how to do the corridor sequences; I was swift on the words (such as they were); and I knew I had to give the audience a bit of variety.

'So sometimes a director might say, "Tom, I think in this sequence ...," and I'd cut in and say, "No, let's not do that, because we did that last week in an identical situation." Sometimes they'd realise I was only trying to be helpful and we'd reverse it, just to get the variation. So because I was the constant factor, I became more and more proprietorial, and in the end it became obvious I had to go.

'I got more and more irascible, and people seemed to think the programme was me, we became so *utterly* intertwined. This was very bad, and a sign that I had to go. Also I didn't find rehearsals as funny as I had done.'
Interviewed by John Freeman in 1991 for *Doctor Who Magazine* Nos. 179-181.

ON THE SERIES' VILLAINS AND MONSTERS:

'I quite liked the Wirrn, as they were grotesque. But the Daleks and the Cybermen I found, from the point of view of playing the Doctor and beating them, insufferably tedious, because they were utterly predictable and witless and not really ingenious. But never mind – it doesn't matter what I feel about them. Undoubtedly the Daleks seized the imagination of the first generation of *Doctor Who* watchers, and of subsequent generations. I never much cared for them really, but I can see it's what the viewers like.'
Interviewed by Dave Dean in 1982. Published in *Private Who* Issue 3.

'I loved some of our monsters because they were so funny. We used to have a regular set of actors who'd play them, so we were all very chummy. I adored the Krynoid – the giant walking vegetable – and I also liked the Wirrn. They were both fun. Then there was the giant rat in *The Talons of Weng-Chiang* – I thought that looked rather good. We also had some superb villains. Michael Wisher was brilliant as the creator of the Daleks. I remember once he was playing a scene and he was also doing the Dalek voices, and I said, "Can we all go home now?", because he was in total control. Some of our villains were quite chilling – I used to try to believe in them so as to communicate their threat to the audience, and often I didn't have to try very hard, they were so good.'
Interviewed by Richard Marson in 1984 for *Doctor Who Magazine* No. 92.

'I must say I did enjoy Davros in *Genesis of the Daleks*, because Michael Wisher did work so seriously and was unbendingly passionate about the character. He used to make us howl with laughter! He's a very accomplished actor, and he had us gripped from the first rehearsal, he was so unselfconscious. When he used to rehearse with a paper bag over his head, that used to crucify me! I used to yelp. He never relaxed, which is very important for an actor. You must *never* patronise your own character – this is what happens if people stay too long or are recalled into cameo parts. Always play a character from his point of view and never be hard on him, because if you do that, it instantly betrays a lack of commitment. You've got to believe absolutely; never give him or her a hard time. You must play it the way you believe it should be played.'
Interviewed by John Freeman in 1991 for *Doctor Who Magazine* Nos. 179-181.

ON LEAVING *DOCTOR WHO*:

'It was in the works for months before. I struggled with all the arguments for and against staying, but seven years is a long time. I'd given the show all I felt I could give it, but I loved it so much that in other ways I didn't want ever to go. I didn't want anybody to start feeling awkward about me being there, so I had to take the initiative and say, "It's time I did something else and let somebody else come in." I had the happiest years of my life with *Doctor Who* – it was such a thrill to be the Doctor.'
Interviewed by Richard Marson in 1984 for *Doctor Who Magazine* No. 92.

'There was a kind of slight fatigue. And also I was becoming neurotically proprietorial about it ... the signs were that it was entirely mine, so in other words it was really time to go, because that meant that I couldn't be influenced. And when you can't be influenced, then it's time to go to another village, isn't it really, another pub from wherever you are. Because once you're cut off from the influences, there'll be no growth in any direction, however slight it may be. You're not going to have a jolly time.'
Speaking at a press conference to publicise the release on video of *Shada*, 11 May 1992.

ON HIS FAVOURITE STORY:

'I do get asked that question a lot, and I don't really know the answer. I didn't watch them all, but sometimes I do remember them. What I enjoyed about *Doctor Who* was the day-to-day work, the grinding routine of rehearsals and trimming and trying to make it witty televisually. I think I did enjoy one called *The Ark in Space*, because I particularly liked the designs on that. I admired the designer, Roger Murray-Leach, very much, and I think that it was very well realised.'
Interviewed by Dave Dean in 1982. Published in *Private Who* Issue 3.

'I can never remember story titles, and I never watched the series, so all I can remember are the sequences I filmed – which were all out of order anyway – and of course rehearsals, which used to go so quickly. My favourite kind of stories were the "different" ones – and the ones I was happy with for personal reasons, like the Renaissance one. That was a good one; I felt quite happy with that. The one set on the giant Ark was another I liked – it had some beautiful, clever sets and quite a good script. Then there was the one with the giant, man-eating plants, which had Tony Beckley, who was such a fine actor, in it.

'I wouldn't want to give the impression that I didn't enjoy making *Doctor Who*, but sometimes it was very, very exhausting, and occasionally I'd be ill, as I was on my last few stories. But usually I used to have so much fun – I'd never have stayed so long otherwise. I was amazed recently when I saw how many episodes I'd made – I thought, "Goodness, was it really that many?" – and the days when I felt I needed to get out were, happily, few and far between.'
Interviewed by Richard Marson in 1984 for *Doctor Who Magazine* No. 92.

ON HIS LEAST FAVOURITE STORY:

'Looking back on it, it would have to be my last one, *Logopolis*. I remember not liking the final shot, because I was leaving by then. I remember I wanted to be gone. I remember thinking the shot wasn't particularly heroic or witty, and they recorded it straight from above with me lying flat. It was very difficult to be heroic in that situation, because, to do that, I should have at least been able to get up on one elbow. But it had to be that way, because they wanted to do that dreary old reverse shot of me looking into a circle of faces. They were stealing the shot anyway, from a film.

'It was all right for them, but not for me, and I went away with that slight niggling disappointment. I can still remember the shot after all these years – I didn't like the images, it wasn't heroic enough.'
Interviewed by John Freeman in 1991 for *Doctor Who Magazine* Nos. 179-181.

ON NOT APPEARING IN *THE FIVE DOCTORS*:

'That was a decision I had to think long and hard about. The original plan was to have me with Lis and have us all come together at the end. I finally decided I wouldn't do it because I simply couldn't face the prospect of going back. I was lucky also to have other offers, but when I say I couldn't face the happiness again, I mean it. I went to see John Nathan-Turner and explained all my reasons, and in spite of the difficulties it caused, he was very understanding. The programme is my past now – it would, I think, have been a mistake to try to turn the clock back even for that one story.'

Interviewed by Richard Marson in 1984 for *Doctor Who Magazine* No. 92.

'Well, it was too close to my leaving really, and I was very impatient. I didn't want to be seen with either new Doctors or old Doctors. In my own mind, I was the most recent. Thinking about it, perhaps that was another good reason for my leaving. I began to lose that sense of fun and silliness I had. I began to take the Doctor very seriously, and I thought, "Who are these guys?" I didn't know them and I didn't care about them. At first I said I would, and then I read the script and John Nathan-Turner tried to be very accommodating – he always was for me – and he was very disappointed that I couldn't bring myself to do it.

'It was simply that I felt there was a danger that it could be very competitive. I felt it would just be a novelty scheme, and I wasn't interested in novelty at the time. I was looking for good drama.'

Interviewed by John Freeman in 1991 for *Doctor Who Magazine* Nos. 179-181.

ON LOVE AND MARRIAGE:

'I have no intimate friends. Not one. Fifty or sixty people are acquainted with me, but nobody knows Tom Baker. I am a secretive soul.

'The price of being an unmarried, middle-aged man tearing around the world is that I am so often alone. I consider myself a bachelor and have been now for many, many years. I enjoy the freedom that being unmarried gives me. I can do whatever I'm offered as an actor and go anywhere – which you can't do with the same ease if you are married. I have only myself to think of.

'I envy people with a happy domestic life, wife and children, a house and dogs, but it is a big weight. I choose to be alone and free to go to Brazil or Egypt or wherever I want. I pay the price – you can't have it every way. I don't think of myself as a confirmed bachelor. I am simply an unmarried man. I am not any kind of woman hater. The marvellous thing about falling in love, or getting married, is that reason plays no part in the process at all.

'When I was married to Anna Wheatcroft, I realised that we were two innocent people who got married and who weren't very good together. It wasn't all that difficult to become unmarried. I think it is rare that it is ended by mutual consent, but that is how we ended our marriage. I see my ex-wife from time to time. Being divorced is always a matter for regret when you've got children because, however you look at it, it is a defeat. But I pay my dues, and I am in touch with them in an official way. My sons are grown up now. One is 20, and about to go to university. The other is 17 and not far behind. I was with them when they were very small, and I enjoyed them a great deal.

'I don't think I would like to start all over again having children, although I really

adore them. Some men start new families well into their middle age, but that is not for me. *Doctor Who* allows me to have all the pleasure of intimacy with lots of children without any of the anxieties of starting all over again.'
Interviewed by Dan Slater in 1979 for the *Sun*.

'We were incredibly aware of each other from the very first moment when Lalla joined the show. She was in one episode with me, then I went away during a break in the series. We came back to work together again and it happened. We fell in love. I realised that after she left the programme I couldn't envisage living without her.'
Interviewed by Jack Bell in 1980 for an unknown newspaper.

'I know a good thing when I see it. It's a great pleasure to go home now! Lalla's a super cook. She laughs a lot at me – she finds it amusing that I'm so chatty at all hours, even in the morning. Well, I'm not *raucous* exactly, but I'm pretty perky first thing. We're always having meals with her parents. We all get along very well. I'm very confident and happy.'
Interviewed by Maureen Patton in 1981 for the *Daily Express*, 21 March edition.

'I do find co-existence very difficult. Marriage is full of mutual irritations, but the only alternative seems to be this punishing loneliness of being on your own.

'I'm not an accomplished bachelor. I'm quite good at the linen and making beds, but I don't like vacuuming and I can't master ironing boards – vicious things that always collapse on you. One of the prices you pay for being on your own is that very swiftly you can become old womanish and over fussy. I've seen it so often in loners and confirmed bachelors. Luckily I'm very gregarious. I still have my old haunts in Soho: the Coach and Horses, the French, the Swiss and the Colony Room.

'I am still optimistic that Lalla and I might get back together again. This separation is just a period to test out attitudes. Lalla wants my happiness and what is good for both of us. Anyway, actors are prone to making gestures. I still believe in marriage, and there are masses of advantages to being with Lalla. She is extraordinarily well-read, witty, and wonderful good company. The trouble is that it's easier to see all that from a distance, rather than as one of the participants in our relationship, in much the same way that agony aunts can be very rational and philosophical about other people's problems because they're not involved.

'Any marriage is difficult, but two jumpy, insecure, freelance actors, flogging themselves at work and desperately seeking approval all the time, have got less chance of making it than most. I ring Lalla up nearly every day to see how she is and what's happening. I don't do it from emotional dependency, but just as a friendly, civilised, polite thing to do. When you are separated, you can't just excise all the nice things about the other person. When you have been very generous to each other emotionally, you must still remember that. The trouble, when you separate, is that although you may be united in times of happiness, it's rare to be united in times of anxiety. So that just as one person says, "I think it would be a good idea to sever things now," the other is thinking, "I'm sure it's starting to get better." So it's not logical and it's very hard to be reasonable. But I ring Lalla anyway to see how her play is going and to see how the cats are. I do miss the cats …

'I often wish that Lalla was with me, when I'm alone in the flat. Thoughts of her float about in my head all the time. But even if we don't get back together again, I would never think of our marriage as a failure. We have been very happy together and that's what matters, not how long it lasted. I always remember Germaine Greer, when asked if she regretted her short-lived marriage, saying "No, it was a huge success – for three days!"'

Interviewed by Jenny Nisbet in 1982 for the *Daily Express*, 8 June edition.

'I wouldn't say I'm close to my children. I wouldn't say I'm close to anyone, except my wife, Sue Jerrard. I don't have much capacity for friendship, because of my self-centredness. I'm not generous enough to give to individuals. These things are heightened in actors, when you are thinking about yourself all the time and worrying about where the next round of applause is coming from.

'I've lost my religion and sometimes I think I've lost everything in life, because I'm a great betrayer. The title of my autobiography is going to be *All Friends Betrayed*. That's made me more anxious to hold onto my dear wife. I used to be very fragmented, and I do need to be adored. I feel this overriding security in her affection; she reassures me constantly. Now that I've located admiration, I'm hanging onto it for grim death.'

Interviewed by Corrina Honan in 1992 for the *Daily Mail*, 28 March edition.

'I do adore my wife. I think about her and phone her every day while I'm away filming, and I couldn't exist very well without her. She guards and protects me, because, as you know, I'm not very good at reality.'

Interviewed by Julia Beasley in 1992 for *Woman's Weekly*, 24th March edition.

ON SPARE-TIME PURSUITS:

'I adore being in pubs – it is my idea of bliss. I spend a lot of time philosophising in ale houses. I go to a pub, and if there are some chums there who are interesting, I stay. If they are not, I just move on.

'I am a joyous drinker. The idea of deliberately going out to get plastered horrifies me. What is the point of doing something that interferes with fundamental functions? I can't bear doing anything that would make me sexually impotent or stop me working or concentrating. I am not saying that from time to time I don't get stinko, but that is an accident – and I love those accidents. You meet a couple of chums, then you meet someone else, and the next thing you know you are as high as a kite. That's lovely.

'I am sometimes unreliable, and my acquaintances know that. People will say, "Come to dinner," and I'll say, "Yes, all right, I'll come if I feel I can contribute, and if you don't like that arrangement, don't invite me." I don't turn up if I suddenly feel on the night that I am not going to make a contribution. Perhaps it is just me licensing myself to be unreliable.

'I like to be in the middle of things. I like to live near enough to the centre of London so that I can walk home from the theatre or a late night jazz concert. I go out to dinner three or four time a week. Recently I had a week off and I went to the theatre every night, saw three movies and read two books.

'Nearly everything I do is related to acting. We are professional pleasers, and that works against deep relationships. To spend a lot of time with an actor like me must be boring for people who want to take the relationship seriously. I am not a good proposition when it comes to deep, private relationships, because I am totally

preoccupied with work. I live a profoundly shallow life – or a deeply superficial one.'
Interviewed by Dan Slater in 1979 for the *Sun*.

'I love reading – I simply couldn't survive without books. I appreciate art, music, poetry – I love beauty of any kind. I like people too – there's so much in life to be enjoyed, I can at least say I'm never bored.'
Interviewed by Richard Marson in 1984 for *Doctor Who Magazine* No. 92.

'I read a lot of escapism. I watch very little television: mainly the news or news comment. I sometimes watch Brian Walden at the weekend and have a glass of wine. I read a lot of newspapers every day; I take four so-called serious newspapers and often two tabloids, which I scour. I read some Dickens every day and Shaw.

'I also have a self-appointed job as a churchyard keeper, in which I look after the dead near my house. There are two cemeteries, and I feel very proprietorial about them. I keep them mown and tidy and I know lots of the dead people there, and I know the names of lots of them. I had a pruning session recently. They're full of sinister-looking yew trees. This time of year is the growing season, so I'm kept busy. Yesterday I was in that cemetery for four hours!

'So if I'm home, I go in and do various odd jobs, a bit of mowing or a bit of weeding or just a bit of looking, keeping things in check. It's nice to think about the dead and wonder what they were like and to speculate on so little evidence. The speculation fires one's imagination, because, as you know, on gravestones it doesn't really say what they were like. You don't know whether they were happy or what their last words were, and some of what's written, well it's downright lies! When they say, "Not dead, only sleeping," well! I had my Honda mower near a fellow's head yesterday and he *definitely* wasn't sleeping, let me tell you!'
Interviewed by John Freeman in 1991 for *Doctor Who Magazine* Nos. 179-181.

ON DEATH:
'Must go out and get the papers. Check the obituaries. If mine's in, I can stop worrying. I've always felt at home with the dead. Dear old things.'
From *Just Who On Earth Is... Tom Baker* video released in 1991 by Reeltime Pictures.

'There is a kind of implacable logic in my life. My early memories are of graveyards, I live by a graveyard and I want a good gravestone as a sign that I existed. I might be frightened to die. But if there were two cameras there, I might make an effort. One for close-ups and one for wide angles!'
Interviewed by Corrina Honan in 1992 for the *Daily Mail*, 28 March edition.

'I've always admired the dead. I find them so uncritical. Where I live in the country, on two sides of my house there are churchyards, and when I wake up in the morning, I look out at the gravestones, and no matter how sorry for myself I feel, I think, well, it could be worse. And so I bought myself a second-hand gravestone, in order to give some money to the parish really. Unfortunately, the man who'd had it before me, well, his name wasn't Baker, but I've had it smoothed down a bit, and just on the top of it, being

modest, there's a star, and underneath it it says, "Tom Baker 1934 -". I didn't have the courage to put in a second date. As for the epitaph – I'll leave that to someone else.'
From *Myth Makers 17: Tom Baker* **video released in 1989 by Reeltime Pictures.**

ON FANS:
'I can't imagine life without fans. So when the fans run out, and the fans of the Doctor run out, and the fans of Tom Baker run out, then what we're talking about is when there's no more love left. And when there's no more love left, there's nothing left. And I'd be nothing then.'
From *Just Who On Earth Is... Tom Baker* **video released in 1991 by Reeltime Pictures.**

'... and I could try, perhaps more convincingly, to demonstrate that I am grateful, and that it all was such fun. And that by and large, if you'll pardon that amazing expression, it goes on being fun. And maybe the fans won't go away, as one of my interrogators suggested so frighteningly a little while ago they would. Perhaps you won't, and if you won't, then I won't. We'll both stay.
'Good health.
'Thank you.'
From *Just Who On Earth Is... Tom Baker* **video released in 1991 by Reeltime Pictures.**

CHARACTER – THE FOURTH DOCTOR

The character of each of the Doctors has been vitally influenced by the personality of the actor playing the role. As Barry Letts, producer of the series from 1969 to 1974, once put it, 'No actor playing the Doctor should be acting *all* the time. There has to be enough of his own personality showing on the screen. It makes life easier for him, for the script writers, in fact for everybody.' Graham Williams, producer from 1977 to 1980, shared this view, maintaining: 'We are utterly dependent on the individual actor's portrayal of that part.' The casting of a new Doctor is therefore one of the most crucial factors determining how the character will come across on screen.

When the third Doctor, Jon Pertwee, reached the end of his time in the series, it was Barry Letts who had the principal responsibility for choosing the next lead actor. One name he considered was that of 39 year-old comedian and former pop singer Jim Dale, well known for his appearances in the *Carry On...* films; but on the whole he favoured casting someone rather older. Amongst those he approached were: Richard Hearne, whom he eventually discounted as the actor was set on the idea of playing the part in the style of the popular Mister Pastry character he had created in the Forties; Michael Bentine, who was quite keen to take the role but decided against it because he would not be happy working on a series without being able to contribute to the scripting; and Graham Crowden, who was also quite enthusiastic but ultimately decided that he would not want to make such a long-term commitment to one particular series.

Many ideas were considered for the image of the new Doctor, including having him look like Albert Einstein and play a violin in the manner of Sherlock Holmes to emphasise his eccentricity. As Letts told *Doctor Who Magazine* in 1981, 'All of us who were involved in the casting wanted a Doctor who would be radically different from Jon Pertwee's style of portrayal. It was no good just turning out a carbon copy, as that would have given the audience the impression that the new Doctor was a watered down version of the previous one, and that would have been unfair to Jon's successor.'

While Letts was still unable to find a suitable candidate for the role, time was marching on and writers had to be briefed to start work on scripts for the fourth Doctor's initial run of stories. In view of the likelihood that the part would eventually go to an actor of advanced years who would be unable to cope with strenuous physical action, the production team decided to introduce a new, young male companion to undertake any 'rough stuff' that might be called for. So was born the character of UNIT medic Harry Sullivan.

With time running short to decide on a new Doctor, Barry Letts received inspiration from another source, as he later explained:

'Eventually it was my head of department, Bill Slater, who suggested Tom Baker. Now, I'd heard of Tom from such productions as *Nicholas and Alexandra*, in which he had taken on the role of Rasputin, so I invited him along to the production office for discussions. I asked him if he had any video tapes of past things he'd worked on, and he said no, but added that just around the corner was a cinema showing his latest film, *The Golden Voyage of Sinbad*. I duly went along to see it, and was impressed. Shortly afterwards, we asked him if he would like to accept the part.'

Speaking on stage at a US *Doctor Who* convention in 1985, Tom Baker recounted his own, rather colourful version of these events:

'I once wrote a letter to the BBC demanding that I be employed. I said that somewhere there, there was a job for me, and it was disgraceful that I hadn't been given it ... The man I wrote to, Bill Slater, had been to a *Doctor Who* casting session that afternoon – the part just happened to be free, that's the way it happens sometimes – and he'd had no ideas. My letter demanding employment was the last letter he read as he was getting into bed. Now, here is a coincidence. I actually knew his wife quite well. No, I don't mean in the Biblical sense; I was acquainted with his wife. I mean, we had sometimes held hands in various canteens – you know, actors are rather extravagant about those sort of things ... Anyway, he was getting into bed, and he conscientiously read his last letter, with a terrifying sigh, and said, "Bloody Tom Baker, demanding employment." And she said, "Oh really, I thought he was doing rather grand things?" He replied, "No, no, he says here I've got to give him a ..." Then he said, "Do you know, I've just come from a casting session this afternoon, for *Doctor Who*." To which Mary Webster – which was his wife's name – said, "Ring him up now, Bill."

'So at eleven o'clock, I was lying on my mattress on the floor, being rather self-consciously bohemian and feeling tragically sorry for myself, which sometimes can be rather a pleasant sensation, and the phone went. He said, "Bill Slater here, BBC. Come and see me tomorrow." And then my life took another change. That's how it happened. I can scarcely believe it myself. And that's the truth – just imagine if I wanted to elaborate on it!'

With Baker cast as the Doctor, the next step was to decide exactly how he would approach the part. He initially had few ideas of his own, and was happy to be guided by Barry Letts and the series' script editor, Robert Holmes. Letts later told the fanzine *In-*

Vision about the preliminary discussions they had:

'Basically, with Tom Baker, we decided to go away from Jon Pertwee. People came up with all sorts of ideas that would have looked like an attempt to duplicate Jon – a poor man's Jon Pertwee. So what we looked for was a strong personality in its own right. We had a meeting in the Balzac wine bar – there was Tom, Philip Hinchcliffe, Bob Holmes and me. This was before Philip took over from me as producer. We discussed the way Tom was going to play the Doctor. The floppy hat and so on was Tom's idea, stemming from me saying that the one thing he mustn't be was a dandy, as Jon had played him that way. And what came out of that conference was fed back to costume designer Jim Acheson.'

Philip Hinchcliffe, *Doctor Who*'s producer from 1974 to 1977, also talked to *In-Vision* about these early discussions:

'I had no hand in casting Tom. He was a *fait accomplis*. But I did have a hand in developing the character. Barry was very good about that. I formed a relationship with Tom, and discussed with Barry what the character would be.

'I had quite firm ideas about the Doctor's character. I discussed with Tom what we thought he could do with it. We discussed what he ought to look like. I also did a sort of crash course on the programme – I hadn't really seen that much of it, although luckily I'd seen quite a lot of the Jon Pertwee stuff. That was the first thing I did, in fact. Then I formulated a view of the character, which I suppose was partly from that tradition, and the Sydney Newman 'cosmic hobo' phrase stuck in my mind. I'd read a fair bit of science fiction, not a lot, so I spent my preparation time reading further from writers and authors whom perhaps I knew about but had never really read. I read voraciously throughout the whole genre.

'I got really interested in all sorts of concepts. It was like suddenly discovering a really fascinating area that I had only vaguely known before. Bob Holmes already had a very good background and was very well read. He also had the drop on me, because he could remember all these old movies that I've never seen! So out of all that, we formulated the character. I liked the idea of him being sort of bohemian.

'At the time, heroes were really going out of fashion. Your hero could be a little bit more vulnerable, a little bit more complex. So our Doctor wasn't quite the same moral authority. He was getting a little bit back to the first Doctor – he was irascible, unreliable, and humans were not quite sure whether they should trust him or not. But basically he was an heroic character. He was less powerfully heroic, though. He had to work a bit harder to get out of problems; and we gave him some pretty tough opposition, I think, so he couldn't just "with one bound" be free all the time!

'Tom kept going round saying, "I'm not really human – how do I portray a 500-year-old Time Lord?" And I said, "Olympian detachment, Tom. You're very good at Olympian detachment." So he used to quote this back at me. But basically, the Doctor is a human hero – we all identify with him so easily. He is the ultimate essence of human virtue. But at the same time, biographically as it were, he's got to sort of be non-human. So Tom was quite keen to get some of his "non-humanness" into it. Bob was as well, which is probably why, at times, we showed him being a bit detached.'

Barry Letts' desire to avoid the fourth Doctor being perceived as 'a poor man's Jon Pertwee' was clearly reflected in Tom Baker's debut adventure, *Robot*. Here, the appearance and behaviour of the new incarnation presented a stark contrast to those of the old. Whereas the third Doctor had been the epitome of Seventies elegance in his velvet smoking jacket, bow tie and frilly shirt, the fourth took on the look of a slightly scruffy bohemian eccentric with his baggy jacket, broad-brimmed hat and long, winding scarf. And whereas the popular image of Pertwee's portrayal had been that of a dashing man of action, often using Venusian Aikido – his own brand of unarmed combat – to tackle his enemies physically, Baker's Doctor was introduced as someone whose preferred approach to problems was contemplation rather than action. On the rare occasions in *Robot* when the new Doctor did become involved in a violent confrontation, he seemed to win almost without trying to, his opponents falling over him or tripping over his scarf. Even the scenes immediately following the Doctor's regeneration, as he wanders around in a nightshirt and finds the TARDIS key hidden in his shoe, can be seen as a light-hearted reworking of similar sequences in Jon Pertwee's debut story, *Spearhead from Space* – again emphasising the contrast between the two Doctors.

Comments made by Jon Pertwee and Tom Baker in the numerous interviews each gave while playing the Doctor show just how important the actors' own personalities were in shaping these contrasting interpretations of the role. Pertwee invariably came across as a very active man, often speaking of his love of strenuous sports such as water-skiing and his interest in high-powered vehicles and state-of-the-art gadgetry. Tom Baker, on the other hand, was always reflective and thoughtful, telling of his years as a monk and offering insights of self-analysis.

The script for *Robot* was written by Terrance Dicks, the man from whom Robert Holmes had just taken over as script editor. Talking to *In-Vision*, Dicks confirmed that in his description of the fourth Doctor he had been greatly influenced by Baker's own personality:

'There was very little to go on, except that I had met Tom by then and talked to him, so I had some idea what he was like. And I'd been in on the casting of Tom before I wrote the script. Tom in the flesh does have this type of loony scatter brain, so I played on that very much. I also used the device, which you can always use in the first episode, that the new regeneration is unstable. So he starts off being rather crazy and gradually quietens down and becomes more reasonable by the end of it. So I thought, if they don't like that interpretation, or if Tom doesn't like that interpretation, they could always say, "Well, he was a bit weird then, but he's different now, he's stable." In fact I think they always kept quite a lot of the arbitrary erraticness that I started him off with.

'In any case, the changes are superficial. It's always the same man; his surface mannerisms may change. So the dramatic thing of writing the serious Doctor stuff actually changes very little indeed. The flourishes are different, and the kind of jokes and witticisms.'

The 'flourishes' that Dicks gave the new Doctor included having him, in the words of the script, 'seemingly ignorant of people's conversation, preoccupied with child-like pursuits – although actually deep in concentration.' Another description read: 'He has a general tendency to adopt gawky, sprawling stances. It is characteristic of his new incarnation that he always tends to lie, lean, perch or hang in some unlikely position rather than sitting conventionally.' These characteristics were picked up by Christopher Barry, the director of *Robot*, and faithfully reflected on screen; and, as noted by Terrance Dicks, traces of them were to remain throughout the fourth Doctor's era.

The 'alien detachment' of which Philip Hinchcliffe spoke was also apparent from an early stage. It was highlighted in a speech that Robert Holmes wrote for the Doctor to deliver in his second story, *The Ark in Space*, when contemplating his discovery of a group of humans lying in suspended animation in an orbiting space-station after the apparent destruction of all life on Earth:

'Homo sapiens – what an inventive, invincible species. It's only a few million years since they crawled up out of the mud and learned to walk, puny defenceless bipeds. They've survived flood, famine and plague. They've survived cosmic wars and holocausts. And now here they are, out among the stars, waiting to begin a new life, ready to outsit eternity. They're indomitable ... indomitable.'

It was Holmes again who, in his script for the following season's *Pyramids of Mars*, had the Doctor making specific comment on his alien nature. When his companion, Sarah Jane Smith, chides him on his pensive mood, reasoning that he should be happy to be returning to Earth, he tells her:

'The Earth isn't my home, Sarah. I'm a Time Lord ... You don't understand the implications. I'm not a human being. I walk in eternity ... It means I've lived for something like 750 years.'

In *The Seeds of Doom*, the Doctor refuses to help a group of scientists at an Antarctic base to amputate the arm of a colleague who has been infected by an alien Krynoid. 'You must help yourselves,' he explains, and one gets the impression that he is referring not just to the scientists but to the human race as a whole.

It was this other-worldly aspect of the Doctor to which Tom Baker drew particular attention in interviews he gave shortly after winning the role. 'I want to play him in an individual way,' he told *The Times* in February 1974, 'with the suggestion that although he has a human body he comes from somewhere else.'

Baker did not, however, want the Doctor to seem omniscient or invulnerable. As Peter Haining's 1986 book *The Doctor Who File* quoted him as explaining:

'I came to believe that the Doctor should have an air of naive innocence about him to counter his enormous wealth of knowledge and past experience. He had to seem vulnerable, and therefore more interesting to an audience I felt would quickly tire of the Doctor as Superman!

'My basic approach to new situations was to walk boldly into them and say with a broad grin, "Hello, I am the Doctor." Now the audience may be aware, from previous scenes, that the Doctor is going into a situation of dire peril, but their attention is held, subconsciously knowing that, any second now, he is going to get knocked to the floor!'

Giving the Doctor this air of constant optimism and naive trustfulness – unwilling to think ill of any person or creature until presented with hard and often painful evidence of their villainy – was just one of the ways in which Baker sought to keep his portrayal fresh and interesting.

Before long, the fourth Doctor had become, as Barry Letts had hoped, a very popular character in his own right, and a highly identifiable one with his imposing stature, his extraordinary hat and scarf, his rich booming voice, his broad toothy grin, his bag of jelly babies and his yo-yo. This eccentric image was quickly seized upon by journalists in the popular press, whose standard description of the fourth Doctor was along the lines of 'the gangling, 6ft 3in figure in the floppy hat and the long scarf.'

There were however a number of respects in which the character changed and developed as time went by. While his thoughtful side continued to be apparent – one particularly celebrated instance of this being a scene in *Genesis of the Daleks* in which he questions his right to destroy the Dalek race at birth – he also became more physical in his approach to problems, making the Harry Sullivan character partly redundant. He was at perhaps his most aggressive in *The Seeds of Doom*, the story that closed his second season of adventures. In this story, he was seen violently to assault several of his adversaries, breaking a chair over the head of one of them, and even to wield a gun. None of the previous Doctors had ever been quite so unrestrained as this in his use of force to combat evil.

Although the degree of violence in *The Seeds of Doom* was arguably exceptional, this was by no means the only story in which the Doctor was seen to get heavily involved in forceful action. In *The Masque of Mandragora*, for instance, he at one point lashes out with his feet to try to avoid capture and also takes part in a swordfight, as he does again in *The Androids of Tara*. *The Deadly Assassin* and *The Talons of Weng-Chiang* provided further examples of him tackling his enemies physically. On the other hand, where he did employ such tactics, it was almost always because he or one of his friends was under threat or in imminent danger. For the most part, he showed a clear disposition towards reaching peaceful solutions; and he was certainly committed to preserving life wherever possible. He chastised his companion Leela for her tendency to rely on her hunting knife to get her out of difficult situations, and showed a similar disapproval of violent behaviour by others – for example, private eye Duggan's propensity for throwing punches in *City of Death* (although ironically it is with one such punch that Duggan saves the day at the end of the story).

An equally if not more significant development in the Doctor's character was a growing inclination for him to resort to tomfoolery to confuse and outmanoeuvre his enemies, accompanied by his adoption of a generally more outrageous and amusing disposition. His brooding, contemplative moods came to be offset by bursts of manic activity; he began to assail his opponents with flippant retorts and cheeky wise-cracks; and it became increasingly common for him to be seen staring goggle-eyed into camera. All these things helped to give the fourth Doctor a uniquely zany, off-the-wall persona.

This shift of emphasis was born out of Tom Baker's keen determination to keep the character constantly surprising and engaging – an aim that came increasingly to preoccupy the actor, as he told *Doctor Who Magazine* in 1984:

'The Doctor is a moral being – you know exactly what he's going to do and why. There's very little that's unexpected about him. Character development – well, there's no such thing, because the Doctor is a heroic stereotype who conforms to the patterns of behaviour you expect him to conform to. His character basically stays the same. The challenge is to make that character as diverting and as interesting as possible within the given framework. I'd think, "How can this be made different?" or, "There's something new to be exploited here," but it got harder and harder to keep the character fresh. The scripts often didn't help, either.'

Although the fourth Doctor could never have been considered an entirely conventional hero, being – as Philip Hinchcliffe observed – more 'complex' and 'vulnerable' than that, Baker was frequently frustrated by what he perceived to be a lack of imagination and ingenuity on the writers' part in representing the character. While the actor's own natural inventiveness had been held in check to a degree during Hinchcliffe's time as producer, under Graham Williams he came to demand more and more input into the scripting process, using rehearsals as an opportunity to rewrite, sometimes with the

413

assistance of his co-stars, any action or dialogue with which he was unhappy. This gave him the freedom to make the stories, and especially the character of the Doctor himself, much more tongue-in-cheek and exuberant; a philosophy that he carried through into his performance.

This method of working was taken to perhaps its furthest extent after Lalla Ward joined the series as the second incarnation of the Doctor's companion Romana. In Ward, Baker found a kindred spirit – they were later to be married – and together they frequently made radical amendments to the scripts with which they were provided. 'We used to have the most awful problems with our writers,' Ward told *Doctor Who Magazine* in 1984. 'Tom and I used to have to rewrite most of our dialogue with the director, usually because it wasn't right for the parts we were playing. And it happened from the start. Our actual rehearsal time, which was incredibly tight, was reduced still further as a result. So the programme was always a heavy workload – we had this responsibility for the show, and we were doing so many a year against the problems of a small budget and scripts that we wouldn't have done without at least an element of rewriting.'

On screen, there was an obvious rapport between Baker and Ward, and the dialogue in the scenes they shared together was often highly witty and sophisticated. There was even at times a hint of playful surrealism about it, such as in the following conversation as they prepare to descend from the top of the Eiffel Tower in Paris in the opening episode of *City of Death*:

> ROMANA: Shall we take the lift, or fly?
>
> DOCTOR: Let's not be ostentatious.
>
> ROMANA: All right, let's fly then.
>
> DOCTOR: That would be silly. We'll take the lift.

This exchange is given added significance by a scene at the end of the story in which the pair, having returned to the top of the Eiffel Tower, are then shown back on the ground again only moments later, so that it appears the only way they could have got down so quickly is indeed to have flown!

Speaking to *Doctor Who Magazine* in 1991, Baker said: 'Naturalism isn't my strong point – I'm not even good at coming through doors convincingly! But never mind, even if you can't come through a door convincingly, perhaps you can come through a door interestingly or, dare one say, amusingly ...'

Baker meant this comment quite literally. Such had been his anxiety not to let his portrayal of the Doctor become stale or repetitive that he had indeed tried to find interesting ways of doing such normally mundane things as coming through a doorway or sitting in a chair. At one point in *The Invasion of Time*, for instance, he had insisted on having the Doctor trip whilst walking along a corridor, for no other reason than that it made the scene more unusual and entertaining. And as was so often the case, it also raised a laugh.

At the time, some critics felt that Baker's performance had gone too far in the direction of humour, making the Doctor appear almost a buffoon – just as, during Philip

Hinchcliffe's time, some had felt that too much violence had entered into his portrayal. In his 1984 interview with *Doctor Who Magazine*, Baker explained his attitude both to violence and to comedy in the series:

'I didn't like real violence – the mindless type of thug violence you always get in American police series. I can't say how much that bores me. I always preferred to outwit the baddies – I don't think it's necessary to blow them from here to kingdom come. I mean, it's dull, isn't it? What's new about that? I don't feel we really went too far with the violence in the show. I think if it had been over-the-top, somebody would have said so. The problem in a show where good always wins over bad is how to do it in a new way. Usually our scripts would blow them up.

'As for the comedy, I think a lot of the criticism we got was from people who were used to the old way. The audience expected the old, cliche scripts – the comedy element was only part of it, but I felt it was a wonderful way of winning the children's imagination. I always felt *Doctor Who* was a children's programme, watched by children of all ages. With a comic approach, it was more diverting to laugh our villains into destruction. You can't tell me we lost all our tension – in the comedy there were very serious bits; that contrast is extraordinarily effective. I don't think we overdid either violence or comedy – in fact I think we could have gone further with both elements.'

While the furthest the Tom Baker era went in the direction of violence was probably in his third season of stories, the furthest it went towards comedy was without doubt in his sixth and penultimate season. Baker's final year as the Doctor saw him returning to a predominantly serious characterisation more in line with his original interpretation of the role.

The main reason for this late change of style was the appointment of a new producer in the person of John Nathan-Turner. Nathan-Turner disliked the type of humour that had become a standard feature of *Doctor Who* during his predecessor's tenure and was determined to stamp his own mark on the series – something that initially caused clashes between him and Baker. However, although more serious, Baker's performance in this last season remained as charismatic as ever. It was also, at times, more sombre and brooding than ever before – an impression enhanced by the darker, more subdued costume he was given at this time. This led up to the fourth Doctor's final adventure, *Logopolis*, in which the manifestation of the mysterious figure of the Watcher portended his imminent regeneration. Eventually, in foiling the latest scheme of his arch-enemy the Master, he sacrificed his own life to achieve one last, all-important victory – saving the universe itself from destruction.

REWRITING THE MYTH

In the fourth Doctor's era, countless new monsters, planets, alien races and other elements were added to the *Who*niverse. Some were so important that they would forever change the nature of the series. Yet continuity would seem to have been fairly low in the list of priorities of the successive production teams making *Doctor Who* in the Seventies, as revealed in an interview with Tom Baker and producer Graham Williams in Issue 19 of *Starburst*:

Tom Baker: I meet people who reel off these titles or ask my opinion about certain things and they obviously know more about the history of the programme than I do. Because I'm not really – except in the informed way of not subverting anything – interested very much in what Pat did or Jon did. We're playing it absolutely from moment to moment, holding on by our fingertips with the pressure of time and money and everything.

Graham Williams: I mean, you and I only keep marginally in the back of our minds what we did last year …

Baker: Yeah.

Williams: Let alone five years ago or ten years ago.

Baker: Not interested in that.

Williams: The audience aren't very interested in that either.

Baker: What those fans are conceding is they don't understand actors and programme makers. What's in the past is in the past. Each one you try to make history with – 'This one is the best one'.

Williams: If we stuck religiously to points of continuity, of what we'd done before, the series would still be exactly where it was 15 years ago. You can't change a programme overnight. I don't think any audience could be expected to wear that – it wouldn't be fair on them. But, I think, in my years with the show, the changes we've made have been quite significant. It's changed only 15% or 20% a year, so it's still within the acceptable framework of the programme, but nevertheless it's moved on.

Graham Williams seems to have been suggesting that continuity was often sacrificed in favour of good plots, and that this practice of rewriting *Doctor Who* history was acceptable provided that changes were made gradually so as not to confuse the viewer. It would not however be true to say that this was the policy of all the producers of the Tom Baker era, or – perhaps more importantly – of the various script editors who worked under them. Baker's suggestion that what had gone before his era was ignored does not stand up to close scrutiny. Many links with the series' past were apparent during his time with the series. Even if one chooses to ignore the fact that his first story, *Robot*, was a very typical UNIT tale, which could arguably have slotted in at any point during Jon Pertwee's tenure as the Doctor, there is no denying the fact that the remainder of his debut season also drew heavily on the series' past. His third story, for instance, saw the re-use of a monster race – the Sontarans – that had made its own debut as recently as the previous season. This was clearly an attempt by departing producer Barry Letts and the Sontarans' creator, script editor Robert Holmes, to keep continuity between the adventures of the new Doctor and those of the old.

The Sontaran, Field-Major Styre, in *The Sontaran Experiment* appears identical at first sight to the original Sontaran, Linx, seen in *The Time Warrior*. In fact the same actor – Kevin Lindsay – played both parts. A number of minor differences are however worthy of note, especially as they serve to illustrate some of the factors that can underlie departures from strict continuity.

First, although the Sontarans are supposedly a race of genetically identical clones, Styre's facial features are slightly different from Linx's. These changes were the result of a requirement to make the costume more comfortable for Lindsay to wear; the original mask had been made from heavy fibreglass matting coated with a thin surface layer of latex, and had caused breathing problems for the actor, who suffered from a heart condition. The new mask was lighter and better ventilated. This is an example of a departure from continuity caused by a practical necessity.

Secondly, Styre has five fingers whereas Linx had only three. When asked about this discrepancy at a convention, one-time script editor Terrance Dicks joked that Sontarans probably found it easier to break human bones with five fingers! In truth, however, this change was probably the result of a simple mistake or oversight by a member of the design staff. If this change had been carried forward into subsequent Sontaran stories, it would no doubt have become accepted that Sontarans have five fingers, but in their next appearance, in *The Invasion of Time,* they had reverted to having only three fingers, leaving Styre the odd man (or Sontaran) out.

In *The Sontaran Experiment*, it is also revealed that when exhausted, the Sontarans need to recharge themselves. This new fact is introduced as a plot device that allows the Doctor to defeat Styre, and is an example of a deliberate addition to *Doctor Who* mythology.

In terms of character, Styre and Linx are very similar. This is not surprising, as writer Bob Baker recalled in an interview in *In-Vision* that the Sontarans' creator Robert Holmes had given him and his writing partner Dave Martin a very detailed introduction to the monsters:

'Bob had given us the most incredibly deep briefing on the life and breeding systems and defecation systems of the Sontaran (I think he must have met one at some time). We just had to stop him, he was going on so much. It was very funny actually. He was under a bit of a strain, I felt, and this was manifest in the way he was talking about the Sontaran.

'So he said "There's the character, in you go and put the story for two episodes around that." As far as cramping our style goes, it was just a brief – just like the Doctor is already a character. We didn't feel we were being fobbed off with a Sontaran. A story is a story, and we did get our own little monster in it.

'The script was printed, rushed down to the location, and shot. I think Bob changed three or four words – about the Sontaran. "He wouldn't do that. He wouldn't say that." "Oh all right then, change it Bob. It's your monster."'

In the very next story after *The Sontaran Experiment*, the fourth Doctor encountered another old foe, in fact the oldest of all – the Daleks. Dalek history comprises a major part of the *Who*niverse, and in the twelve years prior to their appearance in *Genesis of the Daleks*, their mythology had already undergone a number of subtle changes and developments. From radiation-spawned mutants trapped inside metal casings, powerless to move outside the confines of their metal-floored city, they had been transformed into a space- and time-faring army, sweeping through the galaxy to conquer and enslave countless other worlds.

In *Genesis of the Daleks*, the Daleks' creator, Terry Nation, sought to tell the story of their origins. Naturally enough, he set the action on the creatures' home world, Skaro, which had first been seen in their introductory story, *The Mutants*, back in 1963. In *The Mutants*, the Doctor and companions had learnt from the history records of the planet's humanoid inhabitants, the Thals, that the Daleks had once been a race of scientists and philosophers called the Dals. A terrible nuclear war between Dals and Thals had led to the creation of the horribly-mutated Daleks. This view of Skaroine history is essentially confirmed in *Genesis of the Daleks*, although the Dals are replaced by the Kaleds as the Daleks' ancestors, and a new character is introduced as the Daleks' progenitor. This character, Davros, creator of the Daleks, stole centre stage from the Daleks themselves and would continue to do so in many subsequent Dalek tales long after the end of the fourth Doctor's era.

It was perhaps inevitable that any story about the origins of the Daleks would focus primarily on the situation that had existed before their creation, showing the transition to the state of affairs on Skaro that viewers had seen in *The Mutants*. Davros was the personification of the transition. Half-human, half-Dalek in appearance, he exhibited the evil cunning that he would eventually instill into his creations. Meanwhile, the prototype Daleks appeared almost inanimate, being switched on and off like radio controlled models. It was only at the end of the story that they revealed their sentience, when they apparently exterminated Davros and seized control of their own destiny.

Although *Genesis of the Daleks* appears to fit fairly well into previously-established Dalek history, a few continuity errors do surface. The most obvious of these is the fact that the prototype Daleks are seen to operate outside the Kaled Elite's bunker, far from any metal floors, and even attack the Thal city. Yet in *The Mutants*, which must have been later in the Daleks' time stream, they were unable to leave their city, a disadvantage that the Doctor was able to exploit. Also, the 'prototype' Daleks from *Genesis of the Daleks* resembled those from much later periods of Dalek history, rather than those seen in their debut story.

In *Destiny of the Daleks*, the Daleks' second and last appearance during the fourth Doctor's era, Davros was resurrected. There was of course no overriding need for him to have reappeared for the sake of continuity, as he had already been established to have died at the very beginning of Dalek history. Yet, although *Destiny of the Daleks* is presumably set many hundreds of years after the events in *Genesis of the Daleks*, the character is brought back to aid his progeny in their battle with the Movellans.

The Movellans are humanoid robots, whose thinking is perfectly logical in all respects, including their battle strategy. The Daleks' battle computers are also totally logical, and the resulting impasse sends the Daleks scurrying back to Skaro to excavate and revive their creator in the hope that he will be able to break the deadlock – a hope that proves well-founded, as Davros realises that the required solution is for one of the sides in the battle to make an intuitive, illogical move. This plotline is flawed, however, as the Daleks should have been able to break the stalemate without Davros's help, simply because they are by nature illogical and emotional, conditioned to respond to situations with hate and anger.

Yet the Daleks in *Destiny of the Daleks* are subtly different from the Daleks of old. Several times during the story they are referred to as robots; and at one point the Doctor himself mentions in passing that they were once organic life-forms, perhaps inferring that they no longer are. Is this the 'destiny' to which the title of the story refers – the evolution of the Daleks into the robots that the general public and media have often mistakenly assumed them to be? Whether this suggestion of a radical change in the nature of the Daleks was intentional on the part of the production office is however uncertain, especially in the light of subsequent stories in which the Daleks reverted to their original nature as organic mutations within metallic casings.

Tom Baker's first season ended with a story featuring a race of monsters that had been absent from the series for some seven years. The Cybermen had last appeared in the Patrick Troughton story *The Invasion*. It is perhaps not surprising, then, that many changes were apparent when they returned in *Revenge of the Cybermen*.

For one thing, there were a number of differences in the Cybermen's appearance. This was not an unusual occurrence as there had been some degree of variation in the costumes in every previous Cybermen story. These variations had ranged from very subtle touches to radical redesigns. The introduction of the Cyber Leader into the Cybermen's command structure was another important innovation in *Revenge of the Cybermen*. Previously the viewer had seen only the Cyberman Controller in *The Tomb of the Cybermen*, the Cyber Planner in *The Wheel in Space* and the Cyber Coordinator in *The Invasion*, the latter two of which had been not even humanoid in shape but more like partly-organic computers.

The concept of the Cyber Leader (his rank denoted by the black colouring of the sides and back of his head – an idea drawn from writer Gerry Davis's novelisations of previous Cybermen stories) was an innovation that militated against a view of the Cybermen as being just a horde of identical silver zombies, raising the possibility of Cybermen trained, or rather programmed, for specific tasks. However, it was in the characterisation of the Cybermen that *Revenge of the Cybermen* differed most from previous stories. Before, the Cybermen had not really had individual characters as such. They were merely machine men, without emotions or personalities to distinguish one from another. In *Revenge of the Cybermen*, the Cybermen – and in particular the Cyber Leader – display a wide range of emotions, including anger, pride and fear.

The premise of the Cybermen being vulnerable to gold dust, which plates the respiratory apparatus in their chest units and effectively suffocates them, was an important development in their history. *Revenge of the Cybermen* can in fact be seen as the final end of the Cybermen, their race having been reduced to a mere handful of survivors by an earlier cataclysmic war with humanity. Their plan to destroy Voga, the 'planet of gold', seems born of desperation, and at one point the Doctor taunts the Cyber Leader over his race's depleted state:

> Doctor: You've no home planet, no influence, nothing. You're just a pathetic bunch of tin soldiers skulking about the galaxy in an ancient spaceship.

It is indicative of the level of emotion with which the Cybermen are endowed in this story that the Doctor's goading seemingly causes the Cyber Leader to lose his temper, to the extent that he physically attacks the Time Lord, even though the latter's survival is, for the time being, essential to his plan.

Reinforcing the impression that these were unusually emotional Cybermen was the treatment of their voices. In previous stories, their dialogue had been delivered by a voice artist who, in most cases, used a small electronic palate device inside his own mouth to give the voices a machine-like monotone; a process that effectively removed any sense of emotion from the resulting voice. In *Revenge of the Cybermen*, however, the actors playing the Cybermen provided the voices themselves, with only a slight electronic treatment. The resulting voices were still very human-like, and in the case of the Cyber Leader, played by Christopher Robbie, a slight trace of a South African accent was detectable.

After the death of Roger Delgado in 1973, it seemed unlikely that the Master, the evil Time Lord he had so memorably portrayed, would ever again return to pit his wits against the Doctor's. In 1976, however, *The Deadly Assassin* did see the Master return, albeit in a much-altered form.

The Master had originally been presented as a character with many similarities to the Doctor; he was of the same race, of comparable intelligence and capable of exhibiting equal if not greater charm. Yet whereas the Doctor had always been driven to help the underdog and to combat injustice wherever he encountered it, the Master saw only the possibilities for exploitation and corruption. During the Pertwee era, viewers witnessed the Doctor thwarting many of the Master's evil schemes. Each successive defeat would no doubt have fuelled his adversary's sense of frustration and resentment. It is not surprising, therefore, that by the time of his reappearance in *The Deadly Assassin*, the Master has become clearly unhinged. Although he retains his cunning and guile, and his penchant for the grand scheme, his veneer of charm has gone. Moreover, nearing the end of his natural life, having used up all his regenerations, he is now a twisted parody of his former self. His body is emaciated and blackened, the result of a terrible accident on the planet Tersurus, and he is clinging to life only by virtue of his amazing willpower and his hatred of the Time Lords – and especially of the Doctor.

Writer Robert Holmes included in his script for this story some evocative stage directions for the Master, describing his features as 'the crawling face of death' and his hands as '... belonging to a skeleton, the remaining withered skin hanging in strips.' The fact that the BBC chose to bring the Master back in this deteriorated form is a testament to the strength of the public's association of Roger Delgado with the role of the evil Time Lord. Producer Philip Hinchcliffe could simply have regenerated the character, in much the same way as the Doctor himself had been transformed on three previous occasions, but would the public have accepted a new actor in the part? The idea of depicting the Master in a decrepit state allowed the production team to resurrect the character in a way that would minimise such audience resistance, while at the same time leaving open the possibility of a proper regeneration at a later date. In the publicity material sent out to the press prior to transmission of *The Deadly Assassin*, the BBC went out of their way to stress that this was not the straightforward return of an old foe:

'Although publicity along the lines of "The return of the Master" will help us, please bear in mind that Roger Delgado who formerly played the Master died tragically in a car accident several years ago. The actor playing the new Master, Peter Pratt, is only ever seen wearing a mask.'

It would be another four years before the Master would return in *The Keeper of Traken*, the penultimate story of the fourth Doctor's era. Still initially in his decayed form, he attempts to gain control of the Keepership of the Traken Union and the vast powers that accompany it. His plan is only partially successful, as the Doctor's intervention forces him to abandon the Keepership. However, the residual effects of his time in the Keeper's chair apparently enable him to steal the body of Keeper-elect

Tremas, giving himself a new lease of life. (This is not explicitly stated in the story, but if he had already possessed the power to take over another person's body, he would presumably have done so before this point.)

The actor cast as the Master's new incarnation was Anthony Ainley, who had also played Tremas. Whereas each successive incarnation of the Doctor had been given a different and distinctive image, Ainley was intentionally chosen and made-up to resemble Delgado. And in *Logopolis*, the story in which the new Master really established himself, it quickly became apparent that Ainley's interpretation of the role also owed much to Delgado's original. The Master seemed to have regained the calm and self-confidence of his earlier incarnation, albeit now tinged with a streak of pure insanity from his degenerated period.

The Master's plan in *Logopolis* involves disrupting the Logopolitans' calculations, which are holding open a number of Charged Vacuum Emboitments (CVEs) – gateways into other universes. This was in itself a clever piece of story continuity, as CVEs had been previously introduced as part of a linking theme to the stories of season eighteen.

As so often before, the Doctor eventually defeats the Master in the story's closing moments. In doing so, however, he sacrifices his own fourth incarnation and regenerates. And this is by no means the end of his troubles with the Master ...

With such interesting characters as the Doctor and the Master, it is hardly surprising that *Doctor Who* viewers and writers alike were fascinated by the society that spawned them. Of all the new elements of *Doctor Who* mythology introduced during the fourth Doctor's era, those revolving around the Time Lords and their planet were arguably the most important in terms of the series' future development.

When first introduced in *The War Games*, Patrick Troughton's final story as the Doctor, the Time Lords had been presented as a mysterious and rather aloof race possessing awesome powers. Then, in their occasional appearances during the Jon Pertwee era, a little more had been learnt about them and they had come to seem rather less alien.

The first season of the fourth Doctor's era added little to this previously-established history of the Time Lords, although a single emissary did appear to the Doctor at the beginning of *Genesis of the Daleks* to assign him the task of attempting to alter the Daleks' future. It wasn't until the next season, the thirteenth, that any significant new information came to light.

The Brain of Morbius cast still further doubt on the original view of the Time Lords as invulnerable, near-immortal beings. In particular, it revealed their need to use a substance known as the Elixir of Life to get them through difficult regenerations. Something else that became apparent during the course of the story was that Time Lord society might not be as idyllic and well-ordered as had been previously suggested. It was recounted that revolutionaries had in the not-too-distant past attempted to overthrow the Time Lords' rulers and their policies of non-intervention in the affairs of other worlds. Morbius, believing that his race should dedicate itself to conquest, had raised a large following to aid him in his quest for power. He and his supporters had however been defeated on the planet Karn, where he had eventually been tried and sentenced to be vaporised.

Morbius was by no means the first renegade Time Lord to have featured in *Doctor Who* – there had previously been the Monk, the War Chief and the Master, amongst others. The fact that so many Gallifreyans want to rebel against their rulers' authority tends to suggest that there is something rotten at the core of their society. This was certainly the view taken by script editor Robert Holmes, who presented his own interpretation of Gallifreyan life in *The Deadly Assassin* – the first adventure to be set entirely on the Doctor's home world.

Holmes's Time Lords were a race gone to seed, more concerned with etiquette and rituals than with the science that had made them so powerful in the first place. Their superior knowledge in fact appears to have allowed them to slip into complacency, spending their time worrying about petty politics rather than about the affairs of the rest of the universe.

This depiction came as a bit of a shock to many fans who had grown accustomed to the idea of the Time Lords as a race of almost omnipotent beings. The President of the fledgling *Doctor Who Appreciation Society* wrote a strongly critical review of the story, condemning it for not following the established Time Lord mythology. In a letter to the fanzine *Gallifrey*, Holmes explained his reasons for departing so radically from previously-perceived notions of the race:

'I'd noticed that over the years they had produced quite a few galactic lunatics – the Meddling Monk, the Master, Omega and Morbius. How did this square with the notion that the Time Lords were an omnipotent bunch of do-gooders? Could it be that this notion had been put about by the Time Lords themselves?'

Holmes claimed that the main inspiration for the plot of *The Deadly Assassin* was the film *The Manchurian Candidate*, from the novel of the same name by Richard Condon. This told the tale of an American war hero secretly brainwashed by the Chinese and sent back to America to assassinate key political figures, including the President. The mention in *The Deadly Assassin* of a secretive Time Lord organisation known as the CIA (Celestial Intervention Agency) is a clear reference back to Condon's tale of political intrigue. *The Deadly Assassin* also has many plot similarities to the real-life assassination of President John F Kennedy in Dallas on 22 November 1963.

The system of Time Lord government as depicted in *The Deadly Assassin* seems to have its basis both in scholastic and in religious organisations. The Lord President is the figurehead, and beneath him are the Chancellor and the Cardinals, the heads of the Time Lord chapters, three of which – the Prydonians, the Patrexes and the Arcalians – are specifically named in the story. Each of the different chapters is distinguishable by the colours of its ceremonial robes: orange and scarlet for the Prydonians, green for the Arcalians and heliotrope for the Patrexes. The Doctor is revealed to be a Prydonian, and this is apparently the most important and influential of the chapters, having provided more Presidents than all the others put together. The true seat of power on Gallifrey however rests within the High Council, a body on which the most high-ranking of the Cardinals sit.

These facts about Time Lord society are presented to the viewer primarily by way of the dialogue of the character Runcible, one of the Doctor's peers from his days at the Prydonian academy. He is a Commentator for public access video, covering the important Presidential resignation ceremony held in the Panopticon, the central chamber of the Time Lords' city, the Capitol.

Below the Cardinals there are other ranks of Time Lords, including the Castellan, an official responsible for law and order, who is in command of the force of Chancellory guards. There is also the Coordinator, whose duties are akin to those of a librarian, watching over the APC Net and the Matrix – the repository of all the knowledge and experience of deceased Time Lords. In *The Deadly Assassin*, it is to Coordinator Engin that Castellan Spandrell goes when he wishes to access the Doctor's biographical data.

Engin comments to Spandrell that the Castellan usually deals with more plebian classes than Prydonian renegades, a remark suggesting that although all Time Lords are Gallifreyans, not all Gallifreyans are necessarily Time Lords. The evidence seems to suggest that the majority of the populace of Gallifrey do not share the great powers of their rulers – a possible cause of the unrest that is hinted at, especially by Cardinal Borusa's insistence that Chancellor Goth's treachery be covered up to avoid the Time Lords being seen in a bad light.

The Time Lords certainly would have looked foolish if it had become commonly known that they had forgotten the true significance of the Sash and the Great Key of Rassilon, which they had believed to be merely symbolic regalia of the Time Lord President. As the Doctor discovers, these artifacts are in truth devices that give access to the Eye of Harmony, a monolith hidden beneath the floor of the Panopticon, which holds stable the core of a black hole and thereby acts as the source of all the Time Lords' power.

Like Omega, Rassilon is described as a legendary Time Lord figure who lived at the dawn of their civilisation. Coordinator Engin reads to the Doctor from the Book of the Old Time, which records that Rassilon was originally an engineer and an architect before the Time Lords abandoned the barren road of technology – a rather strange statement considering that, however ignorant they may be of the workings of the technology that powers their world, they are still very much dependent upon it. It seems odd, too, that although the APC Net supposedly holds the sum total of all Time Lord knowledge, they still have to turn to such obscure texts as the Book of the Old Time to find out about their early history!

Underworld gave viewers a little more information about that history, explaining in the process the reason for the Time Lords' non-interventionist policies. During the story, it is revealed that the Time Lords once aided a race called the Minyans by giving them the technology with which to build an advanced society. The Minyans treated the Time Lords as gods, but were not advanced enough to cope with the new abilities they had been given. They used those gifts to create powerful weapons, and ultimately destroyed themselves in a cataclysmic war. The Time Lords vowed that from that time onwards they would never again interfere in the affairs of other races.

It was in *The Invasion of Time*, the story that immediately followed *Underworld*, that the Time Lords themselves were next seen in *Doctor Who*. This story essentially confirmed the Robert Holmes view of Gallifreyan society, while at the same time adding a number of new elements.

One of those elements was a female Time Lord, Rodan, who – with the sole exception of the Doctor's own grand-daughter, Susan – was the first female Gallifreyan ever to be seen in the series. Rodan was a very junior Time Lord, whose responsibilities included monitoring the approach of spaceships to Gallifrey and controlling the transduction force field barriers that protected the planet from possible invasion.

Another important addition was that of a group of Gallifreyans who had turned their backs on their former comfortable lifestyle and now lived a more primitive existence in the wastelands outside the Capitol. It has often been speculated by fans that these people were the Shabogans, a group of trouble-makers mentioned by Castellan Spandrell in *The Deadly Assassin*, but there is no evidence to suggest that the two groups were connected.

A slight oddity in *The Invasion of Time* is that the rod-like artefact referred to in *The Deadly Assassin* as the Great Key of Rassilon is described here as the Rod of Rassilon, while another Key of Rassilon is introduced that does actually look like a conventional key. The Key proves to be a vital component of the Demat gun, a weapon so powerful that it can remove its target from time and space altogether.

The sixteenth season of *Doctor Who* also introduced a number of important new elements, and the fact that it had an over-arching theme (sometimes referred to as an umbrella theme, or a story arc) was in itself an innovation. The Doctor's search for the Key to Time was initiated by the White Guardian, a being representing the forces of light and order, who was implied to be in an eternal power-struggle with the opposing Black Guardian, representing the forces of dark and chaos. The Guardians were created by *Doctor Who* producer Graham Williams essentially to meet the series' need for a race of powerful, omniscient beings – a role vacated by the now-flawed Time Lords – and they would become an important aspect of the series' development over the next few years.

For one thing, the White Guardian provided the Doctor with a new companion, a female Time Lord by the name of Romanadvoratrelundar – Romana for short. This was the first time the Doctor had had a companion who was his intellectual equal. Romana had in fact gained higher grades than the Doctor at the Time Lord academy! But her aloof nature and her lack of practical experience of the universe outside the transduction barriers of Gallifrey often led her to stumble into dangerous situations.

Romana's relationship with the Doctor was often strained by their competitive natures, and this may perhaps be why, after they had successfully collected all six segments of the Key to Time, she chose to regenerate. This regeneration was quite different from those that viewers had previously witnessed the Doctor undergoing, in that Romana was able to choose her new form. She paraded a number of alternatives before the Doctor, before overcoming the Doctor's resistance to her adopting the likeness of Princess Astra, the living being who had embodied the final segment of the Key. In her new incarnation, her relationship with the Doctor seemed to improve greatly. The Doctor was clearly deeply saddened when she elected to leave him to remain with the Tharils in E-Space at the end of *Warriors' Gate*.

Three stories during season eighteen took place within this mysterious realm of E-Space, a universe smaller than our own, which the TARDIS inadvertently entered through a CVE. It was in one of these stories, *State of Decay*, that a further piece of information about the ancient history of the Time Lords surfaced. The Doctor finds himself battling the last of the Great Vampires, the ancient enemy of the Time Lords from the time of Rassilon. It is revealed that the Time Lords formed a fleet of bow-ships to hunt down and destroy the Vampires, but one of the creatures escaped and fled into E-Space. Rassilon then ordered that a special instruction be placed within all time capsules to the effect that the operator should make every attempt to destroy the Vampire if ever its whereabouts were to be discovered.

Further facts would have been added to Time Lord history in *Shada*, but as industrial action at the BBC prevented its completion, it is arguable whether or not these should be regarded as bona fide elements of *Doctor Who* mythology. For this book, we have chosen not to cover anything that was not televised.

The Doctor's TARDIS had played an important part in the series' history from the first episode onwards. During seasons twelve and thirteen, there were actually very few scenes that took place within the TARDIS, but in *The Masque of Mandragora*, the Doctor was seen to take Sarah Jane Smith on a tour through some of the many rooms of his ship, including the enormous boot cupboard. The most interesting discovery is the TARDIS's secondary control room, a wood-panelled affair with a smaller central console on a raised dais, also in wood. This new control room set was used for the whole of the season, and was intended to be a permanent replacement for the now fairly tatty original console and set. However, the panels of the new set warped whilst in storage, and were unusable come the beginning of the following season. Hence the original control room was rebuilt, and made its reappearance in *The Invisible Enemy*.

Another new fact revealed about the TARDIS, in *The Deadly Assassin*, was that it was a Type 40 TT Capsule, and the only one of its type still in operation.

The greatest tour of the TARDIS ever undertaken was during *The Invasion of Time*, when the Doctor and his friends were chased by the Sontarans through the many rooms of the ship. A laboratory and a swimming pool (described as the bathroom!) were amongst the sections shown.

In *Logopolis*, the existence of the Cloister room is revealed. This is a large chamber containing ancient stone work covered in overhanging plants. Another addition is the Cloister Bell, presumably located somewhere within the Cloister room. The tolling of the Bell indicates the approach of some catastrophe for the TARDIS.

Throughout the fourth Doctor's adventures, new elements were continually added to the evolving myth that is *Doctor Who*. This process of development was the end result of many individual and collaborative decisions by the writers, script editors and producers who worked on the series during this period, each leaving his own personal mark on it. Some writers went to great pains to weave their tales into the existing legend, whereas others ignored the restrictions of established facts in the cause of producing exciting and watchable television.

Doctor Who's strength as a series has always lain in its flexibility. As the Doctor can travel anywhere in time and space, the only limits for a writer are those of his or her imagination. It would be a shame if any writer felt so burdened by the series' past, that he or she could not create new characters and situations because of a fear of contradicting previous stories. If, however, a fact were to be established in one story, only to be contradicted in the next, the viewer would quickly become disorientated and lose interest. As Graham Williams recognised, major changes should be carried out over a period of time to allow viewers to get used to them.

Fans, of course, have a rather different perspective from other, less-committed viewers. They are much more concerned about the minutiae of continuity. However, they themselves have the ability to plug almost any gap, simply by coming up with their own theories to explain apparent inconsistencies. Some even take up their pens to write their own versions of events to link two or more unconnected bits of *Who* mythology. Perhaps if the whole history of *Doctor Who* had been meticulously planned in advance to allow no departures from strict continuity, the series would not still be one of the most exciting to write for, and of course, to watch.

PRODUCTION DEVELOPMENT

The production of a TV drama series relies heavily on teamwork, with many different people – script editor, writers, directors, designers and actors among them – all influencing the form and content of the finished product. Probably the most influential contributor of all, however, is the producer, who has overall responsibility. During Tom Baker's time as the Doctor, *Doctor Who* had four producers – Barry Letts, Philip Hinchcliffe, Graham Williams and John Nathan-Turner – each of whom brought his own particular approach and style to the series.

Barry Letts had been appointed to the producer's job in 1969, and had been in charge throughout all but the first story of Jon Pertwee's successful five-year stint as the third Doctor. In 1974, when he came to cast Tom Baker as the new lead actor, he had almost reached the end of his time on the series; and Baker's debut story, *Robot*, recorded back-to-back with Pertwee's swan song *Planet of the Spiders*, was in fact the last on which he received the producer's credit.

Save for the new Doctor himself, there was little in *Robot* to distinguish it from the *Doctor Who* to which viewers had become accustomed in recent years. It took place in near-contemporary England – the setting used for the majority of the Pertwee stories – and featured not only the Doctor's established companion, Sarah Jane Smith, but also the familiar characters of Brigadier Lethbridge-Stewart, Sergeant (now Warrant Officer) Benton and the UNIT organisation. Interviewed in 1981 for *Doctor Who Monthly*'s Winter Special, Letts explained the thinking behind this:

'Because the audience has not yet accepted the new Doctor, their sympathies are with the characters they know, and they are identifying with these characters as they react to the new and eccentric Doctor. The old characters – the Brigadier, Benton and Sarah – are there to reassure the viewing public that they are still watching *Doctor Who*.'

This was a philosophy that underpinned much of Tom Baker's debut season, season twelve. Although *The Ark in Space*, *The Sontaran Experiment*, *Genesis of the Daleks* and *Revenge of the Cybermen* followed the trend of the latter Pertwee seasons by moving away from the tried-and-trusted UNIT set-up and into more unfamiliar territory, continued viewer reassurance was provided by way of the inclusion of a parade of popular returning monsters – Sontarans, Daleks and Cybermen. Then in *Terror of the Zygons* – planned as the final story of season twelve although ultimately transmitted as the first of season thirteen – the Doctor, Sarah and Harry Sullivan (the new companion introduced in *Robot*) were brought back to Earth for another UNIT adventure.

Speaking in 1987 to the fanzine *In-Vision*, Letts recalled this period of transition between himself and Hinchcliffe:

'The cross-over period was quite lengthy. While I was still producer, Philip hung around; and then, after he became producer, I hung around to hand over. So I was there during *The Sontaran Experiment* and I was there for *The Ark in Space* and made various comments.

'*Planet of the Spiders* was far more my epitaph than *Robot*. I had far more input and directed it myself, and we said goodbye to Jon. With *Robot*, the main thing was to try to get a good, exciting show for the first one of the new Doctor, so that I could hand the success over to Philip Hinchcliffe.'

Although Letts was not physically present for the whole of the season, all the scripts had been commissioned while he was still producer, so his influence continued to be felt. However, much of the responsibility for the content of the season fell to new script editor Robert Holmes, as Philip Hinchcliffe told *In-Vision* in 1987:

'Bob Holmes had quite a large influence. He was very much anti-UNIT – he thought it was all rather silly, running around shooting at monsters. It had had its day.

'When I got there, they'd commissioned a Dalek story from Terry Nation, a Cyberman story from Gerry Davis, and from Bob Baker and Dave Martin they'd commissioned one about a Sontaran – which was a character that Bob himself had invented. Although those stories were not completed – the Sontaran one had been written, and the Dalek one was half written – they were on the go. Bob didn't like the idea of using the old monsters, but he was enough of a showman to know that probably it was a safe bet to beef up the season.'

Despite the presence of some reassuringly traditional elements, these stories contained strong hints that *Doctor Who* was undergoing an important change of style at this time. *Robot*, for all its military hardware, gun battles and explosions, had been essentially cosy, fantasy-based family drama, very much akin to most of the Pertwee-era UNIT tales, but productions like *The Ark in Space* and *Genesis of the Daleks* had a harder, grittier, more realistic quality. *The Ark in Space*, for instance, had a Gothic horror flavour in its portrayal of people becoming physically and mentally possessed by the Wirrn, while *The Sontaran Experiment* depicted what was, in effect, the brutal torture of a group of human spacemen. *Genesis of the Daleks*, with its themes of warfare, racial hatred and genetic experimentation, was even more graphic and disturbing, provoking complaints from some viewers and from TV watchdog Mary Whitehouse's National Viewers and Listeners Association.

The new, more adult style was welcomed and actively encouraged by Hinchcliffe, who shared his script editor's view that there ought to be, in tandem with the change of Doctor, a change of direction for the series as a whole:

'Although we'd got these old favourites in the first season – in the bag, as it were – both Bob and I felt that we'd like to move the show away from what had been the "Barry Letts formula". Not because we didn't rate that – I think Barry was a terrific producer of the show, and Jon Pertwee was a very good Doctor ... But I felt that that was now slightly played out.

'I felt that we could move the show in a different direction – more into genuine science fiction and fantasy. We didn't want to be so reliant on monsters in funny masks all the time, but in a way to take the audience on a genuine journey of fantasy by creating an atmosphere in the stories. And that tied in with Bob's idea of not relying totally on monsters that weren't very interesting and didn't have very interesting motives. I thought we could add a bit more power – I was quite interested in doing something in the science fiction area that, okay, would be *Doctor Who*, but we could balls it up a bit!'

The new, more 'ballsy' style was readily apparent in seasons thirteen and fourteen – the two seasons for which Hinchcliffe was fully responsible. The stories of these seasons are generally regarded as amongst the most frightening in the series' history. Incidents often cited as having been particularly horrific include: the dropping of Morbius's brain on the floor in *The Brain of Morbius*; the man-to-Krynoid transformations and Harrison Chase's death in the compost grinder in *The Seeds of Doom*; the strangulations perpetrated by *The Robots of Death*; and the various grim and violent fates suffered by

4 FOURTH DOCTOR

characters in *The Talons of Weng-Chiang*.

The National Viewers and Listeners Association's earlier condemnation of *Genesis of the Daleks* proved to be just the first of many such attacks on *Doctor Who*; and in one instance, when the Association complained about a scene at the end of *The Deadly Assassin* part three in which the Doctor appears to be on the point of being drowned, they even won a written apology from BBC Director General Charles Curran. Curran wrote that the scene in question had in fact been cut down prior to transmission but that, with hindsight, 'the head of department responsible would have liked to cut out just a few more frames of the action than he did.' Although expressed in relatively mild terms, this apology marked a significant change of policy by the BBC, where at one time Mary Whitehouse had been very much *persona non grata*. It represented a minor landmark in the perennial debate about the portrayal of violence in TV drama, and was to have a long-term and arguably damaging impact on *Doctor Who* itself.

In an interview with *Daily Express* journalist Jean Rook, published on 11 February 1977 under the title *Who do you think you are, scaring my innocent child?*, Robert Holmes answered some standard criticisms of the series' new style:

'Of course it's no longer a children's programme. Parents would be terribly irresponsible to leave a six-year-old to watch it alone. It's geared to the intelligent 14-year-old, and I wouldn't let any child under ten see it.

'If a little one really enjoys peeping at it from behind the sofa, until Dad says "It's all right now – it's all over," that's fine. A certain amount of fear is healthy under strict parental supervision. Even then, I'd advise half an hour to play with Dad and forget it before a child goes to bed.

'That's why we switched the time-slot from 5.15 to after 6.00, when most young kids are in the bath.

'When *Doctor Who* started, as a true children's programme, the monsters were rubber and specific and you saw them almost at once. What horrifies far more is the occasional flash of monster – bits and pieces of one. People are frightened by what *might* come round the corner or in at the window.'

When challenged about the portrayal of death in the series, Holmes told Rook:

'They're strictly fantasy deaths. No blood, no petrol bombs, nothing a child could copy. We're not in business to harm children. We learned our lesson years ago, with some plastic daffodils which killed just by spitting at people. We didn't consider that people actually have plastic daffodils in their homes. They caused screaming nightmares, so we scrapped them. You must never attack the security of a child in its home. If you make something nasty, you don't stick it in a nursery.'

In fact, Holmes was slightly mistaken here: seasons thirteen and fourteen did feature both blood and (in *The Seeds of Doom*) petrol bombs. However, it would be wrong to assume that the impact – and undeniable success – of *Doctor Who* under Hinchcliffe and Holmes relied solely on the presentation of a succession of gory or shocking images. Much more important were the chilling concepts underlying the stories and the realistic and frequently Gothic style in which they were produced.

Hinchcliffe explains what he and Holmes were aiming for:

'We'd already decided that we wanted to take the Doctor away from Earth, to go out there to other worlds. So that was one principle. Alternatively, if Earth was involved in some way, it would not be just a case of having a monster invading and then getting the soldiers out to come and shoot at it!

'What I wanted to do were stories that had a powerful concept behind them. Stories that had depth and menace, in terms of science fiction or horror or literature generally.

'We wanted to develop themes – like nemesis, a man trapped in something he doesn't really understand and he's really fighting himself. Those very basic mythic themes were things that I wanted to try and get in. And Bob and I wanted to incorporate them into things we'd either seen before, or that we had read about.'

This deriving of inspiration and ideas from other sources such as popular myths, literature, TV and, in particular, cinema films was another of the distinctive features of seasons thirteen and fourteen. It had been by no means unknown for *Doctor Who* to draw from such sources in the past – some of the early Pertwee stories, for instance, had paid homage to the BBC's science fiction serials of the fifties featuring Professor Bernard Quatermass, while Tom Baker's debut adventure, *Robot*, had been in some respects a reworking of the *King Kong* idea. In these two seasons, however, the practice was taken further than ever before, as Tom Baker recalled when interviewed in 1991 for *Doctor Who Magazine*:

'We used to see lots of movies at that time and often, like actors and directors do, we adapted scenes from films – recalling a scene from a film and doing our version of it. If anyone out there loved the film as much as we did, we wanted to send them a sort of signal. Likewise, when I had to say the co-ordinates of something, I often used the BBC telephone number and the *Doctor Who* office extension, and no-one ever noticed!

'Of course the stories Philip Hinchcliffe and Robert Holmes worked on were all film pastiches, and of course we spotted them. In fact, sometimes I was extremely rude about it if they didn't come clean about where they were nicking the idea from! Like good comedians, you thrash around anywhere for material and steal and adapt, trying to perform that alchemy, transmuting one thing into another.

'If people recognise the influence, it adds a certain pleasure, it's another little level. You don't have to see those things, but there were lots of little nudges and winks that people who were going through time and space were able to send to their watchers, little signals like an astronaut might send, which mean one thing to one listener and something else to another.'

The eclectic referencing of such sources added great depth and resonance to the stories of seasons thirteen and fourteen, and helped to create the suspenseful and often Gothic atmosphere for which Hinchcliffe and Holmes were aiming. These stories also benefited from the fact that they were made during a period now widely regarded as a golden age of BBC drama, with extremely high production values being achieved across the Corporation's entire range of series, serials and plays. Having reached an almost unprecedented level of popularity, *Doctor Who* was at this time regarded as one of the BBC's flagship programmes, and the production team were able to call upon not only the highest real-terms budget the series had ever had, but also some of the cream of the BBC's considerable creative talent to help bring it to the screen.

Contributors included such experienced directors as Douglas Camfield and David Maloney, both of whom had been responsible for many well-remembered *Doctor Who* stories in the past; costume designers of the calibre of James Acheson, later to win Hollywood Oscars for his work in films, and John Bloomfield; and top-flight set designers like Roger Murray-Leach, another subsequent Oscar winner, and Barry Newbery, a BAFTA award winner. Another important contribution to the series' overall

FOURTH DOCTOR

style was made by composer Dudley Simpson, who supplied a succession of distinctive and acclaimed incidental scores. Amongst the accomplished writers who provided scripts were Robert Banks Stewart, later to be responsible for such hit series as *Shoestring* and *Bergerac*, and Louis Marks, a playwright and later a distinguished BBC producer.

It is perhaps unsurprising, all things considered, that the stories of this period are now generally agreed to have been some of the most outstanding in the series' entire history. However, the long term success of *Doctor Who* has always depended upon change and innovation, and as season fourteen drew to a close, another important development was imminent. Having been offered the job of producer on a new, hard-hitting police series called *Target*, Philip Hinchcliffe left *Doctor Who* at this point, handing over the reins to the man who had earlier created *Target* – Graham Williams.

Williams' arrival marked the start of another change of direction for *Doctor Who*. One important reason for this was that he wanted to tone down the level of violence in the series, as he told *In-Vision* in an interview shortly before his death in 1990:

'With Philip Hinchcliffe, Bob Holmes had been spoofing Hammer films for years, and I saw no reason to discourage this practice. Hammer had been going for years in this country and had hardly drawn a breath of comment from the infamous Mrs Whitehouse. I suppose because so much of it was set in the 19th Century and in foreign countries, it was deemed to be the acceptable face of horror – which was as far down that road as I wanted to go. To me, a lot of what Philip had done went too far. When I learned I was taking the show over, I made special efforts to watch it. One of the ones I saw – *Genesis of the Daleks* – had Lis Sladen climbing up a rocket gantry, being shot at by guards with rifles. She almost falls once, and then on reaching the top she gets caught, and is deliberately tripped by her captors and left dangling in mid-air while they laugh.

'I had by then just become father to our first son, and so was more aware that if children were going to be watching *Doctor Who* at 5.25, then a lot of this sadism and deliberate shock-horror, which Bob and Philip took a particular glee in producing, was not very defensible. I did not think Philip was right to let the drowning sequence in *The Deadly Assassin* go through, because the violence was too realistic and therefore could be imitated. Even on *Z Cars*, you did not show a fight using a broken bottle for precisely that reason.'

Even had Williams not wanted to reduce the level of violence, this was an area in which he had little room for manoeuvre, as senior BBC executives were keen for him to 'clean the series up' following the persistent criticisms that had been made during Hinchcliffe's tenure. As he would later reflect, this was the most difficult problem he had to face during his first year as producer:

'I was happy to tone down the realistic horror and gore. But then the BBC told me to go further and actually clean it up. It was over-reaction, of that I am sure, but it did not help that in my first year I was under a directive to take out anything graphic in the depiction of violence.'

While some of Williams' earliest productions, notably *Horror of Fang Rock* and *Image of the Fendahl*, retained the Gothic quality of the Hinchcliffe seasons, it was not long before his new policy took effect. This gradual removal of the series' more horrific elements left a void that was filled in part by an increased use of humour, particularly after Anthony Read succeeded Robert Holmes as script editor mid-way through production of season fifteen. The lighter tone at first manifested itself mainly in the way stories were directed and acted, Tom Baker taking the opportunity to inject a lot of his own ideas and dialogue into scenes during rehearsals to make them more off-the-wall and amusing. Robert Holmes' own *The Sun Makers* however was an exception to the rule in that the script itself had a distinctly humorous slant, with its satirical references to the British tax system; and as time went by, the series' writers increasingly picked up on the new, less serious approach and tailored their work accordingly, incorporating deliberately comedic scenes and dialogue.

This trend gained an added impetus when humorist Douglas Adams, later to enjoy great success with *The Hitch-Hikers Guide to the Galaxy*, took over from Anthony Read as script editor for season seventeen. It culminated in stories like *The Creature from the Pit* and *The Horns of Nimon*, which came complete with ludicrous monsters, slapstick sound effects and scenes of the Doctor giving K-9 artificial respiration and talking directly to camera.

'It was inevitable that the style of *Doctor Who* would change once Tony Read took on the burning torch,' Williams later reflected. 'But of course one can never predict how in advance. In all honesty, and with no detriment implied either to Tony Read or to Douglas Adams, I have to say that I would have been a very much happier chap had I had Bob Holmes as my script editor throughout all my seasons, as Philip had done. I certainly felt I was on more of a wavelength from the word go with Bob than I was with either of the others. It took working towards with the other two, but Bob truly had found the natural slot for *Doctor Who* in the television universe.'

During Williams' time on the series, Tom Baker's Doctor increasingly took centre-stage and dominated proceedings with his wise-cracking, larger-than-life personality. This is not to say, however, that the producer exercised no restraint at all over his lead actor. Baker's more outlandish suggestions – such as replacing Leela with a talking cabbage perched on the Doctor's shoulder – were instantly discounted, and it was not unknown for major disagreements to occur. Perhaps the most serious of these arose towards the end of production on season sixteen, when Baker threatened to quit unless given script, casting and director approval for the following year's stories – something that Williams, not surprisingly, was unwilling to concede. Fortunately this dispute was amicably resolved when, after high-level discussions and a meeting between Baker, Williams and the BBC's Head of Series and Serials, Graeme McDonald, Baker dropped his demands.

At the time, the change of style that occurred under Williams was viewed less than enthusiastically by some of the series' fans – particularly those who had enjoyed and grown accustomed to the relatively serious Philip Hinchcliffe productions. There were wry suggestions from some quarters that *Doctor Who* ought now to be re-named *The Tom Baker Show*, or even *Tom Baker's Comedy Half Hour*! It would however be a mistake to imply that the stories of these seasons were in any way crass or simplistic. On the contrary, the liberal use of humour often disguised the fact that the scripts were, on the whole, highly literate and intelligent. They exhibited a knowing, postmodern playfulness with the traditional conventions and cliches of *Doctor Who* and of TV drama in general, and were realised with a kind of tongue-in-cheek camp unique to this period of *Doctor Who*'s history.

It is fair to say that the cleverness and sophistication of these stories have become much more widely appreciated in recent years, and that Williams' contribution to *Doctor Who* has been reassessed in a much more positive light. In any case, as far as the general viewing public were concerned, there was never any doubt as to the success of his new approach – they lapped it up!

Although not as consistent as during Hinchcliffe's time, the series' ratings remained

FOURTH DOCTOR

generally high while Williams was producer, often breaking the 10 million barrier and, in the case of *City of Death*, reaching an all-time record story average of 14.5 million viewers per episode, albeit with the help of a strike that blacked out ITV. Clearly *Doctor Who* was still very much a high-profile series, and an important element in the BBC's Saturday evening programming.

On the minus side, many critics felt that there was a decline in production values during Williams' three year stint. What they perhaps failed to recognise was that the further the series moved away from the realms of naturalistic drama, the less appropriate it became for it to have 'realistic' sets, props, costumes and so forth. The visual aspects had to reflect the increasingly larger-than-life, fantastical nature of the stories.

Another important consideration is that in those instances where the production did fall short of expectations, this could almost always be attributed to the sheer scale and ambition of what was being attempted. Take, for instance, the case of *Underworld*, in which whole sequences were created through the use of CSO – by far the most extensive use ever attempted in *Doctor Who* of this electronic effect. These scenes have been widely dismissed as unconvincing, but they could equally well be viewed as a praiseworthy effort to push back the frontiers of the series' visual effects work. During its long history, *Doctor Who* has often been at the forefront of technical advances in television, and if the experiment had proved successful, it would no doubt have been hailed as a great triumph.

A further example is provided by the brick-walled TARDIS interior as seen in *The Invasion of Time*. Again, some have cited this as a lapse in production standards that undermined the credibility of one of the series' most important icons. Looked at in another light, however, Williams' decision to have these scenes shot on location could be regarded as a daring innovation, creating the opportunity for an exciting chase sequence that would have been impossible to achieve within the confines of the television studio. If anyone was at fault here, perhaps it was those critics who were unable to suspend their disbelief during the scenes in question. After all, if the TARDIS's chameleon circuit can change the outer shell of the ship into a mundane, everyday object like a police box, why shouldn't it also change the interior to give it brick walls?

One thing that can certainly be said is that throughout his time as producer, Williams consistently pushed the series to the limits of what could be achieved, striving to make it as good as possible given the various difficulties with which he was faced. A particular problem, as he later reflected, was a shortage of money:

'During those three years, inflation was running at breakneck speed. We were almost hourly being told that costs had just gone up by another ten per cent. The knock-on effect was like compound interest, with everything spiralling up into quite lunatic sums. I had several long and very severe conversations with the bosses upstairs, to the effect that they didn't care how I spent my money, as long as it was money from that year. Once that was gone, there was no question of over-funding. I would just lose episodes – end of argument. Philip Hinchcliffe had not left me with too much of a reputation, because so many of his *Doctor Who*s had gone massively over-budget on scenery.'

Another stumbling block Williams had to face right at the outset was the loss of the story that should have been his first production for the series – Terrance Dicks' vampire tale *The Witch Lords*. This had to be dropped at virtually the last minute on the insistence of Graeme McDonald, who thought it might be construed as a send-up of a prestigious BBC adaptation of *Dracula* that was then in the pipeline.

The loss of *The Witch Lords* not only necessitated the hasty commissioning of a replacement script, which Dicks himself provided in the form of *Horror of Fang Rock*, it also completely disrupted the production schedule for the early part of the fifteenth season. *The Invisible Enemy*, which should have been second into the studio, had to be recorded first, and consequently ended up looking rather rushed. *Horror of Fang Rock* then followed, but had to be recorded at the BBC's Pebble Mill studios in Birmingham – making this the only *Doctor Who* story of the original series to have had its studio work done outside London – as it transpired that no studio space was available at the usual Television Centre facilities on the dates when needed. All in all, as Williams put it, this was 'a punishing baptism of fire'!

Williams' headaches did not end there, either. Throughout his time on the series, he was dogged by problems arising from industrial action within the BBC. Although *Doctor Who* had been affected by such action even as far back as the Sixties – the 1968 story *The Wheel in Space*, for example, had been hit by a scene-shifters' strike, necessitating several last-minute changes of studio – never before had it suffered to this extent. Inevitably this also had an impact on the stories as transmitted.

'On each of the three years I did *Doctor Who*,' reflected Williams, 'at exactly the same point in time (which was about mid-November), we had the *Crackerjack* Clock dispute. *Crackerjack* Clock is the generic title for a dispute, in those days of some fourteen years standing, about demarcation as to whether it was the props department or the electrics department who turned on the clock to start the children's programme *Crackerjack*.'

It was one such dispute that resulted in the cancellation, only part-finished, of what should have been Williams' swan song production, *Shada*; and the preceding story, *The Horns of Nimon*, was also badly hit, making for a somewhat unsatisfactory conclusion to his producership.

Such were the difficulties involved in making *Doctor Who* at this time that Williams had repeatedly requested the appointment of an associate producer to help ease his burden. Although this request had been turned down, Graeme McDonald had instead given former producer Barry Letts a 'watching brief' over Williams' final season. When Williams left, to be succeeded as producer by the inexperienced John Nathan-Turner (formerly Williams' production unit manager), Letts was officially appointed executive producer for season eighteen. His role was however largely advisory, fulfilling a function usually performed by the head of department, and he has since confirmed that Nathan-Turner was fully responsible for the day-to-day production of the season. Letts therefore had only a limited influence on the style of the stories made at this time.

Nathan-Turner later recalled his aims in taking *Doctor Who* into the Eighties:

'I think you really have to look at the expectations of an audience. The late Seventies and the early Eighties, and indeed the late Eighties, have seen a level of sophistication in television and the movies that no-one could have foreseen. Children particularly now, possibly due to the advent of computer games and so on, have very high expectations of television programmes in our genre. My idea was simply not to attempt to compete with the likes of *Star Wars*, but to use the resources that were available to us to the best possible effect. In that way, we would appear to be moving with the times.'

The resources available for season eighteen were in fact greater than for season seventeen as Nathan-Turner was able to win a modest increase in budget. This meant that he could improve the series' production values and give it a noticeably more polished, up-to-date look than in recent years. One aspect of this was his commissioning of a new title sequence and a more modern arrangement of the theme tune. He was also successful in arguing for an extra two episodes to be added to the season – making it the longest since the Sixties – so that he could schedule seven stories at what he regarded to be the optimum length of four episodes each. The direct responsibility for the form and content of these stories fell however to the new script editor, Christopher H Bidmead, who took over from Douglas Adams at this point.

Interviewed by *Doctor Who Monthly*, Bidmead recalled his initial discussions with Nathan-Turner and Barry Letts:

'I had to confess to both John and Barry that I didn't actually want to do *Doctor Who*, as it had got very silly and I hated the show. They agreed with me – Barry wanted to go back to earlier principles and to find a way of familiarising children with the ways of science. You can understand how deeply that idea had been subverted.

'Two things were going wrong, as we saw it. One was the pantomime element and the other was the element of magic that had come in. Magic is entirely contrary to science, and to my mind the Doctor's view of the world is that he looks at a problem objectively and then tries to apply laws derived from experience to reach a scientific solution.

'So often in the past, it had been a case of the Doctor effectively waving a magic wand, which amounted to teaching children that the scientific way of looking at things was nonsense. It was a sort of infusion of late Sixties hippie ideas that derived from Third World cultures, which had filtered its way down into *Doctor Who*. Now, John liked the idea that it was going to be as different from the previous era as possible. In other words, I got the job on the premise that we would go back to basics.'

In line with this approach, and drawing on Bidmead's own writing experience in the scientific and technical fields, the stories of season eighteen had a much firmer scientific basis than those in the earlier part of Tom Baker's era, dealing with such ideas as tachyons, charged vacuum emboitments, E-Space, block transfer computations and, perhaps most significant of all, entropy. *Doctor Who* at this time was certainly more science-fiction than science-fantasy. This season also had an unusually high degree of conceptual and thematic coherence and a greater level of complexity in its plotting than had others in the recent past, suggesting that the series was being aimed at a more adult audience. Consistent with this, K-9 – originally intended to appeal to the younger child audience that Graham Williams felt had been lost as a result of the horrific nature of many of the Philip Hinchcliffe productions – was now written out.

Another feature of season eighteen was its generally sombre mood. The Doctor himself was considerably more subdued than before, and the stories – particularly towards the end of the season – had a dark, brooding atmosphere. Events such as the reappearance of the Master, the destruction of Nyssa's home planet Traken and the manifestation of the mysterious Watcher in *Logopolis* created an air of impending doom. This was in fact quite appropriate, given that they led up to the Doctor's 'death', his latest regeneration.

Although well-received by the series' fans, season eighteen was apparently less popular with the general viewing public: it was by some margin the lowest-rated of the Tom Baker seasons, averaging only 5.8 million viewers per episode. A new era was however just around the corner, which would see *Doctor Who* being moved to a twice-weekly time slot; enjoying a significant ratings revival; and, of course, featuring a new lead actor in the person of Peter Davison.

FROM SCRIPT TO SCREEN: THE BRAIN OF MORBIUS

Introduction

This chapter presents an in-depth look at just one of the fourth Doctor's stories. In doing so it reveals the process of creating a *Doctor Who* story at this point in the series' history, and some of the behind-the-scenes discussions and thought which go into a production, a factor common to every story.

The production chosen for this case study is *The Brain of Morbius*, the penultimate story from the thirteenth season, first transmitted in 1976.

To take our view of the story we are grateful to several people, in particular the director Christopher Barry and the designer Barry Newbery who recalled, scene by scene the work that went into it.

The Scripts

The original idea for *The Brain of Morbius* came from producer Philip Hinchcliffe.

Hinchcliffe had mentioned to his script editor, Robert Holmes, that there had not been an attempt at a serious robot story in *Doctor Who*, and he was keen to try a story that treated the human/robot relationship seriously. Holmes took this basic idea to writer Terrance Dicks, who had been script editor of *Doctor Who* during the Troughton and Pertwee eras and the writer of several previous stories for the show, and discussed it with him.

Terrance Dicks takes up the story: 'We'd been talking about various myths, and one of them was the Frankenstein myth of a man making a monster. I came up with the idea of a galactic super-criminal who has a super robot assistant – a sort of devoted robot Jeeves. The criminal, Morbius, is fleeing from his enemies, and his spaceship crashes.

'Morbius is smashed up to the extent that the robot can save only the head. And having been saved like this, he demands a new body. The robot is well-intentioned, but limited as robots are. Now for some reason, spaceships do crash on this planet. So the robot goes out, scoops up the remaining bits of alien life forms and whacks them together into a roughly-functioning body, onto which he puts Morbius's head. But as Morbius has always been something of a handsome Greek God, he is far from pleased.

'That was the story – it is gruesome, macabre, and funny. But it is also logical: the robot would do that. Bob and I worked out the story, and I wrote a set of scripts which he seemed happy with.'

As Dicks was such an experienced contributor to the series, the usual requirement placed on writers to submit a formal story synopsis, possibly followed by a detailed scene breakdown, before moving on to the scripting stage, was dispensed with on this occasion.

Some of the ideas used by Dicks were actually lifted from his script for the 1974 stage play *Doctor Who and the Daleks in Seven Keys to Doomsday*. These included the name of the planet Karn, together with images such as a single-clawed creature, a brain in a tank, a mind battle and a desolate citadel clinging to a windswept cliff. What happened next was something that, perhaps surprisingly, had happened only once before in *Doctor Who*'s history: the scripts had to be re-written without the writer's consent or input, and the writer objected to the re-writes to the extent that he asked for his name to be removed from the transmitted episodes. The previous time this had happened was on

Mervyn Haisman's and Henry Lincoln's story for *The Dominators*, then under its working title of *The Beautiful People*. The disagreement over this story back in 1968 had caused Haisman and Lincoln to forego any further work on *Doctor Who*, but in Dicks's case, the disagreement was short-lived with – eventually – no bad feelings on either side.

Dicks: 'The mistake I made was in delivering my final scripts on the day I went away on holiday! During subsequent discussions, I was out of the country and could not be contacted. And Philip Hinchcliffe turned against the robot. I can sympathise with him more now that I'm a producer than I could then. He thought that the robot would be too expensive to realise. So Bob was instructed to remove it from the story.

'Now, the robot is the whole core of the story. Poor old Bob, in a state of some desperation, he came up with a mad scientist instead. It was not the most original idea in the world, but it was the only one available. He invented Solon.'

What remained after Holmes had removed the robot was the basic idea of creating a body. He couldn't just replace the robot with Solon, as they would not have had the same motivation. Holmes had to go through Dicks's scripts and re-write every scene in which the robot appeared. This involved a total change of dialogue as well as shifts in characters and plot to keep the whole thing hanging together.

Terrance Dicks was less than pleased when he returned from holiday and eventually received the revised scripts. 'I rang up Bob and shouted at him down the telephone. He was apologetic, but asked what else he could have done. Eventually I said "All right. You can do it, but I'm going to take my name off it." (This was the ultimate sanction!) "Not because it's a bad show, but because it's now much more you than me."

'He asked: "Well, what name do you want to put on it?" I said: "I don't care. You can put it out under some bland pseudonym," and slammed the phone down.

'Weeks later, when I saw the *Radio Times*, I noticed it was "*The Brain of Morbius* by Robin Bland" – that's Robin Bland's only existence in life. By then I'd cooled down, and the joke disarmed me completely.'

Pre-production

While Dicks may not have had much to do with the scripts as they finally appeared, Holmes certainly did, and it seems that he even carried the mythical Robin Bland into the production meetings, as director Christopher Barry remembers:

'The scripts were all there and available by the time I joined the team. And as for Robin Bland; Holmes said: "Oh, well, he's the scriptwriter." As a director, I seldom met the scriptwriters, particularly on a show like *Doctor Who*. On *The Dæmons*, Barry Letts was the scriptwriter as well as the producer, again hiding under another name [Guy Leopold – a pseudonym for Letts and co-writer Robert Sloman]. But the scripts had to be written and virtually finalised long before the director joined, and so generally you didn't get to meet them.'

The director would normally be one of the first people to join the production team for a *Doctor Who* story, but often the producer would have previously sent out scripts to the various design departments for them to be able to allocate resources and to get started on the creative process. Usually the producer would have checked with the intended director to see if there were any specific people he or she wanted to work on the show, and then tried to arrange for them to be available. In the case of *The Brain of Morbius*, Hinchcliffe wanted an experienced director and designer to work together to bring the challenging script to life on a studio-bound production, as there was no location work budgeted for.

Barry Newbery certainly recalls that, 'I was told! I had no choice in whether I wanted to do the show or not, and the gentleman's agreement of the producer, director and designer talking at an early time didn't really come about until later.'

Once the director was appointed, his job initially would be to liaise with all the other departments, as Christopher Barry explains: 'As a director joining, it's really a question of you working out your need to get in touch with all these people with their need to get in touch with you. By the time the director joins the programme, he's one hundred per cent committed. But all these other people are working on other programmes, finishing them off, and like as not, you ring them up and say you need to have a chat and they say they haven't had time to read the scripts yet but they'll look at them over the weekend and see you on Monday for a preliminary check. It really was a case of you having to fit them in when their schedules allowed. Therefore, although it would be sensible to talk to the designer first, it often turned out that this was not possible.'

With all television being made to a strict deadline, both Christopher Barry and Barry Newbery found their work cut out for them from the start.

'Working in the Series and Serials Department,' says Barry, 'we always used to complain about the Plays Department having so much time to put on a play; they seemed to have weeks to rehearse. However in Series and Serials we never had enough time.'

Newbery agrees: 'The usual time given at that point to design the settings for a thirty minute recording was nine days. There would be extra allowed for any filming. This is the time in which all tasks have to be completed if settings are to be created and ready in studio for rehearsal and recording.

'This particular *Doctor Who* story was four episodes without any film. I therefore had just thirty-six days – four of which were spent in the studio – to complete my work. Thinking about all the things that had to be done before the first studio, that is in four weeks, I find it incredible now that I managed to do it. But of course, that goes for everyone else as well.'

Christopher Barry certainly agrees with this view: 'If we'd had filming, things would have been even more difficult.' In fact, *The Brain of Morbius* was atypical in that it had no filming or OB work. Almost every other *Doctor Who* story up to this point had featured some material shot either on location or at the Ealing Film Studios (normally modelwork or sequences calling for fire or water or where the story required sets that were either larger than normal or with other specific requirements – for example in *The Creature from the Pit*, Ealing was used for all the forest scenes and those involving the top of the pit into which people were thrown).

If there was to be some location work, then this would normally be completed prior to the studio recordings. Because of costs, the location filming tended to be within easy travelling distance of London, but occasionally would be further afield (for example to North Wales for *The Abominable Snowmen* and to Paris for *City of Death*) where the additional costs could be contained.

Even though *The Brain of Morbius* did not have location filming, there was still a great deal of work to be completed before the show was ready to be recorded. Christopher Barry recalls putting incredible pressure on Barry Newbery as a result: 'I needed to know all his design thoughts, sizes of sets and complete floor plans in time to do my preparation work: prepare a camera script; prepare for planning meetings, meaning that I had to have the production visualised in my mind: how I was going to shoot it; every effect; everything I wanted to discuss at the planning meetings. Ultimately I needed to produce a pro-forma camera script. I always went into rehearsal, unlike most younger directors, with a camera script that could work if I suddenly fell ill. The reason for this was that I had started my training in live television. If something happened to me, then my production assistant could step in and put the show on. We used to go into rehearsal with a camera script and be utterly willing to adapt that to the exigencies of the rehearsal. If an actor didn't like something for any reason, then you resolved the problem. You'd explain the effect you were after, why people were positioned as they were, and then either arrive at a compromise or change your script. In order to do that effectively, you had to have worked it all out beforehand.'

As part of the process of working out who would be doing what and by when, a planning meeting per episode would be held between all the departments that would be contributing to the show.

These would include the designer (in charge of the overall look of the show, together with all the sets), the director (who has to pull everything together to come up with a transmittable production), the costume designer (responsible for every costume seen), probably make-up (designs and executes all the make-ups on all the cast), the visual effects designer (handling explosions, special props, models and other effects that must be achieved 'live' during the recording), electronic effects designer (looks after Colour Separation Overlay (CSO) and other effects produced electronically rather than on the studio floor), lighting (works out and arranges all the studio and location lighting requirements), sound (handles the sound recording of all the scenes), the technical manager (basically in charge of the studio), the production assistant (secretary to the director, looking after the typing of scripts and continuity), assistant floor manager (another of the director's assistants, supervising the special effects and hand props, the artistes, and generally in charge of the rehearsals, including responsibility for marking up the outline of the sets with coloured tape on the rehearsal room floor, using a different colour for each set) and production manager (acts as a deputy to the director and looks after the studio floor during recording); but not the producer at this stage, unless it was the first episode of a completely new show or there was some specific reason for the producer to be there.

All these people would meet to listen to the director outline his plans for the show and to discuss how to achieve the various things that he wanted doing. Often ideas would be changed and expanded upon as each person was able to suggest other ways of getting the production to meet the director's standard.

Following the planning meeting, the next stage was the outside rehearsal, which took place at the BBC's rehearsal rooms in Acton.

Christopher Barry recalls the process: 'The normal procedure was that about two days before you went into studio, there would be a technical run-through at the rehearsal rooms. All the people who attended the planning meeting would come along, as well as the senior cameraman (responsible for the cameras and their positionings based on the director's plans), the whole camera crew if you could get them, the scenic supervisor (ensures the sets are available when required for studio) and the prop buyer (looks after everything that appears on the set that is not a part of the constructed set or a visual effect). This was to allow everyone to see how the programme was shaping up, and to ask any questions. There would be quite a crowd at the rehearsal rooms, and they would all be wandering around with huge floor plans in their hands, on which all the sets were overlaid. Another point is that you would usually have been rehearsing the show in scene order, but at this rehearsal you may well have put everything into recording order for the first time. This could cause problems, but generally it was very useful and a lot of work got done and time was ultimately saved in the studio.

'About the same time, although not necessarily on the same day, the producer and script editor, and possibly the writer [although, in the case of *The Brain of Morbius*, the writer was not available], would come to see a run-through of the episodes at the rehearsal rooms. This was in story order and would give the actors a chance to show the producer what they could do. The prime purpose from the producer's and script editor's point of view was to check that the performances and story points were being brought out, and to discuss with the director how he or she was intending to shoot certain sequences. From the director's point of view, although some of the comments made could be niggly, this run-through was extremely useful, as it gave the opportunity for someone (the producer) who had been at arm's length on the production to see if things were going right. Often the director became too close to the production to see the overall picture.'

In Studio
Eventually, the programme would go into the studio, and would be recorded over a number of days and a number of recording blocks. *The Brain of Morbius* was recorded in two, two day blocks on 6-7 October 1975 in TC1 and 20-21 October in TC3 respectively, with an additional one and a half minute scene for part four between Solon, the monster and Morbius's voice recorded on 24 October. Recording would be done in an order worked out by the director based on which sets would be available for use in each studio. All the scenes that used one particular set would generally be recorded together, and then the crew would move onto the next set and record the scenes there, and so on. In this way, an actor could find himself performing his big death scene before he had even recorded his entrance. There were two alternative ways of recording in studio. First was the rehearse/record method, where the director would rehearse each scene immediately before recording it. The other involved all the rehearsals being carried out in studio during the day, and the evening then being spent recording them. The method used was generally up to the individual director, depending on the facilities available.

The actual recording of a story was always a very time-restricted process, with much being achieved by all the creative staff in getting the material required by the director actually committed to tape. Recording had to stop in the evening at ten o'clock sharp, and unless the director had sanction to go into overtime (an expense that had to be agreed), at ten o'clock the studio house lights would go on, even if the cast were in the middle of a scene, and the cameramen and other technical personnel would leave for the night. Unless all the sets were required in studio the following day, then the scene-shifters would come in and take down (strike) those sets that were not required, and erect those that were, ready for the following day's work.

To indicate some of the considerations involved in making a *Doctor Who* story during the Tom Baker era, what follows is a scene-by-scene summary of *The Brain of Morbius*, taking in comments from Christopher Barry, Barry Newbery and the costume designer L Rowland-Warne as appropriate.

Part One

We open on an alien planet where an alien, insect-like humanoid (John Scott-Martin) is crawling over a hexagonal rock formation as thunder and lightning crash and flash around. The creature is being watched by Condo (Colin Fay), who rises up from behind the rocks. Condo's left hand is missing, replaced with a metal hook. Raising a small machete knife in his good hand, he falls upon the alien creature, whose screech of surprise and pain is abruptly cut off.

Christopher Barry: 'The insect alien was an old Mutt costume from *The Mutants* back in 1972, which Jim Acheson had designed and I had directed.'

L Rowland-Warne: 'We found the costume in stock, and the Visual Effects Department did quite a few repairs on it for me.'

Inside his citadel, Solon (Philip Madoc) is admiring a bust of Morbius when Condo arrives with his prize – the head of the alien. Solon berates Condo, as the head is not suitable; he needs a warm-blooded humanoid to complete his work.

CB: 'I'd not worked with Philip Madoc before, but I'd seen him in a black and white series, a BBC Sunday afternoon classic serial, probably *The Three Musketeers* or something. I know he was playing a French d'Artagnan-type character. He had a slightly manic quality but didn't overact doing it. It's in his voice and his eyes, a certain intensity. He really is magnificent; I can't think of any other actor who could have played that part so well.'

Barry Newbery: 'I hadn't really paid much attention to Philip Madoc until I worked on this. I'd seen him on films and things, and you're used to a certain competence on television, but with this, I became a fan of Madoc. I think he's terribly under used as an actor.'

CB: 'Colin Fay was an opera singer; he just happened to write in for a job at about the right time. He said he was over six foot, and I wanted a big fellow to play Condo. He hadn't done any television, so he was cheap. He was a huge man, and like so many big men, was incredibly gentle. Yet he played this backward creature who could be both fearsome and vulnerable.'

Elsewhere on the planet, the TARDIS arrives, and the Doctor emerges, shouting angrily to the skies at the Time Lords, who appear to have pulled him off course. Sarah (Elisabeth Sladen) determines to explore and sees a graveyard of spacecraft off in the distance, lit by the flashes of lightning.

BN: 'That shot was comprised of a number of elements. The background was a cyclorama skycloth and a cut-out of the mountains in the distance. In front of that was a four foot stretch of plain, dotted with model spacecraft from other productions, which I obtained from Visual Effects. The plain was seen as middle distance, the nearer part being hidden by foreground rocks and plants on the set.'

The Doctor feigns complete disinterest and Sarah goes off to explore further. When she cries out upon discovering the beheaded alien, the Doctor comes running. Looking about them, they see a castle atop a mountain in the distance illuminated by a flash of lightning.

CB: 'It's a lovely shot, but it's not there long enough … it's under three seconds … it could have been twice that!'

BN: 'The castle was not a model, nor was it painted on the cloth. It was done as a cut out, so that it could be silhouetted against a bright sky.'

CB: 'We could have lit it a bit better – we should have had a tiny spotlight on it or something, just to pick it out. It's such a fine structure, and it helps justify the interior architecture that we're going to see.'

The Doctor and Sarah make their way up to the castle. It starts to rain torrentially, and standing watching their progress is Ohica (Gilly Brown), one of the red-robed Sisterhood of Karn.

CB: 'That's not real rain. We hired a six foot film loop of rain and ran that superimposed onto the main picture.'

In his laboratory, Solon is experimenting on the Mutt head when the generator blows and the lights go out. He calls for Condo to fetch lamps.
   Maren (Cynthia Grenville), the leader of the Sisterhood, is informed of the Doctor's and Sarah's arrival on Karn. Maren fears that they may have arrived to take the Elixir of Life from the Sisterhood. She shows Ohica that the sacred flame that they tend is growing weaker by the day. Soon there will be no flame and no Elixir. The Sisterhood will be no more.

BN: 'Maren's chair had Genoese velvet draped over it. It was actually a curtain pelmet, and I wrapped it around the chair, which had been hired in.'

CB: 'I don't remember any discussions about the colour scheme of the Sisterhood being all red: the girls are dressed in red and the decor is all red too. I don't think it was a coincidence, somebody must have said something.'

LR-W: 'The Sisterhood had hats that were made very cheaply and decorated with coloured latex. The skirt fabric was in two layers, and made ragged and sprayed with wood dyes to give it texture. They wore bodices that were fabric covered in latex, with plastic tea-spoons from Winnie the BBC tea lady, laid into it.'

BN: 'The inspiration for the Sisterhood's flame room came from China. I was working from Chinese wall and panel decoration, and that was where the predominance of the colour red came from. The basic idea derived from the design in Buddhist temples.'

CB: 'The bit when they reveal the sacred flame received its share of criticism, I gather, but it's due as always to the lack of man hours to get the perfect finish. I think the sacred flame needed to be low, as at this point you're trying to show that this fact is desperately

FOURTH DOCTOR

dangerous for them.

'I cast Cynthia Grenville as Maren for her wonderful lined, craggy face and for her strong, but old, voice. She seems to be timeless, and that was the quality I wanted to bring over. Gilly Brown I liked for her suppressed nervous energy, suggestive that she is realising the critical situation that she is in. The other members of the Sisterhood were cast as being good looking women with dancing experience. Janie Kells was brought in by Geraldine Stephenson, who supervised the movement and dances of the Sisterhood, because she was a professional dancer. This comes down to cost again. Because dancers cost more to hire than extras or walk-ons, we had one real dancer and the rest copied her.'

In the main hall of the citadel, Solon finds Condo looking for his missing arm. Solon tells him that he will get the arm back once his work is finished.

BN: 'I decided that the formal structure of Solon's citadel would be unlike traditional Gothic structures, in that it would have supports on the inside instead of buttresses on the outside. Hence the radiating pattern of struts – the sloping columns that leaned towards the walls. I intended it to look as if each had a gigantic steel ball-and-socket joint at their base to allow for movement of the structure.

'It has been said that I based the designs on the work of Antonio Gaudi, but that's not so. I didn't use Gaudi at all – although I did look at his buildings in my research. The only place in which that influence did perhaps show through was in the shape of the window in Solon's laboratory.

'My starting point was to try to think of ways in which a civilisation parallel to that on Earth – one that had the same genetic make-up and lived on a planet nearly identical in its circumstances – would develop at the same rate but solve its problems differently. So the architecture was inside out.'

CB: 'I can remember talking to Barry about it and saying I didn't want Gothic in the terms of ecclesiastical architecture, I wanted Gothick with a k. I thought something like that would have a macabre quality, something out of a Grimm fairytale, or a drawing by Arthur Rackham; that kind of atmosphere.'

The Doctor and Sarah arrive at the citadel, where Solon greets them enthusiastically, commenting on the Doctor's magnificent head. After Sarah has warmed herself at a blazing fire, they sit at a table and Solon orders Condo to get the wine.

CB: 'This time, as they stood outside the door, we used "fully practical" rain – water falling from pierced "sparge-pipes" rigged up over the doorway. They result in a lot of unwanted rainwater noise, because it is uncontrollable, unlike rain noise off disc, and much mess on the floor, and as a result they are commonly resisted by all concerned.'

BN: 'Those chairs were originally made for the designer Norman James, for a television production of *Canterbury Tales* back in 1959.'

CB: 'Designers always give you a table bigger than you want, because they want you to get back wide enough to see the whole set!

'The shot from behind the fire appears very self conscious. But I wanted to get behind the fire to establish it, firstly because it goes out in a minute, and I also wanted to show warmth and hospitality. It wasn't just done to be clever.'

BN: 'Note that Chris wanted to give a feeling of warmth and hospitality because that was the only thing the set deliberately didn't have!'

Back at the Sisterhood's headquarters, the Sisters are chanting and gesturing as Maren concentrates on the Doctor's TARDIS, transporting it to their throne room.

CB: 'The Sisters' movements came in discussion. I remember talking to Geraldine about this and saying I wanted a sort of ritual. The words "Sacred flame, sacred fire" were in the script, but it was my decision to have them delivered as a chant, overlapping the sounds and also overlapping the visuals, cross fading, making it more mysterious.

'The TARDIS's appearance was not achieved with CSO. The camera pulled back and then was fixed in position (locked off) and then we did the superimposition on the side of the shot.'

Having confirmed that the TARDIS is a Time Lord vessel, Maren decides to locate its occupant. The Sisterhood form a circle and begin to chant again.

CB: 'Directing scenes that involve a number of people can be difficult, as you have to work out the positioning. While they're moving there's no problem, as you have choreographed them and it's just a question of where you cut your shots. But when you get to a static position with lots of people, it's then a question of how to make the most of it. You've paid for them to be there, so you don't want the characters to be hidden either by each other or by the scenery and props. That takes time in rehearsal to get the artistes to hit their marks and to be seen. This planning is dead easy with one camera, but when you are involved in a multi-camera shoot, as with all the *Doctor Who*s, you've then got to ensure that all the camera angles are correct.'

Back at the citadel, the Doctor has recognised the bust that Solon was working on as being Morbius. The Sisterhood pay a telekinetic 'visit', making the doors fly open, the fire snuff out and a chandelier fall from the ceiling.

CB: 'I'm rather ashamed of that shot of the chandelier. It wasn't actually dropped, it was run through a gloved hand with baling rope so it wouldn't break itself on the studio floor. Once it hit the ground, they didn't even let go of the rope, so the rest of the chain doesn't come down. In retrospect, I should have cut the shot a few frames earlier.'

The Doctor falls down unconscious; the wine was drugged. Sarah pretends to succumb as well (she had not been drinking). Solon and Condo take the Doctor to Solon's laboratory, where Solon examines him prior to the operation to remove his head.

CB: 'As far as I recall, Solon's laboratory was to be a mixture of what you would find in a fairly well equipped medical laboratory and in a museum. Old and new together. It's plainly a cod laboratory, it's just got a few pipes and tubes bunged in. It's not a physician's lab, nor a physicist's nor a chemist's, but a bit of everything.'

BN: 'Yes. Basically, as a scientist, I saw him as a bit of a wally.'

When Solon and Condo leave to repair the generators, the Doctor is transported to the Sisterhood's headquarters in the same way as the TARDIS. Sarah enters the room just after he vanishes. She notices the curtained-off bed and assumes that the Doctor is on it. She pulls open the curtain to reveal a monstrous headless body (Alan Crisp), which twitches and tries to sit as she stares in horror.

End of Part One

Part Two

CB: 'The intention here was to show the monster as late as possible. It's rather like in the first Dalek story: just show a little bit of it, but hold back from revealing the whole thing. All monsters are better if you only suggest them; let the viewer's imagination build a picture of what it looks like in its totality. Look at Ridley Scott's *Alien* for example.

'The design of the monster came from the script. I think it described it as a pot pourri, a hotch potch. We came up with the idea that it would be built from bits and pieces of other creatures, but that became rather difficult to realise. Rowland-Warne thought we could have panels of flesh without being specific as to their origin. What we specifically didn't want to use were any metallic or non-organic panels, because the only thing we wanted to look false and inorganic was the head that gets fitted later.'

LR-W: 'We cut up lumps of foam and stuck them onto a cotton jumpsuit, which had been layered with textured latex and foam rubber. We then covered the foam with terylene wadding dipped in latex. We built muscles down the spine – which in fact were to conceal the zip – and I used real surgical clips on the body, and also coffee beans to give the skin the right texture.'

Solon and Condo return to find the Doctor missing. Realising that the Sisterhood must have taken him, Solon determines to get him back.
The Doctor awakens in the Sisterhood's throne room to find himself tied up. Maren informs him that he will die at the next sun and that he should confess his guilt. The Doctor realises that Morbius is still alive, but Maren says this is impossible as she saw him die, and that the Doctor will soon join him.
A pyre is prepared, and the Doctor is placed in its centre as the sun bursts through the window.

CB: 'That light flare is a deliberate light, that's the sun coming in and hitting the Hele Stone, like at Stonehenge. It comes through a hole in the set and hits the post where the Doctor is tied. It was a difficult effect to get right.'

The Sisters dance around the Doctor, leading up to his sacrifice. As they dance, their torches

spring into life. The ceremony is interrupted by Solon, who first offers Condo in exchange for the Doctor and then pleads for the Doctor's head to be spared. Maren dismisses him. The sacrifice continues, but this time the dancing Sisters have been joined by Sarah, who followed Solon and Condo. She releases the Doctor's hands before the pyre is lit, and, as the flames leap higher, the Doctor seems to vanish from within them.

CB: 'There's a procedure laid down at the BBC that you must inform the fire department through the studio manager if you will be using any form of flame in the studio. It goes for smoking, too: if someone's going to light a cigarette, it has to be down on paper and agreed. If a fireman hasn't been notified and he happens to be on the set watching somebody light up a cigarette, then he can step in and stop the rehearsal. Studios are strictly non-smoking, cast, crew, everybody.'

BN: 'Because we had fire in the studio, and I was fairly worried about it, I took into the studio a number of those big, black, carbon dioxide fire extinguisher cylinders. The scene boys were standing by with these, and the fireman came in and told us to take them away, as only he was allowed to use extinguishers!

'The fire was designed and built by the visual effects designer John Horton on the scenery podium provided as part of the set. The lower platform was six feet in diameter and the upper central platform three feet in diameter, giving enough room for the Doctor to stand tethered to a central post.

'The flames came from self igniting burners within the brushwood, to which gas was fed through hidden pipes. And of course everything had to be very heavily fireproofed.'

CB: 'Tom was in the middle and there was a gap at the back because Sarah had to come up to cut the Doctor free. There had to be a place where she could crawl up and get close to him.

'In the end, we had to go for two takes on it, because it got out of hand. The flames leapt so high that Tom had to get out early, but not without reason!'

LR-W: 'I wasn't told before we got into the studio that the Sisterhood were going to carry genuine burning torches. So, I had to fireproof their costumes on the day with a substance that could have caused skin irritation.'

As the Doctor and Sarah run from the Sisterhood, Maren fires her ring at Sarah, which blinds her.

CB: 'I wasn't happy with the effect of the ring firing. I would have preferred it to have been more directional, rather than an uncontrolled blast.'

Solon has returned to his citadel, where Condo threatens him with death unless he gives Condo back his good arm and takes the hook away.

CB: 'Colin Fay had quite a lot of make-up on to play this part. He had things behind his lips to plump them out, and I think there was probably a bit of collodian (latex) pulling his eyes down at the sides. He was given big, bushy eyebrows, and I think his nose was slightly disfigured too.'

The Doctor discovers that Sarah has been blinded and realises that the only person to whom he can go for help is Solon.

CB: 'Acting blind is a very difficult thing to do, it's terribly hard to be convincing. Some of it I think Lis (Sladen) does well, some isn't so good. The difficult thing is to not use your eyes. If you watch people who are really blind, like for example David Blunkett, the MP, they're always blinking. But that's somebody who's congenitally blind. Sarah is just temporarily blind, and I thought it would be similar to staring at the sun for too long. You get an after-image burnt on your retina, and I think it makes you stare a bit.'

Solon has descended into a basement laboratory, where he is speaking with an unseen person, eventually identified as Morbius (Michael Spice). Morbius is impatient to be free again, but Solon is reluctant to proceed.

CB: 'I chose Michael Spice to play the voice of Morbius as I'd met him previously when he was working on radio. He had a good, strong voice, and radio actors are used to doing all their acting through their voice. Peter Hawkins, who provided the Daleks' voices for me, was again primarily a voice-over actor.'

Solon returns to the main hall when Condo announces the arrival of the Doctor and Sarah. Solon examines Sarah's eyes and tells the Doctor that there is no hope. He suggests, however, that the Elixir of Life could help, and the Doctor leaves to obtain it. Solon sends Condo on ahead of the Doctor with a message for Maren.

Meanwhile, Sarah, left alone, hears Morbius calling from below. She heads in the direction of the voice. She stumbles down the stairs into the underground laboratory, where she advances on the source of the voice – a flashing brain, bubbling in a tank.

End of Part Two

Part Three

CB: 'The brain in the tank came about because I wanted this Grand Guignol feel. It was partly the settings, the visuals from Barry's design, but wherever I could extend the feeling through details, I did.

'That's one of the things I think is so astonishing about this programme, we always managed it on such a small budget.'

Solon enters behind Sarah and throws her out of the room. She listens while Solon outlines his plan to use the Doctor's head to complete his body for Morbius.

CB: 'This idea of a brain in a tank had featured in another *Doctor Who* before this [*The Keys of Marinus*]. I'm just talking of sources and unoriginality, because this reminds me of the Steve Martin film *The Man With Two Brains*.'

When Solon comments that he has sent the Doctor into a trap, Sarah pulls the door shut and locks it, trapping Solon. Sarah hurriedly makes her way up the stairs and out the main door to warn the Doctor.

CB: 'That is total rubbish! She's never been there before, yet she knows how to shut and lock the door, and she's blind! That's my fault, that's bad direction. Often you get the script and find inconsistencies like this in rehearsal. You stop and discuss it for five minutes, but time is pressing, and eventually you just have to accept it and move on. Either that or you get in touch with the script editor and explain the problem – I've had to do that on occasion as well.

'If you were worried to the point that you couldn't continue rehearsals if it wasn't resolved, then you would telephone the script editor and explain the problem. The script editor would either settle it himself in discussion with the producer or, if he felt it was of prime importance and needed referring to the writer himself, he would get in touch with him and finally let you know. In the meantime, you carried on rehearsing the rest of the scenes. This procedure was used throughout BBC Drama, particularly in Series and Serials.'

Five of the Sisterhood are ritually sipping the last of the Elixir. Maren denies herself the liquid despite Ohica's concern about what will ultimately happen to her.

BN: 'This ritual is fairly typical; many religions have this kind of thing. But look at that! Maren tips that empty cup into the Sister's mouth … Now she does it to the next one, and she doesn't get any either!'

CB: 'The idea was that there's a sticky liquid in there and there's so little of it that they're supposed to put their tongues in and just touch it.'

BN: 'When I first came into television I wondered why they never ever put any liquid into teacups or mugs or whatever. They were either empty or else just had a token amount inside.'

CB: 'Apparently it's because the artiste's hands shake when they pass the saucer! That said, I should have had more liquid in the chalice than I did, but it's the pressure again. Unless you have been there, you just don't appreciate the pressure! I think I'm known as a director who stops for most details, but you simply cannot cover everything all the time.'

Solon's message arrives, and Maren prepares for the Doctor's arrival.
Sarah stumbles through the rocks on her way to warn the Doctor.

CB: 'This is highly unlikely. I'd have loved to have been able to shoot this from very low, looking right up so it would look like she's really up high. Had we had some location budget, I would have shot it outdoors with the sky behind her to make it feel high, but you can't shoot upwards in the studio, because there is no ceiling to the sets – all you would see would be the lights and gantry above.'

The Doctor arrives at the Sisterhood's domain and asks for Maren's help. Maren explains

447

that the blindness is not permanent and that Solon knew this. The Doctor explains that he believes Morbius still lives, and discusses Morbius's crimes with Maren.

BN: 'I have been thinking about the colour of the flame room and Maren's chair. The fact that the chair was also in red was not planned. It was sheer serendipity that on one of my buying trips I found such a chair in red velvet and the cut velvet Italianate pelmet I used to dress it.'

CB: 'The scene of the Doctor and Maren walking round the flame-room whilst talking was difficult to shoot. This whole story is very static, with long dialogue scenes. There are some nice opportunities in that subterranean vault at Solon's citadel: I use the set twice to give movement. Solon walks all the way round the columns and back, and later the Doctor does the same thing. On this scene, I decided to have Maren and the Doctor walk round, complicated by the fact that it's in procession, and additionally complicated by a cutting point in the middle of the scene. What I've done there is to jump frame. The Doctor is on the left as they start the walk, and we left the cut until as late as possible. If you look closely, you can see that one of the Sisterhood masks the Doctor on the cutting point, and what has happened is that Maren and the Doctor have swapped positions. Luckily it works, and you get away with it. I was trying to find movement, because otherwise this whole scene would be completely static, as it is all dialogue.'

The Doctor offers his help to the Sisterhood, but there must be no more drawing of ships down onto Karn to their doom.
Sarah is found by Condo, who picks her up and takes her back to Solon.
The Doctor checks the sacred flame, as he thinks he might be able to solve the problem of the lack of Elixir. He realises that the flame heats the rocks, which produces the Elixir. The Doctor takes from his pocket a small firework, which he lights and inserts into the crack from which the flame emerges. The flame dies, but then there is a small explosion and the flame bursts out anew, higher and stronger than before.

CB: 'That was a firework, an ordinary sparkler, the sort you can get in a Christmas cracker, but Visual Effects produced the little bang at the end. Then there's the big flame, again produced from a gas jet.'

BN: 'The walls of the sacred flame's niche were made from fibreglass, which had been fireproofed pretty heavily.'

Solon secures Sarah in his laboratory and returns to the cellar to inform Morbius of the impending operation. He lets slip that the Doctor is a Time Lord. Morbius is horrified and suggests that the Doctor has been sent by the Time Lords and is working with Maren to destroy him. Morbius insists that Solon gets him into the body as soon as possible, using an artificial brain-case that Solon had earlier constructed and rejected. Solon reluctantly agrees.

BN: 'All the bubbling vials and equipment were provided by John Horton. The bubbles in the bottle were done with air jets, with the air lines out of sight somewhere, controlled by the effects team. John had two assistants, one of whom was John Brace, who later became a designer in his own right, and there was also someone else there who I think was more like a visual effects operator than an assistant.

'The walls on this set were textured with sawdust taken off the workshop floor and mixed in the paint. Another way to create texturing, which I didn't use on this occasion, was to spray glue over the wall and then throw sawdust and Polyfilla at it, painting it once it had dried.'

CB: 'I decided that the brain was going to flash just to indicate that it was talking; a little like the lights on the Daleks flashing for the same reason. I know a flashing brain is crazy, but I'm not a rational man!'

The Sisterhood carry an apparently dead Doctor up to the citadel. Meanwhile, Solon and Condo carry the tank containing the brain up to the laboratory. Condo sees the patchwork creature that Solon has built and recognises his own arm attached to it. Condo attacks Solon, who shoots him in the stomach. They struggle and the brain is knocked off the table onto the floor. Solon carefully picks it up and places it into the artificial brain-case.

CB: 'Now this is the scene that I, in retrospect, regret. I don't regret it for the same reasons as Mary Whitehouse, but I can see what she was getting at. It was in the era of the bloody Sam Peckinpah films, and I knew what Sam Peckinpah was getting away with and I didn't feel that this *Doctor Who* scene was violent at all. But seeing it again, I can see why it is totally wrong, because it suddenly ceases to be science fiction and becomes naturalism. It was an error of judgment. I think somebody explained about Solon having a gun, and then someone else probably suggested seeing a red splat when Condo is hit by the bullet. I agreed without really thinking about it. If the producer had questioned this, then I probably would have argued with him for a moment and then given in. Watching it today, I don't like it any more, and it does seem wrong.

'On the other hand, I have no regrets about when the brain falls to the floor. I loved the effect.'

Solon unties Sarah and forces her to operate a pump while he performs the operation to connect Morbius's brain to the body.

The Sisterhood arrive at the base of Solon's citadel and carry the Doctor up the steps. Thunder and lightning crash about.

CB: 'This is one of my favourite shots in the show. Flashes of lightning can be done various ways. It used to be with two poles and a carbon arc across them, but here it was an electronic flash.'

In his laboratory, Solon finishes connecting the brain-case to the body when he is called away to greet the Sisterhood, who have arrived at his door. Remaining in the lab, Sarah finds that her eyesight is returning as the creature on the operating table (Stuart Fell) begins to stir. It lurches to its feet behind her and moves towards her.

End of Part Three

449

Part Four

CB: 'That claw really is monstrous. Stuart Fell, who played the creature, was marvellous. I always used him for stunts, and he's worked with me on numerous occasions.'

The monster chases after Sarah, knocking over a bunsen burner and setting fire to some liquid and its claw in the process. The creature comes across a mirror and smashes it in frustration on seeing its reflection.

CB: 'The floor was coated in preparation for the flammable liquid spilling on it, and just out behind the camera there are three firemen with extinguishers. After the sequence with the claw alight, we stopped to put out the fire before proceeding with the rest of the scene. You can see the claw still smouldering in the next shot.

'That was real glass in the mirror. Usually you don't have real glass, for obvious safety reasons.'

BN: 'I would probably have had three more mirrors off set, ready for any re-takes.'

Solon enters, and the monster crushes him unconscious before lurching out of the room. The Doctor and Sarah meet it, and it knocks the Doctor down before chasing Sarah again. The wounded Condo comes to her aid, and she falls down the stairs to the basement lab as Condo fights off the creature. It grabs Condo by the neck and throttles him before leaving the citadel.

BN: 'To shoot the scene where Sarah falls down the stairs, we had a crane set up to follow behind her as she fell. The landing at the top of the stairs was twelve feet high, and because there was no handrail around it, the fireman stopped us shooting until one was fitted!'

CB: 'Lis's stunt double, Jenny Le Fre, was at the top of the stairs without handrails, ready to fall down, and the fireman was saying that it was not safe up there.'

BN: 'So many things have to be done even during camera rehearsals to make the sets ready for recording. This was one of those occasions when we didn't actually get it all done in time – the chippy was supposed to have put the handrail in but probably was not allowed time to do it because of other priorities. In the end, we had to wait until the chippy had fixed the handrail before we could continue.'

CB: 'Condo's death here is like opera, and Colin understood the basis – you go on dying for half an hour after you have been mortally wounded. That's straight out of *Rigoletto*, an operatic death!'

Solon recovers, and loads a dart gun with tranquilliser. He recruits the Doctor to help him stop Morbius. They find and immobilise the creature, but not before it has killed Kelia, one of the Sisterhood. The Doctor tells Solon that the brain must be detached and returned to the Time Lords. He picks the creature up and returns to the citadel.

CB: 'This scene is interesting. There is a very slow pace here, long pauses as we see first Solon and then the Doctor, building deliberately until the monster appears, and then a pause as it attacks the Doctor, before Solon comes to the rescue. I love the sequence where Solon is only concerned about his creation, not whether the Doctor has been hurt!'

Back at the laboratory, the Doctor gives Solon five minutes to disconnect the brain, and leaves to check on Sarah in the basement. Solon follows and locks them in. The Doctor explains Morbius's history to Sarah and discovers too late that they are locked in.

CB: 'The Doctor walks around the set again here – I should have had him go the other way round from Solon. This sort of sequence can pose problems for the sound people. They may well have asked me to arrange for Tom to pause behind the column so they could pick the sound up from a microphone on that side, and then pick up the sound on another microphone from the other side, otherwise there would be a dead patch on the soundtrack.

'The columns in Barry's set were a great bonus; you get all sorts of interesting angles and compositions to shoot through and around.'

BN: 'In this instance, it wasn't something I'd consciously thought of. I was simply trying to make the structure of the room echo the constructional principle of internal buttressing. However, Christopher looked at it visually, and two lines at an irregular angle are always going to make the picture look more interesting than two parallel ones.'

CB: 'In terms of past *Doctor Who*, on *The Romans*, the set was full of columns, which gave me ample scope for using them to shoot round and behind. Often in the preliminary discussions about sets with designers, you ask for items to be placed in the foreground, some columns or things like that.'

Solon repairs the brain connections, while the Sisterhood discuss what should be done. Ohica persuades Maren that they should go to the citadel to help the Doctor. Trapped in the basement, the Doctor creates a cyanide gas, which he wafts up a duct to Solon's laboratory. The gas affects Solon just as he puts the finishing touches to the creature, but the creature itself survives, as it has specially adapted lungs. It heads off to the basement as the Sisterhood climb the steps to the citadel.

BN: 'Those poor girls! They all climbed up the steps, but there was nowhere for them to go when they reached the top!'

CB: 'I had to cut the shot before they started backing up on the stairs.'

Morbius arrives in the downstairs laboratory and faces the Doctor and Sarah. The Doctor baits the creature and challenges him to a mind bending contest. They take their places, and the battle commences. As they fight, we see all the past incarnations of, first the Doctor, and then of Morbius, appear on a screen.

CB: 'We got into trouble with Equity, because we used photos of non-Equity people for the images in the mind bending sequence. The photos are of George Gallaccio (production unit manager), Robert Holmes (script editor), Graeme Harper (production assistant), Douglas Camfield (director), Philip Hinchcliffe (producer), Christopher Baker (production assistant), Robert Banks Stewart (writer) and me. The picture of Morbius was a photo of the clay bust upstairs, which was then re-touched. Basically we couldn't afford to hire actors to do it, so we tried to get away with it. In the end, we had to give a fee to Equity's benevolent fund.'

There is a small explosion inside Morbius's brain case, and he staggers out of the room. In the citadel's main hall, he encounters the Sisterhood brandishing flaming torches. They herd him out onto the mountain, where he falls from a cliff and plummets to the ground far below.

CB: 'This fall was quite a remarkable thing for Stuart Fell. He actually fell about eight feet onto mattresses. You see him take one look round to see where he's got to go, and then over he goes! He actually hits the camera, which is why the picture bumps as he goes out of shot, but I didn't mind that. The shot of him falling away into the distance was just one take. We put him on a blue turntable, with a high camera looking down on him, zooming out, so he appears to get farther and farther away, then that image is inlaid on a photograph from the BBC's slide library of a high shot of a canyon somewhere in California.'

Back in the Sisterhood's flame-room, the Doctor is given the few remaining drops of Elixir to prevent him from dying. Maren, having denied herself the Elixir for too long, enters the flame, and as she dies, she appears young again.
The Doctor and Sarah enter the TARDIS, leaving Ohica with another two fireworks. The TARDIS vanishes in a flash of light and a cloud of smoke.

CB: 'I read somewhere that we used a double for this because Maren couldn't get in the flames, but she didn't need to get in the flames, it's a superimposition. What they mean is that the younger girl replaced Maren as her younger self.
'The TARDIS's dematerialisation in a puff of smoke was my little joke. We were using pyrotechnics in the story, the script had the Doctor reciting what was written on the firework – light the blue touch paper and stand clear – and off goes the firework. It was a joke that may offend *Doctor Who* purists.'

Post-production
If one considers that the period from the time a writer first submitted his or her scripts to the time the story was transmitted could be many months, and that the actual recording took about one day per episode, it is clear that the proportion of time spent in studio was very low indeed compared with all the work carried out both before and after that.

The early part of this chapter covered the pre-production work on *The Brain of Morbius*. Now Christopher Barry describes the post-production process: what actually happened once the programme had been recorded.

'While we were in studio recording the scenes, the production assistant, Pauline Silcock, had been keeping a log of every take and re-take and had noted where the best takes were and where the faults were. All the recorded tapes were then put onto a Japanese machine called a Shibaden, an early form of helical scan video recording

452

machine, which could be stopped and started at random and which displayed a time code on the picture. We would go into the Shibaden Room in Television Centre, play through the tapes and note down where the edits needed to come. In those days, this was called Shibadening, but nowadays it is called off-line editing. You basically construct your finished programme as a sort of rough-cut. It wasn't as accurate as cutting on the exact frame; you tended to cut within a second of where you actually wanted.

'With that as your guide, together with all the notes made whilst doing it, you would go in to do the final edit knowing exactly what you were going to do, how all the scenes and takes fitted together, and the exact frames for editing it all together. You might even change what you had previously edited on the Shibaden, because the Shibaden showed the pictures in black and white on a tiny screen and you might have missed small details that rendered a take unusable – say a microphone boom was slightly in shot. You could decide on balance that one of the other takes was better than the one previously chosen.

'Once you had constructed a good edit, time was also a factor. The show had to run for the required time, twenty-five minutes in *Doctor Who*'s case. Therefore you logged where you could make cuts, and you had to offset one cut against another. You traded and juggled your cuts until the running time was as required. That was then the final edit.

'Another Shibaden copy was then run off and given to the composer, Dudley Simpson. I would have talked to him beforehand about where I wanted the music to fall, and as I was preparing the preliminary Shibaden, I would have been noting down the time codes of the sequences where I wanted music. Sometimes specific to the frame. Dudley would then come in to the BBC, because Shibadens were huge machines and were not very portable, and he would play it through and get his exact timings from a new time code that was put on the tape after editing. He would then go away and write the music.

'We would then have a recording session to record the music, at which the director would be present; we'd record each piece, and after each piece we'd play it back. I would make any comments, and so we carried on until all the music was complete. There was always the pressure of time, because of the musicians. You would try and record the score in a three hour session. If you went a minute over time, the musicians would want twice the money.

'Once the music had been recorded, the tape would be given to the sound and grams operators, who would arrange a pre-sypher session. (Sypher stands for *SY*nchronous *P*ost dub with *H*elical scan and *E*ight-track *R*ecorder.) This involves putting the music and other sounds onto the final edited visuals. They would get Dick Mills's special sounds, which had been worked on separately by Dick in the same way as Dudley. The pre-sypher session would probably take place in the morning in a small studio containing tape decks and a monitor, and they would look through and log everything that needed doing in the way of adding music, effects and special sounds. We would then go into the proper sypher suite for probably six or eight hours for one episode. It was a rock and roll procedure, like film dubbing: you'd go backwards and forwards through the story until you had everything right. This process has steadily become more and more computerized over the years, and is now very sophisticated indeed.

'Out of all this work would come your final programme.'

Transmission
The Brain of Morbius was eventually transmitted on consecutive Saturdays from 3 to 24

January 1976, and was well received by the general public. It received an average rating of 9.7 million viewers per episode (compared with the season average of 10.1), which was very respectable, and its position compared with the other BBC and ITV programmes on at the time was on average 28th in the weekly chart.

Complaints were levelled at the show by the National Viewers and Listeners Association (NVALA), in particular because of the scene in which Condo is shot by Solon with an old fashioned pistol and blood is seen to fly from his stomach. *Doctor Who* was always subject during this period to close scrutiny by the NVALA, and there were several instances when their complaints were taken further.

The Brain of Morbius was popular enough to warrant a repeat on 4 December 1976, but rather than repeat the whole story, the BBC edited it down into a one hour omnibus version (thus removing a quarter of its original running time). This edit was done without the participation of the director, and both he and the fans felt that it did not do the story justice, as it lost much of the depth and characterisation of the original.

When *The Brain of Morbius* was chosen as the second *Doctor Who* release from BBC Video in 1984, they decided to use the cut down version. The story was subsequently re-released complete (save for a short piece of incidental music as Sarah enters Solon's laboratory at the end of part one) and unedited in 1990.

The only other area of contention surrounding this story has already been touched upon above. The BBC were taken to task by Equity for their use of photos of non-members during the mind-battle sequence. The BBC had to make a special payment to Equity as a result.

CREDITS

Writer	Robin Bland (pseudonym for Robert Holmes from an idea by Terrance Dicks)
Director	Christopher Barry
Producer	Philip Hinchcliffe
Script Editor	Robert Holmes
Designer	Barry Newbery
Assistant Floor Manager	Felicity Trew
Costume Designer	L Rowland-Warne
Incidental Music	Dudley Simpson
Make-Up	Jean McMillan
Movement	Geraldine Stephenson
Production Assistant	Carol Wiseman
Production Unit Manager	Janet Radenkovic
Special Sound	Dick Mills
Studio Lighting	Peter Catlett
Studio Sound	Tony Millier
Theme Arrangement	Delia Derbyshire
Title Music	Ron Grainer and BBC Radiophonic Workshop
Visual Effects Designer	John Horton

EFFECTIVELY SPEAKING

Doctor Who has always put a great deal of emphasis on its special effects. The creation of the numerous monsters, space craft, explosions and futuristic weaponry has taxed the ingenuity of the programme makers from the series' beginnings. During the latter part of the Seventies, *Doctor Who* benefited not only from an experienced, talented and enthusiastic team of behind-the-scenes technicians, but also from the burgeoning of television technology. This allowed ever more complex effects to be achieved in ever shorter spaces of time. *Doctor Who* was, indeed, at the forefront of these developments, as it was seen by many within the BBC as an important proving ground for new techniques and ideas.

With colour television firmly established in Britain by the mid-Seventies, the BBC's technical staff, having got used to the technology, began to experiment with the possibilities of the medium. It was felt that the area of electronic effects – producing something electronically from the images relayed by the TV studio cameras and recording it directly to tape rather than achieving it through a physical prop or model – was one that could benefit from a greater investment of time and money.

Responsibility for producing the early electronic effects at the start of the Seventies was held by a small group within the BBC called inlay operators. There were only three inlay operators at any one time, and the posts were held by cameramen seconded for a three month period before returning to the main camera department. An inlay operator's job was to combine images from two or more video sources (camera or pre-recorded tape) to create a single, combined image. Traditionally, the technique was used to provide the opening and closing titles for programmes, as well as more elaborate effects when images of models or paintings were combined with live-action.

Many cameramen seconded to the position found the job highly tedious and were only too happy to move on once their allotted time was up. However, particularly with the advent of colour, ever greater demands were made of and expectations placed upon the inlay operators. One of the cameramen seconded at this point was A J 'Mitch' Mitchell, who spent much of his three month stint in the department working on *Doctor Who*'s eighth season. Mitchell remembers this period as chaotic, due to the fact that there was no one person overseeing the production of the electronic and photographic effects and this often led to productions over-running their allotted studio time.

Mitchell became so interested in the possibilities offered by electronic effects that he extended his stay in the department to six months. By the end of his time there, he and his fellow inlay operators had begun to plan out the effects, and things were slowly becoming more efficient. Mitchell eventually returned to his job as a cameraman, but his interest in electronic effects did not end there. He submitted a report suggesting that the BBC create the rôle of special effects cameraman. Four years later, the post was indeed created, although with the title electronic effects operator. Into this embryonic department came Mitchell, together with Dave Jervis and Dave Chapman. The first *Doctor Who* work credited as being performed by the Electronic Effects Department – as opposed to inlay operators – was on *The Seeds of Doom*. Since then, electronic effects have become a staple part of *Doctor Who*'s creative arsenal.

4 FOURTH DOCTOR

During the Sixties, most effects seen on British television were achieved either through inlay or overlay or were of a mechanical nature, being based on the types of trickery the film industry had been using for years. These included glass paintings, mattes, scaled down and forced-perspective models and other forms of trick photography. Some of these effects relied on the nature of celluloid film, which meant that in order to use them for television, the sequences had to be shot on film rather than recorded on video. By the early Seventies, in addition to these mechanical effects, experimentation in the field of video had given rise to a bag of tricks unique to that medium.

Perhaps the best known video effect is Colour Separation Overlay, or CSO, which was used extensively in *Doctor Who* during the Tom Baker era.

CSO, or Chroma-key as it is known by ITV companies, allows one picture to be inserted electronically into another. A colour (usually blue, but any colour can in theory be used) is chosen as the key, and this is used for all the areas of the first picture that are to be replaced with the other picture. If an actor stands on a full CSO set (usually just a large, coloured curtain hung behind and extending over the floor, covering all areas of the image to be recorded) he can be electronically superimposed against a different background provided by any other video source.

The colour information from the camera recording the actor is matrixed to produce a black and white key signal to be fed to a video switch. The nominated CSO backdrop becomes black and all the other colours in the picture become white. This key signal is then used to combine the original CSO camera's picture with any other background, whether it be video of a model, a painting or photograph or an image being taken by another camera. Of course, the actors and any props that are to remain in the combined image cannot contain any of the selected key colour, otherwise they would disappear. This is partly the reason why blue is often chosen, as it does not feature in most human skin tones.

The earliest use of CSO in *Doctor Who* can be found in the 1970 story *Doctor Who and the Silurians*. Subsequently during the Seventies, it was used increasingly as a way of combining monsters and models in scenes with actors, and of creating fantastic landscapes. In *Robot*, it was employed to achieve the effect of Kettlewell's creation growing to mammoth proportions, and this was just the first of many examples from the Tom Baker years. It became the standard way of realising effects involving monitor screens and spacecraft, and was used particularly effectively in a number of stories such as *The Robots of Death*, where it was utilised to provide a buzzing 'live' pattern on the active Laserson Probes and to make the Robots' eyes glow red when they were converted to the cause of Taren Capel. Generally speaking, however, the electronic effects operators were happiest when their work went unnoticed by the viewers, as this meant that they had achieved what they intended – the creation of a totally realistic effect.

In *The Deadly Assassin*, some very clever combinations of camera work and video effects were used to populate Gallifrey, and particularly the Panopticon set. The impression was given of a far greater number of Time Lords than the story's budget could actually stretch to, by mixing together a number of recordings of the same scene with the twelve extras standing in a different area of the set each time. The apparent size of the set was also increased by a similar effect. The upper galleries were a repeat of the lower ones, recorded separately and then electronically grafted on in the appropriate place. More traditional uses of CSO in this story included the inlaying of images onto the Time Lords' wrist communicators.

Video effects were also used for the scene where the TARDIS is transducted to the museum. A pattern generator, originally created by the effects staff for the Saturday morning children's show *Multi-Coloured Swap Shop*, was used. A shot of the TARDIS was fed through the device, which broke the image up into many little squares in primary colours. The police box was then removed and the signal from the pattern generator faded out, giving the impression that the TARDIS had been converted into some form of digital pattern, which had then been transmitted elsewhere. To make the TARDIS appear in the museum, the process was simply reversed.

CSO was a cheap and relatively simple technique, but was also fairly inflexible. It could not be used for panning shots, for example, as anything that had been superimposed onto the picture would remain static. The only way to achieve good results was to have all the cameras locked in position.

This limitation was one of the main reasons why the most ambitious use of CSO in *Doctor Who*, in the season fifteen story *Underworld*, was largely unsuccessful. All the chase and fight scenes had to be recorded with locked-off cameras – there could be no pans, zooms, tilts or tracking shots – and this resulted in a very static production. Added to this, the sheer quantity of CSO used, and the tell-tale blue outline it often left around the actors (a result of interference between the signals from the two camera sources), resulted in highly unconvincing images. *Doctor Who* relies on the suspension of disbelief of the viewer, and in this case that suspension was very difficult to achieve. CSO generally works best when used subtly and sparingly.

These restrictions were later partly overcome with the introduction of a technique that the BBC called Scenesync. This was first used on the *Doctor Who* story *Meglos*, for the CSO-created scenes set on Zolfa-Thura. When General Grugger and his band of Gaztak mercenaries emerge from their ship and walk between the giant screens on the planet's surface, the camera follows their progress – even as they pass behind one of the struts supporting the screens.

The principal of Scenesync is quite simple. There are two sets. The first is a model onto which the actors are to be placed via CSO. The second is the studio set through which the actors will walk in real life. The studio set must match exactly the architecture of the model set, with one important exception – it must all be in the CSO key-colour. The movement of the camera focused on the actors is electronically linked to that of the camera focused on the model, so that they will move in unison. Thus, for the scene in *Meglos*, when actor Bill Fraser, playing Grugger, walked under the blue mask of the screen's supporting strut on the live action set, the camera on the model followed exactly the same movements, providing an overlay image of the model strut.

Ironically, at about the same time as solutions were being found to the problems posed by CSO, the whole process was about to become virtually obsolete.

New developments in computers and in digital technology had resulted in electronic equipment capable of creating effects similar to those achieved through CSO, but without the use of blue screens, and without any of the problems associated with that technique. An added advantage was that digital images could be manipulated in any way conceivable. They could be flipped, reversed, broken up, re-formed and generally tailored to whatever the director wanted. This new technique was called Quantel Image Processing and, once again, *Doctor Who* was one of the pioneers of its use.

In *The Leisure Hive*, Quantel was used to create the effects of the Tachyon Recreation

Generator in the scenes where characters are seen to break into several pieces. A far more subtle use of the technique, however, was witnessed in the scenes where Mena speaks to Brock via an apparently holographic image floating in the centre of a table. Not only did the camera pan past the image as the scene progressed, but people and objects could be seen through the image too. This was a good example of something that worked so well that the viewer could easily forget that it was an effect. Another of this story's claims to fame is that it was the first in which the camera moved during the TARDIS's materialisation – the effect likewise achieved using Quantel.

Tom Baker's regeneration scene was another that benefited from digital effects. As actor Adrian Gibbs, playing the Watcher, moved towards Baker's prone body, the image was distorted to make it appear as if the two figures were merging together. An overall glow was also added to the scene, in which the image of Baker's face slowly dissolves into that of the Watcher's, then blends into a shot of Peter Davison wearing Watcher-like make-up, and finally mixes into Davison's true features.

The advent of video effects might have made life a lot easier in some respects, but for the Visual Effects Department, responsible for all the series' mechanical effects work, the Tom Baker era was very much business as usual. The basic tools of their trade remained essentially the same, tried-and-trusted techniques that they had always used. Apart from advances in film cameras and the increasing miniaturisation of electric and electronic components, the visual effects in *Logopolis* were produced in pretty much the same way as those in *Robot* over six years earlier.

By the mid-seventies, the Visual Effects Department boasted a team of highly-skilled individuals, who were responsible for the great variety of effects seen during the Tom Baker era. Many *Doctor Who* scripts called for spaceships to be seen in flight, including sequences of the TARDIS spinning through space. Visual Effects were also called upon to produce any special props that could not be obtained from stock or brought in from outside the BBC. These included laser guns of all types, communicators, and even futuristic coinage. If weapons had to be seen to cause damage, controlled explosions would be placed to provide the desired effect without endangering the actors involved. Most often, these pyrotechnics would be combined with a ray or pulse of light created via electronic effects to give the ultimate appearance of a laser rifle that really did fire bursts of energy and that could, say, burn a hole in a door.

The contributions of some of the visual effects designers are particularly noteworthy. The stunning model work in *The Invisible Enemy* and *City of Death* came courtesy of Ian Scoones; the numerous effects showcased in *The Stones of Blood* – spacecraft, mobile stone aliens, a flashing wand and a futuristic beam machine that made the first major use of microchip technology in *Doctor Who* – were all provided by Mat Irvine, as was the filmed model sequence of the destruction of the Gateway in *Warriors' Gate*; while arguably *Doctor Who*'s most well-known effect of all was the creation of a designer called Tony Harding. This was K-9, the Doctor's robot dog companion, which was originally built for the story *The Invisible Enemy*. One condition of K-9's continuation as an ongoing character was that Visual Effects had to be able to supply a prop that would function well enough to be used regularly and that would survive the rigours of television production.

When first introduced, K-9 suffered a few teething problems. Difficulties arose because the radio control frequencies used to control the dog interfered with the operation of the television cameras, and vice versa. This led to K-9 going haywire on set and crashing into things. Further problems surfaced when K-9 was taken on location. Camera cables and door sills had been difficult enough for the robot to get over in the studio, but the rougher terrain of grass or quarry floors proved completely insurmountable. In many cases, K-9 was pulled along on a piece of carefully concealed twine, or else wooden boards along which the dog could travel were laid on the ground out of shot.

Following *The Invisible Enemy*, several modifications were made to the dog. The first was to change its drive from rear-wheel to front-wheel. The introduction of newer cameras in some of the studios also coincidentally resolved the problems over the radio control frequencies. However, it is to the credit of the various visual effects designers, and the talents of a radio-control specialist, Nigel Brackley, who was brought in specifically to look after K-9, that it was able to appear in as many stories as it did.

The next major overhaul came during the eighteenth season. Following *The Leisure Hive*, which saw K-9 conveniently write himself out by going for a dip in the sea off Brighton beach, the dog was completely stripped down and re-built internally by a designer called Charlie Lumm, who specialised in mechanical effects work. The wheels were enlarged, with those at the front given independent drives to achieve greater power and control, and the radio control was updated from the AM frequency band to newer FM frequency models.

The first story in which the new, improved K-9 appeared was *State of Decay* – but despite all the time and money that had been invested in the prop, the character was then written out in the following story, *Warriors' Gate*.

The introduction of K-9 coincided with the release of a film that was to have far-reaching repercussions for *Doctor Who* and for television science fiction in general. George Lucas's *Star Wars* redefined the audience's expectations of what could be achieved on screen. With its spectacular visuals and breathtaking dog-fights in space, *Star Wars* made almost everything else pale by comparison. The problem was that, in terms of effects, this film set the standard for all that was to come after it, and to try to match that standard required far more money and resources than the BBC could muster. The effects staff at the BBC did their utmost with the materials and budgets at their disposal, and achieved some remarkable results. The space scenes in *The Invisible Enemy*, *Underworld* and *The Invasion of Time*, and the creatures created for *Full Circle* and *Warrior's Gate*, were arguably every bit as good as those presented by George Lucas's film. However, the advantage of powerful computer control was not available to the BBC at this point, and *Doctor Who* had to wait until technology could provide a cheaper counterpart. This was not to happen until the early Eighties.

It was not only the visual aspect of *Doctor Who* that changed as the series progressed. Technology also improved in other areas, most notably in that of radiophonic sound and music. *Doctor Who*'s signature tune had been realised by the BBC's Radiophonic Workshop back when the show began, but during the Sixties and the early Seventies only a very small proportion of the series' incidental music had been electronic. Rather, it had been realised mainly by freelance composers using traditional instruments and methods. Although Carey Blyton (*Revenge of the Cybermen*) and Geoffrey Burgon (*Terror of the Zygons*, *The Seeds of Doom*) also provided some scores, Dudley Simpson was the principal composer for the fourth Doctor's stories, and his music came to epitomise the feel of *Doctor Who* during this period. For the eighteenth season, however, incoming producer

John Nathan-Turner wanted to get away from the traditional themes and to update the show for the Eighties. One of his decisions was to allow the Radiophonic Workshop to handle the incidental music as well as the special sounds. Therefore the orchestral arrangements of Simpson gave way to the electronic compositions of Peter Howell, Paddy Kingsland and Roger Limb. Their music was generated on the latest synthesisers and complemented the more glossy and hi-tech look Nathan-Turner gave the series.

Another change for the eighteenth season, again intended to update the show's image, was the altering of the title sequence. Ironically, the new titles, showing the Doctor's face being formed from clusters of stars and then disappearing, used a technique that was actually far older and less innovative than that of the version they replaced.

Bernard Lodge's 'tunnel' graphics, first introduced for the eleventh season in 1973, had been completely unlike anything else that the BBC had produced up to that time. Lodge had created the patterns using a version of the technique pioneered by Douglas Trumbull for the film *2001: A Space Odyssey*. This process, called slit-scan, was very time consuming, but gave excellent results. The titles for the eighteenth season, created by Sid Sutton, were simply animation. Numerous cels (sheets of plastic) were created, each showing an advancement of the image from the previous one, and when viewed together they formed the completed title sequence.

The fourth Doctor's era came to an end just as computer technology was revolutionising the creation of both electronic and other effects on British television. The effects created for *Doctor Who* during the fourth Doctor's era were however the most innovative of their time. Without programmes like *Doctor Who*, which has always encouraged innovation, it is doubtful if television as a whole would now be reaping the benefits from ever-more sophisticated technology as it becomes available.

ON LOCATION

There are a number of common misconceptions concerning the physical media upon which television programmes are actually made. During the Sixties, *Doctor Who* was recorded on videotape in an electronic studio, with a small proportion of 16mm or 35mm film inserts generally copied onto the tape during the studio day. These inserts would consist of stock footage; model or live action work specially shot at Ealing Film Studios; or material filmed on location. As the series moved into the Seventies, it started to benefit from more advanced technology. By the time Tom Baker took over as the Doctor, it was possible to record onto video on location (termed Outside Broadcast or OB) as well as in the electronic studio. Despite this, up until the Eighties, it was still normal to take film cameras on location and then transfer the film to video to produce the final programme.

The decision to take a programme like *Doctor Who* on location can be made for a number of reasons. There are artistic considerations – that to try and achieve, say, a forest or a cave system effectively in the studio would simply not work, and that to go to a real forest, or to descend into a real cave, would give far better results in the final programme. There are also budgetary considerations – that studio recording and location filming have different costs, and therefore it can occasionally work out cheaper to go on location than to stay in a studio. This however is the exception rather than the rule, as location costs usually far exceed studio costs.

Of course, on a science fiction production like *Doctor Who*, it is not always possible to find what is required within easy reach in the real world – there are not too many underwater Zygon spacecraft, for example, and snow-blown, bleak ice plateaux are not the most hospitable or accessible of places to travel to in real life. Occasionally, however, an alien planet or citadel can be created from the most mundane of settings, and the humble quarry has become one of the most versatile and popular locations for planets from Gallifrey to Skaro.

When *Doctor Who* started, back in 1963, there was hardly any location filming done. The first season had just a few short sequences filmed for *The Reign of Terror*; but following that, the amount of location work steadily increased.

Part of the problem in the Sixties was that the technical equipment required for filming was big, bulky and expensive to move about, therefore it tended to be far easier to create what was wanted in the electronic studio through clever and imaginative sets and effects. As *Doctor Who* moved into colour at the start of the Seventies, so location work increased, but the locations always tended to be fairly close to the BBC's London base, with only one or two longer journeys made, such as to Cornwall (*The Smugglers, Colony in Space*), Wales (*The Abominable Snowmen, The Green Death*) and Cheshire (*The Time Warrior*).

SEASON TWELVE

The fourth Doctor's debut coincided with the first use of OB cameras for the series' location work. For *Robot*, director Christopher Barry had the use of an OB unit, which could record everything straight to video. One of the major advantages to this was that the whole story could have a uniform look to it – a switch from film-originated material to material recorded directly to tape is always accompanied by a noticeable change in picture quality.

Aside from the more practical advantages of OB over film, that it is cheaper and the results can be viewed immediately, another advantage to using all-video for this particular story was that the script called for the eponymous robot to grow to giant size and go on the rampage. Obviously this could not be achieved in reality, and the use of video enabled the effect to be achieved through Colour Separation Overlay (CSO).

The need to use CSO on *Robot* was, according to departing producer Barry Letts, why a bid was put in to use the OB facility in the first place. The sequences were recorded first on location without the robot present. The actors had to pretend that they were shooting at and running from a rampaging behemoth without it actually being there. Then that video material, some of which had been taken from the giant robot's point of view, was married in studio with the robot, played by Michael Kilgarriff, performing in front of a blue screen. Some scenes also called for a further CSO pass to be done, when the giant robot was in the distance and some foreground action was required. Christopher Barry remembered the set-up when interviewed for *The Frame* in 1987: 'One big advantage we had was that all the backgrounds had been shot on video rather than film, which meant that the colour balances were good and the horizontal hold was absolutely rigid, so the background and foreground fitted together better than usual.'

The only problem with the CSO was that the metallic robot reflected the key-colour from the CSO back-cloth, and occasionally parts of the creature were therefore inadvertently replaced by the background video image.

The location used for *Robot* was the BBC's engineering training centre at Wood Norton near Evesham. It was chosen, according to Christopher Barry, 'because there is an underground bunker there, which I thought we could use as the entrance to the underground area in the story. But suddenly somebody at the BBC clamped up and said, "Sssh, you can't have that seen, it's secret". This was despite the fact that if you drive down the road, you can see it! But we couldn't show it on television. So we had to build a rather unconvincing entrance into the side of a hill, rather similar to what we had done with the tumulus in *The Dæmons*, as a way into the underground area.'

Co-incidentally, *Robot*, the first story to be originated entirely on video, was shortly followed by *The Sontaran Experiment*, the first story to be recorded entirely on location, again using OB cameras. The reason for the move to complete location in this instance was that *The Ark in Space* required a high design budget, as the ambitious sets that comprised the Ark had to be created from scratch; to keep costs down, it was decided to make *The Ark in Space* and *The Sontaran Experiment* almost as one six-parter, with the former all in studio and the latter all on location. Another factor was that usually a six-part story would have just one week of location filming, and so *The Sontaran Experiment* had to be completed in that week. The use of OB cameras allowed the necessary versatility and speed in the recording process. Because this situation was recognised early on, script editor Robert Holmes was able to ask *The Sontaran Experiment*'s writers, Bob Baker and Dave Martin, to keep the costs down and to set it all on location.

The location used, at the writers' suggestion, was Dartmoor. In story terms, it represented Picadilly Circus in the far future, returned to grass and moorland, as they explained to *In-Vision* in 1988: 'We chose Dartmoor because the cast and crew could travel and stay and shoot it there – keeping the cost down to a minimum and therefore invention up. We'd been there many times.'

Although Dartmoor may have been an ideal location from the setting point of view, recording in October did not guarantee the best of weather, as actor Glyn Jones, who played Krans, recalled in the fanzine *Tardis*: 'Filming on Dartmoor in October was enough to freeze the proverbial brass monkey. Looking at it on the small screen, one doesn't realise that, for the most part, the sleet and rain were pelting down. And I wondered why I looked so large until I realised that, under my spacesuit, I had enough tracksuits and sweaters to fit out the entire crew of an oil rig.'

The only other major location shoot during the twelfth season was for *Revenge of the Cybermen*, as the location work for *Genesis of the Daleks* had been restricted to a few scenes shot in a Fullers Earth Quarry near Reigate.

Revenge of the Cybermen made use of Wookey Hole, the world-famous cave system in Somerset. This is the only time *Doctor Who* has been to this particular location, which is perhaps odd as it offers a remarkable variety of backdrops and tunnels that it would be difficult to reproduce within a studio. A story such as *Underworld*, which ended up through budgetary problems being recorded against CSO models of tunnels, would certainly have benefited greatly from use of such a real location. Michael E Briant, the director of *Revenge of the Cybermen*, told *Doctor Who Magazine* an interesting story of one of his visits to check out the location site: 'I wanted to spend about a day in the caves where we were going to film, but the authorities weren't keen on me being down there while they were showing guided tours around. They asked if I would mind going down after closing time, about seven o'clock. I said "fine", but pointed out that I'd have to be there until midnight at least. They agreed, saying that they'd lock both entrances as normal, giving me a key. With my wife, I duly set off into the caverns, and after about two hours of wandering about, taking notes, somebody came up. I thought at first he was a security guy, but then I saw he was dressed in a wet suit. I asked him how he had got in and he said, "Oh, I always come in. Can I borrow your torch?" I refused, because I needed it to see with, and the man said, "Right you are," before going off into the gloom. Shortly afterwards, we heard a little Irish tune whistling from the shadows, and both my wife and I began to feel a bit scared. I decided to call it a night, even though I hadn't finished, but first I asked the caretaker who the man had been and why he had been let in. I was told, "We didn't let anyone in. He was an Irishman who died down there pot-holing, three years ago." Of course I couldn't tell anyone, because my film unit would never have worked there.' Later, during filming of the story, a number of other strange incidents would occur, which some members of the cast and crew would attribute to supernatural causes.

AT-A-GLANCE SEASON TWELVE LOCATIONS

Robot	BBC Engineering Training Centre, Wood Norton Hall, Wood Norton, Evesham, Worcs
The Sontaran Experiment	Hound Tor, nr Manaton, Dartmoor, Devon Headland Warren, nr Postbridge, Devon
Genesis of the Daleks	Betchworth Quarry, Pebblehill Road, Betchworth, Surrey
Revenge of the Cybermen	Wookey Hole Caves, Wookey Hole, Wells, Somerset

SEASON THIRTEEN

The thirteenth season's opening story, *Terror of the Zygons*, was supposed to be set in Scotland, around Loch Ness and the mythical village of Tulloch. It had originally been intended that some filming would actually take place in Scotland, but this was eventually ruled out on cost grounds, so director Douglas Camfield had to find some Scottish-looking locations closer to home.

The place chosen was the small, picturesque village of Charlton, near Chichester in Sussex; and further scenes were shot on a small stretch of beach and sand dunes south of Climping, between Bognor Regis and Littlehampton on Britain's south coast. Charlton was ideal for the village of Tulloch, and Camfield elected to retain the name of the village pub, 'The Fox Inn' (later renamed 'The Fox Goes Free' when the pub became a Free House rather than a pub tied to a single brewery), rather than change it as Christopher Barry had done in a similar situation in *The Dæmons*.

The other major location was yet another quarry, at Storrington in West Sussex, this time with a large lake in it that doubled for the shores of Loch Ness for the scenes of the Zygon spaceship emerging from the water. Actor John Woodnutt, who played the dual roles of Broton, the leader of the Zygons, and the Duke of Forgill, recalled for the fanzine *Shada* his work on the story: 'It was shot just outside Bognor, and in fact one village was very cleverly adapted by the scenic designer, who just stuck bits on that looked Scottish, just on the outsides of buildings. We took all the Sussex signs down and stuck up odd things that made you think of Scotland. It's not a bad location for it, in fact, because outside you do have quite a lot of conifers, which look awfully like those in Scotland. One conifer looks very like another, and when you put a bit of bagpipe music in the background, everyone assumes you're actually in Scotland.'

Another real pub was featured, and retained its original name, in *The Android Invasion*. This was the 'Fleur de Lys' in the picturesque village of East Hagbourne in Oxfordshire. The village and its surrounding countryside became the Kraals' duplicate English village, while the National Radiological Protection Board buildings nearby in Harwell became the base on Earth infiltrated by androids at the story's conclusion.

Both *Pyramids of Mars* and *The Seeds of Doom* called for a large country house to be used. For *Pyramids of Mars*, a private mansion house near Newbury called 'Stargroves', a residence of rock star Mick Jagger, was chosen by the director Paddy Russell. This had the additional benefit of a stable block, which doubled for Laurence Scarman's cottage.

The Seeds of Doom used Athelhampton House, which is about six miles east of Dorchester in Dorset. Again, this is privately owned, although it is open for public viewing. Yet another quarry made an appearance in this story, too. This time, it was a sand and silica quarry near Dorking. Another well known building also featured – surprisingly, one not often used as a location by the BBC, their very own Television Centre in London. The script called for short scenes of characters entering and leaving the headquarters of the World Ecology Bureau, and rather than travel miles, the crew simply used one of their own side entrances.

AT-A-GLANCE SEASON THIRTEEN LOCATIONS

Terror of the Zygons	Climping Beach, Climping, West Sussex
	Ambersham Common, South Ambersham, West Sussex
	Hall Aggregates Quarry, Storrington, West Sussex
	Charlton, West Sussex
	Furnace Pond, Mill Lane, Crabtree, West Sussex
	Millbank Tower, Millbank, London SW1
Pyramids of Mars	Stargrove Manor, East End, Hants
The Android Invasion	National Radiological Protection Board, Harwell, Oxon
	Worsham Quarry, Witney, Oxon
	Tubney Wood, Tubney, Oxon
	East Hagbourne, Oxon
The Seeds of Doom	Buckland Sand and Silica Co Ltd, Reigate Road, Buckland, Surrey
	Athelhampton House, Athelhampton, Dorset
	BBC Television Centre, Wood Lane, Shepherd's Bush, London, W12

SEASON FOURTEEN

The fourteenth season contained more filmed location work than *Doctor Who* had ever had before, with every story bar two (*The Face of Evil* and *The Robots of Death*) featuring a large proportion. The season started with one of the most impressive UK locations used on *Doctor Who*. Portmerion in North Wales is very well known both as a tourist attraction and as a television location, as the Patrick McGoohan adventure series *The Prisoner* was filmed there during the Sixties. Sir Clough Williams-Ellis's baroque mock-Italian village, opened in 1926 and based on the Italian village of Portofino, is situated on a forest-covered headland, which also overlooks the wide expanse of a river delta fed by the Trawsfynydd Lake and the river Glaslyn amongst others, east of Porthmadog.

Designer Barry Newbery recalled working in Portmerion during the making of *Masque of Mandragora* for *Doctor Who Magazine*: 'I was disappointed when I discovered we were to film in Portmerion, mainly because I was looking forward to doing some filming in Italy! But I fell in love with the place when I got there, and it approached how I imagined parts of Italy would look. Since then, I've been to Italy and realise now that it doesn't look like that at all. We built the remains of a temple close to one of the lakes, and Williams-Ellis actually asked if we could leave it there when we finished. We couldn't, because it was stock scenery made of light-weight jablite – if there had been a strong wind, the whole thing would have just blown away.'

Sir Clough Williams-Ellis died in 1978, but Portmerion remains open to the public, and, as it is a holiday village, one can stay and live in what really is a remarkable place.

For *The Hand of Fear*, a power station was required, and the writers, Bob Baker and Dave Martin, as with their previous story, *The Sontaran Experiment*, had already decided on a place that could be used. In this case, they had even gone there to scout it out before writing their scripts. The location chosen was the Oldbury Nuclear Power Station on the Severn Estuary in Avon.

The Deadly Assassin's location footage is well remembered, and so it should be, for over nineteen minutes of part three's twenty-five minute running time was given over to location film. The reason was that Robert Holmes, the writer and script editor, wanted to present: 'a technically innovative script with subjective and surrealist sequences that I felt widened the vocabulary of the programme.' Therefore part three was written as a nightmare dream experience for the Doctor. Sequences at the close of part two, featuring the Doctor falling off a real cliff-edge, a Samurai soldier, a man in surgical gowns holding a huge hypodermic needle, and soldiers on railway lines, were all filmed at Betchworth Quarry and its adjoining goods yard. All the material in the jungle and river was filmed in the gardens of the Royal Alexandra and Albert School, with a short sequence in the school's swimming pool for the scene when the Doctor's face is held under water. Finally, the filming of a bi-plane attack was achieved using miniatures at Wycombe Air Park. It took five full days to film all the required material for this one episode – compare that to the six days it took to shoot two complete episodes' worth of material for *The Sontaran Experiment*.

As previously mentioned, there was no location work for *The Face of Evil* or *The Robots of Death*. However, the production team again pushed the series' resources to the limit to create a gloomy, fog-bound, late 19th Century London for the season's final story, *The Talons of Weng-Chiang*. Wapping and Southwark were lovingly taken back in time and dressed in Victorian style, as director David Maloney remembered in *Doctor Who Magazine*: 'We were due to film in and around a set of Victorian houses in Wapping. We had posted letters to all the owners of the houses, asking them if they'd all please remove their motor cars, because we wanted to bring a carriage through the square. When we got there, there was a Porsche still parked in full view, and it was really going to ruin everything we wanted to do, so Roger Murray-Leach, my designer, had the very clever idea of putting a tarpaulin over the car and covering it with hay.' Other scenes involved the Doctor and Litefoot heading down the Thames in a rowing boat. All the material outside Litefoot's house was filmed in Twickenham.

As well as using film for all this location footage, director David Maloney decided to use OB cameras to record on video the remaining location work, all of which took place indoors. The first port of call was the Northampton Repertory Theatre, which was to become the inside of Henry Gordon Jago's Palace Theatre. This was chosen by Maloney 'because it's still got the original Victorian flying area above the stage, and we had a big chase there.' Philip Hinchcliffe was also impressed by the results achieved in his final credited story as producer: 'All that behind-the-scenes stuff looked really classy, because it was obviously not a studio.' From there, the OB cameras moved to St Crispin's Hospital, where Litefoot's mortuary was set up, as well as the Palace Theatre dressing room where Chang leaves a hypnotised cleaning girl who is found by Leela.

AT-A-GLANCE SEASON FOURTEEN LOCATIONS

The Masque of Mandragora	Portmerion, Penrhyndeudraeth, North Wales
The Hand of Fear	Cromhall Quarry, Cromhall, Wootton-under-Edge, Gloucs
	Oldbury Power Station, Oldbury Naite, Thornbury, Gloucs
	Stokefield Close, Thornbury, Gloucs
The Deadly Assassin	Betchworth Quarry, Pebblehill Road, Betchworth, Surrey
	Royal Alexandra and Albert School, Rocky Lane, Merstham, Surrey
	Wycombe Air Park, Clay Lane, High Wycombe, Bucks
The Talons of Weng-Chiang	Ealing Film Studios
	Wapping Pier Head, Wapping High Street, London, E1
	Clink Street, Southwark, London SE1
	Ivory House, St Katharine's Dock, East Smithfield, London, E1
	St Mary Overy's Wharf, Cathedral Street, Southwark, London, E1
	Bridewell Place, Wapping, E1
	Bankside, Southwark, SE1
	Broad Oak, 24 Cambridge Park, Twickenham, Middx
	East Dock/Centre Basin, St Katharine's Dock, East Smithfield, London, E1
	Northampton Repertory Theatre, Swan Street, Northampton
	St Crispin's Hospital, Duston, Northampton
	Empty Rates Office, Fish Street, Northampton

SEASON FIFTEEN

Compared with that of the previous season, the fifteenth season's location work seems positively frugal. Only one story, *The Invasion of Time*, made major use of location filming, some of it pre-planned but some because a strike at the BBC forced it out of the studios.

Image of the Fendahl was, like *Pyramids of Mars* and *The Seeds of Doom* before it, set in and around a large country house, and the production team returned to 'Stargroves' to carry out the location work required. One particular problem was that *Image of the Fendahl* required a lot of night-filming.

Whereas filming during daylight often requires only a minimum of additional lighting (spotlights for artistes' faces, white boards to reflect the sunlight and so on), when night-filming is called for, the lighting of all the scenes becomes particularly crucial, and the time required to set up each shot is increased accordingly. Elmer Cossey, the film cameraman, recalled for *In-Vision* an incident that occurred while the crew were setting up to film for *Image of the Fendahl* at two o'clock in the morning: 'The Doctor and Leela were running down through this wood, with mysterious lights in the background. We got it all ready to go, and one of the dressers came up and said, "Your generator's on fire." The gaffer said, "Oh don't be silly, a joke's a joke." And the dresser said, "No, honestly, your generator's on fire!" I said, "Hang on a moment," and we looked round. Over the top of this hill was a red glow and smoke. Suddenly there was a bang, and all the lights went out. There were frantic 'phone calls back to London to the lighting company – a little difficult at two o'clock in the morning. But by about 4 am, we had another generator down, and fortunately there was still plenty of darkness.'

The Sun Makers posed its own problems for director Pennant Roberts and his team in scouting out the locations. The scripts called for lengthy corridors along which protracted chases in electric buggies could be staged. Roberts knew that Camden Deep tunnels, which connect various ducts, tunnels and passages between North and West London, would be suitable, as they were far cheaper to rent than London Transport-owned tunnels. However one of the buggies required for the chase scenes was too large to fit through the access doors, so an alternative had to be found for that scene.

The script also called for scenes set on the roof of the Company Megropolis on Pluto, and the production team had assumed that they could use for this any high building in London. However, the script also specified that no other buildings were to be visible, and in London this was impossible. Roberts had almost resigned himself to using CSO to get around the problem, when one of the production team came to the rescue, as Roberts explained: 'My production assistant brought a copy of *The Architectural Review* into the office, with illustrations of the new Imperial Tobacco factory in Bristol. Not a very high roof, but the size of two football pitches. Enormous.' When they scouted the location, they found an unexpected bonus that resolved the problem of getting the large buggy into the Camden Deep tunnels: the cigarette factory had a three hundred foot long underground tunnel, which ran between two halves of the facility.

Underworld has been mentioned previously as having been sorely in need of a decent cave location, but overspending on other sets for the story meant that it had to resort to the less than satisfactory medium of CSO. This left just *The Invasion of Time*, which ended up with more location work than had been originally planned.

The story was already well behind schedule, due to an original story by David Weir (concerning a race of cat-people living on Gallifrey) not working out and a substitute having to be written by producer Graham Williams and script editor Anthony Read. Then, one of a series of wildcat strikes hit *Doctor Who*, causing the loss of some studio time. The only solution was for much of the material to be recorded on location, using OB cameras, rather than in studio. Luckily a partially disused hospital in Redhill was found by the production assistant Colin Dudley, which provided the mixture of required settings, from rooms and corridors for the TARDIS interiors to a boiler room for the control centre of Gallifrey's transduction barriers. There was even a convenient quarry nearby for the filming of the sequences on outer Gallifrey.

This location did not, however, satisfy the requirement for the TARDIS to have a swimming pool, and so the pool at the British Oxygen Headquarters was used, together with the changing rooms. Stuntman Stuart Fell, who was playing one of the Sontarans, remembered the locations in an interview for *Doctor Who Magazine* in 1989: 'We used two contrasting locactions; a cold, damp, disused mental hospital in Reigate, and a luxury swimming pool in Hammersmith. I suggested leaping over the corner of the pool, jumping onto a chair, which collapsed, and then doing a roll.'

AT-A-GLANCE SEASON FIFTEEN LOCATIONS

Image of the Fendahl	Stargrove Manor, East End, Hampshire
The Sun Makers	WD & HO Wills Tobacco Factory, Hartcliffe Way, Hartcliffe, Bristol, Avon
	Camden Town Deep Tube Shelters, Stanmore Place, Camden Town, London, NW1
The Invasion of Time	Beachfields Quarry, Cormongers Lane, Redhill, Surrey
	St Anne's Hospital, Redstone Hill, Redhill, Surrey
	British Oxygen, Blacks Road, Hammersmith Broadway, London, W6

SEASON SIXTEEN

The Pirate Planet was the first story of the sixteenth season to require locations, and production assistant Michael Owen Morris found all that he needed, including a power station, fields and meadows and caves, in Gwent, South Wales. The power station was used as the engine room of the space-hopping planet Zanek, while the fields and meadows were used for scenes where the Mentiads advance on the Captain's bridge, the entrance to which was a disused railway tunnel. The Abercrave Caves at Dan-yr-Ogof became mineshafts deep inside Zanak, the large Cathedral Cavern being used for most scenes.

For the following story, *The Stones of Blood*, a rather unusual requirement had to be met. Rather than needing a location to act as some alien planet, or to give the impression that it was somewhere other than where it really was, the story called for a circle of standing stones that was to be used in the story as precisely that – a circle of standing stones.

The circle used was the Rollright Stones, which can be found just off the main A34 road in Oxfordshire. The circle in real life is small and insignificant-looking, and, as visual effects designer Mat Irvine explained to the fanzine *Temporal Limiter* in 1983, it had to be augmented: 'The stone circle we used was a real one and, as a stone circle, fairly boring. We wanted to make it more interesting, so we added a trinithon [two standing stones with a third stone laying across them] in the middle and things. In a lull during shooting, a party of schoolkids came round, and we let them through. They were going round counting the stones, and counting our dummy ones as well as the real ones. It wasn't until one of the teachers went up and touched one of them that they realised it was a polystyrene one.'

The Stones of Blood's director Darrol Blake also recalled working on the show for *Doctor Who Magazine*: 'I remember we had K-9 running on ploughed fields and various other places. Dear old Mat Irvine said it couldn't be done, so we put planks down and we shot the field through some grass and weeds, which masked the planks the tin dog was on. We got him travelling quite fast to rescue Romana, which took quite a bit of ingenuity.'

One of the most impressive castles in the south of England, Leeds Castle in Kent, was used as the main location for *The Androids of Tara*. Paul Lavers, who played Farrah, remembered the storming of the castle when interviewed for the fanzine *Web Planet*: 'It was about two o'clock in the morning, a night shoot with lots of lights. Just before we were about to start, Michael Hayes [the director] came over with a bottle of whisky to give us all a shot, because it was quite cold by then, and coming across the car park to the castle, [Simon Lack, who played Zadek] slipped, and this bottle of whisky smashed all over the place. Then Michael came up to us and said, "Listen, I know you've got to storm the castle, but could you do it quietly, because there are people inside sleeping."'

The final location used in the sixteenth season was for *The Power of Kroll*, and this time the crew travelled up to Suffolk to a section of flat marshland around Iken. One of the requirements was for the horizon to be flat and low, to facilitate the appearance of the giant Kroll creature in the sky above, and the marshes provided such an environment. Effects designer Tony Harding, interviewed for the fanzine *Fendahl*, remembered the location: 'We were working in a tidal marsh alongside the Maltings in Suffolk. You can imagine the problems this presented. At the beginning of a sequence we would be on dry land, and at the end up to our necks in water. Because of this, there were great problems with continuity, and it just so happened that we chose the few days of the year when the whole area was affected by spring tides. The tide came up twenty or thirty feet further than it normally would have done.' Mary Tamm, who played Romana, also remembered the mud when interviewed for *Doctor Who Magazine*: 'Tom and I got totally stuck in the mud, we just couldn't move until we were rescued. We were miles from anywhere, and it was so bleak. There was absolutely nothing to do between takes, because if you'd wandered off, you'd probably have been swallowed up!'

Terry Walsh, who played the green-skinned Swampie Mensch in the story, also recalled for *Doctor Who Magazine* the location work: 'We were running around in the marshes, and had to wear green waterproof make-up, which had been specially ordered from Germany. At the end of the first day's filming, they told us that they had forgotten to order the special stuff needed to get the make-up off. They sent us down to an American airbase to shower, and we arrived looking like a group of jolly green giants. There were all these black American airmen playing baseball, shouting out, "Hey, now you know how we feel!" We got in the showers, and it still wouldn't come off. We were using brushes, and still nothing happened. We ended up back at the hotel at two o'clock in the morning stark naked in the kitchen, with a group of very embarrassed make-up girls trying to get it off with Ajax. The hotel bedsheets remained green for weeks!'

AT-A-GLANCE SEASON SIXTEEN LOCATIONS

The Pirate Planet	Disused Railway Tunnell, Daren-felen, Gwent, Wales
	Big Pit, Blaenavon, Gwent, Wales
	Coity Mountain, Gwent, Wales
	Monmouthshire Golf Course, Llanfoist, Gwent, Wales
	Bwlch y Garn, Ebbw Vale, Gwent, Wales
	Cathedral Cave, Dan-yr-Ogof Showcaves, Dan-yr-Ogof, Powys, Wales
	Berkley Power Station, Berkley, Gloucs
The Stones of Blood	The King's Men, Rollright Stones, Little Rollright, Oxfordshire

Reed Cottage, Little Compton, Warwickshire
Field belonging to Manor Farm, Oakham Road, Little
    Rollright, Oxfordshire
Little Rollright Quarry, Oakham Road, Little Rollright,
    Oxfordshire

The Androids of Tara   Leeds Castle, Nr Maidstone A20, Kent
The Power of Kroll   The Maltings, Snape, Suffolk
Iken Cliff, Iken, nr Snape, Kent

SEASON SEVENTEEN

The first time the fourth Doctor visited Skaro, he found himself in Reigate Quarry, and for his next visit, in *Destiny of the Daleks*, yet another quarry was used, this time Winspit Quarry near Swanage. The fanzine *Oracle* covered the location filming of this story in 1979 through an interview with visual effects designer Peter Logan. Logan had to build a model that matched the location for the scenes where the Movellan spacecraft landed and then burrowed into the earth. Between the choosing of the location and the taking of the background photograph for matching with the model work, a heavy rainstorm had created an artificial lake just alongside the place where the spaceship was supposed to land. The main problem with the model lake was not the difficulty caused by water's refusal to miniaturise well, but its tendency to seep through sand. Since the lake was always as still as a millpond, and muddy because of the sand, there was no difficulty in making the model look like the real thing. In any event, in many of the model shots, the lake was partially obscured by a strategically placed bank of sand.

The feature went on to reveal that when the TARDIS was buried under rubble at the start of the story, it wasn't the weight of the rocks that was the problem, as they were made of polystyrene; rather it was that a half mile walk around the cliff was necessary to get to a position above the TARDIS in order to drop the rocks. Two or three journeys were necessary for each re-take, as there were so many polystyrene rocks to be dropped.

Destiny of the Daleks was also the first *Doctor Who* adventure to make use of a Steadicam. This is a lightweight, single-operator video camera, finely counter-balanced, giving its operator precise control over the image being recorded. It also allows for smooth tracking shots to be taken over bumpy terrain. Previously, camera tracks had to be laid on the ground, and even then the smoothness of the shot depended on the care of those pushing the camera-dolly along the tracks. With a Steadicam, all these problems are removed, and fast, smooth camerawork is the result.

The next story, *City of Death*, took *Doctor Who* overseas for the first time ever, and the only way that producer Graham Williams managed it was to keep the costs involved down to a minimum, as he explained to *Doctor Who Magazine*: 'No sooner had we settled on Paris [as a setting] than I decided to cost out the script. I felt that we could actually go to Paris at no extra cost, as long as we were clever about it. I gave John Nathan-Turner, then my production unit manager, the list of the cast that I intended taking over and the time we'd be there, and he returned me a costing that was to within about fifteen pounds of what we'd have spent going to Ealing Studios to shoot it.' The reason that this worked out was that at Ealing there would have been the costs of designing and building the sets, buying in the props and other hire charges, whereas by taking a minimum of crew over to Paris – just a film cameraman, a sound man, the director and producer – the costs were minimised on the location. This was the reason why K-9 was written out of this story, as taking him out to Paris would have involved more people in the form of operators and visual effects technicians.

Lalla Ward, interviewed in the fanzine *Eye of Horus*, remembered filming in Paris: 'Tom was a bit annoyed that the French were more interested in me and my schoolgirl outfit than him and his long scarf. Of course, *Doctor Who* isn't shown over there, so the French didn't take too much notice of us. I remember on one location we were to film at the top of the Eiffel Tower, but we couldn't as it was so misty and there was four inches of snow on the ground. We couldn't see a thing!'

As it turned out, this was the last location work seen on screen from the seventeenth season, as both *Nightmare of Eden* and *The Horns of Nimon* were studio-bound stories (although *The Horns of Nimon* was originally planned to include some location work), and the season's final story, *Shada*, was not completed, due to another strike, and was therefore never transmitted.

The location filming for *Shada* was done in and around the streets of Cambridge and Grantchester. Footage was also shot of the Doctor punting on the River Cam. Assistant K-9 Operator Stephen Cambden spoke to *Private Who* fanzine about this sequence: 'Tom Baker, very much a land lubber at heart, managed to move the punt in every conceivable direction except the one indicated by the director! He spun it, pitched it and even jammed the pole into the river bed, while Lalla Ward, a nervous passenger, prayed for deliverance. On the one occasion Tom did steer the punt in for a perfect landing, the cameras were not rolling!'

AT-A-GLANCE SEASON SEVENTEEN LOCATIONS

Destiny of the Daleks	Winspit Quarry, Worth Matravers, Dorset
	Binnegar Heath Sand Pit, Puddletown Road, Wareham, Dorset
City of Death	Eiffel Tower, Parc du Champ de Mars, Paris, France
	Duplex Metro Platform (line 6), Rue August Bartoldi, Paris, France
	Trocadero Metro Platform (Line 6), Place du Trocadero, Paris, France
	Avenue Kleber (Boissiere Metro and Entrance), Paris, France
	Rue de Rivoli (Louvre Museum), Paris, France
	Le Notre Dame Brasserie, Place du Petit Pont, Paris, France
	Place de la Concorde, Paris, France
	Denise Rene Gallery, Boulevard St Germain, Paris, France
	Avenue des Champs Elysees, Paris, France
	47 Rue Vieille du Temple, Paris, France
Shada	Emmanuel College, St Andrews Street, Cambridge;
	The Backs, River Cam, Cambridge;
	Botolph Lane, Cambridge;
	Trinity Lane, Cambridge;
	Garret Hostel Bridge and Lane, Cambridge;
	Portugal Place and Portugal Street, Cambridge;
	King's Parade, Cambridge;

4 FOURTH DOCTOR

St Edward's Passage, Cambridge;
Blackmoor Head's Yard, Cambridge;
High Street and Grantchester Meadows, Grantchester

SEASON EIGHTEEN

Tom Baker's final season reverted to all-British locations. The opening scenes of *The Leisure Hive*, the only location work in that story, were all filmed on Brighton beach, and whereas the script had called for the weather to be dull and overcast, in fact it was bright and pleasant – something of a novelty for *Doctor Who*, as most location work seems to have taken place either in wet, windy and cold conditions, or at the height of a heat-wave.

Black Park near Iver was the location used for two of the stories, *Full Circle* and *State of Decay*. *Full Circle* made use of a lake in the park, as well as some of the forest surrounding it, and director Peter Grimwade told *Doctor Who Magazine* about the alterations the crew had to make to the location: 'The huge, coloured lights taken on location, which made Alzarius seem as though it had a strange sun, were not conceived at an early stage. That came along when the cameraman suggested lighting the foreground as we were setting up the forest scenes. It worked especially well after the designer, Janet Budden, had made the set look even more exotic by dabbing powder paint all over the foliage and trees. It kicked back off the lights and gave a very garish feel to the setting. The only problem was that the stuff got everywhere and we were continually having to clear it up, because the park was National Trust property.'

State of Decay concentrated on Burnham Beeches' forest areas in Black Park. Due to the park's location close to Bray House, the former home of Hammer films in the Sixties and early Seventies, it was also used in many of their horror films. For *Doctor Who* to have filmed sections of its vampire story there seems somehow fitting.

Logopolis, the final story of the eighteenth season and Tom Baker's final story as the Doctor, made use of a number of locations in central London, and also a lay-by and fields lying alongside the A413 road in Buckinghamshire. The production team had originally wanted to use one of the few remaining police telephone boxes still in existence, located along the Barnet bypass, but the box was vandalised in between their taking of reference photos and arriving to film, and so a prop was used instead. Shortly after this, the genuine box was dismantled and removed altogether.

AT-A-GLANCE SEASON EIGHTEEN LOCATIONS

The Leisure Hive	Brighton Beach, Fish Market Hard, Brighton, East Sussex
Full Circle	Black Park, Fulmer, Bucks
State of Decay	Burnham Beeches, Burnham, Bucks
Logopolis	43 Ursula Street, Battersea, London, SW11
	Albert Bridge, Kensington and Chelsea, London, SW3
	Cadogan Pier, Chelsea Embankment, London, SW3
	BBC Receiving Station, Crowsley Park, Blounts Court Road, Sonning Common, Berks
	Lay-by, Amersham Road (A413), Denham, Bucks

The era of the fourth Doctor had seen technology advance by leaps and bounds, with better, lighter cameras, and ever-more realistic effects being achieved through digital technology. Although the budget had not increased to the extent that regular overseas filming was possible, through careful use of resources the production teams were able to make the most of what was available in Britain.

The filming of *City of Death* in Paris proved that locations could be found further afield, as long as the schedules were carefully prepared, and this paved the way for several more trips abroad in the following years. Some lessons were also learnt: K-9 was never successfully used on location, despite having his wheels modified for the eighteenth season, and his appearances were therefore limited mainly to studio-bound stories.

Other stories looked as though they had used locations, but had in fact been made all in studios. *Planet of Evil*, *The Creature from the Pit* and *Nightmare of Eden* all featured realistic forests that had been artificially created. Even *Horror of Fang Rock*'s effective lighthouse interior was a set, created by designer Paul Allen up at the BBC's Pebble Mill studios in Birmingham.

As technology progressed and *Doctor Who* utilised what was available, so the quality of the finished product improved. *Doctor Who* at the end of the Seventies was very different from what had been produced a decade before, and the use of location work more than ever augmented the final product as the integration of film, OB recording and studio recording became flawless.

SELLING THE DOCTOR

Television is the biggest and most popular form of mass entertainment, and a whole industry exists to try and capture and market something memorable, something that will make one particular product or person stand out from all the others. As often as not, it is the unlikely that succeeds, and some products that are hyped up through expensive campaigns fall at the first fence.

When discussing *Doctor Who*'s impact on popular culture, it is impossible not to mention the Daleks, the first great marketing success of the series. Like other cultural icons of the same period, such as Superman, Batman, the Beatles and International Rescue's Thunderbirds, the Daleks were not planned to be a rip-roaring, money-spinning success. Quite to the contrary, the metal monsters from Skaro had been created by an author who conceded to write the story in the first place only because he was strapped for cash at the time; and their look came about through a logical progression by the designer thinking about how best to achieve the effect required on screen. The final element was the voices, and these came about as simply a desire to get away from a human voice.

Three disparate elements: the character, the look, and the voice, but together they captured the imaginations of a generation of children.

If the Daleks were *Doctor Who*'s first commercial success, then its second was the fourth Doctor. This is not to say that the previous three Doctors had been unpopular, but none of them had captured the imagination of the viewing public to the extent that the fourth Doctor did.

While the first three Doctors all had strong characters, and enjoyed a variety of entertaining and memorable adventures, their impact – at least as far as commercial prospects were concerned – was lessened by the far greater impact made by the Daleks.

4 FOURTH DOCTOR

In 1965 and 1966, the Daleks ruled both the television and the toyshops. The other elements that made up the television series in which they appeared were relegated to the background, and so the Doctor, his TARDIS and the many other creatures he met were not given a look in. The manufacturers saw that the Daleks were popular, and if they couldn't have Daleks, then they weren't interested.

One consequence of this was that when the Dalek boom tailed off in late 1966, those responsible for exploiting them commercially moved into other areas. *Doctor Who* had been mined, had been successful for them, but now they wanted another major success, and the Daleks and the Doctor were perceived to be rather old hat. This resulted in a lack of media coverage, made worse by the fact that the second Doctor, Patrick Troughton, rarely gave interviews to the press and kept personal appearances to an absolute minimum. With little backup from the BBC, it was better from the manufacturers' point of view to let *Doctor Who* lie and to try elsewhere.

When Jon Pertwee took on the rôle of the Doctor, all the elements required to make a successful impact on the media appeared to be there. Pertwee had the look: a frilly shirt, velvet jacket and swirling cloak. He had the gimmicks: a sonic screwdriver and his old Edwardian roadster, Bessie. It wasn't that the actor was shy and retiring. Far from it: Jon Pertwee was a true showman and threw his all into promoting the series and the Doctor. While he was playing the Doctor, there was interest in the show, but despite the fact that Pertwee stayed in the part for four years, the popular memory of his era focuses not only on the Doctor himself but also on the other elements that made the early Seventies so successful in *Doctor Who* terms: the Master, the Brigadier and UNIT.

When Tom Baker arrived, it coincided with the phasing out of UNIT and the re-establishment of the Doctor as an enigmatic traveller in time and space. The focus of the programme returned to its central character. What is more, the new Doctor was more instantly recognisable than his predecessors, due to his distinctive looks and his trademark hat and scarf. The highly memorable costume, combined with Tom Baker's eccentric portrayal, helped to fix the character in viewers' minds. The third Doctor had become somewhat predictable and staid, played seriously and with conviction by Pertwee, but Baker's fourth Doctor was an unpredictable maverick. One could never be quite sure how he would react in a situation, or what he would do next. At times the character seemed so packed full of suppressed energy that he would explode at the merest provocation, and at other times he could be so mellow that nothing could perturb him.

Each of the actors who has played the Doctor over the years has brought a little of himself to the part – Pertwee's love of gadgetry being a good example. With Tom Baker's Doctor, there was more than just a little of the actor on show. Baker's unpredictable nature, his tendency toward self-contemplation, his immediate and tangible charisma, all overspilled into the fourth Doctor. Tom Baker was a larger than life character himself, and that quality reinforced the rôle he played, creating a truly memorable Doctor.

MEDIA

Tom Baker was a godsend to the media, and his characterisation of the Doctor resulted in more coverage than any other – including pastiches.

There had been the occasional pastiche based around *Doctor Who* before Tom Baker came along, for example newspaper cartoons in the Sixties, a sketch ending with an appearance of a Dalek on *Crackerjack*, and even pop star Cliff Richard including a spoof of the series in one of his BBC variety shows in the early Seventies. However, the real proliferation of *Doctor Who* parodies on TV started with Tom Baker's immensely visual Doctor. There were a number of parodies during his tenure, and many others followed, so that a *Doctor Who* inspired sketch could be found on the TV shows of most popular comedians.

One of the earliest parodies was presented by *Crackerjack* toward the end of 1975, when Don MacLean played the fourth Doctor, Peter Glaze portrayed the Brigadier and Jacqueline Clarke played Sarah. Set in the control room of the TARDIS, which had landed atop the Post Office Tower, it featured the Doctor knitting his scarf throughout.

Another celebrated example was the 1979 *Doctor Eyes* item featured in an edition of the LWT sketch show *End of Part One*, written by Andrew Marshall and David Renwick. In this, actor Fred Harris wearing an exaggerated version of Tom Baker's costume – complete with huge, bulging 'eyeballs' fixed over his own eyes – romped across a tacky alien landscape accompanied by a female companion, Gloria, played by Sue Holderness and based on Mary Tamm's Romana. Gloria was periodically prodded with a stick from out-of-shot to make her scream on cue, and was preoccupied with when in the script she was supposed to scream or sprain her ankle. The Doctor was forced to regenerate (the new version played by Tony Aitken) because his previous incarnation was getting far too expensive. The regeneration was triggered when a Dalek-like monster shot him through his contract. The skit was set on the planet Chromakey 5 and also featured the Doctor's computerised companion, 'plastic-thing-that's-meant-to-look-like-a-dog'.

Other pastiches around this time were seen on *Emu's Broadcasting Company* and Spike Milligan's *Q6* – a classic 'Pakistani Dalek' sketch. Another example from the realms of TV, although this could hardly be classed as a bona fide pastiche, are the series of tongue-in-cheek futuristic commercials that Tom Baker and Lalla Ward made in 1979 for Prime Computers in Australia, wearing their original *Doctor Who* costumes – something they would never have been allowed to do in Britain!

Another notable *Doctor Who* parody of the period appeared not on TV but in print, in *Mad* magazine. Interestingly enough, although *Mad* originates from America, this was at a time when *Doctor Who* was almost entirely unknown in the States, only a few of the Jon Pertwee stories having been shown on PBS stations. Presumably, then, the *Doctor Ooh* feature that appeared in Issue 161 was for the British edition only.

Mad magazine regularly features accurately caricatured parodies of topical films and TV shows, well drawn but usually with somewhat leaden text. The five page *Doctor Ooh* spoof, written by Geoff Rowley, was no exception. Heavily based on *The Ark in Space*, it had characters similar to the fourth Doctor, Sarah Jane and Harry arriving in a remote, deserted spaceship where, as the Doctor puts it, 'a handful of the chosen few are hovering in suspended animation.'

The strip illustrations by Steve Parkhouse are well-observed, although they obviously owe much to stock photos of the regular cast and the sets used in *The Ark in Space*. What wit there is relies heavily on the well-known limitations of the show's budget – "Doctor! There's a plastic bag full of ping-pong balls crawling towards you!" – and the by-then-established characteristics of the regular cast (re-named Dr Ooh, Squarer and Hairy).

Squarer spends the entire strip snivelling and having her clothes removed, rather like Carol Cleveland in the *Scott of the Sahara* sketch from *Monty Python's Flying Circus*. Hairy is bold, forthright – and transformed, frame by frame, from naval surgeon into full blown, Robert Newton-style buccaneer. The bulk of the humour, though, relies on Tom Baker's scarf – which proves to be his undoing – and incidental appearances by everything from Cybermen to Peter Cushing. Devices that work well are Squarer being eventually reduced to a sniffle emanating from a Kleenex box, appearances by the first three Doctors, and a Dalek using its eyestick as a watering can!

Elsewhere, in the mass-market press, journalists were finding tags for the Doctor: 'the curly-haired Harpo Marx with his wide-eyed projection of the Doctor,' reported one newspaper in 1975; 'intellectual, eyeball-rolling,' said another in 1977.

All through Tom Baker's time as the Doctor, and even after he had left, the press headlined features about him with puns and wordplay such as: 'Who's next as 007?', 'Doc's dilemma', 'Who goes hairless', and 'Yo, ho Who!'. Baker loved to promote the show, and was interviewed many times on television, including on *Nationwide* and *Pebble Mill at One*, discussing his past and his approach to playing the Doctor. The coverage was certainly helped in the latter part of the Seventies by the start of Saturday morning kids TV shows, with Noel Edmonds's *Multi-Coloured Swap Shop* featuring many *Doctor Who* celebrities over the years. Other notable appearances included Tom Baker presenting *Disney Time* in August 1975. This was done in character as the Doctor; at the end of the show, he leaves saying that he must get up to Scotland in time to help the Brigadier – a direct link into *Terror of the Zygons*. There was a specially recorded trailer for the seventeenth season, in which the Doctor is awakened from sleep to hear a warning from the continuuity announcer that he will be up against the Daleks again. After the announcer tells him to forget the warning, the Doctor returns to the TARDIS, placing a 'Do Not Disturb' sign on the door. Another in-character appearance was on Johnny Morris's *Animal Magic*, where the Doctor speaks about some of the animals and creatures he has met on his travels. This sequence was shot during the filming of *The Creature from the Pit*, on the forest set at Ealing Film Studios, and the Doctor is seen wearing the portable stocks placed on him by Lady Adrasta.

At this time, *Doctor Who* had an especially large adult following, and the press interest reflected this. The press seemed to delight in asking Baker about his private life, and he seemed equally to delight in revealing very little to them, with the result that what little they did know (his failed marriage to Anna Wheatcroft, his romance with Lalla Ward) was pounced upon eagerly in practically every interview and feature about him.

Further proof of Baker's incredible popularity came when he started writing a regular column in a weekly newspaper, *Reveille*. The column ran for some nine months from March to November 1975, and was written in a chatty, friendly style, with a very broad range of subject matter. There were stories about Tom's fight against chicken bones that kept getting thrown into his front garden; faces in tree trunks; sponsorship of mountain rescue dogs; people with their heads stuck in pots; a visit to the zoo; Peter Pan; not talking to strangers; a dream in which Tom tap-dances in a London museum; and many, many more.

To give some idea of the scope and style of the writing, here are some examples.

'Last week, dressed as an Egyptian mummy, I bumped into 36 schoolchildren. We were filming in Berkshire. They seemed very intrigued, then nervous, then vastly amused. We finally had a picture taken. The next day, in regular costume, I went to the school. The children were delighted. They all looked so well and cheerful. During the conversation, which was mostly about monsters, the excitement grew and the children teased each other and boasted of fantasy exploits. One lad, all of five, said he liked nettle and snake soup. During a lull, I heard a six-year-old singing: "Whistle while you work, Hitler bought a shirt …" "What's Hitler?" I asked him. "Oh, he was a German, nasty too," he replied. I wondered what programme he watched on television. Could it have been *Colditz*?' (6 June 1975)

'Trees have faces. You didn't know that? But you can find them if you just bother to look. Tree faces aren't like human ones – stuck at the top end and at the front. Sometimes they are halfway up, hidden under a branch. Often they are clown-like with big noses or funny staring eyes. So next time you go for a stroll in the park or through the woods, keep your eyes open and you should spot a few faces looking at you.' (27 June 1975)

'At rehearsal last week, the director asked me if I could do a double loop with my yo-yo. I said: "Of course, watch this." When I swung my yo-yo back it came and hit me between the eyes. Everybody was very amused – except me.' (7 November 1975)

The latter is one of a number of occasional anecdotes that were included about the making of *Doctor Who*, although these were usually very watered down – tending to concern encounters with children or animals while away filming on location.

Other notable press coverage was generated when the production office decided to get rid of K-9. A 'Save K-9' campaign was even waged through the pages of the *Sun* newspaper. This was the first of new producer John Nathan-Turner's many ways of getting additional press coverage for the series, and it worked a treat. The *Sun* had readers writing in with protest letters, and ran a follow up article featuring some of those who wrote in. There was even one girl who had written to the Queen on the subject, but the article did not reveal what her reply said.

Right up until the end of his era, the press followed the fourth Doctor, and when Baker finally hung up the famous hat and scarf and left, John Nathan-Turner, always keen to maximise publicity, arranged for him to 'let slip' that the next Doctor Who might be played not by a man, but by a woman. This masterstroke ensured banner headlines the following day, as Baker was hounded by the press and TV for interviews. After all, he had played the Doctor for close on seven years, the longest continuous run of all the Doctors to date.

COMPANIONS

It was not only Tom Baker who was subject to the tender attentions of the press, but also the actors and actresses who portrayed his companions. During the tenure of the fourth Doctor, the press developed a near-obsession with the Doctor's travelling companions. No-one had ever made a secret of the fact that this mysterious man travelled with a succession of pretty young girls, but neither had anything been made of it. Throughout the Sixties, the press had reported when companions joined and left, but this had always been done in a serious, news-reporting style. Even in the early Seventies, there had been little fuss made when Caroline John (Liz Shaw) joined and left, and even Katy Manning (Jo Grant) was treated with some respect until her decision to reveal all in a set of nude photographs for a men's magazine called *Girl Illustrated*, the cover of which featured Katy with a Dalek.

All this was to change as, in line with general trends in the British tabloid press, reporting became less and less news and more and more sensationalism. When the 'good girl next door' Sarah Jane Smith decided to leave the Doctor and his new travelling companion was announced to be a half-naked savage girl played by the attractive Louise Jameson, reporters pounced on the story eagerly.

'Dr Who's tough new Lady' screamed one headline, accompanied by a press-call photograph of Leela on the set of *The Face of Evil*, brandishing a knife in a very aggressive pose. 'A cave girl with a killer touch' was the description given, and when Tom Baker was asked what he thought of his new assistant, he apparently said, 'You know the Doctor. He doesn't have a sex life.' One can only surmise that the question actually asked was rather different from the one that appeared in print. As usual, it was the *Sun* that made the most of the situation, going as far as to ask, on its TV pages, 'Is sex about to rear its irrepressible head in that most adult of children's shows, Dr Who? I'm getting worried about the Doctor's attitude to his new assistant, Leela (Louise Jameson). It does not fit the pattern.' The writer went to describe the first three Doctors' attitudes to their assistants, and ended: 'But the present Doctor, Tom Baker, is definitely on the dishy side. And while he was purely avuncular towards silly Sarah, he seems to see Leela in a different light. I'm sure I detect the stirrings of something sexual. Perhaps he is turned on by the wash-leather the strange little creature wears on her bum. But this being a children's show, there won't be any hanky panky, I presume. So will it be Dr and Mrs Who?'

After Leela, the next companion to join the Doctor was Romana, played in her first incarnation by Mary Tamm. The press were in their stride by now, and the standard headlines, such as 'Who's next' and 'Who's in Luck', all appeared. This time, the papers had even somehow got hold of several modelling shots of Ms Tamm, one with her hair blowing in the breeze, another with her hair pinned up, wearing classy clothes, holding classic modelling poses. These photographs were featured alongside stories claiming that glamour was boarding the TARDIS, and that as well as being glamorous, Romana was – gasp – intelligent. Obviously a concept that the papers found hard to take, as the introduction of Romana generated a lot of coverage along these lines.

Lalla Ward was the next companion, taking over the role of Romana from Mary Tamm. This time, the *Daily Express* saw fit to give a large centre-page spread to a round-up of all of the Doctor's 'sexy assistants', describing Lalla Ward as the latest 'teatime sex symbol' and encouraging readers to draw their own conclusion as to whether being Doctor Who's assistant was a passport to stardom or a one way hop to obscurity. At the time this article appeared (1979), only Jean Marsh (the first Doctor's short-lived companion Sara Kingdom) had gone on to greater things, and since then, only Louise Jameson, possibly the most stereotyped of all the female assistants in the press, has continued to carve out a high-profile acting career for herself through numerous roles in popular series.

Lalla Ward went on to hit the headlines again when she and Tom Baker announced plans to marry in 1980, apparently confirming to the tabloids that their suspicions had been correct all along and that there was hanky-panky in the TARDIS. The marriage lasted only sixteen months, and the break-up was again the subject of much press coverage.

Pretty much the same level of coverage occurred when Sarah Sutton and Janet Fielding were announced as joining the TARDIS crew towards the end of Tom Baker's tenure. In Fielding's case, the situation was similar to that in Mary Tamm's, in that the papers got hold of some glamorous photographs and ran those, presumably in preference to the BBC supplied photographs.

During the seven years in which Tom Baker played the Doctor, the role of the assistant had been redefined by the popular press, from being a simple acting role, to that of some sexy bimbette cavorting through time with the eligible and desirable Doctor. Certainly in the eyes of the press, *Doctor Who* was no longer an educational tea time series for children and adults alike, but a light-hearted space series, aimed firmly at kids, but with a pretty girl on board to keep the dads interested.

OVERSEAS

Doctor Who had been sold outside the UK since shortly after it started in 1963, but at the time Tom Baker took over the lead role, all that viewers in the USA had seen were occasional re-runs of a range of thirteen Jon Pertwee stories from *Doctor Who and the Silurians* to *The Time Monster*. These were not particularly well received, despite a fair amount of trade advertising, and it wasn't until 1977 that the BBC decided to sell, through its overseas agent Time Life, a new package of Tom Baker stories to that market. This amounted to ninety-eight episodes featuring the fourth Doctor, perceived by the BBC as being marketable as his Doctor was far more eccentric than the serious Pertwee image, and the American market tended to favour eccentrics. In February 1978, there was a press call to announce that the package of episodes was available. Photos were taken showing the Doctor and a variety of alien monsters supposedly waiting for visas outside the American Embassy in London.

What the American audience were faced with when *Doctor Who* Tom Baker-style first hit their screens was a very doctored and Americanised version. For a start, all the episodes had been given a new voice-over introduction by veteran actor Howard da Silva, which often blotted out dialogue to tell the viewers what they already knew or to give away vital plot twists before they were revealed in the story.

Other changes included the addition of a montage of clips from the forthcoming serial at the start of each part one, and a 'next episode' trailer at the end of all bar the final episode of a story – again with narration from da Silva. As the running time had to be around half an hour (including three commercial breaks and all the montages listed above) the actual episodes themselves were also trimmed down to ensure that they didn't overrun.

To give an example of the style of introductory voice-over, the opening episode of *Robot* was accompanied by Mr da Silva saying: 'Doctor Who's face is transformed as his friends watch – instant plastic surgery. But the change goes more than skin deep. The Time Lord, on the brink of death, is inducing a complete physical metamorphosis … Recently returned from a distant planet where he was exposed to deadly radioactivity, Doctor Who enters into his fourth incarnation, thus saving his own life. But his new personality is still erratic and in transition, so the Brigadier has no alternative but to place him in the hands of a mere Earth doctor.'

Another example, which shows how inaccurate the voice-overs could sometimes be, is from *Revenge of the Cybermen*, where 'The Cyberscheme unfolds as a plot to take over the galaxy, but the metal men can succeed only if they regain control of their home planet in order to blow it up. Its core is of pure gold, alluring to human kind but fatal to Cybermen.'

Doctor Who was seen in this form via the Public Broadcasting Service (PBS) stations in America for many years, and despite the detrimental impact on the stories, it quickly became a cult favourite, thanks in part to almost continuous transmission of the stories. Eventually Lionheart, the successor to Time Life, distributed *Doctor Who* in its original, unadulterated episodic form, and also as movie-length story compilations. Fan groups sprung up all over the country, and Tom Baker was being hailed by science fiction writer

479

Harlan Ellison in his introduction to a range of *Doctor Who* novelations published by Pinnacle in 1979 and 1980 as: 'The one and only, the incomparable, the bemusing and bewildering Doctor Who, the humanistic defender of Good and Truth whose exploits put to shame those of Kimball Kinnison, Captain Future and pantywaist nerds like Han Solo and Luke Skywalker. My hero! Doctor Who!'

Tom Baker made his first appearance at a fan convention in America in 1979 when the cancellation of *Shada* meant that both he and producer Graham Williams were free to attend. The event did extraordinarily well, and even after he had finished playing the Doctor on television, Baker remained in great demand to attend further American events. Because of the importance of the American sales to the BBC, Williams' successor, John Nathan-Turner, encouraged this attention, and even arranged whole plane-loads of guests to travel out to attend the events. The same attention was not given to Britain, and fan conventions in this country often lost out, as the British organisers simply did not have the cash to compete with the fees offered by their American counterparts. While *Doctor Who* fandom was at its peak, British fans could forget about any reunion of Doctors in this country – every anniversary, all the actors were in America; and Troughton and Baker, along with some of the companions, were not keen to attend British events anyway.

Meanwhile, in Australia, where *Doctor Who* had been screened since 1965 by the Australian Broadcasting Commission (ABC), Tom Baker's debut season coincided with an attempt by the ABC to stop screening the show as the ratings were poor. Australian fans didn't think much of this, and lobbied the ABC to continue with the show. Luckily they got their wish, and also got a fan organisation, the Australasian *Doctor Who* Fan Club, which was created as a means to get the programme back on the air.

One of the problems *Doctor Who* has had to contend with outside its home territory are stricter rules governing what can be shown at particular times of the day. In Australia, adventures like *The Deadly Assassin* and *The Brain of Morbius* were rated as being for an adult audience, and deemed unsuitable for transmission in a 6.00 pm time slot, while others were edited to remove any material that the Australian general public might have found offensive – for example, two sequences from *The Talons of Weng-Chiang* were cut: one in part three when the giant rat appears to bite Leela, and the other in part four when the rat appears to bite Chang.

New Zealand
By Paul Scoones

The first three Tom Baker stories were initially aired on Saturday evenings at 6.30 pm on the second television channel, South Pacific Television (SPTV), from 4 February to 8 April 1978. The stories were screened in production order, so *The Sontaran Experiment* preceded *The Ark in Space*.

After a gap of four months the series resumed with *Revenge of the Cybermen* through to *Pyramids of Mars* from 12 August to 25 November 1978. *Genesis of the Daleks* was not screened, and the stories were again aired in production order, so *Pyramids of Mars* preceded *Planet of Evil*. The series again screened on Saturdays on SPTV, but at the earlier time of 4.30 pm.

After a month long break, the series returned on Fridays at 6.30 pm on SPTV, with *The Android Invasion*, screened from 29 December 1978 to 19 January 1979. *The Green*

Death followed this, which was one of many stories that had been omitted in the initial run of Jon Pertwee stories.

The series resumed several months later with *The Brain of Morbius* screened from 12 May 1979. SPTV screened every story, in order, up to *The Invisible Enemy* except for *Horror of Fang Rock*, which was omitted. The episodes were once again on Saturdays, but at the earlier time of around 4 pm, though advertised start times varied from week to week, from 3 pm to 4.10 pm.

On 18 February 1980, following a major revamp of the schedules, and a channel name change from SPTV to Television Two, the series moved to Monday evenings at the regular time of 6 pm. *Image of the Fendahl* was the first story screened in this new timeslot, followed by *Underworld*. Both *The Sun Makers* and *The Invasion of Time* were omitted. All six Season Sixteen stories were screened in their correct order, however the first three stories of Season Seventeen were then screened in production order so viewers saw *The Creature from the Pit*, followed by *City of Death* and then *Destiny of the Daleks*. *Nightmare of Eden* and *The Horns of Nimon* screened in January and February 1981, after which the series went off air for four weeks.

Season Eighteen was acquired by Television New Zealand between 12 March 1981 (for *The Leisure Hive*) and 12 April 1981 (for *Logopolis*). Tom Baker's final season was launched on a new day, channel and timeslot. From 23 March 1981 the series aired on Tuesdays on Television One with an earlier start-time of around 5.30 pm. Most of Season Eighteen was screened in this position, but came to a premature end on 1 September 1981 with the final episode of *The Keeper of Traken*. At this point, New Zealand was just one story short of catching up to the UK, but viewers were then left waiting for just over a year to see *Logopolis*, which finally screened from 20 September to 18 October 1982, with a week off midway through the story to accommodate Commonwealth Games coverage, on the same channel, day and timeslot as the rest of Season Eighteen. TVNZ had held on to *Logopolis* for a year, and their rights to screen Season Eighteen episodes expired 31 March 1983.

The first repeats of the Tom Baker era took place several years later. Following on from a run of Jon Pertwee stories, *Robot* was screened from 30 December 1986, marking the beginning of a run of the entire Tom Baker era, including *Genesis of the Daleks*, *Horror of Fang Rock*, *The Sun Makers* and *The Invasion of Time* which had all been omitted during the initial screenings of the Tom Baker stories. *Genesis of the Daleks* was screened out of sequence in May-June 1987, located between *The Seeds of Doom* and *Masque of Mandragora*, but otherwise the stories were transmitted in the correct sequence. The episodes were initially broadcast on TV1, twice a week on Tuesdays and Wednesdays at around 5.30 pm. In February 1987, midway through *Revenge of the Cybermen*, the series moved from TV1 to TV2 but otherwise continued unchanged. In December 1987, *The Ribos Operation* was screened as two double-length episodes from 5 pm. For the last two stories of Tom Baker's era, the series moved to Thursdays and Fridays, and *Logopolis* ended on 19 August 1988. The episodes screened at this time were supplied by the Australian Broadcasting Corporation and consequently in many cases exhibited cuts that had been made by the Australian censor.

Viewer ratings for the 1986-88 period reveal that *The Hand of Fear* Part Four, with a rating of 18.5% (of the potential viewing audience) was the Tom Baker episode with the most viewers, and this episode was placed 45th on the top 50 most watched programmes chart in the first week of July 1987. Part Three of *Horror of Fang Rock*, seen by 15% and charting in 49th position for the third week of September 1987, was second equal with *The Hand of Fear* Part Three. The five top rating stories were: *The Hand of Fear* (14.1%), *The Robots of Death* (13.4%), *The Deadly Assassin* (12.4%), *Horror of Fang Rock* (11.3%) and *The Face of Evil* (10.9%). The time of year would appear to have had an influence on the viewer ratings, with all of the top-rated episodes screened during New Zealand's winter months when television viewing figures are typically higher than in warmer months and correspondingly the lowest rated episodes – including *The Stones of Blood* Part Two (3%), *The Ark in Space* Part Three, *Robot* Parts Three and Four (all 4%) and *The Invasion of Time* Part Six (4.5%) – all screened in December and January, which is New Zealand's summertime.

A further run of Tom Baker era repeats commenced on 9 February 2001 with *Robot*, following on directly from a run of all complete Hartnell, Troughton and Pertwee stories on the UHF and satellite digital channel, Prime Television. The Tom Baker episodes were screened six days a week (Sunday to Friday). Initially two episodes were played each day back-to-back at 6 pm, running until *The Sun Makers* Part One & Two on Friday 30 March 2001. Thereafter the schedule changed to single episodes at 6 pm from *The Sun Makers* Part Three on Sunday 1 April 2001. The run ended with *The Horns of Nimon* Part Four on Thursday 7 June 2001. For the first time on New Zealand television, all of the stories from Seasons Twelve to Seventeen were played in the correct sequence. Prime planned to resume the series with *The Leisure Hive* from Monday 7 January 2002 but around this time the channel changed owners and a major change to the schedules meant that *Doctor Who* was dropped from Prime's programme line-up.

FANDOM

The BBC had for many years acknowledged that *Doctor Who* had a fan following, and the first fan club had been set up and run in 1965 as the William (*Doctor Who*) Hartnell Fan Club. This had survived, following a change of name and several changes of organisers, into the Seventies, but had then folded.

The BBC continued to cater to the wide-ranging interest in the series with numerous competitions, normally of the 'draw a monster' type, with first prize being a trip to the BBC to see *Doctor Who* being made. There seemed to be many of these competitions, with visits made to the sets of *The Masque of Mandragora*, *The Deadly Assassin*, *The Face of Evil* and *The Stones of Blood*. Fans too were invited along to watch the proceedings (usually from the studio gallery, but occasionally from the studio floor), and news of forthcoming stories became much easier to obtain when some fans started working for the BBC and therefore had almost unrestricted access to the observation galleries and other areas of the production process, depending on where in the Corporation they were working – some even worked on *Doctor Who* itself. When John Nathan-Turner arrived as producer in 1980, he was concerned about the fan 'grapevine' and started taking steps to withhold information, leading to his closing the public viewing galleries and stepping up studio security, as well as logging in and out all the copies of the scripts each day when particularly newsworthy stories were being recorded. *Logopolis* was the first story on which the galleries were closed in an attempt to keep the fans away, and to keep the circumstances of the Doctor's regeneration secret.

Backtracking to 1976, this year saw the establishment of probably the most effective, and certainly the best-run, *Doctor Who* fan group in Britain. The *Doctor Who*

Appreciation Society began life as a group at Westfield College in London, but the organisers soon realised that there was a potential wider appeal to be had, and so opened their doors to the rest of the country.

From mid-1976, the Society provided a monthly newsletter (*Celestial Toyroom*) and a magazine (*TARDIS*, which had actually been instigated earlier and was adopted as the Society's publication from issue 7) as well as pooling the respective resources of a number of fans to provide various departments like Reference, Art, Fiction, Photographic, and so on.

Those who ran the DWAS were given information about the stories in production, which was relayed to the members via the newsletter. They were also supported in other ways by the BBC, who generally helped with any photographs, interviews and information the group wanted. When producer Graham Williams commented that they ought to check into clearing the copyrights on what they were doing, they did so and were able to negotiate a deal with the BBC for the reproduction and sale of photos to the Society members. When K-9 was announced as joining the TARDIS crew, Williams was careful to maintain the secret, and would not allow photographs or information out. The Society, however, managed to obtain a photograph, and arranged for an artwork rendition of it to be used on the cover of *TARDIS* to coincide with the transmission of *The Invisible Enemy*. Williams never asked how the Society came by the information, but this incident helped to show the production team that the Society could be trusted to keep secrets. The DWAS was also asked to provide assistance with putting together the first ever *Doctor Who* documentary in 1977, a *The Lively Arts* production presented by Melvyn Bragg and called *Whose Doctor Who*.

The DWAS also organised the world's first *Doctor Who* convention, held on 6 August 1977 at a church hall in Battersea, south London, and it has followed this up with numerous events – almost one a year – ever since.

The original organisers of DWAS decided, almost unanimously, to throw in the towel at the end of 1979, and it was left to a handful of other fans, who had joined the Society and had helped out with the organisation in one way or another, to pick up the pieces and restructure the fan club for the Eighties. The fact that the DWAS has survived to date and is still going strong is down to the hard work and dedication of all the people who have helped in its organisation and running over the years.

The DWAS was not the only British fan group operating, but it was by far the biggest. Perhaps next in line, certainly as far as enthusiasm went, were the Friends of Tom Baker, or FOTB for short.

The FOTB was formed in 1976 as a focus for fans of, naturally enough, Tom Baker, and published a bi-monthly newsletter that contained a multi-part interview with the actor, reports from watching the recording of *The Hand of Fear* and *The Face of Evil*, news, reviews, items on Baker's other roles, transcripts of interviews with Baker from television, and really anything and everything to do with him, including some FOTB members' breathless accounts of fleeting meetings with their idol.

There was also some poetry, and even Baker's horoscope appeared, painstakingly worked out by one of the group's members. It is quite apparent, looking back at the newsletter, that the FOTB's predominantly female membership were far more besotted with Tom Baker as a person than interested in any of the roles he had played, and the mix of material tended to reflect this.

4 FOURTH DOCTOR

It was not only Tom Baker who attracted fans; Elisabeth Sladen, who played Sarah Jane Smith, also had her own fan club called the Elisabeth Sladen Friendship League (ESFL). This club was launched in October 1976, and it too produced a newsletter very similar in format to the FOTB one but lacking the personal 'trembly-kneed' descriptions of encounters with the members' heroine. One disappointing thing for the ESFL was that in their first issue, they had to announce that Sarah Jane Smith was leaving *Doctor Who*. This did not daunt them too much, however, and the newsletter continued regardless. It certainly looks today as though the ESFL was run more out of sheer enthusiasm than anything else, and much of the news and comment contained within the newsletters is of a superficial, rather than informative, nature.

MERCHANDISE

Even before the twelfth season started, there was interest from the merchandisers. It takes anything from six months to several years to get a new product off the ground, and as there were several fourth Doctor-related items on sale in late 1974, early 1975, one can only surmise that the interest had been there almost as soon as Jon Pertwee hung up his cloak.

These early items included a set of photographic jigsaws, the photographs taken during location recording for *Robot*; a series of painting by numbers kits featuring the fourth Doctor; and a set of four pencil sharpeners.

As the Seventies progressed, so more and more merchandise was produced by manufacturers eager to tie their products into the series, and into its star. The Daleks had been supplanted by the Doctor, and although there were a few Dalek items available, the vast majority used other aspects of the series as well.

The *Doctor Who* novelisations published by Target books (an imprint of Universal-Tandem initially in 1975, then of Wyndham Publications, and finally of W H Allen) still formed the backbone of *Doctor Who* merchandising, and with the adventures of the fourth Doctor being novelised, starting with *Robot* in 1975, Tom Baker undertook a great many country-wide signing tours, promoting both the books and the series. As well as the shops, these tours took in schools and hospitals. Baker was often reported in newspapers as being incredibly touched and moved by some of the children he had seen, and he regarded it as part of his job as the Doctor to try to bring a little happiness and wonder into their lives.

As well as the novelisations, there were a great many other books published. World Distributors continued with their *Doctor Who* Annual, and also published a *Terry Nation's Dalek Annual* for four consecutive years. In 1976, Target released an updated version of Terrance Dicks's and Malcolm Hulke's *The Making of Doctor Who* and published the *Doctor Who Dinosaur Book*. Then, the following year, they explored other avenues with a series of titles under the *Doctor Who Discovers ...* banner. They released a second *Doctor Who Monster Book* (1977), two *Junior Doctor Who* books (1980), a *Doctor Who Quiz Book* (1981) and *The Doctor Who Programme Guide* (1981). From other publishers came *Doctor Who and the Daleks Omnibus* (Artus 1976); two Dalek activity books (Childrens Leisure Products 1978); *A Day With A TV Producer* (Wayland 1980), which looked at the making of *The Leisure Hive* in the company of producer John Nathan-Turner; and four titles for young children featuring K-9 (Sparrow 1980).

Aside from the books, many other items were produced. These included a fourth Doctor scarf (Today Promotions 1976), *Doctor Who* underpants (BHS 1981), milk chocolate bars (Nestlé 1975), Candy Favourites (Goodies 1979), two poster magazines (Legend 1975 and Harpdown 1976 respectively), numerous free promotions – including two with Weetabix breakfast cereal (free stand up cardboard figures), and one with Ty-phoo tea (a set of twelve cards to collect, plus a poster and hardbacked annual-type book to send away for). There were several records, including a new *Doctor Who* adventure, *The Pescatons* (1976), starring Tom Baker and Elisabeth Sladen; a *Doctor Who Sound Effects* album (1978); a *Genesis of the Daleks* soundtrack album (1979); and several versions of the theme music, one of which – *Doctor Who* by Mankind – even got into the pop charts in 1978. There was bubble bath (Water Margin 1976); colour-in posters (Salter 1978); greetings cards (DAP 1979); a fourth Doctor costume and mask (Berwicks 1976); transfers (Letraset 1976); jigsaws (Whitman 1977/78, World Distributors 1979); bagatelle (Playtime 1978); TARDIS tin (1980); Viewmaster slides for the story *Full Circle* (GAF 1980); two board games, *Doctor Who* and *War of the Daleks* (both Strawberry Fayre 1975); a talking Dalek (Palitoy 1975); and a range of Action Man-like figures of the Doctor, Leela, the Giant Robot, a Cyberman, a Dalek and the TARDIS (all in 1976) and K-9 (in 1978).

This burgeoning of interest in both the series and its star continued into the Eighties, providing a media boost to the show, something it had been looking for since the Daleks took off in the Sixties.

RATINGS

Part of the success of any television programme depends on the ratings it receives. It is always dangerous to draw conclusions about a programme's popularity from its ratings alone, as there are many different reasons why these can fluctuate. What the weather was like can affect them, as can the time of year, what was on the other channels at the same time, and the pulling-power of other programmes placed before and after it in the schedule. In some cases, other channels might even have been blacked out by a strike, as was the case during the ITV strikes of the late Seventies.

In the case of *Doctor Who* during the fourth Doctor's era, stories from the first three seasons mostly received over ten million viewers on average; then, for the next three seasons, the ratings dropped slightly, while still remaining generally high; then for the final, eighteenth season, a dramatic drop was seen.

The stories at the top of the pile, *City of Death* and *Destiny of the Daleks*, were both transmitted during the ITV strike between August and October 1979. Those of the eighteenth season, by contrast, were up against ITV's offering of a glitzy new space series from America, *Buck Rogers in the 25th Century*. The latter season was also relegated to a 5.20 pm time slot, earlier than that of the more successful stories of the thirteenth and fourteenth seasons, which had tended to start transmission at around 5.45 pm for the thirteenth season and after six o'clock for the fourteenth.

In terms of *Doctor Who*'s popularity relative to other TV programmes at the time, it leaped about a great deal. The highest placed episode in the weekly TV chart was part two of *The Ark in Space*, which came in fifth, with parts two, three and four of *The Deadly Assassin* next at positions 11, 12 and 12 respectively. The lowest placed was part two of *Full Circle*, which was almost at the bottom of the barrel at position 170, with part three of *State of Decay* at 145th and part two of *Meglos* at 139th.

As previously stated, it is very difficult to draw firm conclusions from ratings, but it certainly seems that during his seven year run as the Doctor, Tom Baker took *Doctor Who* from being one of the top rated programmes, with over 12 million viewers, to one struggling near the bottom of the pile, with around 5 million. The reasons for this appear to be an amalgam of poor scheduling on the part of the BBC, an entertaining American import series showing on ITV at the same time, and perhaps even a general public who were beginning to tire of Tom Baker as the Doctor.

TOP TEN RATED TOM BAKER STORIES
(Average viewing figures per episode in millions)

1	*City of Death*	14.5
2	*Destiny of the Daleks*	13.5
3	*The Robots of Death*	12.7
4	*The Deadly Assassin*	12.2
5	*The Android Invasion*	11.68
6	*The Face of Evil*	11.2
7	*The Ark in Space*	11.1
8	*The Hand of Fear*	10.95
9	*The Seeds of Doom*	10.9
10	*The Sontaran Experiment*	10.75

BOTTOM TEN RATED TOM BAKER STORIES
(Average viewing figures per episode in millions)

41	*Meglos*	4.65
40	*The Leisure Hive*	5.1
39	*State of Decay*	5.2
38	*Full Circle*	5.25
37	*The Keeper of Traken*	6.25
36	*Logopolis*	6.7
35	*Warriors' Gate*	7.5
34	*Terror of the Zygons*	7.5
33	*Image of the Fendahl*	7.8
32	*The Invisible Enemy*	7.9

The Fifth Doctor

by

David J Howe

Stephen James Walker

FOREWORD

Television is a medium that seemingly delights in giving people their fifteen minutes of fame. Its very nature is rooted in change, and as the months pass, so new programmes are made and presented, and new stars are born. Some of these shows and individuals go on to win enduring popularity, but far more are never heard of nor seen again.

Since the end of 1974, there had been a single constant for *Doctor Who* viewers across the country: Tom Baker *was* the Doctor.

It had been a period during which the BBC had arguably enjoyed more success with *Doctor Who* than ever before. The ratings had soared to an all-time-high – higher even than in the heyday of the Daleks in the mid-Sixties. The distinctive image of the Doctor – incredibly long, multicoloured scarf, floppy felt hat, bulging eyes, tangled curly brown hair and an engaging and disarming smile – was firmly entrenched in the public's consciousness.

Now, however, after some seven long years in the series, Baker was moving on and a new actor had been chosen to take on the lead role. All those who had watched, enjoyed and indeed grown up with Baker as the Doctor must surely have experienced more than a twinge of sadness at the closing moments of *Logopolis*, the fourth Doctor's final regular story. This truly was the end of an era.

The man chosen to succeed Baker was Peter Davison – an actor totally dissimilar in appearance and temperament. This was nothing new for the series, as each of the previous three Doctors had presented a marked contrast to his own predecessor: Baker's image had been very different from Jon Pertwee's; Pertwee's had been very different from Patrick Troughton's; and Troughton's had been very different from William Hartnell's. There was however a major distinction on this occasion in that Davison, unlike the others, was already very well known to television viewers when he joined *Doctor Who*, principally from his role as Tristan Farnon in the BBC's veterinary series *All Creatures Great and Small.*

This was by no means the only innovation to occur at this time. Davison's era as the Doctor in fact coincided with a significant change of direction for *Doctor Who*, as new producer John Nathan-Turner proceeded to stamp his mark on it. The 20th anniversary was also looming, and the series was taking off in a big way in America. Fandom, too, was becoming increasingly well-organised and sophisticated, and the *Doctor Who* Appreciation Society was losing its virtual monopoly on major conventions and other activities.

Elsewhere in the news, Freddie Laker's airline business fell into a state of collapse; Argentina attempted to reclaim the Falkland Islands, provoking a brief war between that country and Britain; Michael Fagan popped into the Queen's bedroom for a chat with the monarch; the *Mary Rose* was raised from the sea bed; long-time Soviet leader Leonid Brezhnev died and was succeeded by Yuri Andropov, who also died just 15 months later to be replaced by Mikhail Gorbachev; and Stephen Spielberg unveiled his new blockbuster film *ET.*

It was against this backdrop, and the increasing freedom that technological advances like digital processing, fibre optics and microchips brought to television production, that *Doctor Who* marched boldly into the Eighties.

Peter Davison brought a fresh charm to *Doctor Who*. His Doctor was an innocent lost in space and time; an elder brother figure intent on righting wrongs and, if at all possible, getting in a good game of cricket too. His era saw him coming up against a wide variety of foes, both new and old, and travelling with a succession of companions – namely Adric, Nyssa, Tegan, Turlough, Kamelion and Peri. It also saw the series making a successful start to the 1980s, despite a number of factors that were not in its favour, and introducing a new generation to the wonders of the *Doctor Who* universe.

Join us as we revisit the era of the fifth Doctor.

PETER DAVISON: IN HIS OWN WORDS

ON HIS EARLY ACTING CAREER:

'It's a wonderful thing; you don't actually have to do any exams to go to drama school, and all you get at the end is a useless piece of paper which says you have been there! You don't do a degree, you simply graduate from it, and then it's up to you.

'The first part I got after leaving drama school in July 1972 was in *Love's Labours Lost* at the Nottingham Play House. I had one line, which changes the whole play, but I can't remember it now.'

Interviewed by Andrew M Smith on 30 August 1983 for *The Cloister Chamber*, published in October 1983.

ON HIS ROLE AS ELMER IN *THE TOMORROW PEOPLE*:

'It was a fairly silly programme. Very definitely a *children's* programme. I played a space cowboy in a blond wig. My wife, Sandra Dickinson, was in it, too.'

Interviewed by Ben Landman in 1985 for *Starlog* Issue 102, published in January 1986.

'I suppose it was ITV's answer to *Doctor Who*, really, except they tried to get children to relate to it by having children in it, and children are usually terrible actors.

'I don't know if you saw it, but the story we did was not terribly popular with children because we sent the whole thing up. I remember we had this terrible talking ceiling, and I reached up and tickled it and it let out this booming "Ho-ho-ho"!'

Interviewed by Terry and Andy Kerr for *Skonnos* Issue 10, published in March 1985.

ON HIS ROLE AS TRISTAN FARNON IN *ALL CREATURES GREAT AND SMALL*:

'Playing Tristan was a very interesting time for me. I know it's been said to me, so it's obviously in print somewhere, that I think Tristan was the nearest I've ever played to myself, but when I first got the part, I thought I was totally unsuitable for it.

'It sounds a terrible thing to say, but it also helped my role that Christopher Timothy walked in front of a car one Christmas and broke his leg. He couldn't move anywhere for about three months, and that meant that a lot of scenes that should have been Robert Hardy and Christopher Timothy became Robert Hardy and me. So that built the

489

character of Tristan up and did me a lot of good. Poor old Chris.'
Interviewed by Stephen Collins in April 1983 for *Zerinza: The Australasian Doctor Who Fanzine* Issue 30/31, published in August 1983.

ON HIS ROLE AS DISH OF THE DAY IN THE TV VERSION OF *THE HITCH-HIKER'S GUIDE TO THE GALAXY*:

'My wife, Sandra Dickinson, was doing the series as Trillian, and when they were looking for someone to play the Dish, she suggested me.'
Interviewed by David Hirsch for *Starlog* Issue 62, published in September 1982.

'It involved going down to the Visual Effects Department and having a bucket of dental plaster poured over my head. They let me have a straw in my mouth so that I could breathe! This plaster gave them a "face" to work with, so they went away and made the model around it. I didn't initially know what voice to use, but we had the actor Dave Prowse, who speaks with a wonderful West Country accent, in the same episode playing Hot Black Desiato's bodyguard. Suddenly I latched onto this wonderful sound, and it sort of came out like that.'
Interviewed by Stephen Collins in April 1983 for *Zerinza: The Australasian Doctor Who Fanzine* Issue 30/31, published in August 1983.

ON BEING CAST AS THE DOCTOR:

'John Nathan-Turner rang me up one Saturday night and told me that Tom Baker was leaving *Doctor Who*, which I didn't know, and I didn't know why he was telling me that. And then he went on to say, "How would you feel about being the next Doctor?" Well, there was a sort of stunned silence. I didn't know what to say. So I told him to ring me back the next night. I spent 24 hours thinking about it; and also asking close friends, or people whose opinion I respected, what I should do. Then he rang me back, and I still really hadn't made any sort of decision, so he asked me to lunch the following week to discuss it.'
Interviewed by Stephen Collins in April 1983 for *Zerinza: The Australasian Doctor Who Fanzine* Issue 30/31, published in August 1983.

ON FOLLOWING TOM BAKER AS THE DOCTOR:

'Of course I was daunted to be following Tom Baker. It didn't hit me until I sat down and tried to rationalize it. Tom had played the part for seven years and that, I figured, meant that no child under the age of 10 in Britain would ever have known a Doctor other than his. That was one factor. And because he was *so* identified with the role, one tended to forget – even though I had watched *Doctor Who* from the age of 12 – one sort of forgot about the other ones. It wasn't until I sat down and thought that William Hartnell had played it for three years, Patrick Troughton for three years and Jon Pertwee for five, that I saw myself in that context and was able to rationalize it. But it certainly did worry me, yes.'
Interviewed by Stephen Collins in April 1983 for *Zerinza: The Australasian Doctor Who Fanzine* Issue 30/31, published in August 1983.

ON RECORDING THE REGENERATION SCENE FOR *LOGOPOLIS*:

'It took about four and a half minutes! It was meant to take much longer than that, but we ran out of time. I had to lie in shot with white goo in my hair. Then I was thrown

into the Make-up Department, my hair washed, and given make-up. Then I was put onto the set and told to sit up and smile!'
Interviewed by Ian Atkins for *Wholook* Issue 2, published in April 1986.

ON HIS DOCTOR'S COSTUME:

'It seemed to me that in some respects the Doctor is essentially English. So what could be more English than a cricket sweater and a pair of striped trousers like those worn by Victorian cricketers?'
Quoted by Peter Haining in *Doctor Who – A Celebration*, published in 1983.

ON HIS CHARACTERIZATION OF THE DOCTOR:

'I wouldn't say so much that I'd tried to change the role, but maybe I am now getting closer to what I had originally intended. It's always a dichotomy between what you set out to do and what actually comes over, until you find ways in which to play it to your satisfaction. So I don't think my idea of the character has materially changed, but the way in which it is coming over may certainly have done. Because as you gain confidence and knowledge about the part, you get closer to your ambitions.

'I haven't really explored the character to any great extent at the moment. One season, although it seems long when you set out on it, actually is fairly short as far as making the part your own is concerned. So I feel I'm still only on the surface of it to a large extent. I haven't quite decided in my own head yet how the Doctor's mind works. At certain times I can see the line straight through him and know what I'm doing, but at certain other times you rather have to bluff your way through, because you haven't quite got his thinking worked out. After all, it is such a complex character in relation to any other character you might be asked to play, you do have to start from scratch. So I just find things in different stories, and I say to myself, "I could have done that in the last story, and maybe I'll bring it out a bit more from now on."

'Scripts are always changed slightly in rehearsal – especially in a thing like this, which is written by scriptwriters for a character that is in a long-running programme. I don't insist on any radical changes in which I say, "I think we have to change this otherwise I'm not going to do it." It's very much a case of working through and then you say, "I don't like *this* line. I find it a bit awkward. I think it might be better if it was said this way."

'It depends on how much you believe the actor knows best ... Tom Baker did the Doctor for seven years and by that time he really did know the character inside out. However, when you've been doing it for only eight months or so, you still rely very heavily on the back-up from those more involved with the paraphernalia of *Doctor Who*, who were there before me.'
Interviewed by Jeremy Bentham for *Doctor Who Monthly Summer Special*, published in June 1982.

'Any similarities between my characterisation and Patrick Troughton's have never been deliberate. I would say it has more to do with the fact that I am younger than any of the others. I felt, in a way, I had to be more fallible, because I didn't want to play him as a hero as such – like, dare I say it, a Buck Rogers type figure. I was never pushed towards this, but the implication always is that if you get someone younger to play a lead part like that, you tend to try to make him dashing. I felt he should be a sort of anti-hero – not evil so much,

but someone who doesn't go about things in the way a normal hero would.'
Interviewed by Jeremy Bentham for *Doctor Who Monthly Summer Special*,
published in June 1982.

'In the episodes made before *Castrovalva*, I used a technique of playing so blandly that
afterward it can be interpreted as being part of whatever aspect you end up doing.'
Interviewed by Gary Russell and David Saunders in June 1982 for *TARDIS*
Volume 7 Issue 3, published in July 1982.

'My Doctor does lose his temper sometimes, but so did the early ones. William
Hartnell's certainly did. That's really where I picked it up from. Also, I suppose it was
initially a thing to counteract the fact that I was much younger. I think I might have
dived in a bit with the losing the temper in the first few stories, simply because I did not
want to come over as the sort of jolly ex-public school boy – which I'm not, as it
happens. When I was looking at how to play the character, I wanted to pick up pointers
from the other Doctors. Also, the companions I was with were rather frustrating, in
terms of the story, so it was nice to bring that element into it. Probably, looking back on
it, I slightly overdid that bit of it, but when you start off, you're not sure how you're
going to do it, so you gradually have to work through it.'
Interviewed by Andrew M Smith on 30 August 1983 for *The Cloister Chamber*,
published in October 1983.

'Performance wise, I was never very happy with the second season. I think it got just a
bit dull, and the stories a bit over-complex. I didn't feel that I had a lot of room to
embellish the character, and I think this is definitely one of the inherent dangers of doing
Doctor Who – the writers tend to latch onto your first portrayal of the part and stick with
that. For me, that presented too limited a challenge. On the other hand, I think there
was a conscious effort made during the third season to do something about that, which
is why I felt happy about going out on top – or at least at a peak.'
Interviewed by Richard Marson for *Doctor Who Magazine* Issue 106, published in
November 1985.

'When I first took on *Doctor Who*, I did a terrible interview on *Pebble Mill at One*, with
young children suggesting how I ought to play the part, and one little boy said, "I think
you should be like Tristan, but brave". If they want to view my Doctor that way, or
Campion as Tristan with funny glasses, in a way that's OK. To me, they're very different
parts, requiring very different approaches from me. Fortunately, I started off in a very
endearing part as Tristan, but it didn't get me stuck with just that role.'
Interviewed by Graeme Wood, Mark Wyman and Gary Russell for *TV Zone* Issue
16, published in March 1991.

ON THE DOCTOR'S COMPANIONS:

'The character relationships were worked out in rehearsal. The Tegan character was
meant to be abrasive and a little pissed off at things, not to put too fine a point on it. I
think actually the best companions are the ones who scream and say, "Help me! Help
me!" There is a danger that if you give the companions too many personal problems, it

becomes a bit like soap opera.

'Turlough started off well. John Nathan-Turner is a very good ideas man, and promised Mark Strickson a part with a little more meat to it. Mark was very intrigued with Turlough, but, as it turned out, they kept locking him up so he could do no wrong. Mark would often speak to me about this – he was very worried. That's why he wanted to leave.

'With Kamelion, we had a situation where Gerald Flood would record his dialogue prior to the studio recording of a story, and they'd go away and write a computer program to make the robot's mouth move around the words. We'd have to fit our lines *exactly* into the pauses, otherwise he would start talking over us.

'He was terrible. He couldn't move, couldn't do anything. When I first saw him, at the beginning of my second year, or maybe at the end of my first, he was just a head and shoulders mock-up, and his mouth and eyes moved and he looked quite impressive. But when we got the real thing ...'
Interviewed by Terry and Andy Kerr for *Skonnos* Issue 10, published in March 1985.

'I didn't think Janet Fielding's character worked, which is nothing against Janet, who thought maybe I did have something against her! We actually got on very well, but I don't think that kind of aggressive person, who's always getting at the Doctor, works. I think there's got to be a feeling that they're on the same side. OK, the companion gets fed up with the Doctor when he doesn't do something right, but they're basically on the same side. With Janet's character and with Turlough, I think you came very close to having two companions who very definitely weren't. I think that was a frustration for Mark Strickson, too; he couldn't do anything.'
Interviewed by Richard Marson for *Doctor Who Magazine* Issue 134, published in March 1988.

'Nicola Bryant was pretending to be American with everybody. I think it was under instructions from John Nathan-Turner – although I haven't got quite close to the truth as to whether it was her idea or his idea actually to pretend to *everybody*. The trouble was that we had two reporters with us the entire week we were in Lanzarote for *Planet of Fire*, and I think she had to pretend to be American for them, so they didn't let the cat out of the bag.

'I knew that she didn't have a very strong American accent, but I didn't find out for ages she wasn't even American. What she was telling us was that her father was American, or that she'd been brought up in America. It was all lies ... under instruction, but nevertheless, complete fabrication!'
Interviewed by Nicholas Briggs for *Doctor Who Magazine* Issue 215, published in August 1995.

ON THE LENGTH OF HIS STAY IN *DOCTOR WHO*:
'Doing the first season hasn't put me off doing it for any length of time to which I'd envisaged doing it, but exactly how long I'll do it for, I just don't know. I will certainly give it what I consider to be a substantial time, but I think I can safely say I don't want to break any records for duration. At the same time, though, I doubt I'll be the shortest.'
Interviewed by Jeremy Bentham for *Doctor Who Monthly Summer Special*, published in June 1982.

FIFTH DOCTOR

'It seems to me that you either do it for a substantial but short amount of time, or you stay in it for life, because it does follow you around and you have to get away from it. Now, by that I don't mean that I want nothing to do with *Doctor Who*, or that I'm tired or sick of it, but you do have to work in the future. My job is acting. What happened was that when my three years were up, I had the opportunity then to do it for as long as I liked, but I just felt that as I had given myself three years, I should stick to that, because the temptation is always to do another year, and then another, and another ...

'If you did it for endless numbers of years, you could always be developing the character, but at the same time, there has to come a point when you say that's it.'

Interviewed by Liam Rudden for *TARDIS* Volume 9 Issue 2, published in 1984.

'I did find it frustrating towards the end of the last year, for various reasons. I would have liked in many cases for things to have been done better. I mean, we ran out of money on lots of stories, and time. That was frustrating, because I don't think the programme is given enough time to do it.'

Interviewed by Jackie Marshall for *Space Rat* Issue 7, published in 1984.

'Obviously concern about typecasting was a factor when I said I wasn't going to do a fourth year – the fact that I felt that period was about as long as I could do it without becoming too fixed as the Doctor in people's minds. The only thing I really did to avoid typecasting was to stop playing the Doctor fairly soon. As it is, Tristan is the part I'll never quite get away from in anyone's mind. I think it's the first part in which you come to the public's attention that stays with you. So, I was "Tristan playing the Doctor"!'

Interviewed by Ben Landman in 1985 for *Starlog* Issue 102, published in January 1986.

'I hummed and hawed for a long time. I had set myself three years, not knowing how I would feel at the end of those three years. It was touch and go – I almost did a fourth year.

'If I'd been offered *Doctor Who* when I was, say, fifty, then I would have gone on for many, many years. The fact of the matter is that I was still fairly young – still am, I hope – and there were just other things that I wanted to do. I used to have enormous fun doing *Doctor Who*. We used to rehearse at Acton, and I'd see contemporaries of mine doing other things as well, and I thought I'd do a nice stint, enjoy it and leave.'

Interviewed by Ian Atkins for *Wholook* Issue 2, published in April 1986.

'I was quite happy with my first and third seasons, but not really with the second. I had to make my decision to leave after the second season, and that was difficult. I had to gamble on the third season being quite good, because I wanted to go out on a high note. And the good thing is that the best story I did was the last story, *The Caves of Androzani*. So, I was pleased with that. I'm sure there are many things I wish I could have done differently, given different conditions. There's an anxious time when you leave, where you wonder if you're going to be stuck with nothing else but *Doctor Who*. I don't think I have been. Since I've left *Doctor Who*, I've been busy doing other things, and that's good, the security of jobs being offered.'

Interviewed by Juanita Elefante-Gordon in 1987 for *Starlog* Issue 127, published in February 1988.

'Another contributing reason why I left was that, for two of the years, I was doing *Sink or Swim* and *Holding the Fort*, and then an *All Creatures Great and Small* special, during the break between seasons, but after they stopped, I knew there was nothing new that someone would offer me in my three months off.'
Interviewed by Richard Marson for *Doctor Who Magazine* Issue 134, published in March 1988.

ON RECORDING THE REGENERATION SCENE FOR *THE CAVES OF ANDROZANI*:

'Of course, this regeneration scene wasn't done in the same way as the one in *Logopolis*. Most of it starred Nicola Bryant's cleavage, as I recall! I had good fun on *The Caves of Androzani*. We had a good time with Colin Baker. It was quite a jovial time, but sad as well in a way. I wanted to keep the whole thing bright but, yes, it was quite sad. Still, I enjoyed the whole thing.'
Interviewed by Ian Atkins for *Wholook* Issue 2, published in April 1986.

ON OVERSEAS LOCATION FILMING:

'We all leave *en masse* as a sort of huge coach party, and drink the plane out of booze!

'You usually get more of a sense of a unit when you're filming abroad, because there is nothing else for you to do. The filming when it's done in England is usually done within striking distance of London, so you all make your own way home, whereas when we were in Lanzarote, there was a very good feeling of being a unit, very much like a company in the theatre.'
Interviewed by Liam Rudden for *TARDIS* Volume 9 Issue 2, published in 1984.

'It was nice to be able to film sequences abroad, because it inevitably added a bit more gloss to the look of the show. I tend to prefer location film for various reasons, because it looks better than studio-shot stuff. I was never entirely happy when we were totally studio-bound, and studio work is much more concentrated, because you're recording a lot of material in the space of a very short time. Filming gives you a chance to think, to catch your breath and go into it all a bit more thoroughly. Woe betide you if you hadn't done your homework before going into the studio, because there just wasn't time for you to stop and have a quiet think about it all. Filming abroad was a different kettle of fish again. When we went to Amsterdam, I got a lot of recognition because they had *All Creatures Great and Small* running over there – but not *Doctor Who*. So I caused a lot of confusion I think, as well as some shock, wandering about with all that decaying face make-up.

'I think, if anything, it's harder filming abroad, because the onus is on the director to make the location work, and make it show on screen. You become very cliquey in your unit, because it's all a strange land. Socialising in the evening is very "in". I think Lanzarote looked great; it gave that story a very polished look, which was something that I felt we could be proud about. In either situation it's hard work, because you've got to get it all done within the imposed time limits. You can afford a laugh at a rubber monster or a silly line in rehearsals, but when you actually do it, if you're not concentrating 100 per cent then, as likely as not, that's what will go on tape and you'll come out of it looking silly. It can be difficult keeping a straight face in some scenes, but you have to make the effort or chaos would reign.'
Interviewed by Richard Marson for *Doctor Who Magazine* Issue 106, published in November 1985.

'Lanzarote for *Planet of Fire* was great fun, and generally worthwhile as far as foreign filming goes. It would have been a lot nicer to have filmed a lot more than we did – we were there for only a week. But Amsterdam for *Arc of Infinity* I had grave doubts about. I think it just interfered with the story. The trouble was that it highlighted the impossible coincidences of the programme. If it had been in London, then meeting Tegan would not have shown up as being so ridiculous as it did. That Tegan was in Amsterdam was just too absurd.'
Interviewed by Ian Atkins for *Wholook* Issue 2, published in April 1986.

ON PRODUCER JOHN NATHAN-TURNER:

'He's really very, very good, because, unlike some producers, he's there all the time. He's at every day's filming that there is, every studio recording that there is. He takes a hand in everything. That's the way he wants to operate, as total overlord of everything. His dedication to the series cannot be denied.'
Interviewed by Stephen Collins in April 1983 for *Zerinza: The Australasian Doctor Who Fanzine* Issue 30/31, published in August 1983.

ON WATCHING EARLIER ERAS OF *DOCTOR WHO*:

'I was a fan of the *Doctor Who* programme 18 years ago, and it had a very big impact on me. Along with millions of other children, I used to hide behind the sofa every Saturday evening. The stories used to terrify me, and even now I can vividly remember certain parts – in particular, the Hartnell and Troughton eras. For about five or six years, I watched it absolutely avidly.'
Quoted by Peter Haining in *Doctor Who – A Celebration*, published in 1983.

'I had watched *Doctor Who* since 1963, really fairly avidly through the first two Doctors. It had *never* occurred to me, before John Nathan-Turner phoned me, that I might play the Doctor – never in a million years. I mean, it *had* occurred to me that I might one day be in the show, but *never* as the Doctor!'
Interviewed by Ben Landman in 1985 for *Starlog* Issue 102, published in January 1986.

ON *DOCTOR WHO* MERCHANDISE:

'Quite frankly, I think it's got a little out of hand! It wasn't really anything to do with me, more with John Nathan-Turner. There's a line to be trod between making available to the public things that they want, and exploiting the public. Some items did step over the line a bit. I mean, there's now a *Doctor Who Cookbook*! It seems that a lot of people are sort of cashing in on the whole thing.

'At least I never got underpants with my face on them, like Tom Baker did!'
Interviewed by Ian Atkins for *Wholook* Issue 2, published in April 1986.

ON PUBLIC RECOGNITION:

'My total view of *Doctor Who* is that I am playing a part. However, I realise that there is a lot more to it than just acting on the screen. You somehow take on the mantle of the Doctor, and a kind of instant charisma goes with the job. You have a responsibility – it is important to be always polite and cheery in public. Fortunately, I'm not a rabble rouser in my private life!'
Quoted by Peter Haining in *Doctor Who – A Celebration*, published in 1983.

'After I first appeared as the Doctor in *Logopolis*, it was ages before I actually appeared in my own stories. I said to John Nathan-Turner at the start that when I did leave, I would much prefer to go so that someone else had taken over, so really that thing of being the current Doctor had been lifted from me before the end of the season. If I left *Doctor Who* at the end of this season in the last story, although I would be doing other things, I would still be thought of as the Doctor until the beginning of the following year. So from everyone's point of view, it's really much better if one Doctor disappears and the new Doctor appears and does at least one story in the same season.'
Interviewed by Andrew M Smith on 30 August 1983 for *The Cloister Chamber*, published in October 1983.

'People in Britain get the wrong idea about *Doctor Who* in the States. It is very big there with fans – there were 12,000 at the Chicago convention last year, too many really – but as it is shown on Public Broadcasting Service channels, not the big networks, it isn't that well known to the general public. They know me better there from *All Creatures Great and Small*, though even then, I can still walk down the street unrecognised most of the time.

'I very much want to keep in touch with *Doctor Who* and all the fans. I'm not going to cut the ties with the character, but at the same time I intend to keep a low profile for a while so that I don't tread on Colin Baker's toes. It is so that Colin can become established to everyone as the Doctor. That is why it was a shame, in a way, that they didn't do the regeneration as the last few minutes of the season, as has happened before. That way, the former Doctor can sort of fade out in the time that passes to the next season, and the new Doctor has a chance to establish himself. Colin has done one story, which isn't enough to establish his Doctor to everyone, and since mine is still fresh in the memory, it is that much easier for comparisons to be made. And I think it might have been fun if they'd done the regeneration by in some way bringing in Colin's role as Maxil, the Head of Security on Gallifrey, who shot and tried to execute me in *Arc of Infinity*.

'So I don't think I'll be at conventions for a while, for Colin's sake, but after that, of course, I will when I can.'
Interviewed by Wendy Graham for *Space Voyager* Issue 12, published in December 1984.

'I couldn't go into a supermarket or walk down the street dressed as you are. At one point, I took to wearing baseball hats and dark glasses. The first time I was recognised, after *Love for Lydia*, it was quite gratifying, but that was one person along a crowded street. When they all start to recognise me, I don't like it. So I look at the ground mainly. People's behaviour is rather strange, because they rarely come straight up to me and start talking. Mostly they stand a few feet away and say loudly, "I'm sure it's him," as if I'm on another planet or something! Even when I am not recognised, the fear that I might be is always with me. It's often said to me, "You'll be sorry when they stop recognising you," but that's not true. I won't. I'll be very happy, in fact.'
Interviewed by Terry and Andy Kerr for *Skonnos* Issue 10, published in March 1985.

'I know people like autographs, but there's something about someone approaching you and saying, "Oh, will you sign this please?" that somehow brings down a barrier between you. And, suddenly, you are "the celebrity" and they are "the fan". I would rather simply talk to people, because it's a whole different thing. You can talk to them like you might

497

talk to anybody, like a friend; and you don't have this barrier of "them" and "us". I can't tell you how much I like just talking.'
Interviewed by Ben Landman in 1985 for *Starlog* Issue 102, published in January 1986.

'Being invited to conventions was a very new experience. It wasn't a total shock, but still very amazing. You have to accept that the fans have probably got more knowledge of the programme than you ever will have, so I never pretended to be a great authority on it, even though I played the part and also enjoyed the series before I was in it. Before I did the first convention, which was in America, I was fairly terrified. But when I got up there and said, "Hello, it's nice to be here," there was spontaneous applause! It was fine after that.'
Interviewed by Ian Atkins for *Wholook* Issue 2, published in April 1986.

'You do have some idea of what it is you're getting into before you take on the part. I think my most immediate problem was that I had about a year before I actually appeared on television as the Doctor, and John Nathan-Turner was very keen to sell me beforehand. It all happened very quickly, and I began to get mail and recognition extremely quickly too, so it didn't really matter that I was doing this personal appearance and promotion bit as well. Even if I hadn't participated, I think press interest was still there, and of course there's always going to be merchandise if the show is successful.

'What I tried to do was strike a balance. I didn't mind doing all the publicity and so on, but I didn't want *Doctor Who* to totally take over my life. I needed time to myself, time for other projects. Besides, if I'd have overdone it, I think the public would have got pretty sick of my face. When I did personal appearances, I wasn't keen on going in costume – I didn't want to go in character. If somebody asked for my autograph, it would always be signed "Best Wishes, Peter Davison", because if you sign yourself as the Doctor, you're insulting the person's intelligence.'
Interviewed by Richard Marson for *Doctor Who Magazine* Issue 106, published in November 1985.

'I was aware of what I was letting myself in for, which is one reason why I hesitated when the producer, John Nathan-Turner, offered me the part. I finally said yes in my agent's office late one afternoon, and it was agreed we could call a press conference to announce the fact in a couple of days.

'However, no sooner had I driven home than it was obvious that the story had been leaked to the press, for the phone never stopped ringing with calls from journalists.

'On the *Nine O'Clock News* that night, the first story was that Ronald Reagan had been elected President of the United States – while the final story was that Tom Baker was going to regenerate into me! Friends who had been watching with the sound turned down told me later that they had assumed when my photograph was flashed up on the screen that I must have died!'
Quoted by Peter Haining in *The Doctor Who File*, published in 1986.

'I'm always getting "Where's your TARDIS?" – all the time. With *All Creatures Great and Small* it was "Would you have a look at my dog?" These things people actually think no-one has ever said before! With the *Doctor Who* fan thing, in a way I find it kind of sad. A lot of the fans are fine – they like the programme, know everything about it – but there's a small proportion of those fans to whom it is like a religion, and who get terribly offended when you're talking about the programme.

'I remember at the first convention I ever did, they asked my philosophy of *Doctor Who*, and I said "I get the script and learn the words", and they thought that was an awful thing to say. They do care about it, as I did when I was doing it myself, but at the same time, you have to laugh at it, too, or it gets very po-faced.

'I do find that with very few exceptions, you can never become friends with fans, because underneath it all, they are still fans and they are in awe. I remember once I got on quite well with a couple in America, and they then asked me to sign an autograph in a particular way, and you think, "Wait a minute, if you're supposed to be friends with these people, and you invite them into your home ...?" It doesn't work, though they're very friendly and very nice and we've all done a lot of conventions in America.'

Interviewed by Richard Marson for *Doctor Who Magazine* Issue 134, published in March 1988.

'I don't mind at all appearing on programmes like *Blue Peter* and *Nationwide*, as long as no-one expects me to be entertaining. I don't mind *Wogan* or anything like that – indeed especially not *Wogan*, as he likes to take part of the entertaining on himself. A lot of actors you see on *Wogan* are helped out by him.

'What I don't like are the ones where you're the one that has to come out with the anecdotes and be funny. I'm not very good at that at all. The worst one was *Boxing Night at the Mill*. It was very much a parade of guests expected to be funny, and it was just terrible. Hopeless.

'Doing *Blue Peter* was very funny, because they always want you to hold the cat. Every time they cut away to something, they'll shove this cat in your lap, and every time they come back to you, the cat will run away. And this goes on and on.'

Interviewed by Richard Marson for *Doctor Who Magazine* Issue 134, published in March 1988.

ON THE DIFFERENCE BETWEEN BRITISH AND AMERICAN FANS:
'There is a difference. Over here *Doctor Who* is an institution, but in America it is a cult. At the BBC's Longleat convention we had something like 35,000 people – I can't remember the exact numbers – but a lot of those were general viewers; in other words, people who watched the programme, whose children watched the programme, and who had come along to see Doctor Who. There were thousands of people who just liked the programme. At events in America, on the other hand, they were all fans. They all knew about the show, as all the members of the *Doctor Who* Appreciation Society do over here, and were intensely interested in it, so they were easier to handle in groups of thousands. Whereas Longleat became impossible, because general fans just aren't prepared to put up with the sort of thing that a DWAS fan would put up with. In America, the *Doctor Who* fans would queue for hours and hours just for your autograph and a word, whereas the Longleat people were not used to it. They could not cope with queuing up for three hours to get just one word, and tempers did get a bit frayed at Longleat. Of course Longleat was badly organised, there's no doubt about that.

'Unfortunately, the actors involved sort of got blamed for Longleat. I received quite a few rude letters saying how dare I be associated with something so badly organised.

We tried to explain to them that there was no way 25 actors, or indeed only four Doctors, could satisfy 35,000 people. And the organisers insisted on having autograph sessions, which were just an impossibility. One should have spent the whole day simply walking around.'
Interviewed by Liam Rudden for *TARDIS* Volume 9 Issue 2, published in 1984.

ON IIIS 'PUBLIC SCHOOL BOY' IMAGE

'Unless you make a positive move to say, "I will not play any more of these types", you are a bit stuck. It's the luck of the first part that brings you public attention. They kind of label you with that.

'I was never by nature a rebel – I never wanted to offend people, I just wanted to do what I wanted to do, so I'm quite at home being a cosy figure, actually. It's quite nice to be liked by little old ladies. But I do find it disconcerting sometimes when people meet me and they expect me to be wearing blazers all the time.

'I *could* say, "I won't accept any similar parts, I want to play different parts", and I'm sure if I put myself out of work for six months to a year, maybe a part like that would come along. But it wouldn't necessarily be successful, and I wouldn't necessarily be any good at it, and I wouldn't necessarily enjoy doing it, which seems to me to be the most important thing. If I enjoy doing it, I'll do it. So, I've never really had a master plan.

'I find the worst thing about papers is getting them to print what you actually say. Going back to this public school thing, they have this insistence of putting everything I do say into kind of public school language. "Did you enjoy this series?" they'll ask, and I'll say, "Yes", but they'll print it as, "Yes, it was jolly good fun". Loads of "goshes" flow all over the place.

'I'm a bit boring for them really, because they haven't got any dirt at the moment.'
Interviewed by Richard Marson for *Doctor Who Magazine* Issue 134, published in March 1988.

ON THE RELATIVE MERITS OF STAGE AND SCREEN WORK:

'I'm not saying that it's not good to go back to the stage sometimes, but I don't personally feel that the stage is where it's at. I don't see that at all.

'I enjoy doing stage work, but it has tremendous drawbacks. You're doing the same thing several months on end, and you can never quite produce a definitive performance. You think you've done it really well one night – you think, "I've really cracked this performance" – and the next night it's rubbish and doesn't work at all. And of course at the end of it, you have absolutely nothing left, apart from memories. On TV, you've created something that's been recorded for posterity.'
Interviewed by Richard Marson for *Doctor Who Magazine* Issue 134, published in March 1988.

ON *DOCTOR WHO* WITH COLIN BAKER AND SYLVESTER McCOY:

'I have to say, I didn't really watch the show after I left. I watched Colin's first one, as it was at the end of my last season, but I didn't like it much. I think Sylvester is very good, but I think it would work much better if they went back to the older sort of story, because he is eccentric and kind of wacky, but the stories are wacky too, which I personally don't think works. It's kind of university humour. I think it would work better

if Sylvester was the kind of eccentric figure in the middle of a serious story.'
Interviewed by Richard Marson for *Doctor Who Magazine* **Issue 134, published in March 1988.**

ON HIS INTERESTS:
'I read a fair amount of science fiction. Either detective fiction or science fiction; mainly American detective fiction. I like Philip K Dick, when I can understand him! Silverberg I quite like. And English science fiction; the H G Wells and John Wyndham school of science fiction, where it's really based on … in a way, much more normal, everyday life.'
Interviewed by Jackie Marshall for *Space Rat* **Issue 7, published in 1984.**

'I don't find acting all-consuming at all. You do take it home with you a bit, in that if you're playing a really depressing part, then you tend to get depressed, but I never sit at home and talk about a part. Most of the friends I have are not in the business at all – most of them are school friends.

'I've never been in love with acting in the way that some people are. They love going to the theatre and seeing various shows, and a lot of it is the whole thrill of showbusiness, which I don't enjoy at all. I don't object to it, but it's not me.

'There's a very stereotyped image of the business, and it's generally wrong. I've never really understood the total inability of television and films to imitate themselves. When you see a thriller set in a TV studio, no-one ever behaves like that in the real thing.

'My interests. Well, I don't go to the cinema much, though I ought to. I tend to watch videos! My greatest joy is actually doing absolutely nothing – not having to get up and do anything. I can just sit there and let an hour go by. Or spend hours just wandering round the house. I used to play cricket, but people expect too much of you and it ceases to be relaxing.'
Interviewed by Richard Marson for *Doctor Who Magazine* **Issue 134, published in March 1988.**

ON HIS CAREER AFTER *DOCTOR WHO*:
'I did a series called *L Driver* for the BBC, which was in the studio at about the same time as one of Colin Baker's *Doctor Who*s. As a bit of a joke, I went in when they were doing a scene with Pat Troughton and crept up behind Colin to give him the shock of his former lives, so to speak – but he took it all in his stride!'
Interviewed by Richard Marson for *Doctor Who Magazine* **Issue 106, published in November 1985.**

'Things are done differently on different shows. A lot more trouble is spent on *A Very Peculiar Practice* than on *All Creatures Great and Small*, which suffers as a result. As actors, we're just as guilty as the director and producer of being blasé about it and thinking we can come in and just "do it like that", without really needing a rehearsal. Sometimes it works, but you always come a cropper in the end – there's no real substitute for sitting down and thinking it through.

'It's a question, too, of how right the director wants to get it, and that's not an individual criticism. *A Very Peculiar Practice* is very well written, and that's the difference – there's so much to get out of the script. You want to do justice to the script,

5 FIFTH DOCTOR

so you work extra hard.'
Interviewed by Richard Marson for *Doctor Who Magazine* **Issue 134, published in March 1988.**

'I'm open to offers. Of the sitcoms I did, I didn't like *Holding the Fort* and I did like *Sink or Swim*, because one was good and one was bad. The biggest thing I'd like to do would be a film – something I haven't done before. You'd think I could get in there somewhere, wouldn't you?'
Interviewed by Richard Marson for *Doctor Who Magazine* **Issue 134, published in March 1988.**

'Really I guess everything I have done has been fairly visible. I went back to *All Creatures Great and Small*, left it and then went back *again* – Bobby Ewing style, but not via the shower ... I did two series of *Campion* ... I haven't, however, snuck off for years abroad or done great theatre tours.'
Interviewed by Graeme Wood, Mark Wyman and Gary Russell for *TV Zone* **Issue 16, published in March 1991.**

CHARACTER – THE FIFTH DOCTOR

The genesis of the fifth Doctor can be largely attributed to John Nathan-Turner, who became producer of *Doctor Who* following the conclusion of work on the series' seventeenth season at the end of 1979.

Nathan-Turner had never been particularly enamoured of Tom Baker's portrayal of the Doctor. Baker had by this point completed some six years in the role, and the producer considered that his increasingly assured and flippant interpretation made the character seem too dominant and invulnerable, detracting from the dramatic potential of the stories. He also greatly disliked the slapstick-style humour that the previous production team had allowed to flourish, and the general air of jokiness that Baker now tended to inject into the proceedings. During the eighteenth season, he therefore took steps to address these concerns, cutting down drastically the level of humour in the series and prevailing upon his directors to keep a much tighter rein on their leading man – a policy that, at least initially, created a good deal of friction between himself and Baker. Nathan-Turner's preferences could ultimately be met only by the casting of his own, completely new Doctor, and so it was that he reached a mutual agreement with Baker that the actor would bow out of the series at the end of that year's run.

Nathan-Turner's principal requirement for the fifth Doctor was simply that he should present a complete contrast to the fourth. (And despite his teasing of the press with the notion that the series' new lead might be a 'she' rather than a 'he', he never actually contemplated casting a woman in the role.) In this, he was motivated not only by his misgivings about Baker's portrayal, but also by the thought that to cast an actor who was in any way similar to the outgoing star would be to invite invidious comparisons (a consideration that had weighed similarly heavily with past producers who had overseen the Doctor's previous regenerations). He had no definite preconceptions beyond this basic desire for contrast, and no particular actor initially in mind. One candidate he thought about but then discounted was Richard Griffiths, a well-established character actor of portly build who is now perhaps best remembered for his starring roles in the series *Bird of Prey*, *Pie in the Sky* and *The Cleopatras*, and as Mr Dursley in the *Harry Potter* films.

As recounted in his 1985 book *The TARDIS Inside Out*, the producer eventually came up with a 'shopping list' of ideal characteristics that he would like to see in the new Doctor:

1. Heroism – the Doctor must be heroic.

2. Youthfulness – I wanted a younger Doctor for a more youthful audience.

3. Vulnerability – we needed a Doctor who could get it wrong occasionally. This is something the series hadn't had with Tom.

At this point, I began to see that the task wasn't impossible, and my excitement mounted. Fitting together the pieces of a puzzle like this is one of the real pleasures of being a producer.

4. Straight hair – Tom's curly locks had become so famous. We needed an opposite image.

In the end, only one man was ever seriously considered for the role of the fifth Doctor: twenty-nine year old Peter Davison. Pinned up on the *Doctor Who* office wall were an array of stills relating to productions on which Nathan-Turner had worked, including one of Davison taken at a charity cricket match during his time starring as the country vet Tristan Farnon in the popular BBC series *All Creatures Great and Small*. It was this that brought the actor to Nathan-Turner's mind when he happened to notice it while mulling over his choice of Baker's successor, and the suggestion was quickly approved by his BBC superiors.

'He was my first choice,' Nathan-Turner told Jeremy Bentham in a 1981 interview for *Doctor Who Magazine*. 'I had worked with him on *All Creatures Great and Small*, and he was a very talented and capable actor. He had everything I was looking for in the new Doctor'.

Nathan-Turner had realised that Davison would fully meet his list of ideal characteristics. He was younger and slighter in build than Baker and had straight, fair hair as opposed to his predecessor's dark, curly locks. He was also somewhat more reserved and easy-going in manner, and carried with him a large fan following from *All Creatures Great and Small* – a factor that the producer considered a great advantage, given that Baker had become very closely associated with the role of the Doctor and would consequently be very difficult to displace in the public's affections.

Nathan-Turner phoned Davison at his home one weekend in September 1980, told him that Baker was leaving *Doctor Who* – something that had yet to be announced to the public at that point – and asked if he would be interested in taking over. Davison was astonished, considering himself totally unsuitable for the role, and initially felt inclined to turn the offer down. He asked Nathan-Turner to phone back the following week, and then agreed to meet him for lunch one day shortly afterwards, to give the producer a chance to try to change his mind.

When the meeting took place, Davison was further surprised to learn that Nathan-Turner saw him as a 'personality actor' – someone who drew to a large extent on his own personality in bringing to life the various characters that he played, and who would thus imbue the Doctor with the same boyish charm and enthusiasm as he had Tristan. Davison himself had not previously thought in these terms. 'I'd never seen myself in a million years as a personality actor,' he admitted in a 1994 interview with Nicholas Briggs for *Doctor Who Magazine*. Rather, he took the view that he was essentially a character actor who just happened to have come to public attention in one particular type of part. He also felt that the role of the Doctor was best suited to an older man, and that he was too young for it. Again he was left with the distinct feeling that he should decline Nathan-Turner's offer. After several further meetings and phone conversations, however, he decided to accept, almost on a whim, as he could not bear to think that someone else would be given the job instead and that he would then have to remain silent about the fact that he had been the first choice.

Keen to gain as much advance publicity as possible for his new star, Nathan-Turner ensured that the news filtered out to the press almost immediately after Davison agreed to accept the role – indeed, rather more quickly than the actor himself would have liked. An announcement was even made on the BBC's main evening news on 4 November 1980, and a hastily-arranged press conference was held to give eager journalists their first chance to ask questions of the new Doctor.

Later the same month, Davison made his first substantial *Doctor Who*-related television appearance, on the popular BBC children's show *Blue Peter*. Then, on 3 December 1980, he guested on the lunchtime magazine programme *Pebble Mill at One*, discussing with presenter Donny McLeod a number of costume ideas sent in by viewers, ranging from a 'college boy' look, complete with yellow striped blazer, to an outfit consisting of a 'tin foil suit' and a red bow tie. Davison, although reacting diplomatically to these ideas, found little amongst them to spark his interest. There was however a panel of fans on hand in the studio to offer further advice, and a young man named Stuart Unit drew a favourable response when he suggested that the fifth Doctor should be 'like Tristan Farnon, but with bravery and intellect'. The actor was later to cite this as having been one of the most influential ideas in his early thinking about the role.

Nathan-Turner himself offered Davison relatively little advice or guidance as to how he should approach his characterisation of the Doctor – perhaps not surprisingly, given his view that the newcomer was a personality actor who would bring to the series his own distinctive personal qualities and traits.

'I don't think John had much in mind about what he wanted the part to be,' Davison told journalist Ben Landman in a 1985 interview for *Starlog*, 'except for casting me in it. I mean, he didn't say, "I'm offering you the part, and I want you to play it like *this*." The trick of a good producer is to cast someone who is right for the part in the way that they see it, and then let them do it. Which is really what he did. I was very much thrown in and told "You're the Doctor – now do it!"'

The producer did however have some lengthy discussions with the actor as to the type of costume that he should wear. Both men were agreed that it should have, in the tradition of the previous Doctors' images, an air of old-fashioned and slightly eccentric Englishness about it. A sporting motif was also thought to be a good idea. Polo jodhpurs were at one point considered but, in the end, period cricketing attire was decided upon as being a better choice – a suggestion made by Davison, who was himself a keen cricketer, and possibly again inspired in part by the photograph of him on the *Doctor Who* office wall. A test costume fitting was held around the end of the year, in which Davison tried on various cricketing outfits from stock to assess their effectiveness.

Work was meanwhile in hand on scripts for the forthcoming season. The character summary being sent out to freelance writers in the closing months of 1980 gave a general description of the Doctor's background but offered little hint as to the newcomer's intended personality:

THE DOCTOR

The DOCTOR comes from the planet Gallifrey, in the constellation of Kasterborus. His relationship with his fellow TIME LORDs has been portrayed in contradictory ways during the programme's long history; but the original premise is worth bearing in mind: the TIME LORDs were aloof super-creatures who watched the workings of the universe objectively, building up their store of knowledge without interfering. One of their number, unable to remain detached, plunged himself into moral involvement by 'borrowing' a TARDIS from the dry-dock where it was undergoing repairs. This fugitive was the DOCTOR. Subsequent adventures have had him revisiting Gallifrey and redeeming himself in the eyes of the TIME LORDs. There is, however, evidence that at least some of these stories may be forgeries!

Like all TIME LORDs the DOCTOR has two hearts and a normal body temperature of 60 degrees Fahrenheit. He's over seven centuries old, and has the capability of regenerating himself into different appearances – his present form being his fourth regeneration.

Incidentally, he's never referred to as 'DOCTOR WHO' either in speech headings or by other characters. His name is the DOCTOR – 'Who?' is the mystery! The fact that he is always 'DOCTOR WHO' for the purpose of the closing titles is a historical quirk, reminding us that the format has been shaped more by collective intuition than by centralised logic.

The DOCTOR shouldn't be seen as a sort of Superman. He's fallible and vulnerable and only too conscious that life consists largely of things going wrong for well-intentioned people like himself. Note too, that he's only rarely intentionally funny. If many of his responses and solutions make us laugh with their unexpected appropriateness it's because we lack his agility of mind and breadth of experience, and didn't see them coming.

The intention at this point was that the new season should open with a four-part story entitled *Project Zeta-Sigma*, the scripts for which had been commissioned from John Flanagan and Andrew McCulloch on 7 October 1980 under the working title *Project '4G'*, and that this should also be the first of the new block in production order. This would then be followed, both on transmission and in production, by another four-parter, Terence Dudley's *Day of Wrath*. By the beginning of 1981, the writers had been briefed to include cricketing references in their scripts. A considerable degree of uncertainty was still apparent, however, as Flanagan recalled in an interview conducted by John C Smith and Michael McLester in September 1981 for the fanzine *Definitive Gaze*:

'We wrote a scene in which Tegan Jovanka, who is Australian, is saying that the Doctor looks like a cricketer, because of his costume. And Adric says, "That's an Earth insect, isn't it?" "Yes, but it's also a game." "Well, how do you play it?" And we had this thing where the Doctor tries to explain cricket to him. If you've ever tried to explain cricket to an American, you'll know it's virtually impossible, so the more the Doctor explains about it, the more ludicrous it becomes. The whole idea behind cricket is that it's so absurd. We had quite a long section on that. Plus a lot of rather bad punny jokes – sort of like "How's that?" Cricket imagery all the way through.

'Peter had his own ideas, the producer had his own ideas, everyone else had their own ideas. There was quite a lot of discussion about the character, especially the costume. We were phoned up half way through writing the cricket scene and told, "Forget every reference to cricket; he's not wearing cricket gear at all; we're going for something else." Then, later that afternoon, another call came, saying, "Don't scratch it altogether." Two days later, "Look, he's possibly going to wear a morning suit." There was a problem.'

The man charged with the task of giving substance to the costume ideas worked out by Nathan-Turner, Davison and others was Colin Lavers, who had been assigned as costume designer for *Project Zeta-Sigma*. Nathan-Turner gave him the following instructions in a memo dated 10 February 1981:

> Literally about to depart to the USA for a few weeks for a holiday and wanted to give you some information about the new Doctor's image.
>
> As you probably know, Peter Davison and I have been discussing various ideas for several months now, namely as follows:
>
> That the basic costume would be *period* cricket outfit (all the Doctors have reflected Earth's history). I enclose some photos of Peter which we took at a 'stock' fitting some time ago. I do feel the *Doctor Who* shirt with the '?' mark on the lapels is worth hanging onto. Similarly, I am committed to a cricket jersey in terms of *Doctor Who* annuals and other merchandise.
>
> Anyway, here are the latest thoughts – I'm sure you can *vastly* improve them ...
>
> *Doctor Who* shirt, cricket pullover, white cricket shoes, period baggy pants – possibly some colour introduced here, e.g. stripes?, with an optional top coat and hat. One idea we tossed around was a morning suit jacket and collapsible topper.
>
> I shall be returning to the office on 4 March and I wonder if you and I and Peter Davison could have some sort of experimental session on the afternoon of Friday 6 March (Peter Davison is not available any other time and leaves the country around 11 March).
>
> If you would like to come and see me either on 4 or 5 March with any drawings or further thoughts I'd be delighted to see you.

A major change of plan for the new season occurred shortly after this when Nathan-Turner, apparently while on holiday in the USA, decided to drop *Project Zeta-Sigma* from the schedule, possibly with a view to moving it back to a later slot. (Ultimately it was abandoned altogether, although some pre-production work had been carried out on it.) A replacement first story was hastily sought from Christopher H Bidmead, who had until recently been the series' script editor – a post now held on a caretaker basis by newcomer Antony Root. An outline entitled *The Visitor* was commissioned from him on 9 March, shortly after Nathan-Turner's return from holiday, and a full set of scripts under the revised title *Castrovalva* on 8 April.

One consequence of this change of plan was that Davison's first transmitted story could no longer be the first into production, for the simple reason that recording was due to start in mid-April and the scripts for *Castrovalva* could not possibly be completed in time. Consequently *Day of Wrath*, which in late February had been retitled *Four to Doomsday*, was moved forward to fill the production slot previously held by *Project Zeta-Sigma*. *Castrovalva* was meanwhile scheduled to be made fourth in line, after *Four to Doomsday* and two other stories, *The Visitation* and *Kinda*, which would be transmitted fourth and third respectively. Making a virtue of this necessity, Nathan-Turner considered it a positive advantage that Davison would now have a little time to settle into the role before having to record the story that would introduce his Doctor to the public – particularly as the plot of *Castrovalva* would see him experiencing a confused state of post-regeneration trauma, presenting a considerable challenge to the actor. This was a view with which Davison concurred. He still felt somewhat unsure about his approach to the role, and continued to seek advice from Nathan-Turner, executive producer Barry Letts and others, including *Four to Doomsday*'s director John Black.

Recording of *Four to Doomsday* began on schedule in mid-April, at which point a photocall was also held to unveil the Doctor's costume to the press – and, through them, to the public. The design drawn up by Lavers and approved by Nathan-Turner had a highly stylised, uniform look. This was something that Nathan-Turner had particularly favoured – in line with the redesign of the fourth Doctor's costume that he had instigated for the previous season – as he considered that it would give the character a readily marketable image and help to boost interest amongst toy and other manufacturers in producing spin-off items. Davison himself was not entirely happy with this aspect of the costume; as he would later admit in interviews, he would have preferred a more 'off the peg' look, giving the impression that the Doctor had simply picked up an assortment of clothes found in the TARDIS wardrobe, much as his previous incarnations had done.

The finishing touch to the outfit (although this was removed for the purposes of the initial photocall) was a prop stick of celery affixed to the lapel of the coat – another idea hit upon by Nathan-Turner, although he has never revealed the inspiration behind it.

For *Four to Doomsday*, Davison adopted a style of performance that he would later describe as 'bland', his intention being to avoid doing anything that could conceivably clash with his eventual interpretation of the role, once he had refined this to his full satisfaction. By this stage, he had already formed some quite firm views as to how he should approach the part, as he explained in an early press interview quoted by Peter Haining in the 1983 book *Doctor Who – A Celebration*:

'For a start, I will be a much younger Doctor and I'll be wearing a kind of Victorian cricketing outfit to accentuate my youth. I would like him to be heroic and resourceful. I feel that, over the years, the Doctor has become less vital, no longer struggling for survival, depending on instant, miraculous solutions to problems.

'The suspense of "Now how is he going to get out this tight corner?" has been

5 FIFTH DOCTOR

507

missing. I want to restore that. My Doctor will be flawed. He will have the best intentions and he will in the end win through, but he will not always act for the best. Sometimes, he will even endanger his companions. But I want him to have a sort of reckless innocence.'

Davison drew a certain amount of inspiration for his performance from the earlier Doctors – particularly the first and second, as played by William Hartnell and Patrick Troughton respectively. He had been an avid viewer of the Hartnell and Troughton stories as a teenager, and had recently watched a number of them again (along with several Jon Pertwee and Tom Baker stories) after borrowing videotape copies from Nathan-Turner. Some fan commentators would later suggest that his portrayal most closely resembled Troughton's, but he himself felt that it drew more heavily on Hartnell's, as he explained in a 1982 interview with David Hirsch for *Starlog*:

'I was given a completely blank page to do with as I liked. But at the same time, I didn't have the advantage I would have with another part, where I could create the character by saying, "His parents were like this," or, "This is his background". So I thought about what the other Doctors had done and I picked up ideas. I didn't want to dive in with a totally down-the-line character. I think my character has more than I intended to do with that of William Hartnell's Doctor. My Doctor gets cross sometimes, as Hartnell's did. Very gruff. He always has the best intentions in the world but, because of this … He doesn't always make mistakes, but he sometimes *causes* them. When he gets into a dangerous situation, he gets into trouble.'

Perhaps providing some support for this view, Hartnell's widow Heather would later comment that Davison strongly reminded her of her husband as a young man, and that she saw a number of parallels between their respective portrayals of the Doctor (although she also thought that the fifth Doctor's alien qualities were insufficiently emphasised, making him too similar to an ordinary human being).

One major difference between Davison and his four predecessors was that he was already very well known for other TV work at the point when he first appeared on screen as the Doctor – a fact that in the opinion of some critics made it more difficult for viewers to suspend their disbelief and accept him in the role. Not only was he still recognised from *All Creatures Great and Small*, but he was also gaining exposure in two current situation comedy series: LWT's *Holding the Fort* and the BBC's own *Sink or Swim*. *Sink or Swim* would indeed remain in production during the first two years of Davison's time in *Doctor Who*, obliging Nathan-Turner to release the actor between *Doctor Who* stories to work on that series.

The first televised pictures of the fifth Doctor in costume came not in *Doctor Who* itself but in the BBC's outside broadcast coverage of the annual Lord Mayor's Show in London on 14 November 1981, during the course of which Davison and a group of assorted monsters (fans wearing largely home-made costumes) were seen waving to the crowds from a float devoted to the series. After a further round of publicity appearances, including a guest spot on *Boxing Night at the Mill* when Davison was, amongst other things, required to demonstrate his prowess at making chocolate milk shakes, transmission of the new season began with the first episode of *Castrovalva* on Monday 4 January 1982, finally getting the fifth Doctor's era under way on the screen.

This first story saw the Doctor making a gradual recovery from his aforementioned state of post-regeneration trauma. His behaviour was initially confused and erratic, coloured by occasional reversions to the mannerisms of his previous incarnations – Davison essaying brief impressions of his predecessors in explicit recognition of the inspiration that he was drawing from them. He became progressively more stable, however, as the events of the story unfolded in the supposedly healing environment of Castrovalva and as his true character started to emerge.

Many of the qualities that had led Nathan-Turner to cast Davison were immediately evident to the viewer – particularly his relative youthfulness. One early idea, particularly favoured by Bidmead, was that he should give the impression of being an old man in a young man's body, and this also was reflected in the story. It quickly became apparent, too, that the fifth Doctor was to be a less overtly eccentric and off-the-wall character than the fourth. This was partly a consequence of Nathan-Turner's determination to cut down the level of humour in the series – or, as he put it, to concentrate on 'wit rather than slapstick' – but partly also a reflection of Davison's own natural disposition, in keeping with the producer's appraisal of him as a personality actor.

'I'm not a wacky, eccentric person,' noted Davison in a 1988 interview conducted by Richard Marson for *Doctor Who Magazine*. 'If they had wanted a wacky, eccentric person, John would have cast one. He did not want me to do that. I went along with what he wanted – he was the producer – and he wanted me to play it in a certain way. I'm sure if he had wanted me to be wacky and eccentric, I could have done it, but I could never have played the part in the way Tom Baker did. I'm not by nature like that.'

Expanding on this theme, Davison told Ben Landman in his 1985 *Starlog* interview:

'I don't think you ever think too consciously – especially if you're playing someone from Gallifrey, someone 750 years old – *exactly* what parts of yourself you're putting into it. I wanted to change the direction of *Doctor Who* a bit, to make it more believable. The fact of the matter is that it was *me* playing the part. Therefore, bits that are me came over.'

As Season 19 continued, so further aspects of the new Doctor's character began to become familiar. The heroism that had been one of the producer's original requirements was very much to the fore, as was the vulnerability – a quality demonstrated perhaps most vividly in the fact that the Doctor was unable to prevent the death of Adric in a space freighter crash at the end of *Earthshock* – a story written by the series' new permanent script editor, Eric Saward.

The thinking behind this vulnerability was a subject on which Nathan-Turner elaborated when interviewed by David Hirsch in 1982 for *Starlog*:

'I opted for a more fallible Doctor, a more vulnerable character who wasn't always on top of every situation. I felt that, in the past, some of the Doctors had been too dominant. There really had been no threat. Every cliff-hanger ending had left the Doctor in jeopardy of some kind, and we had all known that he was going to get out of it and be back next week. I think that if the role is played infallibly, then, in a way, that's undercutting the drama. If you've got a Doctor who is fallible, I think, hopefully, the viewers can get more involved and seriously believe he might not be back next week.'

The combined qualities of heroism and vulnerability meant that the fifth Doctor was sometimes seen to act rather recklessly, rushing breathlessly into new situations with an air of innocent curiosity and failing to consider all the risks.

'I think he has a certain amount of tunnel vision!' opined Davison in a 1982 interview with Jeremy Bentham for *Doctor Who Magazine*. 'He's not always the wisest of men. Maybe when he sits back and ruminates on the way things have gone he *is* wise, but I think that he's headstrong and he makes more of a mess of things in the short run until he's sorted out his own problems. He doesn't always act for the best. Quite often he'll land in a certain situation and, obviously, the common sense thing to do would be simply to leave – to get out of there because it's dangerous to everyone. But he doesn't get out, he wants to find out what's going on, he's got to explore … and thus he gets embroiled in the story.'

Like all his predecessors, the fifth Doctor was a resolute champion of the cause of good against evil, invariably standing up for the underdog and combating tyranny and oppression wherever he encountered them. He also had a considerable degree of moral courage, as was well illustrated by the following confrontation from *Earthshock*, when he sought to prevent the Cyber Leader from harming Tegan:

> CYBER LEADER: I see that Time Lords have emotions.
>
> THE DOCTOR: Of sorts.
>
> CYBER LEADER: Surely a great weakness in one so powerful?
>
> THE DOCTOR: Emotions have their uses.
>
> CYBER LEADER: They restrict and curtail the intellect and logic of the mind.
>
> THE DOCTOR: They also enhance life. When did you last have the pleasure of smelling a flower, watching a sunset, eating a well-prepared meal?
>
> CYBER LEADER: These things are irrelevant.
>
> THE DOCTOR: For some people, small, beautiful things is what life is all about!

Again, there were echoes of the Hartnell Doctor here, as this exchange was similar to one that he had with an earlier Cyber Leader in the Season 3 story *The Tenth Planet*, as also seen in *Earthshock* by way of a flashback extract:

> THE DOCTOR: Emotions: love, pride, hate fear! Have you no emotions, sir?

Davison was considered by BBC management to have made a great success of his debut season as the Doctor. Nathan-Turner's superior, Head of Series and Serials David Reid, wrote to him in glowing terms on 29 March 1982:

> Sadly we have only said a fast 'hello' to each other in the BBC Club but then your schedule doesn't leave you much free time. I wanted simply to congratulate you at the end of your first season of *Doctor Who* and to express my admiration for the way in which you have taken the part and made it your own. I am delighted with the response from the audience

and I hope very much that you are.

It is, I know, a very demanding schedule and the confidence and expertise achieved is remarkable – so thank you also for the enormous amount of energy, concentration and work that you have put into the series.

What more can I say except to say that the season has been a great pleasure and a success largely due to you and I greatly look forward to the next season.

Season 20 revealed little more about the fifth Doctor's character than had been established in Season 19. This may have been due in part to the fact that Saward, although acknowledging Davison to be a very good actor, considered him miscast in the role and consequently, as he would later admit, felt uninspired to devote much attention to the character's development. Davison, for his own part, was understandably perturbed at this situation and felt that he was being less well served than he should be by the series' scripts. One thing that he was especially keen to do was to inject some elements of flippant humour into his portrayal, but any such suggestions were generally vetoed by Nathan-Turner in what the actor regarded as an over-reaction against the perceived excesses of Tom Baker in this regard. Davison was also rather dissatisfied with his own performance during the course of this season.

Quite apart from these concerns about his own role, the actor harboured a number of misgivings about the general direction in which the series was moving at this point. In particular, he thought that the stories were becoming too reliant on familiar monsters and characters from *Doctor Who*'s past; he felt that there was an increasing tendency for stylish production values to take priority over good plotting; he disagreed with Nathan-Turner's decision to have Nyssa written out in *Terminus*, the fourth story of the season, as he considered her to be the companion best suited to his Doctor; and he disliked the producer's policy of casting 'guest star' celebrities, often best known for comedy or light entertainment work, in supporting roles.

'I was actually very unhappy with the second season, script-wise and concept-wise,' admitted the actor in his 1988 interview with Richard Marson for *Doctor Who Magazine*. 'I just felt that it didn't go anywhere and John couldn't quite decide if he was having old monsters back or bringing in new ones. And I wasn't very happy with me in it.

'It was then – in the second year – that I had to decide if I wanted to do a fourth year, because of the way it works. But I just wasn't sure about the programme.

'John and I have always got on very well, but we did have a creative difference over the direction in which he wanted *Doctor Who* to go, and the direction in which I thought it should go. We talked it through, and I decided I would be better off if I left.

'As far as companions went, I thought there should be one companion, who was a fairly nice person, to work with the Doctor – preferably Nyssa, although I wasn't insisting on her. I also thought it needed to get away from turning into a sort of variety show in space.

'If you look back to the very first season of *Doctor Who*, I know it looked very tacky – sets that wobbled and all that – but it had a kind of mystical quality in it, an atmosphere that was disappearing when I did it, and that I think has completely disappeared now. It was that atmosphere that made the need to compete with special effects unnecessary. Certain effects we did fine, but you've got to know your limitations and you can't expect

FIFTH DOCTOR

to compete with *Star Wars* in BBC television.

'It wasn't a row at all – indeed, I didn't decide until about two months after our discussion that maybe I should leave. It was kind of frustrating coming to the BBC rehearsal rooms every day as well, and seeing people doing other things.'

'I used to meet Peter from time to time for chats and so on,' noted Saward in a 1993 interview, 'and he always used to have this thing at the end of each season: was he going to come back? I know that he felt a little uncomfortable playing the part, and I think he felt it wasn't working as he would have liked. As I recall, before the end of the second season, he was saying more frequently, "I don't know if I'm going to do it again. I don't know if I'm going to do it again". Really he was just saying out loud what he was feeling. So when John came in and said, "Peter isn't doing it again," I wasn't surprised. I don't think anyone was surprised, as he'd been saying it for so long.'

Davison was in fact much happier with Season 21 than he had been with Season 20, and even had second thoughts about his decision to leave. By this point, however, steps had already been taken to write him out and to cast a replacement, so it was too late for a rethink. Thus it was that the fifth Doctor bowed out with the transmission on 16 March 1984 of the final episode of Robert Holmes's *The Caves of Androzani*, bringing to an end an era of the series' history that, for the actor's many fans, had been all too brief.

'The press were all looking for a behind the scenes row,' recalled Davison in his 1988 interview for *Doctor Who Magazine*. 'Indeed the *Daily Mail* printed that I'd been given the elbow because I was too boring! Unfortunately for them, there was no row – in fact John Nathan-Turner tried very hard to keep me on for another season. However, I remembered, when I joined, meeting Patrick Troughton in the BBC car park, and him saying, "Congratulations. Don't stay longer than three years though." And I think he was right. You see, as an actor, I've lived for a long time with the terror of expecting a day to come when there's no work for me. The temptation with doing *Doctor Who* was that I could just have stayed for season after season. But I was risking an association that could have been very damaging career-wise. It was a decision I made through attempting to further my career. It wasn't a happy decision, as in "Thank god that's over". I just wanted to do other things after my time. *Doctor Who* was a lot of fun to do. We had some terrific guest artists, and I wouldn't have missed it for anything. It was very demanding, and strikes delayed my last story so I was too tired to feel sad when it was all finally over, but, yes, one does suffer the odd pang.'

REWRITING THE MYTH

None of the three script editors who worked on the fifth Doctor's era regarded continuity with what had gone before as being of overriding importance, particularly where they felt that it would get in the way of telling a good, entertaining story. There was, however, a conscious effort made by the production team to avoid committing any really major errors; and, indeed, the series' mythology was drawn upon more heavily than ever before as a source of inspiration for new plot ideas and elements, giving rise to many continuity developments.

A number of new facts about the Doctor become apparent right from the outset. In

Castrovalva, the transformation of his physical appearance leaves him suffering after-effects far more traumatic than any experienced by his three predecessors, leading him at one point to think that the regeneration is actually failing. (No reason for this is ever given, but one explanation might lie in the severity of the injuries he sustained in the fall that triggered the process.) As with the regeneration of the first Doctor into the second, the mysterious process has affected not only the Doctor's body but also his clothes – his boots have metamorphosed into shoes, and his scarf is starting to unravel. He quickly decides to discard his old outfit altogether in favour of some period cricketing gear found near a pavilion-like room within the TARDIS. Later in the story, he dons a pair of glasses to read; and in the following one, *Four to Doomsday*, he reveals that he is short-sighted in his right eye and carries a magnifying glass in his pocket.

Also in *Four to Doomsday*, the Time Lord is seen to be able to survive for several minutes in the freezing vacuum of space without the benefit of a pressure suit. It is however possible that the helmet-like apparatus that he is wearing to enable him to breathe is also generating some sort of a protective force field around him. Certainly the cricket ball that he throws during the course of his space walk behaves in a manner that would not normally be expected in the absence of any other forces.

The Doctor's improvised use of a cricket ball reinforces the impression given by his clothing that he has something of an affinity for the sport. This is confirmed a little later on, in *Black Orchid*, when he actually takes part in a match in 1920s England and gives a good all-round performance. As the fourth Doctor was also familiar with cricket (evidenced in stories such as *The Ark in Space* and *The Hand of Fear*) but the first was completely unaware of it (established in *The Daleks' Master Plan*), it might perhaps be logical to assume that the third was introduced to the sport during his period of exile on 20th-Century Earth.

In the Buddhist-influenced *Kinda*, the Doctor appears unaffected by the Box of Jhana, a representation of the power of meditation, suggesting that he is already in touch with his inner self. In its sequel *Snakedance*, however, he is unable to find the 'still point' at the centre of his consciousness without the psychic aid of the elderly shaman Dojjen.

The Visitation sees the destruction by the Terileptil leader of the sonic screwdriver, a multipurpose tool introduced during the second Doctor's era in the story *Fury from the Deep*, moving the Time Lord to comment that he feels as if he has lost an old friend.

In *The Five Doctors*, the Doctor is taken ill and then starts to fade away altogether as his previous incarnations are taken out of time and space by the Time Lord President Borusa, causing him to reflect that 'A man is the sum of his memories, you know – a Time Lord even more so.'

An ability to swim is revealed by the Doctor in *Warriors of the Deep*, when he is knocked into a water tank and forced to make his escape through a hatch beneath the surface. *The Caves of Androzani*, on the other hand, sees two weaknesses disclosed. First, the Doctor confides to his companion Peri that he is allergic to certain gases 'in the praxis range of the spectrum' – hence his habit of wearing a stick of celery on his lapel, as this will turn purple if exposed to the gases in question and so warn him of their presence, following which he will eat the celery. Secondly, he is seen to succumb to spectrox toxæmia after touching some strands of raw spectrox, a substance apparently peculiar to the planet Androzani Minor. It is this that ultimately causes him to regenerate once again, after he selflessly uses the last of the antidote to cure Peri of her similar affliction.

The Doctor's ship, the TARDIS, also gives up a few more of its secrets during this period of the series' history. *Castrovalva* involves the Doctor and his companions venturing into some previously unseen areas of its interior, including the pink-hued zero room – a tranquil environment shielded from all external influences (or supposedly so, at any rate, as an image of the Doctor's young male companion Adric is at one point projected inside). This room is part of the random twenty-five per cent of the ship's interior that the Doctor subsequently jettisons when he adjusts the architectural configuration circuits to provide the extra energy needed to pull the TARDIS clear of imminent destruction at Event One, the primordial hydrogen inrush towards which it has been directed by Adric under the Master's evil influence.

It is another of the Doctor's companions, Tegan, who discovers during the course of *Castrovalva* that the TARDIS has a computerised information system, accessible from the main control console. Although she is later disabused of the notion that she has succeeded in piloting the ship to *Castrovalva* by following instructions from this source, she does manage to initiate a short trip in the following story, *Four to Doomsday*, and proves quite proficient at operating the craft later on, most notably in *The King's Demons*.

In Season 20, *Mawdryn Undead* sees the TARDIS making an emergency landing inside a giant spacecraft after colliding with its warp ellipse field. The same story then brings a reminder of the series' past when the Doctor produces a TARDIS homing device first seen, although in a different form, in *The Chase* during the era of his first incarnation and also used by Adric in the fourth Doctor story *Full Circle*.

Terminus presents further problems for the Doctor when his young companion Turlough, coerced into sabotaging the TARDIS, operates some switches behind one of the wall roundels and then partially pulls out a piece of equipment called the space-time element from beneath the control console. The time rotor starts to jam, leaving the Doctor no option but to operate the cut-out. He then refocuses the scanner screen to show images of the ship's interior – another capability not previously displayed – and discovers that a wall of shimmering light is encroaching on its dimensions. The TARDIS has in fact melded itself to a ship headed for the space station Terminus, and an interface soon appears in the form of a doorway in the TARDIS's laboratory area.

The Doctor completely refurbishes the TARDIS console at the start of *The Five Doctors*, but fails to cure it of its temperamental behaviour. In *Warriors of the Deep*, the ship is revealed to be susceptible to attack by energy weapons fired from a satellite orbiting the Earth around the year 2084, the Doctor being forced to perform a materialisation flip-flop in order to remove it from the area of danger. Then, in *Frontios*, the possibility arises that the ship may actually have been destroyed by the power of a creature called the Gravis and his Tractator drones. In truth, however, it has become fragmented and interspersed with the rock of the eponymous planet's surface, and the Doctor is able to trick the Gravis into reassembling it. No sooner has this crisis been averted than, in *Resurrection of the Daleks*, the ship gets caught in a time corridor operated by his oldest adversaries. Finally, in *Planet of Fire*, the Doctor's short-lived android companion Kamelion resets the ship's destination co-ordinates by plugging himself into the data banks via one of the wall roundels, and Turlough performs some further minor sabotage by pulling out a number of wires from beneath the control console in order to cut off an incoming distress call.

Amongst a host of familiar characters returning to the series during the fifth Doctor's era is Brigadier Alistair Gordon Lethbridge-Stewart. He is first seen in *Mawdryn Undead*, working as a mathematics teacher at Brendon, a boys' public school, after his retirement in 1976 from service in the United Nations Intelligence Taskforce (UNIT). He suffers a nervous breakdown and loses his memory in 1977 as a result of the events of the story, but saves the day after the TARDIS takes him forward in time to 1983, where he meets his future self and, in so doing, inadvertently triggers a release of energy – the Blinovitch Limitation Effect (described in rather different terms in the third Doctor story *Day of the Daleks*) – that enables the Doctor to avoid the threatened loss of his remaining regenerations.

It is also mentioned at one point during *Mawdryn Undead* that the Brigadier's former subordinate Sergeant Benton left UNIT in 1979 and is now working as a used car salesman, and that the Doctor's one-time companion Harry Sullivan has been seconded to NATO and is now doing 'hush hush' things at Porton Down. However, as the dates given in this story are completely at odds with those given during the fourth Doctor's era, from which it was clear that the Brigadier, Benton and Harry were all still serving in UNIT in the early 1980s, it may be that *Mawdryn Undead* takes place in a parallel universe (as did certain of the events of the third Doctor story *Inferno*). An alternative explanation would be that, for reasons unknown, a significant change has since occurred in the course of Earth's history.

The Brigadier's other appearance during the fifth Doctor's era comes in *The Five Doctors*. Here, he is attending a reunion at UNIT's British HQ, now under the command of his successor Colonel Crichton, when he encounters the second Doctor – who has for once been able to steer the TARDIS correctly, albeit at the expense of bending the Laws of Time – and is whisked off with him to the Time Lords' home planet, Gallifrey. At the end of the story, the pair depart in what appears to be an offshoot of the fifth Doctor's TARDIS, presumably on their way to further, undisclosed adventures in time and space.

The Five Doctors sees also the return of the Doctor's other previous incarnations, along with his former companions Susan, Sarah Jane Smith, K-9 and the second Romana – not to mention phantom appearances by Jamie, Zoe, Liz Shaw and Captain Mike Yates of UNIT. The first Doctor and Susan and the third Doctor and Sarah also depart in their own respective offshoots of the fifth Doctor's TARDIS once the crisis is over, again heading for destinations unknown.

It is never stated from what points in their respective lives the Doctor's previous incarnations have been taken by the timescoop device used to transport them to Gallifrey. The fourth could easily have been abducted during the course of an untransmitted adventure from his own era. (In fact, the footage was culled from the abandoned Season 17 story *Shada*, although opinions differ as to whether or not this should be regarded as part of the true *Doctor Who* canon.) Where the first, second and third are concerned, however, this explanation would appear to be ruled out both by their appearance – they all look somewhat older than they did at the end of their own respective eras – and by their circumstances – they are all initially without companions, for instance, and at least two of the three appear to be aware of events that occurred at or after the point when they regenerated into their successors. Another apparent anomaly with regard to the second, third, fourth and fifth Doctors is that none of them has any recollection of having already experienced the events of the story in their previous lives.

Similar continuity problems arose in relation to the Season 10 story *The Three Doctors* (and would arise again in relation to the Season 22 story *The Two Doctors*) and, although various different theories have been advanced by fans as possible solutions to them, it is perhaps safest to say simply that they remain unresolved within the fiction of the series itself.

A further point of note about *The Five Doctors* is that no energy release or other apparent adverse reaction occurs when the different incarnations of the Doctor meet up with one another. Although in line with the events of *The Three Doctors*, this appears on the face of it to be inconsistent with what happened when the Brigadier encountered his future self in *Mawdryn Undead*. It may be, however, that Time Lords are less affected by such temporal displacements than are mere human beings (just as they are less affected by temporal disturbances, judging by events in the third Doctor stories *The Time Monster* and *Invasion of the Dinosaurs*).

The Five Doctors is just one of a number of stories in which the fifth Doctor encounters members of his own race. The Master, having recently taken over the body of Consul Tremas of the planet Traken, makes several return appearances, attempting to ensnare the Doctor in the sophisticated trap of Castrovalva (*Castrovalva*); to gain control of the awesome power of the alien Xeraphin (*Time-Flight*); to prevent the signing of the Magna Carta (*The King's Demons*); and to reverse the effects of an accident that has left him stranded in a miniaturised state on the planet Sarn (*Planet of Fire*). In *The Five Doctors* itself, the Master actually attempts to aid the Doctor – at the behest of the Time Lord High Council, who have promised him a whole new regeneration cycle in return – but is thwarted when his old opponent refuses to trust him.

Even more so than in the incarnation encountered by the third Doctor, the Master demonstrates a remarkable ability to disguise his normal saturnine features, taking on various false identities during the course of these stories. He also makes greater use than ever before of his trademark weapon, now referred to as a tissue compression eliminator, which reduces its victims to miniaturised corpses (as previously seen in the third Doctor story *Terror of the Autons* and in the fourth Doctor story *The Deadly Assassin*). One ability of which he makes rather less use than in the past, however, is that of hypnosis.

Arc of Infinity sees the return of another of the Doctor's old adversaries. This is Omega, the legendary stellar engineer whose work provided the Time Lords with the initial power that they needed to enable them to travel through space and time. In his introductory story, *The Three Doctors*, he was shown to be trapped in a universe of anti-matter beyond a black hole, his physical body utterly destroyed and his existence preserved only by his enormous force of will. In *Arc of Infinity*, he makes a further attempt to escape back to his home universe, and again looks to the Doctor to act as the unwilling provider of the means for him to do so. Enlisting the aid of an Ergon servant (an energy creature presumably similar in nature to the Gel Guards featured in *The Three Doctors*) and Councillor Hedin, a traitorous member of the Time Lord High Council who is apparently responsible for providing him with a TARDIS, he conspires to create a new corporeal form for himself by bonding with the Doctor's. The scheme fails, however, and Omega is apparently destroyed when the Doctor fires a matter converter at him.

The Doctor's old Time Lord teacher Borusa, first seen holding the rank of Cardinal in *The Deadly Assassin* and then that of Chancellor in *The Invasion of Time*, has gone one better and become President by the time *Arc of Infinity* takes place – all three stories featuring different incarnations of the character. Other Time Lords encountered during the course of this latest Gallifreyan sojourn include: Damon (an old friend of the Doctor's, although not previously seen in the series); Chancellor Thalia; the Castellan (either a different incarnation of the Time Lord who held that post in *Invasion of Time* or a different Time Lord altogether); and the Chancellery Guard Commander Maxil (whose physical appearance is subsequently adopted by the Doctor when he regenerates into his sixth form in *The Caves of Androzani*).

Arc of Infinity also involves the Doctor visiting once more the virtual reality of the Matrix – the repository of all Time Lord knowledge – as previously featured in both *The Deadly Assassin* and *The Invasion of Time*. This occurs when, despite capital punishment having been long abandoned on Gallifrey, the Time Lord High Council make an unsuccessful attempt to have the Doctor vaporised in order to prevent Omega from succeeding in his plan.

President Borusa features again in *The Five Doctors* – again in a different incarnation – and it becomes clear as the story unfolds that he has now gone insane. It is he who is responsible for bringing all the Doctors and their companions together on Gallifrey, in an area known as the Death Zone. The grim history of this desolate place and of the Game that was played there is explained by the second Doctor as follows:

'In the days before Rassilon, my ancestors had tremendous powers – which they misused terribly. They set up this place, the Death Zone, and walled it around with an impenetrable force field. And then they kidnapped other beings and set them down here.'

At the centre of the Death Zone lies the Dark Tower – the tomb of Rassilon, 'the greatest single figure in Time Lord history'. Official Time Lord lore maintains that Rassilon was a good man, but the second Doctor recalls many rumours and legends to the contrary:

'Some say his fellow Time Lords rebelled against his cruelty and locked him in the Tower in eternal sleep.'

Later, it is revealed that Rassilon's consciousness does indeed live on within the Tower, although his body lies immobile on a bier, apparently in suspended animation. It transpires however that, in keeping with the official history, he is not a cruel tyrant but a wise and benevolent figure. He set up the Game of Rassilon as a trap for those, such as the deranged Borusa, who would seek immortality. These power-crazed individuals are given what they desire, but not in the way that they expect: they are turned into living statues along the side of Rassilon's bier.

The Castellan puts in a further appearance in *The Five Doctors*, but is killed after being falsely accused of treachery. The Chancellor is now a woman named Flavia, who at the end of the story invites the Doctor to return to the Capitol (which, like the planet itself, appears to be called Gallifrey) as President of the Time Lords. The Doctor, however, beats a hasty retreat in the TARDIS …

The Black Guardian and the White Guardian, introduced in the fourth Doctor's era as awesomely powerful opposing forces superior even to the Time Lords, are featured again in a trilogy of stories comprising *Mawdryn Undead*, *Terminus* and *Enlightenment*. The Black Guardian is determined to avenge himself against the Doctor after their earlier encounter and, unable to intervene directly in the affairs of the universe, co-opts Turlough as a reluctant pawn to bring about his destruction. Ultimately, however, when faced with the choice of handing over either the Doctor or a huge, glowing diamond that he has been offered by the Guardians, Turlough opts for the latter. The Black

Guardian is apparently consumed in flames, but the White Guardian warns the Doctor to remain vigilant: 'As long as I exist, he exists also, until we are no longer needed.'

The fifth Doctor's era also sees the return of a number of monstrous alien races introduced in earlier periods of the series' history. In *Earthshock*, a force of Cybermen under the command of a Cyber Leader is attempting to destroy an interstellar peace conference on Earth in the year 2526. As on a number of previous occasions, the creatures' appearance has quite significantly altered since they last crossed paths with the Doctor. This story also contains the first hint that they may now have acquired a limited time travel capability. Not only do they have visual records of events that took place around the 29th Century in the fourth Doctor story *Revenge of the Cybermen* (as well as of incidents in the first Doctor story *The Tenth Planet* and in the second Doctor story *The Wheel in Space*), but one of their devices causes a spaceship to travel back in time after it is tampered with by the Doctor's companion Adric. Another innovation is their use of two deadly androids to guard a powerful bomb that they have concealed on Earth. The Doctor eventually thwarts the Cybermen's plans, in part by exploiting the fact that, as established in *Revenge of the Cybermen*, gold dust is lethal to them when forced into their chest unit breathing apparatus.

The Doctor's oldest foes, the Daleks, are back in action in *Resurrection of the Daleks*, attempting to free Davros from imprisonment on board a military space station orbiting the Earth. They have lost their long war against the android Movellans – as seen in the fourth Doctor story *Destiny of the Daleks* – and hope that their creator will be able to find a cure for the deadly virus created by their enemies that is wiping them out. They also aim to usurp the power of the Time Lords by infiltrating Gallifrey with android duplicates of the Doctor and his companions. Davros, however, has plans of his own, and begins to inject Daleks with a substance that makes them subservient to his will. This second faction of Daleks then comes into conflict with the one still loyal to the Dalek Supreme (making its first appearance in the series since the third Doctor story *Planet of the Daleks*), although in the end both groups are wiped out when the Doctor releases some of the Movellan virus. Davros, although himself affected by the virus, apparently reaches the safety of an escape pod.

The Five Doctors features a Dalek, a force of Cybermen and also, from the second Doctor's era, a Yeti (which judging from its appearance is a real creature from Tibet, as seen at the end of *The Abominable Snowmen*, rather than one of the Great Intelligence's controlled robots). These creatures have all been transported to the Death Zone on Gallifrey as part of Borusa's scheme, but little new information is revealed about any of them on this occasion.

The Silurians and a force of Sea Devil Warriors – survivors of the reptilian species that ruled the Earth before the rise of humankind – attempt to take over an underwater nuclear weapons facility around the year 2084 in *Warriors of the Deep*. Unlike in *Doctor Who and the Silurians* and *The Sea Devils* – the third Doctor stories that gave them their respective debuts – the creatures are this time identified by individual names: the Silurians are led by Icthar, Scibus and Tarpok, while the Sea Devils are commanded by Sauvix. Icthar is described as being the last surviving member of the Silurian Triad and is already known to the Doctor, indicating that there must have been an earlier, untelevised encounter between them. Like the Cybermen in *Earthshock*, both the Silurians and the Sea Devils have undergone a number of changes since their races last appeared in the series. The Silurians' third eyes – which previously acted as weapons and tools – now flash in synchronisation with their voices when they speak, and their voices are themselves completely unlike those heard in *Doctor Who and the Silurians*. In the Sea Devils' case, however, the changes are confined to their clothing: they now wear Samurai-style armour instead of the blue mesh garments seen in *The Sea Devils*.

Other new developments in *Warriors of the Deep* include the Silurians' use of a huge, amphibious cyborg, the Myrka, to attack the humans' base, and the revelation that exposure to hexachromite gas is lethal to all reptiles.

Many new characters and monsters are introduced during the fifth Doctor's era, but few go on to make return visits. The Terileptils, for instance, appear only in *The Visitation* (although they do subsequently receive one further mention, in *The Awakening*, when the Doctor explains that – as indicated in the earlier story – they mine a substance called tinclavic on the planet Raaga, and also a cameo in *Time-Flight*). One exception to the rule is Lytton, an alien mercenary seen assisting the Daleks in *Resurrection of the Daleks*, who turns up again in a sixth Doctor story, *Attack of the Cybermen*. Another is the Mara, which also features in two stories: *Kinda* and *Snakedance*. As explained in *Snakedance*, this evil intelligence, which manifests itself in the form of a snake, originated on the planet Manussa. The Manussan scientists had used molecular engineering to produce a Great Crystal attuned to the wavelength of the human mind and able to absorb its energy; only the evil aspects were absorbed, however, and when amplified and reflected by the Crystal these brought into being the entity that became known as the Mara.

Significant though the many continuity developments were during the era of the fifth Doctor, they would be equalled and indeed surpassed during that of his successor, when the series would come to rely ever more heavily on the rich heritage of its own mythology.

$@@@@@@@@@@@@@@@@@@@@@@@@@@@@@@@@@@@@$

SCRIPT EDITING

It was in early 1963 that the BBC's then Head of Drama Sydney Newman – one of the creators of *Doctor Who* – set up within the Drama Group a system of production teams, each of which would be responsible for making a particular series, serial or strand of plays. Following the precedent already established in many of the ITV companies, these teams would consist of two permanent staff members, namely a producer and a story editor, along with secretarial support. The producer would be given overall artistic, administrative and financial control of the production, overseeing the work of the different directors who would be brought in to handle individual episodes or programmes, while the relatively junior story editor would have the task of finding and working with freelance writers to come up with the required scripts – a function previously performed by the now-defunct Script Department.

The story editor's role was described in more detail by Drama Group Organiser Ayton Whitaker in a loose-leaf Editors' Guide produced in October 1968 for internal use within the BBC:

The primary function of the editor is to find, encourage and commission new writers. He should concern himself with the details of television scripts so that his producer's horizon can be kept clear. The editor is the writer's representative in the Television Service and is responsible for looking after the writer's interests right through to the time of production. While encouraging writers to practise their art with as much freedom as possible, it is yet the editor's job to guide them on matters of television grammar and the necessary disciplines of the Service, e.g. timing, number of sets, size of cast, amount of film which can reasonably be used ...

The Guide also set out and codified other aspects of the editor's duties, including the need to follow policy guidance on questions of sex, violence and bad language. It went on:

The principles underlying editorial control are based deeply on the assumption that the finding and encouraging of all those creative and wayward and surprising talents that go into making television programmes is a major part of the Corporation's responsibility to the public. But, as every truly professional writer will be aware, it is from the disciplining of creative talent, not from its reckless indulgence, that true art emerges.

Other matters covered in the Guide were: checking names in scripts (e.g. to ensure that they could not be misconstrued as referring to real-life people); preparing scripts for typing; keeping track of amendments; and using the services of the Drama Script Unit (the vestigial successor to the old Script Department) in areas such as copyright, briefing procedures, contractual agreements and staff contributions. Also included were a number of articles written by current story editors, explaining how they saw their own jobs in practical terms.

By the early 1980s, most editors were freelancers working on fixed-term contracts rather than permanent members of the BBC's staff. Little else had changed, however. The Guide was still in use – albeit revised and updated, taking into account amongst other things the switch of formal job title from story editor to script editor that had been instituted in June 1968 – and the basic functions of the job were still essentially the same as they had been back in 1963.

Three different script editors had an influence over the stories of the fifth Doctor. The first was Christopher Hamilton Bidmead, who worked on Tom Baker's last season – Season 18 – and played a major part in setting up Peter Davison's first – Season 19. Having initially studied acting at the Royal Academy of Dramatic Art, Bidmead had since earned his living as a radio and television writer and as a journalist specialising in scientific and technical articles. He had been offered the *Doctor Who* post after being recommended by one of the series' former writers, Robert Banks Stewart, and had decided to accept it after being assured by producer John Nathan-Turner and executive producer Barry Letts that they disliked as much as he did the humorous, fantasy-orientated style that had been favoured by the previous production team.

Bidmead enjoyed the challenge of taking the series in a new direction but found the job a very gruelling one, and it was this that ultimately resulted in him spending only a year on the production team. He told *Doctor Who Magazine* in 1986:

'About seventy per cent of Season 18 was written by me, in two senses. One was quite legitimate: as script editor, I would have brainstorming sessions with each of the writers, and there I would contribute at least half the ideas. The slightly less rewarding side of the job was that far too often writers would come back and, for a variety of reasons, they would fail to achieve what was required, and I would end up working far into the night writing stuff myself. Part of the reason for this was my own failure to communicate to them what was needed, part was that they went away in such a frenzy of enthusiasm that ideas would expand beyond our original strictures. It was also partly through lack of experience. I had to attempt to get writers to hammer the stories back into shape, but we needed to feed the juggernaut of the production schedule, so more often than not, I'd have to do it myself.

'I think the script editor has an impossible job, which is indirectly why I left: I mean, I wanted to stay on, but I also wanted the BBC to pay me the sort of money that recognised the kind of effort I was putting into the show. The BBC didn't feel able to do that, so I left. I think you get what you pay for, and subsequent script editors quite rightly didn't have the time to devote to scripts that fans often rightly criticise.'

Before his departure, Bidmead was heavily involved in discussions with Nathan-Turner about the characterisation of the fifth Doctor and about other aspects of the nineteenth season, for which he commissioned a number of stories. He had by this point prepared a revised format document headed '*Doctor Who*: Notes for New Writers', which was sent out to all prospective writers. The document was updated from time to time to reflect new developments, but its basic contents remained unchanged. The version dated 14 November 1980 began with the following general summary of the series' requirements:

THE NATURE OF THE SHOW

What we're looking for from new writers are *not* complete scripts or even involved scenarios, but fresh and readably presented (i.e. brief) storylines.

We're interested in plots that rise convincingly out of characterisation and well-thought-out situations; in particular, storylines should indicate how the idea fits into the four episode shape in which we (usually) serialise our stories. An example, not intended to be definitive, might be: 1. Exposition, 2. Complication Leading to Crisis, 3. The Real Situation Exposed, Revealing the Awful Truth, 4. The DOCTOR Battles Against the Odds But Finally Wins Through.

This kind of thinking gives rise and fall to the narrative, and should throw up strong cliff-hangers in which characters are forced to deal with changing situations, as opposed to the ad hoc 'in one bound our hero is free' variety.

There is no *DOCTOR WHO* formula, but experience shows that the format allows for three main kinds of story:

a. Space Fiction
Recently the programme has been developing a more solid science-fiction basis, and while we feel this is probably a welcome change we're anxious to avoid importing wholesale the familiar clichés of the genre. Of course it's impossible to avoid the sci-fi icons – exploding supernovae, menacing robots and so forth – but they need to be as far as possible rethought into

5 FIFTH DOCTOR

our unique context.

b. Earth-Bound

The appeal of an Earth-bound story is that it gives both the team and the viewers an opportunity to get out on location for a breath of fresh air. But filming is very expensive, and night filming, immensely appealing though it is as a device to wind up the tension, is almost completely outside the scope of our budget. Writers should try to keep all filming to no more than fifteen minutes in a hundred minute story.

c. Historical

These are probably the most difficult to handle, and new writers are recommended to avoid the genre unless they are particularly sure of their ground. Many new writers seem drawn to Kitsch-History themes (Doctor Who meets Machiavelli), but the result is usually an unhappy pot-pourri of fact and fantasy.

It's a well-understood convention that a Time-Travelling Hero does not change history; additionally we tend to shy away from the sort of story that 'reveals' that the truth about a particular historical event is different from what we always thought it to be. Thus, unless very carefully handled, a story based on the idea that the First World War was actually triggered off by refugees from a coup d'etat on the planet Zorrella, is not going to appeal to us.

Having said this, we are in the business of transmitting 'Science Fiction Adventure Stories', and this element mustn't be overlooked.

The adventures of a time-travelling renegade Time Lord are of course built on a premise of wildest fantasy. But without inhibiting creative ideas, we'd prefer writers to work within this concept in a way that acknowledges the appropriate disciplines. Charged Particle Physics (to pick a topic at random) is mapped territory accessible to many of our viewers (there are *Doctor Who* Appreciation Societies in universities all over the world); and writers who want to bring the topic into the story should at least glance at the relevant pages of the encyclopedia. History of course deserves similar treatment. Imaginative extrapolation of 'the facts' should be preferred to pure gobbledegook.

I should add that having the DOCTOR go back in time to do a fix that solves the problem by not allowing it to arise is a favourite storyline idea we've had to outlaw. If recursive solutions are allowable, our audience will ask why the DOCTOR doesn't always do this, and there'll never be any adventure.

A WORD ON PRESENTATION

Putting characters' names in CAPITALS makes it considerably easier for the reader to track back on plot. Double spacing with proper margins also improves readability. Four pages should be adequate to put across the essence of the idea you want to sell us. I've already suggested that storylines should show clearly how the material fits into the four-part format; but it's sometimes helpful to lead off with a short preface that sets out the premise on which the story is based.

FINALLY

Notes on the DOCTOR, his current companions and the TARDIS follow.

I'm appending a copy of the Introduction to the US edition of a recent *Doctor Who* novel. While it doesn't necessarily represent our official line in all respects, it does give a good overview of what the show is all about.

I'm also enclosing extracts from 'Guide to *Doctor Who* Storylines', written by Douglas Adams when he was script editor of this programme. I think he makes some good points.

Storylines you send in will be warmly welcomed and read. It's always helpful if the writer can include some brief details about his writing history and aspirations. Obviously previous television writing experience is a valuable asset, but we have in the past produced a number of scripts written by newcomers to the medium. A useful book to put you in the picture is *Writing for Television* by Malcolm Hulke (another former *Doctor Who* script editor [sic]), published by A & C Black.

We'll acknowledge all submissions as soon as we can – though experience shows that due to our heavy production schedule our replies are often far from instantaneous. How we proceed from there will obviously depend on the quality and suitability of the ideas submitted.

The US-derived attachment mentioned by Bidmead had in fact appeared as the introduction to all the editions of the Target *Doctor Who* novelisations issued in that country by Pinnacle Books. Written by well-known science fiction author Harlan Ellison, it explained why he considered *Doctor Who* to be the greatest science fiction series of all time.

The appended extract from Douglas Adams's earlier document, headed 'The Script Editor's Guide to *Doctor Who* Storylines', read as follows:

> * *Brevity is the soul of storylines.*
> We don't want to plough through 20 pages of closely-typed prose trying to work out what the story is about. At the initial stage of story ideas, we just want to know what the idea is, how it resolves, and whether it promises sufficient area of conflict to sustain a hundred minutes of tension and drama. If that takes more than two or three pages then the idea hasn't been thought out well enough. There is absolutely no point in working out all the complicated details of the plot mechanics – who is running after whom at what time and with which monkey wrench – until the basic plot concepts have been properly hammered out.
>
> A script writer is basically in the business of selling his ideas. Imagine the reaction of a harassed script editor faced on the one hand with a very lengthy and detailed exposition of a complicated plotline that he can't fully understand on one reading, and on the other hand with a short, pithy idea that is irresistibly concise.

* Daleks

Don't bother to submit stories involving Daleks. Terry Nation invented the beasts, he owns the copyright, and quite properly reserves the right to write Dalek stories himself. In fact the copyright in all monsters and characters is owned by the writer who invented them. It's far better to invent your own.

* Whose Story?

This point seems almost too obvious to mention, but it's surprising how often we get storylines which are quite clearly based on previous *Doctor Who* stories, or at least elements of them. Obviously it's terribly difficult to be thoroughly original after a hundred stories, but no-one ever said that writing *Doctor Who* isn't terribly difficult.

I'm writing these notes on the assumption that most people who submit storylines are seriously interested in tackling the very tough professional job of writing for the programme.

It was not a new writer but Bidmead himself who became responsible for writing the fifth Doctor's introductory adventure when the story originally planned for that slot – *Project Zeta-Sigma* by John Flanagan and Andrew McCulloch – fell through at a late stage.

'With *Castrovalva*,' he noted in his *Doctor Who Magazine* interview, 'it was super to start off a new Doctor. It was written at short notice, because another script had fallen through and it was quite a slow burn. They weren't quite sure how Davison was going to work out, and I was asked to write the script accordingly.'

Following his departure from *Doctor Who*, Bidmead resumed his career as a freelance writer. His successor on the series' production team was Antony Root. Root, unlike Bidmead, was not himself a writer.

'I don't write,' he told Philip Newman in an interview for a 1992 issue of *The Frame*. 'I never write scripts. I suppose I'm one of those old-fashioned script editors who believes that script editors are sometimes better when they don't write, because what they're actually doing is, like a publishing editor, trying to get the best work out of other people; helping them achieve what they want to do. I know *Doctor Who* has a tradition of writer/script editors, but I was not one of those people.

'After I left university, I worked in live theatre for five years, initially as a theatre manager and then as a publicist. Then, at age 25, I decided that I didn't want to stay in live theatre any longer and got a holiday relief job for three months as an assistant floor manager with the BBC. I suppose that must have been in the summer of 1979 – and, funnily enough, the show I did was a four-part *Doctor Who* directed by Ken Grieve [*Destiny of the Daleks*]. At the end of that holiday relief period, they advertised some permanent positions. I applied, and became a fully-fledged assistant floor manager, a job I did for about eighteen months to two years I guess. After that, I started an internal training course as a script editor and subsequently went on to do programmes.

'What happened was that I went to Graeme McDonald, the person who was then Head of Series and Serials, and asked him what the opportunities were. He gave me some advice that led me to approach the TV Drama Script Unit, where I got what was called a "training attachment" as a script editor. This involved a period of time – about three months, I think – at the Script Unit, followed by a spell back in the Drama Series and Serials Department as a trainee.

'At the end of my time at the Script Unit, Chris Bidmead decided to leave *Doctor Who* and they needed someone to plug the script editor job for a limited period while they found a replacement. I arrived back with perfect timing and was asked if I would do it – which, of course, I did.'

'Root was only meant to be temporary,' explained Bidmead. 'I was getting increasingly bogged down with unsolicited scripts and he was working at the Drama Script Unit, where I used to send stuff. He knocked me out by coming back with a beautifully argued, well condensed report on one of the scripts. That was how he came to my attention.'

'Oh yes,' agreed Root. 'It was always going to be temporary. I don't think I commissioned any new work; I inherited a lot of it. I think I was around for about two stories with John Nathan-Turner.'

Root had followed *Doctor Who* since childhood, and remembered hiding behind the sofa to watch stories of the first Doctor's era. It was partly because of the series' long history that he ultimately found the process of working on it a somewhat trying one.

'It was one of the worst jobs I could imagine a script editor having to do, because the weight of history was so great that it was actually totally stultifying. I was used to working to a fairly broad brief about what one might do in a script, and I was very excited about the possibilities of doing almost any story one could envisage and shaping it within the mould of *Doctor Who*. But then, within twenty-four hours of arriving there, I was introduced to the *Doctor Who* mail, which would often come to the script editor to advise on what the reply should be. You know, you would look at fifty letters that said something like, "Sprodget No 5 in the TARDIS cannot be pressed to do the function that you think it can!" It seemed to me that the weight of history wasn't working to the show's benefit. So I approached it with great hopes but found it an extremely difficult thing to engage with.

'John Nathan-Turner had seen out Tom Baker and was seeing in Peter Davison, whom he knew extremely well from having been production associate on *All Creatures Great and Small*. I think that any difficulties were to do not with the casting but with the usual thing in TV series, like "the production starts shooting in three weeks' time – which script are we going to do?" But Barry Letts was executive producer at that time, so he was always there to turn to.

'I remember I spent a lot of time with Eric Saward on his Great Fire of London story [*The Visitation*], though I don't know that I made any real contribution to it. The other story I remember, with great affection, was written by somebody called Christopher Bailey and entitled *Kinda*. I thought that was really a very interesting script indeed, because it had shades of Buddhist philosophies as well as being quite entertaining on the surface. I have vague memories of the first one we did [*Four to Doomsday*], by Terence Dudley, and another about a cricket match set in the 1920s [*Black Orchid*], but that one was done mostly after I'd gone.

'My job at the time was basically to firefight and to make sure that there were scripts ready to achieve the production schedule that was set. It was a very, very intense time of sleepless nights – I do remember that. I felt like I'd been thrown in right at the deep end. But, as always with script editing, it was about delivering up to directors and production crews, on the day they were meant to start, material they could use that fitted the brief. And obviously I wasn't working solo, but with John Nathan-Turner on that.

'My attachment expired at the end of the *Doctor Who* period and I was told that I would have to go back to being an AFM because, after all, that was technically what I was, as far as the staffing of the BBC was concerned. I said that I didn't want to do that and that I would be leaving the BBC if that had to be – although I understood the reasons why, if it did. A couple of days went by, and then they called me in and asked if I'd like to work on *Juliet Bravo*. So I went and worked on that for a season under Joan Clark, who was the doyenne of series script editors. I then went on with the same producer, Terry Williams, to do the second series of *The Chinese Detective*. Following that, I worked for a couple of years on various things as script editor to a former *Doctor Who* producer, Philip Hinchcliffe. I finally left the BBC in 1984 to go to Euston Films, where I'd been offered a job as their script editor.'

At Euston, Root worked as script editor and script executive on a number of programmes, including a five-part gangster series called *Fear*, which he also co-produced. A few years later, he moved to a company called Working Title, where he continued to serve as a producer on such projects as *Newshounds* (a co-production with the BBC), *Lorna Doone* (a co-production with Thames) and the acclaimed Derek Jarman film *Edward II*. Today he continues to pursue a career in film and television production, having always seen script editing as simply a means to that end.

Root's successor on *Doctor Who* was Eric Saward, the writer commissioned by Bidmead to script the pseudo-historical story *The Visitation*. Born in December 1944, Saward had attended grammar school until the age of 18 and then some time afterwards moved to Holland, where he had lived for three years and been briefly married. On his return to England, he had trained and worked for a short time as an English teacher.

'I had started writing by that stage,' he recalled in a 1993 interview, 'and I decided that I didn't like teaching – in fact, the only reason I had gone into it was that there were long holidays and I could spend my time writing, which was what I really wanted to do. I had just started to sell scripts to radio on a fairly regular basis – always drama – and as I had no family commitments, I decided to have a go at being a full-time freelance writer. I had nothing to lose.

'I was about 30 then, and I always managed to stay afloat through one thing or another. I picked up the odd job. I worked in the theatre briefly as a self-taught electrician, including on *Hair* and *The Canterbury Tales* at the Phoenix in Shaftesbury Avenue. I bobbed along like that for a while, and then became involved with *Doctor Who*. Chris Bidmead approached the senior drama script editor at BBC radio and asked – quite boldly – if he could recommend anybody to write for the series. I was doing very well in radio and so, along with a few others, I was recommended. Chris rang me up and asked if I would be interested, and I said "Why not". I hadn't watched *Doctor Who* in years, so I really didn't know what I was letting myself in for.

'I wrote a storyline, *The Visitation*, which John Nathan-Turner disliked, as one of the characters was an actor – John had a thing about not showing actors on television. That was around the March of 1980, I think, and my reaction was, "Well, that's it, I'll just get on with my life". Then, around the September, Chris rang up and said, "Do you remember that storyline you wrote, that John didn't like? Would you like to do us a scene breakdown?" I was initially inclined to refuse, but Chris said that they would pay me a fee, which I think was about £400, and as I needed the money, I agreed to do it. He liked what I came up with, and I think that by that stage they really had to go with it as they needed to fill a slot in the production schedule. I delivered the full scripts about eight weeks later, in January 1981, and that's how I got started in television.'

It was shortly after this that Saward was invited to join the *Doctor Who* production team.

'I went there originally for three months. Antony Root had been working on the series, but unfortunately knew very little about putting scripts together. That's not deriding him; he was just inexperienced. Even after he had done three months on *Doctor Who*, the powers-that-be still wanted him to do something else before they would offer him a staff script editor post – this was how the BBC viewed *Doctor Who*, which in my own view was the most difficult assignment anyone could be given. So Antony went to work on *Juliet Bravo* and then on *The Chinese Detective*, where I gather that he had a really horrible time as it was written by the very distinguished Ian Kennedy Martin, and the producer, Terry Williams, didn't want his star writer to be criticised at all.

'Anyway, there was a lot of humming and hawing, and they kept extending my contract by a month at a time, as they didn't know if Antony was going to be coming back to *Doctor Who* or what was going to be happening. We had this messing around for about three months, which was really very aggravating. In the meantime, I had written *Earthshock*, which went more or less immediately into production. Eventually they decided that I would be staying, and I was then given a nine month contract.'

Like Root, Saward sometimes found himself at odds with the series' fans.

'I remember that when we killed Adric in *Earthshock*, we had just a short scene at the beginning of the next story, *Time-Flight*, where the Doctor was sort of in mourning. This brought a tremendous outcry from the fans. People were saying "Oh god, he should have been in mourning throughout the *whole* story, and the next one as well." Well no, sorry, it doesn't work like that! *Doctor Who* is about the Doctor going off and having adventures. The dramatic impact of Adric dying had been had at the end of *Earthshock*, and that was it. As in life, you move on.'

On questions of continuity, too, Saward felt that many fans were often overly pedantic, devoting their time to picking up small contradictions in the scripts rather than simply enjoying them as entertaining stories.

'You've got an audience with the fans, you see, who know infinitely more about the series than any person working on it can or perhaps even wants to. That accumulation of knowledge can get in the way of telling a good story; you're so busy trying to get the continuity right that the story goes down the tubes.'

Saward was however keen to avoid making any really major continuity errors, and so he – like Nathan-Turner – occasionally sought advice on these matters from prominent fans such as Ian Levine.

'Ian Levine did a hell of a lot of work during that time, all uncredited. I mean, all the clips that were needed for flashback sequences, he sorted them out all in his own time and without payment. He was very, very useful when it came to continuity. I turned to him lots of times, especially when we were using established things like Daleks and Cybermen. We still made loads of mistakes – for which I don't apologise, as there was never any strict continuity on the series – but we tried not to counter massively what had been previously established. So we didn't suddenly have Cybermen who could fly, for example.'

Another aspect of the script editor's job is to check and approve any changes that cast members or directors want to make to scripts during the course of production.

'You don't sit in your office like some demon king, saying "You can't do this" or "You can't do that" to directors. On the other hand, the script editor is obliged to safeguard the rights of the writers – it's in the agreement that the BBC has with the Writers' Guild. Also, he's an independent person in the sense that he's outside the production of the particular story – he's not at rehearsals all the time. Changes will come out of enthusiasm as much as anything else. I was always very strict about any changes that affected the plot, because if it hadn't made sense when it was all cut together then I was the one who was going to be hounded down the corridors by people demanding to know why I had agreed to changes that had ended up ruining it.

'A director is hired to interpret a story, not to rewrite it. In the same way, actors are booked to appear in it, not to rearrange it. If someone comes up with a brilliant line, though, then obviously it's not going to be refused. Lines will also get dropped, because action takes over or because an actor needs only an expression to convey something to the audience.'

Although vigilant about changes being made to scripts after they had been finalised and agreed with the writer, Saward found that – like Bidmead before him – he was often having to carry out a considerable amount of rewriting himself before that stage was actually reached.

'Script editors are a blessing and a curse. I worked for a long time in radio – I still do – and the fact is that, in that medium, what you write is what goes out. I mean, the director will talk to you, if he or she is a little concerned about something, but it's like in the theatre where the writer is viewed as being a little more important than in television series. I think that's a mistaken attitude on the part of television. If you've got lousy writers you've got lousy shows; that's always been so and always will be so. On shows where there is a well known writer – someone like Andrew Davies, for example – I assume that the script editor just makes the tea, because you ain't gonna be playing with his scripts without an awful lot of discussion and an awful lot of reasons why you want to change things. To my mind, that's absolutely right, and most writers will respond to that sort of treatment. I mean, if they know the thing is all right, why the hell should they change it? On a lot of shows, that works. You don't have script editors rewriting or wanting to change the scripts.

'My attitude towards script editing was that what the writer wrote ought to be, wherever possible, what was produced. But *Doctor Who* is one of those old-fashioned shows that is very difficult to write. It requires strong characterisation, strong stories, action, humour, adventure, thrills; the whole gamut. Other shows like *Casualty*, for example, simply aren't that demanding. I'm not knocking *Casualty*, but it's got a stock setting, stock characters and stock situations. The writers just have to weld on their own idea: a road accident, a schizophrenic on the run with a meat axe, or whatever. Half the work is done for them, because they are using the established elements. In *Doctor Who*, the only ongoing characters are the Doctor and the companion. The rest, the writers have to invent for themselves.

'The problem is that modern television writing makes writers very lazy. Up-and-coming writers are used on soaps like *EastEnders*, which have stock characters, and on shows like *Casualty*, which require, to my mind, a limited amount of characterisation and plotting. My experience – and I tried many, many different writers – was that a lot of them just couldn't characterise to the standard that was wanted. Their imagination wasn't developed sufficiently. I mean, imagination is not a gift one is given at birth; it's something that can be developed. The more one works at it, the stronger it becomes. And a lot of writers never have that opportunity. The reason so much rewriting went on by me and by my predecessors was that it was very hard to find people who could do it well.

'Another problem was getting writers to work within the constraints of what could be achieved on our budget. The first hour of my discussion with any writer would always be about the technical limitations: what could be done, what couldn't be done, the number of sets we could have, the number of talking parts. I mean, we would always try to do whatever the writer wanted, but I would have to say things like, "Never give a creature tentacles, because we can't manage that." There were certain things we just couldn't do, because we didn't have the money or the time. The writers had to be realistic about what could be achieved. I assume that Terrance Dicks, Douglas Adams, Christopher Bidmead and all the other script editors down the decades must have said very similar things to their writers, because it's pointless sending a writer away to write something and then finding out that it can't be done.

'I still carry the *Doctor Who* burden, because whenever I write something, I'm always careful about the number of sets I have. I'm always thinking, "Am I justifying the use of this set?" It's good training from that point of view, because one can easily go into fantasy land and have a set for this, a set for that and so on, and it'll never happen, because television just doesn't work like that.'

Saward would generally have three different types of writer in mind when planning each new season: those who had already established a good track record on the series; those who were successful in other fields but had not previously worked on *Doctor Who*; and those who were complete or relative newcomers to television.

'I never drew lines about choosing scripts – there was no prescribed mix between established writers and new ones. I would always use new talent if I could – it was a BBC policy – but at the same time I obviously wanted to go back to writers who had done good work for me in the past. Most of the time it was a case of writers coming to us with original ideas. Occasionally they would come with a thought rather than a fully worked out idea, and then it would be a matter for discussion. And as with any discussion, the original concept would often change drastically.'

A notable feature of the fifth Doctor's era was that more ultimately unused material was commissioned than during any other equivalent period of the series' history. This included the following:

Title	Writer	Commission	Date
Mark of Lumos*	Keith Miles	Storyline 1	
Mouth of Grath*	Malcolm Edwards and Le	Breakdown	18
Farer Nohan*	Andrew Stephenson	Breakdown	18
The Dogs of Darkness*	Jack Gardner	Breakdown	29
S			
Soldar and the Plastoids	John Bennett	Breakdown	10
Psychrons	Terence Greer	Breakdown 1	
Project '4G'	John Flanagan and	Breakdown	15
(aka Project Zeta-Sigma)	Andrew McCulloch	Scripts	07

The Torsan Triumvirate	Andrew Smith	Breakdown	25/11/80
Hebos	Rod Beacham	Breakdown	05/12/80
The Enemy Within	Christopher Priest	Breakdown	05/12/80
		Scripts	06/02/81
Title unknown	Tanith Lee	Scripts	06/02/81
Way Down Yonder	Lesley Elizabeth Thomas	Breakdown	23/04/81
Space-Whale (aka *Song of the Space Whale*)	Patrick Mills and John Wagner	Breakdown Scripts	07/09/81 02/12/81
Parasites (aka *The Parasites*)	Bill Lyons	Breakdown Scripts	22/09/81 16/02/82 23/04/82
*Domain***	Philip Martin	Breakdown Scripts (1) Scripts (2-4)	13/04/82 14/10/82 27/01/83
Poison	Rod Beacham	Breakdown Scripts	27/04/82 27/05/82
The Place Where All Times Meet	Colin Davis	Breakdown	10/06/82
The House That Ur-Cjak Built	Andrew Stephenson	Breakdown	10/06/82
*The Six Doctors****	Robert Holmes	Breakdown	04/08/82
May Time (aka *Man Watch*)	Christopher Bailey	Breakdown Scripts	24/08/82 16/09/82
*Ghost Planet*****	Robin Squire	Breakdown Scripts	05/01/83 20/05/83

*May have been initially envisaged for the fourth Doctor's last season.
**Ultimately reworked as *Vengeance on Varos* for Season 22.
***Ultimately scrapped in favour of *The Five Doctors*.
****May have been envisaged for the sixth Doctor's first season. Robin Squire had previously worked as uncredited assistant script editor on the third Doctor's debut season.

Other writers who had discussions with the production team during 1980 but who (judging from surviving BBC documentation) were not subsequently commissioned during the fifth Doctor's era included John Gribbin, Richard Sparks, Ian Marter (who as an actor had earlier played the Doctor's companion Harry Sullivan), James Follett, David Tebbet and Geoff Lowe (who submitted an outline entitled *Romanoids*).

'I was always looking for new writers,' notes Saward. 'The first problem was finding people who were actually prepared to do it, because – in spite of what the fans think – it wasn't considered a great privilege to work on the show. *Doctor Who* was viewed within the Department as something that just sort of happened rather than as a prestigious show worth looking at. Our budgets were awful – we always had problems with that – and, as I've said before, new writers found it very difficult to come up with the strong characters and plots that we wanted. Really what I needed was six Charles Dickenses. That would have been brilliant. But I never found them. I had Bob Holmes and I had Philip Martin, but it took me several years to get that far.'

Although he enjoyed his first year as script editor, finding it a new and exciting challenge, Saward became increasingly disaffected with the job as time went by. This was due not only to the gruelling nature of the work, but also to a widening divergence of opinion between himself and Nathan-Turner as to the direction in which the series should be moving and the manner in which it should be produced. This eventually resulted in his acrimonious and controversial departure from the production team during the era of Peter Davison's successor, Colin Baker. Since then, he has continued to pursue a career as a freelance writer, including for German radio (his scripts being translated into German for production). Of his involvement with *Doctor Who*, he is now left with distinctly mixed feelings.

'There were script editors in the building who used to come in at 10 o'clock in the morning and be gone by 12, and there was I working weekends, working evenings ... My life was just not my own. And I did five years of it. Bob Holmes had done three and a half years back in the Seventies, and he said that he didn't know how I'd managed to get to the fifth year. He was absolutely right. I was knackered. The only reason I hung on was that it was quite well paid. I mean, I enjoyed talking to the writers, I enjoyed getting things going, I enjoyed seeing the programme being made, but it was really too much for one person, in the end, with all the problems and all John's messing around. It all piled on in an unnecessary way.

'Most of the stories had massive input from me. Not out of choice, I might add, but because I had to pull the thing round. I mean, if you've got a director sitting across the hall and the scripts are still in a thousand pieces, you can't say, "Excuse me, we're waiting for the muse to strike". He's got only a few weeks to prepare for production, and he wants the scripts. You have to come up with something. I didn't enjoy doing it a lot of the time. I always feel that if you rewrite something, you don't necessarily make it better, you just make it different, you make it you, or more you. And I can't be brilliant every day of the week. No-one can, alas.

'During the years that I worked on *Doctor Who*, I could have gone up as co-author on almost every story.'

PRODUCTION DEVELOPMENT

The production of a TV drama series relies heavily on teamwork, with many different people – script editor, writers, directors, designers and actors among them – all influencing the form and content of the finished product. Probably the most influential contributor of all, however, is the producer, who has overall responsibility for the making of the series.

During the 1980s, *Doctor Who* had only one producer, John Nathan-Turner, who consequently oversaw the whole of Peter Davison's era as the Doctor. He was initially aided by one of his predecessors, Barry Letts, who had been appointed as executive producer to the series for the fourth Doctor's last season, Season 18, after acting as such on an informal basis during the previous year. However, Letts's involvement was essentially supervisory in nature – commenting on scripts, giving advice and approving major production decisions at a time when the BBC's Drama Group was undergoing a major reorganisation and the new Head of Series and Serials, David Reid, had yet to settle into his job – and it lasted until only August 1981, by which time the reorganisation was complete and it was clear that Nathan-Turner had fully grasped the reins of the series.

One of Nathan-Turner's chief concerns in planning the fifth Doctor's debut season was to retain the loyalty of *Doctor Who*'s regular audience. Davison's predecessor, Tom Baker, had remained with the series for an unprecedented seven years and built up an enormous following amongst the general viewing public, many of whom were no doubt unaware that there had ever been any other actors playing the Doctor. To recast the lead role in a long-running and popular series is always a high-risk endeavour, and Nathan-Turner felt that Baker's successor would be bound to have an uphill struggle to win the acceptance of *Doctor Who*'s many avid followers.

One way in which the producer aimed to smooth the transition from the fourth Doctor to the fifth was to arrange, in addition to the usual summer reruns (which this year comprised *Full Circle* and *The Keeper of Traken*), a season of repeats from earlier eras of the series' history, thus reminding viewers that there had indeed been other actors than Baker in the lead role. Despite the trouble and expense involved in re-negotiating rights on 'out of time' repeat material – that is, material more than three years old – the powers-that-be acceded to Nathan-Turner's request, and a season of five stories – *100,000 BC*, *The Krotons*, *Carnival of Monsters*, *The Three Doctors* and *Logopolis* – was transmitted in an early evening BBC2 slot in November and December 1981 under the banner title *The Five Faces of Doctor Who*.

Another strategy developed by Nathan-Turner with a view to maintaining regular audience loyalty was to make Season 18's last two stories – *The Keeper of Traken* by Johnny Byrne and *Logopolis* by Christopher H Bidmead – and Season 19's first – *Project Zeta-Sigma* by John Flanagan and Andrew McCulloch – a loosely-linked trilogy of adventures, in which the Doctor's old arch enemy the Master would be reintroduced in a new physical form. Even after the abandonment of *Project Zeta-Sigma* (in which the Master was to have adopted the guise of an alien scientist named Sergo), this plan was followed through with the commissioning of a replacement Master story in the form of Christopher H Bidmead's *Castrovalva*.

To provide still greater incentive for regular viewers to keep faith with the series, Nathan-Turner decided upon the introduction at the end of Season 18 of two new regulars to join the Doctor and his established companion Adric on their journeys – the theory being that these characters would quickly gain their own respective groups of fans who would want to follow their adventures and see how they coped with the new Doctor.

The first of the newcomers, Nyssa, had originally been created by Johnny Byrne as a one-off character for *The Keeper of Traken*, but Nathan-Turner had quickly decided to keep her on for a further three stories. (Even before rehearsals for *The Keeper of Traken* had begun, actress Sarah Sutton had signed a contract for an additional 12 episodes, with an option on the BBC's part for her to appear in a further 16 out of the following 20 – later reduced to 16 out of 18 after Season 19 was allocated a total of 26 episodes instead of the 28 originally planned for.)

The second new regular was Tegan, who made her debut in *Logopolis*. Created by

Nathan-Turner and Bidmead to be a more long-term companion, she was characterised as an argumentative air hostess from Australia – a country of origin chosen by the producer partly in order to break the precedent of exclusively British human companions and partly with a view to increasing the chances of gaining a co-production deal for the location filming of a story in Australia.

One consideration that Nathan-Turner had very much in mind in choosing this mix of regular characters was that it ought to give the series a very broad-based appeal. This he felt was ultimately borne out, as he told journalist David Hirsch in a 1982 interview for *Starlog*:

'The younger viewers have Adric and Nyssa to identify with. Tegan, judging by the fan mail, is very popular with some of the older boys and the dads. Peter Davison is very popular all around, but he has a huge female following. Consequently we have a line-up of people who provide something for everyone.'

There were other reasons, too, why Nathan-Turner was keen to experiment with a three-companion set-up, as he explained to Hirsch:

'I brought in three companions because I liked the original line-up of the first Doctor with the two teachers and the grand-daughter. I thought it worked very well. With four people on board the TARDIS, you can have two storylines going and you can have plenty of dialogue. Or you can have four storylines, with the regulars speaking only to non-regulars. It's a very useful device but, like everything, after a time it begins to bore. Keeping four characters on the air throughout the story can be a difficult responsibility.'

It was partly due to his concerns over the difficulty of ensuring that all three companions were given sufficient to do that Nathan-Turner originally intended to have Nyssa written out in Season 19's second story, Terence Dudley's *Four to Doomsday*. He changed his mind, however, when Davison raised strong objections to this plan. The actor, although sympathising with the producer's desire to dispense with one of the companions and thus make the TARDIS a little less crowded, was keen that the one to go should not be Nyssa, whose pleasant, refined character he considered made her the most suited of the three to accompany his Doctor. Nathan-Turner therefore decided to have Adric written out instead – an arrangement with which Davison was content – and this was achieved in the later Season 19 story *Earthshock*, written by the series' new script editor Eric Saward. Saward himself was similarly pleased to see the number of regulars reduced, as he explained in a 1982 interview with Jeremy Bentham for *Doctor Who Monthly*:

'I didn't like the set-up at all of writing for the Doctor and *three* companions, particularly when they're all together in the TARDIS; it's like doing a crowd scene! All the dialogue seems totally artificial when you consider it's mostly the Doctor who has to come up with all the information and the ideas. The companions are forced more and more to become ciphers – something I totally disapprove of – and I'm pleased that we have in fact now lost one of them. Ideally I think it could come down to just one companion, so we could then take that character and develop a full personality to him or her and not just a stereotype.'

One issue over which Davison and the production team continued to disagree was the relative merits of Nyssa and Tegan. Nathan-Turner's view, as he told *Starlog*, was that Tegan was the stronger of the two characters:

'I think Tegan's one of the most interesting companions that there's ever been. She isn't a typical *Doctor Who* girl. In the old days, they used to say that the two basic requirements of being a *Doctor Who* companion were to be able to run down corridors and to say "So what do we do next, Doctor?" with conviction. Now, here's this bossy lady who stumbled into the TARDIS, who gets irritated by the Doctor, and the Doctor gets irritated by her because she speaks her mind. Tegan, being the outsider, is representing the average viewer's point of view.'

Saward also considered Tegan to be a stronger companion than Nyssa, although he did not always see eye to eye with Nathan-Turner as regards the way her character was used, as he explained in a 1993 interview:

'Of all the companions I was involved with, I thought Tegan was the best, because she was ballsy, she had an energy. There was always a struggle with John, though, because whenever a writer gave her something strong to do, he would say, "No, she's a stupid, dumb Australian". Well, the actress is neither stupid nor dumb, the character she was playing was a strong, independent woman, and I thought it was pointless wasting her as we did. We could have developed her. She could have acquired skills under the tutelage of the Doctor. I mean, we could have taken her wherever we'd wanted.'

Having said this, Saward conceded that there had to be a balance struck between the regulars:

'With Peter Davison we had a Doctor who was a softer, younger, more vulnerable person, so if we'd built up Tegan to be a much stronger, tougher companion, that would have overwhelmed.'

Nathan-Turner explained in the introduction to his 1986 book *Doctor Who – The Companions* why he was wary of making the Doctor's companion too strong a character:

> One of the problems I discovered with companions of my own devising was that the more rounded the character, the more it required development. And development of character takes air-time and this reduces the amount of dramatisation air-time and before you know where you are, a science-fiction adventure series is taking on a soap-opera flavour. So, slowly but surely, writers and script editors *and* producers decide to play down the character development of the companion (in any case after 23 years we know comparatively little about the Doctor) and concentrate on the drama of the story.

Despite Davison's affection for Nyssa, the production team eventually decided to have her written out in the Season 20 story *Terminus*. They also decided to have introduced – in *Mawdryn Undead*, the story immediately prior to her departure – a replacement character: a young, male companion named Turlough. Interviewed by Richard Marson for a 1984 edition of *Doctor Who Magazine*, Saward explained how the creation of a new companion was approached:

'If someone wants to leave or the producer decides it's time for a change, we'll discuss a new companion. Based to a degree on the conversation I've had with John, I'll write an audition piece reflecting the character we want to end up with. Then it's up to the actor in the audition to make it his or her own.

'Turlough in his situation piece was a rather shifty, unreliable young man who at the same time was confused. He was self-centred, but he had reason to be scared. Here he was, stuck on Earth, an alien, and suddenly this hideous creature [the Black Guardian]

comes out of nowhere and orders him to kill somebody [the Doctor] in order to return to his own planet. It's going to disorientate the toughest of individuals, and we wanted to explore that through Turlough. That said, we knew he would have to settle down and become enough of a companion – friendly with the Doctor – for it to be credible, otherwise we'd have had a situation whereby Turlough spends umpteen episodes lurking about the TARDIS sharpening his knives and polishing his stun gun. The Doctor has got to buy Turlough for what he is – a rather selfish, uncertain individual who has only thrown his lot in with the Doctor to some extent. Turlough too has to accept the Doctor ultimately for what he represents.

'A lot was left to the actor, Mark Strickson, who always maintained a slight edge. Whatever he was doing and however much he had to do, he always had an air of menace. The viewer could never be quite certain. I thought he was an excellent companion.'

A return to the three-companion set-up came with the introduction of the shape-shifting android Kamelion in Season 20's final story, *The King's Demons*. This proved less than successful, however, as near-insurmountable problems arose with the robot prop that had first attracted Nathan-Turner to the idea of accommodating the character. Kamelion would thus appear in only one Season 21 story, *Planet of Fire*, and at the end of that would be written out. It was decided that Tegan and Turlough should also make their respective departures during Season 21, and that the Doctor should then go back to having just a single female companion – an arrangement that Nathan-Turner recalled having worked particularly successfully during the third Doctor's era.

Davison still felt that Nyssa was the companion best suited to his Doctor, and attempted to persuade the producer to bring her back into the series.

'I thought Nyssa worked best with the Doctor's character,' affirmed the actor in an interview with Graeme Wood, Mark Wyman and Gary Russell for a 1991 edition of *TV Zone*. 'I did tire of the abrasiveness of arguing with Tegan, getting annoyed with Adric. But Nyssa always seemed down to earth and sympathetic, fulfilling those things an assistant has to. It may be demeaning, but the companion is there to help the Doctor, to be "in this thing together" as friends. I did suggest that John consider bringing Nyssa back miraculously from the lazars' planet, but he didn't buy it.'

It was shortly after this that Davison decided to leave the series once his contract expired.

The new companion devised by Nathan-Turner, Saward and writer Peter Grimwade was Peri, an American botany student who was introduced in Grimwade's *Planet of Fire* – Davison's penultimate story.

'With Peri,' recalled Saward in his 1984 interview for *Doctor Who Magazine*, 'John decided we should have an American girl to break away from the stereotype of the English girls. We talked about her background and what she should be like and, as with Turlough, I wrote an audition piece. Nicola Bryant read for us, made the part come alive and turned out to be the most suitable … Peri is quite a strong girl. She doesn't like to be pushed around, but at the same time she's a gentler character than Tegan.'

Davison had disliked having an Australian on board the TARDIS, feeling that this was simply a misguided attempt on Nathan-Turner's part to increase the series' appeal to Australian viewers, and his initial reaction on learning that her successor was to be an American was one of great disappointment.

'There was the American girl coming in,' he recalled in a 1986 interview with Ian Atkins for *Wholook*, 'which I didn't think was an awfully good idea. I mean, the American aspect; Nicola Bryant was very good, but I didn't feel that the American aspect was a very good idea. Apart from anything else, the Americans like *Doctor Who* because it is *English*, not because it has American elements. I would like to have done more stories with Nicola. I think that if I had made the choice later, then I might well have stayed on, but as it was, I went straight into another series'.

One notable aspect of the fifth Doctor's companions that distinguished them from their predecessors was that – like the Doctor himself – the costumes they were given to wear were essentially uniforms: distinctive, highly stylised outfits that generally remained unchanged from one story to the next. This development was motivated in part by a wish to save money on the series' costume budget. A far more significant factor, however, was Nathan-Turner's desire to help keep the series in the public eye by ensuring that the regulars had recognisable, unvarying images for marketing purposes. This strategy was successful, in that these images – the Doctor in his cricketing gear, Nyssa in her aristocratic Traken garb, Tegan in her air hostess uniform, Adric in his Outler's tunic, and so on – became very familiar to the general viewing audience and often adorned the packaging and contents of spin-off merchandise produced during this period of the series' history. When Tegan and Nyssa did finally have a complete change of costume, in the Season 20 stories *Arc of Infinity* and *Snakedance* respectively, this was actually thought significant enough to be made the subject of a press photocall, and gained considerable publicity.

The same philosophy extended to other aspects of the series. The Master, for instance, generally adopted a disguise in the early stages of each story in which he appeared, whether or not there was any reason for him to do so in plot terms, as this was perceived by the production team to be an established and popular aspect of his character. To many fan critics, however, this new focus on identifiable images had the downside of damaging the series' credibility. Viewers, they argued, found it difficult to suspend their disbelief in characters who never changed their clothes; and the series also took on aspects of the fantastical superhero genre, which had been spawned in American comic books and had since entered popular culture more widely, with its easily recognisable, uniform-wearing characters such as Superman and Batman.

This development went hand in hand with *Doctor Who*'s recent adoption by Marvel Comics in their regular publication devoted to the series, which during the fifth Doctor's era was known variously as *Doctor Who – A Marvel Monthly*, *Doctor Who Monthly* and *The Official Doctor Who Magazine*. Although *Doctor Who* strip stories had been running for many years in titles such as *TV Comic* and *Countdown*, these earlier ventures had been very much a part of the long tradition of British children's comics. Marvel's strips, on the other hand, were principally influenced by the American, superhero-dominated comics genre.

There were other respects, too, in which the Davison-era stories came to resemble aspects of American comic book fare. One of these was their increasing preoccupation with the series' own internal continuity, which manifested itself in numerous continuity references; in frequent return appearances by old monsters and other characters; in 'team up' adventures like *The Five Doctors*; and in plots, such as that of *Planet of Fire*, largely devoted to writing out established regulars and introducing new ones.

This growing reliance on the reuse of popular elements from the series' history was initially discernible in the trilogy of Master stories that saw out the fourth Doctor and introduced the fifth. It was taken to a higher level, however, in *Earthshock*. The Cybermen's return appearance in this story, their first in seven years, was one of the most talked-about and popular aspects of Season 19, and generated considerable publicity – although, in order to preserve the surprise, Nathan-Turner made sure that the Cybermen's involvement was kept under wraps prior to the transmission of the first episode, even to the extent of turning down the offer of a *Radio Times* front cover photograph and article.

The success of *Earthshock* encouraged Nathan-Turner to continue the trend by reviving other popular characters in the following season. Saward would later express the view that the producer was motivated in this regard solely by a desire to appeal to the series' fans. In fact, however, the large amount of press coverage and positive comment generated by *Earthshock* had led Nathan-Turner to suspect that such an approach would be welcomed not only by the fans but also by the general viewing public; and in order to test this hypothesis he had gained agreement to the transmission of a further season of largely 'out of time' repeats under the banner heading *Doctor Who and the Monsters* (amended slightly from *Doctor Who Meets the Monsters* in his original proposal). The good ratings and positive feedback generated by these repeats – edited compilation versions of *The Curse of Peladon, Genesis of the Daleks* and *Earthshock*, transmitted on BBC1 rather than on BBC2 as *The Five Faces of Doctor Who* had been – had convinced the producer that he was on the right track.

The revival of old monsters was initially welcomed by the series' leading man, too. '*Earthshock* was my favourite story from my first season,' noted Davison in a 1983 interview with Stephen Collins for *Zerinza: The Australasian Doctor Who Fanzine*, 'and one of the reasons for this was that it featured the first old enemy I'd faced, apart from the Master. I think old enemies are good. I think that possibly in my second season there weren't quite enough, really, but that was not the fault of anybody except the people behind the standard BBC strike, which seems to come once a year, usually at Christmas time for some reason. Anyway, we were four episodes short, and they would have featured old enemies. I think it's nice to have old enemies back.'

The strike-hit four-parter to which Davison referred was Saward's *The Return*, featuring the Daleks, which was to have been transmitted after *The King's Demons* as the closing story of Season 20. Despite its temporary loss (it would eventually appear in slightly revised form as *Resurrection of the Daleks* in Season 21), Season 20 still drew much more heavily on established *Doctor Who* continuity than had Season 19, making Davison's expression of disappointment seem somewhat surprising. Indeed, there was at least one element from the Doctor's past in every story – a fact that, after it was pointed out to him by fan Ian Levine, Nathan-Turner used as part of his promotion of the series in its 20th anniversary year. The special anniversary story, *The Five Doctors*, itself afforded still further evidence of the series' increasing reliance on its own mythos to provide the inspiration and substance for new stories.

'We drew on the series' past far too much,' reflected Saward in 1993. 'Again it was a case of John wanting to appeal to the fans. I think *Doctor Who* works best when the production team are going for it and inventing their own things. To my mind, the best period of the series' history was in the mid-Seventies when Philip Hinchcliffe and Bob Holmes were in charge. Bob Holmes was the best writer the series ever had, and when he was script editor he – like many others before him and after him – rewrote a lot of the stories. He made them very Bob Holmes, and because he was very confident and very strong, the scripts were very confident and very strong and very inventive. He had

537

in Philip Hinchcliffe a producer who was new to the job and who would go for it; he would be down in the visual effects workshop, for example, trying to get them to do the best they possibly could. He was doing the producer's job, which is to support the script. He had in Tom Baker an excellent Doctor, and he had in Lis Sladen and Louise Jameson two interesting companions, in their very different ways.

'Hinchcliffe and Holmes still used old monsters like the Cybermen and the Daleks, but they also brought a lot of new things to the series themselves. We didn't do that when I was script editor, and I always felt that was a tremendous drawback. We weren't adding to it, we were just living off it. It's always better to invent your own things. That's not just an ego trip; you often do better when you invent your own instead of using somebody else's. Writers shouldn't be told, "I want you to do this, this, this, this and this". They'll say, "No, I'm not interested." They should be given as much freedom as possible. What Peter Grimwade got lumbered with on that awful story *Planet of Fire*, for instance, was utterly lunatic. I mean, I felt embarrassed. Turlough leaving, Peri joining, the Master, Kamelion, the Lanzarote location – it was ridiculous.'

Davison, although more restrained in his comments than Saward, has also in later interviews expressed the view that the series came to rely rather too heavily on its past successes. Despite any doubts that there might have been from these quarters, however, Season 21 saw a continuation of the policy of bringing back old monsters – in particular in *Warriors of the Deep*, which featured both the Silurians and the Sea Devils, and in *Resurrection of the Daleks*, the Dalek story postponed from Season 20.

Notwithstanding Saward's contention that little of substance was added to the series' mythos during his tenure as script editor, the frequent reuse of old characters and concepts in fact gave rise to many new continuity developments. In addition, most of the returning monsters – including the Cybermen, the Silurians and the Sea Devils – appeared in redesigned form. Although many fan critics would later express the view that the new designs were generally somewhat less effective than the originals, these changes were initiated by Nathan-Turner as part of a conscious policy of giving the series a more glossy, expensive and up-to-date look. The phenomenally popular cinema film *Star Wars* had dramatically increased the public's expectations of science fiction in the media, and the producer was keen to counter the commonly-held perception of *Doctor Who* as a cheap series with relatively low production values and substandard visual effects. (The aforementioned reduction of Season 19 from 28 episodes to 26 was made at his request, as he considered that the budget allocated to it was insufficient to support the extra two episodes without sacrificing production quality.)

'Looking back to the time I worked on the series,' commented Saward's predecessor Antony Root in an interview with Philip Newman for a 1992 issue of *The Frame*, 'there was then – and frankly it's still to be resolved – a crisis about what you could actually do with television science fiction post-*Star Wars*. On *Doctor Who*, you used to be able to get away with an exploding wall and a weird monster, but once you'd had the cinema, with its massive special effects pictures, showing people what could be achieved, you had to find something else for the show to do, some other way in.'

Nathan-Turner was expert in budgetary matters – he had been production unit manager, responsible for managing *Doctor Who*'s resources, prior to his appointment as producer – and made it a top priority to ensure that the limited money available to the series was spent in ways that would be readily apparent on screen. This was a policy on which he expounded in his 1982 interview for *Starlog*:

'I removed a lot of the location work, which is very expensive. In a way, it's very restricting, because we try to do it within 25 miles of London, which nearly always *looks* like it's within 25 miles of London! For *Time-Flight*, we had a studio landscape created, which looked absolutely marvellous. Totally alien. Had we more money, I guess we would have gone on location. When you remove the location work, it does put a bit more money at your disposal for things that count. Actors count, designs, costumes, make-up and visual effects. My motto is, "Spend the money where it shows". If it doesn't show, let's stop spending it.'

As one aspect of this policy, Nathan-Turner decided that any major location shoots done for the series should generally be in countries other than Britain, which would automatically tend to give the finished product a more expensive look. Thus trips were made to Amsterdam for *Arc of Infinity* and to Lanzarote for *Planet of Fire*; and both stories featured extensive sequences showing off their respective locations, to guarantee that full value was gained from the money spent.

Another manifestation of the producer's policy was the frequent casting of popular television celebrities in guest star roles, ensuring that the budget allocated to hiring actors had maximum on-screen impact. Amongst the many examples here were Stratford Johns (best known for his work in *Z Cars*) in *Four to Doomsday*; Nerys Hughes (*The Liver Birds*) in *Kinda*; Michael Robbins (*On the Buses*) in *The Visitation*; Beryl Reid (distinguished actress and comedienne) in *Earthshock*; Liza Goddard (*Take Three Girls*) in *Terminus*; and Rodney Bewes (*The Likely Lads*), Rula Lenska (*Rock Follies*) and Chloe Ashcroft (*Play School*) in *Resurrection of the Daleks*.

Nathan-Turner's hopes were certainly borne out as far as press coverage was concerned, as both the overseas location shoots and the celebrity guest stars gained considerable publicity for *Doctor Who*. Again, however, many fan commentators had reservations, feeling that the use of overseas locations was unwarranted by the plots of the stories in question, which consequently had to be adjusted to fit around them, and that the inclusion of familiar television personalities made it even more difficult for viewers to achieve the all-important suspension of disbelief.

Nathan-Turner, in response to the latter criticism, pointed out that the celebrity guest stars, although admittedly best known in many cases for their comedy or light entertainment work, were in fact jobbing actors who had previously played a wide variety of different roles, not only on television but also in radio, theatre and – in some cases – film. He likened *Doctor Who* to *The Morecambe and Wise Show*, in the sense that many distinguished performers were delighted to be asked to appear in it, and prided himself on taking a bold approach to this aspect of his job rather than resorting to type-casting, as was more commonly the case in British television. The critics, however, remained concerned that a higher priority was being placed on achieving a slick, expensive-looking production than on telling well-plotted, convincing stories, and that content was thus being sacrificed in favour of style.

Nathan-Turner was in fact unusual amongst *Doctor Who*'s producers in that he had never been an editor or a writer of scripts and had few aspirations in that direction – a recognition, as he candidly admitted in interviews, of his own limitations. He consequently played rather less emphatic a part than had some of his predecessors in defining the overall dramatic style of the series in story as opposed to production terms, and was more reliant on his script editors to take the initiative in this regard. He did, on the other hand, have strong views about certain aspects of the series' scripting. One example of this was his determination to ensure that humour was used only very sparingly; a point on which he was somewhat at odds with Davison.

'I wanted more humour,' affirmed the actor in an interview with Terry and Andy Kerr for a 1985 edition of *Skonnos*. 'John cut the humour for my first two seasons. You see, prior to that, we'd had quite a lot of humour in Tom Baker's time, and I don't think John quite liked it. Occasionally I'd find the early drafts of scripts, which had a bit more humour in them, and I'd say to John, "I quite like this," and show it to him at the producer's run. Sometimes we'd keep those bits, and sometimes we wouldn't. More often, though, I wouldn't see those earlier drafts.

'I remember watching one of Tom's stories, where the Doctor was about to be executed, and he was laughing and joking and offering everyone jelly babies. I think Tom, Douglas Adams and Graham Williams got together to create this image. I don't think Tom and John saw eye-to-eye about humour.'

When Davison decided to leave the series after his third season in the role, Nathan-Turner again became concerned with the question of retaining audience loyalty over the change of Doctors. The series had done well in the twice weekly weekday evening slot that it had occupied for the past three years, winning very respectable ratings (although more so for Season 19 than for Seasons 20 and 21), and he was keen to ensure that these viewers – many of whom he suspected were fans of Davison from his years in *All Creatures Great and Small* – were given every possible encouragement to 'stay tuned' (a favourite expression of his) for the sixth Doctor's era.

One way in which the producer approached this problem was to introduce, just before the change of Doctors, a new companion character, Peri, who he hoped would help to bridge the gap between the two eras – repeating the tactic he had adopted on the previous occasion with the introduction of Nyssa and Tegan. This time, however, he decided to go one stage further by bringing in the new Doctor himself for the final story of Season 21, thus giving viewers a chance to get acquainted with the newcomer before the series went off the air for its between-seasons break. Thus, in a departure from recent precedent, Davison would make his exit in the penultimate story of the season rather than in the last.

'That was John's idea,' confirmed Saward in 1993. 'He always felt that he wanted to leave the audience with a taste of what was to come. I thought he was worrying unnecessarily, to be honest, because *Doctor Who* is engraved in everyone's minds, and who's playing the lead won't be the reason why people will tune in; they'll tune in because they enjoy *Doctor Who*, or they have memories of it, or they're getting their kids to watch it or something.'

Davison's last story, *The Caves of Androzani*, marked the return to *Doctor Who* of Robert Holmes, Nathan-Turner having been persuaded by Saward to make a rare exception to his long-established policy of using writers and directors new to the series rather than bringing back those who had worked on it during earlier eras of its history. The result was a story considered by many to be the finest of all those in which Davison appeared. The high production values pursued by Nathan-Turner and the strong scripting sought by Saward came together and complemented each other perhaps more successfully than at any other time during the previous three years, ensuring that the fifth Doctor bowed out in considerable style.

FROM SCRIPT TO SCREEN: THE FIVE DOCTORS

Introduction

In many ways, *The Five Doctors* was a typical story of its era, involving location filming as well as studio recording and a large number of complex visual effects sequences to realise. In other ways, it was atypical as, being conceived as a celebration of *Doctor Who*'s 20th anniversary, it had constraints and requirements that other stories did not.

For our view of the production we have turned primarily to director Peter Moffatt and to visual effects designer John Brace, who recall, scene by scene, the work that went into it. We have also incorporated comments from other participants: the producer, John Nathan-Turner; the writer, Terrance Dicks; the designer, Malcolm Thornton; the costume designer, Colin Lavers; the composer, Peter Howell; the sound effects designer, Dick Mills; and some of the cast. The primary source for much of this supporting interview material is a publication edited and published by David J Howe for the *Doctor Who* Appreciation Society in 1984, which looked in detail at the making of this story. We are grateful to Jan Vincent-Rudzki, who conducted the original interviews with Malcolm Thornton and Colin Lavers, for allowing us to reproduce his work here. Thanks also to Patricia Holmes, wife of the late Robert Holmes, for allowing us to reproduce her husband's original synopses for the story.

The Scripts

The idea of a story celebrating *Doctor Who*'s 20th anniversary originated with the series' producer, John Nathan-Turner. He started thinking about this as early as July 1981, and on 3 August that year sent to David Reid, the Head of Series and Serials, the following memo:

> Further to our conversation of the other week, I should like to request that *next* year's *Doctor Who* season transmits in the Autumn of 1982.
>
> We must get back to an autumn transmission in readiness for the 20th anniversary programme in November 1983. (The 10th anniversary programme in 1973 starred all the actors who had played the Doctor up until then (William Hartnell, Patrick Troughton, Jon Pertwee), and if I am still producing the show in 1983, I would like to do something really spectacular!!)
>
> As I have had to release Peter Davison for eight weeks during the current season's production period, it became impossible to transmit this season till Week 1 1982. (In any case Controller of BBC1 did not want *Doctor Who* and *Sink or Swim* to transmit at the same time.) The result of the above is that currently *Doctor Who* is *off the air* for nine months as opposed to the usual six months. As you know, interest has been retained in the programme, as we have a *new* Doctor, in August of this year there are two four-parter repeats on BBC1 and in November of this year a season of repeats – *The Five Faces of Doctor Who* (five four-parters) on BBC2.
>
> I would suggest we capitalise quickly on the anticipated popularity of Peter Davison's Doctor, and have only a six month break between seasons next time.

I am sure I can transmit next year's season from Week 36 1982, *even* if the programme remains bi-weekly – *provided* I do not release Peter Davison for *Sink or Swim* during *Doctor Who*'s production period. *Sink or Swim* could then go into production after my final recording and *still* transmit in Week 1, if required.

To simplify, I suggest next year *Doctor Who* transmits in the autumn, and *Sink or Swim, if required*, in the winter. I do hope this can be achieved, as it would be most beneficial to the programme and its future.

Nathan-Turner's idea was that a celebratory story could be transmitted on the anniversary and within the planned structure of the regular season (something that would happen in 1988 with *Silver Nemesis* for the 25th anniversary).

After discussions with Alan Hart, David Reid replied on 25 August as follows:

Controller of BBC1 is not prepared to change *Doctor Who* transmission to the autumn of 1982. He will think again about 1983 but is not prepared to put undue pressure on Comedy for the release of Peter Davison. He is concerned that *Sink or Swim* might finish up being off the air for too long.

Alan has, however, suggested that he would be interested in, perhaps, a 90 minute special to coincide with the anniversary in November 1983 to trail the series in the winter. This is not a silly thought and perhaps we might discuss it.

As plans for the special developed, Nathan-Turner and script editor Eric Saward decided that they wanted a production that would feature all five of the television Doctors to date, as well as numerous companions and monsters. One early problem was how best to get around the fact that William Hartnell, the first Doctor, had died in 1975. It was felt that the best option was to cast another actor to play the part. In July 1982, a check was made on the last BBC fee paid to actor Geoffrey Bayldon, who had appeared in the 1979 *Doctor Who* story *The Creature from the Pit* and who was considered by many fans and professionals to be an ideal choice for a new Doctor.

To write the anniversary story, Saward and Nathan-Turner had little hesitation in approaching writer Robert Holmes. Holmes had script edited *Doctor Who* for three and a half years during the Tom Baker era, and had seen several of his own scripts for the series reach fruition, the first being *The Krotons* back in 1968.

Holmes was approached, and, despite many misgivings, agreed to have a think and see what he could come up with. In an undated letter to the production office, he outlined three possible scenarios, one in great detail and the other two only sketchily. The entire content of his five-page note was as follows:

The main problem we face is to find a satisfactory and plausible explanation for all the Doctors, plus companions, appearing at the same point in the space-time continuum. I feel that this – dramatically – is what our audience will expect. However, the clash of mighty egos has been mentioned and it is possible for them to appear in the same story without appearing together.

The purpose of this discussion document is to survey the various options open to us.

1) The planet Maladoom. Doctor Will and companion striding across a misty landscape. They've obviously just arrived as he is pointing out various botanical features and making deductions about the nature of the planet.

We pull back to see that the Doctor is being watched on video. Voices of unseen watchers comment admiringly – 'Really remarkably lifelike,' etc. – (Eventually, about an hour from now, we shall learn that Doctor Will and Carol Ann are cyborgs, created by cyber-technology. This will explain why the Doctor is not quite as we remember Hartnell.)

Tardis. The Doctor helpless at the controls. Tells Tegan the machine is being drawn into a time vortex. It could mean destruction. Maybe we do some clever mirror-work and show more than one police box whirling down this sudden fissure in the ordered universe.

Maladoom. The Doctor and Tegan arrive. He is now very angry. Some irresponsible idiot must be interfering with the delicately balanced polarity of time and matter. Incredibly dangerous lunacy that could create chaos. Must put a stop to it.

Now, one by one, the other Doctors arrive with their companions. All have approximately the same reactions – although Doctor Tom may speculate that some other race has discovered the power previously known only to Time Lords. But, anyway, all go off to put a stop to it.

The Doctor and Tegan are heading across rough terrain towards a pulsing light that seems to be coming from inside a distant, craggy hill. In the shadow of a low cliff they see, apparently inset into the rockface, a rectangular panel of some shiny black substance. As they examine this curiously, concealed jets puff out vapour. They collapse unconscious. Then the panel begins to open.

One by one the other Doctors are inveigled into other automated traps.

Cryogenic chamber. The Doctors and companions lie unconscious. The Master comes in for a gloat. At last he has all the time entities that comprise the total Doctor at his mercy. If he turns the freezer down a few more degrees he will achieve final triumph over his oldest adversary. So why doesn't he? Probably because he daren't, at this stage, upset his allies, the Cybermen.

Doctor Pat is carried off to the operating theatre. The Cybermen prepare for surgery. An injection revives the patient for preliminary tests. The Cybermen intend to find the organic mechanism that separates Time Lords from other species. When they find it they will separate it and implant it into their familiar cybernetic machinery, thus turning themselves into Cyberlords.

This aspect of the plot is brought out in conversation between the Master, Doctor Pat and the top Cyberman.

As the operation begins the Doctor goes into terminal collapse. Resuscitation procedures fail. The patient is pronounced extinct. The Cybermen aren't too concerned; they expect to lose a few Doctors before discovering the vital organ. That is why, with the Master's help, they have drawn all the manifestations of the Doctor's form from their various time loops.

Doctor Pat is returned to the cryogenic chamber where he recovers from his self-willed cataleptic state. Fighting against the numbing cold, he disconnects the freezer panels. As the temperature rises the Doctors slowly begin to stir.

In the operating theatre the Cybermen are reviewing their techniques before investing in another patient.

In the cryogenic chamber total bafflement at finding themselves all together. An impossible situation which they resolve by deciding they are trapped in a temporal paradox created by the Master.

The Cybermen come to collect Doctor Jon. Docs and companions take them by surprise and effect an escape.

Film. Trial by ordeal. Cybermen hunting Doctors who are all intent now on their original objective – restoring the time-space continuum to its natural order before permanent damage is done to the universe. And to this end they are heading for the shining hill.

Doctor Will – the fake cyborg – tries to lead them into an ambush. But at the last moment he is spotted as a phoney. He bounces down a cliff and all his springs fall out. Carol Ann, too, is shown to be a cyborg. This is tough on Frazer because he was getting to like her.

They struggle on and finally reach the shining hill. Its core is a mass of technology linked to the Master's Tardis, the effect of which is to raise its power a thousandfold. Projected through the space-time continuum this enormous force has created a time vacuum into which all Time Travellers (principally our Doctors) were inevitably drawn.

The trouble is that it is now feeding upon itself, like a nuclear reactor running out of control, and in a very short while the whole of this part of the universe will implode into a black hole. Unless they can slow the whirligig down and stabilise matters.

We've all been through this one before. The Master will, of course, turn up to provide some last-moment impediment. But, in the end, the Doctors get the machinery into phase before it goes critical. As it slows they, together with appropriate companions, disappear back into their own sectors of time – the relative dimensions effect.

The Doctor and Tegan are alone at the end.

The sharp-eyed reader will ask what happened to the Cybermen. Well, we won't have that many to start with. Some will be blown up when the Doctors escape because, before departing, they sabotage the operating theatre. Others will be disposed of variously – buried under rock falls, sunk in swamps, pushed off cliffs and so on – during the film chase.

* * * * * * * * * * * * * * * * *

2) The other option. Much the same general shape of story but we open with the present Doctor and stay with him until the operating theatre scene.

The effect of the Cybermen tampering with his metabolism, however, is that he starts to regress through his various phases – i.e. turns first into Doctor Tom, then into Doctor Jon and so on.

While doing this, of course, he is also escaping, combating the Cybermen and trying to reach the shining hill. When he reaches his Doctor Will incarnation he knows he is on his last legs. If he doesn't make it before his time runs out, he will be finally dead.

(This, too, offers a possible explanation as to why he doesn't exactly resemble the real Hartnell.)

The attraction of this shape is that it would allow us to have all the Doctors in the story without having them meet up. Its difficulty is in finding a convincing reason for Tegan also to slip back through various companion incarnations. Maybe mental projection? In each of his forms he would see the companion he had at that time?

****

3) We might use the Tardis as a kind of tuning fork. We postulate that within its structure lie the echoes or 'vibes' of all who have ever been aboard. Given the right technology, therefore, it is possible to recreate any or all of the former Doctors and hold them in corporeal form as long as the energy supply lasts.

The present Doctor – perhaps finding himself out of action – might be compelled to activate this 'memory function' in order to seek help from his predecessors.

This could be a battle of wits between the Doctors and the exhausted old computer at the heart of a starship that has been drifting for twenty million years. But I see no Cybermen in it.

The substance of these ideas is of interest as, although Holmes was ultimately not to use them for the anniversary story, the suggestion of an alien race trying to find the organic basis for the Time Lords' power was later used by him in his 1985 sixth Doctor story *The Two Doctors*.

On 4 August 1982, Holmes was formally commissioned to provide a scene breakdown for the 90-minute special, now with the working title of *The Six Doctors*, reflecting the idea that the version of the first Doctor in the storyline was a fake.

Because Holmes was very unsure as to whether or not he would be able to come up with a workable scene breakdown by the delivery date of 23 August, Saward and Nathan-Turner decided to ask another writer to 'stand by' in the event of Holmes being unable to resolve the logistical problems presented by the story. This was Terrance Dicks, another ex-*Doctor Who* script editor with numerous stories to his name.

On 24 August, Saward wrote to Holmes thanking him for keeping the office advised of progress on the breakdown, and requesting that he provide the document a day before their forthcoming meeting on 1 September to give himself and Nathan-Turner a

FIFTH DOCTOR

chance to digest the work so far. On the same day, Saward wrote to Dicks, apologising for the delay and stating that they would be making a final decision on the story once they had seen Holmes' work. Following the meeting with Holmes, Saward again wrote to Dicks, on 2 September, saying that Holmes had decided to try and write the first 20 minutes of the script, despite the fact that he had huge reservations about whether or not he could make it work.

Ultimately, Holmes delivered his scene breakdown on 13 October, and on 18 October, Terrance Dicks was commissioned to provide a scene breakdown as well. Holmes' version was subsequently dropped. Following delivery of Dicks' breakdown on 1 November, at which point the story had been renamed *The Five Doctors*, Dicks was commissioned on 16 November to write the script, which was formally delivered on 20 December and accepted on 27 January 1983.

'I knew from the beginning that the job was going to be appallingly difficult and complicated and full of the most enormous hassles, as indeed it was,' said Dicks. 'Since I was prepared for that, nothing actually threw me. I knew it was going to be like jumping into a combine harvester from the very beginning.'

Dicks was presented with the same set of guidelines that Holmes had been working to. 'My standing joke about it was that it was like that game where you make up a story about objects that come out of a box. This particular box had an awful lot of objects in it!

'First of all, you knew it had to be *all* the Doctors – they had already come up with the idea of having Richard Hurndall as the look-alike first Doctor – and *some* of the monsters – they already knew that they wanted the Cybermen as the lead monster, and as well as the Cybermen, there had to be other villains and other monsters. It wasn't all one way – obviously they wanted my ideas as well. At first they weren't too keen on having Daleks in, but I told them that they'd *got* to have Daleks, even if it's only one Dalek. They weren't too happy about having K-9 either, but eventually they agreed and said he could put his head around the door.

'There was the problem of the companions – who was going to be in it and who wasn't. Some they were sure of, like the Brigadier, Susan and Sarah, but others kept changing. One of the things that kept happening was that they would ring up and say, "Have you written so-and-so in?" I'd say that I had, and they would reply, "Well, write him out again, he can't do it. You can have such-and-such." There was a lot of to-ing and fro-ing with the companions. In fact, it wasn't absolutely set who were going to be the "cameo companions" until almost the last moment. Those bits where they pop up in the corridors on the way to the tomb were almost the last things to be put in the script. They had to be done very simply, because by that time the budget had nearly been used up. The brief was complicated enough, and I still needed a story.

'The problem was to put all these elements together to make some kind of sense. They didn't want a pantomime, they wanted a story that would stand on its own even if it wasn't the 20th anniversary special. The main problem was coming up with a plot to pull all these elements together. It all began to come together for me when I came up with the idea of the game. Almost before anything else, I had this picture in my mind of a black gloved hand picking up this little figure and putting it on a board. Thinking of it as a kind of chess game gave it a basic shape. But this game was against the people on the board. The Player just sat and watched what they did. Then there was the question of who was the Player? The first thought I had was that it was the Master but, quite rightly, Eric Saward said that was too obvious; it would be an anticlimax. You have, however, got to come up with some type of surprise villain as the sting in the tail. If you are going to do that, then it's got to be someone significant, it can't be the third Time Lord on the left. The only candidate was Borusa.

'This happens very often in story writing; things just fall into place. Of course it's got to be Borusa, who else can it be? The thing about Borusa turning into a villain was that you didn't have a saintly character who suddenly went all bad. Borusa had always been a politician and an autocrat, someone who was prepared to be ruthless. I felt that you could believe that he could take that one stage further and say: "Well, I'm the one who knows what's good for everybody; it would therefore be much better for Gallifrey if I were in charge forever!" So you just have to take the existing characteristics and push them a bit further over the edge into madness. It's very difficult stuff to play. I think Philip Latham did extraordinarily well.

'So that was the structure: it was Borusa manipulating the five Doctors in some way, kidnapping them out of time. That became the overall idea, which is the hardest bit. After that, it's just a question of working it all out.'

In the final draft of the rehearsal script, dated 25 January 1983, Dicks had included a scene involving the third Doctor and Sarah encountering several Auton mannequins in a ruined high street. The copyright clearance for this had been checked by the BBC on 14 December 1982, but ultimately the Autons were dropped, and on 11 February 1983, a sequence already in the script, where the second Doctor and the Brigadier were attacked by an underground monster in the caves, was altered to change the attacking creature into a Yeti.

'There just wasn't time to do it,' explained Dicks about the Auton sequence. 'What all that came down to was Sarah going over the cliff, which was a lot simpler.'

There were other aspects of the script and action that were refined as the director mapped out the various practicalities, and these are mentioned as we go through the televised story later in this chapter.

One of the most distinctive and memorable images from the production is the central tower to which all the Doctors are trying to get. Dicks included it specifically as a symbol of evil. 'This is the central citadel of evil; like in *Lord of the Rings*, where Frodo's going with the ring to the tower where the Dark Lord lives. There's also a poem by Browning, called *Childe Roland to the Dark Tower Came*. It's like a little fragment of a non-existent narrative poem. It describes the knight riding up to the old dark castle. There's a horn hanging outside it, and he raises it to his lips and blows. That's all that happens, and I think it was in my mind as an image. After that, I worked Rassilon into it. Again, it had to be Rassilon who was going to resolve it. There was a time when I wasn't sure whether it was going to be a good Rassilon or a bad Rassilon; I trailed that maybe Rassilon had been a monster of evil and that the Time Lords had covered it all up, which was quite fun, as that seemed to be a very Time Lord thing to do – a Bob Holmes type Time Lord thing to do. I quite liked the idea that the Time Lords had some very shabby episodes in their own history that they were ashamed of and hushed up.'

Casting

Whereas normally the casting of a *Doctor Who* story would be carried out by the director in collaboration with the producer, in this instance, many of the parts were returning characters from *Doctor Who*'s history, and therefore the question wasn't so much who could play them, as whether or not the required actors were available.

The first problem tackled by the production team was someone to play the first Doctor. This was resolved when John Nathan-Turner remembered an actor called Richard Hurndall. 'I was asked to play the first Doctor,' recalled Hurndall in 1983, 'because John Nathan-Turner saw me as Nebrox in *Blake's 7* and thought I looked very like William Hartnell.

'I remembered William's approach to the part very well, and decided it would be stupid to try and "mimic" him, so I hope I split the difference between his performance – his personality – and mine.'

'He was marvellous,' opined Nathan-Turner. 'I did offer him tapes of Bill Hartnell to look at, but as he did remember Bill, he decided that rather than view the tapes and try to do a "Mike Yarwood" on it, it would be better if he just went for his instinct.'

Peter Moffatt had asked Hurndall to suggest Hartnell's portrayal of the first Doctor with some of his mannerisms, such as holding his lapels and using his vocal 'Hm? hm?' and then gradually moulding this to his own interpretation. 'I really believe he gave us a beautiful performance and one accepted him on his own merits,' said Moffatt. 'I know he was very nervous of the undertaking, as the other Doctors had only to drop back into their old performances, whereas he, as a newcomer, had to create his, and then not in his own mould but in that created by a very celebrated and much loved actor who had made an enormous impression on the public twenty years ago. However, he really did a wonderful job and succeeded in conveying a vivid impression of Bill and making the part his own at the same time.'

Hurndall agreed to play the first Doctor on 6 October 1982. William Hartnell's original costume was not held by the BBC (it had been hired from the theatrical costumier's Bermans and Nathans) and so a new one had to be created for Hurndall. In designing this, Colin Lavers went by photographs in a magazine published in 1973 by the *Radio Times* to celebrate *Doctor Who*'s tenth anniversary. The original outfit had featured a morning coat, for which it was fairly easy to find a substitute, but the original waistcoat had been an authentic Victorian one, so a look-alike was made. The script emphasised the age of the first Doctor, so Lavers used mittens to make him appear older and slightly feeble. The mittens also hid the fact that he wasn't wearing the first Doctor's blue ring, as it was felt that the colour would be too noticeable. There was also a photograph in the magazine of William Hartnell in a hat and scarf, but Lavers considered that the scarf was by this point associated firmly with the fourth Doctor and the hat with the fifth, so those two items were not re-introduced.

Because Nathan-Turner wanted to have something of the original first Doctor in the story somewhere, he decided to use a clip from *Flashpoint*, the final episode of *The Dalek Invasion of Earth*, as a pre-title sequence trailer.

Patrick Troughton, playing the second Doctor, presented Nathan-Turner with a problem of scheduling. Troughton was working on *Foxy Lady* for Granada television during the original proposed location filming dates for the story in April, and so Nathan-Turner, recognising that the inclusion of the other Doctors, and for them to be played by the original actors, was essential to the production, moved the dates forward to March to ensure that Troughton would be available to appear.

Most of Troughton's scenes in the draft script were on location, and Colin Lavers was keen to develop a costume that would keep the actor warm. The fur coat used in *The Abominable Snowmen* was suggested, but the original could not be used as it was made of real fur, and to have two of them (to allow for the possibility of one getting damaged during filming) would be very expensive, so two close substitutes were used instead.

The trousers worn by the second Doctor originally featured a large, inch-square check pattern. The BBC was in the early Eighties trying to establish a new picture clarity for Direct Broadcast Satellites, and some striped and checked materials had become unsuitable for use. Bearing this in mind, Lavers opted for a light plaid pattern for the trousers.

Jon Pertwee's third Doctor was less of a problem, as the actor was available on the required dates and happy to reprise his role. His costume was a variation on that worn by the actor for a photocall to publicise *The Three Doctors* back in 1973.

Tom Baker, playing the fourth Doctor, presented by far the greatest challenge to the production team.

'I think I first approached Tom in April 1982,' recalled John Nathan-Turner. 'Initially he said that he was interested but would like to see a script. Then our first writer fell through, which meant that we didn't have a script within three months as we had hoped, and the time was going on. Eventually, in the December, we were filming *The King's Demons* somewhere down south, and I knew that Tom was appearing at the Theatre Royal in Brighton, and so I sent him the first seventy pages of the script, which was all we had. I met him after one of his shows to talk about it, and at that time he had agreed to do it. We were then able to contact Terrance and tell him that Tom was to be included. Within about ten days or so, he pulled out and changed his mind.

'That was an extremely big hurdle to overcome, because we were saying up front that it's the *five* Doctors, and really it was four and a bit, and one of those was a re-cast, so suddenly it started to look as though it was falling round my ears.'

In order to ensure that the fourth Doctor was represented in the show, Nathan-Turner had the idea of incorporating into the narrative some scenes from the *Doctor Who* story *Shada*, which had been partially completed in 1979 before industrial action at the BBC forced it to be cancelled incomplete. To this end, on 10 January 1983 he wrote to both Tom Baker and Lalla Ward, who played his assistant Romana in the story, requesting permission to use clips from the cancelled story. Both artistes agreed.

'I knew this sort of thing was going to happen, but I don't think that even I was prepared for that!' exclaimed Terrance Dicks. 'At the start, I asked Eric if they were *sure* that they'd got all the Doctors, and he said they were. But apparently there was some kind of confusion between Tom and Tom's agent and the BBC. Tom believed that he hadn't committed himself and the BBC genuinely felt that he had, and it was passed on to me that Tom was definitely going to be in it. I had in fact just completed my first draft, with Tom playing a major role, and the phone rang – this was happening every day, it was like a hotline to the *Doctor Who* office. It was Eric again. He asked how I was getting on, and I told him proudly that I'd just finished the first draft and it was all ready to go to the typists. He said, "Oh my god!" – not the reaction I'd been expecting. I asked him what had happened now. He said, "You know what we said about Tom ..." He explained about this confusion and was very apologetic. I had no choice but to go back to square one again.

'Tom in fact was going to steal the Master's transportation device and go back to Gallifrey, Davison was going to go to the tower and work his way in through the front entrance, and Hurndall was probably going to stay in the TARDIS with Turlough and Susan – all three would arrive with the TARDIS. There was also a sub-plot so you might feel that Tom was the villain or maybe he was going to ally himself with the villain. I felt that the Tom Baker Doctor was the one that you could believe would go bad, he has a darker side to him. Eric told me about the footage from *Shada*, the sequence in the punt, and so I came up with the idea that we could see Tom kidnapped. But that was all we could do with him – we couldn't have him in the story. Once again, it all fell into place. The obvious thing was to have his kidnap bungled. The equipment was ancient and Borusa wasn't all that good at it anyway. So, we had the fourth Doctor trapped in a time warp. This gave me another menace, with the Baker Doctor being like a hole in the dyke. There was a danger that the Davison Doctor, followed by all the other Doctors, would be sucked in, giving a sense of urgency. If the Doctors didn't solve the problem by a given time, they would disappear together.

'My feeling is that it all worked better the way it ended up. Five Doctors were just too many to handle, but four worked very neatly, and you do at least *see* Tom. The other thing that I found quite amazing was how well the scenes from *Shada* fitted in. I'll swear that if you didn't know, you would think it was written for the special.'

With all the Doctors covered, the remaining problem was the companions. Nathan-Turner was keen to include one companion per Doctor, and the original idea was to team Susan with the first Doctor, Victoria with the second, Jo Grant with the third and Sarah with the fourth. However, despite agreeing to take part quite late in the day, Deborah Watling then had to drop out from playing Victoria as the location filming dates clashed with another commitment, on *The Dave Allen Show* (which was subsequently hit by a strike and never made). Katy Manning could not travel from Australia to play Jo, so Sarah was paired with the third Doctor instead, and the Brigadier was put with the second Doctor.

Nicholas Courtney was actually asked whether he would appear in the special while he was recording *Mawdryn Undead* during August and September 1982. 'When I heard that all my old friends were going to be in it; Terrance Dicks was writing it, and he had been involved with so many of the ones I had been in; I was going to be with Pat; I thought I had to be in it. Having been around with the programme for so long, I couldn't miss being in the special.'

As Dicks mentioned, the 'guest star' companions were confirmed at a very late stage, and among the casualties was John Levene, who was approached to reprise his role as Sergeant Benton but unable to make the dates.

As far as the guest characters were concerned, Peter Moffatt was able to engage most of the actors that he wanted, although Charles Gray was originally considered for the part of Rassilon and Denis Quilley was felt suitable to play Borusa. Richard Bonehill was originally going to play a Cyberman in the studio, but he dropped out, to be replaced by Mark Bassenger.

The costume and make-up fittings for the cast took place between 27 January and 28 March 1983, with actor Richard Mathews, the ultimate choice to play Rassilon, having a face cast made on 24 February 1983. This was to allow another actor (identity unknown) to play Rassilon's body lying on top of the tomb.

'I cast Richard Matthews because he's a splendid actor,' explained Moffatt. 'I'd worked with him years earlier in repertory when I was an actor, and had always been impressed by his presence and his voice, rasping and deep and full of authority. He played a judge for me in an episode of *Lady Killers* for Granada TV, and when I first read the script of *The Five Doctors*, he immediately sprang to my mind. He had a difficult scene to play, as he was, so to speak, disembodied. We did have his effigy lying on the top of his tomb, and maybe he could have sat up out of this, but I felt in the end that he would have more impact by suddenly appearing in space above Borusa's head. After all, he had no longer any connection with that tomb, he was an all-pervading spirit.'

Pre-production

Unlike other *Doctor Who* productions, *The Five Doctors* was being produced in addition to the scheduled season, rather than as part of it, and therefore the money with which to finance it had to be obtained from outside the standard allocation of funds to the series. Realising that the show had a very great potential to be aired outside the UK, the BBC approached the Australian Broadcasting Commission (ABC) with a view to obtaining co-funding. After numerous discussions, an agreement was signed on 7 April 1983 by the BBC and 16 May 1983 by the ABC, which brought in $60,000 in Australian currency towards the production budget – although the agreement stated that no credit to the co-funder would appear. The agreement meant that *The Five Doctors* was effectively pre-sold to the ABC for transmission in Australia.

With work on the script under way, there were several areas of concern in getting this particular programme off the ground, and another early requirement was the appointment of a director. John Nathan-Turner's original thought was to return to the very start of *Doctor Who* and to see if the services of the first director to work on the show could be secured. Waris Hussein was therefore approached about directing *The Five Doctors*, but on 20 December 1982 he declined to take part. The directorial duties were eventually taken up by Peter Moffatt, a freelancer who had already directed the stories *State of Decay*, *The Visitation* and *Mawdryn Undead*.

Moffatt recalled being temporarily confused by the script when he first read it. 'Well, to be quite honest, I didn't really understand why the Doctors were lifted one by one in the time scoop and then prevented from doing what was required of them by so many obstacles being set in their paths – they were enticed and then repelled. But as I began to work on the script, I understood more and more. It was a game set for the satisfaction of Borusa, with the Doctors being reacted upon like pawns in a game of chess, and the more times I read the script, the more I appreciated the basic theme. This is nothing unusual for me, I may be slightly blank about the content of the script on first reading and then, as I begin to visualise it all happening on the screen, the whole concept catches fire, my adrenaline begins to flow, my enthusiasm mounts, and the whole script becomes an intrinsic part of me, and for better or worse we march together, as one, towards the final realisation.'

On Location

For *The Five Doctors*, Peter Moffatt was permitted to travel further afield for location work than might normally have been considered affordable or practicable for a *Doctor Who* production (notwithstanding the recent shooting in Amsterdam for *Arc of Infinity*). He had initially thought that Scotland might offer the various bleak landscapes as described in Dicks' script, but on further consideration felt that this was perhaps too far from London and that travelling time would eat too much into the allocation of filming days. Instead he opted for Wales.

Jeremy Silberston, the production manager, managed to find all the required settings – caves, mountainsides and bleak flat areas – around the Ffestiniog area in North Wales. When Moffatt visited the area with Silberston for a technical recce from 21 to 23 February 1983, everything was covered with deep snow, but when they came to work there, the snow had melted, and in its place were freezing winds, rain and mists, which caused specific problems of their own. Also present on the recce were John Baker (film cameraman), John Gatland (sound recordist), Archie Dawson (lighting), June Collins (production associate), Malcolm Thornton (designer), John Brace (visual effects designer), Pauline Seager (assistant floor manager), Jean Peyre (design effects) and Gavin Birkett (safety officer). A recce of the London locations took place on 24 February.

Following the recce, Gavin Birkett submitted to Jeremy Silberston a report dated 28 February 1983, in which he stated that the 'Wasteland 1' location – Carreg Y Foel Gron – should not present any problems. He also noted the following points with regards to 'Wasteland 2' – the Manod Quarry:

Safety harnesses should be provided for the sequences when the Raston robot fires arrows along lines, and the harnesses themselves should be secured to the ground with special stakes.

Care should be taken with the sequence when a Cyberman's hand grabs the Brigadier's arm through a wall. The production team needed to remove stones from the wall to create a hole large enough, and Birkett noted that the structure should be checked after the stones were removed to ensure it was still stable.

There was a loose slab of stone above one of the caves. This was to be removed and a further inspection carried out to ensure that the cave was safe. A second cave seemed safe, but a further inspection should be made of a ledge above the entrance to ensure that nothing was likely to fall onto the BBC staff working there.

The final part of the report concentrated on the sequences in the caves themselves. Everyone was to be provided with safety helmets. Emergency lighting should be provided, with a separate power supply, and good rechargeable torches should be available. Barrier rope was to be used to cordon off areas not in use by the crew. As radio communication did not work too well underground, a landline telephone system was to be employed to communicate with the outside, in case the walkie-talkie system failed. No gas appliances of any kind were to be taken into the caves, and everyone was to be warned of the dangers of exploring the various sites.

Prior to setting off for the location, there was a read-through of the script for the full cast on Friday 25 February 1983 in a conference room at BBC Television Centre, followed by location rehearsals at the BBC's Acton rehearsal rooms between 28 February and 3 March 1983. Then the unit – comprising some twenty nine cast and crew – set off for North Wales on Friday 4 March 1983, arriving just after midday, so that everything would be prepared and ready for the first section of filming on the following day.

The first location was Plasbrondanw at Llanfrothen, which was to be used for the scenes set at the Eye of Orion and also for the sequence when the first Doctor was picked up by the spinning obelisk from his garden. The scenes with the fifth Doctor, Tegan and Turlough were filmed first, followed by the first Doctor being snatched from his garden.

Filming started on Monday 7 March at Carreg Y Foel Gron, a desolate area just off the B4407 road. This was to become a wasteland area, and the first scenes filmed were of the first Doctor and Susan traversing a rock-strewn area just prior to their discovery of the TARDIS. For this scene, the Doctor had to rest on a rock and, despite the fact that the valley was littered with them, there was not one single piece in the right position for Richard Hurndall to sink upon in an exhausted fashion. Therefore, amongst all the lumps of real rock were two pieces of fake rock supplied by the Visual Effects Department.

The next scene to be filmed was where the fifth Doctor, Susan and Tegan discover the Master and are ambushed by the Cybermen. This sequence was continued the following day, with the Master joining forces with the Cybermen, and finally the scenes where the Cybermen prepare to detonate the bombs they have placed around the TARDIS were filmed. Also on 8 March, a special photographic session for the *Radio Times* took place.

The final filming at this location took place on Wednesday 9 March. The crew had planned to start the day with some glass shots of the tower seen through the mountains, but the bad weather meant that these had to be scrapped. The shots were subsequently created electronically in the studio. The first scenes filmed this day, therefore, were shots of the second Doctor and the Brigadier looking at the tower, as the Doctor realises they are on the Death Zone in Gallifrey. A later scene featuring the second Doctor and the Brigadier was also filmed. Peter Moffatt recalled seeing a wonderful vertiginous view of a mighty cliff face above a rocky path that the two actors had to cross in order to reach the cave mouth for which the characters were heading. 'As the cameras turned over to shoot the scene, down came a thick barrier of mist, blotting all else out of sight. Through the various takes necessary to shoot the scene, there were a brief few minutes when the mist vanished and all was dramatically revealed. Unfortunately the assistant cameraman had been obliged to go back to the car to get a new magazine of film, and though I kept saying to myself, "Come back, come back!", by the time he did (and he could not really have been quicker), the mist had swirled down again and the cliff face was obliterated. It looked all right in the end – bleak, isolated and unwelcoming. But I did miss that rocky precipice!'

The crew then moved to the third location, Manod Quarry, wherein a ruined building would be used for the sequence in which a hidden Cyberman grabs the Brigadier's arm through a hole in a wall. The quarry was also used on the following day to film a sequence set in the caves, where the second Doctor and the Brigadier are attacked by a Yeti but frighten it off with a firework.

By prior agreement, and in order to get all the material they needed to film complete, while Peter Moffatt was supervising the filming of the sequence in the caves, so John Nathan-Turner was elsewhere in the Manod quarry directing a series of visual effects close-ups to be edited into the battle between the Cybermen and the Raston Warrior robot. 'Peter asked me to direct it before we went on location,' said Nathan-Turner. 'It was always scheduled as one day where we had a second unit. Originally Peter had asked me for another day on location, but unfortunately we couldn't run to it, so instead he asked for a second unit and asked me to direct it. I had the most marvellous day, blowing up the Cybermen.

'The night before, Peter and I had sat down with a map and worked out where Jon and Lis would be and which ways all the shots should be and so on. The only real problem with the sequence was that Visual Effects put some substance on one

553

Cyberman's mask to make it smoke, but the smoke blew inside the mask and we had to rip, and I mean rip, the helmet off, as the actor was nearly suffocating. It was almost a very nasty accident.'

The next day, Friday 11 March, Moffatt continued with the wide-angle shots of the Cybermen coming over the cliff edge, the robot materialising and vanishing and then later the moments when Jon Pertwee and Lis Sladen entered the scene and reacted to all that was going on. When edited together, it all worked beautifully, but it had been a close thing, as one day had been misty and the next not, and there was a fear that it might be difficult to join everything up together seemingly continuously. All this unending care over a long period of shooting resulted in about three minutes of final edited footage.

On the same day, some further sequences were filmed with the second Doctor and the Brigadier.

After a day off, the crew returned to the quarry, and on Sunday 13 March filmed the scenes where the third Doctor and Sarah are nearly caught by the Cybermen and become trapped between them and the Raston robot. The following day, and still at the quarry, the scene where the third Doctor and Sarah swing across to the tower was filmed, as well as the short sequence where the third Doctor meets Sarah in the Death Zone for the first time.

The lake Cwm Bychan in Llanbedr was the final Welsh location, on Tuesday 15 March, for the scenes where the Master first appears in the Death Zone and then meets the third Doctor and Sarah.

The shooting in Wales had many problems, not least of which was the weather. Being March, 1500 feet above sea level, it was so cold that, as costume designer Colin Lavers commented, 'teeth hurt and faces turned blue'. Often the crew were working in the clouds, and there was a cutting wind from the sea. As much thermal underwear as possible was worn, and because of the damp, any costumes and props that could get wet had to be duplicated. Obtaining two of nearly every costume caused its own problems. Because of the deepening financial recession, shops were not inclined to stock two items of the same size, and so this dictated in part what could be used. For instance, Lavers found what he wanted for Sarah's costume in John Lewis in Brent Cross, but the shop had to obtain duplicates from branches in Oxford Street and Swiss Cottage.

The amount of water present on the location, both on the ground and in the air, was a constant problem. The Cybermen had to be glued together after they had been blown up with explosive charges. Lavers discovered that no glue would work well in the wet conditions, although eventually one aerosol adhesive was found that just about worked. A large amount of silver paint was used on the Cybermen. The explosive charges would be put on, followed by a quick wipe with the hand, and then the paint spray. By the time the team had finished, they had used four dozen cans!

On Wednesday 16 March, having completed all the filming in Wales, the crew returned to London.

On Thursday 17 March, filming took place at Tilehouse Lane in Upper Denham, Buckinghamshire, for the sequences where the third Doctor is snatched by the time scoop. From there, the crew moved to a Ministry of Defence/YMCA Hostel in Hayling Lane, which was to become the exterior of UNIT HQ, from where the second Doctor and the Brigadier are snatched. This location was the same as that used for the exterior of UNIT HQ in *The Three Doctors*. It was while the crew were at this location that a final photo-call took place, this time for the benefit of the press. Because of the absence of

Tom Baker from the line-up, John Nathan-Turner had arranged for a waxwork effigy of him to be brought from Madame Tussaud's in London, and the other four Doctors dutifully posed with the dummy of the fourth Doctor. This was something of a stroke of inspiration, as it almost ensured good newspaper coverage on the following day, with the papers variously asking readers to spot 'Who' was not 'Who'.

The crew finally moved to outside a house at 2 West Common Road, Uxbridge, Middlesex, where the scenes of Sarah bidding farewell to K-9 and being snatched as she waits for a bus were filmed.

The final day's filming for the production, on Friday 18 March, took place at the Television Film Studios in Ealing, where sets had been erected for the interior of UNIT HQ and for the top of the tower, which the third Doctor and Sarah reach by sliding down a wire. Once all these scenes had been completed, preparation started for the studio recordings, which were, by now, only eleven days away.

In Studio
As soon as they had returned from the location work, the cast were straight into rehearsals for the studio sessions. These took place at the BBC's rehearsal rooms in Acton, up until 28 March.

On 26 March, a technical run-through took place, where any final questions or problems with the technicalities of the studio recording were ironed out and resolved.

Much of designer Malcolm Thornton's planning time before recording was spent in trying to balance only three days of recording with the number of studio settings. There were ten sets to shoot and turn around over the three days – almost as many sets as for a normal four-part story, which would be spread over two studio sessions, one of three days' duration and one of two. The initial studio requirements were: the metal corridors, the Brigadier's office, interior of the tower (three levels), the ante-room with the chequered floor, Rassilon's tomb, the TARDIS interior, and the roof of the tower. The amount of setting and striking overnight dictated how much could be recorded in the time available; this is why it had been decided to do some filming at Ealing in addition to recording at BBC Television Centre.

Another planning problem for Thornton and Moffatt was working out the order of studio recording. All the most important scenes had to be shot early on, so that if anything went wrong, there would be time to correct it. A lot of the scenes in the TARDIS control room with Tegan, Turlough and the Davison Doctor were left to the end, just in case the studio recording did overrun, as it would have been much easier, and less expensive, to recall these actors than most of the rest of the cast.

Thornton decided to use post-production techniques for various wide shots using mattes, such as the roof of the tower and the ceiling of Rassilon's tomb. This technique had been successfully used on *The Hitch-Hiker's Guide to the Galaxy*, and is a method by which it is possible to pre-record, or pre-film, sequences of action and then electronically reduce that action and expand the surrounding background using painted images and the Quantel electronic image processor, to create a composite picture. Another example in *The Five Doctors* was the front door by which the first Doctor and Tegan enter the tower. (The door opening was achieved simply by moving a piece of flat scenery behind an electronic wipe.)

This technique also replaced the glass shots and model shots that had been planned for filming on location but ultimately abandoned due to the bad weather conditions.

The overall style of Gallifreyan architecture and clothing had been established in previous stories, most notably *The Deadly Assassin* and *Arc of Infinity*, so in designing the sets and costumes, Thornton and Lavers had to consider what had been seen before.

The hieroglyphics included on the obelisk in Rassilon's tomb had originated in Piccolo Books' *The Making of Doctor Who*, published in 1972, a copy of which had been supplied to Thornton by John Nathan-Turner. In the book, these symbols had denoted the Doctor's name, but this was not the specific intention here; Thornton simply used it as reference for Time Lord writing.

Thornton also devised a lightning symbol, which he used on the obelisk and all over the interior of the tomb. He and John Brace had been talking about the model of the tower and had remembered the scene in which the Master nearly gets zapped by lightning bolts in the wastelands; they had thought it a good theme to use as a decorative logo, so the inverted lightning flash was used as a device throughout.

The metal corridors in which the first Doctor and Susan encounter a Dalek were described in the script as 'highly polished'. Some thought had initially been given to filming these sequences somewhere on location, but it had been decided that it would cost too much to dress as required, so they were ultimately scheduled to be done in the studio instead. Thornton decided to make the corridors look as confusing as possible, rather than regularly linear with right angles and square panels. He felt it would be much more effective if any recognisable surfaces were destroyed, so stock flattage was used and dressed up using silver-brushed aluminium, polished mirrors and plastics that reflected into each other. The idea was that when the Dalek appeared, it would have three images as it passed. Thornton worked out carefully which surfaces would play onto others, the reflections that would be achieved, and where they would appear. But, scenery being the way it is, by the time it had been moved around and finally put up in the studio during the first night (in place of the tower corridors set), the optical perfection had been lost. However, once it had been lit and patched up, it did exactly what had been intended. Instead of getting optically pure images, there were extraneous and distorted reflections, which made the whole thing look sinister and even more confusing.

The problem with the tower corridors was that, for budgetary reasons, a single set had to be used to represent all three levels – upper, middle and lower. Thornton designed it so that it would look basically different when shot from three different positions, to give the effect of coming up from below, coming down from above and passing through on ground level. He had a few of the lightning symbols switched around, and subtly changed the lighting and dressing, to help create the illusion of three different areas.

Overnight on the second day of the studio recording, the Gallifrey composite (corridors, game control and conference room) was taken down and Rassilon's tomb was put up. It had been decided to use a post production matte to create a high vaulted roof, so when the scenes were recorded the studio lights could be seen above the set walls. The final set had the tomb in the middle, a series of architectural elements around to define the space, the transmat at one end, and the entrance to the tomb at the other. Because this was a long sequence with a lot of action, the production ended up using the whole width of the studio. After the tomb scenes had been recorded, the central raised tomb was then removed to reveal a painted chequer-board, and the architectural elements re-arranged to create the ante-room where the Cybermen were to be destroyed. While this transformation was being effected, the scene with the first Doctor and Tegan entering the tower was being rehearsed and recorded in another part of the studio.

John Nathan-Turner had commissioned Visual Effects to build a new TARDIS control console for this production, and one of the first re-writes to Terrance Dicks' script had been to incorporate a piece of action of the Doctor fiddling with the new console. Thornton therefore felt that there was some justification in re-vamping the console room interior set as well. This was an additional design requirement, but was something that would be carried forward to and benefit many episodes to come. John Nathan-Turner wanted to keep the wall roundels, but knowing the form that the new console would take, Thornton thought that the set could be subtly made more angular. The new TARDIS walls was thus made symmetrical, allowing for the set to be more easily erected in studio than the previous one.

The new design meant that the console could go in only one position, in that each facet of the console corresponded to a particular facet of the walls. Thornton's aim, which he felt he had achieved, was to get more relief interest in the walls. He used fewer roundels and also restyled the main doors slightly. When both doors were open on the new set, it was now not possible to see outside from a normal cross-shooting camera position.

A variety of external hire companies were used to supply all the props required for the various sets. For the main Gallifreyan sets, the armchairs were obtained from Newmans, velvet drapes came from Old Times, the harp was hired from M Plaquet and its pedestal from Giltspur. The ferns and exotic foliage came from a company called Greenery, and the armourer Baptys supplied armour for wall dressing. Finally, the stones and crystals needed to stud the coronets worn by Borusa and Rassilon, as well as to decorate other props, came from a firm called Farley.

To indicate some of the considerations involved in making a *Doctor Who* story during the Peter Davison era, what follows is a scene-by-scene summary of *The Five Doctors*, with comments from some of those involved in the production. The story was made and originally transmitted as a single 90 minute programme. It was split into four, 25-minute episodes primarily for overseas sales, although the four part version was also shown in the UK in 1984. The episode endings for the four-part version are indicated at the points where they occurred.

In the TARDIS console room, the Doctor (Peter Davison) is flicking and polishing the controls with a duster.

Peter Moffatt: This was a new console room, and that's why Peter is polishing it off, so that we can all see how beautiful it is.

John Brace: The new console was designed and built by a team headed by designer Mike Kelt, who was brought in specifically to handle that task.

Tegan (Janet Fielding) enters, concerned that the TARDIS will now work properly.

PM: I had no say in the short skirted costumes for the ladies. John kept saying,

'Something for the fathers ...'.

The Doctor chides her and tries to open the doors. They don't operate, and he bangs the console to make them open.
The TARDIS is at the Eye of Orion, a tranquil stopover point. Turlough (Mark Strickson) is outside, sketching.

PM: This was a lovely location with this wonderful view. I think the building was a ruined abbey.

Meanwhile, in a hidden control room, an unseen, black gloved person is operating the forbidden controls of a time scoop and homing in on the Doctor's previous selves: the first Doctor (Richard Hurndall) is picked up by a black, spinning obelisk in a garden.

PM: That garden was designed and built by Sir Clough Williams-Ellis, the same chap who designed and built Portmerion. Williams-Ellis's widow, Lady Annabel, who owned the house, asked John and me to tea, and it was a real old fashioned affair with cake stands and little scones and everything just so. She was a lovely lady. Her house was Elizabethan, not an Italianate mixture as in Portmerion.

JB: The control consoles were all made from black perspex for the game control room set.

When the Doctor has been snatched, a small model of him appears in a box in the time scoop control room. It is picked up and placed on one of five segments on a games board.

JB: The bulk of the games board was made from vacuum formed plastic, but we had to create the shape of the tower in the middle. It was quite a large model, and it was tricky to tie in all the elements. I think Tony Auger was involved in constructing the model. You always tried to apportion out single items of work to the design assistants and leave them to get on with it, once you had talked with them about the initial ideas and what the prop had to do. This then allowed you to get on with the rest of the work. The game was always seen to be a key element in explaining what was going on, and so we were able to spend a little bit more of the budget on it than on other elements that were perhaps not so key.

PM: Someone outside the BBC was commissioned to make those little figurines, but I don't recall who. I do remember that they were very expensive.

JB: All the miniatures had to be hand crafted and had to be proper caricatures. I remember talking to Julie Jones of BBC Marketing about the models, to see if they could be exploited after the show.

The fifth Doctor suddenly clutches his chest in pain. A twinge of cosmic angst, as if he has lost something.
The second Doctor (Patrick Troughton) and the Brigadier (Nicholas Courtney) are snatched from the grounds of UNIT HQ, where the Brigadier was to be guest of honour at

a UNIT reunion with Colonel Crichton (David Savile), his replacement.

[In the rehearsal script, it is the Brigadier's last day in office before he retires. The Brigadier is handing over command his replacement, Brigadier Charles Crichton.
  The costume for the Brigadier was fairly easy to design, as he was an ex-army type, but Colin Lavers had to keep in mind that he had to be as warm as possible, as he was going to be on location as much as Patrick Troughton.]

PM: The spinning obelisk was put on in post-production. I wish it hadn't been a black triangle. It looks all right once the pictures get in it, but before, it's just a bit blank.

The fifth Doctor again winces in pain and collapses. Two more figurines are placed on the board.
  The third Doctor (Jon Pertwee) is driving in Bessie, his car, when he encounters the scoop. He thinks he has eluded it, but he is snatched.

PM: This sequence had to take place on private land, as Bessie was not properly registered for public roads at that time. It also meant we didn't have problems with other cars.

[Because Bessie needed an overhaul before it could be used in the production, John Nathan-Turner gained agreement that the production would pay the first £250 of the referbishment costs, with the remainder to be covered by BBC Exhibitions, who would be able to use the car thereafter.]

Sarah Jane Smith (Elisabeth Sladen) says farewell to K-9 (Voice: John Leeson) at her front gate, despite the robot's warnings of danger.

[For Sarah Jane's costume, Lavers chose something that would suit the actress's personality but would not clash with the outfit worn by the third Doctor.]

PM: I liked the area of water in front of the house, because it adds interest to the location, which would otherwise have been a little dreary.

John Leeson: When I first started doing the voice of K-9, they used to put it through a ring-modulator or some such device to put a very tinny edge on it, but the treatment's been getting less and less and I've been finding myself sort of growing into the voice of K-9. On the filming of *The Five Doctors*, the sound supervisor came up to me and said, 'Look, no, we don't want any treatment; just do it yourself.' So I did!

The fourth Doctor (Tom Baker) and Romana (Lalla Ward) are relaxing on a punt on the river Cam. As they steer the boat under a bridge, they too are snatched.

PM: That was the footage from *Shada* that John provided. I had nothing to do with the selection of material.

As each person is taken from their own times, the black gloved figure places a large figurine of each on a big, circular games board, split into five zones, each radiating from a sinister castle-like structure in the centre. All except the fourth Doctor and Romana, for they have been caught up in a time eddy and are trapped in the temporal void.

JB: I always enjoyed designing consoles and setting up all the lights to flash underneath. On the consoles here, underneath the perspex were lots of square, egg box shaped compartments with the lights in, so that when they lit up in sequence, you got the little cubes of light appearing on the perspex panel.

The fifth Doctor, in a rapidly weakening state, operates the TARDIS controls and collapses.
Sarah Jane Smith is snatched by the spinning obelisk as she waits for a bus.
In the TARDIS, the fifth Doctor lies on the floor. As Tegan and Turlough watch, he starts to fade from sight.

PM: We wanted a high camera angle on that shot so that he could disappear without getting Janet's or Mark's feet in shot.

The TARDIS materialises on a bleak and windswept plain. In the distance can be seen the tower, and on the games board, the final three figures are placed.
The remaining members of the High Council of Time Lords on Gallifrey – President Borusa (Philip Latham), Chancellor Flavia (Dinah Sheridan) and the Castellan (Paul Jerricho) – are aware that there is evil afoot, for all four Doctors' time traces are found to converge in the newly-activated Death Zone on Gallifrey

PM: With regards to the casting of the Council, Paul Jerricho had been in *Doctor Who* previously as the Castellan. I cast Philip Latham as Borusa mainly because of the final scenes. I considered him to be a very thinking actor and wanted someone with a bit of authority. I had worked with Dinah Sheridan years ago at Yorkshire Television, and loved the experience. She's got an elegance, too, and I also thought she looked authentically aristocratic.

[The standard Time Lord costumes were eight years old, as they had been originally made for *The Deadly Assassin*. Fibreglass, however, has a limited life: after a while, it tightens up and becomes very brittle. This made getting into the formal Time Lord collars very difficult, as they needed to be flexed open to get them over the artistes' shoulders. They were also very heavy and tended to fall back, which meant the actor had to keep his arms around the collar to stop it doing so. This made movement very restricted. As most of the time the Time Lords were sitting down, it was decided that the formal collar should be used only at the end of the story for Flavia.
Borusa's costume was a variation of the standard Time Lord costume, using different fabrics. The colour was pale to make it look bigger, and the costume cut square off the body to maximise the shape.]

JB: We designed the little handsets that the Council members are using. They were supposed to be small machines that you rest your palm on and then use your fingers to tap out the digits. They're nice little props to design and make.

There is only one hope of escape for the Doctor, and for this the Council have summoned the Master (Anthony Ainley). In exchange for a free pardon and a new regeneration cycle, he must enter the Zone and rescue the Doctor.

[With the Master, there was again the problem of two copies of the costume being needed for location, so a second black velvet outfit had to be made. The original one had Victorian embroidery on the neck, which had to be copied as near as possible. This was not too easy, as it had oxidised silver in a North African pattern. The embroidery was done by Locks, who also embroidered for the Queen and Queen Mother.]

In a metallic corridor, the first Doctor meets up with Susan (Carole Ann Ford), his granddaughter. They narrowly escape from a rampaging Dalek (Operator: John Scott Martin; Voice: Roy Skelton) by tricking it into exterminating itself. They then begin the long trek towards the tower.

[In an early draft of Terrance Dicks' script, there was a scene where Susan was picked up by the obelisk while she was walking through an outdoor market in London. This was cut at the scripting stage.

Colin Lavers had originally thought that Susan had been left on present day Earth, and so clothed her as a woman of today. As it turned out, the costume could well be suited for the future time she was left in.]

PM: Working with reflecting corridors can be tricky, but as long as you work it out beforehand and don't point your cameras directly into the mirrors, then there are not too many problems. It was very difficult to light, because of the enclosed space, and it was tricky for the sound booms as well.

JB: The moving Dalek was taken from stock, but we replaced the top half with an exploding version for the shot when it blows up. Malcolm James was one of the assistants on this, and I remember practising the explosion in the effects workshop. The top part of the Dalek had to be created with all the insides in place. The explosions were titanium magnesium flash charges. There would have been eight or nine charges in the Dalek's casing, and they were contained in steel mortars. When these went off, they blew the various outer panels off, revealing the pulsating creature inside. There were airlines in the Dalek creature that is revealed, to make its tentacles thrash and writhe using compressed air from a bottle. The wall behind the Dalek was pre-cut, hinged and held together with some fine line, which was broken with a small charge at the appropriate point.

The other Doctors also begin making their way towards the tower, each hampered by different menaces: the second Doctor and the Brigadier are nearly caught by a lone Cyberman (Emyr Morris Jones); the third Doctor meets Sarah when she tumbles down an incline at the side of a road.

[End of Part One]

PM: There should have been a greater drop there. I think the problem was in trying to find somewhere where the path was on the edge for the car. It would have been better if we had used a stunt girl and a proper cliff. As it is, the Doctor could just have stepped down and helped her up.

JB: We used smoke guns to create some of the mists and smoke that drift across to obscure the roadway. There are a couple of shots here where a smoke effect has been overlaid on the picture afterwards.

The first Doctor and Susan find the TARDIS. On entering, the first and fifth Doctors meet and discuss the situation. The first Doctor suggests that Tegan make some tea while they decide what to do.

PM: Janet nearly had a fit over this. 'Why pick on the woman to make the tea? Why pick on me? Why should I make the tea?' She only agreed to go with the scene when Turlough went with her to help.

[In the rehearsal script, it was Susan who suggested she help Tegan to make the tea.]

The Council give the Master their seal, and a recall device that will bring him back to the conference room when activated. He enters a transmat device and is transported into the Death Zone.

PM: In that scene, it's nice that Dinah Sheridan is in shot when the Master disappears. She had to stand very still while it was being done, and it worked very well.

The second Doctor explains to the Brigadier that the tower is Rassilon's tomb, placed in the centre of the Death Zone on Gallifrey, which was used by the ancient Gallifreyans as a source of entertainment. They would kidnap different races and set them to fight each other in the Zone. This barbaric practice was stopped by Rassilon when he became President. The Zone was closed off and the tomb placed in its centre as a warning.
    The Master comes across a desiccated corpse lying on the ground. He recognises it as one of the Council who had preceded him. A fire bolt shoots from the sky, and the Master moves off.

[The shot of the corpse was edited out of the American version of the story, as it was felt to be too strong.]

JB: I think the body might have been created by Stan Mitchell, another of the workshop assistants.

In the TARDIS, a meal has been laid out, which the companions help themselves to as the Doctors argue.

PM: I don't know what the idea behind all that food was. I think that nobody ever knows what food they have on the TARDIS. It was sort of like manna from heaven, ambrosia, because the Doctor never eats.

The third Doctor and Sarah meet up with the Master but refuse to believe him when he says that he was sent to help them. They drive off when more lightning bolts crash from the skies. The Master runs off, dodging the bolts. Shortly after this, Bessie is hit by a bolt and is immobilised. The third Doctor and Sarah continue on foot.

JB: What we had there were nice balls of flame. We used small camping gas cylinders with a small charge in the dimple at the top. Usually if you wanted a ball of flame, you'd fill up a polythene bag with gas and then ignite that. Under these conditions, that would have been difficult, and you also wouldn't have got the nice spout of gas that takes the flame up into the air.

The fifth Doctor, having gained strength from the presence of the first Doctor, sets off for the tower, along with Susan and Tegan. When they arrive, they plan to deactivate the force field that is holding the TARDIS in place, so that the first Doctor and Turlough can join them there in the ship.

The third Doctor and Sarah are making their way up a mountain when they see a squad of Cybermen (Lee Woods, Richard Naylor, Myrddin Jones, Gilbert Gillan, Emyr Morris Jones) lower down.

PM: It's sometimes tricky to get the timing right when you are directing a group that is far away from the camera and they have to make timed separate entrances into shot.

[There is a big problem with claustrophobia in a Cyberman costume. It takes ten minutes to get into the suit, two more to get the head on, fastened with two large screws. The actors are very aware that they cannot take off the heads themselves, and so Colin Lavers warned the director that if he saw any sign of panic, he'd walk into the shot and stop it. Panic can spread very easily. The main problem with this was that Colin was always looking at the actors, but was never quite sure what the signs of panic would be.]

The second Doctor and the Brigadier find a cave into the mountain. The Doctor remembers an old nursery rhyme about the tower, which mentions three entrances: above, between, below. They are going below. Beside the entrance, there is a flaming brazier and some torches, one of which they take to light their way.

PM: The torches had firelighters in the top so that they would light easily and flame well.

JB: We had to make these up, and used the lightning logo that Malcolm Thornton had worked out. They had to be safe to transport about as well, and reasonably practical to make.

The fifth Doctor, Tegan and Susan make their way across the wasteland.

PM: Poor Janet. John insisted that she wore these ridiculous high-heeled shoes, but you never see her feet! They sank into the mud because it was so wet, and she walked out of her shoes several times. It was awful. She really was shaking with the cold. I felt so sorry for her.

The Master hails the fifth Doctor from a gully, and he goes to speak with him. A Cyber scout

5 FIFTH DOCTOR

(William Kenton) sees them and reports back to the Cyber Leader (David Banks) and the Cyber Lieutenant (Mark Hardy). The Cybermen go to detain them, but the Time Lords run off. The Cybermen open fire, and the Master gets caught in an explosion and is knocked out.

PM: These explosions were tricky to time. Especially the one where the Master was running away.

JB: The action here really gives the whole game away. We wanted it to be very visual, and there is a point when both the Doctor and the Master are looking back at the Cybermen, away from the explosion, and that's when we fired it off. It's the essence of a good explosion. You warn and work with the artistes and tell them what will happen step by step.

The fifth Doctor is trapped as he bends to check the Master's condition. Susan and Tegan run back to the TARDIS, but Susan trips and sprains her ankle. The fifth Doctor takes and activates the recall device that the Council gave the Master, and is transported to the conference room. Meanwhile, the Master recovers and swears allegiance to the Cyber Leader. The fifth Doctor shows the Council the recall device – it has a homing beacon in it, which is how the Cybermen found them so quickly. One of the Council is a traitor! Borusa orders that the Castellan's office and living quarters be searched.

JB: The homing device had a small but bright LED in it, and it also had to contain a battery.

The Cybermen decide to use the Master. When he is of no further use, he will be killed.
The first Doctor and Tegan have already left the TARDIS for the tower when Susan and Turlough hear sounds from outside – they operate the scanner and see Cybermen.

[End of Part Two]

In the cave, the second Doctor and the Brigadier are chased by a Yeti (Lee Woods).

PM: There was this incredible great deep lake in the caves, which was difficult to light because it was so vast. You couldn't see very much of anything.

PM: On a location like this, you work out very carefully in advance where you're going to film, as it can be very dangerous and slippery in places.

The third Doctor and Sarah encounter a Raston Warrior robot (Keith Hodiak) on the mountain slope. They freeze – it is programmed to react to movement.

PM: The robot was played by a dancer, Keith Hodiak, and at one point when he was inside the costume he had to go to the toilet. He ended up with this terrible stain on the costume, which wouldn't dry, and so someone had to hold a fan up against him to try and dry it off before the next take. We had hired a dancer for the leaps because he had to be able to jump high enough not to land straight away.

JB: We designed this robot with a smooth, reflective head. It was made from a vacuum formed silver chrome material that, once you thinned it out, you could actually see through, like a half-silvered mirror. Unfortunately it kept misting up on location.

The Castellan is accused of being the traitor after the Black Scrolls of Rassilon are found in his quarters. The Scrolls spontaneously ignite, and he is led off by the guards (John Tallents, Norman Bradley, Lloyd Williams) to be subjected to the mind probe.

PM: The number of times I tried to get Paul to say, 'Not the *mind* probe.' Yet he insisted on 'Not the mind *probe*.' It doesn't sound like English at all somehow. We did about four takes, but he never got it right.

JB: The box was electronically controlled. We had holes drilled through the table underneath to take the control wires. We had to use some hot coils to make it smoke first of all, and then the flames had to come later. It also had to be self-extinguishing. We rehearsed it under studio conditions, to make sure it worked without the pressures of time.

The Castellan is conveniently killed by the Guard Commander (Stuart Blake) 'whilst trying to escape'. The fifth Doctor does not believe this and suspects that someone else is the traitor.

[Eight year old costumes were being used for the Chancellery Guards. The helmets tended to be too large, but were not too much of a problem. However, the original fibreglass knee and elbow patches were tightening up and had become very brittle, so much so that the elbow patches could not be used.]

JB: We designed the guns you see here. The guard has one and there is another lying beside the body.

The second Doctor and the Brigadier move further into the caves. The Doctor finds a narrow cave and they squeeze in. Luckily it is too small for the Yeti to follow.

PM: There was a huge drop down from the walkway, but you can't really see it. We found a whole area with all these locations in, and it was too good an opportunity to miss, really.

[An original Yeti costume, made of goatskin, was found in the stores rolled up in a box and had to be laid out for two weeks to get it straightened out. Colin Lavers got into the costume to try it out and see what size of person was needed. There was only one foot, so a new pair was made. No nose section was used, as the costume was to be worn in a cave with lots of cables and fireworks, and the field of vision would have been restricted too much to be safe for the actor.]

JB: We used lumps of dry ice in the pool to make it smoke and bubble.

The Doctor pulls from his pockets a firework – a galactic glitter – and, after lighting it from the flaming torch, throws it at the Yeti. Rocks fall from above, effectively trapping them. The

Doctor notices that there is an air-flow, and they move off deeper into the cave.

PM: The section of cave that they were in tailed off to nothing. The next sequence was in a different part of the caves.

JB: We constructed the firework that the Doctor held. It would have been safe for the actor to hold. When the rocks fall here, you can just see that they are attached to a net. We had to close the way out when the rocks fell, and the only way to ensure that was to have a net, which we threw down over the entrance. Unfortunately you can just see it as the net shudders at the end.

Nicholas Courtney: Pat Troughton took one look at the cave mouth and said, 'You're not getting me in there!' But we did. There was also lots of polystyrene rock as opposed to real rock in the little niche that we hid from the Yeti in, and so we had to be very careful with the flaming torch not to set the rock alight. One had to be sure to hold the torch under real rock and not under polystyrene rock, otherwise the whole place would have gone up in smoke.

They find a doorway across the cave and enter the lower section of the tower.

PM: That was built across an existing tunnel by Malcolm Thornton.

Susan and Turlough watch as the Cybermen outside the TARDIS prepare a coffin-like bomb.
   The third Doctor and Sarah are saved when the Cybermen that were following them appear. The robot quickly and efficiently destroys them all, cutting them to pieces with steel bolts and discs (Stunt Cyberman: Stuart Fell, other Cybermen as previously on location). The third Doctor and Sarah take advantage of the diversion and carry on up to the mountain, having taken some of the robot's spare weapons.

Terrance Dicks: The Raston robot sequence came about because we had reached a point in the story where the Pertwee Doctor and Sarah were going to go through into the tower. We needed one last major obstacle. We didn't want another old monster like a Yeti or a Cyberman as we'd already used them, and so this was the place to come up with something new. The robot was planned to be simple and effective; sometimes you write something regardless, and hope the production team do it as well as they can. But by this stage, everyone was screaming about the cost, and also Peter Moffatt was getting worried about the amount of location filming he had to get through. So we planned something that was both practical and good. Something we knew they could do, that at the same time would be effective. It was a kind of martial arts robot. We worked out this business of the smooth egg face and the silver figure and the gimmick that it can practically teleport: it moves at such a speed that it goes from here to there without being seen, and that was it really. An idea that didn't make it to the final version was that the robot was very tidy minded, and would stack all the bits of Cyberman up into a neat pile outside its cave. One bit that was added was the Cyberman being sick, and another – when it came to the studio work – was when the Dalek exploded. I didn't write all that about the dying creature inside, but I was very pleased when they added it.

JB: We had three or four different things that happened to Cybermen. This one loses an arm, this one's head blows up, and so on. It was quite a challenge to put together a battle sequence in an afternoon, when you have the pressure of the weather and all that. It is all so quickly cut together that you don't notice the individual shots and it just creates the impression of overall carnage.

[From a costume design point of view, as the script required the Raston robot to move its hand over one shoulder, it could not be an armoured type and had to be more flexible and plastic. The headpiece had a mirrored visor. When it was light outside, the actor could see out, but in Wales this was not always the case, and often he was almost blind. With so many loose rocks, that was quite dangerous, and often he had to be led on and off the location.]

The fifth Doctor speaks with Chancellor Flavia. The Doctor does not believe that the Castellan was the traitor, and he decides to speak to President Borusa.
　　The third Doctor and Sarah arrive on a precipice overlooking the tower. The Doctor starts to unravel the rope obtained from the Raston robot's cave.
　　The first Doctor and Tegan arrive at the main entrance to the tower. The Doctor activates an electronic bell-shaped device, and the door slides open.
　　The third Doctor lassos one of the tower's cornices with some steel rope. He and Sarah slide down it, much to the dismay of the Master and the remaining Cybermen, who are watching from further down the mountain.

Terrance Dicks: That was originally a hang-gliding sequence. I thought that we could have the third Doctor turn his cloak into a hang-glider and just fly to the tower. But it wasn't possible to do it in the time, so we came up with them sliding down the wire instead. It's always *Star Wars* on a shoestring with *Doctor Who*, and you are always fighting against what's possible and what isn't. I think it's amazing that they do so well. It's always a part of your brief that you must come up with something amazing, astonishing and cheap!

JB: This was originally going to be a bow and arrow idea to fire something across the gap. But we had a bit of a problem with that and it broke, and I think that Pertwee couldn't use it. In the end, we came up with the idea of a lasso. I remember rigging something up in the film studio, so that we could get them swinging along the line to the top of the tower.

PM: There was an enormous pause in filming during this sequence, for over an hour, because Jon Pertwee refused to do the scene. The Doctor was supposed to build a bow and arrow from the bits he had picked up, and I had kept asking and asking how he was supposed to do this, and how this thing should be made, and everyone said it would be all right. When we got to the scene, Jon couldn't see how it could be done. In the end, while the Cybermen were nearly frozen to death in the valley down below, John Nathan-Turner, Pertwee and I went to a car somewhere out of the cold and worked out a way to make the scene work.
　　The scene as it eventually appeared was a great mixture of different shots that we were unable to do all at the same time. Jon threw the lasso on a cliff-top in a howling gale in

Wales; it landed on a pinnacle on a set in the film studio at Ealing; they slid down the wire at Ealing; the Master looking up at it, surrounded by Cybermen, was at the bottom of a valley in Wales; and the high shot of the tower was matted in afterwards. But when edited together, it all worked like a dream.

The Doctor helps Sarah onto the top of the tower.

PM: Sarah's quite high off the ground there. The parapet was about eight feet off the ground. The composite shot there is really nice. It's the film at Ealing plus the painted tower plus the filmed background.

JB: I know we had to make a bigger version of the top of the tower for that. Jean Peyre got involved with this scene as well, to match all the elements together.

The first Doctor and Tegan have arrived in the entrance hall of the tower, only to be confronted by a deadly floor pattern of electrified squares. They hide as the Master, followed by the Cyber Leader, Cyber Lieutenant and a group of Cybermen (Graham Cole, Alan Riches, Ian Marshall-Fisher, Mark Bassenger) enter. The Master, by crossing the pattern, demonstrates to the Cybermen that it is safe. The Cybermen follow, only to be destroyed by bolts of electricity from the ceiling. The Cyber Leader demands to know the safe route, but the Master turns a cyber weapon on the Cyber Leader as it is following him across.

JB: You can't see any wires trailing from the Cybermen to trigger the explosions, because there weren't any. My assistant on the show, Malcolm James, suggested that to avoid the problem of trailing wires, we got the actors playing the Cybermen to trigger the explosions themselves using small battery packs. This was a great idea, and really worked well in the studio.

[There was almost a problem in the studio when the Cybermen were being sprayed with paint to cover up the various explosive charges placed there by Visual Effects. The spray could all too easily drift into the costume and choke the actor.]

The first Doctor deduces from the Master's comment that it is as easy as pie, that the squares have a safe path across derived from the calculation of pi. He and Tegan follow the Master across.
   The fifth Doctor finds that Borusa, who was in the conference room and has not left through the door, is there no longer. He begins to search the room.
   The third Doctor and Sarah move down through the tower. Sarah is feeling scared, so the Doctor checks ahead. He meets phantoms of Mike Yates (Richard Franklin) and Liz Shaw (Caroline John), which vanish screaming when he realises they are not real.

[In the rehearsal script, there were no scenes present with the phantom companions. Instead, Sarah Jane was physically attacked by a phantom of the third Doctor after the real one has left her on her own.

Colin Lavers chose present day clothes for Liz; simply something that suited the actress and was comfortable to wear. Yates wore a costume from stock, but to emphasise that he was a phantom, and that the mind conjuring it was not perfect, there were no

568

UNIT insignia.]

The first Doctor and Tegan pass by a flight of stairs on their way through the tower. The Master comes down the steps behind them.

[End of Part Three]

The second Doctor and the Brigadier encounter phantoms of Jamie (Frazer Hines) and Zoe (Wendy Padbury) on a flight of stairs leading up. The phantoms vanish screaming when the Doctor realises that the real Jamie and Zoe would not have known who they were.

[Colin Lavers again used the 1973 *Radio Times* special for costume reference for Jamie and Zoe. There were two colour photographs of Jamie, each showing a different tartan, but one had been specially shot for the publication rather than taken from the series itself. The actual McCrimmon tartan was mainly blue, but when Frazer Hines saw it, he commented that it was not the right one. Eventually Lavers hired a red and green 18th Century kilt that had been used in the film *Bonnie Prince Charlie*. For Zoe's costume, Lavers wanted to reflect the Sixties plastic look, particularly as Zoe had tended to wear plastic-looking clothes, and so he used packaging material. If Zoe had had to move around, it would have been far too noisy, but it was quite suitable for the short scene. Actress Wendy Padbury was pregnant when this scene was shot, but not to the extent that it showed. Unfortunately she later lost the baby.]

The fifth Doctor notices the Harp of Rassilon by a wall and realises that a musical key must open a hidden door. He begins to experiment on the harp.

PM: Peter played the harp himself at this point, as he's quite musical.

The first, second and third Doctors all meet up in the main hall of the tower. They translate the hieroglyphs on a small monolith: whoever takes the ring from Rassilon's finger will have eternal life. The Master steps forward from the entrance to the room – now he will claim eternal life. He threatens the Doctors with his tissue compression eliminator weapon. The Brigadier jumps him from behind, and he is tied up.
  The fifth Doctor plays the correct tune on the harp, read from a painting on the wall, and a door slides open revealing the forbidden games control room.

PM: Peter didn't play that sequence. We had a lady harpist come in for the sound dub to record the music.

In the games control room, President Borusa is dressed in black and is presiding over the game board – he is quite mad. He is after immortality and has used the Doctors to breach the tomb's defences.

[Borusa's black costume was almost an opposite to his normal costume. It was cut to emphasise height and thinness with converging lines. Various different black materials were used as, if only one had been used, this would have tended to appear on screen simply as a black blob.) Colin Lavers had designed a new collar made out of black wire to give the impression of cobwebs and possibly provide the director with interesting shots through it. Unfortunately Philip Latham found it rather inhibiting and couldn't wear it.]

JB: Some of the consoles in the room were practical and some were dummies. The walls were made from those milk crate things. Malcolm was always up against the budgets, and if he could re-use materials then he would. In this case, the walls look really good with the lighting behind them.

The Doctors find a communication and control system in the tomb, and the third Doctor reverses the polarity of the neutron flow, thus allowing the TARDIS to come through the force field.
   The Cybermen by the TARDIS detonate their bomb just as the TARDIS dematerialises and heads for the tower on pre-set co-ordinates.

JB: The explosion was done with a locked off camera and a cut immediately before the explosion so that the TARDIS could be removed. There's also another of our small props there, which the Cyberman uses to detonate the bombs.

Borusa is wearing the Coronet of Rassilon, and with his mind enhanced by this, he takes over the fifth Doctor's mind. He and the fifth Doctor then go to the transmat, where the second Doctor is trying to make contact.

PM: The sequences on the monitor with the second Doctor were fed through live from the other set, but the Peter Davison sequence was pre-recorded. You can see that the background is different.

The fifth Doctor and Borusa arrive in the tomb, and Borusa freezes the companions in time. The other three Doctors link minds and free the fifth.

PM: To do that sequence of cutting between the Doctors, we just used the normal number of cameras and changed position if we needed to between shots.

The voice of Rassilon booms out that this is the game of Rassilon.

Terrance Dicks: Having put Rassilon at the end to resolve it all, I envisaged him as a kind of Valentine Dyall type actor; tall and gaunt and impressive. I think in the end it worked quite well, because Rassilon didn't look the way you expected him to. I think I had envisaged a more elaborate projection of the giant Rassilon, you would actually see a giant Rassilon towering above at the end of the story, but again it's a matter of time and budget.

Rassilon's face (Richard Mathews) materialises and asks if Borusa wishes immortality. Rassilon asks the Doctors if Borusa deserves immortality, and they all say no – except for the first Doctor, who has realised what is happening. He says that Borusa should get immortality. Rassilon agrees, and tells Borusa to take the ring from the hand of his effigy, which is lying on top of the tomb itself. At this, Borusa is immobilised in stone and set in the base of the tomb with other megalomaniacs who previously sought immortality (Johnnie Mack,

Frederick Wolfe, Charles Milward). He too is now immortal.

PM: All those actors behind the masks were lying underneath the hollow tomb. We had two versions of the side of the tomb – one with transparent faces and one with opaque faces – and we mixed from one to the other.

JB: I remember doing something with the ring on this. We set up a little rig to fire the ring off his hand, but they've done it with a video effect on the final story. Obviously it didn't work too well and it got dropped.

Rassilon returns the first three Doctors and their companions to their respective time zones and the Master to his. The fourth Doctor is freed from the vortex.
The fifth Doctor is proclaimed as President by Chancellor Flavia when she arrives in the tomb. Taking the initiative, the Doctor orders Flavia back to the Council as acting President until he arrives to take over from her later. He then hurriedly leaves in the TARDIS with Tegan and Turlough – a renegade, just like in the beginning.

Post-production

Once the studio recordings were complete, the next stage was to copy them all onto tape for viewing and later editing by Peter Moffatt. This tape-to-tape transfer took place on 18 April 1983, and took around four hours to complete. The footage filmed on location was transferred to video on 13, 19 and 25 May 1983, and took three hours to rehearse, in order to match the studio conditions to the film conditions, followed by an hour to achieve the actual transfer of material.

The video effects, which included the spinning time scoop obelisk, as well as the various ray gun bursts from Dalek, Cybermen and other sources, were created on 16 and 18 May 1983 by video effects designer Dave Chapman using a Quantel 5000 imaging machine in the gallery of studio TC6.

The opening and closing titles were created on 23 May 1983 for both the single part story and the four part version.

The story was finally edited together by Hugh Parson, who had been requested specifically for the job by John Nathan-Turner, on 23, 25, 28, 29 and 31 May and 2 and 3 June 1983 in editing suite B. The final day had originally been booked as a 'safety day', but it was ultimately needed to complete the work.

Two VHS copies of the edited programme were supplied to John Nathan-Turner, one at the end of Sunday 29 May showing the work so far, and one at the end of Tuesday 31 May. These were viewed by Nathan-Turner on Wednesday 1 June for his comments before the final edit on Thursday 2 June.

The dubbing of sound recorded on location to the transferred video footage took place on 30 May 1983, and lasted from 11.15 in the morning until 11.00 at night.

With the final edited version of the story complete, two VHS copies were supplied to the BBC's Radiophonic Workshop for work to start on the music and sound effects for the show. The tapes were delivered over the weekend of 4/5 June 1983 and were viewed on the following Monday by the studio sound technician Martin Ridout and Dick Mills, who as usual would be creating the special sound effects for the story.

The composer allocated to work on *The Five Doctors* was Peter Howell. 'I was actually very pleased to do *The Five Doctors*, as it was rather an exciting idea,' he said when interviewed in 1984.

The Workshop wouldn't start putting music and effects onto a *Doctor Who* until they received a finished tape from the production office, thus making their task a lot easier, as they were able to time exactly how long scenes were and to compose and place the music precisely.

Peter Howell liked to approach the task by getting a lot of inspiration from various pieces of equipment. 'I always like to take a couple of days just setting up the studio using slightly different pieces of equipment in the sort of style that I think is right for the story. In this particular instance I felt that the story really did divide itself into three sections; the first section was the gathering together of the Doctors, with quite a lot of electronic hardware involved with the games board and all that; having got that part over with, you are then into the adventure story with the Cybermen and so on; and the third part of it was the coming together of the characters with the Rassilon sequence, which was to me much more of an epic legend. I found that in my mind I had divided it into three, so consequently when I started off, I was basically interested in setting the place up to do quite a lot of sequenced electronics and things like that, which I felt was right for the electronic hardware in the picture, and then further on I was using the Fairlight computer more. Much of the music in the later scenes was done using the "Rassilon horn", which by the way is the hooter from the Queen Mary, which had been slid up and down and re-sampled into the computer so you that you could play it. It took about a day and a half to make just that one sound, but I felt it was very important. I wanted to link it with the constant view of the tower, and in fact it was quite useful in the culmination of the story as I used it almost as if someone were playing bagpipes until you couldn't stand it any longer. There came a point when Borusa put his hands over his ears just as he was about to disappear into the stone; in fact he was putting his hands up purely as an artistic device, but it occurred to me that he was putting his hands over his ears as the horn beat him senseless, so to speak.'

'I did suggest to the producer early on that bearing in mind that there were five Doctors in this programme, I would like to use the *Doctor Who* signature tune in the incidental music, as that would be quite a nice way of linking it all together, as if ever there was an excuse to use the signature tune in the incidental music, then this was it. I had done it before (in *Meglos*) and enjoyed it, and it is actually a very adaptable piece of music. As a matter of interest, I sampled the original sounds from the original signature tune onto the Fairlight, and during the opening scenes when the Hartnell character is taken, I was actually using the original sounds, only digitally.

'I also considered using some of Malcolm Clarke's excellent music from the previous Cyberman story, *Earthshock*. I borrowed it, but it is incredibly difficult to get pre-written music to sync in with the actual timed sequences that exist. It was very difficult to get it in, but I did try.'

One very notable aspect of the production was that the closing credits rolled over a version of the theme music that combined the original Sixties and Seventies theme with the then current Eighties theme, which Peter Howell had himself arranged. 'I suggested it to the producer, but added that I had no idea whether it would work or not,' said Peter. 'Once I had done it, he came along and listened to it and decided to use it. I personally was very pleased with it. I felt that because the end of the story was not a cliff-hanger, it was not necessary to have the very strong start to the end music. I do have a version of the music that goes from a sort of twenty year old mono with hardly any frequency response to a classy stereo version, and that really blows your mind. I'll tell you a trade secret here: the old signature tune is in E Minor and the new version is in F Sharp Minor, so the two didn't mix very well as they stood, also the new one is slightly faster, so I had to pass the old one through a harmoniser to jack the pitch up to that of the new, and then I had to do a slight speed change on it so that it would match, and it really was a major task. I did it quite a long time before I saw any of the programme, because I had a couple of days at my disposal and I thought I'd try it to see if it worked or not. Most people thought that it was a nice touch. It's probably the right time to do things like that when you are doing a special, as you can get away with it.'

The other aspect of the production handled by the Radiophonic Workshop were the special sounds, created by Dick Mills. Mills had been with the Workshop since the late Fifties, and had been handling the special sound requirements for *Doctor Who* almost single-handedly since the mid-Seventies.

'As with all programmes,' explained Mills at the time, 'we tend to look at each *Doctor Who* story with a view to its complete form, and so our first concern was to make it "moody" and "mysterious" – the actual sound-making part is easy once you've decided where all the sounds are to go.

'We first discussed with the director where sounds would appear and what they would be like. An early decision was to try and make each sector of the Death Zone have its own wind background, so as to give a different location to each Doctor's adventures there. I'm not sure whether this subtlety came off or not in the final version. Another idea was to back Rassilon's presence with sound. Fortunately, with the amount of film material used, there was not a great deal of special sound required, except perhaps to add to the Raston robot scenes.'

One nod to continuity brought in by Mills was the use of established *Doctor Who* sound effects. 'There were the Cybermen and Dalek guns, and the Gallifreyan stasers, in addition to the Yeti roar (from *The Web of Fear*) and the standard TARDIS sounds.

'There is total liaison with the musician on the show, now that both sounds and music are created under one roof at the Workshop. Discussions usually occur over dramatic matters and/or frequency ranges to be used, to avoid clashing with one another. Often just one contribution from either music or sound is eventually preferred at one point in an episode. I usually insist that all dramatic effects in space are covered musically, except for the final obligatory BANG!

'We generally have a ten day space between episode review and the dubbing session, and we always need all ten days. This is particularly true in my case, where I have to visit studios, do reviews or dubs for other episodes as well, once the season has started. The ten days allows for composition, creation, playback to the director and any remaking to occur before the final dub; plus of course all the necessary paperwork (shot lists, dubbing instructions etc.)'

It was during post production that it was noticed that Richard Hurndall had made a mistake in reeling off the numbers that comprised the value pi during the studio scenes set on the ante-room set. The actor was then recalled to perform a short sound recording to be used to overdub the erroneous dialogue. This recording took place on 20 July 1983.

The final sypher dub – the combining of all the aural elements of the programme with the visual elements – for the single episode edition of the programme took place over 14 and 15 September 1983 in the BBC's Sypher II suite. The same suite was used for the final dub of the four-part version, which took place on 22 September and 6 October 1983. This involved the inclusion of several new musical 'stings' created by Peter Howell for the new episode endings.

The final dub marked the completion of production work on *The Five Doctors*, and all that remained was for it to be scheduled for transmission.

With all the work complete, Terrance Dicks was pleased with the final result. 'I was very pleased with it, considering all the obstacles and hassles that had to be overcome. It's difficult to say that without sounding self-praising, but there was nothing that disappointed me, I was very pleased with it; it all worked.

'Having said that, one of the problems with the story was that it wasn't written as four episodes. Normally you only have to hold the viewer's attention for 25 minutes at a time, but when everything is all together, it is very long, so it's much harder to keep it driving along. You have got to have a series of climaxes or at least something happening all the time to keep the viewers interested.'

Peter Moffatt also felt the story worked. 'I think it is a great credit to everybody concerned in the production that it succeeded so well. To John Nathan-Turner for all his encouragement and his ever guiding hand, to Terrance Dicks for his intriguing script, aided and abetted by Eric Saward, to the designers and technicians at the BBC for their wonderful enthusiasm and hard slog of work, to the actors who gave it such life. Everyone gave of his or her best, which is the way that good television is made.'

Transmission

John Nathan-Turner had initially been hopeful that the show would be broadcast in England on the anniversary itself, but this was not to be.

In response to a letter from David J Howe enquiring why this was the case, David Reid, the Head of Series and Serials, wrote on 1 November 1983:

'Thank you for your letter concerning *Doctor Who*. You should know that the original schedule for *The Five Doctors* was indeed Wednesday 23rd November. However, other problems on BBC1 forced the Controller to move it by two days, by which time we had given permission for other countries to transmit on the 23rd. It was not really possible for us to go back on our word, particularly as other countries had already gone to considerable expense to line up simultaneous networking.

'Naturally I would prefer the programme to transmit on the 23rd, but I do assure you that it is not possible and that hopefully the Friday slot is likely to attract a far larger audience.'

The Five Doctors was eventually transmitted in the UK on Friday 25 November at 7.20 pm as a part of the annual *Children In Need* appeal fronted by popular television and radio presenter Terry Wogan. Because the appeal was geared towards raising money via telephone pledges, in some regions of the UK captions were run across the bottom of the screen during the transmission, giving the status of the amounts raised so far by the regions.

After the story had completed, Terry Wogan was joined in the *Children in Need* studio by Peter Davison. This was a pre-recorded sequence, as the actor was at the time travelling to America, along with all the other major cast members, to attend an anniversary convention in Chicago. Davison donated his Doctor's coat for telephone auction to raise funds for the appeal, but it is unknown how much was offered or who finally obtained the coat.

The Five Doctors was actually premiered in Chicago on the anniversary itself, 23 November.

The press coverage was very strong. The BBC placed the story on the front of their press information pack for the Friday, and for the first time since the start of the eleventh season back in December 1973, the BBC's listings magazine, the *Radio Times,* afforded *Doctor Who* a front cover. This was a painting by Andrew Skilleter depicting the five Doctors and the Master around an image of the Dark Tower. Inside the magazine was an article about all the companions who had travelled with the Doctor.

Despite the twin attractions of the 20th anniversary and the *Children in Need* appeal, the UK transmission managed only 7.7 million viewers, which placed it 51st in the week's top rated television shows. This figure, however, matched the highest rated episodes of the twenty-first season.

When the programme was repeated as a four part story in 1984, it managed only a maximum rating of 4.7 million, with the chart position dropping to 88 for the first episode and then falling as low as 107 for the third episode. This was notably lower than the stories in the surrounding seasons.

The press were less than kind about the special. The *Philadelphia Inquirer,* after explaining why two of the Doctors were not 'the originals', said: 'What's left is a silly, occasionally entertaining story in which four Doctor Whos finally converge to solve a mystery and save their individual lives. Like all TV reunion shows, it falls short of the original – but in this case, the original is still running.'

Closer to home, the *Sunday Times* said, 'Just why, in these days of sophisticated, multi-million pound films such as *Star Wars*, *Doctor Who* still attracts a regular audience of some 8 million remains a mystery even to the BBC. Part of the reason is that the viewing habit passes easily from one generation to the next, though that doesn't explain why, in America, *Doctor Who* has become a late-night cult show for adults.'

The *Yorkshire Post* however was slightly more critical. 'Last night's celebratory adventure on BBC1, *The Five Doctors*, was a partial misnomer, as the longest serving, Tom Baker, made no more than a token appearance. Richard Hurndall gave a convincing impersonation of the original Doctor, the late William Hartnell.

'But it did give the opportunity to contrast the styles of the three remaining, and it confirmed my view that Patrick Troughton had the character assessed perfectly.

'Splendid actor that he is, he was able to bring conviction to his highly eccentric and whimsical professor.

'Jon Pertwee took the eccentricity too far, while the latest Doctor, Peter Davison, was too easily recognisable as himself, and he was also too young, barely older than the obligatory mini-skirted female assistants, included to persuade fathers to join their children watching.

'The programme in which the Doctors were stranded in a death zone, which looked like a cross between a fairground hall of mirrors and a slate quarry, also enabled the suavely villainous Anthony Ainley to live up to his description last night as "my best enemy", playing the Master. The deficiencies of some of the Doctor's past adversaries were mercilessly exposed.

'The Daleks, those rubbish bins on wheels which have inspired thousands of children's games, proved inefficient fighting machines as they blew off their own heads, and the Cybermen, predecessors of the *Star Wars* storm troopers, were massacred by a remarkable Jumping Jack Flash character who fired deadly bolts from his fingertips.'

The fans were, on the whole, positive about the show in the *Doctor Who* Appreciation Society's quarterly magazine *TARDIS*. 'A good, traditional *Doctor Who* story, with an excellent dream-like quality. I would label it a classic, but I think sentimentality made that near-inevitable.' (Saul Nasse); 'The show relied too heavily on old material and ideas.' (Christopher Denyer); 'What we got, as nonsensical as it all was, was entertaining stuff.' (Saul Gething); 'I think it deserves a 9.5 out of 10.' (Ian Massey).

The novelisation of *The Five Doctors* was published by W H Allen in their Target range before the show had even been screened; the first time that this had happened for any story. 'They were very keen to get the novelisation out as close to the show as possible,' explained Terrance Dicks, who adapted his own script for book form. 'I finished writing it before I saw the final playback of the programme, which does explain some of the minor differences between the show and the book. For instance, Patrick's furry Yeti coat, which I didn't know he was wearing until I saw the show. It's that kind of thing. When they get to the caves, they had put a little ceremonial entrance outside, with a torch. That wasn't in the script, but it does give them a torch to carry and explains how they could see where they were going in the caves. It's the Brigadier's cigarette lighter that they use in the book. Other things, like Patrick's talking about Zodin the Terrible, came from a Programme as Broadcast script that I got in the last stages of editing the book, so I knew pretty well every line and interjection – but nobody ever mentioned the fur coat! I wish I'd known; I'd have written it into the book!'

CREDITS

Director	Peter Moffatt
	(Shada) Pennant Roberts
	(Inserts) John Nathan-Turner
Producer	John Nathan-Turner
Production Manager	Jeremy Silberston
Production Assistant	Jean Davis
Assistant Floor Manager	Pauline Seager
Floor Assistant	Chris Stanton
Script Editor	Eric Saward
Production Associate	June Collins
Production Secretary	Jane Judge
Designer	Malcolm Thornton
Assistant	Steve Fawcett
Costume Designer	Colin Lavers
Assistant	Peter Halston
Dressers	Carl Levy
	Philip Winter
	Camilla Gavin
Make-Up Artist	Jill Hagger
Assistants	Naomi Donne
	Fay Hammond

Visual Effects	John Brace
	Mike Kelt
Assistants	Malcolm James
	Dave Rogers
Film Editor	M.A.C. Adams
Film Cameraman	John Baker
Assistant	Nick Squires
Sound Recordist	John Gatland
Assistant	Brian Biffin
Video Effects	Dave Chapman
Camera Supervisor	Alec Wheal
Crew	11
Technical Manager	Derek Thompson
Design Effects	Jean Peyre
Graphic Design	Ian Hewett
Videotape Editor	Hugh Parson
Studio Lighting	Don Babbage
Studio Sound	Martin Ridout
Grams Operator	John Downes
Vision Mixer	Shirley Coward
Lighting	Archie Dawson
Grips	Tex Childs
Film Ops	John Rice
	Les Thomas
	Brian Walters
	Eric Levey
Armourer	Tony Chilton
Prop Buyer	Robert Fleming
Film Operations Manager	Graham Richmond
Title Music	Ron Grainer and the BBC Radiophonic Workshop
Incidental Music	Peter Howell
Special Sound	Dick Mills
Writer	Terrance Dicks

SELLING THE DOCTOR

MEDIA

During the first six years that Tom Baker had played the Doctor, *Doctor Who* had consistently maintained a very high level of popularity. The ratings had averaged around nine to 11 million per episode for most of the period, and had even risen to an all-time high of 16 million at one point during 1979 – although this record figure had been attributable in part to a protracted strike that had hit the ITV companies and blacked out the third channel for several weeks across the country. In 1980, however, the programme schedulers at ITV came up with a secret weapon: a glitzy new American science fiction series entitled *Buck Rogers in the 25th Century*. With its slick special effects, cute robots and lycra-clad ladies, this show was a big hit with UK viewers and had the effect of splitting the audience. *Doctor Who* was left with only around five million viewers per episode for most of its eighteenth season, and although there was a slight increase to around six million by the end of the story in which Baker left, this was still less than half the number that had been watching the year before.

There was, nevertheless, a large amount of press coverage generated by the announcement on 24 October 1980 that Baker was shortly to leave the role that had made him famous. Even the national news media covered the story, and speculation was rife that the new Doctor could be played by a woman (although this was in fact a publicity stunt dreamed up by Baker and producer John Nathan-Turner).

In the event, it is doubtful that anyone could have predicted just who would be chosen as the next Doctor. One factor that Nathan-Turner certainly had in mind, however, was the need to cast an extremely popular actor whose presence would help to reverse the series' disastrous ratings decline suffered during Season 18.

Peter Davison's accession to the role was announced to the press on 4 November 1980 and, given that the actor was best known for playing vet Tristan Farnon in the popular series *All Creatures Great and Small*, the subsequent headlines were fairly predictable: 'Dr Moo! TV Vet is New Space Doctor', 'Meet Dr Tristan' and 'TV Vet's the New Dr Who' were typical examples.

Davison could already be seen appearing on ITV as a regular in the comedy series *Holding the Fort* and in the children's story series *Once Upon A Time*, and he was also recording for the BBC a new sitcom called *Sink or Swim*. By the time he made his debut as the Doctor, some pundits were suggesting that it was becoming almost impossible to turn on a television set without seeing him.

The actor was even promoting Websters beer in a series of television commercials. After being announced as the Doctor, however, and only one year into his three year contract with the firm, he was replaced. The advertising agency were quoted as saying: 'As star of a children's programme, there's no way he should be advertising beer.'

The press mentioned that Davison was the youngest actor to play the Doctor, and Ian Black in the *Daily Express* wrote:

> [Peter] said that as a 12-year-old he sat glued to the box watching the original Doctor Who, William Hartnell. And he declared: 'I'm very happy to accept the part.
>
> 'I'm not doing it for the money – in fact I'm getting paid less per episode than I've been used to earning in other shows. But I think it will be enjoyable to do.'
>
> Davison went on to predict that he wouldn't be playing the Doctor for too long:
>
> 'I expect a lengthy, substantial time on the programme, but I believe any show needs that bit of regeneration to keep the interest up.'

John Nathan-Turner, who had worked with Davison on *All Creatures Great and Small*, commented:

'Peter is an ideal actor for the role. He has the right combination of light humour, drama and realism, is very popular with children and has a large following with feminine viewers.'

A number of early publicity appearances followed for Davison, culminating in the unveiling of the fifth Doctor's costume at a press call on 15 April 1981, where the actor was photographed wielding a cricket bat in front of a set of stumps painted on the side of the TARDIS police box prop.

The BBC's announcement on 19 August 1981 of its schedules for the forthcoming autumn season again saw *Doctor Who* featuring prominently, Davison being photographed in costume along with Pamela Stephenson and other stars of the shows included in the promotion. This was all the more remarkable given that *Doctor Who* was not actually a part of the autumn line-up: its new season would not begin until 4 January 1982.

One major change when the series did return was the move from its traditional Saturday teatime placing to its new twice-weekly evening slot, where it was in competition with a wide range of ITV fare including initially the soap opera *Emmerdale Farm* and the holiday programme *Wish You Were Here*. It is unknown what prompted this change of scheduling, which appears to have been decided upon by BBC1 Controller Alan Hart, but it may well have had something to do with the poor ratings gained by the previous season.

Whereas Tom Baker had actively courted the press, Davison was an altogether more private person. Although during his time in the series he attended many conventions and made many personal appearances – which he was quoted as saying that he did because they came with the job of being the Doctor – the total amount of press coverage that he generated was not great. When interviews did appear, the actor's primary concern seemed to be the fact that he was recognised wherever he went and was becoming tired of signing autographs and being nice to people. The extent to which this public attention arose solely from his role as the Doctor is however debatable; Davison was such a prominent figure on television in the early Eighties that he would no doubt have been recognised anyway.

Amongst the shows on which Davison guested during his time in *Doctor Who* were: *Multi-Coloured Swap Shop* (9 January 1982, publicising *Castrovalva*); *So You Think You Know What's Good for You* (11 January 1982, with his wife, actress Sandra Dickinson); *Pebble Mill at One* (March 1982, plugging a newly published anthology of science fiction short stories to which he had lent his name for promotional purposes); *This is Your Life* (recorded 18 March 1982 and transmitted 25 March 1982 with him as its subject); a BAFTA awards show outside broadcast (20 March 1983, presenting awards for children's programmes); *Saturday Superstore* (26 March 1983, with companions Janet Fielding and Mark Strickson); *The Late, Late Breakfast Show* (10 December 1983, receiving a Golden Egg award for a humorous out-take from *The Awakening*); and *Harty* (20 March 1984, with his successor, Colin Baker). He also took part in a number of radio shows, including one on BBC radio in May 1981 when he spoke about his interest in cricket.

As he himself had predicted, Davison ultimately decided to leave *Doctor Who* after only three seasons in the lead role. 'There was a danger of becoming stereotyped,' he told the press after the announcement was made on 28 July 1983. 'And I've always done three years of everything else. It's a nice round figure.' Some quarters of the press tried to suggest that his decision to leave was prompted by some 'backstage bust up' but, as this was not in fact the case, they were unable to get very far with that line of reporting.

Nathan-Turner again generated a certain amount of controversy by dropping false hints that the next Doctor might be played by a woman – 'I'm not ruling out the choice of having a lady Doctor,' he was quoted as saying – but the press seemed equally keen to report the recent decline in the series' viewing figures. While Season 19 had averaged over nine million viewers per episode, Seasons 20 and 21 had managed only just over seven million apiece. This was still a respectable rating, but Nathan-Turner no doubt had in mind the possibility of giving the series a further boost in popularity when he came to regenerate the Doctor once again. On the subject of Davison's successor, he was quoted as saying: 'The next Doctor will be older and a little more eccentric. We want to change the style of the Doctor completely. The new character will be vastly different from Peter.'

Just as press coverage of the series' lead actor seemed to diminish slightly after Davison took over from Baker, so the interest in the actors and actresses who played the Doctor's companions seemed to drop a little.

Matthew Waterhouse (Adric), Sarah Sutton (Nyssa) and Janet Fielding (Tegan) had all made their debuts at the tail end of the fourth Doctor's era, so their novelty value had been all but exhausted by the time that Davison took over. Waterhouse's departure did gain a little coverage, having been publicised by way of a BBC press release issued on 3 December 1981, but the production team were probably less than pleased to see that this focused mainly on the actor's displeasure at their decision to kill off his character. The tabloid press had always shown rather less interest in the Doctor's male companions than in the glamorous 'Doctor Who girls', however, and for much of the fifth Doctor's era, it was actually Fielding who attracted the most attention – especially when she posed on one occasion in black leather gear and on another in a moulded fibre-glass outfit.

Nathan-Turner, well aware of the perceived image of the female companions, contrived to dress Nyssa and Tegan in figure-hugging and impractical costumes throughout their time in the series. Perhaps the most well-publicised event of all, apart from the series' 20th anniversary (of which more below), occurred when the crew visited Amsterdam to do location filming for Season 20's opening story, *Arc of Infinity*, and Tegan was finally given a change of regular costume. No doubt to the delight of the assembled photographers, the new outfit was even more revealing than the old – a pair of culottes and a boob tube.

The recording of *Mawdryn Undead* again saw a number of newspapers running photographs of Fielding and Sutton, although these were rather less glamorous than was usually the case as the pair were showing off the old-age make-up that they were required to wear at one point during the action. The accompanying reports concentrated mainly on that fact that Fielding was getting married that week.

There was little noise made in the press when Sutton and Fielding later made their respective exits from the series. Similarly, the arrival and subsequent departure of Mark Strickson (Turlough) went largely unremarked, in line with the usual treatment of the male companions.

The arrival of Nicola Bryant (Peri) brought something of a resurgence of popular interest in the *Doctor Who* companion. The tabloids went wild, printing numerous photographs and articles about the newcomer, and Bryant made her television debut with an appearance on the BBC's *Breakfast Time* on 6 July 1983. By this time, however, the era of the fifth Doctor was almost at an end. The next story after Bryant joined the series, Davison bowed out, to be replaced by the sixth Doctor, Colin Baker.

THE 20TH ANNIVERSARY

An anniversary is always a good opportunity to make an impression, and with *Doctor Who*'s 20th falling in November 1983, everyone involved was determined to make the most of the occasion – especially as the series had by that point really taken off in America.

A special programme, *The Five Doctors*, was planned to celebrate the anniversary on BBC1. The other major event of the year was a convention organised by BBC Enterprises and held at Longleat House in Warminster, Wiltshire. Longleat had been the home of one of two permanent *Doctor Who* exhibitions in the UK since 1974, and Lord Bath, its owner, was keen to see its profile raised in this manner. The event would be open to the general public and would feature guest appearances by all four surviving Doctors – Patrick Troughton, Jon Pertwee, Tom Baker and Peter Davison – and numerous companions, as well as screenings of rare episodes and displays and talks by some of the BBC departments involved in making *Doctor Who*. Advertising trailers were placed after a number of Season 19 episodes, and other advance publicity for the event included mentions on Ceefax and fliers sent out with specialist publications.

The Doctor Who Celebration: Twenty Years of a Time Lord took place over the Easter bank holiday weekend, Sunday 3 April and Monday 4 April 1983, from 10.00 am until 6.00 pm each day. Admission was £3.50 per day for an adult and £1.50 per day for a child. The main convention area was behind the House, where a number of marquees had been set up. These housed displays by the BBC's Costume, Make-up, Design and Visual Effects Departments and Radiophonic Workshop; a forum in which panel discussions and guest interviews were presented; a cinema in which the complete stories *The Dalek Invasion of Earth* (Hartnell), *The Dominators* (Troughton), *Terror of the Autons* (Pertwee), *Terror of the Zygons* (Baker) and *The Visitation* (Davison) were shown; and a sales area where large quantities of spin-off merchandise were on offer and an auction of *Doctor Who* props and costumes took place – the first time such items had ever been made available to the public to buy. A large conservatory adjoining the House was meanwhile converted into an autograph room.

Everything might have gone smoothly had it not been for the inclement April weather and the fact that far more people than anticipated turned up. The walkways and grass were churned into slippery, mud-caked areas, and queues stretched into the distance as every tent was filled to capacity. The organisers had apparently expected around 50,000 people spread over the two days, but over 35,000 came on the Sunday alone, leading to many disappointed families being turned away at the gate.

The event attracted quite a bit of press interest, and Colin Randall of the *Daily Telegraph* described the situation as follows:

> Long queues formed outside most of the main attractions and senior BBC officials apologised for the delays, saying that the event had proved 'too successful'. Families had to wait up to two hours for autographs from the members of cast, past and present. One visitor, Mr David Southwell, said he had spent more than £20 on the day's outing from Bristol with

his wife and two children. 'We have been here over two hours and all we have seen is a couple of sets,' he said. 'It is a complete rip-off and everybody is entitled to their money back.' Others made similar points, though with more restraint.

Bryon Parkin, Managing Director of BBC Enterprises, was reported as saying:

> We have been the victims of our own success. No one could have conceived that so many people would have come so early. There were queues at 8 am and we have just done our best to cope with it.

Parkin went on to promise that any ticket holders who were unable to get in would have their money refunded, and the BBC also made a statement that only ticket holders would be permitted entry on the Monday.

Interviewed from Longleat by BBC Radio 2 disc jockey Ed Stewart, Peter Davison put a brave face on the organisational shambles. Behind the scenes, however, many of the guests were extremely concerned at the poor treatment the public were receiving, and at the damage this could do to *Doctor Who*'s reputation. Particularly vociferous and forthright in his condemnation of the event's organisers was Mark Strickson, and he later admitted in interviews that this had almost cost him his job on the series.

In addition to several new ranges of merchandise launched to coincide with the anniversary (which are covered in a later section of this chapter), some special celebratory items were also produced.

W H Allen, the publishers of the successful range of *Doctor Who* novelisations, had put out the soft-covered *The Doctor Who Monster Book* and its sequel back in the Seventies but had not so far ventured to produce a large-format illustrated hardback about the series. It was therefore something of a bold step when they decided to commission a celebratory volume of this type, *Doctor Who – A Celebration*, from writer Peter Haining. Haining was an obvious choice for the task as he was experienced at putting together overview-type publications. He had already completed books on Sherlock Holmes and Charlie Chaplin, and was also a good friend of W H Allen's managing director Bob Tanner, who would later become his agent. To ensure a degree of authority, the publishers put Haining in touch with Jeremy Bentham, a well-known fan historian of *Doctor Who*, who worked on a chapter chronicling all the Doctor's adventures to date. The remainder of the book looked at each Doctor in turn; gave brief descriptions of K-9, the TARDIS, Gallifrey and the Master; and presented interviews with Barry Letts, Terrance Dicks and John Nathan-Turner.

The other 20th anniversary publication of particular note was a lavish special published by the BBC's listings magazine *Radio Times*. The precedent of the similar title produced to celebrate the tenth anniversary in 1973 had led to a widespread expectation amongst the series' fans that such a special would be issued, but it was only after pressure from Nathan-Turner that the powers-that-be capitulated and set one in motion. Brian Gearing, the editor of *Radio Times*, took responsibility for the project and commissioned one of his regular researchers, Gay Search, to provide the bulk of the text.

The format of the special stuck very closely to that established by its 1973 forerunner. Opening with a spread of photographs depicting the evolution of the series' title sequence, it continued with illustrated text features on: the Doctors; the companions; the Master; the fans; the aliens; some of the creative behind-the-scenes team; and the merchandise. A specially-commissioned short story by the series' script editor, Eric Saward, told of the Doctor's original departure from his home planet Gallifrey, and also featured the Master and the Cybermen for good measure. Rounding off the whole magazine was a piece by 'devoted fan' Ian Levine (who had been recommended for the job by Nathan-Turner) looking at all the Doctor's adventures to date.

All things considered, the special constituted a very effective skim through the series' 20-year history, and was nicely illustrated and put together. Even the recently-announced sixth Doctor, Colin Baker, was included in its coverage, making it as up-to-date as it possibly could be.

Other activities connected with the anniversary included: a visit by Troughton and Davison, along with K-9 and a Dalek, to the 1 March 1983 edition of the BBC's *Breakfast Time*; a major photocall for *The Five Doctors* on 16 March featuring all the Doctors (Baker being represented by his dummy from Madame Tussauds) and many of the companions; an appearance by Troughton, Pertwee, Davison and former producer Verity Lambert on the 17 March edition of the BBC's evening news digest *Nationwide*; and a further photocall, on 24 March, at which Davison appeared with many of the actresses who had played the Doctor's female companions over the years.

MERCHANDISE

The boom in *Doctor Who* merchandise that had occurred in the late Seventies continued into the Davison era.

The range of novelisations published by W H Allen under their Target imprint progressed unabated, with around eight new titles added to it each year. Other publications from the same company included Jean-Marc Lofficier's *The Doctor Who Programme Guide*, which came initially in two hardback volumes in 1981. This book, although containing numerous mistakes in its earliest editions, was to become one of the most influential and popular works ever written about the series; since its original publication, it has been revised and reprinted several times in rather more accurate versions. Peter Haining meanwhile followed up his *Doctor Who – A Celebration* with *Doctor Who – The Key to Time*, a 1984 book that presented a chronological history of *Doctor Who* but unfortunately contained numerous incorrect dates and other factual errors.

World Distributors continued to produce their regular *Doctor Who Annual* during the fifth Doctor's era, and other publishers also began to exploit the potential of the *Doctor Who* market. Alan Road's *The Making of a Television Series* (Andre Deutsch, 1982) provided a case study of the making of *The Visitation* – the first instance of a single story being subjected to extensive analysis in a professional publication. More in-depth still was *Doctor Who – The Unfolding Text* (Macmillan, 1983) by John Tulloch and Manuel Alvarado. This was a university-level media studies textbook, which many non-academic readers and fans not surprisingly found rather heavy going. It looked at *Doctor Who* from a variety of viewpoints and featured much material about the making of *Kinda*, a story with a suitably deep religious subtext.

As previously noted, a large number of new products were launched to coincide with the series' 20th anniversary in 1983. These included: badges and a paper Cyberman mask from Image Screencraft (a commercial offshoot of Imagineering, the effects house that had created the Terileptils for *The Visitation* and the Cybermen for *Earthshock* amongst many other monsters and special props for the Davison era); sundry mugs, erasers, pencils, bags and balloons produced specifically for the Longleat event; a series of large artwork prints, generically called Profile Prints, showcasing the work of artist Andrew Skilleter (who had provided the covers for many of the W H Allen novelisations) and issued by his embryonic Who Dares publishing firm; and the first in what would become a massive range of *Doctor Who* video releases.

BBC Video had in fact carried out some market research amongst attendees at the Longleat event to discover which titles they would like to see made available in this new medium. The Season 5 story *The Tomb of the Cybermen* had come out top of the poll, no doubt mentioned by many fans as a joke in view of the fact that all four episodes were at that time missing from the archives, but BBC Video reasoned that any other Cyberman adventure would do just as well, and so chose the Season 12 story *Revenge of the Cybermen* to spearhead their range.

Other product lines to start up during the Davison era included a large range of pewter *Doctor Who* figures from Fine Art Castings, and Reeltime Pictures' series of *Doctor Who* interview tapes. Also in the shops were: *Doctor Who* wallpaper, featuring images of Davison, Daleks and Cybermen; a TARDIS tent; *Doctor Who* gloves and tee-shirts; and a Dalek hat. The *Doctor Who* theme record was reissued with a photograph of Davison on the sleeve, and the *K-9 and Company* theme was also released. In addition, the first ever LP of incidental music from the series was put out in the form of the highly-acclaimed, if unimaginatively-titled, *Doctor Who – The Music*.

Marvel Comics' *Doctor Who Monthly* was still going strong, with numerous special publications being produced in addition to the regular monthly magazine; BBC publicity photographs from the series went on sale to the public thanks to a firm called Whomobilia, run by fan John McElroy; and eager fans could even obtain a *Doctor Who* umbrella.

In fact, the merchandise produced during this period almost rivalled that of the Sixties in terms of its range and diversity. There was however one significant difference: whereas in the Sixties almost all the merchandise had been issued by large toy manufacturers, in the Eighties most of the items on sale were produced by small firms acting as cottage industries, or even by fans-turned-professionals. These firms and individuals usually escaped the overheads of the larger companies, but also lacked their sales, marketing and distribution functions. Luckily, the enormous fan interest in the series both in the UK and in America had resulted in a great many conventions being held, newsletters being produced and dealers setting up in business, and this had led to the creation of a ready market on both sides of the Atlantic for all the various items produced.

OVERSEAS

North America

The Peter Davison era saw *Doctor Who* approaching the peak of its popularity in the United States of America, as episodes – albeit mainly those featuring Tom Baker as the Doctor – were shown on an almost daily basis on PBS stations covering over two thirds of the entire country.

By 1981, Time-Life Television, the distributors of *Doctor Who* in the United States, had sold off the syndication side of their business to investors; with the BBC picking up half interest in the new company – Lionheart Television. Many of the stations carrying the show had switched to airing the series in a movie format on the weekends. Because of this, the stations were circulating through the available Tom Baker serials quickly and the PBS stations were anxious to get the latest Peter Davison serials to keep their viewers happy. Lionheart began selling packages of Peter Davison serials before the stories were even available. This led to several problems later as they had not expected season twenty to be short a story or Davison to leave before the end of the next season. This meant they had to scramble to fill the packages they had pre-sold with *K9 and Company* and other specials. Around this time the original Howard da Silva introduced Tom Baker episodes were being replaced in the syndication run with the unedited versions.

Another curious side effect to the "bicycling" method of distribution that Lionheart used to get the transmission tapes from one station to another was that quite often the series was broadcast out of order. In the original Tom Baker syndication, serials were sometimes arranged by story code, but over the years even this method had gone to a much more haphazard format that meant some areas of the country were seeing stories from different seasons mixed together. Initially, Lionheart was only selling syndication packages "by Doctor" which meant a station could purchase all the Peter Davison serials with an option to broadcast each serial a specific number of times. Eventually this would change to a yearly subscription type of syndication.

By 1983 the series was popular enough for several PBS stations to arrange a special Wednesday night screening of *The Five Doctors* on the anniversary – two days before its UK premiere. This was a slightly edited version from the one eventually shown in Britain. PBS stations were also starting to produce their own documentaries on the series, including *Once Upon a Timelord* (KRMA) and *The Whovians* (WOUB/WOUC).

Barely a weekend went by, it seemed, without a large *Doctor Who* convention taking place somewhere in America, and the show's stars, both past and present, were in constant demand to attend these celebrations, with large fees and travel expenses being offered to entice them from UK shores. John Nathan-Turner even began to act as a semi-official guest liaison officer for the organisers of these events. The biggest US convention of all, attended by an estimated 12,000 people, was the Ultimate Celebration, which took place in Chicago over the series' 20th anniversary weekend in 1983 and achieved the unique feat of bringing all four surviving Doctors on stage together, along with many of their companions from the series.

The North American *Doctor Who* Appreciation Society, which like its UK sponsor had been run essentially on a non-profit-making basis, now gave way to professional organisations such as Spirit of Light – who staged the Ultimate Celebration and many other conventions – and the *Doctor Who* Fan Club of America. The latter body was set up by two commercially-minded fans, Ron Katz and Chad Roark, after they met Nathan-Turner at BBC Enterprises' Longleat event. Its members, who would eventually come to number some 30,000, received a regular newspaper entitled *The Whovian Times*, which featured interviews and news items and also numerous adverts for some of the masses of BBC-licensed (and, in some cases, possibly unlicensed) merchandise items produced in the States at this time, including tee-shirts, jackets, mugs, key-fobs, pens, model kits and towels.

Elsewhere on the North American continent, fan support for *Doctor Who* remained strong in Canada, where an organisation called the *Doctor Who* Information Network launched a regular fanzine, *Enlightenment*, around the end of Davison's stint in the series. Circulation of this well-produced publication quickly rose to around 400.

Australia

Doctor Who also remained very popular 'down under' during this period of its history. The Australasian *Doctor Who* Fan Club continued to publish issues of its high-quality fanzine *Zerinza: The Australasian Doctor Who Fanzine*, as well as a more basic newsletter, and attracted a large influx of new members. A number of '*Doctor Who* Parties' and other events were held, with guests including former companion actress Katy Manning, who now lived in Australia. Other groups, such as the *Doctor Who* Club of Victoria, produced fanzines and carried out activities on a more local basis.

The public profile of the series in Australia received a considerable boost during April 1983 when Peter Davison and his wife Sandra Dickinson made a promotional tour of major cities to meet the fans and do a number of book signings at stores in the Myer chain, who had sponsored the trip and arranged an extremely hectic schedule for the two visitors.

One unfortunate aspect of the Australian transmissions of the Davison stories was that – as had also been the case in earlier eras – a number of the episodes were edited by the censors to remove material that they considered unsuitable for a family audience. The most badly affected of all was Davison's swansong, *The Caves of Androzani* part four, which lost over two and a half minutes of material.

New Zealand
By Paul Scoones

Peter Davison's Doctor arrived on New Zealand television screens just over a year after his first story screened in the UK, and as *Castrovalva* Part One screened in New Zealand, Davison's second season was ending on British TV screens.

The series screened on Mondays at 5.30 pm on Television One, beginning 14 March and ending 28 November 1983. This run of episodes covered all seven stories of Season Nineteen as well as the first three stories of Season Twenty. Unusually for New Zealand, *Arc of Infinity*, *Snakedance* and *Mawdryn Undead* were all screened the same year these stories were aired in the UK. After *Mawdryn Undead* ended however viewers had to wait over a year for the series to return but further Davison stories were not seen until five years later.

When *Doctor Who* returned to New Zealand television in April 1985, it was with the Troughton story *The Mind Robber* which launched a long-running series of repeat and first-time screenings. The series reached the Davison era in August 1988, at which time *Doctor Who* was screening twice weekly, on Thursdays and Fridays at 5.30 pm on TV2. Davison's first season, *Castrovalva* to *Time-Flight*, was screened from 25 August to 18 November 1988.

The regular Thursday and Friday screenings were interrupted for one week as Television New Zealand scheduled a 'Silver Jubilee' week of *Doctor Who* special screenings, from Saturday 19 November to Friday 25 November, featuring the first New Zealand broadcasts of five stories. *The Five Doctors* screened Sunday 20 November 1988 at midday, followed by a repeat of the 1965 Peter Cushing movie, *Dr Who and the Daleks*.

Following the 'Silver Jubilee' week, regular screenings resumed. The return was short-lived as just two stories were broadcast before the series took a break. *Arc of Infinity* and *Snakedance* screened from 1 to 23 December 1988.

After three months the series returned 6 April 1989 back on Thursdays and Fridays on TV2, but at the slightly earlier time of around 5.15 pm. The series resumed with *Mawdryn Undead* and then *Terminus*, which saw the regular story sequence pick up where it had left off in New Zealand more than five years earlier. Because it had screened as part of the 'Silver Jubilee' week just a few months earlier, *The Five Doctors* was omitted after *The King's Demons*. *Resurrection of the Daleks* played as a four-part story (as opposed to the two episode format seen in the UK), and the Davison era ended 4 August 1989 with the screening of Part Four of *The Caves of Androzani*.

Many of the Davison episodes screened during 1988 and 1989 were broadcast in a slightly edited form, as the commercial half-hour slot to which they had been allocated allowed for only 23 minutes of actual programme time. Further edits were evident because the episodes had been supplied by the Australian Broadcasting Corporation and cuts had been made by the Australian censor.

The version of *The Caves of Androzani* screened in New Zealand was one that had been heavily edited by the Australian censor to remove sequences deemed too violent, with around two and a half minutes removed from Part Four alone.

Viewer ratings for the Davison era stories screened in 1988 and 1989 show that *Frontios* Part Two was the highest rated episode on 9%, with the first episodes of *Terminus*, *Resurrection of the Daleks* and *Planet of Fire* all rating 8.5%. *The Awakening* and *Frontios* were equally the highest-rated stories, each with a 7.3% average.

UK FANDOM

The *Doctor Who* Appreciation Society continued to be at the forefront of UK fandom during this period, although its dominance was now starting to be challenged by other fan groups and, in the publication field, by independent fanzines.

After its original organisers had bowed out in mid-1980, the Society had effectively been saved from collapse by David Saunders (who became Co-ordinator), David J Howe (who had for some time been running the Reference Department) and Chris Dunk (the editor of the Society's newsletter, *Celestial Toyroom*). Over the next couple of years, the Society's executive body took steps to put its organisation and finances on a sounder footing. Dunk was succeeded as *Celestial Toyroom* editor first by Gordon Blows and David Auger, then by Gary Russell and then, until the end of the Davison era, by Gordon Roxburgh. The Society published much material during this period, including regular editions of the fanzine *TARDIS*, edited by Richard Walter, and the fan fiction periodical *Cosmic Masque*, edited initially by John Peel and then, from early 1981, by Ian K McLachlan.

The Society's membership was boosted considerably by a strong presence at the BBC's Longleat convention in 1983, and managed to top the 3,000 mark for the first time. The Society meanwhile continued to stage its own conventions under the aegis of Convention Department organiser Paul Zeus. In addition to the major PanoptiCon event each year, a number of smaller and more informal Inter-Face and DWASocial gatherings were held. It was however a constant source of irritation to the Society that the PanoptiCons had to be scheduled so as not to clash with major American events, such as the one held in Chicago on the series' 20th anniversary, as with their relatively high fees and travel expenses, the latter would always be more successful in attracting guests. The fact that so many of the series' stars were always overseas on important dates such as the anniversary also meant that numerous opportunities for UK press coverage were lost.

VIEWER REACTION

As previously noted, the Davison era gained very respectable ratings, although they were somewhat higher for Season 19 than for Seasons 20 and 21. One factor that impacted on these figures was the boom in home video recording that occurred in the early 1980s; the ratings system took no account of people who videoed shows to watch later. Another factor was that the UK's fourth terrestrial channel, Channel 4, started transmitting in 1982 and offered people a greater degree of choice about what to watch at any given time.

Further information on viewers' contemporary reactions to *Doctor Who* during this period can be gained from the BBC's own internal audience research reports.

The summary report for Season 19 began by discussing the size of the audience, based on results from the BARB Audience Measurement service:

> Audiences for this series were estimated to range from 16.1% to 20.5% (8.3 to 10.5 million) of the United Kingdom population, giving an overall average of 18.2% (9.3 million). There was no appreciable difference between the Monday and Tuesday audience sizes.

There then followed a section on audience reaction, based on questionnaires completed by members of the BBC's regular Viewing Panel. This recorded that the overall reaction index for the season was 66%.

The report continued:

> Viewing of this 26 part series tended to be rather sporadic although ... the majority of those reporting managed to tune in to at least half ... Fewer than one in ten (8%) reporting deliberately decided to stop watching; frequency of viewing, perhaps predictably, tended to be governed by the convenience of the transmission time to individual respondents ... The timing was only totally suitable for a minority, although only about one in ten (12%) found it completely inconvenient ... Predictably, those who found the transmission time less convenient tended to tune in to fewer programmes. Just under half (47%) of the total sample watched with children under the age of 15, and these viewers tended to find the timing rather more suitable. There were several requests for a return to the old Saturday evening transmission time, albeit from a small minority.

Next came a number of sections relating comments on the actual content of the episodes:

> Although only about one in seven of those reporting found the latest series of *Doctor Who* immensely appealing, the large majority reacted favourably and still enjoy the programme. The episodes in this series were considered well written and not too predictable, and most viewers felt that the storylines had been quite exciting ...
>
> Reactions to the standard of acting were rather mixed, although still generally favourable ... Peter Davison appears to have been accepted as the new Doctor. Although there were a number of unfavourable comparisons with certain predecessors (notably Jon Pertwee) and a

couple of suggestions that he should stick to being a vet, the majority of those reporting clearly feel that he has got to grips with the part and now fits in rather well. There were few comments regarding the performances of the rest of the cast, although these were considered good.

All aspects of the production were thought to have been of a high standard. A number of respondents did feel that the special effects had been unbelievable and obviously false, but their opinions were heavily outweighed ...

As mentioned previously, just under half the sample audience viewed in the company of children aged 15 or under. Boys were slightly predominant (55% : 45%). The children's ages were fairly well spread; all ages between two and 15 were represented, but there was a marked concentration of children (particularly boys) aged between 6 and 10. In general, their comments were succinct ('great', 'brilliant' etc.) and very favourable. Boys tended to be rather more enthusiastic than girls (although both sexes liked the series) but there was a tendency among very small girls (under-sevens) to be frightened. Several children were rather disturbed by the death of Adric, although these were in the minority.

Interspersed with these comments were a number of tables giving detailed breakdowns of the figures in their respective sections. The report then concluded with a final table that the production team must have found particularly encouraging:

Finally, the sample audience was asked whether they would welcome a further series of *Doctor Who*. They responded as follows:

Yes, very much	36%
Yes, quite	42%
Not particularly	19%
Definitely not	3%

The audience research report for Season 20, which was accompanied by a three page computer tabulation of statistics, recorded an average audience of 7.0 million and an average appreciation index of 62. Its text read as follows:

This series of *Doctor Who* received a somewhat mixed but essentially favourable response from the members of the sample audience. Approximately half of those reporting regarded it as an entertaining and enjoyable programme which provided excellent viewing for the whole family. A number of this group thought it especially good for children, whilst others indicated that they had been fans of the Doctor since his portrayal by the late William Hartnell. These reporting viewers (who were most likely to be under 54 years of age) considered the storylines interesting, amusing and gripping, liked Peter Davison's portrayal of the Doctor and praised the other members of the cast.

Another group of respondents (between one quarter and one third of the total sample) liked the series, but were slightly disappointed in it. They tended to criticise the plots ('enjoyable, but stronger storylines needed'), the special effects or the transmission time. Indeed, the time at which the programme was broadcast was noticeably less popular amongst the 35-54 age group.

One in five of those reporting had not enjoyed the series. For 15% this dislike had led them to make a positive decision to stop watching. They were mainly over the age of 55 and criticised the series for being, in their opinion, boring and predictable. They also felt it had weak storylines, poor acting and disappointing special effects. A few ceased watching because their young children had been frightened by the programme.

57% of the sample audience indicated that they wished to see a new series of *Doctor Who*. A further one in three had no strong opinion on the subject. The desire for a new series of *Doctor Who* was strongest in those under 34 and weakest in the 55+ age group.

The average viewer and reaction index figures for Season 21, at 7.2 million and 65 respectively, were both slightly up on those for Season 20, but – although no audience research report is available for this season at the time of writing – it is known that there was a considerable drop in satisfaction levels after Colin Baker took over as the Doctor for the final story. Only 66% of those in the reporting sample thought that the sixth Doctor was a likeable character in this story, and only 54% thought that he was well portrayed by Baker. These figures compared with 73% and 71% respectively for the fifth Doctor and for Davison's portrayal during Season 20. While it was hardly unexpected for a new Doctor to encounter some initial audience resistance, Nathan-Turner must have known that a considerable improvement would be required the following year.

PETER DAVISON STORIES IN ORDER OF AVERAGE VIEWING FIGURES
(Figures in millions of viewers)

Black Orchid	10.00
The Visitation	9.60
Castrovalva	9.57
Earthshock	9.33
Four to Doomsday	8.88
Time-Flight	8.88
Kinda	8.80
The Five Doctors	7.70
Resurrection of the Daleks	7.65
Mawdryn Undead	7.28
The Caves of Androzani	7.28
Warriors of the Deep	7.25
The Awakening	7.25
Arc of Infinity	7.15
Snakedance	7.10
Terminus	7.10
Planet of Fire	6.98
Enlightenment	6.83
Frontios	6.80
The King's Demons	6.50

AFTERWORD

Following his appointment as *Doctor Who*'s producer at the beginning of November 1979, John Nathan-Turner set about transforming the series – his intention being, as he put it, 'to bring it into the 1980s'.

The new producer's influence was first apparent during Tom Baker's final season as the Doctor. A glossy new star-field title sequence and neon-style logo were commissioned; a more trendy theme tune arrangement was introduced; Dudley Simpson's relatively conventional incidental music, for so long a staple ingredient of the series, was dispensed with in favour of fully electronic scores provided by the BBC Radiophonic Workshop; the two established companions – Romana and K-9 – were written out, while three new ones – Adric, Nyssa and Tegan – were brought in to take their places; all the regulars, including the Doctor, were given heavily-designed, uniform-like costumes that went unchanged from one story to the next; and finally, of course, the Doctor himself was regenerated.

All these new approaches were carried forward to Peter Davison's tenure in the lead role. With a new Doctor in place, Nathan-Turner was able fully to realise his ambitions for *Doctor Who*, and the production became increasingly slick and sophisticated.

'I hesitate to say this,' noted the producer in a 1989 interview, 'but what happened in some – and I would emphasise not *all* – of the older episodes was very minimal. There were a lot of very long scenes, a lot of exposition, and not a lot of action or plot development. I like episodes sharply cut, with a strong narrative drive. The optimum length for a *Doctor Who* episode is now 24 minutes 15 seconds and, once you take away the titles, you have about 22 minutes to play with. So you really want to get on with a whole lot of story development – not just to hold the attention of the audience, but to make what you are handing them more substantial.'

Critics, however, expressed concern that Nathan-Turner's attentions were focused principally on cosmetic, essentially superficial aspects of the production, rather than on the dramatic content of the stories. Certainly this latter aspect was determined more by the respective interests and preferences of the series' successive script editors, namely Christopher H Bidmead, Antony Root and Eric Saward. An interesting mix and variety of different story types was achieved – even down to the inclusion, in the form of *Black Orchid*, of the first *bona fide* historical adventure since 1966 – and frequently the scripts matched the production in achieving a level of sophistication and slickness previously unseen in the series. One common feature identified by many fan commentators, however, was an increased emphasis on concepts and imagery at the expense of *Doctor Who*'s more traditional strengths of good, straightforward plotting and solid characterisation. In other words, many felt that style was being given precedence over content.

Notwithstanding these common concerns about its artistic direction, the series gained very respectable ratings during the fifth Doctor's era – particularly so during the first of the three seasons, when it achieved a significant improvement on the previous year's unusually poor performance. One important factor underlying this upturn in popularity was the rescheduling of the series away from its traditional Saturday teatime slot, where it had recently been suffering in competition with ITV's imported American science fiction series *Buck Rogers in the 25th Century*. In its new weekday evening slot, with its episodes going out at the rate of two a week in the manner of a soap opera, it reached a whole new group of viewers, many of whom would no doubt not have counted themselves amongst *Doctor Who*'s traditional audience.

Another factor contributing to the series' improved ratings was the high public profile that it continued to maintain. One thing of which *Doctor Who* certainly did not go short during this period was promotion. Nathan-Turner was very publicity conscious, and – working in conjunction with senior BBC press officer Kevin O'Shea – highly skilled at dealing with the media. This contributed greatly to the series generating extensive newspaper coverage, many television guest spots for its stars, copious quantities of spin-off merchandise and numerous promotional events – undoubtedly the biggest of which was the chaotic twentieth anniversary convention staged by BBC Enterprises at Longleat House.

The Davison era maintained *Doctor Who*'s position as an important and highly-regarded element of the BBC's steadily diminishing output of family programming. It did however provide some portents of the coming fall from grace that would see the series just managing to escape cancellation in 1985 and ultimately failing to do so in 1989. The changes in style and dramatic content that had so concerned many fan commentators would be taken still further during the sixth Doctor's tenure, when the overall look of the series would grow increasingly gaudy and stylised and the stories would become steadily more concerned with continuity and less with straightforward, comprehensible plotting.

The move to a two-episodes-per-week transmission schedule meant that the series was now on the air for only three months each year, rather than for six as it had been in the recent past, providing less of an opportunity for it to become imprinted on the minds of the nation's viewers as a permanent feature of the television landscape. This problem would also be carried forward to later years when, although there would be a return to the more traditional one-episode-per-week format, the number of episodes per season would be effectively halved (with double-length episodes for the sixth Doctor's establishing season and standard-length episodes thereafter).

In many ways, the fifth Doctor's era marked the end of the original *Doctor Who* as a series with a wide popular appeal amongst the general viewing public. In its declining years, despite presenting many good stories and ultimately undergoing something of a creative renaissance, it would find itself playing principally to an ever-dwindling audience of cult science fiction fans.

The Sixth Doctor

by

David J Howe

Mark Stammers

Stephen James Walker

INTRODUCTION BY COLIN BAKER

On 10 June 1983, I went to visit John Nathan-Turner at the BBC at his request, not in any way suspecting that that visit would result in my sitting at this word-processor ten years later reflecting on the fact that the work of this 'jobbing' actor could result in a book containing such meticulous and detailed research as that which follows this introduction.

And certainly when, exactly six months later, I stepped into BBC's Rehearsal Room 202 in Acton, I would have perhaps been a little more unnerved, rather than elated and nervous, had I known the exact course of events that would follow over the next three years, culminating in that 29 October 1986 phone call from John Nathan-Turner informing me of the order from above to 'regenerate'!

Now that the moving finger has written and moved inexorably onwards, it is, I am happy to say, predominantly the happy memories that endure, both in the making of the programme and in the warmth and generosity of many of the people I have met as a result of making it.

Having been a guest actor in other series in the past, I was very aware that the regular performer/performers in a series dictate to a certain extent the working atmosphere at rehearsals and in the studio. I was therefore delighted to have the opportunity of ensuring that the atmosphere during the time of the sixth Doctor should be conducive to everyone giving their best, whilst enjoying themselves at the same time. Arguably we sometimes enjoyed ourselves inordinately, particularly when Pat Troughton and Frazer Hines joined us or when we joined Brian Blessed (it would almost be *lèse majesté* to envisage it the other way round)! But I like to think that the work was enhanced rather than suffered as a result of all the good humour.

I was also extremely lucky in my companion. Nicola Bryant had received a lot of good-natured chaffing from Peter Davison along the lines of 'Colin Baker, eh???' followed by a lot of head-shaking and sucking in of air through the teeth – much in the same way as any *soi-disant* expert does when I tell them what car, computer or lawn-mower I have just bought. (Long suck – 'Oh, I could have got that for you for next to nothing, they're phasing them out because the technology' …. etc …. etc).

So Nicola, whilst being aware that she was being wound up, nonetheless viewed the impending regeneration with a little uncertainty. And, of course, from my point of view, she was the old hand and I was replacing her Doctor! But we very soon realised that we worked well together, after she had discovered that there was a slight difference between the Doctor and the actor. At least I hope there is, even if only in terms of dress sense.

It didn't take long before going to work became like going to another home. There are those, I suppose, who might not find that desirable, but I like to feel surrounded by kindred spirits when working. I found John Nathan-Turner a very supportive producer to work with and whilst he could quite properly crack the whip on occasion, nonetheless he would happily enter into the badinage at other times. He was also very much a part of the team, putting in regular appearances at rehearsals rather than simply turning up for the 'Producer's Run', with that 'Right, let's see you earn your money' attitude, which can be somewhat intimidating when that is the only time a producer puts in an appearance. The crew were also a welcome constant. We developed a great rapport with Alec Wheal and his camera team, which saved a lot of time in the studio and added to the enjoyment.

We had some splendid guests on the show – I have very fond memories of working with Maurice Denham, a gentle and understated genius, and Kevin McNally, with whom we laughed a lot on *The Twin Dilemma*, with the inventive and talented Nabil Shaban, the deceptively effortless Martin Jarvis and the refreshingly charming and unaffected Jason Connery in *Vengeance on Varos*, with Sarah Greene, Faith Brown and David Banks in *Attack of the Cybermen*, the irreplaceable Pat Troughton, the irrepressible Frazer Hines and the irredeemable Jackie Pearce in *The Two Doctors*, with the under-used Anthony Ainley and my former sparring partner from the days of *The Brothers*, the eternally glamorous and versatile Kate O'Mara, in *Mark of the Rani*, with that eschewer of understatement Paul Darrow in *Timelash*, and marvellous William Gaunt, Eleanor Bron and Clive Swift in *Revelation of the Daleks* – not to mention the odd Dalek!

In the Trial season the team was joined by Lynda Bellingham, Michael Jayston and Tony Selby, all of whom became very good friends. I think the memories of Michael's and my attempts to invent rhyming slang to baffle Tony were highlights of my entire time as the Doctor. (As in: 'Me carrots are really giving me gyp today.' 'Carrots?' 'Yeah, carrots and onions – bunions.' Well, you should have been there!!) Michael is one of the great 'twinklers' of this business, with a great talent and refreshing lack of ego combined with a finely tuned humour – *and* he likes cricket! The visiting artists included wonderful Joan Sims, BRIAN BLESSED for whom there are no words that do not draw on the epic, the dashing and perplexed Patrick Ryecart, Trevor Laird with his infectious laugh, splendid Adam Blackwood, the impossibly divine Honor Blackman, the dry and very funny Malcolm Tierney and the ditto Geoff Hughes, who had the added advantage of making me look like a bantamweight!

And, of course, that season brought Bonnie Langford into the long list of companions. I had worked with Bonnie before in *Goldilocks* at Lincoln, when I could only marvel at her sheer professionalism and all round niceness. In a way, she was an easier companion for the sixth Doctor, because she was in a sense less of a 'woman' than Nicola, so it was easier for the Doctor to be protective, in an avuncular way, which might have been susceptible to misconstruction with the undeniably more nubile Peri. And she lacked her predecessor's advantage of being previously unknown. Everyone knows Bonnie, and so she had a hard task to show us a Mel unencumbered by the baggage of her many outstanding previous roles in many areas of the acting profession. That she succeeded so well is a tribute to her.

I was very impressed by another rare quality of John Nathan-Turner's – he spent a lot of time going around drama schools and spotting and encouraging new young talent, resulting in many new faces that have since become well known, making their first appearance on *Doctor Who*. This was a splendid counter-balance against the fact that very popular and 'name' artists were queuing up to appear on the programme. John also had the happy knack of persuading the best directors to take on the very specialised job of directing *Doctor Who*. In the past, highly respected directors had balked at the challenge of bringing to the screen a programme that demanded so much from what, it must be admitted, was not always an adequate budget. Each director with whom I worked rose to the occasion admirably and I am sure the others will forgive me if I single out Peter Moffatt, who made my first story such a delight to do, by trusting me and encouraging me to be my own Doctor. I think he knows how much that helped me through those

6 SIXTH DOCTOR

first few difficult episodes – I imagine that as an actor of no mean reputation himself, he sensed how best to assist those first few faltering steps! Also I must mention Graeme Harper, whom I knew as a young assistant floor manager on *War and Peace* in 1971. He was an amazingly resilient campaigner in a very difficult, whipping-boy position. I was not surprised to find that his energy and enthusiasm had not dimmed over fifteen years and that his boundless appetite for the job and ability to create on the hoof, as it were, made him a delight to work with. And the end results were original and vital.

I cannot recall once during my tenure in the role wishing that I were doing anything else. In a sense, it was as well that Michael Grade and Jonathan Powell decided that three years was the optimum gap between regenerations, otherwise I might have been sorely tempted to try to match my foolishly declared ambition of beating Tom Baker's impressive seven years as the Doctor.

Given the enduring popularity of *Doctor Who*, it is inevitable, I must concede, that I am frequently and sometimes uncomfortably reminded of the less pleasant elements of my brief time in 'the best role on television'. It is still a great sadness to me that there is a handful of people on the fringes of the programme whose misguided devotion to it has led them to engage in behaviour that can at best be described as selfish and arrogant and at worst pathological and vindictive. Whilst I myself have suffered only slightly from the effect of this blinkered obsession, it pains me to see that others have been hounded quite so mercilessly for that great crime – having a different belief. I would draw the attention of those concerned to the effects of intolerance and vendetta on the world around us today and in our daily news. Whilst the plights of Yugoslavia and Salman Rushdie may seem far removed from the subject of this book, and I have no wish to diminish them by this seemingly banal comparison, it is assuredly from the smallest of such seeds of envy and bigotry that grow the forests of hatred and destruction.

It would be inappropriate to end this introduction without paying a tribute to the many members of the *Doctor Who* Appreciation Society and other unaligned fans of *Doctor Who*, worldwide, who have been kind enough not only to write and tell me that they have found my work not unwatchable, but who have also been warm-hearted enough to take on board a charity that means a lot to me. The Foundation for the Study of Infant Deaths has repeatedly benefited from the generosity and industry of fans of the programme who have pushed Daleks, run conventions, held raffles, made films, sold memorabilia and generally harassed people into giving to this very worthy cause. I know that the recent drop in the incidence of cot-deaths is due in part to money raised in this way to fund the research that led to the recognition that sleeping position, temperature, and cigarette smoking in pregnancy were significant and avoidable contributory factors. For that I will be eternally in their debt.

Finally I would like to commend this book to you. I know the authors. They are honourable men. I may not agree with every opinion expressed herein, but like many others before me, I will defend to their last drop of blood their right to hold those opinions. I am grateful to them for the opportunity to write this introduction and hope that you will be as stimulated and intrigued as I have been to read the results of their endeavours. I am amazed how much I didn't know! I know you will find it fascinating and eminently readable.

Colin Baker 20/05/1993

FOREWORD

As the swirling sea of colour dissipated and the burly figure of the new Doctor sat up abruptly on the TARDIS floor, the 21 year-old television series *Doctor Who* was – like its leading character – about to enter the most unsettled and difficult period of its history, which would see changes to its format, weekly slot and season length, as well as the eventual halving of its average viewing audience.

The sixth Doctor in the person of Colin Baker was introduced to the press on 20 August 1983. The event even made the BBC's own early evening news broadcast, which commented on the actor's earlier *Doctor Who* appearance as Maxil in the fifth Doctor story *Arc of Infinity*.

The press quizzed Baker as to how long he would like to play the role, and Baker replied – possibly with tongue in cheek – that as Tom Baker had played the role of the Doctor for seven years, he would have to play the character for at least eight years, as he could not bear the thought of anyone having done it for longer than him.

This statement was ultimately proved to be quite ironic, as events overtook Colin Baker's intentions, and the era of the sixth Doctor turned out to be the shortest of his television incarnations to that date, consisting of only eight individual stories over a period of a little under three years.

After three, fairly successful seasons with Peter Davison in the title role, producer John Nathan-Turner found himself having to choose another actor to carry the programme into the second half of the decade. Davison had decided to leave the series in May 1983 after having asked for an extended period in which to consider whether or not he could accept the offer of a contract for a fourth season. In the meantime, Nathan-Turner had been considering Colin Baker as a suitable replacement in case Davison did decide to leave. Baker's own vibrant and open personality was well suited to the role, and would prove an interesting contrast to Davison's more reserved nature.

Nathan-Turner telephoned Baker directly, asking him to come and see him. The actor assumed he was being asked to open a fête or some-such event, little guessing that he was actually being sounded out for the role that he himself had considered asking his agent to put him up for when the fourth Doctor, Tom Baker, had departed in 1981. Once offered the part, Baker agreed without a moment's hesitation.

The new Doctor's era took place in a Britain in the middle of a prosperity boom. House prices were rocketing, and the mobile phone had become the badge of a new social class nicknamed yuppies. In the world at large, the threat of war had receded as the Soviet Union's new moderate president Mikail Gorbachev discussed the end of the nuclear arms race with US President Ronald Reagan. The Conservative Government was into its second term under the leadership of Mrs Margaret Thatcher, *Spitting Image* arrived on television, and the Duke and Duchess of York were married.

During the mid-Eighties the nature of broadcast television in Britain was entering a state of change. Competition for audience share was growing between the independent television companies and the BBC. Technology had altered the viewing habits of the British public. Instead of being slaves to the programme schedulers as to when they could watch their favourite series, they could choose what to watch and when to watch

6 SIXTH DOCTOR

it, by using the video recorders that were becoming common household items up and down the country. This meant that the often-used ploy of scheduling two popular programmes at the same time on opposing channels, forcing the viewer to choose a channel and then stick with it, no longer worked, as one programme could be recorded whilst the other was being watched live. This fact also made something of a mockery of the audience viewing figures that all television channels used to judge the impact of their output, as no account was taken at that time of programmes watched on video.

The BBC needed to modernise its image, as well as increase its activities into new areas such as breakfast television and daytime broadcasting, where it had not previously competed for viewers. Meanwhile, the BBC was also taking its share of the flak arising from the government's apparent obsession with bias against its policies in news and current affairs programmes. This led to a siege mentality developing amongst the top management of the Corporation.

On the face of it, none of these events would seem to have had any bearing on *Doctor Who*, yet indirectly they all played a part in the cancellation of the original Season 23, and to some extent in the eventual replacement of Colin Baker in the lead role.

We have spoken to many different people involved in making *Doctor Who* during the period in question, although regrettably the producer, John Nathan-Turner, declined to contribute to this book, explaining that, at the time we were researching it, he wanted to distance himself from *Doctor Who*. We also received help from many fans of the series, and we hope that this volume presents a balanced and accurate record of perhaps the most turbulent and controversial period in *Doctor Who*'s long history.

Doctor Who in this period was adult in content, and yet featured a Doctor with a heart of gold – and a tasteless coat! Join us as we re-visit the era of the sixth Doctor.

COLIN BAKER: IN HIS OWN WORDS

ON HIS EARLY LIFE:
'I was born in London – on Waterloo Bridge, which is quite a feat, isn't it? At the south end of Waterloo Bridge there is a hospital called the Royal Waterloo Lying-in Hospital, and in the summer of 1943, I was born in the maternity ward on the top floor of this hospital, during an air raid!'
Interviewed by David Banks in July 1989 for *The Ultimate Interview*, released by Silver Fist tapes.

'I spent the first two years of my life dodging bombs. I was oblivious of the fact, although I do still have a piece of shrapnel about the size of a key, which apparently embedded itself in the back of my infant cot when the house opposite caught a direct hit. But for the six inches by which that missed my head, I wouldn't be sitting here today. Those are the little threads of circumstance that separate life and death. It's quite extraordinary, isn't it? Those little, tiny things.

'When I was two years old, I met my father, who'd been away fighting in the war. He'd come home on leave a couple of times before, which I gather had been quite traumatic for me. At two, I didn't like the idea of this *man* who suddenly appeared and whom Mummy seemed to *like* quite a lot. At least, I've been told that. I don't remember it at all.

'I have an appallingly vague memory of my childhood. I think all the information that I trot out on these occasions is stuff I've been *told*! Memory is half what you do actually remember and half what's been topped up by others through the years.

'When I was two or three years old, after my father came back, he was then moved from London up to Manchester for his work. He was managing director of an asbestos company. So I went up to live in the north of England when I was quite young, and lived there until I was 23. When I said that I wanted to be an actor, that was dismissed by my father as being an unworthy occupation for an intelligent young man, so I was despatched off to law college. I studied law for five years.

'About the time I was due to start practising as a solicitor, I decided I'd had *enough*. It just didn't work. I was anarchic, I'm afraid. I had too exaggerated a sense of justice to work in the law. It's quite interesting, but it does tie in with the Doctor actually. The Doctor isn't about the letter of the law at all – he's about *justice*. Natural justice, intergalactic justice or whatever you like. And I always felt that way. The company I worked for was a big company that always worked for the big man and was always crushing the little man, or so it seemed to me. So I used to be very *unethical*! I used to decide who I thought was in the right and structure the case accordingly! I used to tip people off! I'd ring 'em up and say, "Look, you're about to have a summons served on you – I should make myself scarce if I were you," and things like that.

'I've never regretted studying law, though, because it does mean that, for instance, I can buy and sell my own house without having to hire a solicitor, I can make my own will and I can sue people.'

Interviewed by C L Crouch in 1985 for *Fantasy Empire* Issue 19.

ON HIS EARLY ACTING CAREER:

'I actually made one TV appearance as a child. This was around 1954. It was in a series called *My Wife's Sister*, starring Eleanor Summerfield, Martin Wyldeck and Helen Christie.

'In this particular story, Eleanor Summerfield has met a Frenchman who is very good looking, with a moustache and everything. She then has a dream that she is married to him, and she has three little boys. The viewer then sees the backs of these three little boys gathered around a Christmas tree. They all turn around, and they all have moustaches pencilled on. The middle one, which was me, then says, "*Jolie Noel* Papa."

'I got that part because I came top in French that year! The mother of one of the kids at the school was the casting director at Granada. They wanted three kids, and they asked who was good at French. "Oh, Colin is," came the reply. That set me on the slippery slope.'

Interviewed by Michael Sibley in May 1987 for *The Colin Baker Interview*.

'I was brought up in Rochdale and went to school in Manchester. Then, when I was twelve years old, at St Bede's College in Manchester, I was invited to take part in a production of *Yeoman of the Guard*. They did Gilbert and Sullivan each year at my school. So I was in the chorus for *Yeoman of the Guard*. Then, when I was thirteen, for some bizarre reason known only to themselves, they decided I ought to play the female lead. So I played Phyllis in *Iolanthe*.'

Interviewed by Trevor Ramsay in June 1989 for *Time Lord* Issue 4.

'I got a review in the school magazine that read: "Colin Baker threw himself with verve into the part of Phyllis and rarely strayed more than half an octave from the notes." At the time, I thought that was a good review! Thereafter, I appeared in the Gilbert and Sullivan production every year at school.

'When I left school, I went with my mother to see an amateur production of *The King and I* at the Palace Theatre, Manchester. I said to my mother, "I'd love to do that," and the man sitting in front of me turned around and said, "I'm the president of this society. If you'd like to join, come along next Friday night." So I joined the North Manchester Amateur Dramatic Society, and I got really hooked on it. I was studying law at the time, and after five years I thought, "Blow this for a game of soldiers. I'll have a go at doing what I want to do. I've only got one life, so I'll have a try." So I went to drama school and started acting.'
Interviewed by Paul Duncan in 1984 for *Arkensword* Issue 11.

'On 23 May 1969 I made my first professional appearance on the stage, in a play called *Plaintiff in a Pretty Hat* at the Arts Theatre in Cambridge. This was after completing three years' training at the London Academy of Music and Dramatic Art, or LAMDA for short, which I entered at the advanced age of 23, having already done five years' training as a lawyer and deciding that the law wasn't for me.'
Interviewed by Bob Furnell, Dean King and Janette Taylor in March 1987 for *Time Meddlers of Vancouver*.

'My career stared when I was 26. I did two or three years of repertory theatre, in local theatres all over the country. Then I was quite lucky to get my first television very early on, in a series called *Roads to Freedom*. That set the ball rolling, because the next part I got was in the BBC version of *War and Peace*, with Tony Hopkins as Pierre. It was a 26-part series, but it was stunning. It was beautifully done, and I was lucky enough to play Prince Anatol Kuragin. If you know the story, he's the one who elopes with Natasha. The sort of villain of the piece. That took about a year and a half to do. Then I played Count Wenceslas Steinbock in a thing called *Cousin Bette*, which was a BBC serialisation of the Balzac novel.

'I did a lot of those kind of "classics". Then I did a fair bit of theatre again. I was at the Chichester Shakespeare Festival. I did *Macbeth* and *Hamlet*, things like that. Around 1974, I got the part of a ruthless tycoon, a J R type, in a series called *The Brothers*, which I suppose was a kind of forerunner of soap operas like *Dallas* and *Dynasty*.'
Interviewed by C L Crouch in 1985 for *Fantasy Empire* Issue 19.

ON HIS ROLE AS PAUL MERRONEY IN *THE BROTHERS*:

'I was J R before J R was! In England I was the man you loved to hate, which made me the most unpopular person, but at the same time the most popular.

'It was a series that was on in England from about 1967 until 1976. Halfway through the programme, I came into it. It was about a haulage company – truck driving – which was run by three brothers. And the three brothers all had their own problems. It was a bit like the *Dallas* set-up, only it was set in London and they didn't sit by the pool freezing to death pretending it was hot. Halfway through the series, the company had to expand, so they had to borrow from the bank, and the bank put in a chairman at the company. This young guy was Paul Merroney, a whiz-kid banker. He was totally ruthless, totally unscrupulous, but totally honest, unlike J R. He never did anything anyone could send him up for, he just ruined people's lives.

'He was a very interesting character, and he made my name what it was in England, so much so that when the programme ended in 1976, I was out in the cold a bit. I couldn't do any television for about five years. I did stage work. That's the good thing in England; there's a very vital theatre network, and they're very anxious to get people they've seen on television out into the theatres. So you can earn a very good living working in the theatre. But I missed television, so it's been quite nice to get back in again. It did rather typecast me. I've always got villain parts until now. They always cast me as the heartless, stone-blooded type.

'I enjoyed the success of *The Brothers* while it was happening. I went to Israel and was told that the Arabs would have stood a better chance during the Six Day War if they had attacked on the night *The Brothers* was on. I was at a party and I had a phone call from Moshe Dayan, who said how very upset he was at not being invited and how much he enjoyed the programme. It had that kind of impact. It was the same in Sweden as well.'
Interviewed by Jean Airey in 1984 for *Fantasy Empire* Issue 12.

'I made Paul Merroney totally emotionless and without any sense of humour at all. He didn't drink or womanise, and was interested only in business. He was not an unpleasant person, but if you got in his way he would utterly destroy you – legally, honestly and cleverly, which I thought was a little bit more interesting than the "J R" type. Just by chance, another actor who was playing a pivotal role in the series left, and there was a kind of gap. They thought the character of Paul Merroney was a good one to write up, so they asked me to do the next series, and I stayed for about three series. This got me voted the most hated man on television!'
Interviewed by Michael Sibley in May 1987 for *The Colin Baker Interview*.

'*The Brothers* finished in 1976. We didn't *know* it had finished. What usually happened was that we went away for two or three months and did something else. Then the BBC would get in touch – "OK, we're starting again." This time, though, they didn't get in touch! That's the way they work. No-one says, "We're cutting *The Brothers*." They just don't bother to do anything. That was the end of it.'
Interviewed by C L Crouch in 1985 for *Fantasy Empire* Issue 19.

ON HIS CAREER AFTER *THE BROTHERS*:

'I did very little TV for five years after *The Brothers*. That's the trouble with TV series: they tend to restrict your future employment. So I did a lot of touring. I went to Leicester and did *Macbeth* there, and I toured with productions of thrillers and comedies and all sorts of things. I was pretty constantly employed, I'm pleased to say.

'The first TV I did after *The Brothers* was, I think, an episode of *Blake's 7*, in which I played Bayban the Berserker, an intergalactic space pirate. He was the second most dangerous man in the galaxy, which caused him great annoyance because he wanted to be the *most* dangerous man. It was a great part, an over-the-top role.

'Then I did a series called *For Maddie with Love*, which was an afternoon weepie with Nyree Dawn Porter and Ian Hendry. I played a character a bit like the one in *The*

Brothers, a kind of slightly mercenary but very articulate man. I must have done a couple of dozen episodes of that.'
Interviewed by Kevin Taylor in 1989 for *Timelines* Issue 3.

ON HIS ROLE AS MAXIL IN THE *DOCTOR WHO* STORY *ARC OF INFINITY*:
'After *For Maddie with Love*, I guested in three episodes of *Doctor Who* when Peter Davison played the Doctor [*Arc of Infinity*]. I played Maxil, who was chief of security on Gallifrey, and I got to shoot the Doctor. Many people suggested that that was my audition for the part – if you zap the incumbent, you get to be the next one!'
Interviewed by Kevin Taylor in 1989 for *Timelines* Issue 3.

'I played Maxil, aided and abetted by Esmerelda. For those of you who don't know who Esmerelda was, that was the name I gave to the hat that I dragged around with me in the story. It wouldn't go through any of the doors, so I couldn't wear it; I had to carry it.'
Interviewed on stage in 1985 at a convention in Texas, USA.

'I've never been one to regard a small part as a small part. So this guy Maxil struck me as the most important person in the show. I was doing a fair few things during the producer's run, and at the end of it John Nathan-Turner said to me, "Yes, that's fine, but …. This isn't about Maxil the guard, it's about the Doctor." And I replied, "Is it really? Good heavens, I didn't realise that. I thought it was called *The Maxil Show*." He said, "Could you tone down the reactions, please, and the acting in the background." Ha ha! But because of that, when Peter Davison said a few months later that he was going to leave, JN-T thought of me for the part of the Doctor. So it paid off in the end! Purely by chance.'
Interviewed by Kevin Taylor in 1989 for *Timelines* Issue 3.

'A little rider … is that they asked me to play Maxil again, in *The Five Doctors*, but I couldn't, because I was doing something else. If I had taken the part, it would have been too recent, and perhaps I wouldn't be playing the Doctor.'
Interviewed by Paul Duncan in 1984 for *Arkensword* Issue 11.

ON WANTING TO BE CAST AS THE DOCTOR:
'The extraordinary thing is that when it was suggested that Tom Baker was finishing on the programme, I rang up my agent and said, "Look, I want to do that programme, get onto it." And before he could do anything, Peter Davison was announced as the new Doctor. I was really annoyed. I didn't think I had much chance, but I thought it would be nice to have a go. And this time, it happened the other way around. I didn't even know that Peter was leaving when John Nathan-Turner got in touch with me.'
Interviewed by Jean Airey in 1984 for *Fantasy Empire* Issue 12.

ON THE INITIAL SECRECY SURROUNDING HIS CASTING AS THE DOCTOR:
'It had to be hidden for a long time. In fact, John Nathan-Turner and I were having a sneaky drink at a pub one day when Peter Davison came in quite by chance, and we had to make up stories. He knew he was going, but John didn't want anyone knowing who was taking over until the right moment. So I had to pretend I was there for another

purpose. "I come to clean the windows." It's tough as an actor.'
Interviewed by Jean Airey in 1984 for *Fantasy Empire* Issue 12.

ON HIS INITIAL THOUGHTS ABOUT PLAYING THE DOCTOR:

'It's a bit like Biggles or *Just William* or Dan Dare, isn't it?

'I want to continue the tradition of making him as quirky and as eccentric as possible; to inject a little acid humour occasionally, perhaps. I think what the producers try to do with Doctor Who is to use as much of the actor's own personality as possible, because it's such a high-density rehearsal and performance rate that you don't have time to go out on a limb.

'Hopefully it'll be a combination of my ideas and their ideas … A lot of it depends on scripts, of course. People have to write the scripts before you can do it … An "edge" is a word that is useful to use.

'It's very exciting. There is no other part like it, because there are no other parts where you can actually play the same part as someone else in a television series that has already been created.

'Doctor Who must be nice. "Nice" doesn't mean, necessarily, soft! I think it's important that Doctor Who can be a bit spiky sometimes.

'It is one of those characters that has somehow got into … almost sort of current mythology. You do bracket him with the sort of great folk heroes of literature. And it was, I think, the first of the science fiction, if it can be so called, programmes on television. It transcends the age gap: children love it, adults love it.'
Interviewed in August 1983 for BBC1's *Breakfast Time* – his first ever *Doctor Who* interview.

ON HIS INTEREST IN SCIENCE FICTION:

'I think I have one advantage that perhaps none of the previous Doctors has had, which is that I have always been a sci-fi fan. Which means that there's more to it than just doing a job; it's something extra. So I think I'll enjoy doing it for as long as it's there.

'Obviously in a science fiction show you have to have some special effects, but I think special effects should serve the show rather than the show be a showcase for the special effects. Particularly in a show like *Doctor Who*. When you're making a big movie like *Star Wars*, the special effects play a much larger part, and quite rightly, too. With a programme like *Doctor Who*, what matters most are the story and the characters and the interplay between the characters. Obviously if someone points a piece of twisted plastic at you, you can't just say, "Bang, you're dead." It's got to look as if something's happening, so the effect is put on electronically as an enhancement rather than as the whole.

'I love special effects. I can sit forever and watch that scene in *2001: A Space Odyssey* where the characters are running around inside the spacecraft, exercising. I adore that film, *2001: A Space Odyssey*. It's wonderful. I love all the *Star Wars* stuff. I love *Battlestar: Galactica*.'
Interviewed by Jean Airey in 1984 for *Fantasy Empire* Issue 12.

'I'm not mad keen, but science fiction is what I've read more of than anything else. There are some authors, like Ursula le Guin, Anne McCaffrey and Frank Herbert, whose every book I have got. I've just been reading the Thomas Covenant books.'
Interviewed by Paul Duncan in 1984 for *Arkensword* Issue 11.

6 SIXTH DOCTOR

ON WATCHING EARLIER ERAS OF *DOCTOR WHO*:

'I watched a lot of Hartnell and Troughton, and some Pertwee. Not so much Tom, and not so much Peter, because I was working.

'The ones I watched were in the days when I was younger, before I was an actor. But I've always watched it when I could. I've enjoyed the series and I have memories dotted all along its twenty-four years.'

Interviewed by Penny Holme in 1986 for *Doctor Who Magazine* No. 118.

ON HIS DOCTOR'S COSTUME

'John Nathan-Turner said to me, "What would you like to wear?" and I found that very difficult. My first instinct, which was wrong, was to wear something like the Master wears, all in black, something quite austere. It would have been wrong, I can see that … it's just that I would like to wear slimming black!

'Nothing in Earth's history appealed to me, and you can't really use something futuristic for the Doctor, it's wrong. Then John said, "I think it should be very bad taste." I thought, "Yes, that is rather a good idea for my Doctor. He would just grab something and not care about it. Then, even though he may have realised that it's appalling, he would never admit it, and therefore he would be stuck with wearing it!

'We gave it to a designer, Pat Godfrey, and said, "Give us something in bad taste," and she came back with an exquisitely tasteful design of lots of apparently clashing colours … It's very hard for a designer to design something in bad taste. We said, "No, too good," and sent her away and away and away, until she came back with the present one, which she hated actually putting together, because it was so appalling. But even so, when you get used to it, it has its own entity.

'The only thing I don't like about it is that it's so hot when we're out filming. When we were filming in Spain, it was a hundred and ten degrees, and a couple of weeks ago on Brighton beach, there was no respite from the sun, and it was horrendous.

'But it's lovely on cold locations, when the companions in their skimpy costumes are all shivering and chattering their teeth. So you can't win 'em all.'

Interviewed by Penny Holme in 1986 for *Doctor Who Magazine* No. 118.

'The only things that changed for Season 23 were the waistcoat and the ties; the trousers and the jacket were the same. We did have to have extra jackets made, because of scenes like the one where I had to be submerged in quicksand.

'I did keep saying that I wanted to change the costume, but it's a large expense, unfortunately. John liked it as it was and so was not prepared to waste money, as he saw it. They did let me have new waistcoats and ties, just in order to make the timescale clear. I had a different tie and cat button in each of the different time zones.'

Interviewed by Michael Sibley in May 1987 for *The Colin Baker Interview*.

ON RECORDING THE REGENERATION SCENE IN *THE CAVES OF ANDROZANI*:

'I'd met Peter Davison before on *Arc of Infinity*, but of course I didn't know then that I was going to be playing the Doctor. I was only slightly involved in *The Caves of Androzani*, because I just turned up on the studio day and did it.

'Peter and I didn't have much time to discuss the role, because he was very busy.

'After the recording, I went home, got out of my car, opened my front door, walked in to where my wife was sitting watching television, and stood there and said, "*I am the Doctor.*" She looked at me and said, "Oh yes? Could you take the rubbish out, please."'
Interviewed by Gary Levy in December 1984 for *Doctor Who Bulletin* Issue 17/18.

ON PLAYING THE DOCTOR:

'I've already found that, like all SF TV, *Doctor Who* is good fun off stage, very light hearted.

'Most of the work an actor does tends to be bread and butter, not *Hamlet*. This combines the best of working, as it is so creative.

'As an actor it is marvellous in another way too, for every story has a new cast of guest stars. And, of course, as a devotee of *Doctor Who*, what could be better for me? A fair few years employment in a role that goes round the world and that I've always wanted to do. Wonderful!

'It was exciting to get the role, not daunting. It's not like playing Hamlet. I used to get recognised from my time in *The Brothers* sometimes, but right from the announcement in August, people have been recognising me as the Doctor, and I'm fully aware that I'm going to be unable to go anywhere without being looked at from now on.'
Interviewed by Wendy Graham in 1984 for *Space Voyager* No. 9.

'I believe that Tom Baker was quite right, that whoever plays the Doctor does have a responsibility never to cause any children ever to have the remotest worry about what they see him do in public. So I have no intention of breaking the senses of England as I amble through the streets. I think one does have to be very responsible, one's going into so many homes. To go into someone's home like that is a privilege. To be welcomed as the Doctor in this programme is an even greater privilege.

'I can't get over the fact that there are some actors who say, "Oh, look, this is a real drag, all these people wanting autographs." My answer to that is, "Well, do something else then. Go be a bus driver." If you want to be an actor, you want people to see your work. The more people who see your work, the better you're doing your job. The other side of that is that people are going to want you to sign bits of paper for them. If it makes them happy, why the hell not? It's lovely. What other job do you get where people come up to you and say, "I really like what you do"? The majority of the people around the world never get any feedback on the work they do. They go and they do it nine to five. They go home and nobody says, "You're doing well." It's wonderful, isn't it?

'I also love being the centre of attention. It's really nice. It suits me.'
Interviewed by Jean Airey in 1984 for *Fantasy Empire* Issue 12.

'I want everyone who watches *Doctor Who* not to be disappointed that I'm playing it. I think we all have our favourite Doctor, and it is usually the one who was the Doctor when we started watching it. Each Doctor has left a block of loyalty behind him. There's a huge following for Tom Baker. A strong following for Peter. Maybe in ten years' time, the fans will feel the same way about me. I hope so. That's nice, as long as nobody says, "This is the *only* Doctor," and all the rest of it. That's silly, because they've all brought something to the part. They're all very good actors.'
Interviewed by Paul Duncan in 1984 for *Arkensword* Issue 11.

'The atmosphere is great – we have a good time. We always have the same camera crew in the studio, and I've known them from other programmes – we get on very well. I flatter myself that I'm a fairly easy person to get along with, and I'm not at all autocratic. There are people paid to do jobs: writers to write, directors to direct, producers to produce and actors to act. Of course, we discuss things, but I would hate to be in the position where my power was such that I could say, "No, I want that cut, I want this line in," and all that, because I think when you're this closely connected with it, you are least qualified to know best.'
Interviewed by Gary Russell and Justin Richards in 1985 for *Doctor Who Magazine* Issue 97.

'At no stage does one ever really feel *au fait* with any part. There's always something one can learn and there are always further avenues to be explored. But if the question is, do I feel happy in the role?, then the answer is most emphatically yes. Right from the very beginning, I felt that it was a part for which I – in all humility – was ideally suited, by chance rather than by any great skill on my part. And right from the beginning, I've enjoyed doing it.

'I enjoy the totality of it. There isn't an individual aspect that overrides all the others; it's playing the role that I enjoy. I enjoy the day to day work in rehearsal with other actors, I enjoy the studio work, and I enjoy the moment when the next script pops through the letter box and – a little ahead of the viewer – I find out what's going to happen next.'
Interviewed by Doug Smith in 1985 for *Fan Aid* Issue 2.

'Being associated with something that has such a grip on the imagination of several generations. It really is part of current mythology.

'It's like playing Robin Hood, or King Arthur. It's one of those characters …

'I was already sufficiently impressed with the fact that I was playing it, but I've had a great many, very respected actors who've said to me, "You've got the best part in television." And in a sense they're right.

'It's given me a more secure life – or rather did give me a more secure life until Michael Grade's intervention last year, when the future of the programme seemed a little bleak. But that's beginning to turn over again, and I think everyone is now aware of the value of *Doctor Who* in people's lives.'
Interviewed by Penny Holme in 1986 for *Doctor Who Magazine* No. 118.

'I felt very positive about what I could add to the programme, and a kind of sense of responsibility. It's like when you take the baton and you've got the next 400 metres to run. You don't drop the baton, you don't throw it into the crowd, you don't stop and pick your nose. You actually do something worthwhile while you've got it; you do your best. I was always aware of that responsibility, and not just as a job; it was more than a job. I wanted to honour the tradition that those other five guys had upheld so marvellously before. I just wanted to add another cherry to the cake.'
Interviewed by Nick Briggs in 1990 for the *Myth Makers 19* video, released by Reeltime Pictures.

ON HIS MARRIAGE TO ACTRESS MARION WYATT:

'It was a pretty instant thing. I wasn't looking for a serious relationship at the time. I was having a jolly good time by myself, doing all the things that chaps do when they're younger, like swilling beer, smoking too much and being a bit of a slob.

'The thing was that I'd hardly ever lived by myself. I'd shared flats, lived with girls, then married [to actress Liza Goddard]. So I took full advantage of the situation.

'At first I was hesitant about marriage again. Having had one failure, I wanted to be sure I was doing the right thing. But then I knew this wasn't going to go wrong – and it hasn't. I don't think it's a problem being married to an actress, either. There's extra pressure, of course. But it's people who go wrong, not their jobs.

'Marion isn't career crazy and she's not jealous of my current success, either. She loves the country life we lead with our dogs and messing about in the home. She, like me now, knows what comes first.'

Interviewed by Ivan Waterman in 1984 for the *News of the World*, 29 April.

ON THE DEATH OF HIS SON JACK:

'It was like being hit in the stomach by a steam hammer. That's the only way I can explain it. Everything just stood still. It was totally numbing and draining. Marion and I will never, ever get over it. It's not something you *can* "get over".

'It took me twelve hours to get home [from working on *The Mousetrap* in Malmo, Sweden]. It was the longest night of my life. As I waited for a boat to catch the plane, I was plagued by the appalling thought that Marion was having to cope on her own. I felt so awful that I wasn't there to support her. That I'd been out enjoying myself while our son was lying dead. I kept thinking: "I knew him only four weeks. I never saw my baby smile." I kept asking, "Would it have happened if I'd been at home? Was it something to do with the last time I held him? Were we feeding him right? Was the house too big, too small, too hot, too cold? Why? Why? Why?"

'He just stopped breathing. He wasn't in any discomfort. It was just as if the habit of breathing hadn't established itself firmly enough.'

Interviewed by Mary Peplow in 1984 for *Woman's Realm*, 1 September.

'Jack died almost a year ago this week, when I was about two weeks away from starting work on *Doctor Who*. I got in touch with the Foundation for the Study of Infant Deaths as soon as it happened, because I didn't know anything about cot death and I wanted to find out about it. Then a newspaper wanted to do an article about Jack's death, and the last thing I wanted to do at the time, about a week after it happened, was to talk to a newspaper, but suddenly I thought, "Maybe I can use this to help." Out of something dreadful like that, one can actually derive some good, and the good I could do was to make the newspaper pay an awful lot of money to the Foundation, which they did happily – it's terrifying what they'll just shell out, especially if it's for a charity, as they don't want to appear mean. Also the article publicised the cause of raising money for cot death research. I mean, 2,000 children a year in this country alone is a lot to go, and nobody knows why.

'The Foundation were, commendably, reticent to use me at the beginning. They said, "Look, give yourself a few months, you might change your mind." But I'm now on the fund-raising committee.

'When I do fêtes and things, I get offered expenses and what have you, and I feel a bit embarrassed saying, "Yes, it's £7.42 please," so I just ask them to make a donation to the Foundation.'
Interviewed by Dominic May, David Saunders and Robert Moubert in November 1984 for *TARDIS* Volume 9 Issue 3.

ON THE LENGTH OF HIS STAY IN *DOCTOR WHO*:
'I'm going to have a smashing time, and I'm going to have a long run!'
Interviewed by Wendy Graham in 1984 for *Space Voyager* No. 9.

'My thoughts are long term rather than short term. I am someone who likes to break records, and I understand that someone with a name not dissimilar to mine played the role for seven years. So I'd hate to be known as the second longest-running Doctor.'
Interviewed on stage in 1985 at a convention in Philadelphia, USA.

'I'd like to stay in the part as long as I'm enjoying it and the public want to see me playing it, which may be two years, three years, ten years … I've always stated publicly that it would be nice to equal Tom Baker's number of years and episodes, but that would be quite an achievement, because he did seven years in the show, and made an awful lot of episodes.'
Interviewed by Chris Parnham in 1986 for *The Ribos Operation* Issue 2.

'I think it's probably in other people's hands, rather than my own.
    'Say the choice was mine; when I started doing this, I said that Tom Baker's record of seven years was awfully attractive. I've done it for three years now, even though we've done only two seasons, and I'm enjoying it. So I see no desire on my part in the near future to stop. Also, I'd like to beat the episode tally! In order to do that at the present rate, I'd take about twenty years, because in Tom's day they were making twenty-six episodes a year, now we're down to fourteen.'
Interviewed by Penny Holme in 1986 for *Doctor Who Magazine* No. 118.

ON HIS FIRST *DOCTOR WHO* DIRECTOR, PETER MOFFATT:
'As he was directing the first story, *The Twin Dilemma*, he gave me a lot of room to experiment and try things out, and of course the first script was very strong. I'd never previously worked with Peter. We got on together well and very quickly. Altogether, we had seven days' rehearsal in which we kicked certain ideas around, but it was a very pleasant process. It wasn't at all traumatic.'
Interviewed by Bill Baggs in 1984 for *Time Watcher*.

ON *THE TWIN DILEMMA*:
'*The Twin Dilemma* had the problem of establishing a new Doctor, and the difficulties of regeneration were the prime element of the story. In a sense, the plot of Mestor and Azmael and so on was subsidiary to that. Had the story been too strong, it might have distracted from the main purpose of the first story – that is, to establish that the new Doctor was experiencing problems.'
Interviewed by Doug Smith in 1985 for *Fan Aid* Issue 2.

'When I did it, I had nothing to judge it against. I think first scripts are always very difficult. If you look back at any of the incoming Doctors' first scripts, they tend to be very hesitant, because neither the Doctor nor the writers – nor anybody – knows what is actually going to happen, on the basis that any kind of coming together of talents is an organic process.

'We had made certain decisions about what my Doctor was going to be, and I think they were very brave ones, actually. They weren't just mine; we all agreed that we would go for making the Doctor inaccessible, so that people would think, "This isn't my Doctor. Bring back that nice Peter Davison, who was kind and gentle. This awful man is going around strangling Peri, and being remote and arrogant and conceited!"

'The story itself may well have been a weak one. In retrospect, I suspect it possibly was. In fact, it was one of the weaker stories of the time I was doing *Doctor Who*, and certainly didn't compare with the stories I always remember from the past, such as the great Robert Holmes ones of the Tom Baker era. It wasn't in the same league. But that didn't necessarily matter, because you could actually concentrate on what was happening with the Doctor and Peri, and the whole regeneration thing.'

Interviewed by Nick Briggs in 1990 for the *Myth Makers 19* video, released by Reeltime Pictures.

ON *VENGEANCE ON VAROS*:

'*Vengeance on Varos* is one of my favourite shows out of the first complete season. Like all successful plays – as well as *Doctor Who* stories – there are two elements involved. One is that it's on the surface a ripping good story. It's a good adventure, it's well told and the plot's well developed. It has humour in it and good characterisation. But at the same time, it has an underlying theme, which can be quite simply put as: violence corrupts, and violence as a form of entertainment in the media is not exempt from that corrupting effect.

'It's extraordinary that certain elements of criticism have been levelled at *Vengeance on Varos* because of its violence. That seems to me to have missed the whole point of the show. It's a bit like complaining about *Macbeth* because it glorifies regicide, murder and corruption. And – as a parallel – the whole point of *Vengeance on Varos* is that "video nasties" are not a good thing, any more than manipulation of the population is a good thing. For critics – I use a polite term to describe them – to complain because *Vengeance on Varos* portrayed the very scenes of violence it was condemning, strikes me as faintly ludicrous, quite honestly. It has been pointed out that *The A-Team*, which was shown opposite *Vengeance on Varos* on the other channel, was more successful than *Doctor Who* in terms of viewing figures. That illustrates the point that it's very difficult to cope with that kind of violence. *The A-Team* is surely gratuitous, spectacular aggression, and people find it easier to watch that kind of mindless violence. It's a shame that *Doctor Who* was criticised for making exactly that point.'

Interviewed by Doug Smith in 1985 for *Fan Aid* Issue 2.

ON *THE MARK OF THE RANI*:

'*The Mark of the Rani* was excellent. We had the writers, Pip and Jane Baker, with us most of the time on location. They had to do a lot of rewriting, usually because of the poor weather conditions. We had to kind of scrabble for the last few days, so a lot of cutting and changing went on. Pip and Jane went home of a night and produced another few pages to cope with what we'd had to lose or couldn't cope with the day before. I remember that very clearly.

'The thing I liked about Pip and Jane is that they wrote very well for my Doctor; they understood the sixth Doctor very well.'

Interviewed by Nick Briggs in 1990 for the *Myth Makers 19* video, released by Reeltime Pictures.

ON *THE TWO DOCTORS*:

'I'm afraid Patrick Troughton suffered rather badly at my and Frazer Hines' hands. Frazer is one of the quickest-witted, funniest people I've ever met. I mean, he has a repertoire of jokes that would make Bob Hope's card-carriers worry. A very funny man. I made the mistake of battling with Frazer the first two or three weeks of rehearsals, and then I gave up. I kept saying, "Frazer, I'm the Doctor, I do the jokes," but it was really he who did them. So we used to play practical jokes on poor old Patrick. For example, setting him off in his wheelchair. I don't mean that Patrick himself actually had a wheelchair, but there were scenes in the show where he was strapped into a wheelchair, and as soon as he was strapped into it, he became very vulnerable. So we used to play chariot races with poor Patrick.'

Interviewed on stage in 1985 at a convention in Texas, USA.

ON THE CANCELLATION OF THE ORIGINAL SEASON 23:

'Michael Grade wanted very much to do things *his* way, and there's an old saying – "A new broom sweeps clean." The first thing he did was to cancel *Dallas*. This brought such a storm of protest that there was pressure put on from above (so I understand), and it went back on again. The *second* thing he did was to say, because the BBC is a bit short of money, "We've got to save money, so what we're going to do is *not* produce *Doctor Who* this year. That will save us money to do new drama, because we want to do new things, and the only way we can do that is by cancelling some of the *old* things." That was his logic, and so *Doctor Who* fell under the axe. What then happened was another storm of protest – headlines in the national daily newspapers ... "*Doctor Who* Axed!" *Thousands* of letters have been carried into Michael Grade's office ... First from British fans and then, of course, once they got word of it, from the *American* fans.

'I was *shattered* by the cancellation. I was very upset. I mean, if you put it in the context of someone who had just taken over the part – and at the end of my first season, the programme's taken off! Now, I hope and pray – I think I *know* – that it's not because they think, "My God, he's dreadful! Let's take him off!" But none the less, it could be *interpreted* that way. To someone who's not even slightly interested in *Doctor Who*, it reads: "Colin Baker's taken over the part. Oh, yeah, now they've taken it off ..." The two things are linked together subconsciously in people's minds, and I don't like to be associated with that kind of failure!

'Also, I was enjoying *doing* it! I was geared up for it! I was ready to go on to the next series. We should have been starting next week on a superb story, which I'd read and which I was really excited about – a really good one. It was harking back to something in the past, but a very clever story. So, yes, I'm very, very disappointed.'

Interviewed by C L Crouch in 1985 for *Fantasy Empire* Issue 19.

'I have been very busy during the suspension. I've been to America many times to conventions over there. My wife and I had a baby last March, and I have been around home for the past few months, which has been very pleasant. I've had lots of work to do with the charity I'm involved with, the Foundation for the Study of Infant Deaths, to which the *Doctor Who* Appreciation Society have very kindly contributed quite a considerable amount over the last year. I've been very heartened by the way in which the members of DWAS have taken on the charity I'm involved with as their charity, and it's been marvellous to see the response from all the members.'

Interviewed by Chris Parnham in 1986 for *The Ribos Operation* Issue 2.

'Michael Grade came in as Controller of programmes, and he didn't single out *Doctor Who* as such. In the same breath that he axed *Doctor Who*, he summarily ended some other programmes. These included *Come Dancing* and *The Hot Shoe Show* and things like that, which had their own aficionados. For some reason, *Doctor Who* always seems to be able to attract the tabloid press to write headlines. It seems there is some knack the programme has of attracting those newspapers. So all the other programmes that were axed as part of the new Controller's clearout were not really mentioned, while *Doctor Who* was. I think – and this is only my assumption – that probably Michael Grade was taken as much by surprise by that as by anything else.

'I saw him being interviewed on TV a long time before he came to the BBC. He was saying in response to a question that he thought the BBC had become very old fashioned and was producing anachronistic programmes that were driving viewers away. "For instance," he said, "that terrible, tired old format *Doctor Who*." I remember thinking – and this was before I played Maxil even – "I don't agree with that. I quite like *Doctor Who*." That's why it stuck in my brain.

'So he had a declared aversion to the show. He came along, presumably with far-reaching powers to reshape the BBC, and admittedly it did need it. To a certain extent he was right. It was becoming a sort of tired old machine, turning out tired old programmes. It's all part of the same attitude: "Right, we've got to go for change, so let's get rid of some dead wood. That's been on for a long time, so has that, and so has that, so let's get rid of them and get something new in." It does make a certain amount of sense. But not when you're dealing with a commodity like *Doctor Who*, which earns more money than it costs to make. For that reason alone, it's worth keeping, quite apart from the fact that it has a very strong adherence from a lot of people.

'Counting viewers is one thing, but you can count ten million viewers who sit and watch a quiz show in a sort of mild apathy, turn it off and never give it a thought again, or you can say that there are five million who watch *Doctor Who* and think about it non-stop, and who absolutely love the programme. I think the latter is the more worthwhile type of programme to be making.'

Interviewed by Gill Green and Dominic May in September 1987 for *TARDIS*, January 1988 edition.

ON MAKING SCRIPT SUGGESTIONS:

'I sometimes comment on something if I think that there is a better way of doing it, or if it is inconsistent with something that has previously been said, or if my Doctor – I feel – would not behave in precisely that fashion. But ultimately the producer and the

director are the arbiters of what is best, and my attitude is purely that of an actor who is faced with a problem, sometimes, in bringing to the screen that which is written on the paper. On some occasions the producer and the director will agree with me, and on other occasions they will give a very good reason why my suggestion is not as good as the one of the author. The process of bringing a *Doctor Who* story to the screen is – like all acting – collaborative, so there's very little head-on confrontation. It's basically a question of getting together, working with the material we've got and coming up with the best result.'
Interviewed by Doug Smith in 1985 for *Fan Aid* Issue 2.

ON THE *DOCTOR WHO* RADIO SERIAL *SLIPBACK*:

'I think that *Doctor Who* is ideal for radio, given the fact that a major worry in the making of a series like this is the realisation of special effects and sets and costumes. It was wonderful to be in a situation where that was no longer a problem. We had the best sets, the best costumes, the best-looking actors. My costume was wonderful on the radio – it was a shame you couldn't see it!

'I'd been acting on radio for years. I did quite a lot around 1970 to 1972: several Shakespeare plays, poetry readings, all sorts of things. I do enjoy it. It has that wonderful joy that you don't have to learn the lines. You can have an awful lot of fun doing radio productions. They can be much more imaginative than television or theatre, in the sense that the audience – in this case, the listeners – are much more active participants in the play; they are supplying, with your help, all the things that have been taken away from them because it's not a visual production. Some of my most enjoyable experiences of plays have been plays that I've heard on the radio, in ideal circumstances, very often driving in a car, when you can get really involved in the story.'
Interviewed by Patrick White in 1988 for *Tranquil Repose* Issue 6.

ON HIS SENSE OF HUMOUR:

'There are some people who don't understand my sense of humour. I met someone at a convention recently who told me that I had been extremely rude to her at another convention. What it turned out had happened was that I had been walking through the foyer, seen her standing there wearing a huge Tom Baker scarf and said something along the lines of, "Get rid of that scarf at once! How dare you wear that in my presence?" I think the mere fact of saying that indicates that it's not intended to be serious, but this woman had been distraught for weeks because I had told her to remove the scarf. I would say that was hypersensitivity rather than anything that was my fault.'
Interviewed by C L Crouch in 1985 for *Fantasy Empire* Issue 19.

'I don't think uproarious comedy is a good idea in *Doctor Who*, but I enjoy humour and I always try to put in moments of humour. Sometimes the directors like it, sometimes they don't. I think we have decided that the next season will have more of what you might call comedy in it.'
Interviewed by Chris Parnham in 1986 for *The Ribos Operation* Issue 2.

ON *THE TRIAL OF A TIME LORD*:

'I'm very excited by the new season. The trial has a great many twists. The three stories are all very different, and there are also interconnections between them. There are lots of layers, and it's very, very complicated, which I rather like.

'I like things you can't understand, like *Edge of Darkness*. What I loved about that series was what other people objected to, which was that the viewer hadn't got a clue what was going on. It stimulates your thoughts. It's like doing a crossword. I wanted to make the pieces fit before they told me, and I didn't, but it was all totally consistent.

'There is an awful tendency to let the "game show" mentality take over, which is reducing television to its lowest common denominator … I think we have to get away from viewing figures. The BBC is about providing television for everyone, but not necessarily all at the same time. You can have seven million people watching one programme and then going off and doing something else, and a different seven million watching the next one. I think that is more important than having fourteen million sitting in apathy watching something with no contact, which only sinks them further into the stupor that we are encouraged to descend into. The BBC has stood for quality for so long, it would be a shame to allow it to be watered down.'

Interviewed by Penny Holme in 1986 for *Doctor Who Magazine* No. 118.

'It is very difficult when you're actually doing something on the inside to be objective about it. I read all the magazines sent to me, if I get the time. Some of the criticisms I think, "Well, that's fair, that's somebody's opinion." Others I think, "Oh, you stupid berk! That's just being petty and unpleasant, or you have missed the whole point of it!" Sometimes I think people get it into their heads that whatever one does, they are not going to like it, and they will look for things not to like. I think that's a shame.

'I suppose I was naive when, before the season went out and after we had finished it, I said, "I'm so confident of the new season that I think the future of *Doctor Who* is secure." I even thought my own job was secure, because the "buzz" when we were doing each separate story was really good. People I respected, like Michael Jayston, were all saying, "This is good, this is working really well." Michael enjoyed doing it, and I thought it was excellent.'

Interviewed by Michael Sibley in May 1987 for *The Colin Baker Interview*.

'I thought it was a valiant attempt, a decision by Eric Saward and John Nathan-Turner to mirror what was actually going on – the series being on trial. Unfortunately, they fell out in the final analysis of the last episodes. Rightly or wrongly, I don't know. But I think Pip and Jane Baker did a brilliant job writing a replacement script.

'I loved all the stuff with the Valeyard. I thought that was very good. But it could equally have been the Master, and I know that Anthony Ainley was a little put out at being supplanted – he thought, "This is a part I could've played," and indeed he could. 'That's the sort of stuff I like: the good versus evil; opening doors and stepping out on to the beach; Popplewick and all that kind of weirdness in the Fantasy Factory.'

Interviewed by Guy Wainer, Greg Jones, Neil John and David Greenham in 1990 for *Skaro* Volume 5 Issue 2.

ON DOING HIS OWN STUNTS:

'One thing that I have insisted upon, as far as I can, is doing my own stunts. I always object when I'm watching something if I can see that it's a stunt man. In film it's easier to get away with, because they have more money and spend more time on it, so the

6 SIXTH DOCTOR

double actually looks like the actor. But in television, you can see that it's a double; the head turns and you can see that it's not the actor.

'So far, everything that the Doctor has been seen to do, I've actually done. The most painful stunt was one in *The Mark of the Rani*, where I was dangling on a chain above a 150 foot drop – which, I'm happy to say, there was a board across, so that if I had dropped, I wouldn't have fallen 150 feet! It was a very cold day for filming, and my fingers were so numb that I couldn't actually feel them. I was still holding on to the chain while people were hitting me with poles, trying to make me lose my grip, and I got one of my fingers caught in the chain and ripped all the skin off. In fact, it's still bent, as you can see. That was … irritating.

'In the same story, there's a scene where I'm strapped on to a trolley on wheels. Peri supposedly pushes it in the wrong direction and lets go, and I go rolling down a hill. It's shot very well. Actually, everyone's saying it looked very frightening. I found it exhilarating! It was actually great, and I was really annoyed that they got it in the can the first time, because I wanted to go again!

'In *Vengeance on Varos* there's a hanging scene, and the platform on which I was standing collapsed! The rope around my neck tightened a little, but fortunately the bit that collapsed wasn't actually the bit on which I was standing, otherwise I wouldn't be here today.

'There was a lot more uncomfortable stuff, such as a couple of fights in *Revelation of the Daleks* in the snow – it was horrendous snow.'

Interviewed on stage in 1985 at a convention in Texas, USA.

'The scene in *The Trial of a Time Lord* where I had to be submerged in quicksand was brilliant! It was shot at Camber Sands in Kent. The prop boys got there a long time in advance and dug a huge pit. They made two chambers, so basically it was a pit with a wall across the middle. When we shot the scene, we had a couple of guys standing in the first chamber with their arms protruding through a waterproof rubber roof, which was covered with water and had cork etc floated on top of it so that it looked just like sand. That was how the shot was done of the hands coming up through the sand and grabbing my ankles. In the second chamber, which was about six feet deep and filled with water, was a hydraulic lift, with a central pole and a platform at the top. All I had to do was to fall onto the platform, which again was covered with the cork etc to make it look like part of the beach. The lift was then lowered so that it looked as though I was sinking into quicksand. Once my hands had gone under, I had to grab the sides and force my own head down, otherwise I would just have floated. I had to hold myself under for about ten seconds, then come out and do it all over again for a retake. In fact, I had to do it three times, I think.

'The funny thing was, the pit was so well concealed that the sound man fell into it! He was walking around checking the sound with his microphone, and the poor chap fell straight into this thing!'

Interviewed by Michael Sibley in May 1987 for *The Colin Baker Interview*.

ON HIS FAVOURITE *DOCTOR WHO* WRITERS AND DIRECTORS:

'My favourite writer was Robert Holmes, because over the years he contributed more in terms of imagination and depth of writing than did many other writers. All his stories worked on several levels. They worked on the superficial level of a ripping good yarn, but also he always wrote a story that had an underlying, very significant message. He didn't shirk the more thorny problems of violence, or indeed of cannibalism in *The Two Doctors*. That was a fairly nasty subject to tackle, but he tackled it.

'I liked very much working with an awful lot of directors. Matthew Robinson was very good. He directed *Attack of the Cybermen*. Peter Moffatt, who directed my first and *The Two Doctors*, is a lovely director. Graeme Harper, who did *Revelation of the Daleks*, was a great favourite of mine. He had an enormous amount of energy and was a smashing director.'
Interviewed by Patrick White in 1988 for *Tranquil Repose* Issue 6.

ON HIS FAVOURITE ADVERSARIES:

'I have a liking for the Autons from Jon Pertwee's time. They've only ever had two stories. I enjoyed them. They provoked, I gather, a reaction from Mary Whitehouse, who didn't like telephone lines and daffodils killing people, because it made children frightened of everyday objects. I loved their smooth faces. I find the humanoid monsters more frightening than the totally alien ones – the bug-eyed monster syndrome. That's why the Master is so effective, because he's another Time Lord. There are all sorts of things that can go on between the two. There's almost a pleasure at the confrontation. One thing that I see in my Doctor is that even though the defence of the weak and the championship of right against wrong is uppermost, there is a certain enjoyment of conflict. I want him to think, "Hello, there's something going on here. I'd like to get stuck in and see what it is!"

'What other monsters? There are the old classics. It would be nice to meet the Ice Warriors. They haven't been around for a long while, have they? Oh, and Davros. I must meet Davros.'
Interviewed by Bill Baggs in 1984 for *Time Watcher*.

'My favourite enemy is the Master, because Sherlock Holmes has his Moriarty, and while most monsters have no particular desire to destroy the Doctor – they want to get on with whatever it is they are doing that's particularly evil, and the Doctor gets in the way – the good thing about the Master is that it's a personal matter. So there is a great opportunity for confrontation. I would like, and haven't yet had, a really thundering good Master story.

'I would also love to work with the Rani again. She was a wonderful adversary. But after the Master and the Rani, I would say the Daleks and the Cybermen come joint second, along with Sil.'
Interviewed by Penny Holme in 1986 for *Doctor Who Magazine* No. 118.

'I rather enjoyed working with Sil, particularly because the actor, Nabil Shaban, is such a nice bloke and such a very good actor. I also thought it was a smashing character, and the relationship between Sil and the Doctor developed quite nicely.'
Interviewed by Michael Sibley in May 1987 for *The Colin Baker Interview*.

'My favourite enemy is the Master. I think he's been underused very much in the last few years, and it's a great shame, because the one-to-one Holmes-Moriarty syndrome is a lot of what *Doctor Who* should be about. The Daleks, they're kind of silly, but they're there and they work, and they terrify everybody! The sad thing about *Revelation of the Daleks* was that there wasn't a lot of contact between the Doctor and the Daleks. It wasn't a full-blown Dalek story, because there was so much going on with Davros, the

city and all that. I do like the Cybermen as well. I think it's a shame that they have been reduced in their abilities to an extent over the seasons. I have a slight predisposition towards continuity, wanting it to be good, and once or twice it has slipped.'
Interviewed by Guy Wainer, Greg Jones, Neil John and David Greenham in 1990 for *Skaro* Volume 5 Issue 2.

ON THE LACK OF HANKY-PANKY IN THE TARDIS:

'I don't think the world is ready for Doctor number six and Perpugilliam Brown and hanky-panky! The rule is that there should be absolutely no possibility of any kind of love interest between the Doctor and his companion. The companion is there for the viewer to identify with, so younger people, children, can imagine what it's like for them to be flying in the TARDIS with the Doctor. The one thing we don't want them imagining is …. well … It's the way the show is structured; that's the way it is and has always been. Mind you … I could make an exception for Leela!'
Interviewed on stage in 1985 at a convention in Texas, USA.

ON HIS TWO TV COMPANIONS:

'One problem with Peri is that the scriptwriters think that they're writing authentic American dialogue, but they're not. Nicola tries to get them to change the script, but bear in mind that it's her first job, and in your first job you don't go around trying to tell scriptwriters how to write scripts! She does say, "This is not the way an American would say it; I'd rather say so-and-so," and they reply, "Could you please say the script as it's written." So don't blame her. Also, bear in mind that the programme is made by the BBC initially for showing on British TV. If you have too many words like "faucet" and "sidewalk" you'll confuse the British viewer.'
Interviewed on stage in 1985 at a convention in Texas, USA.

'I think Nicola encountered the problem that an awful lot of companions have, which is that the character isn't ever properly developed by the writers. All they ever do with her is make her say "Oh Doctor!" and fall over. Then they separate her from the Doctor – have her carried off by the monster or something – so that they can get two different story strands going. It's very, very difficult, and considering that this was Nicola's first proper job out of drama school – she'd not even had any theatre experience when she played *Doctor Who* – I think she did wonderfully. She didn't want to do all the whining; it was imposed upon her by the nature of the scripts. Had she been an actress with fifteen years experience behind her, she might have been able to stand up and say, "Look, I won't have this," but like any newcomer, she basically did just what she was asked to do. She was great to work with; I am very fond of Nicola.
    'Bonnie was lucky, because she was a known personality. She's been in the theatre longer than I have! The character of Melanie was very quickly made very specific – she had an interest in keep-fit, she was spunky, she was enthusiastic. The idea was that I would be the one who was always saying, "Hey, let's be careful," because she would always be rushing out and doing things. That's a good, positive thing to grab hold of when you're starting in a role.'
Interviewed on stage in 1987 during a convention at the University of Western Washington, USA.

ON HIS FAVOURITE STORY:

'From the point of view of watching them, I think my favourite would be either *Vengeance on Varos* or *Revelation of the Daleks*, because as complete stories, they stood up extremely well and were different. The one I enjoyed doing most was probably *The Two Doctors*, mainly because of working with Patrick Troughton and Frazer Hines, both of whom are now very good friends of mine. I have a particular regard for Patrick Troughton's Doctor, so it was a great honour for me to work with someone who I believe is a very gifted and versatile actor.'

Interviewed by Doug Smith in 1985 for *Fan Aid* Issue 2.

'Pat I've adored for many years, and I've known him for a long time. I was best man at his son David's wedding, and I shared a flat with David for ten years, so I've known Pat off and on, and always admired his acting, and adored his Doctor, so actually to work with him was a special treat.

'I was a bit in awe actually, but that was dispelled in a couple of days, and Frazer also is a delight. Frazer and I got on extremely well. We larked around a lot, and Pat treated us like an affectionate … I'd say father, but he'd be offended. No, I'll say father anyway, because he calls me Miss Piggy at the moment (a reference to my weight); I call him Gonzo (which is a reference to his physical appearance)!'

Interviewed by Penny Holme in 1986 for *Doctor Who Magazine* No. 118.

'I think in retrospect I was unlucky in that I never really had any great stories; there weren't any that stood out. I think *Vengeance on Varos* was the nearest in that it was very different. Yes, and that was the one that got all the criticism in Britain. It was violent and it was dark and it was gloomy. I liked that. I enjoyed that a lot. I thought it was a good story, and I enjoyed doing it.'

Interviewed by Bob Furnell, Dean King and Janette Taylor in March 1987 for *Time Meddlers of Vancouver*.

ON HIS LEAST FAVOURITE STORY:

'I suppose it was *Timelash*, which never quite gelled for me.

'It was actually much better than I thought it was going to be. Pennant Roberts did a good job directing it. There was nothing intrinsically wrong with it, it's just that, of that particular series, it was the one that didn't work for me. I don't think that the Doctor's element was as strong as I'd have liked.'

Interviewed by Penny Holme in 1986 for *Doctor Who Magazine* No. 118.

ON SCRIPT EDITOR ERIC SAWARD'S RESIGNATION:

'We had a hiccup towards the end of *The Trial of a Time Lord*. I suppose, like all of us, Eric's a complex man. He used to ring me up late at night and moan on about John Nathan-Turner. I would spend an hour and a half or two hours talking on the phone with him – and he'd ring about midnight, so at two in the morning I would say, "Look, Eric, I have to go to bed, I'm tired." I would calm him down and say, "Look, Eric, I think you are being paranoid. I don't think John is trying to do you down. I think all he's doing is disagreeing with you, which he is entitled to do as producer of the programme." Then suddenly I read the interview that Eric did for *Starburst*, most of which he spent slagging off John. Most of it was unfair, and some of it just his opinion. Some of it I don't know about, as I wasn't present.

'What had happened was that dear old Robert Holmes had died before completing his script for the final episode of the season. Eric had been very close to him. He wanted to stick to the spirit of what Robert Holmes had wanted to do. John asked Eric to write it, even after they had fallen out. I've got a copy of the actual script that he wrote. He seemed to be venting his anger in the writing, and he wrote a very strange ending. John turned it down for many reasons.

'Pip and Jane Baker then had to write a new version of the last episode over a weekend, and I thought they did it brilliantly. I think episodes thirteen and fourteen were the best; the characters of Glitz, Popplewick and the Valeyard were wonderful.'
Interviewed by Michael Sibley in May 1987 for *The Colin Baker Interview*.

'The truth is an awful lot of things: there are no absolute villains, there are no absolute good guys. It's certainly true that JN-T and Saward were chalk and cheese, but in the early days that worked extremely well, because they complemented each other. It's only as both of them – and John will admit this himself – have become a bit jaded doing the programme … JN-T wanted to leave the show. He announced that he was leaving, he told all the fans this. Then suddenly the BBC said, "We want you to carry on and do more." He replied, "I don't want to. I want to go and do something else, please." And they said, "Either you do more or you pack your bags." Obviously he wanted to stay at the BBC – he's got a living to make – so he had to do what they told him. I mean, all I know is what he's told me. There may be things going on behind the scenes. But it does strike me as ludicrous that when you have an actor who wants to carry on playing the part and a producer who wants to go, you do exactly the reverse: you keep the guy who doesn't want to do it and get rid of the guy who does!'
Interviewed by Bob Furnell, Dean King and Janette Taylor in March 1987 for *Time Meddlers of Vancouver*.

ON THE SERIES' SCRIPTS:

'Actually, I found there was an awful lot of casual script writing went on during my time in the series. I had terrible trouble with *The Trial of a Time Lord* in particular. I remember that the worst part was the segment written by Philip Martin. I would ask the director, "Is this the Matrix lying, is the Doctor under the influence of the process he's been subjected to, or is he lying for some reason of his own that we'll later discover?" "I don't know," came the reply, "you'd better ask Philip Martin." So I asked Philip Martin, and he said, "I don't know. Eric Saward put that bit in. You'll have to ask him." I asked Eric, and Eric said, "Oh, I don't know. Philip Martin wrote that bit!" I told him, "Look, I need to know, in order to play this scene. When I'm chaining Peri to the rock, is that a Matrix lie or am I behaving like that because I'm being watched?" "Oh, whichever suits you!" The thing is that no-one had ever bothered to work it out. In the end, I decided that most of it was a Matrix/Valeyard lie.

'Small continuity points don't bother me: what bother me are basic mistakes like that, which usually come from a total lack of caring. I wouldn't normally accuse an individual, but because Eric was later so vociferously critical of the programme and of me, I will say this: make sure your own slate is clean before you start criticising other people's dirty slates! He

really was very casual about it. You can't blame the writers, because they get given a brief.'
Interviewed by Stephen James Walker, David J Howe, Mark Stammers and Gordon Roxburgh in August 1989 for *The Frame* Issue 13.

ON THE SERIES' RATINGS:

'Michael Grade said publicly that the ratings for Season 23 were very disappointing. I wrote him a letter in which I said, "Given the fact that you had cancelled us for eighteen months, and given that we were again opposite *The A-Team*, which pulls in 30 million viewers and is the kind of whiz-bang violent programme that you don't want to make … We came on immediately after *Roland Rat – The Series*, which sadly pulled in only two million viewers. Then, halfway through *Roland Rat – The Series*, *The A-Team* started. To get the five million viewers that we did get, I actually thought was bloody good."

'I suppose we did also go out in the hours of daylight, with good weather. These of course are not the factors that people mention when they say that the ratings are poor. So – scapegoat – change the Doctor!

'I would never dream of wishing my successor any ill, but I hope that if he is successful, it's because the programme deserves it, not because of the schedule. I would feel well peeved if the series was put opposite something kind of flabby, and put out at seven o'clock at night, and therefore doubled its figures. Of course, they would say, "Ah, there you are, told you so! Get rid of Colin Baker and you get 10 million viewers!"'
Interviewed by Michael Sibley in May 1987 for *The Colin Baker Interview*.

ON HIS OUSTING FROM *DOCTOR WHO*:

'At the end of *The Trial of a Time Lord*, we left the studio with a party, I had a nice time and we all said, "See you next year." I kept in close contact with John Nathan-Turner because, as you know, we did the conventions and things together. Then when the time came for the option on my contract to be taken up by the BBC, which was the end of October, he rang up and said, "I don't even know if we're doing the programme. They haven't even told me if I'm producing it next year, so I can't take up the option at the moment." So the option lapsed. Then, at the beginning of November, he rang me up and said, "Look, I've got a bit of bad news. The programme is going ahead but Michael Grade has instructed me to replace the Doctor."

'I was quite surprised by this! You know that sort of blood-draining-from-your-veins kind of feeling? John said he had told them that he thought it was a dreadful mistake and he wanted me to play the Doctor, but they were adamant. "Grade says three years is quite enough. He's said nothing derogatory about your performance, he thinks you are fine, but he thinks a new Doctor will give the programme a boost. I have pointed out that you have not done three years, and that you have done only one and a half seasons, but he remains adamant that that is long enough and it's time for a change." So there was nothing much I could do about it.

'Three days later, I got phone call from the BBC asking me to go to America with Grade to publicise *Doctor Who*. I thought that was rather odd, but I agreed to do it on the basis that I might be able to find out some more. However, Grade avoided me very cleverly throughout the whole time I was there. All I've ever got from anybody – and I've seen Jonathan Powell, who is Head of Series and Serials – is that they were happy with my performance but that they had decided that three years was enough.

'It goes against what I was asked to do, when I started the show, by David Reid – Powell's predecessor. He asked me if I was prepared to commit myself to the programme for *four* years. Having said yes in 1983 to four years of 26 episodes a year, I actually did one year of 26 episodes (or the equivalent), nothing at all the next year, and just fourteen episodes the next. Then I was unceremoniously bundled out. So I felt fairly aggrieved.'

Interviewed by Robert Cope in September 1987 for *Doctor Who Bulletin* Issue 48.

'How do I feel about it as we sit here now? As we sit here now, I feel quite calm and unbothered about it. I suppose if I thought about it for a few minutes, I could work myself up into a bit of a lather again, but I think that's rather a waste of time. When it happened, I got cross. I felt I had been treated unfairly and badly. I thought I was a pawn in a game of publicity and power politics, played by Michael Grade. I thought that he had got to a point where he had criticised the show so much that he had to be seen to do something, and the most overt thing he could do was to change the Doctor, because that's the one thing that would get all the publicity. It seems perverse that the Doctor wanted to stay, so he had to go, but the producer wanted to go, so he had to stay. John Nathan-Turner was very keen to move on to something else and wasn't allowed to. That strikes me as the action of someone who doesn't have the programme's best interests at heart.

'Having said all that, this all happened six months ago now. I had had a career for fifteen years before I became involved in *Doctor Who*, and I hope most sincerely that I will have one for another fifteen years afterwards. I am enjoying the play I am doing now.

'Yes, I shall miss the programme. But my connection with it will remain, as long as people like you and all the other smashing people I have met through *Doctor Who* maintain an interest.'

Interviewed by Michael Sibley in May 1987 for *The Colin Baker Interview*.

'I would be dishonest if I was to pretend that suddenly it wasn't the best job on television, because it was. I had a brief spell when I was allowed to play with the best toy there was. And like any little child that has had his biggest and best toy snatched away from him before he is finished with it, I was a little bit *cross*. But my life goes on. I suppose my feelings about *Doctor Who* remain as they were. I loved doing it. I had a great time. Perhaps it is just as well that it was taken away from me. I have done far better than I thought I would this year with the play I am doing. Maybe somebody's done me a favour in some way. I miss it, though.

'I was very irritated about the treatment I received. I could have done what was suggested, which was to pretend that I was leaving for personal reasons, but I don't like to tell lies. I like to tell the truth. It may have been a mistake, I suppose, as I have to talk about it now.'

Interviewed on stage in September 1987 at the *Doctor Who* Appreciation Society's PanoptiCon 8 convention in London.

'I feel that "unlucky" is the word that sums up my tenure, really. A combination of Michael Grade – who changed the schedules, changed the length of the programme, cancelled it in the middle, then put it on after *Roland Rat – The Series* and opposite *The A-Team* – together with the whole Eric Saward business, the upheaval that the BBC itself was going through at that time … all those things conspired to make it very difficult. In a way, it was more frustrating than anything else. If someone had said, "Look, we think you're awful and we're replacing you," I would have had to live with that. But when I know it was just a combination of circumstances, and I was powerless to do anything about it ...

'You know, if someone else had been cast as the Doctor in 1984 and I was doing it *now*, I'd still be in that part for years to come.'

Interviewed by Stephen James Walker, David J Howe, Mark Stammers and Gordon Roxburgh in August 1989 for *The Frame* Issue 13.

ON HIS CAREER AFTER *DOCTOR WHO*:

'The first thing I was offered was a tour of a play called *Corpse* – a brilliant play, set at the turn of the century, in which I got to play murderous twin brothers. It meant a number of quick changes, in that I exited through one door as one brother and, as the set changed, returned as the other. Chaotic at first. That went into the West End for five months and covered the full year after *Doctor Who*.

'Then I did panto at Wimbledon with Dennis Waterman and Rula Lenska. Immediately after that, I did another play, *Deathtrap*, with Anita Harris. Then I did 65 programmes for the Children's Channel, a satellite station. These were co-produced by Longmans, the book publishers, and were scholarly in a *Sesame Street* style, which was great fun. I loved doing that.

'I then did four months of *Run for Your Wife* with Terry Scott, following which I directed a play called *Bazaar and Rummage*. Then it was straight into the *Doctor Who* stage show. So I've been busy!'

Interviewed by Kevin Taylor in 1989 for *Timelines* Issue 3.

ON THE STAGE PLAY *DOCTOR WHO – THE ULTIMATE ADVENTURE*:

'Everyone says it must be pretty painful going back as the Doctor after my untimely removal, but it's not, as I never really took personal umbrage at what happened. It was just an irritant in the same way as if a headmaster at school was to say that one's half holiday was cancelled. One feels a bit cross about it.

'My decision to take the part was based on exactly the same criteria as any other work on offer. What else is available? What would be the enjoyment factor therein? What would be the financial rewards thereof? This role had the advantage of my already knowing the character. I'd seen Jon Pertwee in the show and thought it would be fun to do, because the cast were all enthusiastic and inventive. I've been proved right; it is great fun.

'I think my new costume is very successful. I wanted a complete break from the previous image and to have something that was going to be cool on stage *and* say something different: add another layer to the Doctor, if you like. But for very understandable reasons, Mark Furness, the producer, said he wanted a costume as close as possible to the essence, if not the actuality, of the original. They borrowed the BBC costume for the brochure photographs, as they hadn't made the new one at that point.

'The only brief I gave the designer was that it must be lightweight, because of my being two hours on stage under heavy lights. Even now, it's still heavier than I'd have liked, but I think Yvonne Milnes, the costume designer, did an excellent job. The trousers are similar to the ones I wore on TV. I've got red shoes instead of green, and another jazzy waistcoat, this time with pineapple buttons. But the *tour de force* is the

621

coat, which I think is much better than the TV one. It's got blue in it, which I couldn't have for television because of the electronic effects, and I think the colours blend rather nicely. Worth seeing, folks!'

Interviewed by Dominic May in June 1989 for *Doctor Who Magazine* **tenth anniversary special.**

'Jon Pertwee had been playing the part for ten weeks before I took over, and Terrance Dicks, who wrote the script, wrote it specifically with Jon in mind. So he sent me a copy of the script and asked me what kind of changes I thought I'd want. When I'd read it, I rang him up and – to his great relief, I think – said that there were very few changes I would make. Basically, the Doctor is the Doctor, and it's the mere fact that I'm saying the lines instead of Jon that makes it different. The voices are very different.

'The lines that have been changed are about one or two percent of the script. "Reverse the polarity of the neutron flow," which is a Jon Pertwee trademark line, has been changed, and there are things that've been added in, some by me and some by Terrance Dicks, in consultation with each other. It's a shift of emphasis rather than a change of dialogue. I mean, I'm my usual kind of bumptious, arrogant self, and he was his usual kind of dignified, courteous self, but we're saying more or less the same lines.'

Interviewed by Trevor Ramsay in June 1989 for *Time Lord* **Issue 4.**

'I saw the show in Wimbledon, shortly after it opened, and I wasn't particularly impressed. Then I saw it again four or five weeks later, in Bristol, and it was much, much better. Even when I saw it the first time, though, when it was a bit of a shambles, I realised – with no disrespect whatsoever to Jon – that it was particularly suited to my Doctor. That's because my Doctor is a "stage" Doctor – he's flamboyant and over the top. Jon's dignified portrayal was brilliant on television, but as the centre of a busy show, he had a problem, and the script didn't serve him as well as perhaps it ought to have done. My Doctor, on the other hand, can rush around and do a few things, and I thought, "Maybe I can contribute something to this." So that was one reason why I decided to do it. Obviously the negotiations came into it too – the fact that I was well paid for it. And it fitted in with all the other things that I wasn't doing!

'When I was rehearsing, we took the opportunity to make a few changes to the script. In the swordfight, for example, I wanted to have the Doctor saying, "Now, if you go over there …" – and as he pointed over there with his sword, he deflected one blow – "Or is it over that way?" – and he deflected another one – so that he was totally oblivious that he was actually having a swordfight. Unfortunately, there wasn't enough time to work that out, so in the end we played it as if I was such an expert swordsman that I could actually have a conversation with somebody while fighting behind my back. I mean, it's a terrible gag, but it was a compromise.

'The other scene I particularly wanted to change was the one with the flying ant creatures. When I watched it, I couldn't believe that the Doctor just walked off, consigning these things to a grisly death at the hands of the Cybermen. So now I play it as if I'm trying to stop them from sacrificing themselves, saying, "No, no." And then, as I run off, I say, "Thank you." Otherwise, it made the Doctor look totally callous, actually asking them to fly down and get themselves killed!

'Since rehearsals, we haven't changed anything, apart from the small variations I put in nightly, which keep the rest of the cast on their toes! I see myself, in a show like this, a bit like a soloist in an orchestra. I mean, I've got to play the tune – I've got to say the words – but I'm allowed a little licence. I think the part, and the show, benefit if the Doctor's slightly unpredictable and does something different every now and again. For instance, the business with Zog has grown tremendously since I started doing it.

'The audiences have varied enormously. Usually, if you open to a certain advance booking at a theatre, you can gauge from that how you're going to do during the week, because you know a certain proportion of people will just turn up on the night. With this show, though, it seems we always open quite low, then gradually build and build and build. By the end of the week, we're doing quite well, because the word's got round, but then we go on somewhere else. We just haven't been able to sell it properly in advance, and I don't know why. The hot summer might have had a lot to do with it, or perhaps people have the wrong impression of what *Doctor Who* will be like on stage.

'I learnt quite quickly that I either spend twenty minutes signing autographs at the stage door, uncomfortably jammed against a brick wall, or I formalise it. So I formalise it, and sit at a table in the foyer to sign a few autographs after each performance. Mums, dads and children come up, and the comment I've had consistently from parents is, "Well, we only came because, you know, little Jason wanted to see the show, but we've had a wonderful time, we've loved it."

'Funnily enough, doing this tour has helped to redress the balance. I've had young kids hugging me, in tears, saying, "Why can't you come back on TV? You'll always be my Doctor." I expect every other Doctor has had the same thing, but I personally had never experienced it before. Families, too, have come up and said, "You will always be our Doctor." OK, that's probably because I just happened to be the one who was in it when they started watching, I realise that. But it's nice to know there are people out there who feel that way.'

Interviewed by Stephen James Walker, David J Howe, Mark Stammers and Gordon Roxburgh in August 1989 for *The Frame* Issue 12.

CHARACTER — THE SIXTH DOCTOR

'The light that burns twice as bright burns half as long, and you have burned so very, very brightly ...'

So says Doctor Eldon Tyrell to his android creation Roy Batty in the classic Ridley Scott film *Blade Runner*. Looking back, it seems that the analogy could apply equally well to Colin Baker's Doctor – the most incandescent of the first seven incarnations, but also the shortest-lived.

Peter Davison, the fifth Doctor, had decided in May 1983 that he would not wish to renew his contract when it expired toward the end of production on the following season of stories, the twenty-first in *Doctor Who*'s history. Thus the producer, John Nathan-Turner, was again faced with the difficult task of finding a new leading man. His first instinct was to go for a contrast – a sixth Doctor who would be as different from the fifth as the fifth had been from the fourth – and he was quoted in the press as saying that he was looking for someone older and more obviously eccentric. 'We do want to make the next one a little more eccentric than Peter's been,' he confirmed at a November 1983 convention in Chicago, USA. 'To make him a little more crotchety and perhaps give him a kind of acid wit, which we think would make a nice change.'

He had in fact had Colin Baker in mind since the previous summer, as he later explained in an interview with Peter Haining:

'I got to know Colin during the time he played Maxil, a Gallifreyan guard captain, in a Davison-era story called *Arc of Infinity*. Then we met up again later when we were invited to the wedding reception of my assistant floor manager, Lynn Richards, with whom Colin and his wife Marion had become very friendly. The *Doctor Who* crowd were sitting together on the grass, having a good time, and for the whole afternoon, Colin kept us thoroughly entertained. Even though I wasn't actively looking for a new Doctor then, I thought that if he could hold the attention of fifteen hard-bitten showbusiness professionals for hours, then he could do the same with a television audience.'

Strangely enough, even though she was unaware that Peter Davison was planning to leave the series, Lynn Richards later went to see Nathan-Turner to suggest that Baker would make an ideal candidate for the next Doctor. Little did she know that he was already the hot favourite for the role!

In an August 1989 interview for *The Frame*, Baker recalled how he had first been approached to play the part of the sixth Doctor, and how the character had then been developed:

'John Nathan-Turner rang me up one afternoon and said he'd like to see me. I went in to the office, thinking that he was going to try to talk me into opening a fête or something, and he said, "I'm not offering you the part, but Peter Davison is leaving and I wondered if you would be interested in playing the Doctor?" So I replied, very casually, "Oh, yeah, I wouldn't mind." He said, "Well, I'm going to give you a few tapes and ask you to go away and watch some of the earlier Doctors. We'll meet again in a week's time, and you can tell me how you think *you'd* like to play him." And that's what we did.

'I can't remember all the stories I was given, but they included *The Space Museum*, *The War Games*, *Carnival of Monsters*, *Pyramids of Mars* and *Warriors of the Deep*. Anyway, I watched them all several times, then I went back to see John. He asked me what I thought, and I said, "Well, I would obviously play the part as a kind of distillation of myself, as all the others have done, but one thing I would like to bring out is the fact that the Doctor is an alien – he's not a human being, even though he looks like one."

'I thought it would be quite nice if sometimes he didn't behave in the way we would expect him to behave. So, on one day, if a person was mown down in front of him, he might just step over them and ask somebody the time; on another day, he might go into terrible paroxysms of grief about a sparrow falling out of a tree. Obviously we'd have to be able to explain why, and what it was that was concerning the Doctor; I just didn't want him to behave in an obvious, sentimental, approachable way. I wanted him to be a little bit unapproachable. He could get extremely angry about something – a build-up followed by a sudden explosion, so that the rage might seem to be about one thing when it was actually about something that had happened two episodes ago, perhaps. I think there's a danger with this kind of programme that it's all too pat, all too obvious.

'Now, John liked this idea, and in the end he pushed it further than probably I would have had the courage to do, by making the Doctor *so* unapproachable in my first story, *The Twin Dilemma*. You had to wait for four episodes before finding out if this person had anything remotely *likeable* in him, and I think that was very brave, especially as it was the end of a season. I like that kind of bravery in television. It's all too easy to play safe all the time.

'So that was one thing I wanted. I also saw the Doctor as being rather austere, dressed in black. I wanted a black velvet costume, but it was pointed out to me that the Master had got in there first, so I couldn't have it. And the one aspect of my Doctor that I suppose I do regret is the costume. It works for me now, but I would have liked it to have been something different. Really, though, the costume was, to me, a very unimportant part of the whole enterprise. This was partly because I was inside it looking out – everybody else had to look at it, therefore it meant a lot to them!

'I also suggested that the Doctor should tell excruciatingly bad jokes – you know, the puns. The idea of using quotes was mine, as well. I wanted to use quotes from the English language – obviously, as we were making the programme in English! – but also I wanted to make things up that sounded like quotes from other cultures. So it might be a Venusian quote, or a quote from Aldarberan 4. I thought that was a nice idea.

'There was another thing, too. I have a little bee in my bonnet about the English language. It's the richest language in the world in terms of the amount of words available, but gradually we're losing most of them. I wanted there to be at least half a dozen words in each episode that viewers would have to rush off and look up, because they didn't know the meaning. If you are really hooked on a character and he uses a long word that you don't understand, then you'll go and find out what it means: it's extending people's vocabularies, which I think is nice.

'All these ideas John Nathan-Turner liked, and we both went upstairs to see David Reid, who was then the Controller in charge of BBC1. Fortunately he was watching a Test Match on TV at the time, and I asked, "How's Botham doing?", or something. He said, "Oh, do you like cricket?" and we chatted about cricket for twenty minutes – to JN-T's total perplexity, because he knew nothing about cricket! After that, we talked about the role of the Doctor for a minute or two, and David Reid said, "Well, I think that's great, excellent." Apparently the fact that I liked cricket did it for me!

'I was then asked if I would sign a four-year option, because Peter had left after three years and they wanted to get a bit more continuity. I said, "I'd like that very much!" – I was thinking, "Four years, 26 episodes a year, wonderful!"

'And that's really how it all happened!'

As is apparent from this account, *Doctor Who*'s then script editor, Eric Saward, made relatively little contribution during the meetings when the sixth Doctor's character was being conceived. He now explains that he did not feel inspired to come up with ideas, as he was unhappy with the casting of Colin Baker as the Doctor, considering that although he was a competent character actor, he lacked the screen presence required.

Saward recalls that he took on board Nathan-Turner's idea of making the new Doctor more crotchety and more at odds with the world than the previous one, and also that an attempt was made to reintroduce more humour into the part. Again, however, he considers that Baker lacked the lightness of touch required to bring the humour across on screen.

'The other thing that we were going to try to introduce,' explains Saward, 'which just didn't work, was a sort of Holmesian ability to make extraordinary deductions. Just as Sherlock Holmes might say something like, "I see that you came via Marylebone Road," and then explain that he had deduced this from the distinctive clay on the person's boots, the Doctor would have this wonderful ability to make sense out of highly improbable things. In the real world, of course, it just wouldn't work – the whole of London happens to be built on clay! But that's the sort of thing we were going to try to do. Unfortunately, because of problems with scripts and so on, there were aspects that just got left behind. It takes quite a lot of time to work that sort of thing out; ideally it should be firmly locked into the story.'

When asked by *The Frame* if he felt that he had been given an unusually large say in the development of his Doctor's character, Baker replied:

'Well, in terms of the shape of my character at the beginning, it's not that I had any say as such, it's just that they asked me how I would play it, I told them, and they liked it. I think you'd have to do that with any Doctor. There's no point in hiring an actor for that part and then telling him to play it in a way that is different from how he would naturally approach it. He's got to play it his way.

'After that, though, I certainly wasn't consulted by Eric Saward about scripts, and if ever I made any suggestions about scripts, he didn't respond very warmly to that. He was of the "writers write, directors direct and actors act" school, which to a certain extent I am myself, but I think that when you've got a long-running programme with a central actor, eventually he's going to have more input potential than new people coming in from outside. I could never make any headway with that, though.'

The sixth Doctor's 'unapproachable' debut in *The Twin Dilemma* came as a shock to many of the series' viewers, who had grown accustomed to Peter Davison's sensitive, charming portrayal. Following his regeneration, the Time Lord was seen to suffer a number of violent fits – at one point actually attempting to strangle his companion, Peri – and even during his more lucid periods he appeared to experience a rapid succession of different moods, ranging from disconsolate self-pity through cringing cowardice to narcissistic bravado. Viewers were left uncertain as to whether these bewildering switches of temperament were simply after-effects of the regeneration itself or whether they would continue to be apparent in later stories.

The sheer unpredictability of the sixth Doctor was, indeed, the quality that Colin Baker often chose to emphasise in his earliest *Doctor Who* interviews. 'He has many facets to his personality,' he told the fanzine *Arkensword* in 1984, 'and, bearing in mind that he is an alien, some are difficult for humans to understand. When he's a little bit curt to his assistant. Impatient. Irascible. I think that these are very important aspects for the Doctor to have. For him to behave exactly the same way as a human behaves would be a shame. It would be wasting the character … He's not a slavish follower of anybody. He is prone to reacting very differently to exactly the same situation, according to the way he feels. The one thing he'll always do is to champion the cause of the weak. In casual conversation he won't always be polite. That's an Earthly concept. He can't be bothered with the social graces.'

Talking to the magazine *Space Voyager* shortly before starting work on *Attack of the Cybermen*, the opening story of the twenty-second season, the actor drew a contrast between this alien unpredictability and the comparatively staid behaviour of more conventional heroes: 'My Doctor will be insatiably curious, intolerant, waspish, and kind but cruel … Many times he won't react with the emotions expected. As a rule, the baddies are the more interesting parts. The Doctor is the great exception to that. He is a hero, but not in the bland mould. Baddies generally are best because the writers have found it more interesting to write about people who break the rules, but the Doctor makes and breaks his own rules. He is a galactic buccaneer. Neither good nor bad. A bit of a meddler.'

Not for this Doctor the role of a passive observer, staying quietly in the background until forced to act. On the contrary, as signalled by the garish, tasteless costume that John Nathan-Turner decreed he should wear, he seemed actively to court attention; and the overblown, oratorical way in which he often expressed himself was indicative of an ostentatious, self-important personality.

The mood changes he experienced immediately after his regeneration became less violent and erratic as time went by but never abated entirely, making him a highly capricious character. Flamboyant, pretentious, grandiloquent, overbearing, petulant and egotistical: all these adjectives could be reasonably used to describe typical aspects of his behaviour. With these traits in mind, some critics have ventured the assessment that he was 'unpleasant' and 'unlikeable', but this overlooks the fact that on many occasions he also displayed such admirable qualities as kindness, compassion, humour, courage and moral outrage at the many injustices he encountered. Following the events of *The Two Doctors*, he even became a vegetarian! It could be seen as a tribute to Colin Baker's abilities as an actor that he was able to assimilate so many diverse and apparently contradictory idiosyncrasies and mould them together into a three-dimensional (or should that be four-dimensional?), consistent and believable character.

Another common criticism made of the sixth Doctor is that, particularly during Season 22, he appeared to possess a rather violent streak, frequently resorting to the use of force to resolve problematic situations – for example, shooting Cybermen with a gun in *Attack of the Cybermen*, causing some of his opponents to be killed with poisonous vines in *Vengeance on Varos* and physically tackling and suffocating the character Shockeye in *The Two Doctors*. The introduction of a running thread of black humour was also thought by some commentators to have misfired when the Doctor was seen to crack jokes over the bodies of dead and injured adversaries. Rather than fostering an air of alien aloofness, it was argued, this merely made him appear callous.

Colin Baker was generally unmoved by such objections. 'I personally would probably go a bit further myself,' he said in a 1984 interview for the fanzine *Time Watcher*. 'I'm undecided, to be honest. John Nathan-Turner is very keen that the Doctor should not be a violent person, and of course I agree with that. But I think that it's sometimes naive to expect that one can get out of every situation without being placed in a position where one might have to be violent, or to use violence.

'I think that if one sanitises violence, if one cleans it up too much, it has the effect of conditioning people to it. They become so used to seeing people being shot and falling over and nothing messy happening that it makes violence seem acceptable. Whereas, despite what the critics say, directors who show blood pumping out and severed organs dragging across the ground, things that are horrific and unpleasant to look at, are at least showing what violence really is. Violence is horrible. But it's maybe true that in *Doctor Who* we're dealing in an area that is a bit removed from first-degree naturalism, so it's better if we stay away from showing that kind of direct effect of violence. I think it's always better if the Doctor can get himself out of a situation by using the mind.'

On other occasions, the actor was rather less equivocal. 'I am quite fond of violence,' he told the audience at a US *Doctor Who* convention in 1985. 'I like it a lot. Some people were appalled at the vicious way in which I disposed of the Cyber Controller in *Attack of the Cybermen*. I wanted to go much further, but they wouldn't let me. I wanted to stand over him pumping machine gun bullets into him for hours ... green stuff all over the walls. But they said, "No, that's going too far; three or four will do quite nicely, thank you."'

While remarks like this were made partly tongue-in-cheek, Baker clearly relished the more physical aspects of the role. This was something on which he had commented when discussing his interpretation of the Doctor's character in a 1984 interview for the magazine *Fantasy Empire*:

'Doctor Who is neither a good guy nor a bad guy. He's an apart guy. He has a very strict code. He's always on the side of goodness in the universe, but you couldn't say he was being saintly. He's very rude to people, and apparently quite heartless, although he's not really.

'I think in order to play the Doctor, an actor has to draw on himself very largely. I think the reason John Nathan-Turner asked me to play the part is that he saw things in me that he thought I could usefully bring to it ... An interest in cats, a sense of the ridiculous, a sense of chivalry. I believe in a lot of the great values of chivalry, like a sort of a cross between the Dragonriders of Pern and William Tell ... I hope my Doctor will be cerebral. I certainly want him to be the brightest there is around.

'When John Nathan-Turner spoke to me, he asked me how I felt about the physical stuff, and I said I loved doing it. I've done stage fighting in Shakespeare and all that. There's not a lot of swordplay in *Doctor Who*. I think it might be nice to have a fight between the Master and the Doctor. I'd like to get involved in one of those. I love the physical stuff, and I want to climb the walls and fight the villains.'

Season 22 was, for *Doctor Who*, unusually grim and downbeat in tone, and the depiction of a somewhat harder Doctor can be seen as merely symptomatic of this more general shift in the series' emphasis, the responsibility for which must rest primarily with the production team. The on-screen realisation of a character such as the Doctor is inevitably a fusion of the actor's own qualities with the writers' conception, as reflected in the action and dialogue laid down in the scripts. As Baker put it in his interview for *Fantasy Empire*, this synthesis of performer and script is 'a sort of marriage, if you like. Your own personality plus the page in front of you that tells you what the Doctor says and what he does. All somehow gradually combining over a period of time into something different.'

It should also be noted that the Time Lord's earlier incarnations had been by no means averse to becoming involved in direct physical action: the first Doctor had gleefully indulged in a bout of 'fisticuffs' with the mute assassin Ascaris in *The Romans*; the third had frequently overpowered assailants using Venusian karate; the fourth had launched violent assaults on a number of opponents in stories such as *The Seeds of Doom* and *The Deadly Assassin*; and there are many other examples that could be quoted. So it can be argued that the sixth Doctor's use of force was not an entirely unprecedented departure from established characterisation. The issue was really one of degree.

Having initially studied a number of his predecessors' stories on video, Colin Baker did make a conscious effort to include some of their traits in his own performance, as he told *Arkensword* in 1984:

'It's a lot made up with ingredients of the previous Doctors. Pertwee's adventure sense. I like that, the derring-do, swinging from ropes, and I want Eric Saward to write in things like that, because I enjoy it. Hartnell's irascibility. Tom Baker's irreverence, up to a point. The one thing I don't want to do is belittle the monsters. I think that if you start joking and clowning around when being threatened by a Cyberman or a Dalek, it's so easy to make them look as though they are not very threatening. When analysed, a Dalek is a very difficult thing to be frightened of, because it can't even climb a flight of stairs. And once you start sticking jelly babies in the end of their nozzles, then it makes life difficult, because it has to work for the audience.'

Another influence was Baker's love of cats. He adopted the cat as the symbol of the sixth Doctor's persona, as reflected in various badges that he wore on his coat lapel, and often quoted Rudyard Kipling: 'I am the cat that walks by himself, and all places are the same to me.' (This is actually a paraphrasing of lines from the poem *The Cat that Walked by Himself*: 'The Cat. He walked by himself, and all places were alike to him.') 'Cats,' said the actor in a 1985 interview for the *Doctor Who* Appreciation Society's magazine *TARDIS*, 'do what *they* want to do, *when* they want to do it, and it may fit in sometimes with what you want to do, but that's never a consideration, and I think that's a bit like the Doctor.'

In another 1985 interview, for the fanzine *Fan Aid 2*, Baker was asked how he saw the character of the sixth Doctor developing in future stories. 'I'm afraid it sounds like a cop-out,' he replied, 'but there is no answer to that question. I see it developing, full stop. I wouldn't wish to prejudice that development by saying how I think it should go, because that would imply that the job of the writer and the producer is merely that of a cipher – which is not the case. We work together in a kind of symbiotic way. Very rarely are conscious decisions about development made. It comes out of ideas and developments of ideas.'

In later years, however, the actor asserted that there *had* been a long-term plan for development of the sixth Doctor's character. Talking to the 1989 fanzine *Kroton* about the irritation he had felt at his premature expulsion from the series, he said:

'It was very frustrating, because we had envisaged an overall plan over a few years of how we could learn more about this Doctor, and didn't want to give too much away in the first few seasons. We wanted people to be a little unsure about this person, and then gradually find out "Ah, he's not really like that, that's because of this." All sorts of things and clever nuances that we never had a chance to explore. That's life though.'

In a 1990 interview for the *Myth Makers 19* video, released by Reeltime Pictures, the actor again spoke of his long-term plan for the development of the character, and gave the following literary analogy:

'I always like to compare the idea to that of the character Darcy in *Pride and Prejudice*. For the first 35 per cent of the book you hate him, then you grudgingly come to like him, and then by the end of the book you think he is the best person in it. That's sort of what we wanted to do with the Doctor.'

A degree of progression in the Doctor's character was certainly apparent between the end of the twenty-second season and the beginning of the twenty-third, when the series returned after the 1985/86 production hiatus with the fourteen-part story *The Trial of a Time Lord*. Apart from during a short period when his sanity was called into question for the purposes of a sub-plot, the Doctor as seen in this season was noticeably mellower and less aggressive than before, again reflecting a more general shift in the series' emphasis (and incidentally providing an effective contrast to the season's major villain, the Valeyard – a character intended literally to personify the dark side of the Doctor's nature.)

To a casual observer, the sixth Doctor might still have appeared to be little more than a rather egotistical adventurer with a poor taste in clothes and a tendency towards over-reaction and brash theatricality. Beneath this facade, however, Colin Baker had by this time succeeded in establishing a deeper level to the character, making him more interesting and agreeable. He was now clearly capable of compassion, whilst outwardly continuing to appear off-hand and detached, as illustrated by his habit of offering allusive quotations rather than making direct statements. A distinction was drawn between his superficial image as perceived by others and his true underlying qualities, which were gentler and more concerned. 'I am known as the Doctor,' he would often announce, whereas his predecessors had been content to say simply, 'I am the Doctor.'

This softening of the sixth Doctor's demeanour was very evident in his relationship with his companion, Peri. Up until this point, their conversations had been characterised by ill-tempered bickering and petty point-scoring, Peri displaying a distinct tendency to whinge and whine – a situation that John Nathan-Turner attributed to a lack of ingenuity on the writers' part, as he told *Doctor Who Magazine* in an interview published in May 1986:

'There is a problem that writers face in terms of the show, which is that the initial TARDIS scene between the companion and the Doctor is inevitably preoccupied with its position in setting out where you're going and why you're going there and so forth, in order to lay the foundations for a particular story. One obvious way of getting out of that is by conflict, and often a writer will lapse into unnecessary conflict in order to get that information over. That is just a dramatic device, and one that I would like to see less of.'

In *The Trial of a Time Lord*, this wish was fulfilled, as the Doctor and Peri appeared to be on much friendlier terms. Interviewed for *Doctor Who Magazine* some years later, actress Nicola Bryant explained how she and Colin Baker had modified their performances, sometimes playing scenes against the way they had been written, to help achieve this effect:

'When we came back after so long, we felt we couldn't have the same relationship. We would have parted company on bad terms – either I would have left or he would have dropped me off. The relationship settled down and we had to establish that although they may have their differences, they still cared for each other. Looking back, I think the constant bickering and fighting was taken too far.'

A further change occurred part-way through *The Trial of a Time Lord* when Peri was written out of the series and Bonnie Langford was introduced as her successor, Melanie. Interviewed during a March 1987 convention at the University of Western Washington, USA, Colin Baker spoke of the Doctor's more demonstrative behaviour towards this new companion:

'One change, which was rather nice, was that I was able to be much more openly affectionate towards Mel than I had been towards Peri. This was because Bonnie was very young-looking and wasn't as voluptuous as Nicola, so nobody could misconstrue my actions as having a sexual connotation. If I had put my arm around Nicola and said, "Come on darling," people would have been very taken aback. Bonnie, though, had a kind of asexuality about her in the character of Melanie. As I'm much older than she is, and she's so very girlish, the relationship was obviously paternal or avuncular. So I was able, especially the way it was written, to give her the odd cuddle. That was always very difficult with Nicola's character, and I was constantly being asked by the directors to tone it down; there might have been some suggestion of hanky-panky in the TARDIS, and we couldn't have that! I think the relationship between Melanie and the sixth

Doctor would have worked out very nicely, but sadly it was thwarted in its progression.'

It is perhaps ironic that just as Baker had refined his interpretation of the Doctor and succeeded in winning over many of the viewers who had been uncomfortable with his initial, rather more abrasive characterisation, any further development was abruptly forestalled by the BBC management's decision not to renew his contract. As he recalled in his interview for *The Frame*, he was asked to stay on for just the first four episodes of Season 24 to record a regeneration story, but declined to do so: 'I was offered the chance to do the first four episodes of the following season – that was actually a concession won by John – but I said, "Quite honestly, if I've got to leave, I want to leave now and start making a career." The analogy I've always used is that it's like your girlfriend giving you the push and saying, "But you can come back and spend a night with me next year!" It's just not on.'

This was not quite the end of the road for Colin Baker's portrayal of the sixth Doctor, however, as he returned in 1989 in the Mark Furness Ltd touring stage play *Doctor Who – The Ultimate Adventure*.

Many commentators felt that it was in this production that Baker was at his most assured and engaging yet in his portrayal of the Doctor. As one reviewer put it, 'He gives a great performance, which leaves you yearning for more.' This reflected the actor's own satisfaction with his return to the role, as he explained in his interview for *The Frame*:

'Doing this show has been like putting on a pair of comfy old slippers. I was a little alarmed at how easily I slipped into it again, and how much I enjoyed it, although it's rekindled old sadnesses as well. I won't feel particularly sad when it finishes, mind you, because I've done nearly a hundred performances, and that's enough. But it's been nice to play the part again. In a way, it's laid a ghost, it's added a coda. It's made me believe that my Doctor has a part in the scheme of things.'

In a 1990 interview for the fanzine *Skaro*, Baker looked back on his time in *Doctor Who* and offered the following summation of the sixth Doctor's character:

'I would describe him as embodying all the Doctor's traditional virtues – compassion, kindness, high principles, a crusading spirit and a desire to relieve oppression and deal with the oppressor – but at the same time tinged with arrogance, irritability and impatience, which I got a little bit from the first Doctor. He enjoyed the pursuit of the mind and did not find it necessary to display what he was feeling, and could therefore appear to the Earthling observer to be a little unfeeling. That doesn't mean he *was* unfeeling; he just didn't feel the necessity to display it.'

Controversial though it had been, the era of the sixth Doctor finished all too soon for the many viewers who had come to savour his effulgent, larger-than-life personality – truly a light burning bright.

REWRITING THE MYTH

Is good continuity important in a fantasy-orientated series such as *Doctor Who*? Colin Baker certainly considered that it was, as he told the fanzine *The Colin Baker Interview* in 1987:

'I think it is important not to ignore it totally. I did fall out with the script editor, Eric Saward, on a couple of occasions. For instance, on *The Trial of a Time Lord*, I remember reading the script and saying, "Hang on a minute, Eric. As I recall, from watching the episodes before I came into the series, Peter's Doctor was made the Lord President of Gallifrey at the end of *The Five Doctors*, because of his actions in nobbling Borusa. Don't you think that if you're going to put the Lord President on trial, there should be some mention of that fact? Not only the fans but also the general viewers in this case are going to remember it." Eric's reply to that was, "What do you want me to do then?" I said, "Well, can't we write in a little scene where we explain that he is not the Lord President any more?" So he put in two lines that short-circuited the problem.

'Yes, I do believe that continuity is very important. In the end, one has to recognise the fact that, of the five million people who watch *Doctor Who*, it is only a thousand or so who are going to examine it in detail, and the remainder are going to be perfectly happy. But I think I would agree with a lot of the fans, because I am often put in the position of going to conventions and having to make up excuses for all these things. Whenever I spotted anything in the script and it could be altered, I would alter it. I did not have as much input on scripts as Tom Baker did, but then he played the part for seven years. Towards the end, though, I was putting a few extra bits in.'

In fairness, it should be noted that the Doctor's status as President of the Time Lords was one of the points on which writers were specifically briefed during the initial planning meetings for *The Trial of a Time Lord*. It was suggested that an explanation might be included to the effect that there had been a change in Gallifrey's system of government during the Doctor's absence, and that consequently he had lost his former position. It seems however that this point must have been lost in the translation of the original ideas into script form.

Continuity was certainly not something which Eric Saward or John Nathan-Turner ignored during this period. On the contrary the sixth Doctor's era is often noted for the unusually large extent to which it drew on the series' own established mythology.

Saward, in common with previous script editors, considered that while continuity should not be accorded such an inordinately high priority that it got in the way of telling a good story, care should be taken to keep faith with the series' viewers by avoiding major discrepancies. Consequently he sometimes consulted on such matters with *Doctor Who* fan Ian Levine – whose input, made without payment or credit, he found extremely helpful – as did producer John Nathan-Turner.

Many new facts are learned about the Doctor himself during the eight stories of his sixth incarnation. His first adventure, *The Twin Dilemma*, shows how extreme and unpredictable the after-effects of regeneration can sometimes be, while his last, *The Trial of a Time Lord*, presents a distillation of all his darker aspects in the form of the Valeyard. In *The Two Doctors*, he is seen to suffer a psychic trauma when his second incarnation is apparently put to death, and later he communicates with his other persona telepathically across space.

Viewers are also introduced to a number of old acquaintances from earlier incidents not seen in the TV series. In *The Twin Dilemma*, there is Azmael, a retired Time Lord with whom the Doctor once spent a pleasant drunken evening beside a fountain on the planet Joconda; in *The Two Doctors*, it is revealed that he first met Joinson Dastari while attending an inaugural function as a representative of the Time Lords, before he fell from favour with them; in *Timelash*, the TARDIS materialises on Karfel, where the Doctor is honoured for having saved the population from a disaster during a visit in his third incarnation with Jo Grant and another companion; and in the Vervoid segment of *The Trial of a Time Lord*, he arrives on the space-liner *Hyperion III* too late to save the life of his old friend Hallet, an undercover law enforcement agent, but still in time to come to the aid of Commodore 'Tonker' Travers, a man for whom he apparently caused some trouble during a previous encounter.

In *The Two Doctors*, the second Doctor and Jamie are seen to be undertaking a mission for the Time Lords – something that surprised many fans as, during his own era, this Doctor had not even admitted his origins until the end of his last adventure, *The War Games*. This is an example of a change occurring as a result of a misunderstanding on the part of the writer. Robert Holmes had always been under the impression that it was the second Doctor who had routinely undertaken missions for his own people, as the price of his continued freedom, when in actual fact it was the *third* Doctor who had done so. Some interesting theories have been advanced by fans to account for the apparent inconsistency that arose from this. One ingenious explanation is that after the momentous events of the 1973 story *The Three Doctors*, it was not only the third Doctor who was rewarded by the Time Lords by being given a new dematerialisation circuit for his TARDIS, but also the first and second Doctors, by each being allowed a completely new lease of life. This would certainly account for some of the developments seen in *The Two Doctors*, and also for some of those in the earlier anniversary story *The Five Doctors*, but it is only one of many possible explanations.

The Doctor's trusty TARDIS features prominently in a number of the stories of this period. In *Attack of the Cybermen*, the ship temporarily discards its familiar police box form after the Doctor repairs its chameleon circuits, appearing first as a decorated cupboard, then as a pipe organ and later as an ornate gateway; in *Vengeance on Varos*, it becomes stranded in a galactic void owing to a fault in the transitional elements, requiring the trans/power system to be relined with zeiton 7; in *The Two Doctors*, viewers learn that a TARDIS's briode-nebuliser has to be primed with the Rassilon Imprimatur – a print of symbiotic nuclei within the physiology of every Time Lord – before it can be used; in the same story, the sixth Doctor is heard to express considerable envy on discovering that his second incarnation is now able to operate his TARDIS with a Stattenheim remote control unit, provided by the Time Lords; and in *Timelash*, the ship is used as a deflector shield to neutralise a Bandril missile.

Along with the introduction of a number of new characters who would go on to become returning characters – the evil arms dealer Sil and his fellow Mentors, the exiled Time Lord chemist the Rani and the intergalactic mercenary Sabalom Glitz – the sixth Doctor's era saw the return and development of a number of well-established adversaries from previous seasons.

Attack of the Cybermen could almost be considered a sequel to the Sixties classic *The Tomb of the Cybermen*, as it sees the Doctor being forcibly returned to that story's setting, the tomb complex on the planet Telos. Here he has a new battle with the creatures' ultimate leader, the Cyber Controller, who has apparently recovered from the damage inflicted upon him at the end of his debut story. This time, viewers also meet Telos's original inhabitants, the Cryons – creatures who can exist only in extreme cold – with whom Lytton, the mercenary first encountered working for the Daleks in the fifth Doctor story *Resurrection of the Daleks*, has now allied himself. The Cybermen's plan turns out to involve the use of a time ship, captured from another race, in order to crash

Halley's Comet into the Earth and thereby prevent the destruction in 1986 of their original home planet Mondas, as seen in the first Cyberman story *The Tenth Planet*. In the end, however, their scheme is defeated and the Controller finally destroyed.

It has become traditional over the years for subtle – and sometimes not-so-subtle – changes to be made in the Cybermen's appearance for each new adventure. *Attack of the Cybermen* is one exception to the rule, however, as this time, the creatures' costumes are almost exactly the same as in their previous outing, *The Five Doctors*. The only variations are provided by a black-camouflaged Cyber Scout in the sequences set in the London sewers – the site of the Cybermen's base on Earth, as they were in the 1968 adventure *The Invasion* – and by the Cyber Controller, who looks somewhat bloated in comparison with his underlings and whose helmet is notable for having a domed top and a lack of any side handles, echoing some of the distinctive features of the original helmet as seen in *The Tomb of the Cybermen*. Director Matthew Robinson had also intended that the Cybermen seen on the surface of Telos should wear transparent, globe-shaped space helmets over their heads, but this idea was dropped at a late stage as it was found that the globes had a tendency to steam up and impede the actors' movements.

The Doctor's arch-enemy the Master returned to plague him once more in *The Mark of the Rani* – with no explanation given for his miraculous escape from the apparently fatal predicament in which he was last seen at the end of the Season 21 story *Planet of Fire*. His powers of hypnotism – somewhat neglected during the fifth Doctor's era – are very much in evidence here, as is his familiar tissue compression eliminator weapon, but his characteristically devious scheme is directed towards what seems – for him – a remarkably unambitious end. His main aim is simply to disrupt the course of Earth's history by thwarting the start of the industrial revolution – although in the process he also plans, as usual, to humiliate and kill the Doctor!

The Trial of a Time Lord has the Master setting his sights rather higher as, by revealing to the court the High Council's corrupt deal with the Valeyard, he contrives to bring about their downfall, creating insurrection on Gallifrey and leaving a power vacuum that he intends to fill. He has once again miscalculated, however, and ends up trapped inside his own TARDIS, lodged within the Matrix.

The Sontarans also reappear during the sixth Doctor's era, having their fourth on-screen skirmish with the Time Lord. Little new information is learned about them on this occasion, though, apart from the fact that they are vulnerable to attack with a chemical called coronic acid. They are still as bellicose as ever, still attempting to gain the secret of time travel – something that they were seen to have achieved in rudimentary form in Season 11's *The Time Warrior* and that they tried to take by force in Season 15's *The Invasion of Time* – and still locked in their seemingly endless intergalactic war with the shape-shifting Rutans, described on this occasion as 'the Rutan Host'.

No era of *Doctor Who* would be truly complete without at least one story featuring the series' most famous monsters, the dreaded Daleks. *Revelation of the Daleks* presents viewers with two different Dalek factions: one – with the traditional grey livery – loyal to the Supreme Dalek on their home planet Skaro, the other – with a new, white and gold colour scheme – created by Davros on the planet Necros to do his bidding. Continuity with previous Dalek stories is excellent, the splitting of the Daleks into two opposing blocs being a highly logical development after their earlier clashes with Davros, their progenitor.

The idea of Davros deliberately creating new mutants to serve as recruits for his Dalek army is also a fitting reference back to the creatures' origins on the radiation-soaked Skaro, and provides the opportunity for a particularly memorable image – that of the transparent, partly formed Dalek in the incubation room on Necros. The concept of a transparent Dalek had first appeared in David Whitaker's book *Doctor Who in an Exciting Adventure with the Daleks* – the novelisation of the Daleks' debut story from 1963/64 – but could not have been realised in the TV series at that time, so it is nice to see it reaching the screen here.

Another important development in *Revelation of the Daleks* is the scene where one of Davros's Daleks appears to hover some distance off the ground when exterminating the characters Natasha and Grigory, finally providing the answer to the age-old question as to how the Daleks can conquer a galaxy when they can't climb stairs!

Davros's own evolution is taken a stage further in this story. He is represented for the most part as a disembodied head within a life-support unit, which is actually just a decoy to fool potential assassins – although whether it is a clone or a projection or a mechanical automaton of some sort is never made entirely clear. When the real Davros finally appears, however, it is obvious that he has developed some previously unsuspected powers: he immobilises the assassin Orcini with a stream of blue lightning projected from his forefinger, and – like the Dalek in the incubation room – demonstrates an ability to hover effortlessly in mid-air. A rather more prosaic development occurs toward the end of the story when he has his remaining hand blown off by a burst of gunfire from Orcini's squire, Bostock!

Ever since they were devised in 1969 by writers Terrance Dicks and Malcolm Hulke, the Time Lords have been an increasingly important part of *Doctor Who*. Their contribution to the series' mythology is developed significantly during the sixth Doctor's era, and most notably in *The Trial of a Time Lord*. This is the third time the Doctor has been placed on trial by his own people; in *The War Games* he stood accused of interfering in the affairs of other planets, and in *The Deadly Assassin* he was erroneously charged with the President's assassination.

The trial takes place on a giant space station, into which the Doctor's TARDIS is drawn by the mental energy of the assembled Time Lords, and the evidence is presented on a huge screen linked to the Matrix – the computer that acts as the repository of all Time Lord knowledge, as established in *The Deadly Assassin* and expanded upon in a number of later adventures. In charge of the court is the Inquisitor, and presenting the case for the prosecution is the Valeyard.

At the beginning of the story, the Doctor learns that during his absence from Gallifrey, he has been deposed as President due to his neglect of his duties – the reference that Colin Baker had asked to have inserted, as mentioned at the start of this chapter. At first, he is told that the proceedings are merely an inquiry into his behaviour, ordered by the High Council. The charges are that he is guilty of conduct unbecoming a Time Lord, and that he has broken the First Law of Time – which appears to relate here to interference in the affairs of other planets, although at earlier points in the series' history it was the law that prevented a Time Lord from crossing his own time stream. The Valeyard considers that the sentence imposed upon the Doctor at his last trial – presumably a reference to the one in *The War Games* – was too lenient, and before long, he has had the inquiry changed into a formal trial, with the Doctor's present and future lives at stake if he is found guilty. Later, the charge is changed again, under Article 7 of Gallifreyan law, to one of genocide, the Doctor's own evidence having shown him destroying the Vervoid race in a future adventure. Clearly the Gallifreyan judicial process works rather differently from any here on Earth!

During the course of the trial, it becomes apparent that the Matrix is by no means as inviolable as its Keeper – a figure not featured or referred to in any previous story – asserts. The Master has gained access to it using a copy of the Key of Rassilon and, at his urging, Glitz tells the court that thieves from Andromeda had previously been stealing hi-tech secrets from it for some time, before their actions were finally discovered. The Doctor's trial is in fact part of an elaborate cover-up by the High Council to prevent anyone from finding out about the drastic measures they took to prevent their secrets from getting out; measures that involved moving Earth – the base for the Andromedans' operations – light years across space, devastating it with a fireball. As seen in the opening segment of the story, Earth is now known as Ravolox and inhabited by primitive peoples such as the Tribe of the Free. This continues the trend of previous Time Lord stories in suggesting that their race's hold on power – which the Doctor states has been absolute for ten million years – has had a highly corrupting influence.

Further features of the Matrix are observed in the closing stages of the story as the Doctor, Glitz and Mel enter it through the Seventh Door – a portal, situated just outside the courtroom, which is opened by placing the Key of Rassilon against a sensor pad – and as all three become caught up, along with the Master, in a fantasy domain created by the Valeyard – scenes highly reminiscent of those in *The Deadly Assassin*, also written by Robert Holmes, in which the Doctor battled another adversary within the Matrix.

Considering its relative brevity, the sixth Doctor's era saw some significant changes taking place in, and some important additions being made to, the *Doctor Who* universe: a legacy that would remain with the series and be further built upon in later years.

PRODUCTION DEVELOPMENT

The sixth Doctor's era broke with recent precedent right from the outset, the newcomer's introductory story being placed not at the beginning of a season but at the end of one. This was a consequence of John Nathan-Turner's desire to establish the new Doctor before the series went off-air for the summer. It could therefore be considered rather surprising that the production team then chose to make him mentally unstable in the aftermath of his regeneration, leaving viewers uncertain as to what he would be like in later stories. They took this decision partly with a view to keeping all their options open, but also in a conscious effort to try something new, making the sixth Doctor highly impetuous and unreliable, as Eric Saward explained to *Doctor Who Magazine* in 1984:

'Because the Doctor has always been slightly seedy after regenerating ... and because we wanted to make the sixth Doctor different, we decided to make the regeneration so extreme that it would resemble madness. The swings of mood were amazing – if he had been walking around on the streets, he would have been a strong contender for a psychiatric hospital! So the whole behavioural aspect of the Doctor in *The Twin Dilemma* was quite deliberate – I wanted to explore what happened after the regeneration.'

Saward acknowledges that this idea could not be sustained for long:

'It's an obstacle to developing a story. Personal traits in the way a character approaches a problem are interesting, and a writer can use them, but when a character is utterly unreliable, and one doesn't know how he's going to act or which way he's going to go, it creates endless problems.'

In view of this, the sixth Doctor became noticeably more stable in his first full season, Season 22, allowing the emphasis to be shifted towards the stories themselves. One thing that remained unchanged, however, was his garish, multicoloured costume, the initial inspiration for which had come from John Nathan-Turner.

'John very much wanted to achieve a kind of development from one Doctor to another,' recalled the costume's designer, Pat Godfrey, in *The Frame*. 'He wanted to get the feel of the previous Doctors' costumes by going back to a more Victorian shape, but he also wanted to make the new one look very bizarre, rather fairground and clown-like. He even suggested that I could give the character spotted trousers, but that was a direction we chose not to follow. John wanted a garish costume – his own words were "a totally tasteless costume" – which is actually very difficult to achieve, as one has to be tastefully tasteless.

'The other constraints I was given were that the shirt had to have a question mark on each collar and that there couldn't be any blue anywhere in the costume, as it would have caused problems with the electronic effects.'

This brief continued John Nathan-Turner's policy of giving his Doctors highly stylised, uniform-like costumes, rather than simply eccentric collections of more conventional clothing as had been worn by the Time Lord's earlier incarnations. The very distinctive nature of the sixth Doctor's costume had an obvious impact on the style of his stories, in that it precluded any possibility of him making an unobtrusive entrance into a situation and inevitably meant that he became the centre of attention. It also had another, less obvious repercussion, as Pat Godfrey explains:

'This really arose from a technicality of working in colour television. When colour was first introduced, we were trained in how to design for it. We were shown a scale of 0 to 100, where 0 was black and 100 was white. We were told that the maximum range that video cameras could cope with at that time was only about 30 – in other words, the darkest and brightest colours in the picture could be no more than 30 points apart on the scale. So because the Doctor's costume was very bright, I had to move everything else up the scale accordingly. If the companion's costume had been in very subtle hues, it would have been washed out by the Doctor's, so hers had to be bright as well.'

This knock-on effect extended not only to the series' costumes but also to other aspects of the production, most notably the sets. The end result was that the overall look of the sixth Doctor's stories tended to be very gaudy and unsubtle – a development that John Nathan-Turner later acknowledged to have been to the series' detriment, although he was unaware of it at the time.

Season 22 also saw important changes being made in the style and pacing of the series' scripts. These came about as a direct consequence of the decision – reportedly taken by Alan Hart, the then Controller of BBC1 – to double the length of each episode, with a concomitant halving of the number of episodes per season. The new episode length was originally to have been 50 minutes but was eventually fixed at 45 minutes when John Nathan-Turner pointed out that, with fewer title sequences required, a 50-minute episode would actually have demanded *more* than twice the usual programme content, increasing the strain on the series' budget and resources.

The extended episode length was welcomed by Nathan-Turner. 'I feel that the show lends itself more easily to that formula,' he told the fanzine *Zygon*. 'I know that's a kind of outrageous thing to say, after 21 years of the old format, but it provides an opportunity for us as programme makers to examine the relationship between the Doctor and his companion ... and to find out more about the guest characters, to flesh them out more.'

Notwithstanding this potential advantage, both Nathan-Turner and Eric Saward realised that the transition from the old format to the new would require careful handling. In an interview for *Doctor Who Magazine*, Saward later explained the challenges it had presented:

'It involved, from my point of view, an attempt to talk to our writers about a format of which I had no experience, although obviously I'd written 50-minute things myself for other programmes. While rethinking the format, we were very careful to keep the essence of the show, which is a fantasy/SF adventure story. We couldn't just cobble together two 25-minute episodes, because a compilation of two fast-running parts is very off-putting – it jars. We had time to stop and think a bit more, although we did have to keep on hammering away with the action.'

Saward considered that the transition had been achieved relatively successfully and was disappointed when the powers-that-be decided to revert to the traditional 25-minute format for Season 23, feeling that another season of 45-minute episodes would perhaps have been better. This was a view with which John Nathan-Turner concurred, as he told *Doctor Who Magazine* in the same September 1985 interview:

'Yes, I think it did work. Inevitably when there's a change in something that has been a tradition for such a long time, there's a kind of apprehension from the front office that it won't work. Now we're rethinking again. We've got material that has been written for 45-minute slots and will have to be split up again. Those scripts we do finish up using will have to be restructured. There's more to it than just splitting it down the middle. It would have been lovely to have done one more season in that slot to get it exactly right, but we were both surprised and delighted that we achieved accuracy so quickly.'

Another significant change in storytelling style arose from the fact that, unlike his predecessor, the sixth Doctor had just a single companion. This was a change that Eric Saward actively supported, as he revealed to *Doctor Who Magazine*:

'From my point of view, both as script editor and as writer, you can do much more with just one companion. The Doctor and the companion can have a much stronger, better-defined relationship, and they can relate to each other in a more positive way. When you've got more than one companion, you're farming out lines that could be said by one person. Also, if you've got so many people in a confined space like the TARDIS, it's difficult to give them a lot of positive action. That became very apparent with three companions. It's also a problem to deal with so many sub-plots. Thus the return to the old idea.'

What Saward found rather less appealing was the nature of Peri's character, which he considers to have been weak and 'feminine' in all the worst ways. Neither was he any happier with Peri's successor, computer programmer Mel Bush, whom he recalls to have been conceived purely to fulfil Nathan-Turner's desire to have a companion with red hair – possibly with a view to his intended casting of the part.

The original character outlines for Peri and Mel were both relatively detailed. The former was prepared by Nathan-Turner along with Saward and writer Peter Grimwade, while the latter was entirely Nathan-Turner's work. In his book *Doctor Who – The Companions*, the producer gave his own account of the factors that had shaped Mel's development:

'One of the changes we decided to make [for Season 23] was a change of emphasis in humour. I have always maintained that *Doctor Who* should have a helping of wit rather than slapstick. In order to make this helping more than ample I decided to devise a companion whose basic character gave the writers more opportunity for fun and humour; a character who, by her very nature, placed the Doctor in humorous situations.'

Thus Mel was conceived as a get-up-and-go health-and-fitness fanatic with a mane of red hair, who would rush impetuously into dangerous situations and keep the Doctor on his toes in more ways than one, often chiding him about his tendency towards portliness.

Nathan-Turner did however admit, in his introduction to *Doctor Who – The Companions*, that he was wary of making the Doctor's companion too strong a character:

'One of the problems I discovered with companions of my own devising was that the more rounded the character, the more it required development. And development of character takes air-time and this reduces the amount of dramatisation air-time and before you know where you are, a science-fiction adventure series is taking on a soap-opera flavour.'

When he came to cast the part of Mel in December 1985, almost six months after he had first devised the character (his original outline being dated 5 July 1985), Nathan-Turner made a very surprising choice. He later described to *Doctor Who Magazine* how this had come about:

'I was having a meeting with the agent Barry Burnett, and he said, "Is there any other casting I can help you with; what about the new companion?" and I said, "You have a client who is perfect for it from the way I've described it, but I don't know if she'd be interested, or whether it's really a good idea or not." He said, "Who's that?" and I said, "Bonnie".'

The selection of popular variety artist Bonnie Langford to play Mel was not well received by Eric Saward. In an interview for *DWB* in 1992, he commented: 'Bonnie Langford, I'm convinced, was Nathan-Turner's most cynical piece of casting.' Ian Levine, speaking in the same interview, added: 'I'm not alone in believing he hired her not simply because in his opinion she'd be good for *Doctor Who*, but because he saw her as a big draw for Teynham Productions' pantomimes.' Teynham Productions was an organisation run by Nathan-Turner and others, which mounted regular Christmas pantomimes during this period.

The casting of Bonnie Langford was also unpopular with many fans, who saw it as an extension of the recent policy of featuring 'guest stars', frequently best known for their comedy work, in prominent *Doctor Who* roles. Examples included comedienne Beryl Reid as captain of a space freighter in *Earthshock*, Rodney Bewes of *The Likely Lads* as an android trooper in *Resurrection of the Daleks* and Kate O'Mara, most famous for her roles in the soap operas *The Brothers* (opposite Colin Baker) and *Triangle*, as the Rani in *The Mark of the Rani*.

As some critics saw it, this influx of 'celebrity' actors damaged *Doctor Who*'s credibility, bringing inappropriate 'light entertainment' connotations to serious roles and making it more difficult for viewers to suspend their disbelief – a vital factor in the impact of any science fiction or fantasy series. The *Doctor Who* audience, it was argued, would be unable to dispel from their minds the popular image of Bonnie Langford as a precocious

6 SIXTH DOCTOR

song-and-dance performer, who had come to prominence as a winner of the *Opportunity Knocks* talent contest and as a child star in roles such as that of the obnoxious Violet Elizabeth Bott in London Weekend Television's *Just William* series.

John Nathan-Turner, however, was unswayed by such criticisms, pointing out that Langford's popularity with youngsters could attract many new viewers to *Doctor Who*. 'Bonnie is a terrific little actress,' he told *Doctor Who Magazine*, 'and anybody who has seen her in the West End in *Peter Pan*, which is something a darn sight more recent than Violet Elizabeth, will realise that. I think of myself as ambitious in casting terms, and I know that Bonnie has the potential to make the part totally unirritating, as opposed to Violet Elizabeth.' Nathan-Turner also rejected the more general criticisms of the 'guest star' policy, arguing that it attracted valuable extra publicity for the series.

Another objection to which the production team often had to respond at this time concerned the increasing level of violence in *Doctor Who*, and particularly in the six stories that made up Season 22. This season was, without question, exceptionally bleak and oppressive in emphasis, dealing with such heavy themes as video nasties, genetic experimentation and cannibalism; and, added to this, the plots themselves became rather more gory and horrific in content, featuring disturbing scenes of torture, dismemberment and suffering.

'I've always felt,' says Eric Saward, 'that if you're going to show violence, you should also show the horrific effects of it. If you hit somebody, it hurts; it hurts your hand, for one thing, and it certainly hurts the person you hit. If you hit them in the face, they're going to get a black eye or a bloody nose. Similarly, if you shoot at somebody's hand, they're going to lose fingers, as Davros did in *Revelation of the Daleks*. That's a terrible thing to happen, but if you present an action-adventure story in which there's no apparent consequence to the violence, then I think you're cheating the audience.

'I'll never understand Mary Whitehouse's point of view. She seems to want a bland, safe little world in which everything is quiet and ordered and the traditional class structure is completely in place. That's simply confirming a stereotype, and is an evil portrayal of society. In the same way, if you offer an audience blandness, it's a corrosive thing. I would argue with anybody on this point. To pretend that there's no consequence to violent conflict is to cheat and to deceive.'

This graphic portrayal of violent incidents certainly brought a greater degree of realism to *Doctor Who*. It is also fair to mention that Season 22 was planned on the basis that the episodes would be going out at around 6.20 pm, and not in the 5.20 pm slot to which they were eventually allocated. These factors were of little comfort, however, to the many viewers who remained concerned at the sheer number of violent incidents presented, and at the depiction of gratuitously unpleasant images such as that of the character Shockeye killing and biting into a rat in *The Two Doctors*. The inclusion of such scenes was generally felt to be quite at odds with the series' traditional 'family viewing' appeal – as was the introduction of a blatantly sexual overtone in the form of Peri's titillating outfits and the recurring subplot of aliens lusting after her body.

Some commentators even went so far as to suggest that Season 22 marked a temporary departure from the strong moral standpoint that had previously been one of *Doctor Who*'s most distinctive and popular features. No longer, it was said, was there any clear delineation between good and evil in the stories. The actions of supposedly noble or heroic characters – such as Lytton in *Attack of the Cybermen*, the Governor in

Vengeance on Varos and Orcini in *Revelation of the Daleks* – were criticised as being almost as questionable as those of the villains themselves, and even the Doctor's tactics did not entirely escape reproach. Although *The Trial of a Time Lord* saw the production team making a considerable reduction in the level of violence – a response to a specific instruction from Michael Grade, the Controller of BBC1 – many still consider this arguable lapse in the series' basic morality to have been a major failing of the Colin Baker era.

Eric Saward sees these criticisms as naïve:

'There have never been moral absolutes. The Doctor has been responsible for many deaths throughout the series' history. The portrayal of characters such as Lytton and Orcini perhaps reflected a more accurate image of life than had been attempted before. Remember that soldiers honoured as heroes have often killed many people, an activity that would be seen as totally unacceptable in peace time.'

Another criticism often made of the Colin Baker era was that it placed an excessive reliance on *Doctor Who*'s own history and mythology to provide the inspiration for new plots. Examples are numerous; and in this regard, *The Trial of a Time Lord* was so complex that even many fans, with the benefit of repeated viewing on video, found it difficult to follow. Other, less-committed viewers were probably completely alienated – a supposition supported by the season's comparatively low ratings.

Speaking at a convention in November 1985, during the period when scripts were being commissioned for *The Trial of a Time Lord*, John Nathan-Turner gave a dismissive response to criticisms that the series had been drawing too heavily on its own past:

'I don't think it's been drawing too heavily. I think the mix has been about right. Something that has a 22-year history should not dismiss its heritage. At the same time, it shouldn't pander to it. I don't think we've overdone it. There are facts and figures one can produce to show that the popularity of the Daleks and the Cybermen is above that of all the other old enemies, and it would be totally foolhardy to dismiss them. They constitute the majority of our returning villains.'

Eric Saward, however, feels that the series did indeed become over-reliant on its own mythology at this point, and had indicated to *DWB* in 1988 that he was never in favour of such an approach:

'I think that it was John's idea to feature a past element in every story [of Season 20], but it was something I wasn't very interested in. I mean, we had had the Cybermen in the previous season, and that had worked; but personally I wanted us to move on. Looking back, it was a fault both John and I fell into. The season and the celebration failed because of wanting to relive history. I must say that this was done, certainly on John's part, to please the fans rather than the general public.'

Saward went on to say in the same interview that as far as the scripts went, '*Doctor Who* should have the highest rejection rate in the department ... because they are very difficult things to write well. The writers tried their best and were paid for their efforts, but the scripts should nevertheless not have been made.' However, as Saward explained, Nathan-Turner did not like rejecting material.

Accepting that John Nathan-Turner would very often request stories featuring popular monsters such as the Daleks, the Cybermen and the Sontarans, it might perhaps be asked why the writers could not then have made original and inventive use of them, just as their predecessors had done during other eras of the series' history. Eric Saward puts this down to the fact that the concepts were in many cases very dated:

'Attitudes have changed a great deal in the last twenty years: schoolchildren no longer accept as gospel what is said by their teachers; adults no longer become staid and over the hill at 45; and no-one now believes that the police are like Dixon of Dock Green. It's the same with good, imaginative writers: they prefer to invent their own projects – it inspires them – rather than try to breathe life into a tired old concept like, say, the Daleks. When they are asked to use such concepts, their work often reflects the tiredness of the original idea.'

There is no doubt that during the mid-Eighties *Doctor Who* drew on its own mythos to a far greater extent than at any other point in its history. *The Trial of a Time Lord* came in for some particularly heavy fan criticism for this, and indeed for its general incoherence. Philip Martin, one of the writers of the fourteen-part epic, had a number of reservations about it, as he later told *Doctor Who Magazine*:

'It suffered from being simultaneously commissioned. Bob Holmes died after his second draft, there were problems with the final storyline – there were six or seven writers altogether – and we never knew where we were going. Then the script editor left, and when we reached the final episode, it was all so confusing I couldn't follow it. And I had been there at the beginning! The story as it eventually reached the screen seemed to have little left of our original idea.'

Eric Saward admits that almost all the scripts commissioned during the Colin Baker era were heavily rewritten by him – a fact that he attributes to the difficulties experienced by incoming writers in coping with *Doctor Who*'s especially challenging format and budgetary restrictions. Speaking to *DWB* in 1988, he recounted some of the behind-the-scenes problems encountered on *The Trial of a Time Lord*:

'Bob Holmes wrote the first four episodes, which, given the pressures, were okay on paper. But Jonathan Powell didn't like them. We got this memo saying, "Didn't like this, or that, thought this was too silly …" and all the rest of it. So alterations were made, which he accepted and which went into the final programme.'

The original idea had been that Holmes would also write the final two episodes of the story. These would have ended the season with the Doctor and the Master locked in mortal combat and with a question mark hanging over the outcome. Saward says that this was agreed with Nathan-Turner, and that the writing of the scripts was taken forward accordingly.

A further development then occurred, however, when Saward decided to resign his post as script editor. He had, as the sixth Doctor's era progressed, become increasingly unhappy working alongside Nathan-Turner, rarely seeing eye to eye with him over production decisions, and he decided at this point that it was time he left the series. Despite this, when Holmes fell ill after completing only a draft of the story's penultimate episode, Saward accepted Nathan-Turner's invitation to finish the work on this script and to write part fourteen himself, according to the agreed outline. As Saward recalls, when Nathan-Turner eventually saw the script for the final episode, he reneged on what had been agreed and refused to accept the cliff-hanger ending to the season. Saward consequently withdrew permission for the use of this script – a decision he declined to reconsider, although Nathan-Turner wrote to him in conciliatory terms in an attempt to persuade him to do so. Nathan-Turner then had to commission from Pip and Jane Baker a last-minute replacement.

Following these incidents, Saward gave *Starburst* magazine an interview in which he aired his criticisms of Nathan-Turner:

'I was getting very fed up with the way *Doctor Who* was being run, largely by John Nathan-Turner – his attitude and lack of insight into what makes a television series like *Doctor Who* work.'

He went on to say that his former colleague had, amongst other things, brought pantomime aspects to *Doctor Who*; neglected important tasks in favour of trivial ones, such as making arrangements for and attending fan conventions in the USA and approving merchandise for BBC Enterprises; been reluctant to work with experienced people in case they undermined his authority; taken insufficient interest in the series' scripts; and made poor casting decisions.

As Saward had a day-to-day involvement with the series' production, his comments must clearly be accorded considerable weight; and equally critical opinions of Nathan-Turner's qualities as a producer have been publicly expressed by a number of others involved in *Doctor Who* during the mid-Eighties, including writer and director Peter Grimwade, actor Anthony Ainley (who played the Master) and Ian Levine. It should be noted, however, that Nathan-Turner also has many friends and supporters amongst those who worked on the series at this time. These include stars Colin Baker, Nicola Bryant and Bonnie Langford, writers Pip and Jane Baker, and directors such as Fiona Cumming and Nicholas Mallett, all of whom have given quite the opposite impression of the contribution made by the producer, praising him for his strong support of their work, for his enormous energy and for his fierce commitment to the series. This is not of course to suggest that anyone has been less than truthful in their comments on Nathan-Turner; it is simply a reflection of the fact that there seems to be a very wide divergence of opinion amongst those who worked with him, making him arguably the most controversial figure ever to have been associated with the series.

Despite this divergence of opinion, some fans came to believe that the multitude of problems with which *Doctor Who* was beset during this period were almost entirely the fault of John Nathan-Turner. Whilst it is certainly true to say that all matters pertaining to the production of *Doctor Who* on a day-to-day basis were ultimately the producer's responsibility, it can also be said that some of the difficulties the series faced – the frequent, damaging changes of transmission days, times and episode lengths; the postponement of Season 23; Michael Grade's public attacks on the series and its production team; and ultimately Colin Baker's ousting from the role of the Doctor after *The Trial of a Time Lord* – were matters largely if not entirely beyond the producer's control. While opinions may legitimately differ as to the artistic merits of the sixth Doctor's stories, the vociferous criticisms sometimes directed at Nathan-Turner with regard to scheduling and other decisions taken by BBC management would appear to be unfounded.

If *The Trial of a Time Lord* can be seen as a case of art imitating life – Michael Grade and his colleagues having made it abundantly clear that the series itself was still on trial – then it could be argued that there are certain respects in which, conversely, life imitated art during the Colin Baker era. It was as if the unpredictable, mercurial, explosive character of the sixth Doctor was actually being reflected in the dramatic real-life incidents surrounding the series!

Whatever else might be said, this was undeniably the most troubled and eventful period of production in *Doctor Who*'s long history.

FROM SCRIPT TO SCREEN: REVELATION OF THE DALEKS

Introduction

The production chosen for this case study is *Revelation of the Daleks*, the final story of the twenty-second season, first transmitted in 1985. For helping us to compile our information, we are grateful to several people, in particular the writer Eric Saward, the director Graeme Harper, the designer Alan Spalding and the visual effects designer John Brace, each of whom took the time to speak to us in great detail about their respective contributions, and to costume designer Pat Godfrey, who gave an earlier interview to *The Frame*.

The Scripts

The initial idea for *Revelation of the Daleks* came from producer John Nathan-Turner, who decided that he wanted a Dalek story with which to close the season. He also wanted Eric Saward to write it, as his previous Dalek tale, *Resurrection of the Daleks*, had been very well received.

'I actually went off contract for six weeks to write *Revelation of the Daleks*,' recalls Eric Saward. 'I went away to Rhodes for three weeks round about June/July 1984, had a nice holiday, enjoyed myself, and wrote the scripts.

'I wanted to do something about a planet that specialised in dealing with the dead. I worked out a rough storyline – and it was *very* rough – and went through it with John, and he said "OK".'

The initial inspiration for the story came from an Evelyn Waugh novel. 'When I was on holiday, I re-read *The Loved One*, which is Waugh's skit on how the Americans view the dead. I had first read it many years before, and I remembered that there is a character in it called Joyboy, who is a make-up artist for the dead. He is a very sad character. He is in his thirties, still living with his mother, and is pursued in the novel by an even more lonely and sad woman. I took the idea of Mr Joyboy and made him Mr Jobel, and the poor infatuated woman became Tasambeker. I really should have killed her in the first episode and put her out of her misery!'

Holidaying in Rhodes while writing the scripts provided Saward with the ideas for many of the character names that he used. 'The local goddess of fertility on Rhodes is called Tsambeker, with a silent 'T', and I just took it phonetically as Tasambeker. Stengos ran the local ferry. Cara was a type of potato that we had fresh from the ground out there – I just changed the spelling to Kara. Orcini was the Grand Master of the Knights of St John, who used to be on Rhodes. He defended Rhodes against Suleiman the Magnificent, the Turkish Sultan, and managed to hold out against 100,000 troops for about six months with only 600 Knights and 2,000 auxiliaries. Suleiman was so impressed by their bravery that, when he eventually won, he freed the Knights that had survived. I took the myths rather than the reality and created my warrior Orcini, who is always looking for the mythical "great kill". Of course, there is no such thing as a "great kill" or a "perfect kill", but in his mind there is, because it's noble, it's honourable. Reaching that ideal is what spurs him on to hunt Davros.'

As Saward recalls, there was no pressure from Terry Nation, the Daleks' creator and copyright holder, to include Davros in the story. Rather, this was an idea that John

Nathan-Turner suggested and that he was very happy to go along with:

'Davros was included because I thought someone had to be behind the planet's operations. Davros had decided that he was going to be the self-appointed Great Healer, and I wanted him initially to appear honourable. Kara was meant to be the unpleasant one. But it didn't quite work out in either case.

'The thing about the Daleks is that when you come to write them, they're very boring. They're boring to listen to for any length of time – that stilted monotone. Davros is a much more interesting character. He speaks relatively normally, so he can sustain conversations, which the Daleks can't, and he is therefore convenient to use at the centre of the plot. In which case the Daleks themselves take just a supporting role.

'I believe that nowadays the Daleks can't be taken seriously. They're far too old fashioned to be seen as a deadly and ultimate evil. That's the reality. They're no longer this great, frightening creation that Nation thought they were.

'The plot developed further when I wondered what Davros could be doing running this place. The most heinous thing anyone can do when running a cemetery is to sell the bodies. That seemed obvious, if not particularly original, so I used it.

'The other thing I wanted to do was to take the development of the Daleks one stage further. Their history seemed to me to have been very chequered in terms of what they could and couldn't do. Considering that they're supposed to be so powerful, their early beginnings were very feeble and crude; needing to draw electricity from the floor and so on. I thought that perhaps it was about time for them to be able to reproduce themselves, so that they could go anywhere and be anything that they wanted.'

Perhaps the strangest character in *Revelation of the Daleks* is the DJ. 'The idea for him came about one evening when I'd been out for a meal and was driving back home in my car. I turned on the radio and there was an incredibly boring DJ on the air. Now, prior to this, I'd thought that if one was going to have a super-cryogenic planet, then there would be problems. I've always wondered about the cryogenic idea, because if people could come back after 200 years, imagine what state they would be in! All their technology, their thinking, everything would be redundant. The world would have moved on so far and they would have become so out of touch that they would instantly die of nervous breakdowns! I'd reasoned that there would have to be some way of keeping the frozen people up to date, but hadn't yet decided how. Then, when I heard this lunatic DJ, who was trying to be incredibly serious but at the same time hip, I knew I had to have him! That's how the character was born.

'The DJ is completely at odds with the place. He sits there and plays music and passes on notes from the folks and so on, but he is so cynical about it all. I made him really rather grotesque, and he had to be grotesque.'

Revelation of the Daleks was commissioned to fit the new 45-minute episode format that *Doctor Who* was assigned for its twenty-second season. As Saward explains, this required an approach slightly different from that used in writing the traditional 25-minute episodes: 'A 25-minute episode tends to be rather frenetic, because it's zooming up to the cliff-hanger. The 45-minute ones were paced a little slower. There was never any intention to create an artificial cliff-hanger halfway through. I'm told that *Revelation of the Daleks* was cut up into four parts for sale to America, but I had nothing to do with that.'

Saward recalls that when his scripts for the two episodes were completed and delivered, they were found to be too long and required shortening, but that little other adjustment was called for. 'If the script is there and it's working reasonably well, most of the director's time is spent on the other aspects of the show – casting, designing and so on – and so I didn't have that much to do with the actual process of making it.

'I first saw it performed at the producer's run, and I was in the studio for almost all the recording. The first time I saw it all together was in John's office, when Graeme delivered the rough cut. I thought he'd made a good job of it, and it had come together well.'

Pre-production

Once the scripts have been drafted, the first person to be contracted to work on a *Doctor Who* is generally the director. In the case of *Revelation of the Daleks*, which had been conceived as the grand finale of the season, John Nathan-Turner was looking for someone who could not only convey the story effectively but also bring a sense of spectacle to it. The man he chose was Graeme Harper, whose work on the fifth Doctor's farewell story, *The Caves of Androzani*, had greatly impressed him.

'When we'd finished *The Caves of Androzani*,' recalls Harper, 'John asked if I would come back and do one in the following season, to which I replied, "Yes". At that time, he wasn't sure which story it would be, or where or when we would be filming, but I knew that if I wanted to do another, then the chances were that I would be able to.' It was in fact around June 1984 that Harper was approached by Nathan-Turner to direct *Revelation of the Daleks*. 'At first, I wasn't sure how this would fit in with my other commitments, but about three months later, when I knew exactly what I was going to be doing, my agent went back to John and told him the dates on which I would be free. Fortunately they tied in with John's schedules.'

Once Harper was confirmed in November 1984 as the director, the next task was to bring on board the key creative personnel. Most BBC departments at this time operated some form of rota system whereby staff were allocated to shows for a whole year in advance. Occasionally the director, in consultation with the producer, would specifically request a particular designer, in which case it would then be up to the appropriate department head to say whether or not that designer happened to be free, as would occasionally be the case, or alternatively whether or not he or she could be freed up from a pre-arranged assignment.

To handle the visual effects for *Revelation of the Daleks*, Harper asked for and got John Brace. 'John had worked on several *Doctor Who* episodes throughout his career, and we knew each other anyway, so it was lucky that he was available.'

Brace was equally pleased to be returning to *Doctor Who*. 'Working in the Effects Department, a designer got the opportunity to be involved in many different types of programmes, but to be allocated to *Doctor Who* allowed particular scope for creativity. There were spaceships and monsters, there were explosions, it was a fantasy world. So to have a *Doctor Who* was good news, and everyone wanted to do them.'

The first thing the director does when joining a production is to read the scripts.

'I didn't understand one bit of them at first,' laughs Harper. 'They were quite complex, and I remember going through them suggesting where we might be able to clarify the plot. Even with this, the story was very complicated.

'As an overall fantasy, however, it was well written. I remember it being very wordy, featuring some almost Shakespearean characters. This was one of its strengths, and it worked.

'I saw the story as a pastiche on the 1973 Richard Fleischer film *Soylent Green*, in which the problems of overcrowding and starvation on a future Earth are both solved by making food (the soylent green of the title) from the people.'

In reading the scripts, the director gets many casting ideas, and these are next discussed with the producer.

'The first conversations a director would have after considering the script would be about casting: the areas and the kinds of characters involved, and whether or not there were going to be any guest stars,' says Harper. 'While those discussions were going on for *Revelation of the Daleks*, I was also talking with the designer about the look and feel of the production and about how we could realise it.

'Soon into those discussions would come the Costume and Make-up Departments – but not *too* soon unless there was something very special required. Visual Effects would also be involved quite early on, and all the while John Nathan-Turner would be listening in and occasionally asking how much all this was going to cost!'

The production team had approximately six weeks – which included a break for Christmas – between starting work on the story and going away on location. This timescale meant that many things had to be worked out quickly, always with an eye on the budget.

'I remember discussing the concept for the planet,' recalls designer Alan Spalding. 'It was supposed to be a death planet. It contained a modern cryogenic plant, but at the same time maintained a tradition of death similar to that found in ancient Egyptian society. Designing the modern aspects was fine, because I could make them futuristic and different, but the ancient elements we found difficult to resolve because Graeme argued that there wouldn't be Earth-type graves and all the associated iconography. I therefore had to aim for impressive and different visuals with a very low budget.'

The costume designer, Pat Godfrey, also remembers that money was tight. 'I think the costume budget for this story was, in all, about £5,000. This had been worked out at the beginning of the season, before the scripts had been completed, and as it was a Dalek story, they'd thought that they wouldn't need too many extra costumes. Unfortunately, there turned out to be a lot of characters in the cast, so the money was spread very thinly.'

The scripts also presented some unusually demanding effects requirements, ranging from exploding glass Daleks through to simple prop bombs, guns and knives, all of which had to be realised by the Visual Effects Department. To try to get around the budgetary restrictions, John Brace took a somewhat radical step: 'We needed all sorts of Daleks – grey Daleks and white Daleks, Daleks that blew up and crystal-clear Daleks in an embryonic stage – and also a large polystyrene sculpture of the Doctor. I went to BBC Enterprises and explained that there was no way that the production could afford to have all these constructed, but I knew they had in the past taken visual effects props and other interesting items for exhibition, and they may have had some old Daleks that we could modify. As discussions evolved with the production associate June Collins and Julie Jones of BBC Enterprises, we decided that we could make new Daleks and Enterprises would buy them back from the programme when production was completed.

'Enterprises were fine with the idea, but my own Department's reaction surprised me. They didn't think that I should be able to do this. "What are you doing making deals with Enterprises?" they asked. "You're just an effects designer. We manage the Department! If you have problems with your budgets, come and see us." However I *had* been and seen them, and they had looked and said, basically, that I was stuffed! They had said that this was television, not films. That this was the real world, and that I had to work within my budget.'

Graeme Harper's previous *Doctor Who* story, *The Caves of Androzani*, had consisted of four 25-minute episodes. Although the amount of material required to be shot for the two 45-minute episodes of *Revelation of the Daleks* was the same, the new format placed much greater demands on the director and his team. 'There was a lot to do in the studio,' recalls Harper. 'They'd changed to a 45-minute format, but it felt as though we didn't have the time in the studio. Whereas in the 25-minute format it was just about possible to scrape through with an occasional overrun, on *Revelation of the Daleks* I think we worked until eleven o'clock every night. We just couldn't fit it all in.'

On Location

One way of maximising studio time is to film as much material as possible on location. Like many *Doctor Who*s at this point in the series' history, *Revelation of the Daleks* made quite extensive use of location filming.

Location filming is normally carried out prior to any studio recording and takes place at whatever venue the production team have decided is best suited to the requirements of the story.

It can take many weeks of effort to find a suitable location. The director and the producer will first discuss the most important criteria and then, in conjunction with the production manager and members of the design team, start to think about places where all these can be met. As travelling time must come out of the time allotted for filming, it is usually important that the chosen location should boast all the required features within easy reach of one another, and that it should be fairly close to the production base of Television Centre in west London.

Where *Revelation of the Daleks* was concerned, the team felt that the mortuary complex of Tranquil Repose was the central image of the story and should be the prime location. Alan Spalding remembers that it was quite tricky to find. 'We wanted a building that was very futuristic-looking. Because of the Egyptian death motif, we had in mind something that suggested hi-tech pyramids. We wanted the ancient culture to be reflected in a modern design. We eventually found somewhere by going through lots of books and looking for unusual buildings and architecture. It was the IBM office complex at North Harbour, Cosham near Portsmouth. This fitted the bill perfectly. It had all the right qualities.'

IBM allowed the crew eight hours' filming on their premises and, instead of taking a fee, asked the BBC to make a donation to a local school.

'It was a perfect location,' affirms John Brace. 'It had little tunnel entrances, so that we could establish that the place extended underground, and it was all black glass on top. In our production, the building was supposed to look incredibly nice on top, although underneath it was throbbing with evil.'

The main location having been chosen, all the other requirements were found nearby. The place where the TARDIS lands was represented by a large hill and woodland area of the Queen Elizabeth's Park nature reserve in Petersfield, near Southampton. The scenes when the Doctor and Peri, and later Orcini and his squire Bostock, approach Tranquil Repose, were shot at a disused aerodrome in the Poole area.

The script's description of the planet Necros was quite difficult to realise, as Spalding explains: 'The story was supposed to be set on a bare, stark planet, but we weren't allowed to go too far away to shoot it. It was quite a difficult brief. We couldn't go to the Yorkshire Moors or Fylingdales or anywhere like that, as we weren't originally supposed to have any overnight stays.'

Prior to going on location, a director usually needs to have worked out a detailed schedule for the filming. 'There are some productions on which it's not critical to have worked out all the camera angles and so on beforehand,' says Harper, 'but on something as complex as *Doctor Who*, everything has to be well planned.

'The director is constrained by the requirements of all the various departments – Design, Effects, Make-up, Costume – as to the order in which certain things have to be done, because of construction and setting-up times. Even the availability of certain actors and actresses can sometimes dictate whether their scenes have to be filmed first or last. The whole process must be planned very carefully. You have to know what you're going to do. You have to know all the shots, the angles and how they will develop. This is essential because you haven't got time to try to work it all out when you are already there. It really has to be done in advance.'

With this in mind, the director and his team will normally go on a recce – an advance visit to all the chosen locations – to start working out how the camera will be positioned in relation to the artistes and to any special props or sets required, and also to try to anticipate any problems that might arise.

When on location, the standard method of working is to rehearse each scene immediately before it is filmed, this process being repeated as many times as is necessary until the director is happy with what has been shot. 'I would talk through any major dialogue scenes the night before with the artistes,' says Harper, 'and any changes would be agreed with the writer. Otherwise, it would all have been blocked out and planned beforehand, so I would know what I was hoping to achieve on any particular day.'

The major problem with going on location as opposed to working in a studio is the unpredictability of the weather. In a studio it can be made to rain or snow on cue; gale-force winds can be created, and so can hot, balmy sunshine. Out in the wilds of the English countryside, however, the unit are at the mercy of the British weather, and can encounter considerable difficulties. This was certainly the case on *Revelation of the Daleks*, as Graeme Harper recalls:

'Bearing in mind that we were due to be filming in January, I'm sure we must have wondered what would happen if it snowed. I had never really worried about it, though. Snow can actually give you a longer working day, because it makes things brighter.

'Anyway, we went away on location for four or five days, and the first couple of days went by with no problems at all: everything we had planned to film was done, and all was on schedule. And then the snow came overnight. We were due to film at Queen Elizabeth's Park the next day, and had to try to get there through a foot of snow! In the end, we had to alter the schedule, and as a result we lost one of our major effects sequences.

'At the Park there was a valley where we were going to stage a battle between the Daleks and the two "Don Quixote" characters, Bostock and Orcini. There was going to be a massive gun battle and, as the major feature of this, we were going to prove that the Daleks could fly. This had never been done before, and we had all wondered how they got about so easily over all manner of terrain. During the battle, a Dalek was going to fly up, twenty feet in the sky, and then explode. That was going to be a major effects piece but, once the snow arrived, we couldn't get the equipment up there. It had all been planned and worked out, but the spring-device that was going to launch this Dalek into the air couldn't be set up. I was disappointed to lose that.'

Eric Saward, however, cannot recall this scene at all. 'It might have had something to do with the one in part two where Orcini destroys a Dalek on location, as what was seen on screen was not what was scripted.'

The original script for this scene has two Daleks suddenly appearing on a ridge behind Orcini and Bostock. The mercenaries open fire with bastic-headed bullets, capable of penetrating solid rock, but the Daleks are unscathed. Ducking behind a rock, Orcini manages to blow off the eyepiece of one of the Daleks, which then topples down the bank, allowing him and his squire to slip away.

'I had tried to carry through the idea that Daleks are very difficult to destroy,' explains Saward. 'I had written that Orcini just damaged the Dalek, but this was changed on location so that it exploded.'

Although it caused the abandonment of the planned battle scene, the snow did have certain fortuitous consequences, as Harper notes: 'We had always planned to do the opening sequences of the story at the end of the shoot, and the change in the weather meant that we could have the Doctor and Peri landing in a snowy landscape next to a frozen pond. It really brought over the feeling of icy desolation that we were trying to achieve.'

Mention of the pond reminds Alan Spalding that it had not been easy to find. 'We had decided to use the South Downs area because we wanted the bleakness and the lack of vegetation that you find there. Then we had to try to find a pond, and at first we couldn't, because ponds just don't happen in chalk. Mike Cameron, the production manager, hunted and hunted, but it seemed that there just wasn't one to be found on the South Downs.

'In the end, we found one on a farmer's property. The farmer had built it for his cattle to drink from. There was a little island in the middle and a boat that we used to get out to it. Graeme decided that the boat would be a good place to position the camera for the shot where the alien hand emerges from the water.'

Using a frozen pond in the middle of winter posed particular problems for John Brace and his team. 'There was thick ice all over this pond, and we had to break it up in order to get into the water to set up the effects.

'In view of that fact that we needed to get underwater to achieve the effect of a hand emerging, I asked for my Department's diving section to come out. The diving section was in fact Jim Francis and Dave Barton, two other visual effects designers, and it was difficult to get my management to accept that you could have three designers on one location. I kept explaining to them that it wasn't three designers, it was one designer and two divers.'

The location sequences for *Revelation of the Daleks* were filmed from 7 to 10 January 1985. As a final note, this was the last *Doctor Who* location shoot ever to be done on film. The use of outside broadcast (OB) video cameras had since 1974 become increasingly prevalent, and from Season 23 onwards, all *Doctor Who*'s location work would be done in this way.

In Studio

The first studio work to be undertaken for *Revelation of the Daleks* was one day of filming by the Visual Effects Department to create all the model scenes required for the story.

In keeping with the usual pattern at this point in the series' history, the main studio recordings then took place at Television Centre in two separate blocks, the first of two days' duration, on 17 and 18 January 1985 in studio TC1, and the second of three days' duration, between 30 January and 1 February in TC8. Cast rehearsals were held at the BBC's Acton rehearsal rooms from 3 to 16 January for the first block and from 19 to 29 January for the second.

All the scenes involving the futuristic sets were recorded in the first block and all those involving the underground areas were done in the second, this split being dictated by the logistics of the story. Normally, a certain proportion of the studio space would have to be left empty to meet the BBC's strict safety regulations, but for *Revelation of the Daleks*, Alan Spalding got special dispensation to fill the studio completely, so as to fit everything in.

Recording of *Doctor Who* in the Eighties was invariably done out of story sequence. The exact recording order would be worked out by the director based on which sets were going to be available in each studio. All the scenes that used one particular set would generally be recorded together, then the crew would move on to the next set and record all the scenes taking place there, and so on.

There were two alternative approaches that directors could take to studio work. One, known as the rehearse/record method, involved each scene being rehearsed on camera immediately before it was recorded, just as on location. The other entailed all the rehearsals being completed during the day and then all the recording being done during the evening. The method used was generally a matter of choice for the individual director, depending on the facilities available, and for *Revelation of the Daleks*, it was the latter that Graeme Harper chose.

Each day's studio recording would have to end at 10 pm sharp, the only exception being where the director had – as on this occasion – obtained permission to go into overtime (an expense that had to be agreed). The studio house lights would be switched on at the appointed time, even if the cast were in the middle of a scene, and the cameramen and other technical personnel would leave for the night. The scene-shifters would then come in to take down (strike) any sets that were not required for the following day's work, and to erect any new ones that were.

To indicate some of the considerations involved in making a *Doctor Who* story during the Colin Baker era, we now present a complete scene-by-scene summary of *Revelation of the Daleks*, taking in comments as appropriate from Eric Saward, Graeme Harper, Alan Spalding, John Brace and (from an interview conducted for *The Frame*) costume designer Pat Godfrey. Make-up designer Dorka Nieradzik was unwilling to contribute to this book, but her recollections are also reported, based on an interview by Brenda Apsley that appeared in the 1986 *Doctor Who Annual*.

Part One

A planet in space. The TARDIS arrives on a mist-blown snowy hillside.

John Brace: 'We used three smoke machines here. The tricky thing about this shot was that we had left the TARDIS's blue lamp behind, and we had to knock something up on location.'

Alan Spalding: 'I didn't want to see any trees, but we had to in the end. I wanted it totally blank, but it wasn't to be.'

Graeme Harper: 'I liked it actually, because it got away from the "Dorset sand pit" look.'

Peri (Nicola Bryant) emerges and wanders down to a large pond. She throws into the water the remains of a nut roast roll on which she has been nibbling. The Doctor (Colin Baker) follows her down. They are both wearing blue – the official mourning colour on Necros – as the Doctor intends to honour local customs. The Time Lord has come here to honour the late Professor Arthur Stengos, one of the finest agronomists in the galaxy. As the two travellers turn away from the lake, an alien hand emerges from the icy water and snatches Peri's roll.

JB: 'The hand belonged to Ken Barker, the stuntman who played the mutant creature.'

Alerted by the splash, the Doctor and Peri turn back in time to see the water erupt in a small explosion.

JB: 'We had to have a woofer [a compressed-air device used for simulating explosions by propelling dust and debris with a blast of air] rigged under the water. We had to rig all that up in one day, although we had already put in an underwater scaffold.'

The Doctor and Peri head away, not seeing a ragged figure (Ken Barker) emerge and start to follow them.
  In a mortuary complex elsewhere on Necros, Takis (Trevor Cooper) is putting the finishing touches to the burial mask of the President's late wife, currently lying in state in the main hall. Jobel (Clive Swift), the chief embalmer, congratulates him. Meanwhile other workers are putting the finishing touches to the arrangements of small blue flowers – herba baculum vitæ, or staff of life – and peacock feathers that line the hall

AS: 'A lot of actors won't work with peacock feathers, because they're supposed to be bad luck, but we didn't have any problems here. We had a thousand of the little blue flowers specially made.'

Tasambeker (Jenny Tomasin), a dumpy, unattractive attendant, fawns over Jobel and tells him that the presidential shuttle is on the way. When Jobel has gone, Takis and his friend Lilt (Colin Spaull) tell Tasambeker that she is wasting her time – Jobel isn't interested in her.

GH: 'When I read the script, certain people came straight to my mind. I knew that Takis and Lilt were going to be Laurel and Hardy. If you watch them, even though they're sinister guys, they have this sort of double act going. Trevor Cooper, who plays Takis, does all these kind of Laurel and Hardy things and mannerisms.
  'When it came to Jobel, I just knew that it had to be Clive Swift playing the part. I knew that if I could get him, then he would bring a lot to the character.'

[Dorka Nieradzik decided to give Jobel an obviously Marcel-waved auburn toupée, which deliberately did not match his own grey hair. The intention was to make him appear quite vain, as if he thought that by putting on the toupée he would appear younger, and that everyone would be fooled into thinking it was his own hair – which of course they were not.]

GH: 'I knew that Tasambeker had to be Ruby from *Upstairs, Downstairs*, played here, as there, by Jenny Tomasin.'

AS: 'There isn't actually any set there in the main hall. It's just done with foreground props and a big arch – which was originally made for *Little and Large*. There's virtually nothing on the sides, just space. The idea was to convey a sort of Egyptian high-tech decor.'

As Jobel and the assistants leave to prepare themselves, two outsiders, Natasha (Bridget Lynch-Blosse) and Grigory (Stephen Flynn), cross the hall and, following a map, enter one of the corridors.
The Doctor and Peri are attacked by the creature that has been following them. It is an horrific mutant, its skin peeling from its body, with broken, yellowing teeth and saliva running from its mouth. Peri beats the beast with a stick until it frees the Doctor.

JB: 'We provided a rubber stick for Nicola to use. It was made to look like a lump of wood from the forest.'

GH: 'When *Doctor Who* went over to the longer, 45-minute episodes, I believe the intention was to reach out to a bigger, more family and more adult audience. With the agreement of John Nathan-Turner, we went as far as we dared with the horror, bearing in mind the time-slot and the audience. The intention here was to be a little more frightening.'

AS: 'The make up was by Dorka Nieradzik and was excellent. Prosthetics were her speciality.'

GH: 'Dorka was fairly unknown to me before this story. I'd worked with her when she was an assistant, but I'd never really known what she could do: the talent that was about to burst forth. She really is someone very special in make-up.'

[Nieradzik provided the mutant with some false teeth made by specialist dental technicians to look as if they were in the process of melting away. She left some hair on his head to give him a pitiful look, and also to make him less frightening and more humanoid, thereby conveying the idea that Davros had been experimenting on him and that his mutation was the result of the experiment.]

The fight is being watched on monitor screens by a hippie-like character. This is the DJ (Alexei Sayle), an employee of Tranquil Repose, who is narrating events to the other, less active residents.

GH: 'The DJ was a very difficult character to cast. We could have gone for a real disc jockey, someone like Jimmy Savile or Alan Freeman, a "name" whom everyone would know and love, and just placed him in the story. But would we have got a performance or would we have had to rely on that familiar persona? Alternatively, we could have gone for a character actor, but that would have meant losing the value of some good publicity. 'We went through a whole host of names and eventually started thinking about going for alternative comedy or something. Alexei had just made *The Young Ones* and *Whoops Apocalypse* and had been very good in them, so we knew that he was a talented actor as well as being a comic, not to mention being larger than life, zany and interesting as a character. So we approached him with the idea, and he liked it.'

AS: 'We were going to make the DJ very Sixties-orientated and a collector of Sixties ephemera. As we were doing this in the mid-Eighties, it seemed like the past, but it didn't quite work, because we couldn't get the right objects. The trouble with a lot of Sixties items is that, even now, they look quite futuristic. The idea that he collected things from the past didn't quite gel, because they looked like things from the future! We should maybe have chosen art deco or something that was more obvious. The items were very hard to find as well, which surprised me.'

Eric Saward: 'Alexei Sayle turned out to be very good casting. When I saw him at the producer's run, he was very flat, and I thought, "Oh God, what have we done here?" But that is how Alexei works. He is a very shy man and very awkward – until, that is, it comes to the performance, and then the energy comes and suddenly he's away. I thought he did it very well.'

Elsewhere in the complex, there is a life-support unit containing the disembodied head of Davros (Terry Molloy), who is attended to by a white Dalek. Davros has been watching the DJ on a monitor, but now orders him silenced, and the sound is cut off. Davros then sees on the monitor that the Doctor has arrived, and comments that his lure has worked.

JB: 'Davros was supposed to be just a head, with life support systems surrounding him. Because later there would be explosions going on around it, and Terry Molloy was inside, we had to make it practical. We used techniques to confuse the eye, so that it wasn't obvious that the rest of Terry's body was in there. I think the most difficult thing was trying to make his head spin round. Colin Gory was my assistant, and had been working on this problem in the workshop while I was away filming. He decided to put Terry on a swivel chair such that he had to squeeze himself into position from underneath with the full head make-up on, and the rest of the tank was then put on top of him.'

Natasha and Grigory make their way through the complex. On level seven, they kill a guard. Davros alerts Takis that there are bodysnatchers at large.

GH: 'This was Bridget's first job on television, although she had done some theatre. I met her at an actors' workshop. I knew Stephen from a fringe theatre production that I had directed. I wanted to give him a break.'

The Doctor and Peri talk to the mutant. Before he dies, he tells them that he has been conditioned and is a product of the Great Healer's experimentation.

As Natasha and Grigory penetrate further into the complex, the DJ reads some dedications and Tasambeker orders Takis and Lilt to find the intruders. Davros orders Tasambeker brought to him.

The DJ, now dressed as a Fifties-style leather-clad rocker, is still reading dedications. He picks up on his screen the picture of the Doctor and Peri coming towards the complex.

Davros overhears Takis and Lilt discussing what might be in the catacombs. A Dalek then announces that Kara is ready to speak with him, and an image of the woman appears on his monitor.

Kara (Eleanor Bron) is an industrialist who is helping to finance Davros's operations on Necros. Davros pleads for more money, and Kara agrees to see what she can do. When the communications link is broken, she is obviously ill at ease. She asks her secretary Vogel (Hugh Walters) if Orcini has arrived, and is told that he has.

GH: 'Eleanor Bron was another immediate casting choice on reading the script. I phoned her up and she said yes. Eleanor had some very strong ideas as to how the part should be played, and she was brilliant.'

AS: 'It was quite deliberate that all the parts of the city that weren't to do with death were white, while the catacombs and corridors of Tranquil Repose were either black or had black elements in them.'

Natasha and Grigory have located the cryogenic storage unit for which they were searching. They open it to find it occupied by a mannequin. The body they sought – that of Natasha's father, Stengos – is missing.

AS: 'That unit opened up and was fully operational, but all the rest were just vacuum-formed repeats.'

The two 'grave robbers' are interrupted by guards, who fire on them as they flee.

JB: 'An armoury called Baptys provided all the working guns. The BBC often uses them.'

The Doctor and Peri arrive at a wall, which blocks their path. The Doctor points out to Peri that the occupants of Tranquil Repose are not dead – they are simply resting in suspended animation. He then helps her over the wall.

GH: 'This was filmed at the Goodwood horse racing ground. When they went over the wall, Nicola accidentally kicked Colin between the legs, so his expression of concern over his broken watch is genuine.'

Natasha and Grigory find themselves at a door leading down into the underground areas of the city. They head down into the tunnels to look for a service lift to take them back to the surface. Suddenly Natasha hears a Dalek approaching, and they press themselves into an alcove.

GH: 'I had made a decision that, although we didn't have loads of money, I really wanted to have great lighting effects, which I got from Don Babbage. The idea was to

6 SIXTH DOCTOR

655

light it from the floor and make it reminiscent of the style of *Alien*, with the interesting shadows and dark, dingy passageways.'

AS: 'The under-city corridors were based on Highgate cemetery. The idea was that this was an ancient cemetery that had been buried under the new city, but that elements of the new technology were still represented there. That corridor was so tight and cramped. It was actually a circular set so that we could go round and round and make it look as though there were many long corridors.'

The Dalek, leading some guards with a covered body on a trolley, passes by. Natasha and Grigory continue on and stumble into a red-lit room in which a heartbeat sound can be heard.

GH: 'That room was lit with red gels and also floor-lit, which is time consuming to do because of all the potential shadows.'

Davros is following the progress of Natasha and Grigory on his monitor.
    Natasha and Grigory discover a rack of human brains bubbling in liquid and, in the far corner of the room, a transparent Dalek containing the remains of a human head – it is that of Arthur Stengos (Alec Linstead), Natasha's father. Stengos pleads with Natasha to kill him, becoming more and more Dalek-like with every sentence. She finally raises her laser pistol and destroys her father and the Dalek. As Natasha and Grigory flee from the room, they find Takis, Lilt and some guards lying in wait for them, and are taken prisoner.

GH: 'The shot where Stengos opens his eye was meant to be much more frightening than that. I don't know what went wrong, but it was meant to be really frightening. I think he opens his eye a fraction too soon.'

JB: 'To do a glass/acrylic Dalek was going to be very expensive and time consuming, so I took it to a specialist firm, Denny's, down at Shepherd's Bush. They did a lot of the BBC's plastics work. The main reason I sent that outside was that we had so much other stuff to construct that there was just no time to fit it all in. They supplied us with the three sections – top, middle and bottom – all made out of clear acrylic plastic. Other considerations were that it had to be lit, an actor had to be in it, and we had to be able to see him. We raised it on a platform to get the lights under it.

'I was glad that it wasn't seen very often, because as well as being very fragile, it collected dust like a magnet. By the time we had finished recording, it looked very tacky and damaged. Dorka had a lot of trouble fitting in all the prosthetics and make-up, with the tubes and everything.

'We also had to consider that this Dalek was required to explode. Whatever else we did, we weren't going to be blowing up the perspex one, because the material splinters and is sharp and dangerous. We had to construct another Dalek out of lightweight, vacuum-formed plastic just for the shot where it blows up.'

Kara receives Orcini and Bostock into her office. Orcini (William Gaunt) is a Knight of the Grand Order of Oberon, a hired assassin, and Bostock (John Ogwen) is his squire. Kara is hiring them to kill Davros.

GH: 'I chose William Gaunt to play Orcini because I'd worked with him a couple of times and knew what he could do. I saw the character as a sort of Don Quixote figure, and I find Gaunt a very elegant and classical actor. I'd worked with John Ogwen on *District Nurse* in Wales, but he hadn't worked very much in England. I felt it was time we saw more of his talent.'

Pat Godfrey: 'I wanted to give Bostock and Orcini camouflage jackets, but it was decided that they should be more Che Guevara-type characters, so we hired their costumes from a costumier and just added some small details to them.'

[Dorka Nieradzik decided that, as Orcini was a mercenary who had found fame for his bravery and skill, she would make him up with some scars on his face, as the legacy of a former battle. She also gave him long hair tied back in a leather thong, the aim being to achieve a 'Buffalo Bill' look.]

The Doctor and Peri walk through the outer boundaries of Tranquil Repose. The Doctor explains that he was suspicious when he heard the reports of Stengos's death and of his internment in Tranquil Repose, and this is why he has come here.

JB: 'This was done at an enormous disused airport, which I had to relate to some model shots later. There were strange, monolithic lumps of concrete dotted around, and Alan put statues and painted scenery along one side of the runway. It all gave the impression of huge monuments dotted around the approaches to the mortuary pyramid.'

AS: 'Of the statuary and scenery that we brought with us, the BBC scenic artist handled the painted ones and a guy called Derek Howarth worked on the sculpted ones.'

Jobel gives his workers a pep-talk prior to the President's arrival.

Pat Godfrey: 'The mortuary workers' uniforms were all dentist's tunics, which were specified in the brief. We had to send them all out to be dyed professionally, to make sure that the colour was consistent. As these costumes would have been fairly boring on their own, I came up with the idea of a cap with coloured stripes on it, which would continue down on to the face. I had recently read an article about face painting in an issue of *Vogue*, so I worked with Dorka Nieradzik to produce the right effect.'

Kara gives Orcini a box-like electronic device, telling him that it is a transmitter that he should to use to send her a signal when he and his squire have reached the under-city. Unknown to Orcini, the device is in fact a bomb, with which Kara hopes to destroy Davros and his Daleks.
Tasambeker arrives to see the Great Healer. Davros tells her that he is pleased with her work and that he wants her transferred to his personal staff.
The Doctor and Peri finally arrive at the entrance to Tranquil Repose.

AS: 'The entrance to Tranquil Repose was filmed on location with a glass painting of pyramids over the top. There was a decorative pond outside the IBM building, and the statues were recycled from the ones we had used at the airfield.'

A Dalek passes by behind the two travellers as they enter the complex. Peri catches sight of it, but does not know what it is. She and the Doctor go to investigate, but it has vanished.

JB: 'There wasn't anyone actually inside that Dalek – we pulled it along on a wire.'

Takis and Lilt torture Natasha and Grigory to try to gain information about any co-conspirators. They force the alcoholic Grigory to drink from a flask that he has hanging on a strap around his neck.
In an area that he describes as the Garden of Fond Memories, the Doctor has found a giant gravestone carved with a huge image of his face. As he stands lost in thought, believing that he must be destined to die on Necros in his current incarnation, the gravestone topples forward and falls on top of him.

End of Part One

Part Two

JB: 'The gravestone was carved by Derek Howarth from our specifications. He's a clever sculptor who works with hot wires rather than knives. I would have liked the prop to have been very much thicker, but that would have doubled the price.

'When it finally fell, blood was supposed to come out of the statue's eye.'

GH: 'We did do that but it was cut, I think because it was too grim for the end of an episode. There is a continuity reference to it a little later.'

Peri rushes over to the fallen monument but is intercepted by Jobel, who smarmily tries to ingratiate himself with her. The Doctor is in fact unscathed and pushes his way out from under the lightweight imitation stones. His clothes are marked down one side with fake blood. He determines to find out who had the statue erected.
Grigory is now drunk and Lilt can get no sense out of him.
Inside Tranquil Repose, the Doctor and Peri are met by Tasambeker, who gives them a sales pitch about the facilities it has to offer.
Takis uses a communications screen to find out the ETA of President Vargos's ship. The computer voice (Penelope Lee) tells him that a second ship is also en-route for Necros.

AS: 'The screen was done using inlay rather than overlay, because it was not a blue screen. We just replaced a part of the picture with another image.'

Tasambeker shows the Doctor and Peri a promotional video of the DJ explaining the service he offers of relaying loved ones' messages to the Tranquil Repose residents.

GH: 'The DJ's video was a pre-recorded sequence played in through the small monitor screen on the desk there. It was actually the very first thing we did in studio.'

Bostock and Orcini are nearing Tranquil Repose when they see a white Dalek. Orcini lets rip with his machine gun and the Dalek is destroyed in a violent explosion. Orcini comments with pleasure that the bullets are fitted with bastic heads.

AS: 'This was when we choked everyone as a pall of black smoke from the Dalek blew over the camera crew.'

JB: 'The explosion was rigged up by Jim Francis. As there were other things going on that day, we created the Dalek shell in the workshop and brought it out with us so that we could achieve the effect as easily as possible. However, we had a problem with the wind changing direction all the time, and the smoke from the explosion blew straight at us afterwards. Ideally one would plan the shots so that it blew the other way.

'We had to pre-cut and break the shell of the Dalek. Jim manufactured a number of explosive charges to be set off in sequence: maybe one to lift the thing off the ground, one for light and one for smoke. Sometimes we needed a "pretty" explosion rather than a powerful one. Often, too, when the script said "and it blows up" we had to overstate it, because all you see of an explosion is a subliminal image. The actual effect is always better if it is bigger and more impressive than it would be in real life.'

Davros speaks to Kara via her communications screen and reports that a Dalek patrol has been attacked. He tells her that he is sending some Daleks to 'protect' her against insurrection. Kara thanks him through gritted teeth. Afterwards, Vogel tells Kara he suspects that Davros has realised what they are up to. Kara looks forward to Davros's death so that she will control the provision of food for the whole galaxy.

The Doctor decides to pay a visit on the Great Healer while Peri goes with Jobel to see the DJ. When his companion has gone, the Doctor is captured by two white Daleks and led off. Fighting off Jobel's amorous advances, Peri slips into the DJ's room.

AS: 'The DJ's studio and Kara's office were slightly expedient, and I wasn't too happy with them. They were actually the same set, just changed around a bit. There wasn't enough money to build another set, so we had to make do.'

The DJ is impressed that Peri is actually from America on Earth. He explains that he has based his style of presentation on some recordings brought back from Earth by his great-grandfather.

GH: 'Some of that music playing in the background is genuine. You can't get permission to use most American music as it would cost a fortune, but there are good cover versions and sound-a-likes that you can use.'

JB: 'The DJ's headphones were specially constructed by Andy Lazell.'

Davros congratulates Tasambeker on a job well done. He quizzes her about her feelings for Jobel, encouraging her to watch him on the security cameras and then see if she doesn't hate him enough to kill him.

The Doctor has been placed in a cell with Natasha and Grigory. As he tries to free himself from his manacles, they tell him what they have seen. He gets one foot free.

In Kara's office, a signal is received from Orcini – he has entered the catacombs under Tranquil Repose. Two Daleks enter the office, and, after exterminating Vogel, order Kara to accompany them back to Davros.

GH: 'That is a standard post-production extermination effect. When things have been established over a period of time, you don't just come along and change them for the sake of it.'

Takis and Lilt talk covertly to Jobel about moving against the Great Healer. Jobel is interested but wary.

GH: 'Although Jobel is a slightly camp character, he's real. All the characters are real to me. He's nicely underplayed and, although he's somewhat outrageous, he's real.'

Davros has been watching the discussion on his monitor and is infuriated by Jobel's duplicity. He offers Tasambeker the chance to become a Dalek, and says that to show her total obedience she must kill Jobel.

JB: 'For that shot of the Dalek eyestalk in the foreground, we couldn't get the Dalek close enough to the lens, because the camera was in the way. So we took an eyestalk off a Dalek and moved it in by hand.'

Orcini decides to release the prisoners and use them as scapegoats to divert attention from his own operations.

Tasambeker tries to warn Jobel that he will die unless he leaves. He will not listen, and cruelly snubs her again. In fury, she plunges a filled hypodermic into his chest and kills him.

GH: 'The hypodermic was filled with liquid, and we originally had a shot of it emptying once it had been stuck into Jobel. Again, that was cut as it was too horrific.'

JB: 'The needle was wired with a spring so that it collapsed into the syringe. Jobel was then fitted with a body plate with a needle already attached to it. With careful camera angles and editing, the whole thing came across as effective and real.'

Tasambeker is exterminated by two white Daleks.

Peri uses the DJ's viewing screen to find the Doctor. The DJ shows her how to speak to him. The Doctor responds by telling her that she is in danger. He instructs her to get back to the TARDIS and to warn the President's ship not to land.

Davros has heard this warning and sends his Daleks to bring Peri to him and to kill the DJ.

The DJ bars Peri's exit, saying that it is too dangerous for her to go. He suggests that she uses his own radio transmitter to warn the President's ship.

The Doctor leaves Natasha and Grigory to destroy the incubation room. When Natasha attempts to fire her gun, however, she discovers that its power pack is exhausted. Davros orders

that a specimen be activated, and another transparent Dalek materialises in the room. Grigory changes the controls on the incubator tanks in an attempt to stop the process.

Bostock and Orcini arrive at Davros's base and, killing the guard, burst in. Caught in the crossfire from their machine guns, Davros is killed. Orcini feels it was too easy, however, and he is right. The head in the life support unit was artificial; the real Davros suddenly appears on the steps behind them.

GH: 'The only reason I can think of for my use of close-ups when Davros appears on the stairs is that Terry Molloy might not have been in his base at the time. I suspect, because of time, we just had him standing there, and I took the shots accordingly.'

Bostock throws a knife at Davros, but it thuds into the back of his chair, just missing his neck.

JB: 'We didn't throw the knife, we just had it stuck in there. The cutting from the hand throwing the knife to the knife in the back of the chair gives the impression of it hitting its target.'

Davros's white Daleks enter the chamber and fire at Bostock and Orcini. Orcini's false leg is hit and blown away, and Bostock is winged by an exterminator blast. Davros, in his chair, hovers above Orcini, transfixing him with a bolt of blue lightning from his hand.

JB: 'Gaunt was standing there with one leg strapped up behind him, hopping about, and we rigged a little charge to disconnect his fake leg for the shot where it gets blown off.

'Davros's chair was difficult to recreate. The original didn't exist, so we had to re-build it all without much reference material. It was quite expensive.'

GH: 'The shot of Davros hovering above Orcini was a very complicated one to achieve. We had Davros set up on a block against a black background, and that image was then superimposed on the shot of the room with Orcini down on the floor. The crackling blue light came from a Van der Graff generator, which was also in the studio, and the spark of electricity was added to the main image in post-production, as were the red glow under Davros's chair and the blue glow over the lightning bolt.'

Pat Godfrey: 'Davros's costume was from stock, so we just patched it up and made it re-useable.'

The transparent shell has now converted into a fully formed white Dalek, and it rises up to hover menacingly over Natasha and Grigory. It exterminates them, but then explodes due to Grigory's tampering with the equipment.

JB: 'We got hold of a chap, Stuart Evans, who produced Dalek models commercially, and borrowed one of his kits, so that we could get it up high enough. The problem was that, with the limitations of studio space, we could never have got the depth of field to have had a full-sized Dalek floating up in the air. It wasn't physically possible, because the Dalek needed to be close to the camera. We initially thought that if we went for a model, and put that in front of the camera, it would look as though it was a giant Dalek.'

6 SIXTH DOCTOR

GH: 'We ended up doing the shots of the model Dalek in an effects studio and then adding it to the main picture in post production. It was simply the best and easiest way of getting the effect I wanted.'

JB: 'The model wasn't actually blown up. The explosion was achieved in post-production by using a video effect.'

The President's spaceship has apparently been turned away by Peri's transmitted warning. The DJ has now rigged up in his studio a large gun, which he describes to Peri as firing a highly directional ultrasonic beam of rock and roll. He hopes that this will repel the Daleks.
  Kara arrives in Davros's laboratory. Davros accuses her of trying to kill him, but Kara denies this. Davros gives back to Orcini the communicator device that he earlier confiscated, and instructs him to operate it. Before the Knight can complete the sequence, Kara admits that the device is in fact a bomb. Orcini knifes Kara in response to her treachery, and she falls dead on the floor.

JB: 'The knife worked in a similar way to the hypodermic in the earlier scene; the blade slipped back into the handle.'

The DJ manages to destroy two Daleks with his gun, but is exterminated by a third. The Doctor, listening over the speaker system in the caverns, hears what has happened. Turning a corner, he himself then runs into two Daleks, who escort him away.
  Takis and Lilt monitor the landing on Necros of the second spaceship that was earlier detected approaching.

JB: 'We had a special model filming day to do all these scenes. We built a platform and dressed it with bits and pieces to represent the landing pad, and then the spaceship was built. It descended on an air ram, which was hidden by the tower with the flashing lights.'

The Doctor is taken to Davros, who tells him that he survived their last encounter by using an escape pod. While Davros gloats over his achievements, Orcini and the Doctor have a furtive exchange of gestures, agreeing an unspoken plan. The Doctor then draws Davros's attention, allowing Orcini to retrieve Kara's bomb. When asked about the fate of the Tranquil Repose residents, Davros explains that those whom he considered worthy have been converted into Daleks, while the others have been sent to Kara's processing plant to be turned into a protein-rich foodstuff for sale to the starving masses of this part of the galaxy. When he has created sufficient new Daleks, he plans to invade the neighbouring planets to which the food has been supplied.

JB: 'When we came to get Davros's mask done, we found that the sculptor who had done it the previous time had left, so Dorka took on that responsibility and arranged for it to be re-made.'

Takis and Lilt meet the new arrivals – grey Daleks. Ignoring the two men's attempts to bargain, the Daleks demand to be taken to Davros.

JB: 'Two of these Daleks were originals and two we had built. We got the fibreglass workshop to make up some of the basic components, then the carpenters turned these into final structural pieces and added castors and seats and all that kind of thing. When a designer's got only two or three assistants and so much work to do, then it's useful to be able to get the carpenters to screw and bolt these things together.'

Peri arrives in Davros's laboratory, escorted by a white Dalek. Davros prepares to activate his new Dalek army, but Bostock has revived and manages to shoot his hand off before he can do so. Bostock is then exterminated by a Dalek.

JB: 'We went through a couple of exploding hands getting that shot. The hand was made from brown foam, and we gave him green blood.'

The grey Daleks battle with Davros's white Daleks, eventually defeating them. They sweep into the laboratory and order Davros to return with them to Skaro to stand trial for crimes against their race. The white Daleks will be reconditioned to obey the will of the Supreme Dalek. Davros draws their attention to the Doctor, but they retort that his appearance does not match their records. They intend to hold him until his identity can be verified.
    When Davros has been led away, the Doctor uses Orcini's gun to blind the grey Dalek left on guard. Peri then attaches to it a grenade taken from Bostock's pocket, blowing it up.

JB: 'We always had to be careful not to reveal too much of the insides of a Dalek! All the paper debris that flew into the air after the explosion was deliberate. This was an idea I got from Jim Francis. When you blow something up, it always seems to come down too soon, immediately after it's happened; explosions happen too quickly, and you just get balls of smoke. But if you add these bits of paper, they float down slightly later, and it looks a lot more effective.'

Orcini intends to use the bomb to destroy the complex before Davros and the Daleks can escape, and he tells the others to get out while they can.
    The Doctor tells Takis and Lilt that Davros has created a demand for synthetic protein and they must continue to supply it. They can use the protein-rich staff of life plant as a new raw material – there's certainly enough of it about.
    As everyone races for the exit, the Dalek ship takes off. Orcini detonates the bomb, just too late to stop the ship. Davros has escaped again.

JB: 'The model, constructed by Bill Pearson from my brief, reflected all the elements from the location and from the glass shots: the pyramids, the pool, the statues, the sky. Freon was used for the smoke coming out of the bottom of the ship as it lifts off. There's an awful lot of work goes into a model like this, and then we blow it up! Explosions are especially tricky to do on a small scale.'

As the base rocks with explosions, the workers mill about in the smoke and confusion.

GH: 'The picture shake was all done in post production. It was Quantel shaking the picture electronically rather than us shaking the cameras physically.'

When the excitement has died down, Takis and Lilt prepare themselves for the task ahead – rebuilding the processing plant.

The Doctor decides to take Peri for a holiday, but the picture freeze-frames just as he is about to state the intended destination.

GH: 'The very last word – Blackpool – was cut because the series had been just put on hold and a decision was taken not to trail the following season.'

Post-production

The early part of this chapter covered the pre-production work on *Revelation of the Daleks*. Now Graeme Harper describes the general post-production process: the work that takes place once all the filming and recording has been completed.

'I would sit down with all the recorded material copied on to VHS tapes encoded with a timestamp [a clock with which each frame can be uniquely identified]. From these, I would be able to work out all the "ins" and the "outs" – in other words, the exact frames on which I wanted to cut into and out of each scene – and the order in which I wanted all the shots to come. In the process, I also selected which of the different takes I wanted to use.

'I can't remember whether or not we did an "off-line" edit on *Revelation of the Daleks*. I seem to think that we didn't. An "off-line" edit is where the director supervises a rough cutting together of the show to see how it all fits. Gaps may be left for any post-production work that is still under way, and certain sequences may later be lengthened or shortened by any special video effects that are to be added.

'I think that in this case we went straight to an "on-line" edit – constructing the show from my notes, cutting it according to how I wanted it to be, and to what would hopefully be the correct length.

'It would generally take about two days of work to end up with a basic edit. That would then be shown to John Nathan-Turner, we would go through it with him in the edit suite, and he would suggest changes depending on how he had visualised the show as looking. Any necessary changes would take another day to make.

'We would have to lift off any shots that required electronic video effects and put them on a tape to go over to the Video Effects Workshop. There we would add in John Brace's model work, the Dalek exterminator effects and so on. These treated shots would then be put onto a tape and dropped back into the master tape containing the rest of the programme.

'In the week's gap that had occurred between the end of the location filming and the start of the studio rehearsals for *Revelation of the Daleks*, I had worked with the film editor (Ray Wingrove) to cut together all the film sequences: the fight with the mutant and so on. Once these sequences had been agreed with John, we did a basic film dub [i.e. added the sound] and transferred them all to video. These were also ready then to be dropped into the master tape as and where appropriate.

'Dick Mills at the Radiophonic Workshop would have got a copy of the original "on-line" edit – the one without all the effects added – together with notes showing where and what all the effects were going to be. This was so that he could start putting a basic track of special sounds together. I would go to the Workshop and sit down with him and the composer, Roger Limb, to go through where all the sounds were needed and what I was looking for in the way of music. Eventually Dick would get a copy of the master tape, and he would then be able to add more sounds to complement the effects sequences.

'Dick and Roger would go away and do all their work for two weeks, and when they had finished, I would go and listen to everything that they had done, before we got to the dubbing session. In that way, we could adjust anything that wasn't working. The next time I would hear their work would be at the dub, when we could again make minor changes if necessary.

'I tend not to give detailed instructions to a composer. I think my direction to Roger was simply to make the music big and orchestral. I know the music is electronic but I wanted something huge and orchestral. Roger Limb managed to give me that, and came up with a stunning, electronically produced, orchestral sound. Dick Mills also composed some "death music" for part two.'

Roger Limb, interviewed for *Doctor Who Magazine*, had the following recollections of working on *Revelation of the Daleks*:

'You sit down first with your director, and your relationship with him is crucial for the whole operation. You don't just decide where the music is going to be and what it is going to do in an emotional sense. You also consider the actual sounds themselves. Graeme Harper was very good like that; he really gave me a lot of help in that way. He bullied me a lot, but he knew what he wanted and made me go for it. He made me look for things that I might not have automatically thought of. He was a good director from my point of view. He didn't know anything about music, but he knew exactly what he wanted the music to do. When I played some music, he knew it was something he *didn't* want. The important thing is to find out what the director *does* want.'

Once all the music and special sounds have been dubbed onto the master tape at the sypher dub session, that is then the end of the director's job. All that remains is for the completed programme to be scheduled and transmitted.

Transmission

The two episodes of *Revelation of the Daleks* were eventually transmitted at 5.25 pm on Saturday 23 March 1985 and Saturday 30 March 1985 respectively, bringing to a close the twenty-second season of *Doctor Who*. The closing episode achieved a notable success in attracting 7.7 million viewers, the second highest rating of the season, bettered only by the first episode of the opening story, *Attack of the Cybermen*, which had attracted 8.9 million. The average viewing figure for the story was 7.55 million viewers per episode, slightly above the season average of 7.12 million. Although very respectable, this was still rather lower than the series had been achieving in the recent past. The season as a whole also fared rather less well than most previous ones in the weekly television chart – perhaps the best guide to a programme's success or failure – its average position being a disappointing 61st.

One reason for the lower-than-normal ratings was that HTV/Goldcrest's new film series *Robin of Sherwood* was transmitted by ITV in direct competition with most of the episodes. Word-of-mouth publicity for this new fantasy-orientated show was very good and, given the choice between this and the known quantity of *Doctor Who*, many casual viewers opted for the greenwood forests rather than the desolation of Necros.

Revelation of the Daleks was repeated in 1993 as the sixth Doctor's entry in a series of BBC2 repeats to celebrate *Doctor Who*'s thirtieth anniversary. The repeat was of the overseas four-part version, rather than of the original two-part transmission, and it ran on consecutive Friday evenings from 19 March to 9 April inclusive in a 7.15 pm slot following repeats of *Stingray* and *The Man From U.N.C.L.E.*

Credits

Producer	John Nathan-Turner
Writer/Script Editor	Eric Saward
Director	Graeme Harper
Production Associate	Angela Smith (replaced Sue Anstruther at late stage)
Production Manager	Michael Cameron
Production Assistant	Elizabeth Sherry
AFM	Jo O'Leary (replaced David Tilley at late stage)
Designer	Alan Spalding
Design Assistant	Adele Marolf
Costume Designer	Pat Godfrey
Make-Up Designer	Dorka Nieradzik (replaced Elizabeth Rowle at late stage)
Visual Effects Designer	John Brace
Video Effects	Dave Chapman
Prop Buyer	John Watts
Lighting Director	Don Babbage (replaced Henry Barber at late stage)
Technical Co-ordinator	Alan Arbuthnott
Sound Supervisor	Andy Stacy
Grams	Howard Jones
Camera Supervisor	Alec Wheal
Vision Mixer	Dinah Long
Videotape Editor	Steve Newnham
Floor Assistant	Anna Price
Crew	11
Title Music	Ron Grainer
Incidental Music	Roger Limb
Special Sound	Dick Mills
Film Cameraman	John Walker
Film Sound	Steve Gatland
Film Editor	Ray Wingrove

CANCELLATION CRISIS

Rumours that *Doctor Who*'s twenty-third season had been cancelled by the BBC first began to circulate amongst the series' fans over the weekend of 23 and 24 February 1985, but it was not until the following Tuesday, 26 February, that the first public confirmation came in the form of a report by journalist Patrick Hill in the London evening newspaper, the *Standard*:

> *Dr Who* is being dropped by the hard-up BBC for the first time in 22 years.
> It has decided that *Dr Who*'s adventures are too expensive to produce.

BBC1 Controller Michael Grade has ordered the series, which stars Colin Baker, to be suspended for at least 18 months.

Dr Who fans have launched a campaign to try to persuade Mr Grade to change his mind.

The series has been seen on TV at least every nine months over the past 22 years and regularly attracts nearly eight million viewers.

A BBC spokesman said: 'We intend to make a lot of new drama this year and cannot afford to do that and produce *Dr Who*.

'The Doctor is being rested, but will be back next year.'

The last episode will go out on March 30.

Within hours of Mr Grade's decision, some of the programme's 110 million fans worldwide in 54 countries where it is shown, had begun their campaign.

An army of fans began mustering letters of complaint about the series being rested.

One fan said: 'If public opinion can change the BBC's mind over *Dallas*, then we hope we can do the same.'

London record producer Mr Ian Levine, a lifetime fan and member of the British *Dr Who* fan club, said: '*Dr Who* is now more than just a TV programme. For 22 years it has been a way of life. We are calling on all fans to write to Michael Grade to urge him to change his mind.'

A spokesman for the British branch of the *Dr Who* Appreciation Society, which has over 3,500 members, said: 'This news has been a great shock to us. We will be meeting to discuss exactly what we can do to help save one of the country's favourite programmes.'

A spokesman for the *Dr Who* fan club added: 'We want all our members to write to Mr Grade.

'At present 30,000 letters have already been sent. We have got to save this programme and we are calling on members of the public to help us.'

This short article marked the start of an incredible whirlwind of press coverage and fan activity the like of which *Doctor Who* had never seen before. The first national report came just a few hours later, courtesy of the BBC itself, on the children's news magazine programme *Newsround*, and this was quickly followed by brief items on BBC1's main evening news bulletins at 6 pm and at 9 pm, both featuring a short clip from the most recently transmitted episode, part one of *The Two Doctors*. New developments then occurred daily.

On Wednesday 27 February, the rest of the media eagerly pounced on the story, seeing in it a chance to indulge in their perennial pursuit of knocking the BBC, which had been at the centre of another major furore less than a month earlier when Michael Grade had dropped the popular soap opera *Dallas* and then been forced to reinstate it due to public pressure. David Saunders, the Co-ordinator of the *Doctor Who* Appreciation Society (DWAS), was inundated by phone calls from newspaper journalists, from TV and radio stations – both national and local – and from fans in the UK and in the USA, all desperate for information. Society representatives were even booked to appear on the BBC's *Breakfast Time* programme and on ITV's rival *Good Morning*

Britain, although in the event both appearances fell through – the BBC's because Michael Grade, who was to have responded to the fans' criticisms, was on a skiing holiday in France and reportedly could not be contacted.

On Thursday 28 February, the fruits of all the journalists' endeavours became apparent as the story broke in the national press. Every daily newspaper – not only the tabloids but also the so-called quality broadsheets – devoted space to it, and some – the *Daily Telegraph*, the *Guardian*, the *Daily Express* and the *Sun* – judged it of sufficient interest to merit front page coverage.

The *Sun*'s report, under the banner headline *Dr Who is Axed in a BBC Plot*, was particularly memorable, and was the only one to take a slightly new angle on the story. Wrote reporter Charles Catchpole:

> *Doctor Who* was axed by the BBC last night, and furious fans claimed it was a plot to back up demands for a higher licence fee.
>
> TV bosses say they cannot afford to make any new shows about the famous time-traveller for 18 months.
>
> But even the BBC's own men see the axing of the show – a hit for 22 years – as a cynical bid to whip up support for an increase in the fee.
>
> One official said: 'This is absolute madness. *Doctor Who* is getting around nine million viewers.
>
> 'There's a strong feeling that the high-ups are using it as part of their propaganda campaign.'
>
> Actor Colin Baker, who plays the Doctor, said: 'I was staggered. We were all geared up to start work on the next series.'
>
> And sexy Nicola Bryant – his assistant Peri – was said to be 'very surprised and clearly upset.'
>
> Colin said: 'I am contracted to the series, but the decision will mean the BBC probably having to pay off a lot of other people. It doesn't seem good financial sense.'
>
> Patrick Troughton, 54, who was Dr Who in the Sixties, said: 'I think it is just power politics at work. I'm sure the viewers will make their feelings known.'
>
> BBC1 supremo Michael Grade claimed: 'We intend to make a lot of new drama, and we cannot afford to do that and *Doctor Who*.'
>
> But Beeb insiders say each episode of the sci-fi serial costs only £180,000 – against an average £220,000 for drama.
>
> They claim dumping the Doctor will *lose* the Corporation money from sales to 54 other countries. It has a world-wide audience of 110 million viewers.
>
> With just five new episodes left to be shown, fans were launching a massive campaign to save the Doctor last night.
>
> Jeremy Bentham, co-founder of the *Dr Who* Appreciation Society, said: 'The public won't let it die.'
>
> In America, the show's 40,000-strong fan club pledged themselves to raise one and a half million dollars to keep the programme on the air.

This leader article was followed up by a short editorial comment piece inside the paper which, although written in the *Sun*'s usual lurid style, must surely have struck a chord with many of the series' disappointed viewers. Headed *Who Dunnit?*, it read:

> There can rarely have been a more popular children's TV show than *Doctor Who*.
> Yet this programme is now selected by the BBC to be shelved for 18 months.
> The poor dears say that they cannot afford to make another series. *Dr Who* probably costs less than an average TV drama.
> So what cheap rubbish is going to be put on in its place?
> The life story of Director-General Alasdair Milne? Or just the station signal?
> We can tell the BBC how it can start saving real money.
> By sacking the over-paid fat heads who came up with this nasty little stunt!

It became apparent as the day wore on that the BBC was trying to play down the story. This was clearly a case of swimming against the tide, however, as interest from other sources continued largely unabated, one of the most notable cases being an interview with Ian Levine, one of the leading fan campaigners, on ITN's *News at One*.

Friday 1 March saw further items appearing in the national press, most of them concentrating on fans' reactions to the postponement and on the pledged financial support from those in the States. The *Sun* and the *Daily Star* both took the opportunity to launch 'Save *Doctor Who*' campaigns, the latter giving over no fewer than five pages to its coverage of the series. Reports also started to appear about the possibility of a record being produced, along the lines of the Band Aid famine relief single, to publicise the series' predicament.

The BBC had by this time had an opportunity to formulate a considered response to the situation, having been caught completely off guard by the initial outcry. This belated damage-limitation exercise began on the afternoon of 1 March when Bill Cotton, Managing Director of BBC Television, took the highly unusual step of telephoning DWAS Co-ordinator David Saunders to inform him that the BBC was issuing a press statement to clarify its position over *Doctor Who*'s future, confirming that the series would be returning in 1986 and in its original format of one 25-minute episode per week. Further evidence that the BBC was finally getting its act together came when a planned appearance by Ian Levine on BBC1's early evening chat show *Wogan* was called off at the last minute, denying the fan campaign a valuable publicity opportunity.

The press release that the BBC issued that day was a cleverly worded piece of media manipulation that made it appear that the Corporation had in some way capitulated to public pressure when in actual fact its position remained completely unchanged. Headed 'More *Doctor Who* in 1986 – Another Miraculous Escape for Fiction Favourite', the release read as follows:

> As every follower of *Doctor Who* knows … You can't kill a Time Lord.
> Today Bill Cotton Managing Director of BBC Television phoned David Saunders, Co-ordinator of the *Doctor Who* Appreciation Society, to explain the BBC plans.

He said: 'Doctor Who will be on the air in 1986, as it is in 1985, and as it has been for each of the past 22 years.

'Instead of running in January 1986 we shall wait until the start of the autumn schedule, and then Doctor Who will be a strong item in the mix.

'We are also going to go back to the old tradition and have 25-minute programmes rather than the 45-minute version running at the moment. We think that is what the public wants. So does the producer, and his team.

'The 45-minute series has been a good experiment, but we need to get back to basics, and to established ways. It also means that with a 25-minute length we can run the series for a greater number of weeks.'

Mr Cotton added: 'We appreciate the passionate support of the fan club in this country, and of fans around the world. We ask them to be a little patient while we get the Doctor back onto familiar rails. I am confident that Doctor Who has a great future on BBC1'

The tabloids, perhaps sensing that they had got as much mileage out of the story as they usefully could, seized on this as a chance to claim that their 'Save Doctor Who' campaigns had been a success. The Daily Star of Saturday 2 March repeated sections of the press release verbatim, and went on to add:

A Band Aid style record has been planned to raise cash for the Save Dr Who cause. Fans hope Elton John and Holly Johnson – both Who fans – will take part along with the Village People.

It is the second time in 10 days that Mr Cotton has had to calm angry viewers.

He earlier admitted that the BBC had boobed dropping Dallas in mid-series and announced that it would be back next month.

The Doctor Who news came on the same day it was revealed that the BBC had paid £500,000 – for an American series it hadn't even seen.

Kane and Abel, based on Jeffrey Archer's best-seller, is being made by Embassy Films, which was headed by Mr Grade until 1983.

Mr Grade has a credit on the series as executive producer – but he has no financial involvement in it.

The elusive Mr Grade also entered the fray on 2 March, the Daily Mail's Corinna Honan having actually flown out to the French Alps in order to track him down. His rather brusque comments betrayed a sense of irritation at the sensational coverage given to what he appeared to consider a rather trivial matter:

Of course I care about the Dr Who fans, but I'm only thinking about British viewers. Do you know how many watched Dr Who last week? Six million. Very low indeed. Two or three years ago it was getting 10 to 11 million viewers.

But there's no reason for anyone to make waves. It's not as if I'm cancelling the series. We've got a lot of work to do on it but the show will be back. That's a promise. And it will be better than ever.

The BBC is *not* broke. It's just a question of priorities. A lot of drama shows are reaching their natural end. The writers don't want to write. The actors don't want to act. We need new material.

The policy has been for short-run series in the last couple of years. We hope these new ones will run for more than a year or two.

When challenged to respond to the enormous public outcry that the postponement had generated, Grade dismissed the series' fans as a special interest group and asserted that the rest of the world would barely notice its absence. 'Taking *Doctor Who* off the air is a piece of professional judgment. It is nothing to do with the licence fee coming up. We take a million of these decisions every day of the week. It's just an extraordinary storm in a teacup. Anyway, we've just had our best week in a long time on BBC1 and 2 – over 51 per cent of the total TV audience from 6 pm to closedown every day.'

Sunday 3 March saw the DWAS's executive committee holding a meeting with other prominent fans to discuss their next steps. They decided on two courses of action: first, to send all Society members a photocopied letter explaining the current situation and, secondly, to write to Bill Cotton in response to his phone call to David Saunders, requesting some more meaningful assurances on *Doctor Who*'s future.

Saunders began the following day, Monday 4 March, by taking part in BBC Radio 4's topical *Start the Week* programme, answering presenter Richard Baker's questions about the fan campaign. Then, in the afternoon, he travelled from Broadcasting House to Television Centre to deliver the DWAS's letter personally to Bill Cotton's secretary.

Cotton's reply, sent the very next day, had little to offer in the way of further reassurance, but was interesting in that it marked the first real attempt by the BBC to suggest that the postponement decision had been taken for reasons other than purely financial. Received by Saunders on Wednesday 6 March, it read in part:

> Our intentions are clear. We intend to continue to produce *Dr Who* for as long as we believe the British public enjoy it. There is no decision to drop it after the next series.
>
> As far as money from America is concerned, I regard that with a degree of scepticism, but I will certainly look into it. However the problem is not just financial, it is also about scripts and resources.
>
> The day of the week, the time it is transmitted and the exact number will be decided over the next few months. What is important is that it will be a major offering on BBC1.

On Thursday 7 March and Friday 8 March, recording sessions took place for the much-vaunted record release to draw attention to *Doctor Who*'s plight. Entitled 'Doctor in Distress', it was written and produced by Ian Levine and his songwriting partner Fiachra Trench, who together had previously supplied the theme music for the *Doctor Who* spin-off *K-9 and Company*. The reported original intention of using the proceeds to further the campaign for the series' return had been dropped once it was realised that this might command insufficient support. It had since been decided that any money raised should go instead to a charitable cause, the National Society for Cancer Relief. Although the hoped-for participation by major-league pop stars still failed to materialise, a number of

6 SIXTH DOCTOR

artistes were then assembled by organisers Paul Mark Tams, a long-time *Doctor Who* fan, and Jeff Weston, the Managing Director of Record Shack, the label on which the record would be released, and for whom some of the artistes recorded.

Under the group name Who Cares?, four *Doctor Who* regulars – Colin Baker, Nicola Bryant, Anthony Ainley and Nicholas Courtney – performed the song alongside a whole host of other celebrities and entertainers. The full list ran to some 25 names: Earlene Bentley, comedienne Faith Brown, Miquel Brown, Warren Cann of Ultravox, Hazell Dean, Floid of the Hot Gossip dance troupe, Bobby G of Bucks Fizz, Steve Grant, Julie Harris, Justin Hayward and John Lodge of the Moody Blues, Jona Lewie, Phyllis Nelson, Richie Pitts from the cast of the musical *Starlight Express*, John Rocca of Freeez, actress Sally Thomsett, Basia Trzetrzelewska and Danny White of Matt Bianco, David Van Day of Dollar and Music Academy, and the group Time UK, consisting of the Jam's former drummer Rick Buckler with Ronnie Ball, Fletcher Christian, Jimmy Edwards, Ray Simone and Nick Smith.

The record was pressed and distributed as quickly as possible and released a week later, on Friday 15 March, accompanied by a video directed by Reeltime Pictures' Keith Barnfather after pop impresario Mike Mansfield reportedly pulled out at a late stage. ITV's *The Six O'Clock Show* marked the occasion with a short, very lighthearted item featuring clips from the Aaru cinema film *Dr Who and the Daleks* and interviews with fans and members of the general public. The press, however, showed only limited interest in the record's release, and it received scathing reports and reviews in some of the weekly music papers. BBC radio stations refused to play it, claiming that it was too poor artistically, although it did receive quite good air-play on some of the independent stations.

The next development in the saga came when a fan's letter of complaint about the postponement met with the following reply from Michael Grade in the 23-29 March edition of *Radio Times*:

> The response of *Doctor Who* enthusiasts is bordering on the hysterical given the exact nature of the BBC's decision. *Doctor Who* has not been cancelled, just delayed for a year. The ratings for the current season have been disappointing and we need time to consider the reasons for this. The current series is an experimental 45-minute length and this has not proved as popular as we had hoped. We were looking to make some financial savings in the coming year and it seems that after 21 years a short rest would do the Doctor no harm at all.
>
> Long-running television series do get tired and it is because we want another 21 years of *Doctor Who* that we have prescribed a good rest.

This pronouncement, which again sought to shift the emphasis away from the financial reasons underlying the postponement and towards supposed deficiencies in the series itself, triggered a slight resurgence of press activity. Reports of Grade's comments appeared in several newspapers, most notably in the *Daily Express* of Thursday 21 March 1985, but to the fans' disappointment, these merely followed the BBC line, again asserting that the series' future was safe.

At the beginning of April, further rumours began to circulate within fandom, this time to the effect that Season 23, when it did eventually appear, might be reduced from the then standard length of 26 episodes to only 20 episodes. Ian Levine made an announcement about this at a DWAS convention, DWASocial 5, on Saturday 6 April, but John Nathan-Turner, who was next up on stage, angrily denied that any such decision had been taken.

Throughout the period since the news of the postponement first became public, many thousands of *Doctor Who* fans had written individually to the BBC to make their displeasure felt. Most had received just a standard photocopied letter in response, but DWAS member Gavin French managed to extract a personal reply, dated 17 April 1985, from Head of Series and Serials Jonathan Powell. This offered another slightly different slant on the reasons for the BBC's actions:

> We decided to postpone *Doctor Who* for two reasons. Firstly, we have a financial problem on BBC1 and looking at the programmes we decided that *Doctor Who* would benefit from some breathing space. It seems to me that the show does not work in its new three quarter hour episodes, and would be much better returned to its traditional 25-minute format. To change the format requires time and I believe it to be entirely advantageous that the producer of the programme has some time to consider it in depth.
>
> As yet we have not decided how many episodes we shall make when the show returns. We plan to have it on the screen by Autumn 1986 and the number of episodes will be decided according to our editorial wishes balanced against the financial means.

To add to the fans' bewilderment, Saturday 20 April saw Michael Grade giving yet another explanation, when questioned on the subject during an interview for the Channel 4 chat show *The Late Clive James*. This time, no mention at all was made of any financial problems: 'The truth about *Doctor Who* is that it was a target for a cut, because the show's not doing very well. It's overly violent. It's losing audiences. Its appeal is not what it was. It's not getting new generations of children. We needed time to take it off the air and get it right.'

It was perhaps fortunate for Grade that these statements went unchallenged, Clive James no doubt being unaware that Season 22 had actually achieved quite respectable average ratings of 7.12 million viewers per episode and correspondingly high audience appreciation figures. Nor would anyone with any knowledge of *Doctor Who* have had much difficulty in rubbishing his claim that time was required in order to revamp the series, some quite radical changes having been made in previous seasons without the need for any such delay.

Wednesday 8 June brought further news in the form of a report in the *Sun* stating that Grade, along with Jonathan Powell and BBC Director of Programmes Brian Wenham, had decided to reduce Season 23 to fourteen episodes and subsequently to cancel the series altogether if its ratings failed to improve. The BBC Press Office denied that any such steps were being contemplated, but the fans remained understandably sceptical.

One of the few highlights of this period came with the commissioning of an original *Doctor Who* radio serial, *Slipback*, to go out on BBC Radio 4, in stereo, as part of a new children's magazine programme, *Pirate Radio 4*. Welcome though it was, this was nevertheless regarded by most commentators as being scant compensation for the lack of any new TV stories.

On Saturday 3 August, the *Sun* returned to the subject of the proposed episode count for Season 23, reporting an extraordinary error made by the staff of BBC Enterprises' Sales Director John Harrison:

> A BBC TV boss's blunder has confirmed *Sun* forecasts of *Dr Who* cutbacks.
>
> Beeb chief John Harrison wrote a secret telex message to US distributors, saying next year's series will be trimmed from 26 shows to 14 25-minute episodes.
>
> But someone mixed up the telex numbers – and the message went to the American *Doctor Who* Appreciation Society!

This report was again flatly denied by the BBC Press Office, even though photocopies of the offending telex reportedly began to spread amongst fans both in the US and in the UK.

Having been out of the *Doctor Who* news for a while, Michael Grade returned to controversy in September, using the opportunity of an interview on BBC Radio 2's popular *Jimmy Young Show* to launch another public attack on the series, this time explicitly criticising its production team: 'The people who make it have got rather complacent. The show got rather violent and lost a lot of its imagination, a lot of its wit, and was relying far too much on straightforward on-the-nose violence, and had failed really to capture a new audience. There's no question of it being killed off. There is going to be another series next year. The problem with the programme was that it had been losing its appeal. I decided that it was time to take stock, to look at the show, to rethink the scripts, to rethink the shape of the programme, to think how we might revitalise *Doctor Who* so that it's going to last another 20 years.'

On Wednesday 18 December, the BBC made an announcement finally admitting that Season 23 would indeed be only fourteen episodes long. This time, the disclosure failed to generate any press coverage at all, not even the *Sun* bothering to report the official confirmation of its earlier scoop. It seemed that the phase of media concern over the postponement had finally run its course.

As the glare of public attention moved away from *Doctor Who*, it was left to the series' fans to take a more considered look at the hectic events of this extraordinary ten month period, and to try to assess their long-term implications.

It would later be reported that the original news of the postponement had been leaked to the press by John Nathan-Turner, via Ian Levine.

'The day it was cancelled,' recalled Levine in a 1992 interview for *DWB*, 'John and Gary [Downie, his partner and a *Doctor Who* production assistant] came round to my house and spent the whole evening plotting what to do and how to get the press involved. John got me to phone Charles Catchpole of the *Sun*. He'd told me that there were codenames within the BBC that Catchpole would know, so I phoned him and said that I worked on the sixth floor [of Television Centre] under Michael Grade and that my name was Snowball. I said that there was a plot to get rid of *Doctor Who*. While I was talking, John and Gary were busy scribbling away telling me what to say. I told Charles Catchpole how the show made profits for the BBC, how the series was being used in a plot to defend the licence fee increase – John was even reeling off figures off the top of his head for the number of countries that *Doctor Who* was sold to, and for the millions of pounds [it made], for me to quote at him! John was pulling the strings and using me, because he couldn't risk being identified as being involved. He knew this whole code thing and exactly what to say. Then we did the same thing with Geoff Baker of the *Daily Star*.'

Had Nathan-Turner and Levine not taken this step, the chances are that the phenomenal media outcry would never have occurred, and that the series could indeed have been cancelled altogether. Nathan-Turner himself has since denied that cancellation was ever a real possibility, but Colin Baker, in a 1989 interview for the fanzine *Kroton*, said: 'Originally it was the axe; it was coming off! Grade back-tracked very swiftly when he found out the reaction was as strong as it was, and it turned into a suspension, which was the only way he could get it back without losing too much face, I suppose.'

One thing on which all parties are in complete agreement is that the postponement decision, apparently conveyed to John Nathan-Turner by Jonathan Powell at a meeting on Monday 25 February 1985, came as a severe blow to the morale of the series' production team and cast. Speaking at a convention in Manchester on 16 November 1985, Nathan-Turner described their reaction to the news: 'It's a horrid thing to happen, to be told that the season you've prepared is kind of pulled from under your feet. I think my feeling was that of the rest of my team and of all the actors concerned, and indeed of all the directors who had been engaged. It's all very well to get your money at the end of the week, but it's far, far better actually to earn it. So I think we all felt fairly devastated.'

Eric Saward recalls that Nathan-Turner was in fact particularly demoralised by the decision. Saward himself remains uncertain as to the reasons for the postponement. 'I really don't know what the thinking was,' he says. 'I'm sure that Jonathan Powell hated the show. He was always very hostile to us at playbacks. Very indifferent, whether the show was good or bad. It seemed he'd really decided that he didn't like us. I think it was entirely his decision. I don't think Michael Grade cared one way or the other.'

Fans have often sought to suggest that the postponement was an act of pure vindictiveness on the part of either Grade or Powell, inspired by their apparent dislike of *Doctor Who*. This analysis overlooks the fact that the series had been unpopular with BBC executives throughout much of its history, without ever before having been dropped from the schedules. Programme planners tend to act not on the basis of their own personal preferences but on that of their professional judgment and expertise, weighing up a whole range of different factors before reaching a conclusion. The weight of evidence now suggests that the postponement came about largely as a consequence of the financial problems to which some of the earlier press coverage alluded – and this is a view to which John Nathan-Turner lent support. Two developments were particularly significant in this regard.

First, there was an enormous outlay involved in producing 104 episodes per year of the new soap opera *EastEnders*, which made its on-air debut in the week beginning 18 February 1985 – the very same week that the postponement decision was taken. The need to finance and support this show, which would soon become the BBC's most successful in the ratings, placed a very considerable strain on the budget and resources of the Series and Serials Department and resulted in a permanent reduction in the number of other programmes that it was able to make.

Secondly, and even more importantly, there was a substantial financial shortfall in the 1985/86 accounting year due to a decision taken by top-level management to bring forward by several months the launch of the BBC's daytime TV service, so as to get it up and running in advance of ITV's rival effort. This rescheduling meant that several million pounds had suddenly• to be clawed back from the previously allocated departmental budgets, with cuts being made right across the board. *Doctor Who* was just one of the programmes to suffer, along with others such as *Mike Read's Pop Quiz*, *Come Dancing*, *The Hot Shoe Show* and *Crackerjack*.

It can indeed be considered an astute move on John Nathan-Turner's part to have placed in journalists' minds the idea that there might be a link between Season 23's postponement and the BBC's difficult financial position, as Ian Levine told *DWB*:

'John knew that the story of *Doctor Who* being cancelled alone would not have made the front page, but using the angle that the BBC was axing something popular to draw attention to their efforts to get the licence fee raised was extremely cunning, and it worked!'

A skilled publicist, the producer no doubt reasoned that a fierce public backlash was the one thing that could save the series if Grade and Powell were truly intent on killing it off.

The resulting furore is certainly reported to have caused considerable consternation amongst the BBC's Board of Governors, who saw themselves being drawn into an unexpected and embarrassing controversy. They regarded the postponement as just the latest in a succession of poor management decisions, and apparently took the matter up in forceful terms with Director-General Alasdair Milne. Milne's own view was that Grade, in underestimating the strength of the public's affection for *Doctor Who*, had made a serious error of judgment. On the other hand, however, he admired the way in which his subordinate had coped with the ensuing media circus.

There seemed to be no question of the cancelled season being reinstated, so the production team were left with the difficult task of deciding how to proceed.

The season had been at an advanced stage of preparation when the postponement decision was taken. The scripts for the first story, *The Nightmare Fair* by Graham Williams, had already been distributed to the regular cast and to key members of the production crew, including director Matthew Robinson. This serial, in two 45-minute episodes, would have seen the Doctor and Peri arriving on Blackpool's famous Pleasure Beach (a setting decided upon by John Nathan-Turner after he and Colin Baker made a promotional visit there in 1984 to open a new ride). There they would have discovered that one of the amusement arcades was in fact a deadly trap set by the sinister Celestial Toymaker, a character who had first appeared in an eponymous story in *Doctor Who*'s third season of adventures, way back in 1966.

The second two-parter was to have been *The Ultimate Evil*, written by Wally K Daly and directed by Fiona Cumming. This would have involved the Doctor and Peri arriving in the peace-loving domain of Tranquela with the intention of taking a holiday, only to get caught up in the devious schemes of an unscrupulous arms dealer, the evil Dwarf Mordant, who hopes to provoke a war between the Tranquelans and their neighbouring race, the Amelierons, by causing them to suffer sporadic fits of extreme violence.

Another two-parter for which draft scripts had already been prepared was Philip Martin's *Mission to Magnus* – previously titled *Planet of Storms*. As Martin later recalled in an interview for *Doctor Who Magazine*, this story, set on the female-dominated planet

Magnus, would have featured the return not only of a popular character from Colin Baker's first full season as the Doctor but also of a much more well-established foe:

'I was asked to do a script, again with Sil and maybe involving the Ice Warriors. I'd written a first draft, in which I had the Ice Warriors inside a polar ice-cap, because it suited them being so cold. They were burrowing workshops in the ice-cap, which was beginning to flood the planet, and the people couldn't understand why. This ice environment allowed the Ice Warriors to move freely, because I was always worried about how slow they had been in previous stories.'

The season's longest story, a three-parter, had the working title *Yellow Fever and How to Cure It* (shortened in some later documentation to *Yellow Fever*). Written by Robert Holmes, it was to have been set, and filmed, in Singapore and included return appearances by the Autons, the Rani and possibly also the Master. In the event, Holmes had completed only a brief outline of the adventure before the season was postponed.

One of the two remaining two-part slots would probably have been filled by a Christopher H Bidmead story entitled *In the Hollows of Time*. The other would probably have gone either to a story, title unknown, by Bill Pritchard or to one called *The Children of January* by Michael Feeney Callan.

Following the postponement decision, Robert Holmes, Christopher H Bidmead and Michael Feeney Callan were all asked to continue working on their stories, but in the new 25-minute episode format rather than the old 45-minute one – a request to which all three writers immediately acceded. BBC documentation also indicates that Pip and Jane Baker were commissioned as early as 11 March 1985 – less than three weeks after the postponement decision was taken – to write a story, in four 25-minute episodes, with the working title *Gallifrey*. This is believed to have involved the destruction of the Doctor's home planet. In the end, however, these stories were all abandoned, as were those by Graham Williams, Philip Martin, Wally K Daly and Bill Pritchard, the cancellation ultimately being seen by the production team to imply that they had to start afresh with some new writers and some new ideas.

In any event, the production team decided that a completely different approach was called for, after they learned, in early June 1985, that the postponed season was to be only 14 episodes long. Eric Saward suggested having a season-spanning story in which the Doctor would be seen to be on trial, reflecting the fact that the series itself was still in this situation. This suggestion was readily agreed by John Nathan-Turner, and the two men then set about developing a workable format for what ultimately became *The Trial of a Time Lord*.

The basic premise of the story was that the Doctor would be brought back to Gallifrey by the Time Lords to stand trial for his repeated interference in the affairs of other planets. In a conscious allusion to the structure of Charles Dickens' *A Christmas Carol*, the evidence would be presented in three segments – the first concerning an incident in the Doctor's recent past, the second an incident in his present and the third an incident in his future – before the story was eventually concluded in a fourth and final segment. Two pivotal figures in the proceedings of the court would be the prosecuting counsel, known as the Valeyard, and the judge, known as the Inquisitor, for whom John Nathan-Turner and Eric Saward developed the following character outlines dated 5 July 1985:

THE VALEYARD AND THE INQUISITOR
The Doctor is not very popular on his home planet of Gallifrey. Over the

years, his independence of mind has made him many enemies who would like to see him dead.

So when the Doctor is summoned home to stand trial for crimes that could cost him his life, it is decided, by the High Council, that a judge and a prosecuting counsel must be found who are seen to be both above suspicion and free of prejudice concerning the Doctor.

After close consultation with the KEEPER OF THE MATRIX, the High Council decide to find suitable candidates from their own future.

To avoid any form of prejudicial selection, the Matrix itself is ordered to draw up a list of qualified candidates. To make the selection even more random, the Matrix gives each candidate a code number, and it is from this list that the High Council choose their INQUISITOR (Judge) and VALEYARD (Prosecuting Counsel). This way only the Matrix knows the identity of the candidates concerned.

THE INQUISITOR is female, middle fifties and very learned. She is also a friendly, agreeable soul with a strong sense of humour. (Although it is tempting to parody contemporary judges, I think it would be more interesting and more fun to play against the accepted stereotype.)

THE VALEYARD, on the other hand, is far less agreeable. He is tall and lean with strong angular features, giving him the manner and appearance of a powerful, predatory bird, whose talons are a sharpness of mind and a verbal dexterity capable of dismembering the strongest and most considered of arguments.

As the trial continues, evidence comes to light suggesting that the Matrix has been tampered with and that the list of jurists it produced was far from unprejudiced.

But who has manipulated the Matrix? And who of the two jurists is involved in the deception?

The Doctor has to find out, while at the same time fighting for his own existence.

The intention was that, somewhere around part twelve of the story, the Valeyard would be revealed to be a corrupt future incarnation of the Doctor who had manipulated the whole Trial simply in order to destroy his own former persona. Peri was to be killed off at the end of part eight, becoming trapped in a situation from which the Time Lords were unable to extricate her, and a new companion, Mel, would be introduced in part nine. It was also decided at the outset that the Master should put in an appearance as one of the witnesses in the later stages of the proceedings.

The original writers chosen to provide the scripts for the season were Robert Holmes, Philip Martin, award winning playwright David Halliwell and the late novelist Jack Trevor Story. The idea was that Holmes and Martin would contribute the first two segments of evidence, each in four episodes; that Halliwell and Story would then write two episodes apiece of the third four-part segment, liaising closely to ensure that their ideas dovetailed and could be realised using the same sets; and that Holmes would then provide the final two episodes to form the concluding segment.

On Tuesday 9 July 1985, all four writers travelled to the BBC's Threshold House offices for an initial discussion with John Nathan-Turner and Eric Saward, who explained the format to them and briefed them on their respective contributions.

Despite having made great play in the press of the need for *Doctor Who* to be revamped, Michael Grade had apparently taken no active interest in the formulation of the Trial idea. The only advice he had given John Nathan-Turner, in a meeting reportedly lasting somewhat short of ten minutes, was that the new season should contain less violence and more humour than the previous one. The production team therefore instructed the four writers along these lines, stressing the need to avoid any graphic violence and to make the stories fun and entertaining, albeit with humour arising organically out of the drama rather then grafted on artificially.

While work proceeded relatively smoothly on the segments commissioned from Robert Holmes and Philip Martin, which were given the final working titles *The Mysterious Planet* and *Mindwarp* respectively, the same could not be said of the two-part contributions by Jack Trevor Story and David Halliwell.

Little headway was made on Jack Trevor Story's segment. 'He came up with an idea for his section of the trial,' recalls Eric Saward. 'He said, "I've got an idea of a man sitting in an empty gasometer playing a saxophone." I told him, "That sounds wonderful, but I don't think we can use it in *Doctor Who!*"'

David Halliwell's script – working title *Attack from the Mind* – progressed a little further. Halliwell later recalled the plot when interviewed in 1992 by the New Zealand *Doctor Who* Fan Club fanzine *TSV*: 'It was set on a planet called Penelope, which was inhabited by two rival races; the Penelopeans who were extremely beautiful and poetic, and the Freds who were extremely ugly and plodding. At first it seemed as though the Freds were the aggressors, but later it appeared that this was not the case.'

Attack from the Mind went through a number of drafts before it was eventually dropped, Eric Saward informing Halliwell in a letter dated 18 October 1985 that it lacked the sort of energy and humour that he and John Nathan-Turner were seeking.

Following this, the production team decided that the four-part gap in the season should now be filled by just a single writer. A submission was commissioned from Christopher H Bidmead on 29 October 1985 under the working title *The Last Adventure*, although this would later be changed to *Pinacotheca*. In view of the urgency, Bidmead completed his scripts at a rapid pace, sending in first drafts of episodes one, two and three in mid-November, early December and late December respectively, and personally delivering to Eric Saward a second draft of all four episodes on 9 January 1986. On 7 February, however, Saward wrote to Bidmead to tell him that his story segment was being dropped, as he appeared to have misunderstood the brief he had been given. The script editor later amplified this by explaining that he had found the scripts dull and lacking in substance from the outset, but that he had been reluctant to pass comment until he had seen the complete story.

With the situation becoming ever more urgent, another writer was then approached to provide the missing four-part segment. This was *Sapphire and Steel* creator P J Hammond, whose attempt, commissioned on 10 February 1986, had the working titles *End of Term* and, later, *Paradise Five*.

A fantasy-orientated piece, *Paradise Five* would have seen the Doctor masquerading as a businessman and Mel as a hostess in order to discover the sinister secrets of a planet supposedly designated as a holiday haven for overworked executives, both human and alien. At first sight, the Paradise would have seemed idyllic, being run by two seemingly friendly characters called Michael and Gabriel with the assistance of a host of beautiful girls with names such as Stella and Bella and, to perform the menial tasks, a race of creatures known as Cherubs. However, it would ultimately have been exposed as a brash, artificial front for murderous money-making schemes. The Doctor's task would have been further complicated throughout the plot by the fact that the planet was plagued by a race of evil, ghost-like entities called Angels.

According to Hammond, Eric Saward liked this idea but John Nathan-Turner did not, and it was consequently rejected after he had completed just the first episode in draft.

On 6 March 1986, yet another four-parter was commissioned to fill the gap, and this one – working title *The Ultimate Foe* by Pip and Jane Baker – would finally be accepted. In view of the shortage of time, the writers were asked to have the first episode ready in draft form by 17 March, less than a fortnight later, and the other three by 7 April. In discussion with John Nathan-Turner and Eric Saward, they decided to make their plot a 'whodunit in space', paying homage to Agatha Christie.

In the meantime, on 4 February 1986, Robert Holmes had been commissioned as planned to write the final two episodes of the trial, under the working title *Time Inc..* (It is thought that he was also at this point offered the chance to write the missing episodes nine to twelve, but quickly declined.) The intention was that *Time Inc.* would tie up all the outstanding plot threads from the fourteen-part story and provide a dramatic climax to the season. As things transpired, however, Holmes became seriously ill, and subsequently died on 24 May 1986, having completed only a rough draft of part thirteen. Eric Saward himself then took over the task of writing part fourteen, and in order to facilitate this, he also rewrote completely the latter scenes of Holmes's script, introducing a new character named Mr Popplewick.

This was by no means the end of the season's problems as Saward, who had resigned from the BBC after overseeing the first two segments of the Trial, subsequently had a major disagreement with John Nathan-Turner over the way in which the story was to end. Saward decided to withhold permission for his script for part fourteen to be used, and Nathan-Turner therefore brought in Pip and Jane Baker to write a completely new final episode for the story.

With the eventual transmission of Season 23, it seemed that, at least for the moment, *Doctor Who* had been reprieved.

BEING THE COMPANION

Doctor Who has always placed a great deal of emphasis not only on the enigmatic Doctor himself but also on those with whom he travels. The companion figures have invariably fulfilled the important dramatic functions of facilitating plot exposition and of providing a point of audience identification, but within these basic parameters have ranged from being well-written and interesting characters in their own right to being little more than pretty girls to keep the dads interested.

As one might expect, the attitude of the Doctor (and, more importantly, of the script writers) to the companion has changed over the years. With the changes that occurred during the Seventies and Eighties in social attitudes towards sex stereotyping, the role of the companion in *Doctor Who* was under pressure to develop beyond that of the helpless screamer.

When the *Doctor Who* production team were planning the series' twenty-first season, they were aware that a number of significant changes would have to take place. They knew that Janet Fielding (Tegan) had expressed a desire to bow out along the way, as had Mark Strickson (Turlough). They wanted to lose the Kamelion robot as well, and to introduce a new, female, companion for the Doctor.

In his book *Doctor Who – The Companions*, producer John Nathan-Turner explained that 'the decision to try one solitary companion with the Doctor was an attempt to echo the Pertwee-Jo relationship of the Seventies, which had been so successful'. Of course, the Doctor-companion relationship had gone through many variations over the years, but it is certainly true that, with the third and subsequent Doctors, the one-on-one format had seemed to work well, particularly from the point of view of the female companion. It had started with Liz Shaw and then developed through Jo Grant, Sarah Jane Smith, Leela and Romana. In fact it was John Nathan-Turner again who had broken the, by then, traditional format by introducing three companions – Adric, Nyssa and Tegan – to see out the fourth Doctor and introduce the fifth.

In February 1985, Nathan-Turner, Eric Saward and Peter Grimwade, the author of the new companion's introductory story *Planet of Fire*, devised an outline for the character:

> *Perpugilliam (Peri for short) Brown is a wealthy 18-year-old American student studying Botany. She has long blonde hair which complements her attractive looks. She does not suffer fools gladly and her most charming attribute is an acute sense of humour.*
>
> *We meet Peri for the first time, while she is on holiday in whichever country we decide to film next season's foreign story.*
>
> *Peri's mother, Janine, has remarried a man Peri dislikes – Howard. Peri still treasures the memory of her father who died when Peri was 13, particularly as her mother appears to care more for Howard's three children than for Peri herself. It is because of her respect for her father that Peri thinks so highly of the Doctor – to some extent the Doctor replaces the gap in Peri's life. When he died he was of the same age as the Doctor appears now. This never develops further than admiration and close friendship. Peri is the kind of girl who is popular – not just because of her looks, but because her warmth and sense of fun make her appeal to people of all ages.*

As Eric Saward recalls, it was John Nathan-Turner's decision to make Peri an American. 'John wanted an American,' he says, 'and his brief was simply that: an American.' In Saward's view, this decision was motivated by a desire on the producer's part to curry favour with the American fans of *Doctor Who*. Nathan-Turner has however denied this. According to him, the decision was taken partly because of the popularity of Tegan – another non-British companion – and partly because he wanted to get away from Earth–UK companions in general, as he felt that their former predominance had lacked credibility.

Having auditioned a large number of actresses for the role, Nathan-Turner eventually chose Nicola Bryant, a young woman just out of drama school. Saward considers that the deciding factor for the producer was Nicola's voluptuousness. Having said this, however, he also accepts that she was the best candidate of all those auditioned. Clearly her attractive appearance and vivacious personality were more than sufficient to outweigh the fact that she lacked the blonde hair specified in the character outline. Another respect in which Nicola failed to meet the initial specifications was that she was not in fact an American – although neither producer nor script editor realised this at the time.

Nicola was born in a small village just outside Guildford in Surrey. 'It was the sort of village where everybody knew everybody else,' she explained in a 1992 interview for *The Frame*, 'and you daren't go out and play up because someone would tell your mother what you'd done. My father's central heating company was there, and my mother's family had lived there all their lives. There was no entertainment background at all in my family, except for the fact that my uncle, my father's youngest brother, was very big in amateur dramatics – he actually met his wife while playing in *The Pyjama Game*. I thought he was very funny. I remember as a kid going to see him and thinking "that looks fun", even though I wasn't interested in being an actress at the time. I wanted to be Margot Fonteyn Mk II.

'From as early as I can remember, my very first thoughts were of dancing. I started taking dancing lessons at Bellairs Dance School when I was three, and dancing was all I wanted to do right up until I was eleven, when I told my family that I wanted to go to ballet school. Choosing a career at that age is a very difficult thing to do, and dancing was a very precarious business, so understandably my parents preferred me to stay at my current school, where I could have a better standard of education. This was tough, but they thought it was for the best.

'My mother, being such a wonderful woman, realised that I was very upset at their decision. Having noticed in a newspaper that a local amateur dramatics society were auditioning for parts in *Fiddler on the Roof*, she suggested that I go along, even though you had to be sixteen to join and I was much younger. I went for the audition and when they asked what O levels I was doing, I made them all up. I ended up getting the part of the second youngest daughter, and the lady who played my youngest sister was eighteen! They had absolutely no idea I was so young.

'I took all my O levels and A levels and did well, and my father was very pleased. I worked hard, all through the holidays. Boyfriends used to come round and knock on the door and ask if I could come out, and I'd say, "Oh, not now, I'm doing my Chemistry." I didn't want to go out with boys, I was busy working. I did ten O levels and one O/A level when I was fifteen, then went on to take A levels in Geography, Economics, English and Home Economics.

'Eventually I gave up dancing, because the only classes I could now take were modern dance and tap. I didn't like them very much, as I was classically trained and wanted to be a classical dancer, and as far as I was concerned, anything else was just second best. Either you're going to be Margot Fonteyn or you're not. But I continued to appear in plays put on by the local company. After *Fiddler on the Roof*, I did *The Sound of Music*, *Snow White* … all musicals, simply because I enjoyed them.

'There was an unwritten agreement in our household that once I had done my O and A levels, my parents would support me in whatever I wanted to do. And what I wanted to do was to go to drama school. I wrote to all the accredited schools and got auditions for every one, but they were all sneering about my age. They said, "You can't come here at sixteen or seventeen. We want experienced people, people who have been through things in their life." It seemed that they weren't really interested in how good you were, just in how old you were.

'Now, when I went to the auditions I noticed what type of person each school wanted. You're sitting around waiting before it's your turn to audition, and you see the students going past on their way to classes or whatever. You look at the photographs on the wall and can see who has got which part. It's all a case of how observant you are. After I had been turned down, I reapplied to the schools three months later and was accepted by them all. The reason was that, the second time, I acted my interviews. In other words, I acted the part of the type of person I now knew each of them was looking for.

'The two most extreme were Central and Webber Douglas. For Central I frizzed my hair, put on black eyeliner and wore jeans in which I'd slashed holes long before it was fashionable to do so. Throughout the audition, I talked in a really common accent. At Webber Douglas, in contrast, I wore a full length practice skirt, put my hair in a bun, wore no make up, and was a very classical, serious young lady. When they mentioned my age, I turned to them and said, "I'd just like to ask you … please don't judge someone by the number of birthdays they've had, but by the events that have occurred between them." And that seemed to do the trick.

'I ended up at Webber Douglas. I'm not sure what drama school teaches you, though. I suppose that if you can survive two or three years there, then you can probably survive anything that gets thrown at you in the business. However, I came out after getting my diploma thinking that if that was what the acting business was like, then I didn't want to go into it. I found it so aggressive and bitchy, and it was very hard to strike up real friendships with people, because everyone was so fiercely competitive. Maybe part of my difficulty was that I came from a very close and loving relationship with my mother, very intimate and supportive, and I was as a result much more sensitive. I pick things up about people and what they're thinking. I have very, very acute hearing. I can walk into a familiar room and tell if the battery needs changing in the clock, because I can hear that the ticking is at a different rhythm from the week before. I actually have to sleep with ear-plugs in, because I hear so many sounds. One benefit of this is that I have perfect pitch and can pick up accents easily. The fact that my mother was deaf probably had something to do with it.

'The end-of-term play in my final year at Webber Douglas was the musical *No, No, Nanette*. A director came in from outside the school to audition us, and we had about a week in which to prepare. I looked at the book and thought that I was ideally suited to the lead role: sweet, innocent – I *was* Nanette! But as far as singing went, I thought "forget it", because I had had no training. My fiancé at the time – Scott Kennedy, a singer who had played the lead in two or three Broadway musicals and who was at Webber Douglas doing a post-graduate course – encouraged me and said that of course I could do it. He coached me for a week, and I just went for it. I auditioned and I read the piece and I sang the song. I didn't really think anything of it, because I didn't think they'd give me the part – but they did!

'I was married to Scott at 18, incredibly young, in my final year at Webber Douglas, and then walked straight into *Doctor Who*. I told John Nathan-Turner that I was 21. I was trying to be older than I was, and I think it was odd for someone who looked even younger to be settled down and married. When I played Peri, I wore my wedding ring on another finger, but I never lied about being married. If I was ever asked, I wouldn't say yes or no, I'd simply say that there was just one person in my life.

'I was very lucky that I landed the part in *Doctor Who*, because it gave me back a sense of family. Colin [Baker] and Peter [Davison] were very nice, and so especially was John. John was very paternal and took great care of me. I had three and a half years to develop a thick skin and to realise that there are lots of nice people in the business. I might come across a couple of right so-and-sos, but the majority are all right. I think I was so lucky, because otherwise I might have given it all up and tried to do something else: married the boss's son or something.

'When I auditioned for *Doctor Who*, John had no idea that I was not really American. I do have dual nationality through my marriage to Scott (although we're now separated), and also my room-mate at boarding school was from New York, so I had picked up her accent. I had been playing an American in *No, No, Nanette*, and an agent, Terry Carney, who came in to see it, assumed that I was American. He called me up and asked me to go and audition for *Doctor Who*. He didn't want to take on someone new out of drama school unless they had a job, so this was in his interest as well as mine. I told him that I wasn't strictly American, but he told me to be American anyway. So I did, and I thought that if they weren't happy with my American-ness, they'd just reject me. There was someone from Denver at the office, and I thought that if I convinced him, then I was doing all right.

'I went through several auditions until it finally got down to a choice between me and one other actress. They decided that they wanted me, but then of course I had to get my Equity card, because they couldn't let me have the part unless I was a member of the union. I had to get all my friends together and do cabaret work around some clubs to gain enough work experience to qualify for membership.'

One aspect of *Doctor Who* that makes it unlike other BBC dramas is the large amount of publicity that it often generates, particularly when there is a change of Doctor or of companion. In Nicola's case, this resulted in her first work being an interview for BBC's *Breakfast Time* programme on 6 July 1983.

'That was really bizarre. The first money I ever earned was from an interview on breakfast television! Funnily enough, Terry Carney hadn't wanted to draw up a contract with me at first, but when he saw me on TV in front of the cameras, he rang me that morning asking me to come in and sign a contract.'

Throughout this first interview for breakfast TV, Nicola maintained the pretence of being American. She used her 'Peri' American accent; she talked about driving, and the difference between the UK and the USA; she said she was 'an American playing an American part,' but added (and demonstrated) that she could speak perfect standard English if she wanted to; she even said that she was 21 years old, and then got into a discussion about early *Doctor Who* stories and what she could remember about them.

At the time the interview was conducted, as the interviewers stressed, she had not actually recorded any *Doctor Who*, nor had she even met any of her co-stars, and all she had to go on with regard to the part she was to play was the original character outline. There was therefore only a limited range of questions that could be put to her. One thing that did come up, however, was the suggestion that she might be typecast as playing only American roles. No doubt this concern was justified at the time, but in retrospect Nicola feels very positive about the high profile she gained as a result of playing Peri.

'When I started in *Doctor Who*,' she told *The Frame*, 'I didn't realise how much emphasis the programme would end up placing on me and on my role in it. It was one of those fortunate – for me – bits of timing that the show went through a period of change just before I joined. There had been five companions – Nyssa, Turlough, Adric, Tegan and Kamelion – all working with one Doctor, and in a very short space of time it was back to just the one. Me. So I didn't have to share my dialogue with several others. My first story [*Planet of Fire*], shot in Lanzarote, represented an obvious injection of money and enthusiasm into the show, and it gained a lot of publicity, most of which featured me.'

In interpreting the part of Peri, Nicola was never in any doubt as to how she should be played.

'I knew exactly who she was from day one,' she explained in an interview for *Doctor Who Magazine*. 'I think you've got to. I don't think it's one of those parts that you can go into thinking, "Oh, I'll see how she comes out," otherwise you can get yourself into all sorts of difficult situations. I started to think that there was a lot of me in the part as it was written. That's why I felt sure I could play her. But in the event, I couldn't say really that there's more than half of me in Peri.'

One of the problems in playing a young, 20th Century girl when you *are* a young, 20th Century girl is this great temptation simply to play yourself. How does Nicola see herself as differing from the character she portrayed?

'If it had been Nicola Bryant travelling in the TARDIS rather than Peri Brown, I would not have been so easily *led* by the Doctor. I would have wanted to establish a different kind of relationship with him, and I would have expected lessons on how to fly and operate the TARDIS, amongst other things. I think when I began on the show, Peri and I shared a similar adventurous quality mixed with a certain naïveté, but that's where the similarity really ends. Many of Peri's reactions were actually based on that American friend of mine from boarding school. She too was away from home, on her own, and insecure – but so full of adventure.'

Nicola had envisaged Peri herself as being 'a naïve innocent; quite a spunky kid, but not really experienced, having a pretty sheltered upbringing, with a domineering mother and a stepfather who wasn't exactly a bundle of laughs'.

What happened in practice was that particular character traits were either emphasised or lost by successive writers on the show – a lack of continuity that Nicola found very off-putting: 'I would suddenly find that a writer had highlighted one particular aspect, which might be one that I had never seen as a major part of the character anyway.'

'The part of Peri was very bland,' asserts Eric Saward, when asked about the way the character was treated, 'and writers will never respond to blandness. We did try to use her, but she was generally involved just in a sub-plot. This tends to happen with companions, because, first, it gets them away from the Doctor, so you don't have a constant inane dialogue going on, and, secondly, it means that they can contribute to the story. Peri was used very much in that way, as Nyssa had been before her. She wasn't really developed, because she wasn't very interesting as a character.

'I personally think that the companion should be strong. Of the ones with whom I was involved, I thought Tegan was the best, because she was ballsy and she had an energy. But John Nathan-Turner took a different view, and I always found it a struggle …. We could have developed her, had her acquiring skills under the tutelage of the Doctor, but we weren't allowed to. The same goes for Peri.'

6 SIXTH DOCTOR

Speaking to *Doctor Who Magazine*, writer Peter Grimwade confirmed that he had been asked by Saward to make Peri's debut a strong one, but that this strength had been rather lost along the way: 'The first draft I did, I made Peri a bit wimpish and vague, and Eric said, "This is dreadful. I want her hard and gutsy," and I went away and really re-thought it.

'I came back with a much harder character. They actually used her opening scene as the audition piece, which was very pleasing. I felt I'd cracked it. Then this and other areas were shortened and re-written to accommodate different aspects of the location, because they'd found bits of Lanzarote that they liked.'

Nicola was never consulted by any of the writers regarding Peri's character, but she has a fondness for the scripts written by Philip Martin (*Vengeance on Varos*, *The Trial of a Time Lord 5–8*) and Robert Holmes (*The Caves of Androzani*, *The Trial of a Time Lord 1–4, 13*). 'They had real drama and strength in their episodes,' she explains. She also has no doubts as to which story she liked least. '*Timelash* was my pet hate. Nice ideas, shame about the constant harping back to the Sixties victim role Peri played. It contained the same *Beauty and the Beast* idea as was in *The Caves of Androzani*, but there Peri wasn't weak; she was sick, naïve and inquisitive, but not pathetic.'

Peri certainly starts out well enough in *Planet of Fire*, the first of her eleven on-screen stories, which provides a good establishing framework and sketches in a character with some potential. She thinks nothing of attempting to swim a considerable distance to shore in order to escape from a boat on which she has been stranded – even if she does ultimately get into difficulty and has to be rescued by Turlough – and she stands up to the Master with bravado and bluster. It is obvious that Peri likes the fifth Doctor, and so it is perhaps unfortunate that *The Caves of Androzani*, their first full adventure together, is the last for that particular incarnation of the Time Lord. Here, Peri is initially quietly confident, clearly relaxed and happy in the Doctor's company. As the story progresses, however, she contracts spectrox toxæmia, and gradually descends into fever and delirium as the illness takes its toll – although she still manages to answer back to the unpredictable and unstable Sharaz Jek.

Following this escapade, Peri is faced with an unpredictable and unstable Doctor in *The Twin Dilemma*, and it is probably here that her character really starts to shine through. Her loyalty is very apparent as she stands by the much-changed Doctor – even when, in a fit of temporary insanity, he tries to kill her – and so is her resourcefulness as she takes the lead in exploring on Titan 3 and ultimately as she is left with Hugo Lang to hold the fort while the Doctor disposes of Mestor.

The problems with Peri's character really come to the fore in the twenty-second season. It seems that, perhaps partly as a result of the switch to the 45-minute episode format, the majority of the writers had little idea of what to do with her. She is at times reduced to a cypher, simply the person to whom the Doctor explains the plot.

She certainly shows little bravado or resourcefulness in *Attack of the Cybermen*; and in *Vengeance on Varos*, she becomes the archetypal damsel in distress when Quillam uses her in his transmogrification experiments. Obvious opportunities for use of the character are missed – for example, it is the Governor who persuades Maldak to free him and Peri from confinement, when it could so easily have been Peri herself – and the story is dominated by the Doctor and Sil, who get all the best lines.

Matters improve somewhat in *The Mark of the Rani*, as Peri is again allowed some independence. She suggests making a sleeping potion to help the afflicted miners –

virtually the only occasion on which her experience as a botany student is put to good use – and agrees, albeit nervously, to escort the Master and the Rani as prisoners back to the Rani's TARDIS. She even manages to resist the Master's attempt to hypnotise her – one up to the writers – although she then lets herself down by falling for a rather obvious ploy on the part of the Rani.

Further good material for Peri comes in the next story, *The Two Doctors*, as she has a chance for a fight scene with the temporarily deranged Jamie on board the space station, and later acts as a decoy at the hacienda by posing as a student calling for assistance.

This more effective handling of the character is short-lived, however, as in *Timelash*, it is straight back to the damsel in distress routine. Again, opportunities are missed: Peri simply stumbles upon the Falchan Rocks instead of actively seeking them out after receiving a cryptic message about a rendezvous there; and she has to be rescued by Herbert when it would have been perfectly possible for her to have thought of using a flambeau herself to frighten off the inquisitive Morlox. Perhaps the worst aspect of *Timelash*, though, is the illogical plot point that the Borad falls instantly in love with Peri, and then wants to alter her appearance – the only thing that could have made her attractive to him in the first place, since he had never met her. This whole subtext, that a woman is worthwhile only because of what she looks like, really had no place in a television programme of the Eighties.

The season's final story, *Revelation of the Daleks*, sees some attempt being made to establish a better rapport between Peri and the Doctor. Another plus point is that, as in *The Mark of the Rani*, Peri is not totally the helpless bystander – she beats off the mutant attacking the Doctor, and later manages to elude the fawning Jobel with both verbal and physical rebuffs. Unfortunately, this refreshing self-assurance was never developed further.

What then happened was that *Doctor Who* took an eighteen-month break from the nation's screens, following the decision to cancel the original Season 23. During this longer-than-usual pause in production, Nicola and Colin Baker decided that Peri and the Doctor could not go on as they had been. The whinging American wimp that Peri was becoming was not working, and the two actors decided between themselves that, whatever future scripts be might like, they would do their best to show that travelling in each other's company had changed them both.

The Trial of a Time Lord consequently presents viewers with a slightly mellower Doctor, and with a Peri not quite so at odds with him and with their life together. Peri's final two adventures show her at her best. The first segment of the Trial has her going through some highly emotional situations as she grieves the fate of her planet and then has to face the grim prospect of a life of enforced baby-making at the hands of the Tribe of the Free, while the second gives her perhaps the best characterisation and development she ever had. With the Doctor having apparently lost his mind, it is up to Peri to calm the tempestuous Yrcanos, to talk the strangely bland Tusa around to the fact that they are not his enemies, and to attempt to help her fellow traveller as best she can. For this to be Peri's swan song is fitting, as it illuminates previously unexplored aspects of her character and leaves the viewer wanting more.

The two stories of Season 23 are however overshadowed by the bulk of the previous season, in which Peri was simply a victim to be used in order to generate exciting plot twists as the writers saw fit, or simply as a sounding board to explain proceedings to the viewers. This 'generic companion' aspect of the role is what irritated Nicola Bryant most.

'Having talked to the other girls who had played companions,' she told *Doctor Who Magazine*, 'I realised that we had all had the same problem, that just occasionally we would get a story that didn't really seem to be related to our character, but to the *Doctor Who* "companion of all time".'

Part of the identity of any character, whether on stage, film or television, is established by the costumes they wear. After the departure of Romana in 1980, the *Doctor Who* companions, in common with the Doctors themselves, generally wore 'uniforms' rather than 'clothes'; that is, they tended to wear either exactly the same outfits for every story, or slight variations on a theme. As clothes reflect personality, it is not really surprising that as the clothes became fixed, so did the personalities behind them. Peri was no exception to the rule.

The costumes with which Nicola was presented for Peri were both eye-catching and colourful, but not exactly what she would have chosen herself. The Peri 'look' – generally consisting of figure-hugging shorts and skin-tight leotards – apparently came about because of the clothes Nicola chose to wear to her first photo-call. 'I thought she looked so stunning', relates John Nathan-Turner, 'that I asked our costume designers to echo Nicola's own clothes!'

Nicola, however, recalls that there was slightly more to it than that. 'I was asked to bring several outfits along for the photo call,' she says, 'and "short and very fitting" was the description I was given. I never wore short skirts and clingy-fitting tops myself – all I possessed were a pair of shorts and a leotard. I asked John if this would be okay, and he said "Great!" Unfortunately, he liked it so much that we got stuck with it.'

The result was a succession of costumes that left very little to the imagination, and that were usually wholly unsuited to the weather on location.

'We filmed *The Caves of Androzani* in Devon,' Nicola recalled in *Doctor Who Magazine*. 'But it was very cold, and I had no way of wrapping up, because my costume was in direct continuity from the previous story. I was wearing the same clothes I had worn in Lanzarote. I remember the cameraman saying, "Slap your face, love, you're going blue." I got frostbite, then pneumonia. Then Peter [Davison] fell ill too – it was a pretty rough shoot.

'In *Attack of the Cybermen*, I started out in a shocking pink leotard and shorts, then got into a sort of red jump-suit. In *Vengeance on Varos*, I had a blue leotard and shorts … They went out first and bought the shorts – pink, turquoise and even a pair in yellow – and then tried to find matching leotards. In *The Two Doctors*, I wore a psychedelic thing that glistened nicely in the sun, but filming in Seville the temperature reached 102 degrees, and it was like a thermal blanket – I felt like a roast chicken! I could have used that in Devon!'

She has a pragmatic attitude towards the costumes, however. 'I think that's one of the unfortunate things that comes with the part. The newspapers always want something extra. There's nothing I could have done to escape it, and I wasn't in a position to do so. Other actresses who came into the show often said, "Why don't you put your foot down and say no?" My reply was, "Look, I'd rather be playing Peri and wear that than not be playing Peri." There's just no point in jumping up and down screaming about it. I hoped that a few people would look beyond all that, at the face and at the acting, and judge me on those things, rather than on just the outward appearance.

'I was a lot happier with the more realistic costumes I wore during my last season. It was a relief – especially in Britain's climate. I think the things I wore in that season reflected Peri's character slightly more as I had originally seen her. I still had no choice as to what they were, though.'

So what would Nicola's own choice of costumes have been?

'*Planet of Fire* was fine by me, but afterwards I would have been in jeans, T-shirts, sweat-shirts and sneakers. That's the way I saw Peri. Back to shorts in Seville for *The Two Doctors*, and then of course period costume for *The Mark of the Rani*. Peri should have worn basically the kind of clothes that real American students lived in – casual clothes of the Eighties. I think to have been in jeans and sensible shoes would have added to that more spunky, independent feel that Peri began with.'

Nicola joined the series not long before her original co-star, Peter Davison, left. 'I first met Peter at the studio when I came to watch an episode being recorded. I was amazed at how long the hours were. I remember that when I started the shoot in Lanzarote, the director Fiona Cumming said to me, "Just watch Peter as often as you can," so I did, and in that way, I learned an awful lot about acting in a short amount of time.'

Nicola recalls that she was initially rather nervous and unsure about the new Doctor, Colin Baker, 'mainly because Peter had been winding me up, saying everything and nothing. He would say "So, you're working with Colin Baker … Well, if you have any problems, you just call me. And good luck!"

'After a rather bumpy start, Colin and I turned out to be great mates. As actors, we have the same strong feelings about our characters – something that even now, when we work on video projects together, unites us and makes us a strong team. I think it's also to do with the fact that we trust each other on several levels. Colin was really there for me in a very quiet and special way when my Dad died, and that means a lot.'

Nicola decided to leave *Doctor Who* during the twenty-third season, simply because she felt that three years working on one show was enough. 'As an actor I had to say, "Right, okay, I'm going to get out there and see what else there is." I was happy to do so, in that I felt that I wanted to go and do something else, but sad to be leaving such a nice bunch of people behind.'

If she could give some advice now, to herself as she was then, what would it be?

'I would tell myself to have even more fun that I did. I was a little more serious then than I am now, and perhaps if I had relaxed a little more, then I could have enjoyed it even more than I did.'

It is ultimately down to the production team whether a companion works or fails, and certain key qualities must be present if she is to inspire the writers to use and develop her. Eric Saward's concept of a really strong character was not to see fruition during his tenure on the show, and it subsequently fell to his successor, Andrew Cartmel, to create arguably the true 'Eighties' companion in Ace. It clearly helps if the producer and the script editor are in accord as to the treatment of the character, and this appears not to have been the case where Perpugilliam Brown was concerned. However, the fact that she is still recalled with so much affection by so many viewers must surely be a testament to the skills of all those involved in bringing her to life.

SELLING THE DOCTOR

MEDIA

During the Eighties, *Doctor Who* enjoyed a healthy relationship with the media. John Nathan Turner often played the newspapers at their own game, creating 'news opportunities' at every turn and maximising the impact of those celebrity actors and actresses who agreed to appear in the show with strategically arranged press and photo calls.

During the two-and-a-bit seasons that Colin Baker played the Doctor, almost every story received some news coverage, whether it be because of who was appearing in it, or because of the location, or the monsters, or the companions, or sometimes all of these together.

When Baker's appointment was first announced on 20 August 1983, there was a wealth of press coverage, but, strangely, the *Daily Telegraph* and the *Daily Express* made no mention of the fact that not long before this, they had both announced a completely different actor, Brian Blessed, as having been chosen to play the part. The *Daily Express* report, in the edition dated 1 August, had stated unequivocally that Blessed was to play the sixth incarnation of the Time Lord, had given a brief biography of him, and had even pointed out that his appointment quashed rumours that the next Doctor would be a woman, claiming that BBC chiefs had even described the kind of woman that they had been looking for!

The next major press call was on Tuesday 10 January 1984, when Baker's new costume was unveiled to the waiting lenses of Fleet Street. The following day, 'The Tasteless Time Lord' and 'Who's the height of bad taste?' were the headlines, as John Nathan-Turner was quoted describing the Doctor's outfit as 'totally tasteless'. Almost every newspaper covered the story, many of them in colour. Then, not long afterwards, yet another photo-call was arranged, to publicise the first episode of *The Twin Dilemma*. Such was *Doctor Who*'s press potential for the BBC that their Press Information pack for the week beginning Saturday 17 March 1984 even had a photograph of Baker on the front, promoting his on-air debut.

All in all, Colin Baker probably had more press coverage to launch his Doctor than did any of his predecessors.

A part of this interest was a story run in the *Sun* and the *Daily Star* concerning the fact that Colin and his wife Marion had lost their first child, Jack, to the Sudden Infant Death Syndrome four months previously. Although the *Sun* had run the news of Jack's birth in October 1983, and had also covered the tragic death in November, it considered the story worth repeating, apparently with additional comments from Colin. Colin was determined to use the exposure that *Doctor Who* was to give him to campaign and raise money for the Foundation for the Study of Infant Deaths.

Further media interest was created when John Nathan-Turner 'accidentally' let slip that the Doctor would be getting rid of the TARDIS's familiar shape, as most viewers no longer knew what a police box was. This resulted in a deluge of viewers' letters to the BBC, and in newspapers jumping on the 'Save the TARDIS' bandwagon. One paper even ran a competition to design a new exterior for the Doctor's timeship. In the event, even though the Doctor got the TARDIS to change shape a couple of times in *Attack of the Cybermen*, it otherwise remained in the trusty form viewers knew and loved. The

Sun claimed that this was totally down to its campaign, proclaiming on 17 November 1983 that it had saved the TARDIS from the scrap heap.

For the twenty-second season, there was press interest a-plenty when Prince Andrew's ex-girlfriend, photographer Koo Stark, was announced as featuring in the opening story. This guest appearance was not to be, however, the *Sun* explaining on 18 June 1984 that Stark had been dropped from the role after a row over publicity.

Despite this setback, *Doctor Who*'s aptitude for attracting top names to its cast meant that the BBC soon had further media personalities to parade before the press. On 3 July, comedienne and impressionist Faith Brown was announced as a forthcoming guest star, and on 15 July, Sarah Berger was reported to be replacing Koo Stark as one of the Cryons in *Attack of the Cybermen*. Another Cryon was to be played by ex-*Blue Peter* presenter Sarah Greene. 'Koo missed out on a lot of fun,' said Greene.

Further guest star names announced in the *Daily Star* on 5 January 1985 were Alexei Sayle, Eleanor Bron, Terence Alexander, Martin Jarvis, Frazer Hines, Jason Connery and Jacqueline Pearce. Colin Baker was reported as having the 'best job on television'. 'It's like being a grown-up who is getting paid to play cowboys and indians, it's great fun,' he said.

As the season progressed, *The Mark of the Rani* received coverage because of the presence of the Master, while *The Two Doctors* made the news because Frazer Hines apparently needed hardly any make-up to recreate his role as Jamie.

Of course, while *The Two Doctors* was part-way through transmission, news of a far more dramatic nature broke: *Doctor Who* was being rested for eighteen months. The full story of this turbulent period in *Doctor Who*'s history is covered in its own chapter.

After all the media hype about the postponement had died down, the press turned its attention to publicising the twenty-third season. The series was heralded as coming back 'for a laugh', those anonymous 'BBC chiefs' that the newspapers loved quoting having felt that it was too violent and needed an injection of humour. This approach was apparently confirmed by the casting of *Carry On ...* actress Joan Sims in the first segment of the story. Some interest was also shown because of the Trial theme of the season, which echoed the feelings of those BBC chiefs toward the series itself. The guest cast found themselves the centre of attention, as once again the programme was promoted on its ability to attract star names. This time it was Michael Jayston, Lynda Bellingham, Joan Sims, Tony Selby, Brian Blessed, Patrick Ryecart, Geoffrey Hughes, Christopher Ryan, Honor Blackman and Michael Craig who featured in the reports.

Ultimately, following all the press coverage of the postponement, which included in the *Sun* some damning indictments by Colin Baker of BBC1's Controller Michael Grade, the news broke on 13 December 1986 that Baker had been 'sacked' from the role of the Doctor, reportedly because of these comments. His contract had not been renewed, but Bonnie Langford's had. It later transpired that Baker had been offered four episodes at the start of the twenty-fourth season to make a final story, but had declined them, not wishing to have to forego other work in the interim.

The hunt was now on for Doctor number seven.

COMPANIONS

As always, the press were very keen to feature the Doctor's companions, mainly because they tended to be pretty young women. In the case of Nicola Bryant, the tabloids had a field day.

'Naughty Nicola' screamed a headline in the *Daily Star*, which reported that fans were apparently up in arms because her outfits were too sexy. This outcry came as *Vengeance on Varos* was being screened, and Nicola's tight blue leotard-top and shorts left little to the imagination. 'Red-faced mums and dads want her to wear more modest outfits and hide her ample charms,' said Geoff Baker, writing in the *Daily Star* on 26 January 1985. Sexy the outfits may have been, but the show had again managed to achieve almost a full two page spread, effectively advertising the series, on the day it was transmitted.

When reporting Nicola's departure from the series, some newspapers even found some photographs of her posing with nothing but a smile and a towel. It is perhaps inevitable that the tabloid press will latch on to anything if it is sold to them with a little sex appeal – a fact that the *Doctor Who* production office knew and used to maximise publicity.

When Bonnie Langford was announced on 23 January 1986 as being the replacement for Nicola, the press were, for once, a little confounded. Here they were presented with a 'name', someone of whom they had all heard, and who was arguably more famous than the actor playing the Doctor. There was also no way they could present Bonnie Langford as a sex object, which, given their established attitude towards 'the *Doctor Who* girl', also caused them difficulties. To introduce Langford to the public, the BBC staged a press call at the London theatre where Langford was appearing in *Peter Pan*. Colin Baker, looking somewhat chubby after five or so months with little work, was squeezed into a flying harness, and the two of them were photographed clowning about against a starry background.

Picking up on Colin's apparent increase in weight, the *Daily Record* provided the news that the first thing Langford would do in the series was to put the Doctor on a diet.

The introduction of Langford's character Mel in *The Trial of a Time Lord* was followed up with another press call, this time with Baker sporting a moustache and a beard, grown following his departure from the series. The pair fooled about on this occasion with a pair of garden shears.

PERSONAL APPEARANCES

While *Doctor Who* may not have been as popular with the viewing public at this point as it had been in the past, the producer and his stars were out and about almost constantly promoting the series.

Prior to transmission of *Attack of the Cybermen*, John Nathan-Turner appeared on the BBC1 children's show *Saturday Superstore* talking to presenter Mike Reid about the possibility of the TARDIS's police box shape being replaced. He said that the office was being bombarded with petitions, but stressed that no decision had yet been taken – he and his team were just thinking about it.

The Kenilworth Agricultural Show over the August bank holiday weekend in 1984 played host to a number of *Doctor Who* stars during its three day run. These included Colin Baker and Nicola Bryant, who turned out to promote both the programme and John Nathan-Turner's forthcoming pantomime production, *Cinderella*, in which they would both appear.

The week before part one of *The Twin Dilemma* was transmitted, Colin Baker appeared on *Blue Peter* to publicise the story. A lengthy clip was shown of Mestor in his throne room speaking to Azmael, and of the Doctor and Peri investigating the wreckage of Hugo Lang's ship. This was followed by a further clip, of the Doctor attacking Peri in the TARDIS. Presenter Janet Ellis explained that both stars would be on *Saturday Superstore* that coming weekend. There, the pair answered questions and took phone calls, including one from 'the Master' (actor Anthony Ainley), who warned that he would be coming from the depths of hell to haunt the Doctor. He challenged the Doctor in his new guise to settle their feud once and forever. Baker (as the Doctor) accepted the challenge, and the Master then rang off.

Later in the programme, Baker's handwriting was analysed by an expert in that field. Not knowing whose it was, she came to the conclusion that he was well travelled, well educated and had a very inquiring mind. She recommended a job in which he could do his own thing, as he was too independent to go along with group decisions. She also felt that he saw his rightful place as being at the top, that he had a great sense of timing and presentation and that he appeared to have an affinity for detailed analytical work. She suggested that he would make a good barrister. She added that he liked to work things out for himself, that he liked to cut a dash, and that his clothing would have a certain panache as a result. Baker felt that this summation was partly accurate.

The same week, Baker, together with Peter Davison, also appeared on *Harty*, the weekly chat show presented by Russell Harty; and, on the actual morning of the day of the first episode's transmission, he and Bryant guested on the BBC's *Breakfast Time* show with Selina Scott and Frank Bough.

Take Two, a children's version of the *Did You See* viewers' correspondence programme, spoke to John Nathan-Turner about the series. Children they had interviewed felt that Colin Baker was too young to play the Doctor, and that Peri whined too much and had a disagreeable accent. They didn't appear to be frightened by the monsters, and cited the Daleks and the Cybermen as their favourites. However, the feeling was expressed that *Doctor Who* was shown too early for younger children. Nathan-Turner explained that the show was going out later than it ever had been, and that the intention was not to terrify, just occasionally to scare.

As the twenty-second season got underway, Baker, Bryant, Mary Tamm and Jacqueline Pearce all appeared on the *Saturday Superstore* of 5 January 1985 to promote John Nathan-Turner's *Cinderella* pantomime, which was playing in Southampton at the time. They did, however, find time to answer questions from viewers about *Doctor Who*.

Towards the end of 1985, Lenny Henry turned his satirical eye on *Doctor Who* and presented, in the edition of *The Lenny Henry Show* broadcast on 2 October, a sketch featuring himself as the Doctor. The TARDIS – in fact the Master's TARDIS control room set from *Planet of Fire* – brings the Doctor and Peri to Earth in the future. The planet is now controlled by the most ruthless woman in the universe, Thatchos, who threatens to have them privatised. They escape in the TARDIS, where Peri wants to use the fact that they are no longer on television to get to know the Doctor better.

Shortly after this, on 22 November, the BBC's annual *Children In Need* fund-raising telethon saw no fewer than twenty *Doctor Who* stars presenting a cheque for £1000 to Terry Wogan. The money had been collected earlier in the year at the *Doctor Who* exhibition on Blackpool's Golden Mile, during a special appearance by Colin Baker and Nicola Bryant to sign autographs and meet the fans.

In the studio to present the cheque were Patrick Troughton, Carole Ann Ford, Jackie Lane, Peter Purves, Michael Craze, Adrienne Hill, Jon Pertwee, Caroline John, Nicholas Courtney, Richard Franklin, John Levene, Elisabeth Sladen, Louise Jameson, Ian Marter, Peter Davison, Janet Fielding, Matthew Waterhouse, Mark Strickson, Nicola Bryant and Colin Baker. This was the biggest assembly of *Doctor Who* cast members ever

6 SIXTH DOCTOR

achieved in this country. A cheque for £100 was also presented by Patrick Troughton on behalf of the *Doctor Who* Appreciation Society.

The *Doctor Who* exhibition at Blackpool had been running for ten years, but at the end of October 1985, it closed its doors for the last time. The lease on the building in which it was housed had expired, and many of the costumes and props contained there were needed to fit out a massive *Doctor Who* exhibition bus that was to tour the USA. The new exhibition was contained in a trailer, 48 feet long, that was too large to travel on Britain's roads. It was designed by BBC designer Tony Burrough. Artist Andrew Skilleter created huge *Doctor Who* murals for the sides and interiors, and the whole thing was sent over to America, where, on 9 May 1986, it was launched on its tour by Peter Davison and Michael Grade in New York. The tour was joined at various points by stars from the programme, including Tom Baker and Colin Baker, and was very well received.

Doctor Who appeared on ice in 1986 when, from 14 June until 1 November, an eight minute *Doctor Who* segment was included in the annual *Ice Spectacular* show at Blackpool.

Also in 1986, the French TV network TF1 bought *Doctor Who* to screen in their *Temps X* programme. To publicise the series, they put together a documentary called *Who is Who*, and even arranged for some of the Target *Doctor Who* novelisations to be reissued in French translations, featuring the two presenters of *Temps X* on the covers.

On 25 August 1986, Colin Baker and Lynda Bellingham appeared on *Wogan* talking about Baker's acting career and the new season of *Doctor Who* starting on 6 September. The show also featured a Mandrel (from *Nightmare of Eden*) and a Sea Devil Warrior (from *Warriors of the Deep*) wandering about the studio.

Bonnie Langford made an appearance on *The Saturday Picture Show* on 6 September 1986, primarily to talk about the tour of *Peter Pan*, although *Doctor Who* did get a brief mention. A clip from the end of *Revelation of the Daleks* was shown – strangely, as Langford did not appear in it – leading into a brief clip from the start of the new series.

Colin Baker appeared as the Doctor on 13 September to introduce Roland Rat at the start of that week's episode of *Roland Rat – The Series*.

The next major *Doctor Who* feature on TV was again on *Saturday Superstore*, Sarah Greene and Mike Reid playing host on 29 November 1986 to a TARDIS full of *Doctor Who* monsters and Time Lords to celebrate twenty-three years of *Doctor Who*. To fill the *Doctor Who* costumes, the producers of *Saturday Superstore* contacted the DWAS, and arranged for a group of fans to come along and wander about dressed as Cybermen, Mandrels, Sea Devils and Time Lords. Colin Baker was also in the studio to talk about the series, and the regular 'pop panel' was enlivened by 'Tony the Cyberman' (played by DWAS Co-ordinator Tony Jordan and voiced by David J Howe) commenting on the videos and attempting to destroy Mike Reid in the process. The programme ended with the cutting of a special TARDIS-shaped cake.

OVERSEAS

America

In the mid-Eighties, *Doctor Who* was amongst the top ten bestselling British TV programmes overseas, reaching 54 different countries and attaining world-wide viewing figures estimated at 110 million. One of the series' most important markets was the United States of America.

Since the start of the Eighties, *Doctor Who* had become more and more popular with American fans, and this popularity peaked during the period when the sixth Doctor was appearing on British television screens.

As with Peter Davison and Nicola Bryant before him, Colin Baker's first convention appearance was in the USA, at Panopticon West in Ohio in July 1984, and he also guested at the massive annual convention in Chicago in November of that year, organised by the commercial Spirit of Light company. This frustrated and infuriated the organisers of Britain's *Doctor Who* Appreciation Society (DWAS), who felt that their members were losing out to their American counterparts, as had been the case the previous year when no Doctors had been available for the biggest British fan convention to celebrate the series' 20th anniversary, as they were all being paid to attend the convention in Chicago. *Doctor Who* was, as usual, generally not being repeated in Britain – the latest repeats had been *The King's Demons*, *The Awakening* and *The Five Doctors* in 1984, during the break between the twenty-first and twenty-second seasons – but in America it was being shown almost continuously on Public Broadcasting Service channels. The fact that the American fans were now meeting new Doctors before their British counterparts added to the sense of injustice that many of the latter felt.

What British fans often overlooked, however, was the fact that their fellow devotees in the States outnumbered them by at least ten to one at this point. The *Doctor Who* Fan Club of America boasted some 30,000 members, and could reasonably be considered to have been the hub of *Doctor Who* fandom in the mid-Eighties.

The early US convention appearances by Colin Baker – who would later be extremely generous with his time in attending numerous British events – were partly down to the influence of John Nathan-Turner, who had apparently foregone British fandom in his desire to woo the Americans with the programme and its stars. The BBC themselves were certainly not going to object to this, as they were gaining valuable overseas sales of the show, not to mention a sizeable income from the masses of licensed merchandise being produced in the States. By June 1985, *Doctor Who* was being seen in 146 American markets, covering 70 per cent of the country.

New Zealand
By Paul Scoones

The first the New Zealand television audience saw of Colin Baker's Doctor was nearly two years after the actor had left the role. The first of his stories to be screened was *Revelation of the Daleks*, which was one of five stories all screened for the first time during Television New Zealand's *Doctor Who* 'Silver Jubilee' week of special screenings in November 1988 on TV2. *Revelation of the Daleks* was broadcast in a four episode format over four nights from Monday 21 November to Thursday 24 November 1988 at 5.30 pm. The story gained the highest viewer ratings of all the *Doctor Who* screenings that week, with an average of 6.9%.

The Colin Baker era proper began with *The Twin Dilemma* on 10 August 1988, following on from the end of the Davison era stories. At this point, *Doctor Who* screened twice a week on Thursdays and Fridays at around 5.15 pm. The Season 22 stories were screened in the 25 minute episode format, and the season was also screened in production order, so *The Two Doctors* preceded *The Mark of the Rani*. The series suffered some disruption when it was moved in the schedules at short notice as TV2 realigned its programming to combat the launch of the rival television channel, TV3. *Timelash* Parts Three and Four, which were advertised as screening on Thursday 2 November and Friday 3 November, were moved to Saturday afternoons at 5 pm, with Part Three playing nearly a week earlier than scheduled on 28 October, and Part Four on 4 November 1989.

Viewer ratings for this period show that of the Colin Baker episodes, *The Twin Dilemma* Part One was the most watched, with 9.5% which higher than any of the Davison episodes screened in 1988-89. Part Four of the same story was the second highest at 9%, followed by *The Two Doctors* Part Four on 8%. The average audience ratings for the first six stories of the Colin Baker era are: *The Twin Dilemma* 8%; *Attack of the Cybermen* 6.3%; *Vengeance on Varos* 6.5%; *The Two Doctors* 6.8%; *The Mark of the Rani* 4.5% and *Timelash* 3.4%.

The series resumed with a repeat of *Revelation of the Daleks* followed by *The Trial of a Time Lord* from 27 December to 22 January 1990. These episodes were screened five days a week, from Monday to Friday on TV2 at around 4.30 pm. No episode was screened on the Monday of New Years Day 1990.

Many of the Colin Baker episodes screened in New Zealand were sourced from the Australian Broadcasting Corporation and were quite heavily edited. Cuts had been made by the Australian censor to remove violence and further edits were made in New Zealand, sometimes just to reduce the running time to fit the timeslot. The most edited episodes included *Vengeance on Varos* Part Three, which lost around five minutes, *The Two Doctors* Part Six (three minutes), *Timelash Part Three* (nearly three and a half minutes) and *The Trial of a Time Lord* Part Nine (two and a half minutes). Worst affected of all however was *The Trial of a Time Lord* Part Fourteen, which lost over eight minutes of footage simply to fit the unusually long episode into the available timeslot.

FANDOM

As already noted, the main *Doctor Who* fan activity during the Colin Baker era took place in the USA. In addition to the numerous conventions, the *Doctor Who Fan Club of America* – a commercial organisation run by Ron Katz and Chad Roark – offered their members, reported to number some 30,000, a regular newspaper, *The Whovian Times*. This contained interviews with the series' stars and columns by John Nathan-Turner and, providing all the latest British news, writer Jeremy Bentham. The pages of the newspaper also featured numerous adverts for some of the masses of BBC-licenced (and, in some cases, possibly unlicenced) merchandise items produced in the States at this time, including tee-shirts, jackets, mugs, key-fobs, pens, model kits and towels. Readers were even given regular invitations to join an organisation called the Gallifrey Beach and Body Club!

In Britain, the *Doctor Who* Appreciation Society (DWAS), the only official fan group in this country, was still growing steadily, following publicity gained at the 20th anniversary BBC convention at Longleat in 1983 and subsequent advertising in Marvel Comics' *Doctor Who Magazine*. The Society's newsletter, *Celestial Toyroom*, continued to appear on a regular monthly basis, and the news, as one would expect, covered all the major events of the time.

Apart from Marvel's official *Doctor Who Magazine*, in which news was scant and consisted mainly of brief details about forthcoming stories, the other main source of *Doctor Who* information was a monthly fanzine, *Doctor Who Bulletin*, edited and published by Gary Levy (who later changed his name to Gary Leigh). Levy had started

DWB (as it was generally abbreviated) because he was interested in magazines and their production, and also in *Doctor Who*. He was a member of the DWAS and felt that he could improve on the news aspect of their newsletter. In contrast to *Celestial Toyroom* and *Doctor Who Magazine*, which tended to report news and current events without comment, *DWB*'s editorial style was highly outspoken and controversial. Also unlike the other two publications, *DWB* showed no hesitation in printing information before it had been either confirmed or denied officially. *DWB* started out with a fairly positive attitude towards *Doctor Who* and its producer but, following the postponement of Season 23, the fanzine took on a far more critical and negative stance.

The influence of American fandom made itself known to British fans in July 1984, when the planned annual DWAS convention, Panopticon VI, scheduled for 23, 24 and 25 November 1984, had to be postponed, as on those dates all the potential guests were going to be at the huge commercial Spirit of Light convention in America, which had just had its dates rescheduled from October. The British event was eventually moved to 26, 27 and 28 July 1985 and took place at the Brighton Metropole hotel. The event was notable for featuring the first and only British fan convention appearance of Patrick Troughton. While the convention went ahead and was reasonably successful, when it was all over, the DWAS was left with a hefty bill to pay and insufficient funds to do so. The Society's newsletter reported that the convention's finances had been mismanaged by its organisers.

As the DWAS' Co-ordinator, David Saunders, had resigned just prior to the convention, his successor, Tony Jordan, together with the rest of the DWAS Executive, now had to recover the Society from the brink of bankruptcy, while continuing to provide members with a reasonable service. To this end, the newsletter and the Society magazine, *TARDIS*, were merged, and the membership fee increased from six to eight pounds a year. With these measures in place, planning tentatively started towards the end of 1985 on the next big convention, this time with an edict to put the Society back on a sound financial footing, and with a new team doing the organising.

The resultant convention, Panopticon VII, was praised by many fans as being the best the DWAS had ever organised. There was the added bonus for attendees of being able to watch the transmission of the first episode of *The Trial of a Time Lord* live on a big convention screen, along with 500 of their fellow devotees. This screening was for some the highlight of the event, and was described as 'electrifying' by many of those present.

At the end of 1986, after a great deal of hard work, the Society was again financially stable, and Tony Jordan, feeling that he had done what he was brought onto the Executive to do, moved on. He was succeeded by Andrew Beech, who was to steer the DWAS into yet another new era of *Doctor Who*.

One other UK fan activity of note from this period is Fan Aid. This charitable endeavour was the brainchild of Paul Cornell, who decided to raise money for famine relief in Ethiopia, spurred on by the Live Aid concert and Band Aid record for the same cause. Cornell, along with many other helpers and assistants, organised a very successful convention in Bath, released some interesting and informative fanzines, and managed to raise an announced total of £2,165.

MERCHANDISE

While *Doctor Who*'s popularity might have been slipping somewhat as far as the ratings and the BBC were concerned, from the point of view of the merchandisers, things had

697

never looked better.

There were just over 200 individual items of merchandise issued during the Colin Baker era, which is 100 per cent more than was released in the whole of the Sixties. Whereas in the Sixties, the items were very diverse, in the mid-Eighties, the releases tended to be concentrated in three areas: books, metal miniatures and videos.

W H Allen continued releasing *Doctor Who* novelisations, and when Nigel Robinson took over as editor of the range, he started to look into the past for the stories to feature, as most of the more recent ones had already been tackled. Thus under Robinson's enthusiastic editorship, more novelisations of first and second Doctor stories started appearing, as well as 'gaps' being filled for all the other Doctors.

When W H Allen contacted Baker's agent about using his likeness on the covers of the books, they offered a single fee in lieu of a royalty. Baker's agent asked if a royalty could be negotiated instead, but the publishers refused, and did not contact the agent again. As a result, Baker's face did not appear on any of the first-edition covers of the novelisations of his stories. An illustration of the sixth Doctor that had already been completed for *The Twin Dilemma* was dropped just prior to publication, after proof covers had already been printed up, and artist Andrew Skilleter was asked at short notice to come up with a replacement.

W H Allen, along with all the series' other merchandisers, were reaping the rewards of the increased popularity of *Doctor Who* in America, and all manner of 'factual' books appeared. Some of these had only a very tenuous connection with the series, but this did not appear to matter, as if the product had 'Doctor Who' on the cover, it sold. Hence we saw: the *Doctor Who Cookbook* (recipes provided by numerous *Doctor Who* cast and production team members) compiled by Gary Downie, who had choreographed the dance sequences in *Black Orchid* and had also worked as production assistant on several *Doctor Who* stories; *Travel Without the TARDIS* (an American's guide to visiting *Doctor Who* locations in Britain), written by two American fans, Jean Airey and Laurie Halderman; a number of *Doctor Who* quiz books and similar items; and, perhaps most obscure of all, the *Doctor Who Pattern Book* (knitting and sewing patterns – make your own woolly Cybermat!) by Joy Gammon. Even John Nathan-Turner turned his hand to writing and brought us *Doctor Who – The TARDIS Inside Out*, in which he presented his memories of the actors who had played the Doctor, and *Doctor Who – The Companions*, where he did the same for the companions. While not being as bad as some of the other publications, these volumes were a little slim; and in the case of the companions volume, some additional research on those actors and actresses with whom Nathan-Turner had not worked would not have gone amiss.

There were some highly acclaimed books, too, and top of the pile was J Jeremy Bentham's *Doctor Who – The Early Years*. Published by W H Allen, this told of the design work that had gone into the creation of the Daleks, as well as of other aspects of the early stories, and presented numerous design drawings and photographs from the extensive collection of ex-BBC designer Raymond P Cusick. Bentham had founded and organised the *Doctor Who* Appreciation Society's Reference Department during the late Seventies, and was considered by many to be one of the stalwart historians of *Doctor Who*.

Another worthwhile publication was Mat Irvine's *Doctor Who Special Effects*, published by Beaver Books. Irvine was an effects designer at the BBC and had worked extensively on *Doctor Who*, as well as on many other programmes. This book collected anecdotes and photographs from his own collection and provided an illuminating glimpse into the world of *Doctor Who* special effects.

Lastly on this subject, there were a number of 'game books' released featuring the sixth Doctor. In the US, FASA Corporation in 1986 published *Doctor Who and the Rebel's Gamble* by William H Keith Jr. Described as a 'solo-play adventure game', it involved the Doctor and Peri arriving in the middle of the American Civil War to find that history has been changed. In the UK, meanwhile, Severn House in the same year published six 'Make Your Own Adventure' books. These featured the Doctor alongside a number of TV and original characters in stories written by William Emms, Philip Martin, David Martin and Pip and Jane Baker, all of whom had previously written televised *Doctor Who* stories, and also one by Michael Holt. William Emms's *Mission to Venus* was a particularly notable example, as it was based on a story, *The Imps*, that had been planned for inclusion in Season 4 of the TV series but had ultimately abandoned after the writer fell ill.

The other major *Doctor Who* product type of the mid-Eighties consisted of cast metal miniatures of characters from the series. These were produced by Fine Art Castings out of their small workshop near Andover. The company had previously concentrated on military models, and were keen to branch into another market. There were three basic ranges of *Doctor Who* figures: 80mm figures, 40mm figures and a few 20mm figures, the latter two designed for role-playing games. With the help of David J Howe and Mark Stammers (then involved in running the DWAS' Reference and Graphics Departments respectively), the figures were as accurate as could be represented, given their dimensions. Before long, all six Doctors were available, as well as most of the companions, and a great number of the monsters and villains, from the Daleks and Cybermen right through to the Borad and Drathro.

The company also produced two limited edition bust sets, the first of all six Doctors, and the second of a monster or villain from each of the Doctor's eras. In the three or so years during which Fine Art Castings issued the figures, an impressive total of over 70 different *Doctor Who* characters were made available.

BBC Video decided to release more *Doctor Who* adventures for purchase by the general public, following their successful debut launch of *Revenge of the Cybermen* in 1983. Unfortunately, all the titles from this period presented edited versions of stories. They did however cover a good range of the series' history, even extending back to the black and white Troughton story *The Seeds of Death* and the Pertwee-era's *Day of the Daleks*. Also included were the highly popular stories *Pyramids of Mars* and *The Robots of Death* from Tom Baker's era.

As well as the BBC, another major contributor to the *Doctor Who* video market was a new company called Reeltime Pictures. This was under the aegis of Keith Barnfather, who had previously spent eight years working at the BBC and Channel 4 before leaving to move into business television production for himself. Reeltime Pictures was set up to provide film and video production facilities for corporate customers and, as Barnfather was also a big fan of *Doctor Who*, he decided to put together some video interviews with the stars of that series.

Thus was born the MythMakers range of tapes, which started in 1984 with Michael Wisher (Davros) and John Leeson (voice of K-9) and, when those were well received, continued with such popular actors as Nicholas Courtney (the Brigadier), Janet Fielding

6 SIXTH DOCTOR

(Tegan) and Nicola Bryant (Peri). Each tape improved on the one before as the range became more ambitious in terms of production values, with location recording introduced and limited scope for visual effects. None of the tapes was ever made solely for profit – they were done primarily for fun, and, as the fans seemed to like them, there seemed no reason to stop as long as their production costs were being covered.

Other items of interest released during the sixth Doctor's era included the incredible Dalek hat (a rather sorry felt construction that fell apart rather quickly); the *Doctor Who The Music 2* record, which followed on from the success of the first release and contained incidental music from stories up to *The Caves of Androzani*; more Who Dares Publishing art prints; and, from the same company, a rather nice book celebrating the *Doctor Who* work of artist Frank Bellamy.

There were two sixth-Doctor artwork jigsaws released by Arrow; a set of *Doctor Who* plates from Royal Doulton; and a rubber playmat produced by Sport and Playbase Ltd, which featured a large panoramic illustration of the sixth Doctor and Peri surrounded by Daleks and Cybermen. (As an interesting side note, the latter product was also issued in a slightly different form for the American market, with the fourth Doctor and Leela replacing the then-current UK equivalents.) There were even two computer games – *The Mines of Terror* (Micro Power Ltd) and *Warlord* (BBC Software) released.

Doctor Who merchandise was still selling well and, despite the apparent slump in the series' television ratings, there was no sign of an end to this boom.

RATINGS

During the Eighties, ratings became less and less reliable as a means of gauging the public's reaction to any given television series. For one thing, they didn't take into account the boom in home video that was occurring in UK, as indeed it was across the world. In the past, viewers had only one chance to see a particular programme (unless it gained a repeat), but with a video recorder, they could happily tape their favourite shows to keep, while watching the more transient but still entertaining fare on the other channels.

Towards the end of Tom Baker's tenure as the Doctor, the ratings dropped alarmingly, going from a maximum of 16.1 million viewers in his penultimate season to 8.3 maximum (and 3.7 minimum) in his last. Through the following three seasons – which included the first Colin Baker story, *The Twin Dilemma*, at the end of the Season 21 – the ratings tended to hover around the somewhat lower 6 to 7 million mark.

The twenty-second season, the first full season for the sixth Doctor, maintained this level, receiving between 6 and 7 million viewers per story on average; however, the return of the programme to Saturday evenings with Season 23 proved disastrous in ratings terms.

The main reason for this is arguably easy to identify: ITV had now established an effective and popular line-up of Saturday evening shows, so by the time *Doctor Who* returned to its traditional slot, there was little impact that it could make against this opposition.

The Saturday evening line-up on BBC for the duration of the twenty-third season was: *Roland Rat – The Series, Doctor Who* and then *The Late, Late Breakfast Show* (for the first ten weeks) or a film (a good example being the family offering *One of Our Dinosaurs is Missing*) or *All Creatures Great and Small*. ITV's viewing for the same time period consisted of: *Blockbusters, The A-Team* and *Blind Date*.

The average ratings (and chart positions) for these programmes at this time were as follows:

Blockbusters	7.8 (Pos 48.8)
The A-Team	11.8 (Pos 13.8)
Blind Date	14.8 (Pos 3.9)
Roland Rat –	unrated (Pos >100)
The Series	
Doctor Who	4.8 (Pos 87.3)
Late Breakfast*	8.0 (Pos 45.4)

*figures include the film and *All Creatures Great And Small.*

As can be seen, *Blind Date* was not only ITV's top-rated show, it was frequently in the top three shows on British television. On some occasions, it was second only in popularity to the BBC's flagship soap opera *EastEnders*, which was pulling in around 21 million viewers. There is no way that *Doctor Who* – or any similar programme, for that matter – could compete with this, and as *Blind Date* followed directly on from *The A-Team*, another high rated show, which started ten minutes before *Doctor Who*, viewers tended to be hooked into to ITV for the whole of the early-evening period. If they videoed *Doctor Who* to watch later, then, as mentioned above, this was not reflected in the ratings.

Doctor Who was also not helped by being placed after *Roland Rat – The Series*, a short-lived puppet show that entered the TV chart only once during Season 23's run, polling 4.8 million viewers and coming 91st in the chart for the week of the final episode of *The Trial of a Time Lord*. As this episode was also the highest-rated *Doctor Who* episode of the season, it could be speculated that the Rat's figures were boosted by viewers waiting to see the climax of the Doctor's trial. It may also be significant that *Blind Date* was not shown on that final Saturday, and whatever was shown in its place did not appear in the TV chart at all.

Another factor contributing to the poor showing of the twenty-third season was that *The Trial of a Time Lord* was one long, fourteen part story. It is possible that viewers who had missed earlier episodes were not too motivated to watch later ones – particularly if they did not realise that there were more-or-less self-contained adventures within the story. Despite the voice-over explanations that preceded all but the first two episodes of the season, anyone coming into the story part-way through would have had a hard job understanding exactly what was going on.

Overall, despite an eighteen month break, supposedly to put the show back on the rails, little was apparently achieved except for dramatically lowering the series' ratings. The press coverage cannot be faulted – there was lots of it – and many commentators had wished for a return to the familiar Saturday evening slot ever since the programme had been moved from it back in 1982.

It certainly looked, at least from the ratings point of view, as though *Doctor Who* might have had its day.

TABLE OF SIXTH DOCTOR EPISODES IN ORDER OF VIEWING FIGURES
(Figures in millions of viewers)

Attack of the Cybermen 1	8.9
Revelation of the Daleks 2	7.7
The Twin Dilemma 1	7.6
Timelash 2	7.4
The Twin Dilemma 2	7.4
Revelation of the Daleks 1	7.4
Mark of the Rani 2	7.3
Vengeance on Varos 1	7.2
Attack of the Cybermen 2	7.2
Vengeance on Varos 2	7.0
The Twin Dilemma 3	7.0
The Two Doctors 3	6.9
Timelash 1	6.7
The Two Doctors 1	6.6
Mark of the Rani 1	6.3
The Twin Dilemma 4	6.3
The Two Doctors 2	6.0
The Trial of a Time Lord 14	5.6
The Trial of a Time Lord 11	5.3
The Trial of a Time Lord 9	5.2
The Trial of a Time Lord 12	5.2
The Trial of a Time Lord 7	5.1
The Trial of a Time Lord 8	5.0
The Trial of a Time Lord 2	4.9
The Trial of a Time Lord 1	4.9
The Trial of a Time Lord 5	4.8
The Trial of a Time Lord 10	4.6
The Trial of a Time Lord 6	4.6
The Trial of a Time Lord 13	4.4
The Trial of a Time Lord 3	3.9
The Trial of a Time Lord 4	3.7

AFTERWORD

The news that Colin Baker would not be returning for the twenty-fourth season of *Doctor Who* was broken to the general public in early December 1986. The press once again took an interest in the series, with the *Sun*'s Charles Catchpole interviewing Baker for a rather sensationalist three-part centre-page special. Fan reaction to Colin Baker's departure was, on the whole, muted. Although there was a widespread feeling that he had been very badly treated, many apparently saw the casting of a new Doctor as a sign of hope for the future and an escape from the troubled times of recent years.

This feeling of a bad time best forgotten has perhaps dissuaded fans from looking back and re-evaluating the eight stories produced during Colin Baker's incumbency. It is often forgotten that Season 22 received an average audience of 7.12 million viewers, with a high appreciation rating. It could be argued that, had Season 23 continued as originally planned, Baker would have settled comfortably into the role of the Doctor and viewers would have become used to this flamboyant portrayal of the Time Lord. It is also interesting to speculate what might have happened with the arrival of a new script editor for Season 24. Under Andrew Cartmel's aegis, the sixth Doctor may have taken on a slightly darker nature, a change in characterisation that Colin Baker has indicated he would have been happy with, had it taken place. In fact, this concept was later taken up by the BBC Film Club in a series of video dramas, produced and directed by Bill Baggs, in which Colin Baker played the Stranger alongside Nicola Bryant's Miss Brown. While having no visible connection – other than the casting – with *Doctor Who*, these tapes presented an interesting counterpoint to Baker's tenure as the Doctor.

It is inevitable to conclude that the eighteen-month hiatus in transmission and the public vilification of the series by the Controller of BBC1, Michael Grade, did immense damage to *Doctor Who*. The changes of scheduling and scripting that were supposed to tackle perceived shortcomings in the series' style and direction and increase its popularity with the general public had precisely the opposite effect, leading to a sharp drop to an average viewing figure of 4.8 million.

It is unfortunate that Colin Baker's departure from the role of the Doctor was the only remaining, and highly visible, action that could be taken to give the viewing public the impression that changes were being made to improve the series for the future. In this way, fan and press attention could be diverted from any other reasons for the falling viewing figures, and instead blame, by implication, the series' lead actor for all its woes. Whether this strategy came about by design or by accident is not known, but it worked.

The beginning of Season 24 saw the arrival of a new Doctor in the earthly form of Sylvester McCoy. As Colin Baker had turned down the option of making a regeneration story, the change-over of Doctors was achieved by McCoy donning a blond, curly wig and lying on the floor of the TARDIS dressed in the sixth Doctor's costume. Baker's understandable decision to bow out when he did meant that the last line delivered by the sixth Doctor on screen was the immortal phrase: "Carrot juice, carrot juice, carrot juice!"

A rather less than fitting epitaph.

6 SIXTH DOCTOR

The Seventh Doctor

by

David J Howe
Stephen James Walker

FOREWORD

The era of the sixth Doctor came to an ignominious end. Colin Baker had been fired by the BBC and producer John Nathan-Turner instructed to cast a new actor to star in the twenty-four-year old series. The problem was that Baker, understandably sore at the treatment he had received, had refused to return simply to record a story in which he would be written out, and so, for the first time in *Doctor Who*'s history, a regeneration had to be achieved without the participation of the outgoing Doctor.

To complicate matters further, the only other regular cast member, Bonnie Langford, was a newcomer, who was still settling into her role as computer programmer and health and fitness fanatic Melanie Bush; and the series' long serving script editor Eric Saward had resigned the previous year following disagreements with Nathan-Turner, leaving that post temporarily vacant.

The actor chosen to take over as the Doctor was Sylvester McCoy. Previously known mainly for children's television work and daredevil comedy stunts – including, famously, stuffing ferrets down his trousers in one particular show – he grasped the opportunity that *Doctor Who* presented him to establish himself in a different kind of role with a higher public profile. For the next three years, the Doctor became a lively fellow with dark wavy hair and a faint Scots accent, sporting a paisley-patterned scarf and a question-mark pullover and brolly. McCoy's was a uniquely different interpretation of the nation's favourite Time Lord. Behind his sometimes clownish façade, this was a more introspected and thoughtful Doctor; a more mysterious Doctor; a Doctor who could take command of a situation with simply a suggestion here and a quiet adjustment there.

In the wider world during McCoy's time as the Doctor, the Archbishop of Canterbury's special envoy, Terry Waite, was kidnapped in Beirut, not to be released until some five years later; a car ferry capsized off Zeebrugge, killing two hundred passengers; Margaret Thatcher was elected for a third term as Prime Minister of the UK; hurricane force winds killed seventeen people and left a £300 million trail of destruction across southern England; and the bottom fell out of the London stock market, wiping ten per cent, or £50 billion pounds, off the value of shares on a day forever to be known as 'black Monday'.

Join us as we revisit the eras of the seventh and eighth Doctors, and bring to an end – at least for the time being – our coverage of the ever developing, ever popular chronicles of that mysterious traveller in space and time known only as the Doctor.

INTRODUCTION

Last year I travelled down to Wiltshire to open a small *Doctor Who* exhibition in a museum in Trowbridge. There were all the usual suspects; beautifully crafted Cybermen models, display cabinets stuffed with well treasured boxed sets of monsters, vehicles, Doctors even. And, guarding the entrance to the exhibition, the most menacing and terrifying creation of the lot – poised at the head of the stairs, lethal weapons pointed towards an unsuspecting Mum and her seven-ish year old son who'd popped up from the shopping centre below to see what all the fuss was about.

As I watched, the boy stopped short, pointed and exclaimed; 'Mum, what are those?' 'Daleks, darling,' she replied, 'They had them on telly when I was your age.'

So there we have it. A whole generation growing up without that knowledge we used to take for granted. As I stood there, musing rather sadly, I started wondering how long it's going to take for the *Doctor Who* references to pass out of popular culture altogether. At least at the moment, we can be assured of the odd mention of the TARDIS or Daleks on afternoon game shows and panel games.

But of course there are the fans. You lot out there who keep *Doctor Who* alive by organising and attending conventions, by writing and reading books such as this one, by supporting magazines, keeping *Doctor Who* on the video shelves, introducing new people to the show … the list is endless. And you're doing it not from a sense of duty or loyalty, though that does come into it somewhere along the line, but because you love this programme and these characters and don't want to see them disappear. There's a growing library full of excellent books like this to remind and inform us. There's a lot of stuff in here that I had no idea about, even after all the trawling through my memory banks for my own book on the subject, *ACE!* All the details you could ever wish for, and a bonus chapter on the eighth Doctor, and hope for the future.

So maybe it's not all doom and gloom. Sylvester and I have recently spent a couple of days working together on a spin off audio project created by one of that band of fans who have grown up to become professional writers, directors, production companies and so on. I wondered how it difficult it would be, almost ten years on, to walk back into the relationship, to remember how it was. I needn't have worried. Something that wasn't quite me and wasn't quite acting took over the moment Sylv and I stood together at the microphone; a voice and an attitude that's not quite mine came back to me, like slipping an arm into a familiar old jacket that has been hanging in the back of a wardrobe for some years, waiting and hoping that one day it'll come back into fashion. It's a bit of a saggy old jacket now, lightly faded from lack of use. But the thing is, it's still there … and the badges are nice and shiny.

Sophie Aldred, 1998

SYLVESTER McCOY: IN HIS OWN WORDS

ON HIS EARLY LIFE AND CAREER:

'[I was born in] Dunoon, Argyll, Scotland, on a rainy day, 20 August in the year of Our Lord 1943 …

'I was a lively little lad. I'm sure there were times when people thought I should have been put in prison, but I didn't get caught! …

'I used to go to Saturday cinema and watch those dreadful but wonderful serials like *Flash Gordon* … I collected jam jars, which were worth a ha'penny each, so I could get in to see *Flash Gordon* for four jam jars. The first horror film I saw was *The Beast with Five Fingers*, which I watched through the buttonhole in the top of my school

mackintosh, because I was so scared. I remember Quatermass too, which terrified me.'
Interviewed by Johnny Black in 1987 for *Starburst* Issue 110.

'I was raised by my grandmother and sometimes my aunt ... My father was killed in the War a couple of months before I was born. He was blown up in a submarine. And my mother subsequently had a nervous breakdown. It lasted ... well, it lasted until the end of her life, really. She died when I was twenty-one. She spent most of her life in hospitals.'
Interviewed by uncredited writer in 1988 for *Whovian Times* Volume 17.

'Being a Catholic, I went to the local Roman Catholic primary school, where we used to have vocational talks from people ... We had a priest one day, and they asked if anybody would like to be one. Three of us put our hands up – me, Danny Sweeney and Mary O'Malley. Naturally Mary wasn't called out, but Danny and I were!

'This had never happened before, and we were sent off post haste to see the priest ... When we got there, Danny lost his bottle. Being a cocky little thing, I knocked on the door and said, "I want to be a priest". Next thing I knew, I was on a train to Aberdeen to study for the priesthood. I got so holy, I had housemaid's knee from praying. At first I wanted to be the Pope, then I decided to be much humbler and become a mere monk. I wrote off to the Dominicans, and they replied, a very encouraging letter. When I left [Aberdeen] they all kneeled down and prayed and praised me as a saint, because no-one had ever left to become something even more hard and harsh, a monk.

'Luckily, when I got home, another letter arrived from the Dominicans saying I was too young to start. I was just fifteen. It was the best thing that ever happened, because I had to cram in some education that year, so I was sent off to the local unisex grammar school, where I discovered those wonderful creatures ... girls. I gave up all thoughts of Popes and monks right away.'
Interviewed by Johnny Black in 1987 for *Starburst* Issue 110.

'I worked in the City of London [for a time. It] was much more Dickensian than it is now. It [was] a very uptight place, especially in the matter of attire ... Once I was a trainee executive in charge of the liaison between the computer and auto insurance. In fact, I was more a trainee alcoholic. It was driving me mad. You see, I didn't know I wanted to be an actor. All I knew was that what I was doing wasn't fulfilling, whatever it was. I was very unhappy in that world. You weren't allowed to take your jacket off on a warm day unless you got permission. I knew that this was madness, lunacy, dictatorial and unfair. It wasn't that we were in an office with people coming in to see us. We were just in an office all together, and there was no air conditioning.'
Interviewed by Lou Anders in 1995 for *Dreamwatch* 17.

'I remember once my grandmother – who is Irish – sitting in the bay window of a lovely house we had near the River Clyde, looking out onto a rainy landscape ... Suddenly, in a mysterious kind of way, she turned to me and said I should become an actor. It came from nowhere, and I thought it was a completely barmy, silly idea. But it was there and it took root, I suppose.

'What then happened was that I was working in London for a company that went bust. I ended up working in the box office of the Roundhouse Theatre, and one day Ken

Campbell came in. He was setting up the Ken Campbell Roadshow with Bob Hoskins and various others, and someone had let him down. Brian Murphy was collecting the tickets I was selling ... Ken went to Brian and said, "I need someone for this wild show starting in the North of England," and Brian said, "Well, ask the guy in the box office – he's completely out of his head!"

'So he came up to me – and in those days I was a hippie with a moustache, long hair, beads, the lot – and he asked me to join the Roadshow. I told him I wasn't an actor, and he said, "Do you want to be?" I said, "Yes," and he said he'd come back on Monday. He did – and I became an actor!'
Interviewed by Richard Marson in 1987 for *Doctor Who Magazine* No. 130.

'It was supposed to be for one night, but I stayed with the Roadshow for two years. We toured all over Europe, Britain and Ireland and Israel too, and it became a bit of a cult on the fringe. I left there and went to Joan Littlewood's theatre workshop at Stratford East and worked with her for a while, then from there I went to Nottingham Playhouse with Richard Eyre ... and I worked with him for two or three years. At the same time, television started for me, and a kind of parallel career went on. It was about sixteen years ago I started as an actor and about twelve years ago I started *Vision On* for the BBC ... Then every year I did another television series: *Jigsaw, Eureka, Tiswas, Starstrider* ...

'So I had two careers going on: one in the theatre, [where I was appearing in productions of] Shakespeare, Beckett [and] Brecht and ... having plays written for me by Adrian Mitchell, Ken Campbell and Ken Hill; [the other] paying for my mortgage in a sense by doing television and children's stuff. I also did *The Last Place on Earth*, which was a very adult piece for television – seven one-hour films about Scott's race to the Antarctic, which we actually filmed in the Arctic. [I did] *Tiny Revolutions* for Granada, which was an adult film about a professor stuck in prison in Czechoslovakia for telling jokes against the state.'
Interviewed by Gary Levy and Robert Cope in 1987 for *DWB* 50.

'[At first] I had no idea what sort of actor I was. But because of the nature of working with Ken Campbell and Bob Hoskins, who are both physical performers, I started doing very physical theatre. Then people would come up to me and say I reminded them of Buster Keaton, Stan Laurel or Charlie Chaplin. So I thought I'd better have a look at the work of the comedy pioneers – and by discovering them, I also discovered my own acting "self".'
Interviewed by Graeme Wood and Andrew Lennard in 1992 for *TV Zone* Special # 4.

'The name I used at first was Kent Smith – part of a very long name I've got. There was another actor in America called Kent Smith, and I always had ambitions beyond my ... rights. I thought perhaps I might do something in America, not realising I'd end up doing *Doctor Who*. Also, I thought Kent Smith was more of a matinee idol name, and I didn't think I was that kind of actor. I was doing a show called *An Evening with Sylvester McCoy, the Human Bomb*, and in it, we wanted the audience to believe that there was this little man who could do all these amazing stunts. So we printed a programme stating, "Sylvester McCoy played by Sylvester McCoy," and it stuck, really. I thought it was quite a good name, so I kept it.'
Interviewed by Paul Travers in 1988 for *Doctor Who Magazine* No. 142.

ON WATCHING EARLIER ERAS OF *DOCTOR WHO*:

'I started watching *Doctor Who* with Patrick Troughton when I was about 20 odd, then I watched it with Jon Pertwee and Tom Baker, but when I became an actor – because of the nature of the job – I got out of the habit of watching series and serials ... You can never follow them, because you are working. I really didn't see Peter Davison very much, or Colin [Baker].'

Interviewed by Gary Levy and Robert Cope in 1987 for *DWB* 50.

ON BEING CAST AS THE DOCTOR:

'It was a role I had wanted for some time. I remember that three years earlier, when Colin Baker got the part, I heard about it a bit too late, but I still thought to myself, "I wish I'd known about that – I'd quite like to have tried for it". So though I wasn't actually pursuing it all the time, it was a role that I fancied doing. Then when I heard on the news that Colin was leaving, I phoned my agent and told him that there was a job going at the BBC ...

'Actually, what happened was that my agent phoned John Nathan-Turner, and immediately he had put the phone down, [a producer named] Clive Doig also came on the line and told John he should take a look at me. Apparently John said, "Wait a minute, are you and his agent in cahoots?"'

Interviewed by Peter Haining in 1988 for *Doctor Who – 25 Glorious Years*.

'I was at the National Theatre doing *The Pied Piper*, which was actually a very good audition part for the Doctor. Then I had a two and a half hour interview with John Nathan-Turner.'

Interviewed by Johnny Black in 1987 for *Starburst* Issue 110.

'It was two and a half hours of charm, because you go into these interviews and try to be charming.

'I don't know what I talked about, but I kept thinking, "I hope this interview finishes soon, or I'll run out of charm" ... I managed to con my way through that one. Then I went back and did another two hour interview, and then I met the Head of Series and Serials, Jonathan Powell, who gave me only five minutes, thank god! They decided that they quite liked my quirkiness and humour, but they weren't sure I had the seriousness and the power to overcome the many enemies that I would meet in my time travels.

'So we did two screen tests – two scenes – and one of those was overpowering the enemy, and I passed that, so they gave me the job.

'Janet Fielding did the test with me, and she'd rehearsed this stuff on another day with me and a few others that were also up for the part, so I had to hang around quite a lot. At first I wasn't too bothered one way or the other, as you go up for a lot of parts, but then I began to think, "Oh my god! They're serious!"'

Interviewed by Richard Marson in 1987 for *Doctor Who Magazine* No. 130.

ON THE DOCTOR'S CHARACTER:

'He's someone who loves the Earth, and therefore humanity. But he is also a very wise man who sees the follies of man – and also those in himself. Those are his strengths. But he also has his weaknesses, which are equally interesting. Take his passion for minutiae, and innocently wandering into dangerous situations that perhaps he should see: maybe does, maybe doesn't. He's also a rebel and doesn't really like authority, which is something I like in him. Because, you know, authority has to prove its worth – just because it *is* authority, it shouldn't be accepted. It should be questioned – and the Doctor does, and it gets him into trouble. He's also a bit of an anarchist as well! There is even a bit of Doctor Johnson in him – you know, one of those people you admire who stand up and say what they think.

'In fact, he is a mixture of all sorts of things, but at his most basic, he loves the Earth. He is a man who should not use violence, I believe, but his wits and his intelligence to get him out of any tight corner.'
Interviewed by Peter Haining in 1988 for *Doctor Who – 25 Glorious Years.*

ON HIS DOCTOR'S COSTUME:
'The hat emerged because I wore one to the interviews. I did wear a hat just like that [in my private life], but I can't now, really. Sad. They wanted the hat, though. I wanted my costume to be the sort of thing that could be seen on the street, and that there was only something strange about when people get close. Not too alien. I've actually worn it in the street in Wales when we were [on location] and people who didn't recognise me or realise what was going on didn't notice anything odd. One guy came up to me and said, "I like your jumper; very nice that. Where did you get it from?" I said my mother had knitted it!'
Interviewed by Richard Marson in 1987 for *Doctor Who Magazine* **No. 130.**

'I knew I wanted a baggy jacket with lots of paraphernalia in the pockets. I think the Doctor should be something of an Edwardian character, like in those wonderful Jules Verne novels ... It was basically a combination of various ideas put forward, and I'm really pleased with it.'
Interviewed by Gary Levy and Robert Cope in 1987 for *DWB* **50.**

'The jumper is based on a 1930s golfing sweater. We did consider the idea of the Doctor wearing glasses – as I normally do – but it was decided that my eyes could be seen better without them. The umbrella with the red question-mark handle was all my own idea.'
Interviewed by Peter Haining in 1988 for *Doctor Who – 25 Glorious Years.*

'I like the pullover, but ... the costume is too loud for my taste. I'd like to tone it down. As for the question-marks, they're a nice motif. I don't know whether it matters. I'd miss the [question-mark handle] umbrella if it went ... but I think the scarf could be darker, and the hatband too. Perhaps the jacket could be brown.'
Interviewed by Paul Travers in 1988 for *Doctor Who Magazine* **No. 142.**

'I personally would have liked to have got rid of the question marks on the jumper. I thought that was a bit too much, but I think the umbrella is all right, because at first people don't actually notice it. The pullover I would have preferred to be just plain. I tried to get rid of it last year, along with the jacket change, but the producer said no, really because it was his idea, and the umbrella was mine, so that was fair enough.'
Interviewed by Mark Attwood in 1990 *DWB* **No. 77.**

SEVENTH DOCTOR

ON *TIME AND THE RANI*:

'I had to dress up in Colin's costume with a silly wig, and I looked like Harpo Marx. I had to lie down on my face and then turn over. For just an instant I did look surprisingly like Colin, and then the picture went all funny and [when] it returned to normal, I was me – much to my horror when I looked in the mirror! ...

'Right from the beginning there was a good feeling both in front of the cameras and behind them. No-one made me feel I was the new boy and had to prove my worth. The director of that first story was Andrew Morgan, who had done my screen test for the series. And because I sensed right from that initial meeting that he was the sort of guy who would give me a chance, it was wonderful to work with him on the first story. It felt almost like coming home, and I said to myself, "Hey, I belong here." It was very funny – I didn't worry. I felt relaxed. I just had to learn my lines and not bump into the monsters!'

Interviewed by Peter Haining in 1988 for *Doctor Who – 25 Glorious Years*.

ON *PARADISE TOWERS*:

'There seemed to be so much to learn in the way of words! The Doctor had so much to say! Most of the speaking was on one set, and because we taped it in sets, rather than in order, I was on that set talking non stop. By the end of it, I was completely bored by the sound of my own voice, and exhausted at having to remember all those words. It wasn't all that enjoyable to do, but when I saw it, it really worked. I was surprised by how well it came across, considering the mountain I had to climb.'

Interviewed by Joe Nazzaro in 1993 for *TV Zone* Special # 11.

ON *DELTA AND THE BANNERMEN*:

'It was a fun story to do, and all the people in it were a great laugh. Nobody was trying to act the star – which some of them had every right to do. I was still a bit of a new boy as the Doctor, but they were very welcoming and good fun to be with ...

'We were [recording a] sequence on a rooftop with explosive charges going off all around me. One of them went off a little too early, and this banged my head a bit, but we were able to keep on. Mind you, with the tight schedules we have, we *had* to – and I suppose that I learned right there and then that the one thing one would like more of on *Doctor Who* is time!'

Interviewed by Peter Haining in 1988 for *Doctor Who – 25 Glorious Years*.

ON *DRAGONFIRE*:

'The bizarre thing was, John Nathan-Turner wanted Bonnie [Langford] to stay on for another two stories in the next season. That way, the first story would have us arriving in the new season, and the next story would be about why Bonnie's character had to leave. Because of her commitments in the theatre, she couldn't say, "I'll give you eight weeks," so she said, "I'll give you four, and do the first story".

'I think John felt, "I don't want to do that with the first story in the twenty-fifth season; having someone leave," so he said, "Maybe you should leave now," and we would start afresh. Originally it was going to be a very quick scene, but I said, "We've got to get more into it". The Doctor had been with this character for two personas, and he was obviously very fond of her, so we should have some sort of goodbye scene.

'I'd done a really lovely goodbye scene with that character for my screen test, which had

been written by the script editor, Andrew Cartmel, and I suggested we use that scene to give it more impact. It seemed terribly curt to just say goodbye.'
Interviewed by Joe Nazzaro in 1993 for *TV Zone* Special # 11.

ON *REMEMBRANCE OF THE DALEKS*:

'I didn't feel as if I were a real Doctor until I'd worked with the Daleks. But it's incredibly difficult to move them around – it's also very boring hanging around waiting for them. The new ones have these great round balls, you know, like under those wheelbarrows, and that made them wobbly Daleks! It's like a big joke. I said I'd like to work with the Daleks because I'd like to find out what was underneath their skirts – and now I've found out, they've got three balls!'
Interviewed by Mark Attwood in 1990 *DWB* No. 77.

ON *THE HAPPINESS PATROL*:

'*The Happiness Patrol* was slightly disappointing, because it was done in studio. I think it was a bit over-ambitious.

'If they've got to do a story in studio, it would be better to do something actually indoors. Trying to create a planet, it obviously doesn't work. You have to suspend a lot of [disbelief], especially as the other stories [in the same season] were so successful at creating wherever we were on location.'
Interviewed by Paul Travers in 1989 for *Doctor Who Magazine* No. 154.

'It was a great story, I thought. Really good. It had the underlying theme against the more extreme Thatcherite policies of our time. It had a neo-fascist feel about it as well. The harmonica music and the sense of longing … It would have been great in black and white. Maybe we should encourage everyone to turn their colour off when they watch it and see what it looks like.'
Interviewed by Nick Briggs in 1994 for *Doctor Who Magazine* No. 216.

ON *SILVER NEMESIS*:

'If you ever see the [American] documentary made [on *Silver Nemesis*] … you'll see me sitting on a table, cross legged, with my hair standing up, having a nervous breakdown. The asbestos scare [at the Television Centre studios] had affected us badly. We only had one and a half days' rehearsal left after *The Greatest Show in the Galaxy* to do the story, and we had to make the documentary on the same day. We were just going potty … I didn't know where I was.'
Interviewed by Mark Wyman in 1989 for *TARDIS*, spring 1989 edition.

ON *THE GREATEST SHOW IN THE GALAXY*:

'We had a very difficult time with *The Greatest Show in the Galaxy* because of the asbestos scare at the BBC – we had to [record the studio scenes in a] tent at Elstree. The cameras broke down, we had to stop every time a car went by or a bird whistled. Amazing.'
Interviewed by Paul Travers in 1988 for *Doctor Who Magazine* No. 142

ON *BATTLEFIELD*:

'To work with Nick [Courtney] was lovely! I've always been a great fan of the Brigadier, ever since I watched it when Patrick Troughton and Jon Pertwee were in it. He's a lovely man, and we got on very well. I'd met him at conventions before, but it's not the same as working with someone.

'Jean Marsh was lovely too! ... They're all lovely! I'm a luvvy now! You know how sometimes you just get on with people? The chemistry was great. She could have stayed in *Doctor Who* forever as far as I was concerned. And James Ellis was a great, big-hearted Irishman with all the charm and warmth of that.'
Interviewed by Nick Briggs in 1994 for *Doctor Who Magazine* No. 216.

ON *GHOST LIGHT*:

'I'm enjoying [making] *Ghost Light*. I don't like doing studio work, but I'm happy [that] this one's set inside a building. It will give it much more [credibility]. It's got a brilliant cast, and it's a good story ... once we work it out!'
Interviewed by Paul Travers in 1989 for *Doctor Who Magazine* No. 154.

ON *THE CURSE OF FENRIC*:

'There was a great moment in *The Curse of Fenric* where Sophie [Aldred] and I ran out of a hut and could literally feel the heat of [an] explosion [set off by] the visual effects guys ... I enjoyed that!'
Interviewed by Graeme Wood and Andrew Lennard in 1992 for *TV Zone* Special # 4.

'It was very well written. It made sense and there weren't too many holes in it. I liked it, because it was about another time. Personally, I liked to travel back in time ... My attraction to *Doctor Who* in the beginning was the fact that we could go back in time. I've always been interested in history, so it was rather nice to go back to the time of World War Two.'
Interviewed by Nick Briggs in 1994 for *Doctor Who Magazine* No. 216.

ON *SURVIVAL*:

'We were filming in the deserts of Dorset. There's a big sandpit in Dorset. Vast thing ... It was over 100 degrees in the heatwave, and it was just like doing a spaghetti Western ... It was incredibly hot and all these girls had to be dressed up in catsuits and all this fun fur stuff; I mean it was just too hot for them! Too unbearably hot. But then again, they were very patient, except for one, who suddenly freaked out and ripped all her clothes off and was last seen running for the train. It was a lovely sight though ...'
Interviewed by Bob Furnell, Bonnie Gale, Misha Lauenstein and Pat Burt on 28 January 1996.

'It was lovely to work with Anthony Ainley. It was interesting finding, in acting terms, that he had a way of playing the character. I kept thinking, "Now he's a Time Lord," and so I tried to act similar to him. As Time Lords, when you go round the universe ... you respond differently to different people. But when you meet your own, there would be that kind of similarity of movement, as well as various other things.'
Interviewed by Paul Travers in 1989 for *Doctor Who Magazine* No. 154.

ON HIS DOCTOR'S COMPANIONS:

'Bonnie [Langford] was a specific type of actress, and she was definitely employed to act against [Colin Baker's] coat. It was so colourful! … You needed a very colourful person there, so there was Bonnie. The pairing was excellent for them, but then I came along. I was a different kettle of fish, and so it wasn't the right kind of pairing. Bonnie and I got on really well, 'cause we're good mates, and we'd worked together before on stage, but it didn't work. It was just the state of play; she didn't have to act against such a colourful coat.'

Interviewed by Darren Floyd, Jeremy Taylor and Huw Griffiths in 1991 for *The Global Times.*

'We are developing the relationship between Ace and [the Doctor] … I don't know in depth about the other Doctor/companion relationships, but this is definitely different from [the] relationship with Ace last year, or the one with Mel. It's deeper; and we have arguments – strong arguments.'

Interviewed by Mark Wyman in 1989 for *TARDIS*, **spring 1989 edition.**

'The companion shouldn't be someone who screams all the time, and shouldn't be the token woman. She should be a fully fledged character in her own right. I'm sure that others have been; I'm just going by my own prejudice of what I thought. Sophie [Aldred] is great, and we're great mates.'

Interviewed by David J Howe, Mark Stammers and Stephen James Walker in 1989 for *The Frame* **No. 11.**

ON HIS DEPARTURE FROM THE SERIES:

'To be very, very honest, when the third year actually came up, I was thinking of jacking it in then, thinking that this is maybe too long. I also had at the back of my mind that Peter Davison had told me that Patrick Troughton had told him: "Only do three years." But then John [Nathan-Turner] said, sometime during the negotiations for the third year, "You must agree to do a fourth term." So I thought, "Okay, I'll do it," and decided to go for it.'

Interviewed by Nick Briggs in 1994 for *Doctor Who Magazine* **No. 216.**

'I was upset at the end of *Doctor Who*, but I think, in a way, the fates have taken charge, so perhaps it's right. Otherwise I might have been tempted to stay on for quite a long time; part of me thinks that would have been a bad thing, another part of me thinks I would have enjoyed it. [For my career] as an actor outside … *Doctor Who*, it's been much better that I did only three short seasons … If I'd stayed for a long time, I might … still be typecast. I don't know yet. I'm not that far away from it.'

Interviewed by Darren Floyd, Jeremy Taylor and Huw Griffiths in 1991 for *The Global Times.*

'It was pretty painful for the first couple of years. I was a bit pissed off, really, at the way it had been handled, which seemed to be unfair, but I got used to it as time went on. You just have to carry on.'

Interviewed by Joe Nazzaro in 1993 for *TV Zone* **Special # 11.**

ON THE PLEASURES OF HIS TIME AS THE DOCTOR:

'I enjoyed working on it very much ... Just for purely acting charms, it's a great role to play. You're asked to call upon all sorts of acting in it, from kind of merry to mad, and all the various things in between ... melancholy and manic and murderous ... and all those various things! It's a terrific role and I had a very happy time. I got on incredibly well with all the technicians and the cameramen and also the production staff. My companions were very good friends. One was an old friend, Bonnie, whom I knew before, and Sophie became a good friend ... I felt that our job as the regulars on the show was to make sure that all the other actors who came to it had a very good time, and as far as I know, everyone did.'

Interviewed by Mike Doran, Andrew Gurudata and Kristian LeBlanc in 1993 for *The Chameleon Circuit* **Issue 15.**

'As we only did five months of the year, I had seven months to go off and do other things. So that made the job even more wonderful, because it afforded me the luxury of experimenting. I went off around England with an Iranian theatre group, doing a play about Iran. Because of the wage from *Doctor Who*, I could afford to find out what it was like working in another culture. And, of course, I went back to the National Theatre and did various other things, plays, and *What's Your Story?* for the BBC.'

Interviewed by Nick Briggs in 1994 for *Doctor Who Magazine* **No. 216.**

ON THE PRESSURES OF HIS TIME AS THE DOCTOR:

'It's exhausting in the studio. The first studio I did was with Kate O'Mara, and ... we were on set from ten thirty in the morning to ten at night, just the two of us doing these scenes. By the end of the day, I couldn't stand up, I was completely shattered!'

Interviewed by Richard Marson in 1987 for *Doctor Who Magazine* **No. 130.**

'I don't like the loss of privacy. I get lots of letters. I find it a terrible responsibility trying to answer them, finding the time. I'm delighted to get them, obviously. My family would have preferred that I hadn't done [the series]. I've been on television for twelve years regularly ... People are used to seeing me in the street and saying hello and all that. But *Doctor Who* had a different effect. People do invade your privacy a great deal.'

Interviewed by Mike Doran, Andrew Gurudata and Kristian LeBlanc in 1993 for *The Chameleon Circuit* **Issue 15.**

ON FAN REACTION TO HIS DOCTOR:

'I was told that there were such things as science-fiction conventions, but that's like saying there are bumps on the moon. I didn't know what they were really. Conventions in Britain at that time were very few and far between. My only knowledge of conventions came from the Laurel and Hardy film *Sons of the Desert*, where they run off; their wives don't want them to go, but they end up at a convention. So I had a sort of comedic view of conventions. I had no idea what they were like. I got the job on Monday, and on Thursday I was flown to Atlanta, and there was a convention. People dressed up as various Doctors, companions and monsters from *Doctor Who*. Such great fun.'

Interviewed by Mike Doran, Andrew Gurudata and Kristian LeBlanc in 1993 for *The Chameleon Circuit* **Issue 15.**

'It amazed me at the beginning. I had no idea. At first I was a bit scared, frightened of it. I didn't quite know how to handle it. Then slowly I've grown to like it. I would miss it now. I mean, at one time I used to go to conventions more out of duty – but also because they took me to parts of the world I'd never been to ... But now, you get to know people and various faces and I look forward to going back to places I've been before and meeting people I've met before – seeing old friends.

'In the early days, there were some bad moments, because some fans ... especially in Britain ... became very critical ... before they'd seen a shot I'd done. In a way, Doctor Who is a strange role, because normally you don't have that comparison. The only other similar kind of roles are Shakespearean roles – you [have people talking about] good Hamlets and ...bad Hamlets, [saying one's] not as good [as another, and so on]. In television you really never have that, but with *Doctor Who* you do. So that was a bit of a problem to deal with at first.'
Interviewed by Bob Furnell, Bonnie Gale, Misha Lauenstein and Pat Burt on 28 January 1996.

'There was a tour I did that was on a ship that went from Florida to Mexico and back. [It was] a wonderful convention. But one of the fans, she got a bit emotional, in fact she was so happy that she didn't want to carry on living, and we had to talk her down from jumping off the side of the boat, because she was just so happy! That was a bit sad really.

'There was [once] an American guy who stood up and said [something like], "Excuse me, Doctor, but when you were in your third persona, what were you thinking when you opened the TARDIS door onto the planet Skaro?" He believed it, obviously. Then someone else stood up and said, "Excuse me, Doctor, now you're so universally famous, are you worried about being shot?" That was quite an interesting question. I just said, "Next question, please," and hid behind a chair!'
Interviewed by Mark Attwood in 1990 *DWB* No. 77.

ON THE 1996 TELEVISION MOVIE:
'It's wonderful. The only piece of the original costume is the hat, and when I put that on, I felt, "Oh I'm wearing this hat again. How good!"...

'They've treated me wonderfully. They've been very good to me – treated me with a great deal of respect, which is nice ...

'There's more time and money to it. It's still very British. The director's British. It's a very calm and happy crew as well, and everyone's very enthusiastic ... What is actually lovely is the Canadian crew, who keep saying, "It's wonderful. We're going to get our names up on BBC Television". That's very lovely. They're really excited about it. So there's a great feeling of excitement and joy, and people are really working hard to make it as good as they can, and I'm mightily impressed by the crew. They've been wonderful.'
Interviewed by Bob Furnell, Bonnie Gale, Misha Lauenstein and Pat Burt on 28 January 1996.

ON THE RELATIVE MERITS OF STAGE, FILM AND TV WORK:
'Theatre [is my favourite]. I'm a show-off. I like live theatre. I like standing on the stage and performing to a lot of people. I enjoy it immensely. I like to feel the instant feedback.

'I like doing film. On the stage you paint with a broad brush, and with a film you paint

with a minute brush, sort of like little Chinese miniatures ... Television I sometimes found a bit odd, because the multicamera shoots are very odd. You never quite know which one you're on, and it's like two mediums married together – theatre and film – which doesn't quite gel.'
Interviewed by Bob Furnell, Bonnie Gale, Misha Lauenstein and Pat Burt on 28 January 1996.

ON HIS HOME LIFE:

'I have a family that I love very much, and [mixing private and professional activities] it's like schizophrenia. It's a very schizophrenic profession, and I'm a very schizophrenic person. Someone once read my palm and they said it was the most schizophrenic palm they'd ever seen. I think that's acting all the different parts. I go home and, though I obviously talk about acting, I try to give as much energy there as when I'm working.

'My wife isn't in the business and doesn't really want to be a part of it. She enjoys the fact that I am ... I'm not looking forward to finding a *Sun* reporter in my dustbin. If I do, I'll stick the lid back on and chain it down. I presume people are going to pry, but if they do, they'll get a poke in the eye, or they'll be told in a very Scottish way where to go. They'll no doubt carry on doing it, though, and I'll just have to learn to live with it.

'As for my other interests, I go out to the theatre a lot, I like ballet and I like films and opera.'
Interviewed by Richard Marson in 1987 for *Doctor Who Magazine* No. 130.

'My wife's name is Agnes. We've been married for fifteen years. We have an eleven year old son whose name is Sam and another boy named Joe, who will be ten in November.'
Interviewed by uncredited writer in 1988 for *Whovian Times* Volume 17.

'I like classical music a lot. But I do enjoy all other sorts of music. The other day, I was sailing up the Thames on a barge, and we stopped at this supposedly boring place called Staines. We went into the square [and] there was an opera on at the Town Hall, so I went to the opera ... Then [after the opera I] came out and went across the road ... into [a] pub where they had heavy metal, and I enjoyed that as well ...

'I watch documentaries [and] the news [on television]. I rarely watch series or comedy shows any more. Films if there is a film on. But I have a secret and terrible addiction I must confess ... I don't want anyone to know about it. I watch *Prisoner: Cell Block H* ... I sit there and roar with laughter. It is *so* bad – I love it.
Interviewed by Bob Furnell, Bonnie Gale, Misha Lauenstein and Pat Burt on 28 January 1996.

ON HIMSELF:

'Sylvester McCoy was born at the height of a Scottish summer, i.e. it was raining, it was cold, it was windy. He came out crying. I can't say he's been crying ever since, but he's been trying to make sure that not too many people around-about him cry too much. He's always felt slightly outside society, as if he was looking in and should be commenting on it. He was quite pleased about that. He was delighted to have eventually ended up as an actor, and agrees very much with the idea that actors should be, like gypsies, buried outside the walls of a city. They should not be allowed to be put in consecrated ground. He's delighted by that fact. He finds society comical, cruel,

interesting, and he's sometimes incredibly critical of it. He doesn't want to become a knight, because then he'd know that he'd really been bought by society.'
Interviewed by Nick Briggs in 1994 for *Doctor Who Magazine* No. 216.

CHARACTER — THE SEVENTH DOCTOR

Unlike when he had overseen the transition from the fourth Doctor to the fifth in 1981, or that from the fifth Doctor to the sixth in 1984, producer John Nathan-Turner had no opportunity to lay careful plans to take *Doctor Who* through the difficult process of the departure of the sixth Doctor and the arrival of the seventh. The unexpected nature of Colin Baker's exit from the role in October 1986 – Michael Grade, the then Controller of BBC1, having instructed Nathan-Turner to dismiss the actor after the completion of work on the series' twenty-third season – meant that arrangements for the casting, characterisation and introduction of the seventh Doctor had to be made between seasons. This was a task that Nathan-Turner had not expected to have to manage himself. He had acceded to his superiors' request to inform Baker of his ousting from the series only on the understanding that he would then be allowed to move on to a different project – something that he had been requesting for some time. On his return from a period of extended leave over the winter, however, he was informed that if he wished to remain on staff at the BBC, he would have to continue as producer for the following season.

The most pressing problem requiring attention at this time was the lack of any suitable scripts lined up for production. Nathan-Turner therefore set about urgently finding a new script editor for the series (the previous one, Eric Saward, having resigned amid controversy) and, in the meantime, contacted Pip and Jane Baker – who had written for the sixth Doctor's era – and asked if they would consider contributing the new Doctor's introductory story. They agreed, and on 22 December 1986 were commissioned to provide the scripts for a four-parter entitled *Strange Matter* (adapted from an earlier, unused storyline).

The fact that a new Doctor was required for the series had been picked up by many actors and actors' agents, who were eager to put forward suggestions. On 18 December 1986, Nathan-Turner was contacted by Sylvester McCoy, whose agent subsequently sent in a photograph and information about his client. 'I had endless lists of possible Doctors,' recalled Nathan-Turner in a 1988 interview for Peter Haining's *Doctor Who – 25 Glorious Years*. 'I also got lots of calls from actors' agents suggesting their clients. It really is a plum job, you see, even with all the demands on both private and public life. One of these calls was from Sylvester McCoy's agent, who suggested that I went to see him at the National Theatre in London where he was appearing in *The Pied Piper*. It was 6 January 1987 [when I went], I remember. I was very impressed with Sylvester's performance and decided to meet him. He later came in to my office and we sat chatting for about two hours. There is this wonderful, natural, eccentric quality about Sylvester. There is a sort of disjointed way that he speaks – the gestures are never quite in the right place at the right moment. I found myself riveted, and quite happy to go on listening to him.' Nathan-Turner also viewed videotapes of some of McCoy's television appearances and was particularly impressed by a Channel 4 interview in which the actor had spoken about himself and his role in *The Pied Piper* and exhibited the same kind of fascinatingly offbeat quality that the producer had noted in his office. He was keen from the outset to give the part to McCoy, but his immediate superior, Head of Series and Serials Jonathan Powell, asked him to cast his net a little wider and to carry out some screen tests.

Nathan-Turner and director Andrew Morgan, who had been assigned to handle *Strange Matter* (later retitled *Time and the Rani*), eventually came up with a short-list of actors, three of whom – including McCoy – were subsequently screen tested, as Powell had requested, on 18 February 1987. This involved them being recorded on the TARDIS set performing two short scenes written by Andrew Cartmel, the new script editor found by Nathan-Turner for the series, and directed by Morgan. Former companion actress Janet Fielding was contracted to act opposite them, playing an evil adversary in one of the scenes and a departing companion in the other. 'I did the tests with Sylvester and some other actors,' explained Nathan-Turner, 'and – with no disrespect to the others – Sylvester was the Doctor I was looking for. I had always envisaged a Troughtonesque quality, and here it was. Mind you, I don't think Sylvester and Pat Troughton are madly similar, but there are little characteristics that are the same. I also wanted somebody who was much smaller than Colin Baker.' In addition, the producer favoured casting a relative unknown. The final decision to go for McCoy was made by Nathan-Turner in consultation with both Powell and Grade. The actor's accession to the role was officially announced by the BBC on Monday 2 March, although news of it had leaked to the press over the previous weekend as Nathan-Turner had made his own announcement in the USA on the Friday.

Nathan-Turner had briefed Pip and Jane Baker when they started work on their story to make the new Doctor a more humorous character than the old one. He also wanted to have him behaving 'semi-normally' by the time he had his first confrontation with his adversary the Rani (in contrast to some previous occasions when the Doctor had been seen to act in a decidedly erratic manner for an extended period following a regeneration). 'We were well into writing the story when we were shown a video of Sylvester McCoy,' revealed the husband-and-wife writing team in a 1988 interview. 'We had to find a) a way of regenerating the Doctor and b) a character for him. John asked for a pre-credits teaser. All of us felt that we couldn't go straight into the story. If we had to regenerate in this way, we needed to start with it, then have a full stop and then start the story. It would have been impossible to open with Sylvester's title sequence otherwise; it would have looked silly.'

The apparent implication of the teaser as seen on screen was that the Doctor's regeneration was precipitated by nothing more serious than a fall from an exercise bike when the TARDIS was attacked in flight by his renegade Time Lord adversary the Rani – although it is possible that far more momentous events had occurred before this, of which the viewer was simply left unaware.

McCoy himself was very much in sympathy with Nathan-Turner's wish to bring a degree of humour into the portrayal of the seventh Doctor – at his initial press conference, he told reporters that he wanted to play the part with 'more zest' as a combination of eccentric scientist figures Magnus Pyke and David Bellamy; as someone who was 'madly interested' in everything he did and would get enthusiastic about tiny things amidst mayhem. He was inspired in part by Patrick Troughton's approach to the role, which he recalled as being predominantly humorous, and was in any case naturally inclined toward taking a comedic approach in his work, having been greatly influenced by figures such as Buster Keaton, Stan Laurel and Max Wall, and having started his acting career in madcap comedy roles in Ken Campbell's Roadshow. 'I said in my [initial] discussion with [John Nathan-Turner] that I wanted to be a very Troughtonesque type of Doctor and have the contrast between the comedy and the seriousness,' he told Gary Levy and Robert Cope in a 1987 interview for *DWB* 50. 'He accepted that, but there was one time where he came in and said it was too comedic in the first rehearsal. I think the first story was a learning process for all of us, because it wasn't written for me, it was written for an unknown Doctor and by people who had only written for Colin. Some of the lines are just pure Colin's lines – you can *hear* Colin saying them.'

The 'learning process' of McCoy gradually finding his feet as the Doctor and the writers coming to reflect and cater for his characterisation in their scripts was something that continued throughout the remainder of the twenty-fourth season. 'The first season was just a hotchpotch, really ...' noted McCoy when interviewed by Mark Wyman for the spring 1989 edition of *TARDIS*. 'The writers didn't know who to write for, and I arrived not really knowing ... Although I'd said at the interview, "This is how I want to play the Doctor," I was just talking off the top of my head. I hadn't seen *Doctor Who* for quite a few years, and the memory I had of it was what I was vaguely selling. When I came to do it, half way through the season I suddenly thought, "Now I know what it's about", but by then it was too late and we could only carry on.'

McCoy was in fact able to have a limited degree of input into the scripting of the Doctor's character as the season progressed, as he told an uncredited writer in a 1988 interview for *Whovian Times* Volume 17: 'When the opportunity presented itself, I was able to make a few changes. Very few, but important things. I was even allowed to add a few scenes. If I believed in it and I was enthusiastic enough about it and could get them enthusiastic about my idea, they would put it in.' Another way in which the actor was able to bring his influence to bear was by placing an interpretation on the script that the writer might not have anticipated. Sometimes, for instance, he would deliver a line much more angrily than might have been expected from its immediate context – an attempt, as he later explained, to evoke memories of William Hartnell's Doctor, whom he had been told was often irascible. On other occasions he would endeavour to suggest hidden depths to the Doctor's character, such as through his adoption of a melancholy tone and faraway look when commenting 'Love has never been known for its rationality' in *Delta and the Bannermen*. It was only when work on Season 24 had been completed, however, that he had the opportunity to get together with the series' production team for a detailed discussion of how the seventh Doctor ought ideally to be portrayed. 'We sat down and chatted between seasons,' he told Wyman, 'and I said, "I want him to be more mysterious – to show the inner side of him. He's not just clear cut." Of course, he may have been all those things before that I wanted him to be, but it wasn't clear in my mind.'

The standard brief on the Doctor's character that the production team made available to prospective writers at this time was relatively minimal, and read as follows:

THE DOCTOR

The DOCTOR is a Time Lord from the planet Gallifrey which is in the constellation of Kasterborous. He possesses two hearts, has a body temperature of sixty degrees Fahrenheit and is over seven centuries in age.

7 SEVENTH DOCTOR

He has the capability of regenerating himself into different appearances – his present form being his seventh guise.

He no longer resides on his own planet due to his boredom with his own super-advanced planet and fellow Time Lords – he roams through time and space in his own personalised ship – the TARDIS.

The DOCTOR himself is not infallible. Part of his appeal is his problem-solving capacity when things go wrong, making do with bits and pieces of electronic gadgetry that just happen to be around.

Cartmel, rather than leaving his writers to rely on these basic notes, preferred to talk through with them the way in which the character ought to be depicted, in line with the discussions that he and Nathan-Turner had had with McCoy. The fruits of these discussions became readily apparent in the transmitted stories. In Season 24, the Doctor had been seen to act – particularly at first – in a quirky, somewhat clownish manner, taking near-slapstick tumbles, playing the spoons (an example of McCoy drawing on his own talents for the role – something that Nathan-Turner was keen to take advantage of) and coming out with scrambled adages and mixed metaphors (an adaptation of his predecessor's trait of offering pertinent – and generally accurate – quotations). In Seasons 25 and 26, however, he was shown to be a far more serious, brooding character. He also appeared more able than in any of his earlier incarnations to influence and control events occurring around him; far from being simply an aimless traveller, doing his best to help the underdog and to fight injustice wherever he encountered it, he was now seen to adopt near-machiavellian strategies in order to achieve his objectives, leaving his new companion Ace to handle the more physical aspects of his battles.

The idea emerged of the Doctor being a master strategist, manoeuvring his adversaries and manipulating his allies like a galactic chess player – literally so in the case of Fenric in *The Curse of Fenric*, although the chess motif was also made explicit in *Silver Nemesis*. In *Remembrance of the Daleks*, there were suggestions that, contrary to previous indications, the Doctor might somehow have been a contemporary of Rassilon and Omega – the legendary founders of Time Lord society. Then, in *Silver Nemesis*, the 17th Century sorceress Lady Peinforte claimed to be in possession of momentous secrets about his past 'from the dark time', although in the event, she never had an opportunity to reveal what these were. There were even hints that some aspects of the Doctor's established history might have been deliberate fabrications on his part.

'[We wanted] to increase the mystery,' confirmed the actor in a 1995 interview conducted by Lou Anders for *Dreamwatch* 17. 'The only way we could do that was to make the audience uncertain of him, to find out whether he was this loveable character or he was dangerous. [I wanted to toy with the viewer,] to actually open up another area, peeling an onion, another layer. You'd been given the Doctor that you'd known for the last twenty odd years, and all the mystery had been stripped from him. In order to create mystery, we had to peel another layer and invent another dimension, as it were. Perhaps he was one of the three creators of Gallifrey, and where would that lead you? Well, into a whole new sphere [that] the writers could go and explore.

'[The change didn't happen overnight.] It was like turning a great ship in the ocean. It takes a long time to turn it round, because the scripts have already been written for the next season and all that stuff. It wasn't until half way through ... the second season that the scripts started to arrive that fitted the Doctor that I wanted to do; and by the third season, we were getting there. [Had the series continued, the Doctor's character would have become] much darker, keeping the comedy all the time, but in layers. This was part of the defence system of the Doctor.'

McCoy also felt that the Doctor should be a non-violent person who solved his problems through the use of his wits and ingenuity. 'It's a combination of unarmed vulnerability and eccentric imagination that makes the Doctor so appealing as he confronts evil,' he asserted in an interview for the 5 October 1988 edition of the *Morning Star*.

In gaining agreement to all these changes, McCoy found an enthusiastic and like-minded ally in Andrew Cartmel. 'He's played a hell of a big part,' he admitted to Wyman. 'It's often instant agreement between us. I'll say, "What about …," and he says, "Yes, what a good idea …" We seem to have agreed a lot … I'm getting a trifle worried now about the lack of humour. I have to find the humour as well, because I think it's very important that he has that kind of "front". Now and again, he opens a door, and behind it there is great, dark foreboding, or mystery, and anger, really. The Doctor has spent nine hundred years travelling around, and seen such destruction; love and wonders too, of course, but all that terrible destruction. So I want to bring that out.'

'We certainly did want to build up the mystery,' commented Cartmel in a 1994 convention interview. 'Having said that, we had no agenda. I think that we did say on several occasions that we wanted the Doctor to be more mysterious and also more powerful, because he didn't seem to be this huge, dangerous, interesting alien, and I think we managed to recapture some of that with Sylvester.'

The non-violent aspect of the Doctor's character was reflected in scenes such as the one at the end of *Remembrance of the Daleks* in which he effectively talked the Dalek Supreme into committing suicide by convincing it that it was the last of its kind still alive; this was substituted for a sequence in Ben Aaronovitch's original script in which the Doctor blasted the Dalek Supreme with a gun in a pastiche of a Western shoot-out.

Interviewed in 1994 by Nicholas Briggs for *Doctor Who Magazine* No. 216, McCoy described how he had hoped to take the development of the character further, had he gone on to make a fourth season as the Doctor:

'I wanted to bring a much darker side to the character – not all the time, but I was enjoying mining this part of the character, you know? The misery that the man, this jolly person, carried around. So that's what the fourth term was going to be about.

'He'd been around for, they told me, nine hundred and fifty years – it kept changing. I thought about my grandmother, who'd lived for one hundred years and three months. She got to one hundred and then decided that was it. In the three months left, she took up alcohol and merrily knocked herself out, went to sleep one night and didn't wake up. She'd never drunk throughout the whole of the rest of her life. But she used to tell me that she was tired; not so much physically tired – she was incredibly fit, with a very sharp brain – but all her friends had died; her immediate family had all gone before her. There was that sadness of old age, the sadness of longevity.

'I found that interesting, because the Doctor had lived for all this time. I thought of [the Biblical figure of] Methusalah (who was supposedly nine hundred and sixty-nine years old) and the Ancient Mariner [in Coleridge's poem]. These people who lived for so long … there was a great sadness in their lives. I thought, that ought to be part of the

Doctor's baggage. He goes through all these experiences, and although time is relative and all those kind of things, I felt we had to feel those nine hundred and fifty years. He'd lost so many companions, some happily, but generally it was tragically. He'd seen so much violence and misery! So I wanted to bring that baggage with me – to be part of what he was carrying.'

The discontinuation of *Doctor Who* as an ongoing BBC series denied McCoy the opportunity of exploring these ideas. The seventh Doctor did however make a brief reappearance in the 1996 *Doctor Who* television movie, giving the actor a chance to fulfil a promise he had made to the series' fans that he would return for a regeneration story if ever he was asked to do so, and thereby help to give his successor a smoother introduction than he himself had had. Interviewed by Bob Furnell, Bonnie Gale, Misha Lauenstein and Pat Burt on 28 January 1996, while in the Canadian city of Vancouver to film his scenes for the movie, he summarised the development of his portrayal of the seventh Doctor over the course of his three seasons in the role:

'Starting up in an incredibly naïve way, not knowing really anything about it, diving in the deep end, relying on my own kind of natural bent towards comedy and then realising what the job was, then trying to work towards getting it, not quite achieving it – because really I needed another season to get where I wanted to. And in a sense I kind of arrogantly wanted to bring it back to a more mysterious, dangerous Doctor – not necessarily evil, but questionable. To get back that mystery. I also wanted … I was very interested in the fact of his longevity. I wanted somehow to start carrying that longevity to the screen … I wanted all that. [I wanted to make him darker, but to keep] the comic facade. You know, that kind of Patrick Troughtonesque quality. My first Doctor was Patrick Troughton, and I always remembered him as light and amusing and still at the same time having the ability to switch back and forth. That was the idea. I don't know if I really ever achieved that, but that's what I wanted. I thought [that] *Ghost Light* [had] the best written part for the Doctor. It didn't work on the screen – *Ghost Light* was a bit confusing, you have to read the book to understand what's happening – but I liked what the writer had done for the Doctor … That was really good. I thought, "Oh good! This is how I want to play him. These are the words I want to say."'

REWRITING THE MYTH

In the era of the seventh Doctor, the main developments related to the character of the Doctor himself. The revelations were relatively minor to start with. In *Time and the Rani*, the Doctor's age was stated to be 953 – the same as the Rani's. The last mention of his age, in the previous year's *The Trial of a Time Lord*, had put it at 900, but this sort of discrepancy was nothing new: wildly different figures had been quoted during the course of the series' history. More remarkable was the fact that no real explanation was provided on this occasion for the Doctor's change of appearance, the viewer being left to assume that it was brought on as a consequence of the Rani's attack on the TARDIS.

The new Doctor seems to experience far less post-regeneration trauma than on previous occasions. The situation is complicated by the fact that the Rani drugs him in order to increase his confusion, but nevertheless he instantly recognises his adversary and is immediately on the alert – even if he promptly trips over and performs an impressive pratfall in her laboratory. When the effects of the Rani's drug wear off, he seems stable and fully in control.

Certain aspects of the seventh Doctor's character do, however, seem somewhat at odds with what has gone before. During his visit to Paradise Towers, for example, he seems to have no qualms about killing Kroagnon by pushing him into a mined storeroom (although in the event this task falls to the young man Pex). It is hard to imagine any of the other Doctors, except possibly the sixth, taking such an active part in the destruction of a life-form, no matter how hostile. In *Delta and the Bannermen*, he appears not overly upset at the death of Gavrok – in fact he seems more pleased that Gavrok's trap around the TARDIS has been drained of energy as a result. In *Remembrance of the Daleks*, he blows up a Dalek and deliberately goads Davros into destroying Skaro, and similarly, in *Silver Nemesis*, he arranges for Nemesis to wipe out the Cybermen's fleet in space. In the Dalek story he also tells Ace that lives must sometimes be sacrificed for the greater good, suggesting that his justification for his actions is that the end justifies the means – a philosophy rejected by his earlier incarnations.

These glimpses of a darker side to the Doctor's nature coincide with a deepening of the mystery surrounding the character – a considered policy on the part of the series' production team. In *Remembrance of the Daleks*, the idea is introduced that when the first Doctor came to Earth with his grand-daughter Susan in 1963, he brought with him the Hand of Omega, a remote stellar manipulator device used by Omega – one of the legendary founders of Time Lord society – to detonate stars. Quite how he came by this device is left unexplained, but he is seen to be in total command of it. (It is this that he ultimately uses to bring about the destruction of Skaro.)

There are however a number of apparent inconsistencies between the events of this story and those of the first ever *Doctor Who* episode, *100,000 BC: An Unearthly Child*. A book about the French Revolution is seen lying in the science lab at Coal Hill School, but it looks quite different from the one on the same subject that was lent to Susan by history teacher Barbara Wright, and the latter book was not left in the science lab. A possible explanation for this is that it is simply a different book, and that its presence is a complete coincidence. More difficult to explain away, however, is the fact that the junkyard at Totter's Lane also looks somewhat different this time around. Quite apart from anything else, the owner's name on the entrance gates is spelt differently – in *An Unearthly Child* it was 'I M Foreman', here it is 'I M Forman'. Then there is a scene in which a television announcer is heard to introduce a new science-fiction series on BBC television. Nothing unusual in this – except that the time is stated to be 5.15 in the afternoon, and yet it is still light outside, whereas if this really is November – and a calendar seen on the wall of the café visited by the Doctor and Ace seems to confirm that it is – it should be dark by this time. More interesting still is the strong implication that the series about to start is actually called *Doctor Who*.

One way to rationalise all these apparent quirks is to assume that the action of *Remembrance of the Daleks* takes place in some kind of parallel universe where it is indeed light on November evenings in England, Davros is the Dalek Emperor and the Doctor is a contemporary of Rassilon and Omega, rather than – as implied in previous stories such as season ten's *The Three Doctors* and season fourteen's *The Deadly Assassin* – from a later era of Time Lord history.

The question of the Doctor's origins is further explored in *Silver Nemesis*, when it is hinted that he might not even be a Time Lord after all, or perhaps not *just* a Time Lord (a suggestion also contained in dialogue recorded for *Remembrance of the Daleks* but edited out before transmission). How and why the metal validium fell to Earth in the first place remains unclear, but the viewer learns that after Lady Peinforte fashioned it into a statue of herself, the Doctor was on hand to send it back out into space. It transpires that validium was created by Rassilon and Omega as the ultimate defence for Gallifrey in the 'dark time', and that while in Peinforte's possession, it told her secrets about the Doctor. What exactly those secrets are, however, is not revealed.

'We all knew that there was a mystery as to who exactly the Doctor was,' noted Ben Aaronovitch, the writer of *Remembrance of the Daleks*, in a 1994 convention interview, 'but we all had different ideas about what it was, so that it remained a mystery. I remember that Kevin Clarke [who scripted *Silver Nemesis*] had a completely different idea as to who the Doctor was, and he wasn't telling! So there were two objectives for me: to get more mystery back, and to get the kids back behind the sofa.'

The idea of the Doctor being 'the Other', a mysterious figure associated with Rassilon and Omega, was indeed one of those discussed by script editor Andrew Cartmel and his writers (and ultimately featured in Aaronovitch's novelisation of *Remembrance of the Daleks*), although at least one of the writers, Marc Platt, took the view that 'the Other' was actually a completely different character. Further, arguably more outlandish, ideas considered at one time or another included the Doctor being twice-born (first as a contemporary of Rassilon, then again in his Hartnell incarnation); being more insane than his adversaries; and even being a Christ figure (the idea particularly favoured by Clarke). As scripted, *Survival* had the Doctor explicitly confirming to his old adversary the Master that he had evolved into something more than just a Time Lord (tying in with the loose theme of evolution that had run through the last three stories of the twenty-sixth season). This however was vetoed by John Nathan-Turner and did not feature in the transmitted story. 'Andrew and the writers had all sorts of sensational revelations as to who the Doctor was,' recalled the producer in 1996 in the book *Ace! The Inside Story of the End of an Era* by Sophie Aldred and Mike Tucker, 'none of which I was prepared to entertain. I was prepared to accept the odd hint, but originally it was spelt out. I think that you have to be very careful with what you say to an audience, especially an impressionable one, and I felt that what Andrew and the writers were going to do went totally against making the Doctor more mysterious.' On screen references to the Doctor's mysterious origins were consequently confined to occasional hints and suggestions.

The idea of the Doctor having had untelevised adventures was nothing new for the series; many references to such adventures had been made in the past, often in the form of throwaway remarks about meetings between the Doctor and famous historical figures. In the McCoy era, however, this plot device took on a particular importance. As well as the revelation of the earlier encounter with Lady Peinforte, there are references to the Doctor's hiding of the Hand of Omega on Earth, past battles with the Gods of Ragnarok (*The Greatest Show in the Galaxy*) and Fenric (*The Curse of Fenric*) and a future encounter with the witch Morgaine in an alternate dimension wherein he poses as Merlin and sides with King Arthur (*Battlefield*).

The Doctor during this incarnation is also revealed to have some hitherto unsuspected talents. He is seen to be a consummate magician and acrobat, able to entertain the three demanding Gods of Ragnarok for some time with a seemingly endless succession of conjuring, manipulation and escapology tricks. He is also seen to be able to incapacitate foes with his fingers, apparently transmitting some form of energy to make them sleep (although this could just be a different utilisation of Venusian akido skills that have lain dormant since his third incarnation). More significantly, he is frequently shown to have a degree of foreknowledge about the situations into which he arrives, as in *Remembrance of the Daleks, Silver Nemesis, The Greatest Show in the Galaxy, Battlefield, Ghost Light* and *The Curse of Fenric*. He tends to keep this information to himself, however, leaving Ace – and anyone else unlucky enough to be around – to get caught up in events and learn from the experience.

'This version of the Doctor, I have a lot more respect for him,' Cartmel told interviewer David Bishop in 1994 for *TSV* 40. 'I always hated it when he was zapped on the head or knocked unconscious and tied up. I always thought that was demeaning to him. If he does get tied up, it should be that it was his plan all along ... It all goes back to "Doctor who?" The mysterious, scary, powerful Doctor ... It struck me this was the most interesting way to do the show. You could crack on and do some really exciting television.'

These moves toward restoring some mystery to the Doctor's character went hand in hand with a conscious policy on Cartmel's part, already evident in Season 24, to eschew the continuity-heavy approach of the sixth Doctor's era, in which every story had relied to a greater or lesser extent on the series' established mythology. 'We had a conscious junking of the mythology,' confirmed writer Stephen Wyatt in a 1989 interview conducted by Joe Nazarro for *Doctor Who Magazine*. 'Let's forget about the Master; let's forget about the Time Lords; let's get back to the original idea, which was [that the Doctor was an explorer in] outer space ... There was a clean sweep. [My story] *Paradise Towers* had no cross references whatsoever to any previous *Doctor Who* adventures or characters, and that was quite a conscious decision.'

Given this approach, it is perhaps not surprising that few stories of the McCoy era add anything to the viewer's knowledge of other previously established elements of the series' mythology. The exceptions to the rule are *Remembrance of the Daleks, Silver Nemesis* and *Survival*.

In *Remembrance of the Daleks*, it is revealed that there are, at this time, two rival factions of Daleks: renegades who report to the Black Dalek – otherwise known as the Dalek Supreme – and imperial Daleks who report to the Emperor. They can control human subjects through the use of electronic implants located behind the ear – perhaps a refinement of the Roboman technology previously seen in *The Dalek Invasion of Earth*. It is also explained that the two factions of Dalek creatures are physically different from each other. The imperial Daleks have proper limbs and are fitted with cyborg attachments, whereas the renegade Daleks are little more than blobs with vestigial limbs.

The major revelation, however, is that the Dalek Emperor is none other than Davros, now reduced to little more than a Dalek himself (an idea suggested to Aaronovitch by visual effects assistant Mike Tucker). The Emperor had not previously been seen in this form in the series, although it had appeared in season four's *The Evil of the Daleks* as a static creature housed in and linked to the Dalek city on Skaro. No explanation is provided as to how Davros managed to 'become' the Emperor following his capture by the Daleks loyal to the Dalek Supreme at the conclusion of Season 22's *Revelation of the Daleks*, but the splitting of the race into two rival factions is consistent with the events of that story (in which Davros's Daleks had the same cream and gold livery as the

7 SEVENTH DOCTOR

imperial Daleks in *Remembrance of the Daleks*) and also with those of Season 21's *Resurrection of the Daleks*. It is also quite understandable that the imperial Daleks are more genetically advanced than the renegades, as Davros would no doubt have been continuing his experiments to make them ever more ruthless and efficient.

Another major development in this story is the destruction of Skaro's sun, and with it, Skaro itself, by the Hand of Omega. No time frame is given for this, however, and a Dalek at one point announces that the Hand is entering Skaro's time zone, which might perhaps be taken to imply that it occurs in the very far future.

One well-remembered aspect of *Remembrance of the Daleks* is the scene at the end of Part One in which a Dalek is seen, for the first time, to ascend a flight of stairs. This did not constitute a particularly major development in the series' mythology, however, as even as far back as Season 2's *The Chase: Journey into Terror* it had been implied that this was within the creatures' capabilities, and Season 22's *Revelation of the Daleks* had actually shown that both the Daleks and Davros could hover above the ground.

Earlier stories had been inconsistent in their indications of the Daleks' vulnerability to attack. In Season 9's *Day of the Daleks*, for example, the creatures had seemed impervious to anything that UNIT troops could throw at them, but in Season 11's *Death to the Daleks* one of them had burst into flames on being attacked by spear-wielding Exxilons. *Remembrance of the Daleks* places them at the more vulnerable end of the spectrum, as they are destroyed by Ace's augmented baseball bat and home-made nitro-9 explosives as well as by rockets fired at them from military rocket launchers.

The implied vulnerability of the Daleks is nothing, however, to that of the Cybermen in *Silver Nemesis*. It was well established in *Revenge of the Cybermen* and *Earthshock* that the forcing of gold dust into the Cybermen's chest units could suffocate them by coating their respiratory systems. Here, however, the creatures seem to have an aversion to gold in any form (as vampires have an aversion to garlic, perhaps), and a number of them are destroyed by gold-tipped arrows and by gold coins fired into their chest units by means of a catapult. Paradoxically, however, the Cyber Leader actually survives having a handful of gold dust thrown into his chest unit.

Toward the end of *Silver Nemesis*, the Doctor arranges for the Nemesis statue to destroy the Cyber fleet, which – as hints have been given throughout the story that this is their last remaining force – could be taken to imply that this is the final end of the Cybermen, or at least that they are subsequently reduced to isolated groups scavenging space, as suggested in *Revenge of the Cybermen*.

The final revelations of the McCoy era occur in *Survival*, when the Doctor and the Master become trapped on the dying planet of the cheetah people. The Master has succumbed to the planet's influence and started to transform into a cheetah person himself. It is established that the only way off the planet is for someone affected in this way to lead others back to his or her home world; thus is Ace able to lead the Doctor and her friends back to Earth at one point. At the end of the story, however, as the Master prepares to deal him a killing blow, the Doctor manages somehow to transport himself to Earth. If one supposes that he too has become 'infected' by the planet, this raises the question why he did not return to Gallifrey or perhaps to the TARDIS interior – the only other place that he could legitimately call 'home' – rather than to Earth. Perhaps, though, the answer is something more fundamental; something unique to the Doctor that links him with Earth in a manner previously undisclosed …

PRODUCTION DEVELOPMENT

John Nathan-Turner had not expected to remain as *Doctor Who*'s producer for the seventh Doctor's debut season – his seventh in that capacity. He was asked to do so by his BBC superiors only at the eleventh hour, and agreed with considerable reluctance. He consequently had less time to prepare for this season than for any other that he had worked on, and matters were not helped by the fact that he had to find not only a new lead actor but also a new script editor for the series. 'With regard to the latter,' he recalled in 1996 in *Doctor Who Magazine* Issue 246, 'I had a stroke of luck. Richard Wakely ... [an agent] I had known from the moment I arrived in London ... asked me to meet a young man called Andrew Cartmel, which I duly did, and found him bursting with many ideas and, indeed, firm opinions about the show. Although we didn't always agree, we instantly struck up a rapport – which I do think is a good sign. I invited Andrew to join the team, and I have never regretted it.'

Cartmel had previously been working for a computer company in Cambridge, but had also attended some workshops at the BBC's Television Drama Script Unit and been taken on as a client by Wakely on the strength of some unproduced scripts that he had written. 'The reason John gave me the job was that we got along,' he said in a 1994 interview conducted by David Bishop for *TSV* 40, 'and I didn't impress him as being an idiot. He'd read a script of mine, and obviously saw qualities in there [demonstrating] that I knew what a good TV script should be.'

Pip and Jane Baker had already been asked by Nathan-Turner to write the season opener, *Time and the Rani*, but Cartmel disliked their approach and found the development of the scripts problematic. To provide the other three stories required to make up the fourteen episode run, he commissioned new writers whose way of thinking was more in tune with his own. One of these, Stephen Wyatt, had contacted the production office and been recommended to him by Nathan-Turner (who had had some discussions with him the previous year when the series was temporarily without a script editor) but the other two, Malcolm Kohll and Ian Briggs, were contacts of his from his time at the Script Unit.

Cartmel was a big fan of contemporary comics, and was keen to bring that influence to *Doctor Who*. Collections of Alan Moore's *Halo Jones* stories from *2,000 AD* consequently became virtually required reading for prospective *Doctor Who* writers. 'Alan Moore's *Halo Jones* showed me you didn't have to write comics in a stylised way,' Cartmel told interviewer Tim Robins in 1991 for *The Frame* No. 19. 'You could actually explore interesting aspects of a character's personality.' Another suggestion the script editor frequently made to writers unfamiliar with the series was that they read the 1983 media studies book *Doctor Who – The Unfolding Text* by John Tulloch and Manuel Alvarado. Nathan-Turner meanwhile had decided that, with the series now reduced to only fourteen episodes per season on a permanent basis, a varied mix of stories should be maintained by subdividing each season into two four-parters and two three-parters in a 'traditional-bizarre-kooky-traditional' pattern, with writers selected to fit these styles according to their perceived strengths.

A significant constraint on the production team at this time was pressure from their superiors to avoid the inclusion of any overtly violent or adult content in the stories – a continuing legacy of the controversy that had surrounded the series during the sixth Doctor's era, when it had at one point been taken off the air for eighteen months. 'My basic idea was that I wanted the show to be quite dark and scary,' recalled Cartmel in a 1994 convention interview. 'When I went in to talk to the Head of Drama, one of the first things that he asked me was, "Who is *Doctor Who* for?" I said that it was for everyone – a diplomat's answer – but he said, "No, it's for children." I nodded, but thought, "No it isn't." I never thought that it should be a show that children shouldn't be able to watch, but I thought it should be an adult [show] that was accessible to children.'

Season 24 as it eventually reached the screen had a relatively light, whimsical quality. This, coupled with an avoidance of naturalism in the production and the casting of numerous well-known comedy and light entertainment performers in guest roles, resulted in it coming under fire in sections of the fan press as a further move toward what some saw as a 'pantomime' style of drama in *Doctor Who*. Cartmel found these criticisms misplaced, as he explained to Bishop:

'If we could have just brought the lighting right down, and got really imaginative, moody lighting, I think the whole pantomime thing would have evaporated. That bright, artificial lighting gives a brashness and a lack of depth. That's what made it look like a pantomime. Shooting on video really doesn't help.

'A lot of the problem with *Doctor Who* is that people will say that they don't like a story, the writing is crap, when what they actually mean is that the studio lighting is bad. Frequently the reasons that stories didn't work related to the costumes or the lighting, but fans don't analyse it that way.'

One aspect of the twenty-fourth season that came under particular fire from critics was Bonnie Langford's larger-than-life performance as Mel. Nathan-Turner, speaking to Peter Haining for his book *Doctor Who – 25 Glorious Years*, defended the actress's contribution: 'Bonnie helped bridge the change-over of Doctors very well. She established a very good relationship with Sylvester; they got on extremely well. Actually, they had worked together before on the stage in *The Pirates of Penzance*. I know there are those who love Bonnie or hate her, but to my mind that is the mark of somebody who is making an impact. I think she has been very good for *Doctor Who*.'

Langford had told Nathan-Turner at the start of 1987 that she would probably want to bow out of the series at some point during the course of the season. The production team decided in view of this to keep their options open by ensuring that the last two stories – the ones written by Kohll and Briggs – each featured a character who could if necessary succeed Mel as the Doctor's companion. There were practical considerations to this as well, as initially it was uncertain in which order the two stories would be transmitted. The potential companion character in Kohll's story, *Delta and the Bannermen*, was Ray, played by Sara Griffiths; that in Briggs's, *Dragonfire*, was Ace, played by Sophie Aldred. Cartmel was particularly keen to ensure that the new companion would be a strong and independent young woman: 'We were going for that sort of sisters-are-doing-it-for-themselves kind of thing, which was not Bonnie,' he told Bishop. 'We wanted a post-*Alien* teenage girl.' Ace was a refined version of just such a character, originally called Alf, for whom Nathan-Turner and Cartmel had drafted a rough description dated 26 January 1987, and it was she who was eventually kept on as a regular. A new character outline for Ace was prepared in August 1987 in view of her confirmed status as a companion, and a more detailed set of notes on her character and background were put together by Briggs two months later for inclusion in the guide supplied to prospective writers for the series. The latter read as follows:

Notes on the character ACE

Name: 'Ace' is her nickname. She's ashamed of her real name, and only told Mel in a moment of intimacy. (I feel that she would only ever tell another girl; not a man or a boy – probably not even the Doctor.) Her real name is Dorothy. I didn't specify a surname; it can be either the surname of Dorothy in *The Wizard of Oz*, or something that works in the context of the story it appears in – or, more likely, she'll just avoid the question and keep it secret.

Age: At the point of her appearance in *Dragonfire*, she was meant to be 16 years and 11 months. In fact, she's based on three girls I know, all of whom are 14, so she has the personality and maturity of a young (rather than middling) teenager.

Home: She comes from Perivale, which she regards as the pits of London. As far as she's concerned, the only good thing about Perivale is that it has two tube stations! (One of the girls she's based on actually said this while watching a recording.)

Family: She doesn't have any brothers or sisters. If she did, she'd have mentioned them in her intimate speech with Mel. Besides, she's too much of a loner inside. She didn't get on with her parents, and she gets angry simply at the mention of them. Sometimes she refuses to accept that she even has any parents; at other times she wants to believe that her 'real' parents – the kind, loving ones – are somewhere else, maybe on another planet. But however bad a picture she paints of them, the truth is that her parents are an ordinary middle-class couple who always kept their feelings hidden, and didn't know how to cope with their tearaway daughter.

School: She enjoyed chemistry and was taking it at A-level – although she would probably have failed because she isn't the academic type. She got suspended from school when she blew up the art room.

History: While she was at school she also had a boring evening job working in a fast-food cafeteria. She also used to do experiments with explosives in her bedroom, and it was an accident with one of these that triggered a time storm and carried her to Ice World – where she again found work as a waitress.

Speech: She uses phrases typical of London teenagers: 'Wicked!', 'Well worth!', 'Naff!', and of course 'Ace!'. I don't care if, technically, she left Perivale in early 1987, and so ought still to be using the phrases of that period; the more current and realistic her speech, the better. She coins nicknames for everybody, such as 'Doughnut' for Mel, and 'Bilgebag' for Glitz. And even though it irritates the Doctor, she can't help calling him 'Professor'. The only time she reverts to using real names is when she's frightened, as when Kane was holding her hostage in *Dragonfire*.

Personality: Typical teenager really. Bright and full of life one moment, spiky and argumentative the next. Even though she likes the Doctor, she's bound to come over all moody and complaining with him from time to time. A particular characteristic is her heightened sense of excitement, which sometimes overrides her sense of danger: her immediate reaction on first seeing the Creature in *Dragonfire* was to yell with delight, and only later did she think to run like hell!

The urgency with which stories had been required to be commissioned for the twenty-fourth season had left Cartmel with little time for reflection. In preparing for the twenty-fifth, however, he was able to take a more considered approach. Acting on a fan's recommendation, he viewed a number of highly-regarded stories from *Doctor Who*'s past, including Season 13's *The Seeds of Doom* and Season 14's *The Talons of Weng-Chiang*, and formed the view that the essentially serious and dramatic style of earlier eras had been rather more effective than the relatively light-hearted and comedic one that had prevailed during McCoy's first season. He discussed this with Nathan-Turner, and they decided that the departure of the somewhat lightweight Mel and the arrival of the strong, streetwise Ace should mark the start of a more general shift back toward that more serious and dramatic approach. There would also be a return to a more naturalistic style of production and an increased emphasis on social comment, both overt (such as in *Remembrance of the Daleks*, with its fascist characters in Sixties London and a scene in which Ace discovers a 'No Coloureds' sign in the window of the guest house where she is staying) and allegorical (such as in *The Happiness Patrol*, with its thinly veiled attack on Thatcherism).

Another move that Cartmel was keen to make, in keeping with McCoy's own wishes, was to introduce a greater degree of mystery into the Doctor's character. He felt that over the years, there had been too much revealed about the initially enigmatic time traveller's background, and that this had considerably lessened the appeal of the character. With Nathan-Turner's approval, he therefore briefed the writers of the twenty-fifth season to include in their stories some elements casting doubt on aspects of the Doctor's established history and on the true nature of his character.

Season 25 was also notable for the high degree of emphasis that it saw being placed on Ace. In the past, it had often been the case that the companion characters had suffered from a lack of development after their initial introduction, but Ace by contrast came to take on an increasingly prominent role. McCoy, interviewed by Paul Travers in 1989 for *Doctor Who Magazine* No. 154, explained how this had come about:

'When we chatted between seasons, I thought it would be good for Ace to be educated between adventures. I would be educating her, pointing things out. Each time we got to a story, she would arrive with new knowledge …

'It was a good idea, and the writers went further, and John Nathan-Turner too. They decided the Doctor was trying to make her get over her fears, her weaknesses. The

Doctor, in a very back-handed and subtle way, is trying to put Ace straight, so that eventually, if he does leave her, she'll come back and be Prime Minister ...!'

Cartmel continued for this season to pursue a policy of commissioning enthusiastic young writers who were new to the series and had little or no previous TV experience; something in which he again had Nathan-Turner's full support, as the producer told *Doctor Who Magazine*:

'I think that the new writers that we have encouraged, whether they're experienced or not, are bringing fresh ideas. They challenge the system, and by the system I include myself.

'We have a phrase here: *Who*ed out. Writers get *Who*ed out, they start going over the same territory. We really needed to get a new band of writers, and, as I've been here a long time, it's more challenging and stimulating to have people say "why not?"'

The newcomers this time were Ben Aaronovitch, who had come to Cartmel's attention when fellow BBC script editor Caroline Oulton had passed on to him a script that he had written; Graeme Curry, who contacted the production office after winning a screenplay competition with a play called *Over the Moon*, later adapted for BBC Radio 4; and Kevin Clarke, who was approached by Cartmel on the strength of a script he had written for a series called *Wish Me Luck*. The remaining story was provided by Stephen Wyatt.

Nathan-Turner had been content to remain as *Doctor Who*'s producer for the 25th anniversary season but had again asked his BBC superiors to make this his last year on the series. They refused this request and persuaded him to stay on for Season 26. Cartmel also remained on the series, for his third year as script editor.

This season continued to show the Doctor acting in an increasingly enigmatic light, manipulating events from the background rather than taking centre stage. Even his costume was changed to reflect the darker quality emerging in McCoy's characterisation; his previous, light coloured jacket was swapped for an identical, dark brown one, and his tie and hat band were similarly exchanged for darker versions. Ace, meanwhile, was accorded an ever greater share of the action. She in fact turned out to be effectively the pivotal character in three of the season's four stories, and Sophie Aldred was given an early opportunity to talk to the writers about the development of the part. This was a consequence of Cartmel's preferred approach of working with his writers as a team and involving them more closely in the production than would normally have been the case in the past. Ben Aaronovitch was particularly heavily involved in the development of the season, acting almost as an unofficial assistant script editor, and in addition contributed its first story. Ian Briggs was also commissioned to provide a further story, but the other two writers for the season were again newcomers. Marc Platt had been a long-time fan of the series who had been submitting story ideas to the production office since Robert Holmes's time as script editor in the mid-Seventies; Rona Munro was an up-and-coming writer who had met Cartmel when attending a training seminar at which he was a speaker and had been invited by him to send in some ideas.

The very positive reception given to Season 26 by fan critics suggests that the process of experimentation and development that had taken place during the McCoy years had resulted in the refinement of a highly effective new style for *Doctor Who*, and one that had just started to bear fruit at the point when the series was taken off the air by the BBC. How that achievement would have been capitalised upon in the planned twenty-seventh season, and what other developments would have lain in store, can only remain matters for speculation.

FROM SCRIPT TO SCREEN: DRAGONFIRE

Introduction

This chapter presents an in-depth look at just one of the seventh Doctor's stories – *Dragonfire*. In doing so, it reveals the process of making *Doctor Who* at this point in the series' history and – a factor common to every story – some of the behind-the-scenes discussions and thought which go into a production.

The Scripts

Writer Ian Briggs had been approached to contribute to the series by script editor Andrew Cartmel, whom he had met some months earlier at a writers' workshop at the BBC's Television Drama Script Unit. He had started his career in the theatre after studying drama at Manchester University, and had found work as a script reader – not only for the BBC but also for the Royal Court and some film companies – after several years spent as a theatre lighting and set designer and occasional actor.

Briggs's first idea, submitted in January 1987, was rejected by Cartmel, as the writer admitted to Paul Travers in a 1989 interview for *Doctor Who Magazine*: 'He read it, said it was rubbish, so I started again.' His second attempt – which had the working title *Absolute Zero* and then, when this was deemed too pretentious, *Pyramid in Space* – was judged more promising. 'The first one I'd written had been very old-fashioned, very clichéd SF. After Andrew rejected it, we'd sat down and talked about exactly what he was after, based on [the] new style he'd brought in. *Pyramid in Space* was close, but it went too far. It was too zany, too cartoonish ... A disgusting 14 year old boy who's a financial genius, running [a] huge business empire with an obsequious sidekick called Mr Spewey! Brilliant stuff, but perhaps not *Doctor Who* ... But there were some good ideas in it; the idea of [a] creature living in the cold and itself being the treasure that everyone was hunting for. We hung onto that and constructed another story around it, which was much more serious.'

This more refined idea, which involved a huge pyramid floating through space with a strange creature roaming around its ventilation system, was developed into a detailed storyline bearing the revised working title *The Pyramid's Treasure*. This was commissioned on 9 March 1987, completed on 17 March, delivered on 23 March and formally accepted on 30 March.

The Pyramid's Treasure tells of a villain called Hess, 'whose body temperature is -250° C', running a frozen goods trading centre from a planet-sized pyramid in orbit around a larger planet. The Doctor and Mel arrive looking for refreshment and meet up with 'an intergalactic bounty hunter-cum-pirate called Razorback' who tells them about a treasure hidden in the pyramid, supposedly guarded by 'an ice monster'. The Doctor and Razorback go off to find the treasure, which turns out to be the monster itself, which 'is also the missing component in an opto-electronic circuit – a lens that will focus all the Pyramid's energy and give Hess immense power'. The Doctor realises that Hess's plans for galactic domination will be his downfall. This indeed proves to be the case as, when the pyramid moves out of the shadow of the larger planet, 'the crystalline circuitry ... concentrates and focuses [the heat of the sun] on Hess ..., who melts away'. At the end of the story, Ace, a young human waitress stranded at the trading centre, goes off with

Razorback while Mel continues her travels with the Doctor.

On the strength of this storyline, Briggs was quickly commissioned to write the three part story that ultimately became *Dragonfire*. (Briggs's normal preference, as he confirmed in later interviews, was to prepare a scene breakdown between the storyline stage and the script stage, but this appears not to have happened in the case of *Dragonfire*.) The script for the first part was formally commissioned on 2 April 1987 with a target delivery date of 6 April, and those for the other two on 13 April with a target delivery date of 14 April – the closeness of these dates indicating that Briggs had already started working on the scripts, by informal agreement with Cartmel, prior to being formally commissioned. The three scripts were actually delivered by Briggs on 8 April, 16 April and 13 April and accepted by the BBC on 10 April, 22 April and 20 April respectively. A number of revisions were requested by Cartmel, in particular to remedy the fact that Briggs had overwritten, but these initial drafts were quickly turned into polished rehearsal scripts. Later, during the course of the rehearsal process, these were further refined into camera scripts for the studio recording.

In terms of content, the final scripts stuck quite closely to the original storyline. One of the few significant developments arose when Bonnie Langford, who played Mel, decided during the course of production to make this her last *Doctor Who* story. On 3 August 1987, Briggs submitted a new closing scene in which Mel is the one who goes off with the pirate – changed at producer John Nathan-Turner's request from Razorback to Glitz, played by Tony Selby, from the previous season's *The Trial of a Time Lord* – and Ace, played by Sophie Aldred, who leaves with the Doctor to become the new companion. Sylvester McCoy disliked this version, feeling that the Doctor seemed too unmoved by Mel's departure, and suggested that some lines of dialogue be incorporated from a short scene that Cartmel had originally written for the screen tests carried out in February 1987 for the role of the seventh Doctor. The objection he had raised was recognised to be a valid one, and further work was then carried out on the scene right up until the day of recording.

'Bonnie finally decided that she was going to leave after the first studio recording,' recalled Briggs, 'so that final scene was rewritten during rehearsals for the second studio work. We worked on it ten or twelve times and finally got it right at breakfast on the day it was [recorded]. It's a cliché, but it was genuinely written on a napkin at the breakfast bar in Television Centre.

'I feel it got there, but only by the skin of its teeth. The problem is not so much that it was written at the last minute, but that it could be no longer than three minutes, and it's very difficult to get all the stuff in, that needs to be there, in just three minutes. The biggest problem [was] that it followed straight on from the … death [of the villain] originally, so that it needed a minute – well, perhaps not even that, probably fifteen or twenty seconds – to wind down from the death to the farewell scene.'

Other, more minor changes made between storyline and final script included the alteration of the concept of the trading centre – called Iceworld in the final version – from a planet to a city-like spacecraft on the dark side of another planet; the renaming of the planet (between rehearsal script and camera script stage) from Tartros to Svartos; and the renaming of the villain from Hess to Kane.

'I [originally] wanted [a name for the villain] with lots of sibilants – "s" sounds – in it,' Briggs recalled in a 1989 interview conducted by Michael Proctor for the fanzine

Private Who. 'I thought, "Hiss – what sounds like 'hiss'? Hass ... Hess ..." And I thought, "Hess – that sounds okay". A couple of minutes later, I realised it was the name of [a high ranking Nazi in World War Two], but I thought nobody would notice. [The first time we saw] the design of the [character's] helmet was the point at which we actually changed it. We'd been talking about changing it, because ... something had happened – I think the real Hess had written some letters asking to be released or something. When we saw the costume design, we thought "We can't do it," because it looked like a First World War German helmet, and people would [have thought] there was a connection. I was also [conscious] that there were a lot of foreign names – all the baddies had foreign names, which felt uncomfortably racist. It's a cliché as well – something I wanted to avoid – so I was quite happy to change some of them to more English-sounding names like "Kane" and "McLuhan" ... Three quarters of the stuff [in the scripts] had a reason for being there. Names had a reason, but I can't remember all of them now. Once you begin to piece together the big things, you forget about the small things.'

The name Kane was in fact taken from Orson Welles' film *Citizen Kane*; and many of the other character names in the story also had cinematic connections. Belazs for example was named after Hungarian film theorist and critic Bela Belazs; Kracauer after German film critic Siegfried Kracauer; Bazin after French film critic André Bazin; McLuhan (originally to have been named Eisenstein after Russian director Sergei Eisenstein) after Canadian communication theorist and documentary maker Marshall McLuhan; Anderson (Ace's boss, unnamed in the final dialogue of the story) after British film maker Lindsay Anderson; Pudovkin after Russian film maker and theorist Vsevolod Pudovkin; Arnheim after German/American film and art critic Rudolph Arnheim; and Dorothy, alias Ace, after Dorothy Gale, the lead character in the film *The Wizard of Oz*.

One problem that Briggs encountered in writing the story was that he had only a vague idea of how McCoy was approaching the lead role. The sole example he had seen of the actor's work on the series was his initial screen test. He therefore had to rely on Cartmel telling him whenever he went wrong in his characterisation of the seventh Doctor. He later recalled Cartmel describing McCoy as a 'real-life animated cartoon,' but admitted that he had not understood what this meant until he had actually seen the actor in rehearsals.

Of the writing out of Mel and the introduction of Ace, Briggs told *Private Who*: 'There was always the possibility that Bonnie might not want to continue for another season, and a stand-by companion had to be drawn up. The proposed character was a teenage girl called Alf from North London. Then the season was [reordered and *Delta and the Bannermen* was due to be] the final [story], so I was free to make some changes. I moved the character away from North London – because I had worrying visions of some trendy teenager from Islington! – and ... changed the name, because I never did like the idea of calling a woman "Alf". So Andrew [Cartmel] and John [Nathan-Turner] created the original idea for the character (so the BBC owns the copyright), I created the personality, and Sophie brought the character to life. When my story was moved back to the end of the season, and Bonnie decided to leave, Ace became the new companion.

'I fashioned the personality in a way that I found interesting – she's based on three teenage girls I know. I think it was always intended that she was going to be very contemporary. One of the themes of the story is loneliness, ... people who are lonely and don't have a home – a trait that struck me as fairly typical of teenagers. They feel as though they don't quite recognize themselves and everything isn't as it ought to be.'

Briggs was well satisfied with the story as it eventually reached the screen: 'The finished programme can never be as good as the original idea, because what I saw in my mind was absolutely perfect. It took place in hundreds of places on different planets with different coloured skies ... In that respect, every stage in the scripting and production process is a compromise between the vision and the possible. I don't think there's anything in that programme that anybody working on it need feel ashamed of. There are parts of it that are not the same as I envisaged them, but I don't claim a monopoly on creativity ...'

'Briggs is a really skilled writer,' noted Cartmel in a 1994 interview with David Bishop for *TSV*, 'good on construction. I did have to keep hammering away about the thriller thing, because he came from a background of writing non-thriller material. But he's a really good writer, because he gets passionately committed to things and he writes about people's emotions. When he invents characters, they've got something going for them emotionally.

'A problem was he hadn't written science-fiction before, as a lot of the writers hadn't, and I had to keep hammering that too. It's a thriller, it's a suspense story, it's got to have these punches at certain stages.

'I remember *Dragonfire* has got one of my favourite bits of Briggs's writing, where he has the Doctor trying to go into Glitz's spaceship and discussing philosophy with the guard ...

'The thing I liked about *Dragonfire* was that there were a couple of nice revelations, like there's this monster but it's a synthetic monster and inside the monster is this jewel, which is the McGuffin they're looking for. Then that turns out to be the ignition key for the city, which turns out to be a whole spaceship.'

Direction

The director of *Dragonfire* was Chris Clough. Born in the Yorkshire town of Harrogate in 1951, he had started his working life as an accountant, but then decided on a change of career and studied for a degree in English Literature at Leeds University, where he had also staged a number of student plays. In 1974, he had joined Granada TV as a researcher for current affairs programmes. His real interest lay in drama, however, and he had subsequently gained directing assignments on Channel 4's *Brookside* and on the BBC's *EastEnders*. It was on the strength of the latter than John Nathan-Turner had invited him to work on *Doctor Who*. He had made his series debut on the last six episodes of *The Trial of a Time Lord* and then been invited back to handle Season 24's last two stories, *Delta and the Bannermen* and *Dragonfire*, which were made effectively as two halves of a single production sharing mostly the same designers and behind-the-scenes crew.

The following description by Clough of his general approach to directing *Dragonfire*, and all the quotes attributed to him in later sections of this chapter, have been compiled from interviews that he gave to Richard Marson for *Doctor Who Magazine* (1988), Stephen Payne, David Richardson and Lee Matthews for *Starburst* (1988) and Rod Ulm for *Private Who* (1989), and from comments that he made during an on-stage interview at the PanoptiCon IX convention (1988).

'I leapt at the opportunity to return to *Doctor Who*, despite the fact that I didn't see the scripts beforehand. John Nathan-Turner just asks you whether or not you'd like to come back – you leave him and Andrew Cartmel to sort out the scripts. You certainly don't get approval. Basically, John decides which director will be right for which story and then allocates them accordingly.

7 SEVENTH DOCTOR

'When scripts first arrive, I read them very casually – almost just for enjoyment's sake – which allows me to gauge them as if I'm a viewer. Then I start to think about them more, reread them, tinker with a bit here, fiddle with a section there – just trying to get under the skin of the story really. It's a funny thing about any form of communication; the writer can write something with a certain emphasis in mind, and you can read that same piece and get something completely different out of it. So in those very early stages, I like to have conversations with the writers to discover what precisely their thinking is, and to debate whether there are any holes in the plot or whether I'm just being a bit thick and missing the point. From there, it's a question of trying to inject some style into it – you have to consider what it's going to look like. Okay, the writers have given you some clue as to their ideas, but you have to consider not just that, but a whole range of other options.

'You have to have done your homework before you go into the rehearsal stage. You've got to know what you think the actors should be doing at any particular time in the story and where they should be in the set. Otherwise, all you can say is, "Let's just kick it around for a while".

'I start off with little drawings – he starts there and moves to here, the entrances are here, and so on – and I try to prepare my camera scripts – a very boring job – after I've rehearsed everything at least once. If you do your camera scripts too early, things don't work when you come to rehearsals, and it restricts the actors.

'I like to keep the camera moving – there's an awful lot of boring television around, and I try to avoid the "wallpaper" effect.

'*Doctor Who* is the most difficult thing I've ever done! It is on its own; a mixture of action, adventure, fantasy and nightmare, and you are trying to amalgamate all these different areas to make the plausible out of the implausible. The concept of having a police box flying through space is obviously quite ludicrous, but the fun of it is to be able to turn the accepted form of logic on its head.'

Casting

The casting of any *Doctor Who* story is primarily the director's responsibility. Chris Clough recalled how he went about the task:

'Casting really is a long and complicated procedure. You have to begin by taking the decision to cast one particular part. Then, if that person accepts, it affects who you can offer other roles to. It really is like a jigsaw puzzle – you're constantly trying to mesh together a well balanced ensemble. After all, it's no good having a goodie and a baddie who share similar physical characteristics, because you're in danger of confusing the audience. You have to find a good mix of physical types, so that when any one character comes up on screen, that's that – the audience recognises immediately who it is. You cannot allow for creating shades of, "Is that him, or maybe him …?"; it has to be distinct.

'You have to consider what sort of characterisation an actor will bring to a role, and what qualities he or she possesses. Equally, you yourself have to establish what qualities you perceive within each character – it's no easy task. Whenever I get a script, I go through it and write out a list of casting ideas, which I discuss with John Nathan-Turner. We then see who is available – not everyone is free, and not everyone is willing to do it.'

Amongst the actors considered for the role of Kane were David Jason, who was sent copies of the scripts on 23 June 1987, and John Alderton, who was sent copies on 3 July.

Eventually, however, it went to Edward Peel.

'Kane was a very difficult character to cast,' noted Clough, 'but I chose Edward because I thought the physical height would be good, and I liked the overall acting style. I had seen him in *Juliet Bravo*, and also many years before in Hull in a play called *What the Butler Saw*. I was pleased that he had already shaved off his usual moustache, as I would have asked him to take it off anyway. For one thing, you wouldn't have any surplus hair at -200° C; it would snap off. Also, I did think it made him look rather like a second-hand car salesman!'

Visual Effects

Dragonfire, in common with most other *Doctor Who* stories, had extensive visual effects requirements. The designer responsible for meeting these was Andy McVean of the BBC's own Visual Effects Department; but, as usual for this period of the series' history, he had the support of a number of the Department's assistants, including Mike Tucker, Lindsay McGowan, Paul Mann, Paul McGuinness and Jonathan Clarke, and contracted certain aspects of the work out to freelancers, including the team of Susan Moore and Stephen Mansfield. In the following section of this chapter, all quotes attributed to Tucker, Moore and Mansfield are taken from a 1988 interview conducted by David J Howe, Mark Stammers and Stephen James Walker for *The Frame*.

One of the most important aspects of the effects team's work was the realisation of the dragon – the legendary beast hunted by the Doctor and Glitz. Tucker recalled how this had been achieved: 'The script initially said, "a huge, fire-breathing dragon". It turned out in Part Two to be a biomechanical creature with laser beam eyes, breathing smoke and fire. That was handled almost entirely by one guy in the Effects Department, Lindsay McGowan. Andy McVean came up with some initial design drawings for the head, and Lindsay prepared a rough maquette of the creature – a small plasticine model about twelve inches tall – which was approved by John Nathan-Turner and Chris Clough. Then Lindsay sculpted a full size version, which was a latex and polyurethane foam suit and a fibre-glass head. There was also a separate mechanical head, the mechanics of which were done by Paul Mann, which opened up to reveal the dragon's treasure. That suit was then painted up by Lindsay and Paul McGuinness, another effects assistant who in the previous season was inside Drathro. The head was sat on top of a helmet arrangement on top of the actor's head, and he looked out through the neck.'

'The original maquette of the creature was very beautiful, very menacing,' wrote McVean in *Ace! The Inside Story of the End of an Era* (*Doctor Who* Books, 1996), 'but the actor that they cast was short and fat and we ended up making blocked up shoes for him, to try and get him to look taller. He really couldn't cope at all, because he had a complete rubber body suit on, which was uncomfortable, and because his hands needed to be free and he had to operate the smoke from the nostrils with a blow switch. This meant that when he blew into the mouthpiece, it operated a solenoid, but it also meant that you had to have a battery and a gas canister in the head, so the entire thing was quite top heavy.'

Numerous other creatures were required for sequences set in Iceworld's refreshment bar, where Ace was seen working as a waitress. The intention was that these sequences should be reminiscent of *Star Wars*' famous cantina scene, with examples of a great many different alien life forms gathered together in one place. Moore explained how most of

7 SEVENTH DOCTOR

these had been created:

'The make-up designer asked us if we had any off-the-peg masks that had not be used in any other TV or film production. We had a number of bits and pieces that we'd made over the years – masks and puppets and so on – and I took along a whole collection, including a few masks made by another colleague. Make-up chose a selection and used them on the extras in the background. Luckily, the director was there at the same time, and he spotted a half-mask I'd made for a party and thought that it would be perfect for the scene where the child wears a mask to frighten Mel. He also spotted Eric the puppet, and Eric became a legend in his own lunchtime! (For some obscure reason, every creature we make seems to end up being dubbed Eric – it's a silly name at the best of times, and it seems a suitably ridiculous name to give to anything that's an alien, and supposed to be taken seriously.)

'At one point, the producer called down from the gallery asking if it had a name. I just said, "Eric". It was originally going to be in the background, but then they decided to start the scene with Eric at the table with this fish creature that we provided, and they finished the scene off with him snapping at the Doctor as well. Eric was operated by the man in the green fish mask, and everyone was very pleased with it.'

Dragonfire also featured a certain amount of modelwork, all of which was shot on film rather than recorded on video, owing to the greater controllability of the medium. A major aspect of this work was the realisation of Glitz's ship, the *Nosferatu*. 'Basically we knew it had to have an undocking scene, a take off scene, a flying away scene and an exploding scene,' noted Tucker, 'so two versions were made: one for all the flying work, and a breakable version for the scene where it explodes. The feel of *Dragonfire* was that Glitz's ship should be a rusty old tramp steamer, and that is basically what I used as an influence when we designed it. I had this rusty orange colour and a ship-like conning tower at the back and cargo pods. It just seemed to suit the character of Glitz, that this was the sort of ship he would have.' Another model required to feature prominently in the story was that of Iceworld itself. 'Initially what was wanted,' continued Tucker, 'was a planet with an obvious hot side and an obvious cold side, and on that cold side … an icy, crystalline structure. This would be seen as simply a city, but in Part Three it would be revealed to be a spacecraft. So the initial shots had to disguise the fact that it was going to be a spacecraft, but at the same time it was designed around the fact that it would be taking off into space. Iceworld was designed by Andy and, because of lack of time, had to be made by outside contractors, Derek Hendon Associates.'

The shots in which icy vapour is seen to rise from Kane's hands and from a coin that he places on a desk were achieved, as Tucker explained, by a clever combination of effects: 'When we could, we ran smoke pipes through the costume and out through the cuffs. For the scene where the coin was put down on the desk, we used two chemical substances that, when mixed together, smoke slightly. We sprayed one on the coin, one on the desk top, and when the two were brought into contact, they smoked.'

'The portrait on the coin was meant to be Kane's face,' pointed out Moore, 'so we modelled a likeness of Edward Peel onto it. I hope it looked like him, because originally we were told it was just going to be handed to people in long shot, and we were surprised when it was seen quite close up.'

One of the best remembered aspects of *Dragonfire* is the horrific final sequence in which Kane's face melts away in the light of the sun – another effect achieved by Moore and Mansfield.

'While we were working on the Chimeron baby for *Delta and the Bannermen*,' recalled Mansfield, 'we were told that there was the possibility of a melting head sequence at the end of the final story. At that time, it was not confirmed that we would be handling the sequence, but we were asked whether or not we thought it was feasible. We had to bear in mind the potential complexity of such a sequence and the limitations of a TV studio recording. There were two major stipulations. As the effect had to be done on a live recording day, it had to melt very quickly. In addition, there were to be no red colours on the underskull or any liquid resembling blood.'

'We went off and did a lot of research,' added Moore, 'and found out how the similar melting effect in *Raiders of the Lost Ark* was done. I spoke to some senior effects people in the film industry. Everyone said that it couldn't be done, not on video and certainly not that quickly. In spite of that, we felt the problems as we saw them could be overcome, and that it was certainly a project worth having a crack at. And, as it turned out, a month later, we were offered the job.'

'Edward Peel apparently wasn't keen on the idea of having an alginate face cast made,' noted Mansfield, 'especially as it would have had to have been with his mouth open, which is doubly uncomfortable for the subject. There wasn't really the time, anyway. Andy McVean arranged for us to meet Edward Peel at Visual Effects during a break in rehearsals. We took instant photos of him in the facial position he would assume at the start of the melting scene. I then took caliper measurements of his face, while Sue took more detailed photographs. We set to modelling the head from the instant photos that same afternoon.'

'The head was sculpted in water-based clay, from which a multi-piece plaster mould was taken,' explained Moore. 'From this mould, six wax outer skins were eventually taken. As mould was multi-piece, the original clay bust remained intact – just as the inflexible wax casts had to! Using the teeth and the top of the head as registering points, we started cutting away at the face, taking it back to what it would be if it had melted to the bone. A silicone mould was then taken of this new sculpture, and two fibre-glass skulls were cast. The skulls and the skins were then airbrushed.'

'As the melting had to be done very quickly,' continued Mansfield, 'the wax skins had to be very thin. Therefore when they melted, they tended to give off only a very thin dribble of wax and not much else. To overcome this problem, we fitted the under-skulls with various pipes – in the mouth, in the nose and under the helmet – and through these pumped a liquid coloured to match the molten wax, thus creating a more authentic, head-sized volume of wastage.

'Selected areas of the glass-fibre skull were cast in latex and acted as bladders. These sections, when inflated, helped to distort the face, and generally accelerated the degeneration process by pushing wax away from the skull. The whole lot – six skins, two under-skulls, liquid and so on – was finally completed with hours to spare, at about 4 am on the studio day, 29 July 1987.'

'The head had been fitted to a support post in the studio that was the same height as Edward Peel,' added Tucker, 'and Costume had provided a collar section to go around the neck – they couldn't use a real costume, because all the wax and gunge would have ruined it.

'There were four of us operating it in the end. Steve provided the spit and gunge, while Sue, Paul Mann and I all wielded hot air guns and bladders. Cameras lined up on

7 SEVENTH DOCTOR

it and told us when we were in shot or out of shot. When we were all ready and out of shot, we turned on the hot air guns and away we went.'

'There was a little bit of improvisation when the instruction came from the gallery to start dropping it out of shot,' admitted Moore. 'As the rig was mounted on a huge baseboard we couldn't literally drop it downwards – so we just tilted it backwards.'

'What they were trying to get,' explained Tucker, 'was the effect of a collapsing man; they wanted to see Kane shrivel and deflate as he melted, and they wanted to match this shot with one we had done of the body collapsing from behind.

'Then the electronic effects designer Dave Chapman, in post-production, actually managed to mix in Edward Peel's real mouth, so that it actually screamed as it melted.

'In the end, we did only one take on it, because it all seemed to go well and the gallery was happy with it.'

'Ultimately it turned out to be quite an unsettling effect, in spite of the lack of red colours,' felt Moore. 'At one stage in the middle of shooting it, all this yellow gunge came out in a torrent because of a blockage in the air pipe. Also, one of the wax eyes that were underneath the skin popped and ran down the face. Not a pretty sight. Needless to say, none of this reached the final programme. We were flaterred though to receive a round of applause from the assembled cast and crew.'

'What you saw on screen was a fraction of what was recorded,' reflected Tucker. 'It was shown at about thirty times normal speed, and the melting in real time took about ten minutes, from which they chose a suitable sequence to use.'

'I think on the whole it worked very well on screen,' concluded Moore, 'which is, of course, the ultimate consideration. Apparently it was the first time an effect of that type had been attempted on British television, so it was a first for *Doctor Who* – and of course for us.'

Chris Clough was well pleased with how this effect turned out, as he later confirmed:

'When it came to melting his head, I really did want to make it look realistic, otherwise it would have been awful. At one stage we considered, as an alternative, shooting it from behind Edward, having him pretend to melt, and then cutting to a puddle on the floor. However, that might have looked very laughable, so we decided on going for it, and having the facial close-up, which is what I'd wanted to do from the start.

'For the body, we were going to do a reverse shot. Someone went and bought an inflatable doll from a sex shop, then we dressed it in Kane's clothes [and allowed it to deflate]. However it ended up looking absolutely stupid. Still, there's a lovely photo of it somewhere with its trousers having fallen down, revealing these little [deflated] legs!

'In the end, rather than use the doll, we actually had a shot of Edward Peel sinking to his knees and used that instead, bleached out to give the impression of the blinding sunlight.'

In Studio

Rehearsals for *Dragonfire* took place in the then standard venue of the BBC's custom-built rehearsal block, sometimes referred to jokingly as the 'Acton Hilton', in Acton, West London. Camera rehearsal and recording then took place in two sessions, the first over 28 to 30 July 1987 in Television Centre Studio 1, the second over 12 and 13 August in Television Centre Studio 3.

'I think we had only one week between coming off the OB for *Delta and the Bannermen* and going back into rehearsals for *Dragonfire*,' recalled Chris Clough, 'so everything had to be set up at the same time. I really needed to know that everything was already prepared, so that I could use that free week just to relax and to get my mind clear from the previous story.

'We did have a very tight recording schedule, and fortunately we didn't fall into the trap of letting things drift at the beginning, because if we had fallen behind then, by being too fussy or having things go wrong, it would have been very difficult to make up that time later. There's nothing easy about *Doctor Who* at all. Large chunks of dialogue are very easy to record, but we're dealing with SFX and also a great deal of action, which has to look convincing.

'We did a lot of rehearsal in costume for the scenes involving the dragon – it's unfair on actors to dump them in a costume at the last minute. The worst thing for them is the discomfort, because they sweat buckets.

'With the dragon, I think we had a good design. I tended to put it into half shadow and shoot it to avoid the legs, which never look terribly good on monsters.

'Kane had to be convincing too, without going over the top. That's always the problem with these ultimate foe-type characters – the temptation to go "Aargh!" and all that sort of stuff. And it usually works better if they do less. Then, when they're really angry, they can twitch their eyebrows or something. Edward Peel did that very well.

'And one of the things I enjoyed about *Dragonfire* was having the real cliffhanger with the Doctor and his umbrella at the end of Part One!'

Not everyone was pleased with how the latter scene turned out, however. 'The worst cliffhanger we ever had was the one at the end of *Dragonfire* Part One,' asserted Andrew Cartmel. 'In Ian Briggs's script, the Doctor climbs as far as he possibly can along a path in an ice cliff, then he is forced to climb down the face of the cliff itself. This all makes perfect sense in the script – he's on his way somewhere, the path runs out, he has no alternative, he has to start climbing downwards.

'But the way it's shot! He's walking along, then, for apparently no reason, suddenly he dangles himself over the edge. Someone rang me up and said, "Why does he do this?" The problem is, when you've got the script and you know what's supposed to be happening, when it's expressed on the screen like that, you don't question it. But if you're just a viewer watching this, there's no apparent reason for his actions.

'One of the things the director has to bear in mind is that the viewers don't know the script. Something to do with the essential visual grammar of that scene was missing.'

Ian Briggs himself felt that Clough's pacy, action-orientated style of direction was not entirely well suited to his scripts, which he saw as being very much driven by the characters and their motivations and interactions.

For Sophie Aldred, the recording of *Dragonfire* marked not only her debut as Ace but her first ever experience of acting in front of television cameras; before starting work on the production, she had not even known where Television Centre was. The regular costume that she would wear in the role was inspired partly by some clothes of her own and partly by a couple of photographs of teenage girls wearing club gear that she recalled seeing in an issue (July 1987) of the style magazine *The Face*. She and costume designer Richard Croft went on a shopping trip to the King's Road in Chelsea to choose a collection of suitable items off-the-peg. Some of the many badges and patches that ultimately adorned the jacket were obtained on this trip; others were found by Croft in various Oxford Street shops; and the remainder were supplied by Aldred herself.

7 SEVENTH DOCTOR

'I had every confidence in Sophie Aldred's Ace,' wrote John Nathan-Turner in 1996 in his memoirs for *Doctor Who Magazine*, 'but decided to wait and see her good work in the rehearsal room committed to tape before taking up the option on a full contract … The first studio day went well. Sophie was splendid. I took up the option and, in order to stave off any more leaks to the press, I swiftly organised a press call at TV Centre with Sophie, Sylvester and the TARDIS.'

An interesting contemporary view of the studio work for *Dragonfire* can be gleaned from the following report by *Doctor Who Magazine*'s Richard Marson, who visited the set for the final day's camera rehearsal and recording:

> To an outsider, watching the *Doctor Who* crew at work can be a very frustrating process. Just as a scene gets into its stride, it will either stop, so that [those responsible for] cameras and microphones can ensure their positions are exactly right (according to the director's detailed camera script), or simply because each scene doesn't tend to be longer than a couple of minutes … With all the stops for effects and added camera angles (which increase the pace and tension), as well as for the inevitable mistakes, one might be forgiven for thinking that the cast and crew would be slowly driven out of their minds.
>
> That this isn't so is generally down to the production manager. It is he or she who acts as the director's assistant on the studio floor and maintains the vital discipline that keeps the show on schedule, without the grind wearing down those who are involved. For *Dragonfire* … the production manager was Gary Downie … [who] has captured the ability to have jokes and keep smiling while at the same time letting everyone know what was what and that no slackness could be tolerated.
>
> This discipline showed itself when a confused actor walked off the set before he was cleared to go, and when the busy studio got too noisy …
>
> Making an ice planet convincing has been one of the principal challenges of this production, especially as it has all been taped in the studio, thus losing the added space that can be gained on location work … The sets were of necessity quite flimsy, and looking at them close up, it's a wonder that they look so good on screen. Very often television sets look absolutely dreadful and extremely tacky before they are lit, and this was definitely the case with those assembled for *Dragonfire*. However, on camera they looked fine; as convincing as it was possible to achieve and greatly helped by the acting of the cast.
>
> It was possible to view what was going to be seen on screen in the final stage by looking at one of the monitors carefully arranged around the studio. These are most important to all concerned, and everyone, from make-up and costume [staff] through to lighting men and production manager, [was] glued to what they showed during each run-through of a take. Woe betide anybody who got in the way!

The difficulties of creating a convincing frozen environment in a television studio, with expanded polystyrene 'snow' and sheets of plastic 'ice', were not lost on Chris Clough:

'There is always that problem with something of this nature, but there are no real alternatives to what we used. This was something we gave a lot of thought to in the planning stages, but without the money available, you are always going to be limited to using the same old measures.

'John Asbridge's sets were highly original. We had wanted the cryogenic centre to be very big and very high – an example of pomposity gone berserk – and he did a splendid job. The swirling mists were an absolute nightmare to realise. We had dry ice machines everywhere, but the problem was that the stuff disperses very quickly. We got through literally hundreds of pounds' worth, but it was ultimately very effective. The one real problem though was that we couldn't show the actors' breath. Orson Welles got round this problem by building his sets in a cold storage unit, and Frank Capra put little boxes of dry ice inside the actors' mouths. Others have tried using cigarette smoke, but really, for us, it would have been virtually impossible to show.

'We just had to make sure that the actors kept in their heads the continuity of where they were supposed to be, and didn't start wandering about as though it was the middle of summer. We rationalised it by saying, "Well, it's cold, but it's not *that* cold!"'

Andrew Cartmel also admired Asbridge's sets, but felt that they had been let down by over-bright lighting.

'That's always been a problem in television,' noted Clough. 'Don Babbage, who lit *Dragonfire*, worked with me on *EastEnders*, so we sorted our way through that. He calls me the Prince of Darkness, because I'm always after shadows everywhere and forever shouting, "Turn the bloody lights down!"'

Post-Production

'Once you've recorded it, you go into editing,' noted Chris Clough, 'and you have to let the editor have his input, just like you let the actors have their input. One plays and discusses with the editor – I'll say, "I've shot it with this in mind," and he'll say, "Well, that's a load of crap. Wouldn't it be better if ...", and so on and so forth.

'Editing can be a frustrating process. You often find yourself saying, "Why the bloody hell didn't I shoot it from that angle, or go for a close-up there?"

'Boom shadows are very embarrassing, but if there was a choice between a take where the performance was better with the shadow and one where it was worse without it, I'd go for the better performance and try to edit round the shadow.

'In the case of *Dragonfire*, the main problem was that the episodes overran and had to be cut down to the right length. This meant, for example, that we trimmed a sequence where the Doctor gets trapped under a piece of falling ice and has to be freed by Glitz. In editing, you always have to trim the arty bits, which is very distressing.'

Ian Briggs recalled this trimming process in his interview for *Doctor Who Magazine*: 'Because we were trying to get so much in, we had to cut the "wind down" [between Kane's death scene and the start of Mel's farewell scene]. But when Chris had done a rough cut of the episode, we all agreed that there really was too much of a jump ... Tony [Selby] had to come in and revoice something else, so I [took the opportunity to add an] extra linking scene between the [other] two [– specifically the one with Glitz making an announcement along the lines of] "This is your new captain speaking" – using some spare [visuals that had been recorded.]'

'After the editing,' continued Clough, 'there's the sound dub. We have two days for location stuff and a day for studio stuff, which should be fairly simple. Dick Mills, the special sounds artist, adds his splits and splats, and then there's the incidental music. For *Dragonfire*, the composer Dominic Glynn came down to both studios and we gave it a lot of thought.'

Interviewed by Philip Newman in 1990 for *Doctor Who Magazine*, Glynn recalled that his score for *Dragonfire* had represented a significant development in both style and quality of composition over the ones that he had provided for the previous season's *The Trial of a Time Lord*: 'The music for [those earlier episodes] was done purely on a synthesiser, which made it difficult to get certain "warm", "fat sounding" noises. I had to double track everything. But between seasons, I bought a sampler, which made a huge difference to the range of sounds I could use. I could record a second, or a few seconds, of any instrument, sound or noise and then play it back, at any tone or pitch, on an electronic keyboard. So I was able to sample the jingle-bell sound from a baby's toy, and the biggest church organ in the South of England.'

Speaking to Austen Atkinson-Broadbelt in 1993, also for *Doctor Who Magazine*, Glynn elaborated on his intentions for *Dragonfire*: 'I was attempting to get a more orchestral feel in that story ... I tried to give a feeling of being there on that freezing planet. It was a good story. I think I began to feel more relaxed by the time *Dragonfire* came along. I tried very hard to help build up the atmosphere on that one. I loved doing the music for the soldiers. That's all very metallic. Good stuff!'

Transmission

Dragonfire was transmitted over three consecutive Saturdays in November 1987 as the last story of *Doctor Who*'s twenty-fourth season. Its first episode captured an audience of 5.5 million viewers – the highest individual rating of the season – and it also received good audience reaction figures, reflecting a gradual upward trend during the course of the season. Ace proved to be an instant hit, gaining a higher approval rating than either the Doctor or – by some margin – Mel.

Ten viewers' phone calls about the story were logged at the BBC's duty office. One complained that the story was too childish; six thought that the scene of Kane's face melting was unsuitable for transmission so early in the evening; one considered that the series was great; one felt that the timeslot was wrong; and one was glad to see the back of Bonnie Langford. The production office also received one letter of complaint dated 2 December 1987 from a viewer named Dorothy Barrass, who was upset at a line of dialogue in which Ace had stated that the name Dorothy was 'naff'. John Nathan-Turner replied on 11 December apologising for any offence that had been caused.

'There was something traditional about *Dragonfire* that made me feel it was the right story on which to end the season,' commented Nathan-Turner in his *Doctor Who Magazine* memoirs. 'It was studio-bound, of course, but it also somehow harked back to earlier days of the show, while still using the latest technology. Sometimes innocent, sometimes simple, and yet advanced, moralistic and, hopefully, entertaining. Again, a story of "Hello, goodbye", but with a reasonable degree of optimism for the future.'

CREDITS

Director	Chris Clough
Producer	John Nathan-Turner
Script Editor	Andrew Cartmel

Production Associate	Ann Faggetter
Production Manager	Gary Downie
Assistant Floor Managers	Christopher Sandeman
	Kim Wilcocks
Production Assistants	Rosemary Parsons
	Karen King
Producer's Secretary	Kate Easteal
Designer	John Asbridge
Design Assistant	Hilda Liptrott
Costume Designer	Richard Croft
Costume Assistant	Leah Archer
Dressers	Bob Springett
	Lena Hansen
	Tom Reeve
	Kate Hirst
Make-Up Designer	Gillian Thomas
Make-Up Assistants	Petrona Winton
	Anabela Dellot-Seguro
	Jayne Buxton
Visual Effects Designer	Andy McVean
Visual Effects Assistants	Mike Tucker
	Paul Mann
	Paul McGuinness
	Lindsay McGowan
	Jonathan Clarke
Properties Buyer	Cathy Cosgrove
Sound	Brian Clark
Deputy Sound Supervisor	Mike Weaver
Lighting	Don Babbage
Technical Co-ordinator	Richard Wilson
Senior Cameraman	Alec Wheal
Video Effects	Dave Chapman
Vision Mixer	Shirley Coward
Videotape Editor	Hugh Parson
Film Cameraman	William Dudman
Floor Assistant	Jes Nightingale
Production Operatives	Arthur Stacey
	Dicky Wickes
	Dave Rogers
	Barry Du Pille
Title Music	Ron Grainer, arranged by Keff McCulloch
Incidental Music	Dominic Glynn
Special Sound	Dick Mills
Writer	Ian Briggs

7 SEVENTH DOCTOR

THE WILDERNESS YEARS

After the completion of work on its twenty-sixth season, *Doctor Who* was effectively cancelled as a BBC production. Unlike when it had been taken off the air for eighteen months in 1984, however, there was no official announcement made to this effect. Consequently there was no press coverage of the series' demise and, at least initially, no concerted attempt by fans to get the BBC to change their minds.

Although *Survival* was the last story to be screened in the ongoing series, *Ghost Light* was the last to go before the cameras, the season having been made out of transmission order. Following its completion, there were just two pieces of additional recording undertaken. The first was of a voice-over by actor David Bingham for Part One of *Battlefield*. This was done on 13 August 1989. The second was a voice-over by Sylvester McCoy, consisting of the Doctor's final monologue for the end of Part Three of *Survival*. Whether by accident or design, this was done on a very appropriate date, 23 November 1989 – the twenty-sixth anniversary of *Doctor Who*'s debut transmission.

The BBC's *Doctor Who* production office had already begun to wind down a couple of months before this, and Sylvester McCoy was reported as telling a convention audience: 'The BBC don't want to make *Doctor Who*. They aren't interested in a series that's lasted twenty-six years.'

There had for some time been rumours circulating that the BBC wanted to farm *Doctor Who* out to be made by an independent production company. (At this point in the BBC's history, there was a general move toward outsourcing as many productions as possible; *Doctor Who* was one of the last drama series to be made in-house, and John Nathan-Turner was the last producer on the staff of the Series and Serials Department, all his former colleagues having been obliged to go freelance.) Bids were rumoured to have been made to the BBC by a number of interested companies, including Cinema Verity (run by former series producer Verity Lambert), Saffron Productions (run by former series story editor and writer Victor Pemberton) and Coast-to-Coast Productions Ltd (who were in fact looking to make a feature film based on the series – a subject covered in a later section of this chapter).

In November 1989, prompted by numerous enquiries from concerned fans and a certain amount of press speculation about the series' future, the BBC's new Head of Serials Peter Cregeen issued a statement in which he claimed that *Doctor Who* could easily continue for a further twenty-six years, but added that the BBC was considering the best way to 'take *Doctor Who* through the '90s'. These words were to ring ever more hollow as variations on the same statement continued to be issued by the BBC to anyone who enquired about the future of *Doctor Who* in the years that followed. Another notable occurrence in November 1989 was that Nathan-Turner officially stood down as *Doctor Who*'s producer after some ten years in that post. He remained on the BBC's payroll, however, and would continue to take an active role as the series' 'guardian'.

The following month, former story editor and writer Gerry Davis and writer Terry Nation confirmed in the fanzine *DWB* that they were interested in making a joint bid to produce the series. This, along with approaches from other sources, apparently forced the BBC to reconsider its attitude to the series, to the extent that senior press officer

Kevin O'Shea (who had handled much of *Doctor Who*'s press promotion in the past) made a statement that an announcement on its future was likely to be made soon. Nothing came of this, although two months later, in February 1990, Cregeen was back with another pronouncement, commenting cryptically: 'There will be more changes than people think ...'

1990

The only new *Doctor Who*-related production to be transmitted during 1990 was an edition of the BBC schools series *Search out Science* in which Sylvester McCoy's Doctor and Sophie Aldred's Ace were joined by a John Leeson-voiced K-9 to educate viewers in the wonders of space. There was plenty of old *Doctor Who* to be seen, however, as it became one of the flagship shows on the new satellite channel BSB (which was also available through many cable television suppliers). This began, in April, repeating selected stories from the William Hartnell era onwards; and on 22 and 23 September there was an entire '*Doctor Who* weekend', otherwise known as '31 Who'. This consisted of special screenings, guest appearances and other items put together largely by Nathan-Turner, who had finally left the BBC at the end of the previous month (although he had immediately gained work with BBC Enterprises, producing *Doctor Who* video projects). Nathan-Turner also acted as on-screen co-presenter with Shyama Perera and Debbie Flint.

The stories and individual episodes shown on the Saturday were: *100,000 BC*, *The Mutants* (1963/64), *Inside the Spaceship* (with the second episode accidentally preceding the first), *The Abominable Snowmen* Episode Two, *The Web of Fear* Episode 1, *The Space Museum*, *The Keys of Marinus* and *The Aztecs*. Also shown was the Sixties cinema film *Dr Who and the Daleks*. Interspersed between these screenings were short interviews with: William Russell ('Ian'), Carole Ann Ford ('Susan'), Verity Lambert (producer), Waris Hussein (director), Elisabeth Sladen ('Sarah Jane Smith'), Terry Nation (writer), Raymond P Cusick (designer), Mervyn Haisman (writer), Nicholas Courtney ('the Brigadier'), Sylvester McCoy ('the Doctor'), Andrew Beech (fan), Peter Purves ('Steven'), John Freeman (editor, *Doctor Who Magazine*), Terrance Dicks (script editor and writer), Gerry Davis (story editor and writer), Deborah Watling ('Victoria') and Jennie Linden ('Barbara' from the cinema films). Also presented during the course of the day were a *Doctor Who* 'expert' quiz, a piece on American *Doctor Who* conventions, vox pops of people doing Dalek impressions, an interview with a Cyberman, and the video for the 'Doctor in Distress' single record from 1984.

The stories and individual episodes shown on the Sunday were: *The War Games*, *The Dominators*, *The Mind Robber*, *The Three Doctors*, *The Abominable Snowmen* Episode Two, *The Web of Fear* Episode 1 and *Inside the Spaceship* (with the episodes screened the correct way round). Also shown, between *The Three Doctors* and *The Abominable Snowmen* Episode Two, was the cinema film *Daleks Invasion Earth: 2150 A.D.*. The interviews this time were with: Wendy Padbury ('Zoe'), Frazer Hines ('Jamie'), Pat Godfrey (costume designer), Brian Hodgson (special sound effects), Dick Mills (special sound effects), Sylvester McCoy ('the Doctor'), Stephen Mansfield (visual effects), Susan Moore (visual effects), Raymond P Cusick (designer), Barry Newbery (designer), Peter Hawkins (voice artiste), Terrance Dicks (script editor and writer), Nicholas Courtney ('the Brigadier'), Bob Baker (writer), Dave Martin (writer), David J Howe (collector), Verity Lambert (producer) and Terry Nation (writer). Additional features this time were a special effects demonstration

SEVENTH DOCTOR

and a top ten *Doctor Who* monsters compilation.

BSB spent a great deal of time and effort promoting *Doctor Who* generally, but all this came to an end in November 1990, when it merged with the rival Sky and the *Doctor Who* repeats stopped.

Also in November, one year on from the end of the twenty-sixth season and with no signs of the BBC taking any specific action to revive the series, a 'day of protest' was organised by the fanzine *DWB*. The idea was that on this particular day, Sunday 2 November, fans would bombard the BBC with at least twenty phone calls each in protest at the delay in returning the series to production. In the event, however, only 973 *Doctor Who*-related calls were logged at the duty offices of BBC television and radio. This was certainly far more than on an average day (on the Saturday immediately beforehand, for instance, twenty-three such calls had been logged), but it still fell well below the organisers' hopes; and while the great majority of callers were no doubt sincere individuals genuinely concerned about the series' future, the fact that some gave names very similar to those of well known *Doctor Who* characters and production personnel – 'Mr T Jovka', 'John Turner' and 'Alistair Gordon' amongst them – does raise questions about the motives of a minority. A further problem with this well-intentioned initiative is that, far from increasing the chances of new *Doctor Who* being made, it reportedly had the opposite effect of turning some senior BBC executives against the series altogether, leaving them determined not to let the fans dictate their policy in relation a show that they considered dead.

The following month, the BBC stated that a final decision on the series' future would be made in 1991.

The year did end on a relatively high note, however, when *Doctor Who* was the subject of a *Cult Heroes* documentary on BBC Radio 5 on Christmas Eve. This was produced by Anne Hinds, written by Ed Thomason and presented by comedian Tony Slattery, and featured contributions from John Nathan-Turner (producer), Sylvester McCoy ('the Doctor'), John Collins (DWAS Co-ordinator), Verity Lambert (producer), Dick Mills (special sound effects), Jon Pertwee ('the Doctor') and Elisabeth Sladen ('Sarah Jane Smith'). Also included were interview clips of Tom Baker taken from the 1977 *Lively Arts* documentary *Whose Doctor Who*.

1991

February 1991 saw BBC Chairman Marmaduke Hussey, in response to an enquiry from Sir Hugh Rossi MP, stating that the Corporation was looking 'at all possible avenues before making any long-term decisions' on *Doctor Who*'s future. Other senior BBC figures responded to public enquiries with standard letters along similar lines.

There was no further movement until May, when, following questions from the national press, the BBC finally confirmed that any future series would be made by an independent production company rather than in-house. No particular company was named, however, and nothing of substance seemed to be happening. Some magazines picked up the fact that a new science fiction show was about to be made at Shepperton Studios and leaped to the conclusion that it must be *Doctor Who*. It was actually a completely different production.

Arguably the biggest development during 1991 was the launching by Virgin books of their New Adventures range of original novels featuring the seventh Doctor and Ace. Visitors to London's Museum of the Moving Image (MOMI) were meanwhile able to see 'Behind the Sofa', a major exhibition devoted to *Doctor Who*. This opened on 5 July, following a press launch at which three concept models of creatures from the supposed forthcoming Green Light feature film were on show. Jointly arranged by MOMI, BBC Worldwide and Lorne Martin's company Experience (who were hired by BBC Worldwide to manage all the *Doctor Who* related exhibitions), it proved massively popular and was extended several times, finally running until 23 February 1992 before going on tour to regional venues until November 1992.

Tying in with the exhibition, a company called Teynham Productions, the directors of which were John Nathan-Turner, Gary Downie, Fiona Cumming and Ian Fraser, staged a series of two-day events at MOMI. These involved people associated with *Doctor Who* giving lectures about their work to a group of paying attendees. The dates and speakers were as follows. 6/7 July 1991: Jeremy Bentham (history of *Doctor Who*), Bernard Wilkie and Jack Kine (visual effects), Colin Baker ('the Doctor'), Carole Todd (director, *The Ultimate Adventure* stage play), June Hudson (costumes), Nicholas Courtney ('the Brigadier'), Fiona Cumming (director), Sophie Aldred ('Ace'), John Freeman (editor, *Doctor Who* Magazine), Dick Mills (sound effects), Sylvester McCoy ('the Doctor'); 2/3 November 1991: David J Howe (collecting), Barry Newbery (designer), Sue Anstruther (production assistant), Ken Trew (costumes), Mitch Mitchell (video effects), Barry Letts (producer), Tony Selby ('Glitz'), Ian Dow (lighting), Kevin O'Shea (publicity), Nicola Bryant ('Peri'), Shirley Coward (vision mixer), Elisabeth Sladen ('Sarah Jane Smith'), Ian Fraser (production manager), Jon Pertwee ('the Doctor'); 15/16 February 1992: Andrew Beech (appreciating *Doctor Who*), Gary Downie (choreographer, production assistant), Keff McCulloch (music), June Collins (production manager), Henry Barber (lighting), Jane Wellesley (production assistant), Tom Baker ('the Doctor'), Stuart Fell (stuntman), Lorne Martin and Martin Wilkie (exhibitions), Janet Fielding ('Tegan'), Graeme Smith ('Jason' in *The Ultimate Adventure*), Christopher Barry (director), Denise Baron (make-up), Terry Molloy ('Davros'). Teynham subsequently organised a number of similar events, some of them lasting only one day, in different locations around the UK.

On 26 August 1991, the series' pilot episode had its first ever transmission, some twenty-eight years after it was made, as part of BBC2's tribute to Lime Grove Studios, which were shortly to be demolished. The same month, Peter Cregeen issued another statement to *Doctor Who* Magazine about the series' future:

'There is no question of *Doctor Who* being abandoned. It is still an important programme, and when the time is right, it should return. However, the show's popularity over the years has waned in the United Kingdom, with an average audience of four million. In a competitive market environment, where BBC TV Drama is required to produce a wide range of programmes at an economically viable price, one cannot continue to support a programme that is not able to achieve a substantial audience.

'A decision was taken to rest the programme for an extended period so that when it returns, it will be seen as a fresh, inventive and vibrant addition to the schedule – rather than a battle-weary Time Lord languishing in the backwaters of audience popularity.

'*Doctor Who* is too valuable a property for us to relaunch until we are absolutely confident of it as a major success once again.'

Confused and angered by what they saw as yet another bland statement from the BBC, a group of fans announced plans in October to take the BBC to court for failing to make *Doctor Who* in the face of massive public demand. The consortium included chairman and legal adviser John Giacobbi, Andrew Beech, Steve Wickham, Colin Griffiths and Jonathan Way from the DWAS, Gary Leigh from *DWB* and historian Jeremy Bentham. This well intentioned but perhaps misguided campaign ultimately came to nothing, as a prize competition intended to raise money received only a lukewarm response and insufficient funds were raised to pursue the matter further.

1992

3 January 1992 saw the transmission on BBC2 of a half-hour overview of *Doctor Who* entitled *Resistance is Useless*. This was put together by the production team of the arts programme *The Late Show* (who had also been responsible for the previous August's screening of the pilot episode) and directed by Archie Lauchlan. It consisted mainly of clips from *Doctor Who* compiled into a number of categories and linked by a mysterious character who appeared to be nothing more than literally a talking anorak – the voice for which was provided by comedian Steve Steen. The clips were selected on the basis of responses to a questionnaire sent to a number of fans and on the advice of John Nathan-Turner, who had been engaged as a consultant. Other contributors to the programme included Steve Roberts (a fan who worked in the telecine department at the BBC) and Ian Levine, who along with Nathan-Turner supplied Lauchlan with lists of what was available to be included. The list of categories was: Resistance Is Useless; Thoughts Of An Anorak; Time And Relative Dimensions In Space; Fab Gadgets; Fashion Victims; Leave It To Me, Dear; The Brigadier's Finest Moments; Doc Fax; Behind The Sofa; Doc Fax (again); Effects (Special); Death By Special Effect; Give It All You've Got; Surreal; and Doctor In Charge.

Transmission of *Resistance is Useless* led on to a season of BBC2 repeats, starting with *The Time Meddler*, *The Mind Robber*, *The Sea Devils* and, in a specially restored recolourised version (combining images from a broadcast-standard black and white print with those from a poorer quality colour home video recorded off-air in the USA), *The Dæmons*. This was the first time that the BBC had screened any complete repeats of *Doctor Who* since *The Five Doctors* in 1984. Satellite and cable channel UK Gold also began transmitting regular repeats of the series, following the demise of BSB.

In February, Dark Light Productions was reported by *Doctor Who Magazine* to be the latest independent company bidding to produce a new series. The producer, Alan Jonns, eventually made a statement in the May edition of the magazine, indicating that no episodes had been filmed, no actor had been cast and no contracts with the BBC had been signed. He revealed that his company had simply been carrying out test work to see if their ideas were suitable. Although this work ultimately came to nothing, some of the monster designs created for the company by the Henson Creature Shop were later seen in relation both to the aborted 30th anniversary special *The Dark Dimension* (see below), one test photograph even appearing on the proposed cover of an ultimately unpublished Adrian Rigelsford book about that production, and to a potential Bill Baggs video drama featuring Cybermen and Ice Warriors.

Other notable events during 1992 included as part of the BBC's ongoing programme of *Doctor Who* video releases the cancelled Season 17 story *Shada*, with the missing scenes bridged by narration from Tom Baker, and in May, the Season 5 story *The Tomb of the Cybermen*, all four episodes of which had been amongst a consignment of film prints recently recovered from Hong Kong after being missing for many years from the

BBC archives. In Virgin's New Adventures novels, meanwhile, a new – and ultimately highly popular – companion named Bernice Summerfield made her debut.

1993

The run of BBC2 repeats continued into the early part of 1993 with *Genesis of the Daleks, The Caves of Androzani, Revelation of the Daleks* (in the edited four part version originally created for overseas sales purposes) and *Battlefield*.

In April, the BBC held a press launch, with Jon Pertwee, Peter Davison, Colin Baker, Sylvester McCoy and Nicholas Courtney in attendance, promoting the package of video and audio releases planned for that autumn to tie in with *Doctor Who*'s 30th anniversary. Tony Greenwood, Director of Home Entertainment at BBC Enterprises, also mentioned that, as had been rumoured since the previous December, a script had been written for a special anniversary production – although he added that it might not actually reach fruition, as the necessary agreements had yet to be concluded. (The original aim of BBC Enterprises in holding this press launch had in fact been to announce the making of the special, but they had had to backtrack as it had yet to be given the go-ahead.)

The following month, it was confirmed that the special, entitled *The Dark Dimension* and intended to feature all the surviving Doctors, would be directed by Graeme Harper (who had made his mark on the series with *The Caves of Androzani* and *Revelation of the Daleks*). Then in June, there came the only official announcement that the BBC ever made on the subject, when a ninety-six minute, 16mm film special, referred to as *Doctor Who: Lost in the Dark Dimension*, was listed in its forthcoming drama publicity press release. The special was written by Adrian Rigelsford and Jo McCaul and a production office was set up with Penny Mills (from BBC Enterprises) and newly resigned Head of Drama Peter Cregeen acting as co-producers.

On 9 July, the special was abruptly cancelled. No official reason was ever given, as the BBC denied that it was ever a finalised project. The Managing Director of Network Television, Will Wyatt, blamed over-eager fans for taking it beyond the ideas stage. BBC Video's David Jackson broke the news by saying: 'Due to the constrictions of our budget and the time available, the production has been cancelled.' It is believed that internal BBC politics and objections raised by Philip Segal, the American-based producer bidding for the rights to make a new series, also contributed to the decision not to go ahead with the project. Rigelsford, who had been trying to get his script produced for two years, was reported by *Doctor Who Magazine* to be 'deeply disappointed'. It was also revealed by *Doctor Who Magazine* that Nick Jagels had been brought on board as production associate and that Rigelsford, Harper and Jagels, together with Alan Jonns, had been the 'guiding force' behind Dark Light's earlier attempts to get *Doctor Who* back on air.

Despite future rumours to the contrary, Tom Baker was the only actor ever contracted to appear in the special (and hence the only one to be paid); no other casting was ever agreed (although the other surviving Doctors – who, with the exception of Sylvester McCoy, would have had much smaller roles – were sent copies of the script); no filming or location work was ever carried out; and, aside from Rigelsford writing a draft rehearsal script (of which there appear to have been several different versions, none of them bearing a co-writing credit for McCaul), the only other production work ever carried out consisted of one or two early 'ideas' meetings drawing together interested parties –

including production designer Nigel Jones, visual effects designer Tony Harding and first assistant director Kevan van Thompson – who may or may not have ended up working on the project had it gone ahead. Kevin Davies had also been approached with a view to designing the title sequence, and Mark Russell and Alan Hawkshawe had been under consideration to provide the music.

In August, BBC Radio 5 transmitted a new *Doctor Who* radio serial entitled *Paradise of Death*, written by Barry Letts and featuring Jon Pertwee, Elisabeth Sladen and Nicholas Courtney reprising their roles as the third Doctor, Sarah Jane Smith and Brigadier Lethbridge-Stewart respectively. This had been recorded in May. The serial's producer, Phil Clarke, was also responsible for a documentary, *Doctor Who – 30 Years*, which was broadcast on BBC Radio 2 on 20 November and ran for 55 minutes and 44 seconds. This was narrated by Nicholas Courtney and featured interviews with: Gary Russell (editor, *Doctor Who* Magazine), Katy Manning ('Jo'), John Scott Martin (Dalek operator), Jon Pertwee ('the Doctor'), William Russell ('Ian'), Peter Purves ('Steven'), Louise Jameson ('Leela'), Barry Letts (director, producer and writer), Terrance Dicks (script editor and writer), Terry Nation (writer), Frazer Hines ('Jamie'), Jessica Carney (William Hartnell's granddaughter), John Nathan-Turner (producer), Verity Lambert (producer), Sylvester McCoy ('the Doctor') and Brian Hodgson (special sound effects). Also recorded but unused in the final programme were interviews with Anneke Wills ('Polly'), Elisabeth Sladen ('Sarah Jane Smith'), David J Howe (historian) and Roberta Tovey ('Susan' from the cinema films).

The Season 10 story *Planet of the Daleks* was meanwhile repeated on BBC1 in November and December, with a five minute 'mini documentary' preceding each episode. The themes of these mini-documentaries were as follows: *Bigger Inside Than Out* (Colin Baker narrating a piece on the history of the TARDIS and the police box upon which its external appearance was based); *The Antique Doctor Who Show* (a pastiche of the BBC's *The Antiques Road Show* in which presenter Justin Pressland and collector David J Howe spoke to several fans about their *Doctor Who* collections); *Missing in Action* (a look at the junking of *Doctor Who* episodes and the efforts to retrieve them); *I Was That Monster* (interviews with people who had played monsters); *Crimefile – The Master* (a pastiche of the crime prevention show *Police 5* in which presenter Shaw Taylor warned the public to be on the lookout for the Master); and *UNIT Recruiting Film* (in which Nicholas Courtney encouraged people to join up). At the end of the last of these mini-documentaries was given a telephone number, callers to which could hear Courtney telling them that *The Green Death* was due to be repeated the following year.

Although plans for a proper anniversary story had come to nothing, there was a minor consolation for fans, as the two-part skit *Dimensions in Time* was transmitted as part of BBC1's annual *Children in Need* telethon on 26 and 27 November.

On 29 November, BBC1 also transmitted a more substantial fifty minute documentary entitled *30 Years in the TARDIS* (which was released on video the following year with additional material under the title *More than 30 Years in the TARDIS*). This had suddenly been given the green light in September by the team responsible for the previous year's *Resistance is Useless*. Recorded during October and November, it brought together clips, interviews and dramatic interludes to provide a well balanced overview of the series. Interviews were conducted with: Mat Irvine (visual effects), Mike Tucker (visual effects), Colin Baker ('the Doctor'), Nicola Bryant ('Peri'),

Carole Ann Ford ('Susan'), Verity Lambert (producer), Roberta Tovey ('Susan' from the cinema films), Sophie Aldred ('Ace'), Sylvester McCoy ('the Doctor'), Barry Letts (director, producer and writer), Terrance Dicks (script editor and writer), Elisabeth Sladen ('Sarah Jane Smith'), Delia Derbyshire (theme music arranger), Brian Hodgson (special sound effects), Dick Mills (special sound effects), Jessica Carney (William Hartnell's granddaughter), Jennie Linden ('Barbara' from the cinema films), Deborah Watling ('Victoria'), Frazer Hines ('Jamie'), John Nathan-Turner (producer), Ian Levine (fan), Gary Russell (editor, *Doctor Who* Magazine), Jon Pertwee ('the Doctor'), Eric Saward (script editor and writer), Mary Whitehouse (retired head of the National Viewers' and Listeners' Association), Ben Aaronovitch (writer), Philip Hinchcliffe (producer); Stephen Bayley (academic), Professor Steve Jones (academic); Lowrey Turner (fashion editor); Mike Gatting (England cricketer/celebrity fan), Ken Livingstone (politician/celebrity fan), Toyah Wilcox (pop singer and presenter/celebrity fan) and Gerry Anderson (puppet series producer/celebrity fan). Several of those interviewed were not seen in the broadcast programme, although Davies was able to include some of the unused material in the later video release.

1994

Further repeats – this time of *The Green Death* and *Pyramids of Mars* – were transmitted on BBC2 at the start of 1994. Then, in July, Virgin launched a new range of Missing Adventures books to complement their New Adventures.

On 9 July, listeners to BBC Radio 4 were able to hear *Whatever Happened to ... Susan?*, the fifth in a series of humorous programmes looking at the lives of popular fictional characters, the subject in this case being the Doctor's grand-daughter Susan Foreman, played here by Jane Asher after the original actress, Carole Ann Ford, apparently failed to return the BBC's calls. The programme was produced by Brian King, written by Adrian Mourby and, in addition to Asher, featured James Grout (playing Ian Chesterton), June Barne (Barbara Wright), Eva Haddon (Jo Jones, née Grant), Andrew Sachs (Temmosus Skyedron), Peter Woodthorpe (Joey Oxford), Barry Harrison (researcher) and Claire Rayner (as herself).

Following the success of *Paradise of Death*, a further *Doctor Who* radio serial, *Doctor Who and the Ghosts of N Space*, was recorded in November, although its transmission was ultimately delayed until March 1996, when it went out on BBC Radio 2 (Radio 5 having by this point become an all-news station). Like *The Paradise of Death*, it was produced by Phil Clarke, written by Barry Letts and featured Jon Pertwee, Elisabeth Sladen, Nicholas Courtney and new regular Richard Pearce playing Sarah's young assistant Jeremy.

1995

1995 was a relatively quiet year for *Doctor Who*, although UK Gold continued to transmit repeats and there was still a steady stream of new tie-in merchandise being issued, including the first in a range of BBC audio books featuring abridged versions of the Target novelisations of televised stories read by their respective Doctors. By this point, however, the series' followers were becoming increasingly excited by news reports that seemed to suggest that there might, at long last, be a real prospect of new *Doctor Who* being seen on television for the first time in over six years ...

SEVENTH DOCTOR

MOVIE HELL

Omitted from the preceding sections of this chapter has been any mention of the numerous unsuccessful attempts to get a *Doctor Who* feature film off the ground during the late Eighties and the Nineties – a subject that merits a section all of its own.

There had been serious talk of a *Doctor Who* movie from as early as 1976, when Tom Baker, actor Ian Marter (who played companion Harry Sullivan) and producer James Hill developed an idea, with the working titles *Doctor Who and the Big Game* and *Doctor Who Meets Scratchman*, featuring 'Scratchman', another name for the devil, as the villain. After much negotiation, BBC Enterprises granted James Hill Productions, with effect from 1 November 1978, a one year option to make the film, with no commitment on their part to renew. The project eventually fell through, however, due to difficulties in raising the necessary finance.

In the meantime, numerous other overtures were made to the BBC by parties interested in pursuing *Doctor Who* film projects. On 4 April 1978, Jill Foster Ltd made contact regarding a Douglas Adams film treatment based on the series. An approach came on 12 May 1980 from producer Brian Eastman of Paramount; another on 23 August 1982 from Anthony Williams of Sandfire Productions, based at Pinewood Studios; and another in May 1984 from American producer Norman Rubenstein, who remained in contact with the BBC until October of that year. These all came to nothing. Milton Subotsky, co-producer of the two '60s *Doctor Who* films, contacted Head of Series and Serials Jonathan Powell in April 1984 to indicate that he would like to do a third. This had the working title *Doctor Who's Greatest Adventure* and would have involved two Doctors teaming up to combat some giant monsters. Powell turned the idea down, and confirmed with Head of Copyright Brian Turner that there was nothing in Subotsky's original contracts with the BBC that gave him any rights in this regard. A proposal that progressed a little further was put forward on 15 October 1984 by Edward Joffe of Multivision Communications Ltd. The BBC stipulated as conditions for granting the film rights to Multivision that John Nathan-Turner would have to be involved in the project; that one of the television Doctors would have to be given the lead role; and that a fee of around £50,000 would have to be paid. Peter Davison was subsequently contacted to see if he would be interested in starring in the film, and Christopher H Bidmead was earmarked as a possible writer. In the end, however, this also fell through. On 7 May 1985, Nathan-Turner suggested that *Doctor Who*'s first producer, Verity Lambert, might be a good candidate to make a film based on the series. Then, on 21 June 1985, producer Michael Bond put forward a film treatment entitled *The Crossroads in Time*. This too came to nothing.

It was in March 1985 that Coast-to-Coast Productions Ltd – run by co-directors Peter Litten, George Dugdale and John Humphreys – first entered into negotiations with BBC Enterprises with a view to acquiring the rights to make a *Doctor Who* feature film, having apparently started discussing the idea the previous month. In November of the same year, Litten wrote an undated letter to BBC Enterprises' Director of Business Administration John Keeble, setting out the company's latest proposals for the film and indicating that the budget and scope had recently been increased in all departments. He stated that: actors Denholm Elliott, Steven Berkoff, Caroline Munro, Tim Curry and Laurence Olivier had all agreed to be involved; composer Mike Oldfield had been approached to adapt the series' theme tune and provide the incidental music; make-up artist Christopher Tucker, whose credits included *The Elephant Man* and *The Company of Wolves*, would be creating the creatures and monsters; John Stears, who had won an Oscar for his work on *Star Wars*, would be in charge of visual effects; Rodney Matthews and Anton Furst would be teaming up to design the sets and costumes; Douglas Adams would be acting as script consultant; Robert Holmes would be providing the screenplay; and Richard Lester, the man at the helm of *Superman 2* and *Superman 3* amongst many other projects, was being considered as director. He also stated that Sun Alliance had undertaken to provide financial backing for the film, and that only the BBC's agreement was now required.

Jonathan Powell, when shown Litten's letter, expressed considerable scepticism. In an internal memo to Keeble he wrote: 'With respect, this strikes me as slightly full of baloney. *No* actors would agree without a script. The technicians mentioned would never agree without production dates. Robert Holmes is not an adventurous choice to write the screenplay. Anyone can *consider* Richard Lester. The statement means absolutely nothing in practice.'

Powell went on to state that he believed that the BBC should keep the project for themselves, and that if they did decide to allow it to go ahead outside, then there should be 'some known factor involved'. He concluded by stating that he was unimpressed by Litten's letter, which made many promises and listed many prospective contributors when 'clearly their statements are absolutely meaningless.' He also asked if anyone had any idea as to what Litten had done in the past, or what his production company had actually achieved.

Despite this unfavourable reception from Powell, negotiations with Coast-to-Coast continued, and were eventually concluded around July 1987, when the company was finally granted the rights to make a *Doctor Who* feature film in return for a substantial fee, reported to be £46,000. It was apparently envisaged that the company would need to raise some £1.6 million in backing in order to proceed with the project.

During the latter half of 1987, rumours regarding the film's casting, content and production started to appear with increasing frequency in newspapers and magazines. It was variously reported that actress Caroline Munro would be featuring in the film as the villain; that £5 million was being spent on the effects alone; that Sylvester McCoy was the hot favourite for the role of the Doctor; that the budget was around £9 million; that Tom Conti and Tim Curry had turned down the starring role; and that Tom Baker was the hot favourite to take the lead.

Stage and Television Today carried a short piece on the film on 8 October 1987, headed by a mocked-up image of Munro as the computerised television host Max Headroom (Coast-to-Coast having previously been involved in the production of Chrysalis's *Max Headroom* show). John Humphreys was quoted as saying: 'We intend to make it a big budget film with extensive and advanced special effects – I can promise you we won't be using the BBC's infamous quarry.' The report went on to suggest that the film involved Munro 'in the title role' as a robot who operates a pirate radio spaceship to beam pop videos down to earth. However, as this sounds suspiciously like a description of *Max Headroom* (albeit that Munro did not star in that series), it is possible that the reporter had his or her wires crossed.

Early in 1988, John Cleese was tipped to play the Doctor, and Dudley Moore was also mentioned as a strong contender for the part. Munro was now apparently in line to play the companion rather than the villain, and it was reported that the film's directors would be Litten and Dugdale. £14 million was the latest figure quoted for the budget, and a script was stated to have been commissioned from writer Mark Ezra. In March, another writer, Johnny Byrne, was reported to be under contract to work on the script, and a release date of Easter 1989 was mooted.

In May 1988, fan Ian Levine was confirmed as a consultant on the project. Then, the following month, it was predicted that shooting would commence in January 1989. John Cleese was at this time still being tipped to play the Doctor, and, in a new twist, it was suggested that there would be no fewer than four companion characters. In November 1988, the *Daily Mail* gave over part of the front page of one of its editions to the news that Dudley Moore was to star as the Doctor in a film with a budget of £19 million – the highest figure yet suggested. The following month, however, Moore was reported to be only one of a number of contenders for the title role, others being Donald Sutherland, Ian Holm and Peter Firth. Filming was still reported to be due to start in January, the chosen locations being London and the Canary Islands, but Munro had now apparently reverted to playing the villain.

In April 1989, with no shooting having actually taken place, it was reported that the film had been postponed indefinitely due to lack of finance. In August of that year, however, it was apparently back on again, with filming due to start in March 1990 in Yugoslavia. On 23 October 1989, a number of newspapers reported that Donald Sutherland was to take the lead role, having been cast in preference to Dudley Moore, Michael Caine, John Cleese and Sylvester Stallone, and that – scandalously – the film would show the Doctor boozing, having bar-room brawls, carrying a gun and making love to his assistant. The budget at this time was claimed to be £20 million, and the makers of the Johnny Byrne-scripted film were said to be Pathé.

By the end of 1989, *Doctor Who* fans who had eagerly followed all these reports were understandably totally confused, and many were starting to become highly sceptical that the film would ever see the light of day. Philip Newman, a fan who wrote regularly for several genre magazines and who had apparently been in regular contact with Litten since December 1987, tried to clear the air by explaining in the fanzine *Proteus* what had been really happening. 'Firstly,' he wrote, 'I think it is most important to get one particular message across: *Doctor Who – The Movie* is *definitely* going ahead, and will go into production once all the financial, distribution and other arrangements have been finalised – probably sometime early in 1990.' On the subject of why it had taken so long to get to this stage, Newman indicated that Coast-to-Coast wanted to keep the film as authentic as possible to the original television series and that, with much of the financial backing coming from America, it had 'been hard to keep control of all aspects of the film's production and, moreover, to keep it British.'

As for the scripting of the film, Newman recounted that Mark Ezra had written a first 'rough framework' in 1987 and that this had since been totally reworked by Byrne into a full length script, which had subsequently been through as many as sixteen rewrites. Levine had checked the script for accuracy in terms of the series' mythology, but otherwise had had no involvement in the project. According to Newman, only twelve actors had ever been seriously considered for the role of the Doctor, and just four of these were still seen as possible contenders. At no point had any of the television Doctors ever been under consideration. Newman went on to add: 'Pre-production work is well underway, with twelve conceptual artists, working from different parts of the country, now engaged on producing preliminary designs and plans for all the sets, lighting rigs, creatures and costumes. Several storyboard artists are currently at work on realising the large volume of special effects sequences that the film requires.'

Jean-Marc Lofficier's book *The Nth Doctor*, initially published by Virgin Publishing in 1997, also gives a description of Coast-to-Coast's abortive attempts to get their *Doctor Who* film off the ground, and in some respects this is at odds with the account presented by Newman. According to Lofficier, Ezra had by August 1987 completed not only a 'rough framework' but a full draft script entitled *Doctor Who – The Movie*. Byrne then worked on several different treatments and drafts during 1988 and 1989, and the story gradually evolved away from Ezra's original. The resultant scripts were retitled *Doctor Who – [The] Last of the Time Lords*. The project was sufficiently advanced for the Coast-to-Coast team, now calling themselves Green Light, to prepare an advertising flier for the Moving Pictures International film conference in Milan in October 1990. This showed a re-worked *Doctor Who* logo along with the tag line: 'The Man – The Myth – The Movie'.

As *The Nth Doctor* tells it, Byrne completely rewrote his script in 1991 while Litten and Dugdale brought to fruition another project: a low budget horror feature called *Living Doll*. Green Light, meanwhile, obtained from the BBC another extension of the time period available to them to make the film. This would now expire on 6 April 1994 at which point, if shooting had not commenced, all rights would revert to the BBC.

In 1992, in a further attempt to gain the required finance, Green Light joined forces with Lumiere Pictures and apparently sold on the *Doctor Who* rights to them. One of Lumiere's first acts was to abandon Byrne's work on the project, and instead to commission a totally new script, first from Nicholas Meyer and then, when this did not work out, from a writing partner of Meyer's, Denny Martin Flinn. Lumiere also approached actor and director Leonard Nimoy (famous for his role as Spock in *Star Trek*), and, after reading Flinn's script, he agreed to produce and direct the film. The actor strongly favoured to play the part of the Doctor at this time was Pierce Brosnan. In the event, however, Green Light/Lumiere were unable to commence filming by the deadline date, at which point Lumiere decided to withdraw from the project.

There is one final development to report in this saga. On 10 January 1996, just as news of the Philip Segal/Universal/BBC Worldwide television movie was breaking, the London *Evening Standard* carried a two page exposé on the problems that had beset the earlier feature film project. The report, by Keith Dovkants, stated that Litten, Dugdale and Humpreys were all 'special effects experts' who had worked on *Doctor Who* (it is indeed the case that Litten and Dugdale once worked in the BBC's Visual Effects Department, and it is known that the Morlox creature seen in Season 22's *Timelash* was built by one or other of them, although neither ever received a credit on the series) and had decided to obtain the rights to make a *Doctor Who* film in the late Eighties (sic) as they 'deplored the fact that no-one was tapping the enormous cinema potential'. The report went on to explain that the three men had obtained finance from a consortium of about twenty individuals (including singer Bryan Ferry and, from the band Dire Straits, John Illsley) and formed a company called Daltenreys to take the project forward, pouring in additional money from second mortgages on their homes in the process. Their deal with the BBC was reported to have been with Keeble, and it was stated that Daltenreys had had meetings with Warner Brothers in America, who had

SEVENTH DOCTOR

suggested Jack Nicholson as a suitable actor to play the villain – this was at the time when Tim Burton's *Batman*, featuring Nicholson as the Joker, was flavour of the month – and Bill Cosby, Denholm Elliot, Donald Sutherland and Alan Rickman as potential Doctors.

The problem had come, according to the report, when Keeble had resigned from the BBC and BBC Enterprises had become BBC Worldwide, with a remit from new BBC Director General John Birt to maximise profits. Humphreys was quoted as saying that Daltenreys had signed a deal with Lumiere in 1993; that Lumiere had wanted to make three *Doctor Who* films with a budget of more than $30 million; that Leonard Nimoy had been engaged as director and Alan Rickman 'courted' to play the Doctor; and that after they had heard Stephen Spielberg's name linked to a *Doctor Who* film project (as it had been in the press) they had contacted the BBC and been fobbed off: 'We got the run around'.

The report went on to note that Daltenreys had spent the next few months trying to work out what their position was, and that on 4 March, a month before the filming deadline, the BBC's senior lawyer Rowan Vevers had written to them querying their arrangement with Lumiere on what Humphreys described as a 'technicality'. This had apparently been too much for Lumiere, who according to the report had already spent over a million pounds on the project, and they had withdrawn. This had left Daltenreys high and dry and with no other option but to speak to their own lawyers regarding the legality of the BBC's actions.

The resultant legal action was reported by Joanna Bale in *The Times* a year later, on 15 February 1997. Daltenreys were said to be seeking a million pounds in compensation and £21 million in damages against the potential profits from the three film versions of *Doctor Who* that they had planned to make. They were also said to have paid £440,000 for the rights to make the films. In an interesting aside, Bale reported that the BBC claimed to know nothing about any legal action, but that if it was pursued, they would 'vigorously contest it'.

As of writing, nothing more has been reported about the prospective legal action. Nor have any further proposals for *Doctor Who* feature films been made public.

The Eighth Doctor

by

David J Howe

Stephen James Walker

PAUL McGANN: IN HIS OWN WORDS

ON PUBLICITY
'We've never been Mr and Mrs Showbiz.'
Interviewed by Garry Jenkins for *TV Times* dated 25-31 May 1996.

'I'm fairly private, you know. I don't live in London. I don't do that "showbiz" stuff. I've got family. There's times when I don't want to get involved, and there's times when it's great to be associated with something … Fame is a double-edged sword'
Speaking in Birmingham after a screening of *Withnail and I* on 22 March 1996.

ON TAKING OVER THE ROLE OF THE DOCTOR
'When I saw the casting agent in Los Angeles I kept saying, "You've got the wrong fella." Other actors seemed to fit the image better, so I turned it down. I said, "This is daft, I can't do it." There was no pressure, it's easy to say no.'
Interviewed by Garry Jenkins for *TV Times* dated 25-31 May 1996.

'Taking on such a key role hasn't really sunk in yet. It is just beginning to dawn on me what all this means. Sylvester McCoy is a friend, so he's told me everything I need to know. I loved *Doctor Who* as a kid. William Hartnell used to terrify me. My favourite villain was the Yeti, but the Daleks never did it for me – they couldn't run upstairs.
   'This film will be loyal to the spirit of past series, but will find fresh appeal too.'
Speaking at a press launch on 10 January 1996.

'I was on the *News at 10*! My mum was ringing me up saying, "You're on tonight!" It's like being an ambassador. That's what it feels like for a Brit. It's an honour, but a responsibility as well, which is the part that's beginning to dawn on me.'
Interviewed by Frank Garcia for *Starlog* dated June 1996.

'There was a style to the Doctor that, quite honestly, I didn't think I could live up to. Some of the skills were almost vaudevillian. It was sort of that indoor scarf-wearing, eccentric kind of thing. It wasn't me.'
Interviewed by Mark Nollinger for *TV Guide* dated May 11-17 1996.

'In the past, the Doctors have been rather kooky, manic and zany. I am not a kooky person. When Philip [Segal] initially offered me the role, I said to myself, "What is this person thinking! I'm all wrong for this part."'
Interviewed by Lou Anders for *Sci-Fi Universe* dated December 1996.

'I've signed a contract. I can't go anywhere. I am him. I am Who. He is me.'
Interviewed by Christy Slewinski for the *New York Daily News* dated 14 May 1996.

'I knew I'd have an effect on lots of people, and especially on children. It is a responsibility. But I thought that if I was going to do telly, I may as well do the biggest

telly. And there's no doubt the biggest telly is *Doctor Who.*'
Interviewed by Gary Gillatt in 1996 for *Doctor Who Magazine* No. 238.

'It's like a top posting. It's like being the ambassador to the US or something. It's like getting a mega-top job. The Beeb's equivalent of "our man overseas" or something. I'm just realising the size of the job.'
Speaking on the video *Bidding Adieu* produced by BBV and released in 1996.

ON THE EIGHTH DOCTOR'S CHARACTER

'He's a bit clean, isn't he, old Doctor Who? There's gonna be some changes ... I might put that out on the internet – "There's gonna be some changes ..."'
Speaking in Birmingham after a screening of *Withnail and I* on 22 March 1996.

'There are elements like the jelly babies. There are little bits that have been carried over that have survived. I can't help thinking of Patrick Troughton or Bill Hartnell, but certainly, I'm doing it *my* way. That's easy. It's the only way I *can* do it.'
Interviewed by Frank Garcia for *Starlog* dated June 1996.

'I have been looking for something more edgy. It's like the vampire. You can't have hung around for three hundred years and not feel kind of bitter. There are darker elements to it.'
Interviewed by Garry Jenkins for *The Times Magazine* dated 25 May 1996.

'Playing the Doctor has been strange, trying to find the right level. I spend half the film not knowing who I am, so the character's not even there. It's a learning process for me. I'd like to do more, so I can get my teeth into it, and work with the Doctor.'
Interviewed by Gary Gillatt in 1996 for *Doctor Who Magazine* No. 237.

'Being British and having grown up in Britain you couldn't see past ... the character as he's been represented – that collective popular understanding of what the Doctor is like. So not only was I not convinced that I could hack it, I also couldn't see how they could make it seem remotely interesting for me. I think it was because the names that were being bandied round, pop stars and celebrities rather than actors, created a certain impression about the type of person who would be playing the Doctor. I didn't see that I could fit in with the expectation that a known eccentric should play the part. Much as I loved *Doctor Who* as a kid, I felt I could no sooner play him than I could play, say, Prince Charles. As I said, it's just not what I do.'
Interviewed by Gary Gillatt in 1996 for *Doctor Who Magazine* No. 238.

'What'll I bring to the part? Youth. Glamour. I was going to say "Scouseness", but I'm following in a long line of Scouse Doctor Whos, because Tom Baker's one, isn't he? I shall bring my usual thing. I just do my thing, whatever it is I do.'
Interviewed by Mark Gatiss in 1996 for *Starburst* Special #28.

ON KISSING GRACE

'There are kisses and kisses. There are kisses that are innocently meant. He doesn't kiss

her by mistake. But it is not licentiousness.'
Interviewed by Garry Jenkins in 1996 for *TV Zone* Issue 78.

'I kept my lips together when I kissed Daphne [Ashbrook] because I didn't want the love scenes to be too sexy. It is the first time the Doctor has been seen kissing, and I didn't want to do anything that might upset a family audience.'
Interviewed by Shoba Vazirani for the *Sun* dated 25 May 1996.

'All innocently meant, though, you see … It's an American kiss, it's not a European one … no tonsil-tickling.'
Speaking on the video *Bidding Adieu* produced by BBV and released in 1996.

'It's a magic moment.'
Interviewed by Garry Jenkins for *Inside TV* dated 25-31 May 1996.

'This has been a sore point, hasn't it? I wasn't aware actually that there had never been a … that there was never a … I mean … has the Doctor never had a snog? … So is it going to get the fans' backs up?'
Interviewed by Gary Gillatt in 1996 for *Doctor Who Magazine* No. 238.

ON THE AMERICANISATION OF *DOCTOR WHO*
'We have got mad chases on police bikes – why not? We have had gunfights at the OK Corral in *Doctor Who* before. Who says we can't have *The Streets of San Francisco*?'
Interviewed by Garry Jenkins for *The Times Magazine* dated 25 May 1996.

'This is going off in a new direction. If it goes to a series, I don't know what I'll do, really. It depends whether I've got the bottle to just go with it, embrace it. … Given that it's pitched deliberately as North American, the remnants of the quintessential Britishness of it will have to remain, because they regard that as commercial.'
Interviewed by Mark Gatiss in 1996 for *Starburst* Issue 214.

ON FANDOM AND ATTENDING CONVENTIONS
'The thought of me going anywhere near a convention at the moment makes my flesh creep! I know I'm going to have to. I'm going to get collared at some point, but I want to die when I think about it. Obviously it comes with the job. I can't run and hide forever. Mind you, I can always send one of my brothers …'
Interviewed by Mark Gatiss in 1996 for *Starburst* Special #28.

'It fills me *with absolute dread*, to be honest with you. I know I'll do it. I just know I'll end up doing it at least once, because I like to scare myself. That's very Catholic. I know McCoy does the circuit. But he's very gifted. He can simply stand on a stage and entertain two thousand people for an hour. I'm nervous – the thought of standing there – I won't even do the theatre for the same reason. I'm too scared. I suggested to McCoy that I go along with him in disguise, incognito, to see what it's like, and he said there's no such thing anymore. He said, "You would be eaten alive! They can smell you! You don't stand a chance!"'
Interviewed by Frank Garcia for *Starlog* dated June 1996.

'The fans are very understanding. I've been very pleased and surprised to find that the real fans, the people from the magazine and stuff, have the right amount of "tongue-in-cheekness" about it. It's great, 'cause they love it and they're into it, but it's only a game – they're not going to put someone's nose out of joint! They seem to realise that if I don't want to do something, I won't do it. And recognising that is generally the best way to deal with me. I'm the kid that says "no" to something for ages, then eventually knocks on the door and says, "Well actually, can I join in?" – y'know? I'll do it in my own time though.'
Interviewed by Simon J Gerard in 1996 for *Doctor Who Magazine* No. 246.

ON FAN REACTION
'Sylvester McCoy put it well when he told me that I was basically on a hiding to nothing. He said that some people would love me and some people would hate me, but everyone has their own views of what the Doctor should be like and you can't please all of them. He told me I can't really win, but I can't really fail either.'
Interviewed by Gary Gillatt in 1996 for *Doctor Who Magazine* No. 238.

'There's a lot of people that care a lot – for quite a big group, I'm suddenly the star, there are thousands of people I'm suddenly really important to. But feelings do seem to run very high. People take it all deadly seriously, which is strange, because it's actually quite a light and witty programme.'
Interviewed by Gary Gillatt in 1996 for *Doctor Who Magazine* No. 238.

ON THE FINISHED PRODUCT
'I have a good feeling about it. But who knows, who knows?'
Interviewed by Garry Jenkins in 1996 for *TV Zone* Issue 78.

'When I saw the finished film, I thought it looked amazing. It looks like a major movie.'
Interviewed by John Millar for the *Daily Record* dated 25 May 1996.

'The ratings will be what we're judged by, but the future of the series also seems to be contingent on whether or not the "big cheeses" like it – that's the impression I get. We've been getting good feedback, though; we've been receiving flowers from Hollywood every day, so we must be doing something right. We're getting a good vibe, and we're having a laugh doing it.'
Interviewed by Gary Gillatt in 1996 for *Doctor Who Magazine* No. 237.

ON THE FUTURE
'I'll stay with it. I've got to. I've signed a piece of paper that says I will'
Interviewed by Frank Garcia for *Starlog* dated June 1996.

'Even if it doesn't go any further and I end up being the George Lazenby of the Time Lords, I'll have had a good time. And I'll still get asked to the *Doctor Who* conventions.'
Interviewed by John Millar for the *Daily Record* dated 25 May 1996.

'Well, frankly, it'll be great if it takes off, because I'll be offered more work. That's the first consideration – I won't be sitting on my arse as much as I used to. As for the type of work … I don't know, it's hard to say … I'm not conditioned to think that far ahead. I go out of my mind if I try to do that.'
Interviewed by Gary Gillatt in 1996 for *Doctor Who Magazine* **No. 238.**

'The situation is that we're doing a TV movie but putatively it's a pilot and it might go to a series. But the fact is that the people who run the series are another department altogether. So who knows. If it was all under the same roof, then probably they'd know by now that it was going to go [to a series] and things would be a lot clearer. What's going to be happening in twelve months … who knows? It might not go at all. The chances are dead against it, in fact.'
Speaking on the video *Bidding Adieu* **produced by BBV and released in 1996.**

CHARACTER – THE EIGHTH DOCTOR

It was always the intention of executive producer Philip David Segal to introduce an eighth Doctor in the television movie; no serious consideration was ever given to featuring the seventh Doctor in anything other than a brief appearance leading up to a regeneration. Interviewed exclusively for this book, Segal recalled the qualities that he had been looking for in the new Doctor:

'I don't think my perception ever really changed. I knew the qualities that he had to have. Looking at the series itself, and even at the information gleaned from the books that have been written about it, you can see that a good proportion of what was established with the previous Doctors was stuff that the actors themselves brought to the role. So all we could really do to influence that was to find someone whose appearance and demeanor gave us indications that externally they had the stuff to give us what they might have internally.

'Obviously humour and a dark side and a sort of child-like behaviour along with some alien-like qualities are all important parts of the mixture.

'It influenced the casting in a certain way. I wasn't trying to do anything that I thought was so brilliant that everyone would say it was a work of genius. All I wanted to do was to find somebody who fitted the shoes, so to speak, because whether you like it or not, if you try to go in a direction that moves a long way away from the spirit of who this character is, then I think you're actually damaging the fabric of the franchise. So it wasn't so much that I could bring a unique perspective to this; that wasn't my intention at all. I never felt that I was doing this because I was the one who understood *Doctor Who* better than anyone else in the world. I never felt that way at all. But I was the one who was the keeper of the keys, so I had the opportunity to keep it going, and given that that was an enormous task, I tried to do things that were aesthetically pleasing to me and creatively responsible for the franchise.

'The casting was my responsibility, but I had bosses. I couldn't just wave my wand and have whoever I wanted. Paul McGann was always my first choice, but he joined the project late, and there was a reason for that; it was my responsibility to go out into the field, as it were.'

McGann himself was reluctant to become associated with the project, and in fact initially declined, unable to see himself in the role as it was popularly presented in the media as an outrageously costumed eccentric. In the end, however, he was won over.

Also instrumental in shaping the eighth Doctor's character was writer Matthew Jacobs. 'He had very strong opinions about what the Doctor should and should not be,' acknowledged Segal. 'There was a lot of Matthew's influence in the material ... I specified areas that I felt were very important for us to touch on and that I felt were central to the Doctor's world, and Matthew really ran with it. We had numerous conversations about things that we could and could not touch on. He was terrific, in that he was like a sponge: once he got an idea of the direction I wanted to go, he was very good at picking up the ball and taking it on to the next step. There's very much his imprint on the material. I think he did quite a good job, all things considered.

'When Paul was cast, the thing took on a life of its own. Paul brought his own unique qualities to the role. The first time I saw him on set in his costume, it was pretty uncanny. There was one moment where I didn't think he ever wasn't the Doctor. Once he settled down, I think he felt the same way. I don't know what the general perception was from the audience, but I believe it was fairly positive.'

Any attempt to evaluate the eighth Doctor's character on the basis of just a single adventure is inevitably fraught with difficulty. (To realise this, one need only consider how skewed an assessment would be gained from considering in isolation the debut stories of each of the other Doctors.) Some fan commentators have attempted to do so, however, and a particularly perceptive summation was made by Lance Parkin in *Matrix* Issue 53 dated autumn 1996: 'The eighth Doctor acts impulsively, without planning. He lacks arrogance, instead demonstrating child-like qualities of wonder and boundless energy. Everything is done in earnest, with a passion. He fixes on things and is capable of brilliant improvisation.'

As the Doctor himself says to Grace in the movie: 'I can't make your dream come true forever, but I can make it come true today.'

PRODUCTION DEVELOPMENT

It was in 1994 that Philip David Segal, an Englishman working as head of television production at Stephen Spielberg's Amblin company in the USA, was granted by BBC Enterprises the rights to make a new series of *Doctor Who*. This was an ambition that he had been pursuing ever since the BBC stopped producing the series in 1989, as he explained:

'I wanted *Doctor Who* back. And that took a long time. Simply put, my aim was to rebuild the franchise; that was the object of the exercise, to bring it back. There was a period of time at the BBC where there was a real willingness to do that, so I took advantage of that, and that's essentially how we got *Doctor Who* back.

'That intensified and really became real in 1993; that was when it really became real in terms of actually negotiating a deal with the BBC and wanting to move forward.'

Segal's intention was always to make a television series rather than a feature film, so the fact that the BBC had already granted the *Doctor Who* film rights to the group now known as Daltenreys presented no obstacle. 'We had no interest in making a feature film,' he confirmed. 'That was always the case. I made it very clear from the very beginning that I didn't think that it should be relaunched as a feature film; that there was still a lot of work that had to be done in terms of television; but that ultimately one day it could become the basis of a film ... We had some dialogue with Daltenreys, but nothing that really meant anything significant to me. The sad thing about it is that you don't like to see anyone spend the kind of money they did and not get anywhere, which they did. I feel bad for them in that regard. But it had no bearing on what I was doing.'

The project was initially envisaged as a three-way co-production between BBC Enterprises, Amblin and Universal Television in the USA. Writer John Leekley was commissioned by Segal to put together a 'series bible' – a detailed document outlining, partly for the benefit of potential purchasers, the concept and its intended treatment – and the script for a movie-length pilot episode. The bible turned out to be a lavish affair. Printed on a parchment paper and bound in a real leather cover embossed with the Seal of Rassilon, it purported to be written by Lord Borusa and charted the history and activities of a Time Lord known as the Doctor. By way of illustration, several new pieces of black and white artwork were used (including a sequence of drawings showing some redesigned 'spider' Daleks) along with more familiar (to *Doctor Who* fans) images intended to give an idea of what the characters and settings might look like. To illustrate the section on the Master, for example, Segal used a photograph of Michael Jayston as the Valyard from *The Trial of a Time Lord*, simply because his flowing robes and dramatic appearance matched the style and vision he and Leekley had for the Master. Similarly, to depict an effective alien being, an image was taken from the cover of one of Virgin Publishing's New Adventures novels, *Birthright* by Nigel Robinson.

Leekley's script for the pilot movie featured the Daleks, Davros and the Master in a story set partly on the Doctor's home planet, Gallifrey. Entitled simply *Doctor Who* (although the writer later suggested that *Fathers and Brothers* would have made a good subtitle), it was completed in September 1994, but ultimately failed to find favour. Robert de Laurentis was then commissioned to provide a replacement; his attempt, entitled *Dr Who?*, was completed in December 1994. Segal was at this time attempting to sell the series to the Fox television network, although when problems arose in his negotiations with them, he also entered into discussions with a number of other networks. 'Fox didn't decline it,' he explains. 'There was a situation that happened where there was a distinct split between Amblin and Universal that caused a derailment of the project. It wasn't Fox's fault. But the situation sort of reorganised itself when an executive called Trevor Walton, who is English, came to Fox. We had had serious offers from CBS at that time as well, although they ultimately declined.'

Walton was in Fox's made-for-television movie division, which meant that the project was now seen primarily in that light. 'In our eyes, it was still a pilot for a series,' commented Segal, 'but it was produced through the movie division of Fox and not the TV division. It's not unusual, though, for a two hour movie to be made by the movie division and still end up being treated as a pilot; it's standard in the States. In this situation, you would be canny enough to produce it to look like and feel like and smell like a pilot, so that it had enough story to satisfy a two hour movie audience but at the same time had enough strings so that you could see the character returning. So there were deliberate attempts on our part to package the movie in that way, to give us the basis for hopefully a good series.'

At the Gallifrey convention in February 1995, Segal showed attendees a video featuring some test images of a new computer-generated title sequence (very similar in style to the one used during the fourth Doctor's era) and of a redesigned race of armoured, spider-like Daleks. He also gave a short slide show displaying some early set and prop ideas prepared by one of the movie's production artists.

Segal had always been keen that his version of *Doctor Who* should be true to the spirit of the original, and he found that Walton was much more sympathetic toward this idea than had been his colleagues in Fox's TV division. Walton, for instance, agreed with him that the movie should if possible be explicitly linked to the continuity of the BBC series by opening with Sylvester McCoy's Doctor and leading up to a regeneration, whereas the TV division executives had wanted it to stand completely apart from what had gone before, to the extent that he had considered having dialogue included in the script indicating that it took place in a parallel universe (drawing inspiration from an idea presented in the third Doctor story *Inferno*). A new script was thus required and, although established series writer Terrance Dicks was on the short-list of potential writers, it was eventually commissioned from Matthew Jacobs, another Englishman who already had experience of working in American as well as UK network television.

'It was actually Trevor Walton who had worked with Matthew and asked us to consider him and meet him,' noted Segal. 'The networks rarely make demands over things like that. Usually they will allow you to make a case for a particular writer. However, there were reasons why Matthew made sense to me. When I sat and talked with him at Amblin, it turned out that his grandfather had been an actor in the Wyatt Earp episode of *Doctor Who* [Season 3's *The Gunfighters*, in which Anthony Jacobs played Doc Holliday]. His relationship with his father had been an incredibly rocky one, and when his father had eventually died, they had not been reconciled, so there was this real emotional kind of bridge that this script was going to build for him. And I liked his writing style. He's a very colourful individual and brought a lot of colour and passion to the project, so I was very pleased indeed with the choice.'

Jacobs started working on his script around April 1995, and the first complete draft was dated 18 July. Segal recalled the factors that had influenced its development:

'It was a pretty fast track once we got going. There were a couple of glitches in the story as we went though. Some that I thought were good changes and some that I was disappointed with. Ultimately there was more than one voice in that script, so that's the struggle that I had.

'We knew that the Doctor had to have a companion, simply from the mechanics of the franchise. The problem with the Doctor is that unless he has someone to ask what he's doing or thinking, the audience never gets to know what he's doing or thinking. That's just the flaw of the process.

'I think we first set about trying to think where the location should be. We knew it had to be in the United States for identification reasons, but we also wanted it to be a place that had some universal awareness of it. Most people know of San Francisco, and it's my favourite city in America. The last place I wanted it to be was Los Angeles; it would have felt just so clichéd, for some reason. San Francisco didn't seem clichéd. It had a sort of mystique to it that Los Angeles didn't have. It didn't hurt that Matthew lived in San Francisco. We started to formulate the story out of this, and it changed dramatically as we went along. Matthew's first impressions had a lot more emotionality for Chang Lee than we ultimately ended up with.

'The hospital thing was something that we were also playing around with. We didn't really get all the mileage out of that, really.

'There were several companies that needed specific things, and there was definitely a distinct difference between Fox's need for something with an adult appeal and the familiar perception of *Doctor Who* as a family or children's show. The end product was not necessarily what the BBC wanted, but how far they were prepared to go. They were extremely collaborative with me at various points. Alan Yentob was, and is in my opinion today, this project's best friend. That's just a reality from my eyes. This is the man who, through thick and thin, has supported this project and who still believes in *Doctor Who* as a franchise. He's in a very difficult position. One's philosophy has to be to let management manage, so if you hire someone to do a job, you have to stay out of their way and let them do it; he can make suggestions, but he really has to let people manage.'

Amblin (where Segal had earlier been given a co-executive producer in the person of fellow Englishman Peter Wagg) dropped out of the picture in 1995 after Spielberg joined forces with former Disney executive Jeffrey Katzenberg and music mogul David Geffen in a new company called Dreamworks SKG. Segal left the company in September, and went on to produce the movie independently, as a joint venture between the BBC (eighty percent of whose financial input came from BBC Worldwide, as BBC Enterprises had now been renamed, and twenty percent from BBC Television) and Universal. Fox also had a financial input into the movie.

'The production office was located in the Spelling complex. We leased out some space in Barnerby, just outside Vancouver. That was where the stages were. Locations were in and around Vancouver proper. The production itself was housed in Barnerby, and I had an office there. During pre-production, I was moving backwards and forwards between Los Angeles, Vancouver and London. I also spent some time in New York doing casting. But I worked out of my office on the Paramount lot.

'Universal gave me a boss by the name of Alex Beaton. This was because I was somewhat alienated from the studio – I wasn't somebody they had a tremendous love affair with, let's put it that way – and they wanted to make sure their interests were protected. But Alex and I got on very well. His job was basically to manage the money. He never interfered creatively at all with the production – nobody did, I had the final say in all creative matters – but when it came to the financial side of things, and I fought for what I wanted, I won some battles and I lost some battles.

'Then there was a producer by the name of Peter Ware, who basically managed the physical production. There was also a unit production manager called Fran. He was a fabulous guy. It was his below-the-line crew that worked on the movie.

'Richard Hudolin was the production designer, and was first class. He and I got on like a house on fire. I told him exactly what I wanted to do, and it was done.

'The amazing thing about a lot of these people is that they immediately went out and got every *Doctor Who* book that existed and looked at everything that had been done in the past. So many of them were fans. There was a real passion to get everything right, and sometimes they'd go overboard. The funny thing about it, of course, is that as you dip into *Doctor Who*, you're taking from thirty years of mythology. It's interesting to see people's reactions when you take material from different eras, mixing them up and putting them all in one thing. Some fans look at you and say, "You can't do that!" I thought it was wonderful to take from the cupboard of mythology and just paint a new picture. That's what we did with this production to a certain extent. We painted details throughout it that gave you a taste of the traditions of the show.

'Jo Wright from the BBC was ultimately given the title of executive producer in the end credits; she was the BBC's person.

'Each of the organisations involved had to have its own person; that's the reality of life. Trevor from Fox never got a credit; American network executives don't get credits on movies. He was the big boss. He was the one looking over scripts. I must say he was very supportive of me in the process. What happens is that once a network commits to a project, it goes into a slot and the clock ticks. The pressure is to deliver that project for that time slot, because there's nothing else to fill it; they don't double develop and double produce. So once *Doctor Who* had been given a firm airdate, which we knew at the start was 14 May 1996, we were on a runaway train. Five months to make it, with no excuses. Trevor's job became much more difficult, because the studio wanted to cut corners to save money, it had other agendas; the BBC had its own agenda; and BBC Worldwide had its own agenda – although the truth of the matter is that it was not managing anything.'

The completed movie was delivered to Fox about a week before it premiered. It was promoted with the tag-line 'He's Back – And It's About Time,' and US newspaper critics gave it an almost universally positive reception. In ratings terms, however, the movie ultimately underperformed. This was partly due to the fact that it was up against some very strong competition from the other networks, including a much-anticipated episode of the comedy series *Roseanne* in which the title character's husband, played by John Goodman, suffers a heart attack. In Segal's view, however, there were other underlying political reasons why it did less well than it might have:

'When you really go into the mechanics of why *Doctor Who* didn't get a bigger audience, that would require a two hour dissertation on who the Fox network actually are, who their station groups are, what their demographic audience is.

'If you had put that same movie on a different network, at a different time, with different promotion, away from the sweeps – which is programming designed to hype the network – you may or may not have had a different result. I can't sit here and say to you, "Oh my show would have done a 20 share anywhere else." I don't know that. There may truly have been some problems with the female appeal of the show, the audience awareness of *Doctor Who*, the story itself. There may have been a lot of things working against us.'

In the UK, the movie did much better, winning very good ratings and generally enthusiastic audience feedback. There were over 100,000 copies sold of the BBC's video release of the production, some 55,000 copies of Gary Russell's novelisation and even some 15,000 copies of the script book. Total worldwide sales of the video release were in excess of 150,000 copies. Universal retained an option on *Doctor Who* until the end of 1997, but in the event, did not take it up.

'Several things happened that made it very clear that it wasn't going to be a series,' reflects Segal, 'least of which was the fact that it underperformed. I was also very tired – eighteen hour days, not seeing your family, the stress and the politics, it does take it out of you. There was another regime change at Fox; there were regime changes all the time at the BBC. The movie itself happened for very specific reasons; it wasn't just because I pushed hard enough, there were other reasons, and we got caught up in the tidal wave.

All the fans could really see was that it was coming back, but the truth on the inside was that it was a limited time offer – get it now while it's available. But that's another story.'

Even though the movie did not, in the end, lead on to the hoped-for series, Segal was well satisfied with the end product:

'My job as producer is to bring all the elements together. I think it's ultimately a mistake to try to impose your will on people. That's a dangerous thing to do. I think the object of the exercise is to bring together the best people you can get hold of and give them the room and the opportunity to be the best that they can be. That's something that I take a lot of pride in. I'm very strong when it comes to what I want and don't want, but I also feel that once I've had my two cents' worth, it's very important to take two giant steps back and let people do their jobs. If I feel that the wheels are coming off, then I'm quite happy to jump in and to try and fix that.

'I feel that what you saw there was a chorus of very talented people who came together and made something very special, in my opinion. I'm very proud of it. For all its faults and for all the problems and things like that, I think we did a damn good job, given the rules that we had to play by, I think we did the best we could. I feel that everyone did the best that they could do, and I'm certainly very proud of it.'

As for the future, Segal asserts: 'I really believe that *Doctor Who* will be back again. I really do. Whether it's me or someone else who makes it. You can't kill *Doctor Who*. It will never die.'

REWRITING THE MYTH

Throughout *Doctor Who*'s history, each successive change in the series' behind the scenes team led to a development of its style and content – and of its mythology. Never was this more true than of the 1996 television movie.

The action opens with a seventh Doctor who is visibly older than when last seen. He also seems to have dramatically reconfigured his TARDIS interior, which now has a very gothic, 'Wellsian' look to it – appropriately enough, given that he is seen reading a copy of Wells's *The Time Machine*. The possibility of such reconfiguration had been well established in earlier stories – some of which, including Season 15's *The Invasion of Time* and Season 19's *Castrovalva*, had made explicit reference to it – but the change seen here is the most radical to date. Even more novel is the revelation that the ship contains in its Cloister room an Eye of Harmony. Season 14's *The Deadly Assassin* had suggested that there was just a single Eye of Harmony, the source of all the Time Lords' power, located on Gallifrey; now it seems that every TARDIS must contain a fragment of the Eye. This does make some sort of sense, as it is difficult to see how otherwise the power from a central source could reach the ships, given that they can go anywhere in space and time.

The Eye as seen in the television movie appears to have many properties and functions aside from simply powering the TARDIS. It is somehow connected to the Doctor himself, and can 'see' what he sees. It can also project images of his earlier incarnations and, when correctly set up, can actually transfer one Time Lord's remaining lives to another (as the Master attempts to do here). Perhaps the strangest idea is that it can actually swallow the Master whole, a process that apparently gives the TARDIS 'indigestion'. Also remarkable is the fact that it is able to restore life to both Grace and Chang Lee after the Master has killed them. This could perhaps be viewed as a result of the TARDIS moving back in time to the point before the Eye destroyed the Earth, although an alternative explanation might be that it stored the life essence of the Doctors' two friends when they died and then returned it to them once time had resumed its normal course. The Doctor's own observation is that the TARDIS is sentimental.

The Doctor's regeneration on this occasion is a delayed reaction to him being shot and actually dying on the operating table, his alien metabolism adversely affected by the anaesthetic and by Grace's manipulation of a heart probe. Following the regeneration, the new Doctor goes through the customary period of confusion before recovering fully.

One of the most talked-about aspects of the television movie is its revelation that the Doctor is half-human. This, however, ties in quite well with what has gone before. For one thing, it helps to explain why the Doctor has always seemed to have such an affinity for the Earth and its indigenous people. (The Doctor talks of seeing Gallifreyan skies with his father, and mentions that he is half-human on his mother's side). It could also explain why his grand-daughter Susan wanted to attend school in England. In addition, it provides possible answers to the questions raised about the Doctor's identity in the series' twenty-fifth and twenty-sixth seasons – including the suggestion that he was more than just a Time Lord – and how he managed to return to Earth at the end of *Survival*.

Another fact revealed in the movie is that when a Time Lord reaches the end of his regenerative cycle, he can apparently change species. The Master has become (whether or not by his own choice is left unclear) a reptilian, snake-like creature. With this change, he has acquired the power to change form; to spit a burning venom that can immobilise the victim; and to possess those 'marked' with the venom.

There is arguably only one major aspect of the movie's plot that it is difficult to reconcile with what has gone before. This is the aforementioned idea of the TARDIS travelling back in time to a point before the Eye of Harmony was opened so as to prevent the disaster precipitated by the Master. This flies in the face of many previous assertions made by the Doctor about him being unable to change the course of history – as, for example, when his companion Adric was killed at the end of Season 18's *Earthshock* – and undermines the whole basis of the series' format by raising the question why he does not always simply travel back in time to thwart all his adversaries' schemes before they have even got off the drawing board.

It is a pity that this one less than satisfactory aspect marred what was otherwise an admirable production from the point of view of the use and development of *Doctor Who* mythology.

SELLING THE DOCTOR

MEDIA
by Ian Wheeler

Doctor Who has always been considered newsworthy by the British media, who over the years have expressed both love and hatred for the series – often according to the whims or prejudices of the particular journalist responsible. The Sylvester McCoy era was no exception, and in fact proved to be perhaps the most controversial period of *Doctor Who*'s history as far as press reaction was concerned. In 1985, during Colin Baker's time as the Doctor, the tabloid newspapers had campaigned to save the series when it appeared that it was going to be axed. By 1987, it was clear that things had changed, and that the seventh Doctor was going to get a somewhat rockier ride.

On 28 February 1987, the *Sun* was the first to report the identity of the seventh Doctor. Under the headline 'New Doctor Who is the Unknown McCoy', Charles Catchpole wrote: 'A zany Scot who used to make a living by stuffing ferrets down his trousers is the new Doctor Who'. The paper referred to McCoy as 'a shock choice', adding that other hopefuls had included former companion actor Frazer Hines (who had, in fact, never been under consideration).

The *Sun*'s exclusive was followed by reports in other papers on 3 March (an announcement of the new Doctor's identity having been made on the television news the day before). A number were quick to point out McCoy's lack of celebrity status but, more positively, some also reported that the actor had been awarded a three year contract. In *Today*, McCoy was quoted as saying: 'I might not be all that well-known, but that's going to change. People have been telling me for years that I'd be perfect to play Doctor Who, and I'm going to prove them right.'

The launch of the new Doctor was somewhat overshadowed by the news at the end of March that one of his predecessors, Patrick Troughton, had died following a heart attack at a *Doctor Who* convention in the USA.

The first reports of the new season came at the beginning of April, when a modest number of papers featured the new Doctor in costume on location for *Time and the Rani*. Details were sparse, with particular emphasis being given to the fact that Kate O'Mara was also appearing in the story. A more informative item on the making of the story was however to be seen on the BBC's *Breakfast Time* programme on 5 May. Other TV coverage of the series during this period included items about the location recording of *Delta and the Bannermen* on BBC Wales on 31 July and on BBC1's *But First This … on* 31 August.

It was in September, with the twenty-fourth season now beginning on BBC1, that the new Doctor really began to make his presence felt. The *Star* promised that the new-look show would be 'the glossiest ever', going 'flat out for fun' with stars such as popular comedy actor Richard Briers. Meanwhile, the 5-11 September edition of the BBC's listings magazine *Radio Times* featured the seventh Doctor in full colour on page three with an additional article included as part of the 'John Craven's Back Pages' feature.

The reviews for *Time and the Rani* proved to be less enthusiastic than the pre-publicity. McCoy was nominated 'Wally of the Week' in the *Daily Express* and described as being 'bland' and 'a joke' in the *Sunday Post*. Paul Mount, television reviewer for the monthly science fiction magazine *Starburst*, also expressed dislike for the new series, but at least admitted to McCoy being 'convincing in a way that neither Peter Davison or Colin Baker ever were'.

October began with the *Sun* reporting that the BBC had axed *Doctor Who* after twenty-four years. This 'exclusive' went on to say that the show was losing viewers every week and that the current series would be the last. Days later, the *Sun* was claiming to have saved the show, adding that a new movie produced by Coast to Coast was set to appear in November 1988.

At the end of October, a more encouraging piece appeared in the *Daily Mirror*. The article focused on the appearance of comedian Ken Dodd and actor Don Henderson in Malcolm Kohll's *Delta and the Bannermen*. According to the report, *Coronation Street* had failed to kill off the Doctor, with the Time Lord attracting 'an audience of more than five million'.

The floodgates really opened in November, the month of the series' 24th anniversary. McCoy gave an interview to the *Daily Express* during which he was quoted as saying 'I believe the Doctor is still valid in the *Star Wars* generation'. The week after, the *Star* printed a disturbing article with the headline, 'Who's a Load of Rubbish?'. Fans were said to be dissatisfied with the series and were calling for producer John Nathan-Turner to be sacked. This was prompted by campaigning reports in the fanzine *DWB*, a source to which several newspapers turned for their more sensationalist coverage of the series.

Later the same month, the *Daily Telegraph*'s Charles Spencer reviewed *Dragonfire* Part One, and was generally supportive, referring to McCoy as 'an appealing Doctor with a genuine sense of wonder and a nice line in irony'. He was, however, not entirely without reservations, and felt that the new Doctor could do with 'a little less whimsy and a shade more authority'.

Following *Dragonfire*'s spectacular climax, in which the villain Kane melted on screen, the *Star* reported that angry mothers had phoned the BBC to complain about the sequence. The editor of *DWB*, Gary Levy, was quoted as saying: 'This new controversy will prove more damaging'.

'The Daleks are back!' was the very clear message carried by most of the national newspapers in the spring of 1988. 'Doctor Who has defeated his greatest enemy – former BBC1 chief Michael Grade,' reported the *Daily Express*, 'and when he returns to BBC screens in the autumn, Doctor Who will take on his other deadly foe – the Daleks'. And according to the *Sun* on the same day, 'The Daleks are as evil as ever, but they have swapped their dull grey metal jackets for a gold and white livery'.

A colour article in the *Radio Times* heralded the return of the Daleks as part of BBC1's autumn season: 'Those evil, heartless, cruel, diabolical Daleks are back – and the latest Doctor Who is rather pleased about it!' John Davies' full page feature included comments from Sylvester McCoy, John Nathan-Turner and writer Ben Aaronovitch. Each had his own opinion on the secret of the Daleks' appeal, with Aaronovitch commenting that: 'They are beings within machines rather than just machines. If they were just robots, they'd be boring.'

Following some glowing reviews of *Remembrance of the Daleks* Part One, *Doctor Who* was the subject of an in-depth critique in the *Listener* magazine. 'Sylvester McCoy, the new and promising Doctor', wrote Mark Ball, 'faces the uphill grind of a series hopelessly locked in repetition, unable any longer to break out of its past.' A letter from Dr David M Duckels in the 10 November edition suggested that 'Sylvester McCoy seems set to establish himself as a vintage Doctor'.

A more controversial piece appeared in the *News of the World* on 13 November. 'Bertie Bassett Takes On Doctor Who' was the headline, following a protest from Bev Stokes, chairman of confectionery manufacturers Bassett's, about the alleged similarity between the Kandy Man from *The Happiness Patrol* and the company's famous marketing character, Bertie. 'We would like the programme to do something to restore Bertie's honour', Stokes commented. The Kandy Man's 'death' in Part Three of the story brought the matter to a quiet close.

The week of *Doctor Who*'s 25th anniversary saw the beginning in the *Radio Times* of a new feature called 'My Kind of Day'. McCoy was the subject of the first piece, and was shown sitting in a tree house. As the year drew to a close, the *Weekend Guardian*'s reference to McCoy as 'one of the best Doctors yet' boded well for the venerable Time Lord in 1989.

In May 1989, the *News of the World* asked 'Who's That Evil Parson?', referring to Nicholas Parsons' guest appearance in *The Curse of Fenric*. The actor commented that McCoy had 'been a joy to work with' and that he had 'never had so much fun in [his] life'. Rather less fun was had by Sophie Aldred in June when, as reported by the press, she was nearly killed in a water tank accident during studio recording for *Battlefield*.

The beginning of the twenty-sixth season in September was met with minimal press coverage, and even the *Radio Times*, once the show's greatest supporter, let the side down by running only a brief black and white article about Ace on the children's page. *TV Guide* was far more generous, featuring McCoy on its front cover and a two page report, 'What's Up Doc?', from the quarry location of *Survival*.

Ever a creature of habit, the *Sun* again claimed that *Doctor Who* had been axed on 21 October. Unfortunately, this time, it was true. 1989 came to a close with the series' future uncertain but, according to the BBC, at least safe.

1990 began with the news, on 5 February in the *Daily Express*, that Sylvester McCoy and Sophie Aldred had had their contracts withdrawn, and that the odds were firmly against them returning to play the Doctor and Ace. The paper claimed that independent companies were bidding to produce the twenty-seventh season, and that Dalek creator Terry Nation and Gerry Davis, co-creator of the Cybermen, were the favourites. Again these stories appear to have been inspired by reports in the fanzine *DWB*.

'Doctor Who could be in for a sex change,' suggested the *News of the World* on 26 August. Ex-companion Mary Tamm, who had been the first Romana during the Tom Baker years, was quoted as saying that she would 'love to play the Doctor'.

An interview with McCoy was published by the *Daily Express* on 9 October under the heading 'Doctor Who's the Real McCoy – by Sylvester'. John Munro reported that McCoy had 'fought his way back to the top in theatre' after his 'high-flying career was brought down to Earth when the BBC axed the show' and added that 'when the BBC mandarins finally get round to launching a new series, it's odds on that the flamboyant McCoy will be playing the good Doctor'.

As the years rolled by, there were to be a great number of speculative newspaper articles about *Doctor Who*'s future, many of them bizarre and almost all of them inaccurate. Actors David Hasselhoff, Eric Idle, Pamela Anderson and director Steven Spielberg were just some of the names that were linked with a mooted *Doctor Who* TV series or movie. Fans had to wait many years before concrete news about the series' future was finally to emerge.

THE TV MOVIE
by Ian Wheeler

After years of speculation and many disappointments, the identity of the eighth Doctor was finally revealed to the world on 11 January 1996. All the major newspapers covered the story and reported that a television movie was in production. 'Our man McGann beats the stars to become new Doctor Who,' declared the *Daily Express*, obviously delighted that the role had gone to a British actor rather than an American. Amongst the celebrities whom it claimed had been considered for the part were Bill Cosby, Jack Nicholson and Alan Rickman, while the *Daily Star* reported that Simon Callow and the pop star Sting had both been in the running.

As the first new *Doctor Who* to be broadcast in over six years, the TV movie itself was understandably the subject of considerable media attention. For the first time in its history, *Doctor Who* had the honour of being featured on the front cover of the IPC-published listings magazine *TV Times* (which had at one time covered only ITV programmes). The magazine described McGann as 'the unlikeliest Time Lord – EVER!' and quoted him as saying that he wanted the Doctor to be 'a bit more edgy ... a bit darker. It's also important to me that I have a hoot – and this *is* a hoot. I've got a good feeling about it now.' *Radio Times* also ran a *Doctor Who* cover and rewarded its readers with a free, sixteen page *Doctor Who* souvenir booklet. In addition, there was the promise of a new comic strip based on the series, which would begin in the following issue. This was written by Gary Russell and drawn by Lee Sullivan.

Initial press excitement about the Doctor's return was counterbalanced by a distinct lack of enthusiasm once the movie had actually been transmitted. Reviews were mixed, to say the least. Max Davidson of the *Daily Mail* commented that the movie 'was like a bad memory of childhood. I thought this absurdly inflated character had achieved his final resting place as a line in a knock-knock joke. Seeing the TARDIS again, in a vulgar American reincarnation, was too depressing for words. Do we never grow up?' Others were more positive, and the *Daily Express*'s review by Maureen Paton was fairly typical: 'At last we have a grown up hi-tech *Doctor Who* in Paul McGann ... Only a low-tech Luddite would miss the endearing amateurism of the old teatime serial format ... The makers would be mad not to pursue the option of a series.' Matthew Bond of *The Times* would probably have shared this sentiment, but felt that: 'If the series is to return, it will need stronger scripts than this simplistic offering, which struggled to fill eighty-five minutes and laboured somewhat in its search for wit.'

The general public were also determined to have their say on the movie, and the letters page of *Radio Times* for the week beginning 15 June 1996 was packed with viewers' comments. 'Paul McGann's performance in the new *Doctor Who* film delighted me,' wrote Simon Harries of Dartford. 'He brought an exciting new intensity and intelligence to the character, while still reminding me of Tom Baker at his most "other-worldly" and Patrick Troughton at his most mixed up'. Georgina Scott of Derby was also taken by the new Doctor and claimed that the BBC had given her a 'universally acceptable new sex symbol' in the form of McGann. Sean Coleman of Scunthorpe was more critical. 'The BBC should be exterminated!' he wrote, concluding that the Corporation had 'sold our dear old Time Lord down the Mississippi'.

In the pages of the *Doctor Who* fan press, there was an equally wide range of comments. *Doctor Who* Appreciation Society (DWAS) member Peter Lewis was 'pleasantly surprised and impressed' by the movie, whereas *Doctor Who Magazine* reader Michael Dax found it to be 'a god-awful mess'. Perhaps the best summary was offered in the DWAS's *Celestial Toyroom* newsletter by editor Keith Hopkins, who considered the project to be 'a success ... a qualified success perhaps, but a success nonetheless'. One way or another, the new movie had generated a huge amount of media and public interest, and *Doctor Who* had once again demonstrated its unique ability to make an impact and refuse to go unnoticed.

PERSONAL APPEARANCES
by Ian Wheeler

Of all the actors to have played the Doctor, Sylvester McCoy was one of the keenest to promote and publicise the series. Many people received their first glimpse of the new Doctor on 2 March 1987, when he emerged from the TARDIS on the Monday edition of the children's magazine show *Blue Peter* and chatted with presenter Janet Ellis about his hopes for the role. He also appeared on BBC1's Saturday morning children's show *It's Wicked* on 30 May. When Season 24 began transmission, *Doctor Who* was featured on *Open Air*, the BBC's daytime television discussion programme. McCoy was present, along with companion actress Bonnie Langford and producer John Nathan-Turner, and early viewer reaction to the seventh Doctor seemed to be positive. As his tenure progressed, McCoy was also to be seen on the youngsters' Saturday morning show *Going Live* (in 1987, and again in 1988 for *Doctor Who*'s 25th anniversary), the *Children's Royal Variety Performance* and the 1988 *Tomorrow's World Christmas Quiz*. In 1989, he joined TV presenter Noel Edmonds and comedy actor Jeffrey Holland on *The Noel Edmonds Saturday Roadshow*, and in November participated in the *Children in Need* telethon.

From late 1989 onwards, with *Doctor Who* no longer in production, McCoy tended to avoid wearing his seventh Doctor costume for personal appearances. He did, however, relate a *Doctor Who* anecdote or two to presenter Bruce Forsyth on the ITV game show *You Bet!* in 1990, and briefly stepped back into character for a BBC schools programme, *Search Out Science*, which also saw the return of Sophie Aldred as Ace.

When the ill-fated satellite broadcaster BSB ran a whole weekend of *Doctor Who* episodes and other related material – another first for the series – McCoy was one of the large number of stars to be interviewed about his involvement with it.

In 1993, McCoy joined sixth Doctor Colin Baker and a Tractator (from the fifth Doctor story *Frontios*) on *This Morning*, and the following year he appeared with Baker, fifth Doctor Peter Davison and actors Tim Brooke-Taylor, Bill Oddie and Graeme Garden (otherwise known as the Goodies from the eponymous cult BBC series of the Seventies), for an item on animals on *Good Morning with Anne and Nick*. McCoy was invariably happy to be seen on screen with his fellow Doctors, and good fun and humour were always evident on such occasions.

Perhaps the most unusual appearance for McCoy's Doctor was not on television, but in the pages of one of the nation's favourite children's comics. In the spring of 1988, he was featured in the 'Strange Hill School' comic strip in *The Dandy*, being pursued, rather appropriately, by hideous monsters.

Advertisers were also amongst those eager to utilise McCoy's talents. He played the Doctor in a television commercial for the *Radio Times* in which he claimed to like the travel section of the magazine. On the radio, meanwhile, he participated in a commercial for batteries, which saw the Doctor up against his old enemies, the Cybermen.

This brief summary has highlighted those personal appearances by McCoy that were primarily intended to publicise *Doctor Who* or had an interesting *Doctor Who* connection. It should be noted that throughout his time as the Doctor, and beyond, McCoy was much in demand as a celebrity in his own right. He was frequently to be seen on a variety of light entertainment shows, his contributions ranging from being a mystery guest on the children's programme *Knock Knock* to appearing as a panellist on *The Holiday Quiz*.

Things changed dramatically when Paul McGann inherited the mantle of the Doctor in 1996. McGann was clearly a much more private person than McCoy, and was unwilling to be associated with the role in terms of public appearances. In interviews, he expressed a reluctance to attend any kind of *Doctor Who* convention, claiming that he lacked McCoy's ability to get up and entertain an audience. Consequently, the only appearance of the eighth Doctor in costume was in the television movie itself, and in related press photocalls, and the only on-camera interviews that McGann gave about the role were for the movie's 'electronic press kit', used by the Sci-Fi Channel amongst others to compile behind-the-scenes reports on the production, and the Bill Baggs-produced video documentary *Bidding Adieu*. It was the end of an era in more ways than one.

THE TWENTY-FIFTH ANNIVERSARY
by Ian Wheeler

1988 was a year of growing optimism for *Doctor Who* fans, and the series' 25th anniversary was celebrated in a quiet but enthusiastic manner. There was no special story reuniting old Doctors, as there had been for the 10th and 20th anniversaries, but the Cybermen were brought back in the three-parter *Silver Nemesis*; and, as Cyber Leader actor and sometime writer David Banks remarked in his book *Cybermen*, 'It was thought ... that the Cybermen would make it an appropriately Silver Anniversary'. The season opener *Remembrance of the Daleks* also contained nostalgic elements and included a return to the junkyard in Totter's Lane where the Doctor had begun his televised travels in the winter of 1963.

Production of *Silver Nemesis* was covered by a crew from the US television station New Jersey Network for a programme entitled *The Making of Doctor Who* (one of a series of documentaries that NJN had made about the series). This was not transmitted in the UK, but would eventually be made available in edited form as part of the BBC's *Silver Nemesis* video release.

The British press were also keen to publicise the story, and chose to focus on the appearance of actress Mary Reynolds in a cameo as the Queen. Under the headline 'Her Royal Who-ness!', the *Star*'s TV editor Michael Burke reported on 29 June 1988 that 'new locations and a record budget of £1.5 million mean that the autumn anniversary series will be the best ever for fans all over the world'.

Sylvester McCoy, Sophie Aldred and third Doctor Jon Pertwee appeared on *Daytime Live*, a popular BBC interview show, to publicise the anniversary. The three actors stepped out of the TARDIS and answered questions from the audience (a group of *Doctor Who* fans who had been specially invited). McCoy was asked if he had been approached to take the lead role in the mooted *Doctor Who* feature film. He and Pertwee both seemed keen to be involved and expressed the view that all the surviving Doctors should appear in the film. Aldred meanwhile seemed delighted to be taking on the Daleks and the Cybermen in stories during the anniversary season. Clips of each of the seven Doctors were also shown on the programme.

Radio Times celebrated the milestone by running a retrospective article on the Doctor's many companions. There were also a modest number of merchandise items issued to commemorate the anniversary. These included an album featuring various versions of the theme tune and a selection of Keff McCulloch's incidental music from stories such as *Paradise Towers* and *Remembrance of the Daleks*; *Doctor Who – 25 Glorious*

Years, a W H Allen hardback book by Peter Haining; a special *Doctor Who* playset from Dapol; a badge from the BBC; and two different 'first day covers' featuring the signature of one of the actors to have played the Doctor.

The first episode of *Silver Nemesis* was transmitted in the UK on the actual date of the anniversary. The night before, Noel Edmonds had mentioned the Doctor's birthday on an edition of his *Telly Addicts* quiz show. A trailer had also been extensively shown, utilising scenes from the new story and old footage of William Hartnell from Season 2's *The Web Planet*, to emphasise the series' longevity.

There was also a press call to publicise *Silver Nemesis*. This was held at Space Adventure, a new 'theme ride' located in London's Tooley Street, which boasted an exhibition of *Doctor Who* costumes and props. A photograph from this event of Sylvester McCoy and Sophie Aldred cutting a TARDIS cake appeared in the national press. Shortly after the anniversary, producer John Nathan-Turner was a guest on the afternoon show *Behind the Screen*, talking about the Doctor's past and future. A clip from the forthcoming adventure *The Greatest Show in the Galaxy* was shown, and when asked if there were any plans for a new Doctor, Nathan-Turner replied that he was perfectly happy with McCoy's portrayal.

THE THIRTIETH ANNIVERSARY
by Ian Wheeler

Doctor Who's 30th anniversary in 1993 was a time of surprises and disappointments. The main event planned for the year was *The Dark Dimension*. When this was cancelled, press coverage focused on the fact that Adrian Rigelsford's story had given the fourth and seventh Doctors by far the biggest slices of the action, with the third, fifth and sixth relegated virtually to 'guest appearances' – something that had greatly displeased actors Jon Pertwee, Peter Davison and Colin Baker when they had received copies of the script prior to any formal contract discussions taking place. A number of reports even suggested, incorrectly, that this was the reason why the special had been abandoned.

The two-part skit *Dimensions in Time*, involving characters both from *Doctor Who* and from the popular BBC soap opera *EastEnders*, was transmitted in November as part of the BBC's *Children in Need* telethon. This was featured on the front cover of the *Radio Times*, making it the first *Doctor Who*-related production to be accorded this accolade since *The Five Doctors* exactly ten years earlier. The BBC's popular science programme *Tomorrow's World* ran a report on the new 3-D process and also acknowledged *Doctor Who*'s anniversary by examining the concept of time travel as part of a special feature.

In addition to the *Children in Need* special, BBC1 broadcast the new *Doctor Who* documentary *30 Years in the TARDIS* and repeated the Season 10 story *Planet of the Daleks*, each episode of which was preceded by a five-minute mini-documentary examining one aspect of the series. BBC Radio 2 meanwhile had its own retrospective, *Doctor Who – 30 Years*, produced by Phil Clarke and narrated by Nicholas Courtney.

On the merchandise front, two commemorative video tins were released by BBC Enterprises. The first featured the Daleks and contained videos of Season 2's *The Chase* and Season 25's *Remembrance of the Daleks*, together with a booklet about the Daleks. The other was a TARDIS-shaped tin containing all fourteen episodes of Season 23's solitary story, *The Trial of a Time Lord*. Both tins came in a variety of 'editions' featuring different photographs on their bases. Videos of *Resurrection of the Daleks* and *The Two Doctors* also arrived in the shops, having been designated the 'Fan's Choice' following a *Doctor Who Magazine* poll. Virgin released David J Howe's *Timeframe*, a lavish and colourful collection of photographs and artwork from the series' thirty-year history, which went on to become one of Virgin Publishing's best selling *Doctor Who* titles. Marvel Comics meanwhile produced a special magazine, stylistically based on the *Radio Times* publication in 1973 to celebrate the series' 10th anniversary, with Sylvester McCoy replacing Jon Pertwee in a similar cover photograph. The DWAS published their own glossy booklet with contributions from many of the series' stars, and Dominitemporal Services Ltd organised for them a huge convention in Hammersmith, London, with Doctors Jon Pertwee, Tom Baker, Peter Davison, Colin Baker and Sylvester McCoy attending. All but Tom Baker appeared on stage together in front of a delighted audience. Despite the absence of a new series of *Doctor Who* on television, the 30th anniversary was, all things considered, celebrated in fine style.

MERCHANDISE
by Ian Wheeler and David J Howe

During the McCoy years, the range of *Doctor Who* merchandise available continued to grow at an incredible rate. One notable development was the launching by a company called Dapol of a collection of poseable plastic figures, similar in scale to a famous *Star Wars* range. Early examples included models of the seventh Doctor, his companion Melanie, a Tetrap, K-9 and the TARDIS. They would later be joined by Daleks, Cybermen and an assortment of monsters and other characters. Dapol also manufactured children's versions of the costumes worn by the seventh Doctor and Melanie, and an adult-sized replica of the former's pullover, complete with question-marks.

Of the other new items that became available during McCoy's time as the Doctor, the most noteworthy included: a TARDIS telephone (manufactured by Holdcourt Ltd and costing nearly £100), which had the rare distinction of appearing on popular singer and television presenter Cilla Black's *Surprise Surprise* programme; *Doctor Who* bubble bath (also in the shape of the TARDIS); slippers; the initial volumes of a *Doctor Who* encyclopaedia (written by former *Doctor Who* Appreciation Society Co-ordinator David Saunders and published by Piccadilly Press); and a set of *Doctor Who* logo badges, cloth patches and magazine binders (commissioned by John Fitton Books and Magazines). Not strictly a *Doctor Who* item in itself, but still worthy of mention, is a single record entitled 'Doctorin' the Tardis'. This was based on and sampled 'Rock and Roll Part One' by Gary Glitter and was released in 1988 by a group calling themselves the Timelords, later revealed to be an incarnation of cult band The KLF. It eventually topped the UK music charts for one week in June and also appeared in various remixed forms, including most notably 'Gary in the TARDIS' featuring new vocals by Glitter himself.

The discontinuation of *Doctor Who* as an ongoing series in 1989 did little to decrease its popularity, and new merchandise continued to appear. The BBC video releases of old stories were one of the main growth areas. The number of new titles made available each year increased dramatically in the early Nineties, before decreasing again toward the end of the decade. In addition to 'standard' stories, special extended editions of *The Curse of Fenric*, *Silver Nemesis*, *The Five Doctors* and *Battlefield* were released. The BBC also produced and marketed a series of video documentaries, commonly referred to as 'the Years tapes', each of which featured themed clips and episodes and was introduced by one of the actors who had played the Doctor. The titles issued were: *The Hartnell Years*, *The Troughton Years*, *The Pertwee Years*, *The Tom Baker Years*, *The Colin Baker Years*, *Daleks – The Early Years* and *Cybermen – The Early Years*. Other special BBC video projects included: a completed version of *Shada*, the Season 17 story that had been abandoned due to industrial action, with the missing scenes bridged by narration from Tom Baker and a facsimile edition of the original scripts included in the package as a special bonus; and *More Than 30 Years in the TARDIS*, an extended and re-edited version of the *30 Years in the TARDIS* documentary.

The Nineties also saw major developments occurring in the world of *Doctor Who* publishing. With the appearance of John Peel's *The Power of the Daleks* and *The Evil of the Daleks*, the long-running series of licensed novelisations of the televised stories came to an end. (There remained four transmitted stories – *The Pirate Planet*, *City of Death*, *Resurrection of the Daleks* and *Revelation of the Daleks* – that had not been novelised, but these could not be done as the original scriptwriters had withheld their permission.) In their place, Virgin Publishing launched a range of original seventh Doctor novels known collectively as the New Adventures.

The publishers, at that time W H Allen, had first approached the BBC with the idea of presenting 'further adventures' of the Doctor in a letter dated 18 October 1985 from Nigel Robinson, the then editor of the novelisations, but John Nathan-Turner had replied that he was unwilling to consider such a move until January 1987 at the earliest. The idea had then been reactivated in a letter dated 6 February 1989 from new editor Jo Thurm, and again in one dated 30 August 1989 from her successor Peter Darvill-Evans. Following these approaches, Nathan-Turner had eventually agreed to the principle of the original novels being done. Darvill-Evans then prepared a detailed proposal, which was sent to the BBC on 1 February 1990. It was at this point that W H Allen was bought by Virgin Publishing. A large number of W H Allen staff were made redundant, and existing book ranges sold off to other publishers. The Target range of *Doctor Who* novelisations remained, however, and Darvill-Evans continued working toward his aim of publishing original *Doctor Who* fiction.

On 27 June 1990, Darvill-Evans sent out a press release inviting submissions from authors. One of the first to send in ideas was John Peel, whose work was liked by Darvill-Evans. His *Timewyrm: Genesys* consequently became the lead title in the initial four book 'season' featuring a creature called the Timewyrm. The second book, *Exodus*, was commissioned from experienced *Doctor Who* author Terrance Dicks, while the third and fourth came from ideas submitted by Nigel Robinson and new author Paul Cornell respectively. Robinson's had the working title *The God-Machine* but was renamed *Apocalypse* to follow the Biblical theme now decided upon for the titles of the Timewyrm books. Cornell's, which had the working title *Total Eclipse Rewrite* and was later retitled *Revelation*, was based on a short story that he had previously written for the fanzine *Space Rat*. Nathan-Turner disliked Cornell's submission but, as the television series was by this point no longer in production and the *Doctor Who* office had been closed down, Darvill-Evans decided to publish it anyway. The New Adventures were launched to the public on 20 June 1991. They were initially published at the rate of one every two months, but eventually moved to a monthly schedule starting with Gareth Roberts' *The Highest Science* in February 1993.

In July 1994, Virgin launched a complementary range of Missing Adventures – original novels featuring previous incarnations of the Doctor. The first entry in this range was *Goth Opera* by Paul Cornell, published on 21 July. Further titles followed, again on a bimonthly basis initially but quickly moving to a monthly schedule in September.

Virgin also continued to produce a range of factual *Doctor Who* books. Titles such as *The Sixties*, *The Seventies* and *The Eighties* and the series of Handbooks (of which you are now reading a new, compilation edition!) by David J Howe, Mark Stammers and Stephen James Walker won widespread critical acclaim. *Ace! The Inside Story Of The End Of An Era* by Sophie Aldred and Mike Tucker, which took an in-depth look at many of the seventh Doctor's adventures from the point of view of the authors (Aldred had played Ace and Tucker was one of the BBC's visual effects assistants), was also very popular. Other titles in the range included *The Gallifrey Chronicles* by John Peel, *Monsters* by Adrian Rigelsford, *Companions* by David J Howe and Mark Stammers, *Timeframe* by David J Howe and *Blacklight*, an extensive portfolio of Andrew Skilleter's *Doctor Who* artwork. Jean-Marc Lofficier updated his *Doctor Who Programme Guide* and also produced two further books, *The Terrestrial Index* (which included a chronology of the Doctor's adventures) and *The Universal Databank* (an A to Z of characters and terms from the series). Lofficier also wrote *The Nth Doctor*, a study of several aborted *Doctor Who* film projects; Lance Parkin was responsible for a more comprehensive chronology in *A History of the Universe*; and, for those eager to see the funny side of *Doctor Who*, Paul Cornell, Martin Day and Keith Topping unleashed *The Discontinuity Guide*, and Chris Howarth and Steve Lyons came up with *The Completely Useless Encyclopedia*. Virgin also published one unlicensed *Doctor Who* title called, appropriately enough, *Licence Denied*, a compilation of fanzine material edited by Paul Cornell.

In the spirit of the World Distributors *Doctor Who Annual*, which ceased publication in 1986, Marvel began publishing a series of Yearbooks. This ran from 1991 to 1995. They also launched a *Doctor Who Classic Comics* magazine, which over its twenty-seven issue run reprinted many of the Doctor's comic strip escapades from the Sixties and Seventies (in some cases with added colour) along with related interview and feature material, and a short-lived *Doctor Who* poster magazine.

Virgin's domination of *Doctor Who* book publishing was unsuccessfully challenged by Boxtree, who brought out a number of titles. The *Doctor Who Poster Book* and the *Doctor Who Postcard Book* were straightforward collections of photographs from the series. More ambitious was Adrian Rigelsford's *The Doctors – 30 Years of Time Travel*, which was unlicensed by the BBC and heavily criticised by reviewers for its many factual inaccuracies and major omissions, and its quoting of much interview material of uncertain provenance. Boxtree also published Rigelsford's *Classic Who: The Hinchcliffe Years*, a look at the *Doctor Who* work of producer Philip Hinchcliffe. The 'Classic Who' appellation was adopted in order to avoid the use of the BBC's own licensed *Doctor Who* logo. The BBC was nevertheless displeased that such books were appearing, and brought its weight to bear on the publishers. Consequently Rigelsford's final Boxtree book – *Classic Who: The Harper Classics*, featuring the *Doctor Who* work of director Graeme Harper – although originally intended to be unlicensed, was in fact licensed, and the appropriate credit given to the BBC. After this, Boxtree decided not to continue with further *Doctor Who* titles (four others – *The 500 Year Diary*, *The Making of 'The Dark Dimension'* and similar *Classic Who* books covering the *Doctor Who* work of director David Maloney and producer Barry Letts respectively – having been mooted by Rigelsford).

With no prospect of new *Doctor Who* appearing on television, groups of fans took matters into their own hands by producing on a professional basis a number of independent spin-off dramas designed for video release (although some were subsequently also transmitted on the Sci-Fi Channel, as were various different versions of a video documentary that took its title and cover image from Adrian Rigelsford's book *The Doctors – 30 Years of Time Travel*). The first such project – *Wartime*, starring John Levene as Benton, a character from the third and fourth Doctors' eras – was masterminded by Keith Barnfather and released in 1988 by Reeltime Pictures. Dreamwatch Media followed this up in 1994 with *Shakedown*, featuring established *Doctor Who* monsters the Sontarans and the Rutans. This was scripted by Terrance Dicks and directed by Kevin Davies and starred, albeit not in their familiar television roles, *Doctor Who* regulars Sophie Aldred and Carole Ann Ford and *Blake's 7* regulars Jan Chappell and Brian Croucher. The following year, Reeltime Pictures released *Downtime*, directed by *Doctor Who* veteran Christopher Barry and written by Marc Platt, who had scripted *Ghost Light* for *Doctor Who*'s twenty-sixth season. *Doctor Who* characters featured in this production included the Brigadier (Nicholas Courtney), Sarah Jane Smith (Elisabeth Sladen), Victoria Waterfield (Deborah Watling) and, providing the opposition, the Great Intelligence and its Yeti robots (as seen in the fifth season stories *The Abominable Snowmen* and *The Web of Fear*). 1997 saw the release of *Auton*, written and directed by Nick Briggs and featuring the return of the Nestene Consciousness and its killer plastic Auton mannequins from Season 7's *Spearhead from Space* and Season 8's *Terror of the Autons*. This was produced by Bill Baggs and released commercially by Reeltime Pictures, who also continued throughout the Nineties to add to their range of MythMakers video interviews with former *Doctor Who* cast and crew members.

Other video releases with looser *Doctor Who* connections included, as well as some one-off projects, the *Stranger* series featuring Colin Baker as 'the Stranger' and Nicola Bryant as 'Miss Brown' and several titles about an investigative organisation called PROBE, headed by the third Doctor's companion Liz Shaw (Caroline John), now elevated to the status of a professor. These dramas were produced by Baggs and also starred, in new roles, other well known *Doctor Who* actors including Peter Davison, Jon Pertwee, Colin Baker and Sylvester McCoy.

On the audio front, cassettes and CDs related to *Doctor Who* became more popular. It was possible to buy selected incidental music soundtracks (for *The Greatest Show in the Galaxy*, *Ghost Light* and *The Curse of Fenric* amongst others), talking book versions of certain novelisations, tapes taken from old off-air recordings of television stories otherwise missing from the BBC archives, and even audio equivalents of the spin-off drama videos.

When the *Doctor Who* television movie finally came to fruition in 1996, its transmission precipitated a minor flood of related items. The BBC themselves released a video of the movie (which was actually available to buy about a week before the UK transmission), a novelisation by Gary Russell, and a script book. Other items included posters, a record bag, a watch, a set of postcards and, in 1997, a CD of the soundtrack. This latter item was available only through specialist dealers as it was privately released by one of the composers, John Debney, as a promotional item.

A significant change in *Doctor Who* licensing came in 1996 when, as a direct result of their involvement with the television movie, the BBC declined to renew Virgin

Publishing's long-standing fiction licence. This was so that they could take over publication of the range of original *Doctor Who* novels themselves. The switch came in May 1997, which saw publication of the final novels in the Virgin range, Lance Parkin's eighth Doctor New Adventure *The Dying Days* and Gareth Roberts' fourth Doctor Missing Adventure *The Well Mannered War*. The following month, the BBC's range began with *The Eight Doctors* by Terrance Dicks and *The Devil Goblins from Neptune* by Martin Day and Keith Topping. The BBC also released at this time a Paul McGann-narrated talking book of Gary Russell's novelisation of the movie and a postcard book of images from the movie. Further original novels then followed at the rate of two per month, one featuring the eighth Doctor and his new companion, Sam, the other featuring a past Doctor-and-companion team. Virgin, meanwhile, continued their range of New Adventures minus the *Doctor Who* logo (which they had actually dropped some months beforehand in order to help ensure a smooth transition) and with no BBC-owned characters, concentrating instead on the exploits of the Doctor's erstwhile companion Bernice Summerfield, who had been created for the range by author Paul Cornell some years earlier. From June 1998, these Doctor-less New Adventures moved from a monthly to a bimonthly schedule.

While Virgin retained an interest in factual *Doctor Who* publishing, the BBC also embarked on a programme of such books. The first titles to see print were *The Book of Lists* by Justin Richards and Andrew Martin and *A Book of Monsters* David J Howe. These were followed up by *The Television Companion* by David J Howe and Stephen James Walker and *From A to Z* by *Doctor Who Magazine* editor Gary Gillatt.

Doctor Who merchandise continues to sell well and at the time of writing, and there is no sign of the series' popularity waning. There have been many other items released in addition to those mentioned here – everything from calendars, posters and graphic novels to trading cards, playing cards and model kits. *Who's There?*, a biography of William Hartnell written by his grand-daughter, Jessica Carney, has been published; Tom Baker's autobiography, *Who on Earth is Tom Baker?*, was launched with a nationwide booksigning tour by the actor and sold very well (as did a talking book version); and *I Am The Doctor*, a memoir co-written by the late Jon Pertwee and David J Howe, has been much sought-after. Other products released in the wake of the television movie include a BBC CD-ROM game called *Destiny of the Doctors*.

THE VIRGIN DOCTOR
by David Robinson and Richard Prekodravac

The sixty-one New Adventures novels published by Virgin took the characters and concepts of the television series and used them as the basis for stories, as they put it, 'too broad and too deep for the small screen'. The seventh Doctor as presented in the first sixty of these novels is a complex individual who is defined by his actions, by his relationships with his companions and by his place in the societies he touches. He is a dark Doctor, a clown, a horrifying alien. He is also someone who changes and matures, evolving from an apparently uncaring manipulator of events to a somewhat redeemed and responsible humanitarian. The novels' numerous authors created and developed not only a multifaceted seventh Doctor but also, along the way, a rich tapestry of new *Doctor Who* mythology, adding to that of the televised adventures.

MYTHOLOGY AND TIME'S CHAMPION

The first layer of mythology to be introduced was generically termed 'the Cartmel master plan'. Set out in a format document dated 9 November 1990, this was developed for Virgin by Andrew Cartmel, Ben Aaronovitch and Marc Platt based on ideas devised by them while working on the series' twenty-fifth and twenty-sixth seasons. It postulated the Doctor's origins and his connection with the Hand of Omega and the Other (a character from Aaronovitch's novelisation of *Remembrance of the Daleks*) and described Time Lord society as developing out of an era of superstition dominated by the powerful matriarchal Pythia (as subsequently featured in the fifth novel, Platt's *Time's Crucible*), whose rule fell with the establishment of a lasting curse that transformed Gallifrey into the society as seen in the televised stories.

The second layer of mythology established here was that of the Gallifreyan gods. These are Eternals who exist only as representations of archetypal ideas stemming from the Gallifreyan collective consciousness. Time, Death and Pain are the main gods used by the Gallifreyans as an aid to understanding the ideas they represent; Pain, for example, acts as a reminder of the sacrifice made by betraying friends (*The Left-Handed Hummingbird*, *Set Piece*, *Sleepy*). In order to prevent himself becoming his potential evil incarnation the Valeyard (as seen in season twenty-three's *The Trial of a Time Lord*), the Doctor became Time's champion in a deal with the Gallifreyan god (*Love and War*, *Millennial Rites*). This idea followed a Western literary tradition established by the classical Greeks: the hero as a champion to one of the gods. In this case it was essentially about the Doctor becoming responsible for the actions of his present and past incarnations. It was this acceptance of responsibility that caused him to become a much darker character. The Doctor would use the role of Time's champion as a technique to rationalise his thoughts and actions. Hence he would take up the mantle of someone who not only interceded in the problems of others but was also responsible for the consequences of his actions.

THE DARK DOCTOR

The seventh Doctor in the novels was initially the character as presented on television. This had been firmly established in season twenty-five's *Remembrance of the Daleks* and perhaps best demonstrated in season twenty-six's *The Curse of Fenric*, where the Doctor defeats Fenric by betraying the trust of his companion, Ace. The first twenty-three New Adventures novels concentrated on this dark aspect of his character. He was someone who made deals with Death, Time and Pain and would ride roughshod over the feelings of his companions and friends in order to win the greater battles. Often unemotional and distant, he would sacrifice lives to win. He was described as being 'what monsters have nightmares about'.

The Pit presented perhaps the lowest point of this dark characterisation. In this, the twelfth novel in the series, the villain is a Gallifreyan named Kopyion who has been responsible for the deaths of millions of people on seven planets. The Doctor, controversially, makes no attempt to stop or even condemn his actions; it seems he is unable to take the high moral ground as Kopyion is a reflection of what he himself could become if his character were taken to extremes. The Doctor's development from *Remembrance of the Daleks* to *The Pit* was born out of the culture of the antihero such as in the *Terminator* and *Alien* films; the authors now realised that his character was ultimately self-destructive. This was highlighted in the twenty-first novel, *The Left-Handed Hummingbird*. Then in the twenty-third, *No Future*, the Doctor finally becomes aware that his actions are not only self-destructive but also hurtful to his companions Ace and Bernice.

THE HUMAN ALIEN

Even after the events of *No Future* the Doctor remains aloof, carrying the dark legacy with him. He becomes distant and detached, his alien nature being emphasised as something incomprehensible (*Sky Pirates!*). After Ace departs at the end of the thirty-fifth novel, *Set Piece*, he discovers a need to develop a sense of empathy and humanity. In the thirty-eighth novel, *Human Nature*, he strips all aspects of his Time Lord self away, including his physiology and memories, and becomes the human Dr John Smith. While this allowed author Paul Cornell to set up the Doctor's discovery of human values it also, more importantly, enabled him to explore what it meant to be the Doctor. It firmly established a broader conceptualisation of the Doctor as a whole person comprised of seven distinct personalities: he was not only the seventh Doctor but also *the* Doctor. This idea had been foreshadowed in the earlier novel *Transit*, the tenth in the series, when Ben Aaronovitch had poetically described him as 'all things to all cultures'.

With the arrival of the eighth Doctor on television and imminent loss of Virgin's *Doctor Who* fiction licence, plans were made to bring the New Adventures to a conclusion. The last few novels in the series emphasise the Doctor's redemption. He has carried the burden of blaming himself for the tragedy of his lifetime; he has sacrificed friends and companions, manipulated lives, betrayed friendships and trust, all in the cause of fighting and winning. He is conscious that he looks at the big picture at the expense of the important details (*Bad Therapy*) and knows that he cannot regenerate until he has faced up to the mistakes he has made.

THE HOUSE OF LUNGBARROW

In the penultimate novel, *Lungbarrow*, which picks up on events in *Time's Crucible*, the Doctor is forced to return to Gallifrey and rediscover his neglected family, the people of the strange House of Lungbarrow. *Lungbarrow* sees the Doctor learning of the power of the Hand of Omega and the nature of his identity. He has to accept and come to terms with his past and his family in order to move on. The truth is frightening but it defines the Doctor and, in doing so, heals him.

Commenting on *Lungbarrow* in Issue 14 of the fanzine *Broadsword*, Jonathan Blum wrote: 'Care as he does about what he believes in, fight as he does to do what he sees as right, he is never a tyrant, never in love with his own power, never out of touch with the small beauties and disappointments of life.'

Throughout the course of the New Adventures, the Doctor underwent a far more radical process of change and development than had ever been attempted on television. The novels also bequeathed a legacy of myth and theme that authors and readers alike have delighted in picking up and developing further. The seventh Doctor became an essentially tragic figure imbued with the compassion and eccentricity that can be found only in *Doctor Who*.

OVERSEAS

America
by Robert D Franks

Doctor Who's popularity in the United States was on the wane by the mid-Eighties, having hit its peak earlier in the decade with frequent airings of the Tom Baker episodes by PBS stations. John Nathan-Turner, realising the potential of the American market, was keen to reverse this trend, and actively sought out publicity opportunities. On 28 February 1987, a mobile *Doctor Who* trailer exhibition that had been touring the country for nearly a year made a scheduled stop at Mercer University in Georgia. Here, Nathan-Turner, accompanied by Jon Pertwee and Sylvester McCoy, joined it to announce that McCoy had been cast as the new Doctor. This occurred three days before the official BBC announcement in the UK.

Lionheart Television commenced distributing the McCoy serials toward the end of 1987 as television 'movies' - the episodes of each story being edited together into single 'feature length' adventures. *Doctor Who* was now saturating the American market, with over one hundred PBS stations carrying the series. It was during 1987 that the BBC bought out the remaining investors in Lionheart Television and began shifting the organization to become what is today BBC World Wide Americas.

In 1992, with *Doctor Who* no longer in production and its future up in the air, the fledgling cable Sci-Fi Channel tried to negotiate with BBC Worldwide for exclusive American rights to transmit the series. It ultimately managed to secure a set of Tom Baker episodes. This however had an adverse effect on the PBS stations; when they found that they were no longer able to bill the series as 'exclusive', many started dropping it from their schedules. By the end of the decade, most major markets in the country were no longer showing the series; in fact, only fourteen stations were on the list, which diminished even further as the 2000's began.

The large fan population in America, which had once arguably been the series' most devoted overseas following, continued a slow decline at the end of the '80s and into the 1990s, held together mostly through the Friends of *Doctor Who* organization, the successor to the '80s *Doctor Who* Fan Club of America. FODW, first an independent publication and then a subsidiary of vendor 800-TREKKER, continued to publish newspaper-style newsletters on a quarterly basis, often making contact with fans in far-reaching locations. In fact, through FODW, fans in the USA often found each other and started new fan clubs in their home towns. Through the first half of the nineties, in fact, *Doctor Who* fandom was represented country-wide by large fan groups that continued to meet on a monthly basis across the country: New Jersey, Florida, southern California, Missouri, Arizona and other states boasted large, active fan groups. Nevertheless, by 1995, many of these groups had fallen by the wayside.

1996 was not only the debut of the Fox Television/BBC co-produced *Doctor Who* film starring Paul McGann, it was a year of renaissance in the *Doctor Who* community nation-wide. The film, in fact, achieved quite heavy support from the fan community, as its producer, Philip Segal, scouted out fandom for information about what they wanted to see in the film. The debut of the film in May 1996 in America took place at the Directors Guild of America in Hollywood, California, attended by over 100 fans who had come to support the production.

The same year saw the first major growth of what would eventually revolutionize *Doctor Who* fandom (not to mention the rest of the world): the World Wide Web. Many fans and fan clubs began to post information about their fan gatherings on the Web, having previously been consigned to more tightly-bound but loyal confederations on the CompuServe, America Online and GEnie networks and in the realm of the USENET newsgroup rec.arts.drwho. Websites sprang forth across the country dedicated to the good

Doctor and his travels, many of which continued to grow and flourish throughout the latter half of the decade; one of them, the Outpost Gallifrey website (created by American fan Shaun Lyon) would later develop into the most popular fan-run online *Doctor Who* community in cyberspace. For several years an online mailing list community, the *Doctor Who* Alliance of North America, would take over the banner of the defunct FODW group to link fan clubs together coast to coast. Benjamin Elliott's 'This Week in *Doctor Who*' served as an online "TV Guide" to *Doctor Who* airings, eventually incorporating overseas broadcasts. And there were fan projects across the country that were well served by their 'net connections, from fan videos to episode reconstructions.

Doctor Who conventions, which had been omnipresent throughout the 1980s, also experienced a decline. While the multi-thousand person events in Chicago in the mid-1980s were obviously consigned to the past, other events came forward: Tom Baker's final US convention in Florida, the UNIT reunions at WhoosierCon and so forth. The Friends of *Doctor Who* group held several 'Day with the Doctor' mini-conventions which, although not on the same scale as the earlier Chicago events presented by the commercial Spirit of Light organisation, still attracted a large turn-out.

Chicago itself experienced a rebirth of conventions in 1990 with the foundation of the Visions convenions, which would become the decade's most popular *Doctor Who* events... although in later years they tended to attract far more fans of other genre series than *Doctor Who* fans, and Visions came to an end as the decade did. California, meanwhile, would also see the launch the Gallifrey One conventions in 1990, which went largely unknown to fans outside the West Coast until 1995-96, when it grew dramatically during its association with the Fox/BBC *Doctor Who* film; it would later succeed Visions as the continent's most prominent *Doctor Who* event.

By 2005, *Doctor Who* fandom had largely migrated to the Internet, where many nationalistic divisions fell to the unbridled sense of community its participants shared. Nevertheless, a handful of fan groups still existed in local communities throughout the country; while four annual conventions continued to serve the country's fan population: the long-running Gallifrey One events in Los Angeles; ChicagoTARDIS, the successor to the Visions conventions; Massachusetts' United Fan Con, which developed out of the WishCon charity events near Boston; and Dan Harris' annual Sci-Fi Sea Cruise floating expeditions featuring *Doctor Who* celebrities on vacations to such exotic locations as Mayan ruins and the Atlantic and Pacific coasts. Time will only tell what the future has in store...

Canada
by Michael J Doran

The McCoy era marked a change in the way *Doctor Who* was seen in Canada. From 1976 until 1988, the provincial Ontario-only network TVOntario (TVO) had aired selected Jon Pertwee episodes (several of which, including *The Claws of Axos*, *The Curse of Peladon*, *The Mutants* and *The Time Monster*, were returned to the BBC as 525-line two-inch recordings in the early 1980s as the only broadcast-quality colour versions in existence), all but a couple of Tom Baker stories, and all Peter Davison and Colin Baker stories. With a Saturday evening time slot, the show had been able to develop a following similar to the one it enjoyed in the UK. The first local fan clubs had started up in 1978, and this activity had formed the basis for the *Doctor Who* Information Network (DWIN), established in 1980 and now the longest running *Doctor Who* fan club in North America. The twenty-fourth season was aired on TVO in the usual way, on Saturday evenings with a repeat the following Thursday evening. The run started with *Time and the Rani* Part One on 9 January 1989 and concluded with *Dragonfire* Part Three on 10 April 1989. In July 1989, however, it was announced that TVO had lost the *Doctor Who* rights to the recently launched nationwide youth-orientated cable network YTV. For the first time since 1965 (when the Canadian Broadcasting Corporation had aired the first five William Hartnell serials), *Doctor Who* would be available right across the country for Seasons 25 and 26.

One TVO insider put this development down to the network simply forgetting to renew the rights in time and YTV snatching them up. Nevertheless, it is unlikely that TVO would have been able to continue much longer as a broadcaster of *Doctor Who*, as it had been showing the series in blocks of approximately twenty-six episodes, its 'seasons' bearing no relation to the originals, and with the BBC now producing only fourteen episodes per year, this would soon have become impracticable. As it was, the twenty-third and twenty-fourth seasons were linked together for broadcast in Canada and the latter was aired only seventeen months after its UK transmission, whereas the gap in the past had generally been more than two years.

The twenty-fifth season premiered on YTV on 3 September 1989, in a 7.00 pm Sunday time slot, with *The Happiness Patrol* Part One, the stories being shown out of their UK transmission sequence. Due to a programming error (transmission of *The Greatest Show in the Galaxy* Part Four was delayed by a week as *Remembrance of the Daleks* Part Four was mistakenly rerun in its place), the run lasted fifteen weeks and finished on 10 December. Viewers had only a short time to wait for more new episodes, as the twenty-sixth season went out during the spring of 1990, in a 5.30 pm Saturday time slot. Again the stories were shown out of their UK sequence.

Between September 1989 and August 1994, YTV also aired, in a variety of afternoon, evening, and late night time slots, all the other complete stories that still existed in the BBC archives at the time. Fan reaction to YTV was often negative, particularly in Ontario where many viewers disliked the fact that – unlike on TVO in the past – the episodes were interrupted by commercials. The station nevertheless managed to bring *Doctor Who* to many Canadians who had never seen it before or who had previously had to depend on American PBS border stations. Their screenings were also the first opportunity that Canadian viewers had to see most Hartnell, any Troughton and many Pertwee serials.

Edmonton, Alberta TV station CITV was the first broadcaster anywhere in the world to air the Fox/BBC/Universal *Doctor Who* television movie (which had been filmed in British Columbia, Canada). This was transmitted on Sunday 12 May 1996 at 10.00 pm Canadian Mountain Time. The movie was also aired by CHCH Hamilton on 14 May at 9.00 pm Canadian Eastern Time. Both stations are available on a variety of cable systems across Canada.

In 1998, *Doctor Who* was once again on cable in Canada. 'SPACE: The Imagination Station' purchased a run of episodes and aired the series commercial-free from Monday to Friday. The McCoy episodes were scheduled to follow on from this.

Australia
by Damian Shanahan and Dallas Jones

The arrival of Sylvester McCoy as the Doctor coincided with a change in the way that

Doctor Who was handled by the Australian Broadcasting Company (ABC). Instead of being dealt with by the Drama Department and screened in a 6.30 pm time slot, as had traditionally been the case, the series now formed part of *The Afternoon Show*, run by the Children's and Education Department, and went out an hour earlier. This change was made for two reasons. First, the ABC under the helm of Controller David Hill now had a policy of competing with the commercial networks, and *Doctor Who* was seen as lacking in audience-pulling power in an early evening slot dominated by the networks' current affairs programmes. Secondly, many viewers had actually requested such a change.

The new season was announced in September 1988 and commenced with *Time and the Rani* on Monday 31 October at 5.30 pm, running five nights a week. An ABC spokesperson indicated that the series would receive no publicity and would be cancelled if acceptable ratings were not achieved – a decision that shocked but did not entirely surprise Australian fans, given the new policy that had been adopted. The ABC declined to indicate what it would consider to be acceptable ratings, but there is no doubt that *Doctor Who* had never been particularly popular with the general viewing public in Australia. Its previous best performance had been an 8% share of the viewing audience for the 20th anniversary special *The Five Doctors*. Repeats of Tom Baker's stories, as movie length compilations on Saturday afternoons at 1.00 pm during this period, had received only between 3% and 5% – although this may have understated the series' true popularity, judging by an article in the *Sydney Morning Herald* on 27 February 1988 in which a spokesperson for the ratings company AGB McNair was quoted as saying of the new 'people meter' assessment devices: 'Some mothers tended to conceal the fact that their children were watching *Neighbours* or *Doctor Who*'.

Unknown technical difficulties resulted in a loss of vision for the opening titles of one episode of *Delta and the Bannermen*, but otherwise the transmission of the twenty-fourth season proceeded uneventfully, concluding with *Dragonfire* Part Three on Thursday 17 November. Surprisingly, however, the run then continued with the following season's opening story, *Remembrance of the Daleks*, which aired from Friday 18 to Wednesday 23 November. This was a one-off advance screening arranged – apparently at the behest of *The Afternoon Show*'s host James Valentine – so that the ABC could properly celebrate *Doctor Who*'s silver anniversary. The remainder of the twenty-fifth season was not purchased at this stage, even though the twenty-fourth had won a significant increase on the poor ratings for the Saturday afternoon repeats and the previous 6.30 pm weekday transmissions – *Time and the Rani*, for instance, had gained a 6%-7% share of the viewing audience.

As in the UK, the anniversary period saw the release of the Timelords' 'Doctorin' the TARDIS' single, which entered the Australian music charts on 21 August at No. 8, rose the following week to No. 4, spent the next four weeks at No. 3 and then on 2 October peaked at No. 2. The later 'Gary in the TARDIS' remix failed to enter the Australian charts.

After *Remembrance of the Daleks*, the ABC recommenced screening repeats of the Tom Baker stories. It was not until August 1989 that premiere dates were confirmed for the remainder of the twenty-fifth season, which was to be preceded by a second run of all the earlier McCoy episodes. Originally the ABC planned to start this run on Tuesday 24 October, so that the first episode of *Silver Nemesis* would be transmitted on 23 November – enabling Australian viewers to see the start of the series' 25th anniversary story on the 26th anniversary! It was then realised however that a screening of cricket and golf would interfere with this (sporting events routinely being given priority over Children's and Education Department programmes), so, following consultation with the Australasian *Doctor Who* Fan Club, the ABC brought the start date forward to Friday 20 October and screened the stories in production order rather than UK transmission order. In this way, the first episode of *Silver Nemesis* still went out on the anniversary date, and the season eventually ended with *The Happiness Patrol* Part Three on Monday 4 December 1989. Some regional viewers had the last five episodes of the season delayed by the screening of a cricket match, but only by a few days.

The last three stories of Season 25 were repeated in a run that began on Tuesday 16 October 1990 and led directly on to the premiere screening of Season 26, publicity for which had been planned at a special meeting, as the ABC had viewed all the episodes and been very impressed with their quality. The season began with *Battlefield* Part One on 29 October and ran, as before, five nights a week, Monday to Friday at 5.30 pm, as part of *The Afternoon Show*. It concluded with the final episode of *Survival* on Friday 16 November.

New Zealand
by Paul Scoones

The first the New Zealand television audience saw of Sylvester McCoy's Doctor was during Television New Zealand's *Doctor Who* 'Silver Jubilee' week of special screenings in November 1988 on TV2. *Silver Nemesis* was broadcast as an omnibus edition of all three episodes on Friday 25 November 1988. Part One had been transmitted for the first time in the UK just two days earlier, but New Zealand was the first place in the world to screen Parts Two and Three. The story was scheduled in a ninety minute timeslot from 4.30 pm to 6 pm, with commercial breaks and, between Parts Two and Three, a five-minute break for news headlines. Part One's opening titles were used at the beginning of the story and Part Three's closing credits at the end, and although the other opening and closing titles were removed, Parts Two and Three retained their opening reprises and episode numbers. Part One was cut, with about a minute missing from the point at which a commercial break occurred, although it is unknown whether this was an intentional timing edit or an accidental omission caused by the insertion of the commercials. Viewer ratings started at 7% for the first quarter hour of the story, then dipped to 6% and remained steady up until the last quarter hour when they dropped to 5%.

After experiencing the world premiere of *Silver Nemesis*, New Zealand viewers then had to wait more than a year to see further McCoy stories. The regular screenings (which had reached *Time-Flight* by the time of the 'Silver Jubilee' week) finally caught up to the McCoy era when *Time and the Rani* Part One screened 23 January 1990 on TV2. At this point, episodes were being transmitted Monday to Fridays at around 4.30 pm. This was the timeslot for the Season 24 episodes however from *Remembrance of the Daleks* Part One onwards *Doctor Who* was moved to Sunday mornings, beginning 18 February 1990, with episodes initially starting at 10.20 am and then, after the first two weeks, at 9.35 am. *Remembrance of the Daleks* Parts Two and Three were screened a fortnight apart to accommodate coverage of the Commonwealth Games.

Season 25 stories were screened in their production order, so *Remembrance of the Daleks* was followed by *The Greatest Show in the Galaxy*, *Silver Nemesis* (this time complete and in its original three-part form), and *The Happiness Patrol* in that order.

Season 26 was however screened in its correct story order. An alternative version of *The Curse of Fenric* Part One was screened that lacked on-screen subtitles for the Russian soldiers' dialogue in the opening scenes, but otherwise the episodes were unedited.

The six-and-a-half-year run of *Doctor Who* episodes on New Zealand television, which had begun with *The Mind Robber* in April 1985, finally reached its conclusion with *Survival* Part Three on 16 September 1990. This was coincidentally the same weekend that New Zealand's first national *Doctor Who* convention with guests from the series took place in Christchurch. WhoCon 1990 was run by the New Zealand *Doctor* Who Fan Club and featured guest appearances by Jon Pertwee and Mark Strickson.

The 1996 television movie made its New Zealand debut on Wednesday 30 October 1996 at 8.30 pm on Television Two. TVNZ was offered both the uncut US version and the edited UK version of the movie, and opted to screen the former. It was watched by 13.2% of the potential viewing audience, which placed it higher than the programmes screening opposite on either of the other two channels and eighth in the top ten television movies and mini series screened on New Zealand television throughout 1996.

The TV Movie was repeated on 3 July 1999, screening on a Saturday night on TV2 at 9 pm. The audience rating was 10.5%, which was consistent with ratings for other movies screened in the same timeslot.

FANDOM
by Ian Wheeler

The *Doctor Who* Appreciation Society (DWAS) had been at the centre of fan activity in the UK since its formation in 1976 and was still going strong when the seventh Doctor arrived in 1987. Its long-running newsletter *Celestial Toyroom*, now edited by Neil Hutchings, was a lively and well-presented mixture of news, comment and rather overt humour. Hutchings was succeeded by Brian J Robb in 1988, and although the layout became somewhat untidy, the contents still made for a satisfying read. The next permanent editor, following a short stint by Andy Lane and Andrew Martin in 1989, was Michael Proctor, who arguably inherited the newsletter at the worst possible time, as *Doctor Who* was no longer in production, news stories were hard to find, and the Society's membership seemed reluctant to contribute articles or features. Although Proctor made a brave attempt, it was not until Martin Kennaugh took over in 1990 that things began to improve and *Celestial Toyroom* once again became essential reading. Kennaugh remained as editor for four successful years. His assistant Keith Hopkins then took over, and the newsletter continued to go from strength to strength. Eventually, however, Hopkins left, and a succession of short-term editors then followed before Steve Haywood took over on a permanent basis in 1997. The DWAS's flagship magazine, *TARDIS*, also returned to regular publication in 1997, having made only sporadic appearances during the late Eighties, but somehow lacked the professional and authoritative edge that it had once enjoyed.

The DWAS had been irregularly beset throughout this period by problems in the running of its Membership Department, which had a knock-on impact on the distribution of *Celestial Toyroom* – members frequently received issues late and occasionally even in the wrong order. Another difficulty faced by the Society in the late Eighties was increasing competition in the form of glossy, independent fanzines. *The*

Frame was one of the best examples, and contained a lively mix of rare photographs, interviews, features, fiction, artwork, humour and behind the scenes articles. Created and published by David J Howe, Mark Stammers and Stephen James Walker, it began in 1987 and ran until 1993, when the editorial team reluctantly decided that they could no longer produce the fanzine at the same time as writing their two series of non-fiction *Doctor Who* books for Virgin Publishing. *The Frame* took a balanced approach toward criticism of *Doctor Who*, not least because all three editors had a great affection for the series. *Doctor Who Bulletin*, on the other hand, was probably the most opinionated *Doctor Who* fanzine ever to be produced. Edited and published by Gary Levy (who later changed his name to Gary Leigh), it had been launched in 1983 but became increasingly critical of the series during the Sylvester McCoy years, and was particularly negative about the work of producer John Nathan-Turner.

While the opinions expressed by Levy and his contributors were often extremely harsh, they were not entirely unrepresentative; fandom was deeply split over McCoy's first season in particular. There were indeed some fans who had doubts about McCoy's suitability for the role of the Doctor right from the very beginning, and it was not only in the pages of *Doctor Who Bulletin* that negative comments appeared. After *Time and the Rani* Part One was broadcast, DWAS Co-ordinator Andrew Beech wrote an article for the *Daily Mail* in which he expressed the view that McCoy 'showed the glimmerings of a believable performance [but] the sight of the Doctor grinning inanely, prancing about and doing pratfalls over non-existent obstacles, uttering lines such as "absence makes the nose grow longer" and making a cheap joke of the role does not inspire confidence'. As McCoy settled into the role, however, he gradually began to win over his critics, and by 1989, his popularity was such that he was able to romp to victory in the 'favourite Doctor' category of the *Doctor Who Magazine* readers poll for that year.

Doctor Who Bulletin, or *DWB* as it was called on its masthead, was to remain highly outspoken throughout its long run. In 1989 it transformed into *Dreamwatch Bulletin* (which conveniently also abbreviated to *DWB*) and broadened its coverage to include a whole range of fantasy films and television programmes; then in 1994 it evolved into *Dreamwatch*, a successful, professionally published news-stand magazine.

While *The Frame* and most other glossy fanzines, including *Private Who*, *Proteus* and *NWE* (*New Whovical Express*), slowly faded away in the early Nineties, a handful – most notably *Skaro* and *Matrix* – continued. There was also something of a revival of more modest, photocopied fanzines produced on a tiny budget and supported by a small readership and lots of enthusiasm.

Conventions and other special events remained an important part of the fan scene during the late Eighties and the Nineties. Dominitemporal Services Ltd on behalf of the DWAS continued to hold its large-scale PanoptiCon gatherings, generally on an annual basis, but here too faced increasing competition from independent fan groups organising their own successful events. Smaller-scale gatherings took place under the auspices of an ever-growing network of DWAS and independent *Doctor Who* local groups.

Other fan activities during this period included a number of campaigns to try to persuade the BBC to put *Doctor Who* back into production. These included the 'Target Who' letter-writing campaign directed at *Radio Times* and *Points of View* (a BBC viewers' feedback programme), which failed to make an impact as not a single letter was either published or broadcast. One group of fans even campaigned for funds to mount a legal challenge against the BBC's decision to drop the series, but this was ultimately abandoned.

Off-air audio recordings of Sixties *Doctor Who* episodes, including all those subsequently wiped by the BBC, had long been in circulation amongst the series' fans. In the Nineties, however, much clearer copies became available, mostly from the respective collections of Graham Strong, David Holman and David Butler. These have since been used by a number of fans to create video 'reconstructions' of the missing episodes (the picture usually consisting of a mixture of still photographs and video images, sometimes accompanied by captions describing the action and dialogue), and also in a few instances by the BBC itself, to replace poor quality soundtracks on episodes held in their archives.

The period beginning in 1987 and continuing into the 1990s was, overall, something of a golden age for fandom. Rather than withering away after the demise of *Doctor Who* as an ongoing series, it arguably became stronger and more focused than ever before.

VIEWER REACTION
by Ian Wheeler

Press coverage of McCoy's first season may have been far from enthusiastic, but it would be wrong to say that reaction to the arrival of the new Doctor was entirely negative. The response from the general viewing public – arguably those whose views mattered the most – was often very different. *Radio Times* ran a number of letters of comment from readers who had seen the new Doctor's debut adventure and enjoyed it. S Lancaster from Stoke-on-Trent wrote: 'The real Doctor is back ... For the first time in six-and-a-half years, I can't wait to see the next episode ...' Michael Proctor from Hertfordshire was equally impressed, referring to McCoy as 'an inspired choice'. In Scotland, the *Sunday Post* had some equally positive feedback. 'Sylvester didn't do much for me in the first episode', wrote Miss J Napier of Glasgow, 'but now I have to admit he's got me hooked'. J Robertson of Aberdeen appeared to agree: 'Sylvester is a good new Doctor and the story is fine. The series has definitely improved from last year.'

It wasn't all plain sailing for the series, however, and Margaret Francis of Bristol expressed some strongly negative opinions in the pages of the *Eagle*, the long-running British adventure comic, in January 1989: 'Sylvester McCoy must be the most wimpish Doctor Who ever, as he looks more like something out of a *Carry On* film than what is supposed to be science fiction. *Doctor Who* used to be a super series, but now it's like watching a pantomime, which is a shame'. The comic's fictional editor, a cheerful computer by the name of Max, responded: 'A jokey science fiction series is okay by me. Personally, I preferred *Red Dwarf*, but anyone who takes *Doctor Who* seriously should see a Dalek Doctor!'

Viewers' letters were not the only indication that the BBC had of viewer reaction to *Doctor Who*. They also had hard statistics in the form of an Appreciation Index, or AI, for each individual episode. In much the same way as ratings are compiled by studying the viewing habits of certain households, AIs are an attempt to gauge audience enjoyment in the form of a simple percentage. The higher the percentage a programme gains, the better it was received by those who watched it. The average AI for the twenty-fourth season was 60, with a high of 64 and a low of 57. These figures would generally be considered disappointing, but fortunately things improved over the next two years: Seasons 25 and 26 both gained an average AI of 68. This was still some way below the typical figure for BBC drama – which during the period of Season 26's transmission was 76 – but it should be remembered that *Doctor Who* had always appealed to a somewhat specialist audience and its AI figures were arguably 'diluted' by the reactions of casual viewers with little interest in the series. The AIs for the McCoy stories were, in fact, generally higher than those for the earlier Doctors' eras, although as methods of collecting the data had changed over the years, such direct comparisons can be misleading.

Other forms of statistic were collected by the BBC for Television Audience Reaction Reports. These included 'personal ratings' for the stars of programmes, based on surveys completed by a viewing panel. McCoy's rating was low to begin with, but rose after the twenty-sixth season, when 78% of those questioned found him 'likeable'. One viewer remarked that McCoy was '… naturally charming, not a mannered Doctor'. There were also three 'audience profiles' compiled during the seventh Doctor's era, giving a general picture of viewers' age, sex and social status. These were for *Time and the Rani*, *Remembrance of the Daleks* and the twenty-sixth season as a whole. From these, it would appear that an even greater percentage of *Doctor Who*'s viewers than in the past were adult – 74% for *Time and the Rani* and 78% for both the Dalek story and the twenty-sixth season. There also existed a very even balance between male and female (an exact 50/50 split for the twenty-sixth season). If any conclusion can be drawn from this information, it would arguably be that few programmes have brought together people of different ages, sexes and backgrounds in quite the way that *Doctor Who* managed in the late Eighties.

In 1989, when rumours started to spread that *Doctor Who* was coming to an end, the public were as determined as ever to have their say. The *Radio Times* letters page was once again a forum for debate. 'I hope that Jonathan Powell gets the sack as soon as possible as Controller, BBC1,' wrote Alan Dobbie from London. 'His decision to axe *Doctor Who* at the end of its present series shows that he doesn't understand what people really want. We want *Doctor Who* to continue'. Similar concerns were expressed by a contributor to the BBC's *Points of View*, who was told that there were in fact no plans to cancel the series.

It would be a long time before a new *Doctor Who* project would come to fruition, and viewer reaction to the 1996 Paul McGann television movie is covered elsewhere in this book. Later the same year, however, *Doctor Who*'s many followers finally had a real opportunity to show their appreciation. As part of the celebrations to mark the BBC's sixtieth year of television broadcasting, a telephone poll was held to determine the nation's 'Favourite Popular Drama'. There were twelve nominees to choose from, including such popular successes as *Bergerac*, *Casualty* and *EastEnders*. To the apparent surprise of many, *Doctor Who* won, and McCoy and Peter Davison collected the award as part of the televised *Auntie's All-Time Greats* birthday party. This spectacular victory subsequently attracted some sniping in the press, particularly from disgruntled *EastEnders* cast members, and suggestions were even made that well-organised *Doctor Who* fan clubs had rung in *en masse* to influence the outcome. In fact, there had been no such organised fan campaign to try to influence the vote. In the hearts of many, and by a simple majority vote, the award had gone to the series that most deserved it.

RATINGS
by Ian Wheeler

When considering the viewing figures for McCoy's time as the Doctor, it is important to place the raw numerical data in context. From 1987 to 1989, *Doctor Who* was scheduled against the toughest possible opposition in the form of Granada's *Coronation Street*, the UK's oldest and mightiest soap opera. The ratings were thus bound to be lower on average than for earlier eras of the series' history. It should also be borne in mind that many families are likely to have watched *Coronation Street* and recorded *Doctor Who* on video, a factor not allowed for at this time, as only those viewers who had seen a programme on transmission were counted for ratings purposes.

The ratings for Season 24 were modest but consistent. All the episodes fell within a relatively small range, with a minimum of 4.2 and a maximum of 5.5 million viewers. A notable fall occurred between the first and second episodes of the opening story, but this was nothing new: it had happened on many previous occasions in the series' history, as numerous casual viewers tuned in out of curiosity to see how the season began and then lost interest. The average figure for the season was a somewhat disappointing 5.0 million viewers (although this was still higher than that for the previous run – consisting of the single fourteen part story *The Trial of a Time Lord* – which had had the advantage of a traditional Saturday evening time slot). There are five factors that would seem to account for this rather low figure. First, and most importantly, the scheduling of the series opposite *Coronation Street*. Secondly, the actual transmission time of 7.35 pm, which was rather late for some children and also gave *Doctor Who*'s opponents on other channels a five minute advantage (shows tending to start on the hour or half-hour). Thirdly, McCoy had a relatively low public profile (certainly in comparison with, say, Peter Davison, who had already acquired a major following on *All Creatures Great and Small* before coming to *Doctor Who*). Fourthly, after the hiatus of 1985 (when the series had been taken off the air for eighteen months by BBC1 Controller Michael Grade), people had got out of the habit of watching *Doctor Who* and in many cases simply did not bother to tune in when it returned. And finally, the season itself was arguably of a relatively poor quality, with high levels of humour resulting in negative press reviews. Poor publicity has been cited by some commentators as an additional factor, but this is not entirely valid as *Radio Times* coverage of the series was good, and numerous on-screen trailers were shown.

The ratings for Season 25 were far more respectable, averaging 5.4 million viewers and peaking at 6.6 million. McCoy had by now established himself in the role of the Doctor, and the season had the added advantage of beginning transmission in October rather than September, which was when many new shows made their debut and competition for viewers was more fierce, and running on into January, when ratings are traditionally higher. The combination of an important anniversary and the return of the Daleks and the Cybermen created a considerable 'nostalgia factor,' and the season itself was of a high quality, receiving supportive reviews in the press. Unusually, the second episode of the opening story, *Remembrance of the Daleks*, gained a higher rating than the first, suggesting that there may have been good 'word of mouth' about the quality of the latter and its exciting 'hovering Dalek' cliffhanger.

Season 26 did less well, and in fact received the worst viewing figures of the McCoy era. *Battlefield* Part One was seen by only 3.1 million viewers, *Doctor Who*'s all-time lowest rating. The figures for *Ghost Light* and *The Curse of Fenric* hovered around the four million mark, but only *Survival* gained what could be described as a healthy rating, with five million viewers for Parts One and Three. This time, there can be little doubt that a major factor accounting for the season's relative failure was a lack of publicity.

There was virtually no effort made to promote the series in the *Radio Times*, and, although there had been some press coverage of the stories at the time of their production, a press call (with John Nathan-Turner, Sophie Aldred and Jean Marsh) on 16 August 1989 to publicise their imminent transmission failed to generate any significant interest, and a second one (with Nicholas Parsons) did not take place until 19 October, by which point only *The Curse of Fenric* and *Survival* remained to be transmitted. Given that the viewing figures had been steadily rising during the course of the season, it is tempting to wonder how much more successful it would have become had it continued for a few more episodes. Looking at these figures alone, however, it is perhaps not entirely surprising that *Doctor Who* was taken off the air at this point.

The series bounced back in 1993 when the *Children in Need* special *Dimensions in Time* achieved an average viewing figure of 13.7 million. This, however, was somewhat misleading, as the annual charity telethon had by this point become consistently popular, and the ratings quoted were only for the quarter-hour segments in which the *Doctor Who* skit happened to be transmitted. Rather more impressive was the 9.08 million figure won by the 1996 *Doctor Who* television movie. This placed it ninth in the top one hundred most watched programmes that week, the second highest position attained by a drama show. This was, by any standard, a remarkably good figure, and showed that many of the viewers who had deserted *Doctor Who* in the late Eighties had returned, along with a whole new audience of youngsters.

SYLVESTER MCCOY/PAUL MCGANN STORIES IN ORDER OF AVERAGE VIEWING FIGURES
(Figures in millions of viewers)

Doctor Who	9.08
Silver Nemesis	5.50
The Greatest Show in the Galaxy	5.43
Remembrance of the Daleks	5.35
Delta and the Bannermen	5.27
Dragonfire	5.07
The Happiness Patrol	5.07
Survival	4.93
Paradise Towers	4.93
Time and the Rani	4.63
The Curse of Fenric	4.13
Ghost Light	4.07
Battlefield	3.65

Story titles appear in italics. '*' after a story title denotes a working title; '+' denotes an unmade story.

30 Years in the TARDIS 754, 780, 782

100,000 BC 33, 38, 39, 40, 41, 42, 43, 79, 95, 96, 98, 99, 100, 102, 103, 106, 192, 201, 203, 206, 208, 209, 212, 213, 242, 243, 247, 295, 532, 725, 749

Aaronovitch, Ben 723, 726, 727, 733, 755, 775, 786, 787

Abominable Snowmen, The 221, 236, 239, 249, 288, 289, 293, 295, 301, 380, 437, 461, 518, 549, 749, 784

*Absolute Zero** 734

Acheson, James 338, 339-340, 341, 394, 410, 429, 440

Adam, Kenneth 51, 75, 82, 97, 99, 117-118, 119

Adams, Douglas 431, 434, 523-524, 529, 540, 756, 757

Adams, M A C 577

Ainley, Anthony 421, 561, 575, 595, 613, 643, 672, 693, 714

Airey, Jean 698

Aitken, Tony 475

Alderton, John 738

Aldred, Sophie 706-707, 714, 715, 716, 730, 733, 735, 736, 743, 744, 749, 751, 755, 776, 778, 779, 780, 783, 784, 798

Alexander, Paul 275

Alexander, Terence 691

Allder, Nick 251

Allen, Paul 473

Alvarado, Manuel 583, 729

Ambassadors of Death, The 325, 330, 331, 332, 335, 343, 344, 346, 353, 354, 382, 383, 384, 387

Anderson, Gerry 755

Anderson, Pamela 776

Android Invasion, The 383, 464, 480, 486

Androids of Tara, The 413, 469, 470

Angel, Ray 200

Anstruther, Sue 666, 751

Arbuthnott, Alan 376, 666

Arc of Infinity 495-496, 497, 516-517, 536, 539, 551, 556, 580, 586, 590, 597, 602, 604, 624

Archer, Leah 747

Ark, The 41, 151, 164, 166, 167, 168, 169, 179-200, 203, 205, 207, 208, 209, 213, 295

Ark in Space, The 403, 412, 426, 427, 462, 475, 480, 482, 485, 486, 513

Asbridge, John 745, 747

Ashbrook, Daphne 764

Ashby, Norman 240

Ashcroft, Chloe 539

Asher, Jane 755

Atkins, Ian 65-66, 67, 68, 70, 73, 83, 98, 99, 103

Atkinson, Dave 271

Attack from the Mind+ 679

Attack of the Cybermen 519, 595, 615, 626, 627, 628, 633-634, 640, 665, 686, 688, 690, 691, 692, 696, 702

Atterbury, John 272

Auger, David 587

Auger, Tony 558

Awakening, The 519, 579, 587, 590, 695

Aztecs, The 35, 39, 109, 111, 112, 113, 115, 117, 118, 119, 120, 122, 123, 204, 207, 208, 212, 213, 749

Babbage, Don 577, 655, 666, 745, 747

Baggs, Bill 703, 752, 779, 784

Bailey, Christopher 525, 530

Baker, Bob 417, 427, 465, 749

Baker, Christopher 452

Baker, Colin 224, 495, 497, 500, 501, 579, 581, 583, 590, 594-596, 597, 598-623, 624-625, 626-629, 630-632, 635, 639, 643, 652, 655, 667, 668, 672, 675, 676, 684, 687, 689, 690, 691, 692, 693, 694, 695, 698, 702, 703, 706, 710, 715, 719, 720, 721, 751, 753, 754, 774, 778, 780, 781, 784

Baker, Geoff 675

Baker, George 396

Baker, Jack 607, 690

Baker, John 552, 577

Baker, Jules 337

Baker, Pip & Jane 609-610, 613, 618, 642, 643, 677, 680, 699, 719, 720, 729

Baker, Tom 275, 319, 342, 390, 391-408, 409-410, 411, 412, 413-415, 416, 426, 429, 430-431, 451, 458, 462, 469, 471, 472, 474, 475, 476-477, 478, 479-480, 483, 484, 485, 486, 488, 490, 491, 496, 498, 502, 508, 509, 511, 525, 532, 538, 540, 549, 555, 559, 575, 578, 579, 581, 583, 596, 597, 604, 605, 608, 629, 632, 694, 710, 750, 751, 752, 753, 756, 757, 763, 777, 781, 782, 785, 789

Ball, Ronnie 672

Banks, David 564, 595, 779

Banks Stewart, Robert   80, 430, 452, 520
Barber, Henry   666, 751
Barker, Eric   308-309
Barker, Ken   652
Barne, June   755
Barnfather, Keith   672, 699, 784
Baron, Dee (Denise)   751
Baron, Lynda   169
Barrett, Ray   140
Barry, Anna   353, 363
Barry, B H   280, 285
Barry, Christopher   24, 89, 91, 92, 93, 95,
135-136, 138, 143, 230, 314, 411, 435, 436,
437-453, 454, 461, 462, 463, 751, 784
Barry, Michael   181, 353
Barry, Morris   221, 244
Bartlett, Bobi   334, 336-337
Barton, Dave   650
Baschet, Francois   78
Bassenger, Mark   550, 568
Battlefield   713-714, 726, 727, 748, 753,
776, 781, 792, 797, 798
Baugh, Martin   261, 269, 285
Baverstock, Donald   48, 52, 53, 65, 68, 71,
72, 74, 75, 77, 91, 93-94, 95, 97, 100, 101,
104, 105, 108, 117, 120-121, 125, 127, 128-
131, 132
Bayldon, Geoffrey   542
Bayler, Terence   193
Bayley, Stephen   755
Bayliff, R W   88, 89
Beacham, Rod   530
Beale, Richard   196
Beaton, Alex   770
Beatty, Robert   176, 177
Beautiful People, The*   436
Beckley, Tony   403
Beech, Andrew   697, 749, 751, 752, 794
Bellamy, Frank   374, 378, 700
Bellingham, Lynda   595, 691, 694
Bennett, John   91
Bennett, John (writer)   529
Bennett, Margot   111
Bentham, J Jeremy   582, 668, 696, 698, 751,
752
Bentine, Michael   408
Bentley, Earlene   672
Berger, Sarah   691
Bergman, Christa   73
Berkoff, Steven   756
Bermans and Nathans   335, 336, 548

Bernard, Paul   192, 340, 350-351, 352-353,
356-358, 359-374, 375
Bevan, Stewart   318
Bewes, Rodney   539, 639
Beynon-Lewis, I   98, 99, 250, 251, 255-256
Beyond the Sun*   85, 95
Bidmead, Christopher H   434, 507, 509,
520-523, 524, 525, 526, 528, 529, 532, 533,
591, 677, 679, 756
Biffin, Brian   577
Bingham, David   748
Birkett, Gavin   285, 552
Birt, John   760
Black, Ian Stuart   24, 164, 165, 168, 170
Black, John   507
Black Orchid   513, 525, 590, 591, 698
Blackman, Honor   595, 691
Blackwood, Adam   595
Blake, Darrol   468
Blake, Gerald   111, 220
Blake, Stuart   565
Bland, Robin   436, 454
Blattner, Elizabeth   90, 100
Blessed, Brian   594, 595, 690, 691
Bloomfield, John   429
Blows, Gordon   587
Blum, Jonathan   787
Blyton, Carey   459
Bond, Michael   756
Bonehill, Richard   550
Botterill, Charles   153
Bould, James   70, 73, 76, 77, 78, 81, 87, 94,
99, 113
Bowen, John   80
Bowes, Tony   200
Bowey Group   251
Bowtell, Allister   338-339, 341
Brace, John   448-449, 541, 552, 556, 557-
571, 577, 644, 646, 647-648, 648, 650, 651-
663, 664, 666
Brachacki, Peter   78, 81, 87, 90, 93, 98
Brackley, Nigel   459
Bradley, Norman   565
Bragg, Melvyn   483
Brain of Morbius, The   383, 421, 427, 435-
454, 480, 481
Braybon, John   49-50, 53, 54
Brayshaw, Deborah   362
Briant, Michael   462-463
Briers, Richard   774
Briggs, Ian   729, 730, 731-732, 733, 734-

739, 743, 745, 747

Briggs, Nicholas 784

Bright, Richard 81-82, 83

Briscoe, Desmond 84

Britain 408 AD+ 149

Broadhouse, Lawrence 249-250

Bromly, Alan 341

Bron, Eleanor 595, 655, 691

Brooks, Richard 247

Brosnan, Pierce 759

Brown, Faith 595, 672, 691

Brown, Gilly 441, 442

Brown, Miquel 672

Bryant, Nicola 493, 495, 535-536, 580-581, 594, 595, 616, 630, 643, 652, 653, 655, 668, 672, 681-685, 686, 687-689, 691-692, 692, 693, 695, 700, 703, 751, 754, 784

Bryant, Peter 222, 223, 238, 239, 240-241, 242, 250, 251, 255-256, 265, 284, 304, 323, 324, 343, 344, 377

Buckler, Rick 672

Budden, Janet 472

Bull, Donald 47-48

Bullmore, Jeremy 80

Burdle, Michael 338

Burgon, Geoffrey 459

Burnett, Barry 639

Burrough, Tony 694

Bush, Maurice 361, 366

Butler, David 795

Buxton, Jayne 747

Byrne, Johnny 532, 758, 759

Caffery, E 84, 85, 108, 109, 111-112

Caine, Michael 758

Callow, Simon 777

Cambden, Stephen 471

Cameron, Michael 650, 666

Camfield, Douglas 24-25, 91, 150, 151, 155, 156, 157, 158, 162, 164, 165, 220, 276, 313, 429, 452, 463

Campbell, Neil 285

Cann, Warren 672

Cannon, David 281

Cant, Brian 159

Carney, Ann 25

Carney, Jessica 754, 755, 785

Carney, Terry 76, 684

Carnival of Monsters 327, 340, 382, 383, 386, 532, 624

Carr, Andrew 367

Carrigan, Ralph 272

Carter, Wilfred 359

Cartmel, Andrew 689, 703, 713, 720, 722, 723, 726, 727, 729, 730, 732, 733, 734, 735, 736, 737, 743, 745, 746, 786

Cary, Tristram 66, 75, 138, 155, 158, 169, 183, 200

Casteldini, Ann 73

Castle, Roy 211

Castrovalva 493, 507, 508, 513, 514, 516, 524, 532, 579, 586, 590, 772

Catchpole, Charles 674, 702, 774

Catherwood, Mike 376

Catlett, Peter 454

Caves of Androzani, The 494, 495, 512, 513, 517, 540, 586, 587, 590, 604-605, 646, 648, 686, 688, 700, 753

Celestial Toymaker, The 164, 167, 168, 169, 170, 184, 200, 205, 207, 208, 213, 676

Chafer, Derek 84

Chapman, Dave 455, 571, 577, 666, 742, 747

Chapman, Noel 200

Chapman, Spencer 139

Chappell, Jan 784

Chase, Leonard 61

Chase, The 45, 145, 147, 148, 149, 150, 151, 152, 153, 154, 205, 207, 208, 209, 211, 212, 213, 258, 289, 295, 514, 728, 780

Children of January, The+ 677

Childs, Tex 376, 577

Chilton, Tony 577

Christian, Fletcher 672

Christopher, John 48

Chuntz, Alan 313-314

City of Death 413, 414, 432, 437, 458, 470-471, 473, 481, 485, 486, 782

Clark, Brian 747

Clarke, Jacqueline 475

Clarke, Jonathan 739, 747

Clarke, Kevin 726, 733

Clarke, Malcolm 572

Clarke, Phil 754, 755, 780

Claws of Axos, The 313, 325, 326, 330, 331, 337, 346, 382, 384, 387, 789

Cleese, John 757, 758

Cleveland, Kenneth 82, 84-85

Clock, The+ 169

Clough, Chris 737-738, 742-743, 744-746

Coburn, Anthony 62, 66, 67, 70, 72-73, 76, 77, 78, 79, 81, 82, 83, 85, 89-90, 95, 111, 116

Cole, Graham 568

Collins, John 750

Collins, June 552, 576, 647, 751

Colony in Space 329, 331, 338, 345, 378, 380, 382, 384, 385, 386, 461

Computers, The* 168

Condren, Tim 153, 359

Connery, Jason 595, 691

Conti, Tom 757

Cook, Terence 71, 72, 138, 143, 160, 169, 182

Cooper, Trevor 652

Cornell, Paul 697, 782, 783, 785, 787

Cosby, Bill 760, 777

Cosgrove, Cathy 747

Cossey, Elmer 467

Cotton, Bill 669, 670, 671

Cotton, Donald 37, 164, 166, 169, 175

Court, Jimmy 285

Courtney, Nicholas 241, 305, 317, 318, 359, 550, 558, 566, 672, 693, 699, 713-714, 749, 751, 753, 754, 755, 780, 784

Coward, Shirley 230, 577, 747, 751

Cox, Frank 25

Craig, Gordon 178

Craig, Michael 691

Craze, Michael 25, 173, 175, 179, 235, 286, 693

Creature from the Pit, The 431, 437, 473, 476, 481, 542

Cregeen, Peter 748, 749, 751, 753

Cribbins, Bernard 211

Crisp, Alan 444

Crockett, John 109, 111

Croft, Richard 743, 747

Crombie, Maureen 73

Croucher, Brian 784

Crowden, Graham 408

Crusade, The 145, 146, 147, 148, 149, 195, 205, 207, 209, 213, 295

Cumming, Fiona 643, 676, 689, 751

Cura, John 285

Curran, Charles 428

Curry, Graeme 733

Curry, Tim 756, 757

Curse of Fenric, The 714, 722, 726, 727, 776, 781, 784, 786, 793, 797, 798

Curse of Peladon, The 327, 329, 332, 333, 337, 347, 380, 382, 386, 537, 789

Curse of the Daleks, The 211

Curzon, Jill 211

Cusack, Cyril 76

Cushing, Peter 211

Cusick, Raymond P 25-26, 93, 98, 99, 139, 143, 150, 153, 182, 202, 243, 698, 749

D'Oyly-John, Chris 200

da Silva, Howard 479, 585

Dæmons, The 291, 314, 317, 326, 327, 330, 331, 337, 347, 359, 378, 380, 382, 384, 385, 386, 436, 462, 463, 752

Dale, Jim 408

Dalek Cutaway - see *Mission to the Unknown*

Dalek Invasion of Earth, The 39, 41, 43, 44-45, 111, 125, 127, 130, 131, 132, 133-134, 135, 136, 137, 139, 140, 141, 145, 201, 204, 207, 208, 209, 211, 212, 213, 257, 295, 333, 548, 581, 727

Daleks, The - see *Mutants, The*

Daleks, The* 112

Daleks Invasion Earth 2150 A.D. 211, 287, 378, 749

Daleks' Master Plan, The 39, 40, 41, 43, 45, 154, 155, 156, 157, 158, 159, 160, 161, 162, 163, 164, 165, 166, 180, 182, 199, 203, 205, 206, 207, 209, 212, 213, 258, 289, 290, 295, 349, 513

Daly, Wally K 676, 677

Dare, Daphne 100, 182-183, 200

Dark Dimension, The+ 752, 753, 780, 783

Dark Planet, The+ 146

Darrow, Paul 595

Darvill-Evans, Peter 782

Dator, Jim 382

Davey, Arthur 324, 334

David, Hugh 58, 66

Davies, Ann 132

Davies, Kevin 754, 755, 784

Davis, Colin 530

Davis, Gerry 26, 164-165, 166-167, 168, 169, 170, 174, 175, 176, 178, 179, 200, 226, 227-228, 229, 231, 232, 233, 235, 236, 238, 239, 419, 427, 748, 749, 776

Davis, Jean 576

Davison, Peter 434, 458, 488, 489-502, 503-505, 506, 507-508, 509-512, 524, 525, 533, 534, 535, 537, 538, 540, 541-542, 557, 569, 574, 575, 578-581, 582, 583, 586, 588, 589, 590, 594, 597, 602, 604, 605, 623-624, 625, 626, 684, 688, 689, 693, 694, 695, 710, 715, 753, 756, 774, 778, 780, 781, 784, 796, 797

Dawson, Archie 552, 577

Day, Martin 285, 783, 784
Day, Ray 133
Day of the Daleks 305, 325, 326, 327, 332, 333, 338, 340, 348, 349-376, 380, 382, 383, 384, 385, 386, 515, 699, 728
*Day of Wrath** 505, 507
de Laurentis, Robert 768
Deadly Assassin, The 275, 413, 420, 422-423, 425, 430, 456-457, 465, 466, 480, 482, 485, 486, 516, 517, 556, 560, 628, 635, 636, 725, 772
Dean, Hazell 672
Death to the Daleks 332, 333, 341-342, 382, 384, 385, 386, 728
Debney, John 784
Delgado, Kismet 317
Delgado, Roger 305, 317-318, 319, 328, 336, 349, 390, 420, 421
Dellot-Seguro, Anabela 747
Delta and the Bannermen 712, 721, 725, 730, 736, 737, 742, 774, 775, 791, 798
Denham, Maurice 595
Derbyshire, Delia 87, 454, 755
*Destiny of Doctor Who, The** 227
Destiny of the Daleks 418, 470, 471, 481, 485, 486, 518, 524
Dewhurst, Keith 137
Dickinson, Sandra 489, 490, 579, 586
Dicks, Terrance 234-235, 240, 242, 261, 284, 319, 320, 327, 328, 329, 332, 345, 346, 348, 349, 350, 351-352, 376, 378, 379, 380, 390, 411, 417, 432-433, 435-436, 454, 484, 529, 541, 545-547, 549-550, 557, 561, 566, 567, 570, 574, 576, 577, 582, 622, 635, 749, 754, 755, 769, 782, 784, 785
Dimensions in Time 754, 780, 798
Djurkovic, George 87
Doctor Who (television movie) 384, 717, 776-777, 784, 788, 789, 790, 793, 798
Doctor Who - 30 Years 754, 780
*Doctor Who and Tanni** 134
Doctor Who and the Daleks in Seven Keys to Doomsday 435
Doctor Who and the Ghosts of N-Space 755
Doctor Who and the Monsters 537
Doctor Who and the Silurians 326, 330, 331, 334, 335, 343, 344, 348, 380, 382, 383, 384, 387, 456, 479, 518-519
Doctor Who: Lost in the Dark Dimension+ 753
Dodd, Ken 775
Dogs of Darkness, The+ 529

Doig, Clive 710
*Domain** 530
Dominators, The 233, 240, 267, 287, 288, 289, 291, 294, 298, 300, 301, 436, 581, 749
Donne, Naomi 576
Dove, Ted 251
Dow, Ian 751
Downes, John 577
Downie, Gary 674-675, 698, 744, 747, 751
Dr Who and the Daleks 210, 378, 586, 672, 749
Dragonfire 712-713, 730, 731, 732, 734-747, 775, 790, 791, 798
Driver, Carolyn 375
Du Pille, Barry 747
Dudley, Terence 49, 73, 505, 525, 533
Dudman, William 747
Dugdale, George 756, 758, 759
Dunk, Chris 587
Dunlop, Pat 168
Earthshock 509, 510, 518, 527, 533, 536-537, 539, 572, 584, 590, 639, 728, 773
Easteal, Kate 747
Eastman, Brian 756
Easton, Brian 376
Eden, Mark 109
Edwards, Jimmy 672
Edwards, Malcolm 529
Elliott, Benjamin 789
Elliott, Denholm 756, 760
Ellis, David 169, 175
Ellis, James 714
Ellis, Janet 692
Ellison, Harlan 480, 523
EM-Tech 360
Emms, William 137, 699
End of Term+ 679
Enemy of the World, The 232, 240, 257, 285, 288, 293, 295, 301, 344
Enemy Within, The+ 530
Enlightenment 517, 590
Enoch, Russell - see Russell, William
Erickson, Paul 151, 164, 179-180, 181, 200
Evans, Stuart 661
Evans, Tenniel 323
Evil Eye, The+ 169
Evil of the Daleks, The 233, 238, 239, 247, 248, 258-259, 288, 289, 293, 295, 298, 301, 727, 782
Exelby, Sandra 341
Ezra, Mark 758, 759

Face of Evil, The 464, 465, 478, 482, 483, 486

Faceless Ones, The 233, 236, 238, 245-247, 288, 289, 290, 293, 295, 301, 344

Faggetter, Ann 747

Farer Nohan+ 529

Farhi, Moris 111

Farnon, Robert 183, 200

Farries, Peter 314

Fawcett, Steve 576

Fay, Colin 445-446, 450

Feeney Callan, Michael 677

Fell, Stuart 314, 449-450, 452, 468, 566, 751

Ferguson, Michael 26, 170, 344, 355

Ferriggi, Ann 100

Fielding, Janet 478, 493, 557, 562, 563, 579, 580, 681, 693, 699, 710, 720, 751

Firman, Alec 139

Firth, Peter 758

Fitton, John 781

Five Doctors, The 219, 223, 377, 404, 513, 514, 515-516, 517, 518, 530, 536, 537, 541-577, 581, 583, 585, 586, 587, 590, 602, 632, 633, 634, 695, 752, 780, 781, 791

Five Faces of Doctor Who, The 532, 537, 541

Flanagan, John 505-506, 524, 529, 532

Fleming, Heather 73

Fleming, Robert 577

Fletcher, Maggie 338

Flinn, Denny Martin 759

Flint, Debbie 749

Floid 672

Flood, Gerald 493

Flynn, Stephen 653, 654

Follett, James 530

Ford, Carole Ann 26, 76, 86, 113, 121, 126, 130, 134, 136, 137, 141, 201, 202, 203, 561, 693, 749, 755, 784

Foster, Tony 150

Four to Doomsday 507, 513, 514, 525, 533, 539, 590

Fox, Bernard 365

Francis, Jim 650, 659, 663

Franklin, Pamela 130, 132

Franklin, Richard 361, 568, 693

Fraser, Bill 396, 457

Fraser, Ian 751

Frederick Muller Ltd 108, 112, 117

Fredericks, Scott 363

Freeman, John 749, 751

French, Gavin 673

French, Leslie 76

Frick, Alice 47-48, 49-50, 53-54, 56

Friedlander, John 192, 279, 340, 341, 342

Frontier in Space 331, 333, 340, 348-349, 380, 383, 387

Frontios 514, 587, 590

Full Circle 459, 472, 485, 486, 514, 532

Furness, Mark 320, 621, 631

Furst, Anton 757

Fury from the Deep 135, 233, 240, 258, 265, 288, 289, 291, 293, 295, 301, 513

G, Bobby 672

Galaxy 4 153-154, 155, 156, 157, 158, 203, 205, 207, 208, 209, 213, 295, 300

Gallaccio, George 452

Gallifrey+ 677

Gammon, Joy 698

Gardner, Jack 529

Gatland, John 552, 577

Gatland, Steve 666

Gatting, Mike 755

Gaunt, William 595, 656-657, 661

Gavin, Camilla 576

Gearing, Brian 582

Genesis of the Daleks 402, 412, 417-418, 421, 426, 427, 428, 430, 462, 463, 480, 481, 485, 537, 753

*Ghost Hunters, The** 350

Ghost Light 714, 724, 727, 748, 784, 797, 798

Giants, The+ 64, 66-67, 81

Giacobbi, John 752

Gibbs, Adrian 458

Gilbert, Oliver 364

Gillan, Gilbert 563

Gillatt, Gary 785

Glaze, Peter 475

Glynn, Dominic 746, 747

Goddard, Liza 539, 607

Godfrey, Pat 604, 637, 644, 647, 651, 657, 666, 749

Gorrie, John 111, 112, 113, 125

Gory, Colin 654

Gough, Michael 173

Gould, Robert 88, 95, 107, 113

Grade, Michael 596, 606, 610, 611, 619, 620, 641, 643, 667, 668, 670-671, 672, 673, 674, 675, 676, 679, 691, 694, 703, 719, 720, 775, 797

Grainer, Ron 84, 87, 200, 285, 376, 380,

454, 577, 666, 747
Grant, Steve   672
Greatest Show in the Galaxy, The   713, 726, 727, 780, 784, 790, 792, 798
Green Death, The   314, 326, 328, 340, 349, 381, 382, 383, 384, 387, 461, 480-481, 754, 755
Greene, Sarah   595, 691, 694
Greenwood, John   281-282, 285
Greenwood, Tony   753
Greer, Terence   529
Greneau, David   183
Grenville, Bruce   207
Grenville, Cynthia   441, 442
Gray, Charles   550
Gribbin, John   530
Grieve, Ken   524
Griffiths, Colin   752
Griffiths, Richard   503
Griffiths, Sara   730
Grimwade, Peter   472, 535, 538, 639, 643, 681, 686
Grout, James   755
Grubb, D M B   70, 73
Grumbar, Murphy   364
Guinness, Perry   138
Gunfighters, The   38, 164, 166, 168, 169, 170, 173, 200, 205, 207, 208, 209, 213, 226, 294, 295, 379, 769
Haddon, Eva   755
Hagger, Jill   576
Haggerty, Fred   153
Haining, Peter   582, 583, 780
Haisman, Mervyn   240, 436, 749
Halderman, Laurie   698
Halliwell, David   678, 679
Halls, Clive   200
Halstead, John   193
Halston, Peter   576
Hamilton, Fred   376
Hammond, Fay   576
Hammond, P J   679-680
Hand of Fear, The   465, 466, 481, 482, 483, 486, 513
Hands of Aten, The+   160, 164
Hansen, Lena   747
Happiness Patrol, The   713, 732, 775, 790, 792, 798
Harding, Tony   458, 469, 754
Hardy, Mark   564
Harper, Barbara   80

Harper, Graeme   452, 596, 615, 644, 646-647, 648, 649-650, 651-664, 664-665, 666, 753, 783
Harris, Dan   789
Harris, Fred   475
Harris, Julie   672
Harris, Michealjohn   248-249, 251-252
Harrison, Barry   755
Harrison, John   674
Hart, Alan   542, 579, 637
Hart, Michael   251, 255
Hartnell, Heather   26-27, 37, 176, 508
Hartnell, William   15-30, 33, 36-37, 76, 84, 105, 107, 109, 112, 123, 127, 130, 131-132, 135, 136, 137, 140, 145, 147, 152, 156, 159, 164, 167, 173, 175, 176, 177, 178, 179, 182, 184, 201, 203, 210, 212, 216, 218, 219, 223, 225, 226, 228, 229, 230, 286, 295, 296, 368, 376, 377, 488, 490, 492, 508, 510, 542, 543, 545, 548, 575, 589, 604, 629, 721, 762, 763, 780, 785
Hasse, Camilla   73
Hasselhoff, David   776
Hatts, Clifford   249-250
Hawkins, Peter   446, 749
Hawkshawe, Alan   754
Hayes, Michael   469
Hayles, Brian   137, 146, 160, 164, 165, 167, 168, 174, 236
Hayward, Justin   672
Haywood, Steve   793
Hearne, Richard   408
Hebos+   530
Heddon, Sue   375
Heigham, Pat   285
Helsby, Eileen   193
Helsby, Thelma   193, 200
Henderson, Don   775
Hendon, Derek   740
Heneghan, Maureen   90
Henry, Lenny   693
Henry, Richard   267
Hepton, Bernard   282
Hercules, Evan   261, 268-269, 271-281, 284
Herdsmen of Aquarius, The+   175
Hewett, Ian   577
Hidden Planet, The+   88, 95, 102, 109, 111, 125, 134, 136, 149
Highlanders, The   232, 235, 236, 238, 257, 288, 290, 292, 294, 301
Hill, Adrienne   157, 693

Hill, David 791

Hill, Jacqueline 26, 76, 87, 101, 112, 113, 121, 130-132, 135, 140, 142, 147, 150, 201, 203

Hill, James 756

Hill, Peter 367

Himmelweit, Hilda 291, 297

Hinchcliffe, Philip 394, 395, 399, 410, 411, 413, 420, 426, 427, 428-429, 430, 431, 432, 434, 435, 436, 452, 454, 466, 526, 537-538, 755, 783

Hinds, Anne 750

Hines, Frazer 221, 222, 223, 236, 270, 274, 283, 285, 286, 287, 569, 594, 595, 610, 617, 691, 754, 755, 774

Hines, Ian 275, 278

Hirsch, Henric 125

Hirst, Kate 747

Hoddinott, Derek 130, 139-140

Hodgson, Brian 85, 183, 200, 285, 374, 376, 749, 754, 755

Hodiak, Keith 564

Holderness, Sue 475

Holm, Ian 758

Holman, David 795

Holme, Sally 73

Holmes, John 285

Holmes, Patricia 541

Holmes, Robert 149-150, 330, 350, 409, 410, 411, 412, 416, 417, 420, 422, 423, 427, 428, 429, 430, 431, 435, 436, 452, 454, 462, 465, 512, 530, 531, 537-538, 540, 542-546, 609, 614-615, 618, 633, 636, 642, 677, 678, 679, 680, 686, 733, 757

Holt, Michael 699

Hood, Stuart 117-118, 119

Hopkins, Keith 793

Hordern, Michael 175, 226

Horne, Alan 376

Horns of Nimon, The 431, 433, 471, 481, 482

Horrigan, Billy 314

Horror of Fang Rock 430, 433, 473, 481, 482

Horsfall, Bernard 269, 275

Horton, John 445, 448, 454

Horton, Timothy 275

House That Ur-Cjak Built, The+ 530

Howard, Graham 207, 293

Howarth, Chris 783

Howarth, Derek 657, 658

Howe, David J 587, 694, 699, 749, 751, 754, 781, 783, 785, 794

Howell, Peter 460, 541, 571-573, 574, 577

Hudolin, Richard 770

Hudson, June 394, 751

Hughes, Geoffrey 595, 691

Hughes, Nerys 539

Hulke, Malcolm 80, 88, 90, 95, 102, 109, 111-113, 116, 125, 134, 136, 149, 234-235, 242, 329, 379, 380, 484, 523, 635

Humphreys, John 756, 757, 759, 760

Hurley, John 200

Hurndall, Richard 219, 546, 548, 553, 558, 573, 575

Husband, Mary 338, 376

Hussein, Waris 27, 70, 75, 76, 78, 82, 85, 89, 91, 105, 201, 551, 749

Hussey, Marmaduke 750

Hutchings, Neil 793

Idle, Eric 776

Ice Warriors, The 233, 236, 260, 286, 288, 293, 295, 301, 333

Image of the Fendahl 430, 466-467, 468, 481, 486

Imison, Michael 179, 181-182, 184, 185-198, 199, 200

In the Hollows of Time+ 677

Inferno 313, 325, 326, 330, 332, 335-336, 343, 358, 378, 382, 383, 384, 385, 387, 515, 769

Inside the Spaceship 39, 40, 42, 43, 98, 105, 106, 107, 108, 203, 206, 213, 295, 749

Invasion, The 221, 240, 241, 242, 249, 259, 260, 282, 288, 289, 291, 301, 304, 330, 334, 344, 419, 634

Invasion of the Dinosaurs 326, 328, 331, 332, 341, 383, 384, 385, 386, 516

Invasion of Time, The 414, 417, 423-424, 425, 432, 459, 466, 467-468, 481, 482, 516, 517, 634, 772

Invisible Enemy, The 425, 433, 458, 459, 481, 483, 486

Ireson, Richard 275, 278

Irvine, Mat 458, 468, 698, 754

Jackson, David 753

Jacobs, Anthony 769

Jacobs, Matthew 767, 769-770

Jagels, Nick 753

James, Malcolm 561, 568, 577

James, Sylvia 269, 277, 279, 285

Jameson, Louise 398, 478, 538, 693, 754

Jarvis, Martin 595, 691
Jason, David 738
Jayston, Michael 595, 613, 691, 768
Jerrard, Sue 406
Jerricho, Paul 560, 565
Jervis, Dave 339, 455
Joffe, Edward 756
John, Caroline 318, 335, 477, 568, 693, 784
Johns, Brian 376
Johns, Stratford 539
Johnstone, Norman 376
Jones, Dallas 292
Jones, Elwyn 131-132, 232, 236
Jones, Emrys 269, 272, 274
Jones, Emyr Morris 561, 563
Jones, Glyn 142, 462
Jones, Gwen 47, 48
Jones, Howard 666
Jones, Julie 558, 647
Jones, Myrddin 563
Jones, Nigel 754
Jones, Raymond 139
Jones, Steve 755
Jonns, Alan 752, 753
Jordan, Tony 694, 697
Journey to Cathay, A* 78, 80, 88, 95
Joyce, David 366
Judge, Jane 576
K-9 and Company 585, 671
Katz, Ron 585, 696
Kay, Norman 89
Keeble, John 756, 757, 759, 760
Keeper of Traken, The 420, 481, 486, 532
Keith Jr, William H 699
Kells, Janie 442
Kelt, Mike 557, 577
Kemp, Gypsie 363
Kennaugh, Martin 793
Kennedy, Scott 683
Kenton, William 564
Keys of Marinus, The 40, 41, 42, 43, 107, 108, 109, 111, 112, 113-114, 115, 117, 118, 119, 120, 202, 204, 206, 207, 208, 209, 213, 446, 749
Kidd, Barbara 340-341
Kilgarriff, Michael 461
Killer Cats of Geng Singh, The+ 467
Kinda 507, 513, 519, 525, 539, 583, 590
Kine, Jack 85, 94, 107, 191, 243, 244, 246, 247, 249, 251-254, 255, 285, 751
King, Bill 245, 249, 251

King, Brian 755
King, Chris 376
King, Howard 200, 271, 272, 285
King, Karen 747
King's Demons, The 514, 516, 535, 537, 549, 587, 590, 695
Kingsland, Paddy 460
Kohll, Malcolm 729, 730, 775
Krotons, The 150, 240, 241, 249, 258, 288, 289, 293, 294, 301, 532, 542
L'Epine Smith, Eric 203
Lack, Simon 469
Laing, Roderick 124
Laird, Trevor 595
Lambert, Verity 27, 34, 69, 73-74, 76, 77, 78, 81, 82, 84, 85, 86-87, 88, 89, 91, 93, 94, 95-96, 98-100, 101, 102-3, 104, 106, 107, 109, 110, 111, 112, 114, 115, 118, 119, 123, 126, 127-128, 129, 130, 131-132, 135-136, 137, 138, 139, 141, 142, 143, 144, 146-147, 148, 150, 151, 152, 153, 154, 158, 159, 201, 202, 203, 242, 583, 748, 749, 750, 754, 755, 756
Lambess, Neil 207
Lane, Andy 793
Lane, Barbara 337-338, 338
Lane, Jackie 76, 163, 175, 182, 185, 186, 187, 203, 235, 693
Langford, Bonnie 595, 616, 630, 639-640, 643, 691, 692, 694, 706, 712, 715, 716, 730, 735, 736, 746, 778
Langley, Martin 275
Lasry, Jacques 78
Last Adventure, The+ 679
Latham, Philip 547, 560, 570
Lauchlan, Archie 752
Lavers, Colin 506, 507, 541, 548-549, 554, 556, 559, 561, 563, 565, 568, 569, 570, 576
Lavers, Paul 469
Law, Phillida 73
Lawton, Christina 133
Lazell, Andy 659
Le Fre, Jenny 450
Le Touzel, Sylvestra 275
Learoyd, Barry 151, 153, 161, 163
Lee, Penelope 73, 658
Lee, Tanith 530
Lee, Waveney 73
Leekley, John 768
Leeson, John 399, 559, 699, 749
Leggo, Tony 200

Leigh, Gary (né Levy) 696-697, 752, 775, 794

Leisure Hive, The 457-458, 459, 472, 481, 482, 484, 486

Lenska, Rula 539

Leopold, Guy 436

Les Structures Sonores 78, 84

Lester, Richard 757

Lester, Rick 356, 361, 366, 376

Letts, Barry 233, 242, 304, 311, 314, 316, 318, 319, 324, 327-328, 329, 332, 337, 339, 342, 344-345, 346, 347, 348, 349, 350, 351-352, 356, 358, 361, 375, 378, 390, 394, 395, 399, 408-410, 412, 416, 426-427, 433, 434, 436, 461, 507, 520, 525, 531-532, 582, 751, 754, 755, 784

Levene, John 361, 550, 693, 784

Levey, Eric 577

Levin, Richard 68-69, 70, 73, 75, 81, 91, 268, 354

Levine, Ian 527, 537, 583, 632, 639, 643, 667, 669, 671, 673, 674-675, 676, 752, 755, 758

Levy, Carl 576

Levy, Gary (see Leigh, Gary)

Lewie, Jona 672

Limb, Roger 460, 664-665, 666

Lincoln, Henry 240, 436

Linden, Jennie 211, 749, 755

Lindsay, Kevin 341, 417

Ling, Peter 261-267, 284

Linstead, Alec 656

Liptrott, Hilda 747

Litten, Peter 756, 757, 758, 759

Living World, The+ 84, 111

Livingstone, Ken 755

Lloyd, Innes 27, 164, 166-167, 168, 169, 170, 175, 177, 179, 200, 216, 222, 225-226, 231, 232, 235, 236, 238, 239, 240, 245, 246-247

Lodge, Bernard 86-87, 200, 285, 460

Lodge, John 672

Lofficier, Jean-Marc 583, 759, 783

Loft, Barbara 275

Logan, Campbell 220

Logan, Peter 470

Logopolis 403, 415, 421, 425, 434, 458, 472, 481, 486, 488, 490-491, 497, 532

Lomax, Sid 376

Long, Dinah 666

Lopes, John 285

Lovell, Jack 182, 183, 335

Lovell, John 182, 183, 335

Lowe, Geoff 530

Lucarotti, John 78, 82, 109, 111, 112, 137, 154, 163, 202

Lumm, Charlie 459

Lynch-Blosse, Bridget 653, 654

Lyon, Shaun 789

Lyons, Bill 530

Lyons, Steve 783

MacIntosh, Alex 371

Mack, Johnnie 570

MacLean, Don 475

Macra Terror, The 236, 258, 288, 290, 292, 293, 295, 301

Madoc, Philip 440

Magna Models 251

Mair, John 53, 57, 65, 67, 68, 70, 71-72, 76, 80, 82, 83, 93, 94, 96, 97, 118, 119, 122, 128-129

Making of Doctor Who, The 379, 484, 556

Mallett, Nicholas 643

Maloney, David 200, 220, 261, 267-269, 270-283, 284, 429, 465-466, 783

Man Watch+ 530

Mann, Paul 739, 741, 747

Manning, Katy 314, 316, 318, 328, 336, 338, 360, 365, 368, 378, 379, 390, 477, 550, 586, 754

*Manpower** 261-265, 267

Manser, Kevin 123

Mansfield, Mike 672

Mansfield, Stephen 739, 741, 749

Mansfield-Clark, Pauline 73, 102, 130, 132

Marco Polo 36, 39, 40, 41, 43, 95, 105, 106, 107, 108, 109, 110, 111, 112, 113, 114, 115, 155, 194, 201, 204, 206-207, 209, 212, 213, 295

Mark of Lumos+ 529

Mark of the Rani, The 595, 609-610, 614, 634, 639, 686-687, 689, 691, 695, 696, 702

Markham, Sonia 100, 159, 200

Marks, Louis 113, 122, 350, 351, 352, 353, 376, 430

Marolf, Adele 666

Marsh, Jean 157, 203, 478, 714, 798

Marshall-Fisher, Ian 568

Marson, Richard 744

Marter, Ian 530, 693, 756

Martin, Andrew 785, 793

Martin, Dave 417, 427, 462, 465, 699, 749

Martin, Derek 376
Martin, John Scott 364, 561, 754
Martin, Lorne 751
Martin, Philip 530, 531, 618, 642, 676-677, 678, 679, 686, 699
Martin, Richard 28, 58, 89, 95-96, 98, 105, 111, 131, 144-145, 146, 149, 153
Martinus, Derek 28, 176-178
Maschwitz, Eric 46, 47, 48, 49
Masque of Mandragora, The 403, 413, 425, 465, 466, 481, 482
Massacre of St Bartholomew's Eve, The 37, 163, 164, 165, 166, 167, 183, 199, 205, 207, 208, 213
Masters of Luxor, The+ 95, 111, 116
Mathews, Richard 550, 570
Matthews, Norman 149
Matthews, Rodney 757
Mawdryn Undead 514, 515, 516, 517, 534, 550, 551, 580, 586, 587, 590
May Time+ 530
McCall, Tom 169
McCarthy, Desmond 244, 245
McCaul, Jo 753
McCoy, Sylvester 500-501, 703, 706, 707-719, 719-721, 722-724, 730, 732-733, 735, 736, 744, 748, 749, 750, 751, 753, 754, 755, 757, 762, 764, 765, 769, 774, 775, 776, 778, 779, 780, 781, 784, 788, 794, 795, 796, 797
McCulloch, Andrew 505, 524, 530, 532
McCulloch, Keff 747, 751, 779
McDonald, Graeme 431, 432, 433, 524
McElroy, John 584
McFarlane, Jean 359, 371
McGann, Paul 762-766, 767, 776, 777, 779, 785, 788, 796
McGowan, Lindsay 739, 747
McGuinness, Paul 739, 747
McLachlan, Ian 587
McMillan, Jean 454
McNally, Kevin 595
McVean, Andy 739, 740, 741, 747
Meglos 457, 485, 486, 572
Menzies, Frank 366
Messaline, Peter 364
Meyer, Nicholas 759
Miall, Leonard 72, 83
Miles, Keith 529
Mill, Gerry 245-246
Miller, Alex 137
Miller, Keith 381

Miller, Michael 154
Millier, Tony 376, 454
Mills, A R 108, 112
Mills, Dick 87, 453, 454, 541, 571, 573, 577, 664-665, 666, 746, 747, 749, 750, 751, 755
Mills, Patrick 530
Mills, Penny 753
Milne, Alasdair 676
Milnes, Yvonne 621
Milward, Charles 571
Mind of Evil, The 325, 327, 330, 331, 336, 382, 383, 384, 387
Mind Robber, The 240, 249, 257, 258, 260-285, 288, 289, 290, 293, 294, 300, 301, 346, 586, 749, 752, 793
*Mindwarp** 679
*Miniscules, The** 113, 122
Mission to Magnus+ 676-677
Mission to the Unknown 146, 151, 155, 205, 206, 207, 209, 213, 289, 295, 300
Mitchell, A J 455, 751
Mitchell, Stan 562
Moffatt, Peter 541, 548, 550-552, 553, 554, 555, 557-571, 574, 576, 595-596, 608, 615
Molloy, Terry 654, 661, 751
Money, Stuart 381
Monster of Peladon, The 333, 341, 382, 383, 387
Moody, Ron 323
Moonbase, The 221, 233, 236, 238, 244, 258, 259, 286, 288, 292, 293, 298, 301
Moore, Dudley 757, 758
Moore, Susan 739-742, 749
Moore, Wanda 353
More than 30 Years in the TARDIS 754, 782
Morgan, Andrew 712, 720
Morris, Michael Owen 468
Mourby, Adrian 755
Mouth, of Grath+ 529
Mudie, James 71, 94, 96, 98, 99, 114
Munro, Caroline 756, 757, 758
Munro, Rona 733
Murphy, Peter (see Grumbar, Murphy)
Murphy Grumbar, Peter (see Grumbar, Murphy)
Murray-Leach, Roger 403, 429, 465
Mutants, The (aka *The Daleks*) 34, 37, 39, 40, 42, 43, 44, 83, 85, 88, 89, 91, 92, 93, 95, 96, 98, 100-101, 102, 103, 104, 106, 107, 138, 183, 201, 203, 206, 209, 211, 213,

295, 418, 749

Mutants, The 329, 331, 338-339, 347, 382, 387, 789

Myerscough-Jones, David 350, 353-355, 359-371, 376

*Mysterious Planet, The** 679

Myth Makers, The 155, 157, 158, 159, 160, 205, 207, 208, 213, 295

Nathan-Turner, John 319, 399, 404, 415, 426, 433-434, 460, 470, 477, 480, 482, 484, 488, 490, 493, 496, 497, 498, 502-505, 506-507, 508, 509, 511, 512, 520, 521, 525, 526, 527, 531-534, 535, 536, 537, 538-540, 541-542, 545, 548, 549, 550, 551, 553-554, 555, 556, 557, 558, 559, 563, 567, 571, 574, 576, 578-579, 580, 582, 583, 585, 590, 591, 592, 594, 595, 597, 598, 602, 604, 613, 617-618, 619, 620, 623-624, 625, 627, 628, 630, 631, 632, 636, 637, 638-640, 641, 642-643, 644, 646, 647, 653, 664, 666, 673, 674-675, 676, 677, 679-680, 681, 683, 684, 685, 688, 690, 692, 693, 695, 696, 698, 706, 710, 712, 715, 719-720, 721, 722, 726, 729, 730, 732, 733, 735, 736, 737, 738, 739, 744, 746, 748, 749, 750, 751, 752, 754, 755, 756, 775, 778, 780, 782, 788, 794, 798

Nation, Terry 80, 83, 85, 88, 89, 90, 93, 95, 106, 107, 108, 109, 111, 112, 113-114, 116, 117, 121, 130, 135, 137, 140, 142, 145, 146, 151, 152, 154, 155, 156, 202, 228, 229, 239, 351-352, 374, 376, 379, 418, 427, 484, 524, 644, 645, 748, 749, 754, 776

Naylor, Richard 563

Nazis, The+ 168, 174

Nelson, Phyllis 672

Nesbitt, Derren 109

New Armada, The+ 164-165

Newbery, Barry 91, 93, 151, 160, 169, 179, 182, 185-198, 200, 242-243, 429, 435, 437, 439-452, 454, 465, 749, 751

Newby, Ricky 364

Newman, Peter R 111

Newman, Philip 758-759

Newman, Sarah 352, 376, 381

Newman, Sydney 14, 30, 31, 32, 33, 49, 51-53, 56-57, 58, 61, 65, 66, 67, 68, 74-75, 77, 78, 82, 83, 85, 86, 90-91, 94, 100, 102, 104, 108, 115, 118, 119, 120-121, 123, 125, 129, 136, 137, 141, 159, 164, 219, 226, 228, 229, 230, 235, 239, 283, 410, 519

Newnham, Steve 666

Nicholson, Jack 760, 777

Nieradzik, Dorka 651, 652-653, 656, 657, 662, 666

Nightingale, Jes 747

Nightmare Fair, The+ 676

Nightmare of Eden 471, 473, 481, 694

Nimoy, Leonard 759, 760

O'Brien, Maureen 133, 139, 147, 157, 203

O'Leary, Jo 666

O'Mara, Kate 595, 639, 715, 774

O'Shaughnessy, John 376

O'Shea, Kevin 592, 749, 751

Ocean Liner, The+ 169

Ogwen, John 656-657

Oldfield, Mike 756

Olivier, Laurence 756

Orme, Geoffrey 169

Osborn, Andy 220

Oulton, Caroline 733

Padbury, Wendy 221, 240, 270, 272, 280, 569

Palk, Anna 73

Palmer, Ben 86

Palmer, Gregg 179

Palmer, Valentine 353, 367

Paradise Five+ 679-680

Paradise of Death, The 754, 755

Paradise Towers 712, 725, 727, 779, 798

Parasites+ 530

Parkhouse, Steve 475

Parkin, Bryon 582

Parkin, Lance 767, 783, 785

Parson, Hugh 571, 577, 747

Parsons, Nicholas 776, 798

Parsons, Rosemary 747

Patterson, Bill 71

Pearce, Jacqueline 595, 691, 693

Pearce, Richard 755

Pearson, Bill 663

Pedler, Kit 168, 176, 226, 235, 238, 291, 297

Peel, Edward 739, 740, 741, 742, 743

Peel, John 587, 782, 783

Pegrum, Peter 189

Pemberton, Victor 134-135, 238, 239, 240, 748

People Who Couldn't Remember, The+ 175

Perera, Shyama 749

Pertwee, Bill 306

Pertwee, Hugh 309

Pertwee, Ingeborg 310, 311, 317, 320, 321

Pertwee, Jon 223, 304, 305, 306-324, 328, 334, 335, 338, 342, 343, 349, 360, 365, 368, 376-377, 378, 380, 381, 383, 386, 390, 408, 409, 410, 411, 426, 427, 474, 488, 490, 508, 549, 554, 559, 567-568, 575, 581, 583, 588, 604, 621, 622, 628, 693, 710, 714, 750, 751, 753, 754, 755, 779, 780, 781, 784, 785, 788, 793

Pertwee, Michael 306

Pertwee, Roland 306, 307-308

Pethig, Hazel 338

Peyre, Jean 552, 568, 577

Phillips, Trish 285

Phillipson, Gordon 376

Pilot, the 65, 68, 74, 75, 80, 89, 90-92, 93, 97, 294, 295, 751, 752

Pinacotheca+ 679

Pinfield, Mervyn 51, 66, 76, 78, 84, 86, 91, 95, 105, 111, 113, 137, 138, 144, 201

Pirate Planet, The 468, 469, 782

Pirie, Christine 279

Pitts, Richie 672

Pixley, Andrew 294

Place Where All Times Meet, The+ 530

Planet of Evil 473, 480

Planet of Fire 493, 495-496, 514, 516, 535, 536, 538, 539, 587, 590, 634, 681, 685, 686, 689, 693

Planet of Giants 42, 43, 122, 125, 129, 132, 133, 136-137, 138, 204, 207, 209, 211, 212, 213, 295, 350

Planet of Storms+ 676

Planet of the Daleks 275, 327, 332, 333, 338, 348-349, 383, 384, 385, 386, 518, 754, 780

Planet of the Spiders 326, 327, 328, 330, 331, 332, 342, 382, 383, 384, 385, 386, 426

Platt, Marc 726, 733, 784, 786

Plunkett Green, T 109, 110

Poison+ 530

Pooley, Olaf 313, 336

Pope, Begonia 394

Powell, Jonathan 596, 619, 642, 673, 675, 676, 710, 720, 756, 757, 796

Power of Kroll, The 469, 470

Power of the Daleks, The 229, 230, 231, 232, 236, 256, 257, 258, 285, 286, 288, 289, 292, 294, 296, 301, 333, 378, 782

Pratt, Peter 420

Pressland, Justin 754

Price, Anna 666

Priest, Christopher 530

Pritchard, Bill 677

Proctor, Michael 793

Project '4G'+ 505, 529

Project Zeta-Sigma+ 505-506, 524, 530, 532

Proudfoot, Brian 123

Psychrons+ 529

Pugh, Susan 91

Pulford, Sue 279

Pursuers, The* 141, 142

Purves, Peter 26, 28, 30, 151, 168, 182, 235, 378, 693, 749, 754

Pyramid in Space* 734

Pyramid's Treasure, The* 734

Pyramids of Mars 412, 464, 466, 480, 624, 699, 755

Qualtrough, John 139-140

Quilley, Denis 550

Radenkovic, Janet 454

Radio Times 89, 99, 109, 110, 159, 201, 285, 295-296, 337, 374, 377, 379, 436, 537, 548, 553, 569, 575, 582, 774, 775, 776, 777, 778, 779, 780, 781, 794, 795, 796, 797, 798

Radiophonic Workshop 84, 85, 87, 183, 200, 285, 374, 376, 454, 459, 460, 571, 572, 573, 577, 581, 591, 664

Rae, Dan 376

Raven, John 173

Rawlins, Christine 324, 334-336, 344

Ray, Trevor 242

Rayner, Claire 755

Read, Anthony 430, 431, 467

Red Fort, The+ 90, 95, 106

Reed, Owen 61

Reeve, Tom 747

Reeves, Tony 98

Reid, Beryl 539, 639

Reid, David 510-511, 532, 541, 542, 574, 620, 625

Reid, Mike 692, 694

Reid, Sandra 229, 245

Reign of Terror, The 40, 43, 112, 113, 114, 121, 122, 123, 124, 125, 126, 127, 129, 132, 133, 204, 207, 209, 213, 295, 461

Remembrance of the Daleks 713, 722, 723, 725, 726, 732, 775, 779, 780, 786, 790, 791, 792, 796, 797, 798

Rescue, The 36, 39, 43, 134, 135, 138, 139, 142, 204, 207, 209, 213

Resistance is Useless 384, 752, 754

Resurrection of the Daleks 514, 518, 519, 537, 538, 539, 587, 590, 633, 639, 728,

781, 782
*Return, The** 537
*Return of the Cybermen, The** 244
*Return of the Daleks, The** 112, 121, 123
Revelation of the Daleks 595, 614, 615, 617, 634-635, 640, 641, 644-666, 687, 694, 695, 696, 702, 727, 728, 753, 782
Revenge of the Cybermen 419, 426, 459, 462, 463, 479, 480, 481, 518, 584, 699, 728
Reynalds, Christopher 275
Reynalds, David 275
Reynolds, Mary 779
Ribos Operation, The 481
Rice, John 577
Richards, Justin 785
Richards, Lynn 624
Riches, Alan 568
Richmond, Graham 577
Rickman, Alan 760, 777
Ridout, Martin 571, 577
Rigelsford, Adrian 752, 753, 780, 783, 784
Ritelis, Viktors 158
Road, Alan 583
Roark, Chad 585, 696
Robb, Brian J 793
Robbie, Christopher 280, 420
Robbins, Michael 539
Roberts, Bill 158, 243, 247
Roberts, Gareth 782, 785
Roberts, Pennant 467, 576, 617
Roberts, Steve 752
Robertson, Annette 163
Robinson, Matthew 615, 634, 676
Robinson, Nigel 698, 768, 782
Robot 410-411, 416, 426, 427, 429, 456, 458, 461-462, 463, 479, 481, 482, 484
Robots, The+ 77, 79-80, 81, 85, 88, 89-90, 95
Robots of Death, The 427, 456, 464, 465, 482, 486, 699
Rocca, John 672
Rogers, Dave 577, 747
Romanoids+ 530
Romans, The 40, 43, 133, 134, 135, 138, 139, 140, 141, 142, 143, 144, 204, 207, 209, 211, 212, 213, 295, 451, 628
Root, Antony 507, 524-526, 527, 538, 591
Roslaire, Joan 277
Rowle, Elizabeth 666
Roxburgh, Gordon 587
Rubenstein, Norman 756

Russell, Gary 587, 754, 755, 771, 777, 784, 785
Russell, Mark 754
Russell, Paddy 98, 105, 234, 464
Russell, William 25, 26, 28, 76, 109, 110, 113, 127, 130-132, 139, 145, 150, 201, 203, 749, 754
Rutherford, Norman 46, 69, 71, 72
Ryan, Christopher 691
Ryan, Philip 273
Ryecart, Patrick 595, 691
Sachs, Andrew 755
Salter, Lionel 84
Sandeman, Christopher 747
Saunders, David 587, 667, 669, 671, 697, 781
Savages, The 40, 168, 173, 174, 175, 200, 206, 207, 208, 213, 235, 385
Savile, David 559
Savory, Gerald 152, 164, 167, 226
Saward, Eric 509, 511, 512, 525, 526-531, 533-535, 537-538, 540, 542, 545-546, 547, 549, 550, 574, 576, 583, 591, 613, 617-619, 620, 625-626, 628, 631-632, 636-637, 638, 639, 640, 641-643, 644-646, 650, 651, 654, 666, 675, 677, 679-680, 681-682, 685-686, 689, 706, 719, 755
Sayle, Alexei 653-654, 691
Scoones, Ian 251, 458
Scoones, Paul 207
Scott, Lesley 180-181, 200
Scott, Rod 292
Scuse, Dennis 141
Sea Devils, The 318, 325, 326, 327, 329, 331, 338, 346, 380, 382, 386, 387, 518-519, 752
Seager, Pauline 552, 576
Search, Gay 582
Search Out Science: The Ultimate Challenge 749, 778
Seeds of Death, The 240, 249-250, 260, 288, 289, 294, 301, 333, 344, 699
Seeds of Doom, The 403, 412, 413, 427, 428, 455, 459, 464, 466, 481, 486, 628, 732
Segal, Philip David 753, 759, 762, 766-772, 788
Selby, Tony 595, 691, 735, 745, 751
Sellars, Bill 164, 165
Sensorites, The 36, 39, 40, 41, 43, 111, 119, 122, 123, 124, 125, 126, 204, 207, 208, 213
Shaban, Nabil 595, 615

Shada+ 424, 433, 471, 480, 515, 549, 550, 559, 576, 752, 782

Shallcross, Alan 75

Shanahan, Damian 288-292

Shaw, Colin 245

Shaw, Geoff 71, 91

Shawcraft Models (Uxbridge) Ltd 90, 101, 107, 150, 158, 243, 245-247

Shears, Judy 285

Sheridan, Dinah 560, 562

Sherry, Elizabeth 666

Sherwin, Derrick 233, 240, 241-242, 252, 254-256, 261, 265-266, 267, 274, 284, 304, 323, 343, 344

Shirley, Jane 133

Silberston, Jeremy 552, 576

Silcock, Pauline 452

Silurians, The - see *Doctor Who and the Silurians*

Silver Nemesis 542, 713, 722, 725, 726, 727, 728, 779, 780, 781, 791, 792, 798

Simone, Ray 672

Simpson, Dudley 149, 374, 376, 380, 430, 453, 454, 459, 460, 467, 591

Sims, Joan 595, 691

Six Doctors, The* 530, 545

Skelton, Roy 193, 561

Skilleter, Andrew 575, 584, 694, 698, 783

Skinner, Ernest 200

Sladen, Elisabeth 318, 319, 320, 343, 390, 404, 430, 440, 446, 450, 484, 485, 538, 554, 559, 693, 749, 750, 751, 754, 755, 784

Slater, Bill 409

Slattery, Tony 750

Slipback 612, 673

Sloman, Robert 327, 436

Smith, Andrew 530

Smith, Angela 666

Smith, Graeme 751

Smith, Julia 28-29

Smith, Nick 672

Smugglers, The 164, 175, 176, 178, 206, 207, 208, 211, 213, 299, 385, 461

Snakedance 513, 519, 536, 586, 590

Soldar and the Plastoids+ 529

Song of the Space Whale+ 530

Sontaran Experiment, The 395, 416-417, 426, 427, 462, 463, 465, 480, 486

Souvenir Press Ltd 117

Space Museum, The 36, 41, 42, 142, 146, 148, 149, 150, 151, 205, 207, 212, 213, 292, 624, 749

Space Pirates, The 240, 242, 250-251, 288, 289, 295, 300, 301

Space Trap, The* 150

Space Whale+ 530

Spalding, Alan 644, 647, 648-649, 650, 651-659, 666

Sparks, Richard 530

Spaull, Colin 652

Spearhead from Space 312, 325, 326, 330, 331, 334, 335, 343, 344, 377, 380, 382, 383, 384, 385, 387, 411, 784

Spencer, Valentine 139-140

Spice, Michael 446

Spicer, Joanna 52, 53, 57, 65, 68, 70, 71, 72, 74-75, 91, 94, 96-97, 99, 118, 122

Spielberg, Stephen 760, 767, 776

Spooner, Dennis 35, 112, 113, 114, 121, 133, 134, 135, 137, 138, 139, 140, 145-146, 147, 148, 149, 151, 152, 154, 155, 229

Springett, Bob 747

Squire, Robin 530

Squires, Nick 577

Stacey, Arthur 747

Stacy, Andy 666

Stallone, Sylvester 758

Stammers, Mark 699, 783, 794

Stanton, Chris 576

Stark, Koo 691

State of Decay 424, 459, 472, 485, 486, 551

Stears, John 757

Steen, Steve 752

Stenson, Peter 202

Stephenson, Andrew 529, 530

Stephenson, Geraldine 442, 443, 454

Stewart, Heather 376

Stewart, Norman 357, 375

Stewart, Robert - see Banks Stewart, Robert

Sting 777

Stokes, Bev 775

Stones of Blood, The 458, 468, 469, 482

Strange Matter* 719, 720

Strickson, Mark 493, 535, 558, 579, 580, 582, 681, 693, 793

Stringer, J J 105

Strong, Graham 795

Strutton, Bill 108, 135, 142

Subotsky, Milton 211, 756

Sullivan, Lee 777

Summers, Jill 100

Sun Makers, The 431, 467, 468, 481,

482
Survival 714, 726, 727, 728, 748, 773, 776, 792, 793, 797, 798
Survivors, The* 83
Sutherland, Donald 758, 760
Sutton, Sarah 478, 532, 580
Sutton, Shaun 219, 220, 226, 232, 238, 240, 268, 311, 324, 328, 377, 390
Sutton, Sid 460
Swift, Clive 595, 652
Tallents, John 565
Talons of Weng-Chiang, The 402, 413, 428, 465, 466, 480, 732
Tamm, Mary 469, 478, 693, 776
Tams, Paul Mark 672
Tanner, Bob 582
Tattersall, Graham 380-381
Taylor, Don 69
Taylor, Norman 87, 88, 89
Taylor, Shaw 754
Taylor, Wendy 356
Tebbet, David 530
Tenth Planet, The 38, 41, 45, 176, 177, 178, 179, 206, 207, 208, 209, 213, 216, 226, 229, 230, 235, 256, 259, 295, 300, 510, 518, 634
Terminus 511, 514, 517, 534, 539, 587, 590
Terror of the Autons 325, 329, 331, 336, 345, 346, 347, 348, 349, 377, 378, 380, 382, 383, 384, 387, 516, 581, 784
Terror of the Vervoids - see *Ultimate Foe, The*
Terror of the Zygons 426, 459, 463, 464, 476, 486, 581
Thomas, Barry 72
Thomas, Evelyn M 116-117
Thomas, Gillian 747
Thomas, Les 577
Thomas, Lesley Elizabeth 530
Thomason, Ed 750
Thompson, Derek 577
Thompson, Stephen 286
Thomsett, Sally 672
Thornton, Malcolm 541, 552, 555, 556, 557, 563, 566, 570, 576
Three Doctors, The 223, 286, 326, 327, 329-330, 332, 339-340, 348, 378, 379, 381, 382, 383, 385, 386, 516, 532, 549, 554, 633, 725, 749
Thurm, Jo 782
Tierney, Malcolm 595
Tilley, David 666
Tilsley, Vincent 51

Time and the Rani 712, 720, 724, 729, 774, 790, 791, 792, 794, 796, 798
Time Inc* 680
Time Meddler, The 35, 39, 41, 43, 148, 151, 152, 153, 154, 155, 205, 207, 208, 213, 384, 752
Time Monster, The 327, 330, 332, 337, 347-348, 353, 382, 385, 387, 479, 516, 789
Time Warrior, The 326, 330, 333, 341, 349, 378, 382, 383, 385, 387, 417, 461, 634
Time-Flight 516, 519, 527, 539, 586, 590, 792
Timelash 595, 617, 632, 633, 686, 687, 696, 702, 759
Timelords, The 781, 791
Todd, Carole 751
Todd, Geoffrey 366
Tomasin, Jenny 652, 653
Tomb of the Cybermen, The 208, 233, 234, 236, 239, 248-249, 257, 259, 285, 288, 289, 290-291, 293, 294, 295, 297, 301, 419, 584, 633, 634, 752
Topping, Keith 783, 784
Torsan Triumvirate, The+ 530
Tosh, Donald 29, 148, 149-150, 154, 157, 160, 164, 165, 166, 167, 179, 180, 181, 200
Tovey, Roberta 211, 754, 755
Toymaker, The* 164, 165
Trading Post Ltd 245, 249, 250, 271
Trench, Fiachra 671
Trevor Story, Jack 678, 679
Trew, Ken 336, 454, 751
Trial of a Time Lord, The 612-613, 614, 617-618, 619, 629, 630, 631-632, 634, 635-636, 641, 642, 643, 677-679, 687, 692, 696, 697, 701, 702, 724, 735, 737, 746, 768, 780, 786, 797
- *parts One to Four* 679, 686, 687, 702
- *parts Five to Eight* 618, 679, 686, 687, 702
- *parts Nine to Twelve* 633, 680, 696, 702
- *parts Thirteen to Fourteen* 618, 680, 686, 696, 702
Tribe of Gum, The* 72, 73, 75, 77, 80, 81, 85, 88, 89, 91, 93, 94, 95
Trieves, Frederick 396
Trilogic Game, The* 164
Troughton, David 617
Troughton, Patrick 27, 175, 178, 179, 216, 217-225, 226, 228, 229, 230, 232, 233-234, 242, 251, 252, 270, 283, 285, 286-287, 295-296, 297, 304, 305, 312, 320, 368, 376, 377,

378, 421, 474, 480, 488, 490, 491, 501, 508, 512, 548, 558, 559, 566, 575, 581, 583, 594, 595, 604, 610, 617, 668, 693-694, 697, 710, 714, 715, 720, 724, 763, 774, 777
Troughton, Sheelagh 224
Trzetrzelewska, Basia 672
Tucker, Christopher 757
Tucker, Mike 727, 739, 740,741-742, 747, 754, 783
Tucker, Rex 58, 65, 66, 67, 68, 71, 73, 75, 76, 82, 83, 87-88, 166, 168, 173
Tuckwell, Walter 209-210
Tulloch, John 583, 729
Turner, Brian 756
Turner, Lowrey 755
Twin Dilemma, The 595, 608-609, 624, 626, 632, 636, 686, 690, 692, 695, 696, 698, 700, 702
Two Doctors, The 223-224, 516, 545, 595, 610, 615, 617, 627, 632, 633, 640, 667, 687, 688, 689, 691, 695, 696, 702, 781
Ultimate Adventure, The 320-321, 621-623, 631, 751
Ultimate Evil, The+ 676
*Ultimate Foe, The** 680
Underwater Menace, The 232, 239, 257, 286, 288, 290, 292, 294, 295, 301
Underworld 423, 432, 457, 459, 462, 467, 481
Unna, Harvey 109, 111, 134
Upson, Denise 133
Valentine, James 791
Van Day, David 672
van Thompson, Kevan 754
Vengeance on Varos 530, 595, 609, 614, 617, 627, 633, 641, 686, 686, 688, 692, 696, 702
Verner, Edwina 285
Vevers, Rowan 760
Vincent-Rudzki, Jan 294, 541
Visitation, The 507, 513, 519, 525, 526-527, 539, 551, 581, 583, 584, 590
*Visitor, The** 507
Wagg, Peter 770
Wagner, John 530
Wain, Gerry 282
Wakely, Richard 729
Wakeman, Alan 80, 83-84, 111
Waldman, Ronald 75, 82-83, 141
Walford, R G 77, 82-83, 84-85
Walker, Eddie 158
Walker, John 666

Walker, Stephen James 783, 785, 794
Walmsley, Geoff 285
Walsh, Terry 314, 469
Walter, Richard 587
Walters, Brian 577
Walters, Hugh 655
Walton, Trevor 768, 769, 771
War Games, The 221, 234-235, 240, 242, 250, 251-256, 257, 258, 288, 289, 292, 294, 295, 299, 300, 301, 329, 346, 385, 421, 624, 633, 635, 749
War Machines, The 36, 38, 40, 41, 170, 174, 175, 176, 206, 207, 208, 213, 235, 294, 295, 385
Ward, Albert 138-139
Ward, Jim 335, 376
Ward, Lalla 405-406, 414, 471, 475, 476, 478, 549, 559
Ware, Peter 770
Warne, L Rowland 341-343, 439-441, 444-445, 454
Warriors of the Deep 513, 514, 518-519, 538, 590, 624, 694
Warriors' Gate 424, 458, 459, 486
Warwick, Edmund 29, 135, 152
Waterhouse, Matthew 580, 693
Watling, Deborah 221, 222, 240, 265, 286, 550, 749, 755, 784
Watson, Ian 251
Watts, John 666
Way, Jonathan 752
Way Down Yonder+ 530
Weaver, Mike 747
Web of Fear, The 236, 241, 260, 288, 289, 293, 295, 301, 330, 344, 353, 354, 573, 749, 784
Web Planet, The 41, 42, 45, 135, 142, 143, 144, 145, 146, 147, 148, 153, 201, 205, 207, 208, 209, 211, 212, 213, 780
Webber, C E 31-32, 53, 54-56, 58-65, 66-67, 81
Weir, David 467
Weisener, Bill 272
Wellesley, Jane 751
Wells, Bruce 366
Wenham, Brian 673
Weston, Jeff 672
Wheal, Alec 577, 594, 666, 747
Wheal, Susan 285
Wheatcroft, Anna 404, 476
Wheel in Space, The 233, 235, 236, 240,

249, 258, 259, 265, 269, 288, 289, 291, 293, 298, 301, 419, 433, 518

Whitaker, Ayton 61, 65-66, 68, 69, 71, 72, 75, 76, 80, 84, 519-520

Whitaker, David 32, 34-36, 57, 72, 73, 76, 77-80, 81, 83, 84, 88-89, 91, 92, 93, 95, 98, 101, 102, 106, 107, 108, 109, 111, 112, 113-114, 115-116, 117, 119, 133, 134, 135, 137, 139, 140, 142, 149, 164-165, 211, 227-228, 229, 287, 635

White, Danny 672

White Witch, The+ 160, 164

Whitehouse, Mary 377, 391, 399, 427, 428, 430, 449, 615, 640, 755

Whitemore, Hugh 137

Whose Doctor Who 483

Wickes, Dicky 747

Wickham, Steve 752

Wilcocks, Kim 747

Wilcox, Toyah 755

Wiles, John 29-30, 148, 149, 152, 154, 156-157, 158, 159, 160-162, 163, 164, 165, 166, 167, 169, 179, 180, 200, 226, 235

Wilkie, Bernard 243, 285, 378, 751

Wilkie, Martin 751

Williams, Anthony 756

Williams, Graham 399, 400, 408, 413, 415-416, 424, 425, 426, 430, 431, 432, 433, 434, 467, 470, 480, 483, 540, 676, 677

Williams, Lloyd 565

Williams-Ellis, Annabel 558

Williams-Ellis, Clough 464-465, 558

Wills, Anneke 30, 73, 173, 175, 179, 235, 286, 754

Wilson, Donald 31, 46, 47, 48, 49, 51, 53, 54, 57, 61, 62, 65, 66, 67, 68, 69, 72, 77, 81, 82, 83, 85-86, 91, 93, 94, 96-97, 99, 100,

101, 102, 104, 105, 106, 108, 109, 110, 111, 113, 115, 117, 118, 119, 121-122, 123, 132, 134, 136-137, 141, 142, 147, 148, 152, 181

Wilson, H 91

Wilson, Hamish 276

Wilson, Richard 747

Wingrove, Ray 664, 666

Winston, Jimmy 363

Winter, Philip 576

Winton, Petrona 747

Wiseman, Carol 454

Wisher, Michael 402, 699

Witch Lords, The* 432-433

Witch Planet, The+ 164

Wogan, Terry 693

Wolfe, Frederick 571

Wood, John 153, 250-251

Woodnutt, John 396, 463-464

Woods, Aubrey 353, 361

Woods, Lee 563, 564

Woodthorpe, Peter 755

Worrall, Paul 286

Wright, Brian 193

Wright, Fred 200, 285

Wright, Jo 771

Wright, Terry 272

Wyatt, Marion 607, 690

Wyatt, Stephen 727, 729, 733

Wyatt, Will 753

Wymark, Patrick 175

Wyndham, John 140

Years of Doom* 352

Yeldham, Peter 80

Yellow Fever and How to Cure It+ 677

Yentob, Alan 770

Zenith Film Productions Ltd 82, 83, 84

Zeus, Paul 587